DICTIONARY
OF
BRITISH ARMS

GENERAL EDITOR
SIR ANTHONY WAGNER K.C.B., K.C.V.O., M.A., D.Litt., F.S.A.
Clarenceux King of Arms

Dedicated to the memory of
Lieutenant-Colonel George Babington
CROFT LYONS

DICTIONARY OF BRITISH ARMS

MEDIEVAL ORDINARY
VOLUME ONE

Editors
D. H. B. CHESSHYRE, L.V.O., M.A., F.S.A.
Chester Herald

T. WOODCOCK, B.A., LL.B., F.S.A.
Somerset Herald

Assistant Editors
Hon. G. J. Grant, W. G. Hunt, T.D., B.A., F.C.A.
A. G. Sykes, B.A.

Technical Editor
I. D. G. GRAHAM, Ph.D.

Assistant
J. C. Moffett, Ph.D.

Published by
THE SOCIETY OF ANTIQUARIES OF LONDON

MCMXCII

British Library Cataloguing in Publication Data

Dictionary of British Arms.
  Vol. 1: Medieval Ordinary.
  I. Chesshyre, Hubert, *1940–* II. Woodcock, Thomas
929.60941

ISBN 0–85431–258–7

Typeset by Kudos Graphics, Horsham, West Sussex
Printed by Whitstable Litho Ltd, Whitstable, Kent

CONTENTS

FOREWORD   vii

HISTORY OF THE PROJECT   viii

STRUCTURE OF THE ORDINARY   xv

COMPILERS   xx

SOURCES
  Alphabetical by abbreviation   xxvi

TERMINOLOGY
  Abbreviations and selected word list   xxxviii

INDEX OF HEADINGS   xlvii

THE ORDINARY
  Anchor–Bend   1–396

INDEX OF NAMES   397–530

Acknowledgements

The Papworth Project has been supported by many institutions and individuals. These include:

> The College of Arms
> The British Academy
> Lord Howard de Walden
> The Marc Fitch Fund
> The Leverhulme Trust
> The Institute of Archaeology, University College, London
> The University of Cambridge
> The University of Oxford
> The University of Waikato, New Zealand

The President and Council would wish to record the Society's gratitude for this generous support over many years. Within the Society the project has been steered by the Croft Lyons Committee and supported financially by the Croft Lyons and Research Funds.

Foreword

This volume is the first fruit of a project which has had a particularly long and difficult history. Started as the result of a bequest in 1926 from Lieutenant-Colonel G. B. Croft Lyons for the production of a revised edition of Papworth's *Ordinary of Arms*, it has over the years been worked on by many hands, and undergone many vicissitudes. In 1979 it was decided that a computerised record should be made of some 114,000 of the vast collection of index cards which had been accumulated, and that this should be used, in the first instance, for the preparation of a Dictionary of British Arms, and specifically an *Ordinary*, down to A.D.1530. I am sure that it will be of great use to scholars in a number of different fields, and I should like to take this opportunity of recording the thanks of the Society to all those who have contributed by their labours to the creation of the corpus, and particularly of congratulating the team which over the past few years has brought the Dictionary to the stage of publication. In particular, a special debt of gratitude is owed to Sir Anthony Wagner, who has been intimately associated with the project for so many years and who has acted as guide and mentor to all the heraldic scholars who have been involved in seeing it to fruition.

Barry Cunliffe
President

History of the Project

On 22 June 1926 there died at the age of 71 a man described in *The Times* a few days later as a 'loyal and useful Fellow of the Society of Antiquaries'. He was Lieutenant Colonel George Babington Croft Lyons, a knowledgeable and hospitable antiquary and collector with a special interest in heraldry. Fortunately for posterity he had made his will a few months previously, on 5 January 1926, leaving a sum of about £15,000 to the Society together with a note saying: 'I desire that the income derived from the property left to the Society of Antiquaries of London . . . should be applied to the encouragement of the study of heraldry and in the first instance I wish that a new edition of Papworth's Ordinary should be prepared to be published by the Society.'

John Woody Papworth was an architect who, although he was successful in his profession, is best remembered as the compiler of the *Ordinary of British Armorials* which was completed after his death by Alfred W. Morant and published in 1874. As readers will know, an *ordinary* in this sense is a collection of arms usually arranged in alphabetical order according to their design and accompanied by the names of those who bore them. An *armory* on the other hand is an alphabetical list of names of those bearing arms, accompanied by the arms of each.

There were ordinaries of a simple kind as early as the fourteenth century, but Papworth devised a far more elaborate and comprehensive system of classification than before and the present work is arranged on much the same lines (see next chapter). Papworth's *Ordinary* was in fact based on the third edition of Burke's *General Armory*, which appeared in 1847, and of which the last and fullest edition was published in 1884. Both Burke and Papworth have been much criticized for their failure to quote sources and for their uncritical inclusion of erroneous spellings and spurious coats, but they have nevertheless provided the most comprehensive corpus of heraldic material so far accessible to the general reader.

There is not space here to enlarge on the story of Papworth and Morant's pioneering achievement, but those who wish to know more should consult (a) the introduction to the 1874 edition of the *Ordinary*, (b) 'Papworth and his Ordinary', by S.M. Collins, *Antiquaries Journal* 22 (1942), 1–16, and (c) the reprint of the 1874 edition by Tabard Publications in 1961 which, in addition to the original introduction, includes two new introductory articles: 'Papworth's Ordinary', by G. D. Squibb, and 'The Old Papworth and the New', by A.R. Wagner.

To return to the Croft Lyons bequest, it was realized that a new Ordinary could not be constructed without the previous or concurrent compilation of an Armory. Major Thomas Sheppard, F.S.A. was appointed editor of the new work in 1931, and reported in 1932, recommending the collection of material by counties. However, the work had not progressed very far when he died in 1937 and it was only in 1940, when Messrs S.M. Collins and A.R. Wagner were appointed general editors, that things began to move. They embarked on a nationwide scheme for collecting examples of coats of arms from monuments, seals, rolls of arms and other sources, and the compilation of two complementary card indices, one an Armory and the other an Ordinary, with a view to eventual publication as a *Dictionary of British Arms*. The project was supported by the Chapter of the College of Arms who provided access to its earliest records and collections.

Mr Wagner (who was knighted when he became Garter King of Arms in 1961 and to whom I shall refer from now on as Sir Anthony) would have preferred to see the publication of critical editions of all the early rolls of arms *before* the compilation of the dictionary but realised that this would cause an unacceptable delay. It was not in fact until 1950 that he was able to publish his *Catalogue of English Medieval Rolls of Arms* (Society of Antiquaries, 1950), known as *CEMRA* or *Aspilogia I*, and only in 1967 that the first of a new series of critical editions of early rolls of arms saw the light of day. This was *Rolls of Arms, Henry III* (Society of Antiquaries, 1967). Known as *Aspilogia II*, it consists of editions of the three oldest English rolls of arms, the Matthew Paris Shields, edited by T.D. Tremlett, and Glover's and Walford's Rolls, edited by H.S. London. It also contains Sir Anthony's Additions and Corrections to *CEMRA*. The series has not so far progressed any farther. It was proposed that Professor Gerard J. Brault, author of *Early Blazon* (Oxford, 1972), should continue the task, but other commitments claimed his attention, though he did publish his *Eight Thirteenth Century Rolls of Arms* (Pennsylvania, 1973), which consists of editions of Bigot, Glover, Walford, Camden, Chifflet-Prinet, Falkirk, Nativity and Caerlaverock. As his primary interest is linguistic, these editions do not provide a great deal of biographical information. Also relevant are Cecil Humphery-Smith's *Anglo-Norman Armory* (1973), which contains an edition of the Heralds Roll (Fitzwilliam version), and his *Anglo-Norman Armory Two* (1984), which is a useful ordinary of thirteenth-century rolls.

Editions of other rolls have been published from time to time and details may be found in *CEMRA*. More recently Mr R.W. Mitchell has published transcripts of many rolls (mostly of the thirteenth and fourteenth centuries) under the auspices of the Heraldry Society of Scotland, but these are more or less unedited texts.

To revert to the *Dictionary*, Sir Anthony also perceived at an early stage the desirability of including some genealogical detail, with references to published articles and pedigrees, and as we shall see presently this caused the project to veer towards the production of a dictionary of armorial families rather than a new edition of *Papworth's Ordinary*. The collection of the raw material was a formidable task involving careful selection and briefing of prospective indexers and a highly organized system of administration at the centre. Precise instructions on the compilation of the armory and ordinary cards were given by Sir Anthony in an article entitled 'The Dictionary of British Arms', published in the *Antiquaries Journal* 21

(1941), 299–322. The method differed from Papworth's chiefly in respect of the sources. Whereas he had relied for his raw material largely on *Burke's General Armory*, a work notorious for its errors and omissions, the new project involved a survey of primary sources on an unprecedented scale. The Society owes a great debt of gratitude to the indexers, who were nearly all volunteers, and it is doubtful whether such an ambitious scheme could ever be initiated today.

Progress was rapid in the early stages and by the beginning of 1943 over 61,000 Armory and Ordinary cards had been written, recording crests, badges, supporters and mottoes as well as shields. Furthermore, they included modern material as well as medieval and it was, and still is, the intention to extend the *Dictionary* down to modern times. However, it was decided as early as 1941 that priority should be given to the Middle Ages, which, for our purposes, ended in 1530 with the beginning of the heraldic visitations.

The first published list of sources covered by the *Dictionary* appeared at the end of Sir Anthony's article 'The Dictionary of British Arms: Report of Progress' published in *Antiquaries Journal* 23 (1943), 42–47. In that article Sir Anthony envisaged the production of a self-contained medieval volume or volumes in advance of the main Dictionary. He also stressed the desirability of including genealogical material with a view to producing not only a *Dictionary of British Arms*, but a *Dictionary of British Arms and Families*. He considered the addition of detailed genealogical data to be not a mere luxury, but a necessary key to an understanding of the complex field of medieval arms and surnames. He appreciated the magnitude of the task and compared it with other major projects of a similar sort, the *Complete Peerage* and the *Victoria County History*. However, he pointed out that the main obstacle would be the cost and he went on to say: 'Research of this character and extent calls for collaborative specialization which a staff of one or two could not achieve. In the past expert unpaid full time help might have been hoped for, but it can hardly be looked for in a foreseeable future'. Additional endowment was essential 'unless we are to be content with progress at a snail's pace over a period indefinitely extended'. Such endowment was not immediately forthcoming, but the Society continued to meet the comparatively modest costs of the indexing programme from the Croft Lyons Fund and other sources and in 1945 a grant of £200 for seven years was made by Lord Howard de Walden.

Mr Collins withdrew from the project in January 1944, whereupon Sir Anthony was appointed sole editor. He was helped greatly by Hugh Stanford London (see under 'Compilers'), who gradually took charge of the indexing programme, transcribed many of the most important rolls of arms so that they could be indexed for the *Dictionary*, and was responsible with Sir Anthony for working out the structure of the ordinary (see next chapter). He also made a study of early terms of blazon, and his work in that sphere was acknowledged by Professor Brault (*Early Blazon* (Oxford, 1972), viii). A bibliography of his numerous published works may be found at the front of his *Life of William Bruges* (Harleian Society, 1970); it is preceded by an account of his career by Sir Anthony which includes interesting and often amusing details of their work together on the *Dictionary* during and after the War.

The indexing of sources continued and progress was summarized by Sir Anthony in his paper 'The New Papworth: A Progress Report', dated 26 February 1948. This included a summary of sources indexed from April 1940 to 31 December 1947, during which period contributors had written 74,354 armory cards and 103,866 ordinary cards. The indexing went on until about 1954, by which time it was felt that a halt should be called; most of the major collections had been covered and it was obviously impractical to go on collecting examples indefinitely if publication was to be achieved. The coverage of the *Dictionary* is consequently somewhat arbitrary and incomplete, but one could not hope, with limited time and resources, to record every single surviving example of medieval heraldry.

In his instructions to contributors in 1941 (see above) Sir Anthony asked that 'Every batch of cards sent in should be headed by a Catalogue card showing its contents, the name of the writer, and the date'. These catalogue cards were lost for some years and it was a laborious task trying to ascertain what sources had been indexed for the *Dictionary*. We had to rely largely on Sir Anthony's periodic summaries presented to the Croft Lyons Committee, which were not intended to be detailed, and included such entries as 'Essex 13 parishes'. Fortunately, however, the card index was discovered at Burlington House early in 1985 and, although the discovery occasioned a painstaking revision of the List of Sources, it has enabled us to give a much more accurate picture of the ground covered.

As the collection of primary material slowed down, work began on the writing of articles on the arms of medieval families in the hope of achieving the dictionary of arms *and families* envisaged by Sir Anthony. Many of the early articles were written by Hugh London, and after his death in 1959 the principal author was T.D. Tremlett (see under 'Compilers'), whose contribution to the project was enormous. In 1967 Miss Brigid Allen was engaged as a full-time research assistant, being succeeded in 1968 by Miss Sonia Anderson, who left in 1969 to join the staff of the Historical Manuscripts Commission.

I was introduced to Mr Tremlett in 1971 with a view to my helping him part-time, and after his death in 1972 spent some time sorting and indexing finished and unfinished articles; this index remains in the Society's Library, and supersedes the typed schedules previously maintained by Mrs Daphne Nisbet. I also completed a calendar of Mr Tremlett's papers in 1974 and started writing articles for the *Dictionary*. However, the chief difficulty lay in finding enough time to devote to the work when I was fully employed at the College of Arms. In addition I was not entirely happy about trying to produce definitive articles on the heraldry of every medieval family merely on the genealogical evidence of a few published sources. Existing articles were also of a variable standard. For example, Michael Maclagan, lately Richmond Herald, who has had a lifelong interest in the Clare family, was able to write an article of great authority on the heraldry of that family, whereas other authors were obliged to produce much sketchier articles because they had no previous knowledge of the families concerned.

Meanwhile, I became increasingly unhappy about the rate of progress, as did Sir Anthony and the Society. The help of Thomas Woodcock was enlisted in 1976, but since he was training for an appointment as a Pursuivant his spare time was almost as limited as mine. By February 1977 some 1,200 articles had been completed and about 1,680 were in progress. The number of articles still to be written was variously estimated at between 3,916 and 7,833. Thus the whole *Dictionary* might have consisted of somewhere between 6,796 and 10,713 articles. It was suggested that it might be published in instalments and we therefore recommended a medieval armory of twenty-two volumes, the first volume to include names beginning with the letter A. However, there were difficulties in dealing with those families in isolation: for instance, when quarterings were included for other families whose names belonged elsewhere in the alphabet. On 2 March 1978 the Council of the Society of Antiquaries decided not to approve any further expenditure on the *Dictionary* in the form hitherto proposed. I had earlier suggested the publication of a more or less unedited *Ordinary* and I was asked to explore this possibility in detail, though it was not a course favoured at first by Sir Anthony, who considered that the Society would be jettisoning the valuable work which it had approved and financed over many years.

After much thought and discussion Mr Woodcock and I produced our proposals in a memorandum dated 5 May 1979. We argued that the completion of the Armory in the form envisaged was too ambitious a project without substantial additional endowment and that it would be more realistic to change course at this point rather than to continue at the snail's pace foreseen by Sir Anthony as long ago as 1943. We did not consider the work of 40 years to be wasted, as the articles and armory cards would remain available to readers in the Society's Library.

Instead we envisaged a work on the lines of Joan Corder's 'Dictionary of Suffolk Arms', *Suffolk Records Society*, 7 (1965), which is an Ordinary with a nominal index making it in effect an Armory also, and we mentioned other works of a similar type. We made suggestions about the scope and format of the work and tried to estimate its size. We also made predictions (over-ambitious in the event) about the amount of editorial work likely to be necessary and the possible time-scale and costs. Sir Anthony gave qualified approval and made a number of helpful suggestions in a memorandum of 10 May 1979.

The report was submitted to the Croft Lyons Committee on 14 June following and was sympathetically received. The most significant development arose from a suggestion by Mr Ronald Lightbown that a computer might be used for the work. By a happy chance Professor John Evans, subsequently President of the Society, was a member of the Croft Lyons Committee. He mentioned that the Institute of Archaeology, of which he was the Director, was making increasing use of computers and generously offered us access to his facilities. He put me in touch with Dr Ian Graham, Lecturer in Quantitative Methods at the Institute, to whose attention I drew certain essays on the subject which had already been published, notably 'The Computer and Heraldry', by Dr N.M. Brooke, Department of

Computer Studies, Lancaster University, *Coat of Arms*, n.s. 1 (1974–5), 92–4; and 'Practical Heraldic Computing', by Thomas Stothers, *Proceedings of the Chiltern Heraldry Group* (1975–6).

Dr Graham took an immediate interest in the project and made himself familiar with heraldic terminology and the basic rules of blazon. He arranged for the 114,000 index cards in the medieval Ordinary to be sent in batches of 1,000 to Cambridge, where they were keyed into the University computer by Humanities Computing Consultants, a husband and wife team, who likewise had to familiarize themselves with the language of heraldry.

However, the income of the Croft Lyons fund, even with injections from the Society's Research fund, was insufficient to meet the demands of the new programme and appeals were made to several bodies. Those who responded favourably during the period 1981–4 were the Leverhulme Trust, the British Academy and the Marc Fitch Fund, and their generosity and patience are greatly appreciated. It is hoped that the appearance of the first volume will encourage further benefactions to enable us to complete the task.

It became necessary to enlist additional helpers and we were fortunate in securing in 1982 the part-time assistance of William Hunt, a chartered accountant who has done much work on the compilation of the necessary lists of sources, heraldic terms and abbreviations and on the biographies of the compilers. We have also had very considerable help from Thomas Woodcock's research assistant, the Hon. Janet Grant, and from Alan Sykes, who joined the team for a time in 1983 after graduating from University College, London.

As soon as the data began to come back from Cambridge it was stored on magnetic tape at the Institute of Archaeology and Mr Woodcock and I, who were entirely unfamiliar with computers, were given some basic instruction by Dr Graham and his invaluable assistant Dr Jonathan Moffett, which enabled us to edit the data on screen. A small computer was bought for our use in the summer of 1981 and installed at the Institute and a second in 1982 for use by Thomas Woodcock and Janet Grant at the College of Arms, so that work could proceed more rapidly.

It soon became necessary to embark on a long programme of editorial discussions in order to achieve consistency in our editing. It was agreed at an early stage to retain corrupt spellings, blazons and sources rather than select only the earliest or 'best' source for each coat. There may well be occasions when the inclusion of a corrupt or secondary source can prove helpful in tracing the origins of a later coat of doubtful authenticity, and as almost every source is given, the experienced armorist will be able to decide for himself which are the most reliable.

A number of problems came to light as the editing progressed. For instance, the handwriting on some of the index cards was almost illegible and the compilers had not all been consistent in the way they blazoned the arms and recorded the sources. Thus the editors had to examine every single card to ensure that the details had been keyed into the computer correctly. Even then there were many instances where we would have liked to consult the original source, but this would simply have been too time-consuming. As it was, the preliminary editing took at least an hour for every thirty cards.

Another problem, already mentioned, was the lack of precise knowledge of the sources covered by the dictionary, as the cards were not always explicit. In this connection it was discovered that a good many ordinary cards (e.g. those for Wriothesley's Chevrons and other ordinaries) were still in bundles at Burlington House and had never been fed into the index. It was hoped to devise a programme whereby these could be sorted in by the computer, but this was not possible and they had to be placed manually. There are doubtless other blazons which have become misplaced as a result of the removal of the cards from place to place.

Further laborious tasks proved necessary, such as the alphabetization of surnames within each entry, where special computer programs had to be written in consultation with the editors, and we suffered from computer failures, a shortage of terminals, delays while material was transferred from one system to another, and other setbacks which slowed down the rate of editing. The preliminary round of editing was at last completed by the end of February 1984, but it had produced so many queries that a further, and even more comprehensive, round of editing was called for and embarked on. A deadline was eventually imposed by the imminent departure at the end of 1985 of Ian Graham for a post at the University of Waikato, New Zealand. Janet Grant and Alan Sykes spent long hours at their computer terminals in order to complete the editorial operation and William Hunt somehow found time to finish the lists of sources and abbreviations, with valuable help from Michael Holmes of the Victoria and Albert Museum. Most of the original typesetting program was undertaken at the Institute of Archaeology by Dr Graham himself after urgent discussions with the editors and with Sarah Macready of the Society of Antiquaries, but unforeseen problems arose after Dr Graham's departure. These were tackled by Dr Moffett and his colleague Ian Morton who joined the Institute as computer adviser in 1985 and we are most grateful to them for their help at that time and to the Oxford University Computing Service for typesetting the early proofs. However further difficulties arose and Dr Graham agreed to resume his role as technical editor in order to achieve the completion of the first volume.

The preparation of the remaining volumes still lies ahead but the task will be easier now that the first instalment has at length appeared. Having been fashioned by so many hands over so long a period the final product will be far from perfect, but it will nevertheless fill an important gap in the literature of heraldry.

D.H.B. CHESSHYRE
Chester Herald

Structure of the Ordinary

In a codicil to his will dated 5 January 1926 and proved in the same year Lieutenant-Colonel G.B. Croft Lyons wrote: 'I wish that a new edition of Papworth's Ordinary should be prepared . . . . And that in order that such Edition can be generally useful I desire that the blazon of the Arms in such new Edition shall follow the style of blazon in the present Edition and that the new forms affected in recent years by certain writers be not adopted but that the blazon be full and exact and such that any person can as far as may be understand it.'

Papworth's *Ordinary of British Armorials* was published in 1874 and was the work of two men, John Woody Papworth (1820–70), who edited the first 696 pages, and Alfred William Morant (1828–81), who edited the remaining 429 pages from material left by Papworth.

The initial key to the structure of the present work is Papworth's Introduction to his Ordinary in which he states: 'The Plan of the Work is simply thus: the arms are blazoned (i.e. technically described) and are arranged in alphabetical order by the names of such of the respective charges as are first mentioned in the blazon; so that the inquirer has but to blazon the coat, and the first charge that he names shows under what title in this Dictionary the coat is to be sought . . . some of the charges, such as the ordinaries and others much in use, form heads so comprehensive, that several divisions and subdivisions became indispensable: there it will be seen that further alphabetical arrangements have been observed . . . . This part of the plan will be best learned by inspection.' As Papworth suggested, the best method of understanding the structure of his Ordinary is by inspecting it and this applies to the present Ordinary.

The achievement of Papworth as compared to other compilers of Ordinaries was that he saw the necessity of exact order in the entries. He devised a mode of classification that could extend from the simplest to the most elaborate coats where each had one and only one correct position controlled by the blazon. As the blazon controls the structure there are cases where an ambiguous coat in Papworth occurs more than once blazoned differently.

Papworth's underlying principle is that charges are to be considered in their degree of remoteness from the field or the centre of it. It is also the basis of this Ordinary, though here an exact position is controlled more by linear appearance than in Papworth's Ordinary, where the colour of the field and of the charge determine position within a larger general group.

Papworth gives a few references to sources where these are Rolls of Arms. Other nineteenth-century and earlier Ordinaries give no sources. The present work is devised to lead the user to the original source and a source is given for almost every entry. Any work compiled out of a card index of over 100,000 cards written by many hands over fifty years may contain errors. By the quotation of the original source an error should be discoverable by the user.

An inspection of Papworth shows that Papworth and Morant differed. As already mentioned Papworth placed too much emphasis on colour rather than linear appearance. Papworth has sixty-nine columns of One Lion coats placing together all possible varieties, rampant and passant, statant and couchant, guardant and reguardant, crowned and gorged, charged and uncharged, and worst of all – those which are surmounted by a bend or fess or other charge over all. The contrast between Papworth and Morant can be seen by comparing the subdivision under Bend or Chevron with the more elaborate subdivision under for example Saltire. The present Ordinary has developed from Morant's scheme and, for instance, divides Lions as follows, commencing with the Lion rampant for which the word Lion alone is used:–

(one)   lion no tinctures
       plain field lion plain (i.e. plain as opposed to patterned or charged)
       patterned field lion plain
       lion patterned or charged, fields various, (the lions are categorized by the pattern or charge on them and placed in sequence within each category according to the field)
       lion vulned
       lion coward
       lion dismembered
       lion in umbre
       lion collared
       lion crowned no tinctures
       plain field crowned lion plain
       patterned field crowned lion plain
       patterned lion crowned
       lion crowned and vulned
       lion crowned and collared
       lion queue fourchy or crossed no tinctures
       plain field lion queue fourchy plain
       patterned field lion queue fourchy plain
       lion queue fourchy patterned
       lion queue fourchy vulned
       lion queue fourchy collared
       lion queue fourchy crowned
       lion tail knotted
       lion queue fourchy and knotted
       lion queue fourchy and knotted and crowned
(all up to this point are rampant)
       lion couchant
       lion dormant
       lion passant no tinctures
       plain field lion passant plain

patterned field lion passant plain
lion passant patterned or charged
lion passant collared
lion salient
lion sejant
lion statant
lion rampant guardant no tinctures
plain field lion rampant guardant plain
patterned field lion rampant guardant plain
lion rampant guardant patterned
lion rampant guardant collared
lion rampant guardant crowned
lion rampant guardant queue fourchy
lion rampant guardant queue fourchy crowned
lion passant guardant no tinctures
plain field lion passant guardant plain
patterned field lion passant guardant plain
lion passant guardant patterned or charged fields various (as above
    under lion patterned or charged)
lion passant guardant collared
lion passant guardant crowned
lion salient guardant
lion sejant guardant
lion statant guardant
lion regardant
lion winged
lion with two heads
lion bicorporate
lion tricorporate
lion dimidiating ship
lion holding axe
lion holding other objects
lion pierced by

The above is the overall scheme of subdivision of one lion without another charge or ordinary which is represented in Papworth by pages 62–96. It will be seen that in the present scheme linear divisions take precedence over colour whereas in Papworth *Or a lion passant Vert* is followed by *Or a lion rampant Vert*. Entries are grouped under headings according to the pattern or charges on the lion and then arranged in sequence within each group according to the field.

Unlike Papworth the present Ordinary places the lion at the head of the beasts and follows with one beast other than lion with these latter beasts in alphabetical order whereas Papworth inserts the lion between the leopard and the otter. Like Papworth demi-beasts are placed immediately before a complete beast in each category.

The position of the lion follows an alphabetical sequence with the exception that lions rampant as the most numerous are dealt with before the less frequent lions couchant, passant, salient and statant, which follow in that order. There is one other exception which is that lions guardant, that is with the head turned towards and looking out at the spectator, have been treated as a separate group whether rampant, passant or in some other position. Lions guardant follow lions statant and are subdivided into rampant guardant, passant guardant, and then salient, sejant and statant guardant. Lions reguardant, that is with their heads turned to look back over their shoulder, follow lions guardant.

The English system of cadency marks is thought to have been invented by John Writhe, Garter King of Arms, in about 1500. After 1500 a label in non Royal heraldry denotes an eldest son in the life time of his father. Before 1500 the label did not necessarily indicate this and there are many instances of arms differenced by a label. One beast and a label follows one beast without a label so that all single beasts with a label are grouped together. In a more complicated section such as beast & in chief, the lions & in chief are followed by other beasts & in chief and then all beasts & in chief & label are listed, first the lions then other beasts. Other cadency marks such as crescents and mullets are dealt with according to their position on the shield. A lion charged with a crescent appears under lion patterned or charged and if the crescent is above the lion it is listed under lion & in chief.

The purpose of an Ordinary of Arms is to identify a shield. In many cases, such as a seal or monument, no tinctures are available and for this reason the linear emphasis has been stressed so that this resembles a pictorial Ordinary in arrangement where lions in one position are placed together irrespective of tincture and untinctured examples come at the beginning of each section of coats of a similar linear appearance.

An example of the division in another part of the Ordinary can be seen with chevrons, where a coat with both field and chevron untinctured, as on a seal, is followed by coats with fields of a plain colour or metal and a plain chevron, such as *Argent a Chevron Gules*. Patterned fields (e.g. checky or ermine) with untinctured or plain chevrons follow. Finally, there are patterned chevrons arranged within each subdivision of pattern according to the field, with untinctured followed by plain and patterned fields.

The blazon follows that used by Papworth and is 'full and exact', as required by Croft Lyons. There is a problem of meanings shifting. For example what in the fourteenth century would be called a fess indented might today be blazoned five fusils conjoined in fess. The compilers of the cards were instructed to use an unambiguous modern blazon applicable to the drawing of the Arms and the Ordinary must be used with this in mind, though occasionally compilers did not follow instructions.

Surnames are reproduced exactly as they occur in the original source, even if scarcely intelligible or erroneous, as some errors later led to unwarranted use of arms. In this the Ordinary follows Papworth. The nominal index attempts to catch all variant spellings of a name so that nothing should be lost by repetition of medieval errors, or different forms of the same name such as De Alta Ripa, Dealtry, Dawtrey and Hawtrey.

The Index of Headings and the text contain three sizes of heading. Three degrees of heading were imposed in the interests of simplicity, though there are occasions when a hierarchy of four or more would have been preferable. For instance the heading *Argent billetty 1 lion* should be subordinate to *Billetty 1 lion* but both are of the same size as are cross references (e.g: leopard: see lion passt gard). As far as the structure of individual entries is concerned the blazon is followed by the surname and then by Christian or other names and/or a place of residence. Next comes the source. Editorial comment follows in round brackets and square brackets are used for other material such as speculative attributions, identifications or tinctures. Many abbreviations are used and reference should be made to the list of them.

Many people have worked on the Ordinary, though none for as long as Sir Anthony Wagner. His influence is as important on the structure as in other areas and reference should be made to his articles in *Antiquaries Journal* 21 (1941), 299–322 and 23 (1943), 42–47 and to a progress report written for contributors dated 26 February 1948. These show the development of the structure, though some modifications have been made since 1948. Like Papworth's Ordinary, it is best mastered by inspection and use.

T. WOODCOCK
Somerset Herald

Compilers

By way of acknowledgement of the work of all those who wrote the index cards for the Dictionary, we include brief biographical notes, compiled from reference books, obituaries or personal knowledge. Unfortunately, so long after the groundwork has been completed, it has not been possible in some cases to discover more than the compiler's name. The biographies have been kept as short as possible, but nevertheless contain a career summary and an indication of the journals or publications from which further information might be obtained.

GHA Askew, Gilbert Horden, F.S.A. (1893–1950) of Potters Bar, formed the Enfield Chase Archaeological Society with AM, CRG and COM to compile details of monuments in the churches of Middlesex and Hertfordshire. One-time Keeper of Coins and member of the Council of the Society of Antiquaries of Newcastle-upon-Tyne, he contributed papers to *Archaeologia Aeliana* (an important one on Northumbrian pipes) and *The Numismatic Chronicle*.

MA Ayearst, Dr Morley, Professor of Government and Chairman of the Department of Government and International Relations, Washington Square College, New York University.

FA Ayling, Frederick (1896–1965) of Lee, London, genealogical researcher at the College of Arms, compiled HMC Dorset.

EPB Baker, Revd Eric Paul, M.A. F.S.A. (1906–82), Vicar of Great Milton, Oxfordshire, published a number of papers on English and Continental iconography and ecclesiology, and bequeathed to the Society of Antiquaries his small working library and a fund for the benefit of the Morris Committee.

ENB Baynes, Edward Neil, F.S.A. (1861–1951) excavated the Din Lligwy site in Anglesey, was co-founder of the Anglesey Antiquarian Society, served on the Council of the Cambrian Archaeological Association and the Society of Antiquaries, and was an original member of the Ancient Monument Board for Wales.

RNB Bloxam, R.N., of Warneford, Oxfordshire.

JWPB Bourke, Dr John William Patrick, O.B.E. M.A. D.Phil. (1909–), English Lector, Munich University, author of *Baroque Churches of Central Europe* (1958) and other works including one on English humour.

AB Bracegirdle, A., of Great Casterton, near Stamford, Lincolnshire, supplied details of monuments in the churches of Rutland.

HLB-L   Bradfer-Lawrence, Harry Lawrence, F.S.A. (1887–1965) was a chartered land agent first in Norfolk and then in Yorkshire, where he also became Managing Director of Hammond's Bradford Brewery and ultimately Chairman of United Breweries Limited; he had a great collection of charters, seals and books, and did much for the finances of the Society of Antiquaries, of which he was Treasurer from 1944 to 1964.

AEB   Bradshaw, Alfred E., admitted as a solicitor in 1921 and practised in Blackpool.

EAB   Bullmore, Edward Augustus, F.R.C.S. L.R.C.P. F.S.A. (1875–1948) of Wisbech.

GHB   Burdon, George H., of Darlington.

HDB   Butchart, Hugh Duncan, F.S.A. (1883–1975) of Watlington, Oxfordshire.

WAC   Caffall, William A. (1883–1964), genealogist and archivist at the College of Arms for over 60 years.

DHAC-M   Christie-Murray, Revd David Hugh Arthur, M.A., became a master at Harrow School, having been Rochester Diocesan Youth Organiser and Command Chaplain ATC (SE Area) in Gravesend; author of *Heraldry in the Churches of Beckenham*(1954), *Arms of Schools* (1956); has made interesting contributions to psychical research.

AWC   Clapham, Sir Alfred William, Kt. C.B.E. F.S.A. (1883–1950) served as Secretary and Commissioner of the Royal Commission on Historical Monuments for England, Secretary and President of the Society of Antiquaries, President of the Royal Archaeological Institute and Trustee of the London Museum; author of *Lesnes Abbey* (1916), *Beeleigh Abbey* (1922), *English Romanesque Architecture* (1930 & 1934), *European Romanesque Architecture* (1936).

ACC   Cole, Sir (Alexander) Colin, K.C.V.O. O.St.J. T.D. B.C.L. M.A. F.H.S. F.R.S.A. F.S.A. (1922–), Garter Principal King of Arms, one-time Sheriff of the City of London and a founder member of The Heraldry Society.

AdeCC   Cussans, Anthony de C., M.A. (1924 –) compiled details of monuments in some Cornish churches when evacuated there at school in World War II.

TRD   Davies, Major Thomas R., T.D. F.H.S., (d.1980), 1st Northamptonshire Yeomanry, of Bebington, Wirral; he had an extensive knowledge of the origins and development of English and European heraldry and was a regular contributor to *The Coat of Arms*; past president of the Royal Engineers Association and contributor to its journal, *Sapper*.

FND   Davis, Revd Francis Neville, M.A. D.Litt. F.R.Hist.S. F.S.A., joint editor *Rotuli H de Welles, Bp of Lincoln* (1909); editor *Rotuli R Grosseteste* (1913), *Rotuli R Gravesend* (1920), *Oxfordshire Collections of Wood and Rawlinson* (1920), *Portsmouth Diocesan Calendar* (1928–37); general editor

	Canterbury and York Society (1906–26), *Oxford Record Society* (1919–22), *Proceedings of the Hampshire Field Club* (1928–38).
EED	Dorling, Revd Edward Earle, M.A. F.S.A. (1862–1943), Commissioner of the Royal Commission on Historical Monuments for England, Vice-President of the Society of Antiquaries, Clerk of Epsom Racecourse, heraldic artist for *Victoria County History*; author of *Leopards of England, Heraldry of the Church*.
LD	Dow, Leslie, F.S.A. (1899–1979) read medicine and economics at Cambridge, President of the Suffolk Institute of Archaeology and editor of its *Proceedings* for 22 years; published many notes and papers on Suffolk churches and genealogy.
EME	Elmhirst, Edward Mars "Toby", T.D. M.B. M.S. F.R.C.S. L.R.C.P. (1915–57), né Elmhirst-Baxter, brain surgeon of Ipswich who spent many years abroad with the RAMC and became Surgeon to the Bermudas; a great collector, he wrote articles on daguerreotypes, mourning rings, merchant marks and babies' feeding bottles.
PF	Field, Miss Pamela, of Thornton Cleveleys, Lancashire, assisted H.E.T.
DLG	Galbreath, Donald Lindsay, D.D.S. Hon.F.S.A. (1884–1949), an American who became a Swiss national and practised dentistry in Montreux, President of the Swiss Heraldic Society and a great authority and writer on European heraldry.
CRG	Goodchild, C.R., of north London, assisted GHA with the monumental heraldry of Middlesex and Hertfordshire churches.
DWG	Gurney, Daniel W., M.C., (d.1950s), retired diplomat of Norfolk.
JHH	Harvey, Dr John Hooper, F.R.S.L. F.S.G. F.S.A. (1911 –), a member of the Council of the Ancient Monuments Society for over 20 years and its leading authority on medieval art and architecture; many architectural, topographical and botanical publications.
VH	Heddon, Mrs V., of Iver, Bucks, Assistant Librarian at the Admiralty.
WJH	Hemp, Wilfrid James, M.A. (hon causa) F.S.A. (1882–1962), Secretary of the Royal Commission on Ancient Monuments in Wales and Monmouthshire, founder member of the Council for the Preservation for Rural Wales; an authority on megalithic chambered tombs, not only in Wales but also in the rest of Britain and in the West Mediterranean, particularly the Balearic Islands, he wrote many articles on megalithic monuments, the prehistory of Wales and medieval studies.
CJH	Holyoake, Cedric Jennings, C.Eng. M.I.Mech.E. M.I.Mar.E. F.H.S. F.S.A. (1914 –), of Hornchurch, Essex, author of

	Heraldic Notes on the Great Britain's Issue of Postage Stamps (1976), co-author *English Heraldic Embroidery & Textiles at the Victoria & Albert Museum* (1976), particularly interested in British and continental medieval rolls of arms.
CH	Hordern, Lt. Col. Charles, R.E. (1880 –) of Kendal.
CRH-S	Humphery-Smith, Cecil Raymond, B.Sc. F.H.S. F.S.G. F.S.A. (1928 –), Director and Principal of The Insitute of Heraldic and Genealogical Studies.
WHH	Humphreys, William Herbert, M.A. LL.B. F.S.A. (*c*1884 – 1960)
CHH-B	Hunter-Blair, Charles Henry, M.A. D.Litt. F.S.A. (1863 – 1962), wholesale boot and shoe merchant of Newcastle upon Tyne, where he was President of the Literary and Philosophical Society for 42 years, Chairman of the Diocesan Advisory Committee, member of the University Senate and Excavation Committee, editor of *Archaeologia Aeliana* 1924–61; an authority on Northumberland and Durham seals, he sought to bring to life the history of the North Country and the importance of its great families.
IRH	Huntley, Ivan Roy (1907–72) of South Nutfield, Surrey, for many years Chairman of the Library Committee of The Heraldry Society and an authority on continental heraldry and heraldic bibliography.
GRH	Hutton, G.R., A.R.I.B.A. P.A.S.I., County Architect, Oxfordshire County Council
WPJ	Jeffcock, W.P., of Woodbridge, Suffolk
TEJ	Johnston, T.E., F.S.A. (d.1957), Official Solicitor, Ministry of Town and Country Planning, Ulster.
EMVJ	Jones, Miss Elizabeth M.V., teacher, of Edinburgh, Broughton-in-Furness and Sheffield, recorded some monumental heraldry in those places.
EJJ	Jones, Emeritus Professor Evan John, M.A. D.Litt. d.1977, Department of Education, University College, Swansea, edited and published *Medieval Heraldry* in 1943.
CAK	Kirke, Cecil A., of Milton Clevedon, Somerset.
EAGL	Lamborn, E.A. Greening, of Oxford, schoolmaster, compiled notes on monumental heraldry in Oxfordshire churches and published *Heraldic Stained Glass of Diocese of Oxford*.
HSL	London, Hugh Stanford, M.A. F.S.A. (1884–1979), diplomat, Norfolk Herald Extraordinary, served on the Croft Lyons Committee of the Society of Antiquaries from 1941 to his death; an authority on medieval heraldry in particular, he transcribed over a hundred rolls of arms and wrote more than 10,000 cards for this ordinary; wrote *The Queen's Beasts* (1953), *Royal Beasts* (1956), contributed to many journals.
JCOM	Mack, Col. J.C.O. of Worcester College, Oxford.
JM	MacLeod, John, searcher of records, of Edinburgh.

AM   Manchester, Albert, assisted GHA with monumental heraldry of Herts and Middx.

COM   Marriner, C. Owen, of St John's Wood, London, assisted GHA with monumental heraldry of Hendon.

AWBM   Messenger, Paymaster Commander Arthur William Bryant, R.N. L.R.I.B.A. F.H.S. F.S.A. (1879–1970) of Bideford, Devon; author of *Heraldry of Canterbury Cathedral* (1947).

BRKM   Moilliet, Revd Bernard Rambold Keir, M.A. (c1877–1956) of Wareham, Dorset, brother of HMKM; author of *Pilotage and Navigation* (1948).

HMKM   Moilliet, Capt. H.M.K. O.B.E. R.I.N. of Lympstone, Devon, brother of BRKM.

RABM   Mynors, Prof Sir Roger Aubrey Baskerville, Hon.D.Litt. Hon. Litt.D. F.B.A. F.S.A. (1903 – 1989) of Balliol College, Oxford, Pembroke College, Cambridge and subsequently Corpus Christi College, Oxford; publications include *Durham Cathedral MSS before 1200* (1939), *Catalogue of Balliol MSS* (1963) and many Latin subjects.

JGN   Noppen, John George, F.S.A. (1887–1951) devoted himself to the study of Westminster Abbey and particularly to the problems of its rebuilding by Henry III; member of the Royal Archaeological Institute, on the Committee of the Society for the Protection of Ancient Buildings; author of *Westminster Abbey and its Ancient Art* (1926), *A Guide to the Medieval Art of Westminster Abbey*.

JLP   Peel, John Linley, L.D.S., dental surgeon of Halifax

EWP   Playfair, Sir Edward Wilder, K.C.B. Hon.F.B.C.S. (1909 –) of Chelsea, London, sometime Permanent Secretary, Ministry of Defence, Chairman, National Gallery, Governor, Imperial College of Science & Technology, director of ICL, National Westminster Bank, Glaxo, Tunnel Holdings, Equity & Law.

GWP   Potter, Gilbert Winter, F.H.S. (1915–83), of Gants Hill, Essex, member of the Council of The Heraldry Society for over 20 years, its programme secretary and a lecturer in heraldry.

LP   Powell, Miss Lyn, of Mold, Clwyd.

SWR   Rawlins, Mrs Sophia Wyndham, F.S.A., of Yeovil.

NVLR   Rybot, Major Norman Victor Lacey, D.S.O. F.S.A. (d.1961), of Jersey, Secretary, Société Jersiaise, author of *Heraldry in the Channel Islands* (1928)

TUS   Sadleir, Thomas Ulick, M.A. M.R.I.A., (d.1958), barrister, of Dublin, Deputy Ulster King of Arms to Wilkinson.

CWS-G   Scott-Giles, Charles Wilfrid, O.B.E. M.A. F.H.S. F.S.A. (1893–1982) of Cambridge, Fitzalan Pursuivant Extraordinary, journalist and sometime Chairman of the Parliamentary Press Gallery, founder member of The Heraldry Society, prolific and popular heraldic author who illustrated all his own works.

CJS   Smith, Christopher J., of Cheylesmore, Coventry.

PSS   Spokes, Peter Spencer, B.Sc. M.A. F.S.A., (d.1976), of Oxford
       University, sometime Mayor of Oxford, Chairman, Berkshire
       Archaeological Society, published *Coats of Arms in Berkshire
       Churches* (1939).

GDS   Squibb, George Drewry, L.V.O. Q.C. B.C.L. M.A. J.P.
       F.S.G. F.R.Hist.S. F.S.A. (1906 –), Norfolk Herald Extra-
       ordinary, sometime Chairman, Dorset Quarter Sessions, Hon
       Historical Adviser in Peerage Cases to the Attorney-General;
       publications on legal and antiquarian matters, particularly in
       connection with the Court of Chivalry.

JVS   Stephenson, J.V., of Hove.

EJS   Stuart, Mrs E.J., helped GHA with monumental heraldry of
       Chiswick.

DT   Thomas, Dorothy, (d.1982), assisted HSL and TDT.

BRT   Thompson, Miss Beryl R.

HET   Tomlinson, Harold Ellis, M.A. Ph.D. F.H.S. (1915 –), school-
       master and heraldic designer of Thornton Cleveleys,
       Lancashire; over 500 designs approved by the College of Arms
       and the Court of the Lord Lyon since 1939; publications on
       British civic and corporate heraldry.

TDT   Tremlett, Thomas Daniel, M.A. F.S.A. (1906–72), head of
       Modern Subjects Department, RMA Sandhurst, formerly
       Senior History Master, King's School Bruton, Somerset;
       Assistant Secretary, Society of Antiquaries; palaeographer and
       sigillographer, he recatalogued the heraldic seals in the Public
       Record Office in the course of his work on this ordinary.

AV   Veitch, Andrew, F.S.A. (1887–1970) of Ackworth, near
       Pontefract.

AWV-N Vivian-Neal, Arthur Westall, M.C. D.L. M.A. J.P. F.S.A.
       (1893–1962) of Poundisford Park, Taunton, sometime High
       Sheriff of Somerset whose greatest interests, apart from
       records were mental health and juvenile delinquency; Chair-
       man of the Somerset County Records Committee, Somerset
       Archaeological Society, Somerset Record Society, *Somerset
       and Dorset Notes and Queries*; articles on architecture,
       genealogy, heraldry, manorial history.

ARW   Wagner, Sir Anthony Richard, K.C.B. K.C.V.O. M.A.
       D.Litt. F.S.A. (1908–) of Chelsea and Aldeburgh, Clarenceux
       King of Arms formerly Garter King of Arms and holder of
       many offices connected with heraldry, genealogy and historic
       buildings; appointed editor of this Dictionary in 1940; prolific
       author of heraldic and genealogical works.

GDW   Walton, Miss Grace Dalzell (1895–1989), of Pinner, worked at
       the College of Arms as a secretary and genealogist from 1928–
       75.

JBW   Whitmore, John Beach, T.D. B.A. F.S.G. F.S.A. (1882–
       1957), solicitor of Earls Court, London; compiler, *A Genealo-
       gical Guide* (1953), joint editor, *Record of Old Westminsters*.

Sources

Alphabetically by abbreviation

The list of sources includes only those referred to in this volume. At the end of each entry, the initials of the person who compiled the index cards are given in brackets, where known. Comprehensive records of the sources and compilers were not maintained, and it has not always been possible to give full particulars.

A
Dering Roll, *c*1275
Aldermaston
Aldermaston Deeds [D/ERW.T.1 in Berks CRO]
AN
Antiquaries Roll, *c*1360
Ancestor
Ancestor, Archibald Constable – London, 1902–5 [12 vols] (JGN)
Anstis Asp
Anstis Aspilogia I [1–229] (TDT)
Antiq Journ
Antiquaries Journal, Soc. Antiq.– London, 1921– (JGN)
Arch
Archaeologia, Soc.Antiq.–London, 1779–1933 [vols 1–83] (EPB)
Arch Ael
Archaeologia Aeliana, Soc. Antiq. of Newcastle-upon-Tyne, 1822– (EPB)
Arch Cant
Archaeologia Cantiana, Kent Arch. Soc. – Maidstone, 1858–
Arch Journ
Archaeological Journal, Royal Arch. Inst of GB & Ireland – London, 1845– (HSL)
AS
Ashmolean Roll, *c*1334 (PSS HSL BRKM)
Ash-sls
Seal Matrices in the Ashmolean Museum (TDT)
AY
Ayearst's Roll, 1495 (MA)
AylesburyM-sls
Aylesbury Museum seals (BRT)

B
Glover's Roll, transcr AR Wagner, *c*1255–8 [versions IA, II, III, IV] (BRKM FND)
BA
Ballard's Book, *c*1465–90 [part of Coll Arm MS M3] (HSL BRKM)
Bain
Calendar of Documents relating to Scotland, ed J. Bain, Edinburgh, 1881 &c [only those coats included in HB-SND] (WHH)
Baker Northants
History & Antiquities of the County of Northampton, G. Baker, J.B. Nichols – London, 1822–30 1836–41 [2 vols]
Baker-sls
Seals in the Baker Collection (TDT)
Balliol
Charters & other documents at Balliol College Oxford [only those coats included in HB–SND] (WHH)
Barons Letter
Barons' Letter to the Pope, Ancestor vi-viii, 1301 (JLP)
BarronMS
Loose-leaf Armory of 23 Rolls of Arms, O. Barron [Antiquaries', Boroughbridge, Caerlaverock, Camden, Charles, Dering, 1st Dunstable, 2nd Dunstable, Falkirk, Fitzwilliam, Glover, Grimaldi, Guillim, Harleian, Heralds', Holland, Matthew Paris, Nativity, Parliamentary, St George's, Segar, Walford, Willement] (HET WHH)
Batt
Wiltshire [Revd R. St J. Battersby's MS] (JGN)

BB
   Bruge's Garter Book, *c*1430 (HMKM)
BD
   Book of Draughts, Dugdale–Hatton
   [also called Book of Monuments]
   (BRKM from HSL transcription)
Belcher
   Kentish Brasses, W.D. Belcher, Sprague
   – London, 1888 & 1905 [2 vols]
Bellasis
   Westmorland Church Notes, E. Bellasis,
   T. Wilson – Kendal, 1888–9 [2 vols]
   (CH)
Belvoir
   Deeds at Belvoir Castle, transcr.
   H.H.E. Craster [only those coats
   included in HB-SND] (WHH)
Berks Arch Journ
   *Journal of the Berkshire Archaeological
   Society* (EPB)
BerksCRO–sls
   Berks. Co. Record Office seals (TDT)
Berry
   Armorial de Berry, *c*1445 [Scottish
   Coats therein as published in Stodart's
   Scottish Arms] (AV)
BG
   Basynge's Book, *c*1395 (BRKM)
BGAS
   *Bristol & Gloucestershire
   Archaeological Society Transactions*,
   Bristol & Gloucs Arch Soc – Gloucester,
   1876– (EPB)
Birch
   British Museum Seals, ed. W. de Gray
   Birch, British Museum – London, 1887–
   1900 [6 vols, collated with notes by O.
   Barron, W.H. St. John Hope & H.S.
   Kingsford] (TDT CAK JGN)
BirmCL–sls
   Birmingham Central Library seals [incl.
   Areley Hall, Hagley Hall, Henley Ct]
   (EPB)
BK
   Book of Badges, Sir Christopher Barker,
   ed. T.W. Willement, Coll.T&G III 49–
   76 in 1836, 1522–34 [Harl MS 4632
   ff209–25] (HSL)
Bk of Sls
   Book of Seals, Sir Christopher Hatton,
   ed. L.C. Loyd & D.M. Stenton,
   Clarendon Press – Oxford, 1950 (IRH)
BL
   Balliol Roll A, 1332 (JVS)
Blair D
   Monuments in County Durham, ed.
   C.H. Hunter-Blair, Newcastle-upon-
   Tyne Records Committee, 1925 [from

Coll Arm MS C41] (GHB JCOM)
Blair N
   Northumbrian Monuments, ed. C.H.
   Hunter-Blair, Newcastle-upon-Tyne
   Records Committee, 1924 [includes part
   of Coll. Arm.MS C41] (GHB)
Bow
   Bowditch MS [17 cent sketches of
   medieval sls] (TDT)
Bowes
   Charters & Deeds of the Bowes Family
   [formerly at Streatlam, copy with
   Northd County History Committee, only
   those coats included in HB-SND]
   (WHH)
Bowles
   Annals of Lacock Abbey, W.L. Bowles,
   1835
BR
   Bradfer-Lawrence's Roll, 1445–6
   (TRD)
Brand
   History of Newcastle-upon-Tyne, J.
   Brand, White & Egerton – London,
   1789 [2 vols, only those coats included in
   HB-SND] (WHH)
Bridgwater
   'Bridgwater Borough Archives Seals
   pre. 1550', transcr. T. Bruce Dilks,
   Somerset Record Society 48 & 53 (TDT)
Brindley &W
   Ancient Sepulchral Monuments, W.
   Brindley & W.S. Weatherley, Brooks
   Day & Son – London, 1887
Brit Arch Assoc
   *Journal of the British Archaeological
   Association*, BAA – London, 1846–
   (HSL)
Brooke Asp
   Coll. Arm.MS Aspilogia, J.C. Brooke,
   18 cent (TDT)
Brumell
   Brumell Collection of Charters in Black
   Gate Library [only those coats included
   in HB-SND] (WHH)
Brymore
   Brymore MSS Seal Catalogue pre. 1550,
   T. Bruce Dilks [At Bridgwater, Som]
   (TDT)
BS
   Bruce Roll, *c*1370 (JVS)
BTN
   Coll. Arm.MS B29 Sundries
Burrows
   *Family of Brocas of Beaurepair & Roche
   Court*, M. Burrows, Longman Green, 1886
Burton Agnes
   Burton Agnes Deeds [only those coats

included in HB-SND] (WHH)

BW
Bowyer's Book, c1440 (JLP)

C
Walford's Roll, c1275 [versions I & II]
(CJH)

C2
Visitation of Surrey 1623, Coll. Arm.MS
(WAC HSL)

C3
Visitation of Huntingdonshire 1613,
Coll. Arm.MS (WAC HSL)

CA
Carlisle Roll, 1334 [from transcript by O
Barron and SM Collins] (BRKM FND)

C&WAAS
*Cumberland & Westmorland
Antiquarian & Archaeological Society
Transactions*, Kendal, 1874–

CassPk
Cassiobury Park, Hist.MSS Commission
VII – London (HSL)

CB
Collingborne's Book, c1490 (BRKM
HSL)

CC
Colour on Colour Roll, c1450 [Coll.
Arm.MS Vinc 164 ff222–237b also
known as Domville Roll Copy A] (HSL)

CG
Cotgrave's Ordinary, 1340 [O. Barron's
copy collated with Harris Nicolas edn.]
(FND)

ChesMont
Cheshire Monumental Heraldry [Acton
nr. Nantwich, Backford, Bunbury,
Burton, Chester (Cathedral, Holy
Trinity – Watergate, St John's Old
Cathedral, St Mary-on-the-Hill, St
Peter), Davenham (St Wilfrid),
Eccleston, Farndon, Gt Budworth,
Malpas, Nantwich (St Mary), Neston,
Northwich (St Helen – Witton),
Plemstall, Tarvin, Upton, Waverton]
(HET)

Chron Usk
Chronicon Adae de Usk, ed. E. Maunde
Thompson, Royal Soc of Literature –
London, 1904 (HSL)

CK
Cooke's Book, temp Edw II [Coll Arm
MS Vinc 164 ff22–24b] (FND)

CKO
Cooke's Ordinary, c1340 (TDT)

Clairambault
*Inventaire des Sceaux de la Collection
Clairambault à la Bibliothèque*

Nationale, G. Demay, Paris, 1885 [2
vols, Engl sls therein] (DLG)

Cleeve
Tiles from Cleeve Abbey [now at
Poundisford Park, Somerset] (AWVN)

Clifton
*Proceedings of the Clifton Antiquarian
Club* (EPB)

CN
Clarence Roll, temp Hen 6 (JVS CJH)

Coll T&G
*Collectanea Topographica et
Genealogica*, ed. J.B. Nichols, Nichols –
London, 1834–43 [8 vols]

CombeAsp
Charles Combe's MS Aspilogia, 19 cent
[in possession of H.L. Bradfer-
Lawrence] (TDT)

CR
Clare Roll, 1456 (HSL)

CRK
Creswick's Roll, c1510 [also known as
Creswick's Book II] (BRKM)

CT
Cottonian Roll, 15 cent (BRKM)

CV-BM
Calveley's Book – Becket's Murderers'
Roll, c1350 (BRKM)

CVC
Calveley's Book 3 – Cheshire Roll, 15
cent (BRKM)

CVK
Calveley's Book 4 – Kent Roll, 13 & 14
cent (BRKM)

CVL
Calveley's Book 2 – Lancashire Roll,
temp Hen. IV (BRKM)

CVM
Calveley's Book 5 – Miscellanea
(BRKM)

CY
County Roll, temp Ric 2 [Soc. Antiq.MS
664 iv 1–22 Roll 16] (HSL)

D
Camden Roll, c1280

D4
Visitation of the North 1530, Coll.
Arm.MS (EME)

D5
Visitation of Yorks 1563, Coll. Arm.MS
[includes some arms extinct before Vis]

D9
Visitation of the North 1530, Coll.
Arm.MS (EME)

D13
Visitation of Sussex Kent Surrey

SOURCES

Hampshire Somerset 1531, Coll.
Arm.MS (WAC)

D'Anisy
Chartes Normands, A.L. Lechaude
d'Anisy, Caen, 1834

DerbysAS
*Journal of the Derbyshire Archaeological
& Natural History Society*, Derbys
A&NHS – Derby, 1879

Devon NQ
Devon Notes & Queries, vols 1–12,
Exeter, 1901 (HMKM HSL)

DIG
Irish Gatherings, W. Darell, 1566 [Coll
Arm MS B22] (HMKM)

Dingley
History from Marble, T. Dingley,
Camden Soc – London in 1867–8, temp.
Chas II (AWBM)

Dodworth
Dodsworth MSS [only those coats
included in HB-SND] (WHH)

Drummond
History of Noble British Families, H.
Drummond, W. Pickering – London,
1846 [2 vols, only those coats included in
HB-SND] (WHH)

Dugd 17
Drawings of Seals in Bodleian MS
Dugdale 17 (TRD)

Durham–sls
*Catalogue of the Seals in the Treasury of
the Dean & Chapter of Durham*, W
Greenwell, Soc. Antiq. of Newcastle-
upon-Tyne, 1911–21 (CHH-B RABM)

DV
Domville Roll, *c*1470 (HDB ARW)

DX
Devereux Roll, 15 cent

E
St George's Roll, *c*1285/1450 (BRKM
JVS)

E6
Visitation of the North 1530, Coll.
Arm.MS (EME)

Edinburgh
Book of the Old Edinburgh Club,
Edinburgh, 1916 [vols 1, 2, 4, 8, 14, 15,
17, monumental heraldry of the old
town] (EMVJ)

Exeter D&C
Dean & Chapter of Exeter – Early
Deeds [in Exeter Cathedral Library]

F
Charles Roll, *c*1285

Farrer
Church Heraldry of Norfolk, Revd E.
Farrer, Goose & Co – Norwich, 1887–93
[3 vols] (DWG)

Farrer Bacon
Bacon Charters, Revd E. Farrer, Suff
Inst Arch 21, 1931 [seals formerly at
Redgrave] (WPJ)

Faussett
Faussett MS, 1759

FB
'Friar Brackley's Book', *Ancestor* 10,
*c*1440–60 (IRH)

FC
Furness Coucher Book, *c*1412 (BRKM)

FF
Fife Roll, temp Edw 1 (EPB)

FK
Fenwick's Roll, 1413 [part I] 1471 [part
II] [collated with copy IIa (18 cent)]
(BRKM)

Fouke
Fouke Fitzwarin Poem, ed. L.Brandin,
Paris 1930, *c*1260 [prose version *c*1310
used] (ARW)

Fowler
Memorials of Ripon, JT Fowler, Surtees
Soc 74 (RABM)

Fryer
'Monumental Effigies in Somerset', AC
Fryer, *Som.Arch & Nat.Hist.Soc.Proc.*
76 – Taunton, 1915

FW
Fitzwilliam Version of Heralds' Roll, 15
cent (CRHS)

G
Segar's Roll, *c*1282

G18
Visitation of Cambridgeshire 1575,
Coll.Arm.MS (HSL)

G18
Visitation of Sussex 1570, Coll.Arm.MS
(WAC HSL)

GA
Galloway Roll, 1300 (WHH)

Gelre
Armorial de Gelre, *c*1380 [English and
Scottish Arms therein] (DLG HSL AV)

Gen Mag
Genealogists Magazine, Soc. of
Genealogists – London, 1925–

Gent Mag
Gentleman's Magazine, JH & J Parker –
London, 1731–1877 [only vols 52, 61, 64,
NS 2 & 3] (HSL)

Gerard
Particular Description of Somerset, T.

Gerard 1633, ed. E.H. Bates, Somerset
Record Society 15 – London, 1900
(SWR)
Gerola
   Arms at Bodrum, G Gerola, Riviota del
   Collegio Araldico, 1915 [Engl sls in *Il
   Castello di S Pietro in Anatoli ed i suoi
   stemmi dei Cavalieri di Rodi* 1468, 1493,
   1575, collated with C.T. Newton's *A
   history of discoveries at Halicarnassus,*
   &c, London 1863 and its appendix, R.P.
   Pullen's *Description of the Castle of St.
   Peter at Bodrum*] (DLG)
Goring
   Goring Charters (TDT)
Graveney
   Graveney Kent MS, 1452
Green
   Guide to Nantwich Church, Green
Greenwich
   Greenwich Hospital Deeds – notes on
   seals, H.H.E. Craster [only those coats
   included in HB-SND] (WHH)
GutchWdU
   *History & Antiquities of the Colleges &
   Halls of the University of Oxford,*
   A.à Wood ed. Gutch, Clarendon Press –
   Oxford, 1786–90 (ACC JWPB)
GY
   Gentry Roll, transcr W.H. St. John
   Hope, *c*1480 [Harl MS 6137 ff44–5]
   (TRD WHH)

H
   Falkirk Roll, 1298
1H7
   Visitation of Hampshire 1530,
   Coll.Arm.MS (WAC)
H18
   Visitation of Somerset Dorset Devon
   Cornwall 1531, Coll.Arm.MS (WAC)
H21
   Visitation of the North 1530,
   Coll.Arm.MS (EME)
HA
   Harleian Roll, temp Edw II
Hall-Maxwell
   Hall-Maxwell family seals (EWP)
Habington
   Survey of Worcestershire, T. Habington
   ed. J. Amphlett, Worcs.Hist. Soc, 1895–
   9 [references to Abbey & St. Andrew's
   Ch. Pershore only] (RNB)
Hare
   Coll. Arm.MS Hare I R 36 & 37 [patents
   of arms] (HSL)
Harl 2076
   Harl MS 2076 ff 44–55, temp Eliz I [a

Randle Holme armorial] (JLP)
Harl Soc IV
   Harleian Society Publication 4, ed. G.W.
   Marshall, 1871 [Visitation of
   Nottinghamshire 1569 & 1614]
HB-SND
   Seals of Northumberland & Durham,
   C.H. Hunter-Blair, Soc. Antiq. of
   Newcastle-upon-Tyne, 1923 [includes
   references to sources which have been
   separately indexed & sources which have
   been indexed from this work, the latter
   being abbreviated as follows: Bain,
   Balliol, Belvoir, Bowes, Brand,
   Brumell, J.W. Clay, Dodsworth,
   Drummond, Durham–sls, Greenwich,
   Hodgson, Hodgson MSS, Laing–sls,
   LaingChart, Melros, Merton, Morpeth,
   NCH, Percy, Raine, Ridley,
   YorksChart] (WHH)
HE
   Heralds' Roll, *c*1270–80 (CRHS)
Helyar
   Helyar Muniments Seals pre.1550
   [Coker Ct, Somerset] (TDT)
Heneage
   Button Walker Heneage Muniments
   Seals pre. 1550 [Coker Ct, Somerset]
   (TDT)
Her & Gen
   Herald & Genealogist, ed. J.G. Nichols,
   J.B. Nichols – London, 1862–74
Hill
   Hill MSS [penes Canon Machell, quoted
   by Bellasis in Westmorland Church
   Notes]
Hist Coll Staffs
   Historical Collections of Staffordshire,
   Staffs Record Society, Stafford (1880–)
Hist MSS Comm
   Historical Manuscripts Commission,
   HMSO – London
Hodgson
   History of Northumberland, J. Hodgson,
   Soc. Antiq. of Newcastle-upon-Tyne,
   1858 [6 vols, only those coats included in
   HB-SND] (WHH)
Hodgson MSS
   Transcripts of Deeds relating to
   Northumberland [belonging to J.G.
   Hodgson, only those coats included in
   HB-SND] (WHH)
Hope
   'English Municipal Heraldry', W.H. St
   J. Hope, *Arch. Journ.* 3 – London, 1895
Hutton
   London Burials 1619, M. Hutton
   [Coll.Arm.MS] (HSL FND)

I
Holland's Roll, *c*1310

12[1904]
Coll.Arm.MS 12 temp Hen 8, tracings
T. Willement introdn. Ld. Howard de
Walden, 1904 (HSL)

Inventory
Inventory of Westminster Abbey, Royal
Commission on Historical Monuments –
London, 1924 (JGN)

Isbury
Charity Deeds, Lambourn [D/Q1/T14
Berks CRO]

J
Guillim's Roll, *c*1295–1305

JW Clay
*Extinct and Dormant Peerages of the
Northern Counties of England*, J.W.
Clay, J. Nisbet – London, 1913 [only
those coats included in HB-SND]
(WHH)

K
Caerlaverock Roll, ed. T. Wright, J.C.
Hotten – London, 1864 [Roll in BM of
Arms of the Princes Barons & Knights
who attended Edw 1 to siege of
Caerlaverock in 1300] (BRKM)

KB
Kings of Britain Roll, temp Hen VI
(BRKM)

Keepe
Monumenta Westmonasteriensia, H.
Keepe, Wilkinson & Dring – London,
1682 (JGN)

Kent Gentry
Kent Gentry, *c*1490 [Cotton MS
Faustina E2 Arch Cant XI (folio no and
not Arch Cant ref given)] (HSL)

Kildare AS
Kildare Arch. Soc. vols 1–9, Kildare AS
– Naas, 1895– (AWC HSL)

L
1st Dunstable Roll, 1308

L1
Coll Arm MS L1, *c*1520 (HDB)

L2
Coll Arm MS L2, *c*1520 (HDB)

L9
Coll Arm MS L9, *c*1510 (BRKM HSL)

L10
Coll Arm MS L10, *c*1520 (HSL FND)

Laing-sls
Catalogue of Ancient Scottish Seals,
H-Laing, Laing – Edinburgh, 1850 supp

1866 [2 vols, only those coats included in
HB-SND] (WHH)

LaingChart
Laing Charters, ed. J. Anderson,
Edinburgh, 1899 [only those coats
included in HB-SND] (WHH)

Lambarde
'Coats of Arms in Sussex Churches', F.
Lambarde, *Sussex Arch Collections* 67–
75, 1926–34 (JBW HSL JGN)

Lambeth
Lambeth MS 759

Lamborn
Oxfordshire Church Notes, EAG
Lamborn [Adderbury, Aston Rowant,
Bampton, Beckley, Begbroke, Bicester,
Black Bourton, Bladon, Bletchington,
Brightwell Baldwin, Broadwell,
Broughton Castle, Broughton Poggs,
Broughton St Mary, Bucknell, Burford,
Cassington, Caversfield, Caversham,
Chaddlington, Chalgrove, Charlbury,
Charlton on Otmoor, Chastleton,
Checkendon, Chesterton, Chinnor,
Chipping Norton, Churchill, Clanfield,
Cogges, Cottisford, Cowley, Cropredy,
Crowmarsh, Cuddesdon, Culham,
Cuxham, Deddington, Dorchester,
Drayton, Ducklington, Elsfield, Ewelme,
Eynsham, Fifield, Finmere, Forest Hill,
Fringford, Fulbrook, Garsington,
Glympton, Goring, Goring Heath, Gt
Milton, Gt Tew, Hampton Gay, Hampton
Poyle, Handborough, Hanwell, Harpsden,
Haseley, Headington, Henley-on-Thames,
Heythrop, Holton, Hook Norton, Horley,
Horsepath, Iffley, Ipsden, Islip,
Kelmscott, Kencott, Kiddington,
Kidlington, Kingham, Kirtlington,
Langford, Launton, Lewknor, Lower
Heyford, Marsh Baldon, Merton,
Middleton Stoney, Minster Lovell,
Mixbury, Mollington, Mongewell,
Nettlebed, Newington, Newnham Murren,
Noke, N Aston, N Leigh, Northmoor, N
Stoke, Nuffield, Nuneham, Nuneham
Courtenay, Pyrton, Rotherfield Greys,
Rotherfield Peppard, Rousham, Salford,
Sandford-on-Thames, Sandford St Martin,
Shilton, Shiplake, Shipton-under-
Wychwood, Shirburn, Somerton, Stanton
Harcourt, Stanton St John, Souldern, S
Newington, Steeple Aston, Steeple
Barton, Stoke Lyne, Studley Priory,
Swalcliffe, Swerford, Tackley, Tadmarton,
Thame, Upper Heyford, Warborough,
Wardington, Water Eaton, Waterperry,
Waterstock, Weston-on-the-Green,

Westwell, Wheatfield, Whitchurch, Woolvercot, Wood Eaton, Yarnton] [HET GDW JGN)

Lancs 1533 CS
Visitation of Lancs 1533. ed. W. Langton, Chetham Soc – Manchester, 1876–82 [vols 98 & 110, Harl MS 2076] (JGN)

Lawrance
Heraldry from Military Monuments before 1350 in England & Wales, H Lawrance, Harleian Society 98, – London, 1946 (HMKM)

LD
Lords' Roll, c1495 (JLP)

LE
Letter E Roll, c1510 (BRKM)

Leake
Types of the Garter Plates, S.M. Leake, 1758 [Coll Arm MS SML 39, tricks & blazons of Garter Stallplates in St. George's Chapel, Windsor, collated with W.H. St. John Hope's Stall Plates of the Knights of the Garter] (ACC)

LEP
Letter P Roll (BRKM)

Lethaby
Westminster Abbey Re-examined, W.R. Lethaby, Duckworth – London, 1925

LH
Letter H Roll, c1520 (BRKM)

Llanstephan
Llanstephan MS 46, National Library of Wales, c1560 (HSL)

LM
Lord Marshal's Roll, c1310 (FND)

LMO
Raine-Dunn 2, c1420

LMRO
Lord Marshal's Roll Old, temp Edw 1 & Hen V [parts I & II, Soc.Antiq.MS 664 vol I Roll 6] (HSL)

LMS
Raine-Dunn 1, c1310

LO
London Roll, c1470 (HMKM)

Lockington
Lockington Church Journal (TDT)

LonBH
London Bridge House Deeds seals (BRT)

LonG–sls
London Guildhall Additional MSS seals (BRT)

LP
Legh's Princes, c1446

LQ
Le Neve's Equestrian Roll, c1470 [part of Creswick's Book] (BRKM)

LR
Letter R Roll, c1520

LS
Letter S Roll, c1520

LV
Legh's Visitation of London, 1446–7

LY
Lucy's Roll, temp Hen VI [version A, Coll. Arm. MS Vinc 164 ff194–202b] (FND)

Lyndsay
Sir David Lyndsay's Armorial, 1542 (HMKM)

Lyon
Lyon Register (JM JGN)

M
Nativity Roll, c1300

ME
Merton's Roll, temp Hen VI [collated with Lucy's Roll] (JLP)

Melros
Liber de Melros, ed. C. Innes, Bannatyne Club – Edinburgh, 1837 [2 vols, only those coats included in HB-SND] (WHH)

Merton
Deeds at Merton College Oxford [only those coats included in HB-SND] (WHH)

MGH
Miscellanea Genealogica et Heraldica, London, 1868–1938

Middlewich
Middlewich Cartulary, Chetham Soc 2S vols, 105–8 (TDT)

Mill Steph
Rubbings of all arms on brasses in the British Isles, Mill Stephenson, Headley Brothers – London, 1926 Appendix 1938 [MS at Soc.Antiq.] (HSL)

MK
Meyrick's Roll, temp Hen VII (HMKM)

ML
Mandeville Roll, c1450 [ML I is Strangway's version, ML II Coll Arm version, collated with copy Ib] (HMKM BRKM)

Montendre
Tournoi de Montendre Roll, 1402 (HSL)

Morpeth
Morpeth Town Deeds [in custody of Town Clerk, only those coats included in HB-SND] (WHH)

MP
Matthew Paris Shields, part of Rolls of Arms Hen 3 [*Aspilogia* II], ed. T.D.

Tremlett, Soc.Antiq. – London, 1977
[shields of *c*1244–59]

MP Hist Min
Historia Minora, Matthew Paris, ed. Sir
F. Madden, Rolls Ser. 44, 1866–9 (HSL)

MY
Military Roll, *c*1446 [also called Legh's
Shires [Military] Roll] (EPB)

N
Bannerets Roll, *c*1312 [also called Great
Roll and Parliamentary Roll]

N
Great Roll, *c*1312 [also called Bannerets
Roll and Parliamentary Roll]

N
Parliamentary Roll, *c*1312 [also called
Bannerets Roll and Great Roll]

Namur
Chartrier de Namur, Brussels, 1844
[Engl sls therein] (DLG)

Navarre
Armorial du Heraut Navarre, Paris,
1861 [Engl arms 1368–75 from 16-cent
copy, excludes earls] (DLG)

NB
Nobility Roll[6th], temp Edw III (FND)

NCH
History of Northumberland, Northd
County History Committee – Newcastle,
1893 [vols I–XI, only those coats
included in HB-SND] (WHH)

Neale & Brayley
*History & Antiquities of the Abbey
Church of St Peter Westminster*, J.P.
Neale & E.W. Brayley, Hurst Robinson
– London, 1818 & 1823 [2 vols] (JGN)

Nelson Coll
Nelson Collection [compiled from *Arch.
Journ.* 93]

Nichols Leics
*History & Antiquities of the County of
Leicester*, J. Nichols, J. Nichols –
London, 1795–1811 [4 vols – records
monuments seen by Burton in 1630]
(EPB)

NorfHo
Norfolk House Deeds, R.C. Wilton [MS
calendar in possession of H.L. Bradfer-
Lawrence] (HSL)

North 1558
Visitation of the North 1558, L. Dalton,
Surtees Soc [vol 122, 95–155] (JGN)

NS
Norfolk & Suffolk Roll, 1400 [version A,
Coll. Arm.MS Vinc 164 ff83b–88]
(FND)

O
Boroughbridge Roll, 1322

Ormerod
*History of the County Palatine & City of
Chester*, G Ormerod, Lackington –
London, 1819

OxfAS
Oxford Archaeological Society

OxfRS
Oxford Record Society

P
Grimaldi Roll, transcr. W.H. St. John
Hope, 1350 [collated with Glover's Roll
& Thos. Jenyns's Book] (WHH HSL)

PCL
Portcullis's Book, *c*1440 (FND)

PE
Peterborough Roll, *c*1321–9 (HMKM)

Percy
Percy Seals [only those coats included in
HB-SND] (WHH)

Phillipps
Wiltshire Monuments, Sir T. Phillipps,
1822 (JGN)

Pierpont Morgan
Pierpont Morgan Library New York MS
105

Playfair
Playfair Muniments, E.W. Playfair
(JGN)

PLN
'Peter Le Neve's Book', ed. J. Foster in
Two Tudor Books of Arms, de Walden
Library – 1904, 1480–1500 [Harl 6163]
(AEB)

PlymouthCL–sls
Plymouth Central Library Seals (BRT)

PO
Powell Roll, *c*1350 (FND)

PR(1512)
Parliament Rolls, 1512 (GWP)

PR(1515)
Parliament Rolls, 1515 (GWP)

PRO–sls
Public Record Office Seals, Sir W.H. St.
John Hope [card index by Sir W.H. St.
John hope with additional notes by O.
Barron & T.D. Tremlett] (TDT)

Proc Soc Antiq
Proceedings of the Society of Antiquaries
(JGN)

PT
Portington's Roll, temp Hen VI
(BRKM)

PV
Povey's Roll, temp Edw II (IRH)

Q
Collins's Roll, c.1295 [Soc.Antiq.MS 664] (HMKM)
Q II
Collins's Roll II, 15 cent [excludes those in I) (BRKM HSL)

R
Styward's Roll, temp Edw III (EPB)
Raine
History and Antiquities of North Durham, J. Raine, J.B. Nichols – London, 1852 [only those coats included in HB-SND] (WHH)
RB
Red Book Roll, temp Hen VI (FND)
RH
'Randle Holme's Book', *Ancestor* 3, 5, 7 & 9, c1460 [Harl MS 2169, also published in *Two Tudor Books of Arms*, ed J. Foster] (EED JGN HSL)
Ridley
Charta Ridleana [copies of charters at Blagdon, in custody of Northd. County History Committee, only those coats included in HB-SND] (WHH)
RL
Rawlinson Roll, 15 cent (HMKM ACC)
Roman PO
Inventaire des Sceaux de la Collection des Pièces Originales du Cabinet des Titres à la Bibliothèque Nationale, J. Roman, Paris, 1909 [Engl sls therein] (DLG)
RW
Rous Roll, 1477–91 [also called Warwick Roll] (HSL)
RW
Warwick Roll, 1477–91 [also called Rous Roll] (HSL)

S
Willement's Roll, c1395 [original & revised versions] (FND BRKM HMKM)
S&G
Scrope & Grosvenor Roll, Sir N.H. Nicolas – 1832, 1385–90
SA
Salisbury Roll, c1460 (HSL)
Sandford
Genealogical History of the Kings of England, F. Sandford,Nicholson & Knaplock – London, 1707 (HSL)
SarumC–sls
New Sarum City Deeds seals (BRT)
SarumM–sls
Salisbury Museum seals (BRT)

SarumT–sls
New Sarum Taylors' Guild Deeds seals (BRT)
SC
Scots Roll, c1453 or c1490–1500 (IRH)
SD
2nd Dunstable Roll, 1334
Selborne
Seals from Selborne Charters, ed. W. Dunn Macray, Hants.RecSoc.4 & 7, 1891 & 1894 (TDT)
SES
2nd Segar Roll, c1460 (FND)
SF
Staffordshire Roll, 16 cent
SHY
Shirley's Roll, 15 cent (BRKM)
Sizergh
Sizergh Castle Muniments (CJS)
SK
Starkey's Roll, c1460 (BRKM)
SM
Sherborne Missal Shields, 1405 (HMKM)
Smyth B
Lives of the Berkeleys, J. Smyth, Bristol & Gloucs. Arch. Soc. – Gloucester, 1883 (TDT)
Soc Guern
Transactions of the Société Guernesiaise. ed. N.V.L. Rybot, St Peter Port, 1882– [preheraldic seals] (HSL BRKM)
Soc Jers
Bulletin of the Société Jersiaise, ed. N.V.L. Rybot, 1928 (BRKM)
SomAS
Somerset Archaeological Society Proceedings, Taunton, 1849–
?source
[source reference not noted]
SP
Smallpece's Roll, temp Edw 1 [version A] (JLP)
Spokes
'Arms in Berkshire Churches', ed. P.S. Spokes, *Berks Arch Journal* 35–44, 1931–40 (PSS GRH EPB)
ST
Stirling Roll, transcr S.M. Collins, 1304 [Coll Arm MS M14 ff269–] (FND)
Stamford
St Martin's Stamford – Notes, A. Bracegirdle (BRKM)
Stevenson
Scottish Heraldic Seals, S.H. Stevenson (HMKM JGN HET VH LP)
Steyning
Steyning MSS Seal Catalogue, T. Bruce

Dilks [at Bridgwater, Som] (TDT)

Stodart
Scottish Arms 1370–1678. R.R. Stodart,
W. Paterson – Edinburgh, 1881
[compiled from Armorial de Berry c1445
& Forman's Roll c1562] (AV)

Stoke C
Stoke Coucy Deeds [at Eton College]
(TDT)

Stowe-Bard
Sigilla Antiqua Stowe-Bardolph, ed.
G.H. Dashwood, Stowe-Bardolph, 1847
& 1862 [two series of Engravings from
Ancient Seals attached to Deeds &
Charters in the Muniment Room of Sir
Thomas Hare Baronet of Stowe-
Bardolph] (HSL)

Suff HN
Suffolk Heraldic Notes, Wm. Hervey,
c1560 [Soc.Antiq.MS 676] (LD)

SussASColl
*Sussex Archaeological Society's
Collections*, London & Lewes, 1848–
Sutton's Missal [in BNC Library] (ACC)

T
Rouen Roll, c1410

TB
Talbot Banners, c1442 (JLP)

Tewkesbury
Friends of Tewkesbury Abbey – 31st
Annual Report, 1964

Thornely
Monumental Brasses of Lancashire &
Cheshire, J.L. Thornely, Hull, 1893
[collated with Mill Steph] (HSL)

TJ
Thomas Jenyns's Book, transcr O.
Barron, 1410 [incorporates Jenyns's
Ordinary and Jenyns's Roll, collated
with BM MS Add 40851] (WHH HSL
BRKM ARW)

TZ
Tregoz Roll, 15 cent (EPB)

Uffenbach
Uffenbach Roll, late 14 cent [British
arms extracted by S.M. Collins from
Antiq. Journ. 21]

Ussher
Historical Sketch of Parish of Croxhall,
R. Ussher, Bemrose – London, 1881

Var Coll
Various Collections, Historical
Manuscripts Commission

Vermandois
Vermandois Roll [British arms extracted
by S.M. Collins from *Antiq.Journ.* 21]

Vinc 5
Coll Arm.MS Vincent 5, Vincent's
Chaos, (EPB)

Vinc 88
Coll.Arm.MS Vincent 88, 17 cent
(TDT)

Waiting
Coll.Arm.Old Waiting Book, 1619–99
(HSL)

Wallis
London's Armory, R. Wallis, Wallis –
London, 1677 [as reproduced in Welch]
(HSL)

WB I
Writhe's Book I, c1480 [Coll Arm MS
M10] (BRKM)

WB II
Writhe's Book II, c1530 (FND)

WB III
Writhe's Book III, 15 cent (JVS)

WB IV
Writhe's Book IV, c1435 [excludes
entries in Peter Le Neve's Book] (FND
HSL)

WB V
Writhe's Book V (BRKM)

Welch
*Coat Armour of the London Livery
Companies*, C.A. Welch, London, 1914
[incl R. Wallis's *London's Armory*
(1677)] (HSL)

Wells D&C
Dean & Chapter of Wells MSS (TDT)

WellsM–sls
Wells Museum Seals (TDT)

Wentworth
Wentworth Woodhouse Muniments
(BRT)

WestmAbb
Westminster Abbey [Neale & Brayley,
Keepe & Inventory collated with
existing monuments, bosses & glass]
(JGN)

Weston
Calendar of Weston Charters (HLBL)

WGA
Writhes's Garter Armorial, c1488
(BRKM)

WGB
Writhes's Garter Book, c1488 (HSL)

Whitaker
History of Richmondshire, T.D.
Whitaker, Longman Hurst – London,
1823

Whitmore
Hampshire Monuments, J.B. Whitmore

[J.B. Whitmore's MS re Abbots Ann, Alresford [New & Old], Alton, Alverstoke, Amport, Andover, Appleshaw, Ashmansworth, Barton Stacey, Basing, Beaulieu, Beauworth, Bedhampton, Benton, Bighton, Bishopstoke, Bishops Waltham, Bisterne, Blendworth [New], Boarhunt, Boldre, Botley, Bramdean, Bramshaw, Breamore, Brockenhurst, Broughton, Bullington, Burghclere, Buriton, Bursledon, Catherington Chalton, Charlton, Cheriton, Chilbolton, Chilcombe, Chilworth, Christchurch, Clanfield, Compton, Corhampton, Crawley, Crofton [Old], Crondall, Crux Easton, Damerham, Dibden, Droxford, Durley, E. Dean, E. Meon, E. Tytherley, E. Wellow, E. Woodhay, Ecchinswell, Eldon, Eling, Ellingham, Exbury, Faccombe, Fareham, Farley Chamberlayne, Farlington, Fawley, Fordingbridge, Foxcott, Freefolk, Fyfield, Goodworth Clatford, Gosport, Grateley, Hale, Hamble, Hambledon, Hartley Wespall, Heckfield, Herriard, Highclere, Hinton Ampner, Houghton, Hound, Hunton, Hursley, Hurstbourne Priors, Hurstbourne Tarrant, Ibsley, Idsworth, Itchen, Kilmeston, Kimpton, Kingsclere, Kings' Somborne, Knights Enham, Larham, Leckford, Linkenholt, Little Somborne, Littleton, Longparish, Longstock, Long Sutton, Lower Clatford, Lymington, Lyndhurst, Maplederwell, Martin, Mattingley, Medstead, Micheldever, Michelmersh, Millbrook, Minstead, Monxton, Morestead, Mottisfont, Nether Wallop, Netley, Newnham, N. Baddesley, N. Stoneham, Nursling, Over Wallop, Owlesbury, Penton Mewsey, Plaitford, Portchester, Quarley, Ringwood, Rockbourne, Romsey, Rotherwick, Rowner, St. Mary Bourne, Sherfield English, Sherfield upon Loddon, Soberton, Sopley, S. Stoneham, S. Warnborough, Southwick, Sparsholt, Stockbridge, Stoke Charity, Stratfield Saye, Stratfield Turgiss, Sydmonton, Tangley, Thruxton, Timsbury, Titchfield, Tufton, Tunworth, Twyford, Upham, Up Nateley, Upper Clatford, Upton Grey, Vernhams Dean, Weeke, W. Meon, Weyhill, Wherwell, Whitsbury, Wickham, Wonston, Woodcott] (EPB JGN)

Wilton
Wilton House Archives seals (BRT)
WJ
William Jenyns's Ordinary, c1380 (HMKM)
WK
Writhe's Book of Knights, temp Hen VII)BRKM)
WLN
Sir William Le Neve's Book, c1500 (TRD BRKM)
WNR
Sir William Le Neve's Roll, temp Edw 1 (FND)
WNS
Sir William le Neve's 2nd Roll, temp Edw II [version A, Soc.Antiq.MS 664 vol I Roll 9] (HSL)
Wrottesley
History of the Family of Wrottesley of Wrottesley, 1903 (TDT)
Wroxton
Prophecies of Merlin, ed E.P. Shirley, Her & Gen 7 – 1873, c1510 [penes Baroness North of Wroxton] (HSL)

XB
Prince Arthur's Book – Wriothesley's Beasts, temp Hen VIII (BRKM)
XBM
Selections from BM MS Add 45131, Thomas Wriothesley (HSL)
XC
Prince Arthur's Book – Wriothesley's Crosses, temp Hen VIII (BRKM)
XE
Prince Arthur's Book – Wriothesley's Crosses Engrailed, temp Hen VIII (BRKM)
XF
Prince Arthur's Book – Wriothesley's Fesses & Bars, temp Hen VIII [with Dethick additions c1580] (BRKM)
XFB
Wriothesley's Funeral Banners, c1530 [BM Add MS 45132] (EAB)
XK
Prince Arthur's Book – Wriothesley's Knights, temp Hen VIII
XL
Prince Arthur's Book – Wriothesley's Lions (BRKM)
XO
Prince Arthur's Book – Wriothesley's Crescents, temp Hen VIII (BRKM)
XPat
'Thomas Wriothesley's Roll of Patents', ed. Mill Stephenson & R. Griffin, *Arch*

69, temp Henry VIII [Soc.Antiq.MS 443
664 vol VI] (FND)

XV

Wriothesley's Chevrons transcr HS
London, *c*1525 [Pt I – Norwich Public
Library MS 4406, Pt II – Soc.Antiq.MS
476, 9 pp 322–31]

XX

Prince Arthur's Book – Wriothesley's
Saltires, temp Hen VIII (BRKM)

XZ

Prince Arthur's Book – Wriothesley's
Crosslets, temp Henry VIII (BRKM)

YK

Glover's York Roll, 16 cent [Harl MS
1487, 48b–51b] (BRKM)

YMerch–sls

Merchant Adventurers Seals – York
(BRT)

Yorks Arch Journ

Yorkshire Archaeological Journal,
Yorks.Arch.Soc, 1870–

YorksChart

Early Yorkshire Charters, ed. W. Farrer,
Farrer – Edinburgh, 1915 [vols I & II,
only those coats included in HB-SND]
(WHH)

Yorks Deeds

Yorkshire Deeds,
Yorks.Arch.Soc.Rec.Ser. 111 & 120
(TDT)

Yorks–sls

'Some Yorkshire Armorial Seals', C.T.
Clay, *Yorks Arch. Journ.* 36, 1944
(AEB)

YPhil–sls

Yorks Philosophical Museum seals
(BRT)

Terminology

Abbreviations and selected word list

The list of abbreviations includes abbreviations with the words in full, and vice versa. The full version has been omitted if its inclusion would have placed it next to its abbreviation. The alphabetization of the list ignores apostrophes, hyphens, numerals and spaces.

'Sic' indicates that the word is used in the form given.

'Sic sub' indicates that the word may be used in this form but in a section headed by the alternative word

'Say' indicates that the alternative word is used in preference, particularly in headings, but that the use of the second word is not necessarily precluded.

The spelling of French past participles has been anglicized, e.g. 'semy' rather than 'semé'.

a&l	armed & langued	banded	sic [of garbs etc]
addorsed	sic	bar(s) dancetty	sic
adumbrated	say in umbre	bar(s) gemel	sic
als	alias	barbed & flighted	sic
anct	ancient	barbed & seeded	b&s
antelope	sic sub beast	barnacle	sic sub bray
apaumy	sic	barruly	say burely [for barry unnumbered]
arbalest	sic sub bow		
Archbp	Archbishop	barry	sic [of 6, unless otherwise specified]
arched	sic [of chf etc]		
Arg	Argent	Baroness	Bness
armed	sic [for horns & tusks; say attrd for deer]	barrow	sic
		barrulet	say bar
armed & langued	a&l	basket	sic
arrow-head	say pheon	baston	say bend
ass	sic sub horse	bat	sic
attired	attrd	battleaxe	say axe
attrib	attributed	battled	say embattled
attrd	attired	beacon	sic
axe	sic [includes battleaxe, bill, Danish axe, halbert, hatchet, Lochaber axe, poleaxe &c; see also pick axe]	beaked & legged	b&l
		becket	say chough
		Beds	Bedfordshire
		bend	sic
		bendlet	say bend
Az	Azure	Berks	Berkshire
		betw	between
b	born; verso	bezant(y)	roundel(ly) Or
b&l	beaked and legged	bicorporate	2corp
b&s	barbed and seeded	bill	say axe
badger	sic	billetty	sic

birdbolt	say arrow	cheval-trap	say caltrap
Bishop	Bp	chevron(el)	chev
blackamoor's head	say Moor's head	chf	chief
BM	British Museum	chough	sic
Bness	Baroness	church	ch
boar	sic [includes baconpig, hog, pig, sanglier, swine, wild boar]	Church Notes	CN
		cinquefoil	5foil
		circa	c
		circle of glory	say nimbus
bomb	say fireball	cit	citizen
border	sic [assumed to be overall; & border used, rather than within border]	clarion	sic
		close	sic [of bird &c]
		CN	Church Notes
		Co	County
bouget	sic	coh	coheir(ess)
bourdon	say palmer's staff	Coll Arm	College of Arms
botonny	sic	collared & chained	sic
bray	sic	collared & lined	sic
bro	brother	collar gemel	sic
brock	sic sub badger	combatant	sic [for large animals; say respectant for others]
brother	bro		
Bp	Bishop		
British Museum	BM	compony	say gobony
broad arrowhead	say pheon	coney	sic sub hare
buck	sic	conjd	conjoined
Bucks	Buckinghamshire	contourny	say to sin [i.e. facing to the sinister]
bull	sic sub ox		
burely	sic [barry of many bars, usually 10 or more]	corby	sic sub raven
		Cornish chough	chough
		Cornw	Cornwall
		coronel	cronel
		coronet	sic sub crown
c	circa	2corp	bicorporate
cab	caboshed; cabossed	3corp	tricorporate
caltrap	sic	cotise(d)	sic
Cambs	Cambridgeshire	couchant	sic
camel	sic	counterch	counterchanged
cap of maintenance	sic sub hat	counter-emb	counter-embattled
caparisoned	sic [of horse]	counterseal	c'seal
carbuncle	say escarbuncle	Countess	Ctess
cat	sic	County Record Office	CRO
cat-a-mountain	sic sub cat	couped	sic
Cath	Catherine	covered cup	sic
cent	century	coward	sic [tail between legs]
ch	charged; church	cr	created
chapel	sic	crancelin	crown of rue (Saxony)
chapeau	sic sub hat		
chaplet	sic [wreath of flowers] sub wreath	crane	sic sub heron
		created	cr
charged	ch	crenellated	sic
charger	sic sub dish	cresc	crescent
charter	sic	crest	sic
Chas	Charles	crined	sic [for haired or maned; if minimal say tufted]
checky	sic		
chequy	say checky		
Ches	Cheshire	CRO	County Record Office
chessrook	sic	cronel	sic
chev	chevron(el)	crosier	sic

cross	sic	double queued	2queued
crossbow	sic	double tressure	2tressure
cross crosslet	crosslet [this version is used]	dsp	died sine prole
		dspm	died sine prole mascula
ow	sic sub raven		
crown	sic [for crown of rue say crancelin, for eastern crown say antique crown, for Papal crown say tiara]	dspms	died without male issue surviving
		Duchess	sic
		Duke	D
		E	Earl; east
crusily	sic	eagle	sic
c'seal	counterseal	Earl	E
Ctess	Countess	Earl Marshal	EM
cushion	sic	east	E
Cumb	Cumberland	Eastern crown	antique crown
cup	sic [say covered cup if with lid]	Edm	Edmund
		Edw	Edward
		elephant	sic
d	died	elevated	sic [of wings]
D	Duke	Eliz	Elizabeth
dance	say fess dancetty	EM	Earl Marshal
dancy	say dancetty	embattled	sic [crenellated on upper edge only]
Danish axe	say axe		
dated	dd	embrued	sic
dau	daughter	endorsed	say addorsed
dd	dated	enflamed	sic
debruised	say surmounted (by)	Engld	England
decresc	decrescent [of moon]	engr	engrailed
deer	sic [section includes buck, hart, hind, roe, stag, and the positions: at gaze, courant, lodged, ramp(ant), salient, stat(ant), tripp(ant)]	enhanced	sic
		ensigned	sic
		equestr	equestrian [of seal]
		erad	eradicated
		erased	sic
		Erm	ermine
		escallop	sic
degree	say step	escarb	escarbuncle
demi-lion	demi-lion rampant [unless otherwise specified]	escutch	escutcheon
		estoile	sic
		exec	executed
Derby(s)	Derby(shire)	executor	exor
dex	dexter	executrix	extrix
diapered	sic	exhib	exhibited; exhibition
died	d [see also: dsp, dspm, dspms]	exor	executor
		extrix	executrix
diffce(d)	difference(d)		
dimid	dimidiated (by)	f	father
dimidg	dimidiating	fer de moline	mill rind
dish	sic	fess	sic
dismembered	sic	fess dancy	say fess dancetty
displ	displayed	fetlock	say fetterlock
dog	sic [section includes bloodhound, greyhound, kennett, mastiff, talbot &c]	fimbr	fimbriated
		finch	sic
		fireball	sic
		fired	sic
donkey	sic sub horse	fishweel	sic [sub basket]
dormant	sic	fitchy	sic
double headed eagle	2head eagle	fl	flourished

flamant	say enflamed	grady	sic
flaunches	sic	grand-daughter	gd-dau
fleam	sic	Grand quarter	Gd qr
fleur de lis	sic	grandson	gds
flory	sic [terminating in fleur(s) de lis (of cross, tail, &c)]	grenade	sic sub fireball
		greyhound	sic sub dog
		griece	stay step
flory cf	flory counterflory	gryphon	say griffin
flourished	fl	guardant	gard
3foil	trefoil	Gu	gules
4foil	quatrefoil	gurges	say whirlpool
5foil	cinquefoil	gusset	sic [means small point]
forcene	sic [for horses; salient for other animals]	gutty	sic
formy	sic	gutty de larmes	say gutty Arg
fountain	sic	gutty de sang	say gutty Gu
fourchy	sic	gyron	sic
fox	sic	gyronny	sic [of 8, unless otherwise specified]
fracted	sic		
frase(r)	see 5foil		
fructed	sic	h	heir; heiress
fusil	sic sub lozenge	habited	say vested
fusilly	sic sub lozengy	haft	say shaft
fylfot	sic	haired	say crined
		halbert	sic sub axe
galley	lymphad	halo	say nimbus
gamb	sic	hammer	sic
garb	sic	hamaide(s)	say bar(s) couped
gard	guardant	Hampshire	Hants
garland	sic sub wreath	hank	sic
garn	garnished	Hants	Hampshire; Co Southampton
gauntlet	sic sub glove		
gaze	say at gaze [for deer that are stat gard]	hare	sic [includes coney, leveret, rabbit]
gd-dau	grand-daughter	hart	sic sub deer
Gd qr	grand quarter [i.e. one of the large quarters in a coat which is quarterly quartered. Large Roman numerals are used for grand quarters, Arabic for sub quarters, small Roman for sub sub quarters]	hatchet	say axe
		haurient	sic
		2head	double headed
		headed	sic [for spearheads]
		hedghog	sic sub urchin
		heir(ess)	h
		helmet	sic sub hat
		Hen	Henry
		Heref(s)	Hereford(shire)
		heron	sic [includes crane, stork]
gds	grandson	Herts	Hertfordshire
gemel(s)	see bar(s) gemel	hind	sic sub deer
gem-ring	sic sub annulet	hog	sic sub boar
gilly-flower	sic	hoofed	say unguled
glory	say nimbus	horn	sic [used for animal horns and bugle-horns]
Gloucs	Gloucestershire		
goat	sic		
gobony	sic	horned	say attrd [for deer; armed for other animals]
golpe	say roundel Purp		
gorged	sic		
goutte	sic	horse	sic [includes ass, donkey, mule]
goutty	say gutty		

Hunts	Huntingdonshire	lozy	lozengy
hurst	sic	lucy	sic sub fish
hurt	say roundel Az	lure	sic
		lymphad	[includes galley, but
imp	impaling; impaled;		see ship for other
	impalement		ships]
incensed	sic		
incresc	increscent [of moon]	M	Marquess
indented	sic	m	married
in glory	say irrad	magpie	say pie
in lure	sic	mallet	sic sub hammer
inverted	sic	maned	say crined
IOM	Isle of Man	Margaret	Mgt
IOW	Isle of Wight	Marquess	M
Irld	Ireland	married	m
irrad	irradiated [emitting	mascle	sic sub lozenge
	rays; but for sun, say	masculy	say semy of mascles
	sun in splendour]	masoned	sic
Isle of Man	IOM	mastiff	sic sub dog
Isle of Wight	IOW	maunch	sic
isst	issuant	membered	sic [for male organs
			of mammals; say
jackdaw	sic sub raven		legged for birds]
jamb	say gamb	Mgt	Margaret
Jas	James	Middx	Middlesex
jellopped	say wattled	mill rind	sic
jesst	jessant	molet	say mullet
Jn	John	mont	monument
Jos	Joseph	Moor's head	sic
		mound	say orb
k	killed	mule	sic sub horse
K	King	mullet	sic
knot	sic	mural crown	sic
Kt	Knight	Murrey	sic
ktd	knighted	muzzled	sic
label	sic [of 3 and in chf,		
	unless otherwise	N	north
	specified]	naiant	sic
lamb	sic sub sheep	nd	no date
Lancs	Lancashire	nebuly	sic
langued	sic [see also armed &	negro's head	say Moor's head
langued]		nimbus	sic
		no date	nd
Ld	Lord	Norf	Norfolk
leaping	say salient	north	N
legged	sic [see also beaked	Northants	Northamptonshire
	& legged]	Northd	Northumberland
Leics	Leicestershire	Notts	Nottinghamshire
leopard	say lion pg		
leopard's face	sic	obv	obverse
leveret	sic sub hare	ogress	say roundel Sa
levrier	sic sub dog	Or	sic
Lincs	Lincolnshire	orb	sic
lioncel	say lion	orwse	otherwise
lion rampant	say lion	other	sic
lodged	sic	otter	sic
Lord	Ld	ounce	say leopard
loz	lozenge	ox	sic [includes bull]

pairle	say pall	qr(s)	quarter(s) [large
pallet	say pale		Roman nos for Gd
pall	sic [and per pall]		qrs, Arabic for sub-
pallium	sic [ecclesiastical		qrs & simple qtly
	vestment]		coats, small Roman
palmer's staff	sic		for further sub qrs]
paly	sic [of 6, unless	qtd	quartered
	otherwise specified]	qtg	quartering
panther	sic	qtly	quarterly
papal crown	say tiara	quarter	qr [but say canton
parrot	sic sub popinjay	when alone or over	
part	pt [also used for	all]	
	point]	quatrefoil	4foil
party per pale	say per pale	Queen	Q
paschal lamb	sic sub sheep	queue	sic [qf for queue
passt	passant [pg for		ourchy]
	passant guardant]	queued	sic
paty	say formy	2queued	with 2 tails
pavilion	sic sub tent		
pd	pierced	rabbit	sic sub hare
peacock	sic	radiant	say irrad
pegasus	sic	radiated	say irrad
pelican	sic	ram	sic sub sheep
pellet	say roundel Sa	ramp	rampant [say segr for
pg	passant guardant		griffins; for lion ramp
pheon	sic [for all arrow-		say lion]
	heads]	traven	sic [includes corbeau,
pickaxe	sic		corby, crow, jackdaw,
pie	sic [for magpie]		rook]
pieces	sic	rayonnant	say irrad
pierced	pd	rayonny	say irrad [but for sun,
pig	sic sub boar		say sun in splendour]
pike	say lucy	rebated	say couped
pineapple	say pine cone	regard	regardant
pinson	say finch	rere-mouse	say bat
pl	plate [i.e. picture]	respectant	sic [see also
plate	say roundel Arg		combatant]
point	pt [also used for part]	rest	say clarion
poleaxe	sic sub axe	rev	reverse [of seal];
popinjay	sic		revised
porcupine	sic sub urchin	reversed	say inverted [for
poss	possibly		charges upside down]
powdered	say semy	Ric	Richard
Ppr	proper	rising	sic
pr	proved	Robt	Robert
PRO	Public Record Office	Rog	Roger
prob	probably	rompu	sic
proc	proceedings	rook	sic sub raven or
proper	Ppr		chessrook
proved	pr [of will]	roundel	sic
pt	point; part	roundel barry wavy	say fountain
Public Record Office	PRO	roundelly	sic [charged with or
purfled	say garn		semy of roundels]
Purp	Purpure	rousant	say rising
purse	sic	rowel	say mullet
		rue	say crancelin [for
			crown of rue]
Q	Queen		
qf	queue fourchy	Rutl	Rutland

s	son
S	series; south
s&l	slipped & leaved
Sa	Sable
Saint	St
salamander	sic
salient	sic [say forcene for horses]
Salop	Shropshire
salt	saltire
sanglier	say boar
Sanguine	sic
sans	sic
saracen's head	say Moor's head
savage	say wild man
scallop	say escallop
schl	school
scocheon	say escutch
Scotld	Scotland
scrip	say purse
scroll	sic
seaxe	sic sub sword [but sometimes synonymous with axe]
segr	segreant [for griffins, say ramp for other animals]
sejt	sejant
semy	sic
semy of crosslets	say crusily
serpent	sic
sh	shield [but not usually abbr]
shackbolt	sic
shaft	sic
shakefork	sic
sheaf	sic [for arrows; say garb for corn]
sheep	sic [includes lamb & ram]
ship	sic [for all ships except lymphads]
shldr	shoulder
Shropshire	Salop
sin	sinister
sine prole	sp
sinister	sin
sis	sister
sl	seal
slipped	sic [s&l for slipped & leaved]
Soc Antiq	Society of Antiquaries of London
Som	Somerset
son	s
south	S
sp	sine prole [i.e. without issue]
spear	sic [includes javelin, lance, tilting spear &c]
springing	say salient
spur rowel	say pd mullet
squirrel	sic
St	Saint
staff	sic [includes crozier, mace, palmer's staff, prior's staff, ragged staff, shepherd's crook &c]
Staff(s)	Stafford(shire)
stag	sic sub deer
stalked	say slipped
star	say mullet [or estoile if points wavy]
stat	statant
step	sic
stirrup	sic
stork	sic sub heron
stringed	sic [for instruments, lures, horns, bows &c]
Suff	Suffolk
sufflue	say clarion
sun in splendour	sic
surmounted by	sic
Surr	Surrey
surtout	say over all
Suss	Sussex
swine	sic sub boar
sword	sic [includes dagger, dirk, falchion, rapier, sabre, scimitar, seaxe, skean &c]
syke	say fountain
tabernacle	say tent
tail(ed)	say queue(d); see also 2queued and qf
talbot	sic sub dog
temp	
tempore [in the time of]	
Tenny	sic
tent	sic
Thos	Thomas
throughout	sic
tiara	sic sub hat
tierced	sic [per pall &c]
tiger	sic
tinct	tincture [metals: Argent, Or; colours and stains: Azure, Gules, Murrey, Purpure, Sable, Sanguine, Tenny, Vert; furs: Ermine, Ermines, Erminois, Pean, Vair; also Untinctured, Proper]

tine	sic [points of attires]	w	wife
tipped	sic [unless headed]	W	west
torse	say wreath	Warw(s)	Warwick(shire)
torteau	say roundel Gu	wattled	sic
trefoil	3foil	waves of the sea	say water Ppr
trefly	say botonny	wavy	sic
(2)tressure	(double) tressure	wch	which
tricorporate	3corp	weel	say fishweel
tripp	trippant [for deer; say passt for other animals]	west	W
		Westm	estminster
		Westmld	Westmorland
trussing	say preying on	wheel	sic [say Cath wheel if spiked]
tufted	sic		
tun	sic	whelk	sic
Turk's head	say Moor's head	which	wch
tusked	say armed	whirlpool	sic
		wid	widow
umbre	sic [outline; say in umbre for adumbrated]	wife	w
		wild man	sic
		Wilts	Wiltshire
undy	say wavy	wing(ed)	sic
unguled	sic	winnowing fan	sic
Univ	University	wivern	sic
untinc	untinctured	wolf	sic
urchin	sic for hedgehog	Wm	William
urinant	sic	woodhouse	say wild man
usu	usual; usually	woolpack	sic
		wounded	say vulned
Va	Vair	Worc(s)	Worcester(shire)
vairy	sic	wreath	sic
vambraced	say in armour	wyvern	say wivern
varvel	sic		
verso	say b [not v]	yale	sic
Vert	Vt	younger	yr
vested	sic	York(s)	York(shire)
Vis	Visitation	yr	younger
Visct(ess)	Viscount(ess)		
Vt	Vert		
vulned	sic	zule	say chessrook

Index of Headings

UNCHARGED   1
  Arg plain
  Az &c plain
  Gu plain
  Or plain
  Sa plain
  Vt plain
  Acorn see Fruit

ANCHOR   1

ANNULET   2
  Annulet & in chf &c
  Annulet betw bars &c
  Annulet betw fishes &c
  Annulet betw & in chf   3
  Annulet within
  On an annulet
  2 annulets
  2 concentric annulets
  2 annulets &
  2 concentric annulets &
  2 or more concentric annulets: see
  also Whirlpool
  3 annulets
  3 gem-rings   4
  3 annulets each ensigned with cross
  3 concentric annulets
  3 annulets &c
  3 annulets between or within   5
  3 annulets enclosing
  4 annulets
  4 concentric annulets
  4 annulets &
  5 annulets
  5 concentric annulets
  5 annulets &
  6 annulets   6
  Arg 6 annulets
  Arg 6 annulets Or &c   7
  Az 6 annulets
  Gu 6 annulets
  Or 6 annulets Az &c   8
  Or 6 annulets Sa
  Sa 6 annulets
  6 annulets field patterned
  6 annulets & label
  6 annulets & canton &c
  6 annulets & over all   9
  6 annulets in border
  9 annulets or more

ANVIL   9
  Arbalest: see Bow
  Arm (human): see Hand

ARMS & ARMOUR   9
  Helmet: see Hat
  Gauntlet: see Glove
  Spearhead: see Spear
  Seaxe: see Sword

ARROW   10
  See also Pheon
  Birdbolt
  1 arrow & ...
  2 arrows
  2 birdbolts
  2 arrows or birdbolts & ...
  3 arrows
  3 birdbolts   11
  3 arrows or birdbolts & ...
  4 arrows or more

AXE   12
  See also Pickaxe
  2 axes
  2 axes & ...
  3 axes &c
  Arg 3 axes
  Az 3 axes
  Gu 3 axes   13
  Or 3 axes
  Sa 3 axes
  3 axes field patterned
  3 axes & ...
  4 axes or more
  Barnacles: see Brays

2 BARS   14
  Arg 2 bars Arg   16
  Arg 2 bars Az
  Arg 2 bars Gu
  Arg 2 bars Or &c   17
  Arg 2 bars Vt
  Az 2 bars Arg   18
  Az 2 bars Gu
  Az 2 bars Or
  Gu 2 bars Arg
  Gu 2 bars Or   19
  Or 2 bars Az
  Or 2 bars Gu
  Or 2 bars Sa &c   20
  Sa 2 bars
  Vt 2 bars Or
  Barry &c, 2 bars
  Erm 2 bars
  Per fess &c 2 bars   21

Semy, 2 bars
Vair 2 bars
2 bars patterned
  2 bars Erm
  2 bars fretty
  2 bars per fess indented   22
  2 bars per fess wavy &c
  2 bars semy
  2 bars vairy
2 bars modified   23
  2 bars couped
  2 bars, upper dancetty
  2 bars dancetty
  2 bars embattled   24
  2 bars engrailed
  2 bars indented
  2 bars of lozenges
  2 bars 'tortues'
  2 bars of voided lozenges
  2 bars wavy or nebuly   25
  Arg 2 bars wavy &c
  Az &c, 2 bars wavy &c
  Or &c, 2 bars wavy &c
  Field patterned, 2 bars wavy &c
  2 bars wavy &c Erm   26
  2 ribands wavy & knotted
2 bars & label
  Arg 2 bars & label
  Az &c 2 bars & label
  2 bars modified and label
  2 bars & patterned label   27
2 bars & in base
2 bars & canton
  Arg 2 bars & canton
  Gu &c 2 bars & canton
  Erm 2 bars & canton   28
  2 bars modified & canton
  2 bars & patterned canton
  2 bars & sin canton
2 bars canton & label &c
2 bars canton & bend
  2 bars canton & on bend
2 bars canton bend & label
2 bars & on canton
  2 bars & on canton lion   29
  2 bars & on canton lion passt
  2 bars & on canton lion pg
  2 bars & on canton other beast
  2 bars & on canton bird
  2 bars & on canton buckle &c
  2 bars & on canton cross   30
  2 bars & on canton, cross modified
  2 bars & on canton cushion &c
  2 bars & on canton 3foil
  2 bars & on canton 5foil
  Arg 2 bars & on canton Gu 5foil
  Arg   31

Arg 2 bars & on canton Gu 5foil Or
Arg 2 bars Sa & on canton 5foil
  2 bars & on canton 6foil
  2 bars & on canton garb   32
  2 bars & on canton head &c
  2 bars & on canton mullet
  2 bars & on canton saltire &c
  2 bars & on canton & ...
2 bars & chf
  Or 2 bars & chf   33
  Sa 2 bars & chf
  2 bars & chf patterned
  2 bars & chf modified
  2 bars modified & chf
  For Mortimer &c: see barry chf &
  over all   34
  2 bars chf & label
2 bars (plain, patterned or modified) &
on chf
  2 bars & on chf demi-lion
  2 bars & on chf lion passt
  2 bars & on chf lion pg
  2 bars & on chf other beast   35
  2 bars & on chf bird
  2 bars & on chf castle
  2 bars & on chf crescent
  2 bars & on chf cross &c
  2 bars & on chf fleur de lis
  2 bars & on chf foils &c
  2 bars & on chf roundels
  2 bars on chf ... & label   36
2 bars (plain, patterned or modified) &
in chf
  2 bars & in chf demi-lion
  2 bars & in chf lion passt
  2 bars & in chf lion pg
  2 bars & in chf 2 or more lions
  2 bars & in chf bends   37
  2 bars & in chf bird
  2 bars & in chf crescent
  2 bars & in chf cross &c
  2 bars & in chf escallops   38
  2 bars & in chf estoile &c
  2 bars & in chf 3 fleurs de lis &c
  2 bars & in chf foils
  2 bars & in chf 1 head   39
  2 bars & in chf 2 heads
  2 bars & in chf 3 heads
  2 bars & in chf 3 horseshoes
  2 bars & in chf lozenges &c   40
  2 bars & in chf 1 mullet
  2 bars & in chf 2 mullets
  2 bars & in chf 3 mullets
  Arg 2 bars & in chf 3 mullets
  Arg 2 bars & in chf 3 mullets Sa   41
  Gu 2 bars & in chf 3 mullets

2 bars & in chf pale
2 bars & in chf 1 roundel
2 bars & in chf 2 roundels
2 bars & in chf 3 roundels
Arg 2 bars & in chf 3 roundels   42
Arg 2 bars Az in chf 3 roundels Gu
Arg 2 bars & in chf 3 roundels Gu
&c
Az 2 bars & in chf 3 roundels   43
Gu 2 bars & in chf 3 roundels
Or 2 bars & in chf 3 roundels   44
Purp 2 bars & in chf 3 roundels
Sa 2 bars & in chf 3 roundels
2 bars in chf 3 roundels patterned
or charged   45
2 bars modified in chf 3 roundels
2 bars & in chf wreath &c
2 bars in chf ... & label
2 bars & over all beast
2 bars & over all bend
2 bars & bend sin   46
Arg 2 bars & bend
Az 2 bars & bend
Or 2 bars & bend
Field patterned 2 bars & bend
2 bars patterned & bend
2 bars & bend checky   47
2 bars & bend gobony
2 bars modified & bend
2 bars bend & label
2 bars & on bend
2 bars & on bend cresc
2 bars & on bend foils
2 bars & on bend head &c
2 bars & over all bird &c   48
2 bars & over all cresc &c
2 bars & over all escarbuncle
2 bars & over all escutch
2 bars & over all pile
2 bars & over all saltire
2 bars & over all ... & ...
2 bars on chief ... & over all
2 bars in chief ... & over all
2 bars in chf ... & over all canton   49
2 bars in chf ... & over all head
2 bars chief & over all escutch (e.g.
Mortimer): see Barry &c chief paly
2 bars betw
2 bars betw 3 barrulets &c
2 bars betw birds
2 bars betw 6 birds
2 bars & 8 or more (or orle of)
birds   50
Arg 2 bars Az & orle of birds
Arg 2 bars Gu & orle of birds
Arg 2 bars Sa & orle of birds

Arg 2 bars Vt & orle of birds
Az 2 bars & orle of birds
Gu 2 bars & orle of birds
Or 2 bars & orle of birds   51
2 bars betw chev &c
2 bars betw escallops &c
2 bars betw fleurs de lis &c
2 bars betw insects &c
2 bars betw roundels   52
2 bars betw ... & canton &c
2 bars betw ... & over all
2 bars in border
2 bars in patterned border
2 bars in border engrailed
2 bars in border otherwise modified   53
2 bars border & label
2 bars canton & border
2 bars & in chief ... in border
2 bars betw ... in border
On 2 bars
On 2 bars birds
On 2 bars 6 birds   54
On 2 bars bougets
On 2 bars combs
2 bars upper ch with cresc
On 2 bars crosses
On 2 bars escallops &c   55
On 2 bars heads &c
On 2 bars mullet
On 2 bars 3, 4 or 5 mullets
On 2 bars 6 mullets or more
On 2 bars roundel &c   56
On 2 bars & label
On 2 bars & in base
On 2 bars & canton
On 2 bars & chief
On 2 bars & in chief
On 2 bars between &c   57
On 2 bars within
On 2 bars within & in chief
2 bars cotised
2 bars cotised & ...

3 BARS   57
Arg 3 bars Az   58
Arg 3 bars Gu
Arg 3 bars Or &c   59
Az 3 bars Arg
Az 3 bars Or
Gu 3 bars Arg
Gu 3 bars Or   60
Or 3 bars Az
Or 3 bars Gu
Or 3 bars Vt
Sa 3 bars Arg   61

Vt 3 bars
Field patterned 3 bars
  Erm 3 bars
  Erm 3 bars Gu
  Erm 3 bars Sa
  Gutty &c 3 bars
  Vair 3 bars   62
3 bars patterned
  3 bars Erm
  3 bars Ermines
  3 bars gobony
  3 bars Vair
3 bars modified   63
  3 bars couped ('hamaides')
  3 bars dancetty
  3 bars embattled
  3 bars engrailed &c   64
  3 bars wavy or nebuly
  Arg 3 bars wavy
  Az 3 bars wavy   65
  Or &c 3 bars wavy
  Erm &c 3 bars wavy
  Per pale 3 bars wavy
  3 bars wavy patterned
3 bars & label
  3 bars modified & label   66
3 bars & in base
3 bars & canton
  3 bars modified & canton
3 bars & on canton   67
  3 bars & on canton castle &c
  3 bars & on canton head &c
3 bars & chief
3 bars & on chief
3 bars & in chief   68
  3 bars & in chief beast
  3 bars & in chief bird   69
  3 bars & in chief crescent &c
  3 bars & in chief ermine spots &c
  3 bars & in chief fleur de lis &c
  3 bars & in chief lozenge &c
  3 bars & in chief pale &c
3 bars & over all   70
  3 bars & over all bend
  Arg 3 bars & bend
  Az &c 3 bars & bend
  3 bars & bend patterned   71
  3 bars & bend modified
  3 bars & bend sinister
  3 bars & on bend
  3 bars modified & bend
  3 bars & over all bend cotised
  3 bars & over all chevron &c
  3 bars & over all maunch &c
  3 bars over all ... & label   72
  3 bars canton & over all
  3 bars chief & over all
  3 bars chief & over all escutch (e.g.

  Mortimer): see Barry &c chief paly
3 bars betw
3 bars in border
On 3 bars (i.e. 3 bars, one or more
charged)   73
  On 3 bars bird &c
  On 3 bars crescent &c
  On 3 bars fleur de lis &c
  On 3 bars fruit &c
On 3 bars & canton   74
On 3 bars & chf
On 3 bars & over all
3 bars cotised

4 BARS OR 2 BARS GEMEL   74
  Arg 4 bars or 2 bars gemel
  Az &c 4 bars or 2 bars gemel   75
  Erm &c 4 bars or 2 bars gemel
  4 bars or 2 bars gemel patterned
  4 bars or 2 bars gemel modified
  4 bars or 2 bars gemel & label   76
  4 bars or 2 bars gemel & in base
  4 bars or 2 bars gemel & canton
    4 bars or 2 bars gemel & on canton
  4 bars or 2 bars gemel & chf
    Az 4 bars or 2 bars gemel & chf
    Gu 4 bars or 2 bars gemel & chf   77
    Or &c 4 bars or 2 bars gemel & chf
    Erm &c 4 bars or 2 bars gemel &
    chf
    4 bars or 2 bars gemel & patterned
    chf
    4 bars or 2 bars gemel & modified
    chf
  4 bars or 2 bars gemel chf & label
  4 bars or 2 bars gemel & on chf
  4 bars or 2 bars gemel & in chf   78
    4 bars or 2 bars gemel & in chf
    lion
    4 bars or 2 bars gemel & in chf
    lion pg
    4 bars or 2 bars gemel & in chf
    lion pg crowned   79
    4 bars or 2 bars gemel & in chf
    other beast &c
    4 bars or 2 bars gemel & in chf
    mullet &c
  4 bars or 2 bars gemel & in chf ... &
  label
  4 bars or 2 bars gemel & over all
  4 bars or 2 bars gemel & chf & over all 80
  4 bars or 2 bars gemel betw
  4 bars or 2 bars gemel betw & on chf
  4 bars or 2 bars gemel in border
  On 4 bars or 2 bars gemel

5 BARS   80
  5 bars & label
  5 bars & canton
  5 bars & in chf
  5 bars & over all   81
  5 bars betw

6 BARS OR 3 BARS GEMEL   81
  Arg 6 bars or 3 bars gemel
  Az &c 6 bars or 3 bars gemel
  Field patterned 6 bars or 3 bars gemel   82
  6 bars or 3 bars gemel modified
  6 bars or 3 bars gemel & canton
    6 bars or 3 bars gemel & canton
    patterned
  6 bars or 3 bars gemel & on canton
  6 bars or 3 bars gemel & chf   83
    Az 6 bars or 3 bars gemel Arg &
    chf
    Az 6 bars or 3 bars gemel Or & chf
  Gu &c 6 bars or 3 bars gemel & on chf   84
  6 bars or 3 bars gemel & in chf
  6 bars or 3 bars gemel & over all
    6 bars or 3 bars gemel & over all
    bend &c
  6 bars or 3 bars gemel betw
  6 bars or 3 bars gemel in border

7 BARS   84
  7 bars & over all &c

8 BARS OR 4 BARS GEMEL & MORE   85

BARRY OF 4   85
  Barry of 4 modified

BARRY OF 5   85
  See also 2 bars

BARRY OF 6   85
  Barry of 6 Arg and Az   87
  Barry of 6 Arg and Gu
  Barry of 6 Arg and Sa   88
  Barry of 6 Az &c
  Barry of 6 Gu &c
  Barry of 6 Or and Az
  Barry of 6 Or and Gu
  Barry of 6 Or and Sa   89
  Barry of 6 Or and Vt
  Barry of 6 Sa &c
  Barry of 6 Vt &c
  Barry of 6 including Erm
  Barry of 6 including fretty   90
  Barry of 6 including gobony
  Barry of 6 including per pale
  Barry of 6 including per pale

  indented
  Barry of 6 including semy
  Barry of 6 including Vairy   91
Barry of 6 modified   92
  Barry dancetty of 6 Gu & ...
  Barry dancetty of 6 Or & ...
  Barry indented of 6
  Barry lozengy of 6
  Barry pily of 6   93
  Barry wavy &c of 6 (plain)
  Barry wavy &c of 6 Arg and Az   94
  Barry wavy &c of 6 Arg and Gu
  Barry wavy &c of 6 Arg and ...   95
  Barry wavy &c of 6 Az and ...
  Barry wavy &c of 6 Gu and ...
  Barry wavy &c of 6 Or and ...
  Barry wavy &c of 6 Or and Gu
  Barry wavy &c of 6 Or and Sa &c   96
  Barry wavy of 6 Sa and ...   97
  Barry wavy &c of 6 (patterned)
  Barry of 6 and label

BARRY OF 8   97
  Barry of 8 Arg and Az
  Barry of 8 Arg and Gu
  Barry of 8 Arg and Sa   98
  Barry of 8 Az and Or
  Barry of 8 Gu and ...
  Barry of 8 Or and Az
  Barry of 8 Or and ...
  Barry of 8 Sa and Arg
  Barry of 8 including Erm and Vairy
Barry of 8 modified
  Barry dancetty &c of 8
  Barry wavy &c of 8
  Barry of 8 per   99

BARRY OF 10   99
  Barry of 10 modified
    Barry dancetty &c of 10

BARRY OF 12   99
  Barry of 12 patterned or modified   100

BARRY OF 14 OR MORE   100

BARRY UNNUMBERED   100
  Barry unnumbered Arg and Az
  Barry unnumbered Arg and Gu
  Barry unnumbered Arg and Sa
  Barry unnumbered Or and Az
  Barry unnumbered Or and Gu
  Barry unnumbered Or and Sa   101
  Barry unnumbered Erm and
  Ermines
  Barry & label: see under Label

BARRY &c CHIEF PALY   101
  Barry chief paly & corners gyronny
  Barry &c on chief 2 pales & over all
  escutch
    Barry &c on chf 2 pales escutch
    patterned
    Barry &c on chf 2 pales escutch
    charged
  Barry chief paly corners gyronny &
  over all escutch
    Barry chf paly corners gyronny Arg
    and Az (or vice versa) over all
    escutch   102
    Barry chf paly corners gyronny Arg
    and Sa (or vice versa) over all
    escutch
    Barry chf paly corners gyronny Az
    and Or (or vice versa) escutch Arg
    Barry Az and Or chf paly corners
    gyronny Or and Gu escutch Arg   103
    Barry chf paly corners gyronny Gu
    and Or (or vice versa) escutch Arg
    Barry chf paly corners gyronny Or
    and Sa (or vice versa) escutch Arg   104
    Barry (patterned) chf paly corners
    gyronny over all escutch plain
  'Mortimer' escutch barry
  'Mortimer' escutch Erm
  'Mortimer' escutch semy
  'Mortimer' escutch charged
  'Mortimer' & on escutch label   105
  'Mortimer' on escutch label of 3
  'Mortimer' & on escutch nails &c
  'Mortimer' & base
  'Mortimer' & canton
  'Mortimer' & over all bend   106
  'Mortimer' & over all saltire
  'Mortimer' in border

BARROW   106

BASKET   106

BEACON   106

BEAST (1 LION RAMPANT)   107
  Lion rampant Untinc &c
  Lion rampant to sinister Untinc   122
  Lion rampant (tinctures deficient)   123
  Lion rampant tinctured (to dexter or
  sinister)
    Arg lion Az
    Arg lion Gu &c   124
    Arg lion Purp   125
    Arg lion Sa   126
    Arg lion Vt   127
    Az lion Arg
    Az lion Gu   128
    Az lion Or
    Gu lion Arg   129
    Gu lion Az   130
    Gu lion Or
    Gu lion Sa   132
    Or lion Az
    Or lion Gu   134
    Or lion Purp   136
    Or lion Sa   137
    Or lion Vt   138
    Purp lion Arg
    Purp lion Or
    Sa lion Arg
    Sa lion Or   139
    Vt lion Arg
    Vt lion Or
  1 lion field patterned   140
  Barry 1 lion
  Barry Arg and Az 1 lion Gu
  Barry Arg and Gu 1 lion
  Barry Arg &c and Sa &c 1 lion
  Barry wavy 1 lion   141
  Bendy 1 lion
  Checky &c 1 lion
  Erm 1 lion
  Erm lion Az
  Erm lion Gu
  Erm lion Sa
  Ermines &c 1 lion
  Fretty 1 lion   142
  Lozengy 1 lion
  Paly 1 lion
  Per bend 1 lion
  Per bend sin 1 lion
  Per chev 1 lion
  Per chf 1 lion: see chf & over all
  Per fess 1 lion
  Per pale 1 lion
  Per pale Arg & ...1 lion   143
  Per pale Az & ...1 lion
  Per pale Gu & ... 1 lion
  Per pale Or & ... 1 lion
  Per pale Or and Vt 1 lion
  Per pale Vt &... 1 lion   144

Per pale patterned 1 Lion
Per pale indented 1 lion
Per saltire 1 lion
Qtly lion in dex chf: see Quarterly
(in later volume)
Qtly 1 lion over all
Semy of annulets 1 lion   145
Billetty 1 lion
Arg billetty 1 lion
Az billetty 1 lion
Gu billetty 1 lion   146
Or &c billetty 1 lion
Semy of crescents 1 lion
Crusily botonny 1 lion
Crusily couped 1 lion
Semy of crosslets 1 lion   147
Arg semy of crosslets 1 lion
Az semy of crosslets 1 lion
Az semy of crosslets 1 lion Or   148
Gu semy of crosslets 1 lion
Or semy of crosslets 1 lion
Sa semy of crosslets 1 lion   149
Crusily fitchy 1 lion
Az crusily fitchy 1 lion
Gu crusily fitchy Arg 1 lion
Gu crusily fitchy Or &c 1 lion   150
Or &c crusily fitchy 1 lion
Semy of crosses formy &c 1 lion
Semy of escallops 1 lion
Semy of fleurs de lis 1 lion   151
Arg semy of fleurs de lis 1 lion
Az semy of fleurs de lis Arg lion
Arg
Az semy of fleurs de lis Or lion
Arg
Az semy of fleurs de lis Or lion Or   152
Gu &c semy of fleurs de lis 1 lion
Semy of foils 1 lion
Semy of fruit 1 lion   153
Semy of gouttes &c 1 lion
Semy of pheons 1 lion
Semy of roundels 1 lion
Vair 1 lion
1 lion patterned or charged
Lion head distinguished
Lion barry &c
Lion bendy &c   154
Lion charged with annulet
Lion ch with billets &c
Lion ch with crescent &c   155
Lion ch with fleur de lis
Lion ch with foil &c
Lion ch with mullet   156
Lion ch with roundel
Lion checky   157
Lion Erm

Lion Erm field patterned
Lion Ermines   158
Lion fretty
Lion lozengy
Lion per bend
Lion per bend sin   159
Lion per bend sin modified
Lion per fess
Lion per fess field patterned
Lion per fess Erm &c & ...   160
Lion per fess fretty & ...
Lion per pale &c
Lion quarterly
Lion semy
Lion gutty &c
Lion Vair   161
Lion vulned
Lion rampant coward   162
Lion dismembered
Lion in umbre
Lion holding, supporting or pierced
by: see after lion tricorporate
Lion collared
Az lion collared
Gu &c lion collared   163
Sa lion collared
Lion patterned or charged and col-
lared
Lion with collar patterned or
charged
Lion collared and chained
Lion collared with label &c
Lion crowned   164
Arg lion crowned   165
Arg lion Gu crowned Or etc
Arg lion Or &c crowned   166
Arg lion Sa crowned Or
Az lion Arg crowned
Az lion Or crowned   167
Gu lion Arg &c crowned
Gu lion Or &c crowned
Or lion crowned   168
Purp lion crowned
Sa lion Arg &c crowned
Vt lion crowned   169
Barry lion crowned
Barry Arg and Gu lion crowned
Barry Az &c & Arg lion crowned   170
Erm lion Az crowned
Erm lion Gu &c crowned
Per pale lion crowned
Semy of billets lion crowned
Crusily lion crowned
Crusily fitchy lion crowned   171
Semy de lis &c lion crowned

Vair lion crowned
Lion patterned or charged & crowned
  Lion barry & crowned
  Lion charged with annulet &c and
  crowned
  Lion charged with mullet &
  crowned   172
  Lion checky crowned
  Lion Erm crowned
  Field patterned lion Erm crowned
  Lion per fess crowned   173
  Lion semy crowned
  Lion Vair crowned
  Lion vulned & crowned
Lion crowned with something else
Lion crowned & collared
  Crowned lion holding, supporting or
  pierced by: see after lion tricor-
  porate
Lion queue fourchy
  Demi-lion qf
  Lion qf   174
  Arg lion qf Untinc &c   175
  Arg lion qf Purp &c   176
  Az lion qf
  Gu lion qf Arg   177
  Gu lion qf Or
  Or lion qf Az &c
  Or lion qf Gu &c   178
  Or lion qf Sa
  Or lion qf Vt   179
  Sa lion qf Arg
  Sa lion qf Or
  Field patterned lion qf
  Lion qf charged   180
  Lion qf Erm
  Lion qf fretty &c
  Lion qf vulned   181
Lion qf collared
Lion qf crowned
  Demi-lion qf crowned
  Lion qf crowned
  Az lion qf crowned   182
  Field patterned lion qf crowned
  Lion qf patterned & crowned
Lion tail knotted (not forked)   183
Lion qf & knotted &c
  Patterned field lion qf & knotted
  Lion patterned qf & knotted &c
Lion qf & knotted &c crowned
  Field patterned lion qf & knotted
  &c crowned   184
  Lion patterned or charged qf knot-
  ted &c crowned

BEAST (1 LION COUCHANT &c)   184
  Lion couchant qf
  Lion dormant

BEAST (1 LION PASSANT)   185
  Demi-lion passt
  Lion passt
  Lion passant to sinister Untinc
  Arg &c lion passant
  Barry &c lion passant   186
  Per pale lion passant
  Qtly &c lion passant
  Lion passant patterned
  Lion passant coward   187
  Lion passant collared &c

BEAST (1 LION SALIENT)   187
  Lion salient crowned   188

BEAST (1 LION SEJANT)   188

BEAST (1 LION STATANT)   188
  Lion statant crowned

BEAST (1 LION GUARDANT)   188
  Lion rampant guardant
    Az lion ramp gard   189
    Gu lion ramp gard
    Or lion ramp gard   190
    Sa &c lion ramp gard
    Barry &c lion ramp gard
    Semy of crosses lion ramp gard
    Semy de lis &c lion ramp gard
    Lion ramp gard charged   191
    Lion ramp gard patterned   192
  Lion ramp gard collared
  Lion ramp gard crowned
  Lion ramp gard qf
  Lion ramp gard qf crowned
  Lion passant guardant
    Arg &c lion pg   193
    Gu lion pg
    Or &c lion pg
    Barry &c lion pg
    Lion pg charged or patterned   194
  Lion passant guardant crowned
    Gu lion pg crowned
    Crusily lion pg crowned   195
    Lion pg crowned and coward
  Lion salient guardant
  Lion sejant guardant
  Lion statant guardant
    Lion stat gard crowned

BEAST (1 LION REGARDANT)   196
 Lion rampant regardant
  Lion ramp regard coward
  Lion ramp regard crowned
 Lion couchant regardant
 Lion passant regardant
 Lion sejant regardant

BEAST (1 UNNATURAL LION)   196
 Lion winged
 Lion with 2 heads
 Lion bicorporate   197
 Lion tricorporate
 Lion dimidiating ship

BEAST (1 LION HOLDING &c)   197
 Lion holding axe
 Lion crowned holding axe   198
 Lion in chair holding axe
 Lion holding baton &c
 Lion holding hand &c   199
 Lion holding human being &c
 Lion holding sword &c
 Lion pierced by

BEAST (OTHER)   199
 Antelope &c
 Bear
  Bear passant   200
  Bear rampant
  Bear salient
 Boar
  Boar passant
  Boar passant charged or patterned
  Boar rampant &c
 Camel   201
 Cat
  Coney: see hare
 1 Deer (buck, hart, roedeer, stag, &c)
  Deer (buck &c) courant
  Deer (buck &c) lodged
  Deer (buck &c) passant
  Deer (buck &c) rampant
  Deer (buck &c) salient
  Deer (buck &c) statant
  Deer (buck &c) regardant   202
  Deer (buck &c) holding
  Deer (hind)
 Dog (including alaund, bloodhound,
 dog, greyhound, hound, kennet, levrier,
 mastiff, talbot, &c)
  Dog couchant
  Dog courant
  Dog passant
  Dog salient
  Dog sejant

 Dog statant
 Dog collared   203
  Dog couchant collared
  Dog passant collared
  Dog salient collared
  Dog statant collared
  Dog regardant collared
 Dog holding
 Elephant
 Fox
  Fox holding
 Goat
  Goat rampant   204
  Goat salient
 Hare (including coney, leveret, rabbit)
 Horse (including ass, donkey, mule)
  Horse harnessed   205
  Horse & ...
  Leopard: see lion passt gard
 Otter
 Ox (& bull)
  Sea-Dog, Sea-Lion &c: see under
  Monster
 Sheep (including lamb, ram)
 Squirrel   206
 Tiger
 Urchin (including hedgehog & porcu-
 pine)
 Wolf   207
  Wolf rampant
  Wolf salient
  Wolf collared
  Wolf holding

BEAST & LABEL   207
 Lion & label
  Arg lion & label   208
  Az &c lion & label
  Or lion & label   209
  Sa lion & label
  Erm &c lion & label
  Lion charged or patterned & label
  Lion crowned & label
  Lion qf & label   210
  Lion passt &c & label
  Lion ramp gard & label
  Lion passt gard & label
  Lion & patterned label   211
 Beast (other) & label

BEAST & IN BASE 211
  Lion & in base
  Other beast & in base

BEAST BESIDE OR IN FRONT OF 212

BEAST & CANTON 212
  Lion ramp & canton

BEAST & CHIEF 213
  Lion ramp & chf
  Lion ramp crowned &c & chf
  Lion passt &c & chf
  Other beast & chf
  Beast chief & label

BEAST & ON CHIEF 213
  Lion & on chf escallop &c 214
  Other beast & on chf

BEAST & IN CHIEF 215
  Lion & in chf
  Other beast & in chf &c 216
  Ox &c & in chf
  Beast & in chief & label

BEAST (LION) & OVER ALL 216
  Demi-lion & over all bend
  Plain field lion ramp over all bend
    Lion & bend Untinc
    Lion & bend sin 218
    Arg lion & bend
    Az lion & bend
    Gu lion & bend 219
    Or lion & bend
    Sa &c lion & bend
  Field patterned, lion ramp plain, bend
  plain
  Lion ramp charged or patterned &c
  bend plain 220
    Lion crowned bend plain
    Lion qf bend plain
  Lion passt & bend 221
  Lion guardant & bend
  Lion ramp & bend patterned
    Lion & bend Erm &c
    Lion & bend gobony
    Or &c lion & bend gobony 222
    Field patterned lion & bend gobony
    Lion patterned & bend gobony
    Lion qf & bend gobony
    Lion & bend Vair
  Lion ramp & bend charged 223
    Lion & on bend escallops &c
    Lion & on bend mullets

    Lion & on bend roundels
  Lion ramp & bend modified 224
  Lion & 2 or more bends
  Lion & chevron
  Lion & escutcheon
  Lion ramp & fess 225
    Lion plain, fess plain
    Lion crowned, fess plain
    Lion qf, fess plain
    Lion gard, fess plain
    Lion with fess patterned
    Lion qf, fess patterned
    Lion with fess modified
    Lion with fess charged
  Lion & pale &c 226

BEAST (OTHER) & OVER ALL 226

BEAST & OVER ALL & LABEL 226

BEAST BETWEEN 226
  Lion between
    Lion betw bends &c
    Lion betw 3 crosses 227
    Lion betw 4 crosses or more
    Lion betw escallops &c 228
    Lion betw flaunches, &c
    Lion betw fleurs de lis
    Lion betw flowers
    Lion betw foils
    Lion betw hats &c 229
    Lion betw mullets
    Lion betw pheons
    Lion betw roundels &c
  Beast (other) between
  Beast (lion) in orle of 230
    Lion in orle of crosses
    Lion in orle of escallops &c 231
    Lion in orle of foils
    Lion in orle of 6foils 232
    Lion in orle of mullets &c
  Beast (other) in orle of
  Beast betw ... & label
  Beast betw ... & chief
  Beast betw ... & in chief
  Beast betw ... & over all 233

BEAST IN BORDER   233
  Demi-lion in border
  Lion in plain border
    Az lion in border   234
    Gu lion in border
    Or lion in border
    Field patterned lion in border   235
    Lion crowned in border
    Lion qf &c in border
    Lion gard &c in border
  Lion in patterned border   236
    Lion in border Erm
    Lion in border gobony
    Lion in border party indented
    Lion in border per fess
    Lion in border semy of annulets &c   237
    Lion in border semy of flowers
    Lion in border semy of foils &c   238
    Lion in border semy of mullets
    Lion in border semy of roundels
    Lion collared in border roundelly   239
    Lion crowned in border roundelly
    Lion qf in border roundelly   240
    Lion passant in border roundelly
    Lion in border Vair
  Lion in border modified
    Arg lion border engrailed   241
    Az lion in border engr   242
    Gu lion Arg in border engr
    Gu lion Or in border engr
    Or lion in border engr   243
    Sa &c lion in border engr   244
    Lion in border engr field patterned
    Lion patterned or charged in plain
    border engr
    Lion in patterned border engr
    Lion in border engr gobony &c
    Lion in border engr semy &c   245
    Lion crowned in border engr
    Lion crowned in patterned border
    engr
    Lion qf in border engr
    Lion passant &c in border engr
    Lion bicorporate in border engr
    Lion in border indented   246
    Lion in border wavy &c
  Other Beast in border
    Dog in plain border
    Dog in patterned border
    Dog in modified border
    Goat &c in border
    Ox (bull) &c in border
  Beast & label in border   247
  Beast & in base in border
  Beast & in chief in border   248

Beast & over all in border
  Lion & bend in border
  Lion & fess in border
Beast betw ... & border
  Lion betw ... & border
  Buck or Stag betw ... & border   249
  Hind betw ... & border
  Dog betw ... in border

BEAST IN TRESSURE   249
  Lion in single tressure
  Lion in double tressure untinc
  Arg &c lion in double tressure   250
  Or lion in double tressure Gu   251
  Or lion in double tressure Sa &c
  Lion dormant in tressure   252
  Beast (other) in tressure
  Lion & label in tressure
  Lion & in chief in tressure
  Lion & over all in tressure
  Lion betw ...in tressure
  Lion in tressure in border

BEAST (LION) WITH OTHER BEAST OR
MONSTER   252

2 BEASTS (LIONS)   253
  2 demi-lions
  2 lions rampant
    2 lions combatant
    Field patterned 2 lions combatant
    2 lions combatant coward &c
    2 lions addorsed   254
  2 lions dormant
  2 lions passant
    Arg 2 lions passt Az &c   256
    Arg 2 lions passt Sa &c   257
    Az 2 lions passt
    Gu 2 lions passt   258
    Gu 2 lions passt Or   259
    Or 2 lions passt Az
    Or 2 lions passt Gu &c
    Sa &c 2 lions passt   260
    Field patterned 2 lions passt
    2 lions passt charged or patterned
    2 lions counter-passt   261
    2 lions passt collared
    2 lions passt crowned
    Arg &c 2 lions passt crowned
    Gu &c 2 lions passt crowned
    Sa 2 lions passt crowned   262
    2 lions passt charged or patterned &
    crowned
    2 lions passt crowned holding
  2 lions statant
  2 lions guardant

2 lions pg Untinc
Arg 2 lions pg   263
Az 2 lions pg
Gu 2 lions pg   264
Or 2 lions pg
Sa &c 2 lions pg   265
Field patterned 2 plain lions pg
2 lions pg charged or patterned
2 lions pg coward
2 lions pg collared &c
2 lions regardant

2 BEASTS (OTHER)   266
2 deer
2 dogs &c
2 oxen &c

2 BEASTS & LABEL   267
2 lions passt & label
2 lions gard &c & label
2 lions & charged label   268

2 BEASTS & IN BASE   268
2 lions & in base
2 other beasts & in base

2 BEASTS BESIDE   268

2 BEASTS & CANTON   268
2 lions canton charged
2 lions canton patterned
2 wolves & canton

2 BEASTS & CHIEF   269

2 BEASTS & IN CHIEF   269
2 lions & in chf
2 bears &c & in chf

2 BEASTS & OVER ALL   270
2 lions passt & bend
2 lions passt bend charged or patterned
2 lions pg &c & over all bend
2 lions over all cross
2 lions over all ... & label

2 BEASTS BETWEEN   271

2 BEASTS IN ORLE   271

2 BEASTS IN BORDER   271
2 lions in border
2 lions in plain border
2 lions passt border semy of
martlets: see under Escutcheon
2 lions in patterned border
2 lions in engrailed border
2 lions in border indented   272
2 other beasts in border
2 beasts & label in border
2 beasts & in base in border
2 beasts & over all in border   273
2 beasts betw in border

2 BEASTS IN TRESSURE   273
2 beasts in tressure & label

3 BEASTS (LIONS)   273
3 demi-lions
For demi-lions in the form of lions
pg dimidiated see also 3 lions pg
3 demi-lions ramp
3 demi-lions passt   274
3 demi-lions pg
3 lions rampant   275
Arg 3 lions Gu   276
Arg 3 lions Or &c
Arg 3 lions Sa
Az 3 lions
Gu 3 lions Arg   277
Gu 3 lions Or
Or 3 lions   278
Sa 3 lions
Vt 3 lions
Barry 3 lions
Checky 3 lions   279
Erm 3 lions
Per bend &c 3 lions
Per pale &c 3 lions
Semy 3 lions   280
3 lions charged or patterned
3 lions collared   281
3 lions crowned
3 lions qf
3 lions couchant
3 lions passant
Arg 3 lions passt   282
Az 3 lions passt   283
Gu 3 lions passt
Gu 3 lions passt Or   284
Or 3 lions passt Az &c
Or 3 lions passt Sa
Sa 3 lions passt   285

Field patterned 3 lions passt
3 lions passt charged or patterned
3 lions passt crowned
3 lions rampant guardant
England dimidg another coat: see
under 3 demi-lions
England qtd by France: see in later
volume under fleurs de lis
3 lions passant guardant
Arg 3 lions pg Gu   286
Az 3 lions pg
Gu 3 lions pg Arg   287
Gu 3 lions pg Or (England)
Or 3 lions pg   288
Vt 3 lions pg Arg
3 lions pg field patterned   289
3 lions pg crowned
3 lions regardant

3 BEASTS (OTHER)   289
3 bears
3 boars   290
3 camels
3 cats   291
3 deer courant &c
3 deer passant
3 deer salient   292
3 deer statant
3 deer guardant &c
3 dogs courant
3 dogs courant collared   293
Patterned field 3 dogs courant collared
3 dogs passant
3 dogs passant collared   294
3 dogs statant
3 elephants
3 foxes
3 goats
3 hares, conies &c
3 horses &c   295
3 moles
3 otters
3 oxen
3 rats
3 sheep (lambs)
3 sheep (rams)
3 Squirrels
3 urchins, hedgehogs, &c   296
3 wolves courant
3 wolves passant &c

3 BEASTS (LIONS) & LABEL   297
3 lions rampant & label
3 lions passant & label
3 lions passant guardant & label
Gu 3 lions pg & label Arg &c   298
Gu 3 lions pg Or label Az &c   299
3 lions pg label charged
3 lions pg label semy de lis
England & France qtly label   301

3 BEASTS (OTHER) & LABEL   301

3 BEASTS & IN BASE   301

3 BEASTS & CANTON   301

3 BEASTS (LIONS) & CHIEF   301
3 lions ramp & chf
3 lions passt & chf
3 lions gard &c & chf

3 BEASTS (OTHER) & CHIEF   302

3 BEASTS (LIONS) & ON CHIEF   302

3 BEASTS (OTHER) & ON CHIEF   302

3 BEASTS & IN CHIEF   302

3 BEASTS & OVER ALL   302
3 lions & over all bend
3 lions ramp & bend
3 lions passt & bend
3 lions gard & bend   303
Gu &c 3 lions pg & bend   304
3 lions regard & bend
3 lions & over all bend patterned
3 lions and over all bend charged
3 lions & over all crozier &c
3 lions over all ... & label   305
3 lions over all ... & in chief

3 BEASTS (LIONS) BETWEEN   305

3 BEASTS (OTHER) BETWEEN   305

3 BEASTS IN ORLE OF   305

3 BEASTS BETW ... & IN CHF   305

3 BEASTS IN BORDER   305
  3 Lions in plain border
    3 lions ramp in plain border
    3 lions passt in plain border   306
    3 lions gard in plain border
    Gu 3 lions pg Or border Arg
    Gu 3 lions pg Or border Az   307
  3 lions in patterned border
    3 lions in border Erm
    3 lions ramp in border gobony
    3 lions gard in border gobony
    3 lions gard in border per pale
    3 lions in border semy of birds
    3 lions passt in border semy de lis
    3 lions gard in border semy de lis
    3 lions ramp in border semy of
    roundels   308
    3 lions gard in border semy of
    roundels
  3 lions in border modified
    3 lions ramp in border engr
    3 lions passt in border engr   309
    3 lions in border indented
    3 lions in border invected
  3 beasts (other) in border

3 BEASTS & IN BASE &c ... IN BORDER 309
  3 beasts impaling ... in border
  3 beasts qtg ... in border
  England & France qtly in border

3 BEASTS & ... & LABEL IN BORDER   310

3 BEASTS (LIONS) IN TRESSURE   310

4 BEASTS   310
  4 beasts (lions)
    Qtly 4 lions
    4 lions crowned
    4 lions passt
    4 lions gard   311
  4 beasts (other)
  4 beasts (lions) & ...

5 BEASTS   311
  5 lions & canton
  5 lions canton charged or patterned
  5 lions & on chf &c   312

6 BEASTS   312
  6 beasts (lions)
    Arg 6 lions   313
    Az 6 lions Arg   314
    Az 6 lions Or
    Gu 6 lions
    Or 6 lions   315
    Sa 6 lions Arg
    Sa 6 lions Gu &c
    Vt 6 lions
    6 lions patterned
    6 lions crowned
    6 lions qf   316
    6 lions couchant &c
  6 beasts (other)
  6 beasts & label
    6 lions & label
  6 beasts & canton
    6 lions canton charged
    6 lions canton patterned
  6 beasts canton & label   317
  6 beasts & chief
  6 beasts & over all
  6 beasts in border
    6 lions in border
    6 lions crowned in border
  6 beasts & canton in border

12 BEASTS OR MORE   317

BELL   317
  3 bells   318
  10 bells

BELLOWS   318

BELTS &c   318
  See also buckles

BEND   318
  Per bend
    Per bend modified

1 BEND   319
  Untinc 1 bend
  Arg bend Az   321
  Arg bend Gu   322
  Arg bend Purp &c
  Az bend Arg   323
  Az bend Or
  Gu bend Arg   324
  Gu bend Or &c   325
  Or bend Az
  Or bend Gu
  Or bend Sa &c
  Sa bend Arg &c   326

Vt bend Arg &c

Vairy & bend

1 BEND FIELD PATTERNED   326
- Barry of 4 & bend
- Barry of 6 & bend
- Barry of 6 Arg & Az bend   327
- Barry Arg & Gu bend   328
- Barry Arg & Sa &c bend
- Barry Az &c bend
- Barry Or & Arg &c bend
- Barry Or & Gu &c bend   329
- Barry Sa &c bend
- Barry of 8 or more & bend   330
- Barry wavy or nebuly & bend
- Checky & bend
- Erm & bend   331
- Erm bend Gu
- Erm bend Sa   332
- Gyronny & bend
- Lozengy & bend
- Paly & bend
- Paly Arg & Az bend Gu
- Paly Arg & Gu &c bend Arg &c   333
- Paly Or & Az bend Gu
- Paly Or & Gu bend Arg
- Paly Or & Gu &c bend Az &c
- See also under 1, 2, 3 pales &c and over all
- Per bend sin &c bend   334
- Per pale bend
- Pily & bend
- Qtly bend
- Qtly Arg & Az bend Gu   335
- Qtly Arg & Gu bend Az
- Qtly Arg & Gu bend Gu &c
- Qtly Arg & Gu bend Sa   336
- Qtly Arg & Sa bend Gu &c
- Qtly Arg & Sa bend Sa
- Qtly Az & Or bend Gu
- Qtly Gu & Untinc &c bend Or &c
- Qtly Gu & Or &c bend Arg &c   337
- Qtly Or & Az bend Gu
- Qtly Or & Gu bend Arg &c
- Qtly Or & Gu bend Sa &c
- Qtly Or & Sa &c bend Gu &c   338
- Qtly Sa & Arg bend Arg &c
- Qtly 1&4 fretty &c over all bend
- Qtly 2&3 fretty over all bend
- Qtly 2&3 semy over all bend   340
- Qtly 2&3 Vair over all bend
- Qtly modified & bend
- Semy of billets & bend   341
- Semy of crosses & bend
- Semy of crosses fitchy & bend
- Semy de lis & bend
- Semy of foils &c & bend
- Vair & bend   342

1 BEND PATTERNED   342
- Bend barry
- Bend bendy
- Bend checky or counter gobony
- Erm bend checky &c   343
- Fretty &c bend checky
- Bend chevronny
- Bend Erm
- Gu bend Erm
- Sa &c bend Erm
- Barry bend Erm   344
- Barry wavy &c bend Erm
- Checky bend Erm
- Paly &c bend Erm   345
- Bend Ermines
- Bend fimbriated
- Bend fretty
- Bend gobony
- Barry bend gobony   346
- Checky &c bend gobony
- Paly bend gobony
- Qtly &c bend gobony
- Bend lozengy &c
- Bend per bend &c   347
- Per pale bend counterch
- Bend qtly
- Bend billety
- Bend semy of cross crosslets   348
- Bend semy de lis
- Bend roundelly
- Bend Vair
- Gu bend Vair
- Checky &c bend Vair
- Erm bend Vair
- Fretty bend Vair
- Paly bend Vair
- Qtly bend Vair
- Qtly Gu & Or bend Vair   349
- Qtly Or & Gu bend Vair
- Semy bend Vair

1 BEND MODIFIED   349
- Bend arched
- Bend couped
- Bend dancetty
- Bend embattled
- Bend embattled counter-embattled   350
- Bend engrailed
  - Arg bend engr Az   351
  - Arg bend engr Gu
  - Arg bend engr Purp
  - Arg bend engr Sa
  - Az bend engr Arg &c   352
  - Gu bend engr Arg

Gu bend engr Or
Or bend engr Az
Or bend engr Gu
Or bend engr Sa
Sa bend engr Arg
Sa bend engr Or
Barry bend engr
Barry wavy bend engr 353
Checky bend engr
Erm bend engr Az &c
Erm bend engr Sa
Per pale bend engr
Qtly bend engr
Qtly 1&4 patterned bend engr
Qtly 2&3 patterned bend engr
Billety bend engr
Semy of crosses bend engr
Vair bend engr
Bend engr & patterned or fimbri-
ated 354
Bend flory
Sa bend flory Or
Barry bend flory
Bend fracted or rompu
Bend indented
Field patterned bend indented 355
Bend indented patterned
Bend lozengy
Bend of demi-lozenges
See below for bend of 3, 4 or more
lozenges (number specified)
Bend lozengy
Arg bend lozengy Arg (sic) 356
Arg bend lozengy Az
Arg bend lozengy Gu &c
Arg bend lozengy Sa
Az bend lozengy Arg 357
Az bend lozengy Or
Gu bend lozengy Untinc &c
Gu bend lozengy Or
Or bend lozengy Az
Or bend lozengy Gu
Or bend lozengy Sa 358
Sa bend lozengy Arg
Sa bend lozengy Or
Vt bend lozengy Or
Field patterned bend lozengy
Erm bend lozengy 359
Qtly bend lozengy
Semy bend lozengy
Vair bend lozengy
Bend lozengy patterned
Bend masculy
Bend raguly 360
Bend voided: see bend fimbriated
Bend wavy or nebuly

Arg bend wavy Sa
Gu &c bend wavy

BEND & LABEL 361
Arg bend Az label Gu
Arg bend Sa label Gu 362
Arg bend Sa label Or
Arg bend Vt label Gu
Az bend Or label Arg
Az bend Or label Gu &c 363
Gu bend & label
Or bend & label
Field patterned bend & label
Barry &c bend & label
Qtly Untinc bend & label
Qtly Arg &c bend & label 364
Qtly Or &c bend & label
Qtly 2&3 fretty bend & label
Semy &c bend & label
Bend patterned & label
Bend modified & label
Bend engr & label 365
Bend lozengy & label
Bend & label charged or patterned

BEND & IN BASE 366

BEND & CANTON 366

BEND & CHIEF 366
Bend patterned chief plain
Bend modified chief plain
Bend & patterned chief 367
Bend & modified chief
Bend chief & label
Bend & on chief
Bend & on chief escallops &c
Bend on chief mullets
Bend & on chief roundels &c 368
Bend & on chief & label

BEND & IN CHIEF 368
Bend & in chief bird
Bend & in chief book &c 369
Bend & in chief castle
Bend & in chief crescent
Bend & in chief cross &c
Bend & in chief head 370
Bend & in chief horn &c
Bend & in chief mullet &c

BEND & OVER ALL   370
    Bend & over all cross &c   371
    Bend & over all fess &c
    Bend & over all staff

BEND BETWEEN   371
    Bend betw annulets
    Bend betw 2 beasts   372
    Bend betw 2 lions passt &c
    Bend betw 3 beasts
    Bend betw 4 beasts
    Bend betw 6 beasts (lions)
    Bend patterned &c betw 6 lions   373
    Bend betw 6 other beasts
    Bend betw bendlets: see bend
    cotised
    Bend betw billets
    Bend plain betw 6 billets
    Bend engr &c betw 6 billets
    Bend betw 7 billets or more   374
    Bend betw bird &
    Bend betw 2 birds
    Bend betw 3 birds
    Bend betw 6 birds
    Bend betw 6 eagles
    Bend betw 6 geese
    Bend betw 6 martlets
    Arg bend betw 6 martlets Gu   375
    Arg bend betw 6 martlets Sa   376
    Az bend betw 6 martlets Arg
    Az bend betw 6 martlets Or   377
    Gu bend betw 6 martlets
    Or bend betw 6 martlets
    Sa bend betw 6 martlets   378
    Bend modified betw 6 martlets
    Bend betw 6 owls &c
    Bend betw bougets &c
    Bend betw castles &c
    Bend betw cotises or bendlets: see
    bend cotised
    Bend betw 2 crescents
    Sa bend betw 2 crescents   379
    Bend engr betw 2 crescents
    Bend betw 3 crescents
    Bend betw 6 crescents
    Bend betw cronels
    Bend betw 1 cross &
    Bend betw 2 crosses
    Bend betw 3 crosses
    Bend betw 3 crosses & ...   380
    Bend betw 4 crosses
    Bend betw 6 crosses
    Bend betw 6 crosses botonny
    6 crosses formy &c follow 6 cross
    crosslets fitchy
    Bend betw 6 cross crosslets

    Arg bend betw 6 cross crosslets
    Az bend betw 6 cross crosslets   381
    Gu bend betw 6 cross crosslets
    Or bend betw 6 cross crosslets
    Sa bend betw 6 cross crosslets
    Bend patterned betw 6 cross
    crosslets
    Bend modified betw 6 cross
    crosslets
    Bend betw 6 cross crosslets fitchy
    Arg bend betw 6 cross crosslets
    fitchy   382
    Az bend betw 6 cross crosslets
    fitchy
    Gu bend betw 6 cross crosslets
    fitchy
    Sa bend betw 6 cross crosslets
    fitchy   383
    Bend patterned &c betw 6 cross
    crosslets fitchy
    Bend betw 6 crosses formy &c
    Bend betw 7 or more crosses
    Bend betw 3 cups &c   384
    Bend betw 6 cups
    Az bend betw 6 cups Or
    Bend betw escallops
    Bend betw 6 escallops
    Arg bend betw 6 escallops
    Az bend betw 6 escallops
    Gu bend betw 6 escallops   385
    Sa bend betw 6 escallops
    Bend patterned &c betw 6 escallops
    Bend betw 8 escallops
    Bend betw escutcheons
    Bend betw estoile &
    Bend betw 2 or more estoiles
    Bend betw fish   386
    Bend betw fleurs de lis
    Bend betw 6 fleurs de lis
    Bend betw flowers
    Bend betw foils   387
    Bend betw frets: see qtly 2&3 fretty
    over all bend
    Bend betw garbs
    Bend betw hands
    Bend betw 1 head (beasts) &
    Bend betw 2 heads (beasts)
    Bend betw 2 heads (birds)   388
    Bend betw 3 heads (lions) &c
    Bend betw 3 heads (other beasts)
    Bend betw 3 heads (birds)
    Bend betw 3 heads (monsters)
    Bend betw 4 heads (beasts)
    Bend betw 6 heads (beasts)
    Bend betw 6 heads (monsters)
    Bend betw horseshoes
    Bend betw insects &c   389

Bend betw knives
Bend betw leaves
Bend betw letters &c
Bend betw lozenges or mascles
Bend betw 6 lozenges or mascles
Bend betw monsters
Bend betw mullet & ...
Bend betw 2 mullets
Bend betw 3 mullets   390
Bend betw 6 mullets
Arg bend betw 6 mullets
Az bend betw 6 mullets
Gu &c bend betw 6 mullets
Bend betw nails
Bend betw pheons
Bend betw picks   391
Bend betw roundels
Bend betw 3 fountains
Bend betw 6 roundels
Gu bend betw 6 roundels
Sa bend betw 6 roundels
Bend betw 6 fountains
Bend modified betw 6 roundels   392
Bend betw 10 roundels
Bend betw saltire & ...
Bend betw staves &c
Bend betw wings
Bend betw wreaths

BEND BETWEEN & LABEL   392

BEND BETWEEN & CHIEF   392

BEND BETWEEN & ON CHIEF   392

BEND BETWEEN & IN CHIEF   393

BEND IN BORDER   393
Bend patterned or modified in plain
border
Bend in patterned border
    Bend in border semy &c   394
Bend in border modified
    Arg bend in border engr
    Az &c bend in border engr
    Or bend in border engr   395
Field patterned bend plain in border
engr
Bend patterned in border engr
Bend patterned in border engr &
patterned
Bend modified in border engr
Bend in border indented &c

BEND & IN CHIEF IN BORDER   395

BEND BETWEEN ... IN BORDER   395
    Bend betw ... in plain border
    Bend betw ... in border engr

BEND IN TRESSURE   396

The Ordinary

UNCHARGED

Untinc plain

— *CombeAsp II 158. (qtg 2&3 checky & 4 lion, imp by Jn de Bohun, E of Heref & Northamp).*

— *RH, Ancestor vii 199. (traces of barry Or?Gu?Arg lion crowned Or; shield & name (Sir Hugh Morley) struck out).*

— *Vinc 88, 33. 1361-2. (sl; imp by St Philibert, for Mgt, w of Sir Jn de St P, of Sherborne St John, Hants).*

ASHBURNE, John de, of Lichfield. *Bow L 11a. 1375-6.*

BALIOL, Guy. *D'Anisy V 2, HB-SND.*

KIRKETON, John de, of Balderton Gate Street, Newark. *PRO-sls E40 A9309. 1367-8. (or his w Lucy; imp lily).*

MAUTRAVERS, John. *Birch 11554.* S IOHANNIS MAVTRAVER. *1292. (s&h of Jn M, of Gloucs, Kt).*

MUNCES, Robert de, Lincs. *Birch 12022.* SIG' ROB' D' MVNCES. *c1250-60.*

NEVILE, Walter de. *Birch 12159.* S' WALT'I D' NEVILE. *1253. (?border; s of Jn de N, of Walden, Herts).*

POWER, Michael. *PRO-sls E40 A10298.* ..ICHAEL: PO.... *1444-5. (qrs 1&2).*

WEST, Thomas, Kt, Dominus de la Warr. *(sl). Vinc 88, 48.* +SIGILL' THOME WEST MILITIS. *1534-5.*

Arg plain

Az &c plain

Az plain

— *CB 261.*

CAMVILLE, Geoffrey de. *WLN 490. (unfinished).*

LONGESPEE, le Count de Salisbury. *WLN 192. (unfinished).*

Brown plain

— *MP VIII 17b. (prob the Oriflamme).*

Gu plain

Gu plain

— *CRK 1771. (imp Arg fess Az).*

— *L10 45b, 9. (?unfinished; qtd 2&3 by Chalons).*

AVENEBURY, Osbern de. *WLN 803. (unfinished).*

BRETE, Sr Emenuy de la. *GA 125. ('porte lescu de gueules').*

BRETTE, Edmund de la. *H 58. ('porte tut de goules').*

BRETTE, Eurmenions de la. *K 261.*

ESSEX, Roy de. *RH, Ancestor iii 205.*

GUELDRES, D of. *LO B 58.*

HODERINGO, Barth. *WLN 519. (unfinished).*

KEKITMORE, Piers de. *WLN 530.*

(unfinished).

LAVACHE, Richard de. *WLN 715. (unfinished).*

ORIFLAMME, the. *MP IV 43.*

ST HELYN, John de. *WLN 839. (?unfinished for Gu 6 lions Arg).*

Or plain

Or plain

— *WB II 56, 7. (qtd by Arg salt engr Sa).*

— *ML I 439. ('Le roy de .... He beryth gold. Theys armys to ber gold or sylver alone & no more may be born well & such armys be & have be for such armys wer comyn at the begynnyng').*

Sa plain

Sa plain

— *MP III 13. (dimid by England 'Henry the young King').*

— *CRK 1506. (?Sir Thos Holand, KG).*

BOYDELL, of Ches. *CY 37, 146.*

BRESYNGHAM, John. *RH, Ancestor ix 163.*

DETLING, William de. *WLN 807. (unfinished).*

HOLLANDE. *DV 66b, 2628.*

ST MARTIN, William de. *WLN 741. (?obliterated or unfinished).*

Vt plain

Vt plain

GUNDREINLE, S Gerard. *GA 43. ('ports lescu vert').*

Acorn see Fruit

ANCHOR

Anchor

— *Batt. (on tomb of Sir Ralph Cheney, Erdington Priory Ch).*

ANDERSON, David. *Stevenson 228. (merchant's mark).*

FLESCHER, David. *Stevenson. 1519. (s of Nicholas F, Burgess of Dundee).*

Anchor flukes upward in chf

BAKER, John, of Morpeth. *Morpeth 19, HB-SND. 1361.*

Arg anchor Sa

SKIPTON, John de. *TJ 1500.*

Gu anchor Or

— *ML I 475. ('goules an ankyr gold').*

Anchor betw 3 leopards' heads jesst de lis

BONERES, Robt of, Merchewood Valley, Dorset, priest. *Birch 7589.* S'R-OB'-TI-BO-NE-RS-PE-SB. *1338.*

3 anchors
— *Proc Soc Antiq XVII 2S 46.* (*'sl of Clarenceux who made a grant of Arms in 1452'*).
Arg 3 anchors Sa
KYPLES. *BR IV 72.*

ANNULET

Barry Erm and Gu on dex of 1st Gu bar annulet Arg
BEAUMOND. *DV 52b, 2070.*
BEAUMOND. *L10 26, 7.*
Barry Erm and Gu on dex of 1st Gu bar annulet Or
BEAUMOND. *CC 131, 305.*
Az fretty Arg annulet Or
?ECHINGHAM. *Lambarde 4.* (*N aisle window, Etchingham, Suss*).
Or fretty Gu annulet Az
HAWTON, Sir T. *PLN 1276.* (*qtg 2&3 Arg on bend Sa 3 eagles displ Or*).
MOL, of Codsall, Staffs. *L1 460, 4; L2 342, 7.*
MOLL, Robert, of Codsall, Staffs. *LD 47.* (*qrs 1&4*).
Paly Or and Az on 1st Az pale annulet Or
[GORNAY, M Mauys]. *PLN 1200.*
GOURNAY, Mons Maheu de. *WJ 440.*
Per fess indent Sa and Or annulet Or in dex chf
HARSYK. *L2 244, 10.*
Per pale indent Arg and Gu annulet Arg
HOLANDE, James. *WJ 12.* (*4th s*).
Per pale indent Arg and Gu annulet Or
HOLANDE, James. *WJ B 12.*
Vairy Arg and Sa annulet Arg in dex chf
MEYNELL. *CC 236b, 461.*
Vairy Arg and Sa annulet Or in dex chf
KATHERMA. *L9 23, 8.*
MEYNELL. *L9 54b, 5.*
STANDON. *CRK 1122.*

Annulet & in chf &c

Annulet & on chf indent 2 annulets
AUBERVILLE. *Arch Cant xv 9.* (*?per fess indent 3 annulets*).
Arg annulet & on chf indent Gu 3 annulets Arg
NUNGEDENE. *SK 744.*
Arg annulet Gu on chf Az 2 mullets Or pd Gu
CLYNTON. *SK 330.*
Gu chf Arg annulet counterch & in chf 2 mullets Sa pd Or
— *PO 117.*

Annulet betw bars &c

Az annulet betw 2 bars Arg
VENABLES. *SK 609.*

Gu annulet Or betw 2 bars Vair
TALBOT. *PT 632.*
Sa 2 greyhounds erect back to back heads turned to face each other Or collars ?Arg in fess pt annulet Or
BARNARDE. *SHY 49.*
Annulet betw 3 cocks
COCKAYNE, Edmund. *Mill Steph.* 1515. (*imp Lock; brass to Edm C & w Eliz at Hatley Cockayne, Beds*).
COKAYN. *CC 235, 414.* (*qtg 2&3 Az bend raguly Gu*).
Arg annulet Or betw 3 cocks Gu
COKAYN. *CC 235, 413.* (*b&l Sa*).
Arg annulet Sa betw 3 cocks Gu
COKAYN. *LE 383.* (*b&l Sa*).
COKAYNE. *L10 40, 9.*
Arg annulet Gu betw 3 martlets Sa
CAVERSHAM. *Nichols Leics III 1046.* (*Snarestone Ch*).
Sa annulet betw 3 bougets Arg
— *CRK 556.* (*?Ilderton or Lilburne*).
Annulet betw 6 chessrooks 3, 2, 1
ROKEWODE, William, Essex & Suff. *Birch 13071.* SIGILLUM WILLELMI ROKEWODE. 1413.
Or annulet betw 3 crescs Gu
EDMONSTON, of Duntroch. *SC 74.*
Annulet betw 3 crosslets formy fitchy isst from 3 crescs
CATHCART, James, of Carbiston. *Stevenson.* 1438.
Arg annulet betw 3 crosses patonce Gu
— *PLN 1403.*
Arg annulet betw 3 crosses formy Gu
STAMTON. *L1 599, 2.*
STAYNTON. *CC 234, 387.*
Arg annulet betw 3 crosses formy Sa
STAYNTON. *WB I 33, 19.*
Sa annulet betw 3 covered cups Arg
GRENACRE, Mons Robert. *S 493.*
Sa annulet betw 3 escallops Arg
STRIKELAND. *FK II 371.*

Annulet betw fishes &c

Annulet betw two fishes
LECHE, John. *PRO-sls.* 1330-1. (*shield betw 2 mullets*).
Annulet betw 3 fleurs de lis
BOURSY, Thomas. *Roman PO 2005.* 28 Aug 1427.
BURGH, Thomas. *Clairambault 1734.* 15 Oct 1432.
MONTGOMERY, John, of Eagleshame. *Stevenson.* 1392. (*?gem ring*). (*d1401, m Eliz, heiress of Eglinton*).
Arg annulet Gu betw 3 fleurs de lis Sa
ABELYN. *CC 236, 449.*

Az annulet Arg betw 3 fleurs de lis Erm
  BURGHE. *SK 731.*
Gu annulet Arg betw 3 garbs Or
  COMYN. *CC 231b, 309.*
Per chev Sa and Erm in chf annulet Arg betw 2
  boars' heads couped Or armed Arg
  SANDEFORD. *FK II 464.*
Arg annulet betw 3 boars' heads erased & erect
  Sa
  BOTHE, Sr Robt de, of Ches. *CY 26, 101.*
Arg annulet betw 3 boars' heads couped Sa
  BARTUN. *L2 81, 9.*
Arg annulet betw 3 picks Gu
  PICKWORTH, Mons' Robert. *S 310.*
  PYKWORTH, Robert. *BG 103.*
Gu annulet betw 3 roundels Arg each ch with
  squirrel Gu
  CRESSEWELL, Alexander. *WJ 776.*
Annulet betw 8 roundels
  BLUNDUS, William. *PRO-sls.* 13 cent.

Annulet betw & in chf
Per fess Az and Gu annulet Untinc betw 2 bars
  Or in chf cross formy fitchy Gu
  HOLT. *LH 465.*

Annulet within
Qtly Gu and Or & border Sa roundelly Or in dex
  chf annulet Arg
  RYCHFORDE, Hen. *NS 126.*
Annulet in border engr
  BERDON, Robert. *PRO-sls Anc Deeds B 502,
  HB-SND.* 1412.
Annulet betw 3 crescs tressure flory-c'f
  EDMONSTON, Sir Wm of Duntreath, Justice-
  General of Scotland. *Stevenson.* 1470.
Or annulet betw 3 crescs & tressure flory cf Gu
  SETTOUN, of Tulibody. *Lyndsay 387.*

On an annulet
Per pale Arg and Sa annulet ch with 4 pd 4foils
  all counterch
  NAIRNE. *Lyndsay 230.*

2 annulets
In chf 2 annulets
  KINGSTON, Walter de. *PRO-sls.* 13 cent.
  KYNGESTON, Walter de. *Birch 11173.*
  +SIGILL' WALT'I D' KINGEST'. 1237. *(s of
  Roger de Haya-Ori, of Kingston, Herefs).*
Brown 2 annulets Arg
  GUISNES, Baldwin de. *MP VIII 15b.*
Per chev Arg and Gu in chf 2 annulets Gu
  CRIOLL, Nichole. *FW 678; FW c 676.*
Per fess Or and Az in pale 2 annulets Arg
  GENOESE, the. *MP VIII 18c & d.*

Erm 2 annulets interlaced Sa
  — *PLN 1476. (qtd 2&3 by Southwell).*

2 concentric annulets
Erm 2 concentric annulets Gu
  FYTTON. *Suff HN 6. (qtd by Oxford; Laven-
  ham Ch).*

2 annulets &
Arg 2 annulets & canton Az
  — *SK 251. (& baston Gu).*
  — *SK 250.*
  BRAMBULLE. *CB 222.*
  BREMBER. *L10 77b, 4.*
  BREMBER, Sir Nicol. *CRK 848.*
2 annulets on canton mullet
  BREMBER, Sir Nicholas, Kt. *LonG-sls 36.*
  SIGILLUM: NICOLAI: BREMBRE. 1387.
Arg 2 annulets & on canton Az mullet Arg pd
  Or
  BREMBER. *L1 52, 1; L2 83, 11.*
  BREMBER. *DV 47b, 1876.*
  BREMBURE, Sir Nichol, Middx. *WB III 84b,
  6.*
Erm 2 annulets interlaced in pale & chf Sa
  — *WB II 70, 13. (qtd 2&3 by Southwell).*
Arg 2 annulets interlaced Sa within orle of 3foils
  slipped Vt
  ETTON. *L2 185, 4.*
Per fess Or and Vt 2 annulets Gu border Or
  PISANS, the. *MP VIII 18a & b. (& small
  band of Or betw the Or & the Vt).*

2 concentric annulets &
2 concentric annulets & border ch with 6 leopards' faces
  ASTON, John de, Kt. *Bow LXIX 7.* +Sig Johis
  de Astona.
  ASTON, Sir John. *Dugd 17, 98.* ?1260.
  (?lions' faces).

**2 or more concentric annulets: see also Whirl-
pool**

3 annulets
3 annulets
  — *Bellasis I 102; Hill ii 296. (qtg salt in
  border engr; ?Betham; mont, Beetham Ch).*
  — *Roman PO 7749.* 20 Sept 1545. *(qtd
  2&3 on sl by Jacques, Comte de
  Montgomery; ?escallops).*
  ?DOK, William. *Wells D&C II 648-9, 479-81.*
  S'GVILHEMI DOK (?). 1395. *(used by Jn
  Alhampton, Vicar in Wells Cathedral).*
  [EGLINTON]. *PRO-sls.* 1438. *(qtd by Ld
  Alexander Montgomery).*
  MONDIDIERS, Simon. *PRO-sls.* SIMONIS
  MONDIDIERS. 1367-8. *(2nd of 3 shields on sl*

used by Jn, s of Wm de Middelmor).
[VIPONT]. *Mill Steph.* 1508. *(qtd 2&3 by
Clifford, imp Flint; brass, Aspenden, Herts to
Sir Robt C & w Eliz Darley).*
Untinc 3 annulets Arg
— *ML I 288.* ('*Ther ys i beryth iii annlettes
sylver sanz deperter' ; ?sanz deperter for not
separated; this might be Standish, whose
dishes are represented in some mediaeval
rolls by white roundels marked by 2 concen-
tric black circles).*
Arg 3 annulets Az
RICHES. *LR 101.*
Arg 3 annulets Gu
— *BR VI 48. (qtd by Ld Hilton).*
— *WB I 37, 1. (qtd 2&3 by Ld Hylton).*
Arg 3 annulets Sa
— *CVC 496.*
Arg 3 annulets Vt
HARNALL. *CKO a 520. (addition in margin).*
Az 3 annulets Arg
ANLET. *L1 12, 6; L2 7, 9.*
ANLET. *PT 973.*
ANLETT. *L10 5b, 15.*
Gu 3 annulets Or
DAMOCKE, Sir .... *WB IV 143b, 320.
(painted as 3 cartwheels, another hand has
written an indistinct word over which may be
annulet).*
Sa 3 annulets Arg
DICWARD. *L10 58, 10. (diapered Gu).*
MICHELSTAN. *L1 429, 5.*
Barry on 1st bar 3 annulets
GREY, Reginald, Ld Hastings, Weyford &
Ruthyn. *Dugd 17, 67. 1427.*
Barry Or and Sa each Sa bar ch with annulet Or
URDENBOND, Renaud de. *CA 259.*
Barry Arg and Az on 1st bar 3 annulets Sa
— *PT 726.*
Erm 3 annulets interlaced Gu
— *PT 753.*
Per fess dancetty Gu and Arg 3 annulets coun-
terch
NONGEDEMO. *L2 367, 1.*
Per salt Gu and Az 3 annulets Or
ANNELET. *L1 5, 1.*

3 gem-rings
3 gem rings
— *Stevenson. 1438. (qtd by Ld Alexander
Montgomery; 1st sl).*
— *Stevenson. 1457. (qtd by Ld Alexander
Montgomery d c1461, 2nd sl; & by Hugh M,
1st E of Eglinton d 1545).*
EGLINTON. *Stevenson. 14 cent. (qtd by Thos
Home, ?s of Alexander, 1st Ld H, by his 2nd
w Mgt Montgomery).*
EGLINTON. *Stevenson. c1513. (qtd by
Montgomerie, of Skelmorlie; sl of Eliz*

Houston, w of Cuthbert M, 3rd of Skelmor-
lie).
EGLINTON, Sir Hugh. *Stevenson.* 1357.
*(mounted figure carries square flag
apparently ch with 5 annulets; Justiciar of
Lothian in 1361, d c1376).*
Az 3 gem rings Or gemmed Gu
— *SC 33. (qtd 2&3 by 'the Lord of
Mummgrey').*
[EGLINTON]. *Lyndsay 74. 1542. (qtd by
Montgomery, E of Eglinton).*
Gu 3 gem rings Or gemmed Az
EGLINTON. *Stodart 2. (qtd by 'Le Sr de
Mongoby').*
Per chev Gu and Or 3 gem rings counterch
gemmed Or
GRACE, William. *PLN 881.*

3 annulets each ensigned with cross
Az 3 annulets each ensigned with cross Arg
— *ML I 253. ('Asur iii pleyn crossys
pycchyd in as many annulettys sylver per tri-
angyll').*

3 concentric annulets
Arg 3 concentric annulets Gu
— *PLN 244. (?whirlpool; qtd 2&3 by Arg
bend wavy plain cotised Gu, all qtd IV by Sir
George Carew).*
— *CRK 4. (qtd 2&3 by Lorcy or Lorty).*
Arg 3 concentric annulets Sa
— *PT 740.*
Erm 3 concentric annulets Gu
PECCHE, Sr Thm. *PO 534.*
PECHE, Mons Thos. *CA 179.*
PESCHCHE. *NS 26.*

3 annulets &c
Arg 3 annulets Gu label Az
— *AN 223. (?Monsire Thomas de la fitz
Charreys).*
Sa in chf 3 annulets 2, 1 Or in base 3 crosses
formy fitchy 2, 1 Arg
— *WB I 25b, 5-6. (qtd 3 by Newell).*
3 annulets & canton
BREMBRE, Thomas de, Dean of St.
Cathberga's Coll Ch, Wimborne, Dorset.
Birch 4478. S'COMUNE CATARIE THOME DE
BREBRE IN WYMB. 1350. *(sl of Chantry).*
Arg 3 annulets & on canton Az mullet Arg
BREMBER, Sir Nicholas. *Hutton 86.*
Arg 3 annulets Sa chf wavy Vt
BELLE, Stephen. *SHY 209.*
Sa 3 annulets & chf Arg fretty Sa
HELTONE. *PT 1157.*
Per salt Gu and Az 3 annulets (2 in chf, 1 in
base) Or chf Or fretty Sa
BLANSON. *L1 54, 3; L2 73, 10.*
BLANSON. *DV 60b, 2383.*

BLANSON. *CRK 70.*

Or 3 annulets Sa on chf Arg 3 pd mullets Or
ELLINGTON. *LQ 82. (as painted; mullets prob Sa).*

3 annulets in chf greyhound courant
[RHODES, Prior Robt]. *?source.* c1440. *(formerly at Tynemouth Castle).*

3 annulets in chf greyhound
RHODES, Robert. *Blair N V 215, 439. (on roof bosses in chancel, Cathedral Ch of St Nicholas, Newcastle upon Tyne).*

Sa 3 annulets Or in chf 2 salts Arg
HELTON, John, of Westmld. *TJ 1384. ('... & ii sautours dargent au chief).*
HELTON, John, of Westmld. *LH 338.*

Barry Or and Sa each bar Sa ch with annulet Or over all bend Sa ch with annulet Or
URDENBEND, Corsill de. *CA 260.*

3 annulets between or within

3 annulets in bend betw cotises
— *Gerola 75, 225.* 1468. *(qtg 2&3 helmet betw 3 pairs of lions' gambs; supporters: 2 lions holding pennons [1 with cross, 2 with fess]; stone shield, Bodrum, Asia Minor).*

Gu 3 annulets Or border engr Arg
CORDER, Mons Gauweyn. *CA 135. (rectius angemmes).*

3 annulets enclosing

Gu 3 annulets Arg 1st enclosing lion Arg 2nd wyvern wings displ Arg 3rd King in white robes holding sword & sceptre Or
BRITAIN, K Brecyrall of. *KB 94.*

Gu 3 annulets Or 1st enclosing lion Arg 2nd wyvern wings displ Arg 3rd King in white robes holding a sword & gold sceptre
BRITAIN, K Sewarde of. *KB 103.*

Gu 3 annulets in border Arg 1st enclosing lion Arg 2nd wyvern wings displ Arg 3rd King in white robes holding sword & gold sceptre
BRITAIN, K Saber of. *KB 93.*

Gu 3 annulets Or in border Arg 1st enclosing lion Arg 2nd wyvern wings displ Arg 3rd King in white robes holding sword & gold sceptre
BRITAIN, K Sexrode of. *KB 100.*

Arg 3 annulets Gu each enclosing roundel Gu
— *BA 863. (qtd 2&3 by Thos Chellerey).*

Gu 3 annulets each enclosing fleur de lis Arg on chf Az bugle-horn betw 2 pheons Arg
BARROW. *WLN 284. (imp by Sir Wm Sneyd, d1571).*

4 annulets

4 annulets
— *Durham-sls 2295.* 1361. *(qtd 2&3 by Jn of Stanhop).*

Gu crusily & 4 annulets Or
CONSTANTINOPLE, Emperor of. *LMRO 16. (tricked sans crosses; 'Emperur de Constantinople porte de gules of una croiz passant de or of iiii aneus de or pudre de petis crois de or').*

Per salt Gu and Az 4 annulets Arg
ANLETT. *XPat 10x, Arch 69, 68.*

Per salt Gu and Az 4 annulets Or
ANLETT. *L10 5b, 14.*
ANNELET. *L2 6, 10.*

4 concentric annulets

Arg 4 concentric annulets Az
GORGES, Raf de. *WLN 689.*

4 annulets &

4 annulets 1, 2, 1 canton Erm
[CANTWELL]. *Arch Journ x 126.* c1320. *(effigy traditionally known as 'Cantwell fadha' (Tall Cantwell); Kilfane, co Kilkenny).*

Gu 4 annulets Arg canton Erm
CANTWELL, of Irld. *LQ 3.*

5 annulets

Gu 5 annulets Arg
— *BR V 124. (qtd 2&3 by Sir Robt Burgelon).*
HELBECK, of Helbeck, Westmld. *GutchWdU.* 15 cent. *(qtg checky Or and Sa fess Sa; glass in Balliol Coll Library).*

Or 5 annulets 2, 2, 1 Sa
— *WB I 29b, 10. (imp by Wharton).*

5 concentric annulets

Arg 5 concentric annulets Gu
[CHELLERY]. *ML I 287.*

5 annulets &

Gu 5 annulets 2, 1, 2 Or joined in salt by chains Arg
MARSCHALL. *WB I 18b, 13.*
MARSCHALL. *WB I 18b, 14. (qtg [Smyth] Az bend Arg betw 6 billets Or).*

Gu 5 annulets 2, 2, 1 Or canton Erm
— *SK 866.*
CANTWELL, of Irld. *L2 130, 12. (annulets badly placed; ?might be 3, 2, 1 with 1 hidden under canton).*

Sa 5 annulets in salt & chf Or
— *WB V 78.*

6 annulets

6 annulets

— H21 85. (2, 2, 2; qtd by Perpoynt).

— Durham-sls 2269. early 14 cent.

— Durham-sls 1539 & 1581. (used in 1375-6 by Jn de Lethum, Chaplain & in 1380 by Wm of Lanchester, Vicar of St Oswald's, Durham; crest: 2 annulets interlaced held betw tips of 2 horns isst from helm).

— Antiq Journ xx 1940. (armorial brooch).

— Harl Soc IV 47. 1440-1. (sl; qtd by Hen de Pierpoint).

— Dugd 17, 17. 1339-40. (3, 2, 1; imp by Charleton on sl of Elene de C).

CROMWELL, John. HB-SND.

CROMWELL, John de, of Arnold Manor, Notts, Kt. Birch 9096. 1316. (3, 2, 1).

CRUMBEWELL, John de, Constable of Tower of London. PRO-sls. 1316-17.

GREISELEY, Margaret de. Bow XXX 6. 1334-5. (3, 2, 1; loz, 1 of 3; wid of Geoffrey de G).

LAUTHER, Geoffrey, Esq, of Kent. Birch 11262. ...GALFRIDI.... 1440. (3, 2, 1; martlet in fess pt).

LOUTHIER, John. Birch 11394. [+SI]GNVM SIGILLI IOH'IS LOUT..E. 1338. (3, 2, 1).

[MANNERS]. Harl Soc IV 45. (qtd by Annnora de Pierpoint; sl).

MANNERS, Michael. Harl Soc IV 45. (?semy of annulets; sl).

[?MUSGRAVE]. Bellasis I 51; Hill iv 65. (imp 3 bougets; ?for Mgt dau & h of Sir Wm Ros, m c1384 Sir Thos M; mont, St Michaels Ch, Appleby).

[MUSGRAVE]. Bellasis II 120; C&WAAST i IV 230-2, 1; Hill vii 183. (3, 2, 1; imp [Ward] cross flory; Kirkby Stephen, entrance to belfry).

[MUSGRAVE]. Bellasis II 120; C&WAAST i IV 230-2, 1; Hill vii 183. (3, 2, 1; cresc for diffce; imp by Beauchamp (fess betwn 6 crosses); Kirkby Stephen, entrance to belfry).

[MUSGRAVE]. Bellasis II 130; C&WAAST i IV 178-249, art xvi. (3, 2, 1).

[MUSGRAVE]. Bellasis I 102. (3, 2, 1; 7th of 11 shields, almost certainly Betham, Bellasis says 'Musgrave figures in Betham descent'; Beetham Ch, altar tomb, chancel).

[?MUSGRAVE, of Murton]. Bellasis I 48; Hill iv 65. (Hill says 'most likely Musgrave of Murton' Bellasis says 'very likely Vipont'; on timber at St Michaels Ch, Appleby).

MUSGRAVE, [Sir] Richard. Bellasis II 130; C&WAAST i IV 178-249, art xvi. (3, 2, 1; d9 Nov 1464, tomb in Musgrave Chapel, Kirkby Stephen with w Eliz & s Thos).

MUSGRAVE, Sir Thomas de. Sizergh. Whitmonday 1352. (3, 2, 1; sl).

MUSGRAVE, Thomas of. PRO-sls Ex KR 73/1, 19, HB-SND. 1373.

PLECY, John. Birch 12734. 1372. (3, 2, 1; s&h of Jn Lenueisy of Bucks & Oxfs). PRO-sls.

PLESSETIS, Hugh de. PRO-sls AS 55. S HUGONIS DE PLESSETIS. 13 cent.

PLESSETIS, John de, 8th E of Warwick. Birch 12733. S IOHIS DE ....SETIS....WICHIE. ?1246. (3, 2, 1; d1263).

TOLTHORP, Alice. Birch 13956. 1324. (3, 2, 1; 1st of 3 shields; wid of Thos de T, Yorks).

UNDERHILL, Thomas. Mill Steph. c1530. (& w Anne Drury; brass, Gt Thurlow, Suff).

?VIPONT. Birch 8661. 1417. (qtd II&III 1&4 by Jn, 7th Baron Clifford).

?VIPONT. Mill Steph. 1458. (imp by Stapilton; brass to Wm S, who m Mgt, dau&h of Nich V, Edenhall, Cumb).

[VIPONT]. PRO-sls. 1428-9. (qrs 2&3 of coat imp by Maud of York, Ctess of Camb).

[VIPONT]. Mill Steph. 1458. (imp by Wm Stapilton of Edenhall who m Mgt dau&h of Nich Vipont; brass at Edenhall, Cumb).

[VIPONT]. Blair D II 148, 323. (qtd 2 by Hilton, of Hilton, co Durham; brought in by Stapleton of Westmld; Hilton Chapel, W front).

VIPONT, John de. Greenwich 64a, 3, HB-SND. 1376.

VIPONT, Robert de. Durham-sls 2543. 1347.

VIPOUNT. Birch 12705. 1430. (qrs 2&3 of sin imp of Maud, dau of Thos, Ld Clifford, 2nd w of Ric, E of Camb).

Arg 6 annulets

Arg 6 annulets Untinc

?HERIZ. PLN 1449. (2, 2, 2; imp by Pyrpoynt).

PLECY, Hue de. LM 148.

Arg 6 annulets Gu

— CC 223b, 59. (qtd 2&3 by Hamlyn).

— H18 38. (qtd 4 by Assheley).

— S 466. (qtd by ?Dukinfeld).

— LH 486-593. (qtd 2&3 by Sir Jn Hamlyn).

— CRK 1688. (qtd 2&3 by Hamlyn).

KARDOYLL. L9 22b, 2.

KARDOYLL, Mons Rauf de. WJ 786. (3, 2, 1).

PLAZETIS, Johan de, E of Warwick. BirmCL-sls I 168241.

PLECY. CT 392.

PLECY, Hue de. Q 84.

PLEISE, M de. WNR 152.

PLESCIS, Hue de. G 208.

PLESIS, Sr de. CKO 522.

PLESSETIS, John. DX 21; RW 34. (E of Warw 'by his wiffe').

PLESSIS, Monsire de. *CG 443*.
[PLESSIS]. *CRK 2027*.
PLESSIS, Hue de. *E I 294; E II 296. ('silver 6 rings gules').*
PLESSIS, Sire Hugue de. *J 137*.
PLESSIS, Sir John de. *B 24. ('d'argent ove six fauses roueles de gules').*
PLESSY. *L1 506, 5; L2 411, 9*.
PLESSY. *L9 98b, 9*.
PLESSYS, Mons John. *TJ 975*.
PLESY. *PT 440*.
PLESY, Monsire John de. *AN 293*.
PLESYE. *DV 56b, 2234*.

Arg 6 annulets Or &c
Arg 6 annulets Or
— *I2(1904)139. (2, 2, 2; qtd 2 by Syr Wyllm Pierpoint).*
Arg 6 annulets Sa
— *BD 86. (2, 2, 2; qtd by Sir Hen Pierpont; 4th N window, York Palace Hall, Southwell).*
— *PLN 1449. (2, 2, 2; qtd 2&3 by Pierpoint).*
LEAKE. *CRK 1161*.
LOTHER. *CT 435*.
LOUTHIRS. *RB 241*.
LOUTHRES. *CC 222, 12*.
LOWTHER, William. *WJ 792*.
LOWTHRE. *L9 37a, 6*.
LUZER, Henry. *TJ 982*.
MANNOLT. *WK 441. (2, 2, 2; qtd 2 by Sir Wm Perpont).*
MANOURS. *PLN 1873. (2, 2, 2; qtd 2 by Pierpoint).*
MANVERS. *GutchWdU. 1518. (window, Langtain Chapel, Queen's Coll, Oxf).*
[MANVERS]. *FK II 606. (2, 2, 2; name added by Gibbon; qtd 2&3 by Perpount).*

Az 6 annulets
Az 6 annulets Untinc
MUSGRAVE, Monsire de. *CG 441*.
Az 6 annulets Arg
MOSGRAVE, Ric. *BW 21, 145*.
MUSGRAVE, Mons Thom de. *WJ B 787*.
Az 6 annulets Or
— *WB I 29b, 6. (imp by Wharton).*
— *LD 93. (on chf over all of Mark Ogle, of Northd).*
FOLYOT, of Kent. *CY 157, 627*.
FULYOTT, Sir John. *CVK 719*.
MOSGRAVE. *PT 426*.
MOSGRAVE. *DV 56a, 2220*.
MOSGRAVE, Sir R. *WB I 40, 24*.
MOSGROWE, John, of Westmld. *RH, Ancestor iv 243*.
MOUSGRAVE, Sir John. *WK 75*.
MUSGRAFE, Mons Thomas. *TJ 974*.
MUSGRAVE. *PLN 570*.

MUSGRAVE. *L9 75a, 10*.
MUSGRAVE. *L1 422, 1; L2 325, 2*.
MUSGRAVE, Sr de. *CKO 524*.
MUSGRAVE, Fitz Louis. *BG 386*.
MUSGRAVE, of Hertlaw, Westmld. *GutchWdU. (formerly in Hall, Queen's Coll, Oxf).*
MUSGRAVE, Sir John. *BA 646*.
MUSGRAVE, Sir John, Westmld. *PLN 1736*.
MUSGRAVE, Sir R. *CRK 1862*.
MUSGRAVE, Sir Richard, of Westmld. *WB III 84, 3*.
MUSGRAVE, S Thm. *PO 411*.
MUSGRAVE, Mons Thomas. *WJ 787*.
MUSGRAVE, Mons Thomas. *S 181*.
MUSGRAVE, Thomas. *BG 234*.
MUSGRAVE, Thomas. *WJ 788. ('son fitz').*
MUSGRAVE, of Yorks. *D4 35*.
PECHAM, Johannes de. *FW 693*.
PECHAM, Jon de. *A 58*.
POTHAM, Johan de. *FW 691c*.

Gu 6 annulets
Gu 6 annulets Untinc
CROMWELL, Jon de. *LMS 93. (Jn, Ld Cromwell, 1305-35, m Idonea, coh of Vipont).*
Gu 6 annulets Arg
PLESSY, Mons Hug de. *WJ 790*.
Gu 6 annulets Or
— *D4 31b. (imp by Tonge of Ekylsall, co Durham).*
— *L10 38, 14. (2, 2, 2; qtd II&III 1&4 by Ld Clifford).*
— *D4 46. (qtd by Clifford, E of Cumb).*
— *KB 288. (qtd II&III 1&4 by Ld Clyfforde).*
— *WB I 33b, 14. (qtd I 2 by George Vernon, of Nether Haddon).*
— *RB 96*.
— *CRK 1298. (qtd II&III 1&4 by Ld Clifford).*
CROMELL. *L10 44, 4*.
CROMMVELLE. *SK 379*.
CROMWELL. *CT 363*.
CROMWELL. *SP A 87*.
CROMWELL. *CRK 487. (or Vipont).*
CROMWELL, S John de. *ST 48*.
CROMWELL, Sr John. *M 4; N 122*.
CRUMWELL, Monsr de. *AS 163*.
CRUMWELL, Sr de. *CKO 525*.
CRUMWELL, Mons John. *TJ 972*.
PLESCY. *PLN 483. (3, 2, 1).*
REPOND. *L1 563, 3. (or Wepond).*
VEPOUNT, John de. *P 88. ('de goules a sys anelettes dor').*
[VETERIPONT]. *Bellasis II 143. (imp by [Clifford]).*
VEUPONT, John de. *B 99. ('de gules od six*

fauses roueles d'or').
VIPONT. *Leake. (qtd 6 by Henry Clifford, KG, d1542-3).*
VIPONT. *K 836. (used by Jn de Cromwell, who m Idonea de V).*
VIPOUNT, le Sire de. *WJ 785. (2, 2, 2).*
VITERIE. *WK 539. (qtd 4 by Ld Clyfford).*
VYPOUNT, Wylyam, of the Byschopcryte of Durham. *RH, Ancestor iv 241.*

Or 6 annulets Az &c
Or 6 annulets Az
LONDRES. *PT 424.*
[LONDRES]. *CRK 2061.*
LONDRESS. *DV 56a, 2218.*
VIPOUNTE. *DV 56a, 2219.*
Or 6 annulets Gu
— *WJ 789. (2, 2, 2; Mons Rog de ..., name mutilated & illegible).*
— *D4 35. (qtd II&III 2&3 by Musgrave, of Yorks).*
— *D4 31. (qtd 2 by Hylton, of co Durham).*
CRUMWELL. *L10 41b, 14. (2, 2, 2).*
LOWDER, Sir H. *WB I 40, 6.*
VEPOUND, Sire Nicholas de. *N 121. ('...a vi aneus...').*
VEPOUNT, Sr de. *CKO 523.*
VEPOUNT, Mons John, of Westmld. *TJ 971.*
VEPOUNT, Sr Nicolas. *M 20. ('...sez anelettes..').*
VEPOUNT, S Rob. *PO 573.*
VIPOINTE, Monsire de. *CG 442.*
VIPONT. *CRK 1855.*
VIPOUNT, S Nychol de. *ST 68.*
VIPOUNTES. *L1 661, 1.*
VYPOUNTE. *PT 425.*

Or 6 annulets Sa
Or 6 annulets Sa
LOTHER. *L1 401, 6; L2 310, 7.*
LOUCHER, Monsire. *CG 439.*
LOUDER, Sir Hugh. *WK 299.*
LOUTHER. *SK 756.*
LOUTHER. *PT 1231.*
LOUTHER, Mons Hugh de. *TJ 973.*
LOUTHRE, Monsr de. *AS 160.*
LOUTHRE, Sr Hugh de. *CKO 520.*
LOWDER, Jefferray, of Kent. *MY 193.*
LOWTHER, Mons Hugh de. *CA 158.*
LOWTHER, S Hugh. *GA 83.*
LOWTHER, Sir Hugh. *CRK 832.*
LOWTHER, Mons Robert de. *WJ 795.*
LOWTHER, Sir Robert. *PLN 309.*
[LOWTHER], Robert. *WJ 796. ('son fitz').*
LOWTHUR, Sir Jefrai, of Yorks. *WB III 86b, 8.*
OLOM. *L2 390, 8. (2, 2, 2).*
OLOUTHER, Sire Huwe. *PO 423.*

Sa 6 annulets
Sa 6 annulets Arg
— *WJ B 793. (name mutilated & illegible).*
LOTHER. *CT 434. (?annulets Or).*
LOWTHER. *WJ 791.*
Sa 6 annulets Or
— *WJ 793. (name mutilated & illegible).*
LAKE, Monsire de. *CG 440.*
LEK. *L1 409, 1; L2 302, 1.*
LEK. *L9 42b, 2.*
LEK, Monsr de. *AS 161.*
LEK, Sr J de. *CKO 521.*
LEKE, Mons John de. *TJ 977.*
LOWTHER. *WJ 791.*
LOWTHRE. *L9 37a, 5.*

6 annulets field patterned
Per bend sin wavy Arg and Az 6 annulets counterch
POLLARE, John, of Devon. *WB III 115, 5.*
Or 6 annulets Gu voided Arg
VIPONS. *FK II 838.*

6 annulets & label
6 annulets & label
— *Birch 12725. 1410. (imp in arms of Maud de Plessy).*
LOWTHER, John of. *Durham-sls 1634a. 1327-8.*
6 annulets & label of 4
LOUTHRE, John de. *PRO-sls. 1284-5. (Keeper of the King's viands in the Parls of Carlisle).*
6 annulets & label of 5
PLECY, Nicholas de. *LonG-sls 158.* S': NICHOLAI: DE: PLECY. 1349.
Arg 6 annulets Gu label Az
PLESEY. *PT 441.*
PLESY, Monsire Nichol de. *AN 295.*
Az 6 annulets Or label Gu
MUSGRAVE, Monsr de. *AS 162.*
Gu 6 annulets Or label Arg
HELBEK, S Thomas de. *GA 85.*
HELBEKE, Sir Thomas. *LH 219.*
Gu 6 annulets Or label Az
VEPONT, Sir John de. *PT 1031.*
VEPOUND, Sire Johan de. *N 742. ('...a vi anels...').*
VEPOUNT, Sr John de. *M 71. ('...vi anelettz.-..').*
Or 6 annulets Gu label Az
VIPOUNT, Sr John de. *L 212. ('...a vi annelles...').*

6 annulets & canton &c
6 annulets & canton
NOBLE, William. *PRO-sls. 1386-7.*

Gu 6 annulets Or chf qtly Gu and Or
— SK C 434.
Gu 6 annulets Or chf qtly Sa and Arg
— SK A&B 434.
Or 6 annulets Sa on chf Arg 3 mullets Or
ELLINGTON. LQ 82. (?mullets prob Sa).

6 annulets & over all
Arg 6 annulets Gu bend Az
PLECITE, de. Gerard 3.
PLEICI, Sire Edmond de. L 189. ('...vi aneus
de g...').
Qtly Or and Gu in 2&3 3 annulets Arg over all
bend Sa
BOURGULYON. Suff HN 48. (imp by Shelton;
Mettingham Castle or College).
Gu 6 annulets Or canton Erm bend Untinc
— PT 730. (bend a baston).

6 annulets in border
6 annulets border engr
BEKYSWELLE, John. Stowe-Bard 2s vi 8.
Sigillum iohis bek..elle. 1461-2.
BLEMCANSOP, Sir Thomas of. Hill i 411.
1345. (sl).
VIPONT, John. Stevenson. 14 cent.
VIPONT, John de. Durham-sls 2542.
Arg 6 annulets Sa border engr Gu
BEXWELL. L1 55, 1.
BEXWELL. Suff HN 48. (crest: boar's head
Arg; Mr Spenser's house, Nawnton Hall,
Rendlesham).
BEXWELL, of Norf. ML I 470. (annulets in
orle).
BEXWELLE. L10 29, 15.
BOXWELL. RB 242.
Gu 6 annulets Or border engr Arg
— XF 40. (3, 3; qtd 2&3 by Blenkinsop).
— XF 442. (qtd 2&3 by Robt Blenkinsop).
BLENKENSOP. L1 60, 5; L2 64, 3.
BLENKENSOP, Thomas, de Helbek. TJ 970.
BLENKENSOPPE. PT 1263. (or Hellebecke).
BLENKINSOP. CRK 302. (qrs 1&4).
CROMMEL. L1 136, 6; L2 110, 12.
CRONWELL. L10 39b, 14.

9 annulets or more
9 annulets
VIPONT, Ivo de. D'Anisy XIII 10, 11, HB-
SND 319, 98. early 13 cent. (3, 3, 2, 1).
Arg 9 annulets Gu
— H21 25. (3, 3, 2, 1; qtd by Hilton, of Hil-
ton).
Arg 9 annulets Sa
LOWTHER. DV 42b, 1662. (3, 3, 2, 1; name
added in later hand).

10 annulets
— Antiq Journ vi. (annulets 4, 3, 2, 1; on
chimney piece, Tattershall Castle, built by
Ralph, Ld Cromwell, 1394-1456).
13 annulets
VIPONT, Maud de. D'Anisy X 21, 22, HB-
SND.
Arg semy of annulets Gu
BOULOGNE, Reynold de. MP VIII 7c.

ANVIL
Anvil above it hammer
PURROK, Johannes. Stevenson. 1283.
('dictus Purroc, filius Willi Scoti de Colding-
ham'; not on shield).
Anvil in dex chf joiner's square in sin chf mullet
COCK, John. Stevenson. 1496. (bailie for E
of Errol).
Arg 3 anvils Sa
WOLSTONE. PT 751.

Arbalest: see Bow

Arm (human): see Hand

ARMS & ARMOUR
Az 3 chain shots 2, 1 Or
— Leake. (qtd 2 by Hen Clifford, KG,
d1542-3).
3 clubs
[PATOLE]. Farrer I 337. 1529. (brass to
Robt Clere, d1529, St Mgt's Ch, Norf).
3 maces
— Durham-sls 2618. (used in 1482 by Wm
Whelpdale of Durham).
Sa sling betw 2 broad arrowheads pts down Arg
CURDEN. L2 145, 4.

Helmet: see Hat

Gauntlet: see Glove

Spearhead: see Spear

Seaxe: see Sword

ARROW

See also Pheon

Arrow in pale pt in base
ATTE HALL, William, of Heyemedwestret. *Vinc 88, 3.* 1362-3.

Dart
ROBILARD, Thomas. *PRO-sls.* S THOME DE PRESTONE. 1334-5. *(s of Robt R, of Dorneye).*

Vt arrow in pale pt in base Or feathered Arg
STANPARD, Lord of Shyston. *Lamborn. (corbel in chancel, Shipton on Cherwell, Oxfs).*

Birdbolt

?birdbolt
?BOSON. *Mill Steph. (qtd 3 by Olney; brass to Gadyth B, w of Robt O, Fladbury, Worcs).*

1 arrow & ...

Arrow in bend sin pt down over all on bend 3 buckles
LESLIE, Thomas. *Stevenson.* 1504.

Arg arrow in bend Sa betw 2 pd mullets Gu
— *CRK 131.*

Arg arrow in pale pt down Arg feathered & barbed Or betw 2 pd mullets in fess Sa all betw 3 bugle horns stringed Sa garnished Or
HAULE. *BA 1122.*

Gu arrow Untinc head & barb Arg betw 2 wings Arg
ZINGELL, Stephen. *CC 236, 451.*

Gu arrow erect betw 2 wings Arg
ZINGELL, Stephen. *LS 163.*

Gu broad arrow in pale head & pinions up Arg
ZINGEL. *L1 711, 1.*

2 arrows

2 arrows in salt pts down
?FOREST. *Mill Steph.* 1511. *(over man's effigy on brass to Thos F, Keeper of Dunclent Park, & w Mgt over whom is shield ch with stringed hunting horn, Chaddesley Corbett, Worcs).*

2 arrows in salt pts up
RICHARDSON, Patrick, of Drumsheugh, Burgess of Edinburgh. *Stevenson.* 1507. *(merchant's mark).*

Sa 2 arrows in salt Arg
— *XX 211.*
PEARLE. *XX 98. (pts down, pheon headed; 'Bosan' added by later hand).*

Sa 2 arrows in salt Arg feathered & barbed Or
PERLL. *L9 98a, 7. (pts down).*
PERLL. *L1 504, 3. (arrows broad).*
PERSE. *FK II 808. (pts down; annulet Arg in centre chf).*

2 birdbolts

Sa 2 birdbolts in salt Arg
— *PT 186.*
BOSAN. *DV 64a, 2527.*
BOSAN. *L1 61, 3; L2 52, 5.*

2 ?birdbolts betw 3 crosslets in fess, label
RISHTONE, Gilbert de, of Kent. *Birch 12998.* PREVE SVY. 1288.

2 arrows or birdbolts & ...

Sa 2 arrows pts down in salt Or in chf roundel Arg
PEARLE. *XX 304.*

2 arrows in salt pts down betw in chf estoile in base hunting horn in fess 2 roundels all in border engr
BERY, John de. *Birch 7440.* [S'] IOHANNIS DE BERY. 1364.

Crusily fess surmounting 2 birdbolts palewise
— *Birch 7725.* 1329. *(circular shield; imp by Jn de Bradefeld, s of Robt de B, of Stanningfield, Suff).*

3 arrows

3 arrows in pile pts up
— *Stevenson 229.* 1497. *(qtd 2&3 by Jn Arbuthnot, of Balmakynes).*

3 arrows in pale pts down
— *WB I 25b, 21. ('Anthony the dau of Laurens').*
ARCHER. *CombeAsp II 124.* S' FRATRIS THOME D'ARCHER. *(sl).*
ARCHER, Bro Thos le. *Bow XXXV 10.* Sigillum Fratris Thome le Archer. 1320-1. *(Prior of Hospital of St John of Jerusalem in Engld).*
ARCHER, John of Tamworth, Warws. *Bow XXXV 20.* +SIGILLUM JOHANNIS ARCHER. 1475-6.
ARCHER, Richard le. *PRO-sls.* S 'RICARDI LE ARCHER. 1328.
ARCHER, Richard, Ld of Midleton Hugeford. *Dugd 17, 16.* 1427. *(2, 1).*
ARCHIER, Bro Thos le. *Hist MSS Comm 3rd Rep 45.* 1321. *(Prior of St John of Jerusalem in Engld, with assent of Chapter grts to Wm s of Isabella of Cullon & Matilda in tail 2/- p.a.; sl of Order & on rev of Archier).*
HAYLES. *Batt. (brass Grittleton Ch).*
LARCHIER, Thos. *PRO-sls.* ... Larcher. 1324-5. *(2, 1).*
WENDOR. *Bow XLVII 15b.* S...Wendor. 1361-2. *(2, 1; sl used by Ric Mochet, Chaplain; gt of land in Tutbury).*
WODE, Peter atte. *PRO-sls.* 1368. *(arrows in fess pts down).*

Arg 3 arrows Gu
SANCTUS SEBASTIANUS. *L10 65b, 17.*
Az 3 arrows Arg
ARCHER, Warws. *PLN 1298.*
Az 3 arrows 2, 1 Or pts down Arg
ARCHARD. *CRK 34.*
Az 3 arrows 2, 1 Or
ARCHER, Richard, of Warws. *WB III 113b, 9.*
Gu 3 arrows Or
HALES, Nicolas. *CRK 2014. (pts down).*
Sa 3 arrows Or
— *WB I 25b, 20. (qtd 2 by Jn Clark; in fess pts down, barbed & flighted Arg).*

3 birdbolts
3 birdbolts
BOZON. *Lawrance 7.* 1272 or 1304. *(effigy, Long Clawson, Leics; no arms now visible but Burton deciphered birdbolts).*
BOZOUN. *Farrer III 9. (Mont, Norwich Cathedral).*
BUZOUN, John of Exeter, Devon. *Birch 7713.*
SIGILLUM IOHANNIS BUZON. 1366.
Arg 3 birdbolts Gu
BOSAN. *DV 64a, 2526.*
BOSOM. *L10 86, 8.*
BOSOUN. *CRK 1447.*
BOSOUN, John. *S 417. (in pale 2, 1, pts Sa, at feather end of shaft small ball Or).*
BOSOUN, Sr Jon. *PO 271. (pts Sa).*
BOSOUN, Ralph. *WLN 556. (pilewise, pts down Sa).*
BOSOUN, Rauf. *E I 436; E II 438. (blazoned 'bozons').*
BOULTUM, Rauff de. *L10 34, 7. (pilewise, pts down).*
BOZOME. *PT 185. (pts Or).*
BOZON, Dominus Wm. *Nichols Leics II 134. (glass, Claxton Ch).*
BOZON, Johannes. *Q II 252.*
BOZON, Sire Peres. *N 558.*
BOZON, Raf. *F 158. (pts Sa feathers edged Or).*
Az 3 birdbolts Arg
— *WK 197. (2, 1; qtd 2&3 by Sir Humfrey Fulford).*
— *XV 943. (qtd 2&3 by Fulford).*
BOSOM. *L10 86, 7.*
BOSSON. *BA 1128. (in fess).*
BOSUM, of Devon. *L1 43, 2; L2 52, 4.*
[BOZAM]. *PLN 2048. (qtd 2&3 by Sir Humphrey Fulford).*
SPECCOT, John, of Devon. *WB III 115, 4.*
Az 3 birdbolts Or feathered Arg
[BOZOM]. *DevonNQ VIII i 74. (bolts in fess; imp by [?Southcott]; glass, Chancel, Bridport, Devon).*

Gu 3 birdbolts Arg
— *PLN 2058. (qtd 4 by Sir ... Throgmorton).*
— *I2(1904)134. (qtd 4 by Mayster Frogmorton).*
BAGSSHAM. *PLN 930.*
BAGSSHAM. *WB IV 158b, 589. (alias Bosun).*
BOLTESHAM, Sire Thomas. *N 773.*
BOSAN. *DV 64b, 2557.*
BOSOM. *PT 244.*
BOSUM. *L10 84b, 9.*
BOSUM, of Norf. *L1 42, 1; L2 52, 3.*
[BURGON]. *WK 295. (qtd 4 by Sir Robt Throgmerton).*

3 arrows or birdbolts & ...
3 arrows pts down & chf
ARCHER, Nicholas le. *Bow XXXV 24.* +Sigillum Nich le Archer. 1364-5. *(2, 1).*
3 arrows pts down in chf fillet
FLAGUIERAN, Richard de la. *Bow LX 25.* S Ricardi de la Flaguieran. 1362-3. *(sl used by Eleanor de Schirnok dau of Jn de S, of Kingsnorton).*
Az 3 arrows pts down & chf Or
HEYTON. *CRK 1740.*
Or 3 arrows Sa on chf Az 3 mullets Or
— *GutchWdU. (on roof of Balliol College Chapel).*
3 birdbolts
BELTON, Richard de. *NorfAS III 190 & pl V 28.* 1359. *(over all merchant mark; sl, Norwich Guildhall).*

4 arrows or more
Az 6 arrows pts down Or
ARCHER. *RH, Ancestor vii 214. (name added in later hand).*
Az 11 arrows 5, 4, 2 Untinc
ST URSULA. *L10 66, 1.*
Az flight of arrows pts down Or
STRONDE, Wylyam of Surr. *RH, Ancestor vii 195.*
Gu 3 sheaves each of 3 arrows pts down Arg 2 in salt & 1 in pale
JOSKYN. *WB IV 173b, 857.*

AXE

See also Pickaxe

Az axe-head blade to dex Arg ?embossed Or
— ML I 345. ('asur a pollax hed sylver endorsyd & inewyd wit gold or emboscyd wit gold'; in painting gold is only on edge of socket & 2 vertical lines on shaft; poleaxe).

Gu axe Arg
NEVILL, of France. L2 360, 4. (qtg 2&3 bendy Az and Arg border Gu).

Or axe Ppr
DENMARK, K Sweyn of. MP VIII 21. (banner).

2 axes

2 axes
DENMARK, K Sweyn of. MP VIII 21. (surcoat; blades partly blue, background white).

Gu 2 axes in salt Arg
DENMARK, K of. LMRO 20, 21.
DENMARK, K of. LMO 21.

Sa 2 axes in salt Arg
BYLLYNGFORTH. SHY 140. (bills).

Erm 2 axes in salt Sa
MAIDESTONE, Rychard. LY A 30.
MAIDSTONE. XX 186.
[MAIDSTONE]. XX 61.
MAIDSTONE OF WARDALL. CRK 828.
MAYDESTON. L1 441, 5; L2 338, 9.
MAYDESTONE. SK 592. (mullet Arg on blade of dex axe).
MAYDESTONE. SK 591.
MAYDYSTON, of Middx. RH, Ancestor vii 184.

2 axes & ...

2 axes on chf 2 mullets of 8
BAINBRIDGE, Christopher, Archbp of York 1508-14. Brindley & W (illus). 1514. (qtg 2&3 squirrel sejt erect; incised slab, English College, Rome).

2 axes on chf 2 pd mullets
BAINBRIDGE, Christopher, Bp of Durham 1507-08. Durham-sls 3167. (qtg squirrel sejt).

Az 2 axes & border engr Or
BANBRYG, Edward. PLN 861. (qtg 2&3 Gu ?boar salient Or on chf Or 2 mullets Gu).
BAYNBRYG, Edward. WB IV 169, 783. (qrs 1&4).

Gu 2 axes in salt Or headed Arg enfiled with crown Or
— SHY 599. ('ye Kyng of Tyber').

3 axes &c

3 axes
— Mill Steph. 1420. (fessways in pale; imp by Thos Walysch; brass, Whitchurch, Oxfs).
— PRO-sls. 1335-6. (battleaxes; sl of Philip de Englefeld, ?arms of his w).
DANEYS, Elizabeth. PRO-sls E40 A9640. s.-..EL.ZAB...DANEYS. 1374-5. (1 of 2 shields; 'late the wife of' Ric D).
DANEYS, Elizabeth. PRO-sls E40 A8277. .eys. 1364-5. (2, 1; another coat broken away).
[HACKET]. Mill Steph. 1523. (2, 1; imp by Brugge on brass to Wm B, of Estington & Longdon, Worcs).
HACLUIT, Ralph, d1527. Dingley cxlvii. (hatchets; brass, now destroyed, Leominster Ch, Herefs).
HUSCARL, Thomas, of Beddington, Surr. Birch 10932. SIG' THOME HUSCARL'. (hatchets 2, 1).
LEWESTONE, William, Esq, of Dorset. Birch 11328. SIGILLUM WILELMI LEWSSTON. 1432. (2, 1).
?WYKE, of Northwyke & Cocktree. DevonNQ VIII ii 27. early 16 cent. (paleways in fess; blades to sin; Bench end, Sutcombe, Devon).

Untinc 3 billheads Az
CROKE, Piers. E II 568.

Arg 3 axes

Arg 3 axes paleways 2, 1 Arg each bordered Gu
LYN..., Sir Hugh de. CVC 587. (halberts).

Arg 3 axes Gu
— LH 628. (?doloires; qtd 2&3 by Hector de Harguteville).
CROY, Anthony, Ld de, C of Porcien. CB 433. (hatchets).
CROY, Jehan de, Seigneur de Chimay. CB 435.
DANESTON, of Suff. L1 216, 1; L2 161, 2. (Danish axes 2, 1).
[DENARDSTON]. ML I 552.
DENARDSTON, Sir Thomas, of Suff. WB III 71b, 8.
DENARSTON. L10 59, 16. (qrs 1&4).

Arg 3 axes Sa
CLYFFORD, Wylyam, of Gloucs. RH, Ancestor vii 201. (poleaxes with riven bill heads).
GYBBES. SK A 607.
GYBBYS. BA 1130.
GYBES, of Devon. L1 294, 3; L2 228, 6. (poleaxes 2, 1).

Az 3 axes

Az 3 axes Arg
DENMARK, K Sweyn of. MP VIII 24.
HOSCARLE, Sr Thm. PO 533.
HUMSCHALTES, William. LH 245.

HUMSHALTS, William de. *E II 431.*
HURSTAL, William. *F 355.*
HURSTAL, William. *WLN 427.*
HURSTHALE, William de. *E 429.*
HURSTHALE, William de. *E I 429.*
HURSTHALL, William. *LH 837.*
HUSCARLE, Thomas. *CA 183. (Danish hatchets).*

Az 3 axes Or
ILYS, Ld of. *PCL IV 117. (2, 1; qrs 1&4).*

Az 3 axe-heads Arg
WHIT, John le. *CVC 479.*
WHITE, of Irld. *WLN 928.*

Az 3 axeheads Or
CROKE, Piers. *E I 566. (billheads).*
RYTHRE. *HA 158. (?crescs).*

Gu 3 axes
Gu 3 axes Arg
DENEMACHE, le Rei de. *WNR 6. (2, 1).*
LEWSTON, P. *WB I 44, 9.*
NORWAY, K Harold Hadrada of. *MP VIII 27g.*

Gu 3 brown bills Ppr armed Arg
LEWESTON OF LEWESTON, of Dors. *Gerard 108.*

Gu 3 axes Arg 2 in chf at variance
NEVILL. *L2 360, 7. (qtg 2&3 bendy Az and Arg border engr Gu).*

Gu 3 axes Or
— *LE 377. (qtd 2&3 by Arg bend Az).*
— *WB III 73b, 8. (qtd 2&3 by Sir Emond Blaket, of Gloucs).*
— *Nichols Leics II 758. (qtd 2&3 by Blaket; mont of Mgt d1406, w of Jn B, & dau of Rudolph Hastynges, Naseby Ch).*
— *L10 74b, 1. (qtd 2&3 by fitz Edmund Blaket).*
HACHUTT. *CT 234. (hatchets).*

Or 3 axes
Or 3 axes Sa
NORWAY, K of. *RH, Ancestor vii 210. (Danish axes).*

Sa 3 axes
Sa 3 axes Arg
— *I2(1904)178. (qtd 2 by Francys Hasylden, of Gyldon Mardon, Cambs).*
— *LH 602. (qtd 2 by Francis Haselden).*
— *L10 54b, 1. (qtd 2&3 by Walton, of Walton, Lancs).*
— *L10 95b, 7. (Danish axes; qtd 2&3 by [Walton]).*
DANEYS. *L1 188, 2; L2 148, 8.*
DANEYS. *SK 597.*
DANEYS. *L10 52b, 11. (Danish axes).*
DANEYS. *XFB 36. (Danish axes; qtd 2 by Hasylden, of Gilden Morden).*

DANEYS. *LH 614. (qtd by Haselden).*
[DANEYS]. *LH 611. (imp by Haselden).*
DANYS, Le Sieur. *BG 364. (Danish axes).*
DENNIS, Sir .... *CRK 1237.*
[?DENYS]. *S 598. (hatchets).*
[FITCH]. *PLN 1783. (qtg 2&3 Arg gutty & cross engr Gu annulet Or; battleaxes).*
GIBES. *WB V 66.*
MARTEL, Richard. *WLN 548. (?hatchets).*
THORNETONRUST, Elys de. *P 154. ('...trois haches batantz dargent').*
THORNTON, Mathe. *CT 335. (?hammers).*

Sa 3 axes Or
DANMARCHIE, King. *SM 109, 13.*
EGIPT. *CK a 8. (2, 1; handles Arg).*

3 axes field patterned
Erm 3 axes Gu
DACUS, Thomas. *WK 841.*
DENEIS, of Sock Dennis, Ilchester. *Gerard 208.*
DENYS. *I2(1904)155. (?poleaxes; 'Thomas Denys als Dacus de Holcombe in Devon').*
DENYS, of Devon. *L10 58b, 18.*
DENYS, Thomas, of Holcombe, Devon. *XFB 22.*

3 axes & ...
Gu 3 axes Arg handled Or betw 3 demi-fleurs de lis 2, 1 & 3 pd mullets 1, 2 Or
TREGOLD, Thomas. *LY A 55.*

Sa 3 axes Arg bend Gu
DENYS. *SK 1109. (baston).*
DENYS. *L10 58, 2.*

Erm 3 axes & border engr Gu
DENYE, of Devon. *L1 217, 1. (poleaxes).*
DENYS, of Holcombe, Devon. *L2 162, 2.*
DENYS, Sir Thomas. *PLN 1843. (?Arg gutty Sa; imp Arg chev betw 3 bulls' heads cab Sa).*

4 axes or more
Arg 4 axes Gu
DANESTON, John, of Suff. *MY 41.*

Barnacles: see Brays

2 BARS

2 bars

— *Stevenson. 1491. (2nd sl; qtd by Robt Crichton, of Kinnoul, 1st Ld C of Sanquhar).*
— *Birch 11631. 1407. (qtd 2&3 by Sir Wm de Marny, of Essex & Kent).*
— *PRO-sls. 1317-18. (imp by Wm de Hastings, for his w Eleanor).*
— *Birch 13085. 15 cent. (qtd 2&3 by Robt de Roos, Seigneur de Coudrey, ?Suss).*
— *Birch 10529. 1328. (imp in arms of Alianora de Hastynghes, w (compaigne) of Philippe de Columbers, Chevr, of Holme, Devon).*
— *Vinc 88, 37. (sl).*
— *Vinc 88, 57. (crest: human head full faced wearing brimmed pointed cap; sl).*
— *Proc Soc Antiq XV 2S 18. (on sl betw Archbp & St Katharine apparently adopted by Thos Partier, Dean of Coll of Tamworth 1525-38).*
— *Bk of Sls 456. 1275. (?Lisle, ?Neville or Dodingsells).*
— *?source. 16 cent. (?estoile betw bars; on 4 shields, roof groining, lower lantern, Cricklade, Wilts).*
— *Birch 10121. 1349. (imp by Ric Gobaud, Parson of 2 Parts of Rippingale Ch, Lincs).*
— *Dugd 17, 98. 1237. (imp by Rog de Grafton).*
ASHBY. *Mill Steph. 1492. (upper sin shield on brass to Geoffrey Sherard & w Joice, dau of Thos A, of Lovesby, Stapleford, Leics).*
BINOLE, Lambert de. *Durham-sls 261. (used in 1410 by Jn of Dalton).*
BORHUNTE, William de. *PRO-sls E40 A3217.* S'WILL'I.DE.B..HVNTE. *1259-60.*
BOSCO, Ernaldus de. *CombeAsp II 130. (equestr sl).*
BOYS, Thos, Ld of Manor of Honyng. *NorfHo 3, 10. 27 Jan 1433. (sl on will).*
BRERETON, Joan. *Mill Steph. 1517. (dau of Sir Wm B & w of Ric Cotton; imp by C on brass, Hamstall Ridware, Staffs).*
BURDET, William. *Bow LIX 14.* +Sigillum Willelmi Burdet. *1224-7. (grant of land in Pevele; Test do. Robt. Lupo, tunc vicecomti de Warw. et Leic, Hugone Despensatore, Willelmo Basseth, Radulpho Basseth, Willelmo Charnels, Willelmo Martivall, Reginaldo de Cardoils).*
BURDET, William. *Bow XXXII 6.* +Sigillum Willelmi Burdet. *(grant of land in Pouele, Warws; T Dom. Roberto Lupo, vicecomti Leicestrie et Warr, Hugone Despensatore, Willelmo Basset, Willelmo Charnek).*
BURDET, William. *Dugd 17, 33.*
COCKAYN, Sir John. *Dugd 17, 40. 1420.*
COCKAYN, Sir John. *Birch 8769.* SIGILLUM:

IOH'IS COCKAYN: MILITIS. *1421-2.*
COCKAYNE, Sir John. *PRO-sls. 1421-2.*
COCKAYNE, Sir John. *Brit Arch Assoc vii 380.* Sigillum Johis Cockayn Militis. *1428. (sl; originally arms of Herthull, Sir Jn was s of Edm C, of Ashbourne & Polley by Elizab, heiress of H).*
COLUMBERS, Eleanor de. *PRO-sls.* S'ELIANOR DE GISTING.... *temp Edw 3. (?recte Hastings).*
EYSTON, William, of Istelworth. *PRO-sls E40 AB445.* S'WILLELMI EY.... *1375-6.*
FITZRADULF, Nicholas. *Dugd 17, 77. 1268.*
FITZRALPH. *Cleeve. c1300. (?barry, for Poyntz).*
FOXLE, John de. *PRO-sls. 16 November 1371. (Constable of Queenborough Castle).*
FOXLE, Sir John de. *PRO-sls. 25 October 1313.*
FOXLEY. *Mill Steph; Spokes. 1378. (imp Brocas on brass to Sir Jn F, Bray, Berks).*
FOXLEY, Thomas. *Yorks Deeds I 191. 1436.*
GATESDON, John de. *PRO-sls. temp Hen 3.*
HAKEBECH, Sir Robert, of Norf. *Birch 10368.* SIGILLU: ROB'TI H...EBEK. *1405.*
HAKEBECHE. *Farrer III 148. (St Margaret's Ch, King's Lynn).*
HARCOURT. *Mill Steph. 1415. (brass to Maud H, Kidderminster, Worcs).*
HARCOURT. *Mill Steph. 1500. (mullet on upper bar; imp by Erdeswick on tomb of Hugh E & w Eliz (dau of Jn H, of Ranton), Sandon, Staffs).*
HARCOURT. *Mill Steph. 1415. (imp by Cooksey on brass to Maud H & her husband Walter C, Esq, Kidderminster, Worcs).*
HARCOURT. *Mill Steph. 1415. (imp by Phelip on brass to Maud H & her 2nd husband Sir Jn P, Kidderminster, Worcs).*
HARCOURT, Sir Richard. *Lawrance 21. (fl 1301; effigy, Worcester Cathedral).*
HARECOURT, Alice de. *Bow XXVIII 10. (wid; sl on grt to 'Roberto Noel cognato meo tenam de Holford' etc).*
HARECOURT, Richard de. *Vinc 88, 189. 1232. (sl).*
HARECOURT, Sir Thomas. *Birch 10479.* SIG.- ..DE.HAR.... *1411.*
HARECOURT, Thomas de. *Dugd 17, 7.* Sigillum Thomi Harecourt. *1410.*
HARECOURT, Thos, Esq. *Mill Steph. 1460. (imp 3 bends; brass to Thos H, Stanton Harcourt, Oxfords).*
HARECOURT, Sir William de. *PRO-sls. 1339-40.*
HARECURT, Richard de, of Bosworth. *Bow LV 1.* +Sigillum Ricardi de Harecurt. *(grant of land in Bosworth, Leics; Test Dom Rob de Harecurt, Philippo Lovell, Adamo de*

Wechelburye, Petro Hanendby, Olivero ?Stak).

HARECURT, Richard de, of Staffs. *Birch 10477.* ...GILL': RICARDI.... ?c1250.

HARECURT, Sayer de. *Birch 10478.* +SIGIL-LUM SEERI DE HARECVRT. 1269.

HARECURT, Thomas, Kt. *Bow LVII 11.* +S: Thomae Harecurt. 1410-11.

HERMENVILE, Sir Simon de. *Birch 10653.* S'SIMONIS DE HERMENVILE MILITIS. 1260.

HERTHULL, Sir Richard. *Dugd 17, 40.* 1323.

HERTHULL, Sir Richard. *Dugd 17, 40.* 1378.

HERTHULL, Sir Richard de. *Dugd 17, 73.* 1314.

HERTHULLE, Richard de. *Birch 10662.* 1309. *(Sheriff of Warw & Leic).*

HERTHULLE, Sir Richard de. *Birch 10663.* : CI: GIST: LE: CERF. 1314. *(legend in allusion to design of sl [stag lodged at foot of tree]).*

HERTHULLE, Sir Richard de, of Derbys. *Birch 10664.* SIGIL...RICARDI.DE.HERTHVLL. 1364.

HETON, John de. *Yorks Deeds I 74.* 1419.

[HILTON]. *HB-SND.* 1324. *(1 of 3 shields on sl of Maud, dau of Robt Lascelles & w of Robt Tiliol).*

[HILTON]. *Mill Steph.* 1510. *(fleur de lis for diffce; qtd 2&3 by [Lascelles], all qtd III by Melton on brass to Sir Jn M, Aston, Yorks).*

HILTON, Alexander, Ld of. *Durham-sls 1341.* 1338.

[HILTON, of Hilton, co Durham]. *Blair D II 148, 328. (qtg (2)6 rings [Vipont], (3)3 swords conjd at centre pts outwards [Staple-ton]; on W front, Hilton Chapel, co Durham).*

HILTON, Robt de. *Durham-sls 1346.*

HILTON, Thomas. *Waterford 113, HB-SND.* 1542. *(qtg 2: 3 rings & chf, 3: 3 mullets).*

HILTON, William de, Ld. *PRO-sls.* 1392-3.

[HILTON, William, of Hilton, co Durham]. *Blair D II 141, 305. (qtg 2&3 3 chaplets [Lascelles]; on west front of Gatehouse, Hilton Castle).*

HILTON, Wm of. *Durham-sls 1351.* 1414 & 33.

HILTON, Wm of. *Durham-sls 1352.* 1389.

HORECOURT, Sir Thomas. *Bow LIX 19.* Sig Thome Horecourt. 1406-7. *(grant of Manor of Bosworth, Leics to his s Thos).*

HORECOURT, William de. *Bow XXXI 4. (s of Rich de H; Test: dom Roberto de Halenton, Thome de Kerswell, Phil Noell).*

ISSODUN, Ralph de, Comte d'Eu. *SussASColl viii 150.* c1215. *(rev of equestr sl on grt by the Count to Robertsbridge Abbey).*

LAYS, Philip de, Clerk. *PRO-sls AS 292.* S PHILIPI DE LAYS CLERICI. 1370-1.

MAINWARING, Agnes. *Bk of Sls 45.* 1306-9. *(wid of Warin de M).*

MANWAYRINGS, Joan. *Mill Steph.* 1598. *(wid of Wm M; imp Hurst on brass, Noke, Oxfords to Joan Bradshaw dau&coh of Jn H, of Kingston upon Thames & her 2 husbs Wm M, of E Ham, Essex, d1529, & Hy B).*

MARTIN. *Arch Cant xxi 98. (Altar tomb to Thos Martin, Rich his s & Thomasine his w, S aisle of Chancel, Edenbridge, Kent).*

MARTIN, Constance. *PRO-sls.* SIGILL' CON-STANCE MARTIN. 1393-4. *(used by Robt Martin).*

MARTIN, Margaret. *AnstisAsp I 214, 67.* 1343-4. *(imp maunch).*

MARTIN, William. *Birch 11652.* S' WILL'I MARTINI:. 1301. *(Ld of Camieux, Pembs, 1st Baron).*

MARTIN, William. *PRO-sls, Barons Letter.*

MARTYN, Margaret. *AnstisAsp I 219, 78. (imp maunch). (wid of William M).*

MARTYN, Robert, of Chideock, Dorset. *Birch 11651.* SIGILLVM: ROBERI: MARTIN. 1351.

MAUNWARING, Thomas de. *Bow 12.*

MAYNWARYNG. *Brit Arch Assoc xxiv 382-3.* 15 cent. *(with checky [Calveley] on brass to Dame Margery C, dau of Wm M, sometime w to Philipp Egerton, late of Egerton, Squyer, d 14.. (date incomplete), Ightfield, Salop).*

MEYNWARYNGE, William de, of N Wales. *Birch 11524.* S'G...EM MAYNWARYNGE. 1394.

MORHALL, Thomas, parson of Iverton. *BirmCL-sls 348025.* 1372.

NEVILLE, George. *Birch 12098.* 1499.

NOVEREY, John. *PRO-sls.* 1345-6.

PAGEMAN, Richard. *PRO-sls E40 A2641.* SIGILLVM.RICARDI.PAGEMAN. 1329-30. *(imp by paly of 4).*

PAR, Wil. *Bellasis II 49; Whitaker ii 327; Hill ii 66. (cresc for diffce; qtg [Ros]; 'arma Wil Par militis'; formerly in E window, S aisle, Parr chapel, Kendal).*

PEVENYS, Nicholas. *PRO-sls.* c1395.

POTTERE, Thomas, of Bridgwater. *Bridgwater 409.* 1385. *(?roundels betw bars).*

RIPARIO, Peter de. *Bk of Sls 300.* late 12 cent.

SCROP, Sir Henry le. *Birch 13353.* 1355. *(on triangular flag attached to lance; s&h of Geoffrey le S, Kt, of London).*

SCROPE, Sir Henry le, governor of our seignours. *PRO-sls.* 1363-4. *(in sin half of shield on pennon held by man's hand).*

THELVETHAM, John de, of Norf. *Birch 13898.* S'...ELVETHEM. 1385.

TWYFORD, Robert de, Kt, of Warws. *Birch 14026.* SIGILLUM RO(BERT)I TWY(FOR)D. 1381.

[?UPTON]. *Lawrance 45.* ante 1350. *(effigy, Upton-on-Severn, Worcs).*

VENABLES, Roger de. *Middlewich 97.* 1380.

(cresc for diffce).
VERNON, William de. *Bow LXXIII 3.* ...VT.-
WILELMI.DE.VERN... *(sl rev; grant of rent
from Herlaestuna to Abbey of Polesworth).*
WATTEVILE, Agnes de. *AnstisAsp I 216, 69.*
SIGILL: AGNETE: VXOR: WATTEVILE. 1335-6.
(wid of Wm Martin).
WELLE, Robert. *Birch 14344.* SIGILL'
ROBERTI DE W(EL)LE. 13 cent. *(s of Wm de
W, of Lincs).*
WHITHEVED, Alan of. *Dodsworth 45, 46b,
HB-SND.* 1358.

Arg 2 bars Arg
Arg 2 bars in umbre
    — *ML I 44.* *('sylver barrey. In com' Kancie.
Ye shall say barrey becawse thei apper as
barres & be none'.).*

Arg 2 bars Az
Arg 2 bars Az
    — *I2(1904)85.* *(qtd III 1&4 by Mayster Jn
Mylton).*
    — *PLN 1839.* *(in chf of coat per fess qtg
2&3 Arg 3 chaplets Gu, all imp by Bruarne,
of Lincs).*
    — *BG 124.*
    — *LD 24.*
    — *WB I 39b, 12.* *(qtd 2&3 by Sir J
Cockayn).*
GRAY, of Hilton. *WB IV 184b 1057.* *(qrs
1&4).*
HALSALL. *LH 519.*
HALSALL, S' Gilbert de, Lancs. *CY 57, 226.*
HERON, Messire Jehan. *Montendre 10.*
HILTON. *LH 40.*
HILTON. *PLN 144.*
HILTON. *L1 307, 2.* *(as blazoned).*
HILTON. *DV 65a 2576.* *(Venables crossed
out & H added in later hand).*
HILTON. *LY A 126.* *(qtg 2&3 Arg 3 chaplets
Gu [Lascelles] all in border Sa).*
HILTON. *ME 6.* *(qtg 2&3 Arg 3 chaplets Gu
seeded Or [Lascelles] all in border Sa).*
HILTON. *PLN 668.* *(qtg 2&3 Arg 3 chaplets
Gu [Lascelles]).*
HILTON. *XFB 226.* *(qtd 3 by [Melton] -
name hidden in binding).*
HILTON. *LH 1018.*
HILTON. *L1 342, 2.*
HILTON, Baron. *FK I 128.* *('of Durham'
added by Gibbon).*
HILTON, Baron. *CRK 214.*
HILTON, Baron de. *CV-BM 17.*
HILTON, Ld. *BW 13b, 87.*
HILTON, Ld. *BR VI 48.*
HILTON, Sr de. *CKO 319.*
HILTON, de. *SP A 134.*
HILTON, le Baron de. *TJ 483.*

HILTON, le Baron de. *S 97.*
HILTON, le Sire de. *CG 239.*
HILTON, le Sr de. *AS 118.*
[?HILTON]. *RL 28.*
HILTON, Mons Alex de. *CA 159.*
HILTON, Baro de. *RL 29, 4.*
HILTON, the Barron of. *WK 131.*
HILTON, Die here van. *Gelre 57b.* c1380.
HILTON, ?Edward. *GutchWdU.* *(Fellow,
Benefactor, Queens' Coll, d.1530; Window,
Queen's Coll Chapel).*
HILTON, Sir Jordan. *PCL I 472.*
HILTON, Jurdan de. *Q 151.*
HILTON, Mons Robert de. *WJ 517.*
HILTON, Robert. *LH 239.*
HILTON, Robert de. *XF 961.*
HILTON, Robert de. *LMS 79.* *(fl 1325).*
HILTON, Robert de. *F 472.*
HILTON, Robert de. *E I 293; E II 295.*
HILTON, Sir Robert. *LH 166.*
HILTON, Sr Robert of. *BR IV 31.*
HILTON, Sir Robert, of York. *LH 648.*
HILTONE, Robert de. *H 42a.*
HUYLTON, le Baron de, of Lancs. *CY 47,
188.*
HYLTON, Ld. *WB I 37, 1.*
HYLTON, de. *DV 48b, 1903.*
HYLTON, the baron of. *RH, Ancestor iv 231.*
HYLTON, le Baroun de. *PO 432.*
HYLTON, of Durham. *D4 31.*
HYLTON, Godfrey. *PLN 347.* *(qtg 2&3 Arg
3 chaplets Gu [Lascelles]).*
HYLTON, Baron off. *WB II 50, 10.*
HYLTON, Sr Robert de. *H 42b.*
HYLTONE, Sire Robert de. *N 136.*
MARTYN. *PT 668.*
[VENABLES]. *Lancs 1533 CS 110, 166.* *(qtd
2 by Halsall).*
Arg 2 bars 1st Az 2nd Vt
HALSALL. *LH 702.*

Arg 2 bars Gu
Arg 2 bars Gu
    — *CB 79.*
    — *HA 25b, 136.* early 14 cent. *(tincts
unclear; MS damaged, most of shield & name
gone).*
    — *WK 193.* *(qtd 4 by Sir Rog Neubourgh).*
    — *BA 17.* *(qtd 2&3 by Ld Audley).*
    — *WLN 109; WLN 282.* *(qtd 2&3 by Ld
Cowcy).*
    — *PLN 2041.* *(qtd 3 by Sir Rog Newbor-
ough).*
    — *WB II 69, 15.* *(qtd 2&3 by Sir Jn Danet).*
[BROUGHTON]. *Bellasis B 9.* *(qrs 1&4; E
window, Windermere).*
DAUNDELEGH, Philip. *AN 250.*
HARCOURT. *Farrer I 185.* *(imp by Knyvett;
on font, Ashwellthorpe Ch, Norf).*

MAINWARING. *PLN 731.*
MAINWARING. *ChesMont. (canopied tomb, Acton, Ches).*
MAINWARINGE, de Pevor. *DV 63b, 2513. (name added in later hand).*
MAINWARYNG, Sir John, of Ches. *WB III 93, 5.*
MANWARING, Sir John, of Pever. *XK 164. (qrs 1&4).*
MARTIN. *L1 458, 3; L2 333, 4. (Maveryng of Ches in margin L1).*
MARTIN, Sr, of Devon. *CKO 314.*
MARTIN, Sir John. *CRK 420.*
MARTIN, Sire Willame. *N 100.*
MARTIN, Ld William. *XF 525. (imp Nicole).*
MARTIN, Monsire William. *CG 234.*
MARTIN, S' William. *PO 672.*
MARTIN, Sir William. *XF 584.*
MARTIN, William. *H 44a.*
MARTON, Ser Wyll'm. *CT 273.*
MARTYN, le Sr. *AS 95.*
MARTYN, Sir John, of Devon. *WB III 73, 8.*
MARTYN, le S' R. *WJ 589.*
MARTYN, Monsire Robert. *AN 261.*
MARTYN, Monsr William. *TJ 506.*
MARTYN, Sir William. *WK 333.*
MARTYN, Sir William. *TJ 1235. (also Wm Maudyt).*
MARTYN, Sr William. *H 44b.*
MARTYN, Williamus. *SP A 79.*
MARTYN, S. Wm. *ST 77.*
MARTYNE, Sir William. *BR V 84.*
MAU[DUT], William. *P 126. ('...ove deux fesses de goules').*
MAUDEUT, Wm. *B 65.*
MAUDUIT. *DX 23; RW 35. (E of Warwick, jure uxoris).*
MAUDUIT, Walter. *C 152.*
MAUDUIT, William. *MP II 75.*
MAUDUYT, William. *TJ 1236.*
MAUDYT, Robert, Ld, of Hanslape. *L9 48a, 6.*
MAYNERYNG, Sir J. *WB I 38, 7.*
MAYNWARE', Sir J. *BW 22, 153.*
MAYNWARINGE. *CVC 518.*
MAYNWARRYNG, Sir John. *BA 4.*
MAYNWARYN, Ranulf. *CVC 563.*
MAYNWARYNG, Sir John. *PCL II 46.*
MAYNWARYNG, S' John, Ches. *CY 9, 33.*
MEYNWARYN, Sir John. *WLN 314.*
TAME, William, of Hants. *WB III 78, 1. (qrs 1&4).*

Arg 2 bars Or &c
Arg 2 bars Or
MAYNWARYNG. *L1 430, 5; L2 332, 7.*
Arg 2 bars Sa
— *CC 228, 205. (qtd 2&3 by Sayvill).*
ARCHALL, of Salop. *CY 87, 346.*

BRAILE, Willm de. *WLN 868.*
BREERTON, Sir John. *T b 138.*
BRERERTON. *GutchWdU. c1530. (qtg 2 Berkeley, 3 Arg on salt Gu 5 roses Or; window given by Sir Will Compton, Balliol Chapel).*
BRERETON. *XF 475.*
BRERETON. *RB 251. (mullet Sa in fess pt).*
BRERETON. *SK 527.*
BRERETON, Sir .... *XF 576. (qrs 1&4).*
BRERETON, Sir .... *WK 177.*
[BRERETON]. *WLN 285. (qr 1).*
BRERETON, of Ches. *PLN 135.*
BRERETON, of Ches. *PLN 359.*
BRERETON, Sir John. *WK 263.*
BRERETON, Sir Randolfe. *BA 3b. (cresc Arg on upper bar; qtg Arg 2 'fanons' Sa).*
BRERETON, Sir Randolph. *XF 721. (qrs 1&4; cresc Arg on upper bar).*
BRERETON, Syr Randolf, of Ipston. *I2(1904)207. (cresc Arg on upper bar; qtg Arg chev betw 3 crescs Gu).*
BRERETON, Sir William. *XK 173.*
BRERETON, Sir William. *CRK 177.*
BRERETON, Sir William de. *CVC 549.*
BRERETON, Sr William de. *WLN 328.*
BRERETON, S' William de, of Ches. *CY 18, 70.*
BRERETON, Sir Wylliam. *BA 3b.*
BRERTON, Andrew of. *BA 39b, 383.*
BRERTON, Thomas, of Ches. *WB III 111, 2.*
BRERTON, Mons Will. *WJ 938.*
BRERTON, Sir William de. *PCL II 19.*
BRERTUN, of Kent. *MY 229.*
BRIERTON. *L1 94, 4.*
BRIERTON, of Brierton, Ches. *L1 117, 1; L2 55, 5.*
BRIRTON, Reynold. *BG 244.*
BRYERTON. *L10 77, 9.*
FAYPOW, R'. *WJ 819. ('Mons' Fraunces de Faypow' at side).*
HELAUNDE, Ric' de. *Q 432.*
HETON, Thomas de. *LH 651.*

Arg 2 bars Vt
Arg 2 bars Vt
— *L9 106, 10. (qtd 2 by Thos Palmer, of Warws).*
— *I2(1904)280. (qtd 2&3 by Kokyn).*
— *WB III 83b, 9. (qtd 2&3 by Sir Jn Cokin, of Warws).*
— *BA 32, 323. (qtd 2&3 by Cokyn).*
— *L10 46, 3. (qtd 2&3 by Cokyn).*
— *L10 88, 8. (qtd 2 by Thos, s of Ric Palmer, of Wasperton, Warws).*
HARTHILL. *XF 65.*
HARTHILL. *LH 1057.*
HARTHULL, Sir Richard. *LH 603.*
HERTHILL. *LH 75.*

HERTHILL', Mons de. *AS 464.*
HERTHULE, of Derbys. *L2 269, 1.*
HERTHULL. *LH 801.*
HERTHULLE, Sir Richard. *LH 190.*
HERTHULLE, Sire Richard de. *N 627.*

Az 2 bars Arg

Az 2 bars Arg
— *PLN 2043. (qtd 2&3 by Sir Harry Marney).*
— *CRK 876. (qtg 2&3 Gu lion gard Arg).*
— *PCL II 75.*
— *WGA 135. (qtd 3 by Sir Hen Marny).*
— *XK 68. (qtd 2 by Sir Hen Marney).*
— *XK 150. (qtd 2 by Sir Jn Marney).*
— *WK 192. (qtd 2&3 by Sir Hen Marney).*
— *Kb 342B. (qtd 2&3 by Ld Marney - cancelled with pen strokes).*
— *CY 137, 547. (qtd 2&3 by S' Willm Maryner, Essex, Gu lion pg Arg).*
— *PT 545. (qtd by Marney).*
— *WGA 244. (qtd 3 by 1st Ld Marnay).*
BURDET, Sr Richard. *CKO 332.*
CLIFFORD, Rogerus de. *Keepe. (15 cent inscription, painted shield).*
CRANEBURA. *L10 40b, 17.*
CRANEBURY, Mons Rauf de. *WJ 525.*
HILTON. *L1 307, 2; L2 247, 7. (as painted).*
KINDERTON, Baro de, of Ches. *CY 4, 15.*
KYNDERTON, le Baron du. *BA 1.*
LYGHT, Thewe of, of Lancs. *RH, Ancestor iv 241.*
VENABLES. *L1 657, 3.*
VENABLES. *Leake. (qtd 2 by Sir Hen Marney, KG, d1523-4).*
VENABLES. *PLN 554.*
VENABLES. *DV 67a, 2641.*
VENABLES. *WLN 286. (qr 1).*
VENABLES, Sir .... *CRK 1082.*
VENABLES, Baron, of Hilton, co Durham. *Gerard 68.*
VENABLES, S' Hugh. *PO 657.*
VENABLES, Sir J. *BW 21b, 112.*
VENABLES, of Jersey. *Soc Jers (1928); Soc Guern (1928). ?c1345.*
VENABLES, of Kinderton. *BA 40b, 394.*
VENABLES, Sir Ric'. *PCL II 18.*
VENABLES, Ricardus. *Q II 680.*
VENABLES, Sir Rich le. *WLN 299.*
VENABLES, Richard. *SES 116.*
VENABLES, Sir Richard. *CVC 596.*
VENABLES, Rogerus de. *WestmAbb. 15 cent. (painted shield).*
VENABLYS, Sir J. *WB I 40b, 10.*
VENABYLYS. *WB IV 181, 997. (name struck through in original; field painted Sa but corrected by later hand to 'aseiur').*
WENABLES. *PT 265.*

Az 2 bars Gu

Az 2 bars Gu
MAUDUIT, William de, erle of Warwicke. *BirmCL-sls I 168241.*

Az 2 bars Or

Az 2 bars Or
— *CK a 80.*
— *XF 72.*
ASHBY. *Ussher 32-33, pl xiv. (on incised slab, Croxhall Ch, to Jn Curzon (d1500) & w Anne (d1514) dau of Wm A, of Quenby).*
BLACKHAM, Benet de. *WLN 752.*
BORDET, of Leics. *L2 88, 7.*
BORDIT, Mons Richard. *AS 456.*
BURDEIT, John. *WLN 881.*
BURDET, Sir Oliver. *PLN 639.*
BURDET, Monsire Richard. *CG 229.*
BURDET, Richard. *Q 329.*
BURDET, Sire Willame. *N 812.*
BURDET, Willame. *LM 509.*
[BURDETT]. *Nichols Leics III 116. (window in Woodhouse Chapel).*
BURDEYT, Mons' Richard. *TJ 537.*
CONSTABLE, Sir J. *BW 20b, 141.*
PAUNCEFOT, William. *F 124.*
PAUNCEFOT, Wm. *WLN 632.*
VENABLES, Thos, of Golborne, Ches. *BA 40b, 393a. (4 other qtgs; added by T. Wriothesley).*

Gu 2 bars Arg

Gu 2 bars Arg
— *XK 142. (qtd by Sir Wm Hussey).*
— *WB II 60, 9. (qtg vairy Arg?Gu & Or).*
— *LM 438.*
— *Q II 463. (imp by Or 2 bars & in chf 3 lions Gu).*
BOIS, J. deu. *HA 23b, 116. (tincts unclear). ('Jo. de Borgr' in A).*
DRAYTON, of Salop. *CY 87, 346.*
FOXLE, Mons' John de. *S 554.*
FOXLEY, of Northants. *L1 250, 3; L2 204, 4.*
FOXLLE, Sire Johan de. *N 323.*
KNYT. *L1 294, 9.*
MAINWARING. *XF 722. (qrs 1&4; in fess pt cresc Or).*
MAINWARING, of Ches. *XF 564.*
MAINWARING, John, 'de Pevyr'. *XF 720. (qrs 1&4).*
MANERYNG. *WB I 22b, 2.*
MANWARYNG, of Ichfelde. *I2(1904)254. (qtg checky Arg and Sa).*
MAYNWARING, of Ches. *L9 48a, 7.*
MAYNWARYNG, John, of Peover, Ches. *I2(1904)202. (qtg Gu scythe in bend sin Arg).*
WESTON, Mons Lambert de. *WJ 617.*

Gu 2 bars Or
Gu 2 bars Or
— *PLN 1056. (qtd 2&3 by ?Bracebridge (vairy Arg and Sa fess Gu), all imp by qtly 1&4 Gu chev betw 3 lions Arg, 2&3 Sa chev Erm betw 3 doves Arg membered Gu).*
— *CRK 1459. (qtd 2&3 by Sir Jn Astley).*
— *PT 627.*
— *PLN 1850. (qtd 2&3 by Mayster Astley).*
ARCOURTE, Sr John de. *L 32.*
CHALON. *PLN 1636.*
FOXLE, of Suss. *CY 168, 671.*
HARCOURT. *Leake. (qtd 2&3 by Sir Jn Astley, KG, d1486).*
HARCOURT. *LH 478.*
HARCOURT. *XF 464.*
HARCOURT. *PLN 1484.*
HARCOURT. *GutchWdU. (formerly in window of Master's Lodgings, University Coll, ante 1564).*
HARCOURT. *L10 91, 2. (8 other qtgs, all imp by Bowyer).*
HARCOURT, Sir .... *LH 300.*
[HARCOURT]. *Nichols Leics II 168. (Eastwell Ch).*
[HARCOURT]. *Lamborn. 1460. (Font, Stanton Harcourt, Oxfords, also in contemp glass).*
[HARCOURT]. *PLN 1145. (qtd 2&3 by [Astley], all imp by Sir Jn Cley).*
HARCOURT, of Devon & Cornw. *WJ 549.*
HARCOURT, de, of Guernsey. *Soc Guern (1928).* temp Edw 2.
HARCOURT, Sir Harry. *PLN 340.*
HARCOURT, Sir John, of Staffs. *LH 734.*
HARCOURT, S'r de. *BK 61. (qtg Az estoile of 8 rays Or & imp qtly 1 Arg lion Sa, 2 per pale Or and Vt cross moline Gu, 3 Gu chev betw 3 5foils Or, 4 Or 3bars Gu; sketched in margin opposite standard; for Chris H & w Joan Stapleton).*
HARCOURT, Sir Robard, Oxfords. *RH, Ancestor v 177.*
HARCOURT, Sir Robert. *PLN 2038.*
HARCOURT, Sir Robert, KG, d1470. *Leake. c1461.*
HARCOURT, Sir Simon. *XK 176.*
[HARCOURT, Sir Simon]. *Lamborn. 1547. (Gatehouse, Stanton Harcourt, Oxfords).*
HARCOURT, of Stanton Harcourt, Oxfords. *L1 327, 5; L2 250, 5.*
HARECOURT, Mons de. *AS 225.*
HARECOURT, le Comte de. *TJ 519.*
HARECOURT, Sire Johan de. *N 823.*
HARECOURT, John de. *C 173.*
HARECOURT, Sr John de. *I 33.*
HARECURT, John de. *FW 552.*
HARRECOURT. *SK 903.*
HARRECOURT. *WK 190.*

HARRECOURT, Sir Robert. *WGA 275.*
HARRENCOURT, Sir Robert. *WK 209.*
HAVERCOURT. *Nichols Leics IV 909. (Shakerston Ch).*

Gu 2 bars Vt
MORTYMER, S. Hugh de. *GA 137. (bars rectius Vair).*

Or 2 bars Az
Or 2 bars Az
ASKE, of Aughtone. *PT 1127. (qtg Altaripa).*
HAK-BECHE, Sir Robert. *L1 310, 4.*
HAKBECHE. *DV 64a, 2523.*
HAKEBICHE. *L1 336, 5.*
HAKENBECH, Sir Reynold. *BA 690.*
HAKENBECHE. *C3 13b. (qtd 4 by Drewe, all imp by Clarke, in window of Mr Price's house at Washingby; for Jn C, auditor of Duchy of Lancs, husb of Eliz D, wid of Jn Otter).*
HAKENBECHE, Mons' Reynald. *S 209.*
HAUKBECK, S. *L2 251, 3.*
LEDYS, Mons Esmond, de Kent. *WJ 1000.*
MANNERS. *PT 181. ('after Erle of Rutland'; name added).*

Or 2 bars Gu
Or 2 bars Gu
— *Lyndsay 20. (escutch of K of Denmark).*
— *WB II 58, 12. (qrs 1&4 of coat imp by Blaknall).*
— *BA 838. (qtd 2&3 by Ralph Boteler, Ld of Sudeley).*
BRAMSTON, Hue de. *LM 448.*
BRYTO, Sir Roger. *CV-BM 1.*
DENMARK. *Lyndsay 43. (imp by Jas 3 for his w Mgt, dau of K of Denmark).*
FOXLEY. *CV-BM 116.*
HARCORT, Sire Johan de. *N 147.*
HARCOURT. *LH 90. (qrs 1&4).*
HARCOURT. *PT 460.*
HARCOURT. *DX 17; RW 29. (tinct of bars unclear).*
HARCOURT. *XF 888. (qrs 1&4).*
HARCOURT, Johan de. *G 96.*
HARCOURT, Sir John. *ML II 74.*
HARCOURT, John de, of Ellenhall, d1330. *SF 31.*
HARCOURT, Richard de. *Q 206.*
HARCOURT, Mons Th de. *WJ 582.*
HARCOURT, Sir Thomas. *LH 542.*
HARCOURT, Thomas. *BG 285.*
HARCOURT, Sir William. *LH 304.*
HARCOURT, William. *LH 229.*
HARCOURTE, Sir R.. *WB I 38b, 22.*
HARECOURT, Sr de. *CKO 585.*
HARECOURT, J. *RB 433.*
HARECOURT, John de. *B 69.*

HARECOURT, Richard. *P 124.* (*'dor ov deux fesses de goules'*).
HARECOURT, Mons' William. *TJ 543.*
HARECOURTE. *DV 51a, 2003.*
HARECOURTE, Mons' Thomas. *S 132.*
HARECOURTE, William de. *E 63.*
HARECURT, Richart de. *LM 264.*
HARECURT, William. *F 61.*
HARMANVILLE. *WGA 132.* (*qtd 2&3 by Sir Jn Asteley*).
HERCOURTT. *CT 370.*
SULEE, Bartholomew de. *D 160a.*
SULEE, Munsire Bartholomew de. *D 160b.*
SULL', Monsr de. *AS 224.*
SUYLLY, Mons' Robert. *TJ 511.*
WAKE, Sir John. *ML I 84.* (*3 roundels Gu in chf missing*).
WINTERSHALL, Sir .... *CRK 1022.*
WINTERSHULL, of Surr. *XF 776.*
WYNTURSALL, Sr Symond, of Surr. *WB III 77, 9.*

Or 2 bars Sa &c
Or 2 bars Sa
— *PT 10.*
PEVERE. *ME 86; LY A 211.*
PEVOR. *DV 58a, 2292.* (*name added in another hand*).
Or 2 bars Vt
ACBEECH. *T b 161.*

Sa 2 bars
Sa 2 bars Arg
BRERETON, Sr John. *Harl 6137, 44a-45a (27).*
BRERTON, Sir John. *GY 27.*
HAYME, John, of Irld. *LH 790.*
HAYOE, John, of Irld. *WB III 94, 3.*
VENABYLYS. *WB IV 181, 997.* (*name struck out; tinct of field corrected to 'aseur' in later hand*).
WELLYNG. *BR IV 46.*
Sa 2 bars Or
— *PLN 1326.* (*qtd 2&3 by Ralph Rance*).
BLACKHAM, Bennet de. *XF 384.*
BLAKEHAM, Beges. *F 340.*
BLAKEHAM, Bennet de. *E I 493; E II 495.*
BLAKELIG, Thomas. *WLN 412.*
ORRELL, Sir John, of Som. *WB III 77, 4.*

Vt 2 bars Or
Vt 2 bars Or
COKAIN, Richard, of Derbys. *WB III 101b, 7.*
COKAYN. *L10 46b, 14.*
COKAYN. *L2 142, 7.* (*marginal note: 'Herthull'*).
COKAYNE, Sir John, of Derbys. *PLN 369.*

Barry &c, 2 bars
Barry wavy 2 bars
WALKINGHAM, S Alani. *PE II 23.* (*'filii Joan' de' W; from a sl*).
Checky 2 bars
— *Bow XX 3.* (*trappings on equestr sl*).
Checky Untinc 2 bars Arg
— *LH 59.* (*imp by Huntingfield, but name struck through & coats half erased*).
Checky Arg and Az 2 bars Gu
LECHCHE, John. *CVK 760.*
LECHCHE, John, of Suss. *CY 169, 675.*
Checky Arg and Sa 2 bars Gu
BARE, Sir John, of Herefs. *WB III 121b, 9.* (*qrs 1&4*).

Erm 2 bars
Erm 2 bars Untinc
— Stevenson. c1350. (*qtd by Eleanor Umfraville, Ctess of Angus, & later w of Rog Mauduit*).
BROME, William, Vicar of Bakewell, Derbys. *Birch 7839.* 1428. (*?bar gemel*).
DELAVAL, Robert. *PRO-sls RS 95, HB-SND.* 1322.
DELAVAL, of Seaton-Delaval. *Blair N I 91, 180.* (*over W door of Norman chapel at Seaton Delaval*).
FRERE, Walter, of Sawbridgworth, Herts. *Birch 9957.* 1370.
HUNTERCUMBE, Walter de, Kt. *PRO-sls.* 1274-5.
MARA, William de, Ld of Rendcomb, Gloucs. *Birch 11594.* s' WILLELMI: DE LA MARE. mid Hen 3.
MAUDUIT, Alienor. *Durham-sls 1728.* post 1325. (*w of Sir Rog M*).
MAUDUIT, Sir Roger. *Durham-sls 1729.* ante 1350.
MAUDYT, Roger, Kt. *PRO-sls.* 1323-4.
MAUDYT, Roger, Chev. *Birch 11682.* 1322.
[?VAL, Sir Robert de la]. *Blair N I 22, 50.* (*beneath battlements of Bothal Castle*).
VALE, Robert de la, Kt, of Northd. *PRO-sls.* 1322-3.
WROKESHALE, Sir John of. *PlymouthCL-sls 86, 74.* 1338.
Erm 2 bars Az
VALE, Mons Henry de. *WJ 839.* (*?bars Vt*).
Erm 2 bars Gu
— *PLN 1877.*
— *H21 16.* (*qtd 3 by Husse, of Duffield, Yorks*).
BAVAUNT. *L10 20b, 6.*
BAVAUNT, Mons Waut. *WJ 929.*
BAXBY. *PT 1241.*
HUNTERCOMBE, Sir Walter. *ML I 108; ML II 98.*
HUSE, Mons Mark de. *WJ B 913.*

HUSSEY, Hubert. *LMS 89.*
HUSSEY, Maryon. *WB II 68, 6. (imp by Frances Bello).*
HUYSE, Mons Hug' de. *WJ B 588.*
MARDIT. *L9 50b, 7.*
MAUDIT, Mons Rogere. *WJ 915.*
MAUDUT. *DV 55b, 2200.*
MAUDUT, Sr de. *CKO 313.*
MAUDUT, Monsr R. de. *AS 290.*
MAUDUT, Monsire Roger. *CG 233.*
MAUDUT, of Staffs. *L1 451, 4; L2 337, 12.*
MAUDUTT. *CC 222b, 18.*
MAUDUYT, Monsr Roger. *TJ 510.*
WILL, Johan le fitz. *F 198.*
WROKESHALE, Geffray. *TJ 549.*

Erm 2 bars Vt
DALAVALE, Monsr John. *TJ 1564.*
DALEWELL, of Northd. *CT 456.*
[DELAVAL]. *Blair N I 83, 159. (qtg 2&3 Gu 3 eagles displ Arg; E window, St Nicholas Cathedral, Newcastle on Tyne).*
VAL, Sir Hugh de la. *Lawrance 13.* 1302. *(mullet Untinc for diffce; 2 shields near tomb, Seaton Delaval, Northd).*

Per fess &c 2 bars
Per fess Az and Gu 2 bars Or
HOLT. *LH 852.*
HOLT. *L1 318, 5; L2 253, 6.*
Per fess nebuly Arg and Sa 2 bars counterch
— *PLN 1017.*
Per pale Arg and Gu 2 bars counterch
BARRETT, of Irld. *LQ 59.*
Per pale Or and Gu 2 bars Untinc
— *PT 664. (line crosses bars, but no tincts are marked on them).*
Per pale dex checky Or and Az sin Vt over all 2 bars Arg
COURTENAY, John de. *B 109.*
[OKEHAMPTON]. *PLN 1978. (qtd 4 by E of Devonshire).*
Qtly Arg and Sa 2 bars counterch
CUSACK, of Irld. *LQ 108. (imp Vere; as painted).*

Semy, 2 bars
Semy of martlets 2 bars
FOULISHURST, Matthew de. *Bow XXXV 32a.* 1358-9. *(equestr sl; grant of land in Weston subter Brewood).*
Crusily 2 bars
— *Bow XXXV 14b. (imp by checky; grant of land in Linwood to Fineshade Priory).*
— *Bow XXXV 14a. (sl obv of Vitalis de Engaine on grant of land in Linwood to Fineshade Priory).*
Az crusilly & 2 bars Or
BLAKEHAM, Sire Thomas. *N 479.*
BLAKENHAM, Sr Thomas. *BR V 177.*

Gu crusilly Arg 2 bars Vair
MORTYMER, S. William. *GA 138.*
Arg gutty Az 2 bars Gu
CHAURI. *L10 43, 14.*
CHAURY. *L2 105, 12.*
CHAWRY. *L1 129, 5.*

Vair 2 bars
Vair 2 bars Gu
— *WLN 17. (qtd 2&3 by Ld Coucy).*
BREWIS, Johes de. *L10 24, 10. ('filius et heres Willm de Brewis militis').*
COUCY, de. *PT 411.*
COURCY. *SK 270. (qrs 1&4).*
WALKINGHAM, Sire Johan de. *N 1085.*
WALKYNGHAM, Mons' Aleyn, de Ridmere. *TJ 620.*
WALKYNGHAM, Mons' John de. *TJ 527.*
WALKYNGHAM, Sr John de. *M 72.*

2 bars patterned
Arg 2 bars checky Sa and Untinc
— *GutchWdU. c1514. (qtg 2&4 Gwynbourne, 3&5 Bottetourt, all imp by Sir Wm Fyndern, Kt; window, Lincoln Coll Hall).*
Gu 2 bars gobony Arg and Sa
BARRE, Syr Johne. *BA 17b.*
BARRY, Sir Thomas. *CRK 749. (qrs 1&4).*

2 bars Erm
Untinc 2 bars Erm
— *Clairambault 3487.* 14 Oct 1441. *(qtd 2&3 by Fulk Eyton).*
Gu 2 bars Erm
— *PLN 1391. (imp by Wm Guyton).*
— *CT 151.*
— *CRK 2016.*
BOTELER. *L2 82, 3.*
BOTELER. *SK 809.*
BOTELER. *RB 551.*
BOTTELLEN. *PO 389. (name added in later hand).*
BUTLER, Ralph. *PLN 1494.*
BUTTELER, of Bedmaton. *L1 38, 5; L2 43, 8.*
CHAUNTTE. *WB IV 161, 635. (imp by Bottell'd).*
NYDYAN, Nycolas, Ld of Delven. *DIG 17.*
Gu 2 bars Ermines
PANTON. *XF 807.*
PANTON. *L9 102a, 5. (?fimbr).*

2 bars fretty
2 bars fretty
[CLOPTON]. *Mill Steph.* 1411. *(brass to Thos de Cruwe (d1418) & w Julian, wid of Jn de Clopton, Wixford, Warws).*
CLOPTON, Joan. *Mill Steph. c1430. (imp Besford on brass to Joan C, Quinton, Gloucs;*

brass restored 1739).
CLOPTON, Johanna. *Dugd 17, 18.* 1432. *(w of Wm C).*
PETHERTON, Robert de. *Birch 12601.*
SIGILLV ROB'I DE PETHERTON. 14 cent.
Arg 2 bars Gu fretty Or
CLOPTON. *PT 935.*
CLOPTON. *L1 168, 3; L2 112, 4.*
CLOPTON. *DV 70b, 2798.*
MARSHALL, Thomas de. *Vinc 88, 26.* 1363-4.
SAWTRE PRIORY. *L10 67, 16.*

2 bars per fess indented
Gu 2 bars per fess indented Arg and Az
FRAYN, Monsire de. *CG 238.*
FREN, S' Hugh. *PO 563.*
FRENE. *SK 733.*
FRENE, Sr de. *CKO 333.*
FRENE, Hugh de. *XF 382.*
FRENE, Hugh de. *E I 484; E II 486.* ('two bars of silver indented with azure').
FRENE, Mons' Hugh de. *SD 123.* ('... deus barres endente dargent et dasure').
FREYNEE, Mons' Hugh. *TJ 492.*
TALBOT, Mons John. *WJ 910.* ('de la M'rch de Richards Kastel').
Gu 2 bars per fess indented Az and Arg
FRENE. *AS 112.*
FRENE, Hugh. *CA 220.*
FREYNEE, Mons' Rauf. *TJ 560.*
Gu 2 bars per fess indented Or and Az
FRENE, Walter de. *CT 190.*

2 bars per fess wavy &c
Gu 2 bars per fess wavy Arg and Sa
FRENE, de. *DV 62b, 2504. (name queried).*
Sa 2 bars per fess wavy Arg and Vt
HAKON, Sir Hubert. *BR V 153.*
Sa 2 bars per fess nebuly Vt and Arg
BRACKLEY. *XF 314. (?bars vairy).*
BRAKELEY. *SK 969. (?bars vairy).*
Per pale Arg and Gu 2 bars counterch
BARRETT, S'. *Q 481. (name added).*
Per pale Gu and Arg 2 bars counterch
NORTHFFOLKE, Robarde, of Yorks. *RH, Ancestor vii 185.*

2 bars semy
Arg 2 bars Sa semy of crosses formy Or
DENE, Sire .... *N 753.*
DENE, Sire Johan. *O 177.*
Semy de lis & 2 bars semy de lis
MORTUO MARI, Willelmus de, of Attleborough. *Bow 1.* SIGILLVM WILL: DE: MORTUO MARI. temp Edw 1&2.
Arg 2 bars Gu roundelly Or
MARTIN, of Gloucs. *L1 440, 4; L2 333, 3.*
MARTIN, Sire Wary. *N 100.*

WELLE, Robert de. *B 53.*

2 bars vairy
2 bars Vair
MORTIMER, Isabella de. *Brit Arch Assoc xxiv 288.* ('Domina de Homme Castel' in 1319-20; ?sis&h of Hugh, last M of Ricard's Castle).
TALBOT, John. *PRO-sls.* 1352.
TALBOT, John. *BirmCL-sls 474361.* 1370. ('of the castle of Richard Chindes lord of Coterigge [Worcs]').
TALEBOT, John. *Birch 13831.* SIGILLUM IOHANNIS TALEBOT. 1352.
Arg 2 bars Vair
HERTHILL, Mons' John. *TJ 534.*
Gu 2 bars Vair
— *PLN 1663.*
BEAUMONT, Sir Tomas, of Devon. *RH, Ancestor v 177.*
BEWCHAMP, Sir T. *WB I 40b, 11.*
CASTEL. *L1 131, 3; L2 107, 7.*
CASTELL. *L10 43b, 3.*
COWCYE. *KB 271.* ('Erle of Bedforde'; qrs 1&4).
FREN', Mons Hag' de. *WJ 909.*
FRESNE, Hugh de. *XF 910.*
MORTAMER, Sir Robert. *PCL I 511.*
MORTEMER, Robert de. *FW 147.*
MORTIM(er), Robt de. *Q 58.*
MORTIMER, Hue de. *K 393.* ('... o deus fesses de vair ...').
MORTIMER, Hughe de. *H 91a.*
MORTIMER, Sire Hugue de. *J 93.*
MORTIMER, Roberd de. *HE 123.*
MORTIMER, Munsire Robert de. *D 161b.* ('gules a deus barres verres dazur et dargent').
MORTIMER, Robert. *L9 69a, 8.*
MORTIMER, Robert de. *D 161a.*
MORTIMER, Robert de. *A 160.*
MORTIMER, Robert de. *LM 111.*
MORTIMER, Robert de. *F 118.*
MORTIMER, Robert de. *E 120.*
MORTIMER, Robert de. *WLN 626.*
MORTIMERE. *CT 303.*
MORTON, Mons' Hugh. *TJ 525.*
MORTYMER, Sr Hugh de. *H 91b.*
MORTYMER, Mons' John. *TJ 561.*
TALBOT. *L1 634, 2.* (& de Fren: both names given).
TALBOT. *CRK 1420.*
TALBOT, S' Jon'. *PO 300.*
TALBOT, S' Ric'. *PO 302.* (annulet Or for diffce in fess pt).
TALBOT, William. *TJ 557.*
TALBOTES. *SK 455.*
TALBOTT. *CT 71.* (?vairy Or and Az).
TALEBOT, Sire Richard. *O 6.*

Gu crusilly Or 2 Bars Vair
  MORTIMER, William de. *F 120.*
Gu semy of crosses potent Or 2 bars Vair
  MORTIMER, William de. *WLN 628.*
Sa 2 bars Vair
  HACON, Sir Hubert. *LH 172.*
Arg 2 bars vairy Gu and Arg
  CHAMPAYNE, Mons John. *WJ 810.*
Az 2 bars vairy Erm and Gu
  BREUSE, Reynald. *A a 272.*
  BREUSE, Reynaud. *FW 603.*
Gu 2 bars vairy Arg and Sa
  — *PT 521.*
Gu 2 bars vairy Or and Az
  TALBOTT. *CT 71. (?vair).*
Sa 2 bars vairy Arg and Vt
  HACON, of Norf. *L2 268, 9.*
Sa 2 bars vairy Vt and Arg
  BACON. *L2 44, 8. (marginal note: 'against Brakeley').*
  BRACKLEY. *XF 314.*
  BRAKELEY. *SK 969. (or Sa 2 bars fess wavy Vt and Arg).*
  BRAKELEY. *L1 98, 6; L2 44, 8.*
  BRAKELEY. *L10 77, 25.*
Sa 2 bars wreathed Gu and Arg
  WAY, Rog. *WB I 43b, 12. (wreathed in form of torse).*

2 bars modified

2 bars couped
Arg 2 bars couped in cross Az (in fess) & Gu (in pale)
  — *ML I 480. ('Sylver ii hewmettes in croyse asur & gowles sengylle').*
Gu 2 bars couped Arg
  HELYNGSALE. *WB I 43b, 15.*
Or 2 bars couped Sa
  — *ML I 108. ('Gold ii hewmettes sabylle').*
Sa 2 bars couped Arg
  CAMBRIDGE, Wm. *Hutton 86.*

2 bars, upper dancetty
Arg 2 bars Gu upper dancetty
  HACLUT, Mons de. *AS 264. ('dargent a un fes de goul' a un daunce de goul' en le schef').*
Gu 2 bars Or upper dancetty
  — *Inventory. (qtd by Lewis Robessart, d1431).*
  — *Inventory. (imp by Lewis Robessart, d1431).*

2 bars dancetty
2 bars dancetty
  BASSET, Alan, of Wilts. *Birch 7184.* +SIGILL: ALANI: BASSET. *c1225. (bars ?wavy).*

RYVERE, Sir John de la, Ld of Thormarton, Gloucs. *Heneage 1405.* ...GILLUM: IOHIS: .... 1351.
RYVERE, Thomas de la. *PRO-sls.* 1374.
SEE, Martin del. *Yorks Deeds IX 41.* 1482.
TURBERVILLE, Joan de. *AnstisAsp I 222, 86.* SIGILLVM IOANNE TURBERVILLE. 1375-6. *(loz, 1 of 3; 'quae fuit uxor Ricardi de Beaumont').*
WELLAME, Alexr. *Stevenson.* 1525. *(or Wollome).*
Arg 2 bars dancetty Az
  ?FAUCONBERG. *E II 545.*
Arg 2 bars dancetty Sa
  DOLYNG, Sir J. *WB I 40, 23.*
Az 2 bars dancetty Arg
  STONAR, ... *LO B 18.*
Az 2 bars dancetty Or
  DELAMER, of Berks. *L1 210, 3.*
  DELAREVER, Sir R. *WB I 40, 25.*
  DELAREVER, Tomas, of Berks. *RH, Ancestor v 175.*
  DELARIVIERE, Sir John, of Berks. *L2 158, 5.*
  RIVER, de la. *L9 36a, 7.*
  RIVER, de la. *PT 325.*
  RIVER, la. *BA 795.*
  RIVER, Richard de la. *E I 399; E II 401.*
  RIVER, Richard de la. *XF 355.*
  RIVERE, Sire Johan de la. *N 315.*
  RIVERES, Richard de. *F 393.*
  RIVERS. *XF 307.*
  RIVERS, Richard. *LR 42.*
  RIVERS, Richard de. *WLN 415.*
  RIVVERE, Sr John de la. *L 184.*
  RYUER. *L1 553, 4.*
  RYUER, Sr Jon de la. *PO 245.*
  RYVER, de la. *RB 129.*
  RYVER, de la. *CV-BM 89.*
  RYVER, John de la. *CA 4.*
  RYVER, Mons John de la. *WJ 982.*
  RYVERE, Mons de la. *AS 404.*
  RYVERE, Mons John de la. *TJ 406.*
  RYVERE, Mons' John de la. *SD 32. ('desure ove deux barres dor daunses').*
Az 2 bars dancetty Sa
  METFORD, John. *RH, Ancestor vii 213.*
Or 2 bars dancetty Gu
  DELAMER. *L1 192, 4; L2 152, 1.*
Or 2 bars dancetty Sa
  — *ME 97.*
  — *Inventory.* 1431. *(qtg barry Or and Az). (on mont to Lewis Robessart).*
  SHILFORD. *LY A 222.*
Sa 2 bars dancetty Erm
  — *CRK 1926.*

2 bars embattled

2 bars embattled counter-emb
> BERNERS, Nicholas, ld of Amberden. *PRO-sls.* 1407-8.

Arg 2 bars embattled counter-emb Sa
> BERNERS, Thomas, of Essex. *WB III 105b, 4.*

Gu 2 bars embattled Arg
> COFTYN, Sir T. *WB I 42b, 7.*

2 bars engrailed

2 bars engr
> GUMBERWORTH, Robert de, of Lincs. *Birch 10328.* 1392.
> PRESTON, Laurence de. *Hill 22 E1, 36; AnstisAsp I 14.* 1293-4.
> STAYN, William de, of Lincs. *Birch 13680.* SIGILLU WILL'MI DE STAYN. 1382.
> [STAYNE]. *Mill Steph.* c1405. *(qtd 2&3 by Fitzwilliam on brass to Eliz, dau of Jn Aske & w of Thos F, Mablethorpe, Lincs).*
> [STAYNE]. *Mill Steph.* c1500. *(qtd by Fitzwilliam on mantle of Eliz F, w of Robt Eyre, of Padley; brass to Robt E, Hathersage, Derbys).*
> STAYNE, William de, of Lincs. *Birch 13579.* ...IGILL' WILLELM.... 1355. *(on breast of eagle displd).*

Arg 2 bars engr Sa
> — *WB I 21b, 3. (qtd 2&3 by Sir Geo Fitzwilliam, KB).*
> FAUCOMBERGE, Mons' Henry. *TJ 646.*
> FAUCOMBERGE, Mons' Henry. *TJ 564.*
> FAUCONBERG. *XF 890.*
> FAUCONBREGE. *L1 254, 6; L2 202, 7.*
> FAUCUNBRUGH, Monsr Henry. *AS 268.*
> [STAYNE, de]. *?source. ('MS [c1460] copy of the Statutes').*

Sa 2 bars engr Arg
> ROUS. *CRK 1244.*

Sa 2 bars engr Or
> GRASELL. *L2 233, 11.*

2 bars indented

2 bars indented
> RIVERE, John de la, Kt. *PRO-sls.* 1337-8.

2 bars of lozenges

2 bars lozy
> FAUCONBERG, Sir William, of Catfoss, d1294. *Lawrance 15.* 1294. *(Effigy, Nunkeeling, York).*
> TUDENHAM, John, Kt. *Bow 12.*

Arg 2 bars lozy Az
> FAUCONBERG. *BA 1206. (1st of 5 & 1/2 lozs, 2nd of 5).*
> FAUCONBERG, William de. *WLN 558. (bars of 7 lozs).*
> FAUCOMBERGE. *CV-BM 32.*
> FAUCUNBERG, Wm de. *E I 543. (bars of 7&5 lozs).*
> FAUCUNBERGE, William de. *F 160.*

Arg 2 bars lozy Gu
> — *SK 529. (bars of 5&3 lozs).*
> — *XZ 62. (bars of 3&2 lozs; qtd 2&3 by Trussell).*
> RACELLE, Raf. *WLN 737. (bars of 5 lozs).*
> RATELL, Rauf. *E I c & d 544. (bars of 7&5 lozs).*
> ROCEL, Raf. *F 305.*

Arg 2 bars lozy Sa
> COLEVILE, Willm de. *LM 341. (bars of 5&4 lozs).*
> CONSTABYLL, Tomas, of Cattys fosse, Yorks. *RH, Ancestor iv 240.*
> FAUCOMBERGE. *BA 1287. (bars of 5 lozs).*
> FAUCOMBERGE, Mons' Henry de. *TJ 1024.*
> FAUCOMBERGES. *RB 272.*
> FAUCOMBRIGE, Essex. *L1 260, 5; L2 202, 9.*
> FAUCONBERGE, Sr Henry de. *CKO 438. (bars of 3 lozs).*
> FAUCONBERGE, Mons Waut'. *WJ 1096. (bars of 5 lozs).*

Gu 2 bars lozy Arg
> — *LH 399. (qtd 2&3 by Hartwell).*
> — *BG 89. (bars of 4 lozs; imp by Grenam).*
> — *LH 10. (bars of 5&3 lozs; qtd 2&3 by Sir Wm Hartwell).*
> — *WK 278. (bars of 5&3 lozs; qtd 2&3 by Sir Wm Hartwell).*
> PATEL, Ralph. *BA 1205. (bars of 6 lozs (1st of 5 & 2 halves, 2nd of 6) Arg).*
> PATELL, Rauf. *E II 546. (bars of 7&5 lozs).*
> PRESTON. *BA 1290.*
> PRESTON, Mons Thomas. *S 480. (bars of 5&3 lozs).*
> PRESTONE, Loren de. *LM 563. (bars of 5&4 lozs).*
> RASSTEL, Rauf. *Q 275. (bars of 5 lozs).*
> RATELL, Rauf. *E I 544. (bars of 7&5 lozs).*

Sa 2 bars lozy Arg
> — *LY A 95. (bars of 5 lozs).*

Erm 2 bars lozy Gu
> — *WB IV 138b, 233. (bars of 5 lozs; qtd 2&3 by Sir Jn Copyldycke).*

Qtly Gu and Or 2 bars lozy counterch
> — *D4 25b. (bars of 10 lozs; qtd 6 by Gascoyn, of Galthrop, Yorks).*

2 bars 'tortues'

Or 2 bars bent ('tortues') Sa
> — *ML I 113. ('gold ii barrystortues sabyll' (drawn as flat chevs)).*

2 bars of voided lozenges

Arg 2 bars of mascles Sa
> FAUCONBERGE, Sire Henri. *N 1082.*

Gu 2 bars of mascles Or
　　PRESTON. *L9 106a, 7. (bars of 5&3 mas-cles).*

2 bars wavy or nebuly
2 bars wavy
　　— Stevenson. *1489. (qtd by Robt Drum-mond, Ld of Ardmore).*
　　— Clairambault *1102. 23 Nov 1427. (qtd 2&3 by Thos Blount).*
　　BASSET, Alan, of Wilts. *Birch 7184.* +SIGIL: ALANI: BASSET. *c1225. (or dancetty).*
　　POLE. *Birch 10629. 1403. (imp in arms of Dame Johanna Hemenhale, dau of Jn de la P, wid of Robt de H, w of Reginald Bray-broke, of Essex, Kt).*
　　SAUNFORD, Lawrence de. *PRO-sls. 1256-7.*
　　TEMESE, Thomas. *PRO-sls E40 A146, 168. 1364-5.*
2 bars nebuly
　　BASSET, Simon. *Arch Journ x 148.* S' SIMONIS BASSET. *(?bars nebuly; brass sl matrix; supposed to be sl either of Simon B, of Sapcote, Leics, s&h of Ralph B or his grandson Simon (dc1328)).*
　　CABLE, John, of Frome, Som. *Birch 8007.* ...MERTRS(?). *1381. (or Gable).*
　　CALTHORP, Isabel. *PRO-sls. 1345-6. (1 of 3 shields; w of Sir Wm C).*
　　DRUMMOND, John, 1st Ld. *Stevenson. 1491. (2nd sl).*
　　HANGELTON, Richard de. *PRO-sls. 1334-5.*
　　[POLE, de la]. *Mill Steph; Belcher I 41. (qtg 2&3 ?Peverel, all imp Cobham on brass to Jn de la P & Joane [C], Cobham, Kent).*
　　[POLE, de la]. *Mill Steph; Belcher I 41. 1433. (qtg 2&3 Cobham on brass to Joan, Lady C, Cobham, Kent).*
　　POLE, Sir John de la. *Mill Steph. c1380. (brass to Sir Jn de la P & w Joan [Cobham], Chrishall, Essex).*
　　SPENCER. *Birch 12550. 1527-37. (qtd I 4 by Hen Percy, 6th E of Northd, KG).*

Arg 2 bars wavy &c
Arg 2 bars wavy Gu
　　CHAMPAIN, John, of Kent. *WB III 110b, 8.*
　　GOLDYNGHM, of Norf. *L2 234, 2.*
Arg 2 bars nebuly Gu
　　CHAMPAYN, John, of Kent. *L10 45, 2.*
Arg 2 bars wavy Or
　　CHAMPAYN, John. *Kent Gentry 217b. (sic for bars Gu).*
Arg 2 bars wavy Sa
　　— CB 87.
　　[BASSETT]. *OxfRS I 28. (glass, Banbury).*
　　ELCHEFFELD, Oxfords. *L2 178, 3.*
　　ELLESFELD, Sr Johan. *L 12; N 334.*
　　LOWELL, Ld. *PCL IV 143. (qr 1).*

POLE. *L1 515, 3. (painted nebuly).*
YELVETENE. *PLN 618. (cresc Untinc for diffce).*
ZEVELTON, Mons Robert de. *S 415.*
Arg 2 bars nebuly Sa
　　STAPLETON, Sire Rychart de. *PO 421.*

Az &c, 2 bars wavy &c
Az 2 bars wavy Arg
　　— XF 234. (qtg 2&3 Gu cross moline Arg).
　　PLESENCE, Count of. *WLN 21.*
　　POLE, Mons William de. *WJ 817.*
　　SEE. *L1 582, 5.*
Az 2 bars nebuly Arg
　　SEE, Sir Martyn of the. *BA 619.*
Az 2 bars wavy Or
　　POLE. *L9 108a, 5.*
　　POLE. *L1 496, 4.*
　　POLE. *L9 102b, 2.*
　　POLE, Sr Richard de la. *CKO 639.*
　　POOLE. *XF 710.*
　　POOLE. *LEP 53.*
Az 2 bars nebuly Or
　　POLE, de la. *Arch Cant xi 107.*
Gu 2 bars wavy Or
　　— RL 24. (qtd 2 by [Deincourt]).
　　[LOVEL, Ld]. *WB V 37.*

Or &c, 2 bars wavy &c
Or 2 bars nebuly Az
　　SIGOYNE, M de. *WNR 154.*
Or 2 bars wavy Az
　　POELE, Sir John. *BR V 173.*
Or 2 bars nebuly Gu
　　DAUNTSEY, of Dauntsey. *Batt. (Canopied tomb, Dauntsey Ch, Wilts).*
Or 2 bars wavy Gu
　　FERERS. *WB I 15b, 2.*
　　LOVEL, Ld, of Titchmarsh. *ML I 52; ML II 51. (qrs 1&4).*
　　LOVELL, Ld. *KB 298. (qrs 1&4).*
Or 2 bars wavy Sa
　　BLOUNT, Mons John. *T d 53. (unfinished but apparently qtg 3-towered castle).*
　　BLOUNT, Mons John. *T b 54.*
　　MOWNTEIOYE, Ld. *KB 332. (qrs 1&4).*
Or 2 bars wavy Vt
　　HAWBERK, Sir Nicol. *LH 594.*
Sa 2 bars nebuly Arg
　　YEVELTON, of Ivelton. *Gerard 184.*
Sa 2 bars wavy Or
　　— PLN 1904. (qtd I&IV 3 by Thos Blount).

Field patterned, 2 bars wavy &c
Per pale 2 bars nebuly
　　DAUNDYSLAYE, Mons John. *WJ 544. (unfinished; ?per pale Or and Arg).*

Per pale Or and Arg 2 bars wavy Gu
 DAUNDESEYE, Water. *PLN 685.*

2 bars wavy &c Erm
Az 2 bars wavy Erm
 [HO]LKHAM. *SHY 382.*
 HOLCAM. *PLN 1680.*
 HOLKAM. *L1 300, 4; L2 241, 10.*
 HOLKHAM. *LH 815.*
 HOLKHAM. *LH 506.*
 HOLKHAM, Sir .... *CRK 765.*
 SEE, Mayster Stewyn of the, of Yorks. *RH,
 Ancestor vii 193.*
Az 2 bars nebuly Erm
 — *XF 101.*
Gu 2 bars wavy Erm
 LACY, of Hartre. *Gerard 28.*
Sa 2 bars wavy Erm
 SPENCER. *XF 736.*
 SPENCER, Sir Robert. *PLN 1312.*
Sa 2 bars nebuly Erm
 SPENCER. *BA 1196. (qtd 2&3 by Wm Cary
 [husb of Mary Boleyne]).*
 SPENCER. *L1 602, 1.*
 SPENCER. *BA 1194. (qtd 2&3 by Wm Cary).*
 SPENCER. *BA 1195. (qtd 2&3 by Thos
 Cary).*
 SPENCER, Sir Robert. *XF 737.*
 SPENCER, Sir Robert, of Spencercomb,
 Devon. *Sandford 333. (husb of Eleanor
 Beaufort, wid of Jas Butler, E of Ormond).*
Per pale Gu and Arg 2 bars wavy per pale Or
and Gu
 DAUNDYSE, Water. *WB IV 185b, 1074.*

2 ribands wavy & knotted
2 ribands
 GYGGES, Robert, of Wigton. *PRO-sls E40
 A11071. 1505-6. (narrow wavy bars with
 knot in middle).*

2 bars & label
2 bars label
 — *Yorks Deeds IX 4. (imp by Jn de Eyvill).*
 CORBET, Robert. *Birch 8942.* S' ROBERTI:
 CORBET. *1380. (s of Robt C, Ld of Hadley,
 Salop).*
 HILTON, Robert of. *Durham-sls 1344. 1321.*
 HILTON, Robert of. *BM Harl 1985, 279,
 HB-SND. 1363.*
2 bars label of 5
 BATHE, Eleanor de. *AnstisAsp I 211, 55.
 1349-50. (1st of 3 shields).*
 CAPELL, Henry de, of Denham, Bucks. *Birch
 8322.* SIGILL' HENRICI DE CAPELL.. c1250.
 GARDINS, William de, of Oxfords, Kt. *Birch
 10025.* ...ILL'I DE GARDI.... 1266. *(label
 unclear).*

Untinc 2 bars Gu label of 5 Az
 — *PT 531.*

Arg 2 bars & label
Arg 2 bars Az label Gu
 HILTON, Mons Alex de. *WJ 519.*
 HILTON, Aley de. *Q 225.*
Arg 2 bars Az label of 5 Gu
 GARDYN, Cambs. *L2 234, 6.*
Arg 2 bars Gu label Az
 — *E II 252.*
 MARTIN. *E I 250.*
 MARTIN, Nicholas fitz. *B 202.*
 MARTYN, Nichol Fitz. *TJ 1575.*
 MARTYN, Nichol le fitz. *TJ 539.*
 MARTYN, Willimus. *Q II 134.*
 SEIN MARTYN, Joan de. *E I 244; E II 246.*
Arg 2 bars Gu label of 5 Az
 — *XF 945.*
Arg 2 bars Gu label Vt
 MULTON, Thomas. *TJ 562.*
Arg 2 bars Sa label Gu
 GARDYN, of Cambs. *L2 233, 2.*
 GARDYN, Sire Thomas de. *N 607.*
Arg 2 bars Sa label of 5 Gu
 FITZ MARY. *XF 689.*
 FITZ MARY. *FK II 756.*

Az &c 2 bars & label
Az 2 bars Or label of 5 Arg
 — *CT 387.*
Gu 2 bars Or label Arg
 HARECOURT, le Sire de. *TJ 512.*
Gu 2 bars Or label Az
 HARCOURT, John. *FW 553. ('son fitz').*
 HARECOURT, Sr Jo de, le fitz. *I 43. ('g ii
 fesses d'or un labell dazure').*
Or 2 bars Gu label of 5 Untinc
 [WI]NTERHULLE. *CT 391.*
Or 2 bars & label of 5 Gu
 WYNTRESHULL, John. *E I 591; E II 593.*
Or 2 bars Gu label of 5 Sa
 WINTERSHULL, John de. *XF 399.*
Sa 2 bars Arg label Gu
 HUNGERFORD, Robert de. *GutchWdU. (Ld
 Molynes; [beheaded May 1464]qtg M; form-
 erly in window of Old Hall University Coll,
 built 1450, demolished 1669).*

2 bars modified and label
Arg 2 bars nebuly Sa label Gu
 ZEVELTON, Robert de. *S 420.*
Arg 2 bars wavy Sa label Gu
 ZEBELTON. *L1 710, 3.*
Az 2 bars wavy Or label Gu
 POLE, Sir William de la, le Joesne. *CKO
 641.*

2 bars & patterned label
Arg 2 bars Gu label Az semy of roundels Arg
MARTIN, Willa. *Q 134.*
Arg 2 bars Gu label Az semy of roundels Or
MARTIN, William. *G 171.*
MARTYN, Sr William. *J 60.*
Az crusily & 2 bars Or label Gu semy of roun-
dels Arg
BAR, S Ernaud de. *GA 42.*

2 bars & in base
Arg 2 bars & in base cross botonny Sa
— *CRK 1685.*

2 bars & canton
2 bars canton
— *PRO-sls. 1333. (?border of roses; on
escutch on sl of Jn de Wydeville).*
BOSCO, John de, Kt. *Birch 7614.* SIGILLUM
IOHANNIS D'BOSCO. temp Edw 1. *(s of
Arnulph de B, of Assington, Suff).*
BOSCO, Willim de. *?source.* 1295. *(sl).*
D'AINCURT, Sir Ralph, of Sizergh. *Sizergh.*
c1237. *(sl).*
[DERWENTWATER]. *Proc Soc Antiq II 2S 193.
(on 14 cent font, Crosthwaite Ch, Cumb).*
Untinc 2 bars & canton Gu
— *WB I 24, 4. (qrs 2&3 of coat imp by Sir
Jn Chomley).*

Arg 2 bars & canton
Arg 2 bars & canton Az
— *ML I 39. (canton partly in umbre because
it overlaps the upper bar; 'Sylver ii barres
asur wit a quarter chef of the same parcell in
umbre').*
SCARBURGH. *WB II 64, 1.*
Arg 2 bars & canton Gu
— *WB I 33, 6. (qrs 2&3 of coat imp by
Cholmesley).*
— *WB I 33b, 15. (qtd 2&3 by Or fess of 5
lozs Az).*
— *WB I 29b, 14. (qrs 2&3 of coat imp
Wharton [qrs 1&4: fess of 5 lozs]).*
BERDSEY. *L10 29, 8.*
BOIS, Ernaldus de. *E I 154.*
BOIS, J del. *RB 426.*
BOIS, Jehan de. *E II 153.*
BOIS, Joan du. *Q 36.*
[BOYES]. *Nichols Leics IV 718. (Stoke Ch).*
BOYS. *XF 915.*
BOYS. *PLN 1852.*
BOYS, Ernald de. *MP II 74; MP VII 6; B
105; C 153.*
BOYS, Ernaldi de. *P 110.*
BOYS, Ernaud. *F 85.*
BOYS, Mons Henry de. *TJ 502.*

BOYS, Johan. *D 147.*
BOYS, John. *FW 100.*
BOYS, Sir John. *PCL I 535.*
BOYS, Sir John. *BA 674.*
BOYS, S John, of Essex. *CY 139, 554.*
BOYS, Jon. *A a 211.*
BOYS, Jon. *HE 77.*
BOYS, of Lincs. *L1 53, 2; L2 45, 8.*
BOYS, Sir Reynold de. *WNS 26, 106. ('...
porte dar ou ii barres et un Kantel de gou').*
BOYS, Sir Roger. *T b 156.*
BROGHTON. *CVL 400.*
BROGHTON, of Lancs. *CY 63, 250.*
CORBET. *L1 161, 1; L2 104, 5. (marginal
note in L1: Boyes).*
CORBET. *CB 108.*
CORBET. *SHY 147.*
CORBET, de Hadley, Salop. *CY 86, 344.*
CORBET, R. *AN 102.*
CORBET, S' Rob'. *PO 557.*
CORBET, Robert. *BG 147.*
CORBET, Robert. *S 225.*
CORBETES. *SK 765. ('qtg Corbett' acc Gib-
bon).*
CORBETES. *SK 150.*
CORBETT. *L10 37, 14.*
[CORBETT]. *L10 44, 10.*
SCARBURGH. *CC 223, 46.*
STRIKLANDE, Sire Walter de. *N 1100.*
WODEVILE, Sir Thomas. *PLN 298.*
Arg 2 bars & canton Sa
BOYS, James de. *Q 191.*
BOYS, James de. *XF 373.*
BOYS, James du. *E II 470.*
BOYS, Jamis deu. *Q 419.*
BOYS, Jamus de. *L10 34, 9.*
BOYS, John de. *WLN 694.*
BYNLEY. *L10 32, 7.*
BYNLEY. *FK II 929.*
BYNLEY. *L1 100, 4; L2 59, 9.*
DUBOIS. *F 190.*
PIPARD. *L9 99a, 2.*
[RILBY]. *Nichols Leics IV 477. (Barwell Ch).*
TWIFORD, Monsire de. *CG 242.*

Gu &c 2 bars & canton
Gu 2 bars & canton Arg
DEANE. *XF 61.*
DEDENE. *L1 206, 4; L2 156, 12.*
DENE. *L10 56b, 17.*
DENE, de. *FK II 688.*
Or 2 bars & canton Az
SCARBOROUGH. *XF 261.*
SCARBOURGH. *L1 603, 3.*
WILSON. *CRK 2063.*

Erm 2 bars & canton
Erm 2 bars & canton Gu
  BORS, Nicolas de. *XF 943.*
  BORSE, Nicoll. *L2 93, 7. (canton indistinct).*
  BORSE, Nicoll de. *L10 33b, 13.*
  BOYSE, Nicolas du. *E I 238; E II 240.*

2 bars modified & canton
Arg 2 bars nebuly Sa canton Gu
  FFOLUYLE, S' Matthew. *PO 440.*

2 bars & patterned canton
Untinc 2 bars Untinc canton Erm
  SANCTO JOHANNE, Ld of Plumpton,
  Northants, Kt. *Birch 13225.* SIGILLUM EGIDII
  DE SEYNT JOHAN. 1374.
Arg 2 bars Sa canton Erm
  MARSCHALL, John, d1492. *Nichols Leics IV
  956. (Sibbesdon Ch).*
Gu 2 bars Arg canton Erm
  SEINT JOHN, Mons' Giles. *S 598.*
Or 2 bars Gu canton Erm
  — *SHY 71.*
Gu 2 bars 1st Erm 2nd Arg canton Erm
  [HAROWDON]. *WB IV 159b, 606. (imp by
  Swynerton).*
  [HARROWDEN]. *PLN 947. (imp by Swinner-
  ton).*
  [HARROWDEN]. *PLN 946. (imp Arg 2 lions
  passt Sa).*
Arg 2 bars Gu canton vairy Gu and Arg
  CHASTEL, Wills den. *Q 593.*

2 bars & sin canton
Arg 2 bars & sin canton Gu
  STRICKLAND, Sir Walter. *BR V 88.*
Gu 2 bars Arg sin canton Arg
  — *SK 978.*

2 bars canton & label &c
2 bars canton label of 5
  BOSCO, Ernald de. *Bk of Sls 500.* 1258.
Arg 2 bars & canton Gu label Arg
  CORBET, Sr Johan. *O 196; S 224.*
Arg 2 bars & canton Gu label Az
  CORBET. *XF 697.*
  CORBET. *FK II 861.*
  CORBET, Robert. *BG 145.*
  CORBET, Robert. *S 226.*
Arg 2 bars & canton Sa in chf cresc Sa
  BINLEY, Sir John. *XF 262.*

2 bars canton & bend
2 bars canton bend
  BOYS, John, of Felmingham, Norf. *Birch
  7702.* Sigillu...S: ... : boys: .... 1396.
  BOYS, Roger de, of Farnham, Suff. *Birch

7706.* .....DE.B..... 1383.
  COUPLAND, Alan de. *Birch 9003.* SIG'.ALANI:
  DE COVPLAND. 13 cent.
  COUPLAND, Sir Alan de. *PRO-sls.* [1272-8].
  COUPLAND, Richard. *PRO-sls.* 1230. *(s of
  Alan de C).*
Arg 2 bars & canton Gu bend Az
  — *D4 47b. (qtd by Irton, of Irton, [Yorks]).*
  COPELAND. *XF 700.*
  COPELAND, Alan de. *FC I 68. (baston).*
  COPELAND, Alan de. *FC I 66. (s of Rog de
  C).*
  COPELAND, Sir Richard. *WK B 35. (baston).*
  COPELAND, Sautone. *PT 1083.*
  COPLAND, of Stanton. *L1 166, 4.*
  COUPELAND. *L10 37, 15.*
  COUPELAND. *FK II 892. (baston).*
  COUPELAND, Sir Richard. *XF 259.*
Arg 2 bars & canton Gu bend Or
  COPLAND. *L2 103, 7.*
Arg 2 bars & canton Gu bend Sa
  — *PLN 1905f. (imp by [Southwell]).*
  — *FB 47.*
  BOYES, Ryc'. *NS 134.*
  BOYS. *SHY 122. ('in ye north').*
  BOYS. *PT 651. (baston).*
  BOYS, Johannes de. *Q II 659. (baston).*
  BOYS, Jon de. *Q 408. (baston).*
  BOYS, Roger le. *S 227.*

2 bars canton & on bend
Arg 2 bars & canton Gu on bend Arg annulet Or
  in chf
  BOYS, Hugh. *BG 146.*
Arg 2 bars & canton Gu on bend Sa annulet Or
  in chf
  BOYES, Sir Roger. *WK B 34.*
  BOYS. *CC 224, 77.*
  BOYS. *L10 83b, 7.*
  BOYS. *RB 338.*
  BOYS. *LE 362.*
2 bars sin canton on bend annulet
  BOYS. *Suff HN 22. (Knoddishall).*

2 bars canton bend & label
Arg 2 bars & canton Gu label Sa bend Or
  — *PT 380. (baston Or).*

2 bars & on canton
2 bars on canton destroyed charge
  CORBET, Robert, of Hadley, Salop. *Birch
  8945.* 1363.
2 bars on canton indistinct charge
  LANCASTRE, John de. *PRO-sls.* 14 cent.
Arg 2 bars Sa on canton Erm annulet Sa
  BROWNE, Stephen. *Hutton 86.*

2 bars & on canton lion
2 bars on canton lion
> CORBET, Agnes. *Birch 8935.* SIGILL'
> AGNETIS CORBET. 1334. *(dex of 2 shields; w
> of Jn C, s of Rog C, of Hadley, Salop).*

Arg 2 bars Az on canton Or lion Sa
> — *PT 188.*

2 bars & on canton lion passt
2 bars on canton lion passt
> BOSCO, Ernald de. *Birch 7612.* SIGILL':
> ERNALDI: DE: BO.... 1216-36.
> CORBET, John. *Birch 8938.* SIGILLVM
> IOHANNIS CORBET. 1334. *(s of Rog C, of
> Hadley, Salop).*
> CORBET, Robert, of Ebrington, Gloucs, Chev.
> *Birch 8950.* SIGILLUM ROBERTI CORBET.
> 1371. *(lion unclear).*
> CORBET, Roger, Kt, Ld of Hadley, Salop.
> *Birch 8944.* S' ROGERI.... 1332.
> LONCASTER, John de, of Grisdale. *PRO-sls.*
> S'IOHANNIS DE LONCASTER. 1301.

Arg 2 bars Gu on canton Az lion passt Arg
> LANCASTER, Mr Roger. *PCL I 486.*

Arg 2 bars Gu on canton Az lion passt Or
> LONCASTOR, Rog' de. *Q 112.*

Arg 2 bars & on canton Gu lion passt Arg
> — *CVL 420.*

Arg 2 bars & on canton Gu lion passt Or
> LANCASTER, John de. *FC I 52.*
> LANCASTER, of Milverton. *Gerard 41.*
> LANCASTER, William de. *FC I 57.*
> LANCASTER, William de. *FC I 58.*
> LANCASTRE, Roger de. *E II 266.*

Arg 2 bars Or on canton Gu lion passt Arg
> [BOIS, de]. *Nichols Leics IV 108.* *(Claybrook
> Ch).*

Or 2 bars & on canton Az lion passt Or
> WILSON. *CRK 1645.*

Or 2 bars & on canton Gu lion passt Or
> LANCASTER. *CC 224, 70.*

2 bars & on canton lion pg
2 bars on canton lion pg
> LANCASTER, John of. *PRO-sls Anc Deeds L
> 289.*
> LANCASTER, John of, Ld of Grisdale. *Barons
> Letter.*

Arg 2 bars & on canton Gu lion pg Or
> — *D4 50b. (qtd by [Dacre]; position of lion
> unclear).*
> — *XK 72. (qtd 3 by Dacre, of Gillesland,
> KG).*
> — *L10 52b, 1. (qtd 3 by Dacre de Narthe).*
> — *I2(1904)239. (qtd 3 by Dacre, of Gils-
> land).*
> — *WGA 91. (qtd 3 by Thos, Ld Dacre of
> Gilsland).*
> LANCASTER. *CC 222b, 32.*

LANCASTER. *Leake. (qtd 3 by Thos Dacre,
KG, d1525).*
LANCASTER, Sir .... *CRK 444.*
LANCASTER, J de. *SP A 148.*
LANCASTER, Sir J de, de Helg[ill]. *CKO 581.*
LANCASTER, Roger de. *XF 950.*
LANCASTER, Sir William. *XL 226.*
LANCASTER, William. *BG 148.*
LANCASTER, William de. *MP II 74.*
LANCASTER, William de. *S 228.*
LANCASTRE. *L9 34b, 11.*
LANCASTRE. *CT 384.*
LANCASTRE. *L1 389, 3; L2 301, 8.*
LANCASTRE, Sire Johan de. *N 145.*
LANCASTRE, Mons' John, de Helgill. *TJ 500.*
LANCASTRE, ?Roger de. *AS 92.*
LANCASTRE, Mons' Roger de. *TJ 190.*
LANCASTRE, Mons' Roger de. *TJ 1257.*
LANCASTRE, Wm de. *B 49.*
MOULTONE, Thomas de. *K 176.* *('de argent
a treis barres de goulys. Ses armes ne furent
pas soules de siente en le apparellement Kar-
teles at resemblantment Johans de Langcastre
entremeins mas Ke en lieu de une barre
meins quartier rouge e jaune lupart').*

2 bars & on canton other beast
Sa 2 bars & on canton Arg stag stat Sa attired
Or
> BUKSTON. *L10 85b, 5.*
> BUXSTON, Salop. *CY 88, 351.*

2 bars & on canton bird
Arg 2 bars & on canton Az martlet Or
> BRITCHEBURY, Mons' Avery. *S 279.*
> KATCHEBURY. *L9 23, 12.*
> LATHBURY. *L1 389, 4.*
> [LATHBURY]. *Nichols Leics III 781. (Castle
> Donington Ch).*
> LATHEBURY. *XF 260. (or Katchbury).*
> LATHEBY. *L9 38a, 4. (or Katchbure).*
> LATHEBY. *CC 224, 67.*
> LATHEBY. *L1 411, 5.*

Arg 2 bars & on canton Sa martlet Or
> — *CRK 1859.*

2 bars & on canton buckle &c
Arg 2 bars & on canton Sa buckle Or
> SWYTFORD, Sir Robert, Middx. *WB III 93b,
> 6.*
> TWIFORD, Sir Nicol. *CRK 851. (round
> buckle).*
> TWYFORD. *L1 638, 4.*
> TWYFORD. *PT 630. (round buckle).*

2 bars on canton castle
> CASTELLO, William de. *Dugd 17, 17.* Sy Willi
> de Castello. 1323. *(s of George C).*
> CASTELLO, William de. *Birch 8403.* S'
> WILL'I DE CASTELLO. 1323. *(2towered; s of*

George de C, of Wislaw, Warws).
Gu 2 bars & on canton Arg castle Sa
    CHASTEL. *BA 29b, 227. (3towered).*
    CHASTEL, Sr William. *N 849.*
    CHASTELL, of Berks. *L2 135, 10. (3towered castle).*
Arg 2 bars & on canton Sa chess rook Arg
    BRAYLFORD. *L1 34, 5; L2 46, 1.*
Arg 2 bars & on canton Sa cresc Or
    BILNEY. *FK a 929.*
    BINLEY. *XF 707.*

2 bars & on canton cross
2 bars on canton cross
    ALVINGHAM, Michael. *PRO-sls.* 1230. *(s of Wm de A).*
    FURNES, Michael de. *PRO-sls.* c1227. *(used by his s Wm).*
Arg 2 bars & on canton Gu cross Arg
    — *L10 111, 6. (qtd 2&3 by Ed Osborne, London).*
    BROGHTON, John de. *TJ 1370. ('..deux fees & i quarter de goules & une croice dargent plain el quarter').*
    BROGHTON, Thomas. *LY A 58. (cross ch with annulet Sa).*
    BROUGHTON. *XF 703.*
    [BROUGHTON]. *Bellasis II 306-8. (w of Wm Thornboro; Windermere E window).*
    BROUGHTON, J, of Staffs & Warws. *CRK 1689.*
    BROUGHTON, Nicholas de. *FC I 54.*
    BROUGHTON, Richard. *FC I 48. (s of Simon B, [of Broughton in Furness]).*
    BROUGHTON, Richard de. *FC I 51.*
    BROUTON. *L10 77b, 2.*
    BROUTONE. *FK II 909.*
    BROWTON. *L1 100, 3; L2 49, 6.*
Arg 2 bars & on canton Gu cross Or ch with ram's head erased Sa
    BROGHTON, Nych'. *LY A 59.*
Or 2 bars Az on canton Gu cross Untinc
    ATON. *North 1558 124. (qtd by Eure).*

2 bars & on canton, cross modified
Arg 2 bars on canton Gu cross formy Arg
    BROWTON. *L10 78, 7. (Broughton added in modern hand).*
2 bars on canton cross moline
    [KIRKBY]. *?source.* 13 cent. *(tomb in Kirkby Ireleth Parish Ch, ?of Alexander de K who in 1217 confirmed to Abbot of Furness grant of Kirkby Ch & 40 acres of land; arms mutilated & almost illegible).*
    [KIRKBY, of Kirkby Hall]. *Dodsworth 88, 44. (formerly in glass in Sandys Chapel, Hawkshead Ch, Lancs).*

Arg 2 bars & on canton Gu cross moline Or
    — *CRK 1847.*
    KERKBY. *L9 11, 2.*
    KIRKBY. *XC 121.*
    KIRKBY. *Bellasis II 306-8. (imp barry of 8 Arg and Gu; E window, Windermere).*
    KIRKBY. *PLN 1564.*
    KIRKBY. *XF 704.*
    KIRKBY, Alan de. *FC I 47.*
    KIRKBY, Alexander de. *FC I 46.*
    KIRKBY, Richard de. *S 229.*
    KIRKEBY. *FK II 912.*
    KIRKEBY, John, of Lancs. *WB III 101, 1.*
    KIRKEBYE, Richard. *BG 149.*
    KYRKBY, of Kirkby, Lancs. *D4 47b.*
    KYRKBY, of Lancs. *L2 295, 10.*
    KYRKEBY. *L9 11b, 10.*
    KYRKEBY. *L1 372, 7; L2 288, 3.*
    KYRKEBY, John de. *CA 21. (?millrind).*
Arg 2 bars Sa on canton Arg cross moline Sa
    KIRKBY, Mons' Richard de. *TJ 1498. ('.. a un fees & demy de sable & un fer de molyn de sable').*
Arg 2 bars & on canton Gu cross recercelly Or
    KYRKEBY, S' Jon. *PO 490.*

2 bars & on canton cushion &c
Arg 2 bars & on canton Gu cushion Arg
    DERWENTWATER, Mons' John. *TJ 489.*
Arg 2 bars Sa on canton Gu cushion Arg
    DERWINTWATER, le Sire de. *CG 245.*
Arg 2 bars & on canton Sa voided escutch Or
    — *CVL 413.*
Arg 2 bars & on canton Gu rose Arg
    DERWENTWATER. *L10 58, 14. (seeded Or).*
    DERWENTWATER. *SK 497.*
    DERWENTWATER. *L2 155, 10.*
Arg 2 bars & on canton Gu rose Or
    DERWENTWATER. *L1 201, 6.*
Arg 2 bars & on canton Gu rose Or seeded Gu
    — *PLN 1460.*

2 bars & on canton 3foil
Arg 2 bars & on canton Gu 3foil slipped Or
    WYNSENT, Wylyam, of co Durham. *RH, Ancestor vii 196.*
Arg 2 bars Gu on canton Sa 3foil slipped Or
    — *PT 760.*

2 bars & on canton 5foil
2 bars on canton pd 5foil
    DERWENTWATER, John de, of Cumb, mil. *Vinc 88, 37. (sl).*
2 bars on canton 5foil
    — *Vinc 88, 47.* 1434-5 & 1443-4. *(sl; qtd 2&3 by Jn de Penington, Kt).*
    PIPART, Radulfus. *Vinc 88, 33.* SIGILLVM.-RADULFI.PIPART.. 1300-1. *(sl on grant of lands in Thurvaston, Derbys).*

PIPART, Ralph, of Derbys. *Birch 12652.*
SIGILLVM RADVLFI P[IPART]. 1300.
TWYFORD, John de, Kt. *PRO-sls.* 1323-4.
Arg 2 bars & on canton Az pd 5foil Arg
  PIPARD, M. *WNR 70.*
  PIPPARD. *L9 102b, 1.*
  PYPPARD. *CC 223, 33.*
Arg 2 bars & on canton Az pd 5foil Or
  PIPARD. *SP A 91.*
  PIPARD, Ralph. *WLN 539.*
  PIPARD, Rauf. *E I 247; E II 250.*
  PIPARD, Rauf. *G 165; H 110a.*
  PIPARD, Sire Rauf. *J 48.*
  PIPART, Ralph. *XF 946.*
  PIPART, Sr Rauff. *H 110b.* (*'d'argent ove ung feez et demy feez et le cantell d'azure et en le cantell quintfoyl d'or').*
  PIPPARD. *PT 18.*
  PYPARD, Raf. *F 177.*
  PYPPARD, Ralph. *CV-BM 61.*
  PYPPARD, Ratherfeld. *RH, Ancestor iii 210.*
  PYPPARDE. *DV 58a, 2300.*
Arg 2 bars & on canton Az 5foil Or
  PIPARD, Mons' Rauf. *TJ 526.* (*'d'argent une fees & demy ove un quarter dazure et i quintfoil dor en le quarter').*

Arg 2 bars & on canton Gu 5foil Arg
Arg 2 bars & on canton Gu pd 5foil Arg
  — *PLN 1907.* (*qtd 3 by Az 5 lozs conj in fess Or*).
  — *WGA 119.* (*qtd 2&3 by Sir Ric Radcliff*).
  BEKINGHAM. *L1 46, 5; L2 52, 12.*
  DERWENTWATER. *PLN 979.*
  DERWENTWATER, John. *S 230.*
  PRESTON. *XF 46.*
Arg 2 bars & on canton Gu 5foil Arg
  DERWENTWATER, Adam de. *FC II 142.*
  DERWENTWATRE, John. *TJ 1439.* (*'dargent a une feess & demy fees & quarter de goules & i quintfoil dargent en le quarter').*

Arg 2 bars & on canton Gu 5foil Or
Arg 2 bars & on canton Gu pd 5foil Or
  — *L9 44a, 11.* (*qtd 3 by Sir Jn Lamplough*).
  — *D4 48.* (*qtd by Lamplew*).
  CORBET, S' Rog. *R 94.*
  DERWENTWATER, Sir John. *XF 263.*
  PRESTON. *SK 300.*
  PRESTON. *CRK 1850.*
  PRESTON. *L9 104b, 5.*
  PRESTON. *L1 516, 2.*
  [PRESTON], Eda de. *FC II 78.* (*wid of Wm de Wedacre & dau of Ric de P*).
  PRESTON, Richard de. *FC II 76 & 77.*
Arg 2 bars & on canton Gu 5foil Or
  DERWENTWATER, John. *BG 150.*
  DERWENTWATER, John. *S 228.*
  PRESTON. *CRK 1602.*

Arg 2 bars Sa & on canton 5foil
Arg 2 bars Sa on canton Gu 5foil Or
  — *I2(1904)293.* (*?Twyford*).
Arg 2 bars Sa on canton Or pd 5foil Sa
  RATCLIFFE, Caryll. *LR 63.*
Arg 2 bars Sa on canton Or 5foil Sa
  RATCLIFF. *XF 305.*
Arg 2 bars & on canton Sa 5foil Untinc
  TWYFORDE. *HA 140.*
Arg 2 bars & on canton Sa pd 5foil Arg
  BRAYLSFORD. *L10 78b, 3.*
  FENTON. *CRK 605.*
  PIPART. *CT 188.*
  TWYFORDE, Sr John de, Derbys. *CY 72, 286.*
Arg 2 bars & on canton Sa 5foil Arg
  TWYFORDE. *RB 408.*
  TWYFORDE. *HA 152, 27b.*
Arg 2 bars & on canton Sa pd 5foil Or
  BEWLEY. *CRK 2065.* (*rectius Twyford*).
  PIPARD. *L1 502, 3.*
  TUYFORD, of Leics. *BA 31, 278.*
  TWYFORD, Sr de. *CKO 322.*
  TWYFORD, Sir John. *XF 308.*
  TWYFORD, Sir John de. *PV 11.*
  TWYFORD, S' Jon. *PO 385.*
  TWYFORD, Robert. *S 487.*
  WYFORD, Sir John de. *CV-BM 125.*
Arg 2 bars & on canton Sa 5foil Or
  PIPARD, Sir John. *WNS 26, 69.* (*'Sire Jon Pipard por dar ii barres et un cantel de sa ou un quintefoil dor').*
  PYPARD. *PT 631.*
  SWYNFORD, William. *TJ 1298.*
  TUYFORD, Sire Johan de. *O 11.*
  TUYFORDE, Sire Johan de. *N 829.*
  TWYFORD, John de. *TJ 487.*
  TWYFORD, Mons' John de. *SD 20.*
  TWYFORD, Sr John. *L 99.*
  TWYFORD, Richard. *TJ 529.* (*'dargent ove une barre & demy xi quarter de sable et deins la quarter i quintfoil dor').*
  TWYFORD, Mons' Robert. *S 482.*
  TWYFORD, Monsire Robert. *AN 346.*
  TWYFORDE, Mons John de. *CA 77.*
Or 2 bars & on canton Sa 5foil Or
  [TWYFORD]. *TZ 5.*
Arg 2 bars & on canton Sa 5foil Erm
  TWYFORD, Sir John de, Derbys. *CV-BM 70.*

2 bars & on canton 6foil
Arg 2 bars & on canton Gu pd 6foil Or
  PRESTON, Wm, of Lancs. *RH, Ancestor iv 236.*
Arg 2 bars & on canton Sa 6foil Arg
  SCALEBROK, Willeme de. *LM 218.*

2 bars & on canton garb

Arg 2 bars & on canton Sa garb Arg
  WEUER. *L1 673, 6.*
Sa 2 bars & on canton Arg garb Or banded Gu
  WEBERE, de. *WB II 61, 10.*
  WYVER, Edward de. *LY A 43.*
  WYVERE, de. *DV 48a, 1893.*
Sa 2 bars Arg on canton Sa garb Or
  WEAVER, Sir.... *CRK 1542.*
  WEVER, S' Edwarde, of Ches. *CY 21, 82.*
Sa 2 bars Arg on canton Sa garb Ppr
  WEEVER, S' Edward de. *WLN 359. (garb not Or).*
Sa 2 bars couped Arg on sin canton Sa garb Or banded Gu
  STANLEY, John, 'of Wyver'. *PLN 679.*

2 bars & on canton head &c

Az 2 bars Arg on canton Sa wolf's head erased Arg
  WILBRAHAM, William. *PLN 1933.*
Az 2 bars Or on canton Gu wolf's head erased Arg collared Sa
  HUNT. *LH 986.*
Arg 2 bars & on canton Gu loz Arg
  DERWENTWATER. *L10 57, 20.*
  DERWENTWATER. *FK II 794.*
  DERWENTWATER. *XF 693.*
  DERWENTWATER, Sr de. *CKO 324.*
Arg 2 bars & on canton Gu maunch Arg
  BERDESEY, Gilbert de. *FC I 40.*
  BERDSEY. *L1 60, 4; L2 69, 2.*
  BERDSEY. *PT 1259.*
Arg 2 bars & on canton Gu maunch Or
  [BARDSEY]. *Bellasis II 306-8.* 15 cent. *(?maunch or 5foil; imp [Leybourne] Gu 6 lions 3, 2, 1 Arg; E window, Windermere).*
Arg 2 bars & on canton Gu millrind Or
  KYRKEBY, Mons John de. *CA 21. (?cross moline).*

2 bars & on canton mullet

2 bars on canton mullet
  [LANCASTER]. *Bellasis I 91. (cross with shield [Lancaster] on dex & sword to sin inscr: 'R.N.L. M._...' &c).*
  [LANCASTER]. *Bellasis I 91. (2 shields on arch, 1 in W window recess, & in similar shield opposite, monogram 'LA').*
  NOVEREYE, John, of Burton. *Bow LX 23.* S Johis Novereye. *1378-9.*
Arg 2 bars & on canton Gu mullet Arg
  LANCASTER. *GutchWdU. ?15 cent. (Formerly in Hall, then in Langton's Chapel, Queen's Coll, Oxf).*
Arg 2 bars & on canton Gu mullet Or
  GROUSTEL, Emond. *Q 179.*
  [LANCASTER]. *Hill iv 3, 293; Bellasis II 161. (window, Long Marton).*

[LANCASTER]. *Hill iv 3, 293; Bellasis II 161. (imp by [Wharton]; window, Long Marton).*
Arg 2 bars & on canton Gu pd mullet Or
  TROUSTELL, Ed'us. *Q II 176.*
Arg 2 bars & on canton Sa mullet Or
  TWYFORD. *L1 635, 4.*
Arg 2 bars & on canton Sa pd mullet Or
  PIPARD. *L9 97b, 5.*
Az 2 bars Gu on canton Or mullet Az
  [LANCASTER]. *Bellasis II 152. ('tinctures incorrect'; imp by [Wharton] on corbel, altar, Kirkby Thore).*
Erm 2 bars & on canton Gu pd mullet Or
  GWERRY. *XF 36.*
Sa 2 bars wavy Arg on canton Gu mullet Or ch with annulet Gu
  BROKYSBY, Sir J. *WB I 40, 8.*

2 bars & on canton saltire &c

Sa 2 bars Arg on canton Gu salt Arg
  BRAUNEPATH, John, of Westmld. *WB III 90, 7.*
Arg 2 bars & on canton Sa chaplet of 4 4foils Arg cresc Untinc in sin chf
  [TWYFORD]. *WB I 33b, 20.*
Or 2 bars Az on canton Gu chaplet Arg
  HOLME, Robert, of York. *LH 761. (qrs 1&4).*
  HOLME, Robert, of Yorks. *WB III 117b, 9. (qrs 1&4).*

2 bars & on canton & ...

Arg 2 bars & on canton Sa 5foil Or label Gu
  TWYFORD, le Fitz. *SD 21. (s of Mons Jn de T).*
  TWYFORDE, Mons John de. *CA 78. ('the son').*
Sa 2 bars Arg on canton Sa garb Or label Or
  [WEAVER]. *PLN 1652.*
Sa 2 bars & on canton Arg garb Or banded Gu in sin chf annulet Sa
  WYVER, Geo de. *LY A 44.*
Arg 2 bars Az on canton barry Or and Vt demi-lion isst Untinc in sin chf 3 roundels Gu
  KERNABY. *L2 295, 3.*

2 bars & chf

2 bars & chf
  BYKER, Robert of. *Balliol E 1/3, HB-SND.* 1339. *(?chf charged; sl).*
  [FROGENHALL]. *Mill Steph; Belcher II 54.* 1452. *(imp by [Butler] on brass to Thos Borgeys, Graveney, Kent).*
  [FROGENHALL]. *Mill Steph; Belcher II 54.* 1452. *(imp by [Borgeys] on brass to Thos B, Graveney, Kent).*
  MANNERS, Robert. *LaingChart 80, HB-SND.* 1388. *(qtg 2&3 3 squirrels [Baxter]).*

MANNERS, Robert. *PRO-sls Ex KR 16/26 70.* 1322.

MANNERS, Robert de. *Durham-sls 1698.* (*Sheriff of Norham, d1355*).

[MANNERS, Sir Robert, d28 Sept 1354]. *Blair N II 125, 256. (above great gateway of Etal Castle).*

RICHMOND. *Yorks Deeds VII 142.* early 14 cent. *(imp by Hartforth, for Eliz dau of Robt de H).*

RICHMUNDIE, Roaldus, Yorks. *Birch 5850.* rev: S' RO...RICHMUNDIE; obv: Sigill' Roald'.... early 13 cent. *(s of Alan, Constabularius, equestr sl obv & rev).*

Arg 2 bars Az chf Gu
MANERS, Sr Robert de. *CKO 298.*

Arg 2 bars Gu chf Or
— *PLN 1949. (qtd 3 by Sir Rd Fowler).*

Arg 2 bars & chf Sa
— *WB II 69, 11. (qtd 3 by Burley).*

Az 2 bars Arg chf Gu
DANIEL, Hugh. *TJ 807.*
SAINTTLE, Monsire Hugh. *CG 206.*

Or 2 bars & chf

Or 2 bars Az chf Gu
HAVERS, Sir Robt. *BA 650.*
MAINS, John le. *BG 257.*
MANERS. *L1 422, 3; L2 322, 9.*
MANERS. *L9 52a, 2.*
MANERS, Sir George. *Sandford 395. (m Anne St Leger).*
MANERS, Mons' John. *TJ 521.*
MANERS, Mons' John. *S 204.*
MANERS, Monsr R de. *AS 227.*
MANERS, Mons Rob. *CA 160.*
MANERUS, S' Rob'. *PO 521.*
MANERYS, Robarde, Northd. *RH, Ancestor iv 240.*
MANNERS. *XF 695.*
MANNERS. *FK II 853.*
MANNERS, Monsire de. *CG 212.*
[MANNERS]. *BG 399.*
MANNERS, Sir George. *PLN 2060. (qtg II 1&4 Gu 3 bougets Arg, 2&3 Arg fess double cotised Gu, on escutch Az cartwheel Or, III Arg salt engr Gu, IV Gu 3 cartwheels Arg; Crest: on torse Az and Or peacock in pride Ppr).*
MANNERS, George, Ld Roos, d1513. *Dingley xcv. (Mont, N Transept, St George's Windsor).*
MANNERS, de Ithell, Cumb. *LD 120. (qrs 1&4).*
MANNERS, Sir John. *WB III 85b, 2.*
MANNERS, Sir Robert. *PLN 1283. (qtg 2&3 Vt 3 squirrels sejt Arg).*
MANNERS, Sr Robert de. *M 23.*
MANNERS, Sir Thomas. *CRK 723. (qrs 1&4).*

MENERS, Mons' Robert. *TJ 803.*

ROOS, George, Ld. *I2(1904)76. (qtg II 1 Gu 3 bougets Arg, 2 Az 3 bougets Arg, 3 Gu 3 cartwheels Arg, 4 Arg fess cotised Gu, III 1 England in border Arg, 2&3 Arg salt engr Gu, 4 Or lion Gu).*

Sa 2 bars & chf

Sa 2 bars Arg chf Or
FROGGENHALL, Sir John. *Hutton 3. (d1444; 'Sepelitur in Cancello de Tenham Cantii').*

Sa 2 bars Or chf Arg
FROGENALLE, of Kent. *MY 189.*
FROGHALE. *FK II 567.*
FROGHALL. *XF 683.*
FROGNAL. *L1 264, 5; L2 207, 6.*
FROGNALL, Edmond. *Kent Gentry 216.*
FROGNALL, John. *Kent Gentry 217b.*
FROGNALL, John, of Kent. *WB III 110b, 9.*
FROGNALL, Thomas. *Kent Gentry 216b. ('with his difference').*

2 bars & chf patterned

Or 2 bars Gu chf bendy of 8 Gu and Or
DESPAYNE. *WB I 43b, 1.*

Untinc 2 bars Untinc chf Erm
— *WLN 330. (qtd 2 by Jn Legh of Rudge).*

Untinc 2 bars Untinc chf Vair
HOLME, Robert. *Roman PO 5850.* 26 Apr 1423. *(qrs 1&4).*
[PYMPE, of Nettlestead]. *Gen Mag 14, 19-21.* 1502. *(imp by [Bromston, of Macknade] on brass, Faversham Ch, Kent, to Eliz, d1502, w of Robt Wythiot & dau of Jn B, Esq, of Preston-next-Faversham).*

Gu 2 bars Arg chf Vair
— *ME 127; LY A 252.*
PIMPE. *XF 903.*
[PYMPE, of Nettlestead]. *Gen Mag 14, 19-21.* 1465. *(imp ?Brouning, of Melbury Sampford [Az 3 bars wavy Arg]; stained-glass formerly at Nettlestead Ch, Kent).*
[PYMPE, of Nettlestead]. *Gen Mag 14, 19-21.* 1465. *(imp by [Bromston, of Macknade] Gu gutty Arg fess nebuly Arg; stained-glass formerly at Nettlestead Ch, Kent).*

2 bars & chf modified

2 bars chf indented
LOUCHES, Adam, Kt. *Bow XVIII 15.*

Gu 2 bars Or chf invected Erm
[INGPEN]. *PLN 1030.*

2 bars modified & chf

2 bars dancetty chf
[STONOR]. *Mill Steph.* c1460. *(imp by [Kirby]; brass to [Alice dau&h of Sir Jn K, & w of (1)Thos S & (2)Ric Drayton], Horton*

Kirby, Kent; inscription lost).
STONOR, John de. *Stowe-Bard 1s xii 4.*
S.Iohis.De.Stonore.
[STONOR, Sir John]. *OxfRS IV 116. (Judge of Common Pleas, temp Edw 3; mont, Dorchester, Oxfords).*
STONORE, John de. *BirmCL-sls 489850.* 1331.
STONORE, Thomas de. *BirmCL-sls 494334.* 1415.
Az 2 bars dancetty Or chf Arg
— *I2(1904)209. (qr 1 of 5 on escutch of Syr Adrian Fortescu).*
[ST]ONER, William. *WK 55.*
STANORE, Monsr de. *AS 186.*
STANORE, J, Sr de. *CKO 284.*
STANORE, Mons' John. *TJ 782. ('dazure & deux daunceletz dor a un chief dor').*
STANORE, Mons' John de. *TJ 405. ('dazure a deux dauncelletz dor ove le chief dor').*
STONER. *XF 456.*
STONER. *LS 60.*
STONER, Sir Walter. *XK 267.*
STONER, Sir William. *XF 570. (qrs 1&4).*
STONER, Sir William. *PLN 1735. (qtg 2 Az 5 lions 2, 3 Arg on canton Or mullet Gu, 3 Or 3 roundels Gu).*
STONORE, Robert, of Oxfs. *WB III 101b, 9.*
STONORT. *CC 229b, 245.*

For Mortimer &c: see barry chf & over all

2 bars chf & label
2 bars dancetty chf label
STONORE, John de, Kt. *PRO-sls.* 1358-9.
Arg bar gemel & chf Sa label of 5 Az
WOGAHAN, Johannes de. *Q II 177.*

2 bars (plain, patterned or modified) & on chf

2 bars on chf 3 indistinct charges
PENECESTRE, Margaret de. *PRO-sls.* 13 cent. *(1 of 3 shields in border of lions ramp on sl).*
PENECESTRE, Maud. *PRO-sls.* 1301-2. *(sometime w of Stephen P; 1 of 2 remaining shields (of 3) in border of lions ramp on sl).*
Or 2 bars dancetty Sa on chf Az 3 annulets Arg
BECK, Thomas. *XF 606.*
BEKE, of Berks. *L1 59, 6; L2 76, 4.*
BEKE, Thomas. *WK 622.*
LOCKE, Thos, of Whiteknights, Berks. *L10 98, 5. ('per Tho Feteplac').*
Or 2 bars dancetty Sa on chf Az 3 annulets Or
BEKE. *XPat 59, Arch 69, 73.*
Or 2 bars nebuly Az on chf Gu 2 arrows in salt betw 2 towers 3-turreted Arg
ARCHARD. *L10 7, 18. ('also Fordham' added in modern hand).*

FORDHAM. *L10 74, 11-12. (arrows pts down; alias Archard).*
FORDHAM, Willimus. *WK 412. (arrows pts down; 'alias Archard, Willimus, cellerarius wigorn').*
FORDHM. *XPat 296, Arch 69, 92.*
FOURDHAM. *L2 208, 9. (broad arrows, pts down).*

2 bars & on chf demi-lion
2 bars on chf demi-lion
FREMELESWORTH, William de. *PRO-sls.* 1351.
Az 2 bars wavy Erm on chf Or demi-lion isst Sa semy of flames Ppr
SMYTH, of the Hough, Ches. *D4 51.*
SMYTH, Messire Thomas. *WK 421. ('de la Hoghe en la County de Chesshire').*
SMYTH, Syr Thos, of the Loghem, Ches. *L10 60b, 11.*
SMYTH, Sir Thos, of the Hoghe, Ches. *BA 422.*

2 bars & on chf lion passt
2 bars on chf lion passt
GIFFARD, Sir Osbert. *PRO-sls E40 A252-3.*
..SBERTI.GIFFAR. 1301-2. *(?lion pg).*
GREGORY, William. *Birch 10227.* 1494.
Az 2 bars Arg on chf Gu lion passt Or
— *CT 136.*
2 bars wavy on chf lion passt
AUHNO, Wm de. *Stowe-Bard 2s v 1.* S.W. DE AVHNO. 1418-19. *(appended to deed by Wm Algor, of Fyncham & Matilde his w; legend unclear).*
Az 2 bars nebuly Arg on chf per pale Arg and Sa lion passt counterch
TINGLETON. *XF 228.*
Az 2 bars wavy Arg on chf per pale Arg and Sa lion passt counterch
TINGLETON. *XL 66.*

2 bars & on chf lion pg
2 bars on chf lion pg
[ENGLEFIELD]. *Mill Steph. (qtd 3 by Fowler; brass to Thos F & 3rd w Edith Dynham d1514, Christ's Coll Camb).*
[ENGLEFIELD]. *Mill Steph.* 1496. *(borne in base with Fowler [on canton owl] in chf, all imp on brass to Ric Chamburleyn, of Coobys, Northants, & w Sybyll F, Shirburn, Oxfords).*
Arg 2 bars Az on chf Gu lion pg Or
DENARSTON, Sir Rob, of Suff. *WB III 72, 3.*
Arg 2 bars Gu on chf Or lion pg Az
— *PLN 1806. (in base of coat per fess of Ric Fowler).*
— *PLN 1926. (qtd 3 by Sir Jn Fowler).*

Az 2 bars Arg on chf Gu lion pg Or
  DENARDESTONE, Sr Peres. *N 518.*
  DENARDSTON, Sir Piers. *BR V 205.*
  DENNARDESTON, Suff. *L1 203, 2; L2 158, 1.*
Erm 2 bars & on chf Gu lion pg Or
  GIFFARD, Holekirn. *Q 578.*
  GIFFARD, Osborne. *XF 288.*
  GIFFARD, Osborne. *E I 521; E II 523.*
  GIFFARD, Mons' Oubarne. *TJ 192.*
  GIFFARD, Mons' Oubern. *TJ 480.*
  GYFFARD. *L1 271, 2; L2 217, 1.*
Arg 2 bars wavy Az on chf Gu lion pg Or
  STAPEL. *BG 430.*
Arg 2 bars wavy & on chf Sa lion pg Or
  PERCY, Stewyn. *RH, Ancestor ix 163.*

2 bars & on chf other beast

Gu 2 bars Untinc on chf Or ?greyhound courant
  collared Or annulet Or for diffce
  SKYPWYTH. *Suff HN 41. (imp by Hansard;*
  Mr Rowsse's Roll).
Erm 2 bars wavy Sa on chf Gu bull courant Or
  — *XX 141. (qtd 2&3 by Wm North).*
  — *L9 85b, 8. (qtd 2&3 by Northe).*

2 bars & on chf bird

Sa 2 bars & on chf Or eagle Sa
  — *XF 193.*
  — *L10 104, 8.*
2 bars on chf 2 birds
  MANERS, Robert de. *PRO-sls.* 1323.
Sa 2 bars nebuly & on chf Arg 3 ravens Sa
  — *XF 174.*

2 bars & on chf castle

Sa 2 bars wavy & on chf Arg 3-turreted castle
  Sa
  RAWSON, Richard. *CRK 1776.*

2 bars & on chf crescent

Sa 2 bars Or on chf Arg cresc Sa
  FROGENHALE. *CVK 699.*
  FROGHALE. *FK II 568.*
  FROGNALE, Sir Rychard. *RH, Ancestor ix*
  165.

2 bars & on chf cross &c

Untinc 2 bars Erm on chf 2 crosses moline
  Untinc
  PANTON, Hugh de. *Birch 12374.* 13 cent.
2 bars wavy on chf 3 crosses formy fitchy
  HARVY. *Birch 13721.* ?15 cent. *(imp by*
  Thos de Strata-Villa, Clerk).
Arg 2 bars wavy & on chf Sa 3 crosses formy
  fitchy Or
  HERVY, Nycolas. *WB IV 151b, 460.*
2 bars on chf 3 escallops
  — *Proc Soc Antiq I 2S 354. (on front of*
  castellated building on imperfect tile from

Sandhurst, Kent).

2 bars & on chf fleur de lis

2 bars chf qtly 1&4 fleur de lis 2&3 lion pg
  MANNERS. *Blair D I 80, 211. (qr 1 of 16*
  imp by Hen Neville, 5th E of Westmld; on
  oak tomb in Staindrop Ch).
2 bars chf qtly 1&4 2 fleurs de lis 2&3 lion pg
  MANNERS, Thomas, E of Rutl, Baron Roos of
  Hamlake, Trusbut & Belvoir, KG. *PRO-sls.*
  c1525. *(within garter).*
Or 2 bars Az chf qtly 1&4 Az 2 fleurs de lis Or
  2&3 Gu lion pg Or
  MANERS, of Rutl. *L2 322, 10.*
  MANERS, Sir Thomas. *Sandford 395. (s of*
  Sir George M, augmentation on being made
  E of Rutl in 1525).
  MANNERS, Thomas, Ld Roos, KG. *Leake.*
  (d1543; qtg II 1 Roos, 2 Trusbut, 3 Espec, 4
  Badlesmere, III 1 Plantagenet, 2&3 Tiptoft, 4
  Charlton).
  MANNERS, Thomas, E of Rutl, KG 1525. *XK*
  84. (qrs 1&4).
  [RUTLAND, Thomas, E of]. ?source. 1530.
  (glass, Enfield Ch, Middx).

2 bars & on chf foils &c

Arg 2 bars & on chf Gu 3 5foils Arg
  MORTYMER, Mons' Walran. *TJ 555.*
  ('...iii sytfoilles dargent en le chief').
Arg 2 bars & on chf Gu 3 6foils Arg
  MORTYMER, Mons' Walran. *TJ 1014.*
  ('..iii sytfoilles..').
Az 2 bars & on chf Arg 3 lozs Gu
  FLEMYNGE, de Wath. *PT 1145.*
  FLEMYNGES. *FK II 456. ('of Suffolk' added*
  by Gibbon).
Az 2 bars & on chf Arg 3 maunches Gu
  FLEMING. *XF 887.*
Arg 2 bars & on chf Gu 3 mullets Arg
  — *D9; E6. (qtd by Wm Malore, of Hutton*
  Conyers, Yorks).
  — *CB 75. (mullets of 8 pts).*
Az 2 bars & on chf Or 3 pd mullets Gu
  GUNTHORPE, Thomas. *PE I 4; PE II 3.*
  ('filius Roberti de G').

2 bars & on chf roundels

2 bars & on chf 3 roundels
  GREY, Edward. *PRO-sls.* 1468-9. *(Ld of*
  Ferrers & Groby; used by his sis Elizabeth).
  MORTES. *CT 78.*
Az 2 bars Or on chf Arg 3 roundels Gu
  — *CT 389.*
2 bars dancetty on chf 3 roundels
  STONORRE, William. *PRO-sls.* early 14 cent.

2 bars on chf ... & label
Arg 2 bars Sa label of 5 Gu on chf Az roundel
of St George Ppr irrad Or betw on dex [skull
Arg] in cup Or & on sin basket of cakes Or
BEDLAM HOSPITAL. *L10 67, 4.*
2 bars on chf 3 roundels label
HUNGERFORD, Robert, Chivaler. *PRO-sls.*
1426.

2 bars (plain, patterned or modified) & in chf

2 bars in chf 3 indistinct objects
— *?source. 16 cent. (?6foils or ?roundels;*
imp lion crowned; marshalled with other
charges; roof groining, tower lantern, Crick-
lade, Wilts).
2 bars in chf 3 annulets
NOWERS, John. *PRO-sls E40 A6812.* ...ANNIS
NOWERS. *1369-70.*
Arg 2 bars Az in chf 3 annulets Gu
BASSET, Willimus. *Q II 353.*
Arg 2 bars & in chf 3 annulets Sa
BURDEUX. *L10 81b, 8.*
MILTON. *XF 790.*
MULTON, Mons John de. *WJ 939. ('Meirs*
de Burden').
MYLTON. *L9 67a, 3.*
Gu 2 bars & in chf 3 annulets Arg
ANK, Mons Gregere. *WJ 619.*
ANK, Mons Gregor de. *AS 417.*
AUK, de. *CC 222, 15.*
AUK, Mons' Gregoir de. *TJ 979.*
AUK, Gregoire de. *TJ 533.*
AUKE, de. *DV 55b, 2197.*
SPALDYNG, Michel de. *TJ 509.*

2 bars & in chf demi-lion
Arg 2 bars & in chf demi-lion isst Gu
— *FK II 515.*
DRAYTON. *DV 50a, 1978. (on 1st bar cresc*
Or).
Az 2 bars Or in chf demi-lion isst Arg
MALVESILL. *XL 572.*
MALVESYLL. *XF 685. (in fess pt cresc Arg).*
MALVESYLL. *XF 701.*
MALVESYLLE. *FK a 902.*
MALVOSYLL. *L9 53b, 4.*
Az 2 bars Or in chf demi-lion isst Gu
MALMESHILL, Sir Thomas. *CRK 449. (a&l*
Or).
MALVESYLLE. *FK II 902.*
TREGOYS. *WB IV 1049.*
Erm 2 bars & in chf demi-lion Untinc
[DRAYTON]. *Mill Steph. (qtg 2&3 bend*
between 6 crosslets fitchy all imp by Baran-
tine on brass to Drew B Esq [1453] & wives
Joan 1437, & Dame Beatrix 1446, Chal-
grove, Oxfords).

Erm 2 bars & in chf demi-lion isst Gu
— *SK 258.*
— *CRK 1480. (qtd 2&3 by Barentine).*
DRATON. *CB 228.*
DRAYTON. *L1 213, 2; L2 159, 11.*
DRAYTON. *CRK 1473.*
SEGRAVE, Sir Hugo, of Oxfords. *CV-BM*
142.
Erm 2 bars Gu in chf demi-lion isst Untinc on
1st bar cresc Or
DRAYTON. *PT 307.*

2 bars & in chf lion passt
2 bars in chf lion passt
BURNEBY, George. *PRO-sls E40 A8309.*
SIGILLVM GORGE BVRNEBY. *1404-5.*
BURNEBY, George. *PRO-sls. 1403-4.*
ENGLEFELD, Roger de. *PRO-sls. 1301-2.*
(Ld of Shiplake).
[?TREGOZ]. *Her & Gen I 278. (?gemel bars;*
imp by Fishmongers' Co & qtd by Leather-
sellers' Co; on tomb in Sompting Ch).
Arg 2 bars & in chf lion passt Gu
BORNBY, Thomas, of Northants. *WB III 113,*
4. (qrs 1&4).
BRONEBY, S' Nich'. *PO 335.*
BURNABY. *CRK 1257. (qrs 1&4).*
LOUCHE. *XF 292.*
LOUCHE, Adam. *XL 392.*
LOWCHE. *L9 36a, 11.*
LOWTHE, Mons Adam. *WJ 229.*

2 bars & in chf lion pg
2 bars in chf lion pg
BURNEBY, George. *Bk of Sls 245. 1427.*
ERCEDEKNE, Matilda. *AnstisAsp I 212, 59.*
SIGILL' MATIL LERCE DECNE. *1360-1. (roun-*
del, 2 others round shield).
Arg 2 bars & in chf lion pg Gu
— *ME 116; LY A 241.*
BURNABY. *XF 673.*
BURNABY. *XL 561.*
BURNBY. *L10 86, 5. (a&l Az).*
BURNBY. *FK II 460.*
[BURNBY]. *Nichols Leics IV 108. (Claybrook*
Ch).
Az 2 bars & in chf lion pg Or
TIGOT, Sr Henry. *RB 10. ('Tregose' added*
in pencil by modern hand).
TRAGOSE, Sir John, of Suss. *RH, Ancestor vii*
201.
TRIGOT, Sire Henry. *HA 12b, 6.*
Gu 2 bars Arg in chf lion pg Or
[DENESTON]. *PLN 1649. (or Denardeston).*

2 bars & in chf 2 or more lions
2 bars in chf 2 lions
CALSTON, Thomas. *Heneage 985.* SIGILL
THOM[E] [C]AL[ST]ON. *1409. (deed*

concerning property in All Cannings, Wilts;
'Dat Devyses').
CALSTON, Thomas, of Wilts. *SarumC-sls*
M74/W205 Drawer F. 1392.
Arg 2 bars Gu in chf 2 lions Untinc
— *I2(1904)213. (qtd 2&3 by Sir Edw Dar-*
rel, of Littlecote, Wilts).
Arg 2 bars & in chf 2 lions Gu
— *WK 418. (qtd 2&3 by Sir Edw Darell).*
— *L10 59b, 10. (qtd 2&3 by Sr Edw Darell,*
of Hilcot, Wilts, imp Alis, dau of Joh Flys).
CALSTON. *BA 855 & 857. (qtd 2&3 by Sir*
Edw Darell, of Calston).
Or 2 bars & in chf 3 lions Gu
— *Q II 463. (imp Gu 2 bars Arg).*

2 bars & in chf bends
2 bars in chf 4 bends
SCURES, Robert de. *Bk of Sls 344.* ante
1274. *(Ld of Long Liston, Yorks).*

2 bars & in chf bird
Arg 2 bars Az in chf martlet Untinc
HYLTON. *RB 354. (qrs 1&4).*
Az 2 bars wavy Or in dex chf martlet Gu
POLE, Sr Johan de la. *CKO 642.*
2 bars in chf ?eagle displd annulet for diffce
PAKINGHAM, Robert, Esq. *Birch 12356.*
SIGILLUM ROBERTI PAK....MIGERI. *(imp bend*
dancetty; or Robt Pakeman).
Arg 2 bars & in chf 2 martlets Sa
DENTON. *L10 58, 18.*
2 bars in chf 3 birds
VENABLES, Richard. *PRO-sls.* 1330-1.
WEDON, Ralph de, Kt. *PRO-sls.* 1326.
2 bars in chf 3 cocks
BLAKISTON, Roger of. *Durham-sls 282-4.*
1348 onwards.
BLAYKESTON, Roger de. *Birch 7500.*
S'ROGERI DE BLAYKESTON. 1353.
Arg 2 bars & in chf 3 cocks Gu
BLAUXTON, Wylyam. *RH, Ancestor ix 167.*
2 bars in chf 3 martlets
SMYTH, Thomas, of Hanewell, ?Northants.
Birch 13547. 1392.
Arg 2 bars & in chf 3 martlets Gu
— *FK II 224.*
ANSTABETH, Moles de. *Q II 577.*
DENTONE. *PT 1163.*
MENY. *BA 663.*
Arg 2 bars Gu in chf 3 martlets Sa
WEDONE, Sire Rauf de. *N 353.*
Arg 2 bars Sa in chf 3 martlets Gu
— *C3 41. (annulet Arg for diffce; in St Ben-*
netts Ch, Huntingdon).
PAYNELL. *L9 93a, 11.*
Arg 2 bars & in chf 3 martlets Sa
AGLIONBY, of Aglionby, Cumb. *D4 51b.*
AGLIONBYE. *PT 1169.*

AGLOMBY, Johan. *TJ 1490. ('...a deux fees*
de sable & trois merlotz de mesme au chief').
Or 2 bars & in chf 3 martlets Gu
HARECOURT, Sr Roger de. *CKO 586.*

2 bars & in chf crescent
Arg 2 bars & in chf cresc Sa
BRERETON, Randle, of Brereton. *PLN 198.*
(qtg 2&3 Arg fess betw 3 crescs Gu).
Gu 2 bars & in chf cresc Or
— *PT 500.*
HARCOURT, Anthony, d1541. *Nichols Leics*
IV 575. (mont, Cadeby Ch).
HARECOURT. *DV 63a, 2484. (name added in*
later hand).
Or 2 bars & in chf cresc Gu
HARCOURT. *PT 461.*
Or 2 bars Gu in chf cresc Sa
HARCOURT. *LH 89.*
Gu 2 bars Erm in dex chf cresc Arg
BOTELER. *L10 81b, 9.*
Or 2 bars lozy Gu and Arg in dex chf cresc Arg
LYNCHEFED, Terry de. *CA 143.*
2 bars in chf 3 crescs
NOWERS, John. *PRO-sls AS 9.* SIGILLV
IOHANNIS NOWERS. 1369-70. *(s of Jn de N,*
of Gothurst, Bucks).
Arg 2 bars & in chf 3 crescs Gu
— *SK 329.*
NEWERENE, Bucks. *L2 360, 9. (marginal*
note: 'Nowery').
NOONWERS. *L1 472, 4; L2 367, 5.*
NOUWERS. *L9 85b, 1.*
NOUWERS, Sire ... de. *N 365.*
NOWERS. *XF 832.*
NOWERS, Sir John. *CRK 1338.*
WETESHAM, Mons Robert de. *WJ 761.*
WETESHAM, Robert de. *XO 24. ('Nowers'*
added by Gibbon).
2 bars fretty in chf 3 crescs
NOWERS, John. *PRO-sls E40 A387: A6812*
C4033. SIGILLVM IOHANNIS NOWERS. 1369-
70. *(s of Jn de N, of Gothurst).*

2 bars & in chf cross &c
Gu 2 bars Erm in dex chf cross moline Untinc
PAUNTON, S Hugh de. *GA 139.*
Gu 2 bars & in dex chf cross moline Erm
PAUNTON, Sire Hugh de. *N 1004. ('...en le*
cauntel un fer de molyn de ermyn').
Per fess Az and Gu 2 bars Or in chf cross & in
dex chf annulet Untinc
HOLT. *CC 232b, 349.*
Arg 2 bars Az in chf 3 crosslets fitchy Gu
— *WJ 500.*
Gu 2 bars dancetty Arg in chf 3 cups Or
LAGGAGE, Wylyam. *RH, Ancestor vii 212.*
(Foster says chf should be azure and adds
'imperfectly tricked').

2 bars & in chf escallops

2 bars in chf 2 escallops
HALGHTON, John de, Kt. *Birch 10417.*
S'IOHANNIS DE HAL...ON. *1322.*
HALTON, John of. *Dodsworth 45, 77b, HB-SND. 1321.*
HALTON, John of. *BM Harl 1448, 57b, HB-SND. 1319.*

Arg 2 bars Az in chf 2 escallops Gu
HALTON, Mons John de. *TJ 484.*
HAULTON, Sr de. *CKO 320.*
HILTON, Sir John. *LH 299.*

2 bars in chf 3 escallops
BAYOUS, Sir William, dc1327. *Lawrance 3. (effigy, Careby, Lincs).*
[ERRINGTON]. *Birch 12943.* S'ISABELLE. *1322. (2nd of 3 sh in sl of Isabella ...; used by Thomas, s of Gilbert de Redehough, of Newcastle-on-Tyne, Northd).*
HUNGERFORD, Robert. *Roman PO 5904.* 21 Jan 1428.

Arg 2 bars & in chf 3 escallops Az
ERRINGTON. *CRK 1352.*
ERYNGTON, John de. *TJ 1438. ('...& iii escalops dazure amonte').*

Arg 2 bars Az in chf 3 escallops Gu
HALGHTON, le S' de. *WJ 520.*
HALTON, le Sire de. *CG 240.*

Arg 2 bars & in chf 3 escallops Gu
MELESE, Roger de. *F 47.*
MELESE, Roger de. *WLN 700.*

Arg 2 bars & in chf 3 escallops Sa
PUNE, Sir J de la. *CRK 1640. (?Fitzpen alias Phippen).*

Gu 2 bars & in chf 3 escallops Arg
BAIOUS, Sr de. *CKO 323.*
BAUSE, Sire William. *O 18.*
BAYHUSE, S' John de. *R 122.*
BAYONS. *L10 20b, 5.*
BAYONS, Lincs. *L1 98, 3; L2 45, 12.*
BAYONS, William de. *TJ 488.*
BAYOUES, Sr William. *L 51.*
BAYOUS. *XF 64.*
BAYOUS, Monsire de. *CG 243.*
BAYOUS, Mons Waut' de. *WJ 912.*
BAYOUSE, Sire Willame de. *N 651.*
RAYOUS, Monsr de. *AS 168.*

Or 2 bars Az in chf 3 escallops Gu
CLARK, John. *WB I 25b, 20.*
CLARK, Thomas. *WB I 25b, 21.*
CLERK. *WB I 21b, 15.*

2 bars & in chf estoile &c

2 bars in chf estoile
CHARITE, Henry de la. *Selborne 4, 59.* S' Henrici de Kantate. *1266-7.*

2 bars in chf 2 estoiles
IRELAND, Andrew, burgess of Perth. *Stevenson. 1454. (estoiles of 6 pts).*

2 bars in chf 3 estoiles
MOIGNE, William, Kt. *PRO-sls. 1400-1.*

2 bars in chf 3 estoiles of 6 pts
ESSELINGTON, Robert. *Birch 9512.*
....ESLINGT.... *1323. (s of Robt de E, Chev).*

Arg 2 bars & in chf 3 estoiles Gu
[LOWICK]. *Bellasis II 306-8. (qtg Arg cross wavy Gu; ?3 roundles or lozs in chf; ?Lowick in qrs 2&3, Lawrence in 1&4; E window, Windermere).*

2 bars & in chf 3 fleurs de lis &c

Arg 2 bars & in chf 3 fleurs de lis Gu
SENLYS. *BG 365.*
[ST LIZ]. *Lawrance 27. 1349. (on tomb of Sir Jn Lyons, d1349; effigy, Warkworth, Northants).*
ST LIZ, E of Northants. *DX 141; RW 37.*

Gu 2 bars & in chf 3 fleurs de lis Arg
MORTEMER. *L1 421, 5; L2 324, 8.*

Checky Arg and Sa 2 bars Gu in chf 3 fleurs de lis Or
— *WB I 12, 13. (imp by per fess Arg and Sa double eagle counterch).*

2 bars in chf 3 roses *C3 56b.*
?TRENTHAM. *1321-2. (?roses or 5foils; sl to deed of Thos de T, Ld of Keten).*

Arg 3 bars Sa in chf 3 roses Gu
STERBORGH. *PLN 943. (imp St Leger).*

Az 2 bars & in chf 3 roses Arg seeded Or
— *PLN 922.*
PEWPE. *PLN 573.*

2 bars & in chf foils

Gu 2 bars Erm in chf 5foil pd Sa
— *PLN 1070. (imp by Boteler).*

2 bars in chf 2 5foils
GIMIGIS, Nicholas de. *PRO-sls AS 183.*
S'NICHOLAI: GIMIGIS. 13 cent.

2 bars in chf 3 5foils
KILLINGWORTH, William. *BM Harl 1448, 40b, HB-SND. 1463.*

2 bars in chf 3 voided 5foils
— *Durham-sls 1511. 14 cent. (...ngworth; used in 1556 by Jn Kyllyngworth).*

Arg 2 bars Gu in chf 3 5foils Untinc
DENTTON, Wylyam. *RH, Ancestor ix 173.*

Arg 2 bars & in chf 3 pd 5foils Gu
— *FK II 962.*

Arg 2 bars Gu in chf 3 5foils Sa
DENTON, John. *CA 113.*

Arg 2 bars Gu in chf 3 pd 5foils Sa
DENTON. *CRK 646.*
DENTON. *BG 453.*
DENTON. *L10 57b, 1.*
DENTON. *L1 195, 4; L2 153, 6.*
DENTON, Mons Ric' de. *WJ 590.*
DENTON, S' Ric' de. *PO 396.*
DENTONE. *FK II 870.*

DENTONE. *PT 1252.*

DENTTON, Wm. *RH, Ancestor ix 173.*

Az 2 bars Gu in chf 3 pd 5foils Sa
DENTON. *XF 699.*

Sa 2 bars & in chf 3 5foils Arg
WALDEN. *Hutton 16.* 1523. *(imp by Worse-ley; window in Lambeth Ch [?commemorating Sir Jn Legh]).*

Sa 2 bars & in chf 3 pd 5foils Arg
— *PT 335.*
WALDEN. *XF 246.*
WALDEN. *CRK 1923.*

Sa 2 bars Or in chf 3 pd 5foils Arg
— *WB III 71, 7. (qtd 2&3 by Sir Thos Raunsey, of Norf).*

Sa 2 bars & in chf 3 5foils Or
— *XF 242.*
— *CRK 737. (qtd 2&3 by Sir Thos Rams-ton).*
WELYSHAM. *Suff HN 45. ('Mr Garne's house at Kenton').*

Sa 2 bars Erm in chf 3 5foils Arg
WALDEN, Mons' Alexander. *S 408.*

Sa 2 bars Erm in chf 3 pd 5foils Arg
WALDEN. *XF 245.*
WALDEN, Alexander. *S 413.*
WALDENE. *L1 669, 1.*

2 bars & in chf 1 head

Az 2 bars & in dex chf leopard's face Arg
GOTEHILL. *L2 233, 12.*
[TOTHILL]. *PLN 688.*

Sa 2 bars 1st Erm 2nd Arg billetty Sa in chf talbot's head erased betw 2 chaplets Or
[HUSSEY, of Kenersey Hall]. *WK 587.*

Sa 2 bars 1st Erm 2nd Arg billetty Sa in chf talbot's head erased betw 2 cushions Or voided per salt Sa
KENERSEY. *L2 294, 5.*

Sa 2 bars 1st Erm 2nd Arg billetty Sa in chf greyhound's head erased betwn 2 chaplets Or
HALL. *BA 707.*

2 bars & in chf 2 heads

Gu 2 bars & in chf 2 boars' heads Arg
— *TJ 551.*

2 bars in chf 2 stags' heads cab
[VERNEY]. *Mill Steph.* 1524. *(qtd 2&3 by Danvers, all imp by Fetyplace on brass to Jn F & w Dorothy D, East Shefford, Berks).*
[VERNEY]. *Mill Steph.* 1514. *(qtd 2&3 by Danvers on brass to Sir Jn D, Dauntsey, Wilts).*

Gu 2 bars Arg in chf 2 stags' heads cab Or
— *L10 53b, 12. (qtd 2&3 by Danvers, of Oxfords).*

Gu 2 bars & in chf 2 stags' heads cab Or
— *WK 272. (qtd 2&3 by Sir Jn Danvers, of Dauncy).*

— *RL 31b, 1.*

— *WB II 53, 5. (qtd 2&3 by Davers).*

— *WK 522. (qtd 2 by Danvers, all imp by Hungerford).*

— *WK 857. (qtd 2&3 by Sir Jn Danvers, of Daunsey, North').*

LANGLE, S' Th'm. *PO 546.*

2 bars & in chf 3 heads

Arg 2 bars counter-gobony Gu and Or in chf 3 leopards' faces Az
— *PLN 931. (qtd 4 by Wodhull).*

Arg 2 bars Az fretty Or in chf 3 leopards' faces Or
SENLYS, Sir John, of Lincs. *WB III 82, 2.*

Arg 2 bars Or fretty Gu in chf 3 leopards' faces Sa
— *WB IV 158b, 590. (qtd 4 by Wadhyll).*

Arg 2 bars & in chf 3 wolves' heads Gu
LOU, Sire Johan le. *N 375.*

Arg 2 bars & in chf 3 wolves' heads couped Gu
LOU. *L1 400, 1; L2 309, 5. (?heads erased).*
[?WOLF]. *PLN 959.*

Arg 2 bars & in chf 3 wolves' heads erased Gu
WOLF. *L1 656, 5. (or Volf).*
WOLF. *SK 813.*
WOLF. *XF 893.*
WOLFE. *ME 4; LY A 124. (centre wolf ch with annulet Or).*

2 bars & in chf 3 horseshoes

2 bars in chf 3 horseshoes
BACKPUS, John de, miles, of Barton, Derbys. *Vinc 88, 38.* 1342-3. *(sl).*
BAKEPUIZ, John de. *Bow LVII 5.* Sigillum Johis de Bakepuiz. 1375-6.
BAKEPUS, Emma de. *Birch 7073.* SIGILLVM EMME DE BAKEPVS. 1391. *(imp by paly bend; used by Alicia, dau of Thos Adam, of Ashbourne, Derbys).*
BAKEPUS, Johannes de, dns de Barton. *Vinc 88, 39.* 1339-40. *(sl).*
BAKEPUS, Nicholas, of Barton-Bakepuz. *Vinc 88, 38.* SIGILLVM NICHOLAI BAKEPUS. 1381-2. *(sl).*
BAKEPUZ, Helena. *Bow XXXV 2.* Sigillum Elene Bakepuz. 1384-5. *(dau of Thos B, of Barton Bakepuz, Derbys, imp by [?Long-ford]).*
BAKEPUZ, Helena. *Vinc 88, 38.* SIGILLUM ELENAE BAKEPVS. *(dau of Thos B, of Barton Bakepuz, Derbys; imp by paly bend; sl on deed giving power of attorney for seisin in Barton Bakepuz to Wm Hyde).*
BAKEPUZ, Dame Johanna, of Bailston, Derbys. *Birch 7074.* ...ioha...bakepuys. 1383. *(imp chev betw 3 garbs).*
BAKEPUZ, John de. *Bow XXXV 1.* +Sig Johanis de Barton. 1339-40 & 1342-3. *(dominus de*

Barton [Derbys]).
Gu 2 bars Arg in chf 3 horseshoes Or
BAKEPUCE, Sire Johan de. *N 789.*
BAKPUCE, of Northants & Rutld. *L2 88, 12.*
(horseshoes upright & pd).

2 bars & in chf lozenges &c
Arg 2 bars Az in chf 3 lozs Gu
[FLEMYNG, Bp of Lincoln]. *Stamford 10.*
c1480. *(E Window, Donors' shield).*
Gu 2 bars Arg in dex chf mill rind Erm
PANTON. *L1 527, 4.*

2 bars & in chf 1 mullet
2 bars diapered in dex chf pd mullet
C...hille, Thomas. *PRO-sls.* temp Edw 3.
2 bars fretty in dex chf mullet
MORHALE, Thomas. *Dugd 17, 17.* Sigillii
Thome Morhale. 1372-3. *(sl).*
MORHALLE, Thomas. *Birch 11924.* SIGILLV
THOME MORHALLE. temp Ric 2. *(Rector of
Quenton, Gloucs).*
Gu 2 bars Vair in dex chf pd mullet Arg
— *BG 393.*
TALBOT, Gilbert. *S 200.*
TALBOTES. *SK 456.*
TALBOTT, Mons Gilbert. *S 192.*
Gu 2 bars Vair in dex chf mullet Or
TALBOT. *XF 204.*

2 bars & in chf 2 mullets
2 bars in chf 2 mullets
— *Durham-sls 2726-7. (used by Wm of
Yeland, 1329-46).*
ESLINGTON, Robert of, Kt. *Bk of Sls 225.*
1323.
Arg 2 bars & in chf 2 pd mullets Gu
WASHINGTON, William de. *S 429.*
Arg 2 bars & in chf 2 mullets Sa
MOIGN. *L1 422, 2. (6 pts; painted 3 mul-
lets).*
Az 2 bars & in chf 2 mullets Arg
VENABLES, Sir William, of Bolyn. *CVC 581.*
Az 2 bars & in chf 2 pd mullets Arg
VENABLES, Bolyn. *PCL II 35.*
VENABLES, Sir William, de Bolin. *WLN 300.*
Az 2 bars Or in chf 2 pd mullets Arg
VENABLES, S' William, Bolyn, of Ches. *CY
17, 66.*
Gu 2 bars & in chf 2 mullets Arg
CAUNTON, of Leics. *L2 134, 9.*
CAUNTONE, Sr Johan. *N 830.*
Gu 2 bars & in chf 2 pd mullets Arg
COUNTONE, of Leics. *BA 31, 279.*
Gu 2 bars Vair in chf 2 mullets Or
— *WB I 12, 15. (imp by per fess Arg and Sa
eagle displ counterch).*

Sa 2 bars Arg in chf 2 mullets Or
[SPELMAN]. *WB III 121 & 122. (qtd 2&3 by
[?Peyto]).*

2 bars & in chf 3 mullets
2 bars in chf 3 mullets
AMUNDEVILLE, Ralph de. *Durham-sls 67.*
c1210.
[DENTON]. *Lamborn.* 1487. *(4th mullet in
fess for diffce; imp by Langston; mont,
Caversfield, Oxfords).*
ESLINGTON, Robert of. *PRO Lay Sub roll
158/18, HB-SND.* 1347.
ESLINGTON, Robert of. *BM Add mss 8157,
12b, HB-SND.* 11312-3.
2 bars in chf 3 pd mullets
— *C3 7.* April 1404. *(6 pts; imp lion &
border engr; crest: demi-woman affrontee
holding by both hands a whip with 5 knotted
thongs; ....& Maria his w; mont, Sautrey Ch).*
[?ESLINGTON]. *Blair N I 98, 193. (6 pts; qtg
2&3 blank; wall of hall, Belsay Castle).*
ESLINGTON, Robert, of Eslington, Northd, Kt.
Vinc 88, 66. 1326. *(sl).*
ESSELINGTON, Robert de, Kt. *Bow LV 16.*
+Sigill Roberti de Esselington. 1322-3. *(6 pts; grt
to his sons Robt & Thos de E, seisin of lands
in Everwick).*
[MORTIMER]. *Lawrance 31.* ante 1350. *(this
Kt has not been identified but c1350 Sir Wal-
rand de Mortimer held land here; effigy, Wil-
sthorpe, Lincs).*
MORTYMER, Hugh. *Birch 11958.* S' HUGONIS
MORTYMER. c1410.
MYRIELL, John, Clerk. *Bow LIV 12.* 1464-5.
*(s&h of Wm M, late of Pottersmerston; 1st of
2 shields).*
WASHINGTON, ... *HB-SND.* 1433. *(sl; deed
penes Duchess of Norf).*
WASHINGTON, William of. *Dodsworth 70,
30, HB-SND.* 1349.
WASHINGTON, William of. *HB-SND, deed
penes Duchess of Norfolk 1433.* 1346.
WASSYNGTON, Robert de. *PRO-sls.* S'
ROBERTI DE MASSYNGTON. 1401. *(used by
his s Edm).*
WESSHYNGTON, John. *Durham-sls 3444.*
(prior of Durham 1416-46).
WESSINGTON, Sir Wm of. *Durham-sls 2609.*
1376.

Arg 2 bars & in chf 3 mullets
Arg 2 bars & in chf 3 mullets Az
ESLINGTON, John de. *WJ 504. (6 pts).*
Arg 2 bars Az in chf 3 mullets Gu
BRIDDESHALE, S Gilbert de. *GA 162.*
Arg 2 bars & in chf 3 mullets Gu
— *WB III 100, 5. (qtd 2&3 by Sir Water
Lourance of Lancs).*

— *CRK 1515. (qtd 2&3 by Sir Robt Laurence).*
— *LY A 245. (qtd 2&3 by Edm Lawrence).*
— *L9 42b, 7. (qtd 2&3 by Lawrence).*
BRYDDELSHALE. *L10 79b, 7.*
MOELES, Nicholas de. *B 83. ('trois molets en le chief').*
MORTIMER, Sir .... *CRK 1538.*
PORTYNGTON. *WB I 25b, 16. (cresc Arg on 1st bar).*
[WASHINGTON]. *Bellasis II.* 15 cent. *(qtg [Lawrence]; E window, Windermere; Bellasis gives Lowick; Washingtons, who m Ambrose, heirs of Lowicks, bore these arms).*
WASSYNGTON, Mons ... de, du Count de Lancaster. *WJ 604.*
Arg 2 bars & in chf 3 pd mullets Gu
— *ME 120. (qtd 2&3 by Lawrence).*
[WASHINGTON]. *WB II 59, 13. (qtd by Lawrence).*
WASSINGTON, Mons' William de. *S 424.*
Arg 2 bars & in chf 3 mullets Gu pd Sa
— *WK 292. (qtd 2&3 by Sir Thos Lawrance).*

Arg 2 bars & in chf 3 mullets Sa
Arg 2 bars & in chf 3 mullets Sa
— *PLN 1451.*
ALEIN. *L2 21, 9.*
FOGGE, Sir .... *CRK 1540.*
[GADDESDEN]. *B 108. (name cancelled out).*
MOIGN. *L1 422, 2; L2 325, 3.*
MOIGNE, Mons William. *S 185. (6 pts).*
MOIGNE, Mons William. *TJ 515.*
MOIGNI, William. *BG 260.*
MOINE, Guil Le. *PE II 16.*
MOYELE. *BG 390. (6 pts).*
MOYN. *SK 141. (6 pts; imp Somayne).*
MOYN. *SK 140. (6 pts).*
MOYN, Monsire William. *AN 224.*
MOYNE. *XF 50.*
MOYNE. *CB 16 & 17. (6 pts).*
MOYNE. *L9 70a, 10.*
MOYNE, Mons William. *WJ 934.*
MOYNE, William. *S 187. (6 pts).*
OWGAN, Monsire William. *CG 236.*
Arg 2 bars & in chf 3 pd mullets Sa
BUSY, Sr de. *CKO 316. (6 pts).*

Gu 2 bars & in chf 3 mullets
Gu 2 bars & in chf 3 mullets Arg
— *WB I 34b, 13.*
— *D5 102. (qtd by Conyers alias Norton).*
— *WB III 76b, 2. (qtd 2&3 by Sir Jn Tempest, of Yorks).*
MORTEMER. *L2 324, 9.*
MORTYMER. *PT 427.*
[OGLE]. *Nichols Leics II 282. (Sisonby Ch).*
SAINTLOWE, Mons Thomas de. *AS 402.*

SKELTON. *PLN 1418.*
WASSYNGEDON, Mons Willm de. *WJ 620.*
WESSYNGTON, Mons William de. *TJ 1421.*
Gu 2 bars & in chf 3 pd mullets Arg
[MARTIN, Sir Constantine]. *PLN 308.*
MORTYMER. *DV 56b, 2221.*
WASHINGTON. *CRK 2062.*

2 bars & in chf pale
Az 2 bars Arg in chf pale Vt
— *ML I 326. (bars narrow; 'Asur a pale invectyd in the same vert ii gemellys in barr sylver.The gemellys may not be callyd berulettes for a berulett ys as moche as half a barr').*
Az 2 bars & in chf 2 pales Arg
[?CHURCHMAN]. *ML I 377.*

2 bars & in chf 1 roundel
Or 2 bars in chf roundel Gu
— *FK II 965.*
— *ME 141; LY A 266.*

2 bars & in chf 2 roundels
2 bars in chf 2 roundels
— *Proc Soc Antiq IV 2S 389. (in roundel on sl of Alianor, w of Sir Rog La Warre).*
Sa 2 bars in chf 2 roundels Arg
HUNGERFORD. *XF 455.*

2 bars & in chf 3 roundels
2 bars & in chf 3 roundels
— *Mill Steph. 1433. (?2 bars gemel; qtd 2&3 by Hotoft on brass to Jn H, Treasurer of Household to Hen 6, Knebworth, Herts).*
— *Birch 10055. 1343. (1 of 2 shields in sl of Aundrina de Gayton).*
— *C3 21b. (imp Sa; Stoughton Ch, Hunts on bend Arg 3 conies Sa).*
— *LH 726. (qtd 2&3 by Hungerford).*
BERENGER, Sir Ingelram, Kt. *Wilton 51.* 1332.
COTTINGHAM PRIOR, E Riding Yorks. *Brit Arch Assoc xxvi 214 & pl 12.* early 14 cent. *(on sl of Priory).*
ERCEDECNE, Matilda. *AnstisAsp I 212, 59.* Sigill MATIL LERCE DECNE. 1360-1. *(roundel, 2 others round shield).*
ERCEDEKNE, Matilda. *AnstisAsp I 217, 72.* SIGILLUM MATILDE DE ..... 1360-1. *(?for Moeles).*
GOBAND, John. *Dugd 17, 37.* 1345. *(s&h of Sir Jn G, Ld of Rokeby).*
[HUNGERFORD]. *Arch Journ lxxxiv 382. (imp by Courtenay, mantelpiece, Bps Palace, Exeter).*
HUNGERFORD, Margaret. *Birch 10912.* SIGILLUM MARGARETE DNE DE HUNGERFORD ET DE BOTREAUX. 1462-77. *(imp griffin segr; 1st*

of 2 shields; w of Sir Robt H, 2nd Baron &
dau&h of Wm, Ld Botreaux).

HUNGERFORD, Walter. *Roman PO 5903.* 17
Sept 1423.

HUNGERFORD, Walter, Kt. *Birch 10915.* SIG.-
..HUNGERFORD DOMINI D...BURY DE HO....
1447. *(Ld of Heytesbury & Homet, 1st
Baron, Treasurer of England &c).*

[HUNGERFORD, Sir Walter, of Heytesbury].
Proc Soc Antiq V 2S 177. SIGILLUM OFFICII
MAESCALLIE HOSOICII DOMINI REGIS. *(on sl
attached to transcript of 2 records of
Marshalsea Ct).* c1417.

HUNGERFORD, Walter, Ld of Heytesbury &
Hommet. *PRO-sls.* 1430-1. *(shield betw 2
sickles).*

HUNGERFORD, Walter de, Kt, ?1st Baron.
Birch 10917. ...LL..WALTERI DE HUNGERFORD.
(d1449).

?LATHAM, Richard. *BirmCL-sls 495, 235.*
1504.

MOELS, John de. *PRO-sls.*

MOELS, John de, Ld of Cadbury, Som, 1st
Baron. *Birch 11807.* S IOHIS DE MOLIS.
1301.

MOELS, John de, Ld of North Cadbury.
Barons Letter.

MOLIS, Nicholas de. *PRO-sls.* 13 cent.

MULES, Margaret de. *AnstisAsp I 224, 92.*
SIGILLUM MARGARETE MEOLES. 1347. *(loz).*

PIKOTT, Baldwin. *Vinc 88, 57.* temp Edw 1.
(sl; gt-grandson of Hugh P).

SAUNBI. *PRO-sls.* early 14 cent. *(2 roundels of arms, 1 above shield, other on dex on
sl of Isabell de S on deed of 1390-1).*

SUTTON, William de. *PRO-sls.* late 13 cent.

WAKE. *Mill Steph.* 1466. *(brass, Ingate,
Essex to Mgt, dau of Sir Lewis John or Fit-
zlewes, she m (1) Sir Wm Lucy & (2) ...
Wake).*

WAKE. *Birch 12701.* 1349. *(imp in arms of
Mgt, dau of Jn, Ld Wake & w of Edm Plantagenet, E of Kent).*

WAKE. *WB I 34, 23.*

WAKE. *Birch 3004.* Ceo est le seal labbe e le
covent de Cotingham que vous Thomas Wake singnour
de Lidel avomes founde. 14 cent. *('2 rectangular
flags or shields of arms'; sl of Austin Priory
of Cottingham; Thos, Ld Wake was Founder).*

[WAKE]. *PRO-sls.* 1579-80. *(qtd 9 by Edw
Sutton, Ld Dudley).*

[WAKE, Baldwin de]. *Birch 4264.* 14 cent.
(Founder, sl of Guardian of the Franciscans).

WAKE, Baldwin, d c1282. *Balliol D6, 29,
HB-SND.*

WAKE, Hugh. *Birch 6514.* (obv)SIGILLUM
HUGONIS WAKE; (rev)SIGILL HVGONIS WAKE.
early Hen 3. *(s of Baldewin W, of Haconby,
Lincs; caparisons & shield on equestr sl).*

WAKE, Hugh, of Clifton, Kt. *Birch 14203.*
1359.

WAKE, Hugh, of Clyfton, Kt. *Bow 15.* *(loz).*

WAKE, Roger. *Mill Steph.* 1503. *(brass to
Rog W & w [Eliz Catesby], Blisworth,
Northants).*

WAKE, Thomas. *CombeAsp II 208.* Sigillum
Thome Wake Armigeri.

WAKE, Thomas. *Durham-sls 2547.* 1318.

WAKE, Thomas. *PRO-sls Anc Deeds L 964,
HB-SND.* 1310. *(?Or 2 bars & in chf 3
roundels Gu; used by Jn Wake, f of Thos W).*

WAKE, Thomas, of Blisworth, Northants, Esq.
Birch 14206. SIGILLUM THOME WAKE ARMI-
GERI. 1429.

WAKE, Thomas, Ld of Lidele, 3rd Baron.
Birch 14204. SIGILLUM THOME DNI D'LIDELE.
1317-48.

[WAKE, Sir Thomas, Ld of Lidell]. *Blair N I
20, 42.* *(d1349).* *(beneath battlements of
Bothal Castle).*

WAKE, Thos, Ld of Lavell. *PRO-sls.* 1339-
40. *(Keeper of Tower of London).*

Arg 2 bars & in chf 3 roundels

Arg 2 bars in chf 3 roundels Az
 — *LD 91.* *(qtd 4 by 'Sir Reynald Carnaby in
northumberland Knight').*

CARNABE, Sir Renold. *D5 7.* *(qtg 2&3 Per
pale Gu and Az leopard ramp Or; on canton
Barry Or and Vt bend Gu on chf Or demi-
lion isst Az).*

CARNABY, Mons William. *TJ 1431.* *('... &
trois pelotz dazure amonte').*

HALTON, Mons Robert de. *TJ 541.*

HALTON, Sir Robert. *LH 303.*

KARNABY. *BA 694.*

KARNABY, William de. *WJ 496.*

KERNABY, of Northd. *L1 673, 5.*

WITTISBURY. *XF 176.* *(imp Roos).*

WYTTELBERY. *XPat 258, Arch 69, 89.*

WYTTYSBURY. *BA 487.*

Arg 2 bars Az in chf 3 roundels Gu

Arg 2 bars Az in chf 3 roundels Gu
 — *SHY 457.* *(?Grey imp by ?Calthorpe).*

[GREY OF RUTHEN, Roger de]. *Proc Soc
Antiq XVII 2S 277.* 1290-1330. *(maniple,
Leagram Hall, Lancs).*

Arg 2 bars & in chf 3 roundels Gu &c

Arg 2 bars in chf 3 roundels Gu
 — *CRK 607.*
 — *WB II 49, 15.* *(qtd 2&3 by Ld Bottreff).*
 — *KB 316.* *(qtd 2&3 by Lorde Botreoux).*
 — *CRK 236.* *(qtd 2&3 by Botreaux).*

AUNGEVYN, William de. *SES 32.*

AUNGEVYN, Willimus. *Q II 530.*

BLISSWORTH. *PT 1092.*

COSSINGTON, Stephen. *CA 103. (in error for Johan de Mealos).*

CREKINGHAM. *LY A 232. (cresc Untinc on middle roundel).*

CREKINGHAM. *ME 107.*

KARNABY. *L9 22, 6.*

MARTEL, Sire Will. *HA 20b, 82.*

MARTEL, Sr William. *RB 119.*

MEALOS, Mons John de. *CA 104.*

MELES, Mons de. *AS 349.*

MELES, Mons Roger de. *TJ 542.*

MEOLES. *SP A 118.*

MEULES, Monsire de. *CG 399.*

MEULES, Sr de. *CKO 117.*

MEULES, Mons John. *WJ 975.*

MEULES, Sr Jon. *PO 513.*

MOELES, Nichol de. *B 83.*

[MOELS]. *PV 75.*

[MOELS]. *OxfRS I 22.*

MOELS, Rog de. *Q 153.*

MOLES, Nicholas de. *MP II 75. ('sed quod iii tortelli superius'; above shield of Wm Mauduit).*

MOLES, Roger de. *E 89.*

MOLES, Roger de. *XF 784. (or Wake).*

MOLES, Rogg de. *LM 96.*

MOLEZ, Sir John. *BR V 82.*

MORLENS, Sir Roger. *PCL I 460.*

MORLES. *Gerard 14.*

MOULES. *L2 345, 2.*

MOULES. *L2 347, 6.*

MOULES, Sire Johan de. *N 91. ('...a ii fesses de goules').*

MOULES, Sire Johan de. *J 44.*

MOYLES, Sr John de. *H 63b. ('...iii turteus de gulez').*

MULES, Johan de. *H 63a. ('...trois tourteaux de goules').*

MULES, Sire Johan de. *PV 27.*

MULES, Mons John de. *SD 82. ('... 3 torteux...de goules').*

WAKE. *BA 541.*

WAKE. *CB 117.*

WAKE. *L1 686, 4. (cresc Or on 2nd bar).*

WAKE. *SK 160.*

WAKE, Wylyam, of Northants. *RH, Ancestor v 178.*

WELLE, Mons Robert de. *WJ 924.*

WELLES, Sr de. *CKO 117. (Welles written over Sr de Meules in 16 cent hand).*

Arg 2 bars in chf 3 roundels Sa
— *LH 50. (qtd 2&3 by Sir Thos Hungerford).*

Az 2 bars & in chf 3 roundels
Az 2 bars in chf 3 roundels Arg
HUNGERFORD, Mons Walter. *TJ 566.*

Az 2 bars Arg in chf 3 roundels Or
PYCOTT. *L2 411, 5.*

Az 2 bars Gu (sic) in chf 3 roundels Arg
HOTOFT. *CRK 1848.*

Az 2 bars in chf 3 roundels Or
COLEUILLE, Sire Rob of Blakan. *PO 429.*

DODYTON, Monsr de. *AS 345. (?Pigot, de Dodington).*

PICOT. *L1 513, 4.*

PICOT. *L9 100a, 7.*

PICOT, Monsire John, de Dodington. *CG 397.*

PIGOT, Sr Bawdewyne. *PT 995.*

PIGOT, of Doditon. *XF 892.*

PIGOT, Mons John, de Dodington. *TJ 497.*

PIGOTE. *PCL I 555.*

PYCOT, Sire Baudewyne. *N 704.*

PYCOT, de Dodyton. *BA 521.*

PYCOT, Sr Johan, de Dodington. *CKO 115.*

PYGOT, Mons John, of Doditon. *WJ 818.*

WAKE. *CV-BM 41.*

WAKE. *WLN 827.*

WAKE. *F 457.*

WAKE, M. *WNR 62.*

Gu 2 bars & in chf 3 roundels
Gu 2 bars in chf 3 roundels Arg
— *SK 304.*

EKERYNGE, Mons Rich de. *WJ 618.*

GOBAUD, Sr. *CKO 114.*

MOULES, Sr John de. *CKO 114. (written over Sr Gobaud in 16 cent hand).*

OTTEBY. *L9 90a, 1.*

OTTEBY. *L1 486, 5.*

OTTEBY. *XF 863.*

OTTEBY, Sire Randolf de. *N 693.*

WAKE, Sire Huge, le oncle. *N 703.*

WAKE, Sir Hugh, le oncle. *PT 994.*

Gu 2 bars in chf 3 roundels Or
— *D4 29b. (subqtd 4 by Nevill, E of Westmld).*

GOBAND. *XF 891.*

GOBAND, of Lincs. *L2 231, 11.*

GOBANDE. *BA 517.*

GOBANDE, Mons. *AS 348.*

GOBAUD, Monsire. *CG 396.*

GOBAUD, Johan. *LM 400.*

GOBAUD, Sire Johan. *N 652.*

[GOBAUD, Johannes]. *Q II 495. (names of nos 494 & 495 have been interchanged).*

GOBAUDE, Mons le. *TJ 494.*

GOUBAD, Les Armes. *WJ 550. ('Idem p' Sr Robt Luttrell' added by later hand).*

LOTEREL, Robts. *Q 512.*

LOTERELL, Robert. *SES 25.*

WAKE, Baron. *CK a 53.*

[WAKE]. *Nichols Leics III 1051. (Swithland Ch).*

WAKE, Hue. *D 249a.*

Or 2 bars & in chf 3 roundels

Or 2 bars Gu in chf 3 roundels Untinc
  WAKE, Hugh. *MP IV 50. (d1241 in Holy Land)*.

Or 2 bars in chf 3 roundels Gu
  — *Nichols Leics II 262. (window, Melton Mowbray Ch)*.
  — *E6. (subqtd by Nevill, E of Westmld)*.
  — *PLN 1964. (qtd VI 2&3 by Qtly Az and Gu)*.
  HARCCOURT, S Jeh de. *GA 82*.
  HARCCOURT, Sir John. *LH 217*.
  WAC, Baldwinus. *PE II 8*.
  WAC, Bawdewyn. *FW 102*.
  WAK. *WB II 51, 15*.
  WAK, Badewyn. *HE 79*.
  WAK, Bawldwyn. *ME 85; LY A 210*.
  WAK, Sr Hugh de. *CKO 113*.
  WAK, Sir John. *BR IV 100*.
  WAK, the Lorde. *CT 18*.
  WAKE. *FK I 79. (mullet Arg on 1st roundel; qtd 2&3 by Holand)*.
  WAKE. *WLN 234*.
  WAKE. *SM 329, 57*.
  WAKE. *PO 18*.
  WAKE, Ld. *FK I 145*.
  WAKE, Ld. *BW 11b, 72*.
  WAKE, Ld. *AY 46. (qtd 2&3 by Ld Botreaux)*.
  WAKE, Ld. *WB I 37, 16*.
  WAKE, L. *CRK 1296*.
  WAKE, Le S de. *WJ 581*.
  WAKE, Le Sr. *WB I 32, 2*.
  WAKE, Le Sr. *NB 83*.
  WAKE, M. *WNR 77*.
  WAKE, Monsire de. *CG 395*.
  WAKE, le. *SP A 46*.
  WAKE, le Sire de. *TJ 493*.
  WAKE, le Sr de. *CN 70*.
  [WAKE]. *Nichols Leics II 252. (Melton Mowbray Ch)*.
  [WAKE]. *Neale & Brayley. 1296. (Canopy of Mont to Edm, E of Lancaster)*.
  WAKE, Baldeuuinus. *PE I 9*.
  WAKE, Baldwin. *XF 774*.
  WAKE, Sir Baldwin, of Bucks. *LH 644*.
  WAKE, Baudewin. *A 83*.
  WAKE, Baudewyn. *D 107a*.
  WAKE, Munsire Baudewyn. *D 107b. ('...od treis pelotes de gules')*.
  WAKE, Bawdwin. *E 61*.
  WAKE, Sire Huge. *N 702. (baston Az)*.
  WAKE, Hugh. *B 51*.
  WAKE, Hugh le. *P 77. ('dor ove deux fesses de goules ove troys torteaux de goules en le chief')*.
  WAKE, Joan. *Q 37*.
  WAKE, Johan. *LM 57*.
  WAKE, Johan. *G 55*.
  WAKE, Johan de. *H 25a. ('dor a deus fesses de goules od troys tourteaux de gules en le chef')*.
  WAKE, Sire Johan. *N 16*.
  WAKE, John, Ld. *LMS 41. (d1304, or his s Thomas d1349)*.
  WAKE, Sr John. *BR V 8*.
  WAKE, Sr John. *J 18*.
  WAKE, Sr John de. *H 25b. ('... or iii tortous en le chef')*.
  WAKE, Le Seignr. *AS 33*.
  WAKE, Thomas. *BA 495*.
  WAKE, Thomas, Ld. *Sandford 102 & 110. (d1349, m Blanche of Lancaster)*.
  WAKE, Thomas, Ld of Lydel, Cumb. *Sandford 218*.

Purp 2 bars & in chf 3 roundels

Purp 2 bars in chf 3 roundels Arg
  OTTEBY, of Lincs. *L2 393, 4*.

Sa 2 bars & in chf 3 roundels

Sa 2 bars in chf 3 roundels Arg
  — *BA 820. (qtd 2&3 by Robt, Ld Hungerford)*.
  — *BA 844. (qtd 2 by Sir Thos Hungerford)*.
  — *PLN 1504*.
  — *WK 305. (qtd 2 by Sir George Hastynges)*.
  — *I2(1904)188. (qtd 2 by 'The Lorde Hastyngges')*.
  — *WB I 22b, 1. (qtd 2 by Hungerford)*.
  — *WK 522. (qtd 2&3 by Hungerford, of Dauntsey, Wilts)*.
  — *WB II 56, 9. (qtd 2 by Sir Walter Hungerford)*.
  — *BR VI 41. (marshalled by Ld Moleynes)*.
  FITZJOHN, Lincs. *L2 195, 4. (marginal note: Hungreford)*.
  HONGEFORD, 'Mons Wauter, S de'. *BB 148, 10. (d1449)*.
  HONGERFORD. *WB II 60, 3*.
  HUNGARFORTH, Ld. *KB 326*.
  HUNGERFORD. *BA 462*.
  HUNGERFORD. *LH 29. (qrs 1&4)*.
  HUNGERFORD. *Batt. (in Mere & other Chs in Wilts)*.
  HUNGERFORD. *LH 826*.
  HUNGERFORD. *WK 179*.
  HUNGERFORD. *PT 654. (qtd 2&3 by Per pale indent Gu and Vt chev Or)*.
  HUNGERFORD. *CRK 243*.
  HUNGERFORD. *PT 653*.
  HUNGERFORD, Baron of. *L2 240, 10*.
  HUNGERFORD, Ld. *BA 819. (qrs 1&4)*.
  HUNGERFORD, Ld. *BR VI 40*.
  HUNGERFORD, Ld. *PLN 147*.
  HUNGERFORD, Mons. *AS 506*.
  [HUNGERFORD]. *WB I 16, 4*.

HUNGERFORD, Sir Edw. *L10 100, 9. (qrs 1&4).*

HUNGERFORD, Sir Edward. *BA 469. (qtg Per pale indent Gu and Vt chev Or; imp Childe).*

HUNGERFORD, Sir John. *I2(1904)176.*

HUNGERFORD, Sir John, of Down Amney. *BA 864. (mullet Arg in fess pt; imp Blont, of Mangersfield).*

HUNGERFORD, Robert, Ld of. *GutchWdU. c1460. (qtg 2 Hussey 3 Peverell, all imp Botreux). (qtd 2 Hussey, 3 Peverell, all imp Botreux; window, Old Hall, University Coll).*

HUNGERFORD, Sir Walter. *LH 305.*

HUNGERFORD, Sir Walter. *ML I 57 & 62.*

HUNGERFORD, Sir Walter. *PLN 2019. (qtg 2&3 Arg lion Sa a&l Gu border Az).*

HUNGERFORD, Sir Walter. *ML II 54.*

HUNGERFORD, Sir Walter, KG. *Leake. (d1449).*

HUNGERFORD, Sir Walter, Kt 1485. *WB V 87.*

HUNGERFORD, Walter de, KG. *GutchWdU. c1420. (qtg 2&3 per pale indent Vt and Gu chev Or; garter encircling arms; window, Old Hall, University Coll).*

HUNGERFORD, Walter, 1st Ld. *WGA 250.*

HUNGERFORD, Mons Water. *T b 57. (qtg 2&3 Per pale indent Gu and Vt chev Or).*

HUNGERFORD, Sir Water. *WK 17.*

HUNGERFORDE, Sir ?G. *WB I 38, 4. (cresc Arg in fess pt).*

HUNGREFORD, Ld. *BW 11, 65.*

HUNGREFORDE, Sir Edmonde. *BW 19b, 134. (cresc Arg in fess pt).*

HUNGYRFORDE, Ld. *AY 75.*

JOHAN, Sire Adam le fiz. *N 654.*

JOHN, Mons Adam fitz. *TJ 556.*

REPINGHALE, Johan de. *HE 220.*

Sa 2 bars Or in chf 3 roundels Arg
— *CB 161. (only 1 roundel in qr 2; qtd 2&3 by Ramsay).*
ABEL, John. *TJ 495.*

Sa 2 bars in chf 3 roundels Or
— *SK 207 & 209. (qtd 2&3 by Ramsey).*
— *CB 159.*

2 bars in chf 3 roundels patterned or charged

2 bars in chf 3 roundels each ch with 3 ?leopards' heads
WALEDENE, R. *PRO-sls.* temp Edw 3. *(s of Humphrey de W).*

2 bars modified in chf 3 roundels

Arg 2 bars emb-counteremb in chf 3 roundels Sa
BERNES. *L10 29, 14.*
BERNES. *BA 783.*
BERNES, of Cambs. *L9 29b, 6.*

Sa 2 bars engr in chf 3 roundels Arg
HUNGERFORD. *LH 827.*
HUNGREFORD, Baron. *L1 299, 2. (?or Fitzjohn).*

2 bars & in chf wreath &c

2 bars in chf 3 wreaths
BASSET, Wm. *Durham-sls 167.* 1310.

Arg 2 bars Az in chf 3 chaplets of roses Gu
BASSET. *L2 92, 12.*
BASSET. *L2 87, 6.*
BASSET, S Ric. *PO 581.*
BASSET, Willa. *Q 359.*
BASSET, Sire Willame. *N 1068.*

2 bars in chf ... & label

2 bars in chf lion pg label of 5
BURNEBY, Eustace. *Bk of Sls 245.* 1427. *(s of George B).*

2 bars in dex chf mullet over all label
TWYFORD, John de. *PRO-sls.* 1338-9.

Or 2 bars in chf 3 roundels Gu label Az
MELES, M de. *WNR 141.*

Sa 2 bars in chf 3 roundels Arg label of 5 Untinc
HUNGERFORD, Sir R. *WB I 38, 3.*

Sa 2 bars in chf 3 roundels Arg label Gu
HUNGERFORD, Sir Edward. *XK 137.*
HUNGERFORD, Ld Moleyns. *CRK 1303. (qr 1).*

Sa 2 bars in chf 3 roundels Arg label of 5 Gu
— *BR VI 41. (marshalled by Ld Moleynes).*
HUNGREFORD, Sir R. *BW 19b, 133.*

2 bars & over all beast

Arg 2 bars Az lion Gu
WALTON. *L1 681, 1. (armed Az).*

Arg 2 bars Az lion Gu crowned Or
WILMSCOTE. *XL 489. (a&l Or).*

Az 2 bars Gu lion Or
ALDEHAM. *WB I 18b, 5. (langued Arg).*

Az 2 bars Or lion Gu
HATTELYFF, Lincs. *L2 271, 6.*

Or 2 bars Az lion Gu crowned Arg
[?OXBURGH]. *Farrer II 375. (window, Blakeney Ch, Norf).*

Or 2 bars Sa lion Gu
WALTON. *SK 531.*
WALTON. *XF 270.*
WALTON. *XL 469.*

2 bars & over all bend

2 bars & bend
— *Brit Arch Assoc NS xxiii 8.* ?14 cent. *(qtd 3 by 2 lions passt; mont, S wall of Seaton Ch, Rutl).*
— *YMerch-sls.* 1359 & 62. *(2nd of 3*

shields on sl used by Wm, s of Jn de Newton
& by Ric de Kirkeby).
ASCHTON, Robert de. *PRO-sls.* 1371-2.
(baston).
ASSHEDON, Robert de. *Birch 6953.* Sigill
Roberti.d.asshedon. 1381-2.
ASTON, Robert de. *PRO-sls AS 303.* Sigill.-
..Aschedon. 1381-2. *(baston).*
BATH, Peter of. *Heneage 566.* SIGILLUM
PETRI DE BAA. 1332. *(sl attached to grt by
Robt de Pykeryng, Chaplain, of land in
Twyverton (Twerton, Som), Peter of Bath is
not a witness).*
BOYS, Roger. *PRO-sls.* .OGERI DE BOYS.
1384. *(baston).*
BRAUNDESTON, Hugh de, Ld of Lapmouth.
PRO-sls E40 A7642. ...HUGONIS DE BR....
1359-60.
DANYERS, Thomas. *Ormerod I 473. (roun-
dels round shield; sl).*
HOLSTENE, William. *PRO-sls E40 A2751.*
1403-4. *(baston).*
LYE, Robert. *PRO-sls E40 A4578.* 1374-5.
(bendlet).
NEWBURN, Roger of. *Morpeth 24, HB-SND.*
1363.
SKYPWYTH, William de, of Lincs. *Birch
13509.* SIGILLUM WI... DE SKIPWYTH. 1355.
VENABLES, Alexander. *Bow XXVI 11a.*
1348-9.

2 bars & bend sin

2 bars & bend sin
HARCOURT, William de. *PRO-sls.* 1368-9.
(baston).

Arg 2 bars & bend

Arg 2 bars & bend Az
MONTFORT. *L1 426, 4; L2 323, 10.*
Arg 2 bars Gu bend Az
MARTYDALE. *PT 1246. (baston).*
MARTYNDALE. *L1 433, 2; L2 333, 9.*
Arg 2 bars Gu bend Sa
MILLTONE, Rob de. *Q 454. (baston).*
Arg 2 bars Sa bend Gu
— *PLN 1453. (baston).*
ASCHETON, Mons Robert de. *WJ 940.*
ASHTON, Sir Robert. *CVK 764. (baston;
Constable of Dover Castle).*
ASSHTON, Monsire Robert de. *AN 168. (bas-
ton).*
LINDE. *XF 128.*
LYND. *L1 404, 5; L2 310, 2.*
LYNDE. *L9 39a, 8. (bendlet).*
LYNDE. *CB 101. (baston).*
LYNDE. *SK 143. (baston).*
Arg 2 bars over all bend sin Sa
— *ML I 12. ('silver ii barres sabyll wit a
bastron of the same. This is called a baston*

and every bastard shall ber hys faders armys
wit this over and none but bastardes').

Az 2 bars & bend

Az 2 bars Arg bend Gu
— *CRK 1965. (baston; qtd 2&3 by Legh, of
Both).*
— *BA 4. (qtd 2 by Jn Lee, of the Bothes).*
LEE, John de, de Bothes. *CVC 522. (bas-
ton).*
LEGH. *L1 408, 2.*
[LEGH]. *PCL II 51.*
[LEGH]. *PCL II 50. (baston).*
LEGH, de Bothes. *L9 38b, 11. (bendlet).*
LEGH, of Bothes. *XF 295.*
LEGH, de Boths. *DV 49a, 1922. (baston).*
LEGH, John de, of Bothes. *WLN 650. (bas-
ton).*
LEIGH OF BOOTH. *CRK 625. (baston).*

Or 2 bars & bend

Or 2 bars Gu bend Arg
MONTFORD. *XF 843.*
MOUNTEFORD. *CC 227b, 186. (baston).*
MOUNTEFORD. *L9 72a, 3.*
Or 2 bars Gu bend Az
— *WK 772. (qtd 3 by George Catesby).*
— *LH 381. (qtd 3 by Catesby).*
— *L2 138, 11. (baston; qtd 3 by Catesby).*
— *I2(1904)225. (qtd 3 by Catysbe).*
— *Arch lvi 334. 15 cent. (qtd 2&3 by
[Norreys]; window, Ackwells Manor, Berks
imp qtly [Clitherow & Oldcastle]).*
— *L10 37, 7. (qtd 3 by Catesby).*
— *PLN 1274. (qrs 2&3 of coat imp by Sir
Wm Norreys).*
BRANNDESTON, Hugo de. *Q 484.*
BRAUNDESTON, Hugo de. *Q II 662.*
BRAUNDESTONE, Hugo. *SES 98. (baston).*
[?WAKE]. *WB I 36, 8. (baston).*
WAKE, of Kent. *L1 697, 2.*
Or 2 bars & bend Gu
PALMER, T. *CRK 1935.*
Or 2 bars Gu bend Sa
— *WK 297. (riband; qtd 2&3 by Sir Jn
Philpott).*
WAKE, of Kent. *MY 226.*

Field patterned 2 bars & bend

Erm 2 bars & bend Untinc
DELAVAL, Hugh. *Durham-sls 781.* 1287.

2 bars patterned & bend

Gu 2 bars Erm bend Az
WROKESHALL, Gefferey de. *FW 277. (baston).*

2 bars & bend checky
Az 2 bars Arg bend checky Arg and Gu
    LEIGHE, Mons Thomas de. *WJ 527.*
Az 2 bars Arg bend checky Or and Gu
    LEEGH, Mons William de. *TJ 1430.*

2 bars & bend gobony
Az 2 bars Arg bend gobony Gu and Or
    LEGHE, de Bothes. *CVC 557.*
Az 2 bars Arg bend gobony Or and Gu
    LEE, Sir Robert de, of Adlington. *CVC 577.*
    (gobony of 4).
    LEE, Sir Robert de, de Adlynton. *PCL II 33.*
    (baston).
    LEGH. *L1 408, 1; L2 304, 8.*
    LEGH, of Adlington. *CRK 173. (baston).*
    LEGH, de Adlyngton. *L9 38b, 12.*
    LEGH, de Adlynton. *DV 49a, 1923.*
    LEGH, Sr de Both, Ches. *CY a 11, 44. (bas-ton).*
    LEGH, of the Bouthes. *BA 41, 405.*
Az 2 bars Arg bend countergobony Or and Gu
    — *WB I 36, 11. (qtd 3 by Chykerlye).*
    LEE, of Cumberland. *PT 1258.*
    LEGH. *XF 294.*
    LEGH, of Adlington. *XF 296.*
    LEYGH, of Isel, Cumb. *L9 38b, 5.*
    LEYGH, of Isell, Cumb. *LE 418.*
    LYEGH, William. *LY A 89.*

2 bars modified & bend
2 bars wavy & bend
    DAMORI, Roger. *PRO-sls.* 1315-16. *(?Vair & baston).*
Arg 2 bars nebuly Sa bend Gu
    LEKEBORNE, Robts de. *Q 551.*
Az 2 bars dancetty Or bend Gu
    RYVERE, Mons Rich de la. *WJ 983.*
Sa 2 bars wavy Or bend Erm
    ILSTED, K. *KB 76.*
Erm 2 bars wavy Gu bend gobony Or and Az
    WIDCOMBE, of Widcombe in Martock.
    Gerard 128.

2 bars bend & label
2 bars over all bend & label
    LEGH, Robert. *PRO-sls AS 185.* SIGILLU ROBERTI LEGH. 1374-5. *(used by Thos de Hawkeston, s of Thos de H, Kt).*
    LEGH, Robert de. *PRO-sls E40 A6535, 12153.* SIGILLU ROBERTI DE LEGH. 1374-5. *(used by Geoffrey del Donnes, & Jas, s of Thos de Bagglesham).*

2 bars & on bend
Arg 2 bars Az on bend Gu 3 arrows Arg
    VENABLES, Mons Richard. *S 411.*
Az 2 bars Arg on bend Gu 3 arrows Arg
    DAWNE. *L10 54, 6.*
    DAWNE, John, of Ches. *CY a 29, 113. (bendwise pts down).*
    DONE, Sir John, of Utkington. *PT 986.*
    DOWNE. *CRK 627. (pts down).*
    DOWNE. *SK 1004. (pts down).*
    DOWNE. *LE 220. (pts down).*
    DOWNE, John. *CVC 524. (pts down).*

2 bars & on bend cresc
Az 2 bars Arg bend countergobony Gu and Or in dex chf cresc Or
    LEE. *WB I 20b, 1.*
Az 2 bars Arg on bend Gu 3 crescs Or
    — *WB I 35b, 15.*
    LEGH. *L9 38a, 6.*
    LEGH. *XF 293.*
    LEGH. *RB 265.*
    LEGH. *LE 368.*
    LEGH. *CC 224b, 94.*
    LEGH. *XO 57.*
    LEGH, John A. *PLN 1543.*
Arg 2 bars wavy Gu on bend Sa 3 crescs Or
    GOLLOFFYR, Tomas, Oxfords. *RH, Ancestor iv 250.*
Arg 2 bars wavy on bend Sa 3 crescs Untinc
    GARGRAVE. *RH, Ancestor iv 250. (added in margin by later hand).*

2 bars & on bend foils
Arg 2 bars on bend Gu 3 3foils Arg
    PALMER. *L1 504, 2.*
    PALMER. *XF 702.*
    PALMER. *FK 906.*
Arg 2 bars on bend Gu 3 3foils Sa
    PALMERE. *FK II 906.*
    PALMERE. *FK II 907. (each 3foil ch with annulet Arg).*
Or 2 bars on bend Gu 3 3foils Sa
    PALMER, Thomas. *PLN 544.*
    PALMER, Thomas, of Holt. *WB IV 179b, 969.*
Or 2 bars Gu on bend Sa 5 5foils Arg
    MAPULTON. *L9 52b, 3.*
Or 2 bars Gu on bend Sa 5 pd 5foils Arg
    MAPLETON. *XF 250.*

2 bars & on bend head &c
Arg 2 bars wavy Gu on bend Sa 3 boars' heads couped Arg
    PURCELL. *PLN 538. (qtg 2&3 Arg 3 bends Az on canton Sa lion passt Arg).*
Gu 2 bars wavy Arg on bend Sa 3 boars' heads couped Arg
    PURSELL. *PLN 1558. (3 bars in qr 4; qtg 2&3 bendy of 8 Arg and Az on canton Sa*

lion passt Or).

Az 2 bars Arg on bend Gu 3 pheons Arg
  LEGH. *L1 402, 6; L2 304, 5.*
  LEGH. *L9 40b, 5.*
  LEGH. *XF 297.*
  LEGHE. *SK 678. ('of Betchington, Cestrie'*
  added by later hand).
Arg 2 bars wavy Gu on bend Sa 3 roundels Arg
  — *WB IV 158b, 594. (qr 3 of coat imp by*
  Mantell).
Gu 2 bars wavy Arg on bend Sa 3 roundels Arg
  — *RL 33b, 1. (?Golofre).*

2 bars & over all bird &c

2 bars 2head eagle
  SPEKE, Sir Geo. *Mill Steph. 1528. (eagle ch*
  on breast with annulet; 2nd s of Jn S; brass,
  Dowlish Wake, Som).
Arg 2 bars Az 2head eagle Gu
  — *DIG 41. (qtd by Butler).*
  SPEKE. *XF 468.*
  SPEKE, Sir John. *PLN 2047. (b&l Or).*
  SPEKE, Sir John. *WK 196.*
  SPEKE, Sir John. *L10 96b, 9.*
Arg 2 bars Az 2head eagle Or
  SPEKE, of Whitelackington. *Gerard 140.*
Or 2 bars Az 2head eagle Gu
  — *WB I 16b, 3. (qtd 6 by [Wadham], of*
  West Devon).
  — *WB I 20b, 7.*

2 bars & over all cresc &c

Arg 2 bars Gu 3 crescs Sa
  WATERTON. *XF 168.*
Erm 2 bars 3 crescs Untinc
  [WATERTON]. *Mill Steph. 1538. (qtd 4 by*
  Dymoke & imp by Coffyn on brass to Sir Wm
  C, Standon, Herts).
Erm 2 bars wavy Sa over all crozier in bend Or
  MISSENDEN MONASTERY. *L10 66b, 24.*

2 bars & over all escarbuncle

2 bars & escarb
  BLOUNT, John of Button, Gloucs. *Heneage.*
  1410.
Arg 2 bars Az escarb Gu
  BLONT, of Mangersfield. *BA 864. (escarb ch*
  with roundel Or & another on each of the 8
  rays; imp by Sir Jn Hungerford, of Down
  Amney).
  BLOUNT, of Mangersfield, Gloucs. *XF 411.*
  (escarb ch with roundel Or).
  BLOUNT, Mgt, of Mangersfield. *LH 835.*
  (imp by Sir Jn Hungerford).
Arg 2 bars Az escarb Or garn Gu
  BLOUT, Edmund. *PLN 1788.*

2 bars & over all escutch

2 bars escutch
  HARYETE, Henry de. *PRO-sls. 1389-90.*
Az 2 bars Or escutch Arg
  MORTIMER, Roger de, C of March. *BD 152b.*
  (all that is visible of surcoat; 2nd window, St
  George's Ch, Stamford, Lincs).
Erm 2 bars Gu 3 escutchs Or
  HALL. *L1 318, 1; L2 243, 1.*
  HALL, Pyersse of. *RH, Ancestor vii 189.*
  (?false escutchs).

2 bars & over all pile

Gu 2 bars Or pile counterch
  ALFREYD, Kynd. *L2 20, 3.*
  ELFRIDE, K of England. *BA 897. (pile nar-*
  row).
  ELFRIDE, K in England. *L1 221, 1; L2 169,*
  4.
  ELFRIDUS, Rx. *DV 45a, 1769.*
  ELFRIDUS, K of Britain. *LE 9.*
Or 2 bars Sa pile counterch
  — *SK 601.*
  ENGHAM, William. *CRK 982.*
  ENGHM. *L2 183, 8.*

2 bars & over all saltire

Arg 2 bars wavy Gu over all salt Or
  MALBANKE. *CRK 1186.*

2 bars & over all ... & ...

Arg 2 bars Gu over all 2 serpents palewise undu-
  lant & respecting each other Vt in centre chf
  pd 5foil Gu
  REFFUGE, of France. *L2 428, 5.*

2 bars on chief ... & over all

Arg 2 bars wavy Az over all on chev Sa 3
  martlets Or on chf Gu lion passt betw 2
  anchors Or
  FORMAN. *WB I 14b, 24.*

2 bars in chief ... & over all

2 bars in chf billets & over all bend
  LODELOWE, Robert de, of Norf & Suff. *Birch*
  11357. SIGILLUM ROBERTI DE LO[DE]LOWE.
  1386.
2 bars in chf 3 roundels over all bend
  THRECKINGHAM, Sir Walter. *Lawrance 43.*
  (dc1331; effigy, Threckingham, Lincs).
Untinc 2 bars & in chf 3 roundels Untinc over
  all bend Az
  — *SHY 51. (imp by ?Dills).*
Arg 2 bars & in chf 3 roundels Gu over all bend
  Az
  CREKINGHAM. *XF· 70. (baston).*

CREKYNGHM. *BA 514. (baston).*
Arg 2 bars & in chf 3 roundels Gu over all bend Sa
    CHRIKINGHAM, S Wat de. *R 125. (baston).*
    CREKYNGHAM. *L1 162, 1; L2 118, 3.*
    CREKYNGHAM. *L10 39b, 4. (baston).*
    THREKINGHAM, Sr de. *CKO 118. (baston).*
    TREKINGHAM, Monsire de. *CG 400.*
    TREKYNGHAM, Mons John de. *TJ 496. (baston).*
Or 2 bars & in chf 3 roundles Gu over all bend Untinc
    WAKE, Hue. *LM 162. (baston).*
Or 2 bars & in chf 3 roundels Gu over all bend Arg
    WAKE, Mons Bawdewyn. *WJ 584. (baston).*
Or 2 bars & in chf 3 roundels Gu over all bend Az
    [THREKYN]GHAM, Sr de. *CKO 119. (baston).*
    WAKE, Mons Bawdewyn. *WJ 584. (baston).*
    WAKE, Sir Hugh. *PT 993. (baston).*
    WAKE, Mons T de, of Wynterburne, Yorks. *WJ 583. (baston).*

2 bars in chf ... & over all canton
Arg 2 bars & in chf pale Gu on canton Sa boar's head couped Arg
    PAKEMAN. *L1 520, 6.*
    PAKEMAN. *XF 814.*
    PAKMAN. *L9 102b, 6.*
Arg 2 bars & in chf 3 roundels Az on canton barry Or and Vt baston Gu & isst in chf demi-lion Sa
    CARNABY, Sir Reynald, Kt, of Northd. *LD 91. (qr 1).*

2 bars in chf ... & over all head
Or 2 bars Az over all horse's head erased betw 3 roundels Untinc each roundel ch with an escallop Gu in chf rose Gu betw 2 leopards faces Az
    CLERKE. *XV II 46.*

2 bars chief & over all escutch (e.g. Mortimer): see Barry &c chief paly

2 bars betw
2 bars betw 3 annulets
    ALDINGTON, Henry de. *Goring 249.* 1373.
    [ALDRINGTON]. *Spokes. (qtd 4 by [Waring] & imp by Fettiplace). (qtd 4 by [Waring] & imp by Fettiplace on brass to Wm F, d1528, Childrey Ch, Berks).*
    [RICKHILL]. *Mill Steph.* 1516. *(qtd 4 by Waring on brasses to Wm Fetiplace & w Eliz W, Childrey, Berks).*
    RYKHILL, William. *Birch 13190.* SIGILLUM WILLELMI RYKHILL. 14 cent.

    RYKHULL, William. *PRO-sls.* 1397-8.
Gu 2 bars betw 3 annulets Arg
    RUCKHYLL. *DV 66a, 2610.*
    RYKHYLL. *L1 562, 6.*
Gu 2 bars betw 3 annulets Or
    — *GutchWdU.* c1520. *(qtd 2&3 by [Waryng] & imp by Will Fetteplace (d1529), of Childrey, Berks; Queen's Coll Hall).*
Gu 2 bars Sa betw 3 annulets Arg
    REKELL, Wyllm, of Kent. *MY 199.*
    ROKELYS. *PLN 851.*
    RUKHILL. *PT 803.*

2 bars betw 3 barrulets &c
Az 2 bars betw 3 barrulets Arg
    — *ML I 292.* ('Azure ii barrys departyd & enclosed wit iii closettes sylver. If ther were iiii closettes so that every barr were enclosyd wit ii say he beryth asur ii barrys both severally enclosyd wit as many closettes sylver').
Az 2 bars wavy betw 3 barrulets wavy Arg
    HAVEREYNGDOON, Dominus de. *LO A 39.*
Sa 2 bars betw 3 ?hounds passt Arg
    PADINGTON, Emond, of Essex. *WB III 106b, 5.*

2 bars betw birds
2 bars betw 3 martlets
    ROTHING, S Johis de. *Var Coll vii 327.* 13 Sept 1359. *(3, 2, 1; grant by Wm Straunge to Jn, Rector of Fransham Parva).*
Gu 2 bars Or voided Sa betw 3 owls Arg
    REKELL, William. *Kent Gentry 217b.*
Gu 2 bars Sa betw 3 owls Arg
    REKETT, William, of Kent. *WB III 110, 5.*
Az 2 bars wavy betw 3 swans Arg
    SHIRLEY. *L1 607, 6.*

2 bars betw 6 birds
2 bars betw 6 birds 3, 2, 1
    FOULDON, Simon de. *NorfHo 1, 42.* 1377. *(sl on deed by Simon de F, chaplain, & his fellows re land in Bernham Riskes).*
2 bars betw 6 martlets
    — *Var Coll vii 316.* ..TRIS...ERTI ABBIS DE HAM.... 24 Jan 1317. *(3, 2, 1; shield on sin of full length figure of Abbot with crozier & book in left hand dex shield missing).*
    PAYNEL, Thomas, Kt. *Selborne 84.* Sigill' Thome Paynel. 1311. *(equestr sl).*
Arg 2 bars Az betw 6 martlets Gu
    — *FK II 972. (3, 2, 1).*
Arg 2 bars Vt betw 6 martlets Gu
    MORE, of Wydeford. *XF 89. (3, 3).*
Gu 2 bars betw 6 martlets Arg
    CHALONS, Mons Robert. *BG 52. (3, 2, 1).*

Gu 2 bars betw 6 martlets Or
    ELAND, Sr de. *CKO 582.* *(3, 2, 1).*
Or 2 bars Az betw 6 martlets Gu
    PAYNEL, Sire Will. *HA 4, 12.* *(3, 2, 1).*
    PAYNEL, Sr William. *RB 16.*

2 bars & 8 or more (or orle of) birds
2 bars & orle of martlets
    ELAND, John de, of Wrenthorpe, Yorks, Kt.
    Birch 9439. S IOHIS DE ELAND. 1350. *(3, 2,*
    2, 1).
    PAYNEL, John. *Dugd 17, 77.* 1300.
    PAYNEL, John, Lord of Otley. *Barons Letter.*
    PAYNEL, John, Ld of Otteleye, (?1st Baron).
    Birch 12421. S IOHIS PAYNEL. 1301.
    PAYNEL, William, Ld of Fracyngton. *Birch*
    12422. SIGILLUM WILLELMI PAYNEL. 1303-
    17.
    PAYNEL, William, Ld of Fracynton. *Barons*
    Letter.
2 bars betw 8 martlets
    ELAND, Sir John de. *Yorks Arch Journ xii*
    247. 1326. *(3, 2, 3; sl).*
    ELANDE, John. *PRO-sls.*
    KUC, John, Ld of. *PRO-sls.* late 13 cent.
    (3, 2, 3; on shield & trapper of equestr
    figure).
2 bars betw 9 martlets
    ATMORE, Henry & his w Johanna. *Burrows*
    408. John at More. 1311. *(4, 2, 3).*
2 bars betw 10 birds 4, 3, 2, 1
    — *PRO-sls.* S RICHART P?ONEL. 1387-8.
    (Richard P?onel; used by Edw Swift).

Arg 2 bars Az & orle of birds
Arg 2 bars betw 8 martlets Az
    PAYNEL, Jan. *Q 261.* *(3, 2, 3).*
Arg 2 bars Az orle of martlets Gu
    PAINEL, Hugo. *F 243.*
    PAINELL, William. *E 189.*
    PAINELL, William. *F 409.*
    PAYNEL. *L9 96a, 10.*
    PAYNEL, Willem. *FW 299.* *('...orle of 6*
    martlets gules').
    PAYNEL, William. *TJ 545.* *('.. a merlotz de*
    goules devis la bordure').
    PAYNEL, William. *WLN 505.*
    PAYNEL, William de. *XF 924.*
    PAYNELL, William. *A 125.*
Arg 2 bars Az betw 8 martlets Gu
    PAYNEL, Thos. *Q 259.* *(3, 2, 3).*
    PAYNELLE, Robertus. *Q II 235.* *(3, 2, 3).*

Arg 2 bars Gu & orle of birds
Arg 2 bars Gu orle of martlets Az
    — *FK II 922.*
Arg 2 bars & orle of martlets Gu
    CHALLONS. *WGB 102, 1.*
    CHALONS, Sir Robert. *CRK 1524.* *(qrs*

1&4).
    HOLOND, Sire Huwe. *PO 427.*

Arg 2 bars Sa & orle of birds
Arg 2 bars Sa orle of martlets Gu
    PAYNEL. *L1 529, 4.*
    PAYNEL, Sire Willame. *N 226.* *('de argent a*
    ii barres de sable a les merelos de goules en
    la manere de bordure assis').
    PAYNEL, Willeme. *LM 250.*
    PAYNELL. *FK II 687.*
    PAYNELL, Mons William. *WJ 832.*
Arg 2 bars Sa betw 8 martlets Gu
    PAYNEL, Willam. *Q 258.* *(3, 2, 3).*

Arg 2 bars Vt & orle of birds
Arg 2 bars Vt betw 9 martlets Gu
    MORE. *L9 72b, 7.* *(3, 3, 3).*
    MORE, Hants. *L1 459, 4; L2 342, 1.*
Arg 2 bars betw 9 martlets Vt
    AYLEWARD, Rychard. *RH, Ancestor vii 213.*

Az 2 bars & orle of birds
Az 2 bars Or orle of martlets Gu
    BURDET, Monsire Roger. *CG 230.*

Gu 2 bars & orle of birds
Gu 2 bars & orle of martlets Arg
    CHALONDE. *L1 178, 6.*
    CHALONS. *XF 895.* *(qrs 1&4).*
    CHALONS. *XF 732.*
    CHALONS. *L10 40, 2.*
    CHALOUNS. *CB 158.*
    CHALOUNS. *SK 206.* *(qtg Beauchampe).*
    CHALOUNS. *SK 205.*
    CHALOURS, Sir Robt, of Devon. *WB III 73,*
    3. *(qtg 2&3 Gu...).*
    CHALOUYS, Sir Robt. *WB IV 138b, 228.* *(qrs*
    1&4).
    ELAND, J. *CRK 666.*
    ELAND, Robt, of Lincs. *WB III 104, 3.*
    ELAND, Thomas de. *S 523.*
    EYLANDE. *LE 98.* *(?8 martlets).*
Gu 2 bars betw 8 martlets Arg
    [CHALLONS, of Devon]. *PLN 1468.* *(3, 2, 3;*
    qtg 2&3 Vair [Beauchamp]).
    CHALONS. *L10 45b, 9.* *(qrs 1&4; 3, 2, 3).*
    EYLAND. *L1 229, 6; L2 173, 11.*
Gu 2 bars betw 9 martlets Arg
    — *D4 43b.* *(3, 3, 3; qtd by Savell, of Yorks).*
    AYLAND. *PCL I 575.* *(3, 3, 3).*
    CHALOND, Sir John. *L2 108, 9.* *(3, 3, 3).*
    CHALONS. *BA 1103.* *(4, 2, 2, 1).*
    CHALONS, Devon. *L1 132, 4.*
    SMETHELAY. *WB I 33, 14.* *(orle of martlets).*
    SMETHELEY. *PLN 1316.* *(4, 2, 3).*
    SMETHELEY. *WB I 19, 11.* *(4, 2, 2, 1).*

Gu 2 bars & orle of martlets Or
  BLANDE, Mons John. *TJ 501.*

Or 2 bars & orle of birds

Or 2 bars Untinc orle of martlets Gu
  PAYNEL, Thom. *LM 232.*
Or 2 bars Az orle of martlets Gu
  PAINEL, S Thomas. *GA 166.*
  PAINELL, Thomas. *E 203.*
  PAYNEL. *L1 529, 3.*
  PAYNEL, Sire Thomas. *N 225. ('...a les merelos de goules').*
  PAYNEL, Thomas. *TJ 1273.*
  PAYNEL, Thomas. *TJ 546. ('.. ove merlotz de goules dewis la bordure').*
  PAYNEL, Thomas. *FW 300.*
  PAYNEL, Thomas. *XF 933.*
  PAYNEL, Sire Willame. *HA 12. (6 martlets).*
  PAYNELL. *L9 96a, 2.*
  [PAYNELL]. *Nichols Leics III 116. (window in Woodhouse Chapel).*
  PAYNELL, Hugh. *WLN 459.*
  PAYNELL, Thomas. *G 187. (8 martlets).*
  PAYNELL, Thomas. *A 126.*
Or 2 bars Az orle of martlets Sa
  — *FK II 900.*

2 bars betw chev &c

Sa 2 bars each ensigned by chev Or
  LISLE, Lord John. *BD 158. (?Or fess betw 2 chevs; shield in Garter; E window, St George's Ch, Stanford, Lincs).*
2 bars betw 3 crescs
  HOLEWELL, Lady Johanna de, wid of Sir Walter de H, of Herts. *Birch 10781. ...DNE IOHE D.... 1342. (sin of 2 shields, dex destroyed).*
Or 2 bars betw 3 crescs Gu
  — *CRK 618. (bars narrow). (bars narrow; qtd 2&3 by Davy, of Kent).*
  WODELL, William. *CRK 617. (bars narrow).*
2 bars betw in chf 2 crosslets & in base letter R betw 2 mullets
  MAY, S Reginaldi le. *SarumM-sls. c1280. (from matrix in Nelson's collection).*
Az 2 bars betw 8 crosslets 3, 3, 2 Or
  BLAKENGHAM. *L1 68, 2.*
Az 2 bars betw 9 crosslets 3, 3, 3 Or
  BLAKENGHAM. *L2 70, 6.*
Gu 2 bars Vair betw 7 crosses 3, 3, 1 Or
  MORTIM(er), Willam de. *Q 309.*
Gu 2 bars Vair betw 8 couped crosses 4, 3, 1 Or
  MORTIMER, Willimus de. *Q II 321.*
Or 2 bars Az betw 3 crowns 2 in chf 1 in base Gu
  GENEWELL. *L2 234, 1.*

2 bars betw escallops &c

Or 2 bars & orle of 6 escallops Gu
  HELPISTO', Joan de. *PE II 14.*
Or 2 bars & orle of 8 escallops Gu
  HELPISTONE, Johannis de. *PE I 15.*
2 bars nebuly betw 6 estoiles 3, 2, 1
  CLODSHALE, Richard, Esq. *Dugd 17, 39.* 1423.
Sa 2 bars nebuly Arg betw 5 estoiles 3, 1, 1 Or
  — *WB IV 185b, 1080. (qtd 3 by Sir Water Ardern).*
Sa 2 bars nebuly Arg betw 7 estoiles 3, 3, 1 Or
  — *WB IV 185b, 1080. (qtd 2 by Sir Water Ardern).*
Sa 2 bars nebuly Arg and Az betw 7 estoiles 3, 3, 1 Or
  — *PLN 691. (qtd by Sir Wm Arden).*
Sa 2 bars of clouds Ppr betw 7 estoiles 3, 3, 1 Or
  — *PLN 691. ('2 viores fessways Arg'). (qtd 2&3 by Sir Walter Arden).*

2 bars betw fleurs de lis &c

2 bars betw 6 fleurs de lis
  DAVELL, William. *Blair N I 47, 92. (qtg 2&3 Arg chev betw 3 martlets Gu; lis 2&2). (merchant of Newcastle, d 18 Feb 1521). (qtg 2&3 Arg chev betw 3 martlets Gu; merchant of Newcastle, d 18 Feb 1521; ledger stone, St Nicholas Cathedral, Newcastle).*
2 bars betw 5 'burrs' 3 in chf & 2 in base
  BURTON, Thomas of. *Durham-sls 494.* 1334.
2 bars betw 9 4foils 4, 2, 2, 1
  DUNMERE, Richard de. *Birch 9367.* SIGILLU RICARDI DONMERE. 1323. *(s of Jn de D, of Som, Kt).*
Gu crusily Arg 2 bars betw 6 leopards' heads Or
  HARALDE, Kynge. *RH, Ancestor ix 167.*
Gu semy of couped crosses Or 2 bars Az fimbr Or betw 6 leopards' faces 2, 2, 2 Or
  HARROLDE, K. *KB 223. (of Britain).*
Gu crusily Or 2 bars Az fimbr Or betw 6 leopards' faces Or
  HAROLD, K. *LH 724.*
Gu 2 bars betw 6 leopards' faces Or
  — *ME 104; LY A 229.*
  HARAULDE, King. *WJ 808. (3, 2, 1).*
  HAROLD, King. *XF 313. (leopards' faces 2, 2, 2).*
Gu 2 bars & orle of 6 leopards' heads couped Or
  HAROLD, le Roy. *FW 19. ('...heads gold cut off at the neck').*

2 bars betw insects &c

Arg 2 bars betw 3 bees Sa
  FLEMING. *CC 235b, 443.*
Arg 2 bars betw 3 butterflies volant Sa
  FLEMYNGES. *L1 255, 6; L2 199, 3.*

Arg 2 bars betw 6 voided lozs 3, 2, 1 Sa
  BARNES, Joh. *L10 111, 4. (alias Baron).*
Sa 2 bars Arg betw 2 mullets in chf & in base
  annulet Or
  SPILMAN. *PLN 425.*
Arg 2 bars betw 3 mullets Az
  ESSELYNGTON, Mons John de. *TJ 522.*
  ('port dargent ii barres dazure iii molets
  dazure - drawn in chf').
2 bars betw 3 pd mullets & letter W
  ERLHAM, John de. *PRO-sls.* 1393-4.
Sa 2 bars betw in chf 2 pallets & in base escal-
  lop Arg
  CHERCHEMAN. *L10 37b, 10.*
  CHURCHMAN. *XF 229.*
  CHURCHMAN. *CRK 906.*

2 bars betw roundels
Arg 2 bars Sa betw 3 roundels Gu
  — *L9 106a, 12. (qtd 2&3 by Parker).*
  PARKER. *BA 573.*
  PARKER, Sir James. *XF 601. (qrs 1&4).*
  PARKER, Sir James, Knyght. *WK 585. (qrs*
  1&4; cresc Sa in centre of qrs).
  PERKER. *XPat 168, Arch 69, 81.*
Or 2 bars Sa betw 3 roundels Gu
  PARKER, John. *BA 21b, 179.*
2 bars betw 6 ?roundels
  PENNE, John de la. *PRO-sls.* 13 cent.

2 bars betw ... & canton &c
Gu 2 bars wavy Arg betw 6 roundels 2, 3, 1 Gu
  [sic] on canton Az stag's head couped at
  neck Or
  HALYS, Mastyr. *PLN 620.*
Gu 2 bars wavy Arg betw 6 roundels 2, 3, 1 Or
  on canton Az stag's head couped at neck Or
  HALYS. *WB IV 182, 1009.*
Untinc 2 bars Vt betw 3 chevs Untinc chf Vt
  DALLE, of Wychy.... *SHY 300.*
2 bars betw 6 crosses 2, 3, 1 in centre chf letter
  I
  BURES, Adam de. *PRO-sls E40 A11640.*
  S'AD DE BURES DE. 1385.

2 bars betw ... & over all
2 bars & bend sin betw in chf chessrook & in
  base annulet
  — *PRO-sls E40 A6255.* 1406-7. *(?Wm*
  Bowes, Jn Chirche, or another).
Arg 2 bars betw 3 roundels Gu baston Sa
  CREKYNGHAM, Mons Wauter de. *AS 437.*
  (?or Trekingham).
  THURKINGHAM, Sire Wauter de. *O 75.*
  ('dargent ove ii barres et iii pelotes de gules
  ove i bastoun de sable').

2 bars in border
2 bars & border
  GRIMBAUD, Robt, Ld of Houghton, Northants.
  Birch 6080. S'ROBERTI GRIMBAUT. 1280.
  (equestr sl).
Arg 2 bars Az border Sa
  PAR, Sir Thomas Kt. *Bellasis ii 49; Whitaker*
  ii 327. (on figure of Kt in armour kneeling
  with his lady, on lady's figure is qtly 1&4
  Green 2&3 Maplethorpe; d 11 Nov 1517;
  tomb, Kendal).
Arg 2 bars Gu border Sa
  GIBTHORPE. *CRK 1819.*
  GIBTHORPE. *XF 13.*
  GYBTHORP. *L1 284, 2; L2 223, 7.*
  GYBTHORP. *SK 805.*
Arg 2 bars & border Sa
  RODELEY. *WK 777. (qtd 2&3 by Bourgoyn).*

2 bars in patterned border
Gu 2 bars & border Erm
  DABRICHECOURT. *?source.*
Erm 2 bars Untinc border ?Erm
  [STOKKE]. *Birch 4078. (sl of All Saints*
  Almshouse, alias Browne's Hosp, Stamford;
  name pencilled in margin).
Arg 2 bars Az in border Gu 8 apples (stalks
  upwards) Or
  POMYS. *XF 815.*
  POMYS. *L9 102b, 11.*
2 bars & border roundelly
  — *Blair D II 204, 425.* 13 cent. *(effigy of*
  Kt, Whitworth Churchyard, Durham).
  WHITWORTH, Sir Thomas. *Lawrance 49. (fl*
  1315, or his father). (Effigy, Whitworth,
  Durham).
Erm 2 bars & border roundelly Untinc
  STAMFORD, Hospital of. *HB-SND.*

2 bars in border engrailed
2 bars & border engr
  — *WB I 33, 21. (qtd 2 by Parre).*
  HETHE, Robert de, of Surr. *Birch 10669.*
  ...NDE...US. 1380.
  PAR, William de, Kt. *Birch 12380.*
  S'WILLELMI DE PAR MILITIS. 15 cent.
Arg 2 bars Az border engr Sa
  — *L9 92b, 1. (qtd 2&3 by Pare).*
  — *WK 467. (qtd 2&3 by Sir Thos Par).*
  — *XK 105. (qtd 2&3 by Sir Thos Parr, Kt,*
  1509).
  — *XK 157. (qtd 2 by Sir Wm Parr).*
  — *BA 643. (qtd 2&3 by Sir Wm Par).*
  — *WGA 264. (qtd 2&3 by Sir Wm of*
  Parre).
  — *Sandford 490. (qtd 2 by Q Catherine*
  Parr).
  HALSAL, Sir Gilbert. *CVL 339.*
  PARRE, William, KG. *Leake. (d1571; 10*

other qtgs).

Arg 2 bars Gu border engr Sa
  COTTESFORD. *CB 92.*
  KETTESED. *XF 286.*
  KETTESSED. *L9 22, 7.*
  SUTTON, Sir Benet de. *CVC 498.*
  SUTTON, Sr Benet de, Staffs. *CY a 101, 404.*
Arg 2 bars Sa border engr Gu
  WYVILE, William de. *XF 385.*
  ZEYLONDE, Willm de. *WLN 710.*
Arg 2 bars Sa border engr Or
  — *Suff HN 1. (Braintree Ch).*
  CROMWELL. *L10 46, 10.*
  CROWELL, Thomas, of Herts. *WB III 114, 2.*
  WIVILE, William de. *E I 495; E II 497.*
Per pale 2 bars & border engr
  — *WB I 20b, 21. (qtd by Parr).*
Az crusily & 2 bars Or border engr Gu
  BAR, S Jehan de. *GA 41.*
  BARE, Mons John de. *TJ 523.*

2 bars in border otherwise modified
Arg 2 bars Sa border indent Gu
  LONDE, William del. *TJ 547. ('vel engrelee').*

2 bars border & label
Arg 2 bars & border Sa label of 5 Gu
  — *LM 224.*

2 bars canton & border
Az 2 bars & canton Gu border indent Or
  CORBET, Robert. *CA 216. (?field Arg).*

2 bars & in chief ... in border
2 bars & in chf 3 birds border
  NEVILLE, William de. *Birch 12163.* SIGIL-
  LUM WILLELMI...NEWIL'. 13 cent. *(?martlets; s of Hugh de N, of Lincs).*
2 bars & in chf 3 mullets of 6 pts border engr
  ESSELYNGTON, Thomas de. *Vinc 88, 66.*
  THOMAS.... 1383. *(bro of Robt de E, Kt; sl).*
Arg 2 bars & in chf 3 mullets & border Sa
  BOSARD, Sire Hugh. *O 212.*
Arg 2 bars & in chf 2 roundels Gu border indent
Sa
  WAKE, Thomas. *CA 122.*
2 bars & in chf 3 roundels border engr
  WAKE, Thomas, of Bliseworth, Northants, Kt.
  Birch 14205. 1354.
  WAKÉ, Thomas of Blisworth, Kt. *Bk of Sls 206. 1354.*
Arg 2 bars & in chf 3 roundels Gu border engr
Az
  — *BG 214.*

Arg 2 bars & in chf 3 roundels Gu border engr
Sa
  WAKE. *CB 118.*
  WAKE, de Bleseworth. *BA 542.*
  WAKE, de Bleseworthe. *SK 161.*
  WAKE, de Blisworth. *CKO 116.*
  WAKE, S Thom. *PO 332.*
  WAKE, Mons Thom del. *WJ 923.*
  WAKE, Monsire Thomas, de Blisworth. *CG 398.*
  WAKE, Monsire Thomas, de Bliseworthe. *AN 208. ('...engrailed...').*
  WAKE, Mons Thomas, de Blisworth. *SD 53. ('iii torteux en le cheif ove un bordure engrale de sable').*
  WAKE, Sire Thomas, de Blithesworthe. *O 34. ('iii pelotz de gules').*
  WAKE, Mons Thomas, de Blyseworth. *TJ 498. ('...une bordour recercelee de sable').*
Arg 2 bars Gu in chf 3 roundels & border engr
Sa
  WAKE, Mons Thomas de Depynge. *TJ 499. ('...bordour recercele de sable').*
Arg 2 bars & in chf 3 roundels & border engr Sa
  ALBARTON. *L2 20, 11.*
  ALLERTON. *BA 535.*
  ALLERTON. *L10 5b, 2.*
  ATHERTON. *CC 235b, 444.*
Arg 2 bars & in chf 3 roundels Gu border indent
Sa
  WAKE, Thos, de Bluseworth. *CA 123.*

2 bars betw ... in border
Arg 2 bars betw 3 martlets Gu border engr Sa
  WARDE, John. *Hutton 87.*
Arg 2 bars Sa orle of martlets Gu border Az
  PAYNEL. *XF 872.*
  PAYNEL. *L9 96a, 3.*

On 2 bars
Or 2 bars Sa on 1st bar annulet Untinc
  PEUER, Sir Philip. *BR V 175.*
Or 2 bars Sa on 1st bar annulet Arg
  PENERE. *L1 515, 4.*
2 bars each ch with 3 lions
  HAY, Matilde de la, d1484. *Nichols Leics I 314. (brass formerly in St Mary de Castro).*
Or 2 bars Gu each ch with 3 lions Arg
  — *XF 43.*

On 2 bars birds
Or 2 bars Gu on 1st bar martlet Or
  — *FK II 1013.*
On 2 bars 3 martlets
  — *C2 16. (Streatham Ch, Surr).*

Arg on 2 bars Gu 3 martlets 2, 1 Or
   WARDE. *DV 59b, 2349.*
   WARDE. *PT 67.*
   WARDE, Monsire John. *AN 259.*
Az 2 bars Or on 1st bar 3 martlets Gu
   BORDET, Leics. *L2 88, 8.*
   BURDET, Sire Robert. *N 813. ds BS Arg on
   2 bars Gu 4 martlets 2, 2 Or*
Az 2 bars Or on 1st bar 3 martlets Gu
   WARD. *CRK 1948.*
   WARD. *L1 670, 4.*
Az on 2 bars Or 5 martlets 3, 2 ?Gu
   WRIAELEYE, Pers. *F 113.*

On 2 bars 6 birds
Arg on 2 bars Gu 6 martlets 3, 3 Or
   BURDET, Sir Thomas, of Irld. *WB III 121, 1.*
Arg on 2 bars Sa 6 martlets Or
   TEMPLE, Nicholas, d1551. *Nichols Leics IV
   931. (Shepey Magna Ch).*
Az on 2 bars Arg 6 martlets 3, 3 Gu
   BURDET, Sr Roger. *CKO 331.*
   CRANEBURA. *L10 40b, 18.*
   CRANEBURY, Mons Willm de. *WJ 526.*
   VIGOROUS. *FK II 837.*
Az on 2 bars Or 6 martlets 3, 3 Az
   BURDET, Sir Oliver. *PLN 1812.*
Az on 2 bars Or 6 martlets 3, 3 Gu
   — *WK 541. (qtd 4 by Humphrey Stafford).*
   BORDYT, Mons Roger. *AS 455.*
   BURDEIT, Robt. *WLN 882.*
   BURDET, Syr John, de Bromcot, Warw,
   d1528. *I2(1904)94. (qtg 2 Az lion passt Arg,
   3 Gu fess Or betw 6 martlets Arg).*
   [BURDET]. *Nichols Leics II 570. (Galby Ch).*
   BURDET, Mons John. *S 291.*
   BURDET, Sir John. *XF 726. (qrs 1&4).*
   BURDET, Roberd. *LM 510.*
   BURDET, Robt. *Q 325.*
   BURDETT. *XK 281. (qrs 1&4).*
   BURDETT. *L10 82b, 5.*
   BURDETT, of Bromcot. *L1 89, 3; L2 65, 8.*
   BURDEYT, Mons Roger. *TJ 536. ('dazure a
   deux barres d'or vi merlotz de goules en les
   barres').*
   WRIALLEY, Piers. *WLN 405.*

On 2 bars bougets
On 2 bars 3 bougets
   WHELOBE, Hew. *WB I 20, 16.*
   WILLOUGHBY, Dorothy. *Mill Steph. 1507.
   (dau of Sir Hy W & [1st] w of [Sir] Anth Fitz-
   zherbert; imp by F on brass, Middleton,
   Warws).*
   WILLOUGHBY, Hugh. *Mill Steph. 1513. (&
   w Anne Wentworth; brass, Wilne, Derbys).*
   WILLOUGHBY, Richard, Judge in Assizes,
   Warwicks. *Dugd 17, 7.* Sigillum Rici de Wil-
   lughby. 1334-5.

WILLOUGHBY, Richard de, Kt, jun. *Bow LIX
12.* S Ricardi de Willoughby. *1352-3. (grant of
manor of Engleby).*
WILLOUGHBY, Richd. *Mill Steph. 1471. (&
w Anne [Leck]; brass, Wollaton, Notts).*
Arg on 2 bars Gu 3 bougets Arg
   WYLLYRGHBY, Syr Henry. *I2(1904)92.*
Or on 2 bars 3 bougets Arg
   WYLOUGHBY, of Notts. *D4 23.*
Or on 2 bars Gu 3 bougets Arg
   — *PO 276. ('S Ric de...', original surname
   erased & above is written in Elizabethan
   hand 'Wylowghby').*
   WILLOUGHBY. *DerbysAS XIV 90. (imp on
   tomb of Jn Shelley at Shelley).*
   WILLOUGHBY. *WK 542. (cresc Az).*
   WILLOUGHBY. *XF 458.*
   WILLOUGHBY. *L1 677, 6.*
   WILLOUGHBY. *FK II 640.*
   WILLOUGHBY, Edmond. *S 320.*
   WILLOUGHBY, Sir Hugh. *BD 86. (3rd S win-
   dow of hall, York Palace, Southwell).*
   WILLOUGHBY, Sir Hugh, of Notts. *CRK
   1265.*
   WILOUGHBY, Sir Henry. *WK 211.*
   WYLLOWGBY, Yorks. *MY 243.*
   WYLOGHBY, Richard de. *CKO 583.*
   WYLOWBY, Sir Harry. *WK 74.*
Or on 2 bars Gu 4 bougets 2, 2 Arg
   WILLOUGHBY, of Derbys. *PLN 1385.*
   WYLLUGOB. *WB I 33, 8.*

On 2 bars combs
Erm on 2 bars Sa 3 combs Arg
   LUCAS, Willimus. *Q II 708.*
   LUCAS, Wm. *SES 140.*

2 bars upper ch with cresc
Arg 2 bars Arg (sic) on 1st cresc Az
   MANWARYNG, John, of Peover. *BA 41, 406.*
Arg 2 bars Gu on 1st cresc Or
   MANWARING, Sir John. *XK 235. (qrs 1&4).*
Arg 2 bars Sa on 1st cresc Arg
   — *FK II 370.*
   BRERETON, Sir Randolfe. *BA 3b.*
Gu 2 bars Arg on 1st cresc Az
   MAINWARING, of Ichtfeld. *BA 42, 413.*

On 2 bars crosses
Arg 2 bars Az each ch with 2 crosses formy Or
   DENE, Sr J de. *CKO 584.*
2 bars each ch with 3 crosslets
   DANDELEIGH, Sir Philip. *Lawrance 13.* ante
   1350. *(Effigy at St Mary Bourne, Hants).*
Arg 2 bars Gu each ch with 3 crosses botonny
Or
   DAUNDELEIGH. *DV 59b, 2346.*

Arg 2 bars Gu each ch with 3 crosslets Or
 DAUNDELEGH. *CRK 343.*
 DAUNDELEGH, Mons Philip. *TJ 530.*
 DAUNDELEGH, Mons Philip de. *WJ 926.*
 DAUNDELEGH, Philip. *TJ 1307. ('... a deux barres de goules & vi croiselets dor en lez barres').*
 DAUNDELEIGH. *PT 64.*
 DAUNDELEIGH. *CRK 1949.*
 DAVID. *L10 54, 11.*
Arg 2 bars Sa each ch with 3 crosslets Or
 DEN, of Hunts. *L2 156, 8.*
 DEN, Jan de. *Q 328. (blazon unclear, ?plain crosses).*
Arg 2 bars Sa each ch with 3 crosses formy Or
 DEEN, Johan de. *LM 173.*
 GUNDELL. *CC 233, 357.*
 OUNDLE. *XF 851.*
 OWNDEL. *L1 482, 3; L2 393, 8.*
 OWONDELL. *L9 88b, 1.*

On 2 bars escallops &c

Arg 2 bars Sa each ch with 2 escallops Arg
 FLOTE. *L1 241, 1; L2 200, 1.*
Arg on 2 bars Sa 5 escallops 3, 2 Or
 FLETE. *CRK 60.*
Arg on 2 bars Sa 6 escallops 3, 3 Arg
 — *PLN 1637.*
 FLEET. *XF 678.*
 FLETE. *FK II 524.*
Arg on 2 bars Az 3 5foils Arg
 WELEGBY. *L1 687, 1.*
 WILLOUGHBY. *XF 60.*
Arg on 2 bars Az 3 5foils Az
 WYLEGHBY, Monsr Richard de. *AS 383.*
Arg on 2 bars Az 3 5foils Or
 WILUGHBY, Mons Richard de. *TJ 508.*
Arg on 2 bars Az 6 5foils 3, 3 Gu
 WYLEGHBY, Mons Richard de. *TJ 1015. (5foils painted Gu but blazoned 'dor' which seems an addition in later hand).*
Arg on 2 bars Az 6 5foils 3, 3 Or
 WYLEGHBY, Mons Richard de. *TJ 1016.*

On 2 bars heads &c

Sa on 2 bars Or lion's head couped Gu
 — *XF 148. (imp Bokenham).*
Arg on 2 bars Az 3 lions' heads erased Or
 HARPUR, of Bambery. *WB IV 154, 505. (qrs 1&4).*
Erm on 2 bars Sa 10 holly leaves 5, 5 Or
 ELMES. *L2 181, 11.*
Arg on 2 bars Gu 3 lozs Arg
 — *ML I 259. ('Sylver iii losenges in triangule of the same upon ii barrys goules. Or Sylver ii barres goules iii losenges of the feld upon the same. If the losenges touchyd both the feld and the barres though shuldyst say upon both').*

Sa 2 bars Arg on 1st wyvern isst wings expanded Sa
 [MANFELD, Simon]. *PLN 1320. (1st bar blazoned 'sovereign' bar).*

On 2 bars mullet

2 bars on 1st bar mullet
 LATOUR, William de. *Arch Journ (Norwich 1847) xlvii.* SIGILLU WILLI DE LATOUR. c1370. *(brass sl matrix).*
Or 2 bars Sa on 1st bar mullet Arg
 PEVER. *XF 799.*
 PEVERE. *L9 100b, 10.*
Erm 2 bars Az on 1st bar mullet Gu
 VALE, Mons William de. *WJ 840b.*
Erm 2 bars Az on 1st bar mullet Or
 VALE, Mons William de. *WJ 840.*

On 2 bars 3, 4 or 5 mullets

Arg on 2 bars Gu 3 mullets Arg
 MAYN WARON. *WB IV 150, 436.*
Arg on 2 bars Sa 3 mullets Or
 HOPTON. *L1 305, 5. (mullets missing in trick).*
Arg on 2 bars Sa 5 mullets Or
 HOPTONE. *PT 1192.*

On 2 bars 6 mullets or more

On 2 bars 6 mullets 3, 3
 HOPTON, Nicholas de. *Yorks Deeds III 88.* 1393.
2 bars on each 3 pd mullets
 FILDYNG, William, of Lutterworth. *PRO-sls.* 1396-7. *(on shield betw letters I & H).*
Arg 2 bars Gu on each 3 mullets Arg
 [?MAINWARING]. *CRK 1427.*
Arg 2 bars Sa on each 3 pd mullets Or
 HOPTON. *BA 689.*
 HOPTON. *LH 848.*
 HOPTON, Robert. *TJ 1388.*
 HOPTON, Robert. *LH 339.*
Erm 2 bars on each 3 mullets Untinc
 — *SHY 15. (qtd 4 by Hopton, imp by ...).*
Erm 2 bars Gu on each 3 mullets Or
 BAVANT, Walter. *TJ 554.*
 BAVANT, Walter. *TJ 1169. ('... & sys moletz dor en lez barres').*
Erm 2 bars Sa on each 3 mullets Arg
 HOPTON. *LH 9. (qr 1).*
Erm 2 bars Sa on each 3 mullets Or
 — *LH 65. (qtd 4 by Hopton).*
 HOPTON. *L2 270, 3.*
 HOPTON. *Suff HN 23. (imp by Swillington; Blythburgh Ch).*
Erm 2 bars Sa on each 3 pd mullets Or
 HOPTON. *XF 655. (qr 1).*
 HOPTON. *WK 835.*
 HOPTON. *LH 938. (qr 1).*
 HOPTON, Sir Arthur. *XK 206. (qr 1).*

HOPTON, Mayster. *I2(1904)231. (qr 1).*
Arg gutty & 2 bars Sa on each 3 pd mullets Arg
— *SHY 78. (qtd 4 by Hopptun).*

On 2 bars roundel &c
Gu 2 bars Arg on 1st bar roundel Or
   CHALON. *CC 225b, 114.*
   CHALON. *RB 229.*
Arg 2 bars Gu on each 3 roundels Or
   MARTYN. *Q II 374.*
Gu 2 bars Arg on each 3 roundels Sa
   FOXLEY. *BA 802.*
Arg on 2 bars Gu 9 roundels 5, 4 Or
   WELLE, de. *BA 570.*
Arg 2 bars Gu semy of roundels Or
   WELLE, Rob de. *B 53.*
On 2 bars 3 chaplets
   [GREYSTOCK]. *PRO-sls.* 26 Nov 1527. *(qtd 2 by Wm, Ld Dacre).*

On 2 bars & label
Arg 2 bars Gu on each 3 roundels Or label of 5 Az
   MARTYN, S Water. *Q 380. (surname added later).*
Arg 2 bars Gu on each 3 roundels Or label Or
   — *PLN 1880.*

On 2 bars & in base
Untinc 2 bars Untinc on 1st bar 2 ?Erm spots betw 2 mullets on 2nd bar mullet betw 2 ?martlets & in base salt ensigned with cross Untinc
   BLANSEILE, Robert, burgess of Aberdeen. *Stevenson.* 1478. *(or Blynsele or Blenshiell).*

On 2 bars & canton
Arg 2 bars Gu on 1st bar rose Or on canton Gu cross moline Or
   KIRKBY. *CRK 570.*
Arg 2 bars engr Gu on 1st bar 2 martlets & on 2nd bar 3 escallops Or on canton Az dex hand bendwise appaumy Arg
   TOLL, Christopher, of Cirencester, serjeant at arms. *L10 92, 6.*
Arg 2 bars engr Gu on 1st bar 2 martlets & on 2nd bar 3 escallops Or on canton Az dex hand couped bendwise Arg 4th finger crossed over 3rd
   TOLL, Christopher, of Cirencester, Gloucs. *LS 118.*
Arg 2 bars engr Gu on 1st bar 3 martlets & on 2nd bar 3 escallops Or on canton Az dex hand couped bendwise Arg
   TOLL. *XPat 187, Arch 69, 83.*
   TOLL, Christoffer, seriant at arms. *WK 398.*

Gu on 2 bars Arg 5 voided lozs 2, 3 Gu on canton Or leopard's face Az
   GERY, Willyam. *XF 718.*
Gu on 2 bars Arg 6 voided lozs 3, 3 Gu on canton Or leopard's face Az
   GERY, Willm, de Berkeway. *I2(1904)219. (cresc Or for diffce in fess pt).*
2 bars on each 3 leopards' heads & on canton waxing moon
   SWYDYNGFELD, Tarrimus. *PRO-sls.* 1336-7. *(?leopards' heads or escallops).*
2 bars on 1st bar 5foil on canton wheel of 4 spokes
   KIRKEBY, Robert. *Roman PO 6116.* 14 Dec 1439.

On 2 bars & chief
Arg 2 bars wavy Sa on each 3 roundels Arg on chf Gu gun betw 2 anchors Or
   GONSON. *L1 283, 2; L2 215, 2. (?gun or cannon).*

On 2 bars & in chief
Arg on 2 bars Sa 6 escallops 3, 3 Arg in dex chf annulet Sa
   FLETE. *FK II 525.*
Or on 2 bars Gu 6 3foils 3, 3 Arg in chf greyhound courant Sa
   PALMAR, Thomas. *I2(1904)171.*
   PALMER. *XF 649.*
   PALMER. *L9 104b, 8.*
   PALMER. *XF 652. (cresc Az in fess pt).*
   PALMER. *WK 790.*
   PALMER, of Steyning, Suss. *D13 50.*
2 bars each ch with barrulet in chf 3 estoiles
   MUNDEVILLE, Ralph de, of Durham. *Birch 6827.* S RADULFI D MUNDEVIL. 13 cent.
Gu 2 bars Or on each rose & in chf 3 roses Arg
   DALTON. *LQ 77.*
Gu 2 bars Arg on 1st bar cresc Sa in chf 3 mullets Arg
   — *BG 360.*
Arg on 2 bars Gu 3 martlets Or in chf 3 roundels Gu
   MOILES. *L9 70a, 11.*
On 2 bars betw 4 small birds 6 ?roundels 3, 3
   PAKEMAN, Simon, of Warws & Lincs. *Birch 12349.* ...MONIS PAK.... 1355.
Az on 2 bars Or 4 roundels 2, 2 Gu in chf 3 roundels Or
   — *SP A 106.*

On 2 bars between &c

Gu 2 bars betw 8 martlets 3, 2, 3 on 1st bar
  roundel Or
    CHALONS, Sir Robert. *PLN 227. (qtg 2&3
    Vair [Beauchamp]).*
Arg 2 bars betw 7 fleurs de lis Az on each bar 2
  fleurs de lis Arg
    HAYLARD. *BR IV 65.*
Az 2 bars Untinc betw 3 crosslets ?Sa on each
  bar martlet Untinc & on chf Or an object
  (?pd roundel irrad) betw 2 fleurs de lis Gu
  [?JENKES]. *WB I 24b, 19. (imp by Sir Thos
    Ryche).*

On 2 bars within

Arg 2 bars Gu border engr Sa on dex side of 1st
  bar annulet Untinc
    KOTTISFORDE, Mons Rog de. *WJ 536.
    (annulet ?Arg).*
Or on 2 bars Gu 3 bougets & border Arg
    WILLOUGHBY, Sir R. *SHY 294.*
Arg on 2 bars Az 6 crosses formy 3, 3 Or border
  engr Sa
    OUNDLE, Bucks. *XF 857.*
Arg 2 bars Az border engr Sa mullet Untinc for
  diffce
    PARR, Sir Thomas. *I2(1904)237. (qtg I&II
    2&3 Or 3 bougets Sa, II&III Az 3 chevs
    interlaced & chf Or; father of Q Katherine
    Parr).*

On 2 bars within & in chief

Arg 2 bars Gu on 1st bar 3 pallets Arg in chf 3
  birds & border semy of roundels Untinc
    MARTYN, Willam. *LM 237.*
Arg on 2 bars Gu 6 martlets 3, 3 Or in chf cross
  formy betw 2 fleurs de lis Az border engr Sa
    WARD, Edmund, of Staffs. *XF 640.*
    WARDE, Edmond, of Staffs. *WK 785.*

2 bars cotised

2 bars cotised
    GELDO, Adam de. *PRO-sls. 1312.*
Arg 2 bars cotised Gu
    CARESWALL, Sir Piers de, Notts. *CV-BM
    162.*
    CARYSWALL, of Staffs. *CY a 101, 402.*
    HUNTERCOMBE, Walter. *TJ 517. (blazoned
    Erm 2 bars Gu).*
Erm 2 bars cotised Untinc
    HUNTERCOMBE, Walter de. *BrookeAsp I 19,
    4.*
Erm 2 bars cotised Gu
    HUNTERCOMBE. *TJ 517.*
    HUNTERCOMBE, Walter. *LH 302.*

2 bars cotised & ...

Erm 2 bars cotised & chf Gu
    DYCHANT, Robert. *TJ 550. ('dermyn deux
    barres gemelez & le chief de goules'; bars
    drawn cotised).*
    DYCHANT, Robert. *TJ 549.*

3 BARS

3 bars
    — Stevenson. *1453. (marshalled on 2nd sl
    by Jas, 9th E of Douglas, d 1491).*
    — Durham-sls 918-19. *1322-46. (dex of 4
    shields arranged in cross; used by Simon &
    Rog of Esh).*
    — Birch 7732. S'MABILIE DE BRADESSHAWE.
    1376. (imp by Mabilia de Bradesshawe).
    — PRO-sls. *1354. (qtd by Wm de Garland,
    Ld of Chales).*
    — Birch 3316. *14 cent. (sl of Abbey of St
    Mary, Jervaulx, Yorks).*
    — Birch 2412. *1303. (1 of 2 shields on rev
    of sl of Cathedral Ch of Carlisle, ?of Adam
    de Warwick, the prior).*
    ANDREW, Wm, of Estbury, Glam. *Birch
    6846.* S' Will'i .. Andrew. *1418.*
    ASHWEY, Stephen de. *Bow 10. (1st of 2
    shields; s&h of Mgt).*
    ASK, Conan of. *Bowes 106, HB-SND. 1394.*
    ASKE. *Arch Journ xxv 171. (qtg 2 cross
    engr, 3 fess dancetty [Aughtred], 4 cross, 5
    on chf 3 roundels, 6 on chf bird's head betw
    2 mullets [Hayes]; cresc for diffce over all).
    (on tower, Aughton Ch; inscription: 'Chris-
    tofer le second filz de Robart Ask, Chr, obliar
    ne doyt, 1536').*
    ASKE, Jn of. *Durham-sls 95. 1388.*
    ASKE, Richd of. *Durham-sls 96. 1353.*
    BARETT, Nicholas, clerk. *PRO-sls 15/7.
    1297-8. (imp 3 bars).*
    BENDENGES, Peter de. *PRO-sls AS 109.*
    +S'PETRI DE [BEN]DINGIS. *13 cent.*
    BENDENGES, Peter de. *PRO-sls E40 A14443.*
    S'PET[RI] D. BENDINGES. *13 cent.*
    BENDENGES, Peter de. *PRO-sls. 13 cent.*
    BENDING, Adam de. *Arch Cant v 217-8.*
    SIGILLVM: ADE: DE: BETNEGGIS. *Oct 1225.
    (on deed, Cumbwell Priory charters in Coll
    Arm).*
    BENDING, Peter de. *Arch Cant vi 308, 314.*
    +SIGILL.PETRI.DE.BENDING. *(sls on charters
    dat (a)betw 1206 & 1229 (b)?1237).*
    BERNYNGHAM, Richard de. *PRO-sls. 1323.*
    BUSSY, Sir Hugh de. *Lawrance 9. 1306.
    (Effigy, Hougham, Lincs).*
    BUSSY, John, of Bernardeston & Kedyngton
    Manors, Suff & Essex, Kt. *Birch 7979.*
    +SIGILLUM IO....SSY. *1397.*

CAMERON. *Stevenson.* 1439. *(qtd by Walter Haliburton, Ld of Dirleton & others).*
CAMERON, of Ballegarno. *Stevenson.* 1471. *(qtd by Robt Crichton, of Kinnoul, 1st Ld C of Sanquhar, d 1494-5).*
CAMERON, John, Bp of Glasgow, 1427-46. *Stevenson 112.*
CAMERON, Sir Robert, of Balegrenack, Kt. *Stevenson.* c1296.
CAMERON, Wm, Prior of St Andrews, 1469-82. *Stevenson 98.*
DALLE, Richard. *Selborne 7, 70.* Sigillum Ricardi Da[ll]e. *1375. (?Dawe).*
DENTON, John of. *Dodsworth 45, 102, HB-SND.* 1357.
FECKENHAM, Henricus de, of Kidderminster, Worcs. *Birch 9648.* S' HENRICI .... 1336.
FOREST, Guaston de. *Birch 9868.* S'.-GVASTON.DE.FOREST. *1414. (imp bend cotised; sl used by Jn Philip, of Yundecote, of Exeter, Devon).*
GOCH, Morgan. *PRO-sls.* 1397-8.
HAIG, Peter, Ld of Bemerside. *Stevenson.* c1260.
HAMO, s of Richard. *Bk of Sls 186.* ante 1242-3.
HIDE, Roger de. *PRO-sls.* 13 cent. *(blazon uncertain).*
LEDES, Alexander de. *Yorks Deeds I 196.* 1341.
LUTEREL, Andrew, Ld of Hooton-Pagnel, Yorks. *Birch 11474.* +SIGILL'ANDRE LUTEREL. c1240-50.
LUTTRELL, Sir Andrew. *Arch Journ xxxviii 62. (d1265; sl).*
MANERS, Robt. *Stevenson.* 1388.
?MAUDEYT. *PRO-sls E40 A3, 975.* SIG......ORE . MAUDEYT. *1363. (sl used by Andrew, s&h of Andrew Peverell).*
MAUNDEVILLE, Thomas, Ld of Auescote, Northants. *Birch 11700.* SIGILLUM: THOME: MAUNDEVILLE. 1386.
MULTON, Eliz de. *Birch 7411.* SIGI-LLVM-ELIZ-ABET-DE MV-LTON. *1341. (roundel, 1 of 3 pairs surrounding shield with arms of Bermyngham; w of Walter de B, of Lincs).*
MULTON, Jn de. *PRO-sls.* 13 cent.
MULTON, Thos de. *PRO-sls.* SIGILLUM THOME DE MOULTON. *1301. (shield & trapper).*
MULTON, Thos de, Ld of Egremont, Cumb. *Barons Letter, Ancestor xxxiv.*
PIERRE...nt, John de. *Birch 12636.* SEEL IEHAN DE PIERRE[POI?]NT. *1380. (sl used by Eliz, dau&h of Thos le Breton, of Norf).*
PIPPARD, Joan. *PRO-sls.* 1357.
SELBY. *Mill Steph; Belcher I 77. (brass to Thos, s of Robt S, cit & goldsmith, & w Isoude, dau of Jn Clarke [of Forde in*

Wrotham, Baron of the Exchequer], E Malling, Kent; no shield).*
SPIGURNEL, Ralph. *PRO-sls.* 1360-1.
SPIGURNELL, Dame Elizabeth, Lady of Wigenneure. *PRO-sls.* SIGILLUM ELIZABETHE SPIGURNELL. *1380-1. (dex of 2 shields on sl of Spigurnell).*
SULIE, Sir Remund, of Glam. *Birch 13774.* SIGILL' REMVN DE SVLIE. 1302.
SULLIA, Reimund, of Glam. *Birch 13773.* SIGILL...IMVNDI DE S..LL. *1230. (?field Erm).*
VICCHERCHE, Sir Alan de. *PRO-sls.* S'...NI DE W.... *1218-19. (blazon uncertain; ?Whitchurch).*

Arg 3 bars Az
Arg 3 bars Az
 — E6 25. *(qtd by Aparre).*
ASKE. *BA 1264.*
CYFREWAST. *Nichols Leics III 505. (Wymeswold Ch).*
GREY, Richard de. *B 42.*
MAWRE, John, of Kryke. *BA 21, 177. (qtg 2&3 Az 2 wings ['eylis'] Arg).*

Arg 3 bars Gu
Arg 3 bars Gu
 — CK a 78.
 — XK 79. *(qtd 4 by Radcliffe, Ld Fitzwater, KG temp Hen 8).*
 — XK 95. *(qtd 4 by Robt Radcliffe, Ld Fitzwalter).*
 — WK 681. *(qtd 3 by Sir Ryes Mouncell).*
 — WB I 15, 25. *(qtd 4 by Ratclyffe).*
 — PLN 1840. *(qtd 4 by Ld FitzWalter).*
 — I2(1904)211. *(qtd 3 by Mayster Ratliffe).*
 — I2(1904)212. *(qtd 4 by 'The Lord Fytzwater' [Ratcliffe]).*
 — PLN 1907. *(qtd 2 by Az 5 lozs conjd in fess Or).*
 — CB 433. *(qtd 2&3 by Anthony, Ld de Croy, Count of Porcien).*
 — CB 435. *(qtd 2&3 by Jehan de Croy, Seigneur de Chimay).*
 — WB I 36b, 5. *(qtd 8 by Ric Bolles).*
 — XK 21. *(qtd 4 by Robt Radcliffe, E of Suss).*
ANJOU, Margaret of. *TJ 1. (qr 1 of 6).*
HEULE. *L2 268, 6.*
HOUSE. *L2 241, 5.*
HOUSE. *L1 305, 2. ('Multon' in margin).*
HUNGARY, King of. *RH, Ancestor iii 198. (imp France ancient; ?Ladislas V (1444-57) who m Mgt, dau of Charles 7 of France; however France ancient had ceased for many years to be arms of K of France & note that Hungary is normally barry of 8 Arg and Gu).*
MELTON, Sir Thos. *BR V 61.*
MOLTON. *Leake. (qtd 4 by Robt Radcliffe,*

Baron Egremond, KG, d1542).
MOLTON. *L2 344, 12.*
MOLTON, of Lincs. *L2 347, 4.*
MOLTON, Sir Thomas. *ML I 77.*
MOULES, Wm de. *Q 39.*
MOULTON. *XV I 1217. (imp by Fitzwalter).*
MOULTON. *XF 668.*
MOULTON, le Sire de, de Gillesland. *CG 224.*
MOULTON, of Lincoln. *CRK 90.*
MULTON. *SK 411.*
MULTON. *L9 75a, 6.*
MULTON, le S' de. *WJ 585.*
MULTON, le Sr de. *AS 47.*
MULTON, Sr de, de Gilesland. *CKO 307.*
MULTON, Mons' Rauf, de Egremond. *TJ 504.*
MULTON, Thomas de. *MP IV 38.*
MULTON, Thos de. *LM 133.*
MULTON, Thos de. *K 74.*
MULTON, Thos de. *B 157.*
SOULES, Will' de. *Q II 39.*
SOULES, Wm. (& Multon, both names given). *PCL I 541.*
WALSH. *PLN 1799.*

Arg 3 bars Or &c
Arg 3 bars Or
GRAI, Richard de, of Codnor. *MP II 68. ('album tres fesse auree' [sic for azure], uncoloured).*
Arg 3 bars Sa
ARCULET, Guille. *Berry; Stodart 11.*
BUSCHE, Sir J. *PCL I 565.*
BUSSE. *L10 81b, 7.*
BUSSEBY, Sir Myles, Kt. *I2(1904)75. (qtg 2 Gu fess of 5 lozs Arg border engr Or, 3 Gu fess dancetty Or betw 3 escallops Erm).*
BUSSEY. *L10 83, 10. (qrs 1&4).*
BUSSEY. *SK 788. (qrs 1&4).*
BUSSEY. *L1 97, 2; L2 57, 3.*
BUSSY. *CC 234b, 409.*
BUSSY, Monsr de. *AS 340.*
BUSSY, le Sire de. *CG 235.*
BUSSY, Sire Huge. *N 653.*
BUSSY, Johannes. *Q II 169.*
BUSSY, Mons' John. *TJ 514. ('dargent & trois barrulets sable').*
BUSSY, Monsr John. *S 154.*
BUSSY, Sir John. *S 156.*
BUSSY, Sir Miles. *XF 571.*
BUSSY, Sir Miles. *XF 725. (qrs 1&4).*
BUSSY, Sir Mylys. *WK 432.*
HACCOMBE, Sir Stephen. *LH 188.*
HOGHTON, of Lancs. *CB 71.*
HOURTONE, S' ad'. *PO 255.*
MOIGNE, [Sr] Will. *CKO 317.*
SCHARDLOWE, Mons Willm de. *WJ 933.*
TREUERY. *L1 632, 6.*

Arg 3 bars Vt
FRY. *XF 124.*
FRYS. *L1 244, 1; L2 201, 12.*

Az 3 bars Arg
Az 3 bars Arg
CHAM. *L2 138, 1.*
CHANI, Lucas. *L10 35b, 6.*
CHENEY, Nicolas. *XF 780.*
GREY, of Codnor. *ML I 48.*
PAWNTON. *BG 76.*
TABY, Sir John. *BR V 244.*
TANNE. *CC 222b, 26.*
TANNY, le Seignor de. *WJ 521.*
TANY. *L1 637, 5.*
TANY, Monsire de. *CG 232.*
TANY, Monsr de. *AS 337.*
TANY, Sr de. *CKO 312.*
TANY, Sire Johan. *N 458.*
TANY, Mons' John. *TJ 505.*
TANY, Lucas. *FW 221.*
TANY, Lucas. *CRK 363.*
THANI, Lucas. *E I 66; E II 66.*

Az 3 bars Or
Az 3 bars Or
— *WB I 35, 21. (qtg 2&3 Az fess of 5 lozs Arg).*
— *LO B 15.*
ASKE, Mons Conand d'. *WJ B 1002.*
[ASKE, of Eastrington, Yorks]. *Hare I R36, 163. (qtg Az 3 lozs Arg). (alias Bayley; in chf over arms of Harington, for Wm H, LL.-D., Canon of St Paul's London, confirmation by Wriothesley, Garter & Wall, Norroy 18 Aug 1520.Either patentee or his father m Joan, dau of Wm Aske, of Estrington, unclear from wording of patent which).*
ASKE, Reynold. *PLN 1498. (qtg 2&3 Az in fess of 5 lozs Arg).*
BURDETT. *WB IV 183, 1028.*
CONNSTALB, Sir J, of .... *PCL I 552.*
SPIGNELL, Sir Adam. *WB III 86, 6. (qrs 1&4).*
[SPIGURNELL]. *ML I 572. (narrow bars).*
SPIGURNELL, Sir Richard. *CRK 1001.*
SPINGURNELL. *DV 63a, 2490.*
SPYGURNEL. *L1 617, 2.*
SPYGURNEL, Monsire Rauf. *AN 286.*
SPYGURNELLE. *SK 126.*
TANNE, Sir Lucas. *WLN 317.*
TANNE, Sr Lucas, of Ches. *CY 5, 19.*
TANNE, Sir Richard. *PCL II 43.*
TAUNE, Sir Lucas. *CVC 589.*

Gu 3 bars Arg
Gu 3 bars Arg
— *SK 634-5. (qtd 2&3 by Gra....).*
— *WB III 77b, 5. (qtd 2&3 by Sir Jn Gra...,*

of Lincs).
— *PLN 256. (qtd 2&3 by Sir Thos Gray).*
— *LS 286. (qtd 2&3 by Saville).*
— *PCL IV 18. (qtd II&III 2&3 by Kyng of Sesyle).*
— *WB II 70, 15. (qtd III 1&4 by Arg lion & border engr Gu).*
— *BG 129.*
BENSTEDE. *L1 108, 5; L2 78, 12.*
BENSTEDE, of Essex. *MY 134.*
BENSTEED. *CRK 1841.*
FRAUNKTON, Multon de. *WJ 591.*
HUNGARY. *LMRO 14. (blazoned 'Le Roy de Hugrie porte lescu barre de argent et de gules').*
KARKENTON. *L2 294, 3.*
KIRKENTON. *L9 11, 4.*
MOLETON. *Gerard 92.*
MOLETONE. *L9 69b, 1.*
MOLTON. *CV-BM 33.*
MOLTON, Sire Thomas de. *J 123.*
MOLTON, Thomas de. *Q 80.*
MOLTON, Thos de. *E I 242; E II 244.*
MOLTONE, Thomas de. *F 164.*
[MOULTON]. *Nichols Leics II 237. (Knipton Ch).*
MOULTON, le Sire de, de Fraunkton. *CG 225.*
MOULTON, Thomas de. *WLN 562.*
MOULTON, Thos de. *XF 944.*
MULTON, Sr, de F[raunkton]. *CKO 308.*

Gu 3 bars Or
Gu 3 bars Or
— *L10 23b, 12. (qtd 2&3 by Breyront).*
BLAKEFORD. *CC 230b, 284.*
BLAKEFORD. *L1 78, 4; L2 64, 5.*
ILLE, le Counte del. *C 146. (bars diapered; 'de goules treis barres d'or diaspres').*

Or 3 bars Az
Or 3 bars Az
— *D4 25b. (imp by Stapilton, of Wyghell, Yorks).*
— *Q II 538.*
— *L10 5b, 1. (qtg 2&3 Az fess of 4 lozs Arg).*
ASK, Conan de. *TJ 516. ('dor ove trois barres dazure').*
ASK, Conan de. *P 148.*
ASKE. *PT 1061. ('empres Richmonte').*
ASKE. *LY A 85.*
ASKE. *DV 61b, 2429.*
ASKE. *L1 1, 4; L2 2, 3.*
ASKE. *SK 215.*
ASKE. *L10 5, 19.*
ASKE. *CB 167.*
[ASKE]. *Dingley cccccxv. (imp by Stapleton; Lacock Ch, Wilts).*
ASKE, of Acton, Yorks. *D4 38b.*

ASKE, of Actone. *PT 1035.*
ASKE, Sir John of. *BA 617.*
ASKE, Katherine. *?source. (dau of Rog Aske, & w of Jn de Burgh; E window, Catterick Ch).*
CONSTABYLL, Ser John, Yorks. *RH, Ancestor iv 233. (tricked barry Or and Az but 'vii pecys' written in margin).*
MANDEVILLE, Thos. *CT 162.*
MAUNDEVILLE, Mons' Thomas. *TJ 559.*

Or 3 bars Gu
Or 3 bars Gu
— *SHY 458. (qtd 4 by Arg lion Sa).*
— *SK 974. (qtg 2&3 Az 5foil Erm seeded Gu).*
— *LH 577. (imp by Ld Russell).*
— *BS 22.*
ALAYN, Bryan le fiz. *Q 103.*
ALEYN, Sire Brian fiz. *N 65.*
FITZALAN, Sir Brian. *BR V 48.*
FITZALYN, Bryan. *PCL I 483.*
[HARCOURT, Lo]. *RH, Ancestor iii 203. (name in later hand).*
MARTIN, of Burton. *XF 86. (imp Forde).*
[MOULTON]. *Nichols Leics III 491. (formerly in East Norton chapel).*
MUSCHAMP. *Coll T&G ii 117 & 118. (qtg [Welbeck] & imp [Harmonde] 'Orate pro bono statu Wilhelmi Muschamp armigeri et Agnatis consortis ejus Ano Dom 1528'; in W window of N aisle, Camberwell, Surr).*
MUSCHAMP. *L1 428, 4; L2 331, 3.*
MUSCHAMP. *CC 226, 133.*
MUSCHAMP. *XF 847.*
MUSCHAMP. *DV 43a, 1688.*
MUSCHAMP. *Coll T&G ii 117 & 118. (qtg [Welbeck], no imp; E window of N aisle, Camberwell, Surr).*
MUSHAMPE. *Suff HN 7. (imp by Stapleton; Lavenham Ch).*
MUSTHAMP. *L9 75b, 6.*
PESHALLE, [Sir] Hew. *WK 23. (qtg 2&3 Erm, all in border Az).*
[ROMELY, Alice de]. *Neale & Brayley. 1296. (on canopy of mont to Edm, E of Lancaster).*
SEINT OWEN, Raf de. *F 131.*
SEYNT OWEN. *CV-BM 57.*
ST OWEN, Ralph de. *WLN 471.*

Or 3 bars Vt
Or 3 bars Vt
MOYNE, Mons John le. *CA 148.*
MOYNE, S' Jon. *PO 517.*

Sa 3 bars Arg

Sa 3 bars Arg
— D4 32. (qtd 3 by Brakynbery, of Denton, co Durham).
HAWGHTON, Sir Rycharde, of Lancs. RH, Ancestor iv 238.
HOGHTON. XF 579.
HOGHTON. PT 1173.
HOGHTON. DV 59b, 2343.
HOGHTON, Monsire Adam de. AN 246.
HOGHTON, Sir Adam de. CVL 332.
HOGHTON, Sir Alexander, of Hoghton. BA 35b, 336.
HOGHTON, of Houghton. LH 1001.
HOGHTON, of Houghton, Ches. L1 313, 1; L2 265, 4.
HOGHTON, Mons Ric de. Lawrance 7. ante 1350. (shield on tomb of Sir Jn Bradshaw, Wigan, Lancs).
HOGHTON, Mons' Richard de. TJ 1376.
HOGHTON, Sir Richard. LH 336.
HOGHTON, Yorks. MY 244.
HOUGHTON, Monsire Ric' de. S 140.
HOUGHTON, Sir Richard. CRK 1281.
HOUGHTONE. PT 61.
OSOLVESTON ABBEY, Leics. Arch Journ (Norwich 1847) 104. (Mortuary roll of Abbot Hen Medbourne).

Vt 3 bars

Vt 3 bars Gu
GAYNES. L1 284, 6.
Vt 3 bars Or
— LE 180.

Field patterned 3 bars

Erm 3 bars

Erm 3 bars Untinc
GIFFORD, Jas, of Sheriffhall. Stevenson. 1473.
HUSE, Henry de, Ld of Harting. PRO-sls. 1483-4.
HUSE, Henry, Ld of Harting, Suss, Kt. Birch 10933. S: HENRICI.HUSE.MILITIS.DNI.DE.-HERTYNG. late 15 cent. motto: ?'COR IMMO-BILE'.
HOEUSE, Henry, Kt. PRO-sls. SIGILLUM HEN-RICI HUSE. 1308-9.
HUSER, Henry, Ld of Hertyng. PRO-sls. 1337-8.
Erm 3 bars Az
HUSSEY, Baron of Galltram. DIG 30.

Erm 3 bars Gu

Erm 3 bars Gu
— WB III 74b, 2. (qtd 2&3 by Sir Nicol Huse, of Suss).

— SC 47. (qtd 3 by 'The lord of Zest' [Hay of Yester]).
— WB II 56, 14.
— RB 254. (qtd 2&3 by Huse).
— LH 894. (qtd 2&3 by Hussey).
— LH 746. (qtd 2&3 by Sir Nichol Hussey, of Suss).
FODRINGHAME, of Powrye. Lyndsay 342.
HESE, Henry. FW 639.
HEUSE, Henri. A 94.
HOSEE. WGB 102, 17.
HOSEY. L1 299, 6; L2 241, 3. (or Hussey, of Suss & Surr).
HOUSE, Sir Henry, of Suss. RH, Ancestor iv 407.
HUSE. LH 131.
HUSE, Le S. AS 200.
HUSE, Sr de. CKO 309.
HUSE, Henr'. Q 145.
HUSE, Henry. CVK 747.
HUSE, Mons Mark de. WJ 913.
HUSE, Mons' Thomas. TJ 513. ('dermyn & trois barres de goules').
HUSEE. SK 454.
HUSEE, Sire Henri. N 243.
HUSEE, Mons' Tho. TJ 1605.
HUSEY, Monsire Henry. AN 350.
HUSEY, S' Henry. PO 642.
HUSSEE, Henre, of Suss. CY 174, 695.
HUSSEY. MP II 56. ('Giffardeis et Heusez'; 'scutum de ermine iii benda de gules').
HUSSEY. LH 362.
HUSSEY. WB I 15, 16.
HUSSEY. MP II 113. (Giffardeis et Heusez).
HUSSEY. LH 721.
HUSSEY. LH 817. (imp Brodbridge).
[HUSSEY]. PLN 1614.
[HUSSEY, Sir Harry]. PLN 324.
HUSSEY, Sir Henry. LH 184.
HUSSEY, Sir Henry, of Suss. CRK 1034.
HUSSEY, Sir Thomas. LH 301.
HUSSY, le Sire. CG 226.
HUYSE, Mons Hug de. WJ 588.
LYNDESEYE, Willms de. LM 308.
MARTYN, Waryn. FW 666.

Erm 3 bars Sa

Erm 3 bars Sa
FRANCES, John. WB III 108b, 2.
FRANCIS, John. PLN 533.
FRAUNCEYS. SK 857.

Gutty &c 3 bars

Arg gutty Sa 3 bars Gu
— PLN 1782. (qtd 2&3 by Or 3 hose 2, 1 Sa).
Roundelly 3 bars
— PRO-sls. 1426. (imp by Robt Fitzrobert).

Vair 3 bars
Vair 3 bars Untinc
KEYNES, Sir Robt, d1318. *Lawrance 25.*
(effigy, Dodford, Northants).
Vair 3 bars Gu
— *PLN 1343.*
CANYS. *L1 160, 1; L2 111, 11.*
CAVYS. *L10 44, 8.*
CAYNES. *SK 70.*
CAYNES. *CB 14.*
GAYNES. *L2 234, 3.*
HATHEWICK. *CRK 528.*
KAINES. *SK 96. (imp by Ailsbury).*
KEYNES, Robt. *PLN 476.*
Vairy Erm and Gu 3 bars Az
BREUS. *L10 75b, 3. (or Brens).*

3 bars patterned

3 bars Erm
Untinc 3 bars Erm
GIFFORD, John, Ld of Yester. *Stevenson.*
c1320.
GIFFORD, of Yester. *Stevenson. 1420. (qtd
by Sir Wm Hay, of Lochesworth, & others).*
GIFFORD, of Yester. *Stevenson. 1420. (imp
by Dougal Macdowal, bro of Archibald of
Makerston, & co-lord of Yester).*
HUSE. *Hist Mss Comm 5th Rep 326.* SIGIL-
LUM JOHANNIS HUSE. *(sls on 2 grants by Jn
H, Ld of Charlecumbe, to Nicholas de Lynns
etc).*
Gu 3 bars Erm
— *PLN 1202. (escutch of Jn Bereley).*
— *D4 28. (qtd 3 by Husse, of Herswell,
Yorks).*
— *WK 230. (qtd 2&3 by Sir Jn Husee).*
[ASTROP]. *XPat 13, Arch 69, 70. (qtd 7 by
Sr Hary Amcotts).*
HUSSEY. *LH 363.*
KERKENTON. *DV 51b, 2025.*
KERKETON, Monsr Jehan de. *AS 203.*
KIRKENTON. *L1 383, 4; L2 292, 6.*
KIRKETON. *CV-BM 96.*
KIRKETON. *PT 612. (Kerkinton struck
through & Kirketon written over in later
hand).*
KIRKETON, Mons' John de. *TJ 532.*
KIRKETON, Monsire John de. *CG 228.*
KIRKINGTON, Sir John de. *PLN 251.*
KIRKTON. *XF 287.*
KIRTON, Mons John de. *CA 49.*
KYRETON, Sir John, of Lincs. *PLN 1292.*
KYRKETON. *L9 22, 8. (Hosey added in later
hand).*
KYRKETON, Sr J de. *CKO 310.*
KYRKETON, Mons Joh de. *WJ 592.*
KYRKETON, Robert de. *LM 398.*

KYRKETONE, S' Jon de. *PO 501.*
KYRKETONE, Robert de. *Q 451.*
TATESHALL, le Sieur. *BG 35.*
Sa 3 bars Erm
FYNCHEHAM. *PLN 502.*

3 bars Ermines
Erm 3 bars Ermines
BEDFFORD, James, co Durham. *RH, Ancestor
vii 195.*

3 bars gobony
Az 3 bars gobony of 8 Arg and Sa
— *ML I 476. ('Asur iii barres sylver &
sabyll bylette.Or sylver & sabyll pale').*
Gu 3 bars gobony Arg and Az
BARR, Mons Thomas. *S 465. (qtg 2&3
barry Or and Az bend Gu).*
BARREY. *L10 21, 8. (gobony of 6; qrs 1&4).*
Gu 3 bars gobony Arg and Sa
— *WB IV 139, 239. (qtd 4 by Sir Thos
Barre).*
BAR. *L10 20, 1. (gobony of 6).*
BAR, Mons Thomas. *WJ 844. (gobony of 6).*
BARLE. *L2 51, 6. (marginal note 'against
Barre').*
BARRE. *L1 107, 4.*
BARRE. *FK II 851. (qrs 1&4).*
BARRE, Sir John. *WB IV 169b, 789. (gobony
of 5).*
BARRE, Sir John, of Herefs. *RH, Ancestor
VII 199.*
BARRE, Sir Thomas. *PLN 238. (qtg 2&3
barry Or and Az bend Gu).*
BARRY, Thomas. *S 470. (qrs 1&4).*
Gu 3 bars 1st & 3rd gobony of 5 Arg and Sa
2nd counterch
BARRE. *CT 440-1.*
Gu 3 bars gobony Sa and Arg
BARR, Sir John. *PLN 874. (gobony of 5).*
BARRE, Sir T. *SK 468.*
BARRY. *CV-BM 176. (gobony of 4).*
Or 3 bars Az all semy de lis isst counterch
— *RH, Ancestor ix 174. (blazon unclear;
?for Mortimer, of Attleborough, Norf).*

3 bars Vair
Untinc 3 bars Vair
— *Arch Journ lxxx 4, 42. 1444. (escutch of
Sir Jn Cressy on his tomb, Dodford,
Northants).*
COUCY, Ingelram, Ld of. *Arch Journ xxxv
166. ..DOMINI DE COUCY. 1367. (sl on grant
dd 26 Nov 1368).*
Gu 3 bars Vair
BEMOND, Sir Thomas, of Devon. *WB III 73,
5.*
CASTEN, le Sire de. *CG 246.*
CHASTEL, Rychard, Sr de. *CKO 325.*

(glosses on Say & Mortimer).
CHASTON, Mons' Thomas. *TJ 490.*
GRIMSTEDE, Sire Andreu. *N 199.*
GRYMSTED, of Dorset. *L2 231, 10.*
MURHOIL. *SK 170.*
MURKEIL. *CB 125.*
MURLION. *XF 846.*
MURLYON. *L9 75b, 3.*

3 bars modified

3 bars coupée ('hamaides')
3 bars coupée
[?ARTHUR]. *Mill Steph; Belcher I 29.* 1454.
(brass to Robt A, rector, Chartham, Kent; on sin of effigy & on dex fess betw 3 fir-cones).
Sa 3 bars coupée Arg
RODLEY. *XF 304.*
Erm 3 bars coupée Untinc
DABRICHECOURT, Eustace. *PRO-sls.* 1361-2.
DAWBRICHCOURT, Nicholas. *Birch 9220.*
S'NICHOLAI: DAWBRICHCOURT. 15 cent.
Erm 3 bars coupée Gu
ABRISCOURT. *L2 17, 7.*
ABRISCOURT, Sir Sancett de. *L10 5b, 4.* *(additional gloss 'of Oxford shyre').*
DABREGECOURT. *L1 193, 3; L2 149, 12.*
[DABRICHCOURT]. *PLN 481.*
DABRICHECOURT. *CB 212.*
[DABRICHECOURT]. *WB I 25b, 11.*
DABRICHECOURT, Nicol. *S 322.*
DABRICHECOURT, Sir Sanchet de, KG, d1348-9. *Leake.*
DABRICHECOURT, Sir Sanset. *WGA 122.*
DABRICHECOURT, Sansett. *S 23.*
DABRICHECOURT, Sansett. *S 25.*
DABRIDGCOURT. *PLN 1474. (sometimes blazoned Gu 2 bars & border Erm).*
DABRIDGECOURT. *CRK 1551.*
DABRIDGECOURT, Sir John. *T b 105.*
DABRISCOURTE. *PT 602.*
DABRYCHCORTE, Essex. *MY 170.*
DABRYCHYIRRTTE, Sir Sanset. *BB 77. (d c1345).*
DABRYGECOURT. *BG 131.*
DAPISCORTE. *BW 13b, 85.*
DAVERSCOURTE, Sir J. *WB I 37b, 5.*
DOBRICHECOURT, Sir John. *WGA 143.*
Sa semy of ears of wheat Or 3 bars coupée Arg
STOKES. *CRK 1589.*
Arg gutty Gu 3 bars coupée Az
— *CC 223b, 56.*
AMARLE. *CRK 1931.*
AMARLE. *L10 5, 20.*
AMERLE, le H. *PLN 539.*
AMMARLE. *L1 2, 1; L2 3, 5.*

Erm 3 bars coupée Gu semy of escallops Or
DABRICHECOURT, Nichol. *CA 115.*

3 bars dancetty
3 bars dancetty
— *Lawrance 51.* c1260. *(long supposed to be Geoffrey de Mandeville, e of Essex, d 1144, but more likely to be Balun, Loveday or Rivers; Effigy, Temple Ch, London).*
BALUN, Reginald de, Ld of Magna Markeleyn, Herefs. *Birch 7104.* S' REGINALDI DE BALVN. 1294.
CLERK, John. *Helyar 594.* 1383. *(sl on grant of Gauntesmille, [Gants Mill], Bruton [Som] dated at Albe or Alre [Aller, Som]).*
EDLINGHAM, John. *Dodsworth 49, 9, HB-SND. (s of Jn of E).*
LOVEDAY, Margaret. *Bow XXXIII 3.* 1336-7.
YEDEFEN, Thomas. *Bow XXVII 19.* 1377.
Arg 3 bars dancetty Gu
BALUN, Jon de. *HE 134.*
BASSET. *L10 21b, 14.*
Arg 3 bars dancetty Sa
ENDERBY. *WB IV 184, 1048. (tinct of bars unclear).*
Az 3 bars dancetty Or
DELAMARE. *CC 227, 171.*
LOUEDAY, of Essex. *L1 399, 4; L2 308, 10.*
LOVEDAY, Sire Richard. *N 453.*
Gu 3 bars dancetty Arg
BASSET. *CRK 349.*
Or 3 bars dancetty Az
VALUN, M de. *WNR 136.*
Or 3 bars dancetty Gu
DALARNARE, Peter, Kt, of Parva, Heref. *Bow LX 3.* 1381-2. *(tincts tricked on sl).*
DELAMARE. *Dingley clxiii. (brass to Ric D, d1435, Heref Cathedral).*
DELAMARE. *L10 57, 7.*
MAER, de la. *DV 44b, 1749.*
Or 3 bars dancetty Sa
[SHELFORD]. *CRK 989.*
SHILFORD. *L1 613, 6.*
SHILFORD. *SK 759.*
SHYLFORDE, Tomas. *RH, Ancestor v 182.*

3 bars embattled
3 bars embattled counter-emb
ELSEFELD, Gilbert de, Kt. *PRO-sls.* 1333-4.
Arg 3 bars embattled Gu
BARRE. *CT 449.*
BARRE. *L10 20, 2.*
BARRE, Mons John. *WJ 928.*
Gu 3 bars embattled Arg
BARRE, Mons' Robert. *S 576.*
BARRY, Robert. *S 582.*
WHYTHORSSE, Rychard. *RH, Ancestor vii 210.*

3 bars engrailed &c

Or 3 bars engr Gu

CRESPIN, William. *C 108. (Seigneur de Bec-Crespin, Constable of Normandy, Marshal of France, d1282).*

Or 3 bars flory cf Gu

CARKOWE, Kyng of. *PCL IV 23.*

Az 3 bars indented Arg

TODENHAM, Oliver de, of Lymington. *Gerard 186.*

Gu 3 bars indented Arg

TODENHAM, of Devon. *Gerard 186.*

Arg 3 bars lozy Az

CODENHAM, Oliver. *BA 1208. (3rd bar isst from base, 7 lozs in 1st & 2nd bars).*

Arg 3 bars lozy Gu

CUDEHAM, John. *BA 1212. (3rd bar isst from base).*

SOMERY, George de. *WLN 766. (extra half bar in base; ?for barry indented Arg and Gu).*

3 bars wavy or nebuly

3 bars wavy

— *Roman PO 1612.* 16 Jan 1428-9. *(qtd 2&3 by Thos Blount; sl).*

— *Birch 12644.* temp Edw 1. *(imp by Hen, s of Robt de Pinkeni, of Northants).*

— *Bk of Sls 286.* 1254-6. *(imp by Hen de Pinkeny).*

— *PRO-sls. (qtd 2 by Thos Pigott, of Stratton).*

— *PRO-sls.* 13 cent. *(imp by Hen de Pinkney).*

— *WB I 14b, 21. (qtd 3 by [Stapulton]).*

AMUNDEVILLE, Richard de. *Birch 6830.* +SIGILL'RICARDI DE AMVNDEVILE. early 13 cent. *(decoration on sl; shield is placed over 3 bars wavy). (s&h of Ric A, of Warw).*

BARTON, Robert, of Overbarnton. *Stevenson.* 1519. *(imp merchant's mark).*

BASSET. *Birch 9010.* 1298. *(2nd of 3 shields [Courtenay, Le Despencer & B] on sl of Hugh de C, of Devon).* motto: FRANGE LEGE TEGE.

BASSET. *Birch 1910.* 1298. *(1 of 3 shields in sl of Hugh de Cortenay, of Devon).*

BASSET, Ela, Ctess of Warwick. *Birch 6579.* SIGILLVM: ELE: BASSET: COMITISSE: WAREVYKIE. post 1242. *(dau of Wm Longespee I, wid of Thos de Newburgh, E of Warw & w of Philip B, of Hedendon, Surr, d1297).*

BASSET, Jan Philipp. *PRO-sls.* 1266.

BROWNYNG, John. *Birch 7875.* SIGILL': IOH'IS: BROUNYNG. 1412. *(Ld of Legh near Deerhurst, Gloucs, & of Dorset).*

CHAMPAYNE, Robert. *Birch 8468.* SIGILLVM.-SECRETI. 1294. *(s of Robt de C, of Surr, Kt).*

CHOKE, John. *Clifton vi 214.* 1506. *(qtg*

2&3 *[Lyons]; sl at Ashton Court, Bristol). (supporters: 2 lions; crest: heron's head).*

DRUMMOND, John. *Stevenson.* 1407. *(Ld of Cargill & Stobhall 1403-28, & others).*

MALMIRAN, Mariota dau of, of Glencharn. *Stevenson.* 1365.

NORAIS, Malcolm. *Stevenson.* 1296.

[SAMPFORD]. *Mill Steph.* 1467. *(qtg [Matravers] on tester of tomb of Wm Browning, Melbury Sampford, Dorset).*

[SAMPFORD]. *Mill Steph.* c1470. *(qtd 2&3 by Matravers on tester of tomb of Wm Browning, Melbury Sampford, Dorset).*

[SAMPFORD]. *Mill Steph.* 1467. *(imp [Barset] on tester of tomb of Wm Browning, Melbury Sampford, Dorset).*

SAMPFORD, Roger de, Kt. *PRO-sls E40 A5018, 5054, 5395.* S' ROGERI: DE: SAVFORD. 13 cent.

?SIFREWAST. *Birch 12646.* c1190. *(imp by Robt de Pinkeini, s of Hen de P, of Northants).*

THEBOLD, John, of Merden, Suss. *Birch 13896.* S' PE....... 1462. *(blazon uncertain).*

3 bars nebuly

BASSET, Fulk, Bp of London 1244-1259. *Birch 1909. (sl obv).*

CHAUMPAIGNE, Margerie, Dame de, of Kent. *Birch 8503.* [MARGERIA] DE [CHA]VMPAGNE. 1336. *(loz).*

DRUMMOND, John, 1st Ld. *Stevenson. (4th & 5th sls).*

Arg 3 bars wavy

Arg 3 bars wavy Az

— *CK a 66.*

— *PLN 471.*

BROWNING, of Dorset. *PLN 1720. (qtg 2&3 Sa fretty Or).*

BROWNYNGE. *Suff HN 6. (qtd by Oxford; Lavenham Ch).*

BULBECK, Sir Hugh. *L10 34b, 2.*

SAUNFORDE, Tomas de. *Q 439.*

WALLAR, John. *WB IV 176b, 914.*

Arg 3 bars wavy Gu

CHAMPAYNE, S Jehn de. *GA 193.*

CHAMPAYNE, Johan. *N 290.*

CHAMPAYNE, Robert. *FW 211; A 25.*

CHAMPENEY, of Kent. *L1 136, 5; L2 136, 8.*

CHAMPENEY, Robert. *ME 39; LY A 159.*

CHAMPENEYS. *SK 436.*

CHAMPENEYS. *L2 141, 2.*

CHAMPNEYE, hasard. *L10 38, 9. (name completely erased but retained in index).*

HASARD, Thomas, of Wilts. *LH 492.*

POLMORVA, J. *CRK 779.*

SEDEM, Sir William. *BR V 255.*

Arg 3 bars nebuly Gu
  GOLDINGH[A]M, Aleyn de. *LM 551.*
Arg 3 bars wavy Sa
  — *D5 8b. (qtd by Rog Heyre).*
  BARLE. *RB 281.*
  BARLE. *RB 227. (qrs 1&4).*
  BASSET, Sire Rauf. *J 105.*
  ELKYSFELDE. *WB IV 152b, 486.*
Arg 3 bars nebuly Sa
  BASSET, Symon. *LM 93.*

Az 3 bars wavy
Az 3 bars wavy Arg
  — *CKO 648.*
  [?BROUNING, of Melbury Sampford]. *Gen Mag 14, 19-21. 1465. (imp by [Pympe, of Nettlestead]; stained-glass shield formerly at Nettlestead Ch, Kent).*
  BROUNYNG. *L1 59, 1; L2 42, 11.*
  BROWNYNG. *L10 76, 7.*
  LOVEDAY, Sir Richard. *BR V 234. (?recte 3 bars dancetty).*
  SANDFORD, Tohmas. *PCL I 432.*
  SAUNDFORD, Thomas de. *Q II 426.*
  WAUBOURN ABBEY. *L10 66b, 3.*

Or &c 3 bars wavy
Or 3 bars wavy Untinc
  LOVELL. *CT 28.*
Or 3 bars wavy Gu
  — *BR VI 7. (marshalled by Ld Lovel).*
  DROWMUND, Ld. *SC 49.*
  LOUEL, J. *HA 121, 24.*
Or 3 bars nebuly Gu
  LOVEL, J. *HA 109.*
  [LOVELL]. *D4 23. (qtd 2 by Stapilton, of Notts).*
  LOVELL, Sire Johan. *J 107.*
Or 3 bars wavy Sa
  BLOUNT, Sir Edward. *WK 218.*
Sa 3 bars wavy Or
  BLUNTTE. *PLN 158. (qtd 3 by Arg 2 wolves passt Sa border Or ch with 8 salts Gu).*

Erm &c 3 bars wavy
Erm 3 bars wavy
  BARLEY. *Mill Steph. (imp by Leventhorpe; brass to Thos L, d1588, & w Dorothy B, Albury, Herts).*
  BARLEY. *Mill Steph. 1419. (imp Pateshull; brass from tomb (destroyed) to Jn B & w Joan P, Albury, Herts).*
  [BARLEY]. *Mill Steph. 1508. (imp by Clifford on brass to Eliz d1526 (dau of Wm B), wid of Sir Ralph Joscelin & w of Sir Robt C, Aspenden, Herts).*
Erm 3 bars wavy Gu
  FOLLIOT, Sir Jeffry. *CRK 92.*
  GOLDINGEHAM, William de. *FW 266.*

Erm 3 bars wavy Sa
  BARLE. *WB I 34b, 20.*
  BARLEY. *L10 21, 16.*
  BARLEY. *XF 190.*
  BARLEY, Herts. *L2 51, 5.*
  BARLEY, John. *PLN 1427. (qtg 2&3 Or bouget & border Sa roundelly Or).*
  BARLOW. *L1 40, 6. ('Barlee' in margin).*
  BURLEY. *WB II 69, 11. (qr 1).*
  MARIES. *L1 436, 2; L2 328, 2.*
  MARREIS, William, of Kent. *WB III 110, 2.*
Erm 3 bars nebuly Sa
  BARLEY. *L10 23, 11.*
Ermines 3 bars wavy Arg
  MORES, Wyllyam. *WB IV 180b, 985.*

Per pale 3 bars wavy
Per pale 3 bars nebuly
  DAUNTSEY. *Mill Steph. 1514. (qtd 2&3 by Stradling, all imp by Danvers; brass to Sir Jn D & w Ann, dau of Sir Jn S, Dauntsey, Wilts).*
  DAUNTSEY. *Mill Steph. 1539. (on brass to Dame Ann, cousin & h of Sir Jn Dauntsey & wid of Sir Jn Danvers, Dauntsey, Wilts).*
Per pale Or and Arg 3 bars wavy Gu
  DANDESEY. *L1 187, 3; L2 150, 1.*
  DAUNDESEY, John. *BG 220.*
  DAUNTESEYE, John. *S 366.*
Per pale Or and Arg 3 bars nebuly Gu
  — *WK 522. (qtd 3 by Danvers, all imp by Hungerford).*
  DANDESEY, John. *S 368.*
  DAUNDESEY. *L10 52b, 14.*

3 bars wavy patterned
Gu 3 bars wavy Erm
  [GOLDINGHAM, Sir Walter]. *PLN 708.*
Gu 3 bars nebuly Erm
  GOLDYNGHAM. *L2 234, 5.*

3 bars & label
3 bars label
  — *Stevenson. 1504. (imp by ?Jn Cochrane, of Petcowok).*
  MARTYN, John. *Birch 11642.* SIGILLVM: IOHANNIS: MARTIN. *1356. (citizen & 'Cordarius' of London; shield surmounted by key, handle of which lies partly on shield; above shield estoile & cresc).*
3 bars label of 4
  IFORD, William de. *PRO-sls. 1351-2.*
3 bars label of 5
  CAMERON, Robert, of Balegrenach. *Stevenson. 1296.*
  MOLTON, Alanus de, of Lincs. *Birch 11816.* SIGILL.....DE..... *1341.*

Arg 3 bars Az label of 5 Gu
  GREY, Reynaud de. *Q 32.*
Arg 3 bars Gu label Az
  MULTON. *L9 75a, 7.*
  MULTON, Mons Will de. *WJ 586.*
Arg 3 bars Gu label Sa
  MULTON, Thomas de, Forester. *B 158.*
Arg 3 bars Gu label Vt
  MULTON, Mons Thomas, de Gillesland. *TJ
  507.* (*'Dargent & iii fees de goules lambels
  de vert'*).
Az 3 bars Arg label Gu
  MERTON, Mons Richard de. *CA 87.*
Gu 3 bars Arg label of 5 Az
  MOLETON, Thomas, of Gilsland, Cumb.
  Gerard 92.
Or 3 bars Az label Gu
  SPYGURNELL. *PT 507.*
Or 3 bars Gu label of 5 Az
  — *Proc Soc Antiq XVII 2s 275.* 1290-1330.
  (shield on stole at Leagram Hall, Lancs).
Or 3 bars Vt label Gu
  — *BG 413. (imp by Wake).*
Sa 3 bars Arg label Gu
  HOUGHTON, Monsire Richard de. *S 495.*
Erm 3 bars Gu label Az
  MARTYN, Willame. *FW 664.*
Gu 3 bars gobony 1st & 3rd Arg and Sa 2nd Sa
  and Arg label Az
  BARRE. *SK 305.*
Arg 3 bars Az label Gu roundelly Or
  GREY, Ricard de. *Q 130.*

3 bars modified & label
Arg 3 bars embattled Gu label of 5 Untinc
  BARRE. *CT 451.*
3 bars wavy label
  LOVEL. *Arch Journ xxxvii 328.* SIGNVM EIVS
  CVIVS EGIS. *(sl of Jn, s of Sir Jn L, of
  Suthemere; undated grant).*
Arg 3 bars wavy Gu label of 5 Or
  DAMMORY. *CT 328.*
Arg 3 bars wavy Gu label Sa
  DAUMARY, Robert. *FW 319.*
Or 3 bars wavy Gu label Az
  LOVEL, Jan. *Q 175.*

3 bars & in base
3 bars & in base mullet of 8 pts
  BISSET, John, of Garmouth. *Stevenson.*
  1429.
3 bars wavy & in base mullet
  DRUMMOND, James. *Stevenson.* (*'Atholl
  detached' sl*).

3 bars & canton
Arg 3 bars & canton Gu
  — *CRK 1853. (name blotted out).*
  FULLER. *XF 587.*
  FULLER. *XF 844. (or Fulwer).*
  MOULTON. *XF 669.*
  MULTON. *L9 75b, 9.*
  MULTONE. *FK II 379.*
Sa 3 bars & canton Arg
  RODINGTON. *XF 306.*
3 bars & canton Erm
  [APSLEY]. *Mill Steph. (brass at Thakeham,
  Suss, ?to Jn A, of T, d1507).*
Arg 3 bars Gu canton Erm
  APSLE, John. *PLN 1124.*
  ASPOLE, John. *WB IV 163, 674.*
  MULTON. *L9 75b, 2.*
  MULTON. *SK 323.*
Az 3 bars Or canton Erm
  — *WB IV 161b, 648. (qtd 4 by Spencer).*
  — *PLN 1084. (qtd 4 by Wentworth).*
  SPENSER, Mons Philip. *WJ 815.*
Gu 3 bars Or canton Erm
  MAUNCYLL, John. *WB III 90b, 8.*
  WALSHE. *SK 910.*
Or 3 bars Az canton Erm
  — *BA 853. (qtd 2&3 by Sir Ralph
  Mareschall).*
  — *I2(1904)165. (qtd 5 by Sir Ric
  Wentworthe, of Nettlestead, Suff).*
  GOSELL. *Suff HN 43. (imp Camoys, in Ld
  Wentworth's House, Nettlestead).*
  GOUSSILL.
  — *XFB 82. (qtd 5 by Sir Ric Whitworthe, of
  Nettlestead, Suff).*
Or 3 bars Gu canton Erm
  CANFELD. *L2 233, 6.*
  GAUFELD. *L1 287, 1; L2 225, 7. (marginal
  note in L1 has Gousel or Gonsel).*
  GAWSELL, Nycolas. *RH, Ancestor ix 164.*
Sa 3 bars Arg canton Erm
  MARSHALL, of Notts. *L9 48b, 4.*
Sa 3 bars & canton Erm
  RODINGTON. *XF 256.*
3 bars on canton fret
  MULETONE, Thomas de. *Birch 12019.*
  SIGILLVM THOME DE MVLETONE. 14 cent.
  MULTON, Thomas de. *PRO-sls.* 1229-36.

3 bars modified & canton
Sa 3 bars wavy Arg canton Gu
  BROKYSBY, Notts. *RH, Ancestor v 177.*
Gu 3 bars nebuly Or canton Erm
  LOVELL. *L2 317, 10.*

3 bars & on canton

Gu 3 bars & on canton Arg bull Sa
DENE, Mons J de. *AS 469. ('tarel' for taureau, bull).*
DENE, Mons' John. *TJ 538. ('un torel de sable en le quarter').*

Gu 3 bars Arg on canton Erm bend lozy of 5 Or
WALSALL. *XF 254.*
WALSH. *PLN 1501.*
[?WALSH]. *WB I 35, 23.*

Gu 3 bars Arg on canton Erm bend lozy Or and Gu
WALSALL. *L1 677, 5.*

Gu 3 bars Or on canton Erm bend lozy Gu and Or
VALCHE. *L1 656, 6.*
WALSHE. *SK 833.*

Or 3 bars Gu on canton Erm bend lozy Gu
WALEYS, Estevene le. *Q 320. (4 lozs).*
WALEYS, Stephanus. *Q II 332.*

Arg 3 bars & on canton Az martlet Or
[LATHBURY]. *FK II 314. (name added in later hand).*

Gu 3 bars Or on canton Arg 5 billets in salt Sa
INGLOS, Henry. *XF 257.*

3 bars & on canton castle &c

Arg 3 bars & on canton Sa tower 3-turreted Arg
KARVELL, Robert, of Northants. *WB III 87, 6.*

Erm 3 bars & on canton cresc Untinc
PRENDERGEST, Sir Henry, Kt. *Stevenson. 1275. (s of Adam de P).*

3 bars & on canton cross patonce
[ATON]. *Birch 7840. ....BROMFLET..... 1434. (qtd 3 by Hen Bromflet, chev [?afterwards Baron B, of Vescy]).*

Erm 3 bars Gu on canton Az cross engr Arg betw 4 pheons Or
HUTTOFT, Henry, of Southampton. *L10 61, 6.*

Erm 3 bars Gu on canton Az cross engr betw 4 pheons Or
HUTTOFT, de Southampton. *XPat 373, Arch 69, 97.*

Or 3 bars Az on canton Arg rose Gu
COX. *XF 443. (qtd 6 by Poyntz).*

Arg 3 bars & on canton Gu 4foil Or
[PRESTON, of Preston Patrick]. *Hill ii 305. (imp [Redman] of Burton-in-Kendal, Westmld). (quoted in Bellasis i 167).*

Arg 3 bars Gu on canton Az 5foil Or
PIPART, Rauff. *Q 132.*

Arg 3 bars & on canton Gu 5foil Or
PYPART, Sir Raffe. *PCL I 506.*

3 bars & on canton head &c

3 bars on canton stag's head
RICHMOND, Thos of. *Durham-sls 2084. (used in 1362 by Jn of Aske).*

Arg 3 bars nebuly Az on canton Gu mullet Arg
FOLVILLE. *XF 158.*

Arg 3 bars wavy Sa on canton Gu mullet Or
BROKESBY. *WB I 35, 17. (?barry nebuly of 6 Arg and Sa &c).*

Arg 3 bars nebuly Sa on canton Gu mullet Or
BROKESBY. *Suff HN 5. (in Long Melford Ch).*

Arg 3 bars Sa on canton Gu salt Arg
BRANCEPETH. *XX 250.*
BRANSPATH. *PT 644.*
BRANSPATH. *L1 88, 3; L2 68, 4.*
BRAWNE. *L10 79b, 16.*

3 bars on canton chaplet
HOLME, William de. *Yorks Deeds X 189.*
SIGILLVM WILLILMI D'HOLME. *1370.*

3 bars & chief

3 bars chf
MUSCAMP, Robert of. *Durham-sls 1848. (unclear).*
MYLTON, Richard, of East Greenwich. *PRO-sls E40 A4922. 1446-7. (?4 bars).*

Az 3 bars & chf Or
— *PT 363.*

Untinc 3 bars Untinc chf Vair
— *Birch 9175. 13 cent. (?barry; imp in arms of Galiena de Dammar[tin]).*

Arg 3 bars Gu chf Vair
PIMPE. *CRK 19.*
PYMPE, Sir John, of Kent. *WB III 74, 1.*

Az 3 bars dancetty Or chf Arg
STONER. *L1 574, 1.*
STONORE. *SK 385.*

Arg 3 bars wavy Sa chf per pale Erm and Gu
BARLEE, of Derbys. *WK 837.*
BARLEY. *L10 21b, 8.*
BARLEY. *XF 654.*
BARLEY, Derby. *L2 90, 6.*
BARLEY, Robert, de Barley, Derbys. *I2(1904)146.*

Gu 3 bars Or chf invected Erm
— *LH 677. (qtd 2 by Inkpen).*

3 bars & on chief

Az 3 bars & on chf Arg demi-lion isst Gu
EGRENHALL. *L1 231, 2. (as painted).*
EGRENHALL. *L2 180, 5.*

Az 3 bars Arg on chf Erm lion Gu
EGRENHALL. *L1 231, 2; L2 174, 11.*

3 bars on chf lion passt
ENGLEFELD, Philip de, Kt. *PRO-sls. 1335-6.*

Arg 3 bars Gu on chf Az lion passt Or
INGLEFYLDE. *DV 56b 2238.*
INGLESFIELD. *PT 444.*
INGLISFELD. *L1 361, 5; L2 279, 4.*

Arg 3 bars Gu on chf Or lion passt Az
   ENGELFELD, Sir Thomas, of Berks. *WB III 84, 2.*
   ENGLEFIELD, Philip. *CRK 1986.*
   YNGYLFELD, Essex. *MY 143.*
Az 3 bars Arg on chf Or lion pg Gu
   WALLERRON. *WB IV 173, 851.*
Gu 3 bars Arg on chf Az lion pg Or
   — *CRK 2029.*
Gu 3 bars & on chf Arg greyhound courant Az
   — *PT 256.*
Gu 3 bars & on chf Arg greyhound courant Sa
   — *L10 30b, 7. (name written 'Bekwyth' but 'Bek' erased leaving "wyth", ?for Skipwith).*
   SKIPWITH. *XF 474.*
   SKYPWITH. *CC 228, 204. (tinct of chf uncertain).*
   SKYPWITH, Sir John. *WB I 42, 2-3.*
   SKYPWITHE, Sir John. *WK 252.*
Gu 3 bars & on chf Arg greyhound courant Sa collared Or
   SKIPWITH, William. *CRK 293.*
Sa 3 bars wavy Arg on chf Gu bull passt Or
   — *PLN 907.*
   BULLMAN, John. *WB IV 158, 582.*
Sa 3 bars wavy Erm on chf Gu bull passt Or
   [?BULLMAN]. *WB I 16, 21.*
3 bars wavy on chf peacock in his pride
   [?NEWARK]. *Birch 4631.* 15 cent. *(Birch says variant of Beverley but pencil note says Newark).*
3 bars wavy & on chf 3 birds
   LAVEROK, John. *Clairambault 5742.* 5 May 1432.
3 bars wavy & on chf 3 larks
   LAVEROK, John. *Roman PO 6188.* 15 July 1434.
Or 3 bars Gu on chf Arg 3 fleurs de lis Sa
   NORMAN, John. *LV 56.*
Gu 3 bars & on chf Or mullet Sa
   STODON. *D5 10. (?barry of 8 Or and Gu &c).*
   STODOWE. *PT 1121.*
   STOWDOW. *L1 583, 3.*
3 bars & on chf 3 roundels
   GREY, Ld Edmund, Ld of Hastings, Weysford & Ruthyn. *Birch 10252.* ...: EDMUNDI: GREY. 1442. *(qtg II&III 1&4 maunch [Hastings], 2&3 barruly, orle of martlets [Valence]).*
Gu 3 bars Arg on chf Az 3 cartwheels Or
   LEPTON, of Cornburgh. *PT 1234.*

3 bars & in chief
3 bars in chf 3 annulets
   MULTON, John de, Kt. *PRO-sls.*
Arg 3 bars Sa in chf 3 annulets Gu
   COOK. *L10 39b, 19.*
   COOKE. *L2 141, 10.*

COOKES. *XF 894.*
Sa 3 bars & in chf 3 annulets Arg
   MOULTON. *CRK 1811.*
   MULTON. *L1 423, 2; L2 325, 11.*
   MULTON. *DV 64b, 2547.*
   MULTON, Johannes de. *Q II 583.*
   MULTON, John de. *TJ 531.*
   MULTON, Sir John. *WB III 89b, 1.*
Sa 3 bars Arg in chf 3 annulets Or
   SEYMARKE. *BG 81.*
   SEYMARKES. *FK II 947.*
Sa 3 bars & in chf 3 annulets Sa
   MULTON, John de. *SES 45. (?should bars & annulets be Arg).*

3 bars & in chief beast
3 bars in chf demi-lion isst
   LOUCHES, Adam, of Berks. *Birch 11386.*
   S'ADE.DE.[L]OVCHES. 1352.
3 bars in chf lion passt
   ENGLEFELD, John de. *PRO-sls.* 1401-2.
   ENGLEFELD, Philip de, Kt. *PRO-sls.* 1344-5. *(on shield betw three wiverns).*
   ENGLEFELD, Robert. *PRO-sls.* 1468-9.
   INGLEFELD, Robert, Esq. *PRO-sls.* 1467-8.
Arg 3 bars Gu in chf lion passt Az
   ENGLEFIELD. *XF 477. (qrs 1&4).*
   INGOLFYLDE, Sir Thomas, of Berks. *L9 5, 2. (qrs 1&4).*
Arg 3 bars & in chf lion passt Gu
   ADMER. *L2 18, 2. (?of the Round Table).*
Gu 3 bars Erm in chf lion pass Arg
   GIFFARD, Osbert. *CRK 368.*
Arg 3 bars Gu in chf greyhound courant Az
   ROSCOMMOUR, Cornwall. *L1 564, 5.*
Arg 3 bars Gu in chf greyhound courant Sa
   CORNUK. *L10 46b, 11.*
Arg 3 bars Gu in chf greyhound courant Sa collared Or
   SPYPWYTH, Sir. *PCL I 576.*
Gu 3 bars & in chf greyhound courant Arg
   SKIPWITH, Sir William. *CRK 1756.*
Gu 3 bars Arg in chf greyhound courant per pale Or and Erm collared Az
   SKIPWITH. *XPat 416, Arch 69, 100.*
   SKIPWITH, William. *XF 628.*
   SKIPWITH, Wm, of St Albans, Herts. *LD 80. (granted 20 May 1507 by Wriothesley & Machado).*
Gu 3 bars Arg in chf greyhound courant per pale Or and Erm collared Vt
   SKYPWITHE, William, of St Alban's. *WK 727.*
Arg 3 bars Gu in chf wolf courant Az
   [RESKYMER, of Cornw]. *CRK 1793.*
   ROSCOMOUR. *BA 934. (beast unclear).*
Arg 3 bars Gu in chf ?wolf courant Sa
   RESKMER, Sir Rauf A, of Cornw. *WB III 92b, 7.*

3 bars & in chief bird

Arg 3 bars Az in chf 3 martlets Gu
    PAYNELL, Sr William. *I 34.* (*'dargent 3 fesses dazure iii mereles de g. en chefe'*).
Sa 3 bars & in chf 3 owls Arg
    WAKEFELD. *PT 639.*
    WAKEFELD. *L1 694, 6.*
Sa 3 bars Arg in chf 3 owls Sa
    WAKFILDE. *PT 761.*

3 bars & in chief crescent &c

3 bars & in chf cresc
    LAWRENCE, John, s of. *BM Harl 1885 276b, HB-SND.* 1383.
    LAWRENCE, John, of Seton. *?source.* 1383. (*sl*).
Sa 3 bars & in chf cresc Arg
    GOLDSBOROUGH. *CRK 899.*
    GOLDYSBOROW, of Oxfords. *MY 298.*
Erm 3 bars couped & in chf cresc Gu
    DABRIGECOURT. *WK 682.*
Gu 3 bars Arg in chf 3 crescs Or
    MULTON, Mons' John, de Frankton. *TJ 503.*
Az 3 bars Or centre bar passing through annulet Or in chf cross formy fitchy Or
    [HOLTE]. *WB I 23b, 14.*

3 bars & in chief ermine spots &c

Arg 3 bars dancetty Sa in chf 3 Erm spots 2, 1
    ENDERBY. *PLN 659.*
3 bars in chf 3 escallops
    ERINGSTON, William. *Clairambault 3340.* 10 July 1446.
Arg 3 bars Az in chf 3 escallops Gu
    BRIDESHAL, Gilbt de. *Q 278.*
Sa 3 bars & in chf 3 escallops Arg
    KENNITON, Ine de. *Q 291.*
    KENNTONE, Hue de. *LM 562.*
Erm 3 bars & in chf mullet Untinc
    FOTHERINGHAM, Wm. *Stevenson.* 1461. (*burgess of Aberdeen*).
Erm 3 bars & in sin chf mullet Untinc
    GIFFORD, Alexr, Parson of Newlands. *Stevenson.* 1477.

3 bars & in chief fleur de lis &c

Erm 3 bars & in sin chf fleur de lis Untinc
    GIFFORD, Thomas. *Stevenson.* 1477. (*s of Wm G*).
3 bars in dex chf 5foil
    MORHAM, Adam. *Stevenson.* c1250.
Sa 3 bars & in chf 3 5foils Untinc
    — *PT 652.*
Sa 3 bars & in chf 3 5foils Or
    FILMER. *Hist MSS Comm 3rd Rep 246.* 1520. (*grant by Cooke, Clarenceux*).
3 bars wavy in chf head erased
    DRUMMOND, Harry. *Stevenson.* (*type of head unclear*).

Az 3 bars Arg in chf 3 lions' heads erased Or
    HIKLYN. *L1 319, 5.* (*as painted*).
Az 3 bars & in chf 3 lions' heads erased Or
    HIKLYN. *L1 319, 5; L2 254, 5.*
    HUKLENG. *LH 871.*
Arg 3 bars Az in chf 4 lions' heads erased Gu
    TROIS, Thomas. *WK 315.*

3 bars & in chief lozenge &c

Arg 3 bars Az in chf 3 lozs Gu
    FLEMMYNG, [Rich], Bp of Lincoln. *GutchWdU.* (*in Balliol Coll Lib window, given by Jn Carpenter, Bp of Worcester, d 1476*).
Az 3 bars Or in chf 3 lozs Arg
    — *ML I 139.* (*'iii barres gold in a feld asur wit as many fusewz in the honor sylver'*).
Az 3 bars & in dex chf mullet Arg
    TANY. *SK 118-9.*
Az 3 bars Or in dex chf mullet Arg
    SPIGORNEL, S' Rad'. *PO 378.*
    SPINGURNELLE, Ralph. *CA 60.*
Az 3 bars Or in chf mullet Arg
    SPIGURNELL, Mons' Rafe. *SD 45.*
Or 3 bars & in chf 2 mullets Sa
    [WYBERGH]. *Bellasis I 183; Hill vi 87; C3 g 2 cal 17b.* (*imp [Engayne]; Wm de W. m Elianor, dau&h of Gilbert de E; arms on separate but adjacent slabs, Clifton, Westmld*).
Gu 3 bars & in chf 3 pd mullets Arg
    WESCHYNGTON, Tomas. *RH, Ancestor iv 235.* (*'of ye bysshopperyke of Derham'*).

3 bars & in chief pale &c

3 bars in chf pale
    TWYNHAM, Walter, of Kingston. *PRO-sls BS 54.* SIGILL WALTERI TWYNHAM. 1364-5.
Untinc 3 bars dancetty Untinc in chf pale Erm
    ENDERBY, John, of Stratton, Beds, Esq. *Birch 9466.* SIG......OHANNIS. ENDERBY:. 1427.
3 bars in chf 2 pales
    BURLEY, John de. *PRO-sls.* 1363.
Or 3 bars & in chf 2 pales Sa
    BERELEY, John. *PLN 1202.* (*escutch Gu 3 bars Erm*).
3 bars & in chf 3 roundels
    GOWER. *?source.* c1400. (*unclear; sl of Abbot Richard Gower, of Jervaulx*).
    GREY, Richard, Kt, E of Kent. *PRO-sls.* 1506-7.
    HUNGERFORD. *SomAS LXX 80.* (*imp by Rodney*).
    KNOWT, Nicholas. *Durham-sls 655.* 1376. (*an Errington derivation*).
    TREWICK, Thomas of. *Arch Ael 3S 1, 116, HB-SND.* 1365.

Arg 3 bars & in chf 3 roundels Gu
  ?MOELS. *BR VI 29. (marshalled by Ld Bareny).*

3 bars & over all

Az 3 bars & in fess point annulet Or
  ASKE, John de. *WJ 1003.*
  ASKE, 'son fitz'. *WJ 1004.*
Arg 3 bars Gu lion Sa
  FAIRFAX, Sir Thos. *PLN 2049. (qtg 2&3 Arg chev betw 3 hinds' heads erased Sa [Beckwith]).*
Gu 3 bars Or lion Arg
  PEUEREL. *L1 507, 2.*
  PEVEREL. *L9 99a, 1. (a&l Az).*
  PEVEREL. *XL 183.*
  PEVERELL. *DV 51b, 2032.*
Arg 3 bars wavy Az lion Arg vulned in shldr Gu
  BULBECKE, John, of Kingeston. *L9 25b, 10.*
3 bars lion crowned
  WILLIAMSCOTE, Sir Thomas de. *Dugd 17, 33. 1365.*
Arg 3 bars Az lion Gu crowned Or
  WILLEMESCOTE, Sire Henri de. *N 916.*
Arg 3 bars Az lion Gu collared & crowned Or
  CYPRUS. *Brit Arch Assoc xxxiv 22. ('Scutum regis Cyprie'; on nave ceiling, St Alban's Abbey, c1400-20).*
Gu 3 bars Or lion Arg crowned Or
  LOVENHAM. *L9 42a, 8.*
Sa 3 bars Vt wolf erect Or
  BRITAIN, K Redbald p. *KB 83.*
Or 3 bars Az eagle Gu
  — *XV I 959. (qtd 6 by Wadham).*
  TANFELDE, Dernegan fitz Hugh de. *P 134. (a&l Or).*
3 bars with 3 birds in pale
  MERDISFEN, Roger de. *PRO-sls. 1357-8. (?3 bars with bird perched on each; valet of Aymer de Valence).*

3 bars & over all bend

3 bars bend
  — *PRO-sls. 1313-14. (1 of 4 shields on obv of sl of Wm de Echyngeham, Kt).*
  — *PRO-sls. 1392-3. (baston; dex of 3 shields on sl of Dame Eliz de Clinton).*
  — *PRO-sls. 1441-2. (qrs 2&3 on escutch of Lovell qtg [Holand]).*
  — *Birch 5892. c1307-8. (obv of equestr sl of Wm de Echingeham).*
  DUBU..., John. *Birch 9343.* IEHAN: DUBU..... 1454.
  HAYE, Juliana de la. *PRO-sls.* 13 cent.
  HYDE, de la. *LH 715.*
  MULTON, Thomas de, of Kyrketon, Kt. *Birch 12020.* LE SV SEAL DE AMOVR LEAL. 1345.
  PONYNGES, Sir Robert. *Coll T&G iii 258.*

1416. *(qtg [FitzPayne]).*
[POYNINGS]. *Farrer Bacon 48.* 1357. *(on sl of Joan P, wid of Sir Wm Creketot).*
POYNINGS, Isabella de. *Burrows 409-10.*
Sigill.Isabelle.de.Ponyngges. 1378. *(1 of 3 lozs on sl of Isabella de P, Lady St John).*
SOULIS. *Stevenson.* 1303. *(ribbon over all).*

Arg 3 bars & bend

Arg 3 bars Az bend Gu
  — *XF 198. (bend a baston; qtd 4 by Walton).*
  — *RL 24. (qtd 3 by [Deincourt]).*
  GREY, Robt de. *Q 161.*
  HORBIRI, Johan de. *D a 227.*
Arg 3 bars Gu bend Az
  HYDDE, Wyllyam. *WB IV 156, 541.*
  HYDE, de la. *PLN 824.*
  MOULTON. *XF 845. (bend a baston).*
  MULTON. *L9 75a, 8.*
  MULTON, Mons Robert de. *WJ 587. (bend a baston).*
Arg 3 bars Gu bend Sa
  MULTON. *L1 435, 5; L2 325, 12.*

Az &c 3 bars & bend

Az 3 bars Arg bend Gu
  GREY, of Wilton. *ML I 50; ML II 49.*
Az 3 bars & bend Or
  SCREMBY, Mons' de. *TJ 1515. ('... a trois barres & un bende dor').*
Gu 3 bars Arg bend Untinc
  MOLTON, Mons Thos de. *CA 50. (bend a baston).*
Gu 3 bars Arg bend Az
  MULTONE, S' Th'm de. *PO 502. (bend a baston).*
Gu 3 bars Or bend Sa
  — *SK 906. (bend a baston).*
Or 3 bars Az bend Gu
  — *WB IV 139, 239. (qtd 2 by Sir Thos Barre).*
  GAUNT, Gilbert de. *MP IV 49.*
  PEMBRIDGE, Sir Richard. *Dingley cxliv. 1375. (Mont, Heref Cathedral, S side of nave).*
  PENBRYGE, Sir Rychard, of Herefs. *RH, Ancestor vii 199.*
  QUAPPELAD. *L2 416, 9.*
Or 3 bars Vt bend Gu
  PUNINGE, Lucas de. *FW 244.*
Sa 3 bars Or bend Gu
  HOGHTON. *DV 63b 2515. (bend a baston).*
Erm 3 bars & bend Untinc
  DELAVAL, Robert. *Gen Mag 7, 22, HB-SND. 1294. (Selby Charters).*

3 bars & bend patterned

Untinc 3 bars Untinc bend Erm
FINCHAM, Simon. *Stowe-Bard 1s xii 3 MS ii 103.* SIGILLUM SYMEONIS FYNCH. temp Hen 5. *(betw each word on legend a tiny finch).*
Arg 3 bars Sa bend Erm
FINCHAM. *XF 87.*
FYNCHAM. *L1 246, 5.*
FYNCHAM. *RB 252.*
FYNCHAN. *LE 331.*
Sa 3 bars Arg bend Erm
FYNCHYN. *T b 152.*
Arg 3 bars Az bend gobony Or and Gu
GRAY. *WB IV 158b, 572.*
Az 3 bars Or bend gobony Gu and Arg
LEGH, of Routh. *L2 304, 10.*
Arg 3 bars Az bend Gu roundelly Or
GREY, Richard de. *FW 651c.*
Arg 3 bars Sa bend Vair
FINCHAM. *L2 196, 6.*

3 bars & bend modified

3 bars bend engr
— *Birch 7622.* SIGILLUM: PHIL. 15 cent. *(qtd 2&3 by Philip de Boston).*
[?NEWELL]. *Keepe; Neale & Brayley. (qtd 2 by [Tilney]; brass to Humphrey Bourchier, d1470).*
Arg 3 bars Gu bend engr Sa
MULTON. *SK 589.*
MULTON. *L9 75b, 4.*
ROOS. *XF 152. (& Moulton).*
ROOS. *LR 65. (bend a baston). (Moulton added by another hand).*
ROOS. *L1 564, 1.*
[ROS]. *?source. (glass, Tydd St Mary's Ch, Lincs).*
ROS, Sire Johan de. *N 660.*
ROSSE. *PLN 510.*
Arg 3 bars Az bend indented Gu
GREY, Jan de. *Q 297.*

3 bars & bend sinister

3 bars bend sin
PUSEY, William. *BerksCRO-sls Bouverie Pusey Deeds EBP/T8.* SIG.....M.WILL.P..... 1437-42.

3 bars & on bend

3 bars on bend 3 birds
SCHARD, Roger, of Suff. *Birch 13327.* 1399.
Arg 3 bars Gu on bend Sa 3 escallops Or
WATFORD. *LE 337.*
Gu 3 bars Arg on bend Sa 3 escallops Arg
— *LE 413.*
Gu 3 bars Arg on bend Sa 3 escallops Or
LIGHTFOTE, Sir John, of Essex. *WB III 78b, 1.*
WATFORD. *XF 181.*

Arg 3 bars Az on bend Gu 3 leopards' faces jesst de lis Or
GRAY. *WB IV 146, 365.*

3 bars modified & bend

Arg 3 bars nebuly Gu bend Az
DAUMORI. *L10 53, 3. (bend a baston).*
Az 3 bars wavy Arg bend Gu
HALSWELL, of Halswell [in Goathurst]. *Gerard 44.*
HALSWELL, Nicholas. *GutchWdU. (Fellow of All Souls, fl 1480; imp [?Percival]; formerly in Old Cloister window, All Souls).*
Or 3 bars nebuly Gu bend lozy Untinc
LOVELL, Thomas. *M 500. (?bend Az).*
Or 3 bars nebuly Gu bend lozy Sa
— *LM 455.*

3 bars & over all bend cotised

Or 3 bars Az on bend engr Sa plain cotised Gu 3 escallops Or
SAXBEY. *XPat 183, Arch 69, 83.* temp Hen 7.
SAXBEY. *WK 580.*
SAXBY, of Northamp. *L10 87b, 2.*

3 bars & over all chevron &c

Per pale Arg and Az 3 bars counterch chev Gu
STETHAM, de. *RB 481.*
STODEHAM, M de. *WNR 129.*
Erm 3 bars Gu 3 crescs Sa
WATERTON, Sir Robarde, Yorks. *RH, Ancestor iv 233.*
Arg 3 bars wavy Az over all 2 dolphins hauriant belly to belly Gu
ROWE, Richard. *CRK 972.*
Gu 3 bars Arg over all fleur de lis Untinc
— *WB I 20b, 21. (qtd 5 by Parr).*
3 bars over all 3 cotton hanks
[HAYWARD]. *Mill Steph.* 1523. *(qtd 2&3 by Porter on brass to Rog P, Newent Glos; he m Cath dau&h of Jn H).*
[HAYWARD]. *Mill Steph.* 1524. *(qtd 2&3 by Porter on brass to Wm P, canon, Hereford Cathedral).*
Arg 3 bars Sa over all 3 hanks of cord Or
— *WK 551. (qtd 2&3 by Arthur Porter, alias Gloucester, s of Rog, s of Thos).*
Or 3 bars Sa over all 3 hanks of cord Gu
— *XF 225. (imp Or chev betw 3 ravens' heads erased Sa).*

3 bars & over all maunch &c

Arg 3 bars Sa maunch Gu
MAGNEBY, Hugh de. *P 159. ('...trois barres de sable chargees dune maunche de goules').*
MANBY, Mons John de. *TJ 485.*
MAUNBY, Mons Hugh. *TJ 1044. ('dargent trois barres de sable chargez dune manche*

goules').

Erm 3 bars Sa maunch Gu
OXFORD, Sr John de. *CKO 130.*

Arg 3 bars Gu fretty Or over all 3 piles in pt Az
roundelly Or & over the whole stag stat Sa
attired Or in dex chf sickle Ppr handle Gu
banded Or
— *CB 208.*

Arg 3 bars Gu fretty Or over all 3 piles in pt Az
roundelly Or & over the whole stag stat Sa
attired Or in dex chf sickle Ppr handle Gu
banded Or
HOGHTON, John de. *TJ 1303. ds BS 3 bars
salt lozy*

Arg 3 bars Gu fretty Or over all 3 piles in pt Az
roundelly Or & over the whole stag stat Sa
attired Or in dex chf sickle Ppr handle Gu
banded Or
GREY, Richard de, of Derbys, Kt. *Birch
10276. ...M: RICARDI.... 1282.*

Arg 3 bars wavy Gu salt Or
MABANKES. *WB IV 139b, 247.*
MABANKES. *L1 451, 6; L2 339, 8.*

Arg 3 bars Az 3 chaplets Gu
GREISTOCK. *RL 37.*

Arg 3 bars Az 3 chaplets Or
— *BR VI 57. (marshalled by Ld Graystoke).*

3 bars over all ... & label

3 bars bend sin label
— *Bk of Sls 333. 1369. (dimid by cross
flory on sl of Idanea, former w of Edm
Crawesnerd, of Brook, ?Kent).*

3 bars wavy over all fess checky & in chf label
of 5
STEWART, Alex, 6th E of Menteith (d ante
1306). *Stevenson. 1296.*

3 bars canton & over all

Or 3 bars Gu canton Erm bend Sa
CAUFELD. *DV 61a, 2401.*
GARRFELD, de .... *LH 389.*
GAUFELDE. *PLN 1620.*

3 bars chief & over all

Az 3 bars Arg chf Or over all lion Gu holding
axe Sa shafted Or
— *WLN 104.*

Az 3 bars Arg chf Erm over all lion Gu
EGRENHALE. *XL 502. (or Egrevale).*
EGRENHALE. *LE 79.*
EGRENHALL. *CC 222, 16.*

Gu 3 bars Or over all lion Arg on chf vairy Or
and Vt castle 3-turreted Arg
PEVEREL, Count of Nottingham. *XL 182.
(?bars gemel).*
PEVERELL, Conte. *L9 107a, 6. (middle tower
surmounted by spire).*

3 bars chief & over all escutch (e.g. Mortimer): see Barry &c chief paly

3 bars betw

3 bars betw 8 martlets
LAVINTONE, William de. *PRO-sls.* S'GUIL DE
LAVINTONE. *1345-6. (used by Jn de Fryk).*

3 bars betw 10 martlets (3, 3, 3, 1)
[SOMERVILLE]. *Dugd 17, 45. 1358-9.*

3 bars & orle of martlets
CADURCIS, Thomas de, Kt. *Bow XLIX 11.
1312-13. (9 martlets).*
LAVINTONE, William de. *PRO-sls E40
A6793.* S'GUIL.DE.LAVINTONE. *1345-6. (used
by Jn le Ayk).*

Arg 3 bars & orle of martlets (except in chf) Gu
ROTHING, S Rauff de. *GA 234.*

Arg 3 bars & orle of martlets Gu
RORYNGE. *L1 552, 3.*
ROTHINGE, Sire Rauf de. *N 554. ('de argent
a iii barres de goules od la bordure de
merelos de goules').*

3 bars betw 4 roundels (3 in chf, 1 in base)
WAKE, John. *Clairambault 9638. 29 Oct
1439.*

3 bars in border

3 bars & border
[MOULTON]. *Farrer I 222. (mont at Wick-
hampton Ch).*
PUSEY, Henry. *BerksCRO-sls Bouverie Pusey
Deeds EBP/T8. 1309-10. (?charges in
border; s & h of Ric P, Kt).*

Arg 3 bars Az & border Gu
GRIMBALD. *Nichols Leics II 733. (arms of
Founder, Sir Robt G, used by Ouston Abbey;
Norton Ch).*
PONTIF, le conte de. *XF 310.*
PONTIS, Count of. *L9 104a, 3. (17 cent hand
has struck out P & substituted 'Dammartin').*

Arg 3 bars & border Sa
— *L9 43b, 8. (imp by Litton).*

Or 3 bars Az & border Erm
— *D13 71. (qtd 3 by Suscher).*

Or 3 bars Sa & border Erm
— *1H7 2d.*

3 bars & border semy of roundels
MORTON, Ld Walter de, of Bucks. *Birch
11983.* S' WALTERI DE MORTVN. *temp Hen 3.*

Arg 3 bars Az & border Gu semy of roundels Or
POWYS. *PLN 1574.*

3 bars & border engr
BREDEKIRKE, John of. *Durham-sls 390.
1344.*
[FITZJOHN]. *Birch 9735.* S' GALFRIDI FIL'
IOHANNIS. *temp Hen 3. (Geoffrey fil
Johannis (fil Hugonis), of Fyfield, Berks).*

Az 3 bars Or & border engr Arg
　HAKE. *LH 340.*
　HAKE, Mons' Andreu. *TJ 1399.*
Or 3 bars Az & border engr Arg
　ASKE. *XF 328.*
Or 3 bars Az & border engr Gu
　ASKE, of Yorks. *L2 11, 4.*
Untinc 3 bars Erm & border gobony Untinc
　BURLEY, Thomas de. *PRO-sls.* 1368-70.
　(bro of Hosp of St John of Jerusalem in Irld;
　King's Chancellor in Irld).
Gu 3 bars couped & border Erm
　DABERYCHCORT, Sir Nicoll. *RH, Ancestor ix*
　163.

On 3 bars (i.e. 3 bars, one or more charged)

On 3 bars 9 indistinct charges
　— *PRO-sls.* 1363. *(?3 bars Erm & border).*
　(escutch on sl of Jn de Burley).
Erm on 3 bars indistinct charges Untinc
　DABRICHECOURT, Eustace. *PRO-sls.* 1367-8.
　(charges ?escallops or leopards' heads).
3 bars & on 2nd bar annulet
　ASKE, Elizabeth. *Mill Steph.* *(imp by*
　Fitzwilliam; brass to Eliz, dau of Jn A, & w
　of Thos F, both d1403, Mablethorpe, Lincs).
Gu 3 bars Or & on 2nd bar annulet Sa
　BLACKFORD. *XF 316.*
　BLAKEFORD. *SK 919.*
Or 3 bars Az & on 1st bar annulet Or
　ASKE, of Aughton, Yorks. *L2 16, 3.*
Erm 3 bars couped & on 2nd bar annulet
　DABRIDGECOURT, John. *Birch 9156.* SIGIL-
　LUM: IOHANIS: DABRICHCOURT. ?1409.
Arg 3 bars Az on 2nd bar 2 annulets interlaced
Arg
　MAIDSTONE. *FK II 810.*
Arg 3 bars Az on 2nd bar 2 annulets interlaced
Or
　MAIDSTONE. *XF 694.*
　MAYDESTONE. *L9 52a, 5.*
　MAYDESTONE. *L2 348, 11.*

On 3 bars bird &c

Az on each of 3 bars falcon Arg
　FAWKENER, John. *RH, Ancestor vii 208.*
　(bars like perches).
Arg on 3 bars Sa 3 martlets in pale Or
　— *SK 256.*
Or 3 bars Sa on each 2 martlets Arg
　GORGES. *XF 734.*
Gu on 3 bars Arg 9 birds Untinc
　— *E6. (qtd by Savell, of Yorks).*
Arg on 3 bars Gu 6 bougets 3, 2, 1 Arg
　STRANGE. *LS 150.*
　STRANGE, Sir Peter. *XF 109.*
　STRAUNGE, Pe. *NS 68.*

Arg on 3 bars Gu 6 bougets 2, 2, 2 Arg
　STRAUNGE. *CB 53.*

On 3 bars crescent &c

3 bars on 1st bar cresc
　FREGENHALL, Richard. *Roman PO 4863.* 12
　Oct 1440.
Arg 3 bars wavy Gu on 1st bar cresc Arg
　CHAMPNEYS. *SK 437.*
Arg 3 bars Az on 1st bar 3 crescs Gu
　— *CRK 1942.*
Arg 3 bars Gu & 3 crescs Sa
　— *E6 26b. (subimp by Plumpton, of Plump-*
　ton, Yorks).
Arg on 3 bars Gu 6 crosslets (3, 2, 1) Or
　DAUNDELEY, S' Rob'. *PO 641.*
On 3 bars 8 crosses
　GALLE, John de. *PRO-sls.* 13 cent.
Arg 3 bars Gu on each 3 crosslets Or
　DANNDELEGH. *L1 213, 6; L2 160, 2.*
Erm 3 bars couped Gu on each escallop Or
　DABREGECOURT. *L2 149, 11.*
　DABREGECOURT. *L1 187, 2.*
Erm on 3 bars couped Gu 6 escallops (3, 2, 1)
Or
　DABRYSCOURT. *L10 52b, 10.*
　DAUBRIGCOURT, Mons Eustace. *WJ 534.*
　DAUBRIGCOURT, Mons Gafry. *WJ 535.*
Erm 3 bars couped Gu on each 3 escallops Or
　DABRICHECOURT, John. *S 312.*
　DABRICHECOURT, John de. *S 324.*
Erm 3 bars couped Gu on each escallops Or
　D'AUBECHECOURT, Mons Nichol. *CA 115.*
Erm 3 bars Untinc & on 2nd bar star (?estoile)
Untinc betw 2 Erm spots
　TURNBULL, Wm. *Stevenson.* 1497. *(s of*
　Roland T, of High St, Edinburgh, or
　[Agnes]).

On 3 bars fleur de lis &c

Arg on 3 bars couped Vt 3 fleurs de lis (2, 1) Or
　ROTHELEY, W. *CRK 1190.*
Arg on 3 bars Sa 6 3foils Arg (3, 2, 1)
　TREVRY. *BA 968.*
On 3 bars 6 5foils (3, 2, 1)
　DARELL, Thomas. *Birch 9197.* SIGILLU
　THOME DARELL ARMIGIR. 15 cent.
Arg on 3 bars Az 6 5foils (3, 2, 1) Arg
　— *RB 313. (qtd 2&3 by Pever).*
　— *RB 312.*
　— *XV II 148. (qtd by Peyver).*

On 3 bars fruit &c

Erm on 3 bars couped Gu 11 ears of wheat 4, 4,
3 Or
　STOKES. *XF 889.*
　STOKES. *LS 124.*

Erm 3 bars couped Sa semy of ears of wheat Or
STOKES. *L1 593, 4.*
Arg 3 bars Sa on each maunche Gu
MAGNEBY, Hugh de. *P 159.*
Sa 3 bars Arg on 1st bar mullet Gu
HOGHTON, John. *LH 330.*
Sa 3 bars Arg on each mullet Sa
HOGHTON. *LH 999.*
Gu 3 bars Arg on each 2 pales Sa
BARRE, Sir John. *WB IV 169b, 989.*
Gu on 3 bars Arg 6 roundels (3, 2, 1) Sa
BLANKLEY. *WB I 43b, 13.*
3 bars on each 3 roundels
REVESCROFT, Hugh de. *PRO-sls.* 1357.

On 3 bars & canton

Arg 3 bars Sa on 1st lion pg betw 2 martlets on
2nd 3 pd 5foils on 3rd 3 escallops all Or on
canton Az dove rising wings displ Arg b&l
Gu
THURSTON. *XF 267.*
THURSTON, Joh. *L10 99, 1. (Sheriff & Ald-
erman of London).*
Arg 3 bars Sa on 1st lion passt regard betw 2
martlets on 2nd 3 5foils on 3rd 3 escallops
all Or on canton Az dove rising Arg
THURSTON. *XPat 403, Arch 69, 99.*
Az 3 bars Arg on 2nd bar 3 finches Vt b&l Gu
on canton Gu salt couped Arg
— *WK 809. (imp by Phillip de Carouges).*
FYNCHE, Elizabeth. *WK 808. (loz).*
Sa 3 bars Arg on 2nd bar 3 finches Vt b&l Gu
on canton Gu salt couped Arg
FINCH. *XX 305.*
FINCH. *XF 85.*
FYNCHE, of London. *L2 207, 2.*
Sa on 3 bars Arg 6 finches (3, 2, 1) Vt b&l Gu
on canton Gu salt couped Arg
FYNCHE. *L10 109, 7. (imp by Joh Dawes,
alderman of London, for his w Mgt, dau of
Jas F).*
Sa on 3 bars Or 6 finches (3, 2, 1) Vt b&l Gu on
canton Gu salt couped Arg
FYNCHE. *L10 100, 2. (qrs 1&4 on coat imp
by Joh Dawes).*
Sa on 3 bars Or 6 finches (3, 2, 1) Ppr on canton
Gu salt couped Arg
FYN[CH], Margaret. *WK 571. (imp by Jn
Dawes, Alderman of London).*
Sa 3 bars Arg on 2nd bar 3 popinjays Vt b&l Gu
on canton Gu salt couped Arg
— *PLN 1938. (qtd 4 by [Waring]).*

On 3 bars & chf

Arg 3 bars wavy Sa each ch with 3 roundels Arg
on chf Gu gun-barrel betw 2 anchors Or
GONSON. *XPat 274, Arch 69, 90. ('of Lon-
don' added).*
GONSON, William. *XF 637.*
GONSON, William. *WK 767. (gun fessways).*
GOUNSTON, Mayster. *I2(1904)123.*
Az on 3 bars Arg 3 3foils slipped Sa on chf Arg
3 lions' heads erased Gu
TROYS, Thomas. *1H7 30; D13 104d.*
Gu 3 bars wavy Arg each ch with 3 martlets Sa
on chf Or 3 roundels Sa
MARLAND. *L10 110b, 2.*
MARLAND. *XF 609.*
MARLAND. *BA 512.*
MARLAND. *WK 636.*
MARLANDE. *XPat 347, Arch 69, 95.*

On 3 bars & over all

On 3 bars 8 escallops over all bend
— *PRO-sls E40 A10298.* 1444-5. *(qtd 2&3
by Michael Power).*
On 3 bars 8 ?roses over all bend
— *PRO-sls.* 1444-5. *(charges unclear; qtd
by Michael Power).*

3 bars cotised

Sa 3 bars Erm each cotised gobony Or and Arg
HORWOD, of Hunts. *L1 353, 2; L2 264, 9.*
HORWOD, John, of Hunts. *LD 151.*

4 BARS OR 2 BARS GEMEL

4 bars
MYLTON, Richard, of East Greenwich. *PRO-
sls E40 A4922.* 1446-7. *(?3 bars & chf).*
2 bars gemel
BARRY, John de. *Birch 7173. ...IGILLVM....*
1301. *(s&h of David de B, of Penally,
Pembs).*
BARRY, Sir John B. *Lawrance 1.* c1324.
(effigy, Manorbier, Pembs).
BENESTED, John of. *Durham-sls 198.* 1310.
BENSTEDE, John de. *Birch 7367.* 1310.
FITZRADULF, Nicholas. *Dugd 17, 77.* 1268.
MEINILL, Nicholas de. *PRO-sls.* 1301.
(unclear).
PENEBRUGE, Henry. *PRO-sls.* 13 cent. *(s of
Ralf de P).*

Arg 4 bars or 2 bars gemel
Arg 4 bars Az
FEYCE, William. *PLN 730.*

Arg 4 bars Gu
— WLN 142. (imp by le Roy de Ungarye).
GREECE, King of. PCL IV 65. (qr 1).
HUNGARIE, le Roy de. AS 8.
MOLTON, Sir Thomas. ML 66.
NEAPOLIS, Kyng of. Lyndsay 31. (qtly: 1&4
tierced (a)Arg 4 bars Gu (b)Old France
(c)Jerusalem, 2&3 Or 4 pales Gu).
SOULLY, Sir John. WGA 237.
Arg 2 bars gemel Gu
— ML I 501. ('sylver iiii gemellys in ii
barres gowles').
CROSWELL. L2 145, 6.
Arg 4 bars Sa
NEWPORT, Mr. WB II 70, 8. (qrs 1&4).
TRERYS, Sir .... WB I 41b, 7.
Arg 2 bars gemel Sa
— WLN 621.
— F 151.
CARSWELL. L1 125, 5; L2 110, 9.
GELDEFORD, Johan de. LM 573.
GILDEFORD, Jan de. Q 268.
GUILDEFORD, of Staffs. L2 232, 2.
GULDEFORD, Sire Johan de. N 993.

Az &c 4 bars or 2 bars gemel
Az 4 bars Arg
DELALAWNDE, Thomas. WB IV 175, 888.
Az 4 bars Or
SPRYGONELL, Mons Rauf. WJ 992.
Gu 2 bars gemel Arg
BARRY, Mons' John. TJ 558. ('de goules
deux gemelx dargent en manere de barres').
Gu 2 bars gemel Or
PARRY. CT 127.
Or 4 bars Gu
POINTZ, Hugh. K 204.
Or 4 bars Sa
— Q II 469.
Sa 2 bars gemel Or lower voided Gu
— WB II 68, 3. (qtd 2 by Or eagle Gu sans
beak & legs).

Erm &c 4 bars or 2 bars gemel
Erm 2 bars gemel Untinc
HUNTERCOMBE, Walter of. Barons Letter.
HUNTERCOMBE, Walter of. Barons Letter,
HB-SND.
HUNTERCUMBE, Walter de. Birch 10924. S'
WALTERI DE HVNTERCVMBE. late 13 cent.
Erm 4 bars Gu
SOULLY, Sir John. WGA B 237.
SULLY, Sir John. BB 141, 9. (d c1388).
[SULLY], Sir John, KG. Leake. (d1387-8).
Erm 2 bars gemel Gu
HONTERCOMB. RB 360.
HONTERCOMBE. DV 54b, 2159.
HONTERCOMBE. L2 260, 2.
HONTERCOMBE, Sire Wauter de. N 80.

HONTERKUMBE, Water de. G 161.
HOUERCOMB. L1 342, 3. (or Undercombe).
HOUNTERCOMBE, Sire Wauter de. J 49.
HUNDURCOMBE, Sire Water. PO 614.
HUNT[ER]CUMBE, Wauter de. LM 77.
HUNTERCOMBE. SP A 146.
HUNTERCOMBE. AS 140.
HUNTERCOMBE, Le Sire de. CG 248.
HUNTERCOMBE, Sr de. CKO 327.
HUNTERCOMBE, Ralph. LH 252.
HUNTERCOMBE, Ralph. LH 840.
HUNTERCOMBE, Ralph de. XF 381.
HUNTERCOMBE, Sir Walter. LH 220.
HUNTERCOMBE, Walter. LH 327.
HUNTERCOMBE, Walter. TJ 518. ('dermyne
deux fees gemellez de goules' (drawn as two
fesses cotised)).
HUNTERCOMBE, Walter de. LMS 80.
(d1312).
HUNTERCOMBE, Walter de. K 365.
HUNTERCOMBE, Sir Waut' de. GA 122.
HUNTERCOMBE, Wauter de. H 34a.
HUNTERCUMBE, Walt de. Q II 48.
HUNTERCUMBE, Wautier. TJ 1264.
HUNTERTOMBE, William. PCL I 538.
HUNTRECOMBE, Ralph. E I 482; E II 484.
HUNTYRCOUMP, Sr Waultier. H 34b.
('d' argent d' ermyne or ii gemeus de gulez').
HUNTYRCUMBE, Mons Waut' de. WJ 914.
NORMAVILLE. CT 168.
Erm 2 bars gemel Sa
BUT'COMBE. XF 400. (?Huntercombe?).
HUNTERCOMBE. E I 604; E II 606. (?bars
Gu).
HUNTERCOMBE. LH 995.
Vair 4 bars Gu
COUCY, Earle of Bedford. RH, Ancestor iii
213. (name written in later hand).

4 bars or 2 bars gemel patterned
Untinc 4 bars Erm
FOTHERINGHAM, Margaret. Stevenson. 1511.
(w of Jn Lovell, burgess of Dundee).
FOTHERINGHAM, Thomas, of Powrie Wester.
Stevenson. 1593.
Untinc 4 bars Vair
— LonG-sls. 1432. (unclear; imp by Robt
FitzRobert; Cooper's Co Deeds GLMR 7531).
EPPYNGE, Matilda de. PRO-sls. (w of Peter
de Harewes).
Gu 4 bars Vair
CUSCI, Engelrami de. MP Hist Min iii 84.
(inverted; footnote says 'barry of 8 argent &
vairi gules').

4 bars or 2 bars gemel modified
Or 4 bars dancetty Az
OWLIAMS. L2 393, 6.

Az 4 bars embattled Or
GUINES, Le Conte de. *XF 312.*
Gu 4 bars embattled counter-emb & voided Or
SIRIE, Rex. *RH, Ancestor ix 179.*
Or 4 bars battled counter-emb & voided Gu
MASSYDONIE, Roy de. *RH, Ancestor ix 179.*
Arg 4 bars lozy Gu
THOMAS, le fitz. *BA 1207. (?lozy Arg and Gu).*
Gu 2 bars gemel Or potenty & counterpotenty on inner sides interspaces Sa
ALMAYE, Rex Welmarie d'. *RH, Ancestor vii 199.*
4 bars nebuly
GEOFFREY ATTE HACCHE. *CassPk 307.* 22 May 1369. *(legend defaced; 1st of 2 sls appended to grant by Geoffrey atte Hacche & Wm atte Thome re land at Little Hadham, Herts).*
Gu 4 bars wavy Arg
ARTOYE, Janico de. *TJ 1545. ('... ove quatre fees oundez dargent').*
Erm 2 bars gemel wavy Gu
HUNTERCOMDE, Sir Walter. *BR V 79. (?bars not wavy).*
Sa 4 bars wavy Arg gutty Sa
BARLE. *SHY 264. (imp by ?Walter).*

4 bars or 2 bars gemel & label

Gu 4 bars Arg & label Untinc
— *WB I 17, 6. (qtd 2 by Gernald or Grenald).*
4 bars wavy & label
HENRY, John ap, of Kilpeck. *PRO-sls.* 1422-3.

4 bars or 2 bars gemel & in base

Gu 4 bars Or & isst from base gusset counterch
POYNTZ, Hugh. *XF 472.*
4 bars wavy & in base mullet
DRUMMOND, John. *Stevenson.* 1522. *(Chief Carpenter to Jas 4 & 5).*

4 bars or 2 bars gemel & canton

Arg 4 bars & canton Gu
COWFFOLD, of Essex. *MY A2 177.*
Arg 2 bars gemel & canton Gu
— *XF 881.*
Arg 2 bars gemel & sin canton Gu
STRICKLAND, Sir Walter. *BR V 88.*
Arg 4 bars & canton Sa
CROWHYRST, de Scotney, Suss. *CY 169, 676.*
Arg 2 bars gemel & canton Sa
BUKTON. *SK 524.*

4 bars or 2 bars gemel & on canton

4 bars & on canton lion
ALDER, Robert. *BM Harl 1448, 50b, HB-SND.* 1459.
Sa 4 bars Arg & on canton Arg 4 lozs in bend conjd Sa
GOVYS. *H18 39d. (qtd 3 by Fyldl, of Woodland, Dorset).*
2 bars gemel & on canton 5 billets
INGLOSE, Henry, Kt. *PRO-sls E40 A7907.* 1450-1. *(?billets or roundels).*
Arg 4 bars Gu & on canton Sa cross fourchy Or
ECTON, Sir Milis, of Hants. *WB III 83, 4.*
Gu 4 bars Arg & on canton Untinc cross formy Untinc
ETTON, Sir J of. *WB I 38, 15.*
4 bars & on canton 5foil
— *Birch 4366.* 16 cent. *(doubtful sl of Hosp of St Wolstan, Worcs).*
Arg 2 bars gemel & on canton Gu pd 5foil Arg
BECKINGHAM. *XF 2.*
BEKINGHAM, Thomas. *ME 118; LY A 243.*
BEKYNGHAM. *L10 27, 20.*

4 bars or 2 bars gemel & chf

2 bars gemel & chf
RICHMOND, Joan. *Yorks Deeds VII 60 & 62.* 1320. *(wid of Sir Thos de R; ?bars single).*
RICHMOND, Sir Thomas de. *Yorks Deeds V 124.* 1297. *(?bars single).*
SYFIRWAST, John. *BirmCL-sls 494330.* 1410-11.
SYFREWAST, Sir John. *Burrows 301-2.* Sigillu : Iohannis : Syfrewast. 1384.
SYFREWAST, John, Ld of Clewer. *PRO-sls.* 1434-5.
THORNEHILL, William, Esq. *Birch 13914.* 1438.
THORNHILL, Beatrice. *Yorks Deeds IV 152.* 1322. *(wid of Sir Jn de T; with 2nd unidentified sh: fess betw 3 fleurs de lis).*
THORNHILL, John de. *Yorks Deeds III 35.* 1422.
THORNHILL, William de. *Yorks Deeds III 36.* 1420.
THORNHILL, William de. *Yorks Deeds VII 44.* 1438.
Untinc 2 bars gemel & chf Or
MENIL, Nicol de. *LM 142.*
Arg 2 bars gemel & chf Gu
GIFFARD, Hossebarn. *FW 301.*

Az 4 bars or 2 bars gemel & chf

Az 2 bars gemel & chf Arg
MENILL, Sire Nichole de. *J 80.*
SIFFEWAST, Monsire Roger. *AN 272.*
SYFREWASTE. *DV 56b, 2235.*

Az 2 bars gemel & chf Or
— *XL 218. (qtd 3 by Strangways).*
— *WB IV 177b, 930. (imp by Brekenock).*
— *XL 220. (qtd III 2&3 by Strangways).*
— *WB II 49, 13. (qtd 2&3 by Ld Darcy).*
— *PLN 487. (imp by [Brecknock]).*
— *D4 28b & 34. (subimp by Bulmer, of Yorks).*
CYFREWAST. *CV-BM 93.*
MENILL, Mons Nich. *WJ 821.*
MENILL, Nicolas de. *E II 181.*
MENILLE, Sr de. *CKO 276.*
MEYNEL, Sire Nicholas de. *N 134.*
MEYNILL, Sr Nichol de. *H 77b.*
SIFREWAST. *LS 9.*
SIFREWAST. *LS 311.*
SIFREWAST, Richard. *XF 936.*
SIFREWAST, Richard de. *E I 217; E II 219.*
SYFERWAST. *SK 586.*
SYFFREWAST, de. *F 427.*
SYFREWAST. *WLN 523.*

Gu 4 bars or 2 bars gemel & chf
Gu 2 bars gemel & chf Arg
THORN[HILL], Sr Brian de. *CKO 280.*
THORNHILL. *XF 71.*
THORNHILL. *RH, Ancestor iv 234. (qtd by Sir Jn Saywyle, Yorks).*
THORNHILL, Mons' Bryan. *TJ 781.*
THORNHILL, Monsire Bryan de. *CG 194.*
THORNHILL, Monsr Bryan de. *AS 230.*
THORNHILLE, S' bryan. *PO 507.*
THORVILL, Johannes. *Q II 611.*
Gu 2 bars gemel & chf Or
— *FK II 661.*
RICHEMOND, Sr Rohaut de. *CKO 279.*
RICHEMOND, Rouald de. *P 145.*
RICHEMONDE, Mons' Roald de. *TJ 780.*
RICHEMONNDE, S Thomas de. *GA 245. ('de gueules a ii gymels dor a le chief dor').*
RICHEMUND, Thom de. *LM 251.*
RICHMOND. *XF 354.*
RICHMOND, Briaunt de. *E II 388.*
RICHMOND, Roald, Constable of. *B 209. ('de goules a ung cheif d'or a deus gemeus de l'un en l'autre d'or').*
RICHMOND, Sir Roland. *LR 8.*
RICHMOND, William de. *WLN 719.*
RICHMONT, Monsire Rohaine de. *CG 193.*
RICHMONT, Thomas de. *K 717.*
RICHMUND, Ronant de. *Q 209.*
RUGEMOND, Sire Thomas de. *N 1062.*
RYCHEMOUND, Mons Roland de. *WJ 551.*

Or &c 4 bars or 2 bars gemel & chf
Or 2 bars gemel Gu & chf Arg
— *PT 308.*

Sa 2 bars gemel & chf Arg
MAY, Hew. *BR IV 40.*
MELSANBY, Walter de. *TJ 1457.*

Erm &c 4 bars or 2 bars gemel & chf
Erm 2 bars gemel & chf Gu
DYCHANT, John. *TJ 1565.*
Erm 2 bars gemel & chf Or
DALAVALE, Mons' John. *TJ 520.*

4 bars or 2 bars gemel & patterned chf
4 bars & chf checky of 10
CALETOFT, Philip de. *Birch 8019.* +S' DNI' FILIPPI DE CALETOH'. temp Edw 1. *(s of Eudo de C, of Thoresby, Lincs).*
4 bars & chf paly
MALDON, William de. *PRO-sls.* 1357-8. *(blazon of chf doubtful).*

4 bars or 2 bars gemel & modified chf
Gu 2 bars gemel Or & chf indented Erm
HYNKPENNE. *L1 321, 4.*
INKPEN. *Gerard 184.*
INKPENNE. *LH 1046.*
Gu 4 bars Or & chf invected Erm
— *LH 677. (qtd 3 by Inkpen).*
Gu 2 bars gemel Or & chf invected Erm
— *PLN 1619. (qtd 2&3 by [Inkpen]).*
HYNKEPENNE. *CC 234b, 402. (qtd 2&3 by Colshill).*
HYNKEPENNE. *CC 234b, 403.*
HYNKEPENNE. *L2 254, 10.*
KRYNKEPENE. *L9 10b, 5.*

4 bars or 2 bars gemel chf & label
2 bars gemel & on chf label of 5
RICHMOND, Sir Roald de. *Yorks Deeds VII 61.* 1321. *(?bars single).*

4 bars or 2 bars gemel & on chf
4 bars wavy & on chf demi-lion isst
?MAGGESSONE. *Stowe-Bard 2s iii 4.* 1397-8. *(sl used by Cecilia, dau of Jn M, of Lynn; legend mutilated).*
Untinc 4 bars wavy Az & on chf Untinc demi-horse isst Untinc
[TREVELYAN?]. *WB I 16, 13.*
Arg 2 bars gemel & on chf Gu lion passt Or
— *WLN 178.*
Gu 4 bars Arg & on chf Or lion passt Sa
— *XF 327. (qtd 2&3 by Malyfaunt).*
— *CRK 1156. (qtd 2&3 by Malefant).*
— *WB III 86, 1. (a&l Gu; qtd 2&3 by Sir Jn Malefaunt, of Walis).*
Or 2 bars gemel & on chf Gu lion passt Or
GIFFORDE, Osbarn. *A 220.*

2 bars gemel & on chf lion pg
— *PRO-sls.* 1284-5. *(1 of 3 shields on sl of Sybil, w of Sir Wm Graunsun).*
Or 2 bars gemel Gu & on chf Untinc lion pg Untinc
TREGOS. *CT 91.*
Gu 2 bars gemel & chf Or in dex chf cresc Sa
RICHEMOUND, John de. *WJ 552.*
Az 2 bars gemel & on chf Arg 3 lozs Gu
STERLYNG, Sir T. *WB I 41, 17.*
Gu 2 bars gemel & chf Or in dex chf mullet Sa
STODAWE, John de. *WJ 548.*
STODDAW, John. *LS 179.*
Sa 4 bars & on chf Or 3 roundels Sa on 1st roundel fleur de lis Arg
HILDESLEY. *LH 678.*

4 bars or 2 bars gemel & in chf

Erm 2 bars gemel & in chf demi-lion isst Gu
FREWEN, Fulke. *XL 356.*
FREYNE. *CC 228, 196.*
FREYNE. *L1 259, 3; L2 206, 6.*
FREYNE, Mons Fowk la. *WJ 225.*

4 bars or 2 bars gemel & in chf lion

2 bars gemel & in chf lion passt
— *Birch 10203.* c1286. *(on sl of Sibilla de Grandissono, w of Wm de Gravencon).*
ENGLEFEUD, William de. *PRO-sls.* 13 cent. *(?4 bars).*
GOLDINGTON, William de, Kt, of Essex & Berks. *Birch 10149.* S' WILL'I DE GOLDI.... 1316.
TREGOZ. *A 169.*
TREGOZ, Geoffrey. *Bk of Sls 80.*
TREGOZ, Geoffrey. *Birch 13975.* SIGULLVM SECRETI. mid 13 cent.
TREGOZ, Henry. *PRO-sls.* 1301.
Arg 2 bars gemel & in chf lion passt Gu
FARRYNGES, Richard de. *FW 650.*
FERINGES, Richard. *A 136. (tincts uncertain).*
TREGOCE. *Q II 90.*
TREGOCE, Sir John. *PCL I 542.*
Az 2 bars gemel & in chf lion passt Or
TREGOS, s' Henri. *PO 645.*
TREGOSSE, Henry. *A 90.*
TREGOZ, Henri. *D 198a.*
TREGOZ, Munsire Henri. *D 198b. ('dazure od deus lystes dor a un leun passant dor').*
TREGOZ, Henry. *E II 217.*
TREGOZ, Robert de. *B 113. ('de gules od deux gemelles d'or et un leon [d'or] en le chief passant').*
[TREGOZE]. *WB I 35b, 6.*
Or 2 bars gemel & in chf lion passt Gu
TREGOS, Sire Johan. *J 86.*
TREGOT, Jan. *Q 90.*

TREGOZ, Johan. *LM 159.*
TREYGUS, of Kent. *CY 146, 583.*

4 bars or 2 bars gemel & in chf lion pg
2 bars gemel & in chf lion pg
TREGOZ, Henry. *Barons Letter.*
Az 2 bars gemel & in chf lion pg Arg
NEIVILE, Water de. *E II 263.*
NEIVILE, Water de. *E I 261.*
NEVILE. *L9 82b, 3.*
TREIGOZ, Henry. *HE 101. (?charges Or).*
Az 2 bars gemel & in chf lion pg Or
GREGOR. *L2 231, 2.*
GREGORY, Monsire, de Suss. *TJ 183. ('Gregory an error for Tregoz').*
TREGOLZ. *SP A 120.*
TREGOSE, Ralph. *XL 458.*
TREGOZ. *CRK 1561.*
TREGOZ, Monsire. *CG 553.*
TREGOZ, Henri. *F 334.*
TREGOZ, Sire Henri. *N 115. ('...en le chef un lupard passant de or').*
TREGOZ, Henry. *FW 140.*
TREGOZ, Henry. *WLN 838.*
TREGOZ, Henry. *E I 215.*
TREGOZ, Henry. *XF 935.*
TREGOZ, Sr, of Suss. *CKO 605.*
TREYGOS. *SK 173.*
TREYGOS, Henry. *CV-BM 287.*
TREYGOS, Mons Rauf. *WJ 397.*
Gu 2 bars gemel & in chf lion pg Arg
SPIGURNEL, Thomas. *XL 395.*
Gu 2 bars gemel & in chf lion pg Or
SPIGURNEL. *XF 786.*
SPRYGONELL, Mons Tho. *WJ 369.*
TREGOZ, Robert. *E I 99; E II 99.*
TREVOS, Henre. *WB I 19, 2.*
Or 2 bars gemel Gu & in chf lion pg Az
[TREGOZ]. *TJ 184. ('son cousin', ie of Monsire Gregory de Sussex).*
Or 2 bars gemel & in chf lion pg Gu
— *XF 785.*
TREGOIZ, John. *FW 139.*
TREGOS. *CC 54b, 2146. (name in later hand).*
[TREGOS]. *TZ 1.*
TREGOS, Monsire, de Suss. *CG 552.*
TREGOT, Jan. *Q 185.*
TREGOUS, Jon. *F 48.*
TREGOZ, Geffry. *C 97. ('d'or a un leparde de gules en le chef a ii gymeles de goules').*
TREGOZ, Joan. *E I 97.*
TREGOZ, Johan. *D 106a.*
TREGOZ, Munsire Johan. *D 106b. ('d'or ad deus listes de gules a un leopard de gules').*
TREGOZ, Sr John. *H 78b. ('... en le chef ung leopard passaunt de gules').*
TREGOZE, Sr. *CKO 604.*
TREIGOZ, Sire Jon. *HE 115.*

TREYGOS, Mons' John. *TJ 191.*
TREYGUS. *CVK 672.*
Or 2 bars gemel Gu & in chf lion pg Or
TREGOZ, John. *E II 97.*

4 bars or 2 bars gemel & in chf lion pg crowned
Az 2 bars gemel & in chf lion pg Arg crowned Or
NEVILE, Walter de. *XF 948.*

4 bars or 2 bars gemel & in chf other beast &c
2 bars gemel & in chf greyhound courant
KNOLLE, John, of Bridgwater. *Bridgwater 187, 351.* 1358. *(sl; beast uncertain).*
Arg 2 bars gemel & in chf 2 lions Gu
— *CRK 2.* *('..alston' added in modern hand).*
— *WK 148.* *(qtd 2&3 by Darell).*
Az 4 bars & in centre chf cresc Or
SPRIGONELL, Mons Thom. *WJ 996.*
Gu 4 bars Arg & in chf 3 pd 5foils Or
GRENAM, John. *BG 84.*
Az 2 bars gemel & in sin chf griffin's head erased Or
BYLSDEN. *L1 116, 6; L2 86, 6.*
Az 4 bars & in chf 3 lions' heads erased Arg
NEWARK, of Dalton. *XF 882.* *(narrow bars).*
Az 2 bars gemel & in chf 3 lions' heads erased Arg
NEWARK. *L1 471, 2; L2 359, 7.*
NEWARKE, of Dawlton. *L2 362, 3.*
NEWERKE. *L9 83a, 11.*

4 bars or 2 bars gemel & in chf mullet &c
4 bars & in chf 3 mullets
HYLDESLEY, Wm. *OxfRS II 106.* temp Hen 8. *(brass, Crowmarsh, Oxfords).*
Arg 2 bars gemel Az in chf 3 mullets Gu
BRIDDELESHALA. *L10 79b, 3.*
BRIDESALE, Sire Gilberd. *N 649.*
BRYEYLSHALL, of Lincs. *L2 89, 6.*
2 bars gemel & in chf 3 roundels
— *Mill Steph.* 1433. *(?2 bars; qtd 2&3 by Hotoft on brass to Jn H, Treasurer of Household to Hen 6, Knebworth, Herts).*
Arg 2 bars gemel & in chf 3 roundels Sa
HOLDYCHE. *WB II 62, 13.*
Arg 2 bars gemel & in chf 3 roundels Sa on 1st roundel fleur de lis Or
HOLDYCH. *WB II 62, 14.*
Or 4 bars & in chf 3 roundels Gu
WAKE, Ld de. *BR VI 32.*
Or 4 bars & in chf 3 roundels Sa
HILDESLEY. *LH 679.*
Or 2 bars gemel & in chf 3 roundels Sa
HILDESLEY. *L1 334, 4; L2 248, 3.*
HILDESLEY. *LH 1071.*

HYLDESLEY. *BA 533.*
HYLTUSLE, S' Rob' de. *PO 562.*

4 bars or 2 bars gemel & in chf ... & label
Erm 2 bars gemel & in chf demi-lion isst Gu & label Az
FREYNE, Roger la. *WJ 226.*
Gu 2 bars gemel & in chf lion pg Or & label Az
SPRYGONELL, le fitz. *WJ 370.*

4 bars or 2 bars gemel & over all
4 bars & lion
PIERPOINT, Henry de. *Harl Soc IV 45.* *(barrulets).*
Arg 4 bars Az lion Gu a&l & crowned Or
— *CRK 1398.* *(sin of 3 coats tierced paleways of K of Armenia).*
Arg 4 bars Az lion Or
— *CRK 1303.* *(qtd 4 by Hungerford, Ld Moleyns).*
Arg 4 bars Gu lion Sa crowned Or
WASTHOUSE. *XPat 13, Arch 69, 70.* *(qtd 3 by Sir Harry Amcotts; confirmed by Barker, Garter, 1549, to Sir Alexander A).*
Sa 4 bars nebuly Arg & lion crowned O
CALEYS, [Town of]. *L10 45b, 20.* *(imp Arg on cross betw 4 keys Sa fleur de lis Arg).*
Arg 4 bars Az & 3 lions Gu
WODBURNE, Mons J de. *WJ 228.*
Arg 4 bars Gu & bend Sa
BURTON. *Gerard 90.* *(narrow bend).*
Gu 2 bars gemel & bend Arg
WALEYS, Willame de. *LM 474.*
WALEYS, Wille de. *Q 445.* *(bars gemel widely separated).*
WALEYS, Willimus le. *Q II 433.* *(narrow bend).*
WALEYS, Wm le. *SES 19.* *(narrow bend).*
WALSH, Thomas. *S 278.* *(narrow bend).*
WALSHE, Mons' Thomas. *S 276.* *(narrow bend).*
WELSCHE. *L1 668, 4.*
WELSH, Thomas, d1383. *Nichols Leics III 1099.* *(Wanlip Ch).*
Gu 2 bars gemel Arg & bend Or
QIUTON. *DV 42a, 1653.* *(narrow bend).*
Gu 2 bars gemel & bend Az
— *CRK 1159.* *(narrow bend).*
4 bars & bend engr
CAMERON, Wm. *Stevenson.* 1453.
Arg 4 bars Gu & cross formy Sa
GOWER, of Stydhm. *L2 235, 1.*
GOWER, of Stytenam. *PT 1265.*
Arg 4 bars Gu & cross patonce Sa
GOWRE, of Seydnam, Yorks. *D4 37b.*

Arg 4 bars Az & griffin segr Or armed Gu
    RYSELEY, Sir John, [Kt 1485]. *WB V 74.*
Gu 4 bars Az & griffin segr Sa
    MOPISSON. *WB I 18b, 25. (?barry of 8 Gu*
    and Az etc).
Arg 4 bars Gu & pale Vt fimbr Az
    — *ML I 361. ('A pale vert betwyx ii palettys*
    asur in a feld sylver iiii berulettes upon the
    same goules'; blazon implies that pale is
    cotised, but in painting none of field is visible
    betw green pale & blue pallets).

4 bars or 2 bars gemel & chf & over all

2 bars gemel & chf & bend
    THORNHILL, Thomas de. *Yorks Deeds III 19.*
    1334. *(narrow bend).*
Gu 2 bars gemel & chf Arg bend Sa
    THORNEHILL. *L1 636, 2. (narrow bend).*
    THORNHILL. *CC 228b, 212.*
Gu 2 bars gemel & chf & over all crosier in pale
Or
    ROWALD. *D4 33. (also of St Aggas*
    Monastery, Yorks).

4 bars or 2 bars gemel betw

Gu 2 bars gemel betw 3 annulets Arg
    RIKHILL, Wm. *Arch Cant xxxii 54. (formerly*
    on brass to Wm R & w Katherine, d1433,
    Northfleet, Kent).
Or 4 bars & orle of martlets Gu
    — *PT 592.*

4 bars or 2 bars gemel betw & on chf

Sa 2 bars gemel betw 3 birds close Arg & on chf
Or 3 roundels Az on centre roundel cross
formy & on others goat's head erased Or
    FULLER, Rob, Abbot of Waltham. *L10 90b,*
    1; L10 90b, 2.
Sa 2 bars gemel betw 3 doves Arg on chf Or 3
roundels Az each ch with escallop Or
    [FULLER, Rob, Abbot of Waltham 1526-38].
    XPat 158, Arch 69, 81. (imp by Abbey of
    Waltham Arg on cross engr Sa 5 crosslets
    fitchy Or).

4 bars or 2 bars gemel in border

Az 2 bars gemel & chf Or border engr Erm
    SIFERWAST, Joh'es. *SM 3.*

On 4 bars or 2 bars gemel

Az 4 bars Arg on 1st cresc Sa for diffce
    [LOWND, Thomas de la]. *PLN 445.*

5 BARS

5 bars
    BURDON, Nicholas, Kt. *Bk of Sls 203.* 1261.
    (narrow bars).
    SAMPSON, Henry. *PRO-sls.* 1362.
    SAMPSON, Henry. *Birch 13262.* ..LL'M HEN RI
    SAMPSON. late 14 or early 15 cent.
Arg 5 bars Gu
    HUNGARY, K of. *CRK 1397. (imp Old*
    France).
Or 5 bars Az
    PENBRIG. *BA 19b, 164.*
5 bars engr
    BURDUN, of Gloucs, Kt. *Birch 7925.*
    ...VM: NICHOL.... 1261. *(narrow bars).*
Az 5 bars nebuly Arg
    — *RH, Ancestor ix 170. (attrib by Foster to*
    Wesnam).

5 bars & label

5 bars & label of 5
    EU, Ralph de Yssondin, Count of. *?source.*
    c1200. *(sl, used at Penshurst).*

5 bars & canton

Arg 5 bars & canton Gu
    COWFFOLD. *L1 181, 3; L2 128, 5.*
    COWFFOLD, of Essex. *MY 177.*
Az 5 bars & canton Or
    — *PT 912.*
Az 5 bars & on canton Or martlet Sa
    — *PT 914.*
5 bars & on canton cross
    [?HOO, John]. *Farrer Bacon 82.* 1358.
    (?cross or 4foil; sl on charter of Jn H, re
    land in Foxearth & Pentlow).
Arg 5 bars Gu & on canton Sa cross formy Or
    ELTON, Sir John, of Yorks. *RH, Ancestor iv*
    238.
Arg 5 bars Gu & on canton 3 lozs in fess Untinc
    — *E6. (qtd by [Reresby] of Yorks).*
Arg 5 bars Gu & on canton Arg 3 lozs in fess
Gu
    — *H21 56. (qtd by Reresby, of Yorks).*

5 bars & in chf

5 bars & in chf lion passt
    SAMPSON, John. *PRO-sls.* 1382-3.

5 bars & over all

Arg 5 bars Az & lion Gu
ARMONIE, Rex. *LO B 40.*

Arg 5 bars Az & lion Gu a&l & crowned Or
— *CRK 1354. (qtd 2&3 by K of Cyprus).*

Arg 5 bars Gu & bend engr Sa
— *PT 374. (qtd by Tylney).*

Arg 5 bars Gu & chev Or
STOKE, Stephanus de. *Q II 157.*

Per pale Az and Arg 5 bars counterch & chev Gu
[STALHAM]. *Q 199.*

Arg 5 bars Or & 3 chevs engr Sa
HARPELEY. *WB IV 178b, 948.*
HARPERLEY, of Suff. *L1 350, 4; L2 263, 2.*

Or 5 bars Sa & crancelin Vt
SAXONIE, le Duke de. *WLN 20.*

Gu 5 bars Erm 3 escutchs Or
[?HALL]. *WB III 122b, 1.* temp Eliz 1.

Erm 5 bars Gu 3 escutchs Or
HALL. *LH 400-482.*

5 bars & 3 ?boars' heads
EDYNGTONE, Gilbert de. *PRO-sls.* 1348-9.

5 bars betw

Arg 5 bars Az & orle of martlets Gu
PEMPROU. *SM 311, 52. (martlets facing inwards).*

Arg 5 bars Gu & orle of martlets Sa
BRECKNOCK. *CRK 269.*

6 BARS OR 3 BARS GEMEL

3 bars gemel
— *Clairambault 4008.* 7 May 1432. *(qtd 2&3 by Jn Gayton).*
— *Roman PO 5113.* 12 April 1431. *(qtd 2&3 by Jn Gayton).*
BENSTED, Jane Parnel. *PRO-sls.* 1359-60. *(wid of Jn de B).*
BENSTEDE, Edmund de. *Birch 7366.* 1333. *(s of Jn de B, of Ermington, Devon).*
BENSTEDE, Edward de, chivaler. *PRO-sls.* 1402.
BENSTEDE, Pernella de. *Birch 7369.* S' PETRONELI.DE.BENSTEDE(?). 1359. *(w of Jn B).*
[FITZALAN]. *Proc Soc Antiq XVIII 2S 136. (qtd by Huddlestone, of Melholme on 1 of 6 bosses found in W Cloister walk, Hayles Abbey).*
PELLEGRIN, Hugh. *Durham-sls 1953.* mid 14 cent. *(foreign ecclesiastic holding preferment in Engld).*
PELLEGRIN, Raymond. *Durham-sls 1954.* mid 14 cent. *(foreign ecclesiastic holding preferment in Engld).*

WYTHAM, William de, of Grimsby. *PRO-sls.* 1394.

6 bars
STUTEVILLE, Joanna de. *Brit Arch Assoc i 145.* 1227. *(sl).*

Arg 6 bars or 3 bars gemel

Arg 3 bars gemel Az
DORKALEWE. *CKO 607.*

Arg 6 bars Az
— *XF 956. (altered from Barry Arg and Az).*
MARCH, E of. *MP Hist Min iii 66. (sh rev; 'Hugo cognomento Brun, comes de Marchia, et filius primogenitus ejus' d1249; 'Scutum comitis de Marchis et filius ejusdem').*
WODBRERE. *WLN 823.*

Arg 3 bars gemel Gu
— *WB II 69, 5. (qtd 2&3 by Arg 2 lions pg Sa betw 2 bends Gu).*
HERTLOU, S' William. *PO 638.*

Arg 6 bars Gu
— *PCL IV 65. (qtd 4 by K of Greece).*

Arg 3 bars gemel Sa
CARESSWELLE, S' William. *PO 413.*
CARESVILLE, Jhon. *TJ 1282.*
CARESWELL. *SK 705.*
CAREW, Monsr Pers de. *S 277.*
CARSWELLE. *L10 43b, 17.*
CRESWELL. *CRK 1832.*
ERCALEW, Sir John. *XF 309.*
ERCALEWE, Sr Willame. *O 124.*
ERCALWE, Sire William de. *PV 19.*
KARESWILL, Monsire de. *AN 63.*
KIRKALAYN, Mons William de. *WJ 935.*
KIRKALON, Le sire de. *CG 247.*
KIRKALOU, Mons Richard. *TJ 491.*
KYRKALON, Sr. *CKO 326.*
KYRKLAY, Monsr de. *AS 374.*

Arg 6 bars Sa
— *PT 309.*

Az &c 6 bars or 3 bars gemel

Az 3 bars gemel Arg
— *CRK 294.*

Az 3 bars gemel Or
— *SK 743.*

Gu 3 bars gemel Arg
— *XF 572. (qtg 2&3 Az fess dancetty Erm betw 6 crosses pommy Arg).*
— *WLN 175.*
BARNARDESON. *WK 143.*
BARRY, Sir W. *WB I 42b, 21.*
BENSTED. *PT 305.*
BENSTED. *DV 50a, 1976.*
BENSTEDE, Sir John. *Lawrance 3. (d1323). (glass & tomb, Bennington, Herts).*

Gu 3 bars gemel Or
BARDWELL. *L1 101, 6.*
BENSTEAD, Sir Edward. *XK 197.*

BENSTED. *L1 87, 4; L2 68, 1.*
Or 6 bars Az
— *WB I 14b,22. (qtd by Stapulton).*
Or 6 bars Gu
— *H21 60. (qtd by Savell, of Yorks).*
FOSSADE, Mons Emery de. *CA 124. (or Stossade).*
Or 3 bars gemel Sa
BONYUET. *L10 23b, 6. (qrs 1&4).*
Sa 3 bars gemel Arg
CARESWELL, Mons William de. *WJ 969.*
CARESWOLL. *L10 41, 8.*
Or 2 tierces Sa
— *SK 501. (2 groups of 3 barrulets).*

Field patterned 6 bars or 3 bars gemel
Erm 3 bars gemel Untinc
BROUNZ, Thomas, of Harwell. *Goring 178.*
SIGILL THOME BROUNS. *1359. (sl).*
Erm 3 bars gemel Gu
HUNTERCOMBE. *LH 987.*
HUNTERCOMBE, Sir Walter. *LH 149.*
HUNTERCUMBE, M de. *WNR 119.*
Erm 3 bars gemel Or
— *CRK 1476. (qtd 2&3 by Stokes).*
Per chev Sa and Arg on Sa 6 bars Arg
ALLERTON. *L2 20, 6.*
ALLERTON. *L2 21, 7.*

6 bars or 3 bars gemel modified
3 bars gemel wavy
[BENSTEDE]. *Mill Steph. (drawn 6 bars wavy; qtd 4 by Tyrrell, all imp by Huntingdon; brass to Thos H & w Mgt, dau of Sir Wm T, of Beeches, Hempstead, Essex).*

6 bars or 3 bars gemel & canton
6 bars & canton
— *PRO-sls AS 204. 1318-19. (imp by chf & bend [Sir Jn de Harington]).*
3 bars gemel & canton
BRADEWELL, Thomas, of London, Chev. *Birch 7733.* SIGILLVM: THOME: DE: BRADEVEL:. *1374.*
[BRIGG]. *Farrer II 88. (Sall Ch).*
Untinc 3 bars gemel & canton Arg
BUKTON. *PT 327.*
Arg 3 bars gemel & canton Gu
BRADWELLE, Th. *NS 31.*
Arg 6 bars & canton Gu
PANTON, James de. *WLN 397.*
Arg 3 bars gemel Or canton Arg
FITZAWBERNE. *NS 5.*
Arg 3 bars gemel & canton Sa
FASTOLF. *XF 258.*

Gu 3 bars gemel & canton Arg
— *XK 168. (qtd 2&3 by Sir Ric Jerningham).*
BARDEWELL. *L10 23, 6.*
Gu 3 bars gemel Or canton Arg
— *I2(1904)250. (qtd 2&3 by Edw Jernyngham, de Somerleton in Suffolke).*
— *L9 56, 6. (qtd 2&3 by Jernyngham).*
BARDEWELLE. *SK 203.*
FITZOSBORNE, of Suff & Essex. *L2 209, 5.*
NUSOUN, John. *CA 209. (?name Panton or Fitzoberne).*
Sa 3 bars gemel & canton Arg
— *LR 53. (imp by Robt Rodington).*
BUCKTON. *CRK 1782.*
BUCKTON. *Farrer III 203. (?or Buketon or Beketon; qtd by ?de Boys; St Nicholas Ch, Gt Yarmouth).*
BUKTON. *L1 87, 1; L2 40, 9.*
BUXTON. *L1 87, 6.*

6 bars or 3 bars gemel & canton patterned
Gu 3 bars gemel Or canton Erm
BARDEWELL. *FK II 386.*
BARDWELL. *L2 83, 6.*
BARDWELL. *XF 667.*
INGELOSE. *PO 72.*

6 bars or 3 bars gemel & on canton
3 bars gemel & on canton 5 billets
INGLOSE, Henry, Kt, of Norf. *Birch 10963. 1451.*
Gu 3 bars gemel & on canton Arg 5 billets (2, 1, 2) Sa
[INGLOSE]. *WB II 60, 10.*
Gu 3 bars gemel Or & on canton Arg 5 billets Untinc
FITZOSBORN. *FB 29.*
Gu 3 bars gemel Or & on canton Arg 5 billets (2, 1, 2) Sa
HYNGGELOSE. *PO 57.*
INGELOSE, Monsire John. *AN 128.*
INGHAMES, Sir Henry. *WGB 102, 2.*
INGLONS, Sir. *T b 106.*
INGLOS. *L1 359; L2 276,7; L9 5, 5. ('of Norf' in L2).*
INGLOS. *CB 156.*
INGLOSE. *CRK 1525.*
INGLOSE, He. *NS 121.*
INGLOSSE, of Norf. *PLN 1469.*
YNGELOUE, Sir H. *WB I 37, 25.*
YNGLOUS, Sir Harry. *BW 17b, 117.*
Gu 6 bars Or on canton Arg 5 billets Sa
INGLOSSE, Sir Henry. *PLN 242.*
Gu 3 bars gemel Or on canton Sa 5 billets (2, 1, 2) Or
[INGLOSE]. *SHY 70.*

3 bars gemel & on canton 6 billets
— *Proc Soc Antiq XIV 2S 285. (on wall, Bodrum Castle, Asia Minor).*
Gu 3 bars gemel Or on canton Arg 6 billets (3, 3) Sa
INGLOYS. *T b 158.*
Gu 3 bars gemel Or canton Arg billetty Sa
INGLOSE. *ML I 472.*
3 bars gemel & on canton cresc
[BUCKTON]. *Farrer Bacon 5. (Peter fitz Roger fitz Osbert).*
BUKTONE, Robert, of Newenton, Suff. *Birch 7909.* SIGULLUM: ROBERTI: BUKTONE:. *1403.*
Arg 3 bars gemel & on canton Sa cresc Arg
BUKTON, Robert de. *L10 34, 20.*
BUKTON, Robert de. *WJ 816.*
3 bars gemel & on canton escutch
[?PAY]. *Mill Steph; Belcher II 49. 1419. (upper dex corner of sh on brass to Hen P, Faversham, Kent).*

6 bars or 3 bars gemel & chf

3 bars gemel & chf
— *PRO-sls. 11 Apr 1386. (qtd by Philip Darcy).*
DARCY, Elizabeth. *Vinc 88, 51.* +SIGILLVM.-ELIZABETH.DARCIE.DOMINE.DE.WHERLTON. *1346-7. (sl; imp by crusilly 3 roses & label; loz, 3rd of 5).*
DARCY, Elizabeth, Lady of Wherlton. *BrookeAsp I 31, 2.* SIGULLVM: ELIZABETH: DARCIE: DOMINEE DE: WHERLTON. *(imp by Darcy; loz, 1 of 5; sl drawing).*
[MEINELL]. *Mill Steph. (qtd 2&3 by Darcy on brass to Sir Giles Daubeney d1445 & 1st w Joan Darcy, S Petherton, Som).*
MEINILL, Nicholas de. *Yorks Deeds VIII 88. 13 cent. (poss 3 bars & chf).*
MEYNELL, Nicholas of. *Barons Letter A96, HB-SND.*
MEYNELL, Nicholas, Ld. *Lawrance 31. (d1322). (effigy, Whorlton, Yorks).*
MEYNILL, Nicholas de, Ld of Whorlton. *Barons Letter.*

Az 6 bars or 3 bars gemel Arg & chf

Az 3 bars gemel & chf Arg
CIFREWAST, le Sr. *NB 48. (tinct of chf uncertain).*
[CRESIGNES]. *CRK 1662.*
CYFERWAST, Mons John. *WJ 1156.*
CYFREWAST, le Sr de. *CN 77.*
SCHEPERWAST, Robert. *TJ 1473.*
SIFREWAST, Sr de. *WLN 265.*
SYFREWAST. *PT 442.*
Az 3 bars gemel Arg chf Or
— *I2(1904)65. (qtd 2&3 by Thos, Ld Darcy, KG, beheaded 1538).*

Az 6 bars or 3 bars gemel Or & chf

Az 3 bars gemel & chf Or
— *WB IV 131, 93. (qtd 2&3 by the Lorde Darsy).*
— *BA 729. (qtd 5 by Ld Conyers).*
— *XK 258. (qtd 2&3 by Sir George Darcy).*
— *S 56. (qtd 2&3 by Philip, Ld Darcy of Knaith).*
— *BA 719. (qtd 6 by Strangways).*
— *L10 52b, 2. (qtd 2&3 by Darcy).*
— *BW 10, 57. (qtd by Ld Darcy).*
— *WGA 79. (qtd II&III 2&3 by Sir Jn Conyers).*
— *WK 167. (qtd 2&3 by [Sir Tho]mas [Da]rcy).*
— *CRK 194. (qtd 2&3 by Darcy).*
— *CRK 992. (qtd II&III 2&3 by Sir Jas Strangways).*
— *WK 747. (qtd III 2&3 by Wm, Ld Conyers).*
— *BA 620. (qtd III 2&3 by Conyers).*
— *L10 36, 16. (qtd III 2&3 by Conyers).*
— *BA 595. (qtd II&III 2&3 by Conyars).*
— *WGA 255. (qtd 2&3 by Thos, Ld Darcy).*
— *I2(1904)103. (qtd III 2&3 by 'the Lord Connyas').*
— *KB 337. (qtd 2&3 by Ld Darcey of Menell).*
CRESCQUES, Robert de. *C 176. ('d'azur al chef d'or a treis gemelles d'or').*
MEINEL, M de. *WNR 87.*
[MEINELL]. *AY 59. (qtd 2&3 by Ld Darcy).*
MEMILE. *L9 54a, 5.*
MENALL, Monsire de. *CG 192.*
MENELL. *PT 25.*
MENELL, Ld. *RH, Ancestor iii 212.*
MENIL, Nichol de. *Q 73.*
MENILE, Le Sr de. *AS 42.*
MENILE, le Sr de. *AS 20.*
MENILL, Nicolas de. *E I 181.*
MENILLE, Nicholl de. *H 77a.*
MENYL, Esteven de. *B 125. ('d'asur od trois gemels d'or au chief d'or').*
MENYLE, le Sire de. *TJ 779.*
MENYLL. *DV 58b, 2309.*
MENYLL. *L1 457, 1; L2 322, 11.*
MENYLL. *FK I 96. (qtd 2&3 by Ld Darcy).*
MENYLL, le. *SP A 53.*
MENYLLE. *CT 178.*
MEYNELL, de. *XF 921.*
MEYNILL, Sir.... *CRK 1325.*
MUILL, Nicholas. *PCL I 503.*
Az 6 bars & chf Or
SIFFERWAS, Sir Robert. *WB III 89, 8.*

Gu &c 6 bars or 3 bars gemel & on chf

Gu 3 bars gemel Arg on chf Or lion passt Sa
  MALEFAUNT, Sir Thomas. *BW 19, 129.*
Or 3 bars gemel & on chf Gu lion passt Arg
  — FK II 377.
Az 3 bars gemel & on chf Or greyhound courant Arg collared Gu
  MENILL. *PT 738.*
Az 3 bars gemel & on chf Or 3 escallops Gu
  MEYNEL, M de. *WNR 149.*
Az 3 bars gemel & on chf Or mullet Gu
  MENYLLE. *FK II 185.*

6 bars or 3 bars gemel & in chf

Or 3 bars gemel & in chf lion pg Gu
  TREGOS, Johan. *H 78a.* *('dor od trois jumaux dor de goules en le chef un lupart passant de goules').*
Arg 6 bars Az in dex chf martlet Gu
  [?VALENCE]. *WB V 21. (bars narrow).*
Or 3 bars gemel & in chf 2 martlets Gu
  — SK 933.

6 bars or 3 bars gemel & over all

3 bars gemel & lion
  FAYRFAX, of Yorks. *RH, Ancestor vii 188.* *(name added in later hand).*
Arg 3 bars gemel Gu lion Sa
  FAIRFAX. *Lockington XXX 418. (imp by Waterton).*
Arg 3 bars gemel Sa lion Gu
  MOHAUT, Ad de. *Q 44.*
  MONHAULT, of Lincs. *L1 443, 4; L2 338, 4.*
  MONHAUT. *L9 69a, 11. (a&l Az).*
  MONHAUT, Adam de. *XF 911. (a&l Az).*
  MONHAUT, Adam de. *E I 145; E II 145. (or Rawfe de M).*
  MONHAUT, Sire Jemes de. *N 650.*
  MONTHAUT, Ada de. *A 226.*
  MUHAUT, Adam de. *FW 302.*
  MUHAUT, Mons Adam de. *TJ 54.*
Arg 3 bars gemel & lion Sa
  FOWRYS, S' John of. *BR IV 39.*
Arg 3 bars gemel Sa 3 lions Gu
  — WLN 776.

6 bars or 3 bars gemel & over all bend &c

6 bars & bend
  MARTIGNY, Elyas de. *Bk of Sls 378.*
3 bars gemel & bend
  [POYNINGS]. *Proc Soc Antiq XVIII 2S 136. (qtd by Percy on 1 of 6 bosses, W Cloister walk, Hayles Abbey).*
Arg 6 bars Az bend Gu
  GAUNT. *L1 279, 1.*

Arg 3 bars gemel & bend Sa
  KIRKLAND. *XF 285. (bend narrow).*
  KYRKALAYN. *L9 22, 10. (bend a baston).*
Gu 3 bars gemel & bend Arg
  MARSCAL, Mons John. *CA 233. (bend narrow).*
  WALSHE, Mons John. *WJ 616.*
  WAYLES, John. *CA 94.*
6 bars & on chev 3 estoiles
  MORE, Nicholas de La, of Som. *Birch 11907.*
  S' NICHOLAI DE LA MORE. *1337. (?barry).*
Arg gutty Sa 6 bars Gu over all 3 escutchs Or
  HALL. *L1 340, 6; L2 243, 4.*
Arg 3 bars gemel Az over all 3 chaplets Gu
  — E6. (qtd by [Dacre] subimp by Scrope of Bolton, Yorks).

6 bars or 3 bars gemel betw

Arg 3 bars gemel Gu orle of martlets Sa
  CHAURS, Payn de. *WLN 697.*

6 bars or 3 bars gemel in border

Arg 6 bars Sa over all griffin erect Or border Sa
  — SHY 380.

7 BARS

Arg 7 bars Az
  MOUCHANESY, Willm de. *WLN 552. (?barry Arg and Az).*
Or 7 bars Sa
  ?PORCHESTER. *ML I 241.*
Gu 7 bars Arg label Az
  GUBIONE, Sir Hugh. *PT 1028.*

7 bars & over all &c

7 bars & lion
  STUTEVYLE, John de. *PRO-sls E40 A4767.*
  S'IOH/AN.DE/STOVT/VILE. *1279-80.*
  STOUTEVILE, Jehan de, of Northd. *Birch 13716.* S'IEHAN DE STOVTEVILE. *1280.*
Arg 7 bars Gu & chev Or
  STOKE, Stevin. *PCL I 473.*
7 bars, orle of martlets
  VALENCE, Aymer de. *Dugd 17, 100.* 1309.
7 bars border & bend
  LANCASTRE, John. *PRO-sls.* 1416-17. *(betw 2 lions with eagle above & wyvern below; narrow bend).*

8 BARS OR 4 BARS GEMEL & MORE

Az 4 bars gemel Or
— CRK 1266.
Gu 4 bars gemel & chf Or
RICHEMOND, Sr Thomas de. M 58.
Gu 5 bars gemel Or & canton Arg
— WB IV 173b, 858. (qtd 2&3 by Jn Jer-nyngham).
Gu 11 bars Arg ML I 337. ('Ther ys a frensh Knyght beryth gowles xi barres sylver.At Godstowe in Oxforthsgsher').

BARRY OF 4

Barry of 4 Gu and Or
BRUYS, Ld of Annandale. L2 90, 10.
Barry of 4 1&3 countergobony Arg and Vt 2&4 Sa
— CRK 810.
Barry of 4 Vair and Untinc
— WB I 31b, 2. (qtd III 1&4 by Cheches-ter).
Barry of 4 Arg and Gu per pale counterch
BARET, de belhows in alvithley Essx. L10 23b, 2.

Barry of 4 modified

Barry of 4 indented
MEDFORD, Walter de. Birch 1447. (or Met-ford, Dean of Wells 1413-23; sl of special jurisdiction).
MITFORD, Richard. Birch 2205. (Bp of Salis-bury, 1395-1407; sl ad causas).
MITFORD, Richard. Arch Journ xlv 35. 1396. (Bp of Salisbury, 1396-1407; on episcopal sl).
Barry of 4 indented Arg Sa Arg and Az
MITFORD, of Berks. ML I 584.
Barry of 4 1st & 3rd bars dancetty
MUNCHENSY, Wm de. Bk of Sls 405. 1190-1. (sl re land in Sutton, Norf).
Barry wavy of 4
LOVELL, William, Ld. Dugd 17, 2. 1441.
Barry wavy of 4 Arg and Gu
— RL 34, 2. (qtg 2 Untinc lion Sa crowned Untinc, 3 Gu 9 roundels Az (3, 3, 3), 4 Or fess betw 2 chevs Sa).
Barry nebuly of 4 Or and Gu
— I2(1904)102. (qtg 2 Az fess dancetty betw 10 billets Or, 3 Arg lion Sa a&l Gu border Az, 4 Az semy de lis & lion Arg, all qtd II by Sir Bryan Stapulton).
[LOVELL]. Nichols Leics II 854. (glass, Abbots Chapel, Stoughton).

Barry wavy of 4 Or and Sa
BLUNTTE, Sir J. WB I 38b, 20.
Barry of 4 Arg and Sa on canton Gu mullet Or
TWYFORD. PLN 1924. (qtg 2&3 Or fess Sa betw 3 ravens Ppr).

BARRY OF 5

See also 2 bars
Barry indented of 5 Arg Sa Arg Sa and Az
METFORD, John. RH, Ancestor vii 213.
Barry of 5 each bar Or indented Az
— RH, Ancestor vii 199. (?rectius barry pily of 5 Or and Az; 'An olde lord').

BARRY OF 6

Barry
— Baker-sls. 1365. (Wm ..., Rector of Ruy-ton, Salop; sl on grant of land in Albrighton, Salop).
— Stevenson. 1513. (qtd by Wm Hay, 3rd of Tallo).
— Stowe-Bard 1s vii 3. SEYGLIONIS MALESTES TREPENSIS. 1336-7. (on sl of Katherine, w of Jn Bardolph, of Fretenham, with sh of B).
— Steyning. (imp by Thos Roynon [of Steyn-ing]).
— Gerola 76, 226. 15 cent. (stone sh on English tower, Bodrum, Asia Minor).
— Proc Soc Antiq III 2S 146. 3 July 1362. (sin sh of 3 with pts meeting in centre). (on sl attached to letter of Agnes wid of Ric Fre-bern, of Coventry, making Wm F, of Coventry her attorney).
— WB I 25b, 6. (qtd II&III 1&4 by Sir Jn Sowch).
— Bk of Sls 409. mid 13 cent. (qtd 4 by Dammartin).
APPELBI, Isabella de. Birch 6574. S' ISSABELL'DE APPELBI. 1290. (wid of James A, miles, & w of Wm le Bret, of Appleby, Leics; 2nd of 2 shields).
[ASKE]. Blair D II 125, 281. (imp by Wm Pudsey on table tomb in Gainford Ch, with inscription).
CASTERTON, Geoffrey de. Birch 8405. EN-..ORE...D'AMOVR. 1376. (s of Geoff, s of Rich de C, of Wykstofte, Lincs; blazon uncertain; on 1st of 3 shields conjd at base in triangle on Geoffrey's sl, 2nd indistinct, 3rd salt).
QUEEN'S COLL, Cambridge. Birch 4762. 1575. (Hungary qtg 2 Naples, 3 Jerusalem, 4 Anjou, 5 Bar, 6 Lorraine, all in border; on college sl 1575; arms granted by Robt Cooke

1575).

[CONSTABLE]. *Mill Steph.* 1445. *(imp by St Quintin on brass at Harpham, Yorks to Thos de St Q, Ld of H; he m Agnes, dau of Sir Jn C by Margt dau&coh of Thos Umfreville).*

COUCY, Enquerrand Sire de. *PRO-sls.* 26 Aug 1377. *(held by armed figure).*

ERYNGTON, Gerard, of London. *Bridgwater vi 50, 919. (?3 bars each ch with ?3 roundels; sl fragment).*

FACYNEL, William. *PRO-sls.* 1303. *(betw lion passt in base, 3 fleurs de lis on dex & ?on sin).*

FITZALAN, Brian, d 1306. *Lawrance 17.* 1306. *(effigy, Bedale, Yorks).*

[FITZBRIAN]. *Birch 5942.* SIGILL'ALANI FILII BRIANI. c1250. *('Alanus, filius Briani' [Ld of Bedale, of North Cowton, Yorks]; equestr sl).*

FLOTE, Guillermus. *Birch 9835.* SIGILLVM.-GVILLERMI.FLOTE. early 14 cent.

GANT, Gilbert de, E of Lincoln. *Bk of Sls 297.* c1145-6.

GRAY, John de. *Birch 10215.* 1421.

GREAI, Richard de. *Birch 6078.* SIGILLUM RICARDUS DE GREAI. 1255. *('Consiliarius regis Angliae'; equestr sl).*

GREY, of Codnor, Richard, Ld. *Birch 2577.* 1240. *(sl of Carmelite Priory of Aylesford, Kent).*

GREY, Henry, Ld. *Nichols Leics II 762.* 1436. *(sl).*

GREY, Henry de, Ld of Codnor. *Barons' Letter.*

GREY, Henry de, Ld of Codnor. *Birch 10254.* 1301. (motto): DE LEIAUTE SE ....UNTE(?).

GREY, Henry de, of Codnor. *PRO-sls.* 1302-3.

GREY, John, Ld [of Codnor]. *PRO-sls.* 1421.

GREY, Richard de, Kt. *CombeAsp II 152.* *(drawing of equestr sl).*

GREY, Richard, Ld. *PRO-sls.* 1411.

GREY, Richard, Ld de. *Birch 10277.* SIGIL-LUM DOMINI RICARDI DOMINI DE GREY. 1412. *([of Codnor], 7th Baron).*

GREY, Sir Richard. *PRO-sls.* 1323-4.

HARCOURT, Richard de. *Bow LVII 6.* CLAVIS SEC.......... 1232. *(on sh & trappings on equestr sl, obv & rev on grant of messuage in Frolesworth, Leics).*

[HOUGHTON]. *Birch 7106.* 1392. *(imp by cross flory (Banastre) on sl of Agnes B, wid of Thos B, Kt, of Singleton, Lancs & dau of Sir Adam de Houghton).*

HUSSEY. *Birch 10915.* 1447. *(on standard in sl of Walter Hungerford, Ld of Heytesbury & Homet, 1st Baron, Treasurer of England &c).*

HYDE, Roger de. *Goring 16.* 13 cent. *(sl).*

KIRKETON, Robert de, in Hoyland, Lincs, Kt. *Birch 11094.* ...E.SOI...PE.... temp Edw 1.

LINDSAY, John de. *Stevenson 111. (sl ad causas of Jn de L, Bp of Glasgow 1323-35, h of Sir Philip L, of Strathgorton).*

MAUNDEVILE, Richard. *Vinc 88, 52.* +SIGILL'RICHARDI MAVNDEVILE. 1354. *(sl).*

MERIET, Matildis de. *Birch 11735.* SIGI: MATILDIS: DE: MERIET. 1368. *(imp lion; sl used by Jn, s of Jn de M, Kt, cousin & coh of Sir Jn de Beauchamp, of Som, Chevr).*

MERYET, Sir John de. *Arch Journ xiii 279.* SIGIL': IOHANNIS: MERYOT. 26 May 1374. *(qtg 2&3 Vairy; sl on deed re manors of Comptons, Dundene & Brodemersshtrue, Som).*

MORE, Thomas de la. *Bow LVIII 12.* +Sigillum Thome de la Mori. 1322-3.

MORLEI, Robt de, Kt. *Birch 11933.* SI ROB'TI DE MORLEI. c1250. *(or Morleya; s of Metthew de M, of Norf).*

MURIEHT, Johan. *PRO-sls.* 1363-4.

OYRII, Geoffrey de. *PRO-sls.* SIGILL'GALFRIDI DOYRI. 13 cent.

PAVEILLI, Reinald de. *AnstisAsp I 188, 18.* +S....INAL...VEILLI. *(sh on saddle cloth; equestr sl on grant to St George, of Balcheryvilla).*

PEMBRIGGE, Fouke de. *Birch 12532.* ... DE PEMBRIGG. 1350. *(or Penebrugge; Ld of Tonge, Salop).*

PEMBRUGE, Henry de. *Bow LIX 11.* +S: Henrici de Pembruge. *(Ld of Weston subter Egge; grant of a serf; Test: Rogero de Barcliva, Willelmo de Ragell).*

PEMBRUGGE, Fulk de, Ld of Tonge. *Dugd 17, 11.* Sy.Fulconis de Pembrugge. ?1326-7.

PEMBRYGE, Fulco de, Kt. *Bow XXXV 26.* SIG FVLCONIS DE PEMBRYGE. *(grant rights in manor of Weston Sub le Lesrard (Weston sub Lozard, Staffs)).*

PENBRUGGE, Fulk de. *Dugd 17, 11.* Sy.fulconis de: penbrugge. 1399. *(Crest: soldan's head, capped with conical turban).*

PENNEBRUGGE, Robert de. *Birch 12533.* SIGILL..... 1351. *(Ld of Tonge, Salop).*

SELBY, James. *BM Harl 1448, 24b, HB-SND.* 1362.

SOULIS, Nicholas. *Stevenson.* 1296. *('the Competitor'; 2nd sl).*

SOULIS, Nicholas de. *PRO-sls.* early 14 cent.

SOULIS, William. *Namur.* 1281. *(sl).*

ST ANDOENS, John de, Kt. *Bow 12.*

STUTEVILLE, Robert de. *Yorks Deeds I 55.* 1307.

Barry Arg and Untinc

GREYE, Sir Rechart. *BR V 21.*

Barry of 6 Arg and Az

Barry Arg and Az

— XK 229. (qtd II&III 1&4 by Sir Jn Zouche).

— I2(1904)74. (qtd II 2 by Sir Thos Cornnwall, Kt).

— WB II 70, 8. (qtd 2&3 by Mr Newport).

— I2(1904)163. (qtd II&III 1&4 by 'John Zowche de codnore in com darby').

CODENORE, Mons Henry fitz a. WJ 494.

CONSTABLE, 'de halshame'. PT 1120.

DAMPMARTIN. TB 4. (qtd by Talbot).

GRAI, Henri de. K 6. ('sis pecys .. barree de argent e de asur').

GRAY. CT 185.

GRAY. Nichols Leics II 494. (Market Harborough Ch).

GRAY, Ld. PCL IV 141.

GRAY, S' de. BB 146, 10. (d 1417).

GRAY, Sr de. CKO 304.

GRAY, de. PV 79. temp Edw 2.

GRAY, Codenore. PO 208.

GRAY, le Sr, de Codnore. CN 66.

GRAY, Ld, of Cotenor. BR VI 5.

GRAY, Henri le. H 16a. ('vi pieces dargent et dasur').

GRAY, Henry de. SP A 73.

GRAY, Sr Henry. H 16b.

GRAY, Mons John de, of Codenore. WJ 493.

GRAY, Mons Richard. TJ 569.

GRAY, Richard de. B 42. (of Codnor).

GRAY, Sire Richard de. N 50. ('..barre de sis peces').

GREY. DV 71b, 2840. (name added later).

GREY. SM 66, 358.

GREY, Baron. CK a 42.

GREY, Ld. WGA 248.

GREY, Monsire de. AN 67.

GREY, Munsire de. D 175b. ('barre dazur et dargent').

[GREY]. WB II 65, 5.

[GREY]. WB II 65, 8. (imp [Hastings]).

[GREY]. WB II 65, 7. (imp qtly 1&4 Barry Arg and Az in chf 3 roundels Gu; 2&3 qtly Valance & Hastings (Or maunche Gu)).

[GREY]. WB V 27.

GREY, le Sr, de Codenore. NB 66.

GREY, Ld, of Codnor. ML II 47.

GREY, Ld, of Codnor. WLN 230.

GREY, Ld, of Codnor. PLN 93.

GREY, Ld, of Codnor. KB 284.

GREY, le Sr, de Codnor. S 44.

GREY, of Codnor. CRK 229.

[GREY, of Codnor]. AY 91. ('L[ord] Gray Cotenore').

[GREY, of Codnor]. Nichols Leics II 228. (Kirkby Bellers Ch).

GREY, Ld, of Codnore. FK I 121.

GREY, of Codnore. L1 268, 1; L2 215, 3.

GREY, Henry de. K 65.

GREY, Henry le. BG 286.

GREY, Sire Henry de. J 141.

GREY, Sr Henry de. RB 37.

GREY, Henry, of Codnor, d 1308. LMS 85.

GREY, Joan de. E I 191; E II 191.

GREY, Johan de. F 183.

GREY, John de. XF 931.

GREY, Mons' John [KG]. S 13.

GREY, le S'r de. T c 16.

GREY, Reynaud de. G 100.

GREY, Ricardus de. Q II 130.

GREY, Richard de. HE 111.

GREY, Richard de. A 209.

GREY, Richard de. MP II 68.

GREY, Richard de. FW 135.

GREY, Richard, Ld, of Codnor. S 46.

GREY, Richard, of Codnor, KG. Leake. (d 1418-9).

GREY, Sir Richard, Ld, of Codnor, KG. Proc Soc Antiq XVIII 2S 148.

GREY, Richart de. D 175a.

GREY, Le Sieur. BG 44.

GREY, Ld, de Wilton. WLN 242.

[GUY]. Nichols Leics II 278. (Eye Kettleby Chapel).

LUSIGNAN, Hugh le Brun, Seigneur de, Count de la Marche. MP I 86; MP II 63; C 71.

[MORE]. PLN 619. (qtg 2&3 Az fretty Arg).

[VALENS]. Bellasis II 306-8. (or [Grey]; qtd, in E window, Windermere).

Barry of 6 Arg and Gu

Barry Arg and Gu

— WGA 21. (qrs 1&4 of sh on breast of eagle in arms of Emperor Maximilian).

— C2 16. (qtd 5 on 2nd sh; MI chancel wall, Streatham, Surr, to Edmond Tilney of Leatherhead).

— PLN 1887. (imp by Jn Moreton).

ARAGON, King of. PLN 28. (on 1st of, 3 pales: 2 Jerusalem 3 Naples, all qtd 2&3 by Or 4 pales Gu).

BARREY, Viscount of. DIG 7.

BARRY, of Irld. L2 80, 8.

BAYONS. RB 368.

BAYONS. DV 55a, 2167.

BAYOUS, le, de la Marche. WJ 927.

BAYOUSE. L10 20, 20.

BAYOUSE, Mons Rauf. WJ 613.

CHAURSEY, Patrick de. B 56.

FITZ ALEYN, Bryan de. LM 87.

FOULTES, Willame de. LM 114.

HUNGARIE, le Roy de. P 15.

HUNGARY. LMRO 14. (painted Gu 3 bars Arg; 'le Roy de Hugrie porte lescu barre de argent et de gules').

HUNGARY, King of. BR I 10. (qrs 1&4).

MOLETON, de. SP A 74.

MOLTON, Sire Thomas de. *J 99.*
MOLTON, Sr Thomas de. *H 46b.*
MORAZ, Sir Bayous de. *Q 590.*
MULTON, Thomas de. *H 46a.*
SECILIE, Kyng of. *BR I 16. (qr 1).*
SENLES, le sr de. *BL A 21.*
TALBOT, Gilbert. *XF 311.*
TALEBOT, Gelebert. *FW 168.*
TALEBOT, Gilleberd. *HE 141.*

Barry of 6 Arg and Sa
Barry Arg and Sa
— *WLN 926.*
— *BA 837. (qtd 4 by [Peniston]).*
— *BA 835. (qtd 2&3 by Sir Wm Harpeden).*
— *I2(1904)298. (qtd 4 by Sir Ric Penyston).*
BUSSE, Mons William de, of Lincs. *WJ 937.*
FOULS. *Gelre; Stodart E 15. (or Foulis;*
prob arms of Auchinleck).
HOSTERLE. *SK 342.*
HOSTERLEY. *L1 315, 6; L2 253, 2.*
HOSTERLEY. *LH 865.*
HOSTERLEY. *LH 108.*
OSTERLEY. *XF 319.*
TONKE, Sr Robert. *CKO 318.*
TOUK, Sire Robert. *N 614.*
TOUKES. *L1 637, 4.*
TUKE, S Robert. *GA 207.*
VERNIM. *T b 167.*

Barry of 6 Az &c
Barry Az and Arg
COTENOR, Ld G'y. *BW 7, 35.*
ENGLAND, William I. *ML I 309.*
GRAY, le Sr de. *AS 98.*
GRAY, Monsire Richard. *CG 221.*
GREY, Robert de. *E II 287. (?tincts*
reversed).
Barry Az and Or
BACON. *Suff HN 42. (Mr Rowsse's Rolle).*
CONESTABLE, Mons le, de Holdrenesse. *AS*
247.
MULTON, Rauf fitz Rauf de, de
Richmundshire. *TJ 567.*
PENBRIGE. *Q II 311.*
PENBRIGGE, Mons Fouke de. *WJ 813.*
SPIGURNELL, Radulphus, miles. *Bow 10.*
(tincts tricked in later hand).

Barry of 6 Gu &c
Barry Gu and Arg
— *PLN 1346.*
— *CB 94.*
— *WB I 32, 17.*
[ANJOU, Margaret of]. *RL 19. (imp by Hen 6*
'le Roy et Roigne iontly'; qtg 2 Old France
& label indistinct, 3 Jerusalem, 4 Old France
& border Gu, 5 Az 2 barbels addorsed Or, 6
Arg bend Gu).

MULTON, Sir Edward, of Lincs. *WB III 84b,*
7.
Barry Gu and Or
SAYNT OWEN, Joan de. *E 286.*
ST OWEN, John de. *XF 959.*
Barry Gu and Erm
HESE, Henry. *E II 224.*
Barry Or and Arg
— *CT 441. (tincts indistinct; qtd 2&3 by*
Barre).

Barry of 6 Or and Az
Barry Or and Az
— *WK 488. (qtd 4 by Jn Vernon).*
— *I2(1904)216. (qtd 4 by Thos Vernon, de*
Stokesay, Salop).
— *PLN 2030. (qtd 4 by Sir Harry Vernon).*
— *PLN 1624. (qtd 2&3 by Sir Ric Vernon).*
— *PLN 1628. (qtd II&III 1&4 by Sir Ric*
Vernon).
— *I2(1904)272. (qtd 4 by Syr Hen Vernon).*
— *WB I 33b, 14. (qtd 4 by George Vernon,*
of Nether Haddon).
— *WK 152. (qtd 4 by Sir Harry Vernon).*
CONESTABLE, Robert, de Holdrenesse. *TJ*
574.
CONSTABLE. *PT 846. ('of Holdernesse'*
added in later hand).
CONSTABLE, of Holderness. *PLN 569.*
CONSTABLE, of Holderness, Yorks. *L1 159,*
2; L2 101, 7.
CONSTABLE, of Holdernesse. *L10 36b, 17.*
CONSTABLE, Mons John, [of] Halsham. *WJ*
998.
CONSTABLE, Sir John, of Holderness. *XF*
596.
CONSTABLE, Sir John, of Holderness. *BA*
624.
CONSTABLE, Sir John, of Holdernesse. *WK*
446.
CONSTABYLL, Sir John, Yorks. *RH, Ancestor*
iv 233. ('vii pecys' in the margin).
FOULKES, de Penebrugge. *HA 122, 24b.*
GREY, Ld. *WB I 32, 8.*
HOLNERNES, le Conestable de. *CG 231.*
PANEBRUGE, Henry de. *FW 167.*
PENBREGGE. *CC 228, 201.*
PENBRIGE. *CB 52.*
PENBRUGE, S' Folco, of Staffs. *CY 96, 384.*
PENBRUGH, Sir Fulke de. *CV-BM 72.*
PENEBRIGE, Henr' de. *Q 357.*
PENEBRUGE, Foulk de. *RB 438.*
PENEBRUGGE. *CT 63.*

Barry of 6 Or and Gu
Barry Or and Gu
— *WLN 50.*
— *Lyndsay 129. (qtd by Haliburton, Ld of*
Dyrltoun).

— *SC 31. (qtd 2 by Ld Halybarton).*
— *Neale & Brayley; Inventory.* 1431. *(qtd by Or 2 dances Sa; painted on canopy of mont to Lewis Robessart).*
[?BERY]. *CRK 913.*
BRUCOURT, John de. *WLN 747.*
BRUCURT, John de. *CV-BM 55.*
CAMERON, E of Gowrye. *Lyndsay 84.*
FITZ ALAN, Brian. *K 355.*
FITZ ALAN, Bryan. *A 228.*
FITZ ALAYN, Sr Bryan le. *H 30b.*
FITZ ALEYN, Brian le. *H 30a.*
FITZ ALEYN, Sire Bryan le. *J 26.*
FITZ BRIAN, Alein le. *B 141. (Fitzalan, of Bedale).*
[FITZALAN, of Bedale]. *Dingley cccccxv. (qtd by Stapleton, all within Garter, on mont of Sir Bryan Stapleton KG, Lacock Ch, Wilts).*
GRANDPRE, Henry, Count of. *C 35.*
POINTZ, of Curry Mallett. *Gerard 151.*
POINTZ, Hugh. *K 358.*
POINTZ, Hugh, Ld. *LMS 52. (d 1307).*
POYNIS. *PO 311.*
POYNS, Hugh. *H 111a.*
POYNS, Sr Hugh. *H 111b.*
POYNS, Sire Nicholas de. *N 114.*
POYNTZ, de. *SP A 67.*
PUYNES, Monsire de. *AN 178.*
SAINT HOWEYN, Les Armes. *WJ 545.*
SAVAGE, Robert le. *B 191.*
SAYNTOWYN, Ra'. *CT 361.*
SIMOUND, Hugh le. *CA 7.*
ST OWEN. *LS 294.*
ST OWEN. *XF 452.*
TALEBOT, Robert. *A 224.*
TRACY, Sir Wylyam. *RH, Ancestor vii 198.*

Barry of 6 Or and Sa
Barry Or and Sa
— *PT 815. (qtg Gu chessrook Arg).*
— *WLN 853.*
— *FK II 851. (qtd 2&3 by Barre).*
BOKELAND, S Jehan de. *GA 27.*
EMRIK. *L2 183, 3.*
EMRYK, Mons John. *WJ 833.*
GORGYS. *BA 1169.*
MERICK, of Som. *PT 263.*
MERIELT, of Merielt. *Gerard 73.*
MERIET. *XF 793.*
MERIET, Sire Johan. *N 207.*
MERYET. *L9 66a, 2.*
MERYET, de Somersett. *DV 65a, 2574.*

Barry of 6 Or and Vt
Barry Or and Vt
— *PLN 1339.*
BRAYE. *L10 76, 4.*
BRAYE, Mons Reynald de. *WJ 483. (name*

written in another hand).
POYNINGES. *PT 683.*

Barry of 6 Sa &c
Barry Sa and Arg
— *CRK 2041.*
ILLESLEY. *E17 122, 116. (qtd 3 by Brackenbury).*
TOUK, Robert. *TJ 576.*
TOUKE, Monsire Robert. *CG 237.*
Barry Sa and Or
— *C2 4. (escutch barry Erm and Untinc; all encircled by Garter in glass window in N aisle of Carshalton Ch, Surr 5 Apr 1623).*
MERYOT, John de. *Bow XVI 10. c1380. (s of Sir Jn de M, [of Merriott, Som]; imp [Arundel]; tincts tricked in later hand).*

Barry of 6 Vt &c
Barry Vt and Arg
HERTTYLL, Tomas. *RH, Ancestor vii 190.*
Barry Vt and Gu
COUCI. *L1 30, 4; L2 39, 9. (or Baymont).*

Barry of 6 including Erm
Barry Untinc and Erm
FOTHERINGHAM, Sir Hugh, Kt. *Stevenson. c1370.*
FOTHERINGHAM, Thos. *Stevenson. 1475.*
LINDSAY, Sir Wm. *Stevenson. 1293. (s of Sir David L, ancestor of Es of Crawford).*
Barry Gu and Erm
BEAMONT, le Sire de, of Devon. *CG 244.*
BEAUMOND, le, of Devon. *TJ 575.*
BEAUMOND, Mons J de, of Devon. *AS 483.*
BEAUMOND, Mons' John, of Devon. *TJ 540.*
Barry Sa and Erm
FYNCHAM. *WB IV 178, 945.*
Barry Erm and Untinc
— *Birch 13754. 1355. (enclosed in 2 circular panels forming part of sl of Hen Styrmy alias Esturmy, Ld of Figheldean, Wilts).*
— *PT 337. (name illegible).*
— *C2 4. (escutch on Barry Sa and Or; window, N Aisle, Carshalton Ch, Surr).*
GIFFORD, James, of Sheriffhall. *Stevenson. 1405.*
HERRING, Patrick. *Stevenson. 1425. (may not be his sl).*
HUSEE, Matilda. *Vinc 88, 5, 6. 1304. (wid of Sir Hen H; grant of mill in Corsley, Wilts, to her s Jn H; Dat Stapelford).*
HUSEE, Matilda. *Vinc 88, 6, 12. (wid of Sir Hen H; grant of mill in 'parva Corsleye' [Wilts] to her s Jn Husee).*
HUSEY, Margaret. *Vinc 88, 6, 12. 1319. (dau&coh of Hubert H, Ld of Stapelford; 1st of 3 sh; grant of mill in parva Corseleghe).*
HUSSEY. *Birch 10917. 1449. (on standard*

in sl of Walter de Hungerford, Kt, ?1st Baron).

Barry Erm and Gu
— *SC 47. (qtd-2 by 'The lord of Zest' [Hay of Yester]).*
— *WK 420. (qtd 6 by Pawlet).*
— *F 178.*
— *I2(1904)120. (qtd 3 by Ld Husse).*
— *BA 1325. (qtd 4 by [Dymoke], all imp by Wm Coffyn).*
— *D5 113. (qtd by Husse, of Yorks).*
— *WB I 22b, 1. (qtd 6 by Hungerford).*
BEAMONT, Ld, of Devon. *PLN 252.*
BEAMOUNT, Ld, of Devon. *PLN 148.*
BEAUMONT, Sr J de, de [devensh']. *CKO 329.*
[GIFFORD, of Yester]. *Lyndsay 122. (qtd by Ld Hay, of Zester).*
GYFFERT, Ld, of Auld. *Lyndsay 156.*
HESE. *LH 1135.*
HESE, Henry. *E I 222.*
HUSE. *WLN 540.*
HUSEE. *GutchWdU. (qtd 2 by Robt de Hungerford, [c1460] in window of Old Hall, Univ College, built 1450, demolished 1669).*
HUSSE. *XFB 128. (qtd 4 by Sir Robt Dymoke).*
HUSSEY. *Leake. (qtd 6 by Wm Paulet, KG, d1571-2).*
HUSSEY. *L9 22, 8.*
HUSSEY. *LH 818.*
HUSSEY, Sir .... *CRK 1252.*
[HUSSEY]. *ML I 328. (ermine spots 4, 3, 2).*
HUSSEY, Henry. *LH 364. (said to be living temp Edw 1).*
HUSSEY, Henry de. *XF 938.*
HUSSEY, Hugh le. *C 161.*
KIRKETON, Mons John de. *SD 55.*
Barry Erm and Vt
— *CV-BM 85. (Sir Robert Ha...).*
Barry Ermines and Erm
BRADWARDYN. *L1 78, 3; L2 64, 4.*

Barry of 6 including fretty
Barry Or & Gu fretty Arg
WEEDE, Bernard le. *C 77.*
Barry fretty & Untinc
BERY, Raynald de, Kt. *PRO-sls.* 1 Nov 1352.
GAUNT, Gilbert de, E of Lincoln. *BrookeAsp I 50, 1.* SIGILLVM: GILBERTI: DE: GAVNT: COMITIS: LINCOLNIE. *(equestr sl).*

Barry of 6 including gobony
Barry Gu & gobony Arg and Sa
— *I2(1904)74. (qtg 2&3 barry Or and Az bend Gu, all qtd III by 'Sir Thomas Cornwall Knight').*
BARRE, Sir Thomas. *WB IV 139, 239. (qr*

1).
Barry gobony
PYGOT, Walter. *PRO-sls.* 1357-8. *(triangular sh used by Wm Yuwel or Geoffrey Hamond).*

Barry of 6 including per pale
Barry Az and Arg Arg bars couped in pale
— *ML I 524. ('iii barres sylver invectyd in azure per my').*
Barry per pale Untinc
PEYTO, William. *Clairambault 7138.* 1 Jan 1440. *(qrs 1&4).*
Barry Arg and Gu per pale counterch
BARET. *L10 20b, 1.*
BARET, Wm. *WJ 615.*
Barry Arg and Sa per pale counterch
CUSACK, of Irld. *LQ 108. (imp Vere).*
Barry Az and Arg per pale counterch
— *ML I 116. ('Sylver & asur barr invecte. On sylver & asur invecte barr. Thou nedest not say that he beryth sylver & asur invecte barr per pale for they may not be all invectyd but per pale').*
Barry Gu and Or per pale counterch
— *CRK 1337.*
Barry Or and Az per pale counterch
STODHAM, Simon de. *E II 580. ('barre dasur et dor contrechaunge').*

Barry of 6 including per pale indented
Barry per pale indented
PEITO, William de, senior. *Bow LIII 9.* Sigill Willelmi de Peito. 1379-80.
PEYTO, William. *Dugd 17, 16.* Sigillum Willemi de Peyto. 1331.
PEYTO, William. *Dugd 17, 17.* Seel: mesire guille: peyto. 1431. *(qtg 2&3 fess in chf 3 roundels). (crest: on torse 2 wings elevated).*
PEYTO, William de. *Dugd 17, 1.* 1346-7.
Barry Arg and Gu per pale indented counterch
PETO. *XF 873.*
[PETO]. *ML I 144.*
PETOWE. *BA 31b, 292.*
PEYTO. *L9 97a, 5.*
PEYTO. *L1 519, 2.*
PEYTO, Sir Wylyam. *RH, Ancestor vii 189.*

Barry of 6 including semy
Barry 9 ?charges 4, 3, 2
CAYNES, Robert de. *PRO-sls.* 1301-2.
Barry Gu and Sa on Sa bars 8 billets (3, 2, 3) Arg
— *PLN 1068. (qr 2 of coat imp by Sir Thos Bourchier).*
Barry semy de lis
[MORTIMER, of Ricards' Castle]. *Brit Arch Assoc xxiv 288.* S...LLE DE MORTIMER. *(sl of Isabella de M 'Domina de Homme Castel';*

dau of Robt de M (dc1235) of Ricard's Castle & sis&h of Hugh. Barry &c is old coat of
M, of Ricard's Castle but Caerlaverock
assigns Gu 2 bars Vair to Hugh de M).

Barry Az and Arg semy de lis Or
  GRAY, Sr Richard de. M 14. ('... flurette
  d'or').

Barry Or and Vt semy de lis counterch
  MORTIMER, of Richard's Castle. C 89.
  MORTIMER. XF 103. (lis 6, 5, 4, 3, 2, 1; 'of
  Richardes Castell').
  MORTIMER, Robertus de. C 89. ('barrey dor
  e de vert flurete del une e de aultre').

Barry Arg gutty Gu & Gu
  — PLN 1908. (qtd 5 by St John).

Barry gutty & Erm (mullet for diffce)
  BOWER, Matthew. Arch Journ xciii 42.
  +Sigillu mathei boure. c1440. (sl Matrix Nelson
  colln 93).

Barry Sa gutty Arg and Erm
  — I2(1904)253. (qtd 4 by 'Sir Rychard Gar-
  non als Caundyshe').
  BRADEWARDYN. L10 76, 6.

Barry Sa and Erm on Sa bars 8 oval charges 3,
3, 2 Untinc
  BRADWARDYN. CC 230b, 283.

Barry Arg and Az roundelly Or
  GREY. Nichols Leics II 558. (Evington Ch).

Barry on 1, 3&5 bars 14 roundels (6, 5, 3) on 2
bar ?leopard's head
  KYNGESTONE, Thos of. Exeter D&C 94. (or
  Jn Gyst).

Barry Vair and Untinc semy of sprigs Untinc
  COUCY, Ingram, sire de. PRO-sls. 20 Nov
  1365.

Barry of 6 including Vairy

Barry Untinc and Vair
  BRAUSA, ... de. BrookeAsp I 17, 2. ...: DE:
  BRAUSA.
  GUARNE, Sir Raynold. Brit Arch Assoc xxx
  200. +S'RAYNALDI: GVARNE: MIL'TIS. (bronze
  sl matrix found on site of Old Palace of Bri-
  dewell).

Barry Gu and Vair
  CUYSY, Thomas. TJ 618.

Barry Az & vairy Gu and Erm
  BREWES, Mons' Reynald. TJ 621.
  BREWES, Mons' Reynald de. TJ 535. (Gloss
  on Mons' Jn Grisley).
  GRISLEY, Mons de. AS 468.

Barry Vair and Untinc
  — BrookeAsp I 16, 2. 1433-4. (qtd 2&3 by
  Wm, Ld Fitzhugh).
  [BEAUMONT]. Mill Steph. 1539. (qtd 2 by
  by Sir Jn Basset, of Umberleigh, brass, Ath-
  erington, Devon).
  BEAUMONT, Johanna. Birch 7291. S'.dne.
  iohanne. beau...nt. 1381. (imp [Corbet?]; wid of

Jn de B, of Parkham, Devon).
BEAUMONT, Thomas. AnstisAsp I 227, 98.
SIGILLVM: THOM: BEAUMONT. 1430.
BEAUMONT, Thomas, miles. Vinc 88, 38.
1439-40. (sl).
CAYNES, Robert de, Kt. PRO-sls E40 A5848.
1301-2.
COUCY, Engeram de. PRO-sls AS 257.
S'engeram Comitis: de: bedeford: et: Sire: de : coucy.
1367-8. (Ld of Coucy & E of Bedf).
COUCY, Enguerraud de, E of Bedford. PRO-
sls Anc Deeds AS 257. 1369.
COUCY, Ingelram. PRO-sls. 1367-8. (betw
2 lozs each ch with fess; Ld of Coucy & E of
Bedf).
COUCY, Enguerraud, Sire de. PRO-sls WS
576, HB-SND. 1365. (E of Bedford).
COUCY, Ingeham, Ld of, E of Bedford. Bk of
Sls 247. 1366-8.
COUCY, Ingleram de. Birch 8998.
S'ENGERAM: COUNTE: DE: BEDEFORD: ET: SIRE:
DE: COUCY. 1369. (Ld of Coucy, 2nd E of
Bedford, KG, son-in-law of Edw 3).
FORD ABBEY, Devon. Brit Arch Assoc xviii
198. S'.commvni: Monasterii: beate: Marie: de: Forda.
(recte arms of Beaumont; sin sh on sl of
Abbey, dex Courtenay).
KAYNES. Nichols Leics III 328. (imp by
Chaworth on brass to Sir Thos C (d1458),
Laund Ch).
KAYNES, John de. Birch 11032. SIGILLVM....-
... 1357. (Ld of Dodford, Northamp, Kt).
MONCHENSY. Birch 14079. ...LVM SEC ....
1301. (dimid Valence (barry of 12, 8
martlets in orle) on sl of Johanna de V, Ctess
of Pembroke, dau&h of Warine de Mon-
chensi, niece of Anselm Marshal, 6th E of P
& wid of Wm de V, 1st E of P).
[MUNCHENSI]. PRO-sls E40 A11553-8.
1299-1300. (dimid Valence on sl of Joan de
V, nee Munchesy, Ctess of Pembroke).
MUNCHENSI, Joan. Bk of Sls 115. 1301.
(Ctess of Pembroke, w of Wm de Valence).
[MUNCHENSY]. HB-SND. 1300. (dimid
barry, orle of martlets [Valence] on sl of
Joan de Warin de M, m Wm de VE of Pemb).

Barry Vair and Gu
  — WK 301. (qtd 2 by Sir Jn Bassett).
  — CN 97. (qtd 2&3 by le Sr de Coucy).
  — XF 479. (qtd 2 by Bassett).
  BAYMONT. L10 21b, 1.
  BAYMONT. BA 1094.
  BAYMONT. L1 30, 4; L2 39, 9. (L2 adds
  'Devonshire').
  BEAUMOND. Gerard 7.
  BEAUMONT. XF 733.
  BEAUMONT. L10 30, 2.
  BEAUMONT, John. S 499.
  BEAUMONT, Mons John. S 494.

BENUS, Robert de. *Q 155*.
BEWMONT, Sir T. *WB I 39, 12*.
CONEY, Robert de. *E I 252*.
COUCI. *Lawrance 47*. 1323. *(on tomb in Westm Abbey of Aylmer Valence, E of Pembroke, d1323)*.
COUCY, Ingelram de. *Sandford 178*. *(m 1365, Isabel, dau of Edw 3)*.
COURCY, Ld. *L1 139, 5; L2 121, 11*.
COURCY, E of Bedford. *CRK 280*. *(qrs 1&4)*.
COUSI. *L10 43, 13*.
COUSSY. *L1 129, 4*.
KEMIS, Robertus de. *Q II 155*.
KENEL, Robert de. *XF 947*. *(recte Kennis or Kemys?)*.
KENEZ, Robert de. *E I b 252*.
KEVELL, Robert de. *E II 254*.
KEYNES, S' Jon. *PO 342*.

Barry vairy Arg and Gu & Az
BREWES, William de. *WLN 707*.
Barry vairy Erm and Gu & Az
BREUSE, William. *F 57*.
BREUSE, William de. *E I 30*.
BREWES, William de. *XF 763*.

Barry of 6 modified
Barry dancetty
BALUN, Sir Walter de. *Lawrance 1*. c1322. *(effigy, Arley, Worcs)*.
BASSET, Alan. *PRO-sls E40 A4821*. +S........-L.ALANI...... 13 cent.
DELAMARE. *Mill Steph; Brit Arch Assoc xxvii 92, pl 6*. 1435. *(cresc in dex chf for diffce; qtg Untinc fess Erm, border engr on brass to Rich D & w Isabel, Hereford Cathedral)*.
DELAMARE. *Mill Steph; Brit Arch Assoc xxvii 92, pl 6*. 1435. *(cresc in dex chf for diffce; brass to Rich D & w Isabel, Hereford Cathedral)*.
DELAMARE. *Mill Steph; Brit Arch Assoc xxvii 92, pl 6*. 1435. *(cresc in dex chf for diffce; imp Untinc fess Erm border engr on brass to Rich D & w Isabel, Hereford Cathedral)*.
LOVEDAY, John. *Goring 185*. S'IOHIS FILII .... 1336.
LOVEDAY, John. *Goring 196*. SIOHIS FILII ROB...DAY. 1331.
LOVEDAY, William. *Goring 23*. 13 cent.
MARE, Richard de la. *PRO-sls E40 A5974*. SIGILLV RICARDI DE LA MARE. 1423-4. *(qrs 1&4)*.
OSTERWIC, Baldwin de. *Bk of Sls 404*. early 13 cent. *(s of Baldwin de O)*.
TODENHAM, John de, of Suff, Kt. *Birch 13952*. S' IOHANNIS DE TODENHAM. 1379.

Barry dancetty Arg and Az
TODEHAM, Oliver de. *E I 627; E II 629*.
Barry dancetty Arg and Gu
BALUN. *L10 19b, 15*. *(or Basset)*.
BALUN, John de. *FW 175*.
BALUN, Walter de. *XF 920*.
BALUN, Water de. *E I 170; E II 170*.
BASSET, of Cornw. *ML I 578*.
BASSET, of Cornw. *L1 42, 3; L2 38, 4*.
BASSET, S' Laur'. *PO 319*.
BASSET, Thomas, of Cornw. *TJ 393*.
BASSET, Mons W de, de Cornaile. *AS 480*.
BASSET, Sr William, de Cornwail. *CKO 536*.
BASSETT. *XF 479*. *(qrs 1&4)*.
BASSETT, Sir John. *WK 301*.
BASSETT, Thomas, de Cornewaille. *TJ 394*. *('port une dauncee dargent & de goules de sys')*.
CASSATT. *BA 936*. *(recte Bassett)*.
SAMORY, Sir Richard. *CV-BM 175*. *(or d'Amory)*.
TODENHAM. *PT 60*.
TODENHAM, Monsire. *AN 264*.
TUDENHAM, John. *E I 645; E II 647*.

Barry dancetty of 6 Gu & ...
Barry dancetty Gu and Arg
TODENHAM. *DV 59b, 2342*.
TODMHAM. *L1 645, 5*.
Barry dancetty Gu and Or
BALOUN, Thomas. *TJ 409*.

Barry dancetty of 6 Or & ...
Barry dancetty Or and Gu
MAR', S' Reginal de la. *PO 310*.
MARE, Mons Piers de la. *S 556*. *('dancy gold & gules')*.
[VALOYNES]. *CT 125*.
Barry dancetty Or and Sa
LOVEDAY. *L9 35a, 7*.
LOVEDAY, Roger. *E I 473; E II 475*.
LOVEDAY, Roger. *XF 377*.
LOVEDAY, Roger de. *WLN 578*.
SHYLFORDE, Tomas. *RH, Ancestor v 182*.

Barry indented of 6
Barry indented Arg and Gu
SOMERY, George de. *WLN 766*. *(otherwise Arg 3 1/2 bars of lozs Gu)*.
Barry indented Arg and Sa
SOMERFIELD. *ML I 255*.

Barry lozengy of 6
Barry lozy Untinc
JUSTICE, Reginald, of Kent. *Birch 11029*. ...REGINA...IARII. late Hen 3.
Barry lozy Arg and Gu
FITZ WILLIAM, S' Will'. *PO 80*.

Barry pily of 6
Barry pily
— *PRO-sls.* 1379-80. (*qtd by Theodore Robersart, alias Canoune*).
[D'EVEREUX], Amauricus or Almaric, 4th E of Gloucester. *Birch 9538.* ...ILLVM ALMAR.... ante 1226. (*?party indented; Kingsford substitutes De Montfort for D'Evereux*).
Barry pily of 6
PESHALE, Ralph de, of Essex. *Birch 12596.* SI...DV...DE PESEHALE. 13 cent.

Barry wavy &c of 6 (plain)
Barry nebuly
— *PRO-sls.* 1358-9. (*imp by Gilbert Celsefeld for his w Joan*).
— *Birch 8988.* 1383. (*imp by fess betw ?6 martlets in 1 of 2 shs in sl of Jn, s of Rich de Cotewyke, of Over Stretton, Norf*).
— *WB I 29b, 2.* (*qtly I&IV qtg 2: lion crowned border roundelly, 3: 2 lions passt ?gard; II&III per pale (a) qtly Untinc and Erm border, (b) cross formy on canton lions head erased & crowned*).
BLOUNT, John le, of ?Sheprigge, Wilts. *Birch 7507.* 1343.
BURCESTER, Austin Priory of St Edburga, Oxfords. *Birch 2773.* 14 cent. (*or Burencester; 2nd sl; Birch's attribution is uncertain*).
COSTER. *WB I 12, 4.*
DAMORY, Richard, Chevr, of Bucks. *Birch 9173.* SIGILLVM.RICARDI.DAMORI. 1340.
?DRUMMOND. *Stevenson.* 23 June 1372. (*under sin supporter on sl of Mgt D, 2nd Qu of David II*).
GOLDINGHAM, Walter. *Birch 10142.* SIG'.WALTERI.GOLDINGHAM. 1417-18.
GOLDYNGHAM, Walter, Kt. *PRO-sls.* 1417-18.
LOVEL, John. *Birch 11402.* SIGILLUM: IOHANNIS: DOMINI: DE: LOUEL. 1409-14. (*qtg 2&3 Holand (semy de lis lion); 10th Baron L, of Tichmersh*).
LOVEL, John, Ld. *Bk of Sls 384.* 1404.
LOVEL, Matilda, Lady. *Birch 11403.* SIGILLUM: MATILDIS: DNE: LOUEL: ET: DE: HOLAND. 1387. (*imp H (lion gard betw 6 fleurs de lis); dau&h of Robt de Holand, 2nd Baron, & w of Jn, 5th Ld L*).
LOVEL, Maud. *Bk of Sls 388.* (*wid of Jn, Ld Lovel & Holand*).
LOVELL, John. *Birch 11401.* ...DE...UEL. 1385. (*imp Holand (semy de lis lion gard); Ld L & H, 5th Baron*).
LOVELL, John, Ld. *Bk of Sls 314.*
LOVELL, Robt. *Birch 11404.* SIGILLU[M]: ROBERTI: LOUEL. 14 cent. (*qtg 2&3 crusily lion*).

LOVELL, William, Ld Burnell & Holand. *PRO-sls.* 1447-8.
STURY, Alice. *PRO-sls.* SIGILL' ALICIE STAFFORDE. 1408. (*wid of Sir Ric S*).
Barry wavy
— *Birch 3237.* 13 cent. (*blazon uncertain; ?signet sl of Haghmond Abbey, Salop*).
— *Vinc 88, 84.* Sigillum thome Maunsell. 1448. (*imp by Thos Maunsell on deed concerning hundred of Barstaple, Essex*).
— *WB I 22b, 5.* (*qtd 3 of escutch on coat imp by Sir Geo Putnam*).
— *WK 744.* (*qtd II 1 by Sir Brian Stapilton*).
BASSET, Fulk. *HB-SND, sl-Cast BG.* (*Bp of London 1244-50*). ('*a bracket carved in wavy lines representing barry wavy shield of Basset'*).
BASSET, Gilbert. *PRO-sls E40 A6783.* +SIGILL....... 13 cent.
BASSET, Gilbert. *PRO-sls AS 36.* +SIGILL: GILBERTI: BASSET. (*bro of Philip & Thos B*).
BASSET, Helewisa. *PRO-sls E40 A13961.* SIGILL: HELEVISIE: BASSET. [1266]. (*on dress; w of Philip B*).
BASSET, Philip. *PRO-sls E40 A13954.* SIGILLVM PHILIPPI BASSET. [1266].
BASSET, Philip. *Birch 7191.* +SIGIL....HILIPPI.-BASSET. 1258.
BASSET, Philip. *BrookeAsp I 41, 2.*
BASSET, Philip, of Little Stambridge, Essex. *Birch 7193.* +SIGILL': PHILIPPI: BASSET. 1260.
BASSET, Ralph, of Chedle, Kt. *Bow XXXI 2.* (*T. dom Will de Cavereswell, dom Phil de Draicote, dom Willelmo de Chetilton, dom Will Weier, Will Coyne, Ricardo de Caverswell*).
BASSET, Simon, Kt. *Bow LIV 4.* LA SIGILL SIMON BASSET. 1325-6. (*Dominus de Sapcote, Leics*).
BASSETH, Alan. *PRO-sls.* 13 cent.
BASSETH, Symon. *Birch 7199.* ...SIMON'B.... temp Hen 3. (*s of Ralph B, of Sapcote, Leics*).
[BASSETT]. *Birch 7045.* Sigillum: iohannis: de: ayllesbury. 1376. (*qtd 2&3 by Jn de Aylesbury, of Beaconsfield, Bucks, Kt, s of Sir Thos de A, of Milton Keynes, Bucks & Joan dau&coh of Ralph, Ld B, of Weldon*).
BASSETT, Gilbert. *PRO-sls.* late 13 cent.
BLOUNT, Walter, chev, of Burton-on-Trent, [Staffs]. *Vinc 88, 38.* 1392-3.
BLOUNT, William le. *Vinc 88, 38.* 1340. (*sl on grant of land in Hamslape, Bucks to Sir Jn le B & Eliz his w*).
BLUND, William le. *Birch 7517.* S' WILL'I.-LE.BLVND. temp Edw 2.
BLUNT. *Bow 12.*
BLUNT, William le, Kt. *Bow XXXV 3.* Sig Willmi le Blunt. 1340-1. (*grant of lands in*

Hanslop, Bucks).

BOURG, Elizabeth de, Lady of Clare. *PRO-sls AS 29.* 1356-7.

[D'ARTOIS?]. *KildareAS III 301.* 1496. *(qtd 2&3 by Roland Eustace or FitzEustace, Ld Partlester, of New Abbey, Kilcullen, Kildare).*

DAUNTESEY, John, Kt. *Vinc 88, 50.* +SIG'IOHANNIS DAVNTESEY. *(qrs 1&4).*

HASTINGS, Edmund de. *Birch 10531.* 1301. *(Ld of Enchimeholmok, 1st Baron).*

HASTINGS, Edmund of. *Barons Letter; PRO-sls. (Ld of Enchimeholmok).*

LOVEL, John, Ld. *PRO-sls AS 293.* Sigillum Iohannis domini de Lovel. 1412-13. *(qrs 1&4).*

LOVEL, Maud. *PRO-sls AS 278.* Sigillum: Matildis: dne: lovel: et : de: holand. 1408-9. *(imp [Holand]; w of Sir Jn L).*

LOVEL, Robert, esq. *PRO-sls AS 278.* Sigillu roberti lovell. 1408-9. *(qtg [Holand]; mullet for diffce in qr 1).*

LOVELL, John, Kt. *Bow XXXIII 9.* Sigillum Johannis Lovell Chev. 1333-4.

LOVELL, Robert, Esq. *PRO-sls.* 1408-9.

MENTIETH, Earldom of. *Stevenson.* 1301. *(on sl of Sir Edm Hastings, Ld of Inchmahome, 2nd husb of Isabella, dau of Isabella, Ctess of M).*

SANDEFORDE, Lore de. *Bow 1.* SIGILLVM: LORE: DE: SANDEFORDE. temp Hen 3. *(on shield & dress).*

SANDFORD, Nicholas de. *PRO-sls E40 A4871.* +.....DE SAVNFORD+. 13 cent.

SANFORD. *Bow XXVI 11b.* 1348-9. *(imp by fretty (Venables) for Johanna, w of Alexander V, wid of Jn Makevre & dau of Laurence S).*

SAUNFORD, Lawrence de. *PRO-sls E40 A199.* S: LAVRENCII: DE: SAVNFORD. 1256-7.

[SPENCER]. *PRO-sls E40 A4104.* 1528-9. *(qtd 4 by Hen Algernon Percy, 6th E of Northd (1489-1527) on sl used by his successor).*

[SPENSER]. *PRO-sls.* 1528-9 & 1536-7. *(2 bars wavy; qtd I 4 by Hen Algernon Percy, 6th E of Northd [1489-1527]).*

ST JOHN, Arnaud de, de Gartre. *PRO-sls.* 1336-7. *(Keeper of the King's horses).*

STRADLING, Joan. *Vinc 88, 51.* +S iohan Stradling domina de Dauntesey. 1436-7. *(w of Jn S, Kt; sl).*

[THOMER]. *Bridgwater 643 & 682.* SIGILLVM WILLMI THOMAS ARMIG. 1428. *(qtd 2&3 by Wm Thomas, of Bridgwater, Constable of Codnor Castle, Derbys).*

THOMER, William de, of Bridgewater. *PRO-sls.* 1398-9.

THOMER, William, of Bridgewater. *Bridgwater 404.* SIGILLUM WILLELMI THOMER. 1385.

TRAFFORD, Alice. *PRO-sls.* 1401-2. *(wid of Ric Stury).*

Barry wavy &c of 6 Arg and Az

Barry nebuly Arg and Az
— *PT 524.*

Barry wavy Arg and Az
— *XK 89. (qtd 6 by Jn Vere, E of Oxford, KG 1527).*
— *Hutton 24. (qtd 7 by Ric Wingfield, N window of Gray's Inn).*

BASSET, Symon. *FW 610.*

PERCY, Sire Nichol. *O 109. ('a Samford coat').*

SAMFORD. *Leake. (qtd 6 by Jn Vere KG, d 1539).*

SAUNFORD, Gilebert de. *F 111.*

STANFORD. *WK 526-8. (qtd 4 by Vere).*

STANFORD. *WK 529. (qtd 6 by Vere).*

STANFORD, Gilbert de. *WLN 404.*

STANFORT. *WK 531. (qtd 6 by Vere).*

Barry wavy &c of 6 Arg and Gu

Barry nebuly Arg and Gu

AMMARY. *L10 5, 16.*

BASSET, Lawrence. *XF 365.*

D'AUMERY. *GutchWdU. (imp by [Gaynesford] on tomb of Sir Geo Nowers, Christ Church Cathedral).*

Barry wavy Arg and Gu
— *BA 551. (qtd 2&3 by Caraunt).*

ACHART, Piers. *TJ 1587.*

AMMORI, Sire Richard. *N 328.*

AUMARY. *L1 23, 5; L2 12, 12. (L2 adds baston in bend Sa).*

AUMARY, de. *RB 149.*

BASSET. *L10 19b, 5.*

BASSET, Laurence. *F 114.*

BASSET, Laurence. *E I 444; E II 446.*

BASSET, of Leics. *L1 28, 3; L2 38, 1.*

CHAMPAINE, Robert de. *WLN 406.*

CHEYNE. *CVK 740. (& Champayne; both names given).*

DAMMARI. *PV 8.*

DAMMORY. *CT 432.*

DAMORY, Sir Richard. *CV-BM 123.*

DAUMARY. *AS 124.*

DAUMARY, Monsire. *CG 427.*

DAUMARY, Sr. *CKO 510.*

DEAUMARY. *DV 16b, 621.*

GOMER. *SK 525. (or Tomer).*

[GOMER]. *FK II 437. (alias [Tomer], names added by Gibbon; qtd 2&3 by Carauntes).*

SANDFORD, Nicholas de. *MP IV 81; B 116; C 140.*

SANDFORD, Nicholas de. *MP IV 81. ('a young & fair Knight who died 20 Jan 1251/2 of grief for loss of his sister Cicely de Sandford, widow of William de Gorham').*

SANDFORD, William de. *B 115.*

Barry wavy &c of 6 Arg and ...
Barry nebuly Arg and Sa
— *WLN 859.*
— *Nichols Leics II 281. (Freby Ch).*
BASSET, Simon. *Q 96.*
BASSET, Simon. *XF 364.*
BASSETT. *L2 92, 5.*
ELEFETE, of Oxon. *L2 181, 3.*
ELESFELD, s'gilberd. *PO 633.*
POKKEBORN, Roberd de. *LM 262.*
Barry wavy Arg and Sa
— *WB I 33b, 19. (qtd 6 by [Vere], E of Oxford).*
ASSHEFELD. *L1 25, 2; L2 13, 10.*
BARLE. *CC 225, 113. (qtg 2&3 Or stool Az border Sa roundelly Or).*
BARLE. *CC 225, 112.*
BASSET. *HA 113. (superscribed: 'Sapcote').*
BASSET. *L10 19b, 6.*
BASSET, de Sapecote. *RB 434.*
BASSET, Simon. *PCL I 467.*
BASSET, Simon. *E I 437; E II 439.*
BLOUNT, William. *F 290.*
[BLOUNT?], William le. *WLN 722.*
CHAMPAINE. *Nichols Leics IV 997. (N window, Thurleston Ch).*
DELLESFELDE, Mons' Gilbert. *TJ 594. (base Sa; '... pee de sable').*
ELCHEFELD. *L1 225, 4.*
ELCHESFELD, of Oxfords. *LE 32.*
ELESFELD. *CKO 516.*
ELKESFELD. *PLN 781.*
ELLESFELD. *CT 51.*
ELLESFELD, Sir. *SK 352.*
ELLESFELD, Sr Gilbert. *O 111.*
ELLESFELD, Sr Johan. *N 332.*
ELLESFIELD, Monsire de. *CG 429.*
ELSEFELD, Sire Gilbert de. *WNS 26, 85. ('... por undee dar et de sable').*
ESTBURY. *WB IV 153, 487.*
MACHELER, Sir Grede. *WB I 17b, 17.*
Barry wavy Arg and Vt
— *PT 619. (qtd by Peverell).*

Barry wavy &c of 6 Az and ...
Barry wavy Az and Arg
SAUNFORD, Mons' Thomas. *TJ 599. (base Az; 'port undee dazure & dargent pee dazure').*
Barry wavy Az and Gu
BREUSE, William de. *E II 30.*
Barry wavy Az and Or
FAYRFORD. *Suff HN 40. (imp by Sulyard; at Sir John Sulyard's house, Wetherdon).*
POLE. *CC 223b, 62.*

Barry wavy &c of 6 Gu and ...
Barry nebuly Gu and Arg
DARTEYS, of Irld. *L2 162, 5. (marginal note: Dalby of Warws).*
Barry wavy Gu and Arg
— *WB I 19b, 19. (qtd by [Warneford]).*
DAMARY, Mons' Richard. *TJ 592. (base Gu: 'undee de goules & dargent pee de goules').*
DAUMARY, Mons Richard. *AS 287.*
HAMMORE, Sr Richard de. *L 66.*
PELMORBA, John. *RH, Ancestor ix 160.*
Barry wavy Gu and Or
— *Gelre; Stodart D 8. (name missing: ?Drummond).*
— *PLN 969. (qtd 5 by Ld Strange).*
BASSET, Mons' William. *TJ 596.*
FERRERS, Erle of. *BR V a 14.*
FERRERS, Erle of. *BR IV 88.*
LOUVELL, Ld John. *WGA 190.*
LOVELL. *WLN 264.*

Barry wavy &c of 6 Or and ...
Barry wavy Or and Untinc
PYNKENY, Johan de. *LM 205.*
Barry nebuly Or and Az
BLOUNT. *I2(1904)289. (qtg (2)Arg 2 wolves passt Sa in border Or 10 salts Gu; (3)Or castle 3towered Az; (4)Vair; (5)Arg 3 fleurs de lis Az; (6)Arg fess & in chf 3 covered cups Gu; name added in later hand).*
Barry wavy Or and Az
SAMFORD. *L1 597, 5.*
SAMFORD, de. *RB 475.*
SANDFORD. *LS 263.*
SAUNFORD. *CT 128.*

Barry wavy &c of 6 Or and Gu
Barry nebuly Or and Gu
— *WB I 31, 4.*
— *WK 417. (qtd 2 by Stapylton).*
— *D4 23. (subqtd by Wyloughby, Notts).*
— *WK 416. (qtd I 2 by Stapylton).*
BASSET. *DX 19. ('nowe Lovell').*
BASSET, M. *WNR 143.*
BASSET, Philip. *XF 767.*
LOUEL, S' Jon. *PO 516.*
[LOVEL]. *XF 302. (qr 1).*
LOVEL, Johan. *LM 153.*
LOVEL, Ld John, of Tichmersh. *S 64. (qrs 1&4).*
[LOVEL, Wm, Ld, d1455]. *OxfRS IV 215. (qtg [Deincourt, Holland, Grey of Rotherfield, Burnel, Sydenham, Zouch]; tomb, Minster Lovel, Oxfords, restored 19 cent).*
[LOVELL]. *Neale & Brayley. 1296. (canopy of Mont to Edmund, E of Lancaster, Westm Abbey).*
[LOVELL]. *OxfRS I 28. (glass at Banbury).*
LOVELL, Francis, Ld, KG (d1483). *Leake.*

(qtg 2 Az billetty & fess dancetty Or (Deyn-court), 3 Az semy de lis & lion gard Arg (Holland), 4 Barry Arg and Az bend Gu (Grey of Rotherfield), on escutch Arg lion Sa crowned Or (Burnell); all within Garter).
Barry wavy Or and Gu
— *SHY 124.*
— *WK 500. (qtd III 1&4 by Hen Parker, Ld Morley).*
— *WB I 14b, 22. (subqtd by Stapulton).*
— *WB II 53, 6. (qtd 2&3 by Stradlynge).*
— *L10 94, 4. (qtd II 1 by Norreys).*
— *WJ 797. (name illegible).*
— *I2(1904)180. (qtd 2 by Syr Rychard Grenevile Knyght; added by Jos Holland c1630).*
BASET, Phelip. *F 69.*
BASSET, Gilbert. *MP II 34.*
BASSET, Gilbert. *MP II 34; MP IV 44.*
BASSET, Phelip. *FW 108.*
BASSET, Phelipe. *D a 138a.*
BASSET, Philip. *E I 43.*
BASSET, Philip. *B 93. ('ounde d'or et de goules').*
BASSET, Philip. *HE 85.*
BASSETT. *L10 19b, 3.*
BASSETT, Phillip. *P 106.*
BASSETT, of Umberleigh, Devon. *Gerard 7.*
DRUMMOND, Ld. *Lyndsay 120.*
DRUMMOND, Anabell. *Lyndsay 40. (w of K Robt III).*
LOVEL, Ld. *PLN 97. (qtg 2&3 Holland).*
LOVEL, Sr. *CKO 509. (banner).*
[LOVEL?]. *PV 45.*
LOVEL, Le Sr de, et de Holland. *S 62. (qtg 2&3 Az semy de lis lion Arg [Holland]; 'wavy gold & gules, quarterly with azure flowered silver with a leopard rampant silver').*
LOVEL, J. *RB 437.*
LOVEL, Johan. *H 13a.*
LOVEL, Sire Johan. *N 59.*
LOVEL, John. *CA 125.*
LOVEL, John, Ld. *LMS 47.*
LOVEL, of Oxfords. *L1 389, 1; L2, 301, 3.*
LOVEL, of Titchmarsh. *ML I 52.*
LOVELL. *SP A 110.*
LOVELL. *CRK 284.*
LOVELL, Ld. *FK I 98. (qrs 1&4).*
LOVELL, Ld. *WB II 50, 16. (qrs 1&4).*
LOVELL, Monsire. *CG 428.*
LOVELL, le Sr. *CN 94.*
[LOVELL]. *RL 28b, 4; RL 34, 1. (qtd 2 by Deincourt).*
LOVELL, Francis, Ld. *WGA 229.*
LOVELL, Mons' John. *SD 128.*
LOVELL, S John. *ST 57.*
LOVELL, Sr John. *H 13b.*
LOVELL, John, d1408. *BB 117, 5.*

LOVELL, Mons Thomas, de Tychemersshe. *TJ 593.*
LOVELL, William. *CA 64.*
LOVELLE, le S'r de. *T c 24. (qrs 1&4; qtg Az semy de lis & lion gard Arg).*
LOWELL, Ld. *RH, Ancestor iv 228.*
LOWELL, Ld. *BW 8, 44. (qrs 1&4).*
LOWELL, S'g'r, de Tichemerch. *RB 176.*
LOWELL, L[ord]. *AY 34.*
VALOYNES, Thebaude de. *P 146. ('Sys pences oundees dor & de goules').*

Barry wavy &c of 6 Or and Sa &c
Barry nebuly Or and Sa
— *Leake. (qtd 3 by Walter Blount, KG (d 1474-5)).*
BLONT, Sr William. *R 7.*
BLOUNT. *BA 1052. (imp Saye).*
BLOUNT. *BA 1053. (imp by Courtenay, E of Devon).*
[BLOUNT]. *Neale & Brayley. 1296. (canopy of Mont to Edmund, E of Lancaster).*
BLOUNT, Walter, Ld Montjoy. *WGA 117.*
BLOUNT, William. *XF 363.*
[BLUNT]. *Nichols Leics IV 434. (Appleby Magna Ch).*
ELLESFELD, M de. *WNR 69.*
Barry wavy Or and Sa
— *WK 60. (qtd 3 by Sir James Blount).*
— *WB V 72. (qtd 3 by Sir James Blount (Kt 1485)).*
— *WK 7. (qtd 3 by James Blont).*
— *WGA 180. (qtd 2&3 by Sir Jn Blount; Coll Arm MS says qrs 1&4).*
— *BB 111, 4. (qtd 2&3 by Mons' Joh'n Blontte, d1418).*
— *BA 778. (qtd 2&3 by Eliz Blunt, all imp by Stanley, of Wiston).*
BLOUND, Walter. *BG 379.*
BLOUNT. *SK 433.*
BLOUNT. *CT 173.*
BLOUNT. *FK II 190.*
BLOUNT, Baron Mottoye. *L1 38, 2; L2 41, 5.*
BLOUNT, Sir Thomas. *WK 91.*
BLOUNT, Mons' W. *SD 100.*
BLOUNT, Sire Willame. *N 837.*
BLOUNT, Mons William. *TJ 597. (base Sa; ' ... pee de sable').*
BLOUNT, Monsire William. *CG 430.*
BLOUNT, Sr William. *CKO 512.*
BLOUNT, Sr William. *L 44.*
BLOUNT, William. *XK 85. (Ld Mountjoy, KG, 1526).*
BLUNT, Ld Monjoie. *WK 460.*
BLUNT, William le. *E I 433; E II 435.*
BLUNTTE, Sir J. *WB I 38b, 21.*
Barry wavy Or and Vt
HAUBERK, Sir Nicol. *CRK 714.*

Barry wavy of 6 Sa and ...
Barry wavy Sa and Arg
> [BASSETT]. *OxfAS 80th Report (1934). (also Bicester Priory; late 13 cent shrine, Stanton Harcourt, Oxfords).*
> BLOUNT, Sir Thomas, of Staffs. *RH, Ancestor v 182.*
> DELAFIELD, Sir Gylberd. *RH, Ancestor ix 166.*
> ELEFELD, Monsr Gilbert de. *AS 286.*
> STAPILTON, Mons' Richard. *TJ 595. (base Arg; '... pee de argent').*
> WARDE, Robert de la. *TJ 600. (base Arg).*

Barry wavy Sa and Or
> — *PLN 1985. (qtd 3 by Sir Jas Blount).*
> MONCHORY, the Lorde. *WB IV 134b, 156.*

Barry wavy &c of 6 (patterned)
Barry wavy Gu and Erm
> LACY, Sire Johan de. *N 791. ('oundee de goules & de ermyne').*
> LACY, of Northd. *L1 402, 2; L2 308, 4.*

Barry wavy Erm and Untinc
> MAREYS. *Mill Steph. (Brass to Thomas M, Rector 1472, Stourmouth, Kent).*
> [MAREYS]. *Arch Cant xxiii 117. (on Mont to Joh'na (d1431), w of Wm M, Sheldwich, Kent).*

Barry nebuly Erm and Gu
> GOLDINGHAM. *XF 37.*
> GOLDINGHAM, Alexander. *S 425.*

Barry wavy Erm and Gu
> — *WB I 12, 2. (imp by Sir Geffray Foliot).*
> — *WB I 12, 3. (imp by [?Dengayne]).*
> FILIOT. *SK 679.*
> FOLLIOT, Sir Geoffrey. *WNS 26b, 104. ('...porte undee de ermine et de gou').*
> GOLDINGHAM, Mons' Alexander. *S 420.*

Barry wavy Erm and Sa
> BARLE. *FK II 684.*
> BARLEY, of Herts. *CRK 1131.*
> MAREIS, William. *Kent Gentry 217b.*

Barry wavy per pale Or & Arg and Gu
> DAUNTESEYE, Sr Richard. *N 898. ('Parti de or e de argent e oundee de goules'; tricked by Glover & Gibbon as Per pale Or and Arg barry wavy Gu).*

Barry wavy Arg & Sa gutty Arg
> MORRIS, W. *CRK 1944.*

Barry nebuly Arg & Sa roundelly Or
> BASSETT, S' Joh. *PO 333.*

Barry of 6 and label
Barry Arg and Az roundelly Or label Gu
> GREY. *Nichols Leics II 558. (Evington Ch).*

BARRY OF 8
Barry of 8
> — *Birch 11534. 1315. (1 of 6 coats in sl of Nicholas Malemayns, of Lincs).*
> — *WB I 23b, 12. (imp by Dutton).*
> — *WB I 20, 15. (qtd 2 by 'Matravers').*
> BLOUNT, Felipa. *Birch 7505. S'FELIPE BL...T. 1428. (sl used by Hen Engehurst, of Merden, Suss).*
> CHAORCIIS, Paganus de. *Birch 5802. SIGILL'PA[G]ANI DE CHAORCIIS. early 13 cent. (equestr sl).*
> [HUNGARY]. *Birch 4758. 1448. (qr 1 for Mgt of Anjou; founder's sl, Queens' Coll, Camb).*
> POYNES. *CT 46.*
> POYNES, John. *Birch 12826. .....YN..... 1424. (Ld of Manor of Northwokyndon, Essex).*
> QUEENS COLL CAMB. *Arch Journ li 312. 1448. (?tincts reversed; qtg 2 Naples, 3 Jersualem, 4 Anjou, 5 Barre, 6 Lorraine; sl on Hamonds map of Camb, 1592).*

Barry of 8 Arg and Az
Barry of 8 Arg and Az
> — *Bellasis II 7. (qtd by Az 4 lozs conjd in fess Untinc [Aske], all imp by [Bellingham] qtg [Burneshead]). (Window, Bellingham Chapel, Kendal).*
> GREY. *PO 28.*
> GREY, [L]ord. *SHY 322.*
> MONCHENEY, Sir William. *BR V 278.*

Barry of 8 Arg and Gu
Barry of 8 Arg and Gu
> — *WGA 168. (qtd 2&3 by Fernando, K of Naples).*
> — *WGA 19. (marshalled by Ferdinand, K of Naples).*
> — *XK 29. (qtd II&III (a) by Alphonso, K of Naples, KG, temp Hen 7).*
> — *Dingley cxlv. (on calvary cross engraved on mensa of Easter sepulchre, Erdestland Ch, Heref).*
> — *WGA 159. (qtd 2&3(a) by Alphonse, K of Naples).*
> — *L10 94, 6. (qtd 2&3 by Joh Stubbe, of ?Shelton, Norf).*
> — *Bellasis II 306-8. (w of .... Kirkby, in E window, Windermere).*
> — *Dingley cxlv. (imp Untinc pile ?Sa; 1 of 3 shs above Easter sepulchre, Erdestland Ch, Heref).*
> ANJOU, Q Margaret of. *LH 783. (imp by Hen 6).*
> ANJOU, Q Margaret of. *CRK 1395. (qr 1).*
> ANJOU, Q Margaret of. *LH 782. (qr 1).*
> ANJOU, Q Margaret of. *RL 28, 3. (qtg 2 Naples, 3 Jerusalem, 4 Anjou, 5 Barr, 6*

[Lorraine]; all imp by qtly France modern & Engld).
ANJOU, Q Margaret of. *ML I 382. (qr 1, all imp by Hen 6).*
FITZALURED, of Irld. *L2 194, 12.*
GILBERTUS, Canonicus. *PCL IV 7.*
HUNGARIE, K of. *KB 25. (imp Old France).*
HUNGARY. *WLN 8.*
HUNGARY. *Sandford 299. (qr 1 of Mgt of Anjou, w of Hen 6).*
HUNGARY. *Neale & Brayley. (qr 1 of sh for Lorraine imp by Scotld on mont erected c1612, for Mary, Q of Scots).*
HUNGARY, King of. *PLN 20.*
HUNGARY, King of. *FK I 26. (imp Old France).*
HUNGARY, Roy de. *WJ 65.*
LORRAINE. *Lyndsay 46. (imp by Jas V for his 2nd w Marie de Lorraine).*
SECILIE, K of. *BR I 16a. (qtd 1 on 2nd sh).*
STUTEVILE. *ML I 266.*

Barry of 8 Arg and Sa
Barry of 8 Arg and Sa
BOCHE. *SHY 317.*
MERIET. *PO 187.*

Barry of 8 Az and Or
Barry of 8 Az and Or
ASKE, Mons Conand d'. *WJ 1002. (or Az 3 bars Or; lowest bar Or very small & may be accident).*

Barry of 8 Gu and ...
Barry of 8 Gu and Arg
HUNGRY, Ye Kyng of. *SHY 598. (qtg 2&3 Az 3 suns Or, 4 Barry of 10 Gu and Arg).*
Barry of 8 Gu and Or
— *L10 91, 2. (qtd 7 by Harcourt, all imp by Bowyer).*
FITZ ALAN, Brian, de Bedale. *P 136.*
FITZ ALAN, Brian, de Bedale. *TJ 553.*
LOVELL. *PLN 1538.*
POINTZ, Sir Robert. *BA 846.*
POYNES. *WB I 20b, 12.*
POYNTZ. *XF 443. (qr 1).*
POYNTZ. *XF 481. (qtg Acton).*

Barry of 8 Or and Az
Barry of 8 Or and Az
— *WB I 21b, 10. (qtd 2&3 by Thos Treheyron, Somerset Herald, [1532-42]).*
PANEBRIGGE, Henri de. *A 223.*
PEMBRIDGE, Henry de. *XF 937.*
PEMBRUGE. *LEP 5.*
PENBRUGGE, Sir Richard. *WGA 175.*
PENBRUGGE, Staffs. *CY 97, 386.*
PENEBREGGE. *HE 133.*
PENEBRUGE, Henri de. *E I 221; E II 223.*

PENEBRUGE, Henry de. *D 55a.*
PENEBRUGGE, Fouke de. *HA 110.*
PENEBRUGGE, Henri de. *D 55b.*
PENEBRUGGE, of Mouneshull Gamage. *BA 18b.*
PENNEBREGGE. *L9 104a, 8.*

Barry of 8 Or and ...
Barry of 8 Or and Gu
— *Dingley cxlv. (window, Erdestland Ch, Heref).*
POINZ, Hue. *K 29.*
POYNTZ. *L1 530, 2.*
[POYNTZ]. *DevonNQ VIII ii 33. c1500. (imp by Prideaux, in E window of N aisle, Sutcombe, Devon).*
POYNZ, Sr Nichol. *L 9.*
PUYNES. *SK 575.*
WNGARIE, the Kyng off. *Lyndsay 26.*
Barry of 8 Or and Sa
SAXONY, Henry, D of. *Sandford 69. ('the Lion').*

Barry of 8 Sa and Arg
Barry of 8 Sa and Arg
HOGHTON, of Yorks. *MY A2 244.*

Barry of 8 including Erm and Vairy
Barry of 8 Arg & vairy Gu and Arg
COUCY, Enguerrand de. *MP I 95.*
Barry of 8 Erm and Gu
[?KIRTON]. *ML I 331.*

Barry of 8 modified

Barry dancetty &c of 8
Barry dancetty of 8 Arg and Gu
BALUN, John de. *A a 159.*
COTENHAM, John de. *TJ 399.*
Barry dancetty of 8 Gu and Arg
TOTENHAM. *SK 1104.*
Barry of 8 Or and Gu embattled counter-emb
— *RH, Ancestor ix 179. (on 1 of Or bars is written 'the feld sene thorowe' and 'the feld' is said to be Gu (cf K of Macedonia, RH 1147)).*
Barry lozy of 8 Arg and Gu
TUDENHAM, Jorge de. *F 99.*

Barry wavy &c of 8
Barry nebuly of 8
[BASSET?]. *Birch 1909.* SIGILL': FULCONIS: BASSET: DE[C]ANI: EBOR. *(in space over niche on countersl of Fulk B, Bp of London 1244-59; his sl as Dean of York, temporally used as London countersl).*

Barry wavy of 8 Arg and Gu
  MOWERES, Sir Symond. *BR V 123.*
Barry wavy of 8 Or and Az
  BASSET, Simon. *A a 222.*
Barry wavy of 8 Or and Gu
  BASSAT, Adam. *LO A 28. ('dominis de Wyeub').*
Barry nebuly of 8 Or and Sa
  BLOUNT, Sir Walter. *S 190.*
Barry wavy of 8 Or and Sa
  BLOUNT, Mons Walt. *S 188.*
Barry nebuly of 8 Sa and Or
  [SELBY]. *ML I 465.*
Barry wavy of 8 Sa and Or
  [BLOUNT]. *ML I 522.*
  [BLOUNT]. *AY 65. (qtd 3 by [Blount], Ld Mountjoy).*
  MORLEY. *SHY 237. (imp Marty).*
  MORLEY. *SHY 236. (imp by Marty).*
  MORLEY. *SHY 235. (imp by Yelverton).*
Barry wavy of 8 Erm and Sa
  BARLYE, Essex. *MY 164.*
Barry wavy of 8 Ermines and Arg
  MARREYS, William. *PLN 524.*

Barry of 8 per ....
Barry of 8 per pale counterch
  BARET, William. *Birch 7140.* [S]IGILLVM WI[LL]ELMI BARET. 1331.
  BARRET, William. *PRO-sls.* 8 Jan 1332.

BARRY OF 10
Barry of 10
  BALSHAM, R de. *PRO-sls.* 1370-1.
  FREVYLLE, Baldewine. *Birch 9960.* SIGILLU: BALDEWYNI: FREUILE. 1393. *(coat unclear - ?bendy of 10 for Montfort; qtg 2&3 cross botonny; s of Baldewine F, Chevr, of Tamworth, Warws & Staffs).*
  LUCY, Sir Wm. *WK 126. (marshalled in dex half of qr 1).*
  LYLE, John, of Suss, Kt. *Birch 11484.* 1464. *(coat unclear; sl used by Andrew Theccher, or his w Isabella).*
  [MONCHENSEY]. *Mill Steph.* 1528. *(shield tierced per pall (a) Bures, (b) per fess Waldegrave & [M], (c) [Drury] on brass to [Hen B], Acton, Suff).*
  MONDIDIERS, Simon. *PRO-sls.* SIMONIS MONDIDIERS. 1367-8. *(1 of 3 shs on sl used by Jn, s of Wm de Middelmor).*
  MONTFORT, Peter de. *Dugd 17, 6.* Sigillum Petri de Monteforti. 1325-6.
Barry of 10 Arg and Az
  — *WK 281. (qtd 2&3 by Sir Wm Walgrave).*
  — *PO 12. ((the martlets gone); qtd 3&4 by [Valence], Counte de Pembroke).*

CYPRUS, King of. *LO B 43.*
[LUSIGNAN, Comte de la Marche]. *DX 33.*
MANCHESTER. *L9 53b, 6.*
MANCHESY. *FK II 549. ('potius Monchensy' added by Gibbon).*
Barry of 10 Arg and Gu
  STOTEVILE. *LS 198.*
  STOUTEUILLE. *L1 592, 5.*
  TALBOT. *Dingley cclxxvii. (window, All Hallows Ch, Evesham).*
Burely Arg and Sa
  ASCHFELD, of Suss. *MY 333. (9 to 11 bars).*
Barry of 10 Arg and Sa
  MOUNMAREYN. *CV-BM 300.*
Barry of 10 Or and Az
  — *I2(1904)170. (qtd 4 by Edw Beltnap).*
  CONSTABYLL, Sir J. *WB I 39b, 9.*
  MONFORD, Sir John. *BR V 45. (?bendy).*
Barry of 10 Or and Gu
  — *WLN 66.*
  — *I2(1904)44-5. (qtd 2 by 'Therll of Arundell'; Foster calls it 'Flaal').*
  — *WLN 60.*
  ELEANOR, Queen. *WB I 34, 1. (w of Hen 2).*
  NAPLES, Alphonse, K of. *WGA 159. (qrs 1&4).*

Barry of 10 modified

Barry dancetty &c of 10
Barry dancetty of 10
  MARE, John de la. *Birch 11600.* S' IOHANNIS: DE: LA MA[RE]. temp Edw 1. *(Ld of Little Hereford, Herefs).*
Barry wavy of 10
  LOVELL. *Suff HN 3d. (imp by Crane; Chilton Ch).*
Barry wavy of 10 Arg and Az
  BULBECK, de Sandfort. *L10 34b, 1.*
Barry wavy of 10 Or and Gu
  LOWELLE, Sir John. *BR V 29.*

BARRY OF 12
Barry of 12
  — *WB I 35b, 1. (qtd 4 by E of Shrewsbury).*
  — *Birch 3004.* 14 cent. *(sl of Austin Priory of Cottingham).*
  MONCHENSY, Wm de. *Farrer Bacon 42.* late 13 cent.
  MONTCHENISY, Thomas de, of Suff, Chevr. *Birch 11864.* 1361.
Barry of 12 Arg and Gu
  HUNGARY. *PLN 606.*
  STOTEVILE. *RB 480.*

Barry of 12 Arg and Sa
    MOUNMAREYN. *CV-BM 98.*
Barry of 12 Gu and Arg
    STUTTEVILLE, Mons Robert. *TJ 1231.*
Barry of 12 Or and Az
    BEAUBRAS, Mons Robert de, S' de Porchestre. *WJ 1155.*
    ROANBRAS, Sir Robt, Ld Porchester. *LR 6.*
Barry of 12 Or and Vt
    ARNALE, M de. *WNR 130.*

Barry of 12 patterned or modified
Barry of 12 Or and Az per pale counterch
    BARNS. *L10 22, 14.*
    BRANE. *L1 79, 4; L2 65, 5.*
Barry nebuly of 12
    — *Birch 11703.* 1448. *(imp by Thos Maunsell, of Essex, Esq).*

BARRY OF 14 OR MORE
Barry of 14 Arg and Az
    MONCHENSY, of Herts. *L1 439, 1; L2 336, 7.*
Barry of 14 Arg and Gu
    HUNGARY, K of. *?source. (on ceiling, St Alban's Abbey).* c1450.
    ESTOTEVILLE, Robert d'. *XF 923.*
Barry of 14 Arg and Sa
    PORCHESTER. *R 105.*
Barry of 14 Gu and Arg
    [BADLESMERE]. *PLN 1165. (imp by Lacy; HS London says middle red stripe is twice as wide as others).*
Barry of 14 Or and Sa
    SELBY, S' Will'. *PO 555.*
    THORPE, Sire William de. *PV 47.*
Barry of 18 Arg and Gu
    PERPOUNT, S'John, of Norf. *CY 124, 493.*
Barry of 20 Arg and Sa
    SAMPSON. *LS 271.*

BARRY UNNUMBERED
Burely Untinc
    CHAWORTH, Pain de. *Bk of Sls 470.* 1233-7.
    MUNCHENSY, Thomas. *Birch 12024.* [S T]HOME MUNCHENSY. 1401. *(s&h of Thos M, of Suff).*
    SELBY, John. *BM Harl 1448, 24b, HB-SND. (?barry of 14).*
    STUTEVILE, Johanna de. *Birch 6719.* .....-..EVIL.... 1265-75. *(wid of 1 Hugh Wake, 2 Hugh le Bigod, of Hesele, Yorks).*

Barry unnumbered Arg and Az
Burely Arg and Az
    — *XK 189. (qtd I&IV 2 ii&iii by Sir Edw Grey; orle of martlets omitted).*
    FITZRAUFFE. *L1 263, 4; L2 194, 6.*
    HORBUN, of Yorks. *L1 327, 4; L2 257, 1.*
    HORBYN. *LH 889.*
    [LUSIGNAN]. *WLN 143. (qtd 2&3 by K of Cyprus).*
    MARCHE, [Count] de la. *WJ 1149.*
    MARCHE, Ingraham de la. *XF 415. (& Monchensy).*
    MONCHANESY, William de. *WLN 552.*
    MONCHENSI, Sire Willame de. *N 402.*
    MONCHENSY. *XF 421.*
    MOUNCHENSY, Mons' William. *TJ 588.*
    MUNCHANESI, William de. *F 216. ('barry silver & azure').*
    MUNCHENSY, Walter de. *E I 281.*
    MUNCHENSY, Wm de. *E II 281.*
    PENBROKE, Le count de. *WLN 216. (unfinished).*
    SAINCT B[RIDE], Nicholl de. *FW 192c.*
    SEIN B[RIDE], Nichole de. *FW 192.*
    VALENS, erle of Penbroke. *WB IV 154, 508.*
    WODBRERE. *WLN 823. (?Arg 6 bars Az).*

Barry unnumbered Arg and Gu
Burely Arg and Gu
    BARRY. *Gerard 152.*
    CHAWORTH, Patrik. *FW 129.*
    HUNGARY. *Brit Arch Assoc xxxiv 22.* c1400-20. *('Scutu[m] regis Hungari'; nave ceiling St Albans Abbey).*
    SARTEVILLE, S', de Cotyngham. *WJ 1161.*
    STOTEVILE, Robert de. *E 186.*
    STUTTEVILLE, Mons' Rob't. *TJ 1232.*
    STUTTEVILLE, Mons' Robert. *TJ 590.*

Barry unnumbered Arg and Sa
Burely Arg and Sa
    SAMPSON, Mons Robert. *WJ 1168.*
    WALDEMOND, le Counte. *C 32. (Henry I de Vaudemont (1246-79)'... burle de une grose burlure d'argent et de sable').*

Barry unnumbered Or and Az
Burely Or and Az
    — *BR VI 34. (marshalled by Ld Darcy of the North).*

Barry unnumbered Or and Gu
Burely Or and Gu
    BRILIANS, S Galiard de. *GA 24.*
    HANSBERCH. *LH 210. (qrs 1&4).*

Barry unnumbered Or and Sa
Burely Or and Sa
   SELBY, Walter de. *CA 215.*
   SELBY, Water de. *XF 420.*
   SELBY, Mons Waut' de. *WJ 1167.*
   THORP, Mons' W de. *SD 46.*
   THORP, William de. *CKO 578.*

Barry unnumbered Erm and Ermines
Burely Erm and Ermines
   BEDFORD, Wylyam. *RH, Ancestor ix 165.*

Barry & label: see under Label

BARRY &c CHIEF PALY

Barry chief paly & corners gyronny
Barry chf paly corners gyronny Or and Az
   — *BW 5, 17.* *(2 bars; qtd 2 by [Richard] le Duke de York, [1415-60]).*

Barry &c on chief 2 pales & over all escutch
3 bars on chf 2 pales & over all escutch
   PORTEES, Richard de. *PRO-sls.*
   ....DE PORTES. 1323-4.
Barry on chf 2 pales over all escutch
   [BURLEY]. *PRO-sls.* 1388-9. *(imp in sin of tierced shield by Lady Beatrice de Roos).*
Barry Sa and Or on chf Or 2 pales Sa over all escutch Gu
   BEUERLEY. *L10 27b 18.*
   BEUERLY. *L1 102, 4; L2 57, 9. (3 bars).*
   BEVERLEY. *SK A 1103. (2 bars).*
   BEVERLEY. *SK B&C 1103.*

Barry &c on chf 2 pales escutch patterned
Barry Sa and Or on chf Or 2 pales Sa over all escutch barry Gu and Erm
   BEVERLEY. *PT 776. (on dex pale mullet Or).*
   BURLEY. *L1 93, 4; L2 54, 12.*
   BURLEY, Sir John, KG. *Coll T&G iii 329. (N window, nave, Carshalton, Surr).*
   BURLEY, Sir John. *WGA 210.*
Barry Sa and Or on chf Or 2 pales Sa over all escutch Erm
   BURLEY. *L10 84b, 12.*

Barry &c on chf 2 pales escutch charged
Arg 2 bars Sa on chf Arg 2 pales Sa over all on escutch Gu 3 bars Sa
   BURLEY, Simon, KG d1388. *BD 181b. (mont, N wall, St Paul's Cathedral).*

—

3 bars on chf 2 pales on escutch 3 bars Erm
   ROOS, Beatrice de. *Yorks Deeds X 93.*
   SIGILLUM....CIS DE ROOS. 1404. *(for [Burley]; imp by [Stafford]).*
Barry Or and Sa on chf Sa 2 pales Or over all on escutch Gu 3 bars Erm
   BERLAY, Mons' John, d1383. *BB 126.*
   BEURLY, Mons' reschard, d1387. *BB 108.*
   BURLEY, Mons'r Symond, d1388. *BB 79.*
Barry Sa and Or on chf Or 2 pales Az over all on escutch Gu 3 bars Erm
   BERELY, John. *WB IV 171b, 825.*
Barry Sa and Or on chf Or 2 pales Sa over all on escutch Gu 3 bars Erm
   BURLY, Sir Simon. *MK 3.*
Barry Sa and Or on chf Or 2 pales Sa over all on escutch Erm 3 bars Gu
   BURLAYE, Mons Simon. *WJ 1031.*
   BURLAYES, Mons Joh de. *WJ 1034.*
   BURLEY, Mons Rich. *WJ 1035.*
   BURLEYE, Sir John. *L10 34, 15.*

Barry chief paly corners gyronny & over all escutch
3 bars in chf two pales corners gyronny over all escutch
   PORTES, Richard de, Ld of Bromesbergh. *PRO-sls E40 A8250. ...ICA.... c1302.*
Barry chf paly corners gyronny escutch
   — *BB 28. (qtg Burgh, all qtd 2&3 by Ric, D of York, 'duc de orke conte de Marsche & de olvester reschard' [d1460]).*
   BOSCO, Richard de, Kt. *PRO-sls.* SIGILLUM RICARDI DU BLOIS [recte BOIS?]. 1298-9. *(barry of 8; on shield betw 3 oak sprigs).*
   BOSCO, Richard de, Kt. *PRO-sls.* 1383-96.
   BOYS, Richard du, of La Seete Manor, Ludlow, Salop. *Birch 7704.* SIGILLUM: RICARDI DV BOIS. 1292. *(barry of 8).*
   MORTEMER, Roger de, 4th E of March & Ulster. *Birch 11969.* 1397. *(qtg Burgh).*
   MORTIMER. *(qtg 2&3 Burgh, qtd IV by qtly Engl & France modern, all imp by France mod & Engld qtly for Hen 7 & Elizabeth of York; mont to Mgt, Ctess of Richmond, d1509; S aisle, Hen 7 chapel). WestmAbb.*
   MORTIMER. *Mill Steph.* 1419. *(3 bars; imp by Camoys on brass to Thos, Ld C, [d 28 Apr 1421] & his w Eliz dau of Edm M, E of March & wid of Sir Hen Percy KG, [d 1417], Trotton, Suss).*
   [MORTIMER]. *Inventory. (imp by Sir Jn Harpedon (d1457) on brass).*
   [MORTIMER]. *BirmCL-sls Areley Hall Deeds 35.* 1522. *(qtd 4 by Sir Thos West, Kt, Ld of manor of Martley).*
   MORTIMER, Edmund, E of March. *Stowe-Bard 2s iii 131. (sl, legend mutilated, on*

charter to Abbey of W Dereham).
MORTIMER, Edmund, E of March. *PRO-sls AS 195.* 1378-9.
MORTIMER, Edmund, E of March, Ld of Wigmore. *Bow 11.* S'Edmundi mortuomari: com marchie Dm Wigmore.
MORTIMER, Edmund de, 3rd E of March. *Birch 11956.* S'EDMUNDI .....MARI COM' MARCHI. 1372.
MORTIMER, Edmund de, 1st Baron, of Wigmore. *Birch 11955; Barons Letter.* S'EDMVNDI DE MORTUO MARI. 1301.
MORTIMER, Hugh de. *Dugd 17, 51.* 1343-4.
MORTIMER, Hugh de, of Salop, Kt. *Birch 11957.* S'HUGONIS DE MORTVOMARI. 1344.
MORTIMER, Hugo de. *Dugd 17, 18.* 1320.
MORTIMER, John de, Kt. *Birch 11959.* S'IOHANNIS D'MORTIMER. 1297.
MORTIMER, Margaret. *AnstisAsp I 223, 90.* +SIG: MARG: VXORIS: EDM: MORTIMER. *(imp lion; 'qui fui uxor Edmund de Mortuomari').*
MORTIMER, Maud de. *Bridgwater 43.* S'....DE MORTUOMARI. 1298.
MORTIMER, Roger de. *PRO-sls.* 1300, 01 & 15-16. *(?semy de lis).*
MORTIMER, Roger de. *Birch 11965.* 13 cent.
MORTIMER, Roger de. *Bow XLIV 1.* 1376-7. *(qrs 1&4). (E of March & Ulster, Ld of Wigmore, Clare & Conaght, Marshal of Engld).*
MORTIMER, Roger de, E of March & Ulster. *Bow 1.* 1381-90. *(qrs 1&4).*
MORTIMER, Roger de, Ld of Pentkellyn, 2nd Baron. *Birch 11968.* ...D(E MORTVO....D)E PENKETLYN. 1301.
MORTIMER, Roger de, Ld of Wigmore, Herefs. *Birch 11963.* SIGILL ....ERI DE MORTVO MA. late Hen 3.
MORTUO MARI, Walter de, Constable of Beaumaris. *PRO-sls.* 1311-2. *(blazon uncertain).*
MORTUOMARI, Edmund de. *Bow XLIV 3.* S: EDMVDI: DE MORTVO: MARI: COM: MARCIE: DOM: DE WIGMORE.
MORTUOMARI, Roger de. *Bow XXI 2.* S Rogeri de Mortuomari.

Barry chf paly corners gyronny Arg and Az (or vice versa) over all escutch
Barry chf paly corners gyronny Arg and Az escutch Arg
MORTIMER, Edmund de. *LM 107.*
Barry chf paly corners gyronny Az and Arg escutch Arg
— *L9 9b, 3. (3 bars).*
KENULFUS, Rx. *DV 45a, 1768. (3 bars).*
KENULFUS, King in England. *L2 287, 1. (3 bars).*
KENULPH, King. *BA 896. (3 bars).*

Barry chf paly corners gyronny Az and Arg escutch Or
[BRITAIN], K Kemelyn. *KB 183.*
[BRITAIN], K Kenwolff. *KB 179. (gyrons narrow piles isst from dex & sin chf corners, pts touching bottom of chf but not reaching central pale).*

Barry chf paly corners gyronny Arg and Sa (or vice versa) over all escutch
Barry chf paly corners gyronny Sa and Arg escutch Arg
— *SHY 504. (2 bars).*
Barry chf paly corners gyronny Sa and Arg escutch Or
— *FK II 556. (3 bars).*

Barry chf paly corners gyronny Az and Or (or vice versa) escutch Arg
Barry chf paly corners gyronny Az and Or escutch Arg
MAERTSE, Die Grave van der. *Gelre 56b.* c1380. *(3 bars).*
MARCH, Count de. *FK I 81. (qtg Burgh).*
MARCH, E of. *I2(1904)46. (3 bars; qtg [Burgh]; on banner).*
MARCH, ...le, [Le Co.]. *NB 7. (3 bars).*
MARCH, Edmund, Count de, d1424. *FK I 56. (3 bars).*
MARCHE, Counte de. *CN 6. (3 bars).*
MARCHE, le Cont de. *WB V 11.*
MARCHE, Comit de la. *WJ 1009. (3 bars).*
MARSCHE, Roger, Conte de la, d1360. *BB 4, 104.*
MORTEMER, Sir Roger. *BR IV 101.*
MORTEMERE. *CT 23.*
MORTIMER. *PLN 62. (3 bars; qtg 2&3 Burgh).*
MORTIMER. *PO 26. (3 bars).*
[MORTIMER]. *CB 392. (3 bars).*
[MORTIMER]. *TZ 19. (3 bars; drawing of chf is unusual, could be blazoned gyronny of 7 Or and Az).*
MORTIMER, Earls of March. *RH, Ancestor iii 200.*
MORTIMER, Edmund, E of March. *CRK 1377. (qrs 1&4).*
MORTIMER, E of March. *ML II 13.*
MORTIMER, E of March. *PLN 1162. (3 bars).*
MORTIMER, E of March. *ML I 554.*
[MORTIMER, E of March]. *XB 26. (qr 1).*
MORTIMER, Roger. *XF 760. (3 bars).*
MORTIMER, Roger. *L9 69a, 1. (3 bars).*
MORTIMER, Sr Roger de. *RB 58. (2 bars).*
MORTIMER, Roger, E of March. *S 33. (3 bars; qrs 1&4).*
MORTMER, Sir Edmund. *PCL I 516. (3 bars).*

MORTUMER, Ld of Wigmore. *L1 422, 6; L2 322, 1. (2 bars).*

MORTYMER, Mons Geffray. *WJ 1014.*

MORTYMER, S' Hug de, of Salop. *CY 83, 330.*

MORTYMER, Erle of Marche. *KB 244.*

MORTYMER, Mons' Roger le. *TJ 1097. (3 bars).*

MORTYMER, Sr Roger. *BR V 4. (3 bars).*

Barry chf paly corners gyronny Or and Az escutch Arg

  — *XK 8. (qtd 4 by Eliz of York, w of Hen 7).*

  — *XK 78. (qtd 4 by Arthur Plantagenet, KG, temp Hen 8).*

  — *Leake. (qtd 3 by Arthur Plantagenet, KG, d1542).*

MARCH, E of. *SHY 131. (barry of 10).*

MARCH, Erle of. *BR II 39. (qrs 1&4).*

MARCH, B[aron] of. *AY 21. (qrs 1&4).*

MARCH, Edward, E of. *Sandford 371-3 & 403-4. (afterwards Edw 4; qtg Burgh).*

MARCH, Roger, E of. *WGA 173.*

MARCHE, Erle of. *RH, Ancestor v 181.*

MARCHE, Erele of. *PCL IV 85. (2 bars).*

MARSCHE. *SM 286, 43. (2 bars).*

MORTEMER, Emounde. *G 153.*

MORTEMER, Roger de. *FW 94; FW 621.*

MORTEMER, Sire Roger de. *J 24.*

MORTIM[ER], Edmund de. *Q 63.*

MORTIMER. *Dingley cxlvi. (N window, Eardisland Ch, Herefs).*

MORTIMER, E de. *SP A 45.*

MORTIMER, M de. *WNR 60.*

MORTIMER, de. *F 28.*

[MORTIMER]. *WK 496. (qtd by Arthur Plantagenet, Visct Lisle).*

[MORTIMER]. *I2(1904)184. (qtd 4 by Ld Laware).*

[MORTIMER]. *WestmAbb. c1510-20. (qtd 4 by qtly France modern & Engld, all imp by the same; top tier of lights of window in E chantry of Hen 7 chapel, destroyed by enemy action 26/27 Sept 1940).*

[MORTIMER]. *Lambarde 290. 1421. (imp by Camoys on mont to Thos, Ld C, Trotton, Suss).*

MORTIMER, Anna. *CR 9. (3 bars; dau & eventual heir of Rog, 4th E of March).*

MORTIMER, Anne. *Sandford 384. (w of Ric, E of Camb, [exec 1416]).*

MORTIMER, Edmond. *Sandford 223. (husb of Philippa of Clarence, grand-dau of Edw 3).*

MORTIMER, Edmund. *CR 8. (3 bars; s&h of Rog de M, & 5th & last E of March).*

MORTIMER, Edmund, E of March. *CR 6. (2 bars).*

MORTIMER, Sir Hugh, of Salop. *CV-BM 170. (2 bars).*

MORTIMER, Sir John. *PLN 1983.*

MORTIMER, E of March. *DX 35. (barry of 4).*

MORTIMER, Munsire Roger de. *D 111b.*

MORTIMER, Roger de. *D 111a.*

MORTIMER, Roger de. *B 32.*

MORTIMER, Roger de. *HE 71.*

MORTIMER, Roger of. *Keepe.* ROGERUS DE MORTUO MARI. *(15 cent inscription; painted shield).*

MORTIMER, Sire Roger de. *N 18.*

MORTIMER, Roger, E of March. *S 6.*

MORTIMER, Roger, E of March. *CR 7. (3 bars).*

MORTIMER, Ed'us de. *Q II 63.*

MORTYMER, Roger. *P 73. ('dazure ove troys barres dor ove trois peus recopez deux dazur un dor ove les corners gerunes ove un escuchon dargent').*

MORTYMER, Roger de. *E I 22; E II 23.*

MORTYMER, Roger de. *C 102. (of Wigmore).*

Barry Az and Or chf paly corners gyronny Or and Gu escutch Arg

Barry Az and Or chf paly corners gyronny Or and Gu escutch Arg

  — *WLN 860. (3 bars).*

Barry chf paly corners gyronny Gu and Or (or vice versa) escutch Arg

Barry Gu and Untinc chf paly corners gyronny Or and Gu escutch Arg

CRESTY, Sir J. *WB I 38b, 18.*

Barry chf paly corners gyronny Gu and Or escutch Arg

  — *WB I 16, 16. (qtd 2 by [Faconberge or Wondesford]).*

  — *WB I 16, 16. (qtd 3 by [Faconberge or Wondesford]; barry of 8).*

  — *PT 11. (3 bars).*

  — *L10 45b, 6. (qtd 2&3 by Sir Joh Cressy, of Northd).*

HAGLEY. *L1 308, 6; L2 249, 3. (2 bars).*

MORTEMER. *CT 147. (2 bars).*

MORTIMER, Hugh. *L9 69a, 7. (3 bars).*

MORTIMER, John de. *XF 779. (3 bars).*

MORTYMER, Mons Hugh. *WJ 1030. (3 bars).*

MORTYMER, Mons' Hugh. *TJ 1098. (3 bars).*

MORTYMERE, Sir Humfrey, of Salop. *WB III 80, 4. (barry of 8).*

Barry chf paly corners gyronny Or and Gu escutch Arg

  — *L10 92, 1. (qtd 3 by Hall, of Grays Inn).*

MORTEMER, John de. *FW 624.*

MORTIM[ER], Jan de. *Q 305.*

MORTIMER, Sire Henri de. *N 935.*

MORTIMER, Henry de. *LM 527.*

MORTIMER, Jehan de. *E 65.*

MORTYMER, Monsire de. *AN 10.*
MORTYMER, Sir Hugh. *O 162.* (*'i fauz escu-chun'*).
MORTYMER, Sire Hugh de. *O 189.*

Barry chf paly corners gyronny Or and Sa (or vice versa) escutch Arg
Barry chf paly corners gyronny Or and Sa escutch Arg
BOYS, Ricard. *FW 625.*
BOYS, Ricard de. *Q 301. (3 bars).*
BOYS, Richard du. *LM 234. (2 bars).*
Barry chf paly corners gyronny Sa and Or escutch Arg
MORTIMER, Raf de. *F 87.*

Barry (patterned) chf paly corners gyronny over all escutch plain
Barry Az and Or per pale counterch chf paly corners gyronny Or and Az escutch Arg
PARTENEY, le Sire. *WJ 1017. (3 bars).*
Barry Or and Az per pale counterch chf paly of 8 corners gyronny Az and Or escutch Arg
[MORTIMER]. *Dingley cclxxvii. (6 bars). (window in All Hallows Ch, Evesham; draw-ing gives appearance of silver shield with gobony border).*

'Mortimer' escutch barry
Barry Or and Untinc chf paly corners gyronny Or and Az escutch barry Erm and Gu
EDEFYN, Sir E. *WB I 41b, 19.*
Barry chf paly corners gyronny Sa and Or escutch barry Gu and Erm
BURLEY, Sir Simon. *WGA 125.*

'Mortimer' escutch Erm
Barry chf paly corners gyronny escutch Erm
MORTIMER, Roger de. *PRO-sls.* 1311-12 & 15-16.
MORTIMER, Roger de, Ld of Pentkellyn. *Barons Letter. (3 bars).*
Barry chf paly corners gyronny Arg and Az escutch Erm
MORTIMER, Rogg' de. *LM 109.*
Barry chf paly corners gyronny Az and Or escutch Erm
MORTEMER, Sir John. *WK 16. (3 bars).*
MORTEMER, Roger de. *G 155.*
MORTIMER. *CT 39.*
MORTIMER. *XF 761. (3 bars).*
[MORTIMER]. *Arch lvi 333.* 15 cent. *(3 bars; window, Ockwells Manor House, Berks).*
MORTIMER, Roger. *L9 69a, 2. (3 bars).*
MORTIMER, Roger de. *H 69a.*
MORTIMER, Roger de. *E 24.*
MORTIMER, Sir Roger de. *GA 185.* (*'dasur a iii barres dor en le chief pale on les corners*

geroune a ung escusson dhermyne').
MORTIMER, Sire Roger de. *N 19.* (*'le oncle'*).
MORTIMER, Roger, of Chirk. *ML I 15.*
MORTIMER, Roger, of Wigmore, d 1328. *LMS 66.*
MORTYMER, Sire Roger de. *J 54.*
MORTYMER, Sr Roger de. *H 69b.*
MORTYMERE. *DV 46b, 1833. (3 bars).*
Barry chf paly corners gyronny Gu and Or escutch Erm
— *L10 38, 17. (3 bars; qtd 2&3 by Sir Jn Cressy, Northants).*
Barry chf paly corners gyronny Or and Az escutch Erm
— *WK 540. (qtd 3 by Thomas, Ld Lawarre).*
— *WK 427. (qtd 19 by Ld Ambros Dudeley).*
MORTEMER. *L2 322, 2.*
MORTEMER, John. *WK 63.*
MORTEMER, Roger de. *SP A 47.*
MORTEMER, Rogiers de. *K 72.*
MORTIMER. *Dingley xxxvi.* 1517. *(imp by Beauchamp, for Thos B, E of Warw, who m Katherine, dau of Rog M; Baynton Mont, Bromham Ch, Wilts).*
MORTIMER, Baron. *CK a 22.*
MORTIMER, Ld. *PLN 1435. (3 bars).*
[MORTIMER]. *Lambarde 264. (imp by West on mont to Thos West, Ld La Warr & w Eliz Bonville, Boxgrove, Suss).*
[MORTIMER]. *Lambarde 263. (qtd 3 by West on mont to Thos West, Ld La Warr & w Eliz Bonville, Boxgrove, Suss).*
MORTIMER, Sir John [Kt 1485]. *WB V 84.*
MORTIMER, Rog de. *Q 121. (barry of 8).*
MORTIMER, Roger de. *K 438.*
MORTYMER. *WB I 35, 5.*
MORTYMER, S Roger. *ST 25.*
Barry chf paly corners gyronny Sa and Or escutch Erm
BOIS, Richard de. *E I 213. (3 bars).*
BOIS, Richard du. *E II 213.*
BORS. *L2 93, 6. (barry of 8).*
BŌRS, Richard de. *L10 33b, 12.*
BOYS, Richard. *F 386. (?escutch Arg bil-letty Sa).*

'Mortimer' escutch semy
Barry chf paly corners gyronny Or and Az escutch Arg billetty Sa
MORTIMER, Henri de. *F 375.*

'Mortimer' escutch charged
Barry chf paly corners gyronny Sa and Or on escutch Gu 2 bars Erm
BURGHE. *RH, Ancestor vii 204. (3 bars; 'K of the Garter' added in later hand).*

Or 3 bars & in chf 2 pales Sa on escutch Gu 3
  bars Erm
   BURLEY, Sir.... *CRK 761.*
Barry chf paly corners gyronny Or and Sa on
  escutch Gu 3 bars Arg
   BURLAY, Mons' Symon. *TJ 1396. ('dor ove
   iii barres de sable iii peus recopez deux de
   sable & un dor ove lez corners geronnez &
   un escucheon de goules & trois barres dar-
   gent').*
   OWERBY, John, of Kent. *CY 154, 616.*
Barry chf paly corners gyronny Sa and Or on
  escutch Gu 3 bars Erm
   — *PT 774. (cresc Or in dex chf for diffce).*
   BEVERLEY, Richard. *PT 771. (sable pales
   adjoin sable gyrons on chf).*
   BEVERLEY, Simond de. *PT 772. (pile Arg on
   dex Sa pale).*
   BUERLY, Sir Simon de. *CVK 718. (2 bars).*
   BURLEY. *LS 52. (imp Stafford).*
Barry chf paly corners gyronny Or and Az on
  escutch Arg lion Purp
   MORTIMER, Sr Roger de, le fitz. *L 171.*
   MORTYMER, Sire Roger de. *N 934.*
Barry chf paly corners gyronny on escutch 3 bil-
  lets
   BOYS, Richard du, Kt. *AnstisAsp I 188, 19.*
   SIGILLVM: RICARDI: DV: BOIS. 1292-3.
Untinc 3 bars Untinc on chf paly corners
  gyronny Or and Untinc on escutch Untinc 6
  billets Sa
   MORTIMER, Henry de. *WLN 433.*
   (unfinished).
Barry chf paly corners gyronny Sa and Or on
  escutch Arg 6 billets Sa
   BOYS, Richard de. *WLN 434. (3 bars).*
Barry chf paly corners gyronny on escutch 3
  birds
   PORTEES, Richard de. *PRO-sls E40 A243.*
   ...DE PORTES. 1323-4.
Barry chf paly corners gyronny Az and Arg on
  escutch Arg crosslet fitchy Gu
   KENELMUS, Sanctus. *L10 65b, 16. (3 bars).*
   WINCHCOMBE, Abbey of. *PR(1515)32.*
Barry chf paly corners gyronny Sa and Or on
  escutch Arg 6 gouttes Sa
   BORS, Richard de. *XF 934. (3 bars).*

'Mortimer' & on escutch label
Barry chf paly corners gyronny Az and Or on
  escutch Arg label Gu
   MORTYMER, Mons Th. *WJ 1015. (3 bars).*
Barry chf paly corners gyronny Az and Or on
  escutch Arg label Or each pt ch with 3 chevs
  Gu
   MARCH, 'le second fitz'. *WJ 1010. (3 bars).*
Barry chf paly corners gyronny Az and Or on
  escutch Arg label Or each pt ch with cross
  Gu

   MARCH, 'son fitz eisne'. *WJ 1013. (3 bars).*
Barry chf paly corners gyronny Az and Or on
  escutch Arg label Or fillet ch with 6 roundels
  & each pt with cross Gu
   MARCH, 'son fitz eisne'. *WJ B 1013. (3
   bars).*

'Mortimer' on escutch label of 3
Barry chf paly corners gyronny Sa and Or on
  escutch Gu 3 bars Erm & label Arg
   BEVERLEY. *PT 773.*

'Mortimer' & on escutch nails &c
Barry chf paly corners gyronny Az and Or on
  escutch Arg 3 nails Sa
   MORTEMER, Roberd, of Essex. *WB IV 174,
   872. (2 bars; qrs 1&4).*
Barry chf paly corners gyronny Or and Gu on
  escutch Or serpent Az
   — *LH 632. (serpent ondoyant in pale; qtd 3
   by Jn Hall).*
Barry chf paly corners gyronny Or and Gu on
  escutch Arg Milan viper Az swallowing child
  Gu
   MORTIMER, of Herefs. *L1 353, 4; L2 244, 3.
   (qtd 3 by Edw Hall, of Grays Inn).*
   MORTYMER, Sir Henry. *L9 48a, 11. (escutch
   for Milan).*
Barry chf paly corners gyronny on escutch salt
   MORTUO MARI, John de, Kt. *PRO-sls. 1298.*
Barry chf paly corners gyronny Az and Or on
  escutch Arg salt Gu
   MORTYMER, S John de. *GA 186. (3 bars).*
   MORTYMER, Sire Johan de. *N 933.*
   MORTYMER, Mons Rauf. *WJ 1011. (3 bars).*
Barry chf paly corners gyronny Or and Az on
  escutch Arg salt Gu
   MORTYMER, S John. *ST 26. (bro of Rog M).*
Barry chf paly corners gyronny Or and Gu on
  escutch Arg salt Gu
   MORTEMER, Sir John, of Herefs. *L2 322, 3.*
   temp Edw 2.

'Mortimer' & base
Az fess Or chf & base both paly & corners
  gyronny Or and Az over all escutch Arg
   PRISSONY, the Lorde. *RH, Ancestor vii 200.*

'Mortimer' & canton
Barry chf gobony over all escutch & canton
   HAGLEY, Henry. *PRO-sls. 1372-3. (3 bars).*
Barry chf paly corners gyronny Gu and Or
  escutch Or & canton Gu
   HAGELEY. *SK 547. (barry of 4).*
   HAGLEY. *LH 430. (barry of 4).*
   HAGLEY, T. *CRK 782. (3 bars).*

'Mortimer' & over all bend

Barry chf paly corners gyronny Az and Or
  escutch Arg bend Untinc
  MORTEMERE. *CT 55. (bend narrow).*
Barry chf paly corners gyronny Az and Or
  escutch Arg bend Gu
  MORTIMER. *FK II 160. (3 bars; bend narrow).*
  MORTIMER. *RB 225. (3 bars).*
  MORTIMER, William. *L9 69a, 3. (3 bars).*
  MORTIMER, William de. *XF 777. (3 bars).*
  MORTIMER, William de. *E I 38; E II 38. (bend narrow).*
Barry chf paly corners gyronny Or and Az
  escutch Arg bend Gu
  MORTEMER, Willame de. *FW 622.*
  MORTIMER, Will' de. *LM 316.*
  MORTIMER, Willam de. *Q 299. (2 bars).*

'Mortimer' & over all saltire

Barry chf paly corners gyronny Az and Or
  escutch Arg salt Gu
  MORTIMER, Geffrey de. *FW 623.*
  MORTIMER, Gefrai de. *E I 40; E II 40.*
  MORTIMER, Geoffrey. *XX B 5. (3 bars).*
  MORTIMER, Geoffrey de. *XF 765. (3 bars).*
  MORTIMER, Jefray. *L9 69a, 4. (3 bars).*
  MORTYMERE. *CT 371. (2 bars).*
Barry chf paly corners gyronny Or and Az
  escutch Arg salt Gu
  MORTIMER. *Dingley clxxxv. (window in Heref Cathedral).*
  MORTIMER, Geoffrey de. *XX 103.*

'Mortimer' in border

Barry chf paly corners gyronny Or and Az
  escutch Arg border Erm
  BLAUNFRONT, Sire Thomas. *O 150. (otherwise Erm over all escutch of Mortimer).*

BARROW

2 barrows palewise in fess
  — *Birch 4893. 15 cent. (imp in qrs 2&3 on sl of Droitwich, Worcester).*

BASKET

Arg 3 ?fish-weels Sa
  FALLAGE. *CRK 1760.*
Az 3 baskets of cakes Arg
  MEDELTON ABBAY. *L9 48a, 4.*
Gu 3 eel-butts Or
  — *RH, Ancestor ix 163. (?fish weels).*
Sa 3 ?baskets Arg
  LYTTYLBORNE, Sir J. *WB I 42b, 25.*
Sa 3 baskets of bread Arg
  [MILTON ABBEY]. *SM 78, 71.*
Sa 3 baskets of cakes Arg
  MILTON ABBEY. *L10 68, 11.*
Sa 3 baskets Arg each replenished with 3 loaves Or
  MILTON ABBEY. *?source. 1470. (in window of Ilchester Ch, Dorset).*

BEACON

Or 3 hand cressets Sa
  — *WB I 23b, 16. (qtd 4 by Geofrey ?Hyll).*
Sa 3 beacons flaming Or
  DAUNT, T. *CRK 1898.*
Sa 3 cressets Or
  — *RL 52. (?or capitals of columns). See also under TORCH.ds 1S BEAST (DEMI-LION)*

BEACON

Demi-lion
  MALORE, John, of Welton. *Vinc 88, 29. 1407-8. (sl on grant of land in Whelton, to Elena, his dau & heirs of Elena & Jn, s of Jn Swinerton, of Welton).*
  MALORRE, John. *PRO-sls E40 A7664. 1317-18. (couped).*
  MALORY, John, of Welton, Northants. *Bow XXVI 5.* Sigillum Jo Malory. *1407-8. (Legend written above drawing).*
Demi-lion facing to sin
  MUNFICHET, Wm, 'Ld of Kergill'. *Stevenson. 1287. (or Mushet or Montefixo, [Cargill, Perths]).*
Arg demi-lion Gu
  MALORY. *L1 451, 3. (a&l Gu). ('Denet' added in margin).*
  MALORY. *XL 280. (couped).*
  MALORY. *XL 501. (couped; a&l Az).*
  MALORY. *L2 329, 8. (a&l Gu).*
  MALORY. *DV 55b, 2187. (armed Az).*
  MALORY, B. *PLN 855. (couped; a&l Sa).*
  MALORYE. *CC 222, 4. (with demi-tail).*
Arg demi lion erased Gu
  — *ML I 153. ('Sylver a lyon contre rampaunt rasyd per my gowlys enarmyd of*

hymself).
Az demi-lion Arg
— *ML I 220.* ('a lyon cope, or a lion
isawnt').
PULHAM. *CRK 308.* (couped; a&l Gu, tail
turned outwards).
Gu demi-lion Arg
BENET, Betkyn. *WJ 234.* (couped).
BETKYNDENET. *L10 26, 14.* (a&l Az).
DENET. *XL 278.* (couped).
DENET, Betkin. *XL 364.* (couped).
MALORY. *L9 51a, 10.* (couped).
Barry of 4 in chf demi-lion
LOUCHES, Adam de. *PRO-sls.* 1373-4.
Per fess embattled Az & Gu masoned Or in chf
demi-lion isst Or
— *ML I 211.* ('a castell gowlys symentyd
gold in a feld asur wit a lyon issaunt ram-
paunt of the second').
Az flory Or demi-lion couped Arg
MORVILE. *XL 283.*
MORVILE, Bernard de. *XL 598.*
Az demi-lion couped Arg about its neck chain
Arg fastened to field in sin flank by peg (or
staple)
— *ML I 310.* ('asur a lyon issant countre-
gorgyd wit a cheyn fyxyd in the feld sylver').

BEAST (1 LION RAMPANT)

Lion rampant Untinc &c
Lion ramp
— *?source.* 13 cent. (qtg checky, font, Holt,
Denbigh; also elsewhere on font, alone & not
on shield).
— *AnstisAsp I 223, 90.* +SIG: MARG: VXORIS:
EDM: MORTIMER. (imp by Mortimer for Mgt
M 'que fuit uxor Edmund de Mortuomari').
— *Antiq Journ vi 449-50.* (on shield on
steelyard weights).
— *Antiq Journ xiii 307 & 308.* ([13 cent]
pendant found in Egypt near Memphis, ?for 1
Guy de Chabannes c1250 took part in 7th
crusade when Louis IX was captured at Man-
sourah & bore Gu lion Erm crowned Or; 2
Jean, Comte de Montfort l'Amaury, d in
Cyprus 1249, bore Gu lion qf).
— *Antiq Journ xvi 292.* (qtg 2&3 cross
flory; object found near Wyke Lane, Chiches-
ter).
— *Arch Cant ii 108.* (qtg 2&3 fret in qrs
II&III of Browne, all imp by Rogge on brass,
formerly in Ashford Ch, to Thos R (d1512) &
his w Eleanor B).
— *Arch Journ xviii 81.* 1574. (qtd 4 by
Gervays on brass to Ric G & w Jane

Trefusis, Constantine, near Helston, Cornw).
— *Birch 10015.* 1418. (imp on shield of
Jakelyne, w of Jn ?Gales).
— *Birch 10599.* 1300-12. (dimid by
Johanna, w of Jn de la Haye, of Lincs).
— *Birch 10809.* 1475. (qtd 2&3 by Thos
Hos, Esq).
— *Birch 11735.* 1368. (imp by Matildis de
Meriet).
— *Birch 11905.* 1405. (imp by Geo de la
More, of Nailsea, Som).
— *Birch 2545.* (on sl of Jn Sante, D.D.,
Abbot of Abingdon, Berks, 1469-1495, Papal
Commissary & Ambassador from Engld to
Court of Rome).
— *Birch 3636.* late 14 cent. (on sl of Priory
of Holy Trinity de Bosco, Merkyate, Beds).
— *Birch 3642.* 14 cent. (sl of St Mary's
College of Secular Priests, Mettingham, Suff).
— *Birch 3693.* 1427. (sl of Prior Wm de
Waketone, of Priory of St Paul, Newenham,
Beds).
— *Birch 3795.* 15 cent. (2nd sl of Nutley
Abbey, Bucks).
— *Birch 7050.* +S' IOHAN LE B...R.... 1367.
(name unclear, Jn le B..r..(?); sl used by Ric
ate Hamme, of Goudhurst, Kent).
— *Birch 7403.* 1392. (imp by Eliz, w of
Laurence Bercrols or Berkerolles).
— *Birch 8722.* S'. IO[HA]NNE.DE.C[OB]EHAM.
1364. (?for Johanna de Cobeham).
— *Birch 9345.* 1521. (qtd 5 by Jn Dudley,
D of Northd &c).
— *Birch 9519.* 1329. (imp by Elena, wid of
Wm de Esthalle, of Warws).
— *Birch 9889.* 1433. (imp by Jn Forthey,
of Denham, Bucks).
— *BirmCL-sls Areley Hall Deeds 35.* 1522.
(qtd II 1; III 1&4 on sl of Sir Thos West, Kt,
Ld of Manor of Martley).
— *Bow 10.* 1411-35. (qtg Warenne, all imp
by Beauchamp on sl of Johanna B 'nuper
dna Burgavenny').
— *Bridgwater 284.* 1373. (Robt ..., of
Bridgwater; imp by ...).
— *Brit Arch Assoc xxiv 384-5.* 1464. (qtg
2&3 10 roundels). (imp by Chambre, on
brass to Arthur C, & w Mgt, Middle Ch,
Salop).
— *Clairambault 6744.* 16 Jan 1438. (qtd
2&3 by Wm Nevill, Ld Fauconberg).
— *Dugd 17, 77.* 1304. (1 of 3 shields on sl
of Isabella de Bermyngham).
— *Dugd 17, 91.* 1325. (imp by Alice de
Clinton).
— *Durham-sls 250.* 1447. (used by Thos
Billingham).
— *Durham-sls 2504.* (Rob[ert] ...; used,
1349, by Alan of Ulkyston).

— *Durham-sls 479.* 1356. *(used by Thos of Burdon).*

— *Durham-sls 565.* 1373. *(used by Rog of Catterick).*

— *Durham-sls 884.* 1340. *(used by Robt of Elwick, but perhaps not true arms).*

— *Durham-sls 94.* 1321. *(used by Emma, w of Conan of Ask).*

— *Durham-sls 981.* *(used by Jn of Fery).*

— *Durham-sls 820a.* *(imp 3 bougets in pale; no legend; used in 1313 by Jn of Durham).*

— *GutchWdU.* *(qtd II&III 1&4 by 3 fleurs de lis Erm; window, Balliol Library; given by Tho Harrow or Harrope, Rector of Hesely, Oxfords, c1522).*

— *Inventory.* *(13 cent tile, gallery, W end of St Faith's Chapel).*

— *Lawrance 51.* ante 1350. *(effigy, Halton Holgate, Lincs; ?for Fennes).*

— *Mill Steph.* 1439. *(imp by Juyn on brass to Sir Jn J, Chief Justice, St Mary Redcliffe, Bristol, Gloucs).*

— *Mill Steph.* 1472. *(qtd 2 by Robt Ingleton on brass to him & 3 ws, Thornton, Bucks).*

— *Mill Steph.* 1440. *(stone shield on tomb of Thos Rolf, serjeant-at-law, Gosfield, Essex; ?for his son-in-law Jn Greene).*

— *Mill Steph.* 1439. *(imp fess engr betw 4 unicorns' heads couped 3, 1, border engr on brass to Sir Jn Juyn, Chief Justice, St Mary Redcliffe, Bristol, Gloucs).*

— *Mill Steph; Belcher II 46.* 1507. *(estoile in dex chf for diffce; qtd by Gay on brass to Christopher G & his ws Agnes & Johan, Elmsted, Kent).*

— *Mill Steph; Belcher II 46.* 1507. *(estoile in dex chf for diffce; imp by Gay on brass to Christopher G & his ws Agnes & Johan, Elmsted, Kent).*

— *PRO-sls.* S'IDE DE LA WARDE UX' HUGON' DE NEVILE. 1357-8. *(1 of 4 roundels; on sl of Ida de la Warde, Lady Nevile).*

— *PRO-sls.* 1393-4 & 1394-5. *(imp by Eliz de Julers, Ctess of Kent).*

— *PRO-sls.* 1360. *(?bear; qtd by Peres de Novyl, Esq).*

— *PRO-sls.* 1415-16. *(imp by Robt Hulle, Ld of ?Aijlij & w Isabel).*

— *PRO-sls.* 1392. *(imp by Eliz Stapilton, sometime w of Sir Brian S).*

— *PRO-sls.* 1 Dec 1336. *(imp to sin by Soyer Bouce).*

— *PRO-sls.* 1363-4. *(on roundel; sl of Anne Despenser, wid of Edw le D, Kt).*

— *Roman PO 5850.* 26 Apr 1423. *(qtd 2&3 by Robt Holme; sl).*

— *SHY 573.* *(...yngham, name unclear).*

— *Stevenson.* 1482. *(qtd by Sir Archibald Hamilton, of Innerwick, Kt).*

— *Stevenson.* 1461. *(qtd 2&3 by Celestin Macdonald of the Isles, Ld of Lochalsh &c).*

— *Stevenson.* 1482. *(qtd by Sir James Liddel, Kt).*

— *Stevenson.* 1490. *(qtd by Sir Alexr Guthrie of that ilk, Kt; & by Hen Guthrie, Bp of Dunkeld c1665-67).*

— *Stevenson.* 1519. *(qtd by Geo Leslie, 4th E of Rothes, [d1558]).*

— *Stevenson.* 1508. *(qtd by Sir Alex Boswell, of Glassmont & Balmuto [k at Flodden, 1513]).*

— *Stevenson.* late 13 cent. *(marshalled by Lady Agnes de Vesci; c'sl).*

— *Stevenson.* 1492. *(qtd 2 by Alex Stewart, 2nd E of Buchan, d1505).*

— *Stevenson.* 1511. *(qtd by David Somerville, of Plean).*

— *Stevenson.* 1445. *(qtd by Murdach Stewart, D of Albany, d1458, on sl of his wid Isabella, Ctess of Lennox).*

— *Stevenson 89.* *(charge uncertain; on 3rd sl of Jas Stewart, Archbp of St Andrews, d1504, 2nd s of Jas 3).*

— *Stowe-Bard 1s ix 1.* NICHOLAI. 1342-3. *(sl appended to various deeds from different individuals temp Edw 3).*

— *Stowe-Bard 1s ix 1.* NICHOLAI. temp Edw 3. *(sl on various deeds).*

— *WB I 15b, 9.* *(qtd 2&3 by Courteney as qtd by Mohun).*

— *WB I 38b, 1.* *(qtd 2&3 by Sir J Pylke).*

— *WLN 288.* *(qtg 3 leopards' faces reversed jesst de lis).*

— *XF 525.* *(imp by Ld Wm Martin).*

— *YMerch-sls.* 1359 & 1362. *(3rd of 3 shields on sl; used by Wm, s of Jn de Newton 1359 & by Ric de Kirkeby 1362).*

ABBERNON, Rogo de. *Birch 5594.* SIGILL' ROGO DE ABBNO. late 12 cent. *(equestr sl).*

ABERNETHY, Sir Geo, 4th of Saltoun. *Stevenson 224 & 226.* c1346-70. *(imp Eliz Airth, Lady of Plean).*

ACTON, Lawrence of. *PRO-sls Wards & Liveries 4016, HB-SND.* 1362.

ACTON, Maud of. *Dodsworth 45, 78, HB-SND.* 1348.

AIRTH, Elizabeth. *Stevenson.* 1511. *(sin coat; imp by fess; her 2nd husb was Thos Somerville).*

ALBANY, Robert, D of. *Brit Arch Assoc xlv 239.* *(qtg 2&3 fess checky & over all label; Regent of France 1406-19; 1st sl as Regent).*

[ALBENI, William de]. *Birch 5604.* c1180. *([E of Sussex & Arundel, 1172-1222]; obv of equestr sl).*

ALCMADE, Florencius. *PRO-sls E40 A5809.* ...masd?. 1415-16.

ALDEBURGH, Elizabeth. *Birch 6801.* 1368. *(dex of 2 shields; w of Wm de A).*

ALDEBURGH, Ivo de, Kt. *PRO-sls.* 1321.

ALDEBURGHE, William de, of Kirkby Overblow Manor, Yorks, Kt. *Birch 6799.* Sigillum: willelmi: de: aldeburgh: militis. 1363.

ALINGTON, John. *Roman PO 158.* 17 Apr 1410. *(qrs 1&4).*

ALTOBOSCO, Peter de. *CombeAsp II 156.* SIGILL PETRI DE ALTO BOSCO. *(imp by ...).*

ARONDELL, Richard de, of Brandon Manor, Warws, Kt. *Birch 6932.* ...gi....dar... 1415. *(& Wychampton Manor, Dorset; qrs 1&4).*

ARRONDELLE, the erle of. *CT 10.*

[ARUNDEL]. *Bow XVI 10.* c1373-86. *(imp by [Meriet] for Jn de Meryot, s of Jn de M, Kt, [of Meriott, Som]).*

ARUNDEL, Beatrice, Ctess of Arundel. *Harl MS 4840, 650: Coll T&G i 83-86.* SIGILLUM BEATRICIS COMITISSE ARUNDELIE ET SURREIE. 1432. *(qtg 2&3 checky; imp Portugal; illegitimate dau of John I, K of Portugal, she m 26 Nov 1405 Thos Fitzalan, E of Arundel & Surrey).*

ARUNDEL, Edmund de. *Birch 6927.* s': Edmudi ....aru..el. 1368. *(qrs 1&4; 2nd s of Edm Fitzalan, [10th] E of Arundel).*

ARUNDEL, John, Earl of. *AnstisAsp I 182, 11.* 1433-4. *(qrs 1&4).*

ARUNDEL, John de, of Ayno, [Aynho, Northants]. *Vinc 88, 33.* ARUNDELL. 1377. *(qrs 1&4; sl).*

ARUNDEL, John d'. *Birch 6931, HB-SND.* 1388. *(for [Fitzalan]; qtg 2&3 fret [Maltravers]).*

ARUNDEL, Ricardus, E of. *Birch 5931.* SIGILLUM RICARDI COMITIS DE ARONDEL. 1301. *(equestr sl).*

ARUNDEL, Rich E of. *Bow 11.* 1381-90. *(qrs 1&4).*

ARUNDEL, Richard, E of. *PRO-sls.* 1347-8.

ARUNDEL, Richard, E of. *BrookeAsp I 10, 2.* Sigillum Richardi comitis de Arundellia. *(qtg Warenne).*

ARUNDEL, Richard, E of. *PRO-sls.* 1358-9. *(qrs 1&4).*

ARUNDEL, Richard, E of. *PRO-sls E40 A6953.* SIGILL.......SURREYE. 1382-3. *(qrs 1&4; & E of Surrey).*

ARUNDEL, Richard d'. *Birch 6932, HB-SND.* 1415. *(for [Fitzalan]; qtg 2&3 fret [Maltravers]).*

ARUNDEL, Thomas, Archbp of Canterbury. *Birch 1239.* 1412. *(qtg checky [Warren], all in border engr; privy sl).*

ARUNDEL, Thomas, Archbp of Canterbury. *Vinc 88, 32.* +THOMAS.D.G.CANTVAR.EPISCOP. 1411. *(qtg 2&3 Maltravers, all in border engr & imp by Canterbury; sl).*

ARUNDEL, Thomas, Archbp of Canterbury, 1397-1414. *Birch 1238.* *(qtg checky [Warren], all in border engr).*

ARUNDEL, Thos, Archbp of Canterbury, 1397-1414. *Birch 1239.* 1412. *(qtg Warren, all in border engr on small or privy sl).*

ARUNDEL, William, E of, & Ld Mautravers. *AnstisAsp I 182, 12.* 1447-8. *(qrs 1&4).*

ARUNDELL, Sir Edward de, Kt. *Vinc 88, 40.* +SIG'EDWARDI.ARUNDELL.MILITIS. *(qrs 1&4; sl).*

ARUNDELL, Sir John. *PRO-sls.* 1377.

ARUNDELL, Ric, E of. *PRO-sls.* 1382-3. *(& E of Surrey; qrs 1&4).*

ARUNDELLE, John, Kt. *Birch 6931.* ....nis darondell. 1388. *(qrs 1&4; s&h of Sir Jn Arundelle).*

ARUNDELLE, William de, chivaler. *Birch 6939.* .....de arundel. 1397. *(s of Jn de A, chivaler, of Brandon Manor, Warws; qtg [Maltravers]).*

ASK, Conan of. *PRO-sls Ex KR 16/20, 73, HB-SND.* 1323.

ASTERLEY, Alice de. *Dugd 17, 77.* 1352.

ASTLEY, William de. *Bow LII 8.* Sigillum Willmi de Astley. 1500. *(qrs 1&4; s&h of Thos A).*

ATTEWODE, John. *Birch 7011.* SIGILL'IOHANNIS.ATTEWODE. 1416-17.

AUBREY, Thomas, of Walton, Surr. *Birch 7015.* S' PH....O..VN'. temp Edw 1. *(2nd of 3 shields).*

AUCHTERGAVIN, Robert of. *Stevenson 233.* 1296. *(not on shield).*

BACHEPUIS, John de. *Bk of Sls 78.* ante 1259. *(father of Nicholas & bro of Robt).*

BAKEPUZ, Johan de, of Allexton, Leics. *Birch 7075.* +SI[GIL]LVM IOH[A]NNI...Z. early Hen 3.

BAKER, Jennequin. *Clairambault 581.* 8 June 1446. *(qrs 1&4).*

BALLIOL, Edw. *Brit Arch Assoc xlv 237.* 1332-5.

BALLIOL, John. *Brit Arch Assoc xlv 110.* 1292-6. *(1st sl).*

BATHE, John, of Wallington, Surr. *Birch 7211.* ...IV..H..CI... 1390. *(or Matilda his w).*

BEAUCHAMP, Johanna de, Lady of Abergavenny. *Dugd 17, 51.* 1416. *(qrs 1&4 of sin imp).*

BEAUMONT, Isabel de. *BrookeAsp I 37, 2.* S' ISABELLE: DE: BEAVMONT: DNE: DE: VESCY. 1333. *(imp by Vescy).*

BEAUMONT, William. *Yorks Deeds III 32.* 1319. *(s of Wm de B).*

BEAUMONT, William de. *PRO-sls.* 13 cent.

BEAUUER, William de. *Yorks Deeds V 117.* early 14 cent. *(imp by 3 escallops in pale).*

BECKER, [Lambert]. *PRO-sls.* 1479-80.

BENGES, John de. *Bow XVIII 12. (s of Adam de B, of Drenchestun, [Drinkstone, Suff]).*

BENINGEWRD, Walter. *Birch 7359.* +SIGILL'WAL[TE]RI D'BENINGEWRD. late 12 cent. *(s of Matthew de B, of Lincs).*

BENINGWORTH, Walter de. *PRO-sls.* 13 cent.

BEREWYK, Hugh de, of Beaconsfield, Bucks, Kt. *Birch 7379.* SIGILL.HVGONIS.DE. BEREWYK. 1375.

BERKELEY, Thomas, of Yorks, Kt. *Birch 7460.* 1516. *(shield betw initial letters [..] & B).*

BIGOD, Roger [7th] E of Norfolk, Marshall of England. *Birch 7471.* SIGILLVM.ROGERI.- BIGOD. 1301.

BLUNDEVILLE, Ranulph de, E of Chester. *Brit Arch Assoc v 249.* c1220. *(on 1 of his sls; Planche suggests this may have been his family coat, as distinct from 3 garbs of earldom of Chester).*

BLUNDEVILLE, Ranulph, 7th E of Chester. *Birch 7520.* +SI......ANVLFI COMITI......IE. 1180-1232.

BOHUN, Henry de, E of Hereford. *Heneage 2145.* temp John. *(small privy sl; impression on rev of greater sl, not on shield).*

BOKESELL, Alan de. *?source.* 1317. *(sl at Penshurst).*

BOLBEC. *Durham-sls 1536.* 1284. *(sl of Philippe of Lancaster, dau & coh of Hugh Bolbec; ?lion Erm).*

BONDE, Simon, Citizen of London. *Birch 7585.* ...onis..bonde. 1362.

BOTREAUX, Elizabeth. *PRO-sls.* 1417-18. *(late w of Sir William B).*

BOYS, Walter, of Aldham, Yaldham Manor, Kent, Kt. *Birch 7711.* S WALTERI BOIS DE MVSSEDEN. 1275.

BRABANT, Duke de. *SP A 23. (in all 4 qrs).*

[BRABANT, John, D of]. *WestmAbb. (imp lion on small shield in white marble in 4foil panel under empty niche on S side of tomb of Philippa of Hainault, w of Edw 3, d1369).*

BRABANT & Louvain, Ancient Duchy of. *Birch 2043.* 1366. *(on sl of Thos Percy, Bp of Norwich 1356-69).*

BRAIOSE. *Bk of Sls 397.* 1328.

BRAKINBERI, Cecilia de. *Durham-sls 364.* 1392.

[BRAMPTON]. *Mill Steph.* 1462. *(brass to Sir Sampson Meverell, Tideswell, Derbys).*

BRANC, Robert le, of Magna Shepey. *Bow XLIX 9. (grant of land in Shepey. Test dom Petro le Pore de Syblesdon, dom Adam de Wellesburrowe, Hen de Templo, Rob Overton).*

BRET, Ralph le, of Crockerne Stoke, ?Dorset. *Helyar 303.* 1349. *(sl).*

BREWOUSE, John de, Ld of Buckingham, Kt. *Birch 7793.* SIG.RO.......V.... 1335. *(very indistinct).*

BRIDGE, John at the. *PRO-sls.* S'IOHIS ? OUSE ?. 1341.

BRIENE, Alice. *PRO-sls.* 1396-7. *(on shield slung from bush; w of Guy de B).*

[BROCAS]. *Mill Steph.* 1378. *(imp by Foxley on dress of effigy of Maude, dau of Sir Jn Brocas, of Beaurepair & 1st w of Sir Jn Foxley; on brass to Sir Jn F, Bray, Berks).*

BROCAS, John. *PRO-sls E40 A149.* SIGILLVM: IOH....BROKAS. 1364-5. *(?gard).*

BROCAS, John de. *PRO-sls.* 9 May 1351. *(on shield betw wheel & letters AHEN).*

BROCAS, John, of Basing, Hants, Kt. *Vinc 88, 41.* +SIGILL'IOHANNIS.DE.BROKAS. *(sl).*

BROKUNBERWG, Edmund de. *Heneage 1412.* SIGILL.EDMUNDI BROKUNBERWG. 1356. *(or Brokenborough, Wilts; on grant of land in West Kyngton in Wroxhale).*

BROWN, David, of Cumbrycolstoun. *Stevenson.* 1374. *(& others, down to 1584).*

BRUCE, Peter, 1st of Skelton. *Stevenson.* c1200. *(& others).*

BRUCE, Robt. *Brit Arch Assoc xlv 236.* 1306-29. *(on King's surcoat on 2nd c'sl).*

BRUMPTON, John de. *Dugd 17, 11.* Sigillum Iohis de Brumptone. 1343-4. *(supported by griffin segr).*

BRUNNE, John, of Wyvelingham, [Willingham, Cambs]. *Birch 7886.* SIGILLUM: IOHANNIS: BRUNNE:. 1307.

BRUNTOFT, Philip of. *Durham-sls 431-2.*

BRUS. *Bk of Sls 134.* 1276. *(imp by Ros).*

BRUS, Peter. *Guisboro' Ch II 138 in Surtees Soc 89, HB-SND.*

BRUS, Peter of. *Durham-sls 442.*

BRUS, Peter, d1272. *Birch 15643, HB-SND.* 1256. *(Guisboro' Ch II 162 & 281; Dodsworth 95, 58).*

BRUYN, Robert. *PRO-sls.* 30 May 1364.

BURGO, Eliz de, Lady of Clare. *PRO-sls E40 A14054.* 1323. *(on 1 of 2 3foils).*

BURNEL, Alicia. *Bk of Sls 358.* 1316. *(wid of Edw B).*

BURNELL, Hugh de, Kt. *Bow XXXV 22.* 1410. *(qtg [Botetourt]; crown & border of Burnell not shown in drawing).*

BURNELL, Hugh de, Kt, Ld of Holgate & Weolygh. *BirmCL-sls Hagley Hall 351332.* 1417. *(qrs 1&4).*

BURNELL, Hugh, Kt, Ld of Wyleye. *PRO-sls.* 1416-17.

BURNELL, Hugo. *Dugd 17, 36.* 1405. *(qrs 1&4).*

BURTON, Wathyn. *PRO-sls.* 24 June 1401. *(on shield betw 2 5foils).*

BUSCY, William de, kt. *Yorks Deeds IX 130.*

... DE BVSCI. 1315-16.

CALFOURE, Hugh de, of Bathequelle, [Bakewell], Derbys. *Birch 8015.* S'HUGONIS DE CAL..OVER. temp Edw 1.

CAMERA, Johannes de. *Arch Journ (Norwich 1847) 50.* S'IOHANNIS DE CAMERA. 15 cent. *(silver sl matrix).*

CAREW, Robert of. *Newcastle Liber Cartarum 60, HB-SND.* 1177-9.

CHALMERS, Robert. *Stevenson.* c1296. *(not on shield).*

CHAMBRE, Ambrose del. *BM Harl MS 1985, 288, HB-SND.*

CHARLETOUN, Eliz. *PRO-sls.* 1421-2. *(w of Sir Edw C).*

CHARLTON, Edward, Ld Powis. *Dugd 17, 35.* 1415.

CHARLTON, of Powys. *Mill Steph.* c1470. *(brass to Joice C, Lady Tiptoft, d1446, Enfield, Middx).*

CHARLTON, of Powys. *Birch 13948.* 1451. *(qtd 2&3 by Jn Tiptoft, E of Worcester, Ld Tiptoft & of Powys).*

CHERLATON, John de. *PRO-sls.* 1315-16. *(shield betw 2 wyverns).*

[CHERLETON]. *PRO-sls.*

[CHERLETON]. *PRO-sls.* c1525. *(qtd III 4 by Thos Manners, E of Rutl).*

CHERLETON, Humphrey de, Archdeacon of Richmond. *PRO-sls.* 1376.

CHERLETONE, John de, Ld of Powys, Montgomers. *Birch 8527.* SIGILLU: IOH'IS: DE: CHERLETONE: DNI: POWISIE. 1368.

[CHERLTON]. *Blair D I 80, 211.* *(imp (12th of 16) by Hen Neville, 5th E of Westmorland on oak tomb, Staindrop Ch).*

CHESTER, Ralph, Earl of. *Durham-sls 584.* 1181-1232. *(?wolf passt).*

CHESTER, Ranulph, E of. *Birch 8530.* +SIG..... 1180-1231. *(?wolf).*

CHETEWODE, John, Kt. *Bow XXV 2.* +Si Johis Chetewode militis. 1386. *(grant of mill in Stannern, Northants).*

CHETEWODE, John, of Warkworth, Northants, Kt. *Birch 8536.* +S'IO'HIS: CHETEWODE: MILITIS. 14 cent.

CHETEWOOD, Thomas. *Roman PO 3090.* 4 Aug 1429. *(qrs 1&4).*

CHEVERSTUN, John de. *Birch 8543.* S': IOH'IS: DE: CHEVERSTVN. 1385. *(used by Jn Hende, Cit & Clothier of London or his w Katharine, & by Thos de St Edmund or his w Isabella).*

CHICHE, Ralph, of Kent, Gent. *Birch 8566.* 1488. *(in oval on sl, in allusion to arms of Chiche, viz 3 lions).*

CHISHULLE, William de, of Grant Lawefare, [?Great Laver, Essex]. *Birch 8584.* S'WILL..... ..HVLLE. temp Edw 1.

CLEDFORD, Richard de. *Middlewich 284.* 1366. *('his seale a lyon rampant verie fayre').*

CLERVAUS, John de. *PRO-sls E40 A5158.* S'IOHIS D'CLERVAVS....CLERVAVS. 1272. *(not on shield).*

CLERVAUX, John. *(sl on Langstaffe pedigree).* HB-SND. 1349.

CLIFFORD, Robert de. *PRO-sls.* S'ROBERTI DE CLIFFORD. 1380-1. *(imp bend; used by Ric Bengeworth, chaplain).*

CLINTON, Alice de. *BrookeAsp I 2, 3.* SI.- ALICIE DE CLINTONE. 1325-6. *(imp by 3 piles Az canton Erm).*

CLYVEDON, Edmund de. *PRO-sls.* 1375-6.

COOVIN, Bartholomew de. *?source.* c1200. *(sl at Penshurst).*

CORBET, Nicholas. *LaingChart 9, Liber de Melros I xxv, HB-SND.*

?CORBETT. *Birch 12282.* 1328. *(imp in arms of Emma, w of Sir Jn de Oddyngseles, alias Odingseles, of Long Iginton, Herts).*

CRAWFORD, Reginald. *Stevenson.* 1292.

CRESSY, Hugh de. *PRO-sls.* 1354-5. *(on shield betw letters ABC).*

CREWE, Thos de [d1418] & w Julian [Sesin] 1411. *Mill Steph.* *(brass, Wixford, Warws).*

CRICHTON. *Stevenson.* 1454. *(qtd by Janet Dunbar, dau of 4th E of Moray, & w of James 2nd Ld Crichton).*

CRICHTON, Edw, of Kirtilhous. *Stevenson.* 1436. *(& others).*

CRICHTON, Robert, 2nd Ld C of Sanquhar. *Stevenson.* 1518. *(qtg 2&3 2 water bougets & in chf, over all roundel in fess pt; d1513; 3rd sl).*

CROYDON, Joan. *PRO-sls.* 1403-4. *(wid of Nicholas C).*

D'ACHERES, Rigaud, Bp of Winchester, 1320-23. *Durham-sls 3213-14 & 3685.* *(on sl with another coat; & on his brother's sl).*

DANBY, Thomas. *PRO-sls E40 A6219.* 1404-5. *(imp cresc betw 2 mullets of 6 pts, 1 in chf, 1 in base).*

DAREL, Marmaduke. *?source.* 1322. *(sl).*

DARELL, John. *Yorks Deeds X 50.* SIGILLVM IOHANNIS DAREL. 1343. *(s of Sir Wm D, of ?Ceszai).*

DARUNDELL, Sibilla. *Birch 6938.* 1368. *(qtg [Warrenne] & imp [Montagu]; within arabesque design containing 4 roundels in cross).*

DAVY, John, of Multon, Suff. *Birch 9216.* 1499.

DERBY, John de. *PRO-sls.* 13 cent.

DESPENSER, Anne. *PRO-sls AS 21.* S ANNE LE DESPENSER. 1363-4. *(on roundel; wid of Edw le D, Kt).*

DEVEREUS, John, Ld of East Harptree. *PRO-*

sls. 1371-2.

DEVON, Amicia, Ctess of. *?source. (founder in 1278 of Cistercian Abbey of SS Mary & Benedict, Buckland, Devon; sl of Cistercian Abbey, Buckland).*

DEYSTERE, Richard. *BirmCL-sls Hagley Hall 351270.* 1382. *(s of William D, of Halesowen).*

DOMVILLE, John. *Baker-sls. ... MVIL....* 1334. *(grant of land in Brunstath & Oxton, Ches).*

DOMVILLE, John. *Baker-sls. ... MVIL.....* 1334. *(grant to R del Cros of manors of Brunstath [Brunstock, Cumb] & Oxton [Ches]).*

?DONET, Matilda. *Birch 6625.* S'MATILDIS.-DONET. 1313. *(1st of 2 shields; or Ronet; w of Jn Winchester).*

DONEWYCO, John. *Birch 9372.* 1344. *(s of Rog de D, Suff).*

DOUGLAS, Gavin, Bp of Dunkeld. *Stevenson 143.* 1520-2. *(3rd son of Arch, E of Angus; qtg 2) lion bend, 3) 5 piles in point, 4) fess checky on bend 3 buckles; over all on escutch heart & on chf 3 stars).*

DOUGLAS, Wm, 2nd E of Angus (1402-37). *Stevenson.* 1427.

DOUGLAS, Wm, 2nd Earl of Angus (1402-1437). *Stevenson. (2nd sl; qtg 2&3 heart & on chf 3 mullets & in base of shield cross c'gobony & over all on bend 3 mullets).*

DOUNWILE, John. *Birch 9313.* S'IOHIS: DOUNWILE. 1377.

DRUEL, John, Sheriff of Northants. *Birch 9333.* [C]EST LE SEAL IOH FIZ IOH DERVEL. 1300. *(dex of 2 shields; sin qtly 1&2 cresc, 2&3 unclear charge).*

DUNBAR, Patrick, E of. *Bain II pl V7, HB-SND. (& E of March).*

DUNBAR, Patrick, 5th E of Dunbar (1182-1232). *Stevenson.* c1200. *(& others).*

DUNDAS, James of that ilk. *Stevenson.* 1449. *(& others).*

DUNHEUED, John de. *Dugd 17, 77.* 1286. *(?border).*

EDLINGHAM, Walter of. *Greenwich 117, HB-SND. (on 1st of 2 shields, 2nd being bend wavy & canton).*

EDLINGHAM, Walter of. *Durham-sls 841. (beside an undeciphered coat).*

ESSEX, John of. *Heneage 2573.* S'IOHIS FILII IOHIS DE ESSEX. 1339. *(s of Jn of E, sometime cit & apothecary of London).*

ESTHEYE, Andrew de, Kt. *PRO-sls BS 27.* late 13 cent.

[?ETHEL]. *Stowe-Bard 1s viii 12 MS ii 59.* 1329-30. *(imp cross formy; 2nd sl on deed poll executed by Richd de la Lee, Rector of Bradewelle, & Gilbert de Ethill, rector of Westbrigge).*

EUGEYS, John d'. *PRO-sls.* 14 cent.

EURE, Hugh of. *Dodsworth 49, 43b, HB-SND.* 1280.

EVERINGHAM, Sir Adam de. *Yorks Arch Journ xiii 79.* 1388. *(sl; crest: stag's head).*

FAUCOMBERGE, John de. *PRO-sls.* 1347.

FAUCONBERG, Sir John de. *Yorks Deeds VIII 17.* 1341.

FAUCONBERG, Thos. *Yorks Deeds VIII 85 & 107.* 1366. *(s of Sir Walter de F).*

FAUCONBERG, Sir Water de. *Yorks Deeds VIII 70.* 1361.

FAUCONBERGH, Isabella de. *BrookeAsp I.* Sigillum Isabelle de Fauconberge. 1383-4. *(centre of 5 shields).*

FELBRIDGE, George. *Bow 11.* 1381-98.

[FELBRIGG]. *Farrer II 444. (on font, Sustead Ch, Norf).*

FELBRIGG, Robert de. *Bow XXIV 3d.* Sigillum Roberti Felbrigg. 1396.

FELBRIGG, Simon de, Kt. *(of Lincs, Warws &c).* SIG': SIMONIS: DE: FELBRIGG'. *Birch 9653.* 1406.

FELBRIGG, Simon de, Kt. *Bow XXIV 1c.* Sig: Simonis de felbrigg. 1396.

FELBRIGGE. *Bow XXIX 5.* SIGILLVM.-MARGERIE.FELBRIGGE. 1439-40. *(imp by cross checky fimbr; sl of Margery, w of Thos Sampson, of Brettenham, Norf).*

FELBRIGGE, George de, of Mildenhall, Suff. *Birch 9651.* S': GEORGII: :FELBRIGGE. 1375.

FELBRIGGE, Simon de, of Felbrigg, Norf, Kt. *Bow XXVII 1.* Sig: Simonis de Felbrigge. 1415.

FELBRYGGE, Sir Simon, Kt. *Farrer II 426. (d1400; brass, Felbrigg Ch, Norf).*

FIFE. *Stevenson 37.* 1406. *(qtg Stewart on obv of Great Sl of Robt, D of Albany, Governor of Scotld).*

FIFE. *Stevenson 37.* 1420. *(qtg Stewart on obv of Great Sl of Murdoc, 2nd D of Albany, Governor of Scotld).*

FIFE, Duncan, 10th E of Fife. *Stevenson.* ?1360.

FIFE, Mary, Ctess of. *PRO-sls.* 1336-7. *(on shield held in right hand of lady).*

FITZ-alan, Alianora. *Birch 9704.* SIGILLUM: ALIANORE: DE: ARUNDELL:. 1404. *(imp by fret; dau of Jn Maltravers & wid of Jn F, of Arundel, Kt).*

FITZ-alan, family of. *Birch 9703.* 16 cent. *(qtg 2&3 fret (Maltravers)).*

FITZ-alan, Jn, 16th E of Arundel, Captain of Rouen, &c. *Birch 9708.* ...LL': ....UNDELL: E: DNI: ..... 1431. *(qtg 2&3 fretty (Maltravers); lion enraged).*

FITZ-alan, Richard, 10th E of Arundel & Surrey. *Birch 9716.* SIG...RICARDI....ITIS: ARUND..LE: ET: SURREYE. 1375. *(qtg 2&3 checky).*

FITZ-alan, Richard, 9th E of Arundel. *Birch*

9715. SIGILLUM: RICARDI: COMITIS: DE: ARUN-DEL:. 1359. *(qtg 2&3 checky).*
FITZ-alan, Richard, 9th E of Arundel. *Birch 9714.* S' RICARDI: COMITIS: DE: ARVNDEL. 1330-75. *(sl includes 3 circular checky or fretty shields).*
FITZ-alan, Thomas, 11th E of Arundel & Surrey. *Birch 9717.* 1412. *(qtg 2&3 checky; lion enraged).*
FITZALAN. *Birch 7540.* 1393. *(qtg Warrenne & imp by Bohun on sl of Johanna de B, Ctess of Heref, Essex & Northampton, dau of Ric F, E of Arundel & wid of Humphrey de B, E of Heref).*
FITZALAN. *Mill Steph.* 1412. *(qtg 2&3 fretty [Maltravers]; imp by Echingham (this half lost) on brass to Sir Wm E (1412), his w Joan, dau & coh of Jn, Ld M (1404) & their s Sir Thos E (1444)).*
[FITZALAN]. *Birch 7239-41.* Sigillu: iohann[e]: de: bello: campo: dne: de: bergevenny. 1424. *(qtg 2&3 Warrenne, imp by Beauchamp for Johanna B, Lady of Bergavenny, dau of Rich Fitzalan, sis & coh of Thos Fitzalan, E of Arundel).*
[FITZALAN]. *Birch 3463.* late 14 cent. *(sl of Lewes Priory).*
[FITZALAN]. *Proc Soc Antiq X 2S 98.* 1367. *(qtg [Warren] on sl of Thos Percy, Bp of Norwich 1355-69, on deed).*
FITZALAN, Edmund, E of Arundel. *PRO-sls.* 1322-3.
FITZALAN, John, E of Arundel, Marshal of Engld. *PRO-sls.* 1378.
FITZALAN, Richard, E of Arundel. *Barons Letter.*
FITZALAN, Richard, E of Arundel. *PRO-sls.* 1358-9.
FITZALAN, Thomas, Archbp of Canterbury. *PRO-sls AS 2.* 1403-4. *(qtg checky, all in border).*
FITZALAN, Thomas, of Arundel, Archbp of York, 1388-96. *Birch 2325.* 1392. *(qtg 2&3 checky, all in border engr).*
FITZSIMON, Hugh. *PRO-sls.* 13 cent. *(on shield betw cresc & star).*
[FLANDERS]. *WestmAbb.* *(qrs 1&4 of coat imp by qtly France & Engld on tomb of Simon Langham, d1376).*
FLAUNDERS, Louis. *PRO-sls.* 15 May 1351. *(used by Isabel of Woodstock, eldest dau of Edw 3).*
FLEMING, Gilbert. *(chaplin; on shield betw cresc & 2 stars).* 1323. *PRO-sls Ex KR 16/26, 23, HB-SND.*
?FOLIOT, Richard. *Birch 9852.* S'.ARMORU.-RICAR[D]I.FOLIOT (?). 15 cent.
FOX, William, of Colde Ascheby, Northants. *Birch 9919.* +SIGL....DE..TAYER...T..

1391. *(imp cresc betw 2 estoiles in pale).*
FRANCIS, Wm. *Stevenson.* c1296.
FRASER, Wm, of Philorth. *Stevenson.* 1504.
FRAUNCEYS, Nicholaus le, of Wridelyngton, or Worlington, Suff. *Birch 9942.* S' NICH'I.-LE.FRAVNCES. 1328.
GALLOWAY. *Stevenson.* 1446. *(qtd by Euphemia Graham, Ctess of Douglas).*
[GALLOWAY]. *Birch 5261.* *(sl of Balliol College, Oxf).*
[GALLOWAY]. *Stevenson 20.* *(on sin side of obv of great sl of Jn Balliol, awarded crown of Scotld 17 Nov 1292).*
[GALLOWAY]. *Stevenson 31.* *(shield on dex side of obv of great sl of Edw Balliol, K of Scotld, 1332).*
GATEGANG, John. *Bowes 43, HB-SND.* 1323. *(s of Gilbert G).*
GERARD, Thomas. *Clairambault 4037.* 8 Oct 1439.
GLADSTONE, John. *Stevenson.* 1472. *(?of Roxburghs).*
GODALE, William, of St Albans. *PRO-sls E40 A1127.* 1369-70.
GOLAFRE, Isabella. *BirmCL-sls 492716.* 1379-80. *(imp by cross engr; wid of Jn G, Kt).*
[GOLDWELL]. *Farrer III 37.* *(stone shield outside St Andrews Ch, Norwich).*
[GOLDWELL]. *Farrer III 4.* *(qtg 2&3 6 columbines, on chf 3 golden wells; on boss, Norwich Cathedral).*
[GOLDWELL]. *Farrer III 3.* *(mont, Norwich Cath).*
GOSEHALE, Margaret de, of Kent. *Birch 10190.* S' MARGARETE [D]E GOSEHALE. 1333. *(dex of 2 shields).*
GOURLAY, Wm, of Bagally, Angus. *Stevenson.* 1296.
GRAMARY, Sir William. *Yorks Deeds VI 62.* 1346.
GRAY. *CC 38.* *(?vulned on shldr Gu).*
GRAY, Janet, lady of West Wemyss. *Stevenson.* 1529.
GREY, Henry, 2nd E of Tankerville. *Birch 10255.* S' HENRY GRAY .......TANCARUILLE.ET.-POWYS.WALL....GRANT CHAB'LAIN...
...D'NORMAD. 1421-9. *(in qrs 1&4 for Mowbray; qtg 2&3 Cherleton of Powys; over all escutch of Tankerville).*
GUISNES, Bailieship of the Town. *PRO-sls E40 A6320.* c1490. *(qrs 1&4).*
GUTHRIE, John. *Stevenson.* 1509. *(qtg 2&3 garb; ?ermine spot in fess pt).*
HAGGELEYE, Robert. *BirmCL-sls Hagley Hall 351193.* 1349. *(blazon uncertain; s of Edm, Ld of H).*
[HAINAULT]. *WestmAbb.* *(qtg lion, all imp by qtly France & Engld on tomb of Philippa*

of Hainault in 4foil panel under niche containing headless female figure; Confessor's Chapel).

HALUGHTON, Thomas de, Kt. *Bow XXXI 8.* 1362-3. *(of Halloughton, Warws).*

HANDLO, John de, of Borstall, Kent, Kt. *Bow XVIII 7.*

HANSAKER, John. *Roman PO 5671.* 16 March 1442.

HARCOURT, Simon de. *?source.* +SIGILLVM.-SIMONIS.DE.HARVCVRT. *(not on shield; grant of land in Brocheleia praeter Hennecroft et Clippescroft &c).*

HARTLINGTON, William. *Yorks Deeds VI 84 & 122.* 1349. *(s of Hen de H).*

HARTLYNGTON, Henry. *Birch 10513.* S': HENRICI: HARTLYNGTON. 14 cent.

HASTANG, Sir Robert de. *Yorks Deeds VI 34-5.* 1337. *(imp fess betw 3 lozs [Cleasby]).*

HASTANG, Thomas, of Warws. *Birch 10527.* S' THOME.HASTANG. 1329.

HASWELL, Wm, of Roxburghs. *Stevenson.* 1296. *(rose shaped shield).*

HATTON, Elena de. *Birch 10557.* SIGILLUM ELENE DE HATTON. 1382. *(imp by uncertain coat; sl used by Mgt, dau of Wm fil Robt de Horneby, Lincs).*

HAUDLO, John de, Kt. *PRO-sls.* 1334.

HAUDLO, John de, of Essex, Kt. *Birch 10565.* [S] IOHANNIS DE HAWDLO. 1336.

HENHALE, Edmund de. *PRO-sls.* 1340-1.

HERTFORD, William. *PRO-sls.* 1376-7. *(s of Thos de H).*

[HETON], Sir Henry, of Heton]. *Blair D II 192, 402.* *(qtd 2&3 by Middleton, of Silksworth at end of table tomb, Bishopwearmouth Ch).*

HETSCHETE, Agneta. *Birch 10670.* 1333. *(w of Thos de H of Heyshott, Suss, Clerk).*

HEYWARD, John. *Bridgwater 295, 364.* 1375. *(s of Jn H, of Bridgwater).*

HIDE, Thomas de la. *Dugd 17, 44.* 1325.

HILTON, Adam. *Clairambault 4680.* 9 Apr 1440.

HILTON, Hochequin. *Roman PO 5836.* 5 Feb 1369. *(sl).*

HILTON, Maykin. *Clairambault 4682.* 11 Sep 1440.

HINETONE, John de. *PRO-sls.* 1328-9.

HOLAND, Maud de. *PRO-sls.* 1335-6.

HOLAND, Robert de, Kt. *PRO-sls.* 1309.

HOLANDSWAYN, Robert de. *Yorks Deeds IX 105.* 1393. *(s of Thomas H).*

[HOLLAND]. *WestmAbb.* *(qrs 2&3 of coat imp by qtly France & Engld on tomb of Simon Langham, d1376).*

[HOLLAND]. *WestmAbb.* *(qtd by [Flanders] for [Hainault], all imp ditto for [Jn, D of Brabant] on small shield of white marble in 4foil panel under empty niche on S end of tomb of Philippa of Hainault, w of Edw 3, d1369; Confessor's Chapel).*

[HOLLAND]. *WestmAbb.* *(qtd by [Flanders] for [E of Hainault] on small shield of white marble in 4foil panel under empty niche on E end of tomb of Philippa of Hainault, w of Edw 3; Confessor's Chapel).*

HOLME, Roger. *Birch 2002.* S': ROGERI: HOLME. 1369-89. *(Preb of Kentish Town, Chancellor of St Paul's).*

HOME, Sir Alex, of that ilk, d c1460. *Stevenson.* 1437.

HOTUN, Richd of. *Durham-sls 1390.* 1353. *(imp by fess; used by Wm of Hilton).*

HOUEL. *Lawrance 25.* c1300-20. *(?wolf; effigy, Wrexham, Denb).*

HOWARD, Sir John. *AnstisAsp I 33.* 1308-9.

HOWARD, Thomas, E of Norf. *PRO-sls.* THOME COMITIS SURREY. 1524.

HUBAND, John, Ld Ipsley. *Dugd 17, 2.* 1345-6. *(?badge).*

?HUME, Patrick. *Stevenson.* 1513.

HUTTON, Robert. *Stevenson.*

HYDE, Alan, Kt, of Beds. *Bk of Sls 329.* ante 1350.

INCHMARTIN. *Stevenson.* 1441. *(borne by Andrew Ogilvie, of Inchmartin, & his w Marjorie).*

INCHMARTIN, Sir Henry, Ld of that ilk. *Stevenson.* post 1304.

INSULA, Baldwin de, E of Devon. *PRO-sls AS 67.* S BAL[D]EWINI DE I[NS]ULAE. 1261-2.

JACHLE, John. *Birch 10976.* S IOHANNIS IACHLE(?). 1360. *(sl used by Gilbert de Hagham, of Lincs).*

[JULIERS]. *(imp by Guelders, all imp by Scotld; 1st sl of Marie of G, w of Jas 2 & dau of D of Guelders, marr 1449, d1462). Panmure, Stevenson.* 1459.

JULIERS, William, Marquess of. *PRO-sls E40 A6957.* +WILLELMUS DEI GRA. 1353-4.

KAMVILE, Idonia de. *BerksCRO-sls, Isbury Charity Deeds Lambourn.* SECRETUM YDONIE D'KAMVILE. c1225. *(sl rev; s of Wm Longespee).*

KELLAWE FAMILY. *Durham-sls 1467, 1469, 1470, 1472, 1477 & 1479.* c1284-1370. *(not all of these are heraldic).*

KENDAL, Peter de. *Sizergh.* 1281. *(sl).*

KEVELIOC. *Brit Arch Assoc vii 433.* S'HAWISIE DNE DE KEVEOLOC'. *(dex shield on sl of Hawisia, dau of Owain de K, Princess of Powys, temp Edw 1 & 2, de jure proprietress of Kevelioc by inheritance from her father Owain).*

KEVEOLOC, Hawisia, Domina de. *Birch 6670.* S HAWISIE DNE DE KEVEOLOC. early 14 cent. *(1st of 2; Cyfeiliog, ?Merionethsh; Birch wrote Hawisia was dau of Owen de la Pole & w of Sir Jn Charlton of Powys; marginal note corrects this: 'dau of John le Strange & w of Gruffyd ap Gwenwynwyn, Ld of Powys (Gruffyd de la Pole) who d1289').*

KILKENNY, William. *BM Eg Ch 565, HB-SND.* 1340. *(?lion Erm; imp 5 lozs in fess each ch with roundels; s of Wm K).*

KINGSTON, Sir John. *Stevenson.* 1321.

KINROSS, Sir John, Kt. *Stevenson.* c1310.

KIRKEBY, John de, of Wygenthorp. *Yorks Deeds X 116.* IOHIS DE KERKEBY. 1355.

KNIGHTCOLE, Walter de, of Leics. *Bow Ll 5.* 1343-4. *(grant of rights in manor of Church Waver).*

KYNGESTON, Matilda de. *Vinc 88, 6, 11.* 1329-30. *(on 1st of 3 shields; w of Thos de K, s of Jn de K; sl on Power of Attorney to give seisin of manor of Foxcote).*

KYNGESTON, Thomas. *Roman PO 6122.* 5 Sept 1433.

LACI, Henry de. *Birch 11193.* SIGILLUM HENRICI DE ...ACI. 14 cent.

LACY, Alice. *?source.* 1324. *(sl; w of E... Lestrange).*

LACY, Hen de, E of Lincoln, Constable of Chester. *Bk of Sls 406.* 1285.

LACY, Henry de, E of Lincoln. *Bow XLVIII 14.* ...LINCOLN.... *(on shield, surcoat, trappings; Constable of Chester, Ld of Roos & Roveynok; equestr sl on grant of land in Lwenni).*

LACY, Henry de, E of Lincoln. *PRO-sls.* 13 cent. *(& Constable of Chester).*

LACY, Henry de, E of Lincoln. *Arch Journ (Lincs 1848) 274.* S' HENRICI DE LACI COMITIS LINCOLNIE ET COSTABULAR' CESTR'. 1272-1331.

LACY, Henry de, E of Lincoln. *PRO-sls.* 1297.

LACY, Henry de, E of Lincoln. *PRO-sls.* 1303-4.

LACY, Henry de, E of Lincoln. *PRO-sls.* 13 cent.

LACY, Henry de, E of Lincoln. *Dugd 17, 71.* 1293.

LACY, Hy de, E of Lincoln. *Bk of Sls 69.* 1292.

LANCASTER, Alice. *PRO-sls.* 1322-3. *(wid of Thos, E of Lancaster & dau of Hen, E of Lincoln).*

LANGMAN, Robert. *PlymouthCL-sls MTD 1/56.* 1474. *(or Robt Hilling).*

LANGTON, John de. *Stevenson.* 1292. *(Chancellor of Scotld).*

LANGTON, Thos of. *Durham-sls 1550.* 1435.

LARGE, Christina le. *Bridgwater 165, 80.* 1352. *(sl; imp by 3 leaves; wid of Wm, s of*

Wm le L, of Bridgwater).

LASCI, Henry de, E of Lincoln. *BrookeAsp I 44, 1.* S: HENRICI: DE: LASCI: COM: LINCOLN:. 1306-7.

LASCY, Henry de, E of Lincoln. *Bow 10.* temp Edw 1 & 2. *(& Constable of Chester).*

LASCY, Margaret de, Ctess of Lincoln & Pembroke. *AnstisAsp I 215, 68.* ...RGARETE: DE...... *(2nd of 2 shields).*

LASCY, Margaret de, Ctess of Lincoln. *PRO-sls.* 13 cent. *(2 similar shields supported by standing lady).*

LASCY, Margareta de, Ctess of Lincoln & Pembroke. *Birch 6676.* ..[MA]RGARETE... post 1245. *(on 1st of 2 shields; dau of Robt Quincy, E of Winchester, wid of 1 Jn, E of Lincoln, & 2 Walter, E of Pembroke).*

LAYSNE, Robert. *?source.* 1383. *(sl).*

LENTHALL, Roland, Ld of Haverfordwest, Pembr, Kt. *Birch 11302.* SIGILLUM..OFFICIL-.DOMINI HAUER FORDIE. 1449-50.

LEO, Master Henry, Physician. *Birch 11303.* S MAGRI HENRICI LEONIS PHISICI. late 14 cent.

LEON. *PRO-sls AS 3.* Sigillum Privatum Iohannis dei Gra Regis Castelie et Legionis Ducis Lancast [ri]e. 1372-3. *(qtd by castle; on roundel for Leon & Castile imp by Lancaster; sl of John, D of Lancaster & K of Castile).*

LEON. *Bow LX 16.* S: Johis Aquitania et Lancastria Seneschalli Angliae. 1390-1. *(qtd by Castile, all imp by France & Engld qtly, label Erm, on sl of Jn Plantagenet, D of Guienne & Lancaster).*

LEON. *WestmAbb.* *(qtd by Castile for Eleanor, Q of Edw 1, d1291; carved stone shields in niches on sides of tomb).*

LEON. *Bow LX 16.* S: Johis Aquitania et Lancastria Ducis Seneschalli Angliae. 1390-1. *(qtd by Castile, all imp by Jn of Gaunt, D of Lancaster & Guienne).*

LESCOT, Walter. *Birch 11305.* S WALTERI LESCOT(?). 1401. *(alias Le Scot; sl used by John Edward, Chaplain, of Northants).*

LESTRAUNGE, Alesia. *PRO-sls AS 253.* 1344-5. *(imp 6 lions; w of Ebulo; running scroll of vine leaves & bunches of grapes with A above & L below sl).*

LESTRAUNGE, Alesia. *PRO-sls.* 1324-5. *(on shield surrounded by 3 wiverns; w of Ebulo L).*

LEYBURNE, Roger de. *PRO-sls AS 34.* SIGILLUM ROGERI DE LEYBURNE. 1270-1. *(on banner).*

LINDLAWE, William de, of Beverley. *Yorks Deeds IX 65.* 1341.

LISLE, Robert. *Dodsworth 49, 34b, HB-SND.*

LISLE, Robt de. *Durham-sls 1610.* 1460.

LISLE, Robt de. *Durham-sls 1611.*

LISLE, Walter de. *Durham-sls 1613. (not heraldic).*

LODELOW, John. *PRO-sls. 1394-5.*

LOLT, Gundreda. *Birch 11365. (w of Jn Schapman, of Wyttone, Suff).* 1369.

LORAINE, John. *Stevenson.* 1507.

LOUND, John de, of Hayton, Notts. *Birch 11392.* S'P.... 1339. *(dimidg 3 eagles & border engr; or his s Peter).*

[LOVEL]. *PRO-sls AS 496.* 1438-9. *(qtd by [St Maur] & all qtd by Wm, Ld la Zouche & Seymour).*

[LOVEL]. *Vinc 88, 45.* 1409. *(qtd 2&3 by Ela de St Maur, wid of Rich de St M, Kt, of Castle Cary, Som; sl on seisin of lands in Swanskote to her s Nicholas).*

LOVETOT. *Birch 11413.* 1309. *(1 of 3 shields on sl; used by Dame Johanna de L, wid of Lord John de Lovetot, jun, of Suff).*

LUTTLETON, Matilda. *BirmCL-sls Hagley Hall 351327.* 1417. *(imp blank shield; w of Thos L).*

LUVETOT, John de. *Bk of Sls 96.* late 13 cent.

LUVETOT, John de, of Suff. *Birch 11480.* S IOHIS DE LUVETOT. late Hen 3.

LUXEMBOURG. *Bk of Sls 22.* 1466. *(used by Eliz Woodvile, w of Edw 4; qtg Baux &c & Woodvile in qr 6).*

LYELL, Sir John. *Stevenson.* 1323. *(or Lisle, alias Del Isle or De Insula; 2nd sl).*

LYONS, Sir John. *Lawrance 27. (d1349; effigy, Warkworth, Northants).*

MACDOWAL, Dougal. *Stevenson.* 1420. *(bro of Archibald of Makerston, & co-Lord of Yester).*

MACINTOSH, Farquhar, of Keppoch. *Stevenson.* 1505. *(12th of Mackintosh; & others).*

MAITLAND, Robert, of Netherdale. *Stevenson.* 1424. *(& others).*

MALLORY, John. *PRO-sls.* 1427-8.

MALONY, John, of Welton. *PRO-sls E40 A6372.* 1409-10.

MALORRE, John. *PRO-sls.* 1317-18.

MALORY, John, of Welton. *PRO-sls E40 A7612.* 1428-9.

MAN, Wm. *Stevenson.* 1594. *(?Burgess of Dundee).*

MANTON, Joan. *PRO-sls.* 1403-4. *(wid of Wm de M).*

MARCHE, Sir Wm, Kt. *NorfHo 7, 47.* 1394. *(on grant by Sir Wm M, chivaler, re land in Walpole).*

MARMION, Robert. *Bow LXXV 1.* ...IGILL.....OBE.... *(equestr sl on trappings; confirmation of gift of Abbey to Polesworth, made by his Kt Robt de Koili, of mill of Fresele).*

MARMYON, John, of Kyesby, Lincs. *Birch 11618.* ...ANNIS : MARM..... 1408.

MARNEY, Robert, Kt. *PRO-sls.* 1372-3.

MARNY, William de, of Essex & Kent, Kt. *Birch 11631.* SIGILLU: WILLELMI: DE: MARNY: MILIT. 1407. *(qtg 2&3 2 bars).*

MATRAVERS. *WB I 20, 15. (qr 1, imp Grey, M of Dorset).*

MAUFE, William de. *?source.* c1220. *(sl at Penshurst).*

MAULEON, Wm de. *Bk of Sls 351.* 1199. *(dimidg 3 crescs).*

MELVILLE, Robert. *Stevenson.* 1296.

MENVILL, Ralph. *Durham-sls 1753.* 1399.

MERKES, William le. *Birch 11742.* 1292. (motto): CREDE : MANDATO.

[MESCHINES], Rannulf de, E of Chester. *Bk of Sls 116.* 1207-17.

METTINGHAM COLLEGE, Suff. *Arch Journ (Lincs 1848) xlvi. (dex shield on sl, matrix made 1405-06).*

MEURIC. *Lawrance 29.* 1330-50. *('filius Ynyr Fychan'; effigy, Dolgelly, Merioneth).*

MIDDELTON, Margery. *PRO-sls.* 1357-8. *(1st of 2 shields held by lady on sl; w of Jn de M).*

MIDDLETON, John, of Kilhil. *Stevenson.* 1588.

MIDDLETON, Margery. *PRO-sls AS 149.* 1357-8. *(1 of 2 shields; w of John de M).*

MIDDLETON, Patrick. *Stevenson.* 1528. *(Chaplain of Collegiate Ch of St Salvator).*

MIKLEYE, Adam de. *PRO-sls.* 1373.

MOHAUT, Millicent de. *Bk of Sls 137.* 1287. *(dau of Wm de Cantelupe, wid 1st of Jn de M, 2nd of Eudo la Zouche).*

MOHAUT, Robert de, Ld of Hawarden. *Barons Letter.*

MOHAUT, William. *PRO-sls.* S WILLI DE ...ALTO. 1337.

MOMFORD. *PLN 873. (qtg 2 Arg chf Az, 3 Or 3 bend Az, 4 Sa pale Arg).*

MONHALT, Millisent de. *Bow 14. (1st of 2 shields on sl).*

[MONHAUT]. *Bk of Sls 45.* 1306-9.

[MONTALT]. *WestmAbb. (over all escutch on qtly coat of Stanley; mont to Mgt, Ctess of Richmond, d1509, who m 3rd Thomas Stanley, E of Derby; Henry 7 Chapel).*

MONTALT, Robert de. *PRO-sls AS 251, A 10949.* S ROBERTI DE MONTALT. 1327-8.

MONTE ALTO, Emma. *PRO-sls.* 1322-3. *(1 of 2 shields hanging from tree on sl; w of Robt de M).*

MONTE ALTO, Emma. *PRO-sls E40 A3980.* ..EMM..OR'.R....IS. 1322-3. *(2nd of 2 shields; w of Robt de M).*

MONTE ALTO, Emma de. *PRO-sls E40 A10948.* 1331-2. *(2nd of 2 shields; wid of Robt de M).*

MONTE ALTO, Milisenta de, of Barby, Northants. *Birch 6684-5.* S MILISENTE [DE]

MONTE ALTO. temp Edw 1. *(1st of 2 shields; dau of Wm de Cantilupe, 2nd w of Jn de M, Seneschal of Chester).*

MONTE ALTO, Robert de. *PRO-sls E40 A10949.* ROBERTI DE M...... 1327-8. *(Steward of Chester).*

MONTE ALTO, Robert de, Ld of Hawardyn, Flints, 2nd Baron. *Birch 11863.* S': ROBERTI: DE: MOVNALT. 1301.

MONTE ALTO, Rogerus de, Seneschal of Chester. *Bow XXXIV 12. (grant in Rosliston, Derbys).*

MONTE ALTO, Wm. *Stevenson.* c1300. *(or Mowat).*

MONTFORD, John de, Ld of Lunmeth. *Stevenson.* 1390.

MONTFORT. *?source. (sl of Simon de M).*

[MONTGOMERY, Roger de]. *Birch 5484.* 15 cent. *(on sl of Wenlock, Salop).*

MORE, Thomas, clerk. *PRO-sls.* 1394-5.

MORLEE, Robert de, Kt. *PRO-sls E40 A5565.* ROBERTI MORLEE DE .... 1356. *(blazon uncertain).*

MORLEE, Sir Wm de. *NorfHo 8, 67. (chirograph grant by Sir W de M re messuage at Hengham).*

MORLEY. *Farrer I 97. (on porch, Aldeby Ch, Norf).*

MORLEY. *Farrer II 29. (Cawston Ch, Norf).*

[MORLEY]. *Farrer I 276. (mont, Hingham Ch, Norf).*

MORLEY, Robert de, 2nd Ld. *Durham-sls 1816. (d1360).*

MORTIMER, Thomas, burgess of Dundee. *Stevenson.* 1444.

MORTON, Edward. *Clairambault 6530.* 30 Sept 1415.

MORTON, John de. *Bow XXVI 13. (witness with Ric de Pickford to charter of Thos de Laffide).*

MOWBRAY. *Birch 12000.* 1442. *(separate shield in sl of Jn M, 3rd D of Norf, EM &c).*

MOWBRAY. *Bk of Sls 450.* 1426. *(arms of M & Brotherton together form arms of Byland Abbey).*

MOWBRAY. *Bow XXII 1. (1 of 3 shields).*

MOWBRAY. *Proc Soc Antiq IV 2S 389.* 23 Aug 1359. *(imp by La Warre on sl of Alianor, dau of Jn, 4th Ld M & w of Sir Roger La Warre).*

[?MOWBRAY]. *Lawrance 33.* c1318. *(?Roger, 1st Ld M, d1297, & Jn, 2nd Ld, d1322, but ?Percy tomb; effigy, Fountains Abbey, Yorks).*

[MOWBRAY]. *Vinc 88, 154.* SIGILLUM IOANNIS HOWARD MILITIS. *(qtd 2&3 by Jn Howard, Kt; sl).*

MOWBRAY, Alicia de. *Bk of Sls 397.* 1328.

MOWBRAY, Jn, E of Nottingham & D of Norfolk. *Vinc 88, 180. (sin supporter on sl).*

MOWBRAY, John de. *Yorks Deeds V 129.* 1318.

MOWBRAY, John de. *Yorks Deeds II 16 & 88.* 1310.

MOWBRAY, John de. *?source.* 1241. *(sl on deed).*

MOWBRAY, John de. *Bk of Sls 315.*

MOWBRAY, John de. *Yorks Deeds VII 129.* 1335.

MOWBRAY, John, Ld. *Blair N I 13, 29. (beneath battlements of E tower of inner gateway, Alnwick Castle).*

MOWBRAY, John de, Kt, Ld of Isle of Axholme. *PRO-sls.* 1318-19.

MOWBRAY, John de, Ld of Isle of Axholme. *Bk of Sls 398.* 1348.

MOWBRAY, Roger. *Stevenson.* 1320.

MOWBRAY, Roger. *PRO-sls.* late 13 cent. *(s of Rog de M).*

MOWBRAY, Roger de. *Birch 2789.* 14 cent. *(sl of Hosp & chief House of Order of St Lazarus of Jerusalem in England, Burton St Lazarus, Leics, founded by Rog de M).*

MOWBRAY, Roger de. *Dugd 17, 70.* ?1283. *(s of 'late' Rog de M).*

MOWBRAY, Roger de. *WestmAbb.* Rogerus de Mowbraye. 15 cent.

MOWBRAY, Thomas, D of Norfolk, E of Nottingham, E Marshal. *Bow XLIV 2.*

MOWBRAY, Thomas, E Marshal & E of Nottingham. *PRO-sls.* 1388-9.

MOWBRAY, Thomas, E Marshal & E of Nottingham. *PRO-sls Ex Misc 46, 1.* 1388.

MOWBRAY, Thomas, E Marshal & E of Nottingham. *PRO-sls.* 1391-2. *(qtd by 3 lions passt & label of 5).*

MOWBRAY, Thomas, E of Nottingham. *Birch 2574.* 1450. *(cr D of Norf 1397; sl of Carthusian Priory of Visitation of the Virgin, Axholm, nr Epworth, Lincs).*

MOWBRAY, William de. *Yorks Arch Journ viii 284.* early 13 cent.

MUBARI, Roger de. *Birch 12005.* S' ROGERI DE MVBARI. 1255. *(alias Moubray alias Mubray; s of Wm de M, of Lincs).*

MUCEGROS, Agnes de, dame de Chenmore. *AnstisAsp I 213, 62.* ...MUSSEGROS..... *(1st of 3 shields; dau of Mgt de Ferrers, Ctess of Derby).*

MUHAUD, Wm. *Durham-sls 1843. (used in 1339 by Robert Boys & Agnes of Menville).*

MUMBRAY, William de, of Yorks. *Birch 12009.* late 13 cent. *(not on shield).*

MUSARD, Malcolm. *PRO-sls E40 A4683 & 4685.* 1307-8.

· MUSARD, Malcolm. *PRO-sls E40 A947.* post

1290.

MUSARD, Malcolm. *PRO-sls.* 1300-1.

MUSCEGROS, Agnes de. *BrookeAsp I 4, 4. (1 of 3 shields; Dame de Clenmere, dau of Mgt de Ferrers, Ctess of Derby).*

NARFORD, Thomas de, Kt. *PRO-sls E40 A6895.* Sig' thome de Ner.o.d.milit'. 1375-6.

NERFORD. *Birch 12073.* S' ALICIE DE NER-FORD. 1379. *(imp chf indented for Alice N, wid of Jn de Neville of Essex).*

[NERFORD]. *Farrer II 381. (Cley Ch, Norf).*

NERFORD, Thomas de, Kt. *PRO-sls E40 A2749.* 1340-1.

NERFORD, Thomas de, Kt. *PRO-sls.* 1375-6.

NESSEFIELD, Margaret. *Birch 12077.* 1389-90.

NEUVIL, Margaret de. *Brit Arch Assoc vi 139.* 1315. *(sin shield on sl; 2nd w of Jn, Ld Gifford of Brimsfield; attached to BM Add Ch LFC xxiii l6).*

NEVILE, John de, Kt, of Essex. *PRO-sls.* 1357-8.

NEVILL, Lady Margaret de. *PRO-sls.* 1314-5. *(1 of 2 sh on sl).*

NEVILL, Margaret de. *AnstisAsp I 218, 77.* +SIGILLVM: MARGARETE: DE: NEVILL. *(3rd of 3 shields; wid of Jn N; Witnesses to deed: Reginald de Gynges, Baldwin de Fina, Richard de Southchurch, William de Cloville, Kts).*

NEVILLE, Hugh de. *PRO-sls.* 1267. *(sl on will).*

NEVILLE, Hugh de, Kt, of Darnall, Notts. *PRO-sls.* 1330-1.

NEVILLE, John de. *Yorks Deeds V 176.* 1301.

NEVILLE, John de, Kt. *Birch 12121.* S'IOHANNIS NEVILE D' CO ......(?). 1357.

NEVILLE, Margaret. *HB-SND.* 1315. *(2nd sh on sl [1st 3 lions passt]; w of Jn Neville of Essex).*

NEVILLE, Richard de. *Birch 12145.* ....ICARDI DE NEVEVILE. 14 cent. *(alias Neuevile).*

NEVYLE, Dame Margareta de. *Birch 6690.* S'MARGA.... 1315. *(1st of 2 sh).*

NEWPORT, John. *Mill Steph.* 1522. *(qtg 2 [Pateshull], 3 on cross 5 leopards faces, 4 i&iv chf indent, ii&iii 3 martlets, imp Aling-ton & Argentine qtly; brass Furneux Pelham, Herts).*

NEWTON, Wm, of Newton. *Stevenson.* 1520.

NICOL. *AylesburyM-sls E93, 11.* ..IGILLUM; M......LIS; NICOL. 1379-80. *(sl used by Jn Besevylle).*

NORFOLK, Duchess of. *Baker-sls.* *(Fitzalan qtd by Warenne, imp by Engld & label).*

NORFOLK, Eliz, Duchess of. *Baker-sls.* 1416-17. *(qtg Warenne, imp by Engld & label; grant with others of manors of*

Troghford [Trafford], Stonydunham & Hole, Ches).

NORTHTOFT, Edmund de. *PRO-sls.* 1360-1.

NORTHUMBERLAND. *WB I 20, 6.*

NORTON, James de, Kt. *Bow LIII 13.* Sigill Jacobi de Norton. 1327-8. *(grant of land in Tisted).*

NORTONE, Joames de. *Selborne 4, 75 & 79.* S'... de Nortone. 1290-1300.

NORWICH, Sir John, Kt. *Stowe-Bard 1s xiii 5.* LE SEAL JO NORWYC. 1352-3.

NORWICH, of Mettingham. *Farrer Bacon 7.* [13 cent]. *(sl).*

NORWICH, Wm de, Abbot of W Dereham. *Stowe-Bard 2s viii 2.* 1519-20. *(dex shield on sl).*

NOUYK, Peter de. *PRO-sls.* 1373.

O'BRYN, Captain Donagh. *PRO-sls.* S DONATUS OBRYN CAPIT. 1425-6.

OLDHALLE, WIlliam. *Clairambault 6845.* 6 Aug 1425.

OLDHALLE, William, Kt. *PRO-sls BS 37.* Sigillum Will... dhalle militis. 1456-7.

OLDHALLE, Sir Wm. *?source.* 1440. *(sl).*

OLDHALLE, Sir Wm. *Arch 37, 335-6.* 10 & 22 July 1440. *(sls attached to 2 deeds to which Sir Wm is party re land in Mugwell (Monkswell St), Psh of St Olave, London; 2nd also re land at Thorpe Salveyne. Glover &c give arms of Oldhall as per pale lion Erm. No trace on these sls of party line or Erm spots. Though similar, sls appear to be from difft matrices).*

ORMESBY, Ralph. *Birch 12316.* S' RADVLFI FIL' SIMONIS. 13 cent. *(otherwise FitzSimon; s of Symon de Ormesby, of Lincs).*

OVER, Hugh de, Ld of Ketenes. *Stevenson.* 1292-4.

PACHE, John, of Lawford. *PRO-sls E40 A13725.* 1338-9. *(or Jn Holebrok).*

PANTOUF, Roger de. *PRO-sls.* late 12 cent. *(kite shaped sh).*

PANTULF, William. *Birch 12375.* SIGILL'WILL'MI PANTVLF. 1240. *(s of Rog P, of Warws).*

PARYS, Hugh de. *PRO-sls.* 1312-13.

?PAVILLY, Robert de. *Bk of Sls 400.* 1246. *(imp 6 lions; ind of 2 sls on Charter of Robt de P & Maud his mother).*

PAYNEL, William. *Bow 12.*

PAYTEVYN, Thomas, Kt. *PRO-sls.* 1377.

PENLE, Elizabeth de, ?of Herts. *Birch 12540.* S ELIZABETHE DE PENLE. 1335.

PERCI, Henry de. *Birch 6294.* SIGILLUM HEN[R]ICI DE PERCI. 1301. *([Ld of Topcliffe & 1st Baron P]; obv equestr sl, sh & caparisons).*

PERCY. *Durham-sls 1965.* *(qtg Lucy, over all label; used by Hen de P, later 3rd E of*

Northd, vivo parente as Warden of the East
Marches, 1446).

PERCY. Gerola 76, 226. 15 cent. (qtg 2&3
3 fishes; Bodrum, Turkey).

PERCY. Mill Steph. 1503. (qtg 2&3 [Stra-
bolgie], all qtd II&III by Burgh on brass to
Robt Borrow & w Alice, Stanford Rivers,
Essex).

[?PERCY]. Lawrance 33. c1318. (?Hen, Ld
Percy, d1315 [but l'Anson considered it a
Mowbray tomb]; effigy, Fountains Abbey,
Yorks).

PERCY, Hen Algernon, 6th E of Northd
(1489-1527). PRO-sls E40 A4104.
ALGERNNVS PERCY COIT NO..ONBRIE HONORV
DE COKERMOTH ET PETWORTH DNS NRI.
1528-9. (qr 1; sl used by his successor).

PERCY, Hen de, E of Northd. Yorks Deeds VI
113. 1381. (imp Maud de Lucy, Ctess of
Northd).

PERCY, Henry. PRO-sls WS 369, HB-SND.
1341. (d1351-2).

PERCY, Henry. Percy 16, HB-SND. 1376.
(cr E of Northd 1377, k Bramham Moor
1407/8).

PERCY, Henry. BM Harl 1985, 274, HB-
SND. 1329. (d1351-2).

PERCY, Henry. Barons Letter. (d1315).

PERCY, Henry. PRO-sls BS 422, HB-SND.
1358. (d1368).

PERCY, Henry. Percy 13, HB-SND. 1355.
(d1368).

PERCY, Henry de. Yorks Deeds V 144. 1330.

PERCY, Henry de. Birch 12556. SIGILLVM
HENRICI DE PERCI. 1296. (afterwards 1st
Baron [1299-1315]).

PERCY, Henry Algernon, 6th E of Northd,
KG(?). Birch 12553. ?1527-37. (poss c' sl;
not on shield). (motto): TOUT LOYAL.

PERCY, Henry Algernon, 6th E of Northd,
KG. Birch 12550. ...HRI ALGERN'NVS PERCY
COIT N.....HONBRIE HONORV DE COKERMOTH ET
PETWORTH DNS. (qr 1 of 5, 2 in chf, 3 in
base, qtg France modern, Engld in border,
Lucy, Spenser, Percy ancient, Poynings &
Brian). (motto): ESPERANCE.

PERCY, Henry Algernon, 6th E of Northd.
PRO-sls BS 405, HB-SND. 1528-9. (qtly of
5: I Qtly 1 lion [Percy], 2 France & Eng qtly
in border [?Beaufort], 3 3 luces [Lucy], 4
Barry wavy [Spenser], II fess of 5 lozs [Percy
ancient]; III Barry & baston [Poynings]; IV
3 lions passt & baston [Fitzpayn]; V 3 piles
[Bryan]).

PERCY, Henry Algernon, 6th E of Northd.
PRO-sls. 1528-9 & 1536-7. (qr I 1; used by
his successor, perhaps in default of sl of his
own).

PERCY, Henry de, 2nd Baron (1315-52).

Birch 12557. SIGILLVM HENRICI DE [PE]RCI.
1335.

PERCY, Henry, 2nd Ld, of Alnwick, d1351.
Durham-sls 1960-61 & 1970.

PERCY, Henry de, ?2nd E of Northd, Ld of
Honour of Cockermouth. Birch 12566.
SIGILLUM HENRICI PERCY COMITIS
NORTHUMBR & DNI HONORIS COKIRMOUTH.
1414-55. (qtg 2&3: 3 lucies hauriant).

PERCY, Henry, E of Northd. Blair D II 141,
302. (on W front of gatehouse, Hilton Castle).

PERCY, Henry de, E of Northd. PRO-sls.
1379-80, 1383-4 & 1527-8.

PERCY, Henry, E of Northd. PRO-sls.
1238-9. (sl rev).

PERCY, Henry, E of Northd. Bow XXXIX 2.
S Henrici de Percy Comitis Northumbriae et dmi de Cok-
ermouth. 1396. (qrs 1&4).

PERCY, Henry, E of Northd. PRO-sls Ex QR
531/29, HB-SND. c1380. (k 1407-8).

PERCY, Henry, E of Northd. PRO-sls.
1358-9.

PERCY, Henry, E of Northd. PRO-sls.
1341-2.

PERCY, Henry, E of Northd. Bow LV 17a.
Sigillu Henrici de Percy Comitis Northumbriae. 1379-
80. (shield & lance flag).

PERCY, Henry, Ld of, 3rd Baron. Birch
12558. SIGILLUM HEN ......DOMINI DE PER.....
1376. (Kingsford says 4th Baron).

PERCY, Henry de, (3rd) E of Northd, Warden
of East Marches towards Scotld. Birch
12567. S' HENRICI DE PERCY COMITIS
NORTHUMBRIE CUSTODIS EMARCHIE VERSUS
SCOTIAM (?). 1455-61. (qtg 2&3: 3 lucies
hauriant; arms ch on banner-flag held in
right forepaw by lion sejt gard, tail betw hind
legs & erect over back; Kingsford says 2nd
Earl & dates it 1446).

PERCY, Henry de, 1st E of Northd & Ld of
Cockermouth, Cumb. Birch 12562. S' HEN-
RICI DE PERCI COMITIS NORTHUMBRIE 9AC
DONI DE COKIRMOUTH. 1408. (qtg 2&3: 3
lucies haurient for Lucy).

PERCY, Henry, 1st E of Northd. Durham-sls
1963. (qtg Lucy jure uxoris).

PERCY, Henry de, 1st E of Northd. Birch
12560. [SIG]ILLUM HENRICI DE PER ....COMITIS
NORTH....... 1390. (on each side of shield a
sprig of broom, for Plantagenet).

PERCY, Henry, 6th E of Northd. PRO-sls BS
421, HB-SND. 1536. (qtly of 5: I Qtly 1
lion [Percy], 2 France & Eng qtly ?in border
[Beaufort], 3 3 luces [Lucy], 4 Barry wavy
[Spenser]; II fess of 5 lozs [Percy ancient];
III Barry & baston [Poynings]; IV 3 lions
passt & baston [Fitzpayn]; V 3 piles
[Bryan]; sh surrounded by Garter with

motto).

PERCY, Henry, Ld of Topcliff. *Barons Letter.* *(sl & c'sl).*

PERCY, Sir Thomas de. *PRO-sls.* 1383.

PERCY, Thomas. *PRO-sls Ex KR 68/10, 230, HB-SND.* 1383-4. *(beheaded 1403).*

PERCY, Thomas. *Percy 17, HB-SND.* 1393. *(beheaded 1403).*

PERCY, Thomas. *Birch 2043, HB-SND.* 1366. *(1st of 2 sh on sl; Bp of Norwich 1356-69).*

PERCY, Thomas de. *Birch 12576.* SIGILLUM THO .....RCY. 1393.

PERCY, Thomas, Kt. *Bow 14.*

PERCY, Thomas, Lord Egremont. *PRO-sls.* 1451-2.

PERCY, Thomas de, of Essex, Kt. *Birch 12574.* 1383.

PERCY, Thomas, Bp of Norwich. *Stowe-Bard 1s xiv 4.* 1361. *(sin sh on sl, dex indecipherable).*

PERCY, Thomas, Bp of Norwich. *AnstisAsp I 209, 52.* 1366. *(1st of 2 shields).*

PERNESTEDE, Richard de. *PRO-sls.* 1285.

PERSEY. *Bow 11.* 1381-90.

PHELIPS, Francis, of London. *PRO-sls.* 1609-10.

PICKERING, John. *Woodman 19, HB-SND.* 1374.

[PIERPOINT]. *DerbysAS XIV 90-1.* 1500. *(imp by Shelley on tomb of Jn S, at Shelley).*

PLESSY, John of. *Dodsworth 45, 33b, HB-SND.* 1315.

PLESSY, Richard of. *Ridley 85, HB-SND.* 1346.

PLUGENCY, William de, of Lambourne, Berks. *Proc Soc Antiq IV 2S 407.* S WILLI..

PLOGENE. late 12 cent. *(attached to undated Deed Poll in which Wm, s&h of Wm de P confirms grants by his ancestors to Church of Stanley, Wilts).*

[POITOU]. *Proc Soc Antiq II 2S 143. (on 2 of 3 sh, 3rd bears 2head eagle attrib to Ric, K of Romans, or [Marshal]; on steelyard weight dug up at Toddington, Beds).*

POLE, de la, Ld of Keveoloc. *Arch Journ x 143-4.* late 13 cent. *(shield held in effigy of Hawise, Lady of Keveoloc, on silver sl matrix).*

POWER, William le, Kt. *PRO-sls E40 A8605.* S...WILLIDAL..S. 1280-1. *(blazon uncertain).*

PRESTON, William. *Yorks Deeds IX 63.* W.-LLELMI PRESTON. 1352. *(s of Rog de P).*

PRILLY, Hugh. *Bow LXX 5.* Sigillum Hugonis Prilly. 1320-1. *(deed concerning land in Craneford).*

PULL, Sir John de. *PCL II 29. (unpainted).*

PYCCEN, John. *PRO-sls. (alias Bridde).* 1368-9.

PYKERING, Sir James. *Sizergh.* 1369. *(sl).*

PYLKYNGTON, Sir John, Kt. *NorfHo 1, 61.* 1404. *(sl on deed of manumission by John P, Chivaler & Mgt his w, dd at their manor of Bressingham, Norf).*

REDHAM, William de, of Norf. *Birch 12946.* SIGILLUM WILMI DE REDHAM. 1324.

REDVERS. *Birch 9022.* 1514. *(qtd 2&3 on dex imp of sh of Katharine, w of Wm Courtenay, E of Devonshire, dau of Edw 4).*

REDVERS. *Brit Arch ....Assoc xi 223-4.* Non caret effectu quod voluere duo. 1293. *(imp by de Fortibus (de F dimid, but R not so) on sl of Isabella, w of Wm de Fortibus, E of Aumerle & dau of Baldwin, 3rd E of Devon).*

REDVERS, de. *?source.* c1275. *(sl of Isabelle de Fortibus at Winchester).*

[REDVERS]. *BrookeAsp I 68, 2. (imp by Fortibus on sl of Isabella de F, Ctess of Albemarle & Devon; 'Isabella de Fortibus Comitisse Albemarlia et Devon, et Dna. de Insula, remisit Dno Rico de Affeton 13 s Anni reddit, pro uno molendino aquatic in Affeton').*

REDVERS, Baldwin de. *BrookeAsp I 69, 1.* BALDWINI: DE : RIDVARIIS: CO: DEVON: ET: DNS: INSVLE. *('Omnibus Christi fidelibus psens. scriptum visuris vel audituris B de Redvers, com Devon salt. Noverint univ'sitas vestra me concessisse Alfaro filio Ricardi. Notatorum &c. Hiis testibus Johe. de Brummoru').*

RENTON, David. *Stevenson.*

RIPAR, B de, E of Devon. *PRO-sls.* S BALDEWINI DE INSULA. 1261-2.

RIPARIIS, Alicia de, Ctess of Devon. *AnstisAsp I 223, 88.* +SIG: ALICIE: DE: RIPAR: COA: DEVON. 1277-8.

[RIVERS]. *PRO-sls. (qtd 4 on sl of Henry Courtenay, E of Devon).*

ROBERSART, Theodore, alias Canoune. *PRO-sls.* S LE CANOUNE DE ROBIERSART. 1379-80. *(tail turned over).*

ROBERSART, Theodore, Canon. *PRO-sls E40 A6960.* S LE CANOINE DE ROBIERSART. 1379-80. *(qrs 1&4).*

ROBESSART, Lewis, Ld Bourchier, d1431. *Neale & Brayley; Inventory. (qtg Bourchier on mont; carved banner).*

ROBESSART, Roger. *PRO-sls.* 1422.

ROBESSART, Terry, Kt. *PRO-sls.* 1422-3.

RODES, John de. *PRO-sls.* S DNI WALGERI DERODEN. 1299. *(rev of sl).*

ROOKES, Richard, of Bucks. *Birch 13065.* 1375. *(dex imp; sin imp destroyed except fleur de lis in base).*

ROSELIS, John de. *Durham-sls 2117.* c1270.

ROWLAND, John. *BirmCL-sls 494214.* 1405. *(Parson of Stevenage, Herts).*

RUSSELL, John, of Grafham, Hunts. *Birch 13174.* IE SV SEL DE SMOVR LEL. 1348.

SCHOTE, John. *PRO-sls.* 1413-14.

SCOTENAY, John de. *Proc Soc Antiq IV 2S 391.* SIGILLUM JOHANNA DE ...E. 1 Aug 1342.

SCOTLAND, Alexander II of. *Brit Arch Assoc xlv 108.* 1214-49. *(c' sl).*

SCOTLAND, K Alexander II. *Stevenson 13.* 1214-49. *(Great Sl on pear-shaped sh suspended from shoulders of king on horse-back on rev of sl).*

SCOTLAND, Alexander III of. *Brit Arch Assoc xlv 109.* 1249-86. *(c' sl).*

SEGRAVE, Christina de. *Birch 6712.* S.... DE.-S..RAVE. 1280. *(dau of Hugh de Plessets, Kt & w of Jn de Segrave, after 5th Baron de S).*

SEGRAVE, John of. *Barons Letter, HB-SND.* *(d1325).*

SEINTGEORGE, William, Kt, of Warws & Dorset. *Birch 13224.* 1439. *(in allusion to arms of St George, not a shield).*

SENINGVEAM, Elgenardus de. *Birch 6428.* +SIGILLVM EL.ENARDI DE SENINGUEAM. early 13 cent. *(equestr sl).*

SIBBALD, Isabella, of Balgony. *Stevenson.* c1470. *(w of 1 Geo Douglas, 4th E of Angus (d1462), 2 ?Jn Carmichael, of Balmadie, 3 Robt Douglas, of Lochleven).*

SKOT, Robert, of Whitley, Ches. *Middlewich 278.* 1322. *(sl).*

SLAKE, Nicholas, Rector of Yeovil. *PRO-sls.* 1389-90.

SMYTH, Thos, of Kymberle. *NorfHo 9, 51.* 1370. *(prob not on shield; sl on grant re land).*

SNETESHAM, Thomas de. *PRO-sls.* 1338.

SOREWELL. *Mill Steph; Belcher II 128.* *(brass, Stone, Kent to Master Jn Sorewell, Rector, 1439; inscr now lost; Belcher ascribes it to Jn Dew, c1530).*

ST EDMUNDS, Thomas of. *LonG-sls 419/491, 15.* 1381. *(cit of London).*

STANLOWE, Sir Radulf de. *Dugd 17, 42.* 1328.

STANTON, John, of Wolvelay, Yorks. *Birch 13668.* S' RIC ... LE ...E. 1426.

STAPELEGH, Peter de. *Birch 13670.* IEO SV SEAL...PELES LEAL(?). 1319. *(or Ric de Fouleshurst, of Ches).*

STAPELTON, Brian de, Kt. *Yorks Deeds X 189.* 1370.

STAPELTON, Miles de. *PRO-sls.* 1363.

STAPELTON, Milo de, of Yorks, Kt. *Birch 13671.* MILIS..... c1313.

STAPILTON, Brian de, Kt. *PRO-sls.* 1382.

STAPILTON, Sir Brian. *WK 744.*

STAPILTON, Nicholas. *PRO-sls.* 1327-8. *(s of Sir Miles de S).*

[STAPLETON]. *Farrer I 355.* [1466].

(Ingham Ch, Norf).

[STAPLETON]. *Proc Soc Antiq XVIII 2S 136.* *(qtg [Fitzalan]all imp by [Huddlestone] on 1 of 6 brasses found in W walk of cloister at Hayles Abbey in 1899).*

[STAPLETON]. *Bellasis II 120; C&WAAST i, iv 230-2; Hill vii 183.* *(imp by maunche [Wharton]; shield IV, entrance to belfry, Kirkby Stephen).*

[STAPLETON, Sir Miles]. *Birch 3314.* 14 cent. *(sl of Coll Ch & Priory of Order of Holy Trinity, Ingham, Norfolk, Sir Miles de S was founder, 1360).*

[STAPULTON]. *WB I 14b, 21.* *(qr 1 of 8).*

STAUBERT, Jehen de. *Birch 13675.* S' JEHEN DE STAVBERT. c1385. *(imp cresc betw 2 estoiles; sl used by Wm Deyster, of Northampton, Mason, & (in 1394) by Jn Grene, Chaplain of Draughton, Northants).*

STEWART, Andrew, 2nd Ld Avondale. *Stevenson.* 1501. *(qtg fess gobony; all in border gobony).*

STEWART, Robert. *Stevenson.* 1397. *(3rd son of K Robt II; E of Fife in 1371, D of Albany 1398, d1420; 3rd & 4th sls).*

STONHOUSE, Thos de. *Hist MSS Comm Report 1871 2, 20.* 1306-7. *(grandson of Thos FitzRalph; sl on grant by T de S).*

STRACCHE, John, Kt. *PRO-sls.* 1375-6.

STRATHEARN, Robt, 4th E of. *Stevenson.* c1224.

STRECHE, John, of Norf, Kt. *Birch 13726.* SIGILLVM IOHANNIS STRECH. 1344. *(qtg 2&3 crosslet).*

STURMY, John, Kt. *PRO-sls.* 1333.

SUMERI, Radulfus de. *Birch 6455.* ante 1211. *(of ?Merlege, Berks; equestr sl).*

SUSSEX, William, E of. *BrookeAsp I 48, 1.* *(equestr sl on grant of Ofham to Hugo Esturmi).*

SUTTON, Nicholas de, of Threak. *PRO-sls.* 1323.

SWEYN. *MP VIII 3.* *(s of Rigan).*

TOPCLIFFE, Nicholas of. *Durham-sls 2452.* 1311.

TRAU, Soudan de la. *PRO-sls AS 261.* S [L]E SOLDAZ DE LA TRAUE. 1381-2.

TUDOR, Margaret. *Stevenson.* *(imp France & England qtly; Q of Jas 4 & dau of Hen 7).*

TURBERVIL, John de, Kt. *PRO-sls.* 1263. *(blazon uncertain).*

UTLAGE(?), William. *Durham-sls 2518.* *(used 1340 by Robt of Durham).*

VANDERNOOTT, Jn, of London. *PRO-sls.* 1545-6.

VEAUTRE, Simon. *PRO-sls.* 1418.

VENABLES, William de, Kt. *Middlewich 281.* 1260-77. *('a lyon rampant his seale').*

VENABLES, Wm de. *Middlewich 67.* Sigilum

Willelmi de Venablis. ante 1226. *(on roundel).*
VENIS, ... de. *PRO-sls.* 1405-6. *(1 of 3
shields on sl).*
[VERDON]. *Farrer I, 25. (qtd by [Pilking-
ton]; Bressingham Ch, Norf).*
VERDON, John de, of Norf, Kt. *Birch 14143.*
SIGILLVM IOH'IS DE VERDOVN. 1377. *(chess-
rook above sh in allusion to arms of another
family of Verdon viz: on chf 3 chess-rooks).*
VERDON, Thomas de. *Stowe-Bard 1s iv 8.*
S'THOME: DE VER..N. ?1327-8.
VERDOUN, Thomas de, of Northants, Kt.
Birch 14147. 1349. *(shield betw 2 chess-
rooks, in allusion to arms of another family
of Verdon, viz on chf 3 chess-rooks).*
VERDUN, Thomas de, of Norf, Kt. *Birch
14146.* S' THOME DE VERDOVN. 1315.
VESCY, Isabella de, senior of Scorby, Yorks.
Birch 6727. SI...L...LE.D...C... 1289-1311. *(2nd
of 2 shields; wid of Sir Jn de Beaumont).*
VIEL, Thomas. *PRO-sls. (s of Rich V).*
1284-5.
WA...s, John. *PRO-sls.* 1290.
WAFRE, Alan. *NorfHo 2, 118.* 1298-9. *(sl
on Quitclaim by A.W. & Gilly his w &c re
windmill &c in Hardale).*
WALDEVE, John, s of. *Durham-sls 2552.*
WALKFARE, Richd. *Stowe-Bard iii 128.*
SIGILL.RICARDI.DE.WALKEFARE.
WALKFARE, Robt de, of Cambs, Kt. *Birch
14220.* S' ROBERTI DE WALKFARE. 1332.
WALLACE, Duncan, Laird of Sundrum.
Stevenson. 1371.
WALTON, Robert de. *Birch 14244.* SIGILLV
ROBERTI DE WALTO. 1396. *(sl used by Simon
Palgrave, of Stecheforthe, Cambs).*
WANCY, Wm. *Stowe-Bard 1s xii 8.* 1282-3.
*(sl, no legend, on deed by Wm, s of Sir Wm
de W, Kt).*
?WARKWORTH. *Bk of Sls 463.* 1284. *(sl of
Robt, s of Rog, s of Jn, s of Robt, Ld of
Warkworth, by Ada, sis of Jn de Baliol, K of
Scotld).*
WARRE, Thos la. *Arch Journ xxxvi 82. (on
tomb of Thos La Warre KG, d1525, Broad-
water Ch, Suss; ?missing orle of crosslets
fitchy).*
WARTHYLL, Nicholas. *YMerch-sls Advow-
sons.* 1412. *(s of Jn W).*
[WASTNEYS]. *Mill Steph.* c1475. *(qtd 2&3
by [Gresley] as imp by Kniveton; brass to
Nicholas K & w Joan ?Mauleverer, Muggin-
ton, Derbys).*
WATLINGTONE, Joceus de, of Suss. *Birch
14312.* S' IOCEI DE WATLINGTONE. 1313.
(qtg 2&3 fretty).
WELLS, Alex. *Stevenson.* 1296. *(Warden of
Hospital of St John of Jerusalem in Scotld).*
WEMYSS, Andrew. *Stevenson.* 1468. *(qtg*

another lion; in fess pt 5foil).
WEMYSS, David, of Wemyss. *Stevenson.*
?1423. *(qtg another lion).*
WEMYSS, John. *Stevenson.* 1490. *(s of
Andrew W).*
WEMYSS, John, of Wemyss. *Stevenson.* 14-
15 cent.
WEMYSS, of Reres. *Stevenson.* 1473. *(borne
by Mgt Vaus, w of Sir Thos W, of Reres, Kt).*
WESTONE, John de. *Birch 14421.* S' IOH'IS
DE WESTONE. 1343. *(sl used by Jn Joudy, of
Hepw(o)rth, Suff).*
?WHITTINGHAM. *Mill Steph.* 1471. *(imp
?Buckland on tomb of Sir Robt W, Aldbury,
Herts).*
WILLIAMSCHOTE, Eleanor de. *PRO-sls.* S'
ELINANORE DE WILLIAMSCHOTE. 1362-3.
(used by Thos de W, Kt).
WINCHESTER, Thomas. *Stevenson.* 1296.
(not on shield).
WIRHALE, John de. *PRO-sls.* SIG...IOHANNIS
DE WIRH.LE. 1350-1. *(used by Simon de
Bonde).*
WODYLL. *Birch 8537.* SIGILLUM: ....:
WODYLL': UXOR': THOME: CHETHEWOD. mid
15 cent. *(imp by Thos Chethewod, of Reyes
or Rus, Ches, Esq).*
WUCY, Hugh. *PRO-sls.* 1368-9.
WYKEN, William de, clerk. *PRO-sls E40
A8347.* ..O.DE..ON. 1405-6. *(or others).*
WYLE(s), John. *Heneage 2176.* +SIGILLUM:
IOHANNIS: WYLE. 1397. *(grant of land in
Wodebergh, [Wilts]).*

Untinc lion Arg
MONTALT, Roger of. *WestmAbb.* ROGERUS
DE MONTE ALTO. 15 cent inscription. *(span-
dril, Bay 11, S aisle, Nave).*

Untinc lion Gu
BRET, Walter le. *Gerard 104.*

Untinc lion Sa
DENTON. *North 1558 122, 116. (qtd 4 by
Brackenbury).*
TEDUR. *XK A 28. (descendant of
Cadwalader).*

Lion rampant to sinister Untinc
Lion to sin
— ?source. c1500. *(roof corbel, Stanlake,
Oxfords; imp bugle-horn; another corbel has
bugle-horn imp lion).*
— *Stevenson.* 1491. *(1st sl; qtd by Jn
Lindsay, 6th E of Crawford, d1513).*
ANDREW, Ralph, of Burenham. *PRO-sls AS
18.* +S'R...FI: FIL: A..: E:. 1240-59.
ARDENA, William de, of Hampton-in-Arden,
Warws. *Birch 6896.* ...GILL'WILL. 1188-98.
[ARUNDELL]. *Farrer III 37. (Stone shield
outside St Andrews Ch, Norwich).*

BAUSE, Thomas de. *Heneage 535.* +SI:
THOME: DE: BAUSE. 1289. *(lease of land,
Twiverton, Som).*
BELEBOCHE, Alexander. *Exeter D&C 294.*
S'ALEXANDRII.BELEBVCH. c1286. *(not on
shield).*
BERNARDUS, Clericus Episcopi. *Stevenson.*
*(not on shield; temp Pope Urban IV, 1261-
64).*
BRUNTOFT, Philip de. *Birch 7888.* +S' PHI-
LIPI: DE: BRVNTOFT. 13 cent. *(s of Robt de
B, of Bruntoft, ?co Durham).*
BRUS, Peter de. *YPhil-sls 29.*
CANBELLANUS, Philip. *Birch 8303.* +S PHI-
LIPI CANBELLANI...LES. 1249. *(or le Cham-
bellene).*
CONSTABLE, John the, of Chester. *Bk of Sls
519.* c1175-90. *(c'sl).*
DUNBAR, Patrick, 7th E of, 1248-89. *Steven-
son.* *(1st sl & c'sl).*
ENGLAND, K Richard I. *Sandford 73.*
GYFFARD, Richard. *PRO-sls E40 A8858.*
S'RICARDI GIFORD. 1312-13. *(not on shield).*
HANMEL, Gilbert. *Stevenson.* *(not on shield).*
LACY, Henry de, E of Lincoln. *PRO-sls.* 13
cent. *(on trapper of equestr seal).*
MACKINTOSH, Duncan. *Stevenson.* 1467.
(Chief of Clan Chatton).
MALLORE, Robert, of Welleton, Kt. *PRO-sls
E40 A13119.* S ROBERTI MALLORE. 13 cent.
(not on shield).
[MARESCHAL]. *Birch 6726.* *(3rd of 3 shields;
sl of Agnes de Vesey [dau of Wm de Ferrers,
E of Derby & 2nd w of Eustace de V, 4th
Baron, d c1216]).*
MORTIMER, James. *Stevenson.* 1465. *(s of
Robt M, of Balandrow, Kincardine).*
MUCEGROS, Agnes de, Lady of Chinnor. *Bk
of Sls 95.* 1281 or later. *(wid of Robt de M
& dau of Wm de Ferrers, 7th E of Derby).*
[OXENBRIDGE]. *Lambarde 52-3.* *(outside E
window, S Chapel, Brede, Suss).*
SIMONIS, Hugh, fil. *Birch 9764.* +S'HUGONIS
FILII SIMONIS. 13 cent.
SUTHORMESBY, Simon de, of Lincs, Kt.
Birch 13783. ... MILE .... 1308.
WALDEVE, John, s of. *Stevenson.* c1220.
WASTENEYS, William. *Birch 14303.* 1331.
(not on shield; s of Edm de W, of Lincs, Kt).
(motto): SVM LEO FORTIS.

Lion rampant (tinctures deficient)

Untinc lion Or
ARUNDEL, E of. *Wroxton A 17; Her & Gen
vii 338.* *('The erle of Arundell is ye lyon
rampand in gold').*

Az lion Untinc
BEAUMONT, Le Sr. *NB 68.* *(?lion Or & field
semy de lis Or missing).*
Gu lion Untinc (?Vair)
EVERYNGHAM, Robert de. *LM 571.*
Or lion Untinc
[CARTMEL PRIORY]. *Bellasis B 15.* 15 cent.
*(E window, Windermere; ?for Wm
Mareschal, founder of Cartmel Priory).*
MOHAUT, Johan de. *LMR 113.*

Lion rampant tinctured (to dexter or sinister)

Arg lion Az

Arg lion Az
— *PLN 1689.* *(qtd 2&3 by Percy).*
— *BR II 3.* *(qtd 3 per pale by D of Bur-
goyne).*
— *WB II 50, 1.* *(qtd 2&3 by [Nevill], Ld
Fawconbryg).*
— *WB I 16, 14.* *(a&l Gu).*
— *PLN 187.* *(qtd 2&3 by [Neville] with
mullet of 6 pts Gu on salt).*
— *I2(1904)103.* *(langued Gu; qtg 2&3 Gu
on salt Arg roundel Sa, all qtd II by Ld
Conyers).*
— *XK 134.* *(qtd II 1&4 by Sir Thos Borough
or Burgh).*
— *BA 729.* *(qtd 3 by Ld Conyars).*
— *XX 97.* *(qtd 2&3 by Nevile, Ld Faucon-
bridge).*
— *ML I 249.* *(armed Sa; 'Sylver a lion ram-
pant asur enarmyd sabyll').*
— *BA 719.* *(qtd 4 by Strangwayes).*
— *BA 1053 & 1054.* *(qtd 4 by Courtenay, E
of Devon).*
— *XL 220.* *(qtd II 2&3 by Strangways).*
— *L10 36, 16.* *(qtd II 2&3 by Conyers).*
— *BA 620.* *(qtd II 2&3 by Conyers).*
— *D4 28b & 34.* *(subimp by Bulmer, Yorks).*
— *BR VI 37.* *(marshalled by Ld Falcon-
berg).*
— *KB 293.* *(qtd 2&3 by Nevyll, Ld Fawcon-
berge).*
— *WK 747.* *(qtd II 2&3 by Wm, Ld
Conyers).*
— *('Le C de ...'; coat unclear). NB 12.*
BRAYTOFT. *L10 79, 12.* *(a&l Gu).*
BRAYTOFT, Le bone W. *WJ 280.*
BRAYTOFT, William. *XL 136.* *(langued Sa).*
BRUITOFT, William. *PCL I 547.*
BRUS, Piers. *P 96.*
BRUS, Piers. *B 48.*
BRUYS, Mons', de Skelton. *TJ 22.* *(& Fau-
comberge).*
BRUYS, Ld of Skelton, Yorks. *L2 90, 9.*
(a&l Gu).

BYRNELL. *L10 31b, 11. (a&l Gu).*
CLAVERYNGE, Jhon de. *Q 438.*
CREICHTON, Ld. *Lyndsay 117.*
CRETHON, the Lord. *(a&l Gu). SC 38.*
CREYCHTOUN, of Strathurde. *Lyndsay 349.*
[CRICHTON]. *Lyndsay 121. (qtd by Ld
Creichtoun of Sanquhar).*
[CRICHTON, of Cairns]. *Berry; Stodart 7.
(qtg 2&3 [Ceulx de carmes, ie Cairns]).*
CRICHTON, of Nachtane. *Lyndsay 209.*
CRISTON, ceulx de. *Berry; Stodart 7.*
CROCHTON, of Sanchar. *SC 103. (a&l Gu).*
EGREMOND. *L2 179, 12. (?langued Or).*
ESPAINE, le roy d'. *C 4. (qtg Gu castle Or).*
FACOMBERGE, Monsire de. *AN 86.*
FACONBERGE. *ME 78; LY A 203.*
FACONBERGE. *PT 354.*
FACONBERGE, Monsire de. *CG 44.*
FACONBREGE, Le Sr de. *AS 21.*
FALCONBRIDGE, Wm Nevil, Ld. *WGA 239.*
FAUCO(n)berge, S Walter. *BR IV 30.*
FAUCONBERG. *PV 69.*
[FAUCONBERG]. *CKO 81.*
FAUCONBERG, Walter de. *XL 128.*
FAUCONBRIDGE, The Lorde. *LD 10.
(qrs1&4).*
FAUCOUNBERGE, Sire Wauter. *N 133.*
FAUKONBERGE, Le Sr de. *S 78.*
FAWCOMBRYGE. *Ll 245, 1; L2 202, 6. (a&l
Gu).*
FAWCONBERGH, Ld. *RH, Ancestor iv 231.
(qtg [Nevill]).*
FFAUCONBRGE, Mons Waut. *WJ 269.*
FFAUCUNBERGE, Sire Walter. *PO 194.
(langued Gu; 'facombrige' superscribed by
slightly later hand).*
GALLEWAIT, Le Cont de. *FF 9.*
GONNEBY, S Robert de. *GA 84.*
HANLON, Sir John. *LH 181.*
NEVIL, Ld Fauconberg. *CRK 282. (qrs
1&4).*
[NEVILE], Ld Facombriges. *BW 10b, 62. (qtd
2&3).*
NEVILL, Sir Wm, KG. *Leake. c1440. (qtd
1&4 by Sir Wm N in right of w Joan, d&h of
Thos, Ld Fauconberg).*
[NEVILL, Sir Wm, Ld Fauconberg], KG.
*Leake. (qtg 2&3 Gu on salt Arg pd mullet
Gu for Nevill). (d1463-4).*
PERCY. *Brit Arch Assoc xl 400. (qtd 2&3
Gu 3 lucies Arg; effigy of Anne, w of Sir
Lawrence Reynsford (d1490) & dau of Hen,
2nd E of Northd). (window, Long Melford,
Suff).*
PERCY, E of Northd. *XB 15. (qr I 1).
(?d1537, but prob his f who d1527).*
VELDENS, Count of. *XL 435.*

Arg lion Gu &c
Arg lion Gu
— *WK 478. (qtd 2&3 by Sir Jn Treveynon).*
— *PLN 157. (qtd 3 by Sir Ric Wydevill).*
— *LE 261. (lion poss Purp). (qtd 4 by Dns
Johes de ?Tinan).*
— *Lyndsay 19. (qtd by The King of
[Spain]).*
— *WB IV 158b, 590. (qtd 2 by Wadhyll).*
— *LE 257. (qtd III 2 by Phle duc de Bour-
goigne).*
— *XF 598. (qtd 2&3 by Sir Jn Trevannion).*
— *I2(1904)180. (qtd 13 by 'Syr Rychard
Grenevile, Knyght' added by Jos Holland
c1630).*
— *Lyndsay 21. (qtd by The Kyng of [Cas-
till]).*
— *Lyndsay 27. (qr IV 2 of coat imp by The
Kyng off Romanes).*
— *CRK 576. (qtd II&III 1 by Montferrant).*
— *Keepe 241. 1296. (enamelled sh formerly
on ledge of tomb, of Wm de Valence).*
— *WB I 33, 16. (qtd 2&3 by Boteler).*
— *PLN 931. (qtd 2 by Wodhull).*
— *PCL IV 89. (D of ?Nawelis).*
— *PCL IV 143. (escutch of Ld Lowell).*
— *PLN 1918. (qtd 6 by K of Spain).*
— *WGA 32. (qtd III 2 by Duc Charlis Vic-
torious, of Burgoigne).*
— *L10 104, 10. (qtd 2&3 by De La Mote).*
— *LD 122.*
— *Nichols Leics II 262. ('a bishop is kneel-
ing near these arms'; window, Melton
Mowbray Ch).*
— *WB I 33b, 14. (qtd 3 by George Vernon,
of Nether Haddon).*
— *XK 116. (qtd 2&3 by Sir Jn Trevanion,
Kt, 1509).*
— *WB II 58, 15. (qtd 4 by [Mychell]).*
— *CB 428. (qtd 2&3 by Regnault, seigneur
de Brederode).*
— *Gelre 58b. (imp lozy Gu and Arg; 'die
here van der SR...').*
— *LD 97. (imp by Caston).*
— *KB 33. (qtd III 2 by D of Burgon).*
— *LD 25. (qtd 2&3 by [Butler]).*
— *PLN 157b. (qtd 3 by Master Jn Wyde-
vill).*
— *PLN 155. (qtd 3 by Wydevill, all imp by
Bourchier, E of Essex).*
— *PLN 154. (qtd 3 by Wydevill, all imp by
E of Arundel).*
ARMONIE, K of. *KB 29. (dex of coat tierced
in pale).*
ASTELEY. *L10 2, 17. (a&l Or).*
ASTELEY. *CB 221. (Legh of High Lee added
in Elizabethan hand).*
BOKYNGHAM, of Suff. *Ll 111, 1; L2 76, 6.
(armed Or).*

BOKỲNGHAM, of Suss. *MY 332.* *(a&l Or).*
CASTILE, K of. *Llanstephan 46 105, 7.* *('dan lew mywn arian a dan dwr sieckroc mywn sabl nei liw du dygỳmysg' (2 lions Arg & 2 towers checky Sa or pure black); qtg 2&3 Sa tower checky Untinc; 'Roi de Kastilion vel de Leons' alias "Grenin Kastel nei y llewod").*
DONDAS, Ceulx de. *Berry; Stodart 7.*
DUNDAS, o yt ilk. *SC 88.* *(a&l Az).*
DUNDAS, of that ilk. *Lyndsay 243.* *(armed Az).*
ESTLE. *LE 20.* *(a&l Az).*
HAUERING. *L1 326, 1.*
HILTON. *ME 103; LY A 228.*
HOUNS, John. *CA 224.* *(?recte Horn).*
HYLTONE. *FK II 707.*
LAMERE. *CT 438.*
LASCY. *L9 36b, 6.*
LEGH, of High Legh. *L2 304, 7.* *(a&l Vt).*
LEGH, John de, de Legh. *PCL II 88.*
[LEINSTER]. *DX 49.* *(armed Az).*
LEVERYCH, Duk, de la Marche. *WJ 31.*
LEVERYCHE, Duc, de la Marche. *XL 403.*
LEVERYCHE, duc de la Marche. *L9 34a, 6.*
LOVETOFT. *Leake.* *(?per fess Gu and Sa; qtd 9 by Francis Talbot, KG, d1559).*
LYONS. *L9 36a, 9.* *(a&l Az).*
LYONS, Mons J de. *WJ 201.*
LYONS, John de. *XL 339.*
LYONS, Sir John de, of Northants. *WB III 82, 1.* *(a&l Az).*
LYOUNS. *SK 247.*
LYOUNS, Mons John de. *SD 131.*
LYOUNUS, S Jon. *PO 336.*
MAHAWTE, Costantyne. *RH, Ancestor iv 245.* *(?surmounted by fess).*
LA MERE. *L9 37b, 4.* *(a&l Az).*
MERE, le. *RB 489.* *(lion ramp embelif).*
MONHAUT, Adam. *Q II 44.*
NONAUNT, Willame de. *LM 501.*
NOROVAIGE, le roy de. *LM 27.*
OGILWY, of Ochterhouss. *Lyndsay 336.*
PETIT. *L1 497, 1.*
PETIT. *XL 256.* *(a&l Or; tail turned outwards).*
PETYT. *BA 957.* *(a&l Or).*
POROCE, le rey de. *LM 24.*
STRECH. *PT 324.*
STYWARD. *L1 584, 1.*
TALBOT, John. *PLN 710.* *(a&l Az).*
TERBERVILE, Hue de. *F 35.*
TORBEVILE, Huge de. *A 156.*
TURBERVILE. *CV-BM 120.*
TURBERVILE, Hue. *D 96a.*
TURBERVILE, Hue. *D 77.*
TURBERVILE, Munsire Hue. *D 96b.*
TURBERVILL, Hawe de. *LM 85.*
TURBERVILL, Herre. *PCL I 476.* *(a&l Or).*
TURBERVILL, Hue de. *LM 147.*

TURBERVILLE. *CV-BM 317.*
TURBERVILLE, de. *Soc Jers 1928.* *(Warden of Jersey 1268-70).*
TURBERVILLE, Hugo. *Q II 122.*
TURBERVILLE, Sr Hugo de. *WLN 366.*
VIVIAN. *BA 955.* *(a&l Sa; traces of wavy marks Az in base).*
VUIYAN, of Cornw. *L1 661, 4.* *(a&l Sa).*

Arg lion Or
LYNDE. *ML I 540.*

Arg lion Purp
Arg lion Purp
— *SP A 6.* *(qtd 2&3 by Spain).*
— *CRK 1401.* *(a&l Az; lion embelif; qtd 2&3 by K of Spain).*
— *WGA 161.* *(qtd I 2&3 by [Ferdinand 5, K of Castile]).*
— *Lancs 1533 CS 98, 101.* *(qtd 2 by Sir Alexr Osbaldeston).*
— *XL 420.* *(a&l Az; qtd 2&3 by K of Spain).*
— *PLN 1918.* *(qtd 2 by K of Spain).*
— *XB 28.* *(qtd by Catherine of Aragon).*
BALDERSTON, Mons Richard. *TJ 147.* *(gloss on Mons Robt le fitz Roger).*
BALDIRSTONE. *PT 1178.*
BALDRESTON, Mons Richard de. *TJ 79.*
CLEVISBY, Sir Johan, de Dene. *N 801.*
DENE. *BA 576.*
DENE, Sr Johan. *N 831.*
DENE, of Leics. *L1 204, 6; L2 156, 6.*
DENE, of Leics. *BA 31, 280.* *(a&l Az).*
LASCY, John de. *XL 439.* *(a&l Gu).*
LEON. *PLN 596.* *(qtg 2&3 Castile).*
LEON. *Sandford 70.* *(qtd 2 by Alfonso IX, K of Castile & Leon).*
[LEON]. *FK I 21.* *(qtd 2&3 by K of Spain).*
[LEON]. *WestmAbb.* *(?lion Gu; qtd by [Castile] imp France ancient qtg Engld, for [Joan de la Tour, w of Pedro of Castile, dau of Edw 3]; small enamelled shield on tomb of Edw 3, d1377).*
[LEON]. *TJ 2.* *c149.* *(qtd 2&4 by le Roy de Espayne).*
[LEON]. *WLN 5.* *(qtd II & III by Le Roy de Spayne).*
[LEON]. *Neale & Brayley.* 13 cent. *(qtd by [Castile] for [Eleanor of Castile]; mont to Aveline of Lancaster d1273).*
[LEON]. *Neale & Brayley.* 1296. *(?lion Sa; qtd by [Castile] for Q Eleanor on mont of Edm, E of Lancaster).*
LEON, Isabel of Castile &. *Sandford 377-8.* *(m Edm, D of York, d1402; qtd by Castile & all imp by Plantagenet).*
NYCHOLLE, E of. *BR V a 4.*
ROGER, Mons Robert le fitz. *TJ 147.*
ROGER, Sire Robert le fitz. *J 25.*

ROGER, Robt le fiz. *Q 137.*
SPAIN. *LMS 4. (as painted; qtg Gu castle Or).*
SPAIN, K of. *PLN 1161. (qtg 2&3 Gu tower triple towered Or).*
STORY, Sr Robert. *Kent Gentry 217b. (armed Az).*

Arg lion Sa
Arg lion Sa
— *SC 36. (a&l Gu; qtd 2&3 by The lord Lassly).*
— *WK 474. (qtd 2&3 by Sir Thos Metam).*
— *CB 394. (imp by [Mortimer]).*
— *SHY 478. (...eynt; qtg.... & imp Hastings).*
— *SHY 454. (lion unclear; qtg of 4 lozs). (....nyell; qtg... & imp Letice).*
— *ML I 202. (lion's mouth closed; '[Miles] ix us. Argent un lion le bowche muett comme rampaunt sabill').*
— *CRK 1154. (qtg 2&3 Per pale Vt and Or cross moline Gu).*
— *ML I 208. (lion biting forepaws; '[Miles] XV us. Argent un lion son dextre pe mordaunt comme rampaunt sabill').*
— *SC 22. (a&l Gu; lion shd be Az; qtd 2 by [Crichton], E of Caithness).*
— *BA 696. (qtd 4 by [Moresby], imp by Pikering).*
— *WB I 41, 16. (qtd 2&3 by Sir G Clyfton).*
— *BA 20, 167. (qtd 2&3 by Whittyngton of Stannton).*
— *1H7 1. (qtd by Pyckeryng at Master Westons).*
— *I2(1904)284. (armed Or, langued Gu; qtd 5 by Sir Rychard Cromwell alias Rechar Wylliams Knight).*
— *I2(1904)180. (qtd 3 by Bamfeld of Poltemore in Devon; added by Jos Holland c1630).*
— *XK 112. (qtd 2&3 by Sir Thos Metham, Kt 1509).*
— *Arch Journ (Chichester 1853) 95. c1530. (?one of the Sibyls; Amberley Castle, Suss).*
— *XL 581. (qtd 2&3 by Sir Gervaise Clifton).*
— *PLN 1638. (qtg 2&3 Sa mullet Arg). (qtg Breton).*
— *SHY 458. (imp by [?Calthorpe]).*
— *BG 341. (qtd 2&3 by K of Spain).*
— *D4 29b. (qtd3 by Clyfton, of Durham).*
— *PLN 1868.*
— *H21 21. (qtd by Clyfton).*
— *Dingley cxlvi. (S chancel window, Eardisland Ch, Herefs).*
— *WLN 503.*
— *WLN 18. (escutch of Burgundy).*
— *PCL IV 16. (qtd 2&3 by K of Spayne).*
— *LD 40. (a&l Gu).*

— *D4 38b. (qtd by Meytam, of Meytam, Yorks).*
— *L10 92, 3. (qtd 5 by Cromwell als Williams).*
— *Lyndsay 68. (qtd by Leslie, E of Rothes).*
BLAKE, John 'of the [Walysh]'. *PLN 1171.*
BURNEL, Philippus. *Q II 154.*
BURNELL, Phelip. *LM 151.*
[CRESSY]. *Brit Arch Assoc 3S 207-8; MGH 5S, 167. c1330. (glass, S Newington, Oxfs).*
DESMAREYS, Sr Herbert. *L 190.*
DESPAGNE, Le Roy. *P 5. (qtg 2&3 Gu castle Or).*
FENES, Sire Johan de. *N 1053.*
FINEUX, of Essex. *L2 209, 4.*
FRESNES. *PLN 586. (armed Gu).*
GENEVA, Peter de. *MP I 87. (small sh below 1 of normal size [Sa lion Arg]). (d1249).*
HAILL. *XL 625.*
[LEON]. *OxfRS I 29. (qtd by Castile; glass, Banbury, Oxfs).*
LODELAWE, S Th de. *R 26.*
LUDLOWE. *PT 646.*
LUDLOWE, S John de, Salop. *CY 84, 334.*
LUDLOWE, Sir John de, of Salop. *CV-BM 165. (both eyes visible, triple tongue - ?tyger).*
MONPEYZON, Sir Gyles. *BR V 130. (shd be ch on shldr with 'pinson' or finch).*
MONPYSSON, John. *PLN 529.*
MONTPYNSON, of Norf. *L1 425, 3; L2 327, 11. (a&l Gu).*
MORLEY, Le Sire de. *TJ 85. (painted with crown Or).*
MORLEY, le Sire de. *TJ 86.*
NICOLE, le counte de. *LM 42.*
ROGER, Roberd fiz. *FW 606.*
ROGER, Robert fitz. *A 164.*
RYHULL, Michel de. *LM 339.*
SPAIN. *LMS 4. (qtg Gu castle Or; as blazoned).*
SPAIN. *LMRO 4. (lion painted Purp; qtg 2&3 Gu castle Or; 'Roy daspanie porte lescu quartile de arget et de gules a deus leonces de sabel e deus cha... de or').*
SPAIN, King of. *LO B 36. (qrs1&4).*
SPAYNE. *CK a 59. (qrs 1&4).*
STAPALTON, Mons Miles de. *S 120.*
STAPELLTON. *DV 63a, 2489. (armed Gu).*
STAPELTON, Sire Milis de. *PO 231. (langued Gu).*
STAPELTON, Monsr Nichol de. *AS 157. (armed Gu langued Or; 'dargent lion rampant de sable flote dor arme de goul'; 'flote' here reads to mean "tongued", for in CG we find "Monsire Nicholas de Stapleton port dargent a une lyon rampant de sable langue dor ungle et arme de gules").*
STAPELTON, Mons Nicol de. *TJ 30. (armed*

Gu).

STAPELTONE, Sire Miles de. *N 726.*
('...rampaund...').

STAPILLTON. *CT 154.*

STAPILTON, Sir Bryan. *WK 430.*

STAPILTON, My. *NS 119.*

STAPILTON, Mons Myles, de Haddilsay. *WJ 309.*

STAPILTON, of Notts. *D4 23.*

STAPILTON, of Wighill, Yorks. *D4 25b.*

STAPLETON. *PT 505.*

STAPLETON. *LS 61. (a&l Gu).*

STAPLETON. *L1 614, 3. (a&l Gu).*

STAPLETON, Sir. *BB 57. (d1364).*

STAPLETON, Sr de. *CKO a 39.*

[STAPLETON]. *BK 61. (qtg 2 Per pale Or and Vt cross moline Gu [Ingham], 3 Gu chev betw 3 5foils Or [Bardolf], 4 Or 3 bars Gu [Fitzalan]; , mp by Harcourt (for Joan S, w of Chris H whose s was knighted 1513-4) in margin beside standard of S'r Harcourt).*

[STAPLETON]. *Coll T&G i, 40, note. 1503. (imp by Peyrs Freshevile; mont, Staveley, Derbs).*

STAPLETON, Sir Brian. *XL 223.*

STAPLETON, Sir Brian. *BW 17b, 118.*

STAPLETON, Bryan. *PLN 1198.*

STAPLETON, Sir Bryan. *XL 187.*

STAPLETON, Sir Bryan, KG. *Dingley cccccxv. (qtg Barry Or and Gu for [Fitzalan of Bedale]; all within Garter; Lacock Ch, Wilts).*

STAPLETON, Sir Bryan & his bro Sir Miles S, KG. *S&G II 290. (ch on shldr with pd mullet Gu).*

STAPLETON, Miles. *BG 312.*

STAPLETON, Miles de. *CV-BM 99.*

STAPLETON, Miles, Ld. *S 122.*

STAPLETON, Sir Miles. *PT 1015.*

STAPLETON, Sir Miles. *CRK 1006.*

STAPLETON, S Miles de, of Norf. *CY 113, 450.*

STAPLETON, Monsire Nicholas de. *CG 83. (armed Gu langued Or).*

STAPULTON. *WB I 14b, 22. (with many qtgs).*

STAPULTON, Mons Bryan. *BB 100, 3. (d1394).*

STAPULTON, [Sir Bryan]. *I2(1904)102. (langued Gu, qtg II qtly 1 Barry nebuly of 4 Or and Gu, 2 Az fess dancetty betw 10 billets Or, 3 Arg lion Sa a&l Gu border Az, 4 Az semy de lis lion Arg, III Qtly 1, 2&3 [imperfect], 4 qtly Gu and Or, IV Arg chev Sa in dex chf pd 5foil Sa).*

STAPULTON, Sir Miles. *Leake. c1421. (founder KG; d1364).*

STAPULTON, of Suss. *MY 326.*

STAPULTONE, Brian. *Q II 626. (a&l Gu).*

STAPULTONE, Sir Bryan. *BA 601. (a&l Gu).*

STAPYLTON. *WK 416-7.*

STAPYLTON, Sir M. *WB I 37b, 6.*

STAPYLTON, Sir Bryan of. *WB IV 144b, 341. (a&l Gu; qrs 1&4).*

TRISTRAM, Sir. *PLN 999.*

VAUGHAN, John. *GutchWdU.* temp Hen 7. *(Fellow of All Souls; formerly in window, Old Cloister, All Souls).*

WAKEFARE, Sr de. *CKO a 49.*

Arg lion to sin Sa

— *ML I 205. ('[Miles] xij us. Argent un lion endorsed comme rampaunt sabill').*

STAPLETON, Ld Miles. *BD 159b. (within Garter; 2nd window to W, St Geo's Ch, Stanford, Lincs).*

Arg lion Vt

Arg lion Vt

— *SussASColls xxix 26, 38. (qtd 2&3 by Robert Sherborne, Bp of Chichester 1508-36).*

SCHERBOURNE. *L1 580, 6.*

SHERBURN, Sir Richard, of Stonyhurst. *XL 251. (qrs 1&4).*

SHERBURNE, Sir Rich, of Stonyhurst. *BA 36b, 3&8. (qtg [Bailey]).*

SPRING. *GutchWdU.* c1530. *(qtd 2&3 by Robt Sherburne, Bp of Chichester, d1536; window, Hall, New College).*

SPRING, Sire Johan. *N 727.*

SPRING, John. *XL 448.*

SPRING, Sir John. *XL 194. (a&l Az).*

SPRINGE. *L1 614, 4.*

SPRYNGES, Mons J. *WJ 356.*

TOWCH, of that ilk. *Lyndsay 388. (armed Gu; other Mss make lion passt or salient).*

Az lion Arg

Az lion Arg

— *WB I 38b, 25. (qtd 2&3 by Sir J Colvyle).*

— *ML I 217. ('a lyon rampawnt').*

— *WB I 17, 15. (qtd by Corwyn).*

— *L10 71, 6. (escutch of Ld Jas Stanley, Bp of Ely).*

— *DX 53. (?Fitzhamon).*

— *WB IV 127b, 33a. (escutch of 'the Erle my lord of Darby').*

— *BA 34b, 331. (a&l Gu; escutch of Ld Jas Stanley, Bp of Ely).*

— *WGA 203. (escutch of George (Stanley), Ld Strange).*

— *A 212.*

— *BA 34b, 329. (a&l Gu). (escutch of George (Stanley), Ld Strange).*

— *WB I 36b, 5. (qtd 5 by Richd Bolles).*

— *WK 186. (escutch of Sir Thos Stanley).*

— *WB IV 157, 562. (qtd 2&3 in dex imp of Thos Marnett [or Garnet]).*

— *WK 157. (escutch of Stanley).*
— *CRK 1838. (qtd 2&3 by Sir T Tring).*
— *(?Grey). ML I 40.*
ATLEE. *L2 9, 2. (a&l Gu).*
ATTELLE. *CB 116. (a&l Gu). ('Atte Lle').*
BOYLOND, Sir Robert, of Suff. *WB III 72, 5. (a&l Gu; qtg 2&3 Sa eagle Arg baston Gu).*
BRIAN, M de. *WNR 166.*
BRUN, Sire Richard. *N 1063. (armed Gu).*
BRUNE, Monsire de. *CG 53. (tail erect).*
COLEVILE, John. *S 165.*
COLVILE, John. *BG 112.*
COLVYLE, Sir John, of Norf. *WB III 74b, 6. (a&l Gu; qrs 1&4).*
DALTON. *L10 53, 12. (a&l Gu).*
DALTON. *PT 1109.*
FITZSYMOUND, Mons Rauf. *WJ 283.*
[GALLOWAY]. *Lyndsay 90. (qtd by Douglas, E of Wigtown).*
[GALLOWAY]. *Lyndsay 59. (qtd by Douglas, E of Douglas).*
GERRADE, Thomas. *WB III 102, 3.*
GREY, Ld. *ML II 39.*
HETON, Mons Henry de. *S 169.*
KYNARDESLEY. *L2 289, 4.*
LEE, W Atte. *SK 159.*
MOAUT. *NS 6.*
MOHANT, Roger. *PCL I 520.*
MOHAUD, Sire Robert. *PV 44.*
MOHAUT. *CT 37.*
MOHAUT, de. *CV-BM 74.*
MOHAUT, le Sire de. *WJ 281.*
MOHAUT, Robert de. *H 15a.*
MOHAUT, Robert de. *SP A 81.*
MOHAUT, Sr Robert. *H 15b.*
MOHAUT, Rog de. *Q 87.*
MOHAUT, Roger de. *G 61.*
MOHAUT, Roger de. *HE 95.*
MOHAUTE, Robert le. *FF 22.*
MONALT. *Sandford 329. (escutch of Thos Stanley, E of Derby, 3rd husb of Mgt Beaufort, d1509).*
MONHALT, D of Kent. *CRK 583.*
MONHAUT. *L9 69a, 6.*
MONHAUT. *WLN 225.*
MONHAUT, Le Sr de. *CN 49.*
MONHAUT, Sr R de. *RB 30.*
MONHAUT, Sr Robart. *BR V 16.*
MONHAUT, Robert de. *K 7.*
MONHAUT, Sire Robert de. *N 48.*
MONHAUT, Roger le. *B 98.*
MONHAUTE, Roger de. *E 52.*
MONHAUTE, Sr Roger de. *I 11.*
MONTALT. *Leake. (escutch (as local feudal arms) of Sir Edw Stanley, KG, d1524).*
[MONTALT]. *Farrer II 324. (window, Snetis-ham Ch, Norf).*
MONTALT, Robert de. *K 70.*
MONTALT, Robert de. *LMS 64. (d1329).*

MONTEALTY. *Gerard 152.*
MONTHALT, Sr de. *CKO a 34.*
MONTHAULT, Baron. *CKO a 36.*
MOUHAUT, Robert de. *F 188.*
MOUNTHAULT. *L2 322, 12. (a&l Gu).*
MUHAUT, Roger de. *FW 124.*
MUHAUTE, Mons Robert de. (or Jn de Orton). *TJ 51.*
MUNHAUT, Roger de. *D 228a.*
OCHTERLONYE, of Kellye. *Lyndsay 353.*
PALGRAVE. *L9 93b, 1.*
PALGRAVE. *L1 501, 2.*
PULL, S John de, of Ches. *CY 15, 57.*
WIKES, Richard de. *F 480.*
WYKES, Richard de. *WLN 495.*
WYKES, Richard de. *CV-BM 234.*

Az lion standing on dex paw Arg
— *ML I 226. ('A lyon rampaunt per pee cynestre or one pe cynystr' [standing on right hind paw with left raised]).*

Az lion to sin Arg
— *ML I 228. ('a lyon rampaewnd endorsed').*

Az lion Gu
Az lion Gu
[BARRES, Jean de, Seigneur d'Oissorey]. *MP I 89. (dimidg Or cross recercly Sa; 'Per unum istud scutum accipe scuta Barrensium, scilicet nobilium Francorum'; death on Crusade of many French nobles in Cyprus &c, 1249).*

Az lion Or
Az lion Or
— *WLN 107.*
— *PT 474.*
— *BD 158b. (Garter badge on mantle; ?for Sir Otes Holand; 2nd W window, St Georges Ch, Stanford, Lincs).*
— *WJ 113.*
— *WJ 109.*
— *BR II 3. (qtd 2&3 by D of Burgoyne).*
— *Proc Soc Antiq XV 2S 267.* 13 cent. *(Limoges enamelled plate).*
— *BR VI 2. (marshalled by Ld Beaumont).*
— *WGA 51. (imp by Wm, D of Gelder).*
BILNEVOWE, S Piers de. *GA 127.*
BRAMPTON. *L1 39, 6; L2 50, 5. (a&l Gu).*
BRAMTON. *L10 80, 12. (a&l Gu; dex imp).*
BRAMTON. *L10 76b, 25. (langued Or, sans claws).*
BREWS, S Tho de, of Norf. *CY 125, 500.*
[BURGUNDY, Palatinate]. *Proc Soc Antiq XXXII 2S 134.* post 1309. *(on leg of candlestick originally enamel of which presumably enough remains to identify colours).*
CHAMPNEYS. *L2 111, 4. (a&l Gu q.f.).*

CHAMPNEYS. *L1 149, 6. (a&l Gu).*

DARELL, Sir Jorge. *WB IV 139, 245. (& Carowe; qr 1).*

DARRALL, Sir Emonde, of Yorks. *RH, Ancestor iv 238.*

DARRELL. *GY b 18.*

LEYTON, Sir J. *PLN 1759. (qtg 2 Or lion Gu border engr Az, 3&5 qtly per fess of 2 indents Gu and Or lion pg Arg in dex canton, 4 Gu 6 pears 3, 2, 1 pendant slipped Or, 6 Arg 3 boars' heads couped Sa).*

NEIVILE, Joan de. *E 56.*

NEVELL, Sir John, of Essex. *WB III 78b, 3. (a&l Gu).*

NEVILE, Hugo de. *C 133.*

NEVILL, Monsire le, of Essex. *CG 39.*

NEVILL, S Hugh de. *GA 99.*

NEVILL, Sr Hugh de, de Essex. *CKO a 31.*

NEVILL, Monsr J, de [?Essex]. *AS 369.*

NEVILLE, Mons John, de Essex. *TJ 55.*

NEVYLE, Sir Jon, of Essex. *PO 398. (langued Gu; 'of' interpolated in Elizabethan hand).*

NEVYLL. *L9 82a, 2.*

NEYVILE, Sire Hue de. *N 113.*

NEYVILLE. *L2 359, 1.*

PAYLLE, Syr Raff. *WB IV 167, 746.*

PERCIE, E of Northumberland. *KB 264. (qrs1&4).*

PERCY, William de. *XL 407.*

PYKENHAM. *WB IV 154, 507.*

PYKKYNHAM. *L2 402, 3.*

SCROPE, Lord, Kt 1509. *XK 96. (qrs 1&4).*

SNOWDEN. *BG 449.*

SNOWDUN, Hugh, of Ches. *WB III 111, 3.*

STEPELTON. *CT 171.*

SURIE, le Roy de. *LM 11.*

TALBOT, 'Erle of Shesbury'. *ML II 15. (qr 1).*

WILFORD. *CRK 1184.*

Gu lion Arg

Gu lion Arg

— *KB 61. (qtd 2&3 by Malgo, K of [Britain]).*

— *WB IV 173, 848. (qtd 2&3 by Ryther of Yorks).*

— *BR VI 31. (marshalled by Ld Delaware).*

— *XB 7, 38. (qtd by Howard).*

— *XK 66. (qtd 4 by Thos Howard, KG, temp Hen 8).*

— *PLN 2034. (qtd 3 by Sir Edmond Gorge).*

— *E 290. (?lion salient; arms of Mowbray, but probably leaping lion of Merk).*

— *PLN 1565. (qtd 2&3 by Ryther).*

— *CC 230, 270. (qtd 2&3 by Beauchamp [Gu fess betw 6 billets Or]).*

— *WK 464. (qtd 4 by Sir Morice Barkeley).*

— *PLN 1108. (qtd 2&3 by ҫtly 1&4 Arg cross moline Gu, 2&3 Az fretty Or).*

— *BA 696. (qtd III 1&4 by [Moresby] imp by Pikering).*

— *WB I 14b, 22. (qtd I 4 by Stapulton).*

— *S 35. (qtd 2&3 by Thos, Ld Mowbray).*

— *WB II 58, 16.*

— *XK 102. (qtd 4 by Sir Maurice Berkeley, Kt 1509).*

— *WB I 31, 5. (qtg 2 Arg 2 bars Az, 3 ?Erm salt Untinc).*

— *XK 257. (qtd 3 by of Sir Edm Howard).*

— *WB I 25b, 7. (qrs 2&3 of Gu 9 roundels & chf Or). (coat imp by Lymogys).*

— *1H7 1. (qtd 4 by Dennys; at Master Westons).*

— *WB IV 144b, 341. (a&l Az; qtd 2&3 by Sir Bryan of Stapylton).*

— *PV 72. (?field Or).*

— *L10 26b, 10. (qtd 2&3 by Beawchamp).*

— *L10 6b, 24. (qtd 2&3 by Cusack).*

ANGUS, E of. *SC 7.*

ANGUS, Le Conte de. *Berry; Stodart 1. (qtd 2&3 by Douglas).*

ARUNDELL, le counte de. *LM 43.*

BOULOGNE. *MP I 93. ('Comitis Bolonie').*

[BRITAIN], K Engest panim. *KB 51. (coat per fess, in base Arg on bend Sa 3 martlets Arg).*

DOUGLAS, E of Angus. *Lyndsay 60. (qr 1).*

DOUGLAS, E of Angus. *XFB 23. (a&l Or; qr1).*

[DUNBAR], le Counte Patriz. *C 61. (d1289).*

[FITZALAN]. *PLN 1971. (qtd 2 by E of Surrey).*

GARNONS, Sir Randol. *CVC 444.*

GERNONS, Randle, E of Chester. *TJ 11. (tail estant).*

GERNONS, Randolf. *TJ 1225. ('le quart Conte de Chestre son fitz').*

GERNUZ, Ranulph. *CY 2, 7. (3rd E of Chester after Conquest).*

GRAY, Master of. *Berry; Stodart 3. (border engr omitted).*

GRYFFYTH, Mathew, of Herts. *WB III 90, 8. (qrs 1&4).*

[HOME], ceulx de dunegles. *Berry; Stodart 6. (qtd 1&4 by Pepdie; Gu lion Arg is coat of Dunbar, E of March, from whom the Homes claim descent, but the Homes have long borne field Vt).*

KENAN, Blethyn ap. *WK A 31.*

LAWARRE, Baron. *L2 302, 2. (a&l Az).*

MARCHALLE, le Count. *WLN 201.*

MARE, Mons John de la. *TJ 199. ('de goules a un leon leopard rampant dargent'; 'leon inserted above line').*

MAREYS, Geoffrey de. *MP I 68. ('Patris Willelmi [de Marisco] scilicet Galfridi'; d 1245).*

MAUBREY, Sir Roger. *FF 12.*

MERC, Will de. *F 445. (?lion salient).*

MERK, Ingram del. *C 154.*

MERKE, Willm de. *WLN 792. (lion is nei-ther rampant, salient, passt nor sejt; in F 445 lion is apparently salient).*

[MONTFORD], Erle of Leycetr. *BR IV 87. (should be qf).*

MOUBRAY. *CT 116.*

MOUBRAY. *WJ 141.*

MOUBRAY. *L1 630, 3. (armed Az).*

MOUBRAY, Le Sr de. *AS 34. (armed Or).*

MOUBRAY, Monsire de. *AN 29.*

MOUBRAY, Sr Jo de. *L 130.*

MOUBRAY, Sire Johann de. *J 87.*

MOUBRAY, Robert de. *F 38.*

MOUBRAY, S Robt de. *WLN 369.*

MOUBRAY, Rog de. *Q 35.*

MOUBRAY, Roger. *P 85.*

MOUBRAY, Sir Roger. *PCL I 454.*

MOUBREY, D of Norfolk, of Leics. *L1 421, 3; L2 321, 4. (armed Az).*

MOUBRAY, Roger de. *C 131. (d1297).*

MOUMBRAI. *SM 340, 60.*

MOUNBRAY, Sire Johan de. *N 40.*

MOWBRAY. *Leake. (qtd 4 by Thos Howard, KG, d1554).*

MOWBRAY. *L9 69a, 5. (a&l Az).*

MOWBRAY. *FC II 104.*

MOWBRAY. *PLN 1186. (a&l Az).*

MOWBRAY. *D13 104. (a&l Az). (qtd 3 by Howard).*

MOWBRAY. *Sandford 415. (old coat, dis-carded later for Brotherton).*

MOWBRAY. *WB II 51, 14.*

MOWBRAY, Ld. *BR VI 63.*

MOWBRAY, Ld. *ML I 23; ML II 24.*

MOWBRAY, Ld. *PLN 63.*

MOWBRAY, Ld. *CRK 1310. (a&l Az).*

MOWBRAY, Ld. *DX 24. (armed Az).*

MOWBRAY, Monsire de. *CG 40.*

MOWBRAY, Sr de. *CKO 32.*

MOWBRAY, de. *SP A 57.*

[MOWBRAY]. *Gelre 57. (die grave van Notingen).*

MOWBRAY, of Axholme. *Sandford 110.*

MOWBRAY, C of Nottingham. *XL 648.*

MOWBRAY, Dukes of Norfolk. *Sandford 205, 208.*

[MOWBRAY, Dukes of Norfolk]. *RH, Ances-tor iii 202. (armed Az; 'armyd wt azeure'; 'Erle Marchal Mowbray').*

MOWBRAY, John. *FC II 113.*

MOWBRAY, John, Ld. *Sandford 208. (d1369).*

MOWBRAY, Sr John. *M 2.*

MOWBRAY, John, Ld, E of Nottingham. *Sandford 208. (d1382).*

MOWBRAY, Nigel. *FC II 109.*

[MOWBRAY], Cont de Notingham, Count Marshall. *CN 20.*

MOWBRAY, Mons Roger de. *TJ 23.*

MOWBRAY, Roger de. *E 35.*

MOWBRAY, Roger de. *B 74. ('de gules od un leon d'argent').*

MOWBRAY, Roger de. *FC II 114.*

MOWBRAY, Roger de. *G 101.*

MOWBRAY, Roger de. *G 51.*

MOWBRAY, Roger. *LMS 62. (Roger M, d1297 or his s Jn, d1327).*

MOWBRAY, [Thomas Lord], E of Nottingham. *FK I 64.*

MOWBRAY, 'Sir Tomas, contte de Notynge-ham'. *BB 7, 127. (d1399).*

MOWBRAY, William de. *FC II 112.*

MOWBRAYE. *WB II 52, 14.*

MOWBRAYE, E of Nottingham. *KB 261.*

MUMBREY, Roger de. *A 203.*

MUNBRAI. *PO 20.*

MUNBRAY, Roger de. *FW 596.*

NERFORD, S' John, of Essex. *CY 136, 544.*

NOTTINGHAM, E of. *WLN 211.*

NOTYNGHAM, Le C de. *NB 21.*

NOTYNGHAM, Erl of. *BR II 48.*

[OLDHALL]. *PLN 1240. (a&l Az).*

OOKYNDONE, Nicol de. *Q 479.*

RYDER, Sir Ralph. *PLN 2042. (qtg Az 3 crescs Or).*

RYDER, Sir Robert. *XL 253. (qrs 1&4).*

RYDER, Sir Robt. *BA 626.*

SABARNE, D of. *WGB 138. (pedigree of Eliz Widvill).*

[SABRAN, D of]. *PLN 601. (a&l Az).*

SWELINGTON. *LD 31. (a&l Or; qr 2).*

WALES, of Cragy. *SC 68. (a&l Or).*

WALLACE, of Craigie. *Lyndsay 456.*

WARRE, Lord de. *WLN 219.*

WARRE, le Sr de la. *NB 57. (should be semy of crosses Arg but crosses have disappeared).*

WEKYNDON, ... de. *LM 261.*

Gu lion Az

Gu lion Az

[REVERS]. *PLN 1978. (qtd 2 by E of Devonshire).*

Gu lion Or

Gu lion Or

— *L9 44a, 9. (imp by Rowland Lenthall).*

— *I2(1904)97. (qtg Sa fret Or all qtd III by 'The Lord Wyllowby').*

— *WJ 388. (Mons'..., name erased).*

— *Hutton 24. (qtg Checky Or and Az). (qtd 4 by Ric Wingfield). (in N window of Gray's Inn c1619).*

— *WK 80. (qtd II&III 1&4 by Sir Antony Browne).*

— *KB 61. (sin imp of Malgo, K of Britain).*

— *PLN 2010. (qtg Sa fret Or; all qtd 2&3 by Sir Anthony Browne).*
— *Lambarde 253. (?Fitzalan).*
— *(?Fitzalan). Lambarde 210-213. (qtg [Maltravers]).*
— *PV 58. ([?Arundel]).*
— *XK 264. (cresc Untinc for diffce; qtd III 1&4 by Sir Jn Willoughby).*
— *WGA 171. (?Fitzalan; qtg 2&3 Sa fret Or).*
— *XK 132. (cresc Arg for diffce). (qtd III 1&4 by Sir Christopher Willoughby).*
ALBANY, d'. *WK 542. (later Arundel; qtd II 1&4 by Willoughby). MP Hist Min ii 477. ('Comes Harundeliae Hugo de Albineto', d 1243).*
ARANDELL, E of, of Suss. *MY 309.*
ARENDEAL, Die Grave van. *Gelre 56b. (qtg Warren).*
ARONDEL, Richart, le Conte de. *K 79.*
ARONDELL, Conte de. *CKO 29.*
ARONDELL, le Counte de. *L 151.*
ARONDELLE, E of. *PCL IV 84. (qrs1&4).*
ARRONDELL, E of. *RH, Ancestor iii 201.*
ARRONDELL, Co de. *DV 45b, 1798.*
ARRUNDELL, Count le. *RH, Ancestor iv 227.*
ARUNDEL. *SM 299, 48.*
ARUNDEL. *SK 50. (qrs 1&4; in qr 1 lion ch with annulet Sa on shldr).*
ARUNDEL. *(qtg Mautravers; various imps). L10 7, 6-9.*
ARUNDEL. *PO 9. (qtg [Warren]).*
ARUNDEL. *L10 2, 5. (qtg Checky Or and Az; qtg Maltravers, Sa fret Or).*
ARUNDEL, Counte de. *Q 20.*
ARUNDEL, E of. *BA 745.*
ARUNDEL, E of. *BR II 41. (qrs 1&4).*
ARUNDEL, E of. *BR V a 8.*
ARUNDEL, E of. *XL 211-3. (qtg Warren & Mautravers).*
ARUNDEL, E of. *BR IV 81.*
ARUNDEL, E of. *PLN 1967. (qtg 2&3 Sa fretty Or).*
ARUNDEL, E of. *WNS 25, 19. ('le Cunte de aendsle porte de gou ou un lion rampt dor').*
ARUNDEL, le Counte de. *RB 3.*
ARUNDEL, le Counte de. *N 12.*
ARUNDEL, Comes de. *LMO 47. (qtg checky Or and Az; Jn Fitzalan, Ld Mautravers, succeeded to Arundel Castle, 1415 but was not called E of Arundel & ref may be to one of his predecesors).*
ARUNDEL, E of, KG 1525, d1544. *WGA 206.*
ARUNDEL, le Conte d'. *E 13; F 24; HE 38; FW 55; G 41.*
ARUNDEL, le Count d'. *WJ 237.*
ARUNDEL, Edmund Fitzalan, E of. *LMS 33. (d1326).*
ARUNDEL, John, Count of. *FK I 57. (qrs 1&4).*

ARUNDEL, John, E of. *WGA 224.*
ARUNDEL, off Warren. *L10 2, 2. (qtg Checky Or and Az). WGA 247.*
ARUNDEL, Richard, E of. *K 495.*
ARUNDEL, Thomas, E of. *WGA 69. (qtg Matravers).*
ARUNDEL, Thomas Fitzalan of, Archbp of Canterbury 1397-1414. *GutchWdU. (a&l Az; qtg 2&3 Warren; all in border engr Arg; S window, Merton Coll Chapel).*
ARUNDEL, Thos, E of. *XB 13. (qrs 1&4; succeeded 1488, KG 1474, d1524).*
ARUNDEL, Sir William of. *WGA 14. (qtg Mautravers).*
ARUNDEL, Sir William of, KG. *XK 13. (qrs1&4).*
ARUNDEL, William, E of. *WGA 57. (qtg Matravers).*
ARUNDEL, William, E of, KG. *XK 82. (qr 1).*
ARUNDEL, Sir William, KG, d1400. *Leake. (qtg Maltravers).*
ARUNDEL, S Willm de, d1400. *BB 16.*
ARUNDELL. *CKO a 46.*
ARUNDELL. *L10 2, 1.*
ARUNDELL, Cont de. *CN 12.*
ARUNDELL, E. *L1 0, 3; L2 1, 1. (a&l Az).*
ARUNDELL, E of. *AY 22. (qtd by [Matravers]).*
ARUNDELL, E of. *BW 6, 25. (qrs1&4).*
ARUNDELL, E of. *WB I 48, 6.*
ARUNDELL, E of. *KB 246.*
ARUNDELL, de. *SP A 35.*
ARUNDELL, Comes de. *LMRO 20b, 47. (qtg Checky Or and Az).*
ARUNDELL, le Comte d'. *B 18.*
ARUNDELL, Le Counte d'. *TJ 14.*
ARUNDELL, Fitzallen. *RL 31, 2. (qtg Warren).*
ARUNDELL, Sir John of. *WK 56. (qrs 1&4; cresc Az in centre of qrs).*
ARUNDELL, Mons Rich. *T b 56. (qtg Sa fret Or; cresc Az over all).*
ARUNDELL, Thomas, E of. *I2(1904)175. (qtg 2 Barry of 8 Or and Gu, 3 Sa fret Or).*
ARUNDELL, Thomas, Archbp of Canterbury. *CVK 669. (qtg checky Or and Az, all in border engr Arg).*
BOHEMIA, K of. *LO B 44.*
BOLMEER, Die here van. *Gelre 58.*
BOURNUS, of Seygraw. *LO A 36.*
BREUUSE, M de. *WNR 105.*
[BRITAIN], K Gowan Saracin of. *KB 47. (qr1).*
BRITAIN, K Hungan of. *KB 200. (marshalled in base).*
BRITAIN, K Knoght of. *KB 221.*
BRITAIN, K Sweyn of. *KB 219.*

[BURGHERSH]. *DX 59.* *(armed Az).*

BURWACHE. *CT 448.* *(?qf).*

BYGOT, Hugh' le. *B 89.* *(tricked passt in B II).*

COLYNGRYGGE, W. *WB IV 152b, 483.* *(also Rafe Arondell; qrs 1&4).*

COMBLANDIE, Comes. *RL 42.* *(qtg checky Or and Az).*

DARONDELL, le Count. *CY 159, 633.*

DARONDELL, le Conte de, et de Warren. *S 32.* *('Fitzalan quarterly with Warenne').*

DARRUNDELL, le Counte. *AN 22.* *(qtg Warenne).*

DARUNDEL, Le Conte. *P 54.*

DARUNDEL, le Conte. *AS 31.* *(a&l Az).*

DARUNDEL, le Conte de. *AS 9.* *(armed B).*

DARUNDELL, le Counte. *CG 36.*

DARYNDELL, Le Cont. *WB V 13.*

DAUBENY, Hugh. *MP I 72; MP II 5; MP IV 57.*

DAUBENY, William. *MP I 36; MP IV 18.*

DAVERS, of Beds. *PLN 1778.* *(qtg 2 Arg on cross flory Az 5 fleurs de lis Or, 3 Gu chev betw 3 mullets Or, 4 Sa fess wavy Arg betw 6 martlets Gu).*

ESTOUN, John de. *WLN 774.* *(langued Arg).*

FELLBRUGGE, Sir Symon. *MK 8.*

FITZ ALAIN, Sr Richard, Counte de Arundell. *H 100b.*

FITZ ALEIN, Joh le. *B 88.*

FITZALAN. *Leake.* *(qtd I 2&3 by Sir Antony Browne, KG, d1548).*

FITZALAN. *Leake.* *(qtd by Maltravers in arms of Wm Arundel, KG, d1400).*

FITZALAN. *PLN 90.* *(qtg 2&3 Maltravers).*

FITZALAN. *Lambarde 3.* 1412. *(sin imp on brass to Sir Wm Echingham, & w Joan, dau of Jn Arundel, Ld Maltravers; dex imp lost; brass, Chancel, Etchingham, Suss).*

[FITZALAN]. *Neale & Brayley.* 1294. *(canopy of Mont to Edmund, E of Lancaster).*

FITZALAN, 'Le Count de Arondelle'. *WLN 191.*

FITZALAN, E of Arundel. *D13 52d.*

FITZALAN, E of Arundel. *CRK 1376.*

FITZALAN, E of Arundel. *PLN 154.* *(qtg 2&3 Warren over all label Arg & escutch of Maltravers, all imp Wydville).*

FITZALAN, E of Arundel. *PLN 70.* *(qtg 2&3 Warren).*

FITZALAN, E of Arundell. *I2(1904)45.* *(qtg 2 Haal, 3 [Wydvile], 4 qtly Maltravers & Clun). (banner).*

FITZALAN, 'Contte de Aronde' John', d1436. *BB 8, 137.* *(qtg Sa fret Or).*

FITZALAN, 'Contte de Arundell Reschard'. *BB 10, 145.* *(qtg Checky Or and Az). (d1397).*

FITZALAN, Henry, E of Arundel. *Lambarde*

210-213. 1579. *(qtg [Fitz Flaald, Woodville & Maltravers]).*

FITZALAN, Henry, KG, E of Arundel. *Leake.* *(qtg Muschamp, Woodville & Maltravers qtg Clun).*

FITZALAN, John, E of Arundel. *ML I 55; ML II 10.*

FITZALAN, Richard. *Sandford 225.* *(2nd husb of Philippa Mortimer, 2nd dau of Edmond, E of March).*

FITZALAN, Richard, E of Arundel. *Sandford 111.* *(qtg [Warren]; husb of Eleanor, dau of Hen (d1345) E of Lancaster).*

FITZALAN, Thomas, E of Arundel. *Lambarde 210-213.* *(qtg [Maltravers & Clun] & imp [Woodville]).*

FITZALAN, 'Tomas Conte de Arondell'', d1415. *BB 30.* *(qtg Checky Or and Az).*

FITZALAN, William, KG. *Leake.* *(qtg Muschamp & Maltravers).*

FIZ ALAIN, Jon le. *A 86.*

FIZ ALEYN, Richard le, Counte Darundel. *H 100a.*

FYF, le conte de. *BL A 2.*

FYNEUX, John. *MY 209.* *(& Wm F).*

FYTZ ALLYN, E of Aroundel. *I2(1904)44.* *(qtg 2 [Haal], 3 [Maltravers], 4 Clun; banner).*

GRAS, de. *DV 55b, 2186.* *(crined Arg).*

LINCOLNE, le Cont de. *CN a 11; CN b 2.*

MATREVERS, le S'or de. *T c 45.* *(qtg Sa fret Or).*

MESCHINES, de 'Le Count de Lincolne'. *WLN 190.*

PASSELE, Mons Robert de. *S 259.*

POWES. *L1 530, 3.* *(Cronndell written in another hand).*

[ROPE]. *Green.* 14 cent. *(glass, Nantwich, Ches).*

SKRYMZOUR, Ban' Man. *SC 50.*

Gu lion Or head erased Arg

    GRACE. *L1 289, 2; L2 222, 12.*

Gu lion Sa

Gu lion Sa

    STAUNTON. *LQ 96.*

Or lion Az

Or lion Az

    — *XK 69.* *(qtd II&III 1&4 by Edw Aborough).*

    — *WB I 16b, 2.* *(qtd by [Courtenay]).*

    — *SHY 130.* *(qtd 2&3 by Percy, E of Northd).*

    — *XB 17.* *(qtd by Courtenay).*

    — *WLN 47.*

    — *WB I 43, 2.*

    — *XL 321.* *(qtd 2&3 by Courtenay, D of Devon).*

— XK 74. (qtd 4 by Hen Courtenay, E of Devon, KG temp Hen 8).

— XK 35. (qtd 2&3 by Courtenay, E of Devon, KG, temp Hen 7).

— XK 158. (qtd 2&3 by Courtney).

— PLN 2000. (qtd with others by [Sir Edw Borough]).

— PLN 536. (qtd 2&3 by [Sir Thos Borrow or Borough, Ld of Gainsborough]).

— L10 35b, 3. (qtd 2&3 by 'Courteney, erll of Devynshyre').

— GutchWdU. (qtg Lucy, imp Gu salt Arg (Nevill); in library window, Balliol Coll).

— WGA 253. (qtd II&III 1&4 by Sir Thos Borough).

— T c 7. (qtd by Or 3 roundels Gu; qtd by Courtenay).

— WB IV 136, 188. (qtd 2&3 by Ld Faconbrege).

— I2(1904)251. (qtg 2&3 Or 3 pales Sa; qtd 2 by Thos Bourght de Gaynsbourght, lyngcot).

— PLN 1134. (qrs II&III 1&4 of coat imp by [?Tirwyt]).

— BA 1092. (a&l Gu; qtd 2 by 'Sayne Mooer' [St Maur]).

ALGERNOUNS, Baron Erll Percy. L1 1, 6; L2 2, 1. (a&l Gu).

ALGERNOWE. L10 2, 6.

ARDEN, Waukelynus de. SES 3.

BOXHILL, Monsire. CG 78.

CHARLILTON, le Sr. WB I 32, 1.

COURTENAY, E of Devon. CRK 1378. (qrs 1&4).

DEUESCHIRE, Erle of. BR IV 90.

DEVENYSCHIRE, le Counte de. N 1040.

DEVON, E of. BA 1076. (a&l Sa; qtg 2&3 Courtenay).

DEVON, E of. BR V a 16.

DEVON, E of. Neale & Brayley. 1296. (mont to Edm, E of Lancaster; charges on shield were modelled in gesso, painted & gilt).

DEVON, Earl of. PLN 75. (qtd 2 by [Courtenay]; lion in unusual slant).

DEVONSCHIRE, le Conte de. TJ 19. (& le Sire Percy).

ILDLE, Cunte del. D 134a & b; D 214a.

LILLE, Cunte de. G 42.

LINCOLN, E of. WNS 25, 15. ('Le Cunte de Nichole porte dor ou un lion rompat de pt ar').

LOVEL, Richard. B 168.

LOVEL, S' Richd. BR IV 29.

LYLE, E de. E I 10; E II 10.

MUSEGROS, M. WNR 78.

NICHOLE, C de. WNR 37.

NICHOLL, Co. DV 45b, 1795. (Lacy, E of Lincoln).

NORTH'LAND, le Counte de. RL 12. (qtg 2&3 Gu 3 lucies hauriant Arg).

NORTHD, Hen, E of, KG. Leake. (qtg Lucy; d 1526-7).

NORTHD, Hen, E of, KG. Leake. (qtg Lucy; d 1488-9).

NORTHEHUMBERLAND, E of. WK 138.

NORTHMBRLAND, Comes. RL 27, 4. (qtg Lucy).

NORTHUMB'LAND, le Count de. WLN 208.

NORTHUMBERLAND. SHY 435. (qtg Lucy & imp ?Herbert).

NORTHUMBERLAND, Conte de. CN 17.

NORTHUMBERLAND, le Conte de, Sr de Lucy. S 39. (qtg Gu 3 lucies hauriant Arg [Lucy]).

NORTHUMBERLAND, Hen, E of. WGA 99. (qtg Lucy).

NORTHUMBERLAND, Hen, E of. WGA 228.

NORTHUMBERLAND, Hen, E of. WGA 216.

NORTHUMBERLAND, Hen, E of. WGA 186.

NORTHUMBERLAND, [Hen Percy] E of. FK I 59. (qtg Lucy).

NORTHUMBERLAND, Therll of. I2(1904)50. (many qtgs; banner).

NORTHUMBERLANDE, E of. PCL IV 88. (qrs 1&4).

NORTHUMBERLOND, Count de. RH, Ancestor iv 227.

NORTHUMBLOND, E of. AY 26.

NORTHUMBRIA, Comes. Q II 22.

NORTHUMBRYELAN, Comes. I2(1904)258. (qtg Lucy, Poynings, Fitzpayn, Bryan).

NORTHUMBURLAND, Erle of. BW 5b, 23. (qrs 1&4).

PERCI. PO 19.

PERCI, Henri de. K 18.

PERCY. WK 553. (qr I 1).

PERCY. CT 101.

PERCY. Suff HN 44. (qtg 2&3 Gu 3 fishes hauriant Arg; imp Mortimer in 'Ld Wentworth's house at Netelstede').

PERCY. GutchWdU. (in chf, Lucy in base, all imp Nevile; window of Old Hall, Univ Coll, built 1450, demolished 1669).

PERCY. CRK 1306. (qtd I&IV 1&4).

PERCY. ML I 18; ML II 19.

PERCY. FK I 132 & 136. (qtg Lucy, over all label of 3 or 5 per pale Gu and Sa).

PERCY. DX 14. (armed Gu).

PERCY, Baron. CK a 26.

PERCY, Ld. Sandford 225. ('Hotspur', d1403).

PERCY, Monsire de. AN 12.

PERCY, le Sr de. AS 35. (armed Gu).

PERCY, le sire de. Navarre 1470.

[PERCY]. Neale & Brayley. 1296. (on canopy of mont to Edm, E of Lancaster).

[PERCY]. Lambarde 210. (qtg Lucy, Poynings &c, all imp by Howard on tomb of Thos,

E of Arundel, Norfolk Chapel, Arundel, Suss).
[PERCY]. *WGA 207.*
[PERCY]. *Blair D I 2. (Window, Branspeth Ch).*
[PERCY]. *Blair D I 5. (imp [Booth]; window Branspeth Ch).*
[PERCY]. *XF 741. (qrs I 1&4).*
[PERCY]. *WJ 93.*
PERCY, Algernon, E of Northd. *XL 405.*
PERCY, Comes Northumbria. *LMO 45. (qtg Gu 3 lucies hauriant Arg; E of Northd 1414-55).*
PERCY, Hen' *FC II 120.*
[PERCY, Hen Algernon, 6th E of Northd]. *Blair N I 100, 211. (qtg Beaufort, Lucy, Poynings, Percy ancient, FitzPayne & Bryan, all within Garter; Hexham Priory, Northd).*
PERCY, Hen, E of Northd. *S 41. (qrs 1&4).*
PERCY, Hen, E of Northd. *GutchWdU. (qtg Lucie; benefactor, 1442; formerly in window of room next to old chapel door, Univ Coll, Oxf).*
PERCY, Henr' le. *FF 16.*
PERCY, Sire Henri de. *N 28.*
PERCY, Henry de. *K 158.*
PERCY, Henry, Ld. *Sandford 111. (m Mary, dau of Hen (d1345) E of Lancaster).*
PERCY, Henry, Ld, 1299-1315. *LMS 59.*
PERCY, Sir Henry de. *WNS 25b, 27. ('... por dor ou un lion ramp dazur').*
PERCY, Sire Henry de. *J 41.*
PERCY, Sire Henry de. *PV 39.*
PERCY, Sr Henry de. *H 102b.*
PERCY, Henry Algernon, E of Northd. *N 47. (qtg Lucy, Poynings, Fitzpayn & Bryan).*
PERCY, Henry, E of Northd. *XK 47. (KG temp Hen 7; qrs I 1&4).*
PERCY, Henry, E of Northd. *XK 90. (qr I 1; KG 1531).*
PERCY, Sr Herry. *BR V 7. (tinct of lion unclear).*
PERCY, E of Northd. *BA 586.*
PERCY, E of Northd. *CRK 1374. (qrs 1&4).*
PERCY, E of Northd. *LD 2. (qrs 1&4).*
PERCY, E of Northd. *PLN 77. (qtg 2&3 Lucy).*
PERCY, Sir Thomas. *S 82.*
PERCY, Mons'Thos de. *S 80.*
PERCY, Thos, E of Worcester. *GutchWdU. (qtg Lucy; in window given by Hen Percy, E of Northd, Balliol Coll Library).*
PERCY, Sir William. *XK 256. (cresc for diffce; qrs I 1&4).*
PERCY, William de. *FC II 107.*
PERCYE, Monsire de. *CG 38.*
PERCYE, de. *SP A 62.*
PERSY, Henry de. *H 102a.*
PERSY, E of Northumberland. *BR II 40. (qrs 1&4).*

PIERREPOINT-Roucy, John III Count of. *C 33.*
REDVERS. *1H7 8d; D13 77. (qtd by Courteney).*
[REDVERS, Baldwin, E of Devon]. *Neale & Brayley. 13 cent. (mont to Aveline of Lancaster, d1273).*
[REVIERS]. *RH, Ancestor iv 227. (qtd by Courtenay, Count of Dowenechyre).*
REVIERS, Baldwin de, E of Devon. *MP II 17; MP IV 35; MP IV 60.*
RIDVERS, E of Devon. *Gerard 34.*
RIPARIIS. *L2 428, 1.*
RIVERS. *Leake. (qtd 2&3 by Edw Courtney, KG d1509-10).*
RIVERS. *Sandford 419. (qtd 2&3 by Wm Courtney, E of Devon, d 1512).*
[RIVERS]. *Sandford 420. (qtd 4 by Hen Courtney, M of Exeter, exec 1538).*
?SINOPIS, Queen. *Arch Journ xxii 67. (a&l Gu; on 1 of 3 female figures painted c1530 in Queen's room at Amberley Castle, Suss; legend beneath reads 'The excellet qwene Sinopis to magnify which ruled the hole coutre of Ennay').*
ST BEYSSE ABBEY, Yorks. *D4 48. (Founded by Wm Myschen).*
ST BEYSSE MONASTERY, Yorks. *H21 93b. (qtg 2&3 Gu 3 lucies Arg).*
STEPULTON. *CV-BM 67.*
SUTTON. *L1 617, 1. (armed Gu).*
SWESIE, Rex. *FK I 37.*
SWETHYN, Kyng of. *PCL IV 66. (or Swechyn).*
WYGHT, de. *SP A 41.*
YLE, Le Comte del. *B 12.*
YLE, le Cunte del. *FW 59.*
YLLE, Cunte del. *HE 42.*

Or lion Gu
Or lion Gu
  — *XF 575. (qtd 2 by Sir Wm Tyndale).*
  — *Sandford 113. (qtd by D of Bavaria, temp Edw 3).*
  — *CRK 277. (qtd 2&3 by Tiptoft, E of Worc).*
  — *L10 42b, 6. (qtd III 2&3 by Dudley, baro).*
  — *1H7 7d. (qtd 4 by Arg salt Gu (Fitzwilliams)).*
  — *WK 122. (qtd III 2&3 by [Sir Edw Sutton] Ld Dodeley).*
  — *XK 155. (qtd 2 by Sir Wm Tyndall).*
  — *SC 64. (qtd 4 by Sir Andrew Stewart).*
  — *BW 12b, 80. (qtd 2&3 by Ld Poweys).*
  — *WB IV 174b, 875. (qtd 2 by Samson).*
  — *XK 86. (qtd III 4 by Wm Fitzwilliam, KG 1526).*
  — *XK 84. (qtd III 4 by Thos Manners, E of Rutland, KG 1525).*

— *XK 64. (qtd III 2&3 by Edw Sutton, Ld Dudley, KG temp Hen 8).*

— *CRK 576. (escutch of Montferrant).*

— *XK 23. (qtd II 4 by Edw, Ld Dudley).*

— *BR VI 46. (qtd by Ld Powis).*

— *WGA 100. (qtd III 2&3 by Edw, Ld Dudley).*

— *SHY 198. (imp by [Scales]).*

— *SHY 15. (imp Hopton).*

— *LS 24. (qtd III 2&3 by Sutton, Ld Dudley).*

— *WB I 34b, 14.*

— *LD 140. (Crest: 2 lions' paws Gu armed Arg each garnished outside with 3 balls Or tasselled Arg).*

— *PLN 1318. (a&l Az; qtd 2&3 by Sir Thos Butler).*

— *LS 211. (qtd 4 by Sir Andrew Stewart).*

— *PLN 2033. (a&l Az; qtd 2 by Sir Wm Tyndall).*

— *CRK 212. (qtd 2&3 by Powys).*

— *Lyndsay 139. (qtd by Stewart, Ld of Meffane).*

— *Lyndsay 133. (qtd by Stewart, Ld of Avyndale).*

— *LO B 48.*

— *PLN 969. (qtd 3 by [Ld Strange]).*

— *WB IV 130b, 82. (qtd 2&3 by 'the Erle of Worseter Typtot').*

— *WGA 153. (qtd 2&3 by Wm, E of Ostrevant & D of Holland).*

— *BB 70 & 96. (qtd II&III 1&4 by Wyll'm duc de Holland, conte de osterwantte; elected c1390, d1417).*

— *XFB 23. (qtd 2 by Douglas, E of Angus).*

[ABERNETHY]. *Neale & Brayley. (qtd 2 by [Douglas] on mont erected 1606 to Qus Eliz & Mary).*

ABERNETHY, The Ld, of Alton. *SC 39. (a&l ?Az).*

ABIRNETHY, Ld Saltown. *Lyndsay 151.*

ALBANACTUS, K of Britain. *BW 2, 3.*

[ALBANIACO, Francis de]. *Neale & Brayley. 13 cent. (Mont to Aveline of Lancaster, d1273).*

[ALBANIACO, Francis de]. *Neale & Brayley. 1296. (Canopy of mont to Edm, E of Lancaster).*

ALBANY, Duc of. *SC 3.*

ARMENIA, K of. *FK I 38. (tierced per pall, qr 1).*

BREDERODE. *XL 632.*

BRETT. *Gerard 177.*

BRITAIN, K Brutus. *BA 889 & 908. (qtg 2&3 Az 3 crowns in bend Or).*

CHARLETON, Sr de. *CKO 30.*

CHARLETON, of Kent. *MY A2 236.*

CHARLETON, Baron of Powis, Wales. *L2 129, 4. (a&l Vt).*

CHARLETON, Ld Powys. *PLN 915. (a&l Az).*

CHARLTON. *Leake. (qtd 4 by Sir Antony Browne, KG, d1548).*

CHARLTON. *L1 405, 6.*

CHARLTON. *Leake. (qtd III 4 by Thos Manners, KG, d1543).*

CHARLTON, Monsire de. *AN 58.*

CHARLTON, le Sr de. *S 61.*

CHARLTON, Edward, Ld Powis, KG. *Leake. (d 1421-22).*

CHARLTON, Mons J de. *WJ 261.*

CHARLTON, John de. *XL 375. (a&l Az).*

CHARLTON, John, Ld, of Powys. *S 63.*

[CHARLTON, Ld Powis]. *?source. (Glass (1530) of T.R. [Thos E of Rutland], Enfield Ch, Middx).*

CHARLTON, le S'r de. *T c 44.*

CHERLETON, Humfrey, of Yorks. *RH, Ancestor vii 198.*

CHERLETON, Sire Joh de. *PO 196.*

CHERLETON, Ld Powys. *BA 17. (a&l Az).*

CHERLETON, mons'r Eduard, s'r de powis. *BB 34. (d 1421).*

CHESTER, Ranulph, E of. *Sandford 47. (tail erect).*

CHEYNE, Mons John. *T b 49. (qtg 2&3 Checky Or and Az fess Gu fretty Arg).*

CHORLETON, of Salop. *CY 86, 341.*

DELAFELD, of Irld. *L2 162, 7.*

DELAFELDE. *Suff HN 7. (imp by Scales; Lavenham Ch).*

DELAPOLE. *L2 164, 6.*

ERMENYE, le Roy de. *WLN 67. (a&l Az).*

FELBRIDGE, Sire Robert de. *J 92.*

FELBRIGE, S' Roger. *R 107.*

FELBRIGG, Sy. *NS 122.*

FELBRIGGE. *PLN 1419. (a&l Az; ?embelif).*

[FELBRIGGE]. *MY 236. (blazoned embelif).*

FELBRIGGE, Simon. *S 173. (a&l Az; blazoned embelif).*

FELBRIGGE, Sir Simon. *PLN 209. (a&l Az; blazoned embelif).*

FELBRIGGE, Sir Simon. *CRK 418. (blazoned embelif).*

FELBRIGGE, Sir Simon, KG. *Leake. (d1442-3).*

FELBRIGGE, Sir Symond. *BW 14, 89.*

FELBRYDGE. *Suff HN 47. (in Garter). ('Mr Gonfylde's house at Gorleston').*

FELBRYDGE, Mons. *T b 70.*

FELBRYDGE, Sir. *T b 102.*

FELBRYG, Emond. *BG 120.*

FELBRYGGS, Sir S. *WB I 37, 24.*

FIFE, le Comte de. *Gelre; Stodart pl E2.*

FIT, le Conte de. *Berry; Stodart pl 1. (Macduff).*

GRIFFITH, Jeovan ap. *WLN 365.*

GRIMOND, 'de la seure'. *XL 68. (qrs 1&4).*

HOKELEY. *WB I 33, 9.*

HOKELEY. *PLN 1386.*

HOLANDE, D of. *BR I 34. (qtg 2&3 Or lion Sa).*

HOLANDIAE, Willelmus, Comes. *MP Hist Min iii 23. ('... eligitur in regem Alemanniae', 1247; on 2nd shield: Az on chf Gu lion isst Or; beneath both is written: 'Scutum Willelmi comitis. Primum scutum ejusdem de Holandiae, aspirantis ad imperium').*

HOLLAND. *Sandford 316. (qtd by Jacqueline of Bavaria, 1st w of Humphrey, D of Glouc, s of Hen 4).*

[HOLLAND]. *WLN 38. (qtd 2&3 by Hainault).*

HOLLAND, John I, E of. *Sandford 143. (d c1300, husb of Eliz, dau of Edw 1).*

HOLLAND, William, Count of. *MP I 82; MP II 89.*

HOLLONDE, D of. *KB 35. (coat per fess, Holland in chf, in base Or lion Sa).*

HOLONDE, D of. *AY 13. (qtg 2&3 Or lion Sa).*

JEVAN AP GRIFIT. *F 33.*

LEE, of Lee. *BA 5b.*

LEGH, John, of Legh. *WLN 850.*

LEGH, John de, de Legh, Ches. *CY 22, 86.*

LEGH, de Legh. *DV 49a, 1928.*

LEGH, de Legh. *L9 39a, 2. (a&l Az).*

LEGH, of Legh. *CVC 625.*

LEGH, of Legh. *CRK 359.*

LEIGH, of Leigh. *XL 525. (a&l Vt).*

LYNCOLN, Counte de. *Q 8.*

[MACDUFF], E of Fyfe. *SC 12.*

MAKDUFF, erle of Fyffe of auld. *Lyndsay 55.*

MARCHAM, Sir Richard. *BD 86. (5th N window, Hall of York Palace, Southwell).*

MARESCHALE, le Conti de. *J 9.*

MESCHENES, of Copland, Cumb. *Gerard 34.*

MESCHINES, Randle, 1st E of Chester. *TJ 10. ('la cowe estant').*

MESCHINES, Sir Randol. *CVC 445.*

MESCHINES, Randolf le tierce, Conte de Chestre. *TJ 1224.*

MESCHYNES, Ranulph. *CY 2, 8. ('comes Cestrie post Conquestum').*

MICOLL. *FK II 575. (armed Arg, langued Az).*

MICOLL. *L9 67b, 2. (a&l Az).*

MUSCEGROS, Munsire Robert de. *D 187b.*

MUSCEGROS, Robert de. *D 187a.*

MUSSEGRES, Robert. *PCL I 489. (a&l Az).*

MUSSEGRES, Robt de. *Q 107.*

NICHOL, Erl of. *BR IV 76. ('lion schuld be purpul').*

PAVYS, Edward Ld. *WGA 41. (a&l Az).*

POLE, Le Sr de la. *AS 79.*

POLE, Griffith ap Owen de la, Ld of Powis. *LMS 70. (d1317).*

POLE, L'y Sire de la. *N 1051.*

POLE, Seignior de la. *BR IV 27.*

POLE, Mons' William. *TJ 26. (& Jn Musegros & Griffitz le fitz Wenunwen).*

POOLE, Monsire de la. *CG 37.*

POUWES, le Sr de. *NB 79.*

POWES. *WB II 52, 6.*

POWES, Ld. *KB 299.*

POWES, The Lorde. *WB IV 134b, 155. (a&l Az).*

POWIS. *LS 111. (imp Stafford).*

[POWIS]. *PLN 83. (qtd 2&3 by Tiptoft, E of Worc).*

POWYS. *Leake. c1450. (qtd 2&3 by Sir Jn Tiptoft, E of Worc, KG d1470).*

POWYS, Ld. *FK I 106.*

POWYS, Ld. *WLN 238.*

POWYS, Ld. *PLN 1279. (a&l Az; qtg 2&3 Gu lion Arg a&l & border engr Az; in pretence Vt escutch in orle of 8 escallops Arg).*

POWYS, le Sr de. *CN 74.*

POWYS, le S' de, of Salop. *CY 80, 318.*

STRECH. *LS 162. (qrs 1&4).*

STRECHE. *XL 527. (qrs 1&4).*

STRECHE. *L1 587, 6.*

STRECHE. *DV 49a, 1937.*

TRAUE, Sir Sandich de. *MK 6. (temp Hen 4).*

WEMIS, of Reraff. *SC 67.*

[WEMYSS], of that ilk. *Lyndsay 164.*

WENUNWYN, ... ap. *L10 2, 8.*

WENUNWYN, Griffid ap. *E I 75; E II 75.*

Or lion Purp

Or lion Purp

— *RH, Ancestor iii 201. ('lyone of purpull'; [Lacy, Hen de, E of Lincoln 1257-1311]).*

BROOKE. *CRK 1587. (a&l Gu).*

LACY. *PLN 42.*

LACY, Baron. *CK a 29.*

[LACY]. *Neale & Brayley. 1296. (Canopy of mont to Edm, E of Lancaster).*

LACY, Hen, E of Lincoln. *K 37.*

LACY, Henry de, E of Lincoln, 1257-1312. *LMS 29.*

LACY, Henry, E of Lincoln. *Sandford 108. (his dau Alice m Blessed Thomas of Lancaster).*

LACY, Henry de, Counte de Nichole. *I 1b.*

LACY, Henry de, Conte de Nichole. *I 1a.*

LACY, Count of Lincoln. *XL 180. (a&l Az).*

LACY, Count of Lincoln. *CRK 258.*

LACY, erle off Lyncolne. *WB II 48, 15.*

LINCOLN, Comes. *Q II 8.*

LINCOLNE, le Counte de. *TJ 15.*

LINCOLNIE, Comes. *SM 161, 31; SM 252, 42.*

LYNGCOLN, Erelle of. *PCL IV 129.*

NICHOL, Erl of. *BR IV 76.*

NICHOLE, Cunte de. *G 33.*

NICHOLE, Cunte de. *FW 593. ('gold [a lion] purple').*

NICHOLE, Cunte de. *HE 46.*

NICHOLE, Cunte de. *FW 46a.*

NICHOLE, le Conte de. *J 3.*

NICHOLE, le Conte de. *P 49.*

NICHOLE, le counte de. *N 4.*

NICHOLL, de. *SP A 27.*

NICOLE, Enris li bons quens de. *K 1. ('Baner out de un cendal safrin o un lioun rampant purprin').*

PEULE, s' Rich'. *PO 666.*

WHALLEY ABBEY. *D4 46b. (arms of its founder Lacy, E of Lincoln).*

Or lion Sa

Or lion Sa

— *LMRO 20b, 43. (qtg 2&3 Or lion Gu, all qtd I&IV by Dux de Aubert).*

— *KB 33. (on escutch of D of Burgon).*

— *L1 183, 3. (langued Gu; qtg 2&3 Gu fess dancetty betw 6 crosslets Or, all qtd II 2 by Sir Nich Carow, of Bodington, Surr).*

— *LH 8. (qtd 2 by Strange).*

— *Lyndsay 42. (imp by [Gueldres], all imp by Marie qwyne [of Scotld] w of K Jas 2).*

— *Sandford 113.* temp Edw 3. *(qtd by D of Bavaria).*

— *WGA 22. (qr 1 of escutch betw qrs II&III of Philip, K of Castile).*

— *KB 318. (qtd 2&3 by Ld Mawley).*

— *LO B 59. (escutch of D of Burgundy).*

— *PLN 1328. (qtd 2&3 by Simon [Maure]).*

— *BR II 3. (escutch of D of Burgoyne).*

— *Neale & Brayley.* 13 cent. *(Mont to Avelme of Lancaster, d1273).*

— *1H7 13d; D13 81d. (qtd II 1&4 by Carew).*

— *WGA 32. (escutch of Duc Charlis Victorious, of Burgoigne).*

— *LE 257. (escutch of Phle, duc de Bourgoigne).*

— *Lyndsay 27. (escutch of The Kyng off Romanes).*

— *L10 91, 2. (qtd 3 by Harcourt, all imp by Bowyer).*

— *PCL IV 68. (escutch of D of Bourgyn).*

— *CB 435. (qrs 2&3 on escutch of Jehan de Croy, seigneur de Chimay).*

— *LE 248. (escutch of D de Borgoyne).*

— *KB 35. (qtd by D of Holland).*

— *BB 70; BB 96. (qtd II&III 2&3 by Holland, duc de, conte de osterwantte, Wyll'm, elec c 1390, d1417).*

— *XK 94. (qtd III 1&4 by Sir Nich Carew, KG 1536).*

— *WGA 161. (qr 1 of escutch betw qrs III&IV of Ferdinand V, K of Castile).*

— *PLN 1918. (qtd 8 by K of Spain).*

— *WB V 63.*

ARDEN, Waukelinus de. *Q II 369.*

ARDERNE, Baudebyn de. *Q 375.*

BRITAIN, K Erpewolde. *BA 906.*

BROMWICH. *CRK 86. (tail turned inwards).*

CLIVEDON, Reginald de. *WLN 388.*

CLYVDONER. *CV-BM 38.*

ENGLAND, K Erpewold in. *L1 221, 4; L2 170, 6. (a&l Gu).*

FFLAUNDRES, le Count de. *WLN 96.*

FLANDERS. *Sandford 312. (on escutch of Anne of Burgundy, w of Jn, D of Bedf, 1423).*

FLANDERS. *Sandford 371 & 402. (on escutch of Chas, D of Burgundy, d 1477).*

FLANDERS, Count of. *MP II 79.*

FLANDERS, Count of. *XL 425.*

FLANDERS, Count of. *PLN 581.*

[FLANDERS]. *?source.* 1324. *(Mont to Aymer de Valence, E of Pembroke).*

FLANDERS, Guy de Dampierre, Count of. *C 29.*

FLANDERS, Philip of Alsatia, E of. *Sandford 16.*

FLANDERS, Robt the Frison, E of. *Sandford 16.*

FLANDRES, C de. *WNR 28.*

GELDER, Wm, D of. *WGA 51.*

HAINAULT. *LMO 43. (qtg Or lion Gu, all qtd by Aubert, lozy bendy Arg and Az; [Aubert, called D of Bavaria, Count of Hainault & Holland 1388-1404]).*

HAINAULT. *Sandford 316 & 319. (qtd by Jaqueline of Bavaria, w of Humphrey, D of Gloucester, s of Hen 4).*

HAINAULT, Philippa of. *XK 1. (qtg Or lion Gu). (w of Edw 3).*

HENAUDE, le Count de. *WLN 38. (qrs 1&4).*

[HOLLAND, E of Ostrevaunt]. *WGA 103. (qtg Or lion Gu).*

HOLME COLTRAN ABBEY, Cumb. *D4 50. (imp by Az cross moline Or).*

JULERS, le Counte de. *CA 240. (?Wm 4 or 5, Count of Julich).*

JULIERS. *Dingley ccclxiii. (imp by Engld & border Sa; for Jn, E of Kent, husb of Eliz, dau of D of Juliers; window, Lichfield Cath).*

JULIERS, Eliz. *Sandford 216. (w of Jn, E of Kent, gds of Edw 1).*

JULIERS, of Gulick. *Sandford 489. (qtd 2 by Q Anne of Cleve).*

[LACY]. *D9 24; E6. (imp by Thos, E of Lancaster).*

LACY, E of Lincoln. *H21 91b.*

LODELOWE, Mons Thomas de. *WJ 333.*

LODLOWE, Mons' John de. *S 440. (tail erect).*

LUDLOW, John. *Sandford 319. (of Stokesay & Hodnet, Salop; husb of Eliz, sis of Jn, Ld Grey of Powis, d1497).*

LUDLOW, John de. *S 445. (tail erect).*
LUDLOWE, Mons' John. *TJ 116. (tail erect).*
LUDLOWE, Mons' John. *TJ 99. (tail erect).*
(*'... la cowe estant'*).
MAREYS, William de. *MP I 67. (s of Geoffrey).*
MARISCO, de. *MP Hist Min ii 462.* (*'arma Willelmi de Marisco, de proditioni convicti, deprehensi, et Londoniis suspensi'; shield is cut in half & reversed, & below it is broken spear & banner with broken staff).*
NORTHUBRIE, Comes. *LMRO 20b, 45. (qtg 2&3 Gu 3 lucies Arg).*
OSTREVANT, Wm E of, & D of Holland. *WGA 153. (qrs 1&4).*
POLEY, Monseur de. *AS 495.*
SLANLOW, Monsire de. *CG 96.*
WAKESAYE, of Norf. *L1 221, 4. (a&l Gu; name in margin).*
WELLE, Adam de. *LM 271.*
WELLES. *ML I 26; ML II 27. (should be lion qf).*
WELLES. *XL 472. (tail turned out).*
[WELLES]. *SussASColl lxix 75. c1500. (imp by [Hoo] on armorial glass formerly at Horselunges Suss & now penes HW Devenish, Mount House, Parkestone, Dorset).*
WELLES, Wills de. *Q 524.*

Or lion Vt
Or lion Vt
ARDERNE, M de. *WNR 132.*
ARDERNE, Waklin de. *G 140.*
ARDERNE, Waukelyn de. *LM 492.*
BERTRAM. *RB 494.*
BERTRAM. *XL 112. (a&l Gu).*
BERTRAM. *L1 56, 5; L2 74, 11. (a&l Gu).*
BERTRAM. *L10 25b, 10. (a&l Gu).*
BERTRAM, Robert. *E I 367; E II 369.*
BRIQUEBEC, Bertram, Sire de, Constable of France. *Soc Guern 1928. 1338.*
DUDELLEY, Ld Ambros. *WK 427. (1st of 20 qrs).*
MUKTAN, Mons Rob de. *WJ 353. (?Multane).*
MUKTON. *L9 75a, 9. (a&l Gu).*
POLTIMORE, Richard de. *F 303.*
POLTIMORE, Richard de. *WLN 735.*
ROBESART. *R 112.*
ROBSARTE, Sir J. *BW 14, 92. (armed Gu).*
SOTTONE, Sire Richard de. *N 110.*
[SUTTON]. *?source. 14 cent. (glass, Broughton Castle Chapel, Oxfords).*
WALKYNGTON, Aleyn de. *WJ 357.*

Purp lion Arg
Purp lion Arg
WYMBYSH, Thomas. *SES 26.*
WYMBYSSH, Thomas. *Q II 498.*

Purp lion Or
Purp lion Or
[PAYLE, Sir Raf]. *PLN 259.*
PAYLE, Sir Robt, of Kent. *WB III 86b, 1. (a&l Az).*
PAYLEN. *L9 102b, 10.*
PAYLEN. *L1 520, 3.*
PAYLEN. *DV 60b, 2385. (armed Az).*
PAYLOW. *XL 516. (a&l Gu).*

Sa lion Arg
Sa lion Arg
— *Lyndsay 27. (qtd & imp by 'The Kyng off Romanes').*
— *PLN 235. (cresc Gu for diffce; qtd 2&3 by Sir Thos Gresley).*
— *L2 211, 4. (qtd 2 by Frye, of Devon).*
— *LH 433. (qtd 2&3 by Holme).*
— *PCL II 98.*
— *PLN 436. (armed Or langued Gu [or ?Az]).*
CROMWELL. *L10 92, 3. (a&l Gu; alias Williams; 1st of 6 qrs).*
CROMWELL, Sir Richard. *I2(1904)284. (a&l G; & several qtgs; alias Reshard Wylliams, Kt).*
GENEURE, Petrus de. *MP Hist Min iii 66. (d1249; beneath is another small shield Arg lion Sa).*
GENEVA, Peter de. *MP I 87a. (shield reversed).*
GENEVRE, Eble de. *B 104.*
KINKESTON, Sire Johan de. *J 81.*
KIRCKBY, Mons de. *AS 502.*
LELBENSTEYN. *XL 622.*
MARTEINE. *GutchWdU. (window, new chapel, [c1720], Queen's Coll; ?perhaps removed from Langton's chapel [1518]).*
[MORLEY]. *Farrer I 269. (Brandon Parva Ch, Norf).*
[NITHSDALE]. *Lyndsay 161. (qtd by Douglas, Ld Nithsdale).*
NYDDISDAILL, Ld of, of auld. *Lyndsay 158.*
PENEDELE, Henry de. *E II 389.*
PENEDOKE, Henry de. *E I 387.*
SCURMY. *XL 497. (tail turned out).*
SEG[RA]VE, Johan de. *Q 29.*
SEGRAVE, Nichole de. *FW 595; A 204.*
THORNY. *WB IV 148b, 410.*
V[ER]DON, S' Ch. *R 78. (ch on shldr with chess rook ?Gu; shield badly smeared & discoloured).*
V[ER]DON, S' Jo de. *R 77.*
VERDON. *WB IV 165b, 719. (a&l Gu).*
VERDON, Monsire de. *AN 44.*
VERDON, Sr de. *CKO a 40.*
VERDON, John de. *XL 140.*
VERDON, Mons John de. *WJ 293.*
VERDON, Mons' John. *TJ 82. (armed Or).*

VERDON, Mons' John de. *D 41.*
VERDON, Monsire John de. *CG 84. ('ungle et arme dor').*
VERDON, Sir John de. *CV-BM 228.*
VERDON, Sir John, of Northants. *WB III 75, 1. (a&l Az).*
VERDONE. *FK II 585.*
VERDOUN. *FK II 181.*
VERDOUN, Jo. *NS 13.*
VERDOUN, Sire Thomas de. *N 760.*
VERDOUNE. *PO 328. (langued Gu; name added in later hand).*
VERDUN, Sr Thomas de. *L 187.*
WARDON. *L1 675, 1. (a&l Gu).*
WARDON. *L1 674, 6. (a&l Or).*
WASTENEY, Sr William. *I 22.*

Sa lion Or
Sa lion Or
— *XV I 552. (qtd 2&3 by Bromham).*
— *WGA 22. (qtd II&III 4 by Philip, K of Castile).*
— *WGA 32. (qtd II 2 by Duc Charlis Victorious, of Burgoigne).*
— *XV 552. (qtd 2&3 by Bromhall).*
— *CVK 741. (qtd 2 by Sir Thos Aldon).*
— *CC 233b, 369. (qtd 2&3 by Bromhale).*
— *WLN 86. (qtg 2&3 Arg lion qf in salt Gu).*
— *WJ 345. (Mons Rauf de Som....).*
— *L10 76, 23. (qtd 2&3 by Bromhale).*
— *BA 4b. (armed Gu; qtd 2 by Damport, of Bromalle, Ches).*
— *CV-BM 283. (qtg 2&3 Or 3 roundels Gu).*
— *WGA 161. (qtd IV 2 by [Ferdinand V, K of Castile]).*
— *PLN 1106. (imp by qtly 1&4 Arg cross moline Gu, 2&3 Az fretty Or).*
— *PCL IV 68. (qr 2 of coat imp by D of Bourgyn).*
— *KB 33. (qtd II 2 by D of Burgon).*
ARCHER. *L10 2, 9.*
ARCHER, Nicholas le. *E I 369; E II 371.*
BEWYS, Ld. *BR VI 16.*
BRABAN, D of. *PCL IV 97.*
BRABANT. *Sandford 402 & 371. (qtd by Chas, D of Burgundy, d 1477).*
BRABANT, Henry, D of. *MP II 43.*
BRABANT, John, D of. *C 46.*
BRABANT, Margaret, Duchess of. *Sandford 143. (3rd dau of Edw 1, she m 1290 Jn 2, D of Brabant).*
BROMHALE. *L10 77, 21.*
BROMHALL. *L1 48, 6; L2 45, 2. (a&l Gu).*
BROMHALL. *CRK 48. (tail inwards).*
FLANDERS, Thomas, Count of. *MP II 37; MP VII 11.*
KETERICH, Richard, of Cambs. *WB III 91b,*

4. (a&l Gu).
KYNGESTON. *CT 152.*
[KYNGSTON]. *Neale & Brayley. 1296. (Canopy of mont to Edm, E of Lancaster).*
NARTOFT. *L1 472, 1.*
NEYRMYST, of Essex. *L2 359, 4. (& Nartoft).*
NORTOFT, Sire Adam de. *N 440.*
PULT[ONOR], Richard. *A 192.*
PULTIMOR, Richard. *FW 322.*
RHEINFELDT. *XL 629.*
RICHINGFELD, Mons de. *CA 255.*
SAMBORNE. *XL 169.*

Vt lion Arg
Vt lion Arg
— *PLN 1465. (a&l Gu).*
— *CRK 1095. (a&l Gu; tail outwards).*
— *BA 36, 340. (qtd 3 by Sir Thos Molyneux, of Sefton).*
— *XK 89. (qtd 7 by Jn Vere, E of Oxf, KG 1527).*
— *WB I 33b, 19. (qtd 7 by [Vere], E of Oxf).*
ARDREN. *L10 2, 16.*
BOLBEK, le Baron Sr Hugh de. *TJ 49.*
BOLEBEC. *WK 531. (qtd 7 by Vere).*
HETON. *LH 1122.*
HETON, Alain de. *XL 444.*
HETON, Mons Aleyn de. *WJ 355.*
HOME, of Aittoune. *Lyndsay 309.*
HUME, Ld. *Lyndsay 115.*
HUMME. *CRK 554. ('head & paws fleshed' [ie Gu the division as though erased]).*
SANDFORD, Baron. *LS 299.*
SPRINGES, Sir John. *PT 1016.*

Vt lion Or
Vt lion Or
— *L2 139, 12. (qtd 2&3 by Chaulx).*
— *L10 46, 17. (qtd 2&3 by Chaulx).*
— *WB III 114, 3. (qtd 2&3 by Jn Chanci, of Herts).*
[ARD]ERNE, [Sr Wakelyn d']. *CKO 64.*
ARDERNE, Monsr' Wakelyn a. *AS 179.*
ARDERNE, Mons' Wakelyn d'. *TJ 31.*
GRENEFERD, Mons John. *TJ 150. (tail erect).*
HETON, Aleyn de. *CKO 64. (written over '[Sr Wakelyn d'Arde]rne').*
MONTENACK, Robert. *XL 440.*
MOUNTENAK, Mons Robt. *WJ 354.*
MOUNTENAKE. *L9 70b, 5. (a&l Gu).*
NORTON, Robt de. *Soc Jers 1928 & 1929. (Warden of the Isles, 1326-7).*
NORTON, Robt de. *Burrows 329. (Keeper of Jersey 1326-7).*
NORTONE. *L9 85a, 7.*
NORTONE. *L1 473, 2.*

NORTONE, Sire James de. *N 233.*
ROBASSAET. *DV 46b, 1831. (armed Arg).*
ROBSARD, Sir John. *RH, Ancestor vii 201.*
ROBSARDE, Ld Bowrcher. *RH, Ancestor iii
211. ('wert a lyone of gold'; qtg [Bour-
chier]; [Lewis R, Ld Bourchier, 1425-9]).*
ROBSART. *LR 71.*
ROBSART. *CRK 252.*
[ROBSERD, Sir John]. *WGA 154.*
ROBSERT. *WB II 59, 12.*
ROBUSSARD, Mons' John. *BB 97, 2.
(langued Gu; d1450).*
WALENS, S' Jon. *PO 441.*

1 lion field patterned

Barry 1 lion
Barry lion
LATHE. *C3 13b.* S.Thoma atte Lathe. *1353-4.
(sl on charter of Thos att Lathee, de
Wygenhale, Hants).*
MOUNGUMBRY, Thomas, Ld of ?Lonlond.
Bow XLVIII 4. 1377-8.
PEMBRUGE. *Lawrance 35. c1285. (lion
unclear; on tomb of Sir Jn Pitchford, d1285,
Pitchford, Salop).*
SAUCOIO, Ralph de. *Birch 13283.* SIGILLVM
RADVLFI DE SOCOIO. *c1220. (?foreign).*
STOTEVILLE, John de, Ld of Ekyntona, Der-
bys. *Birch 13715.* S......OTEVILE. *1314.*
STUTEVILLE, John de. *BM Harl 2044, 144,
HB-SND. 1280.*
STUTEVYLE, John de. *BrookeAsp I 49, 3.
1334.*
Barry of 10 lion
[BRANDON]. *Mill Steph. 1516. (imp by
[Glemham] on brass (for Anne's parents) to
Hy Palgrave & w Anne [G], Barningham
Northwood, Norf).*
Barry of 12 lion
ESTOUTEVILLA, Jn de. *Birch 5901.* SIGILLUM
IOH[A]NNIS DE ES[TOU]TEVIL..... *1255.
([miles, of Eckington, Derbys]; equestr sl
obv).*
Burely lion
SUFFOLK, D of. *WB I 20, 13.*

Barry Arg and Az 1 lion Gu
Barry of 8 Arg and Az lion Gu
CYPRES, K of. *KB 28. (qrs 2&3).*
Barry of 10 Arg and Az lion Gu
— *XK 6. (qtd 3 by Eliz Wydvill, w of Edw
4).*
— *XB 20. (qtd by Wydevill).*
CYPRES, Rex de. *LMRO 20, 19.*
LUSIGNAN, Cipaus. *Sandford 374 & 407.
(qtd 3 by Eliz Widvile, w of K Edw 4).*
SYPRES, Rex de. *LMO 19. (arms of*

Lusignan, Ks of Cyprus from 1192).
Barry of 12 Arg and Az lion Gu
— *CRK 1319.*
LUXEMBOURG. *PLN 584.*
Barry of 14 Arg and Az lion Gu
LUXEMBOURG, Count of. *XL 426.*
MARCHE, Pain de la. *XL 336. (a&l Or).*
Burely Arg and Az lion Gu
— *AS 16. (qtd 2&3 by le Roy de Cypre,
1&4 being 'les arme jadis le roy de
Jherusalem').*
CHYPRE, le roy de. *LM 2.*
CYPRESS, The Kyng off. *Lyndsay 28.*
CYPRUS, K of. *FK I 27. ('of the house of
Lusignan' added by Gibbon).*
CYPRUS, K of. *TJ 4.*
CYPRUS, K of. *FK I 28. (qtd 2&3 by K of
Jerusalem).*
[CYPRUS]. *FK I 38. (qtd 3 on tierced coat of
Armenia).*
ESCOTEVILL, Baron. *CK a 41.*
LUXEMBURG. *CA 121. (qrs 1&4 of
Ghistelles).*
LYGNY, Sr Waleran de. *CKO 98.*
MARCHE, Mons Payn de la. *WJ 1150.*
MARCHE, Payn de la. *XF 416. (a&l Or).*

Barry Arg and Gu 1 lion
Barry Arg and Gu lion Az
SHERLAND. *Nichols Leics II 558. (Evington
Ch).*
Barry of 10 Arg and Gu lion Sa
— *L10 24, 1. (qtd 2&3 by Bleset).*
LESTOUTEVILLE, Robert de. *B 200. ('le Nor-
mant').*
Barry of 12 Arg and Gu lion Sa
— *Keepe 241. 1296. (Enamelled shield
formerly on ledge of tomb of William de
Valence, St Edmund's Chapel).*
ESTOTEVILE, Robert, of Norf. *LE 22.*
Barry of 14 Arg and Gu lion Sa
STUTEVILE, Robert de. *XL 335.*
STUTVYLL, Mons Robert de. *WJ 1159.*
Burely Arg and Gu lion Sa
ESTOTEVILLE, Estond de. *Q 174.*
OSTOTENILE. *L2 394, 2.*
STUTEVILLE, Robert de. *XF 419. (a&l Or).*
STUTTEVILLE, Robert de. *P 109.*

Barry Arg &c and Sa &c 1 lion
Burely Arg and Sa lion Gu
CHAUSI, Thomas de. *G 166. (?rectius Cha-
worth).*
Barry Az and Or lion Gu
GERNEGAN FIZ HUGHE. *FW 592.*
Barry Gu and Or lion Arg
PEVERELL. *PT 619.*

Barry of 14 Gu and Sa lion Or
— *FK II 751.*
Barry Or and Az lion Gu
MOWNS. *L9 70b, 1.*
MOWNS, Ralph de. *XL 125. (a&l counterch of field; ?rectius Mohun).*
MOWNS, Mons Rauf de. *WJ 260.*
Barry of 12 Or and Az lion Gu
LISENIAN, Sr Geffrey. *F 5.*

Barry wavy 1 lion
Barry wavy Arg and Az lion Gu
— *CB 32.*
Barry wavy Arg and Sa lion Gu
ELSTED, Mons Gilbert de. *CA 107.*

Bendy 1 lion
Bendy of 8 Arg and Az lion Or
SWETHERIK, le Roy de. *AS 20. (armed Gu).*
Bendy Az and Gu lion Untinc
OCTOMEN. *KB 347.*
Bendy Az and Gu lion Or
— *LE 269. (a&l counterch of field).*
Bendy sin Gu and Az lion Or
OCTANION. *L2 387, 4.*

Checky &c 1 lion
Checky Or and Az lion Gu
ARMENTERS, Johan de. *D a 123.*
ARMENTERS, Munsire Johan de. *D b 123.*
Chevronny of 4 Sa and Arg on 1st Arg chev lion Sa
— *CRK 1440.*

Erm 1 lion
Erm lion Untinc
— *?source.* c1500. *(qr 3; on capital, Mold, Flints).*
ACTON, Richard de. *Birch 6786.* S' R[ICA]RDI D'ACTO...
LEGET, Thomas, esquire. *PRO-sls.* 1391-2.
[LISLE, Sir Humphrey, of Woodburn & Felton]. *Blair N I 25, 59. (qtg 2&3 Athol, all imp Ogle & Bertram; sculptured shield at Bothal Castle).*
LISLE, John de. *PRO-sls Ex KR 16/26, 45-49, HB-SND.* 1323.
LISLE, Robert de. *Dodsworth 68, 18, HB-SND. (d1367).*
LISLE, Robert de. *Dodsworth 49, 35, HB-SND.*
LISLE, Robert de. *Dodsworth 68, 17b, HB-SND.* c1299.
LISLE, Thomas. *Dodsworth 68, 18, HB-SND.* 1438-9.
[PICKERING, Theophilus, Rector of Sedgefield]. *Blair D II 184, 390a.* 15 cent. *(qtg 2&3 3 chaplets; font, Sedgefield Ch).*

Erm lion Az
Erm lion Az
— *BG 118.*
CREIGHTON, Robt, Bp of Bath & Wells. *Fryer 37. (mont, St John Bapt Chap, Wells Cath).*
LILLE. *L9 36b, 2. (a&l Gu).*
LISLE, Sir Robt, of Woodburn. *Blair N II 139, 279. (St Andrew's Ch, Newcastle-on-Tyne).*
LYLE, of Northd. *CT 454.*
LYLLE, Mons J de. *WJ 272.*
MEDEHOP. *TJ 40. (gloss on Sir Thos Pickering).*
[PICKERING]. *Dingley ccccxv. (imp by Stapleton; Lacock Ch, Wilts).*
PICKERING, James. *S 173. (blazoned embelif).*
[?PICKERING], Robert. *S 172.*
PIKERING, Mons' Robert. *S 170.*
PYKERING, Mons' James le. *S 171.*
PYKERYNG. *PO 290.*

Erm lion Gu
Erm lion Gu
— *WJ 364. (blazon added in different hand).*
ESTENGRAVE, Sire Johan. *J 95.*
ESTENGREVE, Joan de. *E I 184; E II 184.*
ESTENGREVE, Mons' John. *TJ 56.*
ESTINGGREFE. *CT 416.*
FELBRYDGE, Mons. *T d 70.*
LEGAT. *L1 394, 3; L2 305, 8.*
LEGAT. *PT 364.*
LEGAT, Thomas, de Herts. *LY A 79.*
SEGRETY, Symon. *TJ 135. (blazoned passt).*
STANGRAVE. *LS 86. (a&l Az).*
STANGRAVE. *RB 477.*
STEYNGRAVE, Joan de. *Q 163.*
STRANGRAUE. *L1 592, 6. (a&l Az).*
TURBERVILE, Thomas. *XL 346.*
TURBERVILE, Thomas de. *FW 355.*
TURBURVYLLE, Mons Th. *WJ 205.*

Erm lion Sa
Erm lion Sa
— *SK 348.*
MARAIS, Denys de. *Q 585.*
STAPULTON, Willm, of Yorks. *WB III 104, 2.*
TOCHET, S' Tho', of Derbys. *CY 69, 274.*

Ermines &c 1 lion
Or ermined Gu lion Az
LUNEBURGH, le Duke de. *WJ 92.*
LUNEBURGH, D of. *XL 404. (?rectius semy of hearts).*
Ermines lion Or ch on shldr with cresc Sa
— *L10 29, 13. (qtd 2&3 by Browne).*

Fretty 1 lion
Gu fretty & lion Arg
    DEYWELLE, Sir John. *BR V 90*. *(?rectius*
    flory).
Gu fretty & lion Or
    BULMER, Sir Ralph. *CRK 1945*.

Lozengy 1 lion
Lozy lion
    BOGREBARIN, William (called). *PRO-sls*.
    S'WILL'I DICTI BOGREBARIN. 30 Apr 1350.
    GOLDWELL, James. *GutchWdU*. *(Bp of*
    Norwich, d1499 [see Bedford's Blazon of
    Episc 12&93]; imp 6 columbines 3, 2, 1 in
    chf 3 wells (or fountains); on screen (pulled
    down 1664) All Souls' College Chapel).
Lozy Erm and Gu lion Or
    WELLES. *XL 492*. *(a&l Az)*.
Lozy Erm and Vt lion Gu
    WELLES. *XL 562*.
    WELLYS. *FK II 218*. *(a&l Or)*.
Lozy Vt and Erm lion Gu
    WELLIS, John, of Middx. *WB III 111b, 6*.
    WELLYS, W. *RH, Ancestor vii 189*.

Paly 1 lion
Paly of 8 Arg and Gu lion Sa
    GLENDOUR, Owen. *Sandford 224*.

Per bend 1 lion
Per bend lion
    [BEESTON, Ralph de]. *Yorks Deeds IV 113*.
    1398.
Per bend Or and Gu lion Sa
    BUTTON, Rodger. *PLN 1770*.
Per bend Sa and Arg in chf lion Or
    [BRITAIN], K Leyr panim. *KB 65*.
Per bend Erm and Sa lion Or
    — *BG 339*.

Per bend sin 1 lion
Per bend sin lion
    TRABOME. *SussASColl xxii 272*. S.I.DE TRA-
    BOME. ?13 cent. *(HSL thinks it should be*
    lion & over all bend sin; sl found at Lewes in
    1874).
    WYREHAM, Ivo de, of Thetford. *PRO-sls*.
    1421-2.
Per bend sin Az and Arg lion counterch
    — *ML I 473*. *('Sylver & asur party per bas-*
    tron a lyon rampawnt contrecoloryd').
Per bend sin Or and Sa lion counterch
    FRANCEYS, Sir Thomas. *DX 74*.

Per chev 1 lion
Per chev Gu and Or lion Arg
    LANGLEI, Robt, of Northants. *WB III 87, 2*.
    (lion poss Vair; 'Painting not completed').
    LANGLEY, Robert, of Northants. *XV I 1165*.

Per chf 1 lion: see chf & over all

Per fess 1 lion
Per fess lion
    MERLAGE, Wm, of Derby. *Birch 11746*.
    1491.
Per fess Arg and Gu lion Sa
    BOTERELL. *FK II 561*.
Per fess Gu and Az lion Arg
    ROTHYNG, ... de. *SK 465*.
Per fess Gu and Az lion Or
    HASTYNS, Sir Robert. *PCL I 477*. *(drawn as*
    per fess but usually blazoned Az chf Gu &
    over all ...).
    SALLEY. *FK II 655*.
Per fess Or and Arg lion Az
    THORNBURY. *XL 508*.
    THORNEBERY. *CC 234b, 405*.
Per fess Or and Az lion Gu
    SANCTUS REYNOLDUS, Myles. *RH, Ancestor*
    ix 180.
Per fess Vt and Gu lion Arg
    — *FK II 886*.
Arg base wavy of 6 Az and Arg lion Gu
    VIVIAN. *XL 255*. *(a&l Sa)*.
Per fess dancetty of 2 Arg and Az in chf lion Az
    SKYPTON. *DV 44a, 1738*.

Per pale 1 lion
Per pale lion
    — *Mill Steph*. 1519. *(qtd 2 by Agmondes-*
    ham; brass to Jane A, w of Sir Jn Iwarby,
    Ewell, Surr).
    — *SHY 40*.
    — *Mill Steph*. 1519. *(imp by Agmondes-*
    ham; brass to Jane A, w of Sir Jn Iwarby,
    Ewell, Surr).
    BIGOD, Roger. *PRO-sls*. 1301. *(E of Norf)*.
    BIGOD, Roger. *Vinc 88, 72*.
    BIGOD, Roger. *Barons Letter*. *(E of Norf &*
    Marshal of Engld).
    BIGOD, Roger, of Scotld. *Stevenson*. 1292.
    (dex side bears marks like rings of mail).
    BLODWELL. *Mill Steph*. 1462. *(blazon un-*
    certain; brass to Dr John B, Dean of St
    Asaph & Rector of Balsham, Cambs at Bals-
    ham).
    BYGOD, Roger le. *PRO-sls*. 1295-6. *(dex*
    half of shield pounced). *(E of Norf &*
    Marshal of Engld).
    BYTHEMORE, William, of Nailsea, Som.
    Birch 8004. SIGILLU[M] WILL'I BY THE
    [M]ORE. 1484. *(imp barry on chf chev)*.
    MARSHALL. *Lawrance 27*. ?1231. *(Effigy,*
    Temple Ch; poss for Wm Marshall, E of
    Pembroke, d 1231).
    NEWPORT, John. *Mill Steph*. 1522. *(brass,*
    Furneux Pelham, Herts).
    NEWPORT, Robert. *Mill Steph*. 1518. *(brass*

to Robt N & w Mary [Alington], Furneax
Pelham, Herts).
NEWPORT, Robt. *Mill Steph.* 1518. *(imp
Alington; brass, Brent Pelham, Herts).*
Per pale lion to sin
[MARSHALL]. *Durham-sls 2537. (sl of
Agnesde Vesci, d1290, dau of Sibyl, dau of
Wm the Marshall, E of Pembroke, with
shields of her husb, father & grandmother).*

Per pale Arg & ...1 lion
Per pale Arg and Gu lion Sa
— *CRK 1839. (qtd 2&3 by Sulyard).*
BLADWELL. *Suff HN 3. (imp Notbene; All
Hallows, Sudbury).*
HUGHES. *LH 450.*
KIRKEBY, Wills de. *Q 393.*
KYRKBY, Wm. *SES 8.*
PYRLY. *DV 63a, 2498.*
PYRLY. *PT 515.*
ROBERT, Hewe. *RB 520.*
ROBERTES. *L1 541, 3. (armed Gu).*
Per pale Arg and Or lion Sa
PIRLY. *L1 507, 5.*
PYRLY. *L9 99a, 4.*
Per pale Arg and Sa lion Gu
KYRKEBY, Willam de. *LM 353.*
Per pale Arg and Sa lion Or
BIGHAM. *L1 103, 4; L2 59, 3. (a&l Gu).*
BYNGHAM. *L10 32, 18. (a&l Gu).*
Per pale Arg and Vt lion Gu
MARESCHAL, le counte. *LM 36.*
PUNDELARD, Robert. *FW 241.*

Per pale Az & ...1 lion
Per pale Az and Gu lion Arg
— *PT 22.*
ARDERNE, of Irld. *L2 14, 4. (a&l Gu).*
STORWYCH, Sir .... *CV-BM 76. (rectius
Norwych).*
Per pale Az and Sa lion Arg
— *PLN 442. (a&l Gu). (imp Sa 3 spear-
heads erect Arg).*
TREMARGAN. *WB IV 175, 885. (a&l Gu;
imp ...).*

Per pale Gu & ... 1 lion
Per pale Gu and Untinc lion Untinc
FITZ MABEU, ... le. *WLN 411. (unfinished).*
Per pale Gu and Az lion Arg
— *RL 29.*
NORWYCHE, Sir W. *WB I 37b, 11.*
ROWSWELL. *CRK 1779. (a&l Az).*
ROWSWELL, of Lymington, Som & of Devon.
Gerard 187. (tinct of lion unclear).
Per pale Gu and Az lion Or
DRAYTON, Jane. *XC 321. (qrs 1&4 of coat
imp by Wriothesley).*
OWLTIM. *L2 392, 8.*

Per pale Gu and Sa lion Untinc
[BELER]. *Nichols Leics II 228. (Kirkby Beler
Ch).*
Per pale Gu and Sa lion Arg
— *I2(1904)215. (qtd 2 by Jn Villars, of
Brokesby, Leics).*
— *WK 855. (a&l Or; qtd 2 by Villers).*
— *XC 235. (qtd 2 by Villiers).*
— *Nichols Leics II 262. (Melton Mowbray
Ch).*
— *L10 99b, 1. (qtd 2 by Villers).*
BELLER, Jacobus. *Q II 261.*
BELLER, James. *SES 7.*
BELLERS. *PT 777.*
BELLERS. *L10 26, 10. (a&l Az).*
BELLERS. *XFB 15. (qtd 2 by Sir Jn Villers,
de Brokesby, Leics).*
BELLERS, James. *BG 382. (armed Or
langued Az).*
BELLERS, James. *S 170. (armed Or langued
Az).*
BELLERS, Mons' James. *S 168.*
BELLERS, John, of Kettleby. *CRK 1418.
(a&l Az).*
BELLERS, of Leics. *PLN 1059. (a&l Sa).*
BELLERS, Mons' Rog' de. *WJ 191.*
BELLERS, Roger de. *XL 342.*
BILLERS, of Leics. *RH, Ancestor vii 185.
(name & tincts added in later hand).*
KIRBY. *L2 288, 6. (a&l Sa).*
KIRKEBY. *L1 377, 4; L2 288, 6.*
LEEK, of Leics. *L2 317, 5. (or ?Fitz-kyrke).*
NORWICH. *L1 475, 1.*
Per pale Gu and Vt lion Arg
BENGHAM, Sire Thomas. *O 159. (?Banham
fam of Norf, tenants of E Marshal?).*
BEVERIDGE, Sir John. *PLN 360.*

Per pale Or & ... 1 lion
Per pale Or and Az lion Arg
— *RL 29b, 1.*
Per pale Or and Az lion Gu
BYGOD, of Setterington, Yorks. *H21 49.*
BYGODE, of Setteryngton, Yorks. *D4 39b.
(name subsequently crossed out in ink).*
MARSHALE, Counte de. *Q 6.*
Per pale Or and Gu lion Arg
PLAYS, Sire Richard de. *O 79.*
Per pale Or and Gu lion Sa
PYRLEY, John. *RH, Ancestor vii 213.*

Per pale Or and Vt 1 lion
Per pale Or and Vt lion Arg
MARSHAL, Gilbert, Earl. *MP IV 47.*
Per pale Or and Vt lion Gu
BASSET, Gilebertus. *MP Hist Min ii 371. (to
whom the K gave 'virgam marescalciae
curiae suae' 11 June 1234).*
BIGOD, Ld. *CRK 1313. (a&l Az).*

[BIGOD], Erle Marshal. *BR IV 95.*
BIGOD, Mon' Roger, le Counte de Northfolk. *TJ 16.*
BIGOD, Rauf. *E II 303.*
BIGOD, Roger, E of Norfolk, Marshal of England. *LMS 31. (1189-1245).*
BIGOT, Erle. *RH, Ancestor v 181.* ('Count de Norfolk Erle Bigot'; 'Bokyngham' struck out & Norfolk added in later hand).
BIGOT, Roger, Conte de Norfolk. *TJ 1228.*
BYGOD, erll Marishall. *L10 31b, 1.*
BYGOD, E Marshal. *L1 36, 4; L2 47, 4.* (a&l Az).
BYGODD, of Setteryngton, Yorks. *D9 & E6.*
BYGODE, erle of Norfolk. *CT 15.*
BYGOT, Comes. *PT 6.*
BYGOT, Duke of Northefolk. *RH, Ancestor iii 202.* ('gold & wert party'; Roger le Bigod, E of Norf 1270-1306, Hereditary Marshal of Engld, last of Bigod line & prob 1st to bear these arms for the marshalship).
BYGOT, R, comit mareschall. *WJ 265.*
BYGOT, Richard, Count Marshall. *XL 376.* (a&l Az).
BYGOTT. *Suff HN 7.* (Lavenham Ch).
BYGOTT. *WB II 59, 1.*
BYGOTT. *WB I 34, 24.*
BYGOTT, Erle of Cambre. *KB 279.*
BYGOTT, Comes. *DV 58a, 2288.*
CARTMELL MONASTERY, Yorks. *D4 47.* (founded by Bygott, E Marshal).
MARCHAL, Cunte. *HE 26.*
MARCHAL, E. *BR V a 22.*
MAREESCALLUS, Gilebertus, Comes. *MP Hist Min ii 451. (d1241).*
MARESCALLE, Comes. *Q II 6.*
MARESCALLUS, Comes. *SM 165, 33; SM 314, 53.*
MARESCALLUS, Willelmus, comes de Penbroc. *MP Hist Min ii 331. (d1231).*
MARESCHAL, Counte. *F 21.*
MARESCHAL, le Counte. *N 1043.*
[MARESCHAL]. *Bellasis II 306-8.* (& Cartmel Priory; Windermere E Window; Machell & Hill add chf Az).
MARESCHALL, Cunte. *G 35.*
MARESCHALL, le Conte. *B 17.*
MARESCHALL, le Bygod. *SP A 28.*
MARESHAL, le Conte. *P 47.*
MARISCALE, Cunte. *E 18.*
MARSCHAL, C le. *WLN 43.*
MARSHAL, Anselm, Earl. *MP IV 67.*
MARSHAL, Gilbert, Earl. *MP I 65; MP II 18.*
MARSHAL, John. *DX 22.* (armed Az; E of Warwick, jure ux).
MARSHAL, Walter, Earl. *MP IV 66; MP V 2.*
MARSHAL, William, Earl. *MP I 47; MP IV 14; MP IV 30.*
MARSHALL, le Cunte. *FW 41.*

[MARSHALL]. *Neale & Brayley.* 1296. (Canopy of Mont, Edmund, E of Lancaster).
MARSHALL, William, E of Pembroke. *Sandford 87 & 96.*
NORFFOLKE, Cont de. *CN 9.*
NORFOLK, Erle of. *CK a 13.*
[NORFOLK], le C de. *NB 39.*
NORFOLKE, le Count de. *WLN 188.*
PEMBROKE, le Conte de. *C 143.*

Per pale Vt &... 1 lion
Per pale Vt and Gu lion Arg
[FELTON?]. *CRK 1996.* (tail outwards; a&l Or).
Per pale Vt and Or lion Gu
BIJGOT, S' Water. *CY a 114, 453.* (langued Arg).
BYGOT. *FB 70.*

Per pale patterned 1 Lion
Per pale Az and Gu billetty & lion Or
VERCHI, M' Giup de. *XL 594.*
Per pale Erm and Sa lion Or
BINGHAM. *XL 45.*

Per pale indented 1 lion
Per pale indented lion
— *PRO-sls.* 11 July 1540. (qtd 2 by Thos Wriothesley).
Per pale indented Az and Gu lion Or
DRAYTON, of London. *L1 216, 6; L2 161, 7.*
DRAYTON, Robard. *LD 159.*
Per pale indented Gu and Az lion Or
— *XFB 245.* (qtd 2 by the lorde Wryotesley, Chancellor of Englande).
— *WB I 33b, 7.* (qtd 2 by [Sir Thos] Wryotesley [E of Southampton]).
— *Leake.* (a&l Az; qtd 2 by Sir Thos Wriothesley KG, d1550).
DRAYTON. *XPat 109, Arch 69, 77.* (a&l Az).
Per pale indented Gu and Sa lion Arg
BELLERS. *L1 110, 3.* (7 indents).
BELLERS, Harry, of Stoke. *CRK 1332.* (a&l Az).

Per saltire 1 lion
Per salt Or and Erm lion Gu
BAGENHOLT, Sr Raulf, of Staffs. *L10 90b, 6.* (a&l Gu).
Per salt Sa and Erm lion Or
GRAFTON, of London. *L9 28a, 3.* (a&l Gu).

Qtly lion in dex chf: see Quarterly (in later volume)

Qtly 1 lion over all
Qtly lion
[OULTON]. *Mill Steph.* c1526. (qtd 2&3 by Starkey on brass to Hugh S, of Oulton,

d1526, Over, Ches).
[OULTON]. *Farrer II 403. (qtd 3 by [Heydon], Salthouse Ch, Norf).*
Qtly Arg and Gu lion Arg
OLTON, John de. *PCL II 76.*
Qtly Az and Gu lion Arg
— *BA 435. (qtd 2&3 by Hugh Starky).*
OLTON, John, of Olton, Ches. *L9 90a, 4. (a&l counterch).*
Qtly Az and Gu lion Or
OLTON, John de. *XL 604.*
REGINALDUS, Scs. *CV-BM 297.*
Qtly Gu and Az lion Arg
NEWPORT. *XL 520. (a&l counterch).*
NEWPORT. *L9 83b, 3.*
NEWPORT, of Essex. *L1 474, 4; L2 370, 2. (a&l counterch).*
Qtly Or and Vt lion Gu
BYGOD, Count Marshall. *XL 181.*
Qtly Vt and Gu lion Arg
OLTON. *L9 89a, 10. (a&l Az).*
OLTON. *L1 483, 5.*
OLTON, Johannes de. *Q II 718.*
OLTON, John de. *SES 148.*
OLTON, John de. *WLN 644.*
OLTON, John de. *CVC 562.*
OLTON, John de, Ches. *CY a 23, 90.*
OSTON. *CRK 691.*
OULTON. *XL 30.*
Qtly Gu & vairy Or and Vt lion Arg
[PEVEREL]. *XL 184. (tail outwards).*

Semy of annulets 1 lion
Arg semy of annulets Gu lion Sa
PERPOYNT. *H21 85.*
Sa semy of annulets lion Arg
FULTHORP. *L1 239, 1; L2 197, 6.*

Billetty 1 lion
Billetty lion
— *WB I 12, 9. (qtd III 3 by Lucy of Warwick).*
BULMER, Hugh of. *PRO-sls Ex KR 16/26, 10, HB-SND. 1322. (in roundel on dex, salt in roundel on sin).*
BULMER, Sir John. *Lawrance 7. (d1268; effigy, Bulmer, York).*
BULMER, Ralph of. *Durham-sls 454. 1400.*
BULMER, Sir Ralph of. *Durham-sls 455. 1485-6. (Hunter-Blair gives 'in an orle of 6 billets').*
BULMER, Tiphaine. *Dodsworth 49, 63b, HB-SND.*
BURGHERSH, Margaret de. *Birch 7952.* SIGILLUM: MARGARETE: DE: BURGHERSH. *1339. (field poss crusilly; imp by lion qf; sis of Ld Badlesmere, w of 4th Baron Burghersh).*
INCHMARTIN, John of, Ld of that ilk. *Stevenson. 1320.*

[PLANCHE], Matilda de. *Bow LI 4. 1305-6. (dau of Nicholas de Haversham, Lady of Claybrok Magna, & wid of [James de la P]).*
PLANCO, Jacobus de. *Bow LI 3.* Sigillu Jacob de Planco. *1297-8. (dominus de Claibrok [Claybrooke]).*
Untinc billetty & lion Or
BULMER, Sir R. *WB I 38b, 7.*

Arg billetty 1 lion
Arg billetty lion Gu
BOLMERE. *L2 87, 5.*
BULMER, Sire Roger. *N 1066.*
GRAMARYE. *ME 89; LY A 214.*
SAPI, Thomas. *F 196.*
SAPY. *LS 276.*
SAPY, John de. *E I 550; E II 552.*
TURBERVILLE, Mons' Thomas. *TJ 70.*
TWRBYRWYLE, Sir Tomas. *RH, Ancestor vii 214.*
Arg billetty lion Sa
— *I2(1904)82. (qtd III 3 by Mayster Lusey).*
— *XK 280. (qtd III 3 by Sir Thos Lucy).*
[PLANCHE, de la]. *PLN 953. (a&l Gu).*
[PLANCHE, de la]. *Nichols Leics IV 108. (Claybrook Ch).*
PLANCHE, John de. *XL 166.*
PLAUNCE, Jake de la. *G 145. (billets drawn as gouttes).*
PLAUNCHE, Sire ... de la. *N 363.*
PLAUNCHE, Sire Jak de la. *HA 30. (?lion crowned).*
PLAUNCHE, S Jakes de la. *ST 17.*
PLAUNCHE, Sire Jakes, de la. *HA 21, 14.*
PLAUNK, Mons J del. *WJ 320.*

Az billetty 1 lion
Az billetty lion Or
— *CRK 187. (tail turned in; qrs 2&3 of coat imp by Hoo).*
— *WB III 89b, 8. (qtd 2&3 by Sir Thos Burstetur).*
— *WLN 89.*
— *LE 257. (qtd II 2 by Phle duc de Bourgoigne).*
— *CRK 745. (qtd 2&3 by Sir Jn Burcester).*
BRIENNE. *PLN 592.*
BRUCE, Sir Robert. *CV-BM 113.*
BRUN, Mons William. *S 261.*
BRUNE, Mons' William. *TJ 169.*
BUR. *L10 86b, 5.*
BUR, William. *S 263.*
COFFLAN, Hugh de. *WLN 748.*
EU, le Counte d'. *C 28. (arms of Alphonse de Brienne, dit d'Acre, m Marie d'Issoudun, dau & co-h of Raoul de Lusignan & d'Issoudun, Count of Eu).*
GELLERS, le Conte de. *TJ 166.*
GELLERS, le conte de. *TJ 165.*

GELRE, le Duc de. *P 41.*
GISORS. *XL 67.*
JEFORS. *L2 278, 6.*
JESORE. *SK 88. (Gibbon adds 'alias Gisor';
qtg Bersetter).*
JESORE. *SK 89.*
JESORS, Sir John. *WB III 89b, 9. (a&l Gu).*
NASSAU, Count of. *XL 430.*

Gu billetty 1 lion
Gu billetty lion Arg
GRAMARY, Sr de. *CKO 89.*
Gu billetty Or lion Arg
CREPPINGE, Johan de. *LM 542.*
CREPPINGE, Sr Johan. *N 688.*
CREPYNG, of Lincs. *L2 134, 5.*
CREPYNGE, Jon de. *Q 429.*
GRAMARY. *L1 275, 2; L2 220, 12. (armed
Az).*
GRAMARY, Sr de. *CKO a 89.*
GRAMARY, Mons' William. *TJ 76.*
GRAMARY, Monsire William. *CG 57.*
GRAMARYE, Mons W. *WJ 148.*
GRAMMARY, William. *XL 270.*
GRAMORI, s'Welliam. *PO 663.*
Gu billetty lion Or
BOLMER, Sire Rauff. *PO 603.*
[BOULMER], Sr de. *CKO 45.*
BOWLMAR, Sir Rowfe, of Yorks. *RH, Ances-
tor vi 183.*
BULLMER. *CT 364.*
BULMER. *L1 95, 2; L2 55, 10.*
BULMER. *D4 27. (used by Marton
monastery, Yorks, founded by Bulmer).*
BULMER. *L10 81b, 15. (a&l Az).*
BULMER, Sir de. *Q II 574.*
BULMER, Mons' John, de Bulmer. *TJ 75.*
BULMER, Ralph. *BG 211.*
BULMER, Ralph, Ld. *S 107.*
BULMER, Sir Ralph. *XL 221.*
BULMER, Mons Rauf de. *WJ 257.*
BULMER, Monsr Rauf. *S 105.*
BULMER, S Rauf. *ST 89.*
BULMER, Sire Rauf. *N 1065.*
BULMER, Sir Rauff. *BA 599.*
BULMER, Sr Rauff. *M 51.*
BULMER, of Yorks. *D4 28b.*
CHATEAUVILLAIN, John de. *WLN 756.*

Or &c billetty 1 lion
Or billetty lion Az
[D'ANGLE], Sir Gyggard, Count de
Hon[tingdon]. *RH, Ancestor iv 243.*
HUNTINGDON, le Cont de. *WJ 96. ([Guis-
card d'Angle]).*
KICHARD. *CRK 468.*
SOLMES, Count of. *XL 432.*

Or billetty Sa lion Az
KYCHARD. *PLN 1187.*
Sa billetty lion Arg
— *Q 269.*
NARSTOFT, of Bucks. *L2 358, 4.*
NEIRMUST, of Bucks. *L9 82b, 10.*
NEYMYSTE. *CT 424.*
NEYRMYST. *L1 472, 5.*
NEYRNUYST, Sire Johan. *N 378.*
[?UFFORD], Johannes. *Q II 210. (name illegi-
ble).*

Semy of crescents 1 lion
Semy of crescs lion
[LISTER]. *Mill Steph. 1472. (?semy of
decrescs; brass to Robt Ingleton & 3 wives,
Thornton, Bucks; arms of 2nd w ?Isabel or
Clemens [Lister]).*

Crusily botonny 1 lion
Crusily botonny lion
BREAUS. *CT 27.*
BREWES. *CT 208.*
Arg crusily botonny Sa lion Gu
— *CT 413.*
Az crusily botonny lion Arg
KYNARDESLEYE. *CT 110.*
Az crusily botonny lion Or
BRAOSE, Sir Thos. *Lambarde 95. 1395.
(Mont at Horsham, Suss).*
BREWSE, Sir John, of Suss. *RH, Ancestor iv
247.*
Gu crusily botonny lion Arg
GRAMARY, Mons' Henry. *TJ 168.*
DE LA WARE, John. *CT 269.*
Or crusily botonny lion Az
LOVEL, Sire Richard. *PV 29. temp Edw 2.*
LOVELL, Rycharde. *CT 135.*
Or crusily botonny Gu lion Sa
VACHE, de la. *CT 378.*
Sa crusily botonny lion Arg
HAUTEVILE, Sir Jeoffrey. *WNS 26, 67. ('Sire
Jeffrei de Hauteuile por de sable croisete de
croiz botonez dar ou un lion rampant dar').*

Crusily couped 1 lion
Crusily couped lion
BREOUSE, William de, Ld of Gower. *Barons
Letter.*
LOVELL, Richard. *Stevenson. 1297. (in cir-
cle, not on shield; 1st Baron L, of Kary, s of
Hugh L).*
Arg crusily couped Az lion Gu
MOUNFORT, de. *WNR 48.*
Az crusily couped lion Untinc
— *BR VI 7. (marshalled by Ld Louel).*
Az crusily couped Or lion Arg
BREWES, Willa de. *Q 166.*

Az crusily couped lion Or
BREWES, William de. *WLN 692.*
Sa crusily couped lion Or
GOSEHALE, Johan de. *LM 498.*

Semy of crosslets 1 lion
Crusily lion
— *WB V 95. (qtd 2 by Sir Thos Cokesey
[KB 1485]).*
— *Birch 7952.* SIGILLUM: MARGARETE: DE:
BURGHERSH. 1339. *(?billetty; imp by Mgt de
Burghersh, sis of Ld Badlesmere, w of 4th
Baron Burghersh).*
— *Birch 11404. 14 cent. (qtd 2&3 by Robt
Lovell).*
BRAND, Robert. *Birch 7744.* SIGILLVM.-
ROBERTI..... 1370.
BRAOSE, William de. *PRO-sls.* 1301. *(slung
from branches of tree).*
BREOUSE, William de. *Birch 7794.*
+S.WILL'I.DE.BREOUSE.DN'I.HONOR'.DE
BREMBR' & DE.GOER'.. 1301. *(Ld of Honours
of Brember, Suss, & Gower Glam; sl obv).*
BREOUSE, Wm de. *Birch 7795.* S' WILLELMI.-
DE.BREAVSSE. 1322-6. *(on loz; Ld of
Honours of Brember, Suss & Gower, Glam).*
BREWOS, Wm de, Ld of Bramber & Gower.
Bk of Sls 315. 1318-20.
BREWYS. *Mill Steph.* 1426. *(brass to Sir Jn
de B, Wiston, Suss).*
BYRTE. *WB V 61.*
CHARLTON, Thomas, Bp of Hereford. *Birch
1608.* S....M.THOME.DE.CHERLETON. 1344.
(1327-44).
[?FLAMANK], Peter. *Birch 9824.* SIGILL':
PETRI..... 1366. *(used by Jn, s of Peter
Flamank, of Nanstallan, ?Cornw).*
KYNARDESLEYE, Hugh de, of Herefs, Kt.
Birch 11168. +S'HVGONIS.DE.KYNARDISLEY.
1311.
LENFANT, Walter. *PRO-sls.* 1302.
LIVET, John. *Birch 11355.* SIG'.IOHANNIS.-
LIVET. 14 cent.
LIVET, John. *Arch Journ viii 78.*
SIG'IOHANNIS.LIVET. *(sl prob of the Jn L
certified Ld of township of Firle, Suss in
1316 [Parl Writs ii (2) 335]).*
[LOVEL]. *Mill Steph. (qtd 2&3 by Seymour
as imp by Zouch; on brass to Wm, Ld Zouch
of Harringworth, d1462, & 2 wives Alice
Seymour & Eliz St John, Okeover, Staffs).*
[LOVEL]. *Bow XXX 28.* 1434-5. *(subqtd by
[St Maur] & all qtd by Wm, Ld Zouche, of St
Maur, Totnes & Haringworth).*
[LOVELL]. *Mill Steph.* 1485. *(brass to Jn
Seyntmour & w Eliz, Beckington, Som).*
SNETTON, Simon de. *PRO-sls.* 1377-8.
VEUTER, Simon. *PRO-sls.* 1406-7.
WARRE, Thomas la. *Birch 14285.* SIGILLUM

THOME LA WARRE. 1389.
WARRE, Thomas la, of Lincs, Clerk. *Birch
14286.* SIGILLUM THOME LA WARR. 1396.
Crusily lion to sin
BRAOSE, Sir Gilbert. *Lawrance 7.* ante
1350. *(Effigy, Horton, Dorset).*

Arg semy of crosslets 1 lion
Arg crusily lion Az
BORNELL, Sr de. *CKO 43. (Sr de Lovell in
copy A).*
LOUEL. *L2 315, 10.*
SEYMOUR, Sir .... *PLN 2057. (qtg 2&3 Arg
2 chevs Gu).*
Arg crusily Gu lion Az
— *WLN 515; F 417.*
BUKES, Walter. *TJ 69. (gloss on Wm
Giffard).*
FALCONBRIDGE. *BG 372.*
GIFFARD, William. *E I 559; E II 561.*
MONTFORD, Thomas. *S 179. (?lion embelif).*
MONTFORD, Sir Thomas, of Yorks. *CRK
1456.*
MOUNFFORT, s' Laurence. *PO 571.*
MOUNFORD, Mons' Thomas. *S 177.*
MOUNFORT, Sire ... de. *N 203.*
MOUNTFORD, Sr de. *CKO 91.*
MOUNTFORD, Thomas de. *P 163.*
MOUNTFORT, S. Alexander de. *ST 56.*
MOUNTFORT, Mons' Thomas. *TJ 94.*
MOWMFORD, of Yorks. *MY A2 250. (lion Or
in original).*
Arg crusily Gu lion Or
MOWMFORD, of Yorks. *MY 250.*
Arg crusily Gu lion Sa
LIVET, Robert. *A 137.*
LYVETT, Robert. *FW 660.*
Arg crusily Sa lion Gu
GIFFARD, William. *F 204.*
Arg crusily lion Sa
BOKMONSTRE, Sire William. *O 68.*
[BREWSE]. *Farrer II 86. (shield, Sall Ch,
Norf).*
HAUTEUILLE. *L2 245, 2. (a&l Gu).*
HAUTEVILLE, Sir Thomas. *LH 277.*

Az semy of crosslets 1 lion
Az crusily lion Arg
— *PLN 2029. (qtd I 2&3 by Sir Wm
Griffith).*
— *XK 156. (qtd I 2&3 by Sir Wm Griffiths).*
— *SK 785.*
— *BA 18. (qtd 2 by Sir Ric Delabere).*
— *XV I 942. (qtd I 2&3 by Griffith).*
BRAYTOFT, Mons de. *CB 100.*
BRAYTOFT, Sr de. *CKO 44.*
BRAYTOFT, of Braytoft Hall, Lincs. *L10 76b,
11. (a&l Gu).*
BRAYTOFT, of Braytoft Hall, Lincs. *XL 202.*

BRAYTOFT, Jane. *XL 203. (imp by Massing-berd).*

KINARDSLEIE, Jehan de. *E II 288.*

KINARDSLEIE, Richard de. *E I 287.*

KYNARDESLE, Sire Huge de. *N 966.*

KYNARDESLEY. *L1 378, 5.*

Az crusily Gu lion Untinc

BREWES, Sir Brian. *BR V 76. (crosses & lion prob Or; 10 crosses).*

Az crusily Gu lion Arg

MONFORT, s'Ailsander. *PO 636.*

Az crusily Or lion Arg

DALTON, Monsire de. *CG 55.*

HOULAND, Mons Henry de. *AS 443.*

Az semy of crosslets 1 lion Or

Az crusily lion Or

— *XE 113. (qtd 2 by Cooksey).*

— *WB I 31, 10. (qg 2&3 Az 3 garbs Or).*

— *L9 22b, 4. (qtd 2 by Kokesey).*

— *L10 38, 2. (qtd 2&3 by Cokesey).*

— *BA 843. (qtd 2 by Sir Thos Cokesey).*

— *L9 10, 3. (qtd 2&3 by Kokyssey).*

— *PLN 1988. (qtd 2 by Sir Thos Cokesay).*

— *WK 31. (qtd 2 by Sir Thos Cokesey).*

— *WK 57. (qtd 2 by Sir Thos Cookesey, alias Grevell).*

BRAOSE, Ld. *CRK 1312.*

BREUSE. *PT 565.*

BREUSE, Monsire de. *AN 76.*

BREUSE, Monsr Thomas. *S 438.*

BREUSE, Willem. *HE 86; FW 109.*

BREUSE, Munsire William. *D b 148.*

BREUSE, Sire William. *J 82; N 66.*

BREUSE, William. *F 1; D a 148; A a 87.*

BREUSE, Wm de. *B 55. (10 crosses).*

BREWASE, William de. *E I 58; E II 58.*

BREWES, le Sire de. *XL 638.*

BREWES, le Sire de. *WJ 110.*

BREWES, S Wm de. *ST 73.*

BREWOSE. *L10 75b, 4. ('de Maningford brewse Will Dns berkeley heres m').*

BREWOSE, Monsr de. *AS 274.*

BREWS. *WB II 52, 16.*

BREWS, of Bucks. *L2 52, 6.*

BREWSE, Sir John, of Suss. *RH, Ancestor iv 247.*

BRWS. *DV 67a, 2660.*

JORDAN. *Gerard 117 & 137. (of Jordans in Ilminster).*

[JURDEYNE]. *D13 151. (qtd 3 by Trenchard).*

Gu semy of crosslets 1 lion

Gu crusily lion Arg

LAWARE. *PO 327. (name in later hand).*

WARE, de la. *PT 875.*

LA WARE, Sir John. *BR IV 19.*

WARE, Mons' John la. *TJ 57.*

WARE, Sir John la. *CKO 94.*

WARR, John de la. *GutchWdU.* c1390. *(formerly in N window, old chapel [demol 1620], Oriel Coll).*

Gu crusily Arg lion Or

ESMTON. *LE 105.*

ESTONE, Johan. *F 270.*

ESTONE, John de. *E I 453; E II 455.*

Gu crusily Or lion Arg

BREWES, S' John de. *R 14.*

Gu crusily lion Or

HOPETON, Water de. *E I 276; E II 278.*

HOPTON, Sir Walter. *LH 204.*

HOPTON, Walter. *LH 821.*

HOPTON, Walter. *LH 237.*

HOPTONE, Walter de. *F 257.*

HOPTTON, of Gloucs. *L2 271, 2. (a Kt Marshall).*

KNEL. *L1 380, 5; L2 291, 8.*

OPTON. *L1 485, 2.*

OPTON. *L2 392, 4. (Hopton in margin).*

OPTONE. *L9 90a, 3.*

OPTONE, Sire Walter de. *N 918.*

LA WARRE, Thomas. *ML I 32.*

Or semy of crosslets 1 lion

Or crusily lion Az

— *I2(1904)198. (qtd II 2&3 by Jn Zowche 'sone and heyer of The Lord Zowche' Arg 2 chevs Gu).*

BREWSE. *WB II 49, 16. (qrs 1&4; Brewse struck out & Stuwre added in later hand).*

LOUVEL, Sr Richard. *L 25.*

LOVEL. *Proc Soc Antiq XVII 2S 56. (qtd by Seymour in dex part of tierced shield with Zouch (centre) & St John of Bletso (sin), on Oker mem brass at Okeover, Staffs).*

LOVEL. *XL 9.*

LOVEL, Sire Richard. *N 127.*

LOVELL. *FK I 117. (name added by Gibbon; qtd 2&3 by Ld Seymour).*

LOVELL, Ld, of [Castle] Cary. *Gerard 54.*

LOVELL, Mons' Richard. *TJ 84.*

LOVELL, Monsire Richard. *CG 85.*

LOVELL, Monsr' Richard. *AS 273.*

MONTFORT, Alexander de. *CG 102.*

SEYMOUR, Ld. *PLN 118. (qg 2&3 Arg 2 chevs Gu).*

ST AMOUND, Ld. *LD 15. (qrs 1&4).*

ST MAUR. *CRK 195. (tail turned inwards; qrs 1&4).*

Or crusily lion Gu

[LONG]. *WB II 59, 7.*

Or crusily Gu lion Sa

— *CRK 1336.*

LA ROCHE. *SP A 126.*

Or crusily lion Sa

ARDARN, Randulf de. *F 248.*

ARDERN. *L10 2, 10.*

ARDERN. *RB 453.*

ARDERNE. *XL 105.*
ARDERNE, Randolf de. *E I 527; E II 529.*

Sa semy of crosslets 1 lion
Sa crusily lion Arg
— *LH 357. (qtd 2&3 by Hanham).*
— *WB I 30, 4. (qtg 2: Arg on chf Gu ?roundel betw 2 ?stags' heads cab Or 3: Gu 2 wings conjd Untinc).*
HANTEUILLE. *L1 326, 3. (armed Gu).*
HAUTEVILE, Sire Geffrei de. *N 183.*
HAUTEVILLE, Sire Geffrey. *O 57.*
HAUTEVILLE, Sir Geoffrey. *LH 189.*
HAUTUILE, de. *CC 225, 129.*
HAUTVILE, de. *DV 43a, 1683. (armed Gu).*
LONG, of Draycot. *XL 242.*
LONG, of Draycott. *BA 827. (a&l Gu).*
LONG, Sir Henry. *XK 149. (qrs 1&4).*
LONG, Mayster Henry, Miltes. *I2(1904)200. (qg 2: Arg on chf Gu roundel betw 2 stags' heads cab Or 3: Gu 2 wings reversed Or).*
LONGE. *L9 41b, 4. (a&l Gu).*

Crusily fitchy 1 lion
Crusily fitchy lion
[HOBURY]. *Mill Steph. (qtd 2 by Manfield on sundry brasses 1455-1617, Taplow, Bucks).*
KNELLE, Edmund de. *PRO-sls E40 A6785.* 1356.
KNELLE, Edmund de, of Suss, Kt. *Birch 11096.* S'.EDMVNDI.DE.KNELLE. 1346.
LIVET. *SussASColl V 202.* SIG'.JOHANNIS LIVET. early 14 cent.
TUCHET, William. *PRO-sls.* IESU SEL DE AMUR LEL. 1301.
WALTON, Henry de. *PRO-sls.* 1351 & 1359-60. *(Archdeacon of Richmond, keeper of the King's wardrobes).*
WALTON, Henry de. *PRO-sls.* 1359.
WARR, John, Ld la, Kt. *Bk of Sls 246.* 1393.
WARRE, Sir Roger la. *Proc Soc Antiq IV 2S 390.* 15 June 1391. *(sl of Joan West, dau of Sir Roger la Warre & w of Sir Thos West; attached to charter of feoffment).*
WARRE, Sir Roger la. *Proc Soc Antiq IV 2S 389.* SIGILL'ROG[ERI L]A WARRE. 23 Aug 1359. *(sl attached to indent).*
WESTON, William de. *Birch 14425.* SIGILLUM WILLELMI ...ON. 1376. *(of Kentwell Manor, Suff).*
WESTONE, John de. *PRO-sls.* 1317-18. *(formerly King's chamberlain in Scotland).*
Arg crusily fitchy lion Az
BRAYTOFT. *L10 76, 8. (a&l Gu).*
Arg crusily fitchy Gu lion Az
MONFORD, Mons Laur'. *WJ 279.*
MONTFORT. *BA 622.*
MONTFORT. *XL 230.*
MONTFORT, Dorset & Som. *L1 430, 2; L2*

323, 11.
MOUNFORD. *L9 70b, 2.*
Arg crusily fitchy lion Gu
BRET. *L10 78, 5.*
BRETT. *Gerard 104. (of Sandford Brett, Yeovil & Whitestaunton).*
BRIGHT, William. *CRK 1144.*
BRYTTE, Wyllm. *PLN 357. (HSL says crusily botonny fitchy).*
Arg crusily fitchy Sa lion Gu
HARTELYNGTON. *L2 259, 7.*
Arg crusily fitchy lion Sa
CORBET. *BG 349 & 350.*
HAUTEUILLE, Cornw & Devon. *L1 337, 6; L2 245, 1. (a&l Gu).*
HAUTEVILE. *XL 498.*
HAUTEVILE, Monsire de. *CG 92.*
HAUTEVILL, Monsr de. *AS 365.*
HAUTEVILLE. *LH 77.*
HAUTEVILLE. *LH 802.*
HAUTEVILLE, Mons' Thomas. *TJ 129.*

Az crusily fitchy 1 lion
Az crusily fitchy Or lion Arg
BRAYNE, conte. *L10 23b, 9.*
Az crusily fitchy lion Or
— *XK 259. (qtd 6 by Sir Thos Berkeley).*
— *WGA 80. (qtd 6 by Sir Thos Howard, D of Norf).*
— *WK 464. (qtd 6 by Sir Morice Barkeley).*
— *XK 102. (qtd 6 by Sir Maurice Berkeley, Kt 1509).*
BRAYNE, de Ponzet. *L10 23b, 10.*
BREHOUSE, de. *SP A 83.* temp Edw 1.
BREWES, Sire Thom'. *PO 201. (langued Gu).*
BREWES, Thomas le. *S 443.*
BREWSE, Monsire de. *CG 86.*
BREWSE, Mons' Thomas. *TJ 85.*

Gu crusily fitchy Arg 1 lion
Gu crusily fitchy lion Untinc
[WEST, Ld De La Warr]. *Hutton 30. (qtg 2&3 3 fleurs de lis; mont of Ctess of Worc in St Jas Garlickhythe, London, in 1619; ?poss for Eliz, dau of Ld de la Warr, 2nd w of Chas Somerset, cr E of Worc 1614; Hutton calls qrs 2&3 'France sans differentia' but HSL says is it not Cantelow?).*
Gu crusily fitchy lion Arg
— *LS 298. (qtd 2&3 by West, all imp by St Amand).*
— *I2(1904)184. (qtg 2&3 Az 3 leopards' faces reversed jesst de lis Or, all qtd II&III by 'The Lord Laware').*
— *KB 306. (crosses in orle; qtd 2&3 by Cantilop, Ld Delaware).*
— *WK 427. (qtd XVIII 1&4 by Ld Ambros Dudeley).*

— *D 158a; HE 172.*
— *WK 540. (qtd II 1&4 by Thos, Ld Lawarre).*
DALAWARE, Ld. *PCL IV 119.*
DELAWARE. *L10 59, 14. (qrs 1&4).*
[DELAWARE]. *Lambarde 163. (small diamond pane of old glass in S window of nave, Twineham, Suss).*
DELAWARR, Ld. *PLN 991. (qtg 2&3 Az 3 leopards' faces reversed jesst de lis 1, 2 [Or?]).*
DELAWARRE. *L1 206, 6.*
LAWARRE. *L1 390, 1. (armed Az).*
LAWARRE, Ld de. *RH, Ancestor iv 228.*
WARE, Monsire de. *CG 46.*
WARE, Monsire la. *AN 73.*
WARE, Monsr le. *AS 275. (crosslets 'peagon' ie fitchy).*
WARE, Johan de la. *G 186.*
WARE, Sire Johan de la. *N 108. ('de goules crusule de argent a un lion rampaund argent').*
WARE, Mons' Robert de la. *TJ 120.*
WARE, Mons Roger le. *WJ 153.*
WARE, Roger de la. *K 183.*
WARE, Roger la. *FW 157.*
WARE, Roger la. *A 103. ('gules crusilly silver & a lion silver').*
WARE, Rogers de la. *K 23.*
LA WARR. *Lambarde 262-4. (qtg [Cantelupe]; Boxgrove, Suss).*
WARR, Ld de la. *CRK 1295.*
WARR, Ld de la. *XL 216.*
WARR, John, Ld de la. *S 55. (a&l Az).*
WARR, Thomas La. *XK 67. (qrs 1&4; KG temp Hen 8).*
WARR, [Thos] West, Ld La. *PR(1512)61. (qtg Cantelupe).*
LA WARRE. *Lambarde 262-4. (qtd by West; Boxgrove, Suss).*
LA WARRE. *Lambarde 262-4. (qtg [Burgh, Gresley & Thornley], all imp by West; Boxgrove, Suss).*
LA WARRE. *Lambarde 262-4. (imp Bonville; Mont to Thomas West, Ld La Warre & w Eliz Bonville, Boxgrove, Suss).*
WARRE, Ld de la. *PLN 1722. (qg 2&3 Az 3 leopards' faces reversed jesst de lis Or).*
WARRE, le Sr de. *CN 43.*
WARRE, John de la. *E I 164; E II 164.*
WEST, Sir Thomas. *WK 150. (crosslets fitchy at foot).*
WEST, Sir Thomas, Ld de la Warre. *BA 746.*
WEST, Thomas, Ld La Warre. *WGA 289.*
Gu crusily fitchy Arg lion Or
HOBURY. *XL 48.*
HOBURY. *LH 867.*
HOBURY. *LH 113.*
HOBURY. *SK 958.*

WARRE, le Sr la. *S 53.*

Gu crusily fitchy Or &c 1 lion
Gu crusily fitchy Or lion Arg
PENGELLI. *L9 108b, 1. (a&l Az).*
WARD, S' William de la. *R 84.*
WESTON, Mons Roger de. *WJ 176.*
WESTON, Roger de. *XL 350. (a&l Az).*
Gu crusily fitchy lion Or
— *WB IV 174b, 877. (qtd 2&3 by Sir Rychard Corbett).*
CAPEL. *L1 160, 4; L2 107, 2.*
HOPTONE, S' Water. *PO 660. (armed Az).*
HUTTON. *LH 979.*
KNELL. *L9 11b, 1.*
KNILL. *XL 15.*
Gu crusily fitchy Vt lion Arg
BAIOUSE, Mons Goselyn de. *CA 9.*

Or &c crusily fitchy 1 lion
Or crusily fitchy lion Az
LOVEL, Richard. *XL 645.*
LOVELL. *L9 35b, 8. (a&l Gu).*
LOVELL, Mons Rich. *WJ 112.*
Sa crusily fitchy lion Or
[CA]PELLE, [Sir] William. *WK 37.*
CAPELL, Sir William. *PLN 1992. (HSL says ends of crosslets are not carefully squared in MS).*

Semy of crosses formy &c 1 lion
Az semy of crosses formy lion Arg
— *WK 154. (qtd I 2&3 by Sir Wm Gryffith).*
Az semy of crosses formy lion Or
FROME. *H18 39d. (qtd 2 by Fyloll, of Woodland, Dorset).*
Or semy of crosses formy Az lion Sa
SAYMORE, Ld. *KB 310. (qrs 1&4; crosses in orle).*
Semy of crosses formy fitchy lion
TOUCHET, William, Ld of Levenhales. *Barons Letter.*
Gu semy of crosses formy fitchy lion Arg
MOBRAY. *L9 73b, 4.*
Or semy of crosses potent lion Sa
ARDERNE, Randolph de. *WLN 464.*

Semy of escallops 1 lion
Arg semy of escallops Gu lion Sa
MANBE, William. *A 115. ('This should go with Maufe').*
MAUFE, William. *D 255a; FW 256.*
MAUFE, Sr Wm, of Suss. *ME 100; LY A 225.*
MAUFEE, Sire Willame. *N 253.*
MAUSE. *L1 442, 1; L2 330, 10.*
Az semy of escallops lion Arg
?COMALE, Robarte. *FW b 154.*

Az 3 escallops Or lion Arg
POUTONE, S William de. *GA 17*. *('dasur a ung lyon rampant darge ou iii escalopes pudre dor')*.

Az semy of escallops Or lion Arg
?COMALE. *HE 174*. *(tinct of escallops uncertain)*.
?COMALE, Robart. *FW c 154*.

Sa semy of escallops lion Arg
HOLLAND, Sgr Richard de. *CKO a 68*.

Semy of fleurs de lis 1 lion

Semy de lis lion
— *Dugd 17, 2*. 1441. *(qtd 2&3 by Wm, Ld Lovell)*.
— *WK 744*. *(qtd II 4 by Sir Brian Stapilton)*.
— *PRO-sls*. 1408-9. *(imp by Maud, w of Sir Jn L)*.
BEAUMONT. *Mill Steph*. 1507. *(qtg 2: Comyn 3: Phelip 4: Bardolf; brass to Wm B, Visct Beaumont & Ld Bardolf, Wivenhoe, Essex)*.
[BEAUMONT]. *?Mill Steph*. 1391. *(brass to Margery [Zouch, 2nd] w of Robt de Willoughby Ld of Eresby, Spilsby, Lincs)*.
BEAUMONT & Folkingham, John, Visc. *Dugd 17, 2*. 1441.
BEAUMONT, Henry de, Kt. *PRO-sls*. 15 Oct 1316.
BEAUMONT, Henry, Ld. *Birch 7289*. 1366.
BEAUMONT, Henry de, Count de Buchan. *PRO-sls*. 27 March 1337.
BEAUMONT, John de, 4th Baron. *Birch 7292*. Sigillu: iohis: dni: de: bellomonte. 1383.
BEAUMONT, John, Visc. *Bk of Sls 55*. 1441.
BEAUMONT, Lewis de. *Birch 2459*. *(Bp of Durham 1318-33; obv & rev)*.
BEAUMONT, Lewis, Bp of Durham 1318-33. *Durham-sls 3130*.
BEAUMONT, Thomas de. *Clairambault 797*. 4 Nov 1432.
BEAUMONT, Thomas, Ld of Basqueville. *PRO-sls*. 1435-6.
BELLO MONTE, Henry de, Kt. *PRO-sls E40 A2489*. ...IGILLVM..CI.... 1368-9.
HOLAND. *Bk of Sls 384*. 1404.
HOLAND. *Birch 11402*. 1409-14. *(qtd 2&3 by Jn, 10th Baron Lovel of Tichmersh)*.
[HOLAND]. *PRO-sls AS 293*. Sigillum iohannis domini de lovel. 1412-13. *(qtd 2&3 by Jn, Ld Lovel)*.
[HOLAND]. *PRO-sls AS 278*. Sigillum: Matildis: dne: lovel: et: de: holand.. 1408-9. *(imp by Lovel, for Maud, w of Sir Jn L)*.
[HOLAND]. *PRO-sls AS 278*. Sigillu roberti lovell. 1408-9. *(qtd by Robt Lovel, esq)*.
[HOLAND]. *PRO-sls*. 1447-8. *(qtd by Wm Lovell, Ld of Burnell & Holand)*.
HOLAND, Maud de. *Bk of Sls 20*. 1337.

LUMLEY, Margaret de. *BrookeAsp I 76, 2*.
Sigill: Marggrete: de: Lumley.. ?1365. *(imp by 6 martlets; on shield betw 4 roundels)*.
[POOLE]. *Dingley cccccxiv*. *(imp by Baynard on mont of Edw Baynard, Lacock Ch, Wilts)*.

Arg semy of fleurs de lis 1 lion

Arg semy de lis Az lion Gu
THORP. *L1 631, 6*.

Arg semy de lis & lion Sa
ARCHBOLD. *LQ 84*.
BOCKEMESTRE, S' Will'. *PO 348*.
BOCKMINSTER, Monsire. *CG 93*.
BOCMESTRE, Mons William de. *CA 92*.
BOKMONSTRE, Sire Willame. *N 662*.
BOKMYNSTER, Monsr de. *AS 267*.
BUCKMASTER, William. *XL 156*. *(a&l Az)*.
BUCKMOUSTZ, Sr de. *CKO a 48*.
BUKMENSTER. *L1 45, 1; L2 72, 1*. *(armed Az)*.
BUKMYNSTER. *L10 81b, 16*. *(a&l Gu)*.
BUKMYNSTER, Mons Willm. *WJ 312*.

Az semy of fleurs de lis Arg lion Arg

Az semy de lis & lion Arg
— *I2(1904)102*. *(qtd II 4 by [Sir Bryan] Stapulton)*.
— *I2(1904)180*. *(qtd 8 by Bamfeld, of Poltemore, Devon; added by Jos Holland c1630)*.
— *PLN 784*. *(imp by vairy Arg and Sa)*.
— *PCL IV 143*. *(qtd 3 by Ld Lowell)*.
— *WB IV 153, 489*. *(imp by Morderrett)*.
— *PLN 2051*. *(qtd 2&3 by Sir Piers Edgcombe)*.
HOLAND, Sir Robert. *ML I 85; ML II 75*.
HOLAUND, Robert de. *CA 161*.
HOLLAND. *CT 256*.
[HOLLAND]. *OxfRS IV 215; OxfAS 83, 13*. 1455. *(qtd 3 by Lovel; tomb [restored 19 cent], Minster Lovel, Oxfs)*.
[MARCHALL, John?]. *RH, Ancestor vii 210*.
POULLE, Thomas. *BA 5*.
PUL. *L1 523, 6*. *(armed Gu)*.
PULL, Sir John de. *CRK 1086*. *(a&l Gu; or Pole)*.
PULLE, Sir John de. *CVC 575*.

Az semy of fleurs de lis Or lion Arg

Az semy de lis Or lion Arg
— *WLN 287*. *(qtd 2&3 by Wm Whorwood, d1545; an addition)*.
DALTON. *CC 233b, 374*.
DALTON. *L1 194, 1; L2 152, 11*. *(armed Gu)*.
DAULTON. *L10 53, 7*. *(a&l Gu)*.
POLE, Sir William. *XK 240*. *(qrs 1&4)*.
POOLE, Sir Thomas of. *BA 40, 388*.
POOLE, Wm. *I2(1904)196*. *(qtg 2&3 Arg*

chev Sa betw 3 stags heads cab Gu; 'Wyllm Poole in Wherhall Chestershyre & Poole').
POOLL', Sir Thomas. *WK 67.*
POOLLE. *L9 106a, 10.*
PULL', Sir John de. *WLN 335.*
SELEYDEN, de. *XL 624.*

Az semy of fleurs de lis Or lion Or
Az semy de lis lion Or
— *WB I 14b, 22. (qtd II 3 & III 1 by Stapulton).*
— *L10 94, 4. (qtd III 1 by Norreys or Norres).*
— *XFB 207. (qtd III 1 by Sir Bryan Stapylton).*
— *KB 283. (qtd 2&3 by Ld Beamond).*
— *WK 416. (qtd III 1&4 by Stapylton).*
BARNARD, le S'r de. *T c 25. (qtg 2&3 Az 3 garbs 'de comyn' Or).*
BEAMONT, Sir Jean, Viconte. *WGA 274.*
BEAMOUNT. *WK 173.*
BEAUMOND, Le Sire de. *TJ 101.*
BEAUMOND, La Wyscount de. *RH, Ancestor iv 228.*
BEAUMONT. *L1 36, 6; L2 39, 10. (a&l Gu).*
BEAUMONT. *BB 162, 12. (a&l Gu; 'le fycontte de Bemond', d1460).*
BEAUMONT. *?source. c1320. (sl of Bp B, of Durham).*
BEAUMONT. *L10 25b, 5. (qrs 1&4).*
BEAUMONT. *L10 25b, 16.*
BEAUMONT. *BB 83. (a&l Gu; 'Sir Jn de Bemond', d1396).*
BEAUMONT, Ld. *PLN 100. (a&l Gu).*
BEAUMONT, Ld. *FK I 107.*
BEAUMONT, Ld. *ML I 35.*
BEAUMONT, Ld. *D4 23b.*
BEAUMONT, Le Sr de. *S 46.*
BEAUMONT, Visct. *XL 641.*
BEAUMONT, Visct. *CRK 217. (tail turned in).*
BEAUMONT, le Sr de. *CN 64.*
[BEAUMONT]. *D4 23. (qtd 3 by Stapilton, of Notts).*
[BEAUMONT]. *Nichols Leics III 116. (Window in Woodhouse Chapel).*
BEAUMONT, Hen, Ld. *Sandford 113. (his dau Isabel m Hen, D of Lancaster d1361-2).*
BEAUMONT, Jn, Ld. *WGA 127. (qtg Az 3 garbs Or).*
BEAUMONT, Jn, Ld. *S 48. (or his s Hen).*
BEAUMONT, Sir John, KG. *Leake. (d1396-7; qtg Comyn).*
BEAUMONT, Vicecomes. *Q II 26.*
BEMOUNDE, Ld. *PCL IV 121.*
BEMOUNT, Ld. *BW 7b, 38. (qrs 1&4).*
BEMOUNT, Vicount. *AY 87. (qrs 1&4).*

Gu &c semy of fleurs de lis 1 lion

Gu semy de lis lion Arg
DEWILLE, Devon. *L2 163, 2.*
DEYVILE, Sr Johan. *N 1108; G 40. (tincts unclear).*
Gu semy de lis & lion Or
BEAMOUND. *WB II 51, 12.*
Sa semy de lis Or lion Arg
[HOLLAND]. *?source. (qtd by Lovell; Glass Banbury, Oxfords).*
PHILIPPE. *XPat 387, Arch 69, 98.*
Vt semy de lis lion Or
REISTON, Mons Raufe de. *WJ B 363.*

Semy of foils 1 lion
Semy of 3foils lion
— *Roman PO 2168. 26 May 1445. (qtd 2&3 by Robt Brews).*
WARRE, Thomas la, clerk. *Baker-sls. 1389-90. (Power of attorney to deliver seisin of manor of Albrighton [Salop]).*
Untinc semy of 3foils Or lion Arg
— *Nichols Leics I 495. (glass in Wigston's Hospital).*
Semy of 4foils lion
BAUD, John, Rector of St Nicholas Cole Abbey. *PRO-sls E329, BS 22. S'IOH'BAUD.-CDQT. .ORDE?. 4 Oct 1376.*
Semy of 5foils lion
CLIFTON, Sir Gervis. *Mill Steph. 1491. (s&h of Sir Robt; brass at Clifton, Notts).*
CLIFTON, Sir Robt. *Mill Steph. 1478. (brass at Clifton, Notts).*
PIERPOINT, Sir Robert. *Lawrance 35. c1260. (Tomb, Hurstpierpoint, Suss).*
Arg semy of 5foils Gu lion Sa
PERPOUNT, le Seigneur de. *CKO 58.*
PIARPOUNT, Syr Wyllm. *I2(1904)139. (qtg 2: Arg 6 annulets (2, 2, 2) Sa 3: Az 3 hedgehogs Or).*
[PIERPOINT]. *Nichols Leics IV 187. (Mont of Robert Walshall (d 1508) & his w, Frolesworth Ch).*
Arg semy of pd 5foils lion Sa
CLYFTON, Sir Gereys of, of Notts. *WB III 77, 8. (a&l Gu).*
PERPENT, Ed'us. *Q II 587.*
Sa semy of 5foils lion Arg
[CLIFTON]. *Nichols Leics IV 872. (Peckleton Ch).*
CLIFTON, of Barrington. *Gerard 122.*
CLYFTON. *H21 21.*
Sa semy of pd 5foils lion Arg
CLYFTON, Gervasius de. *Q II 608.*
Sa semy of 5foils slipped lion Or
— *Nichols Leics II 228. (Kirkby Beler Ch).*

Semy of fruit 1 lion
Semy of acorns lion
    ACTON, Richard de. *Durham-sls 24 & 25.*
    1333. *(Mayor of Newcastle-upon-Tyne).*
Gu semy of acorns Or lion Arg
    PENGELLY. *BA 985. (a&l Az).*
    PENGELLY. *XL 257. (a&l Az).*
    PENGELLY. *LEP 40.*
    PENGELLY. *L1 497, 4. (a&l Az).*
    PENGELLY. *L9 92b, 4.*

Semy of gouttes &c 1 lion
Arg gutty Gu lion Sa
    TOUCHET, Sir Thomas. *XL 608.*
Arg gutty Or lion Sa
    TOCHET, Sir John, of Derbys. *CV-BM 181.*
Az gutty Gu lion Arg
    BREWNE, Sir Tomas. *RH, Ancestor vii 213.*
    BRUNE, Mons Thomas. *TJ 49. (tail 'estant';*
    blazoned Az lion Arg queue gutty Gu).
Az gutty Or lion Arg
    ARABIE, le roy de. *LM 18.*
Gu gutty Or lion Arg
    CREPPINGE, Johan. *G 119. (prob an error*
    for billetty).
Gu gutty lion Or
    BULMER, Johan. *G 114.*
Or semy of hearts Gu lion Az
    LUNEBURG, le Duke de. *WJ B 92.*
Az semy of lozs lion Untinc
    BEAUMONT, Ld de. *WLN 252. (unfinished).*
Arg semy of mascles Or lion Purp
    HERTFORD, Sir Thomas, of Badesworth. *LH*
    273. (a&l Az; tincts of field & mascles un-
    certain).
Arg semy of mullets Gu lion Sa
    PIERPOINT. *PLN 1449. (qtg 2&3 Arg 6*
    annulets 2, 2, 2 Sa).
    PYRPOYNT. *PLN 1448. (imp Arg 6 annulets*
    Sa; Le Neve notes against it 'Nott & Heriz').

Semy of pheons 1 lion
Semy of pheons lion
    — *Bow XXX 1. (qtd 4 by Samson Meverell,*
    Kt, of Throwley, Staffs).
Arg semy of pheons Sa lion Gu
    ROOP, ... de. *WLN 680.*
    ROOPE. *BA 3.*
    ROOPE. *CRK 366.*
    ROOPE. *XL 50.*
    ROPE. *L1 550, 5.*
    ROPE. *SK C 1001.*
Arg semy of pheons lion Sa
    ROPE. *SK A&B 1001.*
Gu semy of pheons lion Arg
    ROOP. *CVC 636. (pts down).*

Semy of roundels 1 lion
Roundelly lion
    KYLKENNI, William de. *Birch 11071.* 1340.
    (imp 5 lozs in fess [dimidiated?] each ch with
    ?5 roundels in pale; s of Wm de K, Kt, of co
    Durham).
Az roundelly & lion Arg
    — *WLN 148.*
Az roundelly & lion Or
    — *RH, Ancestor v 182. (Yorks).*
    — *RH, Ancestor vii 205.*
Gu roundelly Or lion Arg
    — *D4 28. (a&l Az; qtd 2&3 by Ardyngton,*
    of Ardyngton, Yorks).
    HEWICK. *LH 1116.*
    HEWICK, Monsire de. *CG 72.*
    HEWICK, Nicol. *XL 267.*
    HEWICK, Sir Nicol, Ches. *LH 647.*
    HEWIKE, Sir de. *Q II 581.*
    HEWYK. *D4 26b. (qtd by Hungate).*
    HEWYK. *H21 12b.*
    HEWYK, Mons' Nichol. *TJ 39. (Gloss on*
    'Malhom pt Ratclif').
    HEWYK, Mons Nicol. *WJ 147.*
    HEWYK, s' nicole. *PO 655.*
    HEWYK, Monsr Nychol de. *AS 205.*
    HEWYK, Sir Nycoll. *RH, Ancestor vii 214.*
    HEWYKE, Sir Nicol. *LH 268.*
Or roundelly Gu lion Az
    SWEDEN, K of. *LO B 50.*

Vair 1 lion
?Vair lion Untinc
    REYDON, Eliz. *PRO-sls.* 1340. *(w of*
    Ralph).
Vair lion Or
    — *WLN 169.*

1 lion patterned or charged

Lion head distinguished
Az lion Arg head, mane, paws and tail tuft Gu
    NONYS APPRES. *XL 602. (a&l Or).*
Gu lion Or head, mane and dexter forepaw Arg
    GRACE. *XL 500. (a&l Az).*
Gu lion Or head and mane Arg
    GRAS, de. *CC 222, 3.*
Gu semy of 5foils lion Or head erased Arg
    GRACE. *L1 282, 4; L2 222, 10.*

Lion barry &c
Gu on lion Arg 3 bars Az
    WOKYNGDON, Sir Michael. *BR V 245.*
Gu on lion Or 3 bars Az
    DESNEY. *L10 58b, 17.*
Erm on lion Arg 5 bars gemel Sa
    — *ML I 188. ('Hermyn a lyon rampaunt*
    sylver sablyd come gemellys in berulettes').

Gu lion barry Arg and Az
    WOKINGDONE, Sire Thomas. *N 417.*
    WOKINGTON, Thomas de. *XL 322. (a&l Az).*
    WOKYNGTON, Mons Th de. *WJ 152.*
Gu lion barry Or and Az
    WOKYNGDONE. *L1 679, 4.*
Az lion barry of 8 Arg and Gu
    HESSE, Landgrave of. *XL 429.*
Gu lion burely Arg and Sa
    HULTON, William. *CRK 488. (a&l Az).*

Lion bendy &c
Sa lion bendy of 5 Arg and Gu
    HOLME. *LH 387.*
Sa on lion Arg 3 bends Gu
    HOLME. *LH 869. (a&l Or).*
    HOLME. *CRK 1788. (a&l Or).*
    HOLME. *L1 318, 2; L2 242, 5.*
Sa lion bendy of 8 Arg and Gu
    HOLME, of Suff. *MY 54.*

Lion charged with annulet
Arg lion Gu ch on shldr with annulet Untinc
    HILTON. *RB 514.*
Arg lion Gu ch on shldr with annulet Arg
    HILTON. *L1 348, 2; L2 248, 6. (armed Az).*
Arg lion Sa ch on shldr with annulet Untinc
    STAPILTON, Mons' Bryan de. *TJ 145.*
Arg lion Sa ch on shldr with annulet Arg
    — *D4 44. (imp by Copley, of Yorks).*
    — *D4 49b. (imp by Wharton, of Wharton, Westmld).*
    STAPILTON, Mons Bryan de. *TJ 144. (annulet blazoned sans tincts).*
    STAPLETON. *PT 506.*
Arg lion Sa ch on shldr with annulet Az
    STAPELTON, Sr Miles. *PO 181. (langued Gu).*
    STAPILTON, Mons Myles de, de Bedale. *WJ 313.*
    STAPLETON, Monsire Miles de, de Bydal. *AN 91. (name Hecheleslegh struck out).*
Arg lion Sa ch on shldr with annulet Or
    STAPLETON, Miles. *XL 149.*
Gu lion Or ch on shldr with annulet Sa
    ARUNDEL. *SK 50.*
Or lion Az ch on shldr with annulet Gu
    PERCY, W. *WJ 107. (uncle au Count).*
Or lion Az ch on shldr with annulet Or
    PERCY. *FK I 139. (qrs 1&4).*
Or lion Gu ch on shldr with annulet Arg
    POMEROY. *DevonNQ VII ii 27. 15 cent. (2nd window in N wall, Ashton, Devon).*
Sa lion Or ch on shldr with annulet Sa
    BROMHALE. *PT 572.*
Gu crusily fitchy lion Arg ch on shldr with annulet Az
    LA WARE, Mons John. *WJ B 155.*

Gu crusily fitchy lion Arg ch on shldr with annulet Sa
    LA WARE. *L9 35b, 9. (a&l Az).*
    LA WARE, Mons John. *WJ 155.*
Gu lion Vair ch on shldr with annulet Gu
    EUERYNGHAM, S' Edmund. *PO 259.*

Lion ch with billets &c
Arg lion Az ch on shldr with 3 billets Or
    — *E6. (qtd by Curwyn of Wyrkyngton, Cumb).*
Arg lion Sa billetty Or
    — *XC 284. (qtd 2&3 by Moresby).*
    ASCHEBY. *L2 15, 7.*
    ASHEBY, Sir Robert. *BR V 116. (blazoned 'ausyny' for billetty).*
    ASKBY, Mons W de. *WJ 330.*
    ASKBY, William de. *XL 163.*
    ASKEBY, Monsire Robert de. *CG 89.*
    ASKEBY, Mons' Roger de. *TJ 35.*
    ASKEBY, Monsr Roger de. *AS 182.*
    ASKEBY, Sir Roger de. *RH, Ancestor vii 213.*
    ASLEBY, Sgr de. *CKO a 67. ('Hashely vel Asleby').*
    ASSCHEBY, Sire Robert de. *N 1103.*
    ASSKEBY, s' Rob'. *PO 635.*
Az lion Arg ch with 3 billets Or
    — *D4 50. (qtd by Curwen of Wyrkyngton).*
Arg lion Sa ch on shldr with finch Or
    MONPINZON, Sire .... *N 563. ('de argent a un lion de sable a un pinzon de or en le espaudle'; Sire Gilys in Lans MS 855).*
Arg lion Sa ch with martlet Arg
    — *L10 80, 13. (a&l Gu; martlet unclear ch on shldr; qtd 2&3 by Wayt all imp by Brunyng).*
    MONPEUCON, Edmond, of Battington, Wilts. *D13 123. (qtd 2 by Wayte all imp by Norton).*
Arg lion Sa ch on shldr with martlet Or
    MEMPYNSON. *WB I 14b, 9.*
    MOMPESSON. *XL 285.*
    MONPISSONE. *FK II 911.*
    MOUNPYNSSON. *L9 73a, 9.*
    MOUNPYSSON, Sir John, of Essex. *WB III 78b, 7. (a&l Or).*
Arg lion Az ch on shldr with bouget Or
    [CRICHTON, of Sanquhar]. *Berry; Stodart pl 4. (a&l Gu).*
Sa lion Arg ch on shldr with chessrook Gu
    VERDON, Mons Th de. *WJ 295.*
    VERDON, Sr Thomas de. *CKO 92.*
    VERDON, Mons' Thomas. *SD 42. (son frere; '... ove une rockes de goules en lespaule de leon').*
    VERDOUN, Thomas de. *CA 198.*
Lion ch on shldr with 2 chevs
    RUSSELL, Gilbert, of Thorentone, Lincs. *Birch 13173.* S' GILB'TI RVS[S]ELL' DE

THORENTONE. 14 cent.
RUSSELL, Gilbert, of Thornton. *PRO-sls.*
c1300.
Or lion Gu ch on flank with 3 chevs Arg
BAWDE, John. *CRK 490. (a&l Az).*
Sa lion Or ch on flank with 3 chevs Gu
PORINTONE, Gilbert de. *LM 583.*
Arg lion Sa ch with 3 chevs Erm
— *ML I 527. ('Sylver a lyon rampaunt
sabyll iii cheverons upon the same hermyn.
Yf the cheverons towchyd the feld than thou
shuldes say iii chevrons upon both harmyn').*

Lion ch with crescent &c
Arg lion Sa ch on shldr with cresc Untinc
STAPILTON. *L9 5, 9. (a&l Gu; imp by
Ingelby qtg Rowclyff & Mowbray).*
Gu lion Arg ch on shldr with cresc Az
[MOWBRAY]. *WJ 146. ('s'frere au count';
cresc poss Sa).*
Or lion Az ch on shldr with cresc Or
PERCY. *FK I 138. (qrs 1&4).*
PERCY, de. *WJ 102. (fitz a count).*
Or lion Gu ch on shldr with cresc Arg
CHARLTON. *FK II 708.*
Sa lion Or ch on shldr with cresc Gu
BROMEHALL. *DV 67b, 2666.*
Az semy of fleurs de lis lion Or ch on shldr with
cresc Sa
BEUMONDE. *SK 44.*
Arg lion Sa ch on breast with cross formy Arg
NEWTON, of Swell. *Gerard 213.*
Arg lion Sa ch on shldr with estoile Or
WALKEFARE. *PT 69.*
Arg crusily fitchy lion Gu ch on shldr with
estoile Or
BRET. *DV 48a, 1896.*
BRETT. *L1 51, 3; L2 53, 5. (a&l Or).*
BRETT. *XL 523. (?crosses not fitchy).*
Vt on lion Or fess Gu
JEU, Mons' Richard le. *TJ 32.*
JEU, Sr Richard le. *CKO 65. (copy A has
'Sr Roland Lessen').*
JON, Monsr Rich le. *AS 178.*
Or on lion Vair fess Gu
DEN, Monsire Richard le. *CG 68.*
Arg lion Sa ch on shldr with dolphin hauriant Or
ELLIS. *L2 181, 10. (a&l Gu).*

Lion ch with fleur de lis
Lion ch on shldr with fleur de lis
EGREMOYNE, Ld. *RH, Ancestor iv 231.*
Arg lion Az ch on shldr with fleur de lis Gu
CLIFTON, Mons' Gervaise de. *TJ 34.*
CLIFTON, Monsr Gervays de. *AS 181.*
Arg lion Az ch on shldr with fleur de lis Or
FALCONBRIDGE, Roger. *BG 371.*
FAUCONBERG, Roger. *S 178.*
FAUCONBERGE, Mons' Roger. *S 176.*

Arg lion Gu ch on shldr with fleur de lis Or
LYOUNS. *SK 249.*
Arg lion Sa ch on shldr with fleur de lis Arg
WALKFARE, Sgr de. *CKO a 69.*
Arg lion Sa ch on shldr with fleur de lis Or
BARYNGTON, of Leics. *L2 88, 6.*
STAPILLTON. *PO 123.*
WALKEFARE, Mons. *AS 454.*
WARINGTON. *L1 685, 3. (a&l Az).*
WARYNGTON, Mons de. *AS 413.*
Az lion Arg ch on shldr with fleur de lis Gu
MAHAUT, Mons Robt de. *WJ 288.*
MONHAUT, Robert. *XL 146.*
Gu lion Arg ch on shldr with fleur de lis Untinc
[MOWBRAY]. *Nichols Leics ii 252. (Melton
Mowbray Ch).*
Gu lion Arg ch on shldr with fleur de lis Az
— *D4 26b. (qtd 2&3 by Redman, of Yorks).*
— *PLN 358. (qtd 2&3 by [Sir Brian Staple-
ton] Arg lion Sa ch on shldr with mullet Gu).*
— *CRK 1007. (qtd 2&3 by Sir Bryan Sta-
pleton).*
— *D4 23. (qtd 4 by Stapilton, of Notts).*
DALDEBURGH, Mons Hugh. *WJ 151.*
RYDER, Sir Rauff. *WK 194.*
Gu lion Arg ch on shldr with fleur de lis Sa
ALDBURGH, Hugh de. *XL 268.*
Gu lion Or ch on shldr with fleur de lis Az
MANDEUYT, Mons Th. *WJ 250.*
MANDEVYLL. *L9 50b, 8.*
Or lion Az ch on shldr with fleur de lis Or
PERCY. *FK I 69. (qrs 1&4).*
PERCY, T de. *WJ 98. (frere a count).*
Or lion Gu ch on shldr with fleur de lis Arg
CHARBONE, Johan de. *CA 169.*
Az semy of crosslets lion Or ch on shldr with
fleur de lis Gu
BREUSE, Sire Giles. *N 348.*
BROWES, Sir Giles. *BR V 283. (8 crosslets).*
Az semy de lis lion Or ch on breast with fleur de
lis Sa
BEAMOND. *DV 52b, 2072.*
BEAUMONT. *CC 231b, 307.*
Arg lion per fess Gu and Sa ch on shldr with
fleur de lis Or
LOVETOD, Jhon de. *Q 486.*
LOVETOT, Johan de. *LM 283.*

Lion ch with foil &c
Arg lion Gu ch on shldr with 5foil Arg
ECHELASTONE. *L2 174, 5.*
ESTELEY, Sr Andrew de. *H b 48.*
ESTHELASTON. *L2 184, 4. (pd 5foil).*
ESTLEE, Sire Nicholas de. *N 107.*
ESTLEYE, Andreu de. *H a 48.*
Arg lion Gu ch on shldr with 5foil Or
[WALKFARE]. *CKO 83.*

Arg lion Sa ch on shldr with 5foil Or
  WAKEFORD. *Suff HN 39. (imp Baskerfylde;*
  'Mr Stotevyle's house at Dallam').
Erm lion Gu ch on shldr with 5foil Or
  [ESTELEY, Ld]. *Nichols Leics IV 909. (Shak-*
  erston Ch).
Arg lion Gu ch on shldr with 5foil Erm
  ASTELE, Mons' Thomas. *TJ 88.*
  ASTLEY, Monsire Thos de. *CG 74.*

Lion ch with mullet
Lion ch on shldr with mullet
  FELBRIGG. *Mill Steph. 1400. (on jupon of*
  effigy, brass to Sir Geo F, Playford, Suff).
  WALKEFARE. *Mill Steph. 1506. (qtg*
  Morieux; imp by Strange on effigy of 'John
  lestrawnge Knig. Walkefare & Morieux';
  brass to Sir Roger le S, Hunstanton, Norf;
  also qtg 3 Strange on Sir Roger's own effigy,
  same brass).
Arg lion Az ch on shldr with mullet Gu
  FFAUCONBERGE, Rog'. *WJ B 271.*
Arg lion Az ch on shldr with mullet Or
  FFAUCONBERGE, Rog'. *WJ 271.*
Arg lion Gu ch on shldr with mullet Arg
  HILTYN. *WB I 18b, 11.*
  PETIT, of Cornw. *CRK 1213.*
Arg lion Gu ch on shldr with mullet Or
  LEIGH, of Leighe. *L9 27a, 7. (a&l Or).*
  LYOUNS. *SK 248.*
Arg lion Sa ch on shldr with mullet Arg
  — *WB I 17, 3. (imp by Haydon).*
  [STAPLETON, Sir Bryan]. *PLN 328. (mullet*
  of 6 pts).
  STAPLETONE, Messire Bryane. *PT 1208.*
  STAPULTON. *PT 756.*
  STAPYLTON, Sir B. *WB I 41, 10.*
  WALKEFARE, Robert. *XL 159.*
Arg lion Sa ch on shldr with pd mullet Az
  — *SHY 56. (imp by Calthorp).*
Arg lion Sa ch on shldr with mullet Gu
  STAPILTON, Brian. *BG 216.*
  STAPILTON, Mons Bryan de. *WJ 315.*
  [STAPLETON, Sir Brian]. *PLN 358. (qtg 2&3*
  Gu lion Arg ch on shldr with fleur de lis Az).
  STAPLETON, Sir Bryan. *CRK 1007. (qrs*
  1&4).
  STAPLETON, Sir Miles. *WGA 83. (a&l Gu).*
Arg lion Sa ch on shldr with pd mullet Gu
  STAPELTON, Mons' Bryan de. *S 113.*
  STAPLETON, Sir Brian de, of Wighill. *S 115.*
  WALKEFAR, Monsire Richard. *AN 117.*
Arg lion Sa ch on shldr with mullet Or
  STAPILTON, Mons' Myles [KG]. *S 15.*
  STAPLETON, Sir Brian. *WGA 164.*
  STAPLETON, Miles. *S 17.*
  WAKEFAYRE. *DV 59b, 2351.*
  WALKEFARE. *L1 678, 6. (a&l Gu).*
  WALKEFARE, Mons. *AS 454. (corrected*

version).
  WALKEFARE, Sire Robert de. *N 578.*
  WALKFARE, Mons Rich. *WJ 323.*
  WALKFARE, Mons Robt. *WJ 321.*
  WALKFARE, Ry. *NS 51.*
  WALKFARE, Tho. *NS 99. (pd mullet).*
  WARRINGTON. *XL 468.*
Az lion Arg ch on shldr with mullet Sa
  CREWE. *PT 933. (armed Or).*
  CREWE, of Northants. *CRK 518. (a&l Or).*
  CRWE. *DV 70b, 2796. (pd mullet).*
Az lion Arg ch on shldr with mullet Sa pd Or
  CREW. *L1 159, 5; L2 114, 12. (armed Or*
  langued Gu).
Az lion Or ch on shldr with mullet Sa
  HETHERSET, Sir Edmund. *CRK 669.*
Or lion Az ch on shldr with mullet Gu
  PERCY, Mons Roger. *WJ 104. (le uncle;*
  mullet of 6 pts).
Or lion Az ch on shldr with mullet Or
  PERCY. *FK I 137. (qrs 1&4).*
  PERCY, Ralph. *S 126.*
  PERCY, S' Rauf de. *WJ 106. (fitz a count).*
  PERCY, Mons' Rauff. *S 124.*
Or lion Gu ch on shldr with mullet Untinc
  BOTBARNE. *CC 235, 421.*
  FELBRYDGE. *Suff HN 22. (imp Walgrave;*
  Playford Ch).
Or lion Gu ch on shldr with mullet Arg
  BOTBERNE. *DV 60a, 2372.*
  CHARLTON, Howell de. *WJ 263.*
  FELBRIGE, Mons' George. *S 174. (pd mul-*
  let).
  FELBRIGGE, George. *S 176. (blazoned*
  embelif).
Or lion Gu ch on shldr with mullet Az
  CHARLTON, de Appllee, Salop. *L10 41b, 13.*
Or lion Gu ch on shldr with mullet Or
  BOTBARNE. *L10 83b, 12. (langued Gu, sans*
  claws).
  BOTBARNE. *L1 54, 4; L2 73, 11.*
  CHARLTON, Howell de. *WJ B 263.*
  HOLLAND. *LH 981.*
Or lion Vt ch on shldr with mullet Arg
  [SUTTON]. *Nichols Leics IV 500. (Market*
  Bosworth Ch).
  SUTTON, Sir Richard. *Sutton. (a&l Gu; co-*
  founder, BNC, d1524-5; qtg 2&3 Southworth
  qtg Sutton [bugles coat]; 4 Worsley).
Sa lion Or ch on shldr with mullet Gu
  BROMHALE. *SK 972.*
Arg lion Sa billetty Or ch on shldr with mullet
Arg
  TYLIOLL. *DV 46a, 1804.*

Lion ch with roundel
Arg lion Gu ch on shldr with roundel Or
  VEILLEVYLLE, Sir Rouland de. *WK 254.*

Or lion Sa ch on tail with 3 roundels Arg
  [BRITAIN], K Erpenwolde. *KB 99.*
  [BRITAIN], K Sygbert. *KB 105. (a&l Arg).*
Or lion Gu ch on neck with 5 roundels Or betw
  2 bars collarwise Or
  MALORY. *L9 49b, 8.*

Lion checky
Lion checky
  COBHAM, John. *PRO-sls BS 23. ....C...BhA....*
  1359-60. *(s of Ctess Marshall).*
  COBHAM, John de. *Birch 8736.* SIG[IL]LVM.-
  IOHANNI[S].DE.COBHAM. *1359. (s of Mary,*
  Ctess of Norf, Ctess la Marescall, wid of
  Thos Brotherton, E of Norf; in points of tra-
  cery a series of initial letters: T.I.L.B.E.Y.M.-
  A.Y.B.C.A; ?indicating sentence or text).
  COBHAM, John de. *PRO-sls. 1359-60. (s of*
  Ctess Marshal).
Arg lion checky Az and Or
  COKEHAM. *L1 159, 1; L2 114, 8. (a&l Gu).*
Arg lion checky Or and Az
  COBHAM, Mons J de. *WJ 273.*
  COBHAM, John de. *XL 129. (a&l Gu).*
  COBHAM, John de. *AN 195. (le filtz Madame*
  de Mareschal).
  COBHAM, s' Jon. *PO 409.*
  COBHAM, Sir Rawfe de. *RH, Ancestor ix*
  160.
  COKHAM. *PT 566.*
  COKHAM. *DV 67b, 2661. (armed Gu).*
  COOKHAM, J. *CRK 1468. (a&l Gu).*
Arg lion checky Or and Sa
  COBHAM, Sir Rauf. *O 108.*
Arg lion checky Or and Vt
  COKHAM. *L1 176, 2. (marginal note*
  'Goryng').
Az lion checky Arg and Gu
  WEEKS, Richard de. *XL 478.*
  WIKES, Richard de. *E I 628; E II 630.*
Gu lion checky Erm and Sa
  — *RH, Ancestor ix 174.*
Gu lion checky Erm and Ermines
  ?DUNDUN. *CRK 63. (a&l Or).*

Lion Erm
Az lion Erm
  — *WB I 42, 2-3. (qtd 4 by Sir Jn Skypwith).*
  ERMENIE, Rex. *SM 17, 120.*
  FITZRAUF, Sir Symon. *PCL I 550.*
  GERARD. *L2 229, 8. (a&l Gu).*
  JERARD. *L1 360, 6. (a&l Gu).*
  MAUSLEY, Sir Symond. *PCL I 550.*
  PECCHE, Sir John, of Kent. *WB III 74, 5.*
  (a&l Gu).
  SIMON, Ralph Fitz, of Ormesby. *XL 134.*
  SYMON, Sire Rauf filz. *N 682.*
  SYMOND, Fitz. *PT 614.*
  SYMOUND, Mons Rauf fitz. *WJ 283.*

Gu lion Erm
  — *MY 238.*
  — *NS 28.*
  — *XK 262. (qtd 3 by Sir Edw Gorges).*
  — *WK 161. (a&l Az; qtd 3 by Sir Edw*
  Gorge).
  — *(Thomas de ...). XL 332.*
  — *(Willame de ...). FW 336.*
  BROMTON. *L10 79, 9. (sans tongue or*
  claws).
  BROMTON, Th de. *WJ 167.*
  HAMELYN. *CT 114.*
  HOLDHALLE. *LH 922.*
  MEUFORD. *L2 345, 11.*
  MEWFORD, Norff. *L2 347, 1.*
  NEIRFORD, Mons John de. *SD 37.*
  NEIRFORD, Sire Willame de. *N 550.*
  NEIRFORD, Mons William. *TJ 130.*
  NEIRFORD, Mons William de. *TJ 61.*
  NEIRFORDE, Monsr de. *AS 367.*
  NEREFORD, William de. *A 283.*
  NEREFORD, William de. *E I 372; E II 374.*
  NEREFORD, William de. *F 404.*
  NERFORD. *PO 125.*
  NERFORD, Monsire de. *CG 64.*
  NERFORD, Sr de. *CKO a 52. (name written*
  over Sr de Schyr...).
  NERFORD, S' John de. *R 83. temp Edw 3.*
  NERFORD, Wille de. *Q 455.*
  NERFORD, Sir William de. *CV-BM 271.*
  NERFORD, William de. *WLN 452.*
  NEWFORDE. *L2 359, 3.*
  NOWFORD, Norff. *L2 365, 12.*
  OLDCALL. *L9 88a, 6.*
  OLDEHALE, Sir William, of Norf. *WB III*
  74b, 4. (a&l Az).
  OLDEHALL, Norf. *PLN 1556.*
  OLDHALL, Sir William. *CRK 1000. (a&l*
  Az).
  SALLE, Sir Robert. *XL 90.*
  SALLEY. *LS 287. (a&l Az).*
  SCHYR[INGHAM], Sr de. *CKO 52.*
  SHERLYNGHAM. *Suff HN 24. (imp*
  Stenecourt; Chedeston Ch).
  TINNGLEY, Kent. *MY A2 238.*
  VERIFORD, Sir William. *BR V 146.*
Vt lion Erm
  BOLEBEK, Hugh. *B 174.*

Lion Erm field patterned
Barry Az and Gu lion Erm
  WAKELYN. *XL 466.*
  WAKELYN. *XF 222. (a&l Or).*
  WALKELYN. *L1 667, 3. (a&l Gu).*
Checky Or and Gu lion Erm
  SCARLET. *XL 524. (a&l Az).*
Per fess Arg and Vt lion Sa crined Erm
  — *ML I 437. ('vert & sylver partyd per barr*
  a lyon rampant upon both sabyll le chef

hermyn').
Per pale Untinc lion Erm
    NORWICH. *Arch Journ vi 66 & 68.* 1405-6.
    (dex shield on sl of Chantry of St Mary of
    Mettingham founded 1342 by Sir Jn de N).
    NORWICH, John. *Farrer Bacon 8.* 1343.
    NORWICH, of Suff, Chevr. *Birch 12245.*
    ...SEAL....
Per pale Arg and Gu lion Erm
    NORWYZ, Monsire de. *CG 99.*
Per pale Az and Gu lion Erm
    — *XE 112. (qtd 2&3 by Haute).*
    — *WK 175. (qtd 2&3 by Hawte).*
    — *WK 319. (qtd 2&3 by Sir Thos Haute).*
    — *WB I 14b, 10. (qtd by Nycholas Haute).*
    ?CAWNE. *LH 745. (qtd 2&3 by Sir Nicol*
    Haute, of Kent).
    HAUTTE, Sir Wm, of Kent. *MY 188. (qtg*
    2&3 cross engr).
    NORROY. *NS 89. ('Peter' added in margin).*
    NORTHWICHE, Monsire de. *AN 35.*
    NORTHWYCHE. *SK 520.*
    NORTWYCHE, Mons John de. *SD 11.*
    NORWICH, Sir John. *CRK 587. (a&l Or).*
    NORWITZ, Monsr de. *AS 190.*
    NORWYC. *PO 40.*
    NORWYCH, Jo. *NS 59.*
    NORWYCH, Sir John. *RH, Ancestor vii 213.*
    NORWYCHE. *Suff HN 27. (Sotterley Ch).*
    NORWYCHE, Mons John. *TJ 36.*
    NORWYCHE, Sir John, of Norf. *WB III 71, 1.*
    (a&l Gu).
    OLDHALL, Sr de. *CKO a 73.*
    ROUS, Thos le, Ld of Walsall. *SF 23.*
    (d1345).
Per pale Az and Purp lion Erm
    OLDCHALL. *L2 388, 2.*
Per pale Gu and Az lion Erm
    CAWNE, Mons Th. *WJ 196.*
    COWNE. *L10 41, 9.*
    COWNE, Sir Thomas. *XL 337.*
    NARWI, Sir. *T b 103.*
    NORWICH, John de. *XL 337.*
    NORWICH, John de. *XL 276.*
    NORWICHE. *L2 370, 1.*
    NORWICHE, Mons John de. *WJ 193. (both*
    eyes of lion showing).
    NORWICHE, John of Essex. *L9 85a, 12. (a&l*
    Or).
Per pale Gu and Sa lion Erm
    NORWICH. *FK II 221.*
Per pale Sa and Gu lion Erm
    — *PT 707. (qtd by Haut).*
    NORWICHE. *L2 365, 7.*
Arg semy of crosses botonny fitchy Sa lion Erm
    HACHETON. *LH 513.*
Gu crusily fitchy Arg lion Erm
    LAWARRE. *L9 42b, 4. (a&l Az).*
    WARR, de la. *XL 8.*

Lion Ermines
Arg lion Ermines
    — *I2(1904)180. (qtd 6 by Hillersdon, of*
    Memlane, Devon; added by Jos Holland,
    c1630).
Gu lion Ermines
    TYMPYRLEY, Tomas. *RH, Ancestor ix 160.*
Checky Or and Gu lion Ermines
    SCARLET. *LY A 15.*

Lion fretty
Or lion Az fretty Arg
    BOKESHULL, Sire Alan. *O 107.*
    BOKESHULL, Sire Alleyn. *N 262.*
    BOKESHULL, Monsire Mayn. *AN 258.*
    BOKSELLE. *SK 100.*
    BOXHILL, Mons Alain de. *AS 368.*
    BOXHILL, Mons Rauf. *TJ 81.*
    BOXHUL, Suss & Surr. *L1 93, 5; L2 53, 9.*
    BOXHULL. *L10 84b, 13. (a&l Gu).*
    BUXHULLE, Mons allen. *BB 99, 3. (d1381).*
    BUXHYLL, Sir Alen. *PLN 306.*
Or lion Az fretty Or
    BOXHYLL, Sir Robard. *RH, Ancestor vii 214.*

Lion lozengy
Arg lion lozy Or and Gu
    ASHWAY, Stephen. *XL 340. (a&l Az).*
    ASSH'WY, Mons Esteven. *WJ 202.*
Or lion lozy Arg and Az
    LYNDE, Wylyam. *RH, Ancestor v 186.*
    ('other wyse called Adame Boxhull, Barkes
    chyre').

Lion per bend
Arg lion per bend Gu and Sa
    LOVET, Joan de. *F 171.*
Gu lion per bend Erm and Ermines
    TYMPERLEY, Suss. *MY 342. (?per fess).*
    TYMPURLEY, Suff. *L1 647, 5.*
Per bend Arg and Sa lion bisected bendways
counterch
    — *ML I 308. (2 halves of lion do not touch*
    party line).
Per bend Gu and Arg lion counterch
    — *RH, Ancestor ix 175.*
Per bend Or and Sa lion counterch
    FRAUNCEYS, Mons Adam. *TJ 100. ('port*
    dor & de sable partie enbelif a un leon de
    lun en lautre rampant').
    RYTFORD. *PT 1064.*
Per bend Sa and Arg lion counterch
    RATFORDE, Sir H. *WB I 41b, 22.*
Per bend Sa and Or lion counterch
    FRANCEIS, Mons Adam. *S 164.*
    FRAUNCEYS. *XL 271. (imp by Montagu).*
    FRAUNCEYS, Sir G. *WB I 41b, 21.*
    FRAUNCEYS, Mabell. *SA 24. (dau of Sir*
    Adam F & w of Jn, E of Salisbury).

Per bend Sa and Arg lion per bend Arg gutty Sa
& Sa
KELYNGEINCHE. *BG 416.*

Lion per bend sin
Per bend sin Arg and Sa lion counterch
ROTE. *RH, Ancestor iii 190.*
Per bend sin Or and Sa lion counterch
FRAUNCYS, Sir Adame. *RH, Ancestor v 184.*
Per bend sin Sa and Arg lion counterch
— *RH, Ancestor v 187.*
Per bend sin Sa and Or lion counterch
FRANCIS, Sir Adam. *PLN 255.*
FRAUNCES, Adam. *BG 111.*
FRAUNCES, Sir Adam. *CRK 739.*
FRAUNCEYS. *SK 132.*
FRAUNCEYS. *XL 98.*
FRAUNCEYS, Adam. *S 166.*
FRAUNCEYS, Sir Adam, of Middx. *WB III
84b, 5. (a&l Gu).*
Per bend sin Arg and Sa crusily lion counterch
ATTLODGE, of Chardstock, Dorset. *Gerard
117.*

Lion per bend sin modified
Per bend sin nebuly Arg and Az lion counterch
VENOR. *PT 296.*
Per bend sin wavy Arg and Az lion counterch
VENOR. *DV 50a, 1967.*
VENOUR. *L1 661, 2.*

Lion per fess
Lion per fess
— *WB I 35b, 1. (qtd 10 by E of Shrews-
bury).*
[LOVETOFT]. *Mill Steph. 1521. (imp by
[Seymour] on brass to Jn Aschefeld & w
Eleanor S with 4s & 4d, Heythrop, Oxfords).*
[LOVETOT]. *Mill Steph. 1467. (qtd 2&3 by
[Cheyne] on brass to Jn Boville & w Isabel
?C, Stokerston, Leics).*
Arg lion per fess Gu and Sa
LENTOFT, Sire de. *AS 272.*
LOUELL', John de. *WLN 533.*
LOVETOFFE. *L1 403, 3; L2 308, 11.*
LOVETOFTE, Sgr de. *CKO a 75.*
LOVETOFTES. *SK 400.*
LOVETOFTES, Mons J. *WJ 220.*
LOVETOT. *CRK 453. (Lovett also given).*
LOVETOT. *L9 35b, 3. (a&l Az).*
LOVETOT, Jan de. *Q 249.*
LOVETOT, Johan de. *LMRO 281.*
LOVETOT, John. *XL 354.*
LOVETOT, John. *E I 608; E II 610.*
Arg lion per fess Sa and Gu
LOVETOT, John. *TJ 166.*
LOVETOT, John. *TJ 167. ('dargent a un leon
rampant demyce de sable et de goules').*

Az lion per fess Arg and Sa
— *ML I 223. (2 blazons given).*
Gu lion per fess Arg and Az
VENNOR. *CRK 1984. (a&l counterch).*
Or lion per fess Gu and Sa
— *C3 18. (in Southoe Ch, Hunts).*
CHEYNE, Mons John. *T c 48. (qtg checky Or
and Az on fess Gu fret Erm).*
Or lion per fess Gu and Vt
— *L10 34b, 4. (qtd 2&3 by Borurbar).*
— *L10 23b, 15. (qtd 2&3 by Bouchare).*
Or lion per fess Sa and Gu
— *WGB 102, 9. (qtd 2&3 by Cheney).*
— *CRK 1026. (qtd 2&3 by Sir Jn Cheney).*
— *PLN 199. (qtd 2&3 by checky Or and Az
fess Gu fretty Erm; note says S Jn Cheynye).*
— *WB I 15, 18. (qtd 2&3 by Cheyne, of
Bucks).*
— *SK 724. (qtd 2&3 by Chayne).*
— *SK 725. (qtd 2&3 by Chayny).*
— *WB III 89, 2. (qtd 2&3 by Sir Jn
Cheine).*
WORSOP PRIORY. *L10 67b, 15. (a&l coun-
terch).*
Vt lion per fess Or and Arg
GRENFERD. *L1 275, 6; L2 221, 5.*

Lion per fess field patterned
Erm lion per fess Az and Gu
LISLE, John de. *XL 135.*
Per fess lion per fess
SUTTON, Dean Robert. *Mill Steph. 1528.
(brass, St Patrick's Cath, Dublin).*
Per fess Arg and Gu lion counterch
— *PT 395.*
Per fess Arg and Sa lion counterch
— *WB I 25b, 2. (qtd 2 by Arg on fess betw
6 crosslets Sa 3 escallops Or).*
— *D13 150. (qtd by Basket, of Dulish, Dor-
set).*
Per fess Az and Gu lion per fess Arg and Or
— *L9 25b, 2. (qtd 3 by Ingram).*
Per fess Az and Or lion counterch
— *PLN 650. (a&l Gu).*
FRAUNCEYS, Mayor of London. *L1 253, 1;
L2 203, 7. (lion to sin).*
MECHELL, Hary. *WB IV 183b, 1039. (a&l
Gu).*
Per fess Gu and Arg lion counterch
— *FK II 761. (ch on shldr with crosslet
fitchy Gu).*
Per fess Or and Az lion per fess Gu and Or
HASTANG. *LH 419.*
Per fess Sa and Arg lion counterch
— *CRK 1694. (a&l Gu).*
BALLARD, Tomas. *RH, Ancestor vii 192.
(later hand added Tannatt).*
LOVETOT, M. *WNR 124.*

Per pale Az and Or lion per fess Gu and Sa
 STANBERY, Harry. *PLN 987.*
Gu billety Or lion per fess Or and Arg
 BULMER, of Yorks. *L2 55, 11. (bastard).*

Lion per fess Erm &c & ...
Az lion per fess Erm and Gu
 — *FK II 335.*
Gu lion per fess Erm and Ermines
 TYMPERLEY, of Suss. *MY 342. (?per bend).*
Checky Gu and Or lion per fess Erm and
Ermines
 SKARLET. *DV 48a, 1898.*
Checky Or and Gu lion per fess Erm and
Ermines
 SKARLET. *L1 597, 1.*
Per fess Arg and Sa lion counterch ermined Or
 SULBYRNE. *WB I 18b, 18. (langued Gu).*
Per fess Erm and Ermines lion counterch
 KILLINGMARCH. *GutchWdU.* ante 1500.
 (formerly in Hall, Queen's Coll, Oxf).
 KILLINGMARCH, J. *CRK 401.*
 KYNNELMARCH. *GutchWdU. (in window of*
 Old Hall, Univ Coll, Oxf, built 1450 demol-
 ished 1669).
Per fess Ermines and Erm lion counterch
 KELYNGMARCH. *WB I 17b, 22.*

Lion per fess fretty & ...
Per fess Or and Erm lion per fess Az fretty Arg
and Gu
 FORDE. *XF 86. (a&l counterch; imp by*
 Martin, of Burton).
 FORDE, of Kingston on Thames. *BA 770.*

Lion per pale &c
Az lion per pale Or and Gu
 — *PT 878.*
 LORTY. *Gerard 136.*
 TOMSYN, Bartholomew. *CRK 55. (tail*
 turned in; a&l Gu).
Per pale Arg and Gu lion counterch
 PYRELY. *L1 502, 6.*
Per pale Arg and Or lion per pale Sa and Vt
 — *ML I 293. ('Argent & or a lyon rampant*
 upon the same sabyll & synopyll both partyd
 per pale').
Per pale Or and Vt lion per pale Or and Gu
 PENNEBROK, le counte de. *C II 143.*
Per salt Arg and Sa lion counterch
 PAYN, Sir Thomas. *WGB 165. (Secretary to*
 the Q of Portugal, temp Edw 3).
 PAYON. *L2 402, 2.*
Per salt Or and Az lion counterch
 GOLDE, of Suff. *L2 233, 4. (a&l Gu).*
 GOULD. *XL 84.*

Lion quarterly
Qtly Arg and Gu lion counterch
 — *L9 73b, 11. (a&l Az; qtd 2 by Masone).*
 LANGSTON. *PT 979.*
Qtly Gu and Arg lion counterch
 MASON. *L2 349, 8.*
Qtly Or and Gu lion counterch
 [MANSTON]. *BA 784. (imp by Abingdon*
 Abbey).
Qtly Sa and Arg lion counterch
 — *RH, Ancestor ix 172.*

Lion semy
Lion semy of indistinct charges
 — *SHY 544. (imp by Goldwell on shield*
 ensigned by ecclesiastical hat).
Az lion Arg billety Gu
 — *PLN 681.*
 — *PT 218.*
 BRUYN, J of Cumb. *CRK 1861. (a&l Gu).*
 BRUYN, John, of Cumb. *XL 144.*
 BRUYNE. *L10 79, 13. (a&l Gu).*
 BRUYNE, Johan, of Cumb. *WJ 291.*
 JACSON. *WB IV 185, 1070.*
Gu lion Or billety Sa
 BULMER. *L10 86b, 3.*
 BULMER, Mons Ansketil, de Shirefhoton. *TJ*
 74.
 BULMER, of Sherriff Hutton, Yorks. *L2 90,*
 11.
Or lion Sa billety Or
 ASKEBY, S Robert de. *ST 51.*
Or lion Vt billety Or
 PUGEYS, S Ernaud William de. *GA 25.*
Per fess Or and Az lion billety Untinc
 GOLDWELL. *Suff HN 2. ('In the Colledge of*
 Sudbury').
Arg lion Sa semy de lis Or
 BARRINGTON, William de. *XL 167.*
Or on lion Az 5 ?fleurs de lis
 BREYSY, Sr Peres de. *L 34.*
Sa lion semy of 5foils pd Arg
 CLIFTON, Sir Gervaise. *PLN 2037. (?rectius*
 Sa semy of 5foils pd & lion Arg; qtg 2&3
 Arg lion qf Sa).

Lion gutty &c
Arg lion Az gutty Or
 BURNELL, Sir .... *CRK 586. (a&l Gu).*
 BYRNELL, Mons Nicoll de. *WJ 277.*
 HALOM. *LH 79.*
 HALOM. *L1 337, 4. (a&l Gu).*
 HALOM, Sr de. *CKO a 63.*
 HALOM, Mons Johan de. *AS 197.*
 HALON, Monsire John. *CG 63.*
 HAMLON, of Oxfords. *L2 259, 6. (a&l Gu).*
 HANDLON, Sir John. *XL 246.*
 HANLON, Sir John. *LH 267.*
 HANLOW, Monsire John de. *CG 100.*

HAULON, Sire Johan de. *N 336.*
HAULOU, Mons John. *TJ 161.* (*'...degoutee dor'*).
HAULOU, Mon John. *TJ 37.*
HAULOW, Sir John. *RH, Ancestor vii 213.* (*?or Hanlow*).
HAULOWE, Sr John de. *L 65.*

Arg lion Gu gutty Or
— *SK 980.*

Arg lion Sa gutty Arg
MORTYMAR, of Fowlis. *Lyndsay 365.* (*a&l Gu*).

Az lion Arg gutty Gu
BRUN. *L2 87, 4.*
BRUN, Sr de. *CKO 87.*
BRUNE, Mons Thomas. *TJ 50.* (*tail erect*).
BRUNE, Mons Thomas. *TJ 49.* (*painted with field gutty, not lion*).
BRYME. *L10 77, 14.*

Gu lion Arg gutty Sa
FORESTER, Mons John Neville le. *TJ 98.* (*'de goules a un leon dargent rampant degoute de sable'*).
HAMELYN, Sr. *CKO 90.* (*later hand gives Sr de Brampton*).

Gu lion Or gutty Sa
HAMLYN, Monsire. *CG 56.*

Or lion Gu gutty Or
BRONWYCHE. *SK 233.*

Or lion Sa gutty Or
BROMWECHE. *CB 183.*
BROMWICH. *L10 76, 9.* (*a&l Gu*).
BROMWICH. *L1 81, 1; L2 66, 1.* (*de Herref added in margin*).
BROMWICH, John de. *XL 174.* (*a&l Gu*).
BROMWYCH. *BA 18b.* (*armed Gu*).
BROMWYCH, Mons John de. *WJ 335.*
BROMWYCH, Sir John. *RH, Ancestor vii 212.*

Sa lion Arg gutty Sa
NEWYLE, Sir John. *RH, Ancestor vii 214.*

Erm lion Gu gutty Or
ROUS. *L1 555, 3.* (*& 'Tombervil'*).

Arg lion Purp semy of mascles Or
HERTFORDE, Mons Thomas, de Baddesworthe. *TJ 80.*
HERTFORDE, Sir Tomas. *RH, Ancestor vii 214.*

Or lion Sa semy of roundels Gu
LUDLOWE. *L2 305, 10.*

Or lion Sa semy of ?wounds or ?flames Gu
LODELOWE. *L9 36b, 5.*
LUDLOWE. *L1 394, 4.* (*blazoned 'torteaulz' but painted wounds resembling labels of 3*).

Lion Vair
Lion Vair
[EVERINGHAM]. *Mill Steph.* 1455-1617. (*qtd 4 by Manfield; brasses, Taplow, Bucks*).
EVERINGHAM, Sir Adam de. *Lawrance 15.*

1341. (*Effigy, Laxton, Notts*).
LASCELLES, Thomas de, Kt. *Birch 11241.*
+SIGILL'+THOME.[DE].LA[SCEL]LES. 1259.

Arg lion Vair
CALTOFT, Monsire de. *CG 77.* (*blazoned 'Argent a lion vair a une ...'*).
FAUCOMBERGE. *L2 209, 3.*

Gu lion Vair
— *D4 25.* (*qtd 2&3 by Evryngham of Byrkyng, Yorks*).
— *LE 57.* (*qtd 2&3 by Etton*).
— *PO 651.* (*[S'Weliam]; surname illegible & struck through with pen; written over it in Elizabethan hand is 'Eueringham'*).
— *WLN 159.* (*a&l Or*).
EVERINGHAM. *DV 64b, 2548.*
EVERINGHAM. *LE 108.* (*temp Ric 2*).
EVERINGHAM. *L1 225, 1; L2 172, 6.* (*armed Or*).
EVERINGHAM. *DV 63a, 2486.*
EVERINGHAM. *CRK 446.* (*a&l Or*).
[EVERINGHAM]. *RH, Ancestor iv 236.* (*qtd by Robarde Elys of Yorks*).
EVERINGHAM, Adam. *XL 330.* (*a&l Or*).
EVERINGHAM, Adam. *F 307; M 44; N 129.*
EVERINGHAM, Adam de. *WLN 739.*
EVERINGHAM, Sir Adam. *ML I 86.* (*lion untinc*).
EVERINGHAM, Sir Adam. *ML II 76.*
EVERINGHAM, Raynold de. *S 89.* (*qrs 1&4*).
EVERINGHAM, Reynold. *S 87.* (*qtg Sa bend betw 6 crosses Arg*).
EVERINGHAM, Robert, of Devon. *WB III 115b, 5.*
EVERYGHAM, Mons Reyn'. *WK B 3.* (*a&l Or*).
EVERYNGHAM. *PT 502.*
EVERYNGHAM. *AS 123.*
EVERYNGHAM, Mons Ad. *WJ 161 & 163.*
EVERYNGHAM, Sire Ad'. *PO 222.*
EVERYNGHAM, Adam. *LE 21.*
EVERYNGHAM, Adam de. *TJ 1250.*
?EVERYNGHAM, Sir John. *WK 445.*
EVERYNGHAM, Mons John de. *TJ 27.*
EVERYNGHAM, Robts de. *Q 507.*
EWERYNGHAM, Sir John. *RH, Ancestor vii 213.*
MARMYON, Mons William. *TJ 156.* (*de goules a un leon verre rampant*).

Or lion Vair
DARDERN, Monsire Wakehide. *CG 67.*

Per fess Gu and Or lion Vair
— *CRK 384.* (*a&l counterch of field; qtd 2&3 by Langley*).

Lion vulned
Az lion Arg vulned on shldr Gu
— *ML I 376.* (*'Asur a lyon rampaunt sylver the shwldre fresh woundyd'*).

Gu lion Arg vulned on shldr Gu
GRAY. *CC 38.*
GREY. *L1 287, 5.*
Or lion Az vulned on shldr Gu
PERCY, le fitz. *WJ 101.*
Or lion Sa vulned on shldr Gu
LANGTON, Thomas, de Wyngarde. *TJ 1437.*
('dor a un leon rampant de sable nafree sur
lespaule devant').
Or lion Sa with 7 wounds Gu
LUDLOW, Thomas de. *XL 168.*
Sa lion Arg vulned on shldr Gu
WASTNES, of Stowe. *PT 1048.*
Vt lion Arg vulned on shldr Gu
— Hutton 24. *(qtd 6 by Ric Wingfield; in N*
window of Gray's Inn).
BULBECKE. *Suff HN 7. (qtd by Oxford;*
Lavenham Ch).
Vt lion Or vulned on shldr Gu
ROBESART. *L1 554, 4.*
ROBESART, Sir Lowis, Ld Bourghshier. *WGA*
223.
ROBESSART, Sir Lewis, KG. *Leake.* c1421.
(d1450; qtly with Bourchier).
ROBSART. *XL 517. (a&l Gu).*
ROBSART, Ld. *PLN 191. (a&l Gu; qtg 2&3*
Bourchier).
ROBSERD, Sir John. *WGA 154-5.*
Vt lion Or vulned on shldr Sa
ROMSERT, Sir Gery. *WB IV 136, 192. (qrs*
1&4).
Az lion Or ch on shldr with crosslet fitchy &
vulned Gu
DARELL, Sir Edward. *WB II 56, 4.*

Lion rampant coward
Lion coward
— *ML I 194; ML II 129.*
Arg lion coward Sa
— *ML I 194. ('Miles primus.Il port argent*
un lion cowarde comme rampaunt sabill').
Az lion coward Arg
— *ML I 219. ('A lyon cowarde').*

Lion dismembered
Or lion couped in all joints Gu armed Az
MATELAND, of Lethyntown. *Lyndsay 250.*

Lion in umbre
Or lion in umbre
— *ML I 230. ('a lyon rampawned in umbre,*
quasi in umbra').
KENAN, Grefithe ap, P of Gwemothe. *WK A*
30.
NAMUR, Sir Robert. *WGA 219. (a&l Gu).*

**Lion holding, supporting or pierced by: see
after lion tricorporate**

Lion collared
Lion collared
— *G18 21b. (qr 6 of coat imp by Sir Robt*
Peyton, of Lulham, Cambs).
DOUMUILL, John, of Modberlegh. *Vinc 88,*
49. +SIG'IOHANNIS.DOVMVILL. 1392-3.
[GASTNEIS]. *Bow XXXIV 11.* Sig: Thome Greis-
ley de Drakeslowe. temp Hen 4. *(qtd 2&3 by*
Thos de Greisley, of Drakeslowe, Staffs).
GASTNEIS, John de. *Bow XXXIV 2.* +Sigill
Johannis de Gasteneis. *(bro of Sir Thos de G).*
GASTNEIS, John de, Rector of Cranewik. *Bow*
XXXIII 11. 1336-7. *(grant to his nephew*
Thos de G, s of Wm de G, Kt, & to Joan his
w of the manor of Brasingburgh, Carleby, &
lands in Lincs).
GASTNEIS, Thomas de, Kt. *Bow XXX 5.*
1344-5.
GASTNEIS, William de, Kt. *Bow XXXII 21.*
1309. *(grant of land in Colton).*
Arg lion Gu collared Az
— *LH 602. (qtd III 2&3 by Francis Hasel-*
den).
Arg lion Gu collared Or
ASHDOWN. *XL 264. (a&l Or; tail turned*
outwards).
ASHENDEN. *L10 2, 15.*
ASHENDEN. *L1 6, 3; L2 4, 1. (a&l Az).*
ASHENDENE. *FK II 337.*
AYSSELDON. *BA 1179. (a&l Or).*
EYSSELDONE, of Devon. *L1 233, 2; L2 175,*
11. (a&l Or).
HAVERING, Sr John de. *H 89b.*
HAVERINGE, Johan de. *H 89a.*
RADICH, John, of Lancs. *WB III 101, 2.*
STAKEPOL. *HA 65.*
STAKEPOL. *HA 52, 17b.*
STAKEPOL. *RB 92.*
STAKEPOL, Sire Richard de. *N 902.*
Arg lion Sa collared Gu
— *H21 27b. (qtd by Brakynbery, of Denton,*
co Durham).
— *AY 27. (qtd 2&3 by [Butler], E of*
Urmount).
— *BR II 45. (qtd 2&3 by [Butler], Erl of*
Urmonde).

Az lion collared
Az lion Arg collared Arg
SAUMVYLE, John. *PCL II 47.*
Az lion Arg collared Gu
— *PT 936.*
DOMMVIL, John, of Modberlegh. *Dugd 17, 9.*
1392. *('azure avc une leon rampant d'argent*
acesq une collir de gulez').

DOMVILE. *CRK 354. (a&l Gu).*
DOMVILE, de Lymme. *DV 70b, 2799.*
(armed Gu).
DOMVILLE, John de. *WLN 651.*
DOMVYLE, John, of Ches. *CY 23, 89.*
DONNVILE, of Limme, Ches. *BA 2.*
DONNVILLE. *L10 62b, 18. (a&l Or).*
DOUMVYLE. *CVC 519.*

Gu &c lion collared
Gu lion Arg collared Gu
WASTENEYS, Thomas. *XL 148. (a&l Or).*
Gu lion Arg ?collared Sa
DURAS, Gaillard, Ld. *WGA 287.*
Gu lion Or collared Az
BOXWORTH, Sir Wm, of Cambs. *CRK 524.*
Or lion Gu collared Arg
BOGWRTH. *L1 70, 6.*
BOXWORTH, Sir William. *BR V 200.*
BOXWURTH. *L2 70, 11.*
BOYWORTHE, Sire Willame de. *N 597.*
MALLORE, Johan. *LM 408.*
MALLORY, Sir Wm. *S&G II 323.*
MALORE, Joh. *Q 537.*
MAYLORRE, Christfr. *WJ 267.*
MAYLORRE, Esteven. *WJ 266.*
Or lion Gu collared Az
MAYLORRE, Esteven. *WJ B 266.*
Or lion Gu collared Or
BOXWORZE. *L10 86b, 14. (a&l Az).*
Or lion Gu collared Sa
MALORY, Stephen. *XL 377. (a&l Az).*
Or lion Purp collared Arg
BOLKEWORTH, Sr William de. *L 221.*

Sa lion collared
Sa lion Arg collared Gu
— *PLN 1384. (a&l Gu; qtd 2&3 by Wm Gresley).*
— *WB I 33, 7. (qtd 2&3 by Greseley).*
— *CRK 1042. (a&l Gu; qtd 2&3 by Sir Thos Grelley).*
— *FK II 806. (qtd 2&3 by Grysley).*
WASTENEIS, Sr William. *L 140.*
WASTENEY, Edmun. *G 78.*
WASTENEYS. *L1 680, 5.*
WASTENEYS. *SK 431.*
WASTENEYS. *CRK 362. (a&l Gu).*
WASTENEYS, Johan de. *LM 215.*
WASTENEYS, S' Th'm. *PO 503. (langued Gu).*
WASTENEYS, Mons Thomas. *CA 52.*
WASTENEYS, Sire Willame. *N 983.*
WASTENEYS, William. *E I 361; E II 363.*
WASTENEYS, William le. *WLN 847. (?collar Or).*
WASTENEYS, Willm de. *WLN 450.*
WASTENSIS, M.le. *WNR 126.*
WASTENYS, Jan le. *Q 234.*

WASTERNEYS, William le. *F 402.*
WASTNEIS. *Nichols Leics III 505. (N window, Wimeswould Ch).*
WASTNESSE, Mons Th.. *WJ 296.*
WASTNEYES. *Nichols Leics IV 313. (qtd 2&3 by Greiseley; Misterton Ch).*
WASTNEYS. *CT 217.*
WASTNEYS, William le. *CVC 495.*
WASTNEYS, William, of Ches. *CY 22, 85.*
WATENYS, Willame le. *FW 344.*
Sa lion Arg collared Or
WASSENES, of Heydon, Notts. *D9 10b, 3; E6.*
WASTNEIS, Wm, of Colton. *SF 28.*
Sa lion Or collared Arg
VEST. *WB I 18b, 10.*

Lion patterned or charged and collared
Sa lion Arg collared Gu on shldr cresc Gu
WASSTNESSE, J. *WJ 300.*
Arg lion Sa collared Gu on shldr estoile Or
WALKEFARE. *PT 70.*
Arg lion Sa collared Gu on shldr pd mullet Gu
— *CB 206. (a&l Gu).*
WALKEFER, Monsire Thomas. *AN 111.*
Arg lion Sa collared Gu charged with mullet Or
WAKEFAYRE. *DV 59b, 2352.*
Gu lion Erm collared ?Gu
NERFFORDE. *PO 127.*
Arg lion Sa gutty Arg collared Or
DAVID, [Gwillim] ap, of Sengheuyth. *XL 209. (a&l Gu; tail turned out; field ?Ermines).*
DAVID, [Gwillim] ap, of Sengheuyth. *XL 210. (imp Herbert).*

Lion with collar patterned or charged
Gu lion Arg on collar Az 3 roundels Or
— *Q 563.*
Arg lion Sa collared gobony Gu and Or on shldr mullet Or
WALKFARE, Mons Th. *WJ 324.*
Arg lion Sa collared per pale Gu and Or on shldr mullet Or
WALKFARE, Mons Th. *WJ B 324.*

Lion collared and chained
Or lion Sa collared & chained Or
BLEDERYKE, Thomas phyllyp ap, of Wales. *I2(1904)144. (a&l Gu; qtg 2 Az 3 bulls' heads in fess Arg armed collared & chained Or, 3 Az 3 hawks Ppr each with bell on tail & both legs Or).*

Lion collared with label &c
Az lion Arg gorged with label Gu
COLVILE, Sir Jn, of Norf. *L10 44b, 9. (qrs 1&4).*

Per fess Arg and Gu lion per fess Gu and Sa
  gorged with chain Az
  GRYNE. *BA 662.* *(a&l Az).*

Lion crowned
Lion crowned
— *(?source).* early 16 cent. *(on 2 shields in
roof groining of lower lantern, Cricklade,
Wilts).*
— *WB I 20b, 17.* *(crown uncertain; qr 1 of
shield borne in pretence by Knevet).*
— *WB I 29b, 9.* *(imp by Wharton).*
— *Stevenson.* 1282. *(marshalled by Devor-
gilla of Galloway, w of Jn Balliol).*
— *Stevenson.* c1460. *(Crown uncertain; qtd
by Wm, 8th E of Douglas dl452 & Jas, 9th E
of D dl491).*
— *Birch 12414.* 1472. *(qtd 2&3 by Thos
Pauncefot).*
— *Durham-sls 2249a.* 1325. *(used by Wm
of Silksworth).*
— *SHY 571.* *(imp by [Hastings]).*
BEAUCHAMP, Sir Jn, of [Fifiel]d. *Farrer
Bacon 54.* 1335. *(?& border).*
BELLOCAMPO, Ric de. *Birch 7257.*
+S'RICARDI.DE.BELLO CAMPO. 1411. *(rown
uncertain; sl used by Jn Donewych of Hunts).*
BURNEL, Edward. *PRO-sls.* 1314-15.
(shield betw 2 wyverns).
BURNELLE, Hugh, of Great Bradley, Suff, Kt.
Birch 7961. : SIGILLUM: HUG .... 1390. *(qtg
2&3 salt engr).*
DARELLE, Marmaduke, Ld of Sesay, Yorks.
Birch 9196. S...ADUCI: DARELL'. 1401.
DESPENSER, Anne le. *PRO-sls E40 A4785,
4792 & 4795.* S'ANNE LE DESPENSER. 1363-
4. *(wid of Edw le D; 1 of 4 roundels around
shield).*
ERMONYE, Roy de. *RH, Ancestor iii 191.*
FFYENLL, Jn. *Birch 9996.* +S'.IEH ....NLES.-
CHL'R. early 14 cent. *(Alias Ffenll or
Fienles, Ld of Carshalton, Surr).*
GALLOWAY. *Stevenson.* c1430. *(qtd by
Walter Stewart, dl437, 2nd s of Robt II, E of
Atholl; 3rd sl).*
GALLOWAY. *Stevenson.* 1393. *(imp by Sir
Archibald, dl400, 3rd E of Douglas; 4th sl).*
GALLOWAY. *Stevenson.* 1400. *(imp by
Johanna Murray who m 2nd Sir Archibald
Douglas 'the Grim', Ld of Galloway, & 3rd
E of D).*
GRAPER, Peter. *Vinc 88, 68.* +SIG...... 1369.
*(s of Peter G, Burgess of Newcastle-upon-
Tyne).*
HALE, Frank de, Kt, Ld of Rocheford. *PRO-
sls.* S' FRANCONIS DE MIRABEL ...NI ...SFOART.
1351-2 & 1355-6.
KIRKBY-Beller. *Birch 3358.* S'ECCLESIE

BEATI P[ETRI DE] KIRKEBI SUPER WRYTHEK.
14 cent. *(sl of ancient Priory of St Peter,
Kirby-Bellars, Leics).*
MARMYON, Agnes. *Birch 11617.* motto:
?MOYR I WOL BE. 1408. *(w of Wm of Leics,
Kt).*
MARYON, William, Kt. *PRO-sls.* VOINE
FOYRI. 1321-2. *(shield betw 2 words of
legend).*
MIRABIEL, Symon de. *PRO-sls.* 1347.
MORLAYE, die here van. *Gelre 58.*
MORLE, Robt de, King's Admiral in the
North. *Birch 11934.* 1340.
MORLE, Wm de, Marshal of Irld (3rd Baron
M). *Birch 11941.* ....MI DE....... 1362.
MORLEE, Robt de. *PRO-sls AS 247.*
S'ROBERTI DE MORLE. 1334-5.
MORLEE, Sir Robt. *Proc Soc Antiq I 2S 156-
7.* *(sl, [only upper half of lion remains]
attached to deed of 16 June 1336 being
power of attorney by Robt de M, Marshal of
Irld, to receive seizin of manor of Framsdon,
Suff from Lady Isabella, Q of Engld).*
MORLEE, Robt de, Admiral of the Fleet of the
North. *PRO-sls.* 1362-3.
MORLEE, Robt de, Marshal of Irld. *Bow XVII
4.* temp Edw 3.
MORLEE, Robt de of Suff, Kt. *Birch 11935.*
...MILITIS. 1368.
MORLEY. *Mill Steph.* 1470 onwards. *(cresc
for diffce; brasses, Morley, Derbys).*
MORLEY. *CT 61.*
MORLEY. *SHY 371.* *(imp by ...).*
MORLEY. *Farrer III 5.* *(shield on stalls,
Norwich Cath).*
[MORLEY]. *Farrer II 7.* *(on font, Aylsham
Ch, Norf).*
[MORLEY]. *Farrer II 87.* *(Sall Church,
Norf).*
MORLEY, Anna, Lady de. *Birch 11927.*
SIGILLUM ....MINE DE MORLE. 1425. *(w of
Sir Thos, 4th Baron M & dau of Edw, Ld
Despenser; imp Despenser).*
MORLEY, Isabella, Lady de. *Birch 11928.*
...ABELLE DNE DE MOR....MICH NUPER COMITI....
1449. *(w of Thos, 5th Baron M, & dau of
Michael de la Pole, 2nd E of Suff; imp qtly
1&4 de la P, 2&3 indistinct; not on shield).*
MORLEY, Thos de, Kt, Marshal of Ireld. *Bow
XXXIV 3.* Sig Tho de Morley Maresch Hybern.
1382-3. *(grant of land in Colton).*
MORLEY, Thos, Kt, Ld de M (4th Baron).
Birch 11937. ?...THOM.... 1403.
MORLEY, Thos, Kt, Ld de M (4th Baron),
Marshal of Irld. *Birch 11940.* .....ARESCALL
HIB'N. 1387.
MORLEY, Wm de, 3rd Ld. *Durham-sls 1817.*
1363.
MOUBRAY, Jn de, 3rd Ld M. *Birch 11996.*

SIGILLVM IOH ... DE ... RA.... 1339. (Ld of Isle of Axeholme & of honours of Bramber & Gower).
MOUBRAY, Jn de, Ld of Island of Axholme, Lincs, 2nd Ld. Birch 11994. S'IOHANNIS DE MOVBRAY. 1319.
MOWBRAY. Bow XXII 1. (1 of 3 shields on sl).
MOWBRAY, Jn, of Barnbougle. Stevenson. 1511.
OGILVIE, Alexr, Sheriff of Angus. Stevenson. 1417.
[ORTON]. Mill Steph. 1551. (qtd 3 by Blenerhasset on brass to George Duke & w Anne B; Frenze, Norf).
[ORTON]. Mill Steph. 1475. (qtd 2&3 by Blenerhasset on brass to Ralph B; Frenze, Norf).
[ORTON]. Mill Steph. 1587. (qtd 4 by Blenerhasset on brass to Mary B, w of (1) Thos Culpeper & (2) Francis Bacon; Frenze, Norf).
[ORTON]. Mill Steph. 1510. (qtd 3 by Blenerhasset on brass to Jn B; Frenze, Norf).
PAUNCEFOTE, Jn, of Hasfield, Gloucs. Vinc 88, 3. 1305-6.
SCOT, Walter, Justiciar. PRO-sls. 1340-1.
SEGRAVE. CT 53.
SEGRAVE, Jn de. ?source. (fl 1300).
SEGRAVE, Jn, Ld of. PRO-sls. 1301 & 1352-3.
[SEGRAVE, Jn Ld]. Blair N I 12, 23. (Beneath battlements of W.tower of inner gateway, Alnwick castle).
SEGRAVE, Jn de, 2nd Baron. Birch 13396. S'IOH'IS DE SEGRAVE. 1301. (on shield betw 2 garbs in allusion to another Segrave coat: 3 garbs).
SEGRAVE, Jn, Ld de, ?3rd Baron. Birch 13397. SIGILL'IOHANNIS DNI DE SEGRAVE. (on shield betw 3 garbs).
TORBURVILE, Richd, of Dorset. Birch 13962. S'RICARDI TORBVRVILE. 1351. (or Tourbervile).
TURBERVYLLE, Jn. PRO-sls. 1329-30.

Arg lion crowned
Arg lion Az crowned Gu
— CRK 1619. (a&l Gu).
— WB I 32b, 8. (qtd 2&3 by Arg chev Sa betw 3 mullets Gu).
Arg lion Az crowned Or
— PLN 1362. (qtd 2&3 by Dennys).
— PT 854.
HANLO. CV-BM 84.
JAUNEBY, S.Robert de. ST 70.
Arg lion Gu crowned Untinc
HYLLTUN, of Lancs. WB I 19b, 21.

Arg lion Gu crowned Arg
— Sandford 489. (qtd 6 by England, Q Anne of Cleves).
HYLTON, Thos, de Farworth, Lancs. CY 55, 219.
Arg lion crowned Gu
ERELINGTON, Monsire d'. CG 42.
HARTLINGTON, Sir Henry. LH 266.
HERTLYNGTON. L1 337, 5. (a&l Az).
HERTLYNGTON, Monsr Herry de. AS 237.
HILTON, Sr de. CKO a 33.

Arg lion Gu crowned Or etc
Arg lion Gu crowned Or
— L10 80, 13. (crown unclear; qtd 4 by Brunyng).
— BA 20, 166. (qtd 2&3 by Thos Pansfout).
— Neale & Brayley. 1431. (painted on canopy of mont to Lewis Robessart, now defaced).
— L10 61, 9. (qtd 4 [of 6] by Brunynge, of Segre, Wilts).
HERTLYNGTON, Mons Henry. TJ 37. (tinct of crown unclear).
HILTON. BG 408.
HILTON. XL 1.
HILTON. LH 1094. (or 'Hulton of Hulton of Faquenorth').
HULTON, of Farneworth. LH 701.
HULTON, Thomas, of Farnworth. XL 607.
LEUSANDBERGH, Cardynal. RH, Ancestor iii 189. (Cardynall of Ro... [Louis of Luxembourg cr Cardinal by Eugene IV 1439]).
[LUXEMBOURG]. Neale & Brayley. 1606. (qr 1 of coat imp by France mod & England qtly on mont to Qs Eliz & Mary, Hen 7 Chapel).
[LUXEMBOURG]. I2(1904)6. (qr 1 of 6; imp by Engld on banner of Edw 4).
PEYTENEY. CRK 1712. (a&l Az).
POITOU. Sandford 95.
TRUBLEVILE, Sir David. CRK 463. (much mutilated).
[TUR]BREVILLE, John. WK 21. (a&l Or).
TURBERUYLE, Suss. L1 648, 6. (a&l Az).
TURBERVIL, Hugh. CT 252.
TURBERVILE, Sir John. WB V 91. (Ktd 1485).
TURBERVILE, Robert. CA 149.
TURBERVILL, Thom de. LM 382.
TURBERVILLE. PLN 1089. (a&l Az).
TURBERVILLE, Hue de. Q 122.
TURBERVILLE, Sir John. PLN 1728.
TURBERVILLE, Mon' Hugh de. TJ 53.
TURBEVILE, Huge de. HE 164. (crown unclear).
TURBEVILE, Huge de. FW 178.
TURBULVYLE. DV 57a, 2257.
WYDEVILL. XB 20. (qr 1 of coat imp by

Edw 4).
Arg lion Gu crowned Sa
— BA 21, 176. (armed Sa; qtd 3 by Sir Jn
ap Morgan, of Tryggyn Morgan).
LOVETOFT, Monsire de. CG 87.

Arg lion Or &c crowned
Arg lion crowned Or
FITZRERY, Irld. L2 194, 11. (a&l Or).
Arg lion Purp crowned Or
CLEMSBY, Leics. L2 134, 10.
CLEVISBY, Sire Johan. N 832.
Arg lion Sa crowned Arg
— BG 356.
Arg lion Sa crowned Az
BURNEL, Phelip. Q 154. (a&l Az).
Arg lion Sa crowned Gu
— L9 90b, 4. (qtd 2&3 by Ormonde).
— WGA 136. (qtd 4 by Thos, Visct Roche-
ford).
— XK 17. (qtd IV 2&3 by Engld, for Q
Anne Boleyn).
— XK 76. (qtd 4 by Sir Thos Boleyn [Visct
Rochford KG]).
— WB I 20b, 11. (qtd 3 by St Leger).
— WK 499. (a&l Gu; qtd 4 by Sir Thos
Boleyn).
— LS 344. (a&l Gu; qtd 3 by Sir George St
Leger).
HAB, Monsire Godard de. CA 263. (?or
griffin; name unclear, ?for Boppard).
POWELL. CRK 321. (& Rochford).
POWELL, John. CRK 289.
ROCHFORD. Sandford 487. (qtd IV 2&3 by
Q Anne Boleyn).
ROTCHESFORD. CT 131.

Arg lion Sa crowned Or
Arg lion Sa crowned Or
— WB V 22. (qtd 2&3 by Butler, E of
Ormond).
— SHY 472. (armed Or langued Gu; imp by
Hastings).
— WK 482. (qtd 3 by Sir Hen Sacheverll).
— WK 500. (qtd 2 by Hen Parker, Ld Mor-
ley).
— WB II 48, 1. (qtd 2&3 by Butler, E of
Ormond).
— FB 63. (?imp by Kerdiston).
BORNEL. SM 349, 63.
[BURNEL]. OxfRS IV 215; OxfAS 83, 13.
1455. (qtd 5 by Lovel; tomb, Minster Lovell,
Oxfords).
BURNEL, S. Edward. BR IV 15.
BURNEL, Sire Edward. N 99.
BURNEL, Philip. G 65.
BURNELL. Leake. (escutch of Francis Lovell,
KG, d1483).
BURNELL. L2 49, 7. (a&l Or).

BURNELL, Sir Edward. BR V 70.
BURNELL, of Staple [Fitzpaine, Som]. Gerard
145.
BURNELLE. BR VI 64.
FOLIOT, Bishop. Dingley ccli. (on Ledbury
Hospital, Herefs, founded by Bp, 1232).
MORLAY, Ld. RH, Ancestor iv 229.
MORLAY, Tomas, Sir de. BB 75. (a&l Or;
d1416).
MORLAYE, Mons Robt, of Norf. WJ 317.
MORLAYE, Mons Willm de. WJ 319.
MORLE. CC 232, 323.
MORLE. PO 38.
MORLE, Ld. AY 43. (a&l Or).
MORLE, Ld de. WLN 272. (?crowned Arg).
MORLE, le Sr de. CN 84.
MORLE, Sire Roger de. O 37.
MORLE, William de. G 71.
MORLEE. NS 114.
MORLEE, Monsire de. AN 14.
MORLEE, le Sr de. NB 53.
MORLEY. CRK 223. (a&l Or; tail turned in).
MORLEY. PV 81.
MORLEY. PLN 137. (membered Gu).
MORLEY. L9 70b, 4. (a&l Gu).
MORLEY, Ld. Gerard 126.
MORLEY, Ld. FK I 103.
MORLEY, Ld. KB 300.
MORLEY, Ld. WB V 36. (a&l Gu).
MORLEY, Ld. WB I 37, 13.
MORLEY, Ld. BR VI 35.
MORLEY, Ld. XL 188.
MORLEY, Le Sr de. S 60.
MORLEY, Sr de. CKO 37.
MORLEY, le Sire de. TJ 85. (blazoned sans
crown).
MORLEY, le Sr de. WB II 51, 4.
MORLEY, le Sr de. AS 119.
[MORLEY]. Farrer I 191. (imp by [Shelton];
in window, Hardwick Ch, Norf).
[MORLEY, of Kent]. MY 234. (a&l Or).
MORLEY, Lorde. BW 9, 51.
MORLEY, le Sr de, of Norf. CY 111, 443.
MORLEY, le S'or de. T c 23.
MORLEY, Robert de. XL 152.
MORLEY, Thomas, Ld. S 62. (armed Or
langued Gu).
MORLEY, Thomas, Ld. WGA 112.
YORKE, Sir Robert de. WNS 25b, 30.

Az lion Arg crowned
Az lion crowned Arg
DARELL, Sir John. XL 234.
[M'DOUGAL]. Lyndsay 426. (qtd by Kenna-
dye, of Blairquhane).
Az lion Arg crowned Gu
— WLN 28.

Az lion Arg crowned Or
— *PLN 857.* *(qtd 2&3 by Thos Garnett).*
— *SC 10.* *(escutch of E of Douglas).*
— *Leake.* *(escutch of Jas, E of Douglas,*
KG, d1488).
— *WGA 240.* *(escutch of Jas, E of Douglas).*
— *WLN 152.* *(armed Or langued Gu).*
ARMENIA, K of. *TJ 3.*
ARMYNE, Le Roy de. *AS 9.*
BESTON, Sir T. *WB I 40b, 1.*
DALTON, Sir John. *CVL 333.*
DALTON, S'Thos, of Lancs. *CY 59, 236.*
DAREL. *SK 808.*
GALLOWAY, ye lord of, of auld. *Lyndsay*
145.
GALWAY, Alan, Sire de. *?source.*
[MACDOWALL]. *Berry; Stodart 4. (a&l Or).*
('Ceulx de mandoel').
[MCDOUAL]. *Neale & Brayley. 1600.*
(escutch of [Douglas, qtg Abernethy, Wishart
& Stuart of Bontill]; Mont to Q Eliz & Q
Mary in Hen 7 Chap).
SAXNEIE, Le Snre. *WNR 23.*

Az lion Or crowned

Az lion Or crowned Arg
CAREW, Sir George. *PLN 244. (membered*
Gu; qtg 2 Sa 3 lions passt Or, 3 Sa 6 lions
Or, 4 qtly i&iv Arg bend wavy plain cotised
Gu, ii&iii Arg 3 concentric annulets Gu).
DARELL, Sir Edward. *PLN 2053.*
DARELL, Sir Edward, of Littlecote, Wilts.
I2(1904)213. (qtg 2&3 Arg 2 bars Gu in chf
2 lions Untinc).
DARELL, Sir John. *BA 661.*
DARELL, of Suff. *MY 51.*
DARREL, Sir Richard. *Sandford 334. (2nd*
husb of Mgt Beaufort).
DARRELL. *T b 128. (lion ch with 4foil Sa).*
DARRELL. *CRK 1733. (a&l Arg).*
DARRELL, Thomas, of Yorks. *WB III 117b,*
5.
GYLDER, D of. *KB 36.*

Az lion Or crowned Gu
— *PLN 1715. (qtg 2&3 paly Or and Az can-*
ton Erm [Shirley-'2nd coat i.e. of augmenta-
tion']).
GUELDRES. *Neale & Brayley. 1612. (lion to*
sin; a&l Gu; qtd 6 by Lorraine imp by
Scotld; Mont to Mary, Q of Scots, d1587 in
Hen 7 Chap).

Az lion crowned Or
GUELDRES, Duke of. *XL 408.*
[GUELDRES]. *Lyndsay 42. (lion to sin; imp*
Or lion Sa; imp by Mary Q of Scotld, w of
Jas 2 & dau of D of Gueldres).
PYKERYNG, Sir R. *WB I 39, 3.*
SCHWARZENBERG. *Sandford 489. (qtd 3 by*
Q Anne of Cleves).

Gu lion Arg &c crowned

Gu lion Untinc crowned Or
TURBERVILE. *PT 95.*

Gu lion crowned Arg
CLISSON. *WLN 24.*
CLISSON. *WLN 280.*
CLYSSON, le Sr de. *CN 96.*
MALTON, Roger de. *XL 266.*
PASSELEY, S'Robert de, of Suss. *CY 170,*
679. (langued Az).

Gu lion Arg crowned Or
— *KB 63. (marshalled in base by K*
Osemonde).
— *KB 47. (qtd 4 by [Britain], K. Gowan*
Saracin).
BEWME, The Kyng off. *Lyndsay 29.*
(Bohemia).
[BRITAIN], K Engest Panim. *KB 58. (shield*
per fess, in base Arg on bend Sa 3 martlets
Arg).
DALTON. *L10 54, 10. (a&l Gu).*
DALTON, Mons Rog de. *WJ 143.*
GRAY, Mons Thomas de. *AS 357. (armed*
Or).
HAIWARDE, de. *XL 633. (a&l Or).*
HALEWETON, S' Thomas de. *R 85.*
HALOUGHTON, Mons Thomas de. *SD 114.*
HALWETONE, s'th'm. *PO 658.*
LAYSETER. *PV 22.*
[MARMION]. *Nichols Leics II 570. (per fess,*
in base Arg 2 lions passt Sa; Galby Ch).
MOUBRAY, Sr de. *BL A 17.*
MOWBRAY. *SC 59. (a&l Or).*
[MOWBRAY OF BARNBOUGAL]. *Berry; Stodart*
7. (a&l Or; Ceulx de Bernbaquel).
MOWBRAY, of Barnbwgall. *Lyndsay 247.*
(a&l Or).
WOKENDONE, Nichol de. *G 196.*
WOKINDON, Sire Thom de. *HA 53, 17b.*
WOKINDON, Sire Thomas de. *HA 66.*
WOKINDON, Sr Thomas de. *RB 93.*
WOKINGDON, Monsire de. *CG 43.*
WOKINGDONE, Sire Nicholas de. *N 416.*
WOKINGTON, Nicol. *XL 269.*
WOKYNDON, Monsr Thomas de. *AS 358.*
(armed Or).
WOKYNDONE, Nicholaus de. *Q II 460.*
WOKYNGTON. *FK II 169.*
WOKYNGTON, Mons Nich. *WJ 144.*
WYFRINGDON, Sr Nicho. de. *L 3.*

Gu lion Or &c crowned

Gu lion Or crowned Az
— *WJ 249.*
MOUNCEUDYT, Mons W. *WJ 251.*

Gu lion crowned Or
— *XFB 240. (?lion per fess Arg and Sa; qtd*
2 by Sir Thos Toye).
— *KB 214. (marshalled in base by K*

Garfryd).

FITZALAN, John, E of Arundel. *ML I 11.*
(?crowned mistake for enarmed).

Gu lion ?Sa crowned Or
BURNELL. *PLN 1840. (qtd 3 by Ld Fitz Walter).*

Or lion crowned

Or lion Az crowned Arg
DARELL. *WK 148.*

Or lion Az crowned Gu
— *WLN 71.*
CLEUEDON. *L2 133, 10. (langued Sa).*
CLIVEDON, Sire Johan. *N 1080.*
CLYVEDON, Sir John de. *Soc Jers 1928.*

Or lion Gu crowned Arg
— *Farrer II 375. (?for Melton or Constable, in window, Blakeney Ch).*

Or lion Gu crowned Or
ARMENIA, K of. *CRK 1398. (a&l Az; dex of 3 coats tierced paleways).*
CHEYGNE. *GY b 19.*
ERMENYE, King of. *PLN 22. (dex imp of Jerusalem; imp barry of 10 Arg and Az lion Gu crowned a&l Or).*

Or lion Sa crowned Arg
BAA. *Arch Cant xxi 208. (formerly in window of S transept, Bay chapel, Ickham, Kent for Thos de B, of Ickham, Kt of Shire for Kent 1334-5).*
CLEVEDON, Mons Hugh de. *WJ 334.*

Or lion Sa crowned Az
CLEUEDON. *L10 41, 12. (a&l Gu).*
CLEVEDON, Hugh de. *XL 170. (a&l Gu).*

Or lion Sa crowned Gu
— *CRK 2031. (a&l Gu).*
BEAUCHAMP, S Jehan, of Essex. *GA 108.*
BEAUCHAMP, Sire Johan de, of Fifelde. *N 441.*
BEAUCHAMPE, John. *PCL I 445.*
BEUCHAMP, of Essex. *L1 71, 2; L2 39, 2.*
BEUCHAMP, of Fyfelde. *L10 28b, 14. (a&l Gu).*
BEUCHAMP, Johan de. *LM 557.*
BEUCHAMP, Sir John. *BR V 240.*
BEUCHAMP, Jon de. *Q 382.*
BREDERODE, Regnault, seigneur de. *CB 428.*
CLIFDONE, S'Edmond. *PO 244. (langued Gu).*
CLIFFDON. *L1 157, 1. (armed Gu).*
CLIVEDON, Esmon. *AN 307.*
CLIVEDON, Sr Jo. *L 219.*
CLIVEDON, Renaud de. *E I 363.*
CLYFDON. *DV 68a, 2682. (armed Gu).*
CLYVEDON, Mons' Reymunde de. *TJ 71.*
ELYSDON. *PT 448.*
JULIERS. *Neale & Brayley. (qtd 7 by Lorraine imp by Scotland; mont erected c1612 to Mary, Q of Scots, d 1587 in Hen 7 Chap).*

NAMUR. *L2 358, 3.*

Or lion Sa crowned Or
CLIVEDON, Renaud de. *E II 365.*
WELLES, Ld. *BW 13, 81. (armed Arg).*

Or lion Vt crowned Arg
ENTWISLE, Sir Bertyn of. *CRK 704. (qrs 1&4).*

Purp lion crowned

Purp lion Or crowned Gu
PASHELEY, Sr John. *Kent Gentry 217b. (armed Gu).*

Sa lion Arg &c crowned

Sa lion crowned Arg
SEG[RA]VE, Nichol de. *LM 67.*

Sa lion Arg crowned Or
— *WB II 65, 14. (qtd 2&3 by Arg cross Arg fimbr & fretty Sa).*
— *XK 102. (qtd 5 by Sir Maurice Berkeley, Kt 1509).*
— *WK 464. (qtd 5 by Sir Morice Barkeley).*
— *XK 259. (qtd 5 by Sir Thos Berkeley).*
— *WGA 80. (qtd 5 by Sir Thos Howard, D of Norf).*
— *C3 19b. (lion to sin; Alconbury Ch, Hunts).*
LOVEYN, Henr'. *WLN 750.*
PETER, Nychol. *LY A 97.*
SEAGRAVE, John, Ld, d1354. *Sandford 122, 207 & 208.*
SEEGRAVE, Monsire de. *AN 16.*
SEG'F, Sir Joh' de. *FF 17.*
SEGRAUE. *L1 614, 6.*
SEGRAUE, L[ord]. *AY 48. (langued Or).*
SEGRAUE, le Sour de. *PO 203. (langued Gu).*
SEGRAVE. *WB I 15b, 5.*
SEGRAVE. *PV 77.*
SEGRAVE. *DV 65b, 2600.*
SEGRAVE. *PT 289.*
SEGRAVE. *DX 25. (armed Gu).*
SEGRAVE, Ld. *WB I 37, 2.*
SEGRAVE, Ld. *CRK 1311. (a&l Gu).*
SEGRAVE, Ld. *BR VI 10.*
SEGRAVE, Ld. *CRK 1769. (a&l Or).*
SEGRAVE, Ld. *XL 123.*
SEGRAVE, Le Sire de. *TJ 24.*
SEGRAVE, Le Sr de. *WJ 297.*
SEGRAVE, Le Sr de. *AS 81.*
SEGRAVE, Monsire de. *CG 50.*
SEGRAVE, Sr de. *CKO 36.*
[SEGRAVE]. *D13 18. (armed Gu; qtd by Thwaytts).*
[SEGRAVE]. *OxfRS I 28. (Glass, Banbury, Oxfs).*
[SEGRAVE]. *Nichols Leics II 163. (Little Dalby Ch).*
SEGRAVE, Anne, Abbess of Barking, Essex.

Sandford 208.
SEGRAVE, J de. *SP A 70.*
SEGRAVE, Sr J de. *RB 28.*
SEGRAVE, S Joh. *ST 37.*
SEGRAVE, Johan de. *K 16.*
SEGRAVE, Johan de. *H 7a.*
SEGRAVE, Sire Johan de. *N 41.*
SEGRAVE, Sr Johan. *H 7b.*
SEGRAVE, John de. *K 120.*
SEGRAVE, John, Ld. *LMS 40. (d1325).*
SEGRAVE, Sir John. *BR V 62.*
SEGRAVE, Sir John. *ML II 67.*
SEGRAVE, Sir John de. *WNS 25b, 40. ('Sire
Joh de Seg've por de sa ou un lion rampant
dar coron dor').*
SEGRAVE, Sire John de. *J 20.*
SEGRAVE, Lorde. *KB 313.*
SEGRAVE, Sr Stephen de. *RB 48.*
SEYGRAVE. *WB II 52, 15.*
VACHE, Sir Philip de la. *CV-BM 127.*
Sa lion Gu crowned Or
NORTON, Mons Gerveis de. *CA 151. (?cor-
rupt).*
Sa lion Or crowned Gu
HEIDELBERG, Count of. *XL 427. (qrs 1&4).*
ROCHYNGE, Rauf de. *LM 466.*
Sa lion crowned Or
SEGRAVE. *ML I 78.*
Sa lion Sa (sic) crowned Or
RENE, Count Palatine de. *BR I 33.*

Vt lion crowned
Vt lion crowned Untinc
— *SHY 296. (qtd 3 by Untinc chev cotised
Sa).*
Vt lion Arg crowned Gu
BEESTON. *XL 507. (a&l Gu).*
BESTON. *L1 91, 6; L2 58, 5. (a&l Gu).*
BESTON, Myles de. *LY A 279.*
BOFTON, Milis de. *ME 159. (a&l Gu).*
MENIRLE, Rauf. *TJ 91. (gloss on Mons' Jn
Beeston).*
Vt lion Arg crowned Or
BEESTON. *XL 28.*
BOSTON. *CC 224, 73.*
BOSTON. *L10 83b, 6. (a&l Gu).*
BOSTON. *RB 377. (armed Or).*
EIRLIEHEYM. *XL 621. (a&l Gu).*
[GERRARD]. *PLN 1961. (a&l Or; in chf with
in base Arg on cross Sa 5 roundels Or imp
Yeuxlley, Arg chev Sa betw 3 mullets of 12
Gu).*
RESTONE. *PT 1047.*
Vt lion Or crowned Gu
ARDERN. *L1 10, 2; L2 5, 6. (a&l Gu).*
Vt lion crowned Or
BESTON. *L10 29, 5. (a&l Gu; crown
apparently painted Gu but repainted Or).*

Barry lion crowned
Barry of 10 lion crowned per pale
[BRANDON]. *I2(1904)37. (qtg II&III qtly
1&4 cross moline [Bruyn], 2&3 Lozy [Roke-
ley]; Banner of 'The duc of Suff Charles
Knyght the Gartier').*
Barry Arg and Az lion Gu crowned Or
— *PLN 22. (barry of 10; a&l Or; sin imp of
Jerusalem, dex imp being Or lion Gu
crowned Or[K of Ermenye]).*
ARMONIE, K of. *KB 29. (barry of 10; sin
coat on shield tierced in pale).*
CIPRES, le Roy de. *P 12.*
CYPRUS. *WLN 33. (barry of 8; a&l Or).*
CYPRUS. *WLN 56. (armed Or).*
CYPRUS, King of. *PLN 30. (barry of 8 in qr
2 & of 10 in qr 3 ; a&l Or; qtd 2&3 by
Jerusalem, all crosses potent).*
[CYPRUS]. *Neale & Brayley. (barry of 10; in
qr 3 of coat imp by France modern & Eng
qtly on mont erected 1606 to Queens Eliz &
Mary in Hen 7 Chap).*
LUCENBURGHT. *AS 19. (qtd 1&4 by le Roy
de Boeme).*
LUXEMBOURG. *WGB 138 & 140. (barry of
10; a&l Or). (qtd 3 by Eliz Widvile).*

Barry Arg and Gu lion crowned
Barry of 8 Arg and Gu lion Sa crowned Or
— *XF 96. (qtg 2&3 Or fess Gu 6 fleurs de
lis 2, 2, 2 counterch).*
Barry of 10 Arg and Gu lion Or crowned Gu
BRANDON, Sir William. *PLN 1726.*
BRANDON, Sir William. *WB V 75. (Kt
1485).*
Barry of 10 Arg and Gu lion crowned Or
BRANDON. *I2(1904)255. (qtg II & III, qtly
1&4, Az cross moline Or; 2&3, lozy Arg and
Gu; 'Syr Charles Bramdon Vycount lysle').*
Barry of 10 Arg and Gu lion Or crowned per
pale Arg and Gu
BRANDON, Charles, D of Suff. *Sandford 536.
(2nd husb of Mary, 3rd dau of Hen 7).*
BRANDON, Sir William. *WK 12.*
BRANDON, Sir Charles, KG. *Leake. (d1545;
qtg Bruin & Rokesley).*
BRANDON, Sir Thomas, KG. *Leake. (ch on
shldr with mullet Sa; d1510).*
Barry of 10 Arg and Gu lion Or crowned per
pale Gu and Arg
BRANDON. *XL 122. (a&l Az).*
BRANDON. *XK 70. (Visct Lisle, KG; qrs
1&4).*
BRANDON, Charles, D of Suff. *XB 8. (KG
1513, d1545; qr 1).*
BRANDON, Sir Charles, D of Suff. *WGA 196.*
BRANDON, Sir Robert. *WK 105. (ch on shldr
with cresc Sa).*
BRANDON, Sir Thomas. *WGA 286.*

BRANDON, Sir Thomas. *WK 220. (a&l Az).*
BRANDON. *L10 76, 15.*
BRANDON, D of Suff. *L1 29, 1; L2 37, 4.
(a&l Az; qtg II&III qtly 1&4 as above, 2 Az
cross moline Or [Bruyn], 3 Lozy Erm and Gu
[Rokeley]).*
Barry of 10 Arg and Gu lion Or crowned per
pale Gu and Or
BRANDON, Sir William. *XF 453.*

Barry Az &c & Arg lion crowned
Barry Az and Arg lion Gu crowned Or
CIPRES, Kyng of. *BR I 17.*
LUXEMBURG, Duke of. *TJ 8.*
SYPRESSE, K of. *AY 103. (langued Or).*
Barry of 10 Gu and Arg lion crowned Or
?BRANDON. *SHY 135.*

Erm lion Az crowned
Erm lion Az crowned Gu
BOYLAND. *XL 83.*
Erm lion Az crowned Or
MYTHOP, Roger de. *FC II 69.*
PECKERINGE, Sr. *RB 181.*
PEKERING. *L1 490, 3. (armed Gu).*
PICKERING. *BK 64. (qtg II qtly 1&4 per
bend Gu and Arg lion Az, 2&3 Or cross
moline Sa chf Gu ch with cross Arg, III Arg
3 chaplets Gu).*
PICKERING, Sir Edward. *PLN 2008. (a&l
Gu).*
PICKERING, Sir Edward. *XL 222.*
PICKERING, Sir James. *CRK 1323. (a&l Or).*
PICKERING, Sir James. *CVL 378.*
PICKERING, Sir Jamys, of Yorks. *RH, Ances-
tor iv 233.*
PIKERING. *BA 696.*
PIKERINGE. *L2 408, 11.*
PYCKERING. *1H7 1. (langued Gu; tinct of
crown uncertain. 'At Master Westons').*
PYKERING, Mons' Thomas. *TJ 40.*
PYKERINGE, de Illertone. *PT 1154.*
PYKERYNE, Mons James de. *WJ 276.*
PYKERYNG. *L9 107a, 4. (a&l Gu).*
PYKERYNG, Sir Edward. *WK 76.*
PYKERYNG, Monsr Thomas de. *AS 204.*
PYKERYNGE, Sir Edward. *BA 621. (a&l Gu).*
PYKERYNGE, James. *BG 116.*

Erm lion Gu &c crowned
Erm lion Gu crowned Or
PAITSULL. *L9 109a, 9. (a&l Az).*
PATESHILL, Monsire de. *CG 49.*
PATESHULL. *XL 4.*
PATESHULL. *L9 96b, 10.*
PATESHULL, Mons' John. *TJ 126.*
PATISHILL', Monsr J de. *AS 234.*
TURBERVILE, Richard. *XL 348.*
TURBERVILLE, Sr de. *CKO a 62.*

TURBERVYLE, Sir Thomas of Herefs. *WB III
76, 7. (armed Or, langued Az).*
TURBURVYLE, Mons Rich. *WJ 207.*
TURBURVYLE, Monsire Richard. *AN 260.*
Erm lion Purp crowned Or
PAYTESHUL. *L1 500, 4.*

Per pale lion crowned
Per pale Untinc and Erm lion crowned
HADERSETT, Nicholas de. *PRO-sls.* 1334-5.
Per pale Gu and Az lion Arg crowned Or
NORTHAM. *L2 365, 8.*
Per pale Gu and Sa lion Arg crowned Or
BELLERS. *SK 578.*
BELLERS. *L10 26, 11. (a&l Az).*
BELLERS, of Leicester. *L1 83, 5; L2 66, 8.
(armed Or).*
BELLERS, Roger de. *XL 343. (langued Az).*
BELLERS, Mons Roger de, le fitz. *WJ 192.*
BELLERYS, Sir J. *WB I 40, 10.*
BILLERS. *RH, Ancestor vii 203. (name
added in later hand).*
NORTHAM, Thomas de. *TJ 95.*
NORTHAM. *L9 86a, 8. (a&l Az).*
NORTHAM, Thomas de. *TJ 140.*

Semy of billets lion crowned
Billety lion crowned
— *CombeAsp II 171.* Sigillum Willelmi Lucy dni
de Averssum. 1491-2. *(qtd by eagle displ
[Lucy]).*
— *Dugd 17, 21.* 1491. *(qtd by Wm Lucy).*
PLANKE, William la. *Dugd 17, 21.* 1292. *(s
of Sir William de la P).*
Arg billetty & lion Sa crowned Gu
PLAUNKYS. *L1 522, 3. (a&l Gu).*
Arg billetty & lion Sa crowned Or
DELAPLAUNCHE, of Bucks. *L2 165, 5.*
PLANK, Sr Jake de la. *RB 66.*
PLAUNCHE. *L9 101a, 6.*
PLAUNCHE, Sir Johes de la. *HA A 21.*
PLAUNKE. *RB 249.*
Az billety Or lion crowned Arg
BURGOGNE. *L10 86, 12. (a&l Gu; crown
may be Or).*
Az billetty & lion crowned Or
— *WLN 46.*

Crusily lion crowned
Crusily lion crowned
BREEUS, Johanna le. *Birch 7788.*
+SIGILL'IOHANNE LE BREEUS. 1348. *(sl [with
3 roundels barry nebuly of 6] used by Jn,
s&h of Jn de Breouse, of Boyton Manor,
Wilts).*
BREWES. *Mill Steph.* 1506. *(imp by Strange
on effigy of 'John lestrawnge ar and Brewes',
brass to Sir Roger le S, Hunstanton, Norf).*
SHIRLEY, Ralph de, Kt. *BrookeAsp I 64, 5.*

Sigillum: Radulphi: de: Shirley: militis:. 1432-3.
(Dat apud Radeclyf super Soram).
Arg crusily Gu lion Untinc crowned Or
— *PT 587.*
Arg crusily & lion Gu crowned Or
BARRET, Sire Stevene. *O 137.*
BREWSE OF SUSS. *MY 339. (a&l Or).*
Az crusily & lion Or crowned Gu
BREUSE, Monsire Peres. *AN 200.*
BREWES. *L10 75b, 10. (langued Gu; sans claws).*
BREWS, Mons Piers de. *WJ 115.*
Az semy of crosses trefly & lion Or crowned Gu
BREUX. *SK 32.*
Az crusily & lion crowned Or
BREWES, Piers de. *XL 643.*
BREWSE. *Nichols Leics III 781. (imp by Shirley; Castle Donington Ch).*
Gu crusily & lion Or crowned Az
— *PLN 986. (qtd 2&3 by Shirley).*
Or crusily & lion Az crowned Gu
BRUCE OF SKELTON. *XL 204.*
Sa crusily & lion crowned Or
GOSHALL, Sir John. *Lawrance 21.* c1310.
(arms no longer visible; effigy, Ash by Sandwich, Kent).

Crusily fitchy lion crowned
Crusily fitchy lion crowned
MOUBRAY, William, Kt. *PRO-sls.* 1336-7.
Gu semy of crosses pommy fitchy & lion Or crowned Arg
MONTENDRE, William. *XL 371. (a&l Az).*
Gu semy of crosses pommy fitchy & lion crowned Or
MOUNTENDRE. *L9 71a, 2.*

Semy de lis &c lion crowned
Az semy de lis Or lion Arg crowned Or
STIENE, Conrand de. *CA 241. (Conrad IV, Herr von Schleiden, d1345).*
Az semy de lis & lion Or crowned Gu
REYSTON, Ralph de. *XL 446.*
ROYSTON, Sir Ralph. *LR 13.*
Vt semy de lis & lion Or crowned Gu
REISTON, Mons Raufe de. *WJ 363.*
Arg gutty Sa lion Az crowned Or
PYKRYNG, S'Jacob de, of Lancs. *CY 58, 231.*

Vair lion crowned
Vair lion Arg crowned Gu
BASTON, Monsire de. *CG 54.*

Lion patterned or charged & crowned

Lion barry & crowned
Gu lion barry Arg and Az crowned Or
WOKINDON', Sire Nicol de. *HA 54, 17b.*
WOKINDON, Sire Nicol de. *HA 67.*
Gu lion barry Az and Arg crowned Or
WOKINDON, Sr Nicol de. *RB 94.*
Gu lion barry wavy Arg and Az crowned Or
MARMION, Sir Mansell. *CRK 993. (a&l Or).*
MARMYON, of Suff. *MY 45. (a&l Or).*

Lion charged with annulet &c and crowned
Erm lion Az crowned & ch on shldr with annulet Or
PEKERYNG, of Therkele, Cumb. *D4 49.*
Sa lion Arg crowned Or ch on shldr with 3 billets Gu
— *D4 48b. (qtd by Thoattes of Thoattes).*
Az lion Or crowned Arg ch on shldr with cresc Gu
DARELL, Sir Edward. *WK 87.*
DARELL, of Littlecot. *BA 825. (a&l Gu).*
Az lion crowned Arg ch on shldr with crosslet fitchy Sa *L10 53, 10. (a&l Arg).*
Az lion Or crowned Arg ch on shldr with crosslet fitchy Untinc
DARELL. *WB I 23b, 7.*
Az lion Or crowned & ch on shldr with crosslet fitchy Arg
DARRELL, William. *CRK 3. (a&l Arg tail turned inwards).*
Az lion Or crowned Arg ch on shldr with crosslet Sa
DARREL, of Kent. *L1 196, 2; L2 153, 8. (armed Arg).*
Arg lion Sa crowned Or ch on shldr with estoile Arg
— *XFB 51. (qtd 2 by Ric Sacheverel of Sadyngton).*
Arg lion Sa crowned Or ch on shldr with fleur de lis Or
WALKFARE, Robe. *NS 130.*
Gu lion crowned Or ch on shldr with fleur de lis Sa
MANDEVILE, Thomas. *XL 369. (a&l Az).*
Sa lion Arg crowned Or ch on shldr with fleur de lis Gu
SEGRAVE, S Esteuen, s of Joh. *ST 38. (tinct of fleur de lis uncertain).*
SEGRAVE, Sire Estevene de. *N 795.*
SEGRAVE, Sr Estienne de. *L 124.*
SEGRAVE, Jan de. *Q 205. (armed Or).*
SEGRAVE, Johan de. *LM 163.*
SEGRAVE, Johan de. *G 104.*
SEGRAVE, Mons Nicholl de. *WJ 305.*
Sa lion Arg crowned Or ch on shldr with rose Gu
SEGRAVE, Mons Esteven de. *WJ 301.*

Lion crowned & ch on shldr with 3foil slipped
DARELL. *Mill Steph; Belcher II 28. 1438.*
(imp Chicheley; brass, Little Chart, Kent to
Jn D & w Florence dau of Wm C, bro of
Henry C, Archbp of Canterbury).
Arg lion Gu crowned Or ch on shldr with 3foil
Untinc
CHEYGNE. *GY a 19.*
Az lion Or crowned Arg ch on shldr with 3foil
Untinc
DARELL. *Suff HN 47. (imp by Jennegan in*
Mr J's house at ?Somerleyton).
Az lion Or crowned Untinc ch on shldr with
3foil slipped Arg
DARELL. *WB I 19, 6-8. (?3foil Or).*
Az lion Or crowned & ch on shldr with 3foil
slipped Arg
DARELL. *SK C 855. (a&l Arg).*
DARELL, John. *Kent Gentry 216. (armed*
Arg).
Az lion Or crowned Arg ch on shldr with 3foil
slipped Sa
DARELL. *SK A 855.*
DARELL, Sir John. *WK 234. (a&l Gu).*
Sa lion Arg crowned Or ch on shldr with 4foil
Gu
SEGRAVE, Mons Esteven de. *WJ B 301.*
Az lion crowned Or ch on shldr with cresc on
loz Gu
DARELL, Sir Edward. *BA 855. (a&l Arg).*

Lion charged with mullet & crowned
Arg lion Az crowned Or ch on shldr with mullet
Arg
— *L10 97b, 3. (qtd 3 by Sir Hen Sacheurel).*
Arg lion Sa crowned Or ch on shldr with mullet
Arg
— *XK 120. (qtd 3 by Sir Hen Sacheverel, Kt*
1509).
MORLE. *DV 53b, 2104. (armed Gu).*
Arg lion Sa crowned Or ch on shldr with mullet
Or
— *XX 117. (qtd 3 by Sacheverel).*
Barry of 10 Arg and Az lion Or crowned per
pale Gu and Arg ch on shldr with mullet Sa
BRANDON, KG. *XK 60.*
Barry of 10 Arg and Gu lion Or crowned per
pale Arg and Gu ch on shldr with mullet Sa
BRANDON, Sir Thomas. *WGA 233. (a&l Az).*
Barry of 10 Arg and Gu lion Or crowned per
pale Gu and Arg ch on shldr with mullet Sa
BRANDON, Sir Thomas. *WGA A 286.*
Sa semy de lis Or lion Erm crowned Or ch on
shldr with mullet Gu
PHILLIPPS, Matthew. *CRK 966.*

Lion checky crowned
Gu lion checky Sa and Erm crowned Or
DENDUN, John. *RH, Ancestor vii 209.*
Gu lion checky Erm and Ermines crowned Or
BLACBORNE, Nycolas, of Yorks. *RH, Ances-*
tor v 189. (armed Or).

Lion Erm crowned
Untinc lion Erm crowned Untinc
[BOLBEC]. *Blair N I 91, 181. (Over W door*
of Norman chapel at Seaton Delaval).
GERARD, Piers. *Mill Steph; Thornley 63.*
1492. (on effigy's tabard; brass, Winwick,
Lancs).
GERARD, Piers. *Mill Steph. 1492. (qtg*
[Bromley]; brass, Winwick, Lancs).
GERARD, Piers. *Mill Steph. 1492. (imp*
[Bromley]; brass, Winwick, Lancs).
Az lion Erm crowned Or
GERARD, Sir Pers. *CRK 1003. (a&l Or).*
GERARD, Sir Thomas 'of the Brymme'. *XL*
250. (a&l Gu).
— *D13 2b. (qtd by Hart).*
BRINN. *Gerard 177. (qtg Gerard, of Trent*
Arg salt Gu).
DALTON, of Lancs. *CY 58, 230. (original*
legend is 'S' John de Dalton', but Garratt
appears in later hand over Dalton).
GERARD, Sir Thomas. *CVL 368.*
GERARD, Sir Thomas, of the Brym. *BA 35b,*
338.
JERARDE. *L9 5b, 12. (a&l Gu).*
PECHE. *FK II 438.*
Gu lion Erm crowned Or
— *CRK 1405.*
HAMELYN. *Nichols Leics II 316. (Scalford*
Ch).
HAMELYN, Sire Joham. *N 806.*
HAMELYN, Sire Johan. *O 16.*
HAMELYN, Sr John. *L 43.*
HAMELYN, S'Jon. *PO 624.*
HAMELYN, of Leics. *L1 327, 6; L2 251, 10.*
NERFORD. *L9 83a, 1. (a&l Az).*
NERFORD, John de. *XL 333.*
NERFORD, Reynald de. *WJ 168.*
NERFORD, Waut' de. *WJ 172.*
PECHE, Sr de. *Q 395. (name added).*
Vt lion Erm crowned Untinc
BOLEBEC. *Lawrance 13. (mullet for diffce;*
2nd shield nr tomb of Sir Hugh De La Val,
d1302, Seaton Delaval, Northd).

Field patterned lion Erm crowned
Per pale Az and Gu lion Erm crowned Or
NORWYCHE. *Suff HN 48. (arms of founder,*
Mettingham Castle or College).
NORWYCHE, Roger. *NS 93.*
OLDHALL. *PO 137. (name in modern hand).*

Per pale Gu and Az lion Erm crowned Or
  NORWICH, Roger. *XL 275.*
  NORWYCHE, Mons.Rog.de. *WJ 195.*
Per pale Gu and Sa lion Erm crowned Or
  NORTHAM. *L9 86b, 8.*
Untinc semy de lis Untinc lion Erm crowned
  Untinc
  PHELIP. *Mill Steph.* 1464. *(brass, Herne,
  Kent to Dame Christine w of Sir Matthew P
  cit & goldsmith, mayor of London; she d 25
  May 1470).*
Sa semy de lis Or lion Erm crowned Or
  PHILLIP, Sir Matthew. *XL 71.*

Lion per fess crowned
Lion per fess crowned
  GREENE, John. *Mill Steph.* 1473. *(brass,
  Gosfield, Essex; husb of Edith, dau of Thos
  Rolf).*
Gu lion per fess Arg and Sa crowned Or
  GREEN. *XL 87. (tail turned outwards).*
  GREEN, Sir John. *PLN 1858. (imp qtly, 1
  Arg on chev Sa 3 escallops Arg, 2 Arg cross
  betw 4 escallops Sa, 3 Sa 6 lions coward 3,
  2, 1 Arg, 4 Arg chev betw 3 choughs Sa).*
  GREENE. *Brit Arch Assoc 3S ii 233. (imp
  Rolf; on brass to Jn Greene, barrister, d1473,
  Gosfield).*
  GRENE. *CC 236, 452.*
  GRENE, Sir John, of Essex. *WK 249. (tinct
  of crown uncertain).*
  GRENE, of Saufford, Essex. *L1 288, 5; L2
  222, 2.*
Per fess Gu and Or lion counterch crowned Az
  HAYE, Balthasar de la. *LH 627. (a&l Az).*

Lion semy crowned
Arg lion Az gutty Or crowned Az
  HANDLE. *LH 386.*
Arg lion Az gutty & crowned Or
  BURNEL, Sire Nich'. *PO 199. (langued Gu).*
  HANDLO. *L1 347, 1.*
  HANDLO, Sire Jon de. *WNS 25b, 33.*
Az lion Or gutty Gu crowned Arg
  COSYN, of Dorset. *D13 152. (Arms
  confirmed 15 Apr 1452-3).*
Gu lion Sa gutty & crowned Arg
  BLAKBORNE, Richard, of Lancs. *WB III 90,
  9. (armed Arg).*

Lion Vair crowned
Gu lion Vair crowned Or
  — *CG 48.*
  EVERINGHAM, Sr de. *CKO a 61.*
  [EVERINGHAM]. *Nichols Leics II 570. ('there
  is upon the shldr of the lion a stirrup Sa. To
  this coat the crest is a bull's head'; Galby
  Ch).*
  EVERINGHAM, Adam. *LE 118.* temp Hen 3.

EVERYNGHAM, Adam de. *E I 626; E II 628.*
MARMIEN, Sr William. *L 199.*
MARMIENN. *BA 31, 277. (a&l Or). ('Ever-
  ingham' added in later hand).*
MARMION, William. *XL 334. (a&l Or).*
MARMYON. *L9 49a, 3. (a&l Or).*
MARMYON, of Lincs & Leics. *L1 433, 5; L2
  333, 11. (armed Or).*
MARMYON, Mons W. *WJ 164.*
MARMYOUN, Sire Willame. *N 828.*

Lion vulned & crowned
Az lion Or vulned in shldr Gu crowned Arg
  DARELL, Sir Edw, of Hilcot, Wilts. *L10 59b,
  10. (?crown Erm. Qtg another & imp
  another, for Alis filia Joh. Flys).*
Vt lion Arg vulned crowned & langued Gu
  BULBEC. *Leake. (qtd 7 by Jn Vere, KG,
  d1539).*
  DARELL, Sir Edward. *WK 418.*

Lion crowned with something else
Or lion Arg crowned with branch Ppr
  — *Nichols Leics II 285. (Welby Ch).*
Arg lion Purp crowned with castle Or
  SPAYN, King of. *BR I 7. (qrs 2&3; castle
  has one turret, port open & 3 round loo-
  pholes; lion painted Gu but note says 'lion
  should be purple').*

Lion crowned & collared
Sa lion Arg crowned Or collared Gu
  SEGRAVE, Mons Hugh de. *WJ 307.*

Crowned lion holding, supporting or pierced
  by: see after lion tricorporate

Lion queue fourchy

Demi-lion qf
Gu demi-lion with 2 tails Arg
  STOKES. *LS 90. (a&l Az).*
  STOKES. *DV 44b, 1743. (couped; armed Az).*
Gu demi-lion qf Arg
  STOKES. *CC 227, 168.*
  STOKES. *L1 616, 5.*
  STOKES. *XL 281. (couped).*
Or demi-lion qf couped Gu
  MAILORY. *L9 49b, 7.*
  MALURE, William. *E I 589.*
Per fess Az and Or demi-lion qf Gu
  MALURE, William. *E II 591.*

Lion qf

Lion qf

— *PRO-sls.* 16 Dec 1346. *(2queued; qrs 1&4 of coat imp by Philippa de Cergeaux, Lady of Chipping Norton).*

— *Mill Steph.* 1491. *(qrs 2&3 of brass to Sir Jervis Clifton, Clifton, Notts).*

— *Mill Steph.* 1478. *(qrs 2&3 of brass to Sir Robt Clifton, Clifton, Notts).*

— *Mill Steph.* 1483. *(qtd by fess betw 3 martlets; qtd 2&3 by Metford, all imp by Weston on brass to Jn W & w Mgt M, Ockham, Surr).*

— *Birch 12753.* 1467-87. *(qtd 2&3 by Jn de la Pole, E of Lincoln, Lieutenant of Irld etc).*

— *?source. (floor tile, Pershore Abbey Ch, Worcs).*

— *Durham-sls 2269.* early 14 cent. *(tail unclear).*

— *PRO-sls.* 1417-18. *(imp by Margery, Lady de Scrope & of Masham).*

— *Mill Steph.* 1587. *(qtd I&IV 3 on brass to George Clifton, Clifton, Notts).*

BAVENT, Robert de. *PRO-sls.* 1302-3.

BOYS, John, Kt. *PRO-sls BS 36.* Sigillum Iohannis boys. 1375-6.

BREWSE, Johanna le. *Birch 7791.* S' IOH'E L' BREWSE. 1356. *(sl used by Ric le B, of Suff, Chev).*

BROUNFLETE, Henry, Kt. *Yorks Deeds IX 24.* *(2queued).*

BRUMPTON, John de. *Bow LIX 6.* Sigillum Johis de Brumpton. 1369-70. *(2queued).*

BURGHERSH. *PRO-sls.* 1447-8. *(qtd by William de la Pole, E of Suff).*

BURGHERSH. *Arch Journ xxxvii 82. (imp by by Sir Jn de Mohun KG, for his w Joan (d1404) dau of Sir Bartholomew B).*

BURGHERSH. *Birch 9283.* 1397. *(subsidiary on sl of Thos le Despenser, E of Gloucs).*

BURGHERSH. *Birch 9274.* 1401. *(imp with arms of Eliz, Lady Despencer, dau of Bartholomew, 4th Baron B & wid of Edw, Baron D).*

BURGHERSH. *PRO-sls.* 1466-7. *(imp by Alice de la Pole, Duchess of Suff).*

[BURGHERSH]. *Soc Antiq Cast F 33.* late 15 cent. *(qtd 2&3 by Jn de la Pole, 2nd D of Suff).*

[BURGHERSH]. *PRO-sls.* 1397-8. *(2queued; loz hanging from tree; imp by [Clare] on sl of Thos le Despenser).*

BURGHERSH, Bartholomew de. *PRO-sls AS 238.* ....mei de burg.. urchi. 9 July 1353. *(2queued; hanging from leopard's head).*

BURGHERSH, John de. *PRO-sls E40 A3250.* ...ASCH. 1374-5.

BURGHERSH, John de, Kt. *PRO-sls E40*

A3232. SIGILLVM: IOHIS: DE: BVREHASCH. 1371-2.

BURGHERSH, Margaret de. *Birch 7952.* SIGILLUM: MARGARETE: DE: BURGHERSH. 1339. *(imp billety or crusilly, lion). (sis of Ld Badlesmere, w of 4th Baron B).*

BURGHERSH, Robt. *BD 98. (tomb St Mary's chapel, Lincoln Cathedral; tombs to Bp Hen B & Bartholomew B do not show qf).*

BURGHERSSH, Bartholomew de. *PRO-sls.* 1315-16. *(2queued).*

BURGHERSSH, Bartholomew de, Kt. *PRO-sls.* 1366-7. *(2queued; swan above shield & crested helm on each side).*

BURGWASHE. *Habrington ii 244. (imp by le Despencer; glass formerly in St Andrew's Ch, Pershore, Worcs).*

BURWASH, Henry. *Birch 1734. (alias de Burghersh, Bp of Lincoln 1320-40).*

BUSSCHON, Bartholomew de. *Arch Journ (York 1846) 23.* 14 cent. *(2queued; sl matrix).*

CHAUCER. *Birch 12746.* 1439. *(imp in arms of Alice, Duchess of Suff, dau of Thos C).*

[CHAUCER]. *Birch 3120. (imp by de la Pole; sl of Ewelme Hosp, Oxfords, founded 1437 by Wm de la P & w Alice C).*

[CHAUCER]. *PRO-sls.* 1466-7. *(2queued; imp by Alice de la Pole, Duchess of Suff).*

CRESEY, Esmond de. *PRO-sls.* 1291-2.

CRESSY, Sir John. *Arch Journ lxxx 4, 42.* 1444. *(qtg Mortimer). (alabaster tomb, Dodford, Northants).*

DEVON, Amice, Countess of. *PRO-sls.* 1273-4. *(2queued; 'Lady of the Island').*

DUDLEY, John, Ld. *Bow XXX 13.* 1443-4. *(2queued; 1 of 3 shields).*

HAVERING, John de. *PRO-sls.* 1301. *(2queued).*

HAVERING, John de, Baron. *Birch 10588.* +SIGILLVM.IOHANNIS.DE.HAVERING. 1301.

HAVERING, John of. *Barons Letter.*

HERCEBOY, Martin. *Birch 8851.* SIGILL' MARTIN HERCEBOY(?). 1529. *(sl used by Anna Colepepyr, wid of Walter C, of Kent & dau of Jas Aucher, of Kent).*

HERTECOMBE, Richard. *PRO-sls.* 1421-2. *(2queued).*

KEMPSER, Petronilla. *Birch 11045.* 1272-3.

KINGESTON, John de. *PRO-sls.* 1301. *(2queued).*

KINGESTON, John, Ld of. *Barons Letter.*

KINGSTON. *Mill Steph.* 1514. *(imp Fettiplace on brass to Jn K & w Susan F, Childrey, Berks).*

KINGSTON. *Mill Steph.* 1514. *(brass to Jn K & w Susan Fetiplace, Childrey, Berks).*

KINGSTON. *?source. (imp Fettiplace; brass to Jn K, d1516, Childrey Ch, Berks).*

KINGSTON, John de. *Vinc 88, 6, 13.* 1329. *(sl; power of Attorney to give seisin of manor of Foxcote to Thos de K, his son, & Matilda his w, dau of Jn de Clyvedon).*

KINGSTON, John de. *Vinc 88, 150.* 1384-5. *(2queued).*

KYNGESTON, John, Ld. *Birch 11171.* SIGILLVM IOHANN ....ON. 1301. *(Constable of Edinburgh Castle).*

KYNGESTON, Sir John de. *Heneage 2126.* SIGILLUM JOHANNIS: KYNGESTONE. 1347. *(grant of toft in Warminster, Wilts).*

KYNGESTON, Thomas. *Clairambault 4998.* 27 Nov 1437.

KYNGESTON, Thomas de. *Vinc 88, 6, 11.* 1329-30. *(s of Sir Jn de K; power of Attorney to give seisin of manor of Foxcote).*

[LAURENCE]. *Mill Steph; Thornley 203.* 1531. *(qtg, 2 cross emb counter-emb, 3 illegible; imp Ashton, of Middleton on brass to Alice A & her 3 husbands, (1) Jn L (2) Rich Radcliff & (3) Thos Booth, Middleton, Lancs).*

LEYCESTRIE, Alianore, Comitissa. *Birch 6686.* *(wid of Simon de M, E of Leics, d1264 & dau of K John).*

MALORRE, Anketil. *PRO-sls.* SIGILLUM ANXCILLI MALORRE. 1371-2. *(2queued).*

MONTFORD, Simon de, E of Leicester. *Birch 11296, HB-SND.* 1258.

PASSHELEY, John, Esq. *Birch 12396.* SIGILLU IOH'IS PASSH...MIGER. 1458. *(2queued; qtg 2&3 checky escutch semy of roundels, salt; s&h of Jn P, Kt, of Suss).*

PECHAM, Lora. *Birch 12448.* S[IGIL]L' LORE ....E. 1377. *(imp on chev 3 lions; w of Jas de P, of Kent).*

POLE, Edmund de la, 3rd D of Suff, KG. *Birch 12750.* 1495.

POLE, John de la, D of Suff. *PRO-sls E40 A10952.* 1476-7. *(not on shield).*

POLE, John de la, D of Suff, KG. *Birch 12751.*

SEGRAVE, Christina de. *Birch 6712.* S...DE.S.-RAVE. 1280. *(dau of Hugh de Plessets, Kt & w of Jn de S, afterwards 5th Baron de S).*

STANLOW, John de. *PRO-sls.* 1334. *('inditem anglicum').*

STANLOWE, Ralph de. *PRO-sls E40 A6061.* 1322-3. S'RADVLPHI DE STANLOWE.

STAPLETON, Sir Robert. *Lawrance 41.* *(Effigy, Aldridge, Staffs).*

STONTEVILLE, John, Ld of. *PRO-sls.* 1417.

STURI, William, Kt. *PRO-sls.* 1346-7 & 1350-1.

SUFFOLK, John, D of. *PRO-sls E40 A10952.* 1476-7. *(not on shield).*

WAGGE, Nicholas, of Rothewell, Northants. *Birch 14201.* 1390. *(imp cresc betw 2 estoiles).*

WASTNEYS, Edward, Kt. *Vinc 88, 21.* 1301.

WELFFORD, Thomas, of Kent. *Birch 14334.* 1529.

WELLE, Adam de, 1st Baron. *Birch 14335.* SIGILLVM DOMINI AIDE DE W[EL]LE. 1301.

WELLE, John de. *Birch 14336.* SIGILLVM IOHANNIS DE WELLE. 1359. *(s&h of Ld Adam, 4th Baron W).*

WELLES. *Mill Steph.* 1391. *(brass to Margery Zouch, w of Robt de Willoughby, Ld of Eresby, Spilsby, Lincs).*

WELLES, Adam of. *Barons Letter, HB-SND.*

WELLES, Adam, Ld. *PRO-sls.* 1301.

WELLES, Adam, Ld of. *Barons Letter.*

WELLES, John. *Birch 14338.* SIGILLU IOHANNIS DE WELLIS. 1373. *(s&h of Jn de W, Kt, later 5th Baron W).*

[WELLS]. *Mill Steph.* 1538. *(qtd 2 by Dymoke, all imp by Coffyn on brass to Sir Wm C, Standon, Herts).*

WODE, John atte. *Baker-sls.* Sigillum Johannis ... 1377. *(2queued; grant of power of Attorney in manor of Albrighton, Salop).*

YEDELISSH, Sir John. *PRO-sls.* 1416. *(2queued).*

Lion to sin qf

PYCOTT, Baldwin. *Vinc 88, 57.* temp Edw 1. *(2queued; Ld of North Clifton, Hardby & Kirtlington; gt-grandson of Hugh P).*

Arg lion qf Untinc &c

Arg lion qf Untinc
— *CT 108.*

Arg lion qf Az
— *WB I 25b, 19.* *(qtd 2 by qtly Gu fret Arg & Arg on fess Az 2 mullets Arg; qtd by .... of Lancs).*
— *WB I 16, 16.*
CRESSY, Sir Joh, Northants. *L10 38, 17.*
CRESSY, Sir John, Northd. *L10 45b, 6.* *(qrs 1&4).*

Arg lion qf Gu
— *KB 79.* *(marshalled in base by K Hertner).*
— *PLN 2030.* *(qtd 3 by Sir Harry Vernon).*
— *WLN 86.* *(qf in salt; qtd 2&3 by Sa lion Or).*
— *FK II 749.* *(qtd 2&3 by Boteler [of Salop]).*
— *LY A 4.* *(qtd 2&3 by Butler, of Bewsey, Lancs).*
— *C2 4.* *(2queued; imp by Arg 3 roses Gu (Nicholas Gaynsford) in Chancel of Carshalton, Surr).*
— *I2(1904)178.* *(qtd III 2&3 by 'Francys Hasylden de Gylden Morden Cambrygeshyre').*
— *CRK 254.* *(qtd 2&3 by Butler, of*

Warrington).
— *Neale & Brayley.* 1296. *(2queued; qtd by Kingston; canopy of Mont to Edm, E of Lancaster).*
— *L10 23b, 7. (tail forked at tip; qtd 2&3 by Borbon, de Saint Pol).*
— *PO 418. (original name erased apart from S' but 'Momford' written above in later hand).*
BANESAR, Wat' de. *WLN 772.*
BAUESAR, Walter de. *F 268.*
BOKENHAM. *Q II 651.*
BUTLER, Sir John. *CVL 397.*
HAVERING. *XFB 36. (qtd 2&3 by Turbervile as qtd by Hasylden, of Gilden Morden).*
HAVERING, Mons Rich. *WJ 215.*
HAVERING, Richard. *LH 264.*
HAVERING, Sir Richard. *LH 548.*
HAVERING, Sir William. *LH 269. (qf in salt).*
HAVERING, Wilts. *L1 325, 6; L2 256, 8.*
HAVERINGE. *PT 879.*
HAVERINGE, Monsire de. *CG 70.*
HAVERINGES. *L1 345, 3.*
HAVERYNG. *SP A 63.*
HAVERYNG, Monsr de. *AS 314.*
HAVERYNG, Mons' Guilliam de. *TJ 42.*
HAVERYNGES, Monsire Richard. *AN 211.*
HAVERYNGES, Richard de. *E I 660; E II 662.*
HEWERING. *LH 132.*
HILTON. *FK 707. (a&l Sa, qf in salt).*
HILTON, Sir Bartholomew, Cumb. *LH 643.*
HILTON, Lancs. *LH 1084.*
HULTON. *LH 693.*
HULTON. *LH 955.*
HULTON, of the Park, Lancs. *XL 571. (qf in salt).*
LIMBURG, Count of. *XL 424. (qf in salt).*
MALLO, Anthony. *BG 199.*
MALLORY. *PLN 1706.*
MONTFORD, Guy de. *MP I 31.*
MONTFORD, Simon de. *MP I 13; MP II 6.*
MONTFORT, 'de Nony'. *XL 44.*
MONTFORT, Symon. *MP Hist Min ii 239. 1219. (& brother).*
MOUNFORD. *L1 449, 1; L2 323, 12. (a&l Or).*
MOUNFORD, Sr de. *CKO 50.*

Arg lion qf Purp &c
Arg lion qf Purp
BALDYRSTON, Rycharde. *RH, Ancestor vii 193.*
STORY, S' William. *PO 654.*
STORY, William. *XL 447. (a&l Az, qf in salt).*
STORYE, Mons Willm. *WJ 352.*
STURY, Sir William. *Soc Jers 1928. (Warden of Jersey 1354-7).*

Arg lion qf Sa
— *XK 132. (qtd 4 by Sir Christopher Willoughby).*
— *PLN 2037. (qtd 2&3 by Sir Gervaise Clifton).*
— *I2(1904)265. (qtd 3 by Markham).*
— *XZ 158. (qtd 3 by Copley).*
— *WK 189. (qtd 2&3 by Sir Gerveis Clyfton).*
BARANTYNE. *CT 445.*
BURNELLE, Le Sr. *NB 74.*
CRECY, Mons Thomas. *TJ 41.*
CRESSI, Monsire de. *CG 66. (Seigneur de Hodesake).*
CRESSIE, Sr de. *CKO a 38.*
CRESSY. *PT 479.*
CRESSY. *Nichols Leics IV 187. (mont to Wm Stanesmore, d1504 & his w, Frolesworth Ch).*
CRESSY. *CRK 1151.*
CRESSY. *DV 51a, 2020.*
CRESSY, Monsr. *AS 222.*
CRESSY, John de. *XL 153.*
CRESSY, Mons John de. *WJ 311.*
CRESSY, Sir John de. *XL 190.*
CRESSY, William. *N 146.*
CRESSY, William de. *E I 594; E II 596.*
CRESSY, Willm de. *WLN 875.*
CRESSY, Yorks. *L1 142, 4; L2 119, 11.*
MORLAYE, Willam de. *H 107a.*
MORLE, Sir Robert. *BR V 101.*
MORLEY, Sr William de. *H 107b. (tricked crowned Or).*
STANLOWE, Sr Raufe. *CKO a 76. (qf in salt).*
STORYE, Mons Willm. *WJ B 352.*

Az lion qf
Az lion qf Arg
— *CT 205.*
— *PLN 1970. (escutch of E of Derby).*
ATLEE. *L1 15, 4; L2 9, 2. (a&l Gu).*
?CROMWELL, Sir John. *Blair N I 928, 63. (S end of Chancel, Morpeth Ch).*
Az lion qf Or
— *D4 29b. (2queued; qtd 2 of Clyfton, of co Durham).*
— *WB I 36, 12. (qtd 3 by [Hurd]).*
— *H21 2i. (2queued; qtd by Clyfton).*
CHAMPNEYS. *RB 504.*
CHAMPNEYS. *L2 111, 4. (a&l Gu).*
HAROLD, K of Engld. *MP I 1.*
STAPELTON, Robert de. *RB 428.*
STAPELTONE, Robert de. *HA 99, 22.*
STAPILTON, Monsr de. *AS 375.*
STAPLETON. *Nichols Leics IV 941. (Ratcliffe Culey Ch).*
STAPLETON. *LS 77. (a&l Gu).*
STAPLETON, Monsire de. *CG 61.*
STAPLETON, Robert de. *E I 623; E II 625.*

STAPLETON, Robt de. *SF 22. (Ld of Aldridge).*
STAPULTON, Robert. *PCL I 439.*
STEPELTON, Sr. *CKO 59.*
STEPELTONE, Sire Robert de. *N 982.*
STEPLETON, Mons John. *TJ 44.*
STEPLETON, Roberd de. *G 159.*
STEPULLTON, Robert de. *Q 442.*
STEPULTON. *L1 585, 6.*
STEPULTON. *DV 41b, 1634. (armd Gu).*

Gu lion qf Arg

Gu lion qf Arg
AT WOD. *PO 595. (name in later hand).*
ATTE WODE, Mons John. *S 167.*
ATWOD. *L1 15, 2; L2 8, 12.*
ATWODE, Sr. *CKO 51. (written over 'Sr Burghersh'; ?Arg should be Or, now discoloured).*
ATWOOD. *XL 20.*
ATWOOD. *Nichols Leics II 1038. (2queued; Swepstone Ch).*
ATWOOD, John. *D 169. (qf in salt).*
ATWOOD, [of Worcs]. *Habrington ii 242. (glass formerly in Pershore Abbey Ch, Worcs).*
BEHAIGRE, le Rey de. *LM 19. (qf in salt).*
BRYNTONE. *L10 75b, 17. (a&l Az).*
LEICESTER, E of. *WNS 25, 22.*
LEICESTER, Earl of. *WLN 185.*
LEICESTRE, le Conte de. *CN 4.*
LEICESTRIE. *SM 51, 309.*
LEYCESTR, Conte de. *DV 45b, 1785.*
LEYCESTR', le Comte de. *B 4. (banner in margin: per pale indented Arg and Gu).*
LEYSETR, E of. *BR V a 19.*
MALORY. *H21 6b. (2queued; imp by Slingsby, of Scrivin, Yorks).*
MOMFORD. *WB IV 169b, 788. (qr 1).*
MONFORT, Syon, Conte de Leicestre. *TJ 18.*
MONTFORT. *Proc Soc Antiq XVII 2S 277.* c1310. *(2queued; shield on stole at Leagram Hall, Lancs).*
MONTFORT, le Counte de Leicestre. *F 2.*
MONTFORT, le Counte de Leycestre. *N 1037.*
MONTFORT, Counte de Leycestre. *F 6.*
MONTFORT, Cunte de Leycestre. *G 44.*
MONTFORT, Simon de, Earl of Leicester. *RH, Ancestor iii 204.*
MONTFORT, Simon de, E of Leicester, 1230-65. *LMS 25. (as blazoned).*
MONTFORT, Simon de, E of Leicester. *Keepe.* c1260. *(2queued).*
MONTFORT, Simon, E of Leicester. *Sandford 87 & 91.*
MONTFORT, le Cunte Symund. *FW 47.*
MOUNFORD, ... de. *WJ 145.*
MOUNFORD, Conte de Leycester. *L9 69b, 12.*
MUNFORD, Monsire Symun de. *D 137b.*

MUNFORT, Symun de. *D 137a.*
NUNFORT, Symon de. *HE 30.*
PASSELE. *L9 93a, 8.*
PASSLE, S' Rob de, Kent. *CY 148, 590. (2queued).*
PAYNE, Mons' Walter. *TJ 955. (qtd by Az cross flory Or).*
PAYNE, Wautier. *TJ 1324. (qtd by Az cross floretty Or).*
STOKES. *L1 668, 3. (armed Az).*
STRACHEY, Walter. *CRK 102. (qrs 1&4).*

Gu lion qf Or

Gu lion qf Or
— *PLN 1824. (qtd 4 by Stokes).*
— *WLN 149. (qf in salt).*
— *LEP 72. (qf in salt).*
BAREWASSHE. *L10 20b, 7. (a&l Az).*
BERGHERSH. *Sandford 383. (imp by Mohun; mont to Philippa, Duchess of York, St Nicholas Chapel, Westm Abbey).*
BEROHERSSH, S' Barth, Kent. *CY 157, 625.*
BOREWASCHE. *L1 29, 3; L2 45, 10. (armed Az).*
BOREWASSHE, Bertelmo de. *CA 48.*
BOREWASSHE. *SK 152.*
BORWASTHE. *WB I 15b, 6.*
BOURGHERSHE, Sir Bartholomew. *CVK 691.*
BUREWASH, Mons Bertelmew de. *WJ 245.*
BUREWASSHE. *L10 81b, 13. (a&l Az).*
BURGHASCH, Barth. *NS 110.*
BURGHECHE, Monsr de. *AS 330. (tinct of lion unclear).*
BURGHERSH, Mons Barthelmew. *S 8.*
BURGHERSH, Bartholomew. *S 10.*
BURGHERSH, Bartholomew. *BD 154. (3rd N window St George's Ch, Stanford, Lincs).*
BURGHERSH, Bartholomew de. *XL 365. (a&l Az).*
BURGHERSH, Sire Berth. *O 72.*
BURGHERSH, Sire Bertilineo. *N 284.*
BURGHERSH, Sr Esteven. *L 79.*
BURGHERSH, Hereberd. *FW 656.*
BURGHERSHE, Mons John. *TJ 43.*
BURGHERSSH, Bartholus. *Q II 203.*
BURTRESSE, Monsire Bartholomew de. *CG 71.*
BURWASSHE. *CB 110.*
D'AUBIGNY, William, E of Arundel. *MP Hist Min ii 249.* 1221.
D'AUBIGNY, William, E of Arundel. *MP I 36.*
FERRERS. *CRK 204. (both tips of tail turned in; a&l Az).*

Or lion qf Az &c

Or lion qf Untinc
LACY, Earl of Lincoln. *CT 7.*
WELLES. *?source.* 14 cent. *(stained glass, N*

transept, Empingham Ch, Rutl).

Or lion qf Az

    BUXHYLL, Sr Aleyn, Suss. *CY 165, 657.*

    LILE. *SM 49, 302.*

    PERCY, William of. *Keepe.* (*2 queued*).

    REVIERS, Baldwin de, E of Devon. *MP I 75.*

    WANDESFORD. *XL 467.*

    WANDISFORD. *L1 673, 2.*

    WANDYSFORD, of Kirklinton, Yorks. *D4 34b.* (*2queued; a&l Gu*).

Or lion qf Gu &c

Or lion qf Gu

    — *C3 41.* (*2queued; in St Bennetts Ch, Huntingdon*).

    — *PO 415.* (*armed Az; name erased apart from 'S'' & written over erasure in Elizabethan hand is [Malyverrei], above this in modern hand is written [of Kirkby Malory]*).

    BOROWASH. *WB II 50, 13.*

    BOROWASHE, Sir Bartholomew. *WGA 187.*

    BOURGHEYCHT. *L10 86b, 4.* (*a&l Az; name erased from over sh but retained in index*).

    CAUNDYS. *L1 130, 1; L2 102, 10.*

    CHANDOS, Monsire de. *AN 60.*

    CHANDOS, Ches. *L2 102, 12.*

    CHANDOS, Sr Roger. *L 28; N 951.*

    CHANDOYS. *L10 43, 16.*

    CHAUNDAS, Mons John. *TJ 117.*

    CHAUNDOS. *CT 74.*

    DEVON, Baldwin, E of. *MP Hist Min ii 509.* (*buried 1245*).

    HOLLAND, William of. *MP VII 8.* (*K of Germany*).

    MALLERY. *DV 59b, 2356.*

    MALLORY, Anthony. *BG 406.*

    MALLORY, Antony. *S 458.* (*a&l Az*).

    MALLORY, Mons Antoyn. *S 453.*

    MALOIR, John. *Nichols Leics III 499.* c1490. (*mont in Walton on the Woulds Ch*).

    MALORE. *L2 329, 6.* (*a&l Az*).

    MALORE, of Hutton Conyers, Yorks. *D4 35.* (*2queued*).

    MALORY. *PLN 1684.* (*a&l Az*).

    MALORY. *PT 74.*

    MALORY, Sir Wm, Hunts. *CRK 428.* (*a&l Az*).

    POWES, Ld. *RH, Ancestor iv 229.* (*armed Az*).

    TRANE, Sir Sandich de la. *WGA 283.*

    TRANE, Sir Sandich de, KG. *Leake.* c1384.

Or lion qf Or

    — *WK 270.* (*sic; ?lion salient; qtd 3 by Ld Wm Wiloughby*).

Or lion qf Sa

Or lion qf Sa

    — *L10 37, 12.* (*qtd 3 by Coppley*).

    — *WK 842.* (*qtd 3 by Rog Copley*).

    — *WB I 42, 3.* (*qtd 2 by dau of Sir Robt Demock; tinct of field unclear*).

    — *CV-BM 95.* (*head 3/4 face*).

    — *L10 59b, 8.* (*qtd 2 of 6 by Dymoke*).

    — *I2(1904)218.* (*qtd 3 by Rog Coppley, of Roughway, Suss*).

    — *I2(1904)182.* (*qtd 2 by 'Mayster Dymmoke'*).

    — *XK 196.* (*qtd 2 by Sir Lionel Dimock*).

    — *WK 542.* (*qtd 3 by Willoughby*).

    — *XFB 27.* (*qtd 3 by Rog Coppley, of Roughway, Suss*).

    — *XK 264.* (*qtd 4 by Sir Jn Willoughby*).

    — *I2(1904)97.* (*qtd 4 by 'The Lord Wyllowby'*).

    STANLOWE, Mons de. *AS 412.*

    STANLOWE, Mons Gerard. *TJ 45.*

    VALLES, Sr Adam de. *H 68b.*

    WELLE. *PO 212.*

    WELLE, le Sr de. *AS 52.*

    WELLE, Adam de. *K 48.*

    WELLE, Adam de. *H 68a.*

    WELLE, Monsire Adam de. *CG 98.*

    WELLE, S Adam de. *GA 86.*

    WELLE, Monsire John de. *AN 204.*

    WELLES. *SP A 121.*

    WELLES. *XFB 128.* (*qtd 2 by Sir Robt Dymoke*).

    WELLES. *WLN 256.*

    WELLES. *CRK 221.* (*both ends of tail turned in*).

    WELLES. *WLN 233.*

    WELLES, Ld. *XL 121.*

    WELLES, Ld. *AY 71.* (*2queued*).

    WELLES, Ld. *FK I 109.*

    WELLES, Ld. *WGA 115.*

    WELLES, le S' de. *WJ 337.*

    WELLES, le Sire de. *TJ 25.*

    WELLES, le Sr de. *S 63.*

    WELLES, le Sr de. *NB 56.*

    WELLES, le Sr de. *CN 69.*

    WELLES, Adam de. *K 335.*

    WELLES, Sir Adam. *BR V 55.*

    WELLES, Sire Adam de. *N 94.*

    WELLES, John, Ld. *S 65.*

    WELLES, John, Visct. *XK 36.* (*KG temp Hen 7*).

    WELLES, le S'or de. *T c 43.*

    WELLES, S Phelip de. *ST 22.*

    WELLES, Willimus de. *Q II 442.*

    WELLIS, Visct. *WK 2.*

    WELLS, Ld. *PLN 1973.* (*qtg 2&3 Gu fess dancy betw 6 crosslets Or [Enganie]*).

    WELLS, Ld. *PCL IV 122.*

    WELLS, Ld. *KB 290.*

    [WELLS, Viscount]. *WB V 68.* (*Kt 1485*).

    WELLS, John. *Leake.* (*qtg Engaine; KG, d1498*).

    WELLS, John, Ld. *Sandford 417.* (*2queued;*

d1498, m Cecilie of York).
WELLS, John, Visct. *WGA 231. (a&l Gu).*
WELLYS. *L1 668, 2. (a&l Gu).*
WELLYS, Ld. *BR VI 51.*
WELLYS, Ld of. *RH, Ancestor iv 229.
(armed Gu).*
WELLYS, Sir. *WB IV 143, 311.*
WELLYS, Sr de. *WB I 32, 4.*
WELLYS, the Lord. *WB IV 134b, 154.*

Or lion qf Vt
Or lion qf Vt
DODELEY, the Lord. *WK 122. (Sir Edw Sut-
ton).*
[DUDLEY]. *WB I 27b, 2. (or Sutton).*
DUDLEY, Edw, Ld. *WGA 100.*
DUDLEY, Edward, Ld. *XK 23. (qf in salt).*
DUDLEY, Sir John. *XK 303. (cresc Gu for
diffce).*
DUDLYE. *D13 51. (2queued; crest: out of
ducal coronet Or jewelled Az and Gu lion's
head Az ch with cresc Or).*
SOUTON. *L1 605, 4.*
SUTTON. *LS 23-4. (a&l Gu qf in salt).*
SUTTON, Sr de. *CKO 55.*
SUTTON, of Dudeley. *XL 586.*
SUTTON, Edward, Ld Dudley. *XK 64. (KG,
temp Hen 8).*
SUTTON, Edward, Ld Dudley. *Sandford 338.*
SUTTON, Sir Edward, Ld Dudley.
*PR(1512)66; PR(1515)41. (a&l Gu, tail in
salt; qtg Somery, Lexington, Tibetot & Charl-
ton of Powys).*

Sa lion qf Arg
Sa lion qf Arg
— *LY A 42. (qtd 2&3 by Holme).*
— *LH 972. (qtd 2&3 by Holme).*
— *WB III 117b, 9. (qtd 2&3 by Robt Holme,
of Yorks).*
— *LH 761. (qtd 2&3 by Robt Holme, of
York).*
[GENEVRE, Piers de]. *MP II 82. (no name
against blazon).*
MOULENT. *L9 70b, 11. (a&l Gu).*
MOULENT. *RB 464.*
MOULENT. *L1 449, 5; L2 328, 8.
('Wastemye, Staffs' in L1 margin).*
STAPELTONE, Miles. *HA 22b, 105.*
STAPLETON, Miles. *RB 432.*
WASTENEI, Edmund de. *LM 366.*
WASTENEYS, le Sr de. *AS 82.*
WASTENEYS, Mons Arnold de. *D 126.*
WASTENEYS, Sire Edmon. *N 984.*
WASTENEYS, Mons Robert de. *TJ 59.*
WASTNES, Monsire de. *CG 65.*
WASTNEYS, Tomas, Notts. *RH, Ancestor vii
197. (armed Gu).*
WASTYNGES. *FK II 774.*

WASTYNGES. *FK II 773. (qtd by Holme).*

Sa lion qf Or
Sa lion qf Or
— *I2(1904)111. (qr 1 of escutch of Lisle).*
KINGESTON, Sr de. *CKO a 54.*
KINGGESTONE. *PT 477.*
KINGGESTONE, J de. *HA 103.*
KINGGESTONE, J de. *HA 22b, 104.*
KINGSTON, Thomas de. *XL 173. (a&l Or).*
KYNGESTON, de. *SP A 131.*
KYNGESTON, J de. *RB 431.*
KYNGESTON, Johan de. *LM 413.*
KYNGESTON, Mons John de. *SD 78. ('sable
ove un lyon rampant d'or ove la queue
forche').*
KYNGESTON, Sir John. *BR V 95. (lion
poorly coloured).*
KYNGESTON, Sir T. *WB I 40, 19.*
KYNGESTON, Mons Th de. *WJ 346.*
KYNGESTON, Mons Thomas. *TJ 118.*
KYNGGESTON, Monsire de. *AN 165.*
KYNGGISTON. *L1 377, 5; L2 289, 2. (armed
Gu).*
KYNGSTONE. *DV 51a, 2018.*
KYNKESTONE, Sire Johan de. *N 109.*
POWLEY. *Suff HN 2. (St Peter's Ch, Sud-
bury).*

Field patterned lion qf
Barry lion qf
BRANDON, Charles, D of Suff. *PRO-sls E40
A4755. 1516-17. (qrs I & IV).*
Barry Az and Arg lion qf Or
TAYS, the Kyng of. *SHY 593. (a&l Gu).*
Erm lion qf Gu
BREUS, Sir Richard of. *BR V 137.*
MORLEY, Nicholas. *XL 80. (qf in salt).*
Per fess Gu and Arg lion qf Or
— *WGA 34. (qtd 2&3 by Jn de la Pole, D
of Suff).*
Per pale Arg and Gu lion qf Arg
CAWNE, Sir Tho, Staffs. *CY 98, 389.*
Per pale Az and Gu lion qf Arg
CAWNE, S Tho. *CY 172, 685.*
CAWNE, S Tho, Staffs. *CY 98, 392.*
CAWNE, Sir Thomas. *XL 609.*
CAWNE, Sir Thomas. *CVK 748.*
Per pale Az and Purp lion qf Arg
PONDESHAM, S de. *WLN 588.*
Per pale Gu and Az lion qf Arg
ROUS, Roger le. *E I 311; E II 313.*
ROUS, Roger le. *WLN 545.*
ROUSWELL, Roger. *LR 41.*
RUS, Roger le. *F 209.*
Per pale Gu and Vt lion qf Arg
MARSHAL, Walter. *MP Hist Min ii 509. (2
shields both rev; EM, d1245 & his bro
Anselme d1245).*

Per pale Or and Vt lion qf Gu
    MARSHAL, Gilbert, E. *MP I 51.*
    MARSHAL, Richard, E. *MP I 50; MP IV 32.*
    MARSHAL, Richard. *MP Hist Min ii 369.*
    (d1234).
    MARSHAL, William, E. *MP I 29.*
    MARSHAL, William, senior. *MP Hist Min ii*
    232. (d1219).
Gu billetty lion qf Arg
    PETERSHEYN. *XL 635. (qf in salt).*
Sa billetty lion qf Arg
    MEULAN, Amaury de. *C 109. ('de sable a*
    un liun d'argent raumpaunt a la cowe furche
    l'escue bylete d'argent').
Crusily lion qf
    BREWS. *Farrer II 87. (2queued; Sall Ch,*
    Norf).
Crusily fitchy lion qf
    — PRO-sls. *1322-3. (sin imp; sl of Mgt,*
    wid of Hen le Tyayt).
Arg crusily lion qf Gu
    BRYS, Monsr Richard. *SD 119. (dargent ar*
    un lion rampant de goules or la queue doble
    tresse et croissele).
    VENNER. *XL 490.*
    VENOUR, Sire Robert le. *N 647.*
Arg crusily fitchy lion qf Gu
    BREUSE, Monsr John. *S 537.*
    BREWES, John. *S 543. (2queued).*
Az crusily lion qf Or
    BREUSE, Willam. *H a 31.*
    BREUSE, Sr William. *H b 31.*
?Gu crusily formy fitchy lion qf Untinc
    WALLYS, Symon fili. *LO A 27. ('borno de*
    Montte..').
Gu crusily lion qf Or
    — XK 119. *(qtd 2 by Sir Goddard Oxen-*
    bridge, Kt, 1509).
    — WK 481. *(qtd 2 by Sir Godard Oxin-*
    bridge).
Or crusily fitchy lion qf Az
    — CRK 1469. *(qf in salt).*
Or crusily lion qf Sa
    BREAUSE, Gloucs. *L2 89, 9.*
Semy of 4foils lion qf
    BREWOSE, John de, of Hasketon Manor, Suff,
    Kt. *Birch 7792.* S' IOHANNIS DE BREUSE.
    1335.

Lion qf charged

Lion qf ch on shldr with baton in fess
    HASTINGS, Sir Robert. *Stevenson.* 1304.
    (2queued).
Or on lion qf Gu 2 chevs Arg
    RANDE. *L2 428, 3. (2queued).*
Arg lion qf Purp ch on shldr with cross formy
    Or
    STORY. *LS 67. (a&l Az qf in salt).*
    STORY, Mons Richard. *S 446.*

    STORY, Richard. *S 451. (qf in salt).*
Arg lion qf Sa ch on shldr with fleur de lis Or
    BARINGETUN, Sr Phil de. *L 94.*
    BARINGTONE, Sire Felip de. *N 803.*
    BARYNGTON, Leics. *BA 30b, 252. (a&l Gu).*
    BARYNGTON, S Phelip de. *ST 83.*
Az lion qf ch on shldr with fleur de lis Or
    STAPELDOWNE, Sr Robert de. *L 95. ('de*
    azur une lion ramp de or le courve forche
    une fleure deliz de or en l'espante').
Az lion qf ch on shldr with 3 gouttes Or
    CHAMPNEYS. *XL 116.*
Gu lion qf Arg ch on shldr with mullet of 6 pts
    Sa
    WODDE, Mons J de. *WJ 184. (2queued).*
    WOOD, John de. *XL 338. (a&l Az).*
Or lion qf Vt ch on shldr with mullet Arg pd Gu
    SUTTON. *LS 7.*
    SUTTON, Ric, Steward of Syon. *WK 516.*
    (a&l Gu qf in salt; qr 1, martlet Az over all).

Lion qf Erm

Gu lion qf Erm
    — WB I 23b, 4. *(qtd II&III 2 ii by Baker).*
    — WB I 23b, 3. *(qr 4 of coat imp by Baker).*
    — WB I 20, 18. *(qtd 4 by 'Sir John Baker's*
    wife').
    BRINTON, Adam de. *WLN 795.*
    BRINTON, Adam de. *E I 374; E II 376.*
    BRINTONE, Adam de. *F 279.*
    NEREFORD. *L9 82b, 5.*
    NERFORD. *CRK 1674. (a&l Az).*
    NERFORD, ... de. *WJ 171.*
    OLDHALE, Sir Wylyam, Lincs. *RH, Ancestor*
    v 177.
    STOKES. *L1 594, 5.*
    STOKES. *LS 161. (a&l Az).*
    STOKES, of Brinton, Berks. *XL 514. (a&l*
    Az).
Per pale Az and Gu lion qf Erm
    — WB III 74, 2. *(a&l counterch; qtd 2&3*
    by Sir Nichol Hawte, Kent).
    — D13 22b. *(2queued; qtd by Sir Wm*
    Hawte, of Shelvingborne, Kent).
    — 1H7 12b. *(2queued; qtd by Hawte, imp*
    by Gaynsford).
    — WB IV 178b, 951. *(qtd 2&3 by Wm*
    Hawte).
Per pale Sa and Gu lion qf Erm
    — PT 958.

Lion qf fretty &c

Or lion qf Az fretty Arg
    BOXHILL, Alan de. *XL 265.*
    BOXHILL, Sir Alan. *CRK 740. (tufts of tails*
    turned towards each other).
    BOXHULL, Sir Alan. *WGA 163.*
    BUKCULL, Mons Aleyn. *WJ B 108.*
    BUKCYLL, Mons Aleyn. *WJ 108.*

BUKESHYLL, Sir Alleyne de. *L10 34, 14.*
(a&l Gu).
Arg lion qf per fess Gu and Sa
— *RH, Ancestor ix 170.*
BRANTYNTHORPE, Laur de. *Q II 274.*
Lozy Az and Or lion qf per fess Arg and Gu
WEST. *XL 475.*
Per pale Untinc and Gu lion qf counterch
— *WB I 30, 6. (qtd 2&3 by ...).*
Per pale Or and Sa lion qf counterch
— *SK 347.*
Arg lion qf Sa semy de lis Or
BARRENKTON, Mons W de. *WJ 328.*
BARYNGTON. *L10 20b, 92. (a&l Gu).*
Arg lion qf Sa ?gutty Arg
STAPELTON, Milys de. *LM 290.*
Barry of 6 Arg and Gu spotted leopard 2queued
Or
BRANDON. *Arch Journ xxv 253. (on minia-
ture of Alice Brandon, 1st w of Nicholas Hill-
yard (miniaturist); 'Alicia Brandon Nicolai
Hillyardi, qui propria manu depinxit, uxor
prima').*

Lion qf vulned
Or lion qf Sa vulned Gu
LUDLOW, Sir Richard, Salop. *PLN 1771.
(a&l Az).*

Lion qf collared
Lion qf collared
WASTENEYS, Edmund de, Kt, of Lincs. *Birch
14302. 1331.*
Arg lion qf Gu collared Arg
— *WK 488. (qtd 3 by Jn Vernon).*
Arg lion qf Gu collared Az
HAVERING, Sir John. *LH 187. (a&l Az).*
HAVERINGE, Sire Johan de. *N 216.*
Arg lion qf collared Gu
— *D4 32. (a&l; 2queued; qtd 4 by Brakyn-
bery, of Denton, co Durham).*
Arg lion qf Gu collared Or
— *I2(1904)272. (qtd 3 by Sir Hen Vernon).*
— *WK 152. (qtd 3 by Sir Harry Vernon).*
— *I2(1904)216. (qtd 3 by Thos Vernon, of
Stokesay, Salop).*
HAVERLEY, Johan de. *LM 377.*
Arg lion qf Sa collared Or
CRESCY, Sir Edmond. *CV-BM 226.*
Gu lion qf Or collared Arg
BURGHERSH. *Nichols Leics III 340. (Loseby
Ch).*
Or lion qf Gu collared Arg
— *L10 28b, 13. (a&l Az).*
BEMCLER, Suff. *L1 68, 4; L2 70, 7.*
MALORE. *L1 426, 3. (armed Az).*
MALORE, Sir Willm. *BA 615. (a&l Az).*
SEINCLER, Sire Johan de. *N 509.*

SENCHER, Sir John. *BR V 193.*
ST CLER, Guido de, Kt. *Bow 2. (tincts indi-
cated in later hand).*
Or lion qf Gu collared Or
MALORY, Sir William. *XL 219. (a&l Az).*
Sa lion qf Arg collared Gu
— *XF 690. (qtd 2&3 by Holme).*
WASTENEYS, Thomas. *XL 145. (a&l Or).*
WASTNESSE, Mons Esmoigne. *WJ 299.*
Sa lion qf Arg collared Or
WASSENES, of Heydon, Notts. *D4 24.
(2queued).*
Sa lion qf Or collared Arg
WASTENES. *CT 124.*

Lion qf crowned

Demi-lion qf crowned
Gu demi-lion 2queued Arg crowned Untinc
STOKYS, John. *WB III 104, 7.*

Lion qf crowned
Lion qf crowned
BOHEMIA. *WestmAbb. (2queued; imp by
France ancient qtg England; canopy of effigy
of Anne of Bohemia d1394, w of Ric 2,
Confessor's Chapel).*
BOHEMIA. *WestmAbb. (2queued; qtd by the
Empire, all imp by France ancient qtg Engld;
on support of tester of tomb of Ric 2 d1399
& Anne of Bohemia d1394, Confessor's
Chapel).*
MUSARD, John. *Birch 12041.* S' IOH'IS
MUSARD. *1350. (annulet for diffce; s&h of
Malcolm M, of Warws).*
STANLOWE, John de, Kt. *PRO-sls AS 162.*
S'IOHIS DE STANLO[WE MILIT]IS. *1351-2. (qf
twisted together).*
Lion to sin qf crowned
GUELDRES, Marie of. *Stevenson. 1459.
(2queued; w of Jas 2 & dau of D of Guildres,
m1449, d1462; imp Juliers, all imp by by
Scotld; 1st sl).*
Arg lion qf Gu crowned Or
— *Sandford 489. (qtd 4 by Anne of Cleves).*
— *XK 92. (qtd 2 by Philip, Ld Chabot, KG,
1533).*
— *XL 40. (qtd 3 by Edw Wydevill, KG temp
Hen 7).*
— *WGA 230. (qtd 3 by Sir Edw Widevile).*
LEMBOURE. *PLN 585. (a&l Or; qf in salt).*
LUXEMBOURG. *Leake. (qtd 3 by Anthony
Widville, KG, d1483).*
LUXEMBURG, Jaquetta. *Sandford 313. (qrs
1&4; 2nd w of Jn, D of Bedford, 3 s of Hen
4).*
ST PAUL. *1402-3. (imp by Chetwynd on sl of
Alyna, wid of Wm C; 'Orate pro Dno Will :*

Chetwynd et Dna Alina uxore ejus').
WIDVILE, Elizabeth. *Sandford 374 & 407.*
(w of Edw 4).
WYDVILL, Elizabeth. *XL 6. (qf in salt; w of
Edw 4; qr 1).*
Arg lion qf Purp crowned Or
STORY. *XL 499. (a&l Az; ch on shldr with
cross formy Or; qf in salt).*
STORY, Sir Richard. *CRK 717. (a&l Or, qf
in salt).*
Arg lion qf Sa crowned Gu
MORLEY, S Robt. *BR IV 36.*
Arg lion qf Sa crowned Or
— *CT 200.*
BURNELL, le Sr, Salop. *CY 80, 320.*
MORLEE, Sire Robert de. *N 536.*
MORLEY, Norf. *L1 420, 2; L2 323, 2.
(armed Or).*
MORLEY, Norf. *L2 345, 12. (armed Or).*
MORLEY, Sir William. *PCL I 427.*
MORLEYE, Will de. *Q 397.*
Arg lion qf Vt crowned Gu
BESTON, Sr de. *CKO 88.*

Az lion qf crowned
Az lion qf Arg crowned Or
CROMWELL, John. *K 101.*
CROMWELL, John de. *K 836.*
CRUMWELL, S Jeh de. *GA 81.*
PECCHE, Sir John. *CRK 1010. (a&l Or; qf
in salt).*
Az lion qf Or crowned Arg
MONTRYVEL, Monsire de. *CG 91. (armed
Arg).*
[MONTRYVEL]. *CKO 82.*
Az lion qf Or crowned Gu
DARELL. *CRK 1778. (a&l Gu).*
Az lion qf crowned Or
GELDERS, Reynald II, E of. *Sandford 155.
(m 1332 Eleanor, 2nd dau of Edw 2).*
PEECHE, John. *S 168. (a&l Or; qf in salt,
boths ends erect).*
STAPLETON, Hugh. *XL 72.*
Gu lion qf Arg crowned Or
BEAMME, King of. *AY 6. (ducal crown; a&l
Or).*
BEAUME, le Roy de. *WLN 35.*
BEME, K of. *KB 24.*
BOHAYME, le Roy de. *WJ 37.*
BOHEMIA. *XK 2. (qf in salt; qtd 2&3 by
Anne of Bohemia, w of Ric 2).*
BOHEMIA. *Sandford 194. (qtd 2&3 by Anne,
w of Ric).*
BOHEMIA, K of. *CRK 1396. (qf in salt).*
BOHEMIA, King of. *RH, Ancestor iii 197.*
BOHEMIA, King of. *XL 419. (a&l Az qf in
salt).*
?SUEBERR, le Roy de. *RL 11.*

Purp lion qf Or crowned Arg
PASHLEY, John. *XL 600. (?crowned Or).*
Purp lion qf Or crowned Gu
PASHELEY. *L1 491, 6. (a&l Gu).*
PASHLEY, Sir John. *CRK 1013. (armed Or
langued Gu).*
Purp lion qf crowned Or
PASELEY. *L9 107a, 9. (a&l Gu).*
Sa lion qf Arg crowned Or
KYNTZBUULER, de. *XL 630.*

Field patterned lion qf crowned
Barry of 10 lion qf crowned
BRANDON, Charles, 1st D of Suff, KG. *Birch
7745.* ... BRANDON DVX SVFFOLCHIE INCLIT....
1514-45. *(qtg Bruyn & Rokeley).*
Bendy of 12 ?Purp and Arg lion qf crowned
Untinc
MONTFORT. *LO A35. (Monnifort de Weths).*
Per pale Gu and Sa lion qf Arg crowned Or
BELLERS. *PLN 1142. (imp Gu fretty Erm).*
Billety lion qf crowned
HOYCOURT, Walran de. *Birch 10890.* +S':
WALRAN: DE: HOYCOURT:. 1349. *(used by Jn
de Claveryngge, of London).*
Arg crusily lion qf Gu crowned Or
BRAOSE. *CRK 903. (qf in salt).*
BREWES, John de. *XL 357. (a&l Az, qf in
salt).*
Arg semy of crosses Or lion qf Gu crowned Or
— *PLN 1661. (ends of crosses irregular -
painted with free brush strokes sans outline).*

Lion qf patterned & crowned
Untinc lion qf Erm crowned Untinc
— *WB I 19b, 11. (qtd 2&3 by Sir Perceval
Hert).*
PECCHE. *Mill Steph. 1487. (qtg 3 unicorns'
heads couped; brass to Sir Wm P, Lullings-
worth, Kent).*
PECCHE. *Mill Steph. 1487. (imp checky
fess; (lead) brass to Sir Wm P, Lullingworth,
Kent).*
PECCHE, Sir Wm. *Mill Steph; Belcher I 75 &
II 82.* 1487. *((lead) brass, Lullingstone,
Kent).*
Az lion qf Erm crowned Or
PECCHE, Mons John. *S 166.*
PECEHY, Sir John. *RH, Ancestor vii 201.*
PECHCHE, Sir William. *CVK 733.*
PECHE, Sir John. *WK 237. (armed Or legged
Gu).*
PECHE, Sir John. *Arch Cant xvi 102-3.
(Constable of Dover, d1522; tomb, St
Botolph's, Lullingstone, Kent).*
PECHE, Sir John. *XL 249. (qf in salt).*
PECHE, Sir John, Kt. *I2(1904)236.*

Arg lion qf Az gutty & crowned Or
    BURNELL. *L10 86, 16. (a&l Gu).*
    BURNELL. *CRK 1709.*
    BURNELL, Ld. *PLN 1138. (a&l Gu).*
    [PROFETT, 'D']. *FK II 198.*
Arg lion qf Sa gutty & crowned Arg
    BURNELL, Ld le. *WLN 248.*
    BURNELL, le Sr de. *CN 60.*
Az lion qf Or gutty Gu crowned Arg
    COSYN, Dorset. *XPat 112, Arch 69, 77.*
    (a&l Arg; qtd 2&3 by Erm chev per pale Or
    and Sa).
    COSYN, Thomas. *PLN 439. (a&l Arg).*
Per pale Az and Gu lion qf Arg gutty Sa
    — *PLN 508. (qtd 2&3 by Wm Hawte).*

Lion tail knotted (not forked)
Arg lion tail knotted Gu
    LIMBURG, D of. *TJ 9.*
Az lion tail knotted Or
    HETERSETE. *LH 1111.*
Gu lion tail knotted Arg
    — *AS 19. (qtd 2&3 by K of Bohemia).*
    BOHEMIA, King of. *TJ 6.*

Lion qf & knotted &c
Lion qf & knotted
    SEYNCLER, Guydo de. *Birch 5212.* 1357.
    (Sheriff of Norf).
Lion qf in salt
    — *PLN 821. (qtd 2&3 by Melesford).*
Arg lion qf & knotted Gu
    BREWES. *FK II 196.*
    BREWS. *L10 79, 2.*
Arg lion qf in salt Gu
    — *PCL IV 68. ('queue fourchie et croise';*
    qr 3 of coat imp by D of Boureyn).
    BREWS. *L1 104, 3; L2 52, 7. (armed Or).*
Arg lion qf in salt Purp
    — *PT 280.*
Arg lion qf in salt Sa
    CRESSE, Hew. *WB IV 169b, 790. (imp ...).*
Arg lion qf & knotted Sa
    DESTANLADE, Sire Rauf. *L 209. ('dargent*
    un lion ramp de sa fourchie envourve').
    STANLAWE, Sire Rauf. *N 985. ('de argent a*
    un lion de sable ad la courve forchie e
    renourve').
Gu lion qf in salt Arg
    — *PLN 225. (qtd 2&3 by Sir Jn Beau-*
    champ: Gu fess betw 6 billets Or).
    WODE. *CB 26.*
Gu lion qf & knotted Arg
    ATWOOD, John. *BG 381.*
Or lion qf & passed fretways through mascle Az
    BACONTHORP, S' Barth, Norf. *CY 120, 478.*
    (tincts noted in pencil).

Or lion qf in salt Gu
    LEGE, D of. *PCL IV 95.*
Or lion qf in salt Sa
    — *BA 1325. (qtd 2 by Dymoke, all imp by*
    Wm Coffyn).
Or lion qf in salt Vt
    DUDLEY, de Dudeley, Baro. *L10 62b, 6.*
    (a&l Gu; qrs 1&4).
    SUTTON, Sr Richard. *L10 92b, 6. (a&l Gu;*
    martlet Az for diffce).
Sa lion qf & knotted lozengewise Arg
    — *CRK 1129. (a&l Or; qtd 2&3 by Met-*
    ford).
Sa lion qf in salt Arg
    KYNGGYSTON, of Chelvey, Berks. *L9 12, 2.*
Sa lion qf in salt enclosing fleur de lis Arg
    — *MY 163. (qtd 2&3 by Metford, Essex).*
    METFORD. *L1 461, 1; L2 342, 11.*

Patterned field lion qf & knotted
Erm lion qf & knotted Gu
    BREOUSE, Norf. *L1 65, 4; L2 52, 9.*
    BREUS. *PO 135.*
    BREUSE, Sire Richard. *N 549.*
Arg crusily lion qf & knotted Gu
    BREUSE, Sir Giles. *N 162.*
    BREWS, Mons John de. *WJ 233.*
    BROUSE, Mons John de. *CA 203.*
Arg crusily fitchy lion qf & knotted Gu
    HAVERYNG, S' John. *PO 133.*
Or crusily lion qf & knotted Sa
    BREUSE, Sire Peres. *N 896.*
Gu semy of acorns Or lion qf in salt Arg
    ATTWOOD. *L10 2, 11.*

Lion patterned qf & knotted &c
Gu lion qf & knotted Erm
    NEREFORD. *L1 471, 5.*
Az lion qf in salt Arg gutty Sa
    PECHE. *FK II 536.*
Or lion qf in salt Sa vulned on shldr & on each
hind leg Gu
    LUDLOW. *L9 41b, 10.*

Lion qf & knotted &c crowned
Lion qf lozengeways crowned
    BREWS. *SHY 406. (imp by Paxton).*
Lion qf & knotted crowned
    BOHEMIA, Anne of. *Neale & Brayley II 151.*
    (qrs 2&3 of coat imp by qtly France &
    Engld; tomb Simon Langham, d1376).
    STANLOWE, John de, Kt. *PRO-sls.* 1352-3.
Arg lion qf in salt Gu crowned Arg
    SEINT POULE, Earl of. *WLN 130.*
Arg lion qf in salt crowned Gu
    ST POL, Count of. *RH, Ancestor v 180.*

Arg lion qf in salt Gu crowned Or
— WGA 78. (qtd 3 by Anthony Widvile, E of Rivers).
SEYNT POWLE, Earl of. WLN 110.
WIDVILE, Elizabeth. WGB 140. (knot of tail Or; w of Edw 4).
Gu lion qf knotted & crowned Arg
— WK 126. (qtd 2&3 by Sir Wm Lucy).
Gu lion qf in salt Arg crowned Or
— BG 340. (qtd 2&3 by the Empire).
— FK I 23. (qtd 2&3 by K of Bohemia).
BEME, K of. BR I 11. (qf twisted in spiral).
BEME, Ye Kyng of. SHY 597. (a&l Or).
BOHEMIA. L10 86, 3.
BOHEMIA, K of. FK I 22.
BOHEMIA, K of. PLN 29.

Field patterned lion qf & knotted &c crowned
Crusily lion qf in salt crowned
[BREWSE]. SHY 43.
BREWES. Mill Steph. 1489. (imp [Jenney] on brass to Wm B & w Eliz, Fressingfield).
BREWES. Mill Steph. 1489. (imp [Swillington] on brass to Wm B & w Eliz, Fressingfield).
BREWES, Thos. Mill Steph. 1514. (& w Jane Scroop; brass, Little Wenham, Suff).
BREWES, Wm. Mill Steph. 1489. (brass, Fressingfield, Suff).
Untinc crusily lion qf in salt Untinc crowned Or
— SHY 57. (imp by Pastun).
Arg crusily lion qf in salt Gu crowned Or
BREWES. RB 205.
BREWS. L10 75b, 8. (a&l Az).
BRWS, Suff. L1 104, 4; L2 52, 8. (armed Or).
Arg crusily Or lion qf knotted Gu crowned Or
BREWES. FK II 197.

Lion patterned or charged qf knotted &c crowned
Arg lion qf in salt crowned Purp ch on shldr with cross formy Arg
STORYE. L1 601, 1.
Arg lion qf in salt Purp crowned Or ch on shldr with cross formy Or
STORYE. RB 224.
Az lion Arg qf lozengewise Erm crowned Or
PECHE. ML I 367.
Az lion qf in salt Erm crowned Or
PECCHE, Sir John. PLN 344.
PECCHE, William. BG 380.
PECHCHE, S' Willm, of Kent. CY 156, 622.
PECHE. L1 490, 2; L2 408, 12. (armed Or).
PECHE, John. Kent Gentry 216. (langued Gu).
PECHE, Sir William. ML II 96. (queue fretted).

Gu lion qf in salt Erm crowned Or
PECHE. L9 107a, 3. (a&l Gu).
Az lion qf knotted in salt Or gutty Gu crowned Arg
COSYN. L10 109b, 11. (qrs 1&4).

BEAST (1 LION COUCHANT &c)
Lion couchant
CHAUCER, Henry. Arch Journ (Lincoln 1848) xlvi. S' HENRICI CHAVCER. 14 cent. (not on shield; sl matrix found at Higham Ferrers).
DESPENSER, Anne. PRO-sls. 1363-4. (roundel; wid of Edw D, Kt).
Arg lion couchant Sa
— ML I 204. ('[Miles] xi us. Argent un lion cowchaunt sabill' (lying down with head on the forepaws but not asleep)).
— ML I 206. (mouth open & dex forepaw raised). ('[Miles] xiii us. Argent un lion seyaunt in corsche ove bousche & dextre pe comme rampaunt sabill, ou dextre pe rampant; est bien dit, eligas').
Az lion couchant Arg
— ML I 215. ('A lyon cowchawnt' (head down on the forepaws but eyes open)).

Lion couchant qf
Or lion couchant qf Gu
BARTHOLUS, of Saxo Ferrato. ML I 124. (ends of tail curl away from each other like ends of cross recercely).

Lion dormant
Lion dormant
CARLIOL, John of. PRO-sls Ex KR 16/26, 18, HB-SND. 1323-4.
DESPENSER, Anne. PRO-sls AS 21. S' ANNELE DESPENSER. 1363-4. (sl, roundel, 1 of 4; wid of Edw le D, Kt; ?lion couch).
HERRING, Hugh & William. PRO-sls Ex KR 16/26, 17, HB-SND. 1322.
NORTONE, Richard de, of Waddeworth, Yorks. Birch 12237. 1357.
Arg lion dormant Sa
— ML I 200. ('[Miles] vii us. Argent un lion dormaunt sabill' (curled round like a sleeping cat)).
Az lion dormant Arg
— ML I 229. ('A lion dormawnt').
Sa lion dormant Arg
— ML I 201. ('[Miles] viii us. Sabill un lion dormaunt argent').

BEAST (1 LION PASSANT)

Demi-lion passt
Demi-lion passt
HILTON, Alexander of. *Durham-sls 1340.*
STRAFFORD, William de. *Birch 13729.*
SIGILL' WILLELMI DE STREFORD. mid 13 cent.
(or Streford; s of Wm de S, of Bucks; not on shield - preheraldic).

Lion passt
Lion passt
— *PRO-sls.* c1525. *(qtd by Thos Manners, E of Rutl).*
— *Stevenson.* 1476. *(qtd by Jas Stewart, cr E of Buchan 1469, d1498-9; 2nd sl).*
— *BrookeAsp I 25, 1.* S.IOHANNIS: HOWARD: MILITIS. 1396-7. *(qtd 2&3 by Jn Howard, Kt; drawing Bibl Cott Jul C VII).*
— *Birch 4366.* 16 cent. *(?sl of Hosp of St Wolstan, Worcs).*
— *Stevenson.* 1505. *(qtd by Wm Macintosh, of Dunachton & 13th of M).*
ADAM, Thomas, fitz. *PRO-sls E40 A5126 & 5201.* SIGILLVM: TOME: FIL: ADE. c1234. *(not on shield).*
ASCHWELL, Elyanora. *Birch 6965.*
S'ALIANORE: ASCHWELL'. 1368. *(wid of Hen de Lay, of Aschedon, Essex).*
BARDULF, William. *CombeAsp II 127.*
+SIGILLVM WILLELMI BARDULF. *(above shield).*
BIGOT, Roger, E of Norfolk. *Bk of Sls 337.* 1189-1205. *(sl & countersl both on shield).*
BOTEVILLE, Richard. *Stevenson.* 1250. *(not on shield).*
BROWN, Gilbert, Bailie of Perth. *Stevenson.* 1465.
BURDETT, Nicolas. *Clairambault 1369.* 1425. *(qtg 2&3 on fess 3 martlets, escutch fess, 6 marlets in orle, label overall).*
CAUNVILL, Richard de. *Dugd 17, 73.* 1254.
CHESTER, Ranulph E of. *CombeAsp II 141.*
+SIGILLVM: RANVLPHI: COM: CESTRIE.
DURRANT, John. *Farrer I 267.* 1514. *(?talbot; qtg semy de lis; brass, Barnham Broom Ch, Norf).*
HALGHTON, le Sieur de Shasta de. *LH 547.*
HAROLD, King of Man & the Isles. *Bk of Sls 428 & 432.* 1246.
MONTE CANISY, Dionisia de. *Birch 6685.* S' DIONISIE: DE: MONTE: CANISY. late 13 cent. *('on the right [of the shield] in the field... a lion passant'; [Domina de Anesty, Surr d1313]).*
MUSCAMP, Robert, Berwicks. *Stevenson.* c1240. *(not on shield).*
NORMANVILLE, Leo de. *Stevenson.* c1227. *(not on shield; Parson of Maxton,*

Roxburghs).
OGILVY, Patrick, of Easter Kelor. *Stevenson.* 1465. *(& others).*
PASSELEWE, John. *PRO-sls.* 13 cent.
PLAIS. *Birch 10868.* 1431. *(qtd 2&3 by Jn Howard, of Essex, Kt).*
PLAIZ, Hugh de. *PRO-sls.* SIG... DE PLAIT. 1236-7.
PLAYS, John. *Farrer Bacon 11.* 1383.
RIDEL, Patrick. *Stevenson.* c1170. *(not on shield).*
RUSSEL, Adam. *PRO-sls E40 A11652, 11656 & 11789.* SECRETVM ADE RVSSEL. 1310-11 & 1313. *(not on shield; s of Elias R).*

Lion passant to sinister Untinc
Lion passt to sin
BOVILE, John de, of Ardleche. *PRO-sls AS 16.* +S'IOHIS DE BOVILE. *(not on shield).*
ECCLES, John de. *Stevenson.* *(not on shield).*
ESTWODE, Richard. *PRO-sls.* ?c1200. *(s of Thos de Estwode).*
ESTWODE, Richard. *PRO-sls BS 10.* SIGILL RICARDI FILII THOME:. c1200. *(s of Thos E).*
FLEET, Richard, Ld of. *Bk of Sls 185.* temp Hen 2. *(not on shield).*
FOKINGTONE, Hugh de. *PRO-sls E40 A4209.* SIGILL'HVGONIS DE FOKINGTONE. 12 cent. *(not on shield).*
MORVILLE, Wm. *Stevenson.* c1170. *(s of Ric de M, Constable of Scotld; 1st sl, not on shield).*
NIDIN, Hugh de, Perthshire. *Stevenson.* c1210. *(not on shield).*
RIDEL, Patrick. *Stevenson.* c1175. *(not on shield).*
STRETTUN, Richard de, Kt. *Birch 13739.* SIGILL' RICARDI DE STRETTVN. mid 13 cent. *(Ld of Onestona, Derbys).*

Arg &c lion passant
Arg lion passt Gu
HER..., le Roy de. *LM 4.*
OGILVY, of Findlater. *Lyndsay 378.*
QUERZETON, Mons Robt, Sr de. *WJ 217.*
Arg lion passt Sa
— *L2 211, 4.* *(qtd 2&3 Sa mullet Arg, all qtd III by Fyfe, of Devon).*
Az lion passt Arg
— *I2(1904)94.* *(qtd 2 by 'Syr John Burdet de Bromcot Warwyk' [d1528]).*
— *WLN 153.*
— *XF 726.* *(qtd 2 by Sir Jn Burdet).*
— *ML I 218.* *('a lyon passawnt').*
— *XK 281.* *(qtd 2 by Burdett).*
Az lion passt Or
LIBAND, Thomas. *CA 88.*

Gu lion passt Arg
   HETON, Thomas. *LH 278.*
   HETON, Thomas de. *TJ 165.*
   NELLO. *L2 359, 2.*
Gu lion passt Or
   BIGOD, Hugh. *B 89.*
   BIGOD, Hugh. *C 91. (Justicier of Engl, d 1299).*
Or lion passt Gu
   — *PLN 1938. (mullet Arg for diffce; qtd 3 by Waring).*
   ANGLIA. *L10 frontispiece. (qrs I 1&4).*
   BREWTE. *RH, Ancestor iii 192. ('the fyrst that ever conqueryd Yngeland').*
Or lion passt Vt
   TIPAUT. *XL 599.*
Sa lion passt Or
   — *GutchWdU.* post 1440. *(formerly in Old Chapel, Lincoln Coll).*

Barry &c lion passant
Barry of 8 in chf lion passt to sin
   ENGLEFELD, William de, of Englefield, Berks. *Birch 9485.* +SIGILL': WILLELMI: DE: ENGLESFELD. 1230.
Barry in chf lion passt
   ENGLEFIELD. *Lamborn.* 1493. *(per fess with Barton, all imp by Chamberlain; brass, Shirburn, Oxfs).*
Erm lion passt Untinc
   BOWELS, John, of Colmorde, Beds. *Birch 7690.* Sigillu: iohan .... 1374.
   BOWELES, John, of Colmorde, Beds. *Birch 7691.* ...igillu....nis..bowels. 1374.
   DRU, Thomas. *Vinc 88, 50.* +SIGILLVM THOME DRU. 1368-9. *(release of lands in Dauntesey).*
Erm lion passt Gu
   SEGRE, Simon de. *E I 486; E II 488.*
   SEGRETY, Simon. *TJ 135. (painted ramp).*
   DAWES, of Sharpham, Devon. *L10 54b, 2. (qr 1).*
   DREW. *XL 42.*
   DREW, Mons de, of Devon. *AS 501.*
   DREWE, of Sharpham, Devon. *L2 149, 9.*
   DRW, of Devon. *L1 206, 2.*
   LEGRE. *CT 390.*
   SEGRAVE, Monsire Simon. *AN 300.*
   SEGRETY, Symon. *TJ 153.*
   SEGRETY, Symond. *TJ 136.*
Erm lion passt Sa
   WINTER. *XL 483.*
   WYTER, Thomas. *ME 135; LY A 260.*
Paly Or and Vt lion passt Untinc on centre pale
   ATHOL, Sir Aymer of. *Blair D II 136, 277. (imp by Stewart; in St Andrews Ch, Newcastle on Tyne, as recorded by Wm Flower at Visit 1575, from MS in Queen's Coll, Oxf 166, 79).*

Per pale lion passant
Per pale lion passt
   PLAIZ, Hugh de. *Birch 12660.* SIGIL.....GONIS DE PLAIZ. ?c1200.
   PLATZ. *Birch 14119. (qtd 3 by Elizabeth, wid of Jn de Veer, E of Oxf).*
Per pale Az and Gu lion passt Arg
   PLAYS, John. *XL 389.*
Per pale Or and Gu lion passt Untinc
   — *SHY 196. (qtd 2&3 by Gu bend Arg, all imp by Scales).*
Per pale Or and Gu lion passt Arg
   — *LH 599. (qtd 2&3 by Howard).*
   — *SK 748. (qtd 2&3 by Hauward).*
   PLACE. *PT 59.*
   PLACE, Mons John. *WJ 175.*
   PLACE, Monsire Richard. *CH 95.*
   PLAICE, Sr. *CKO 97.*
   PLAICE, Mons Richard de. *AS 366.*
   PLAIS. *Farrer I 200. (imp by Shelton; Shelton Ch).*
   PLAYCE, Monsr Richard. *TJ 93.*
   PLAYS. *L1 515, 1.*
   PLAYS. *L9 108a, 3. (armed Az langued Gu).*
   PLAYS. *L1 496, 2. (a&l Gu).*
   PLAYS. *XL 200.*
   PLAYS, Sir J. *WB I 41b, 14.*
   PLAYS, Joh. *PO 61.*
   PLAYS, John. *BG 313. S 539.*
   PLAYS, Mons John. *S 533.*
   PLAYSE. *DV 59b, 2341.*
   PLAYSE. *FB 19.*
   PLESE, Monsire Richard. *AN 262.*
   PLEYS, Sir Rychard. *RH, Ancestor vii 208.*

Qtly &c lion passant
Qtly Gu and Arg lion passt Arg
   NECHE, Sir Wilham. *BA 2b. (or Nethe).*
Qtly Or and Gu lion passt Arg
   PLACE. *Suff HN 49. (Mettingham Castle).*
Qtly Or and Sa lion passt Gu in dex chf
   BOYVILE, William. *C 100.*
Qtly Or and Vt lion passt Gu
   — *(...Count Marshall). XL 391.*
Billety lion
   HAYTON, Robert. *Mill Steph.* 1424. *(brass, Theddlethorpe, Lincs).*
Gu crusily lion passt Arg
   IDLE, Sire Johan del. *O 8.*
Vairy Or and Gu in chf lion passt Or
   — *BA 721. (qtd IV 1&4 by Ld Dacre).*
Per salt chf & base barry of 8 Arg and Az flanks Arg over all lion passt Gu
   — *XF 197. (a&l Az).*

Lion passant patterned
Vt lion passt Arg, head, paws and tail tuft Gu
   WHITWELL. *XL 488. (a&l Or).*

Gu lion passt Erm
> BAYENAM. *BA 19b, 165.*
> NEREFORD. *PLN 1485. (a&l Az).*

Arg lion passt paly of 26 Arg and Az
> — *ML I 505.* (*'Goules a lyon passaunt sylver & asur palee. On a lyon passaunt sylver asuryd in endocerys').*

Per fess Arg and Az lion passt per fess Gu and Or
> LOCHERAYN. *L9 43b, 4. (a&l Az in chf & Gu in base).*

Per pale Arg and Sa lion passt counterch
> — *LM 272.*

Per pale Az and Arg lion passt counterch
> — *ML I 232.*

Lion passant coward

Lion passt coward
> ST LIZ, Symonde, 2nd E of Northampton. *Birch 6403.* +SIGILL': COMITIS: SIMONIS. 1147. *(oval countersl rev of equestr sl).*

Lion passt to sin coward
> VERNON, William de. *Bow LXXIII 2.* ..IGILL W.LELMI D.... *(sl, not on shield; grant of rent from Herlaestuna to the of Polesworth, Test dom Robt de Grendon, dom Nich de Nuers, dom Robt de Thoke, dom Ada de Herthil, Roberto de Vernon, Roberto de Dunes, Ricrado de Thamenhorne, Ricardo Roffo, Ada Manuallet).*

Arg lion passt coward Gu
> THLOD, John, of Wales. *CRK 1637. (a&l Az).*

Lion passant collared &c

Arg lion passt Gu gorged with crown Or
> OGILWEY, Ld. *Lyndsay 127.*

Lion passt crowned
> — *Brit Arch Assoc NS xxiii 8.* early 14 cent. *(mont of ?priest; Seaton, Rutl).*
> GERARD. *Birch 9345. (qtd 5 by Jn Dudley, D of Northd).*
> LISLE. *Bk of Sls 229.* 1446.
> LISLE, de. *Birch 13848.* 1456. *(qr 2 of escutch of 2nd of 2 shields on sl of Mgt, wid of Sir Jn Talbot, 1st E of Shrewsbury).*
> MOWBRAY, David, of Barnbougle. *Stevenson. (to sin).*
> OGILVIE, David. *Stevenson. (to sin).*

Arg lion passt Az crowned Or
> OGILVY, of Auchterhouse. *Berry; Stodart 3. (a&l Or; ?pg; 'Mosr de Quohon'; qtd by Ramsay of Auchterhouse).*
> TUNES, le Rey de. *LM 28.*

Gu lion passt Arg crowned Or
> — *WK 428. (qtd 7 by Visc Lisle).*
> IDLE, Sire Warin del. *O 5.*

ILE, Gerard del. *TJ 135.*
LISLE, Sir Gerard. *Lawrance 25.* 1288. *(effigy Stowe Nine Churches, Northants).*
LYLE, Ld. *RH, Ancestor iv 230.*

Erm lion passt Gu crowned Or
> SEGRETTY. *XL 38.*
> SEGRETY. *L1 589, 4.*

Lion passt to sin tail ending in 3 pts
> MORVILLE, Wm. *Stevenson. (not on shield; s of Ric de M, Constable of Scotld; 2nd sl).* 1186-96.

BEAST (1 LION SALIENT)

Lion salient
> ADAM, John. *Stevenson 224.* late 13 cent. *(s of Adam, juror at Ayton).*
> BOURGERISE, Poinsars. *PRO-sls.* 13 Dec 1360. *(shield betw 3 3foils).*
> FELBRIGGE. *Farrer I 355.* 1466. *(imp by Stapleton; Ingham Ch).*
> FELBRIGGE, Simon, Kt. *PRO-sls.* 1411-13. *(2 impressions, 1 without right side, other without left side).*
> FELBRIGGE, Symond de. *Mill Steph.* c1380. *(& w Alice Thorpe & s Rog & 2nd w Eliz; brass, Elsing, Norf).*
> FELBRYGGE, Sir Symon, KG. *Mill Steph.* 1416. *(& 1st w Mgt, dau of D of Taschen; brass, Elsing, Norf).*
> STANFORD, Simon de. *PRO-sls BS 11.* +S'SIMONIS DE STANFORT. early 13 cent.

Arg lion salient Gu
> TURBERVILE. *TZ 7.*
> WERDON. *XL 474. (lion embelif).*

Az lion salient Untinc
> — *ML I 221. ('a lyon salyawnt').*

Az lion salient Arg
> — *BG 115.*

Gu lion salient Arg
> — *E II 292. ('de goules a un lyon saleaunt dasur').*
> BOHEMIA, King of. *BR I 31.*
> MERC, Mons Robert de. *TJ 67. ('de goules a un leon rampant sautant embelif dargent').*

Or lion salient Gu
> — *WK 330. (qtd 2&3 by Sir Thos Sampson).*
> FELBREKE, Sir Symond, d1442. *BB 166. (embelif).*
> FELBRIGE, Mons Gorg. *WJ 252.*
> FELBRIGE, Norf. *L1 248, 3; L2 204, 1.*
> FELBRIGG. *FB 39.*
> FELBRIGGE. *XL 543. (embelif).*
> FELBRIGGE. *SHY 30.*
> FELBRIGGE. *FK 231. (ch on shldr with mullet Arg, lion embelif).*
> FELBRIGGE, George. *XL 373. (embelif).*
> FELBRIGGE, Mons John. *TJ 139. ('dor a un*

leon embelif rampant de goules').
FELBRIGGE, Sire Rogert. *N 579.*
FELBRIGGE, Sir Simon. *WGA 284.*
FELBRYG, George. *BG 121.*
FELBRYG, Sir Roger. *BR V 126.*
FELBRYGGE. *SK 1056. (ch on shldr with fleur de lis Arg).*
FFELBRIG, S Sim. *PO 89.*
FILBREGGE. *SK 621. (embelif).*
Sa lion salient Arg
— *CG 94. (Monsire John de ....).*
SCURMY, Monsr. *AS 318.*
SEURMY. *L1 596, 2. (a&l Gu).*
STORMY, John. *CA 123.*
STURMY, Mons John. *TJ 83.*
Sa lion salient Or
REYNE, Count Palentine of de. *BR I 25.*
Paly Erm and Ermines lion salient Arg
LAURENS AP WM AP DAVID. *BA 23b, 201.* (*'paly of 6 E & armynle lioness sayland A').*
Or crusily lion salient Az
— *WK 332. (qtd 2&3 by Sir Wm Seintmore).*

Lion salient crowned
Sa crusily lion salient Arg
LONG, Sir Thomas. *WK 329.*
Arg lion bendwise Sa crowned Gu
ROCHFORD, John, Ld. *XL 191. (embelif).*
ROCHFORT. *XL 566.*

BEAST (1 LION SEJANT)
Lion sejt
LEWYS, Geoffrey. *Birch 11333.* IOHANNES.-
..UUEY. 1496. *(sl, not shield; Citizen & Tailor of Exeter, Devon).*
Az lion sejt Arg
— *ML I 214.* (*'a lyon sesawnt or sejaunt' on a rocky mount).*
Lion sejt with cresc about neck
PERCY, Thos, Ld Egremont. *?source.* 1454.

BEAST (1 LION STATANT)
Lion statant
CAMVILLE, Willelmus de. *Bow LIV 15.*
+SIGILL WILLI DE CAUMVILL. *(sl, not on shield).*
HEYWARD, John, of Cannington, Som. *Bridgwater 279, 346.*
Az lion statant Arg crined Vt a&l Gu
— *ML I 344.* (*'Asur a lyon estaunt sylver ove test pez & tufte del cue cynople langued & enarmyd goules').*
Az lion stat Or
LEBAUD S THOM. *PO 347.*

Gu lion stat Arg
— *WJ 197. (...Shef....ghton).*
HALGHTON, le Sieur de Shasta de. *XL 390.*
Per pale Arg and Gu lion stat Or
PLAYS, Sir .... *CRK 348. (a&l Az).*
Per pale Or and Gu lion stat Arg
PLEYS, Sir Richard. *RH, Ancestor vii 208.*

Lion statant crowned
Az lion stat open mouthed Arg crowned a&l Or
— *ML I 370.* (*'Asur a lyon estaunt brayng sylver crownyd langyd & enarmyd gold la cur hersle. Thys lyon may not be callyd rampaunt but when he ys in hys most ferseness that he can be devysed & therfor se the diversite in blasyng & se a lyon rampaunt also'; tail waved in S shape).*

BEAST (1 LION GUARDANT)

Lion rampant guardant
Lion gard
— *Mill Steph.* c1475. *(qtd 4 by [Calverley or Scott] on brass to Nicholas Kniveton & w Joan [Mauleverer], Mugginton, Derbys).*
— *Birch 4388.* early 14 cent. *(not on shield; 1 on each side of enthroned Virgin; uncertain sl of St Mary's Abbey, York).*
— *Mill Steph.* c1480. *(imp by Frechwell; tomb & brass to Peter Frechwell, d1503; ?arms of his mother).*
BROCAS, Bernard. *Mill Steph.* 1488. *(qtg [Roches]; brass, Sherborne St John, Hants).*
BROCAS, Sir Bernard. *Burrows 351.* 1361.
BROCAS, Bernard, of Little Weldon, Northants &c, Kt. *Birch 7806.* ....BROCAS: MILIT'.. 1390.
BROCAS, John. *Mill Steph.* 1492. *(qtg [Roches]; brass, Sherborne St John, Hants).*
BROCAS, Sir John de. *Burrows 295.* 1363. *(unclear whether lion is gard).*
BROCAS, Oliver. *Burrows 418.* Sigillu .liveri.- brocas. 1420.
BROCAS, Wm. *Mill Steph.* c1540. *(qtg [Roches]; d1506; brass, Sherborne St John, Hants).*
BROKES. *Mill Steph.* 1487. *(brass to Joan, wid of Wm B, patron of the Ch, (formerly w of Jn Addirley, Mayor of London), Peper-Harow, Surr).*
FITZHAMON, Robert. *Tewkesbury Abbey (1964) 11-12.* *(Ld of Tewkesbury in early 12 cent; imp Tewkesbury cross [Tewkesbury Lordship or Abbey]; on tiles, Tewkesbury Abbey).*
GUBWARTON, Ralph of. *Dodsworth 45, 95,*

HB-SND.

HEDERSET, John de, of Wymondham, Norf, Kt. *Birch 10613.* SIGILLVM.IOHANNIS.DE.- HEDERSETE. 1347. *(above shield maunch Erm).*

HEPKALE, John de. *PRO-sls.* 1323-4.

[HETHERSETT]. *Farrer II 418. (imp by [Winter]; brass, Barningham Winter Ch, Norf).*

HORNEDEN, Sir Wm, of Horneden, Berwicks. *Stevenson.* 1256. *(not on shield).*

JERMY, [Sir] John. *Mill Steph.* 1504. *(brass to him & w Isabel [Wrath], Metfield, Suff).*

LANGTON, Nicholas of. *YMerch-sls.* 1334.

MARNEY, Robert de, Kt. *Bow 14.*

MARNY, Robt de, of Essex, Kt. *Birch 11626.* S.: ROBERTI: DE: MARNY. 1365.

QUEMYN. *Vinc 88, 44.* 1313-14. *(sl).*

WESTBURY, William. *Vinc 88, 45.* +S'ARMORUM.WILLIMI.WESTBURY. 1439. *(grant of lands in Westbury & Honibregge, Wilts, 'quae nuper fuerunt Aliciae uxoris Willimi White de Bromham [Wilts]').*

Arg lion gard Gu

— *RL 24. (lion is pink; qtd 4 by [Deincourt]).*

GERMEYN, Joh'n, of Suff. *MY 15.*

GERMIN, John, of Suff. *WB III 109, 4.*

GERMYN. *SK 660. ('Germy' added by Gibbon).*

GERMYN, of Suff. *L1 284, 1; L2 223, 3. (a&l Gu).*

HORNE, Gerard. *XL 456.*

HORUM, Mons Gerrarde. *WJ 384.*

HOURUN, Gerard. *PO 145. (armed Az).*

JERMY. *L9 4, 4.*

JERMY. *SHY 39.*

JERMYN. *XL 549.*

JERMYN. *L1 359, 4; L2 277, 1. (armed Az).*

Arg lion gard Purp

PASCY, Mons J de. *WJ 350. (head 3/4 face).*

Arg lion gard Sa

PASCY, Mons J de. *WJ B 350. (head 3/4 face).*

Arg lion gard Vt

WALTON. *XL 461. (tail turned out).*

WALTON, les Armes de. *WJ 412.*

Az lion ramp gard

Az lion gard Arg

— *SK 530.*

— *RL 28b, 4; RL 34, 1. (qtd 4 by Deincourt).*

DALTON, Robert de. *TJ 202.*

HOLLAND. *PLN 97. (a&l Gu; qtd 2&3 by Ld Lovel).*

HOLLAND, Sir John. *PLN 1670. (a&l Gu).*

HUM. *XL 539. (crined Purp).*

HUM, Maister. *SK A 344. (crined tawny).*

HUM, Maister. *SK B&C 344. (crined Purp).*

HUMES. *LH 916. (crined Purp; Hun [in calendar]).*

Az lion gard Or

ETHERESSETE. *L1 231, 5; L2 175, 8.*

FITZHAMON, Robert. *Sandford 45. (f of Mabel, w of D of Gloucester, nat s of Hen 1).*

HEDERISHEVED, Sir John de. *LH 656.*

HEDRISHENED, Mons Johs de. *WJ 399.*

HEDRISHEVED. *LH 1123.*

HETHERFEL. *L1 314, 2.*

HETHERSET. *CRK 2058.*

HETHERSET, John de. *XL 460. (tail turned out).*

HETHERSETE. *PO 148. (a&l Gu).*

HETHERSETT. *FB 5. (imp by Wachesham).*

HETHIRSETE. *FK II 395.*

HETIRSETE, Ed'. *NS 21.*

PALGRAVE. *L9 106a, 3.*

PALLGRAVE. *SHY 100.*

SWARTENBORCH, Count of. *XL 434.*

Gu lion ramp gard

Gu lion gard Arg

— *Mill Steph. (old glass, Houghton Conquest Ch, Beds).*

— *CRK 876. (qtd 1&4 by Az 2 bars Arg).*

CORBET. *L10 43, 5.*

MARE, Mons' John de la. *TJ 199. ('de goules a un leon leopard rampant dargent'; 'leon' added above line in MS).*

MARNAY, [Hen 1st Ld]. *WGA 244.*

MARNE. *DV 65a, 2575.*

MARNER. *DV 66b, 2640.*

MARNEY. *PT 264.*

MARNEY. *L9 49a, 5.*

MARNEY. *Suff HN 7. (Lavenham Ch).*

MARNEY, Ld. *KB 342b. (name cancelled with pen strokes; qrs 1&4).*

MARNEY, Sir Henry. *XK 68. (KG temp Hen 8; qrs 1&4).*

MARNEY, Sir Henry. *WK 192.*

MARNEY, Sir Henry, KG. *Leake. (d1523-4; qtg 2 Venables, 3 Sergeaux).*

MARNEY, of Layer Marney, Essex. *L1 421, 2; L2 323, 1. (armed Az).*

MARNEY, Richard de. *XL 455.*

MARNEY, Robert. *S 163.*

MARNY, Sir Henry. *WGA 135.*

MARNY, Mons' Robert. *S 161.*

MARYNER, Robert. *BG 108.*

MARYNER, S' Willm, of Essex. *CY 137, 547. (qtg 2&3 Az 2 bars Arg).*

MERNY, Mons R de. *WJ 382.*

MOWBREY, John. *WB III 118, 7.*

Gu lion gard Or

— *ME 140; LY A 265.*

KNOUGHT, K. *WJ 1612. (or Swaye).*

MARNEY. *PT 545.*

Or lion ramp gard
Or lion gard Gu
> — Leake. (qtd 2 by Sir Wm Fitzwilliam, KG, d1543).
> — PLN 1957. (qtd IV 3 by Sir Wm Fitz Williams).
> HOLANDE, Sir John. WJ 1312.

Or lion gard Purp
> NYCHOLL, Count de. WJ 349. (head 3/4 face).

Or lion gard Sa
> ERPEWOLD, King. XL 616.
> ERPEWOLD, Rx. DV 45a, 1778.
> LODELAWE, Sir La.... CV-BM 184. (head 3/4 face).
> LYNCOLNE, Erle of. KB 272.
> NYCHOLL, Count de. WJ B 349. (head 3/4 face).

Sa &c lion ramp gard
Sa lion gard Arg
> — WLN 887.
> BROCAS, Monsire Bernard. AN 240.
> BROCAS, Monsire John. AN 238.

Sa lion gard Or
> — Nichols Leics IV 186. (imp by Staresmore; Frolesworth Ch).
> BROCAS. WB IV 175b, 894. (qtg Waren).
> BROCAS. CRK 1663.
> BROCAS. PLN 451. (qtg 2&3 Warren).
> BROCAS. L10 77b, 10. (qrs 1&4).
> BROCAS, Sir .... CRK 754. (qrs 1&4).
> BROCAS, Bernard. PLN 1217.
> BROCAS, Monsr Bernard. S 162.
> BROCAS, Sir Bernard. BA 749.
> BROCAS, Sir Bernard. XL 238. (qrs 1&4).
> BROCAS, Wm, of Beaurepaire. 1H7 43; D13 117d. (imp by Rich Pexsall, of Beaurepaire, who m Brocas' dau Edith).
> BROCKEYS. L2 41, 9. (a&l Gu; Bromhall in margin).
> BROCKEYS. L1 29, 2. (a&l Gu).
> BROCUS, Barnard. PLN 452. (qtg 2&3 Sa 2 lions coucht gard coward Arg membered Gu).
> BROKAS. DV 57a, 2258.
> BROKAS, Bernard. BG 109.
> BROKAS, Mons' John. TJ 188. (187 & 188 marked in margin of MS to be transposed).
> BROKES, Mons. WJ 409.
> BROKEYS. SK 136. ('of Bedfordshire' added by Gibbon).
> BROKEYS, Barnard. WB IV 175b, 895. (qtg Morrell).

Vt lion gard Arg
> SHERBURN, Richard de. XL 178.
> SHIRBURNE, Mons R de. WJ 411.

Vt lion gard Or
> — FK II 514.
> RANDES, Robert. CRK 61. (a&l Gu).

STORMY, S' John. R 27.
STURMYN, Do'. NS 20.

Barry &c lion ramp gard
Burely Arg and Gu lion gard Or
> ?PALGRAVE. SHY 261.

Lozy Arg and Az lion gard Arg
> HOLLAND, Robert de. XL 606.

Lozy Or and Gu lion gard Arg
> GYL, [of] Devon. L1 275, 5; L2 221, 4. (armed Az).

Lozy Or and Vt lion gard Arg
> GILL. XL 262.
> GYLLE. BA 1176.

Per fess Vt and Arg lion gard Untinc
> — XFB 172. (qtd 2 by Kelefield on pennon).

Per pale Gu and Az lion gard Or
> — LD 91. (qtd 2&3 by 'Sir Reynald Carnaby in Northd, Kt').
> — BA 694. (qtd 2&3 by Karnaby).
> HALTON, Henry de. XL 450.
> HALTON, Sir Henry de. LH 552.

Semy of crosses lion ramp gard
Crusily fitchy lion gard
> WESTONE, Thomas de. PRO-sls. 1370-1.

Az crusily lion gard Arg
> DALTON, Mons R de. WJ 379.
> DALTON, Richard de. XL 452.
> DALTUN. L10 54, 13.
> HOLANDE, Sir Henry de. CV-BM 251.

Az crusily fitchy lion gard Arg
> BRAYTOFTE. PLN 265. (lower limbs of crosses are formy).

Az semy of crosses botonny lion gard Arg
> BRAYTOFTE. WB IV 167b, 752. (a&l Gu; lower limbs of crosses are formy & attached to rectangular blocks).

Az crusily Or lion gard Arg
> DALTON, Sr de. CKO 96.
> DALTONE, S' Rob'. PO 520.

Az crusily fitchy Or lion gard Arg
> [DALTON]. CRK 1854. (a&l Gu).
> [DALTON]. CB 207. (lower limbs of crosses are formy).

Gu crusily lion gard Arg
> AGENALL. L2 18, 9.

Gu crusily Or lion gard Arg
> ASTELEY. L2 3, 7. (a&l Az; lion sans mane).

Semy de lis &c lion ramp gard
Semy de lis lion gard
> HOLAND. Birch 11401. 1385. (imp by Jn Lovell, Ld Lovell & Holand, 5th Baron).
> [HOLAND]. PRO-sls. 1412-13. (qtd by Jn, Ld Lovel).
> [HOLAND]. PRO-sls. 1447-8. (qtd by Wm Lovell, Ld Burnell & Holand).
> HOLLAND, Robt of. Durham-sls 1364-5.

(2nd Ld, d1373).

HOLLAND, Robt of, 1st Ld. *Durham-sls 1367.* (imp Zouche; &/or Thos his son).

HOLLAND, Thos of, E of Kent. *Durham-sls 1366. 1340 & 43. (2nd s of 1st Ld H).*

Az semy de lis lion gard Arg
— WB II 50, 16. *(qtd 2&3 by Ld Lovell).*
— XF 302. *(qtd 4 by [Lovel]).*
— RH, *Ancestor iv 228. (qtd by Ld Lowell).*
— L10 94, 4. *(qtd II 4 by Norreys or Norres).*
— D4 23. *(qtd 3 by [Lovell]).*
— BW 8, 44. *(qtd 2&3 by Ld Lowell).*
— WK 500. *(qtd III 2&3 by Hen Parker, Ld Morley).*
— WGA 229. *(qtd 3 by Francis, Ld Lovell).*
— WGA 190. *(qtd 2&3 by Ld Jn Louvell).*
— KB 298. *(qtd 2&3 by Lorde Lovell).*
— FK I 98. *(qtd 2&3 by Ld Lovell).*
— T c 44. *(qtd by le S'r de Lovelle).*
— WK 417. *(qtd 6 by Stapylton).*

HOLAND. *CRK 234.*

HOLAND. *LH 814.*

HOLAND. *PO 329. (name in later hand).*

HOLAND. *S 64. (qtd 2&3 by Jn, Ld Lovel of Tichmersh).*

HOLAND. *PT 94.*

HOLAND. *LH 69.*

HOLAND, Monsire de. *AN 74.*

[HOLAND]. *Antiq Journ II 143-4.* [14 cent]. *(shield on 4foil shaped copper armorial pendant, in each lobe wyvern in red enamel; found c 1921).*

HOLAND, Sir Alan de. *CVL 379.*

HOLAND, Sir Aleyn de. *CV-BM 82.*

HOLAND, Mons' Henry de. *TJ 189.*

HOLAND, Mons' Otes [KG]. *S 21.*

HOLAND, Sir Otis. *LH 727.*

HOLAND, Robert de. *XL 451.*

HOLAND, Sir Robert. *LH 164.*

HOLAND, Mons Robt de. *WJ 373.*

HOLAND, Mons' Thomas [KG]. *S 12.*

HOLAND, Wylliam. *I2(1904)180. (with 7 qtgs; 'of Weare in the county of Devon'; name added by Jos Holland c1630).*

HOLAUND, Mons Robert de. *CA 161.*

HOLLAND. *L1 300, 3; L2 241, 8. (armed Gu; border roughly outlined).*

HOLLAND. *Leake. (qtd 3 by Francis Lovell, KG, d1483).*

HOLLAND. *WB I 33b, 3.*

[HOLLAND]. *AY 34. (qtd 2&3 by L[ord] Lowell).*

HOLLAND, Earls of Kent. *Sandford 205. (descended from Edm of Woodstock, 2nd s of Edw 1; old coat, discarded in favour of Woodstock, [Engld & border Arg]).*

HOLLAND, Sir John, of Thorpwater, Northhants. *RH, Ancestor v 178. (cresc for*

diffce).

HOLLAND, Sr Robert. *L 96. ('azure un leopard rampant darg fleuretie de a').*

HOLLAND, Sir Thomas, E of Kent. *Sandford 217. (1st husb of Joan 'Fair Maid of Kent').*

HOLLANDE. *DV 57a, 2253.*

HOLLANDE, Mons' John de. *S 160.*

HOLLANT, Her Thomas van. *Gelre 57.*

HOLOND, Sir Thomas. *WGA 208. (shield added post 1506).*

HOLONDE, John de. *BG 107.*

HOLONDE, Sir Ottes. *WGA 109.*

HOLONDE, Robt de, of Lancs. *CY 48, 190.*

HOYLANDE, Sire Robert de. *N 128. ('de azure flurette de argent a un lupard rampaund de argent').*

Az semy de lis Or lion gard Arg
DALTON. *CRK 795.*
DALTON, of Yorks. *MY 260. (a&l Gu).*

Az semy of lozs lion gard Arg
HOLAND, of Lancs. *CY 54, 213.*
HOLLAND. *LH 959.*
HOLLAND. *LH 699.*

Lion ramp gard charged

Az semy de lis lion gard Arg ch on shldr with annulet Sa
HOLANDE, Mons Th de. *WJ 377. (Count de Kent).*

Az semy de lis lion gard Arg ch on shldr with cresc Sa
HOLAND, Mons Otes de. *WJ 376.*

Az lion gard Or ch on shldr with mullet Sa
ETHERESSETTE. *PT 224.*
ETHRESSETT. *DV 56a, 2210. (armed Gu).*
HEDRISHENED, Mons Esmon. *WJ 400.*
HEDRISHERED, Sir Estienne. *LH 657.*
HETHERESSETE, Monsire Esmon. *AN 139.*

Az lion gard Or ch on shldr with pd mullet Sa
HETHERSETTE. *PO 150. (a&l Gu).*

Sa lion gard Or ch on shldr with mullet Arg
BROCAS, Sir Bernard. *Neale & Brayley. (d1400; mont St Edmund's Chapel, Westm Abbey).*
BROKEYS. *PT 96.*

Sa lion gard Or ch on shldr with mullet Sa
BROKAS, Mons Bernard. *WJ 410.*

Vt lion gard Arg ch on shldr with mullet Gu
COTTON, Thomas, of Staffs. *CRK 1416. (a&l Gu).*
COTTUN. *L1 181, 5; L2 128, 7. (a&l Gu).*
COTTUN, Yorks. *MY 281.*

Az crusily lion gard Arg ch on shldr with mullet Gu
DALTON, W de. *WJ 408.*

Az semy de lis lion gard Arg ch on shldr with mullet Sa
HOLAND, Mons Aleyn de. *WJ 375.*

Lion ramp gard patterned
Gu lion gard Erm
    BRIUYS, Mons Robert de. *TJ 192. (blazoned 'leopard passant').*
    FREMLINGHAM, Ralph de. *XL 453.*
    FREMLINGHAM, Mons Rauf de. *WJ 368.*
Per fess Vt and Arg lion gard Erm
    MARCH. *XL 86.*
Arg semy of crosses pommy fitchy Sa lion gard Erm
    HACHETUN, Henry de. *XL 603.*
Per pale Or and Az lion gard counterch
    STONNE. *RH, Ancestor xi 169. (name added in later hand).*
Az lion gard Or spotted Sa
    HETHERFIELD. *LH 1033. (or Hethersett).*

Lion ramp gard collared
Az lion gard Or collared Gu
    HETYRSETT, Tho'. *NS 105.*
Gu lion gard Or collared Az
    LANCASTER. *L9 36b, 7. (a&l Az).*
    LANCASTER, Thomas de. *XL 454. (tail turned outwards, armed Az).*
    LANCASTER, Mons Th de. *WJ 367.*
Gu lion gard Or collar per pale Az and Or
    — *PT 601.*
Gu lion gard Or collared Az semy de lis Or
    LANCASTRE, Monsire Thomas de. *AN 302.*

Lion ramp gard crowned
Lion gard crowned
    [GRIERSON, Gilbert, of Lag?]. *Stevenson. 1418. (arms of Ld of Galloway).*
Az lion gard Arg crowned Or
    ORTON. *L2 394, 1.*
    ORTON, Mons J de. *WJ 406. (crown jewelled Gu).*
    ORTON, John. *L9 90a, 11.*
Gu lion gard Arg crowned Or
    FITZ GERARD. *XL 495. (tail turned out).*
    FITZGERARD. *L1 255, 4; L2 192, 11.*
    MARNEY, Sir Harry. *PLN 2043. (qtg 2&3 Az 2 bars Arg).*
Sa lion gard Arg crowned Or
    HUGRIE, le rey de. *LM 15.*
Per pale Sa and Gu lion gard Arg crowned Or
    [BESTNEY]. *L9 29b, 6. (ch on breast with cresc Sa; qtd 2&3 by Bernes, of Cambs; Bestney added in 18 cent hand).*
    BESTNEY, Mons Edward de. *AS 489.*

Lion ramp gard qf
Gu lion gard qf in salt Arg
    SEYNE, Count of. *XL 433.*
Or lion gard qf in salt Gu
    CATZENELENBOGEN, Count of. *XL 431.*
Gu crusily pommy lion gard qf Arg
    WARE, Ld de la. *BW 9b, 55. (qrs 1&4).*
Gu lion gard Arg qf Erm
    [STOKES]. *PLN 1824. (a&l Az; qtg 2&3 Sa 2 lions pg Arg [Brocas] & 4 Gu lion [?ramp] qf Or).*
Gu lion gard qf in salt Arg
    SEYNE, Count of. *XL 433.*

Lion ramp gard qf crowned
Gu lion gard qf in salt Arg crowned Or
    BEAUME, le Roy de. *WLN 32. (armed Or langued Gu).*

Lion passant guardant
Lion pg
    — *Brit Arch Assoc NS xxiii 8. ?14 cent. (?lion passt crowned; on old mont now let into S wall of Seaton Ch, Rutl).*
    ANGUS, Malcolm, 5th E of, 1214-42. *Stevenson 229.*
    ASHWEY, Stephen de. *Bow 10. (s&h of Mgt; 2nd of 2 shields).*
    BALBIRNY, Alexr, of Inverychty. *Stevenson. 1517. (blazon uncertain).*
    BEK, Anthony. *Birch 2452. c1292. (Bp of Durham, 1284-1311).*
    BOELLES, ... de. *Soc Jers 1929. 1240. (Keeper of Jersey).*
    BOHUN, Humphrey de. *Birch 7534. ....SSE.... 1349. ([10th] E of Hereford [12th] E of Essex, Ld High Constable; decoration on sl).*
    [?BRIWES, Robert de]. *Bk of Sls 411. 1269.*
    BRIWES, Robt de. *PRO-sls. 13 cent.*
    BRUCE, Robt. *Stevenson. 1296. (1st E of Carrick, d1304; privy sl).*
    BURDET, Nicolas. *Roman PO 2334. 12 Feb 1434. (sl; qrs 1&4).*
    DAMMARTIN, Galiena de. *Bk of Sls 409. post 1242.*
    FITZAERUS, Sir John. *Dugd 17, 61. ?1286.*
    FITZBALDWIN, Gilbert. *PRO-sls. 12 cent.*
    FORDWICH, Kent, Mayor of. *Birch 4944.* S'MAIORIS DE FORDWICO. *13 cent. (not on shield).*
    GALLOWAY, Thos of. *Stevenson. (yr bro of Alan, 4th E of Atholl, 1223-31).*
    HAYTON, John of. *Durham-sls 1229. 1370.*
    LONDON, Diocese of. *Birch 1987. c1355. (on sl used by officials of Archdeacon).*
    MAUNDEVILLE, Ralph de, of Essex. *Birch 11692.* S' RADVLFI: DE: MAVNDEVIL'. *temp*

Hen 3.

OGILVIE, Walter, of Beaufort. *Stevenson.*
1446. *(1st sl & others).*

OGILVY, James. *Stevenson.* c1516. *(qtg
2&3 3 crescs; Commendator of Dryburgh).*

Lion pg to sin

BRUS, William. *Dodsworth 7, 56, HB-SND.*
(in roundel on sl).

CHESTERFIELD, Richard. *Yorks Deeds IX 103.*
+SIG ...A....TIRE...RI. 1372. *(Canon of Beverley).*

MUSARD, Ralph, of Derby. *Birch 12043. ..-*
.LFI...AR.... 1220-30.

Arg &c lion pg

Arg lion pg Gu

JERMYN. *L9 6, 5. (a&l Az).*

QUARLTON. *L2 416, 1.*

QUERLETON, le Sr de. *WJ 395.*

Arg lion pg Sa

STONE, William de. *F 172.*

STONE, Willm de. *WLN 534.*

Az lion pg Arg

— *WLN 103.*

ASTLEY, Mons Gye de. *WJ 405.*

Az lion pg Or

THOMPSON. *CRK 1553.*

THOMPSON. *XL 130.*

THOMSON, Joh, Esq. *L10 98, 4. (qr 1).*

TOMSON. *L10 63, 19. (a&l Gu).*

Gu lion pg

Gu in chf lion pg Arg

— *WB I 21b, 2. (qtd 4 by Ld Tayboys).*

— *D4 27b. (qtd 6 by Nevell, Ld Latimer).*

— *FK II 942.*

BRETT, Bernard le. *XL 394.*

LYLE, Sr Gerard. *ME 145; LY A 270.*

REDESDALE, le S' de. *WJ 381.*

Gu in chf lion pg Or

BRETTE. *L10 76, 10. (a&l Az).*

BRETTE, Mons Bernard le. *WJ 365.*

Gu lion pg Or

— *XK 17. (qtd 3 by Anne Boleyn, Q of Hen
8).*

— *CB 396. (qtg 2&3 Arg plain, all imp by
[Mortimer]).*

ENGLAND. *Neale & Brayley. (?for Eleanor
of Guyenne?; on mont erected 1606 to Qus
Eliz & Mary).*

GUYAN, Duk off. *WB II 48, 8.*

GUYANE, D of. *AY 9. (a&l Az).*

GUYEN. *Sandford 487. (qtd 3 by Q Anne
Bullen).*

GUYENNE. *CRK 264.*

GUYENNE, D of. *PLN 41. (a&l Az).*

GWYEN, Duke of. *KB 227.*

GYAN, the armys of. *RH, Ancestor iv 226.*
('an armyd with aseure').

Or &c lion pg

Or lion pg Gu

— *WK B 48. (qtd 3 by Hen 7).*

BRITAIN, Brut, 1st K of. *L2 37, 1. (qtg 2&3
Az 3 crowns in bend Or).*

BRITAIN, Brutus, K of. *L10 76b, 1-2. (a&l
Az).*

BRITAIN, Brutus, 1st K of. *BW 1, 3. ('Arma
Bruti primi regis Britanie').*

BRUTE, K. *WJ 1607.*

BRUTE, Rex. *BR I 32.*

Sa lion pg Arg

?STURMY. *RL 35, 1.*

Barry &c lion pg

Barry of 4 Arg and Gu in chf lion pg Gu

BURNEBY, T. *PLN 1760. (qtg 2&3 Erm on
chf Az 2 mullets Or pd Gu).*

Barry Az and Or in chf lion pg Or

TRYGOWS, Sir Bernard, of Hants. *WB III
72b, 4.*

Paly of 12 in sin canton lion pg

[LONGCASTER?]. *Farrer II 252. (Battlements,
Harpley Ch, Norf).*

Per chev Gu and Or in chf lion pg Arg

LEYTON, Sir Thos. *PLN 1282. (imp per chev
Or and Gu; ?qtly per fess dancetty Gu and
Or &c).*

Per chev Sa and Arg in chf lion pg Or

WILLESBY, John. *TJ 1463. ('dargent arnpty
de sable a un lepard passant dor au chief';
drawing shows upper portion Sa).*

WILLESBY, John. *TJ 1462.*

Per pale Gu and Or lion pg Arg

— *Hutton 24. (qtd 12 by Ric Wingfield, N
windows, Gray's Inn).*

Per pale Or and Gu lion pg Arg

PALIS PERCIE, Sir Gylis. *BR V 140.*

PLACEY. *Suff HN 6. (qtd by Oxford, Lavenham Ch).*

PLAYS, Sire Gyles. *N 568.*

Crusily lion pg

— *I2(1904)180. (qtd 6 by Bamfeld, of Poltemore, Devon; added by Jos Holand c1630).*

Semy of crosses pommy lion pg

TYLNEY, Ralph. *Hutton 90. (mont of Ralph
T, Alderman & Grocer, for his wife Johanna,
d1500; Mercer's Chapel).*

Untinc crusily Untinc lion pg Arg

AGENALL. *PT 1041.*

Az crusily Or lion pg Arg

ASTEL. *L10 2, 14.*

ASTELEY, Robert. *TJ 187.*

ASTLEY. *XL 6.*

[ASTLEY], Sr Robert de. *CKO 458.*

ASTLY. *L1 8, 5; L2 9, 9.*

ASTLY, Mons Robert de. *AS 389.*

DALTON, Sr Robert. *O 54.*

HOLLAND, Monsire Henry de. *CG 474.*

Gu crusily lion pg Or
  LISLEY, Monsire Gerard de. *CG 473.*
Gu crusily fitchy Or lion pg Arg
  LISLE, Monsire Gerard de. *TJ 182.*
  [LISLE], Sr Warin de. *CKO 457. (8 crosses).*
Semy de lis lion pg
  BRET, Simon le. *Bridgwater 303, 665.*
  S'SIM[O]NIS LE BRET. *1376. (sl used by
  Agnes, wid of Walter Palmere, of Bridgwa-
  ter).*
Az semy de lis lion pg Arg
  HOLLAND, Sir Henry. *LH 279.*
Az semy de lis Or lion pg Arg
  POLLE. *L1 492, 2.*
Erm lion pg Gu
  SEGRE, Simon. *F 109. (lion unclear; or Jon
  de S).*
Vairy Or and Gu in chf lion pg Or
  FERRERS, Mons' Robert, Baron de Wemme.
  *TJ 624. ('..a une leopard dor a soverein
  point de escu').*

Lion pg charged or patterned
Arg lion pg Gu ch on breast with mullet Arg
  OGILWY, of Straheryne. *Lyndsay 377.*
Gu in chf lion pg Erm
  BRIUS. *L10 75b, 5.*
Gu lion pg Erm
  BRIUS, Roberte. *E I & II 180.*
  BRIWYS, Mons Robert de. *TJ 192. (lion
  painted ramp gard).*
  BRIWYS, Mons' Robert de. *TJ 193.*
Qtly Erm and Sa lion pg qtly Sa and Arg
  — *RH, Ancestor vii 209.*
Az lion pg Arg semy of scallops Untinc
  HOULAND, Sir Richard de. *Gen Mag NS I
  117; Antiq Journ ii 144. (arms borne at bat-
  tle of Boroughbridge).*

Lion passant guardant crowned
Lion pg crowned
  DORCHESTER, Bailiffs of. *Birch 9594. 1368.
  (sl used by Margery, wid of Thos Fairsted, of
  Denham, Bucks).*
  DORCHESTER, Bailiffs of. *Birch 4876.*
  S'BALLIWORUM DORCESTR'. *1368.*
  DUDLEY, John. *Birch 9346. 1537. (tail
  flory; D of Northd, E of Warwick, E Marshal,
  Visct Lisle, KG; ?for Gerard).*
  GEROLDI, Warinus filius. *Bow 15.*
  [LEGH]. *Mill Steph. 1524. (qtd II&III 2&3
  by Fetyplace; brass to Jn F, & w Dorothy
  Danvers, E Shefford, Berks).*
  [LEIGH]. *?source. (qtd 2&3 by [Bessels], all
  qtd II&III by Fettiplace; on tomb of Jn F,
  d1534, E Shefford old Ch, Berks).*
  LORAINE, Patrick. *1428. Stevenson. (s&h of
  'Robyn Lorane, lord of homylknow').*

?MAUDEYT. *PRO-sls E40 A3975.* SIG... ORE.-
  MAVDEYT. *1363. (2nd of 2 shields; sl used
  by Andrew, s&h of Andrew Peverell).*
  OGILVIE, Sir David, Kt. *Stevenson. 1428.*
Untinc lion pg crowned Or
  [SOUZA, de]. *Proc Soc Antiq XII 2S 87.
  (ancient glass transferred from old to new
  church at E Shefford, Berks).*
Arg lion pg Gu crowned Or
  LILE, S' Waren de. *R 29.*
  LYLE, Waryn de le. *Q 304.*

Gu lion pg crowned
Gu lion pg crowned Arg
  FITZGERARD, Warin le. *B 159.*
  [LISLE]. *RL 15. (qtg 2&3 Arg chev Gu, all
  imp [?Wise]).*
Gu lion pg Arg crowned Or
  — *PLN 2028. (qtd 5 by Ld Latimer).*
  — *WB I 21b, 8. (qtd 5 by [Nevill], Ld Late-
  mer).*
  — *WK 139. (qtd 5 by Nevil, Ld Latymere).*
  — *XX 99. (qtd 5 by Nevile, Ld Latimer).*
  — *WK 427. (qtd 14 by Ld Ambros Dudeley).*
  FITZGERALD. *Gerard 34.*
  ILDLE, Munsire Gerard de. *D 43b.*
  ILDLE, Gerard del. *D 43a.*
  LILE, Gerard de. *A 150.*
  LILE, Jo[hn]. *RL 27b, 3. (qtg 2&3 [Tyes]
  Arg chev Gu & imp Sa 3 chevs Erm).*
  LILE, S' John de. *R 28.*
  LILLE, Sr Girard de. *L 122.*
  LISELEY. *L1 391, 1; L2 300, 2. (armed Az).*
  LISLE. *XL 17. (qtg Tyas).*
  LISLE, le Sr de le. *S 59.*
  [LISLE]. *DX 58. (armed Az).*
  LISLE, Gerard, Ld. *Sandford 448. (qtd 6 on
  escutch of Arthur Plantagenet, Visct Lisle,
  d1542).*
  LISLE, Warren, Ld, of Kingston L'Isle. *S 61.*
  LISLE, S Waryn de. *ST 9.*
  LYLE. *WB IV 154b, 518.*
  LYLE. *DV 57a, 2242. (armed Az & ch with
  annulet Sa).*
  LYLE. *PT 80. (ch on breast with annulet
  Sa).*
  LYLE. *SK 57. ('Gerald Lord', added by Gib-
  bon; qtg Tyes).*
  LYLE. *L9 39a, 6.*
  LYLE, Monsire de. *AN 161.*
  LYLE, of Northants. *L2 316, 2.*
  LYLE, Sr Warin de. *RB 65.*
  LYLE, Monsire Waryn de. *AN 297. (ch with
  annulet Sa).*
  LYLLE, Sr Warren de. *L 57.*
  YLE, Sire Fouk del.
  LISLE. *HA 31. ('Gules a leopard silver
  crowned gold').*
  YLE, Sr Fouke del. *RB 67.*

YLE, Sire Foukes del. *HA 14b, 22.*
YLE, Gerard de. *HE 132; FW 166.*
YLE, Sire Warin del. *HA 14, 20.*
YLE, Sire Waryn del. *N 765.*
Gu lion pg crowned Or
— *WLN 63.*
LISLE. *Leake. (qtd 6 by Grey on escutch of Arthur Plantagenet, KG, d1542).*

Crusily lion pg crowned
Crusily lion pg crowned
CHASTILOUN, Hugh. *PRO-sls.* 1357.
GARNON. *Mill Steph.* 1506. *(so named on brass; imp by Tilney on brass to Regenold T, Leckhampstead, Bucks).*
Gu crusily lion pg Arg crowned Or
LISLE, S Gerard de. *ST 10. (bro of S Waryn).*
LYLLE. *L9 36b, 9.*
YLE, Sire Gerard del. *N 766.*
Gu crusily Or lion pg Arg crowned Or
LYLLE, Mons Gerrard. *WJ 385.* c1380.
LYLLE, Mons Henry. *WJ 387. (ch on shldr with cresc Sa).*
YLE, Sire Robert del. *N 767.*
Sa crusily lion pg Arg crowned Or
CHASTELON. *L10 41, 15.*
CHASTILEON, Mons Maklou. *WJ 403.*

Lion pg crowned and coward
Lion pg to sin coward & crowned
DYVA, William de. *Bow 15. (not on shield; s of Randolph de D).*

Lion salient guardant
Sa lion salient gard Arg
— *PO 186.*
STORMY, Mons John. *CA 123.*

Lion sejant guardant
Lion sejt gard
BALDERSTONE, Richard de, of Preston, Lancs. *Birch 7086.* R.balderston. 1429. *(not on shield).*
BEAUFORT, Thomas de, 2nd D of Exeter. *Birch 7288.* ....o.... 1420. *(octagonal signet).*
HARDRYS, John, of Kent. *Birch 10468.*
S'IOHANNES HARDRYS. 1372.
Lion sejt gard right paw raised collared & lined
EXETER. *Birch 4922.* S'MAIORIS STAPULAE CIUITATIS EXON'. 14 cent. *(not on shield but in castle doorway under portcullis; sl of Mayor of the Staple).*

Lion statant guardant
Arg lion stat gard Gu
OGILWY. *L2 396, 9. (qtg 2&3 Arg eagle displ Sa armed Gu).*
OGILWY. *L2 393, 12.*
OGYLWY, of Balefan. *SC 66. (ch on breast with mullet Arg).*
QUARLTON, le sieur de. *XL 399.*
Az lion stat gard Arg
ASTLEY, Guy de. *XL 400.*
Az lion stat gard Or
ORRETONE, M de. *WNR 125.*
Gu lion stat gard Arg
REDESDALE, Ld. *LR 15.*
REDESDALE, Ld. *XL 397.*
Or lion stat gard Gu
BRUT. *BK 51. (qtg Az 3 crowns in bend Or).*
BRUTUS, King. *XB 10. (qrs 1&4).*
BRUTUS, K of Britain. *XL 409.*
BRUTUS, K of Britain. *XL 410. (qtg another).*
BRUTUS, le roy. *I2(1904)30. (qtg Az 3 crowns in bend Or; on banner).*
Erm lion stat gard Gu
SEGRE, John de. *WLN 402.*
Sa crusily lion stat gard Arg
— *WB I 33b, 13. (imp by on chev betw 3 griffins' heads annulet).*

Lion stat gard crowned
Lion stat gard crowned
INSULA, Gerard de. *PRO-sls AS 123.*
....ARDI.... 1355-6.
Gu lion stat gard Arg crowned Or
— *XK 223. (qtd 5 by Nevile).*
— *XK 78. (qtd 6 on escutch of Arthur Plantagenet, KG temp Hen 8).*
— *XK 303. (qtd 8 by Sir Jn Dudley).*
— *CRK 255. (qtd II 1&2 by Lisle).*
LISLE. *TB 26. (armed Az langued Gu).*
LISLE. *TB 12. (armed Az langued Gu; qtd by Talbot).*
[LISLE, Gerard, Visct]. *1H7 27d; D13 102. (qtd 6 by [Grey] on escutch of Sir Arthur Plantagenet).*
LYLE, s' Gerard. *PO 351.*

BEAST (1 LION REGARDANT)

Lion rampant regardant
Lion regard
— *ML I 196; ML II 131.*
SARESBERIE, Ela, Ctess of. *Birch 6678.*
post 1226. *(dau of Wm d'Evereux, 2nd E of Salisbury, wid of Wm Longespee I, s of Hen 2; 'in the field on each side a lioncel rampant reguardant in allusion to the arms of Longespee').*
WALKFARE, Richard. *Stowe-Bard 2s ii 5.*
SIGILL.RICARDI.DE.WALKEFARE. *1363-4.*
Lion to sin regard
— *ML I 195; ML II 130.*
Arg lion regard Purp
ROUTH, Amand. *XL 443. (a&l Az).*
ROUTH, Sir Amand. *LR 14.*
ROUTHE, Mons Amand de. *WJ 351.*
SEINT QUINTYN, Mons' Herbert. *TJ 155.*
('dargent a un leon rere regardant de sable autrement de purpre').
Arg lion regard Sa
— *ML I 196. ('Argent un lyon comme rampant regardaunt sabill').*
ROUTHE, Mons Amand de. *WJ B 351.*
SEINT QUINTYN, Mons' Herbert. *TJ 155.*
('dargent a un leon rere regardant de sable autrement de purpre').
Arg lion to sin regard Sa
— *ML I 195. ('Argent un lion endorsed comme rampaunt regardaunt sabill').*
Az lion regard Arg
— *ML I 222. ('A lyon rampawnd regardaunt').*
Gu lion regard Arg
— *I2(1904)90. (qtd 3 by [Fitz Uryan] 'Syr Griffithe ap s Res').*
Az semy de lis Or lion regard Gu
DALTON. *L1 194, 1. (painted looking forward).*
Gu semy of acorns Or lion regard Arg
ATWOOD. *CRK 1112.*
CHEYNDUYT. *XL 592.*
Per fess Or and Gu lion regard counterch
KIRKE, Adam de. *Q II 613.*
KYRKE, Adam de. *SES 66.*

Lion ramp regard coward
Arg lion coward regard Purp
AMANDE. *L2 21, 10.*

Lion ramp regard crowned
Gu lion regard Arg crowned Or
— *XFB 211. (qtd 3 by Sir Griffithe ap Sir Res Fitzurian).*

Az lion qf regard Arg crowned Or
CHALTON, Thomas. *LV 40. (a&l Or).*

Lion couchant regardant
Lion couchant regard
DAVID II. *Stevenson. 1358-9. (not on shield).*

Lion passant regardant
Lion passt regard
[ALBENI, William de]. *Birch 5604.*
[SIGI]LLUM SECRETI. c1180. *([E of Sussex & Arundel 1176-1222]; on rev of small round countersl; not described as on shield).*
CHEDNEDUIT, William de. *PRO-sls E40 A5434. ...LLELMI.DE.CHE. temp Hen 3.*
DOYN, Artaut de. *Arch Journ xciii 1936. (device on ring sl, Salisbury Museum II D42).*
Or lion passt regard Gu
— *KB 64. (marshalled in base by K Gurmond).*
Erm lion passt regard Untinc
LEGER, Joan. *Heneage 771. 1336. (w of Roger L; lease of tenement in Boxe, which Alice, sis of Sir Hen de la Boxe sometime held; Dat Boxe [Wilts]).*
Arg crusily formy fitchy Gu lion passt regard coward Sa
BAWLE, Sir H. *WB I 38, 23.*

Lion sejant regardant
Lion sejt regard
DRU, Thomas. *Vinc 88, 34. +SIGILLVM.-THOME......DRV. (sl on grant of land in ?Crutlintone [Grittleton, Wilts], etc).*

BEAST (1 UNNATURAL LION)

Lion winged
Lion ramp winged
GLADSTONE, Sir Wm, Kt. *Stevenson. 1358.*
Arg lion passt winged & haloed Gu
VENYS, D[uke] of. *AY 14. (lion of St Mark).*

Lion with 2 heads
2-headed lion
— *PT 535.*
Arg 2-headed lion Gu
— *CB 264.*
[MASON?]. *CRK 1641. (a&l Az).*
MASSON. *RH, Ancestor vii 211. (in later hand).*

Arg 2-headed lion Az vulned in shldr Gu
MASONE, Sire John. *L9 73b, 11.*
Or 2-headed lion Az vulned in shldr Gu
MASSON. *PT 978.*
Or 2-headed lion Az with dex head cleft in 2 &
blood dripping over breast & belly Gu
MASON, T. *CRK 612.*

Lion bicorporate

Lion 2corp sejt affronty crowned
[COMBERTON]. *Mill Steph. (imp by
[?Fenwick]; effigy of lady, inscription lost,
Langley Marsh, Bucks).*
Lion 2corp combatant crowned
NORTHAMPTON, John de. *PRO-sls. 1375-6.*
Arg lion 2corp combatant gard per pale Gu and
Sa
HOWELL, Davy. *LY A 111.*
Az lion 2corp Arg
— *ML I 231. (blazon torn away).*
Az lion 2corp sejt gard crowned Or
NOTTINGHAM. *RH, Ancestor vii 194. (name
added in later hand; rectius Jn de Northamp-
ton, Ld Mayor of London, 1381-3).*
Gu lion 2corp sejt gard coward Or crowned Arg
NORTHAMTON. *L9 86a, 7.*
Gu lion 2corp sejt gard Or crowned Az
COMBERTON. *L1 155, 5; L2 107, 5.*
NORTHAMPTON, John. *XL 588.*
Gu lion 2corp sejt coward Or crowned Az
CUMBERTON. *FK II 321. (rectius Northamp-
ton, Mayor of London 1381, notes J Gibbon).*
Gu lion 2corp sejt combatant gard coward Or
crowned Az
NORTHAMPTON. *CRK 1814.*
Sa lion 2corp Untinc
COMBERTON. *RH, Ancestor ix 186. (name
added in later hand).*
Sa lion 2corp Arg crowned Or
— *PLN 1176.*

Lion tricorporate

Lion 3corp
FERIBY, Wm de. *PRO-sls. 1 Aug 1362.
(Keeper of King's Wardrobe).*
LANCASTER, Edmund, E of. *Merton 435,
HB-SND. 1274-5. (d1296).*
PLANTAGENET, Edmond. *Birch 12663.*
SIGILLVM EDMVNDI FILII REGIS ANGLIE. 1273.
*(not on shield; E of Lancaster, Leicester,
Derby & Champagne, Ld of Monmouth, Ste-
ward of Engld, ('Crouchback'); d1295, 2nd s
of Hen 3).*
Arg lion 3corp Gu
— *RH, Ancestor vii 194. (bodies passt,
salient & ramp respectively conjd to single
head passt in dex chf; Sharingbury added in*
later hand).
Az lion 3corp Arg head Or
— *BA 1082. (drawn as 3 lions in pall conjd
to single head gard in fess pt).*

Lion dimidiating ship

Stern of ship on dex conjd to demi-lion passt to
sin on sin
[?CINQUE PORTS]. *Mill Steph. 1525. (on
brass to Thos Pownder, Ipswich, St Mary
Quay, Suff).*
Demi-lion pg conjd to demi-hulk of ship
DOVER, Mayoralty of Port of. *Birch 4885.*
SIGILLUM MAIORATUS PORTUS DOVORIE. *(not
on shield but described as in each spandril of
3foiled gothic 4foil of tracery).*
FAVERSHAM. *Birch 4934.* SIGILLUM: CUR.-
PORTMOT.DE FEVERSHAM. 16 cent.
On waves in base demi-lion pg conjd to demi-
hulk
HYTHE, Kent, Customs of. *Birch 5008.*
SIGILLU CUSTOM DE HETH. c1400.

BEAST (1 LION HOLDING &c)

Lion holding axe

Arg lion Az holding axe Sa
— *ML I 447. ('Sylver a lyon rampaunt asur
embatellyd wit a pollax sabyll. Or al defence
ove pollax sabyll').*
Arg lion holding axe Gu
NORWAY. *Brit Arch Assoc xxxiv 23. ('Scu-
tum regis Norwa'; nave ceiling, St Alban's
Abbey, c1400-20).*
Arg lion holding axe Or
— *WNS 25, 3.*
Az lion Arg holding axe Or
— *WB I 16b, 7. (imp by ?Lymsey; Danish
axe).*
ALEXANDER THE GREAT. *Llanstephan 46,
111, 24. (2nd Conqueror [of the 9]; 'Alex-
ander Mawr yr ail gwnkwerwr...assur a llew
rrampant o arian a bwyall ac arvan o aur yn
gwinadd y llew').*
Gu lion Or holding axe Arg
DENMARK, K of. *CRK 1358. (qr 4; battle
axe).*
DENMARKE, K of. *KB 22. (Danish axe; qr 4
of qtly shield with cross Arg over all).*
NORTHEWAY. *L2 357, 4. (battle axe with
long curved shaft).*
NORTHWAY. *CK a 10.*
NORWAY. *SP A 13.*
NORWAY, K of. *L9 86b, 12. (Danish axe).*
NORWAY, K of. *XL 415. (holds Danish axe
with both forefeet & dex hind foot).*

NORWAY, K of. *FK I 35.*
NORWAY, K of. *LO B 42. (shaft straight).*
NORWAY, Rex de. *SM 19, 126.*
ST OSWOLDE .... *WJ 1403.*
Gu lion Or holding axe Arg shafted Az
  NORWAY, K of. *PLN 31. (shaft curved).*
  SCANDINAVIA, K of. *PLN 32. (qtd 4 by Or 3 lions pg Az).*
Gu lion Or holding axe Arg edged & shafted Az
  — *WLN 126.*
Gu lion Or holding axe Arg shafted Or
  NORWAY, Roy de. *WJ 68.*
Gu lion holding axe Or
  — *WLN 154.*
  NORWAY, K of. *TJ 5.*
  [NORWAY]. *RH, Ancestor iii 192. (qtd 4 by Roy de Dacye).*
Gu lion & in sin flank axe erect Or
  [ALEXANDER THE GREAT]. *LO A 9.*
Or lion Gu holding axe Arg
  CYTRIK PANYM, King. *KB 204.*
  CYTRYK, King in England. *L2 100, 11.*
  CYTRYL, King. *L10 45b, 18. (Danish axe).*
  ILDEVER P., King. *KB 209.*
  NORWAY, K of. *?source. (blade ch with roundel Sa?; ceiling, St Alban's Abbey, c1450).*
Sa lion Or over left shldr axe Arg
  NORWAY, K of. *XL 423.*
Gu lion pg Arg supporting with all 4 paws axe in pale Or & holding over shldr another axe Arg
  — *BR I 8. (?2nd axe error: traces of painting out; qtd 3 by Kyng of Denmark).*

Lion crowned holding axe

Gu lion crowned & holding axe Arg
  NORWAY, le Roy de. *WLN 75.*
Gu lion Or crowned & holding axe Arg
  NORWAY. *LMS 9.*
  [NORWAY, K of]. *LMRO 9. ('... porte de gules a un lion rampt de or corone de argent of un ha...').*
  NORWAY, le Roy de. *P 10. (' ... ovec un coronne & une hache dargent en lez pees').*
Gu lion crowned Or holding axe Arg
  NORWAY. *Sandford 276. (qtd by Denmark; Jn, K of Denmark & Norway, m Philippa, dau of Hen 4).*
Gu lion crowned Or holding axe Arg shafted Or
  — *Lyndsay 20. (qtd 3 by K of Denmark).*
  — *Lyndsay 43. (marshalled by K of Denmark as imp by Jas 3 for his w Mgt dau of K of Denmark).*
  NORWAY, the Kyng off. *Lyndsay 25.*
  OLAV, King. *PCL IV 20. (qtd 2&3 by 'Kyng of Norway').*
  OLAV, King. *PCL IV 5. ('Scus Olauus rex').*

Gu lion crowned Or holding axe Az
  — *ML I 276. (qtd 4 by Sweden; poleaxe).*
Or lion Gu crowned Az holding axe Arg edged & shafted Az
  — *WLN 123.*
Or lion Gu crowned Az holding axe Az
  DE .... *SP A 16.*

Lion in chair holding axe

Az lion sejt in chair holding axe Arg
  — *ML I 216. ('A lyon seyawnt in a cheyr' [brandishing a pole axe]).*
Gu lion sejt Or in armchair & holding axe Arg
  ALEXANDER THE GREAT. *ML II 113.*
  ALEXANDER, King of Macedon. *L2 16, 9.*
Gu lion Or in chair & holding axe Arg
  ALEXANDER THE GREAT. *BG 22. (a&l Az & holding axe with all 4 paws).*
Gu lion Or in chair Arg holding axe Az
  ALEXANDER THE GREAT. *RH, Ancestor iii 194.*
Gu lion sejt Or in chair Arg holding axe Sa
  ALEXANDER THE GREAT. *ML I 130.*
Az lion sejt crowned Or in chair & holding axe Arg
  ALEXANDER [THE GREAT]. *KB 8.*
Gu lion sejt crowned Or in chair & holding axe Arg
  ALEXANDER. *Lyndsay 10.*

Lion holding baton &c

Arg lion Sa holding baton Az tipped Sa
  [WILLISLEY]. *PLN 1028.*
Lion pass to sin holding in mouth a bird
  RUFFUS, David, of Forfar. *Stevenson.* 1201.
Gu lion Or holding tower Arg
  — *Lyndsay 139. (escutch of Stewart, Ld of Meffane).*
Az lion passt on its back tower Or
  — *RH, Ancestor ix 167. ('A beryth ascure a lyon passant of gold a towre pynakelyd and embataylyd of the same' [on his back]).*
Sa lion Arg holding in paw chessrook Gu
  VERDON, Monsire Thomas de. *CG 104.*
Az lion Or holding betw forepaws cresc Or
  BONNEVAL. *L10 24, 3.*
Az lion Or supporting cross formy fitchy Arg
  RYSUM. *BA 682.*
Az lion holding cross formy fitchy Or
  — *XL 237.*
  PICKINGHAM. *CRK 31. (tail turned in).*
  PYKNAM, of Essex. *MY 154. (a&l Gu).*
  PYKUAM. *L1 531, 4. (a&l Gu).*
  THORPE. *XL 41.*
Arg lion Sa holding in paw fleur de lis Or
  WALKFAYRE, Monsire. *CG 90.*
Az lion Arg holding in paw fleur de lis Gu
  CLIFTON, Monsire Jervis de. *CG 45.*

Az lion Or crowned & holding 3foil Arg
    DARRELL. *ME 31; LY A 151. (field untinct
    in LY).*

Lion holding hand &c
Lion devouring a sin hand
    ARDERN, John de. *Bow XVII 19.
    (confirmation to Sir Ric de Rupella).*
Lion passt regard holding human hand in mouth
    ROSEI, Baldwin de. *Arch Journ x 142 & 147.*
    +SIGILLVM BALDEW DE ROSETO. *c1200. (dev-
    ice on sl appended to undated deed in Bar-
    rington muniments).*
Lion holding hunting horn stringed
    ELLEM, Alexr. *Stevenson.*
Or lion Purp in mouth horseshoe Gu
    NYCOLL, counte. *PO 599. (langued Gu;
    name added in later hand; ?rectius tyger).*

Lion holding human being &c
Lion holding child in jaws
    MONTEFORTE, Wellisburne Bellator. *Combe-
    Asp II 178.* +S WELLISBVRNE.BELLATOR.FIL
    SIMONIS DE MONTEFORT. *(print of equestr sl).*
Crusily fitchy lion qf holding child in jaws
    MONTFORD, Sir Richard. *Lawrance 31.* ante
    1350. *(effigy, Hughenden, Bucks).*
Lion 2queued holding child in jaws
    MONTEFORTE, Wellesburne de la. *CombeAsp
    II 178.* S.WELLESBVRNE.DE.LA.MONTEFORTE.
Per bend Az and Gu lion regard qf Or holding
    harp Arg
    — *RH, Ancestor ix 172.*
Arg lion with pavise on its back Sa
    — *ML I 207. ('[Miles] xiiii us. Argent un
    lion le targe paveysed comme rampant
    sabill'; ie rampant with pavise slung on its
    back).*
Arg lion behind pavise Sa
    — *ML I 203. ('[Miles] X us. Argent un lion
    paveysed comme rampant sabill'; ie rampant
    with pavise covering snout & paws).*

Lion holding sword &c
Lion holding sword in sin forepaw
    SCRYMGEOUR, Sir James.
    SCRYMGEOUR, John. *Stevenson. Stevenson.*
    1406. 1471. *(Constable of Dundee, d1411;
    burgess of Dundee).*
Lion holding in dex paw sword in bend sin
    SCRYMGEOUR, John. *Stevenson.* 1494.
Lion to sin holding sword in dex paw
    SCRYMGEOUR, James. *Stevenson.* 1468. *(s
    of Sir Jn S, Constable of Dundee, d c1478;
    2nd sl).*
Gu lion Or holding in dex paw dagger Arg
    SKRYMGEOUR, of Dudupe [Dudhope].
    Lyndsay 333. 1542.

Lion holding sword in sin paw in chf label of 4
    SCRYMGEOUR, James. *Stevenson.* 1456. *(s
    of Sir Jn S, Constable of Dundee, d c1478).*

Lion pierced by
Arg lion passt to sin pd through neck with arrow
    Sa
    — *ML I 209. ('[Miles] xvi us & ultimus.
    Argent un lion passaunt endorsed le targe de
    sa gorge plaged ove sett' sabill' (passt to sin
    pierced with arrow through back of neck with
    arrow)).*
Lion with sword piercing its back
    MORE, Thomas. *PRO-sls.* 1404-5. *(Keeper
    of the King's Wardrobe).*

BEAST (OTHER)
Quadruped
    — *PRO-sls.* 14 cent. *(imp by Tyes).*
Beast ramp
    MEAUX, Thomas de, Kt. *PRO-sls E40 A420.*
    1378-9.
Horned beast
    — *PRO-sls E40 A6785.* 1356. *(qtd 2&3 by
    Jn Dalmaigne, Echevin of Calais).*
Beast passt regard with sword piercing back
    IRELAND, Master John. *Stevenson.* 1518.

Antelope &c
Antelope (or goat) passt
    WALTER, Thomasina. *Birch 14237.* 1460.
    *(not on shield; wid; dau of ... Mullyng, of
    Essex; in allusion to arms of M).*
Heraldic antelope collared chained & ringed
    SCOT, John, of Essex. *Birch 13338.* MI
    TRYSTE. 1480. *(not on shield).*
Ape
    EDE, Majory. *PRO-sls E40 A10716.* 1410-
    11. *(not on shield; w of Rog of Skemyng).*
Bat
    HAMPTON, John. *Hist Coll Staffs 1928, 88.*
    1460. *(not on shield; signet sl; Wodehouse
    Deeds, Wombourne).*
Arg bat displd Sa
    STAYNING, of Suff. *LS 207.*

Bear
Bear
    FITZURSE, Reginald. *Stoke C 5.* temp Hen 2.
    (not on shield; of Weleton [Williton, Som]).
    FITZURSE, Robert. *Stoke C 6.* temp Hen 2.
    *(not on shield; sl on confirmation to Priory of
    Stoke Courcy of gifts of his ancestors).*

Or bear Sa muzzled Untinc
    FIZ URS, Reygnald. *HE 142.*
Or bear Sa muzzled Arg
    FIZ URS, Reynold. *FW 169.*

Bear passant
Bear passt
    APHOEL, Cygnen. *Roman PO 386.* 11 Aug 1409.
    BRUEN, Roger de, of [Bruen] Stapleford. *Middlewich 379.* 1346-7.
Arg bear passt Sa muzzled Or
    BARNARD, Jhon, of Suff. *WB III 109b, 9. (qrs 1&4).*
    BARNARD, Jonh'n, of Suffolk. *MY 44. (qrs 1&4).*
Bear passt muzzled & lined
    VINCENT, William, of Essex, Gent. *Birch 14175.* 1440. *(not on shield; in allusion to crest of Vincent).*

Bear rampant
Bear ramp muzzled
    BERNARD. *Mill Steph.* 1518. *(qtg [Lilling]; brass to Eustace B, Ingatestone, Essex).*
Arg bear ramp Sa
    APPULTON. *L10 6, 8.*
    BARFORD, Master. *WB II 68, 2. (qrs 1&4).*
    BARWARD, S' Johan. *BR IV 70.*
    BER, of Cornw. *L1 64, 4; L2 63, 7.*
Arg bear ramp Sa muzzled Or
    BARNARD. *L10 21, 14. (qrs 1&4).*
    BARNARD, Sir J. *CRK 725. (qrs 1&4).*
    BER. *L10 29, 10.*
    BERNARD, Sir John, of Jersey. *Soc Jers 1928. (Bailiff of Jersey 1447).*
Per fess Sa and Arg bear ramp counterch muzzled Gu
    LYNDESEY. *L9 41a, 1.*
    LYNDSEY. *CC 230b, 285.*
    LYNDSEY. *L1 405, 2; L2 306, 1.*
Arg bear ramp Sa collar Or
    BARNARDE. *CT 444. (qrs 1&4).*
Arg bear ramp Sa muzzled collared & chained Or
    BERESFORD. *L10 34b, 8.*
Arg bear ramp Sa crowned Or
    [APLETON]. *Arch Cant xxxii 50. (imp by Wm Hesill, Baron of the Exchequer, d1425, & Agnes his w, Northfleet, Kent).*
    APPELTON. *L10 6, 9.*
    APPELTONE. *FK II 324. (ch on shldr with 5foil Arg seeded Or).*
    APPELTONE. *FK II 323.*
    APPOLTON. *L1 12, 2; L2 7, 5.*

Bear salient
Arg bear salient Sa
    BERE. *BA 975. (langued Gu).*
Arg bear salient Sa muzzled Or
    BARNARD. *L1 63, 5; L2 56, 4.*
Sa bear salient Arg muzzled Gu
    — *PLN 1711. (qtd 2&3 by Peyton, all imp by [Ashby]).*

Boar

Boar passant
Boar passt to sin
    SWINTON, Alan, of that ilk. *Stevenson.* 1271. *(not on shield).*
Arg boar passt Gu
    TREVARTHEAN. *L1 643, 6. (armed Or).*
    TREWARTHEN. *PLN 1522. (armed & unguled Or).*
Arg boar passt Sa armed Gu
    PEROTE. *L1 502, 2; L2 403, 5.*
Gu boar passt Arg
    BOOR. *FK II 883. (armed, unguled & membered Or).*
    BORE. *L1 107, 6; L2 63, 2. (armed Or).*
    BORE. *L10 85, 13.*

Boar passant charged or patterned
Boar passt around neck banner undy ch with lion ramp
    CALAIS, Mayoralty of. *HB-SND.*
Arg boar passt Sa armed Gu ch on flank with cresc Or
    PEROT. *LEP 24.*
Per pale Arg and Sa boar passt counterch
    BARE, Tomas, de Calays. *RH, Ancestor vii 187.*

Boar rampant &c
Or boar ramp Sa tusks & hooves Arg
    [BRITAIN], K Ida pa'. *KB 75.*
Gu boar salient Arg collared & chained Or
    EYRE. *XPat 120, Arch 69, 77.*
Boar stat
    — *Mill Steph.* 1510. *(qtg 2&3 Or helmet Untinc, all qtd IV on brass to Sir Jn Melton, Aston, Yorks).*
    BAKON, Maut. *Birch 7084.* 1449. *(not on shield; w of Jn B, & dau of Sir Thos Bedingfield, Kt).*
    GOSWICK, John of. *PRO-sls Ex KR 16/26, 35.* 1322.
Untinc boar Az
    LAWELLYN, andorch. *WK A 32.*
Arg boar stat Gu armed Or
    TREVARTHEAN. *DV 61a, 2405.*

Arg boar stat Sa
  PEROTE. *L9 97b, 4.*
Arg boar stat Sa langued hooved & membered
  Gu ch on shldr with cresc Or
  PEROT. *SK 1086.*

Camel

Arg camel passt Az
  — *WK 485. (ch on hump with mullet Arg;
  qtd 2 by Edm Mydwynter, of Som).*
Az camel passt Arg
  CAMAYL. *L1 130, 2; L2 106, 4.*
  CAMELL. *FK II 623. (qrs 1&4).*
  CAMELL. *L10 43, 17.*
  CAMELL. *FK II 622.*
  [CAMELL]. *PLN 1553. (qtg 2&3 lozy Az and
  Arg).*
Camel stat
  — *Helyar 925. 1418. (sl; qtd 2&3 by Jn
  Cammel of Quene Camel [Som]).*
Sa camel Arg
  CAMELL, of Queen Camel, Som. *Gerard 197.
  (& of Sherborne & Shapwick Plecy, Dors).*

Cat

Vt semy of 3foils slipped Or cat passt Arg
  MORGANBAGHAN. *L2 339, 2. (cat unclear).*
Vt semy of 3foils Or cat pg Arg
  VAGHAN. *L1 657, 6. (langued Gu).*
Vt semy of 3foils slipped Or cat stat gard Arg
  VAGHAM, Morgan. *LE 108, 23.*

Coney: see hare

1 Deer (buck, hart, roedeer, stag, &c)

Deer (buck &c) courant
Gu hart courant Or
  MACKHARTYMORE, erle of Clemkerne. *DIG
  29.*

Deer (buck &c) lodged
Stag lodged
  STRACHAN, Andrew. *Stevenson.* 1506.
Az stag lodged Arg
  DOWNES. *L10 63b, 15.*
Or hart lodged Az
  TREDERFFE, John. *RH, Ancestor ix 165.*
Sa hart lodged Arg
  DOWNES, of 'Shrigley'. *BA 2b.*
  DOWNYS, de Chest. *L10 64, 6.*

Deer (buck &c) passant
Roedeer passt
  RAE, Alexr. *Stevenson. (depicted like an ass
  & placed vertically on shield; lorimer,*

burgess of Edinburgh).
Stag or heraldic antelope
  ROTHEWELL, Thomas. *Birch 13137.* 1449.
  *(not on shield; in allusion to crest of
  Rothewell).*
Stag
  BARNARD CASTLE, Richard of. *Durham-sls
  557-8 & 3274.* 1355 & later. *(Archdeacon
  of Northd 1362-9).*
  PAYNEL, Thomas, Kt. *PRO-sls.* 1372-3.
Stag passt
  — *Birch 5484.* 15 cent. *(sl of Wenlock,
  Salop).*
  BOWCLES, Clo. *Burrows 399.* 1338. *(grant
  by Wm Terry).*
Stag passt
  — *Burrows 388.* 1409. *(qtd by vase; grant
  by Oliver Brocas).*
Arg hart Untinc
  — *RH, Ancestor vii 198. (Yorks).*
Arg stag Or
  ULTONIGEN, Graf von. *Uffenbach, Antiq
  Journ xxi 408. (repealed, but presumably for
  Munster).*
Arg hart passt Ppr
  HOLME, of Yorks. *L1 353, 1; L2 264, 8.
  (attrd Or).*

Deer (buck &c) rampant
Buck ramp
  BUCKTON, John. *Yorks Deeds II 65.* 1375.
  (s of Wm de B).

Deer (buck &c) salient
Buck salient
  WARNETT, John. *Mill Steph.* 1486. *(?rectius
  fretty, frets not visible in rubbing; attired &
  unguled Or; brass to Jn W, of Furnival's Inn
  & w Joan, Buxted, Suss).*
Stag salient
  WARNETT. *SussASColl ix 216; Lambarde
  101.* 1496. *(prob Jn W, of Furnival's Inn,
  d1486 & w Johanna d1496, brass, St
  Margaret's, Buxted).*
Arg stag salient Gu attired Or
  [KIRCH]. *WB I 27b, 11.*
Az stag salient Arg
  DOWNES, of Ches. *CY 39, 155.*

Deer (buck &c) statant
Roedeer stat
  ROWLEY, Thomas. *Mill Steph.* 1478. *(brass,
  St John's, Bristol; prob a rebus).*
Stag stat
  STRACHAN, Alexr, of Knox. *Stevenson.*
  1459.
Untinc stag stat Purp
  HOLME, of Yorks. *LD 147. (attired Or;
  Purp may be error for Ppr; qrs 1&4).*

Arg buck stat Gu attired Sa
— *SK 900*.
Az stag stat Ppr
STRAICHAUCHIN, of Thorntoun. *Lyndsay 359*.

Deer (buck &c) regardant
Vt stag lodged regard Arg armed ducally gorged
& chained Or
— *D4 29b. (on escutch of Clyfton, [of co
Durham])*.
Vt stag passt regard Arg ducally gorged &
chained Or
— *H21 21. (escutch of Clyfton)*.

Deer (buck &c) holding
Gu buck lodged regardant Or holding in mouth
bunch of ivy leaves Arg
— *ML I 426. ('Goules a buck cowchaunt
regardaunt gold la bouch degoute ove iii
foylz d'yvy argent'; no painting)*.

Deer (hind)
Hind
BISE, John de la. *CombeAsp II 130*. +S'IO.-
..DE LA BISE. *(not on shield)*.
Gu hind passt Arg
BADSULL, John. *L10 30b, 18. (qr 1)*.
Or hind Gu
TIERSTEIN, Count of. *C 120*.

**Dog (including alaund, bloodhound,
dog, greyhound, hound, kennet, levrier, mastiff, talbot, &c)**

Dog couchant
Bloodhound coucht
MARTIN, John, of Canterbury, Kent, esq.
*Birch 11644. 1478. (not on shield but allud-
ing to arms of Martin)*.

Dog courant
Barry of 8 in chf greyhound courant
SKIPWITH. *Mill Steph. 1597. (imp by Har-
ington; brass to Eliz, dau of Hen S, of
Kethorpe, Leics, & w of Thos Harington,
South Witham, Leics)*.
Barry of 8 Arg and Gu in chf greyhound courant
Sa
SKYPWITH. *L1 588, 2*.
SKYPWITHE. *WK 506. (imp by Henege)*.

Dog passant
Talbot
BOTERWYK, John. *PRO-sls. 1371-2*.
Talbot passt
BURGOYNE, John. *Mill Steph. 1505. (brass
to Jn B & w Mgt, Impington, Cambs)*.
COMBERFORD, John. *Dugd 17, 45. 1387*.

COMBERFORD, John de. *Bow XXVII 20*. +S
Johannis de Comberford. 1377.
CUMBERFORD, John de. *Bow XXVIII 17b*.
+Sigillm Johannis de Cumberford. 1364-5. *(party
to grant of mill in Cumberford & of 'sectam
molendini' in Serescole, Staffs)*.
Talbot passt to sin
DRUMMOND, John, 1st Ld. *Stevenson. 1484.
(?not on shield)*.
Arg greyhound passt Sa
HOLFORD. *L1 341, 4; L2 258, 5*.
HOLFORD. *CRK 679*.
HOLFORD, John de. *CVC 574*.
HOLFORD, Sir John. *XK 243*.
HOLFORDE. *WB I 44, 10*.
Az bloodhound passt Arg
BURGOIGN. *L1 91, 1; L2 68, 11*.
Gu talbot passt Arg
TALBOT, Ld Furnival. *ML I 60. (a&l Az;
original blazon crossed out, & Furnival arms
substituted)*.
Sa greyhound Arg
HOLFORD. *BA 2b*.
Barry Arg and Gu hound passt Sa
SKIPWYTH, Mons Will de. *WJ 1163*.

Dog salient
Arg greyhound salient Sa
ATTWODE. *L10 6, 10*.
Sa greyhound salient Arg
POWERTON. *CRK 51*.
Dog salient looking backward at crosslet fitchy
LOUTH, [?Nicholas de]. *PRO-sls. c1364-5.
(?wolf)*.

Dog sejant
Dog sejt
AULDMAULDEN, Wm. *Stevenson 233. 1292.
(not on shield)*.
Greyhound sejt to sin
CUTTE, John, Kt. *Birch 9154. 1507.
(Under-Treasurer of Engld)*.

Dog statant
Arg greyhound stat Sa
HALFORD, John de, of Ches. *CY 25, 97*.
HOLFORD. *DV 49a, 1924*.
HOLFORD. *LH 692*.
HOLFORD, Sir George. *BA 40b, 399*.
HOLFORD, William de. *PCL II 67*.
HOLFORDE, John de. *WLN 640*.
Az talbot stat Arg
BURGOYNE. *L10 82b, 10. (?passt)*.

Dog collared

Dog couchant collared
Hound couch collared & lined
— *Birch 9248.* S' HVBE.......IOL. *1367.*
(Hubert ...iol; used by Ric, s of Nicholas de
Denham, of Denham, Bucks).

Dog passant collared
Dog collared
BOYNTON, William of. *Burton Agnes Deeds,*
HB-SND. c1270.
Hound passt collared
DURANT, Peter, Esq. *PRO-sls.* 1433 & 1438.
Gu greyhound passt Arg collared Az studded &
ringed Or
— *PLN 1243.* *(imp 4 by Jn Wrothe).*

Dog salient collared
Greyhound salient collared
LEWKENORE, Sir Roger, of Suss. *Birch*
11330. 1524. *(not on shield; alluding to*
crest of L: greyhound courant collared).
Arg alaund salient Sa collared Or
WOODE, John, of Kent. *RH, Ancestor vii 185.*
('or wolfe' added in later hand; alant or
alaund is sort of mastiff or wolfdog).
Az hound salient Arg chained about neck Or
KYDWELLE. *L9 11, 9.*

Dog statant collared
Talbot stat collared
BURGOYNE. *Mill Steph; Belcher II 146.*
(brass to Jas Peckham & w Mgt dau of Thos
B, of Impington, Cambs & Wrotham, Kent).
BURGOYNE. *Mill Steph; Belcher II 146.*
(?couch; imp by Peckham on brass to Jas P,
& w Mgt dau of Thos B, of Impington,
Cambs & Wrotham, Kent).
Arg greyhound stat Sa collared Gu
MOORTONE, Ric' de. *WLN 658.*

Dog regardant collared
Greyhound sejt regard collared & ringed
LEVERER, Richard, of Suss. *Birch 11319.*
RICARDI .... 1401.

Dog holding
Gu demi-greyhound erect couped Arg holding
betw paws crown Or
— *ML I 146.* *('goules a grehound assen-*
daunt, issaunt & apparaunt doustr my sylver
pe portaunt un coron').

Elephant
Elephant & castle
COVENTRY, Town of. *Proc Soc Antiq II 2S*
156. SIGILLUM COMUNITATIS VILLE DE
COUENTRE. 20 Jan 1424. *(sl attached to*
deed for transfer of property by Wm Babyng-
ton & Wm Botener to Mayor & Com-
monalty).
Per pale elephant & castle
[COVENTRY CITY]. *Mill Steph.* 1600. *(brass*
to Jn Whithead, Holy Trin, Coventry).
[COVENTRY CITY]. *Mill Steph.* 1568. *(plate*
containing conditions of lease of
Cheylesmore Park granted to city by D of
Northd, St Mary's Hall, Coventry).
[COVENTRY CITY]. *Mill Steph.* 1512. *(brass*
to Jn Onley & w, Withington, Salop).
Per pale Arg and Vt elephant & castle Or
[CORBET]. *Nichols Leics III 116.* *(window,*
Woodhouse chapel).
Per pale Gu and Vt elephant & castle Or
COVENTRY CITY. *FK II 152.* *(name in later*
hand).

Fox
Az fox ramp Arg
CLYSE. *CC 234, 385.*
Per pale Sa and Az fox ramp Arg
FRENCH. *CC 231, 303.*
Fox salient
CALVERLEY, Walter, of Stanley, Yorks.
Birch 8284. 1568. *(or other animal).*
LOUTHE, Robert, of Herts. *PRO-sls.* 1408-9.
(or wolf).

Fox holding
Or fox ramp Gu holding in his paws uncertain
charge Untinc
ORTON. *L2 388, 12.*
Az fox salient carrying off goose Untinc
— *RH, Ancestor ix 166.*

Goat
?Goat
— *Durham-sls 1828.* *(legend illegible; used*
in 1365 by Thos of Morpeth).
— *Durham-sls 157.* *(goat unclear; legend*
illegible; used in 1356 by Jn of Barthen,
clerk).
Goat passt
BOWES, John of. *Durham-sls 329.* 1358-63.
Az goat passt Arg armed & unguled Or
— *Nichols Leics II 262.* *(window, Melton*
Mowbray Ch).

Goat rampant

Arg goat ramp Sa head & mane Arg armed Vt
　BUKTON, John de. *TJ 1523.*

Az goat ramp Arg
　— *ML I 247. ('Asur a gote mowntant [erect]*
　silver. Lyons be rampand, other bestes be
　mowntaunt, berdes be ascendaunt or volaunt,
　fyshes be eyraunt').

Gu goat erect Arg
　BARDEWELL. *L10 22, 20.*
　BARDEWELL. *SHY 110.*
　BOUGHTON. *L10 86b, 6.*

Gu goat ramp Arg armed Or
　— *I2(1904)270. (unguled Or; qtd 3 by*
　'Darsy Essex', ie Darcy).
　— *WB III 103, 1. (qtd 2&3 by Jn Boyntun,*
　of Yorks).
　— *WB I 40b, 9.*
　BARDEWELL, Wyll'm, of Suff. *MY 12.*
　BERDEWELL. *DV 51a, 2014.*
　BERDEWELL. *PT 473. (unguled Or).*

Sa goat ramp Arg
　BOLEGH, of Cornw. *L1 112, 3; L2 77, 3.*
　TREDEK, Sir J. *WB I 41b, 6.*

Goat salient

Goat salient
　[BARDWELL]. *Mill Steph. 1528. (brass to*
　Sir Ric Fitzlewes on sin side of mantle of his
　1st w Alice [dau of Jn Harleston, by Mgt,
　dau&h of Wm B], Ingate, Essex).
　BERDEWELL, William, of Bardwell & Norton.
　Farrer Bacon 23. 1413. (sl).
　BERDEWELL, Wm. *Mill Steph; Farrer I 45.*
　c1490. *(brass to Wm B, esq, & w Eliz, dau*
　of Edm Wychyngham, W Harling, Norf).
　BERDEWELL, William. *Birch 7126.* Sigillum:
　will'i: berdwell':. *1404. (of Gasthorpe, Norf &*
　Thelvetham, Suff, Kt).
　BUCKTON. *Yorks Deeds V 132. 1369.*
　(?poss buck ramp).
　BUCTON, John de. *Birch 7907.* SIGILLUM.-
　IOHANNIS.DE.BVCTON. 14 cent.
　CAPELLA, John de la. *Birch 8324.* S'IOHAN
　DE LA CAPELLA. 1398.
　CAPRAVILLA, Wm de, of Reydon, Suff. *Bk of*
　Sls 347. late 13 cent. *(countersl).*
　CHEFREVILL, Sir Adam, of Reydon, Suff.
　Farrer Bacon 25. c1290, 1304 &c. *(sl).*
　LAC..., John. *Bk of Sls 90.* 1398.

Gu goat salient Arg
　BOUGHTON, Piers de. *S 331.*

Gu goat salient Arg armed Or
　BARDWELL, of Norf. *L1 87, 5; L2 83, 7.*
　(goat bendways).
　BERDEWELL. *DV 46a, 1813.*
　BERDEWELLE, Wy. *NS 138.*
　BERDWELL, Whilliam, of Suff. *WB III 109,*
　2.

BERDWELL, Sir Wm. *PLN 313. (goat*
　embelif; qtg 2&3 Pakenham).
　BUCTON, Sir W. *BW 20, 137. (unguled Or;*
　blazoned 'gootbuk').

Gu goat salient Or
　BOUGHTON, Mons' Peris de. *S 329.*

Sa goat salient Arg
　TRETHEK. *BA 1008.*

Hare (including coney, leveret, rabbit)

Rabbit feeding
　MAXWELL, John. *Stevenson. 1292. (s of*
　Herbert).

Arg coney ramp Gu
　TARSSE, Rex. *FK I 42. (or K of Thrace).*
　THARS, K of. *KB 32.*

Or coney ramp to sin Gu
　TARSUS, King of. *LO B 46.*

Arg hare salient Gu
　TARS, le roy de. *LM 12.*

Az hare salient Arg
　THARSE. *SP A 9.*

Az hare salient Or
　— *WLN 121.*
　TARSUS, King of. *LMS 15.*
　TATE, Roy de. *RH, Ancestor iii 193.*

Az rabbit salient Or
　— *WNS 25, 5.*

Gu hare salient Arg
　CONNIBRE, le Roy de. *LM 10.*

Gu hare salient Or
　TRACE. *CK a 11.*

Sa hare salient Arg
　— *WLN 145.*

Az hare salient Arg hunting-horn Vt suspended
　from collar by sling Gu
　KNELAND, of that ilke. *Lyndsay 409.*

Hare riding on dog
　ACTON, Nicholas. *PRO-sls Ex KR 16/26, 15.*
　1323.

Horse (including ass, donkey, mule)

Ass passt
　BRAYE, Gilbert de. *Birch 7753.* S'GILBERTI.-
　D'.BRAY. 1324.

Horse
　AVENEL, William. *Melros pl IX 10, HB-SND.*

Horse passt
　DELAVAL, Robert. *Waterford, HB-SND.*

Arg foal Sa
　FALYNGBROME. *BA 2b. (blazoned 'foole').*

Gu colt passt Arg
　POULEINE. *L9 93a, 1.*
　POULEINE, Rex. *FK I 46. (blazoned*
　'poulain').

Horse harnessed

Gu horse saddled Or
NORWAY. *C 17.*

Gu horse stat saddled & bridled Arg
P..lie... *LMO 12. (?colt).*

Gu horse Arg saddled & bridled Or
POLERENE, le Roy de. *P 18.*
POM[ER]AN, le rey de. *LM 16.*

Gu horse forcene Arg saddled & bridled Or
— *WJ 78.*

Gu horse forcene Arg bridle Sa
HAAG, Baron Sigismund. *LH 371.*

Gu horse forcene Arg saddled & bridled Sa garnished Or
LETTOWE, le Roy de. *WLN 34.*

Sa horse forcene Arg bridle & reins Or
[CABELL]. *Mill Steph. (stained glass, baptistry, St John Baptist's, Frome, Som).*

Horse & ...

Horse in dex & cock in sin both erect & to sin
TROUP, John. *Stevenson.* 1454. *(portioner of Wardrys-flemyng).*

Leopard: see lion passt gard

Otter

Otter salient
MELDRUM. *Stevenson 133.* 1468. *(official sl of Brechin temp Bp Wm M).*

Otter erect crowned
MELDRUM, George, of Petcarrie. *Stevenson.* 1503. *(imp paly).*

Ox (& bull)

Ox
BERNARDCASTIELL, Richard de, Clerk. *PRO-sls.* 1365. *(?or stag; shield below Virgin & Child seated under canopy).*
BEWET, John. *PRO-sls.* 1417.

Arg bull passt Gu
— *I2(1904)180. (armed Or; qtd 7 by Syr Rychard Grenevile).*
BEBYLEY. *L2 91, 12. (armed & unguled Or; marginal note: 'Gowerris').*
BEVILLE, Joan. *DevonNQ V ii 61.* c1404. *(a&l Or; w of Wm Wynard; in Wynard's Chapel, Exeter).*
GOWOWRIS, of Cornw. *L1 293, 5; L2 228, 2. (armed Or; marginal note in L1: 'Beleyley').*
RYDLEY. *L1 556, 5.*
TORRELL, of Ilchester. *Gerard 208. (armed Or).*

Or bull Gu
DENMARK, Eric V, K of. *C 18.*

Erm bull passt Gu
BEVYLLE, of Woolston. *L1 64, 3. (armed Or; as blazoned).*

Erm bull passt Sa
WYTER. *L1 688, 2. (a&l Gu).*

Per fess Vt and Or bull erect counterch
HASTINGS, Sir Drewe. *LH 347. ('before the Conquest').*

Per pale Vt and Or bull ramp counterch
HASTYNG, Mons Dreuve de. *TJ 1530. ('devant le Conquest').*

Arg bull stat Gu
BEVYLEY, ?of Gowlowris. *BA 994. (armed & unguled Or).*
BOOLS. *WB I 44, 14.*
RYDELY. *DV 49a, 1921.*
TORELL, Sir Wm. *WB V 82. (tincts unclear, ?Vt bull stat Arg; armed Or).*

Az bull stat Gu
BOLE. *BA 1171. (armed, unguled & membered Or).*

Gu ox stat Arg
LEGHVILE, Thom de. *LM 565.*

Erm bull stat Gu
BEUYLLE. *L10 29, 9. (armed & unguled Or).*
BEVYLE, of Wolston. *BA 996. (armed & unguled Or).*

Ox pg
— *Birch 3801.* 13 cent. *(not on shield; 'in allusion to City of Oxford'; 2nd sl of Abbey of St Mary, Oseney, Oxf).*
COLGRYM, Laurence, of Watyndon, Surr. *Birch 8809.* 1319. *(or Ric atten Okette).*

Ox stat gard
BEVILLE, Reginald de. *Bk of Sls 81.* 1308.

Ox in front of bush
OXFORD, Mayoralty. *Proc Soc Antiq IV 2S 392.* [SIGILLU]M [MA]IOR[ATUS VILLE OX[ON]. 19 Feb 1332.

Sea-Dog, Sea-Lion &c: see under Monster

Sheep (including lamb, ram)

Paschal Lamb
AYS, Eustace de, clerk. *Stevenson.* early 14 cent. *(lamb passt regard; or Aths).*
BARBITONSOR, John, burgess of Montrose. *Stevenson.* 1304. *(facing to sinister).*
BARLEY, Ralph. *Durham-sls 53.* 1343.
CARLIOL, Henry of. *Univ Coll P Fasc 6, 1, HB-SND.*
DISSINGTON, Nicholas of. *PRO-sls Ex QR Misc Aug 38/22.* 1323.
FAIRLIE, John. *Stevenson.* 1500. *(Ld of 1/4 of lands of Easter Acolfield).*
?LAMB, Bernold. *Stevenson. (not on shield; regard).*

LAMBE, Alexander, [St Andrews]. *Stevenson.*
1476.
LAMBE, Duncan, [St Andrews]. *Stevenson.*
1469.
TEMPLE, The. *Yorks Deeds IX 168.* SIGILLVM
TEMPLI. c1270. *(not on shield; Imbert de
Perault, Master).*
TEMPLE, Knights of the. *Bow L 13.* SIGIL-
LUM TEMPLI. *(not on shield; on sl used by
Frater Rob de Manford).*
WORTHSTEDE, Simon de. *PRO-sls.* 1349-50.
Az Paschal Lamb Ppr forefoot on chalice Or
CHRIST, 'our Lord Jesus'. *RH, Ancestor ix
176. (banner).*
Ram
— *Birch 2894. 1475. (or goat; not on
shield; on signet of Rog Bemyster, Abbot of
Cerne, Dorset).*

Squirrel
Squirrel sejt
— *Durham-sls 3167. 1507-8. (qtd by Chris-
topher Bainbridge, Bp of Durham 1507-8).*
— *?source. 1514. (qtd 2&3 by Christopher
Bainbridge, Archbp of York 1508-14; incised
slab in English College, Rome).*
CRESSWELL, Robert of. *Balliol E 1/3, HB-
SND.* 1339.
?DARCK, Roger. *Birch 9191.* S' ROGERI.-
DARCK. 1345. *(sl used by William atte
Broke, of Shoreham, Suss).*
LANGTON, David. *Stevenson.*
LANGTON, David of. *PRO-sls Ex QR 37/1.*
1318.
MONTE CANISY, Dionyisia de. *Birch 6685.* S'
DIONISIE DE MONTE CANISY. late 13 cent.
*(Domina de Anesty, Surr, d1313; decoration
on sl).*
TORAUD, John, Rector of Grytelynton, Wilts.
Heneage 1892. S'IOHANNIS TORAUD.
Arg squirrel sejt Gu
— *XK 117. (qtd 2&3 by Sir Wm Cromer).*
— *L10 36b, 18. (qtd 2&3 by Cromer).*
— *XV I 951. (qtd 2&3 by Cromer).*
— *L10 38, 10. (qtd 2&3 by Jn Cromer, of
'fogilston', Kent).*
SQUIRREL. *CRK 981.*
Squirrel sejt eating nut
CRESSEWELL, Robert de. *PRO-sls.* 1323.
HYLLES, William. *Roman PO 5913.* 1 July
1443.
Arg squirrel sejt eating nut Gu
— *WK 479. (qtd 2&3 by Sir Wm Cromer).*
Arg squirrel sejt Gu eating nut Or
SQUYRYE, Suff. *L1 620, 6.*
SQYRYE, of Suff. *MY 76.*

Squirrel sejt holding apple
[HORTON]. *Lancs 1533 CS 98, 84. (qtd by
Holcroft).*
Arg squirrel sejt Gu holding apple Or
— *D13 15. (?apple a roundel; qtd by Cro-
mer, of Tunstall, Kent).*

Tiger
Tiger passt to sin
STAKEPOL, Philip de. *Birch 13646.* S' FILIPE
DE STAHEPOL. early 14 cent. *(not on shield;
in allusion to arms of Stackpoole, heraldic
tiger passt).*
Arg tiger ramp Sa
DANIELLE, John. *BA 2.*
LUDLOWE, Sir John de. *CV-BM 165.*
Or tiger ramp Purp
[LACY], Counte Nycoll. *PO 599.*
Arg tiger Purp ch on shldr with crosslet Arg
STORY, William. *TJ 1462. ('... avec la cowe
tressee').*
Per pale Az and Gu tiger Erm
NORWICHE, Mons' John de. *TJ 1543.
('... a un tigre rampant dermyns').*
Arg tiger salient Sa
— *SHY 106. (uncertain; qrs 1&4; Gonville
in pretence).*
Arg tiger regard Sa
[DARESBURY]. *BA 42, 416. (qtd 2&3 by
Daniel).*
Arg tiger Gu looking at herself Gu in mirror Az
handled Or
SYBILL. *Arch Cant xxvi 804c.* c1500.
*(carved on chimney piece, Little Mote, Eyns-
ford, Kent).*
Arg tiger Gu & mirror Or
SYBILL, John, of Kent. *PLN 1820.*

Urchin (including hedgehog & porcu-
pine)
Hedgehog
FULLERTON, John, of that Ilk. *Stevenson.*
1513. *(?Erm spot; qtg pall).*
HERRES, Robert, of Auchtorabyth. *Stevenson.*
1465. *(?back of hedgehog).*
Gu porcupine erect Arg collared Untinc
— *WB I 33b, 17. (qtd 6 by [Clisold]).*
Gu hedgehog erect Arg collared & chained Or
EYRE, Simon. *LV 27.*
Gu porcupine salient Arg quills barry Arg and Sa
collared ringed & chained Or
EYRE, Symkin. *PLN 485. (Ld Mayor of Lon-
don, 1445).*
Gu porcupine salient Arg collared & chained Or
EYRE, Mayor of London. *L2 177, 1.*

Wolf

Wolf passt
— *Durham-sls 2003. (sl of Richard de ...; used by 1384 by Jn Plumpton, of Durham).*
CHESTER, Ranulf, E of. *PRO-sls.* early 13 cent. *(?lion; tube shaped shield).*
DANYELL, John. *PRO-sls.* 1548-9.
HOUEL. *Lawrance 25.* c1300-1320. *(?lion; effigy, Wrexham, Denbs).*
Wolf passt to sin
KIVELI, Jordan de. *Heneage 2085.* +S ORDANI: KIVELI. temp John. *(not on shield; grant of land in Stanleke, [Wilts]).*
Az wolf passt Arg
SURGEON, J. *CRK 1843.*

Wolf rampant

Wolf ramp
LOUTH, John. *PRO-sls.* 1370-1. *(s&h of Rog de L).*
LOUTHE, Roger, Ld of Wolverton, ?Bucks. *Birch 11393.* SIG.ROGERI.DE.LOUTHE. 1361.
[LOWTHE]. *Mill Steph.* 1518. *(imp by [Goldingham] on brass to Jn G & 2 wives [Joan Lowthe] & Thomasin Leston, Belstead, Suff).*
MESCHINES, Ranulph. *Birch 11760.*
...GILLUM : RAN. temp Ric 1. *(surnamed Blundeville, great-grands of Ranulph, E of Chester; ?lion).*
WOLF, John, clerk. *?source.* 16 Edw .... *(sl).*
Arg wolf ramp Sa
WOLF. *FK II 598.*
WOLFE. *Nichols Leics IV 186. (qtd 2&3 by Gu on cross engr Sa 5 5foils Gu [Amory]; Frolesworth Ch).*
Az wolf ramp Arg
CLICE. *L1 151, 4; L2 124, 4. (a&l Gu; marginal note in L1 'Don').*
DOON. *L10 63b, 19.*

Wolf salient

Wolf salient
DONN, Griffyth. *Clairambault 3207.* 12 May 1438.
KIDWELLY. *?source. (brass to Geoffrey K (d1483), Little Wittenham Ch, Berks).*
LANDALE, Thomas. *Stevenson. (shield shaped sl).*
WOLFE, John, Ld of Frolesworth, Leics. *Bow LVII 7.* Sigillum Johis wulfe. 1412-13.
Az wolf salient Arg
CLYSE. *WB I 32b, 20.*
DON, Sir Edward. *XK 139.*
DON, John. *WB IV 172, 829.*
DOUN. *L1 198, 3; L2 154, 6. (a&l Gu).*
DUNN, Owen. *CRK 288. (embelif).*
[OLIFE]. *PLN 1374.*

THOMAS, Whilliam, of Carms. *WB III 90b, 3.*
Sa wolf salient Or
— *PLN 1001.*
LOUTHE. *FK a 999.*
LOUTHE, Robert. *LY A 83.*
WOULFSON. *FK II 999.*
Per pale wolf salient
KIDEWELLY, Geoffrey. *Mill Steph.* 1583. *(brass to Geoffrey K, Little Wittenham, Berks).*
KIDWELLY, David. *Mill Steph.* 1454. *(qtg 3 spearheads on brass to David K, Little Wittenham, Berks).*
Per pale Sa and Az wolf salient Arg
FRECH. *L1 239, 4; L2 198, 1.*

Wolf collared

Arg wolf ramp Sa collared Gu
WODE. *DV 42b, 1673. (armed Gu; qtg 2&3 Gu on chf Arg 3 pd mullets Sa).*
Arg wolf ramp Sa collared Or
WOD. *L1 693, 4. (a&l Or).*
WODE. *DV 42b, 1672. (armed Gu).*
Arg wolf salient Sa collared Or
WODE, of Batterley, Staffs. *WB IV 156, 548. (langued Gu).*
WOOD. *PLN 832. (langued Gu).*
WOOD, John. *CRK 1423. (armed Or, langued Gu).*
WOODE, John, of Kent. *RH, Ancestor vii 185. (wolf blazoned 'an alaunda').*
Az wolf salient Arg collared checky Or and Gu
KYDEVELLY, Sir Morgan. *WK 276.*
KYDWELLY. *XPat 352, Arch 69, 96. (langued Gu).*
KYDWELLY. *L2 293, 10.*
Az wolf salient Arg chained Or
KYDWELLE. *L1 374, 4.*

Wolf holding

Arg wolf couchant Sa with crown Or between forepaws
BRISBURGH, John, of Suff. *WB III 112b, 2.*

BEAST & LABEL

Lion & label

Lion & label
— *G18 21d. (5th of 6 qtgs imp by Sir Robt Peyton, of Isleham, Cambs, 1575).*
BROOK, Thomas de, Ld of Holditch, Devon. *Birch 7822.* +S' THOME DE ...... 1362.
COLEVILE, Roger de. *Birch 8800.* S' ROG'I DE COLEVILLE D'CARLETON. 1297. *(s of Robt de C of Carleton, Suff).*

COLEVYLE, John de. *Bow 12. (sl).*

DARUNDELL, Sibilla.
Birch 6936. s': SI[BIL]LE: D[ARV]NDEL. 1350.
*(betw lozs of [Montacute & Grandison]; w of
Sir Edm de Arundelle, 2nd s of Edm, 10th E
of Arundel [& dau of Wm de Montacute, E of
Salisbury & Katharine, dau of Wm, Ld
Grandison]).*

HADESTOKE, ...tinus de. *Birch 10362.*
s'...TINI DE HADESTOKE. 13 cent.

HAVERINGGE, Richard of, Archdeacon of
Chester. *Durham-sls 1209.* c1321.

MOUBRAY, Alexander de. *PRO-sls.* 1336-7.
(label unclear).

NEVILLE, John de, of Essex. *Birch 12112.*
...ANNIS...VILL'. 13 cent.

PERCY, Sir Harry. *Blair D II 141, 303.*
*('Harry Hotspur'; on W front of Gatehouse,
Hilton Castle).*

PERCY, Henry. *PRO-sls Ex Treas Rcpt Misc
41/1.* 1392-3. *('Hotspur'; k Shrewsbury,
1403).*

PERCY, Henry. *PRO-sls KR 73/3 29, 41 &
42.* 1392-5. *('Hotspur').*

PERCY, Henry de. *Durham-sls 1962. (4th Ld
Percy of Alnwick, 1st E of Northd).*

ROBSART, John. *Clairambault 7765.* 13 Dec
1441.

STAPILTON, Elizabeth. *PRO-sls.* 1392. *(wid
of Sir Brian S).*

WESTON, William de. *PRO-sls.* 1303.

Lion & label of 4
MORTIMER, Wm. *Stevenson.* 1444. *(s of
Thos M, Burgess of Dundee).*

Lion & label of 5
ASTLEY, Aegidius de. *Dugd 17, 3.*

INSULA, Robert. *PRO-sls.* 1323. *(s of Jn de
I).*

MEISHAM, William de, of Eton & Meisham.
Bow XXXII 5.

MOUBRAY, Geoffrey de. *PRO-sls.* 1292-3.

MOUBRAY, Geoffrey de. *Birch 11993.* s'
GALFRIDI DE MOVBRAY. 1292.

MOWBRAY, Geoffrey of. *PRO-sls Scots 29.*
1392-3.

NEVILE, John de, Kt. *PRO-sls.* 1272.

PEYTEVYN, Thomas, Kt. *Birch 12609.* s'
THOME PETEVYN MILITIS. 1406.

TALEBOT, John, of Gainsborough, Lincs.
Birch 13830. s' IOH(AN)NIS TALEBOT. late
Hen 3.

TRAFFORDE, Stephen, of Northants. *Birch
13972.* s' STEPHANI DE TRAFFORDE. 1345.

Lion & label of 5 on shldr
MOWBRAY, Geoffrey. *Stevenson.* 1292. *(d
before 30 June 1300).*

Lion & label of 7
MOWBRAY, Roger. *Stevenson.* 1249-51.

Arg lion & label
Arg lion Az label Gu
COLVILLE, Mons' John, de Mershland. *TJ 97.*
FFAUCONBERGE, Mons Th. *WJ 270.*

Arg lion Az label of 5 Or
CLAVERYNG, Johannes de. *Q II 428.*

Arg lion Sa label of 5 Untinc
STAPLETON, Sir Nicholas. *Lawrance 41.*
1322. *(effigy, Kirkby Fleetham, Yorks).*

Arg lion Sa label Gu
BURNELL, Willame. *FW 343.*
DANDUERS. *L10 54, 17. (a&l Gu).*
MORLEE, Mons Robert de. *S 547.*
MORLEY, Robert de. *S 553. (a&l Or).*
STAPILTON, Mons Th de. *WJ 310.*
STAPULTON. *PO 121.*

Az &c lion & label
Az lion Arg label Gu
— *CRK 1556. (qtd 2&3 by Sir Jn Colvile).*
— *BW 15b, 101. (qtd 2&3 by Sir J Colvile).*
— *PLN 231. (qtd 2&3 by Sir Jn Colvile).*
— *L10 100b, 3. (a&l Gu; qtd 3 by Regn
Foulesthurst, of Ches).*
COLEVILE, Geffrai. *N 661.*
COLUERLEY, of Marsland, Lincs. *L1 158, 4;
L2 113, 11.*
COLUILE, Geffrey. *PO 139.*
COLVILE, de Mershlande. *PT 689. (qtg Or 3
chessrooks Gu).*
MICHANTE, Monsr John. *L9 68a, 3.*

Az lion Arg label of 5 Gu
— *WLN 439.*

Az lion Arg label Or
MUHAUTE, Mons' John. *TJ 144.*

Az lion Or label Gu
NEVILL, le ffiltz. *WJ 114.*

Gu lion Arg label Az
[MOWBRAY], fittz a Seignr. *WJ 142.*
MOWBREY, Mons Alisant de. *WJ 149.*

Gu lion Arg label Sa
MOUBRAY, Gefrey de. *Q 272.*

Gu lion Or label Arg
ARRUNDELL, Mons Esm d'. *WJ 240.*
DARUNDEL, Monsire Edmon, le filtz. *AN
337. (qtg checky Or and Az [Warenne];
label over all).*

Gu lion Or label Az
— *I2(1904)178. (qtd 2&3 by Arg lion qf Gu
[Franceys Hasylden, of Fylden Mardon,
Cambs]).*
— *S 81. (qtd 2&3 by Thos Mowbray).*
[ARUNDEL], R' filtz au Count. *WJ 238.*
MUCHEGROS, Johan de. *G 202.*
TURBURUILLE. *L1 641, 6.*

Or lion & label

Or lion Az label Arg
　PERCY, Sir Henry. *S 83.*

Or lion Az label Gu
　MOHAUT, Jan de. *Q 110.*
　MOUHAULT, Joan de. *F 336.*
　PERCY, fitz Count. *WJ 94.*
　PERCY, Mons Henry. *S 81.*
　PERCY, Sir Henry de, le Fiz. *CKO 95.*
　PERCY, Thomas de. *Navarre 1471.*
　WORCESTYR, Count de. *RH, Ancestor ix 162.*

Or lion Az label of 5 Gu
　— *WLN 840.*
　MONHAUT. *L9 69b, 9. (a&l Gu).*
　MONHAUT, John de. *E I 520; E II 522.*

Or lion Gu label Az
　BRABANT, Count of. *MP II 80.*
　CHARLTON, J le fitz de. *WJ 262.*
　FILBRIDGE. *PT 215.*
　FYLBREGG. *DV 56a, 2201.*
　SAVOY, Piers of, E of Richmond. *MP II 81.*
　STEWART, Robert, D of Albany, E of Fife & Monteith. *Lyndsay 47. (qtg Or fess checky Az and Arg label Az; 2nd s of Robt II).*

Or lion Gu label of 5 Az
　POLE, Eweyn. *Q 476.*

Or lion Purp label Gu
　PERCY. *CT 64.*

Or lion Vt label Gu
　SOITTONE, Sire Johan de. *N 663.*

Or lion Vt label of 5 Gu
　SUTTON. *LS 1.*

Sa lion & label

Sa lion Arg label Gu
　VERDON, J, le fitz de. *WJ 294.*

Sa lion Or label of 5 Gu
　KYNGSTON. *CT 148.*

Erm &c lion & label

Erm lion Gu label Az
　TURBURVYLL, Mons W. *WJ 206. ('son fitz').*

Billetty lion & label
　PLANQUE, Maillin de le. *Arch Journ xciii 43.*
　c1450. *(sl matric, Nelson Coll 95).*

Gu billetty & lion Or label Az
　BLAMMONSTER, Mons Rauf. *WJ 258.*

Or billetty & lion Az label Gu
　ANGLE, Mons John d'. *WJ 100. ('son fitz').*

Az crusily & lion Or label Arg
　BREWES, J de, le fitz. *WJ 111.*

Gu crusily & lion Arg label Az
　WARRE, Sr John le. *L 177.*

Or crusily & lion Az label Gu
　LOVEL, John. *CA 199.*

Az crusily fitchy & lion Or label Arg
　BREWES. *L10 75b, 12. (langued Gu, sans claws).*

Gu crusily fitchy & lion Arg label Az
　LAVARE. *DV 58a, 2287.*
　VARE, De la. *PT 5.*
　WARE, J son fitz de la. *WJ 154.*

Or crusily fitchy & lion Az label Gu
　LOVELL, Mons Nicoll. *WJ 116.*

Az semy of pd mullets (6 pts) & lion Or label of 4 Gu
　— *WLN 161.*

Lion charged or patterned & label

Arg lion Sa ch on shldr with annulet Az label Gu
　STAPILTON, Mons Miles de. *WJ 314. ('le fitz').*

Gu lion Or ch on shldr with cresc & label Untinc
　— *LH 102. (qtd 2&3 by Haselden).*

Gu lion Or ch on shldr with cresc Untinc over all label Az
　TURBERVIL. *XFB 36. (qtg Havering, all qtd III by Hasylden, of Gilden Morden).*

Gu lion Or ch on shldr with cresc Arg label Az
　TRUBLEVILLE. *CRK 1235.*

Gu lion Or ch on shldr with cresc & over all label Az
　— *LH 602. (qtd III 1&4 by Francis Haselden).*
　TURBERVILE. *LH 578. (qtd 2&3 by Haselden).*
　[TURBERVILE]. *LH 611, 612 & 614.*

Gu lion Or ch on shldr with cresc Sa label Az
　TURBERVILE. *XL 37.*

Arg lion Gu ch on shldr with 5foil Arg label Az
　ESTLE. *L1 227, 4.*
　ESTLE, of Leics. *LE 42.*
　ESTLE, of Leics. *BA 31, 273.*
　ESTLEE, Giles de. *N 824.*

Arg lion Sa ch on shldr with mullet Or label Az
　WALKFARE, Mons J. *WJ 322.*

Per pale Az and Gu lion Erm label Or
　— *PO 136. ('Oldhall' added in modern hand).*

Per pale Az and Gu lion Erm label of 5 Or
　NORWICH, S' John de. *R 82.*

Per pale Gu and Az lion Erm label Or
　NORTHWYKE, Sire Johan de. *O 69.*
　NORWICHE, Mons Water. *WJ 194.*

Gu lion Arg semy of roses Gu label Az
　— *GA 38. ('Sir Patrick le Fitz le Conte').*

Arg lion Az gutty Or label Gu
　BYRNELL, Mons J. *WJ 278.*

Gu lion Vair label Or
　[EVERYNGHAM], Mons W, son filtz. *WJ 162.*

Lion crowned & label

Arg lion Gu crowned Or label of 5 Az
　TURBERVILE, Thom. *Q 373.*

Arg lion Sa crowned Or label Gu
    MORLAYE, R', le Fitz. *WJ 318.*
Az lion Arg crowned Or label Gu
    JUNTROID. *XL 637.*
Gu lion Arg crowned Or label Arg
    CLAPAN, of Glaslogy. *Lyndsay 191.*
Sa lion Arg crowned Untinc label of 5 Gu
    SEGRAVE. *CT 112.*
Sa lion Arg crowned Or label Az
    SEGRAVE, Sr Nichol de. *L 117.*
Sa lion Arg crowned Or label Gu
    [SEGRAVE], J, fitz a seign. *WJ 298.*
    SEGRAVE, Sire Nichol de. *O 21.*
    SEGRAVE, Nicholas de. *H 11a.*
    SEGRAVE, Nicholas de. *G 83.*
    SEGRAVE, Sire Nichole de. *J 27.*
    SEGRAVE, Sr Nicol de. *H 11b.*
    SEGRAVE, Nicolas de. *K 120.*
    SEGRAVE, S Nychol de. *ST 7.*
    SEYGRAVE, Sire Nicholas de. *N 42.*
Sa lion Arg crowned Or label of 5 Gu
    SEGRAVE, Nichol de. *Q 210. (armed Or).*
    SEGRAVE, Nicholas de. *SP A 72.*
    SEGRAVE, Nicol de. *LM 180.*

Lion qf & label
Lion 2queued & label
    [BURGHERSH]. *Soc Antiq Cast F 33. (qtd by Jn de la Pole, E of Lincoln, d1487; sl).*
Arg lion qf Gu label Az
    HAVERYNG, Fitz a. *WJ 216.*
    HAVERYNGES, Fitz a. *LH 549.*
Arg lion qf Sa label Gu
    CRESSY, Sir Roger. *PT 1018.*
    CRESSY, Sr Roger. *N 730.*
Gu lion qf Arg label Az
    MONTFORT, Philip de. *C 183.*
Gu lion qf Or label Az
    BUREWASSH, Mons B le fitz de. *WJ 246.*
    BURGHERSH, Monsire de. *AN 11.*
    BURGHERSH, Barthelmew. *A 133a.*
Or lion qf Gu label Az
    ZWEYNBRUGGE, Count of. *XL 438. (qf in salt).*
Or lion qf Sa label Gu
    WELE, S. Phelip de. *GA 87.*
Sa lion qf Or label Arg
    KYNGESTONE, Sire Henri de. *N 1090.*
Sa lion qf Or label Gu
    KINGESTON, Sire Nicholas de. *N 732.*
    KINGSTON, Sir Nicholas. *PT 1021.*
Sa lion qf Or label of 5 Gu
    KYNGESTON, Nicol de. *LM 414.*
Arg crusily fitchy lion qf & knotted Gu label Az
    HAUIRINGE. *PO 170. (name added in modern hand).*
Arg lion qf Gu crowned Or label Az
    MONTE, le Counte del. *C 116. (Adolphe VIII, Count of Berg, d1296).*

Gu lion qf Arg crowned Or label Vt
    FENER, Monsire Thalman. *CA 251.*

Lion passt &c & label
Barry lion passt label
    ENGLEFELD, John. *Birch 9483.* SIGILLU: IOHANNIS: DE: ENGLEFELD. *1368. (s of Philip de E, of Dunsden, Oxfords).*
Barry in chf lion passt label
    ENGLEFELD, John. *PRO-sls.* 1362-3. *(label unclear).*
Or lion salient Gu label Az
    FILEBRIGG, Monsire Roger. *AN 119.*

Lion ramp gard & label
Arg lion gard Gu label Az
    ?HOURON. *PO 147. (armed Az).*
Gu lion gard Arg label Az
    MERNY, le fitz ... de. *WJ 383.*
Gu lion gard Arg label Or
    MARNEY, Sir John. *XK 150.*
    MARNEY, William. *S 165.*
    MARYNER, William. *BG 110.*
Sa lion gard Or label Gu
    BROCAS, Bernard. *S 555.*
    BROCAS, Mons' Bernard. *S 549.*
Vt lion gard Vt (sic) label Or
    — *PT 731.*
Az crusily & lion gard Arg label Gu
    DALTON, Mons J de. *WJ 380.*
Az semy of crosslets (upper limb trefly, foot formy) & lion gard Arg label Untinc
    DALTON. *PT 417.*
Az semy of crosslets formy at foot & lion gard Arg label Gu
    DALTON. *DV 56a, 2211.*
Az crusily Or lion gard Arg label Gu
    DALTON, John. *AN 245.*
Az semy de lis & lion gard Arg label Gu
    HOLAND, Mons R de, le fitz. *WJ 374.*
Az semy de lis & lion gard Arg ch on shldr with annulet Sa label Gu
    HOLAND. *WJ 378. (s of Thos, E of Kent).*

Lion passt gard & label
Gu lion pg in chf Or label Az
    BRETTE, son fitz de la. *WJ 366.* c1380.
Lion pg crowned & label
    OGILVIE, Sir Patrick, Kt. *Stevenson.* 1422. *(Sheriff of Angus, d1435).*
Lion pg crowned & ch on breast with mullet over all label
    OGILVIE, John. *Stevenson.* 1431. *(s of Sir Wm O, of Landrath).*
Gu crusily Or lion pg Arg crowned Or label Az
    LYLLE, Mons Waryn. *WJ 386.*

Lion & patterned label

Lion over all label each pt ch with chev
HALUGHTON, Thomas. *Dugd 17, 19.* ?1313.
(pts possibly ch with 2 chevs).
Gu lion Arg label Az semy of crescs Or
BEAUMONT, S William de. *GA 90.*
Gu lion Arg label Az roundelly Or
BEAUMOND, W. *WJ 156.*

Beast (other) & label

Gu hedgehog erect Arg collared & chained Or
label Az
EYRE, Thomas. *LV 85.*

BEAST & IN BASE

Lion & in base

Arg lion & base indented Purp
SKYPTON, John de. *TJ 203.* (*'de purpre
argent au pee endentee ove le champie dar-
gent de purper et un leon rampant de
purpre'*).
SKYPTON, John de. *TJ 202.* (*originally bla-
zoned Purp on base indented lion Arg*).
Lion passt on castle 3-towered
?DONCASTER, Borough of. *Birch 2394.*
...DECANAT DE: DONCASTRO. c1310. (*in allu-
sion to Arms of Borough; sl used by Jn
Hubbe of Wlvelaymorhuse, Yorks, for Rural
Deanery of Doncaster, See of York*).
Lion stat in base fleur de lis
MOSSIETO, Peter de. *PRO-sls.* 1361.
Gu in chf lion pg Or & in base castle 3-towered
Arg
NORWICH, City of. *CY 111, 441.*
In chf lion passt in base fish naiant
FULHAM, William, Fishmonger of London.
PRO-sls. 1372-3.
Lion passt regard in base fleur de lis
CHICHESTER, City of. *Hope 183.* (*on old
mayoralty sl*).
Az lion pg & in base fleur de lis Or
FLAWNDRYN. *L1 242, 1; L2 198, 5.*
Lion holding sword erect in right fore-paw in
dex base rose
SCRYMGEOUR, James, of Kirkton. *Stevenson.*
1500.
Lion & in base ?ram's head
PERSEHAY, Henry. *PRO-sls.* 1372-3.
Lion passt in base heart
OGILVIE, John. *Stevenson.* late 15 cent.
Or on mount Vt lion Sa
— *FK II 355.*

Arg on mount Az lion stat gard Gu semy of
estoiles Or
GYBSON, Thomas, Grocer of London. *L9
28a, 6.*
Lion passt in base pastoral staff
CHETEHAM, John. *Birch 2630.* 1426. (*imp 2
lozs in pale; Abbot of Praemonstratensian
Abbey of St Mary, Bayham, in Lamberhurst,
Suss*).

Other beast & in base

Badger on mount
BROCKHULL, Thomas. *Birch 7817.* 1380.
Or on mount Vt boar stat Sa
HENLOYN. *LH 117.* (*mount isolated*).
OHENLOYN. *L2 388, 11.*
Greyhound on mount beneath tree
BROOK, Thomas, of Som, Kt. *Birch 7823.*
IATENS: IMORTALITE. 1415. (*poss Badger*).
On mount stag lodged
METTE, William, of Canterbury, Kent. *Birch
11765.* 1507. (*in field of sl shackle & letters
I.E.*).
Hart lying in water
LYHERT, Walter. *Birch 2056.* 1454. (*Bp of
Norwich 1446-72; signet or privy sl*).
Hart at bay in pool hound on its back
HARTLEPOOL, Town of. *HB-SND.* ?13 cent.
Hart at gaze in pool on its haunches deerhound
HARTLEPOOL. *Birch 4976.* S' COMMUNITATIS
DE HERTEPOL. 13 cent.
Deer lodged in park
DERBY. *Birch 4863.* SIGILLUM COMUNE
WILLE DE DERBI. (*?rebus*).
Talbot passt in chf in base chess rook
PERCHEHAY, Henry, of Devon. *Birch 12547.*
1374.
On mount greyhound courant
— *Birch 14194.* 1461. (*not a shield; sl used
by Jn, s of Wm Nepeker, of Hadlo, Kent*).
Hound collared & tied to stake rising out of
waves in base
LINLITHGOW. *Birch 15577-8.* 15 cent.
(*privy sl ad causas*).
LINLITHGOW. *Birch 17309.* 1357. (*hound
passt to dex with open mouth, pointed ears &
curved tail; 2nd sl*).
Hound passt through waves collared & tied to
stake
LINLITHGOW. *Birch 15575-6.* 15 cent.
(*privy sl*).
Sa on mount Vt goat passt Arg
GOTEHURST. *Gerard 182.*
In chf hare courant in base letter R
WENLOKE, Richard de. *Bow XXVI 3.* 1332-
3.

Arg on mount Vt hare salient Gu
TARSUS, K of. *WLN 26.*
Arg on mount Vt hare sejt Ppr
HARVEY, Thomas. *Nichols Leics IV 873.*
(d1545; mont, Peckleton Ch).
Gu demi-horse Arg isst from water in base wavy
Az and Arg
TREVELYAN. *CRK 661.*
Gu demi-horse Arg isst from water in base Ppr
TRESUYLYON. *L1 632, 2. (shod Or).*
TREVELIAN, Sir John. *WK 331.*
TREVILLIAN, of Nettlecombe. *Gerard 25.*
Gu horse salient Arg dappled Az isst from water
Ppr
TREVYLYON. *BA 952. (shod Or).*
Otter isst from water in base wavy
— *Stevenson. 1503. (qtd 2&3 by George
Meldrum, of Fyvie).*
MELDRUM, Alan. *Stevenson. 1526. (Canon
to Canons Regular of St Andrews).*
Ox passing ford of water
OXFORD, City of. *Birch 5250.* SIGILLUM
MAIORIS OXONIE. 13 cent.
Arg ox Gu crossing ford Ppr
OXFORD UNIVERSITY. *Hope 177. (though
now regarded as arms of the City of Oxf, on
whose early sls ox & ford appear as device,
these arms, in a shield, are on early 15 cent
sls used by Chancellors of University & it is
uncertain whether shield was not first used as
arms of the Univ).*
Bull stat in ford under tree
BOUTHIN, John de. *Birch 7673.* SIGILLUM
IOHANNIS DE BOUTHIN. 14 cent.
Arg on isolated mount Vt bull passt Gu
RIDLEY. *CVC 628.*
RIDLEY. *CRK 1563.*
Arg on terrace in base Arg bull stat Gu
RYDLEY. *PCL II 96.*
Arg on terrace in base Vt bull stat Gu
RIDLEY. *WLN 663.*
Arg on mount Vt ox Gu
RYDLEY. *BA 3. ('Arg ox Gu upon tarage
sinople').*
Arg on field Vt bull grazing Gu
RYDLEY, of Ches. *CY 34, 136.*
Az on mountain sheep Arg burning in fire Gu
ABRAHAM, Patryark. *L1 0, 1; L2 16, 8.*
Sheep standing in water [?ch on flank with roun-
del]
SHEEPWASH, John. *Mill Steph.* c1457.
(brass to Jn S, Hambleden, Bucks).
SHEEPWASH, William. *Mill Steph.* c1500.
(brass to Wm S, Hambleden, Bucks).
Wolf suckling Romulus & Remus
CASTRE, William of. *Waterford 48, HB-SND.*

BEAST BESIDE OR IN FRONT OF

Lion couchant under tree
COLESHULL, Lawrence de. *PRO-sls.* 1340-1.
Or wild boar Gu in front of tree Ppr
[GILPIN]. *Bellasis II 8. (qtg [Burneshead],
all imp by [Bellingham] on mont to Sir Rog
Bellingham, Kt, d 18 July 1533, Bellingham
chapel, Kendal).*
Hart before tree
ROOS, Thomas, of Lutterworth. *PRO-sls.*
temp Elizabeth. *(ornamented shield).*
Horse tied to post on dex
LITHGOW, Patrick, Edinburgh. *Stevenson.*
1526.
Horse courant beneath tree
FREY, William, of Warws &c. *Birch 9961.*
1406.

BEAST & CANTON

Lion ramp & canton
Lion canton sin
FLORIMUND, Ld of Spa.... *Birch 9834.* S'
FLORIMUNDI DOMINI DE SPA.... 14 cent. *(imp
lozy).*
Arg lion Sa on canton Gu wing Or
— *CB 189.*
Gu lion Arg canton Erm
SHERINGBORNE. *XL 228.*
Gu lion Or canton Erm
— *I2(1904)93. (qtd 2&3 by Syr Hen Shern-
borne).*
— *WK 803. (qtd 2&3 by Sharnbury of
Norf).*
— *XV I 967. (qtd 2&3 by Sharnbourne).*
— *XK 279. (qtd 2&3 by Sir Hen Sherborne).*
SCARINGBOURNE. *PO 179.*
SCARNIGBOURNE. *L1 572, 1.*
SCARYNGBOURNE. *DV 59b, 2359.*
SCHARINGBOURNE. *PT 77.*
SCHARYNGBURNE, Mons' Andrewe de. *TJ
138.*
Per salt Or and Az lion counterch on sin canton
Arg Church steeple rising from embattle-
ments Gu surmounted by cross Or betw 2 pot
guns in pale Az banded Or
GOLD, of Stowemarket, Suff. *L2 236, 9.*

BEAST & CHIEF

Lion ramp & chf

Lion & chf
> ROTHELANE, William. *Clairambault 7968.*
> 22 Oct 1426.

Arg lion Az chf Gu
> HUNTINGTON, Waltheof, Erle of. *MK 24.*
> [WALTHEOF, E of Huntington]. *DX 32.*

Arg lion Gu chf Az
> SAMCT GEORGE. *L1 606, 5.*

Arg lion Gu chf Sa
> RUSSELL. *LH 613.*

Or lion Az chf Gu
> SOTTONE, Sire Johan de. *N 1081.* (*'de or od
> le chef de goules a un lion rampand de
> azure'*).

Lion & chf checky
> DUNDEE, John de. *Stevenson.* 1321. (*Jn de
> Glascret, s of Sir Ralph de Dunde*).
> WASTNEIS, William de, Kt. *Bow XXXII 18.*
> (*sl, grant of land in Colton*).

Untinc lion Untinc & chf Erm
> MONCRIEFF, Malcolm of. *Stevenson.* c1460.

Arg lion Gu chf Erm
> MUNCRIEF, of that ilke. *Lyndsay 231.* 1542.

Arg lion Sa chf lozy Gu and Or
> LOWDE, John, of Suff. *WB III 112, 2.*

Or lion Gu chf Vair
> SUTTON, Sr John de. *M 42.*

Lion & chf embattled
> MANTON, Thomas de. *PRO-sls.* SIGILL'
> THOME DE MANTON. 1337-8.

Lion ramp crowned &c & chf

Arg lion Gu crowned Or chf Az
> GEORGE, Mons' Baudewyn Seint. *TJ 96.*

Lion qf & chf
> HASTANG, Sir Robert. *PRO-sls File of Inden-
> tures.* 1302.

Arg lion qf Sa chf per fess dancetty Arg and Sa
> HYETT. *BA 32, 319.*

Lion passt &c & chf

Lion passt & chf
> BLAUNFRONT, Thomas, of Ramenham, Berks.
> *Birch 7499.* 1340.

Az lion passt Or chf Erm
> [BRITAIN], K Albrygh of. *KB 192.*
> [BRITAIN], K Alphened of. *KB 169.*
> [BRITAIN], K Alwolfe of. *KB 171.*
> [BRITAIN] K ARDULFE OF. *KB 173.*
> [BRITAIN], K Eguerd of. *KB 181.*
> [BRITAIN]K MARCELYN OF. *KB 198.*
> BRITAIN, K Mercelyn of. *BA 902.*
> [BRITAIN], K Offred of. *KB 188.*
> [BRITAIN], K Wylden of. *KB 175.*
> MALYN, Rx. *DV 45a, 1774.*
> MERCELYN, Rex. *L9 66a, 4.*

> MERCELYN, King in England. 2 321, 3. (*a&l
> Gu*).
> MERCELYN, Rec. *XL 417.*

Lion passt & chf indented
> ZOWCH, Thomas. *PRO-sls.* 1499-1500.

Other beast & chf

Arg squirrel sejant Gu eating nut Arg chf checky
Or and Az
> HASELWOOD. *LH 383.*

Hedgehog chf countergobony
> LINDSAY, Herbert. *Stevenson.* 1507. (*s&h
> of Michael L of Fairgarth*).

Arg wolf passt Sa chf Gu
> WOODE, Rog, serjeant at law. *Hutton 2.*

Beast chief & label

Vair lion & on chf label Untinc
> WYDEFORD, Richard de. *PRO-sls.* 1353-4.

BEAST & ON CHIEF

Lion on chf 3 indistinct charges
> MYLE, John, Chaplain. *PRO-sls.* 1354.

Lion & on chf lion pg
> ARNALD, Vicar of Ecclesfield, Yorks. *Birch
> 6916.* 1408.

Lion & on chf 3 bells
> DUNBLANE, John, Bp of. *Stevenson 142.*
> (*1355-70*).

Gu lion passt Arg on chf Sa castle 3-towered Or
> CHASTELPER. *RB 470.*
> CHASTELPER. *XL 107.*
> CHASTELPER. *L1 148, 6; L2 123, 4.* (*doored
> & windowed Sa*).

Qtly Gu & vairy Or and Vt lion Arg on chf Az
castle betw 2 stags' heads cab Arg
> — *Sandford 496.* (*escutch of Hen Fitzroy, D
> of Richmond, natural s of Hen 8*).
> [PEVEREL]. *XL 185.* (*attired Or, tail turned
> outwards, middle tower has conical roof*).

Qtly Gu & wavy Arg and Gu lion bendwise Arg
on chf Az castle betw 2 bucks' heads cab
Arg attired Or
> — *PLN 1934.* (*lion embelif, chf Az for Earl-
> dom of Nottingham; escutch of Hen Fitzroy,
> D of Richmond & Somerset*).

Gyronny of 8 Or and Az on lion Erm cresc
Untinc on chf Arg cresc betw 2 fleurs de lis
Sa
> MOKLOW, of Worcs. *L2 349, 4.*

Qtly 1&4 per bend Gu and Arg lion Az 2&3 Or
cross moline Sa over all on chf Gu cross Arg
> — *BK 64.* (*qtd II by Pickering; shield in
> margin*).

Sa lion passt on chf Arg 3 crosslets Sa
— *Phillipps 206. (in nave of Mildenhall Ch).*

Per bend Or and Arg lion Az on chf Gu cross formy fitchy at foot betw 2 mullets Arg
BASQUER. *L2 86, 12. (lion a&l Gu).*
BASQUER. *XL 57. (lion qf in salt).*
BASQUER. *I2(1904)162. (lion qf). ('Mathew basquer de flytte in the ile of Whyght in hamshyre').*
BASQUER, of Fflytte, IOW. *L2 97, 6.*
BASQUER, Matthew. *XPat 69, Arch 69, 73. (lion qf armed Gu).*

Lion & on chf escallop &c

Gyronny of 8 Or and Az lion Erm on chf Untinc escallop Sa betw 2 fleurs de lis Untinc
MOUKELOW, Peter. *WB I 25b, 1. (lion ch on shldr with cresc Untinc).*

Gyronny of 8 Or and Az lion Erm on chf Arg escallop betw 2 fleurs de lis Sa
MUCKLOW. *L2 344, 5.*

Gyronny of 10 Az and Or lion Erm on chf Arg escallop betw 2 fleurs de lis Or
MUKLOW, William, of Worcs. *WK 599.*

Gyronny of 10 Or and Az lion Erm on chf Arg escallop betw 2 fleurs de lis Sa
MUCKLOW. *XPat 342, Arch 69, 95.*
MUCKLOW, Wm, of Worcs. *L10 94, 9. (lion a&l Gu).*

Lion & on chf 3 escallops
COOCUTRE, Walter of. *Stevenson 137.* c1371. *(or of Cambuslang, Bp of Dunblane 1362-3).*
RUSSELL, Jas. *Mill Steph.* 1509. *(imp Wise on brass to Jas R, & w Alice W, Swyre, Dorset).*
RUSSELL, John. *Mill Steph.* 1505. *(imp Frockemer on brass to Jn R, & w Elizabeth F, Swyre, Dorset).*

Arg lion & on chf Gu 3 escallops Arg
RUSSEL, Mons de. *AS 511.*

Arg lion Gu on chf Sa 3 escallops Arg
RUSSEL, Ld John, KG. *Leake. (a&l Az).*
RUSSELL. *L1 566, 2.*
RUSSELL. *CRK 1604. (imp ...).*
RUSSELL, Ld. *LH 577. (imp ...).*
[RUSSELL]. *LH 836. (imp [Tilley]).*
RUSSELL, Sir John. *WB I 42, 6.*
RUSSELL, [Wm, of Chenies]. *I2(1904)226. (qtg Az castle Arg; with 3 other Gd Qrs).*

Lion passt to sin on chf 3 escallops
SPONDON, Agnes de. *Bow XLVIII 2b.* 1316-17. *(w of Wm de S; grant of land in Tutbury).*

Lion & on chf 3 estoiles
INGLIS, Alex, of Tarvet. *Stevenson.* 1497.
INGLIS, Patrick, of Perth. *Stevenson.* 1575.
INGLIS, Thomas, portioner of Duddingston.

Stevenson. 1588.

Arg lion & on chf Gu 3 acorns Or s&l Vt
WOOD, Thomas, of Wood End, Berks. *L9 28b, 8. (lion a&l Az).*

Arg lion Sa on chf Sa 2 pairs of keys addorsed Arg
HYDE ABBEY. *LH 139. (wards interlaced in base).*
HYDE ABBEY. *L10 66b, 12. (keys paleways with bows interlaced).*
HYDE ABBEY. *RH, Ancestor iii 208. ('the Abbey of Hyde in Wynchestyr).*
HYDE ABBEY, Winchester. *PR(1515)34. (a&l Gu; keys wards uppermost the bows interlaced).*

Gu lion passt Arg on chf Az 2 mullets Arg
NEWTOUN. *Lyndsay 474.*

Az lion Arg on chf Az 3 mullets Arg
INGLIS, of Terwat. *Lyndsay 192.*
YNGLIS, of Lochende. *Lyndsay 260.*

Gu lion Or on chf Arg 3 mullets Sa
WICKHAM, of Irld. *LQ 70.*

Arg lion sejt & affronty Gu holding in dex paw thistle slipped Vt & in sin escutch Gu on chf Az salt Arg
LYON KING OF ARMS. *Lyon 1, 2. (imp by Sir Charles Arskine, Lyon King of Arms).*

Bendy lion pg on chf 3 salts
— *Blair N I 24, 55. (qtd 3 by Robt, 4th Ld Ogle; sculptured shield, Bothal Castle).*

Other beast & on chf

Per pale Gu and Arg antelope passt counterch on chf per pale Or and Az 2 crosslets fitchy counterch
— *L2 165, 12.*

Arg bat displd Sa on chf Arg 3 pales Gu
STENINGS, of Honicott [in Selworthy]. *Gerard 31.*
STENYNG. *L9 28b, 5.*

Gu ?boar salient Or on chf Or 2 mullets Gu
— *PLN 861. ('boar' has squirrel's tail & apple in mouth; qtd 2&3 by Edw Banbryg).*

Stag lodged on chf 2 buckles
GUNSTORP, Elizabeth, Dame de. *Birch 6656.* S' ELIZABET DAE DE G...STORP. 1342. *(1st of 2 shields).*

Per bend sin Sa and Or hound courant counterch on chf Az lion pg Or in border gobony Arg and Gu
STAYBER, Sir Lawrence. *XK 289.*

Dog with hare on its back on chf letters IEHS
[AILNER]. *Stowe-Bard ls vi 8. (shield shaped sl appended to deed of Emma, wid of Jn A, of Scoldham).*

Greyhound courant collared & on chf indented 3 roundels
BLACKWALL, Richard. *Mill Steph.* 1505. *(brass to Ric B & w Agnes Tunston,*

Taddington, Derbys).

Sa ox Arg standing on base barry wavy of 10
Arg and Az on chf Sa fimbr on lower edge
Arg 3 demi-nuns Arg crowned Or
ST FRIDESWIDE'S PRIORY. *L10 67, 6.*

Gu squirrel eating nut Or on chf Or 3 fleurs de
lis Az
STOKES, of Devon, Alderman of London. *BA
1318.*

Squirrel sitting on 2 branches issuing from flanks
& crossed saltireways on chf letters LUF ME
GOSPELAWE, Richard de. *Stowe-Bard ls vi 2.*
1305-6. *(shield shaped sl).*

Gu wolf erect & on chf Or 2 mullets Gu
— *WB IV 169, 783. (qtd 2&3 by Edw Baynbryg).*

Arg wolf Sa collared Or on chf Az 3 roundels
Or
WOODE, of London. *L9 27a, 12.*

BEAST & IN CHIEF

Lion & in chf

Billety lion in dex chf two annulets interlaced
[?BULMER]. *Blair D II 134, 293. (on tomb,
Hartlepool Ch).*

Lion in chf 2 bougets
CRICHTON, Laurence, of Rosse. *Stevenson.*

Gu lion pg Or in chf 3-turretted castle Arg
NORWICH CITY. *WLN 932.*

Crusily lion in dex chf cresc
HUNGAYTE, William, of Saxton, Yorks, Esq.
Birch 10907. BYDD.LEW.HER.MYD. *1575.*

Lion holding sword in dex forepaw in sin chf
cresc
SCRYMGEOUR, David, of Fardell. *Stevenson.*
1516. *(3rd s of Jn, Constable 1411-c1460).*

Lion in dex chf cresc
— *PRO-sls.* 1480-1. *(qtd by Thos Hoo,
Esq).*

Lion in sin chf cresc
HILTON, Adam. *Clairambault 4681.* 17 Aug
1446.

Gu lion & in dex chf cresc Arg
SALISBURY. *L1 610, 3.*

Gu lion Or in dex chf cross formy Vair
RESOUN, Sire Johan de. *N 1070.*

Az lion pg sans tail in chf cross formy Arg
DYKESONE, of Ormistoun. *Lyndsay 328.*

Arg lion Gu in chf 2 crosses couped Sa
BOLTON. *CRK 687.*

Lion passt crowned in chf open crown
PUPELPENNE, Geoffrey de, of Som. *Helyar
292.* S. GALFRIDI DE PUP...ENNE. *1347. (not
on shield; quitclaim of lands in Bere nr
Thornford in Hundred of Sherborne).*

Lion holding sword in dex forepaw in sin chf
fleur de lis
SCRYMGEOUR, Walter, of Glaswell. *Stevenson.* 1537. *(3rd s of Jn S of Glassary).*

Lion to sin in chf ?rose (or star)
MACDOWAL, Sir Wm, of Newrlant. *Stevenson.* 1653. *(English resident in Nether-
lands).*

Lion in sin chf 5foil
HERRING, Katrine. *Stevenson.* 1515. *(w of
David Monorgund of that ilk).*

Az lion qf Arg in sin chf goutte inverted Arg
GERARD, T. *CRK 571.*

Lion to sin in dex chf stag's head cab
WALLACE, Lambert, of Shewalton. *Stevenson.* 1493.

Gu lion in chf 2 dragons' heads & necks isst
from shell Or
— *PLN 1960. (qtd 2&3 by Arg 6 billets 3,
2, 1 Sa; all imp by Aylmer, Master of St John
of Jerusalem).*
— *PLN 1694. (qtd 2&3 by Arg 6 billets 3,
2, 1 Sa [Langridge]).*

Gu lion passt & 2 lozs Or
THORNEHAM, Robert. *TJ 1393. ('fondour de
Begham').*

Gu lion Or throwing over its head wyvern Vt
LANGREGE. *L9 42a, 2.*
LANGRISH, Walter. *XL 79.*

Lion holding sword in sin forepaw in sin chf
mullet
SCRYMGEOUR, James. *Stevenson.* 1503.

Lion passt in dex chf mullet
CANT, Sir Charles, parson of Orphir. *Stevenson.* 1496.

Lion passt to sin in chf mullet of 6 pts
FITZODO, Gilbert. *CombeAsp II 148.* +SIGILL
GILBERTI FIL ODONIS. *(not on shield).*

Semy de lis lion & in dex chf mullet
— *PRO-sls.* 1408-9. *(qtd by Robt Lovell,
Esq).*

Lion in chf 2 mullets
MOWAT, John. *Stevenson.* 1404.
NEWTON, Thomas of. *Stevenson.* 1470.
WYDELOCK, John. *PRO-sls.* 1372-3. *(?mul-
lets pd).*

Lion in chf 3 mullets
INGLIS, Master Alexr, Doctor of Decrees &
Master of Requests. *Stevenson.* 1473.

Lion in chf 3 roundels
CRICHTON, Marion. *Stevenson.* 1512. *(w of
Wm Lyon, of 'Estir Ogil').*

Untinc lion passt to sin Untinc in chf 3 roundels
1, 2 Sa
MAULEVERER, Ralph, of Lanarks. *Stevenson.*
1296. *(not on shield).*

Arg lion & in chf 3 roundels Gu
HARNAGE. *BA 557.*
HARNAGE. *FK II 1026.*

Gu lion passt Arg in chf 3 roundels Or
HETON. *LH 1145*.

Other beast & in chf &c
Arg boar & in chf 3 annulets Sa
— *FK II 780*.
Boar passt in chf salt
ST ANDREWS, House of the Friars Preachers.
Ash-sls 57. S-Comune, loci Frii: Predicatorum: civitis:
sancti: Anree.
Stag courant in sin chf escallop
BLAKEBORNE, John de. *Birch 7496*. S'IOH-IS
DE B-LAKEB-ORNE. 1487. *(sl used by Jn
Frensshe, of Chiddingley, Suss)*.
Stag tripp in sin chf 5foil
STRACHAN, John, of Thornton. *Stevenson.*
1470.
Sa mule stat Arg in sin chf mullet Or
MOYLE. *PLN 1752*.
Otter salient in sin chf mullet
MELDRUM, Master Wm. *Stevenson*. 1532.
(mullet pd).
MELDRUM, Wm. *Stevenson 131*. *(qtg 2&3
on chev an uncertain charge; Bp of Brechin
1489-1515/16)*.
MELDRUM, Wm, Bp of Brechin. *Stevenson.*
Otter salient to sin crowned in dex flank mullet
(6 pts)
MELDRUM, David, Canon of Dunkeld.
Stevenson. 1495.

Ox &c & in chf
Untinc bull pass Or in dex chf mullet Untinc
FITZGEFFRY, John. *Mill Steph*. 1480. *(brass
to Jn F & w Elizab, Sandon, Herts)*.
Bull passt to sin in 'flowery meadow' in chf
mullet (6 pts)
MURRAY, John. *Stevenson*. 1250. *(s&h of
Malcolm M, of Moravia)*.
Cow to sin on its back couped salt
CHRISTISON, Richard. *Stevenson*. 1492.
(Canon of Abernethy Collegiate Ch).
Paschal Lamb regard in chf cresc & mullet
BAXTER, Geoffrey, of Lossithe, Co Forfar.
Stevenson. 1296. *(not on shield)*.
Sa wolf salient Arg in dex chf cresc Arg
LOUTH. *Suff HN 41*. *(Mr Rowsse's Roll)*.

Beast & in chief & label
Bat displd in chf 3 pales & label
COLNE, John de, of Steyning, Som. *Steyning
6*. SIGILL IOHIS DE COLNE. 1342.

BEAST (LION) & OVER ALL
Lion & 2 bars
ORMONDE, Anne, Ctess of. *BirmCL-sls
492083*. 1397. *(qtd 2&3)*.
Gu lion Arg 2 bars Or
PLAYSTOWE. *XPat 7, Arch 69, 69*.
Gu lion Arg crowned Or 3 bars Or
LOVENHAM. *XF 153*.
Arg lion Erm 3 bars Sa
— *ML I 55*. *(middle bar passing under &
others over lion; 'Sylver a lyon rampant her-
myn debresyd wit ii berulettes & frett wit the
iiid sabyll')*.
Arg lion Sa 3 bars gemel Gu
FAIRFAX. *XF 467*.
FAIRFAX, Sir Guy. *BA 629*.
FAIRFAX, Sir Guy. *XL 231*.
FAIRFAX, Sir Thomas. *XK 136*. *(qrs 1&6)*.
FAIRFAX, of Walton, Yorks. *D4 35b*.
FAYERFAX, of Yorks. *L2 210, 1*. *(armed
Gu)*.
FAYRFAX, Sir Thomas. *WK 201*.
Arg lion qf Sa 3 bars gemel Gu
FAIRFAX. *CRK 496*.

Demi-lion & over all bend
Demi-lion & bend
MALLORY, John. *PRO-sls E40 A10871*.
1427-8.
MALORE, John, of Welton. *PRO-sls AS 107*.
1417-18.
Az semy de lis Or demi-lion Arg bend Gu
MORELE, Sire William. *O 87*. *('les [armes]
de Fraunce ove i lyoun recoupee dargent i
bende de goules')*.

Plain field lion ramp over all bend

Lion & bend Untinc
Lion & bend
— *Stevenson*. 1442. *(bend a ribbon; qtd by
Jas Douglas, 3rd E of Angus, 1437-46)*.
— *Stevenson*. c1470. *(bend a ribbon; qtd by
Isabella Sibbald, of Balgony who m 1 Geo
Douglas, 4th E of Angus, d1462, 2 ?Jn Car-
michael, of Balmadie, 3 Robt Douglas, of
Lochleven)*.
— *Durham-sls 2304*. *(legend destroyed, used
in 1322 by Jn of Stapleton)*.
— *Fowler I 300*. S. RICARDI HE..VD...(?). 6
May 1390. *(sl on lease in archives of Ripon
Cath; bend narrow)*.
— *Mill Steph*. 1479. *(qtd 2&3 by Chauncey
on remains of brass attributed to Jn C, of
Yedleston, Herts, & w Anne, dau of Jn
Leventhorpe, Sawbridgeworth, Herts)*.
— *Birch 12964*. 1336. *(imp in arms of*

Alice de Raydon).
— Stevenson. 1505. (qtd by Sir Alexr Boswell of Balmuto).
— PRO-sls. 1445. (imp by Benstede).
— PRO-sls. 1340. (imp by Alice de Reydon).
— Stevenson. 1398. (bend a ribbon; qtd by David Lindsay, 1st E of Crawford, d c1407 & many others).
— Birch 10706. late 14 cent. (imp in arms of Rob Hill).
ABERNETHY. Stevenson. 1366. (bend a ribbon; marshalled by Mgt Stewart, Ctess of Angus, d post 1417; 1st sl).
ABERNETHY, Sir Alexander. Stevenson 223-4. 1296. (bend a ribbon).
ABERNETHY, Sir George, 5th of Saltoun. Stevenson 223-4. (bend a ribbon; killed 1388).
ABERNETHY, Laurence. Stevenson 223-4. 1320. (bend a ribbon; s of Sir Wm de A, Kt).
BASTARD, John. Birch 7207. S'.....STARD. 1331. (Warden of Chapel of Holy Cross without walls of Colchester, Essex).
BERMYNGHAM, Isabella de. Dugd 17, 77. 1304. (1 of 3 shields on sl).
BERNER, John. Birch 7421. SIGILLUM IOHANNIS BERNER. 1337.
BERNERS, John, of Bepeden. PRO-sls. 1337-8. (bend a baston; shield betw 2 wyverns).
BLAUPRE, Margaret de. AnstisAsp I 217, 74. +SIGILLUM: MARGARETE: DE: BELLO: PRATO. 1330-1. (wid of Ralph de B, & dau of Mat de Furneaux).
BRAUNCHE, Philip. Birch 7752. Sigillum: Philippi: Braunche. 14 cent.
BRENESIN, Margaret. Stevenson. 1296.
BROWN, Janet. Stevenson. 1461. (charges indistinct; dau of Jn B, of 'ye Kenate').
BRUS, Simon. Dodsworth 95 F62b, HB-SND. (baston).
BUSCY, Oliver de. Bk of Sls 189. early Hen 3.
BUSEY, Oliver de. PRO-sls. 1270 & 71. (bend a baston).
BUZCI, Oliver de, of Notts, Yorks, &c. Birch 7974. +SIGILL'.OLIVERI.BVZCI.. temp Hen 3.
CHARLETON, Alan de. Dugd 17, 17. 1339-40.
CUMBES, Edmund de. Stowe-Bard ls x 4 MS ii 77. 1318-19. (sl appended to indenture by E de Cumbes, of Fyncham).
DEMPSTER, John, of Caraldston. Stevenson. 1509. (ribbon).
DOUGLAS, Gavin, Bp of Dunkeld. Stevenson 143. (ribbon; 3rd s of Archibald, E of Angus).
ELLON, Robert. Stevenson. 1357. (mullet in

sin chf; ribbon).
ESH, Roger of. Durham-sls 917. (d1355).
FAIRLIE, James. Stevenson. 1478.
FICHET, Thomas, Kt. Wells D&C II 616, 313. FIC...T. 1349-50. (grant of tenements in Wells).
FICHET, Thomas, Kt. PRO-sls. 1367-8. (baston).
?FINCHAM, John. Stowe-Bard ls xi 5 MS ii 95. 1342-3. (sl appended to deed whereby Agnes de Kelylston grants Burnham Hall to Jn, s of Adam de F).
FITZPIERS, John. PRO-sls AS 260. +Sigillum Iohannis fitzpiers. 1421-2.
FLETE, Laurence de, of Wisbeach, Cambs, Kt. Birch 9830. SIGILL LAVRENCII DE FLETE. 1347.
FORESTER, John le, of Stony-Stratford, Bucks. Birch 9869. +SEEL HELOUYS. 1330. (imp by cross flory dimid).
FYCHET, Thomas Kt. PRO-sls. temp Ric 2. (baston).
GERARD, John. PRO-sls. 1409-10. (baston).
HAUKWODE, John de, of Sible Hedingham. PRO-sls. 1341.
MALORY, John, of Welton, Northants. PRO-sls E40 A8461. 1427-8.
MERKE, Simon de. Birch 11741. 1334. (bend narrow).
MERTONE, Edmund de. Birch 11754. S' EDMVDI: DE: MERTONE. 1387. (bend narrow; sl used by Ric Robynns of Schobbedon, Herefs & of the Marches of Wales).
NORWYCH, John, of Yoxford, Suff. Birch 12249. SIGILLUM IOHANNIS NORWYCHE. 1420.
PERCY, Henry de, of Wilts. Birch 12555. ....PERCI. 13 cent. (lion uncertain).
RODES, John de. PRO-sls. 1299. (baston; obv of sl).
ROSS, David. Stevenson. 1508. (ribbon).
SCHYRHYLL. WB V 57.
SEGRAVE. CT 161.
SEGRAVE, Hugh de. PRO-sls. 1376-7. (baston).
SEGRAVE, Hugh de, of Berks, etc, Kt. Birch 13393. SIGILLU HUGONIS DE SEGRAVE. 1380.
SULTON, John. Middlewich 285. 1366. (s of Thos de S, of Attcocksfield, Ches).
TILIOL, Robert. PRO-sls Anc Deeds L 989. 1357. (baston; d1367).
TILLIOL, Peter. Durham-sls 2445. 1382. (baston).
[TILLIOL, Sir Peter]. Blair D II 145, 313. (baston; on buttress at dex side of doorway, Hilton Castle).
TOCOTES, Elizabeth, Lady of St Amand. Dingley xxxiv. 1492. (bend baston; imp Braybroke; brass in Bromham Ch, Wilts).

[?TOKETT]. *Dingley cccccviii. (baston; Cloister roof, Lacock Abbey).*

TYLIOL, Robert, Kt. *PRO-sls.* 1357. *(baston).*

WEYLAUND, Sir John de. *PRO-sls.* 1311-12. *(baston).*

Lion to sin & bend

BRISEWORTH, John. *Birch 7802.* SL...ANNIS... 1386. *(s of Jas B, of Thornham Magna, Suff).*

Lion & bend sin

Lion & bend sin

STYWARD, Thomas, of Swaffham. *Stowe-Bard 2s v 6.* Sigillum thome Styward. 1432-3. *(baston).*

Arg lion & bend

Arg lion Az bend Gu

GYSBOROW MONASTERY, Yorks. *D4 28b. (a&l Gu).*

LION, le Sr de. *Berry; Stodart pl 3. ([Ld of Glamis]; ribbon).*

SUTTON, Sir ... de. *CV-BM 103.*

Arg lion Az bend Or

— *E 6. (qtd by Percehay, of Yorks).*

Arg lion Gu bend Untinc

EGBASTON. *L2 180, 2.*

POLE, Lewiz de la. *LM 564.*

Arg lion Gu bend Sa

— *SHY 463. (imp Az 3 5foils Arg).*

BRANCH. *XL 89. (tail turned outwards; baston).*

BRANCHE. *L10 76, 13. (baston; a&l Az).*

BRANCHE. *FB 61. (baston).*

BRANCHYS. *PCL I 574.*

BRANNCHE. *L1 86, 2; L2 67, 5. (baston).*

BRAUNCH. *RL 34b, 3. (imp Arg on bend Gu 3 round buckles Arg).*

BRAUNCH. *RL 34b, 2.*

BRAUNCHE. *RL 70.*

BRAUNCHE, Sir Philip, of Lincs. *WB III 84b, 8. (a&l Az; baston).*

EGBASTON, Mons Rich de. *WJ 203.*

[FLEET], Lawrence de. *XL 345.*

FLETE. *L1 241, 2; L2 200, 2.*

FLETE. *SK 671. (baston).*

OSWALSTER. *PLN 1632. (a&l Az).*

OSWELSTRE. *L2 392, 7.*

Arg lion Or bend Gu

BEUPREY, of Cornw. *BA 949. (baston).*

Arg lion Purp bend Vt

SANDACRE, Monsire de. *CG 80. (baston).*

Arg lion Sa bend Untinc

— *LM 540.*

Arg lion Sa bend Gu

— *FK II 884. (bend narrow).*

BURNEL, Hue. *F 433. (baston).*

BURNEL, Phelip. *FW 342. (baston).*

BURNEL, Phelipe. *D a 241.*

BURNELL, Hue de. *L10 33b, 18. (a&l Gu).*

BURNELL, Hugh. *E I 381; E II 383.*

BURNELL, Hugo. *WLN 781. (baston).*

BURNELL, Philip le. *WLN 522.*

FYNES. *CT 357.*

GEY, Walter de. *WLN 512.*

PIERPOINT, Monsire. *CG 51. (baston; 'le Neveu').*

Arg lion Sa bend Or

PERPONCET, Sr Robert de. *M 45. (baston).*

PERPOUNT. *CKO 57. ('le Nevou').*

PIRPONT, Sr Robert. *L 113. (baston).*

Az lion & bend

Az lion Arg bend counterch

— *ML I 530. ('Asur a lyon rampaunt la cue hersle wit a ryght bastron countyrcoloryd. Or wit a dextr bastron &c. Or wit a primer bastron &c. Or la cue coyraunt &c').*

Az lion Arg bend Gu

— *PLN 1053. (ribbon; qtr 6 (of 7) of coat imp by My Lord of Clarence).*

COLVILE, John de. *XL 132. (baston).*

COLVYLL, Mons J. *WJ 282.*

CORVYLL. *L10 41, 10. (baston; a&l Gu).*

DONEVILL. *L1 191, 6; L2 151, 11. (L1 marginal note 'Colvill of Suff').*

VEILOND, Sire Johan de Veilond. *HA 37. (baston).*

VEILOND, Sir John de. *RB 73.*

WELAND. *L1 685, 4. (a&l Gu).*

WELAND, Monsire de. *CG 88.*

WELAND, Monsr de. *AS 344. (baston).*

WELEND, Roger de. *E I 675; E II 677. (baston).*

WELLAND, Thomas de. *WLN 711. (baston).*

WEYLAND. *XL 2. (baston).*

WEYLAND, Sr de. *CKO a 74. (baston).*

[WEYLAND]. *DX 60.*

WEYLAND, Sr Jo de. *L 119. (baston).*

WEYLAND, S John de. *ST 55.*

WEYLAND, of Radwell in S Petherton. *Gerard 117.*

WEYLANDE, Sire Johan de. *N 506. (baston).*

WEYLAUND, S' Jon. *PO 637. (baston).*

WEYLOND, Sir John. *BR V 202. (bend narrow).*

Az lion Arg bend Or

GERARD, John. *ME 138; LY A 263.*

WAYLAND, Sir Rechard. *BR V 213.*

WEELAND. *LE 131.*

WEYLANDE, Sire Richard de. *N 507. (baston).*

Az lion Or bend Arg

CALTHORP, Mons John de. *WJ 136.*

Az lion Or bend Gu

— *ML I 478.*

Gu lion & bend

Gu lion & bend Arg
— *1H7 1. (qtd II 3 i&iv by Pyckering; bend narrow; At Master Westons).*

Gu lion Arg & bend Az
GRACE. *CC 228, 200. (baston).*
TILLIOL, Geoffrey. *CRK 2000. (a&l Az; bend narrow).*
TILLIOL, Sir P. *CRK 1998. (a&l Az; bend narrow).*
TILLIOL, Mons' Piers. *TJ 1563. (baston).*
TILLIOLL, Mons' Piers. *TJ 90. (baston).*
TILLOL. *FK II 170. (baston; name added by Gibbon).*
TILLYOLF, Sr Robert. *M 39. (baston).*
TILLYOLL, Mons Robt. *WJ 150. (baston).*
TYLIEL. *D9; E6.*
TYLLIOL, S' Rob'. *PO 582. (baston).*
TYLLOL, Sir Robert. *BR V 114. (bend narrow).*
TYLLOL, Sire Robert. *N 1092. (baston).*
TYLYALL, Sir Pyerssa, of Cumb. *RH, Ancestor iv 245.*

Gu lion Arg bend Or
FFYCHET, S' Tho'. *PO 315.*

Gu lion Arg bend Sa
TILIOTT. *D4 31. (tinct of bend unclear).*
WARE, William de. *G 207. (baston).*

Gu lion Or bend Arg
FICHET. *CC 235b, 429.*
FITCHET. *XL 531.*

Gu lion Or bend Az
ABERNYCHEL, Patryk' de. *Q 496.*
[ARUNDEL], J. *WJ 239. (frere au Count).*
STUCLE, Johan de. *LM 161. (tinct of bend unclear).*

Or lion & bend

Or lion Az bend Gu
PERCY, R.. *WJ 103. ('uncle au count').*
VESCQ, Mons William de. *AS 352. (baston).*
VESCY, Mons' William. *TJ 128. (baston).*
VESEY. *XL 5. (baston).*
VESEY. *L1 658, 3. (a&l Gu).*

Or lion Gu bend Az
HOCKLEY. *LH 901. (baston).*
HOCKLEY. *XL 503.*
HOCKLEY. *RB 353. (bend narrow).*
HOKELEY. *L1 343, 6; L2 242, 4. (a&l Az).*
HOKELEY. *LE 366.*
HOKELEY. *CC 224b, 85.*
POLE, Lewys de. *Q 478.*

Or lion Gu bend Sa
— *SC 7. (ribbon; qtd 4 by E of Angus).*
— *SC 6. (qtd 2&3 by [Lindsay], E of Crawford).*
[ABERNETHY]. *Lyndsay 51. (ribbon; qtd by Lindesay, D of Montross).*
[ABERNETHY]. *Lyndsay 172. (qtd by*

Boswell, of Balnowtow).
[ABERNETHY]. *Lyndsay 60. (qtd 2 by Douglas, E of Angus).*
[ABERNETHY]. *Lyndsay 77. (ribbon; qtd by Lindsay, E of Crawford).*
]ABERNETHY]. *Berry; Stodart pl 1. (qtd by Le Conte de Craffort [E of Crawford]).*
ABIRNETHY, the lord of. *Lyndsay 131. (ribbon).*
ABRENTHY, le S'g'r de. *BL A 22. (bend narrow).*
POLE. *L9 101b, 12. (baston).*
POLE, Sire Lowys de la. *N 950.*
POULE. *L1 526, 5.*
WEMYSS. *Berry; Stodart pl 4. (ribbon; qtd 2&3 by Bisset, [Master of Rires]).*

Or lion Sa bend Arg
[HENGEBACH], 'Monsire Johan de Heynbaugh'. *CA 245. (baston; ?bro of Count of Julich).*

Sa &c lion & bend

Sa lion Arg bend Gu
— *BA 1b. (qtd 2&3 by Sir Edw Halle).*
— *I2(1904)180. (qtd 3 by Hilleradon, of Memlane, Devon; added by Jos Holland, c1630).*
CHURCHILL. *CRK 291.*
KYNGESTON. *CT 352.*
MORLEY, Monsire Rob de. *CG 52. (coat unclear).*

Vt lion Or bend Gu
— *LE 403. (baston).*
BEAUPRE. *XL 254. (baston).*
BEAUPRE. *Gerard 31. (bend narrow).*
BEAUPRE, Sr de. *CKO 66. (baston; gloss on Sr de Montenake).*
BEAUPRE, Monsr Rauf de. *AS 180. (baston).*
BEAUPREE. *L10 30b, 8.*
BEAUPREE, Mons' Rauf de. *TJ 33. (baston).*
DIPER. *L1 196, 3; L2 153, 9. (armed Az).*

Field patterned, lion ramp plain, bend plain

Barry of 12 Arg and Gu lion Sa bend Or
RIRPOND, Henry. *LR 47. (baston).*

Burely Arg and Gu lion Sa bend Or
PERPOUNT, Henr' de. *WLN 630. (baston).*
PERPUND, H. *F 122. (baston).*
PIERPONT, Henry. *XF 376. (a&l Or; baston).*
PIRPUND, Henry. *E I 471; E II 473. (baston).*

Per fess Gu and Az lion Arg bend Or
ROCHINGES. *L1 542, 5.*
ROTHING. *XF 670. (a&l Or; baston).*
ROTHYNGES. *FK II 383. (baston).*

Per pale Or and Untinc lion Gu bend Untinc
  BYGOT, Rauf. *LM 559.*
Per pale Or and Sa lion Gu bend Arg
  BYGOT, Rauf. *Q 351.*
Per pale Or and Vt lion Gu bend Arg
  BIGOD, Raf. *F 132. (baston).*
  BIGOD, Rauf. *E I 301. (baston).*
Arg billetty & lion Sa bend Gu
  — *LE 287. (baston).*
Crusily lion & bend
  HAINTON, John le. *Arch Journ lxxix 78.* S'
  johannis de hainton abbatis de Bardenay. *(Abbot of*
  Bardney, Lincs 1385-1404).
  HAYNTONE, John, Abbot of Bardney, Lincs.
  Birch 2586. 1385-1404.
Sa crusily lion & bend Arg
  WAUTEVILL, Sr Geffrey. *L 120.*
Semy de lis lion & bend
  BEAUMONT, Alice de. *Bk of Sls 14.* 1343.
  (formerly w of Hy de B; suo jure Ctess of
  Buchan; imp by Conyer, E of B).
  BEAUMONT, Henry de, Kt. *PRO-sls.* 4 Oct
  1315. *(baston).*
  BEAUMONT, Sir Henry de. *PRO-sls.* 15 Nov
  1326. *(baston).*
  BEAUMONT, Katherine de. *PRO-sls AS 494.*
  SIGILLUM CATHERINE .... 1358-9. *(sin sh of*
  2).
  BELLOMONTE, Henry de. *Birch 7289.* ...rici de
  Bellomonte. 1366. *(3rd B Beaumont, Ld of*
  Loughteburgh).
  BELLOMONTE, Henry de, E of Buchan, 1st B
  Beaumont. *Stevenson.* 1336.
Semy de lis lion & bend sin
  BEAUMONT, Henry de, Constable of Engld.
  Birch 5675. ...L.DE.... 1322. *(equestr sl).*
Az flory & lion Or bend Gu
  BEAUMOND, Sir Hy de. *HA A 1. (baston).*

Lion ramp charged or patterned &c bend plain

Az lion Arg ch with annulet Sa bend Gu
  WEYLOND. *PT 231. (baston).*
  WEYLONDE. *DV 64a, 2539. (baston).*
Arg lion Gu ch on shldr with 5foil Arg bend Az
  ECHEBASTON, Sr Richard. *N 825. (baston).*
  ECLELASTONE, of Leics. *LE 43.*
Arg lion Sa ch on shldr with 5foil Erm bend Az
  ECHEBASTON, Sr Richard. *O 27. (baston).*
Erm lion Gu ch on shldr with 5foil Arg bend Az
  ECLELASTON, of Leics. *BA 31, 275. (bas-*
  ton).
Or lion Erm bend Az
  HAMELYN, S Jehan. *GA 143. (baston).*
  HAMLYN, Sir John. *LH 221. (baston).*
Per pale Untinc lion Erm bend Untinc
  NORWICHE, John. *Mill Steph.* 1428. *(brass,*
  Yoxford, Suff).

Per pale Az and Gu lion Erm bend Or
  NORWICH. *XL 22. (baston).*
  NORWICH. *LE 140. (a&l Gu).*
  NORWICHE. *L9 85a, 11.*
  NORWICHE, John. *Mill Steph. (glass to Jn N*
  & w Maud, E window, Chancel, Yoxford,
  Suff).
Or lion Vair bend Gu
  BEAUPRE, Monsire Ralph de. *CG 69.*

Lion crowned bend plain

Lion crowned & bend
  AUBRAI. *Birch 9844.* IE. SVS'. AVBRAI S' RO
  (?). 1354. *(used by Adam de Foleford, of*
  Newton Abbot, Devon).
  BEESTON, William de. *Birch 7310.* SIGILLUM
  WIL...VN. 1398. *(sl used by Ralph de Bees-*
  ton of Pudsay, Yorks).
  ?CODYNGTON, William de. *Birch 8760.*
  1368.
  SEGRAVE, Henry de, Sheriff of Norf & Suff.
  PRO-sls. 1308-9. *(baston; shield &*
  trapper).
Untinc lion Arg crowned Or bend Gu
  SEGRAVE, Hew. *PT 333. (baston).*
Arg lion Gu crowned Or bend Sa
  CORNEWAILE. *DV 45b, 1787. (baston).*
Or lion Sa crowned Arg bend Gu
  SEGRAVE. *HA 12, 2. (armed Arg).*
Sa lion Arg crowned Untinc bend Or
  SEGRAVE. *CT 181. (bend narrow).*
Sa lion crowned Arg bend Gu
  SEGRAVE, Henr de. *LM 187.*
Sa lion Arg crowned Or bend Gu
  SEGRAVE. *HA 10. (baston).*
  SEGRAVE. *RB 14. (baston).*
  SEGRAVE, Mons de. *Q 464.*
  SEGRAVE, Sire Henri de. *N 793. (baston).*
  SEGRAVE, Henry de. *G 85. (baston).*
  SEGRAVE, 'How'. *PLN 1207. (baston).*
  SEGRAVE, Hugh. *BG 224. (baston).*
Sa lion Arg crowned & bend Or
  SEGRAVE, Simon. *ST 8. (baston; bro of*
  Nychol de Segrave).
  SEGRAVE, Sire Symon de. *N 794. (baston).*
Sa lion Sa crowned Or bend Gu
  SEGRAVE, S Henry. *ST 6. (baston; lion rec-*
  tius Arg).
Gu lion Vair crowned & bend Or
  EVERINGHAM, Sir Thomas d'. *CKO 93.*
  (bend narrow).
  EVERINGHAM, Monsire Thos de. *CG 59.*

Lion qf bend plain

Lion qf & bend
  SUTTON, Margaret. *Stowe-Bard 2s iv 2.*
  SIGILL' MARGARETE D'SVTTVN. 1400-1.

Gu lion qf Or bend Az
  BUREWASSH, Mons J de. *WJ 247.*
  BUREWASSHE. *L10 81b, 14. (a&l Az).*
  BURGHERSH, John de. *XL 370.*
Or lion qf Sa bend Gu
  WELLES. *XL 491. (bend narrow).*
  WELLES, Sire Felip de. *N 669. (baston).*
  WELLES, Mons John de. *WJ 339.*
Sa lion qf Or bend Gu
  KINGESTONE, Sire Walter de. *N 733.*
  KINGSTON, Sir Walter de. *PT 1022. (baston).*

Lion passt & bend
Per pale Or and Gu lion passt Arg bend Az
  PLAYS. *XL 201. (riband).*
  PLAYS. *L9 100b, 8. (baston).*

Lion guardant & bend
Lion gard & bend
  BATHE, Eleanor de. *AnstisAsp I 211, 55.*
  1349-50.
Gu lion gard Or collared Az bend Az
  — *PLN 523.*
  POLDEGREVE, Symond. *WB IV 180b, 984.*
  (a&l Az; baston).
Az semy de lis & lion pg Arg bend Untinc
  HOLAND. *CVL 426. (baston).*
Az semy de lis & lion gard Arg ch on shldr with
  mullet Gu bend Gu
  HOLLAND, Charlis. *LY A 24. (baston).*
Az semy de lis & lion pg Arg ch on breast with
  mullet Gu bend Gu
  HOLAND. *DV 48a, 1892. (baston).*
Az semy de lis & lion gard Arg ch on shldr with
  mullet Sa bend Gu
  HOLAND, of Lancs. *LH 906. (baston).*

Lion ramp & bend patterned

Lion & bend Erm &c
Lion Untinc bend Erm
  — *PRO-sls. 1404-5. (imp by Rob Hull; baston).*
  FICHET, Thomas, Kt. *PRO-sls. 1367-8.*
  (baston).
  FYCHETES. *PT 436.*
  HULL, Robert. *PRO-sls BS 24.* Sigillum rob ...
  hulle. *1404-6. (baston).*
Az lion Or bend Erm
  CALTHORP. *L10 40b, 6.*
Gu lion Or bend Erm
  FALCON. *GutchWdU. (Old Library, Exeter*
  College).
  FALERON. *L1 244, 6; L2 202, 4. (marginal*
  note in L2 'Fuhet').

FICHET. *L1 259, 6.*
FICHET. *CRK 2054.*
FICHET, Thomas. *XL 372. (a&l Az).*
FICHETT, of Spaxton. *Gerard 32.*
FITCHET, Monsire Thomas. *AN 311. (baston).*
FYCHET, Mons Th. *WJ 244.*
FYCHETT. *DV 56b, 2230.*
HALTUN. *PLN 1081. (a&l Az).*
Arg lion Gu bend Vt fretty Or
  SANDIACRE. *LS 218. (a&l Az).*
Arg lion Purp bend Vt fretty Or
  SANDACRE, Monsr. *AS 299. (baston).*
  SANDIACRE. *XL 7. (a&l Az).*
  SANDIACRE, Sr de. *CKO 72.*
Arg lion Sa bend Gu fretty Or
  SANDIACRE, Geoffrey de. *LM 354.*
  SENDIACRE, Galfrs de. *Q 534.*

Lion & bend gobony
Lion bend gobony
  LUCIEN, Warinus, dominus de Brokehole,
  Northants. *Bow XXXV 7.* +Sig Warini Lucien.
  1384-5.
  SUTTON, John, 2nd Ld. *Lawrance 43. 1356.*
  (d 1356; tomb, Sutton-on-Hull, Yorks).
  WESSINGTON, Sir Walter de. *Durham-sls*
  2608. 1318.
Lion Untinc bend gobony Erm and Untinc
  [FULTON]. *Proc Soc Antiq IX 2S 329. (1 of*
  7 shields on cuir-bouilli chalice case, Caws-
  ton, Norf).
Arg lion Az bend gobony Arg and Az
  — *PT 344. (baston).*
Arg lion Az bend gobony Arg and Gu
  LUCYEN, Sr Piers. *CKO 71. (Sr de Fulton*
  overwritten; ?field Or).
Arg lion Az bend gobony Gu and Or
  [FAUCO]NBERGE, Sr de. *CKO 86.*
Arg lion Az bend gobony Or and Gu
  DOKESEYE, S Richard. *N 965. (bend a bas-*
  ton).
  FACONBERGE, Monsire Walter de. *CG 60.*
  FAUCOMBERGE, Sr Waultre. *M 67. (bend a*
  baston).
  FAUCONBERG, Monsr John. *SD 97. (bend a*
  baston).
  FAUCONBERG, William. *XL 131. (bend a*
  baston).
  FAUCONBERGE, Sire Walter. *N 1079. (bend*
  a baston).
  FFAUCONBERGE, Mons W. *WJ 274.*
Arg lion Gu bend gobony Or and Az
  LUCIEN, Mons' Piers. *TJ 89. (bend a bas-*
  ton).
  LUCIEN, Sir Waryn. *SK 603. (bend a baston*
  gobony of 4).
  LUCION, Monsire de. *CG 103.*
  LUCYEN. *L9 40a, 4.*

LUKYN, Warren. *XL 470.*
Arg lion Gu bend gobony Or and Gu
   LUSYON. *PLN 961. (langued Sa).*
Arg lion Sa bend gobony Or and Gu
   DOCKESSAY, of Salop. *L2 164, 3.*
Gu lion Arg bend gobony Arg and Az
   — *BA 672. (imp by Tempest, of Studeley).*
Gu lion Arg bend gobony Az and Arg
   WESSYNGTON, Mons' Wautier de. *TJ 157.*
Gu lion Arg bend gobony Az and Or
   — *CB 41.*
Gu lion Or bend gobony Arg and Az
   AROUNDEL, Johannes de. *Q II 173.*
   ARUNDELL. *CKO a 47.*
   HYLL, Wylyam, of Som. *RH, Ancestor v 177.*
Gu lion Or bend gobony Az and Arg
   AROUNDEL, Hen de. *Q 176.*

Or &c lion & bend gobony
Or lion Az bend gobony Arg and Gu
   — *PLN 112. (qtd 2&3 by Ld Mauley).*
   — *D4 28b. (qtd 2&3 by Bulmer of Yorks).*
   PERCY. *CG 79.*
   PERCY. *CT 282. (or Sutton; tincts unclear).*
   SUTLON, de Hols. *WJ 95. ([sic for Fulton or Sutton]).*
   SUTTON. *SK 79. (baston).*
   SUTTON, Monsr Johan de. *AS 130. (baston).*
   SUTTON, Sire Johan de, de Holderness. *O 134. (baston).*
   SUTTON, Mons John de. *TJ 29. (baston).*
   SUTTON, Monsire John de. *AN 89. (baston).*
   SUTTON, Sir John de, of Holderness. *CV-BM 211. (baston).*
   SUTTONE, S' Jon. *PO 410. (written above in Elizabeth hand is 'Suttone of Holdurnesse').*
Or lion Az bend gobony Or and Gu
   SUTTON, Mons John de. *SD 95. (baston).*
Or lion Az bend gobony Erm and Gu
   SUTLON, T. *WJ 99. (son frere).*
Or lion Vt bend gobony Arg and Gu
   SUTTON. *XL 93. (baston).*
   SUTTON. *XL 642. (?'de Hold').*
   SUTTON, Sgr de. *CKO a 71.*
Or lion Vt bend gobony Erm and Gu
   SUTTON. *LS 28. (a&l Gu).*
   SUTTON. *XL 533.*
Sa lion Arg bend gobony Gu and Or
   MARCHE, Thomas. *WB IV 185, 1065.*
Sa lion Arg bend gobony Or and Gu
   — *PLN 676. (a&l Gu).*

Field patterned lion & bend gobony
Erm lion Az bend gobony Or and Gu
   FAUCONBERG, John de. *XL 133. (baston).*
Az semy of couped crosses & lion Or bend
   gobony Arg and Gu
   BEMUND, S' henr. *BR IV 21. (baston).*

FAUCONBERGE, J de. *WJ 275.*
Az semy de lis & lion Or bend gobony Arg and
   Gu
   — *WJ 121.*
   BEAMONT. *DV 42a, 1655.*
   BEAMONT. *L10 25b, 15.*
   BEAUMONT, Sire de. *XL 639.*
   BEAUMONT, le Sr de. *AS 56. (baston gobony of 6).*
   BEAUMONT, Sire Henri. *N 120. (baston).*
   BEAUMONT, S Henry de. *GA 2. (baston).*
   BEAUMONT, Sire Henry. *O 84. (baston).*
   BEAUMONT, Sire Henry. *HA 9. (baston).*
   BEAUMONT, Sr Henry. *M 3. (baston).*
   BEAUMONT, Henry, E of Buchan. *LMS 71. (d1340).*
   BEAUMONT, Sr Hy de. *WNS 25b, 32.*
   ('... por dazur flurete dor ou un lion rampant dor ou un baston gobone dar et de gu').
   BEMONDE, le Sour de. *PO 204. (baston).*
   GAINCTE, Sir Gylbert of. *PCL I 572.*
Az semy de lis & lion Or bend gobony Gu and
   Arg
   BEAUMOND, Mons' Lowys. *TJ 141.*
Az semy de lis & lion Or bend gobony Or and
   Gu
   BEAUMONT, Monsire de. *CG 41. (gobony of 6).*
Az semy de lis & lion Or bend gobony Erm and
   Gu
   — *WJ 117.*
   BEAUMONT. *L10 25b, 17.*
   BEAUMONT, T de. *WJ 118.*
   BEAUMONT, Thomas de. *XL 640.*
Az semy de lis & lion Or bend gobony Erm and
   Sa
   BAYEMAN. *L10 25b, 19. (?lis Arg).*

Lion patterned & bend gobony
Az lion Or fretty Or (sic) bend gobony Arg and
   Gu
   BEAUMONT, S Henry. *ST 101. (baston).*

Lion qf & bend gobony
Or lion qf Sa bend gobony Arg and Gu
   BAVENT. *L10 20b, 10. (a&l Gu).*
   BAVENT, Mons Rob. *WJ 338.*
   BAVENT, S Robert de. *GA 55. (baston).*
   BAVENT, Robert, of Forsett, Lincs. *XL 171. (baston).*

Lion & bend Vair
Gu lion Or bend Vair
   ASTON. *L1 18, 4; L2 10, 6.*
   ASTONE, Sire Richard de. *N 897.*

Lion ramp & bend charged

Lion & on bend 3 indistinct objects
— *Durham-sls 1685. (used by Wm of Lythepole).*
BURNEL, William, Constable of Dublin Castle. *PRO-sls. 1292. (baston).*

Lion & on bend 3 buckles
SPENS, John. *Stevenson 158. 1503. (succentor of Cathedral, Moray; bend unclear).*

Arg lion Sa on bend Gu 3 buckles Or
BURNELL, Walter. *E II 385.*
GEI, Water de. *E I 383.*
GEY, Walter de. *F 416.*

Lion & on bend 3 crosslets fitchy
[WATTON]. *Mill Steph. 1512. (imp by Peckham on brass to Thos P & w Dorothy [Horne], Wrotham, Kent).*

Arg lion Gu on bend Sa 3 crosslets fitchy Arg
— *PLN 1287. (?crosses botonny; lion a&l Or).*
WATTON, Wylyam, of Kent. *RH, Ancestor v 181.*
WHADDON, William. *CRK 682.*

Arg lion Gu on bend Sa 3 crosses botonny fitchy Arg
WATTON. *PLN 839. (?crosslets).*

Arg lion Gu on bend Sa 3 crosses pommy fitchy Arg
WATTON. *WB IV 156b, 555.*

Gu lion Arg on bend Sa 3 crosslets fitchy Arg
ALDEFELDE, Mons Robert de. *TJ 48.*

Gu lion Or on bend Arg 3 crosses formy Sa
GIBBON. *BA 840.*

Lion & on bend escallops &c

Lion & on bend 3 escallops
HILL, John, of Trill. *Bow XVIII 7.*
HYLLE, John., Ld of Esterpostrugge. *PRO-sls. 1423-4. (baston).*

Arg lion Gu on bend Az 3 escallops Or
MYDDYLTON, of Yorks. *MY A2 251.*

Arg lion Sa on bend Gu 3 escallops Untinc
BURNEL, Phelip. *F 426. ('escallops not visible').*

Arg lion Sa on bend Gu 3 escallops Arg
BURNEL, of Irld. *L2 80, 11. (a&l Gu).*
BURNELL, Philipp de. *L10 33b, 19. (a&l Gu).*

Arg lion Sa on bend Gu 3 escallops Or
BURNELL, Phelip. *E I 385; E II 387.*

Gu lion Arg on bend Az 3 escallops Or
— *WB III 121, 7.*
MIDDILTON, Elias de. *Q II 592.*
MIDDLETON, Sir .... *CRK 1461. (a&l Or).*
MYDDILTON, Elias de. *SES 50.*
MYDDYLTON, of Yorks. *MY 251.*
MYDYLTON. *L1 460, 2; L2 342, 5.*

Arg lion Gu on bend Sa 5foil in chf Arg
BRANCHE. *SK 1062.*

Lion & on bend mullets

Sa lion Arg on bend Gu mullet Arg
[CHURCHILL]. *DevonNQ VIII ii 32. (imp by [de Esse], E Window, Theuborough Chapel, Sutcombe).*

Arg lion Gu on bend Sa 3 mullets Arg
[FLEET]. *CKO 84.*

Arg lion Gu on bend Sa 3 mullets Or
LOURARANCE, Mons. *WJ 204.*

Az semy de lis & lion Or on bend gobony Arg and Gu 3 mullets Sa
BEAUMOND, Andr'. *WJ 119.*

Arg lion Gu crowned Or on bend Sa 3 mullets Arg
CORNUALL. *L10 42b, 19.*
[CORNWALL], S' Geffray. *R 44. (pd mullets of 6 pts).*
CORNWALL, Sir Geoffrey. *WNS 26, 63. ('Sire Geffrei de Cornewaille por dar ou un lion rampant de gou corone dor baston de sable 3 moletz dor'; pd mullets of 6 pts).*

Arg lion Gu crowned Or on bend Sa 3 mullets Or
CORNEWALE, Monsire Jeffrey de. *CG 73.*
CORNEWALL, Sire Geffray. *O 161 & 187.*

Lion & on bend roundels

Lion on bend 3 roundels
STROGUL, Balduin de. *Birch 13741. S' BALDVIN D' STOGVL. 14 cent. (?foreign).*

Arg lion Gu on bend Az 3 roundels Or
BOKENHAM. *XF 148. (imp by Bokenham).*
BOKENHAM, John de. *CA 210.*
BOKNOM. *SHY 280.*

Arg lion Gu on bend Sa 3 roundels Or
EGREVALE, Robert. *XL 353.*
EGREYNALL. *L2 180, 3.*
EGRYNALE, Mons Robt. *WJ 208.*

Arg lion Gu crowned Arg on bend Az 3 roundels Or
[BOKENHAM]. *Farrer I 58. (glass, Old Buckenham Ch, Norf).*

Arg lion Gu crowned Or on bend Sa 3 roundels Or
CORNUALL. *L10 42b, 18.*
CORNEWALE, Monsire Symond de. *CG 76.*
CORNWALL, Sir Edmund. *WNS 26, 62. ('Sire Edmund de Cornewaille po dar ou un lion rampant de gou come dor baston de sa besante de iii besanz dor').*

Arg lion Gu on bend Sa 5 roundels Or
BOKINGHAM, Sgr de. *CKO a 77.*

Arg lion Gu crowned Or bend Sa ch with 5 roundels Or
CORNEWALL, Sire Edmund. *L 211; O 160 & 188.*

CORNWAYL, Sir Edmund. *CVM 798.*

Lion ramp & bend modified
Arg lion Gu bend [embattled] Vt
    STEWARD. *PLN 1912.*
Lion bend engr
    ABERNETHY, Alex, 4th Ld, of Saltoun.
    Stevenson 224. c1512-29. (*qtg 2&3 3 piles
    in pt; mullet in centre chf*).
    FAIRLIE, Wm, of Braid. *Stevenson.* 1520.
Lion to sin bend engr
    FAIRLIE, Archibald, friar of Braid. *Stevenson.*
    1520.
Arg lion Gu bend engr Sa
    ABERNETHY, Jean d'. *Gelre; Stodart pl D3.*
Gu lion Arg bend engr Or
    WESTON, Roger de. *CKO a 53.* (*baston*).
Gu lion Arg bend engr Sa
    MOWBRAY, Sr Phillip de, d'Escoce. *M 53.*
Or lion Gu bend engr Sa
    FAIRLE, of that ilke Braide (sic). *Lyndsay
    294.*
Sa lion Or bend engr Gu
    FLETE, John. *LE 277.* (*a&l Gu*).
Vt lion Arg bend engr Gu
    DYPRE. *L10 58, 15.*
Per fess Gu and Az lion Arg bend engr Or
    ROTHING. *XL 541.*
    ROTHYN, de. *SK 466.* (*baston*).
Gu crusily fitchy Or lion Arg bend engr Sa
    WESTON, Monsire Roger de. *CG 58.*
Az semy de lis & lion Or bend engr Gu
    BEAMOUND, Mons Henry de. *CA 83.* (*bas-
    ton*).
Sa lion Arg crowned Or bend engr Gu
    SEGRAVE, Sr Henry de. *L 126.*
    SEGRAVE, Sire Johan de. *N 796.*
Sa lion Or bend engr Gu ch with 3 annulets Arg
    FLETE, Laurens. *LE 278.* (*a&l Gu; bend
    narrow*).
Lion to sin bend sin engr ch in fess pt with mul-
let
    ABERNETHY, Geo, of Ugstone. *Stevenson
    224.* 1482. (*3rd s of Laurence, 1st Ld Aber-
    nethy*).
    STYWARD, Thomas, of Swaffham, Norf.
    Birch 13767. SIGILLUM THOME STY[WARD].
    1456-7.
    TRABOME. *SussASColl xxvi 272.* S.I.DEI TRA-
    BOME. *?13 cent.* (*sl found 1874 at Lewes*).
Lion bend indented
    BURNEL, Robert, Ld of Hodenhulle. *PRO-sls.*
    1316-17. (*baston*).
Lion bend lozy
    BURNEL, Robt. *Bk of Sls 480.* 1301.
Arg lion & bend of 6 lozs Gu
    VARDES, de. *BA 1204.*

Arg lion Gu bend raguly Or
    STYWARD. *LS 92.*
    STYWARD. *CC 228b 217.* (*?inserted by
    Augustine Styward, temp Eliz*).
    STYWARD, of Norf. *L9 26b, 9.* (*legend in
    later hand; baston*).
Gu lion Or bend raguly Sa
    COMBES, William. *LV 77.* (*baston*).

Lion & 2 or more bends
Lion 2 bends
    THORNBERY, John de, Kt. *PRO-sls.* 1383-4.
    (*narrow*).
    THORNEBURY, Philip. *PRO-sls.* 1402. (*bas-
    tons*).
Arg lion Az 2 bends Gu
    — *FK II 182.* (*narrow*).
Arg lion Az 2 bends Gu chf Or
    — *I2(1904)117.* (*qtd 2&3 by 'Mayster
    Appellyerd'*).
Per fess Or and Arg lion Az 2 bends Gu
    — *SK 445.* (*gemel bendways*).
    — *PLN 456.* (*?bends gemel*).
    BRUSELL, S. Jamys. *WB IV 175b, 899.*
Sa lion Arg 3 bends Gu
    — *RH, Ancestor ix 174.* (*bends narrow*).

Lion & chevron
Lion & chev
    HARDRES, Edmund. *Arch Cant iii 144.*
    1443-4. (*sl*).
    HARDRES, Edmund de, of Kent. *Birch 10467.*
    1410.
Arg lion Gu chev Or
    HARDRES, Robert de. *FW 282.*
Gu lion Arg chev Or
    [HARDRES]. *FK II 683.* (*name in later hand*).
    HARDRES, Edmond, of Kent. *XV I 1147.*
Gu lion Erm chev Or
    HARDES, Edmond, of Kent. *LH 766.*
    HARDIS, Edmund. *Kent Gentry 217b, 397.*
    HARDIS, Emond, of Kent. *WB III 110b, 6.*
    HARDRES, Emond, of Kent. *MY 204.*
    HARDUS, Kent. *L1 351, 2; L2 263, 9.*
Erm lion Gu chev Or
    HARDRES, Robert de. *A 43.*

Lion & escutcheon
Or lion per pale Az and Gu on escutch Gu 3
    female heads Untinc
    — *Arch Journ (Chichester 1853) 95.* c1530.
    (*painting, Amberley Castle, Suss; ?for 1 of
    the Sibyls*).

Lion ramp & fess

Lion plain, fess plain
Lion & fess
  CALVERLAY, John de, of Calverley, Yorks. *Birch 8273.* AMOVRS AHOVRS. *1324.*
  CHALMERS, Wm. *Stevenson. 1528. (s of Robt C).*
  [COOMBES]. *Mill Steph. c1440. (qtd 2&3 by Halsham on brass to Philippa, dau & coh of David de Strabolgi, E of Athol, wid of Sir Ralph Percy & w of Jn Halsham, d1395, West Grinstead, Suss).*
  HAUTE, Henry de. *PRO-sls.* ...NRICUS DE AWTE. *1349-50.*
  MUNDHAM, John de. *SussASColl xl 115. 1375-6.*
  [MUNTHAM, de]. *Lambarde 184, 246. 1390. (or Cumbes; qtd by Halsham & imp Strabolgi on mont to Philippa, w of Jn H, & dau & coh of David de S, E of Athol, West Grinstead, Suss).*
  NUGGE, Peter. *Birch 12267.* S'...ET...E... *1342. (s of Wm N, of Pekenham, Suff).*
  PERCY, Henry. *PRO-sls. 19 May 1385.*
  PERCY, Henry de, Chevr. *Birch 12559.* S' HENRICY DE PERCY CHR. *(?4th Baron, 1368-1377, afterwards 1st E of Northd; bar narrow & in chf).*
  SEGRAVE, Nicholas de, Ld of Stowe. *Birch 13400.* Motto: Bon Ivr eit ke se sel deit (Bon jour a qui ce sceau doit). *1301. (bar narrow).*
  WIGHAL, John. *Birch 6551.* +SIGILLUM IOHANNIS FILI WALTERI DE WIGHAL'. *1286. (equestr sl).*
Arg lion Gu fess Or
  BARBY, Thomas, of Irld. *LQ 68. (as painted; a&l Az).*
Or lion Gu fess Or
  BARBY, Thomas, of Irld. *LQ 68. (as blazoned; a&l Az).*
Crusily lion & fess
  HAWTE, Henry de. S' HENRICUS DE HAWTE. *Birch 16483. (above shield hare in her form). 1343.*

Lion crowned, fess plain
Lion crowned & fess
  — *Mill Steph. (imp by Hoare on brass to Thos Hoore, citizen & mercer of London, & w Alice, Digswell, Herts).*

Lion qf, fess plain
Lion qf & fess
  HASTANG, Robert. *PRO-sls.* BON WR EIT KE SESEL DEIT [motto]. *1301 & 1305. (2queued).*
Lion qf & fess
  HASTANG, Robert. *Birch 10526.* +SIGILLUM ROBERTI HASTANG. *1301. ('Dominus de la*

Desiree').
Or lion qf Vt fess Untinc
  — *WB I 27b, 3.*

Lion gard, fess plain
Az semy de lis & lion gard Arg fess Gu
  HOLAND, Sir Roger, of Lancs. *WB III 73b, 5. (a&l Gu).*
  HOLAND, Sir Roger, of Lancs. *LH 744.*
Vt lion gard Erm fess Gu
  — *WK 296. (qtd 4 by Sir ... Arundell, of Treryse).*
  — *I2(1904)180. (qtd 5 by Yeo, of Heampton, Devon).*

Lion with fess patterned
Lion & fess checky
  GRUWEL, John, sen, of Cawes, Salop. *Birch 10317. 1323.*
Arg lion Sa fess checky Or and Az
  MILDE. *L1 434, 1; L2 333, 12.*
Arg lion Sa fess counter gobony Arg and Sa
  BURLEY, John de, of Salop. *CY 88, 350.*
Arg lion Sa fess counter gobony Or and Az
  BURLEY. *L10 82, 2. (a&l Gu).*
  MILDE. *XL 81.*
  MILDE. *XF 189.*
  MYLDE. *L9 67a, 10.*
Arg lion Gu fess vairy Az and Or
  WYNFLEW. *XL 77.*

Lion qf, fess patterned
Arg lion qf Gu fess vairy Az and Or
  WINSLOW. *XF 167. (1 row of vairy).*
Gu lion qf Arg fess vairy Az and Or
  WINSLOW, Thomas. *LV 86.*

Lion with fess modified
Arg lion Sa fess engr Gu
  POWELL, Benedict. *CRK 292.*

Lion with fess charged
Or lion Az on fess Gu 3 doves Arg
  KAVERNER, Mons' Gerard. *XL 646.*
Arg lion Az on fess Gu 3 ?herons Arg
  TAVERNER, Gerard. *XF 409.*
Gu lion Or on fess Az 3 martlets Arg
  — *XF 32.*
Or lion Az on fess Gu 3 martlets Arg
  DANERNER, Mons Gerard. *WJ 120.*
Untinc lion Gu on fess Or 3 crosslets fitchy Untinc
  — *WB I 33b, 19. (qtd 2 by [Vere], E of Oxf).*
Arg lion Gu on fess Or 3 crosses formy fitchy Arg
  — *I2(1904)257. (qtd 4 by 'Sir John Vere Knyght eryll of Oxinford').*

Arg lion Gu on fess Or 3 crosses formy fitchy Sa
— XK 89. (qtd 2 by Jn Vere, E of Oxford,
KG, 1527).
    COLBRET. WK 528. (imp by Vere).
    COLBRET. WK 531. (qtd 2 by Vere).
Arg lion Gu on fess Sa 3 crosses formy fitchy Or
    COLEBROOKE. Leake. (a&l Az; qtd 2 by Sir
    Jn Vere, KG, d 1539).
Az lion Or on fess Gu 3 fleurs de lis Arg
— WB III 100b, 3.
— CRK 1672.
    FRESLANDE, Roy de. RH, Ancestor vii 204.
Az lion Arg on fess Gu 3 roses Arg
    HEREWARDE, of Suss. CY 170, 678.
Az lion Arg on fess Gu 3 roses Or
    HEREWARD. CV-BM 114.
Az lion Arg on fess Or 3 roses Gu
    HEREWARD. LH 1093. (roses b&s Or).
    HEREWARD. XL 613.
    HEREWARD. LH 720.
Arg lion Gu on fess Or 3 mullets Arg
    CLINTON, of Irld. LQ 73.
Arg lion Az on fess Sa 3 roundels Or
— WB II 54, 5. (imp by [Roberts]).
— WB II 54, 8. (imp by Hastings).
Arg lion Sa on fess Az 3 roundels Or
    THWAITES. XF 169.
    THWAITES. XL 76.
Arg lion & fess Sa ch with 3 roundels Or
    THAWITS. XPat 384, Arch 69, 98. (a&l Gu).

Lion & pale &c

Lion pg & 2 pales
    SALTU, Bernard de. PRO-sls. 1348. (shield
    & trapper).
Lion over all salt
    MAXWELL, Gilbert. Stevenson. 1342. (Ld of
    the half barony of Wilton).
Arg lion Sa salt engr Gu
    GOTISLE. CB 358.
    GOTISLE. L1 291, 4; L2 227, 7. (armed Gu).
    GOTISLE. XX 6. (or Goatley).
Arg lion Sa over all 2 boar spears in salt Gu
headed Sa
    GIBON. L1 276, 6; L2 222, 7.
Arg lion Gu over all ragged staff Or
    STYWARD, Mons Augustine de. AS 488.
    STYWARD, Mons Robert de. AS 496.
Gu lion Arg over all crosier in bend sin Or
    [BYLAND MONASTERY, Yorks]. D4 37.
    NEWBOROUGH MONASTERY, Yorks. D4 27.
    (pastoral staff).
Arg lion Sa over all 2 staves in salt isst from
base Gu upper ends flory Sa
    GYBON. PT 962.

BEAST (OTHER) & OVER ALL

Vt hind erect & fess embattled counter-emb Arg
    PRALL. L9 92b, 7.
    PRALLE. XF 870.
Vt stag salient & fess embattled counter-emb
Arg
    PRALL. BA 1185.
Arg stag salient Sa & over all fretty Vt
    WARNETT, John, of Hempstead, Suss. Suss-
    sASColl iv 298. 1525. (sl on his will).
Untinc bull stat Untinc & pale Erm
    BROKE, Thos. Mill Steph. 1518. (qtg chev
    betw 3 eagles displ; brass to Thos B & w
    Anne [Bulstrode], Ewelme, Oxfords).
    BROKE, Thos. OxfRS iv 37. 1518. (qtg chev
    betw 3 eagles & imp [Bulstrode] & [Shob-
    bington]; Serjeant at Arms to Hen 8; brass
    Ewelme, Oxfords).
Wolf salient over all crozier ensigned with
cardinal's hat
    CAMPEGIUS, Laurence, Bp of Salisbury.
    Birch 2209. c1525-34.

BEAST & OVER ALL & LABEL

Lion fess & label of ?4
    PERCY, Henry. PRO-sls. 12 January 1392-3.
    ('the son').
Az semy de lis & lion Or bend gobony Arg and
Gu label Arg
    BEAMONDE, Mons John. CA 89.
    BEAUMONT. L10 25b, 18.
Az semy de lis & lion Or bend gobony Erm and
Gu label Arg
    BEAUMOND, J de. WJ 122.

BEAST BETWEEN

Lion between

Az lion Arg in dex chf & base annulet Arg
    [?MONTALT]. ML I 343.
Lion ramp betw 2 lions pg in pale
    MOIGNE, Maria. Birch 11809. SEEL: PRIUE.
    1407. (not a shield; wid of Wm M, of Magna
    Ravele, Hants, Kt).
Gu lion salient Or betw 3 ermines salient Arg
tails tipped Sa
    ERMONYE, Kyng of. BR I 21.

Lion betw bends &c

Or lion passt Sa betw 2 bends Gu
    TRACY, Sir J. WB I 41, 14.

Or lion pg betw 2 bends Gu
TRACY, Sir J. *BW 18b, 125.*

Lion passt betw 2 bends each ch with 3 crosslets
MARSAM. *Suff HN 46. (imp Hatfelde; Mr Claxton's house at Cheston).*

Arg crusily Sa lion passt Gu betw 2 bends Az each ch with 3 crosslets Or
MARCHAM. *L10 94b, 1. (a&l Az; ?field crusily fitchy).*

Sa lion passt betw 4 billets Or
WEST. *Suff HN 49. (imp Lewes; Mettingham Castle or Coll).*

Arg lion Vt crowned with twisted wreath Or and Sa betw 5 billets ?Sa & ch on shldr with estoile Or
TRISTRAM, Master Mathew. *Proc Soc Antiq XVI 2S 341. (grant in German by Romerick, K of Arms of Holy Roman Empire, dated, London 24 June 1467).*

Or lion passt betw 6 billets (3, 3) Sa
DEWY. *L10 62b, 14.*

Sa lion Arg betw 3 ?chessrooks Az
GOWSELL. *CRK 575. (?3 cronels).*

Arg lion Gu betw 3 crescs Untinc
PETIT. *L9 108a, 9. (crescs in outline; lions a&l Az).*

Or lion betw 3 crescs Az
BLYTHE, of Blythe, Lincs. *L2 96, 1. (qtd 2&3 Or eagle displd Or).*

Sa lion betw 3 crescs Or
— *XF 957. (qtd 2&3 by West, of Suff).*
— *XL 92. (qtd 2&3 by West).*

Lion betw 3 crosses

Sa lion betw 3 crosslets Or
WALLYS, James. *BA 21, 178. (a&l Arg).*

Gu lion betw 3 crosslets fitchy Arg
WARE, Henry. *SussASColl xxix 4. (Bp of Chichester 1418-1420).*

Gu lion betw 3 crosslets fitchy Or
CAPEL. *XL 16.*
CAPEL, of Stibbyng, Essex. *L2 107, 2.*
CAPEL, Sir William. *Dingley ccccxxxi. (d 1509; crest: demi-lion Or; St Bartholomew's, London).*
CAPELL. *XPat 87, Arch 69, 75. (a&l Az).*
CAPELL. *L10 37, 11.*
CAPELL. *L10 44b, 6. (qrs 1&4).*
CAPELL, Sir Wm. *L10 97b, 9.*

Sa lion Arg betw 3 crosslets fitchy ?Or
FREWKESMERE. *Suff HN 8d. (tinct of crosslets uncertain; Boxtede Ch).*

Gu lion Arg ch with 3 bars Sa betw 3 crosslets fitchy Or
VALLE CRUSIS ABBEY. *L10 68, 18. (a&l Or).*

Az lion Arg collared Gu betw 3 crosses formy Arg
HOLAND, Sir Thomas. *L10 96b, 5. (a&l Gu).*

Sa lion Arg collared Gu betw 3 crosses formy Or
— *D13 21. (qtd 7 by Manyngs, of Kent).*
AYLOFF, of Britsynt, Essex. *L2 14, 10. (a&l Gu).*
AYLOFF, Essex. *XPat 9x, Arch 69, 68.*
AYLOFF, William, of Bretayne, Essex. *XL 101. (a&l Gu).*

Sa lion Arg betw 3 crosses formy Or collar Gu with lozenge shaped ring Arg & ch with 3 roundels Or
AYLOFF, de Britagne, Essex. *L10 6b, 19. (a&l Gu).*

Sa lion betw 3 crosses formy Or collar Gu with lozenge shaped ring & ch with 3 roundels Arg
AYLOFF, William, de Bretains, Essex. *WK 825. (a&l Gu).*

Lion betw 4 crosses or more

Lion betw 4 crosses
RYS, Thoms, of London. *PRO-sls. 1319-20. (loz).*

Lion betw 4 crosses botonny fitchy
WARRE, Thomas la, clericus, Dominus la. *Baker-sls.* Sigillum thomae domini. *1404. (grant of manor of Albrighton, Salop).*

Lion betw 4 crosslets
KENARDESLEYE, Simon de. *PRO-sls. 1319-20. (shield betw 3 owls & in base wivern).*

Lion betw 4 crosslets fitchy
WARRE, Elizabeth. *Birch 14281.* SIGILLU ELIZABETH....... *1393. (imp chf dancetty; shield betw 2 talbots regard addorsed; w of Jn, 4th Ld la W).*
WARRE, John la. *?source. 1390. (sl on record of Durrington Manor, Wilts).*
WARRE, John la, Kt. *Baker-sls. 1389-90. (sl).*
WARRE, John, 4th Ld La. *Birch 14283.* SIGILL(UM) IOH'IS LA WARRE. *1393. (betw 2 lions addorsed each wearing helmet; crest: plume of feathers).*
WARRE, Robert. *PRO-sls. 1455-6.*
WARRE, Thomas, Kt, Ld la. *PRO-sls. 1414-15.*
WARRE, Thomas, Ld la, 5th Baron, clerk. *Birch 14287.* SIGILLUM THOME DOMINI LA WARRE. *1399. (shield held by an angel with open wings inverted; betw 2 lions addorsed each wearing helmet; crest: plume of feathers).*

Gu lion Or betw 4 crosses formy Vair in salt
REASON. *L1 563, 5.*

Sa lion stat gard Arg crowned Or betw 6 crosslets (3, 3) Arg
— *L10 47b, 17. (qtd 3 by Catelyn, of Randes, Northants).*
— *L10 91, 3. (qtd 3 by Rob Catelyn of Rands, Northants).*

Gu lion Arg betw 6 crosslets fitchy (3, 3) Arg
— BA 1037. (qtd 2&3 by West).
Arg lion coward passt regard Sa betw 6 crosses
formy fitchy Gu
HYZHAM. SK A 886.
Arg lion coward Sa betw 7 (4, 3) crosses formy
fitchy Gu
HEIGHAM. LH 1073.
Arg lion coward passt regard Sa betw 7 crosses
formy fitchy Gu
HIGHAM, of Kent. L1 309, 3; L2 249, 4.
(a&l Gu).
HYZHAM. SK B&C 886.
Arg lion stat regard Sa betw 7 crosses formy
fitchy Gu
HIGHAM. XL 554.
Lion betw ?8 crosslets fitchy in orle
WEST, Reginald, 5th B, 6th Baron de la Warr.
Birch 14384. SIGILLUM REGINALDUS ... DELA
.... 1444-5. (qtd 2&3 by West; d1451, grand-
son of Thos West, 3rd Baron W, & Joan, dau
of Rog la Warr, Baron de la W).
Lion betw 9 crosslets fitchy
WARR. Birch 14385. 1470. (qtd 2&3 by Ric
West, 7th Baron de la Warr).
Lion betw uncertain number of crosslets fitchy
WEST, Thomas, 8th Ld la Warr. Birch 14388.
SIGILLUM THOME WEST DOMINI LA WARR.
1515.

Lion betw escallops &c

Gu billetty Or lion betw 2 escallops in fess Arg
BULMER, Wm, of Vppisland, Yorks. L10
110, 8.
Gu billety Or lion per fess Or and Arg betw 2
escallops in fess Arg
BULMER, William, of Uppisland, Yorks. BA
715. (a&l Az; natural s of Sir Rauff B).
Gu billetty Or lion per fess Or and Arg betw 2
escallops Or
BULMER, William, of Uppisland, Yorks. WK
626.
Az lion Arg betw 3 escallops Or
POUTONE, S. William de. GA 17. ('dasur a
ung lyon rampant darge ou iii escalopes
pudre dor').
Per fess lion betw 3 escallops
— PLN 2064. (qtd II 2 by fess dancetty &
label of 5).
Per fess Gu and Arg lion betw 3 escallops
Untinc
— PLN 1890. (qtd 2 by Bartholomew Win-
dowt).
Per fess Gu and Or betw 3 escallops counterch
lion per fess Arg and Az gutty counterch
WINDOUT. XL 158.
WINDOUT, Bartholomew, de Radiswott, Herts.
L10 108, 6. (a&l Az on the Gu & Gu on the
Or).

WYNDOUT, Barthelmew, de Radiswell, Herts.
WK 377.
Sa lion passt Arg betw 3 escallops Arg each ch
with loz Az
HINDE, John. LH 7.
Lion passt betw 6 estoiles
WANDACK, Thomas, dominus de Pillardynton
Herci. Vinc 88, 52. +SIGILL' THOME WAN-
DACK.

Lion betw flaunches, &c

Lion betw 2 flaunches
PRESTWOOD, George, of Whittcombe, Devon.
PRO-sls. 1597-8.
Gu lion Or betw 2 flaunches & gusset in base
Erm
CELY. L10 38b, 20.
CELY. XL 88.
CELY. L2 132, 9. (tomb, Goostham Ch,
Essex).
CELY. XPat 96, Arch 69, 76. (armed Az).

Lion betw fleurs de lis

Lion betw 2 fleurs de lis in chf
MONORGON, Gilbert. Stevenson. 1515, 1519
& 1544. (s of David M, of that ilk).
Lion betw 2 fleurs de lis
— WK 744. (qtd III 1 by Sir Brian Stapil-
ton).
Arg lion passt Az betw 3 fleurs de lis Sa
BRAGDEN. FK II 734.
Az lion passt betw 3 fleurs de lis Or
— LS 141. (qtd 2&3 by Staunton).
Az lion pg betw 3 fleurs de lis Arg
THORPE, Sir .... CRK 1543.
Gu lion Vair betw 5 fleurs de lis Or
EVERINGHAM, Sir John. PLN 1284. (or Sir
Thos; qtg 2&3 Byrkyn Arg fess Az label Gu).
Lion gard betw 6 fleurs de lis
HOLAND. Birch 11403. 1387. (imp in arms
of Matilda, Lady Lovel & Holand).

Lion betw flowers

Lion couchant gard betw 3 double heraldic roses
LUDLOW, Borough of. Hope 180. (on common sl, 1461, when town was incorporated
by Edw 4).
LUDLOW, Salop. Birch 5136, 5139, 5140 &
5142. SIGILLUM BURGENTIUM VILLRE DE
LUDLOW. (in Birch 5142 field described as
'powdered').

Lion betw foils

Lion betw 2 4foils in chf
MONORGON, Gilbert, of that ilk. Stevenson.
1516. (?fleurs de lis).
Az dex chf lion pg Or betw in sin chf & in base
2 pd 5foils Or
[TURBERVILE]. WLN 420. ('Heur'

Habervyle').
Az lion pg Or betw 2 6foils Or 1 in chf & 1 in base
TRUBLEVILLL, of Guernsey. *Soc Guern 1928. 1238. (sl).*
Arg lion Gu betw 3 3foils Vt
LEMESEY. *CC 279b, 256.*
LEMESEYE. *L9 40b, 12.*
LIMESEY. *CRK 1845. (a&l Az; or Livesey).*
LYMESEY, of Lancs. *L1 408, 6; L2 306, 3.*
Lion couchant gard betw 4 3foils
ASTELL, William of. *Birch 6974.* 1412.
Lion betw 5 4foils
BAND, John, Rector of St Nicholas, Cole Abbey. *PRO-sls BS 22.* S' IOH' BAVD...L...T.-..ORDE?. 1375.
Sa lion 2-queued betw 5 5foils Arg
CLYFTON, of co Durham. *D4 29b.*
Arg lion Sa in orle of pd 5foils Gu
PERPONT. *WK 441.*
PERPOUNT. *FK II 606.*

Lion betw hats &c
Lion pg betw 3 helms
[COMPTON]. *Proc Soc Antiq XVIII 2S 136. (qtd by chev in border; on 1 of 6 bosses found in W walk of cloister of Hayles Abbey in 1899).*
Sa lion pg Or betw 3 closed helms Arg
COMPTON. *XL 611.*
COMPTON, of Compton. *L2 137, 5. (a&l Gu).*
COMPTON, Henry. *WK 497. (qrs I 1&4, over all label Gu).*
COMPTON, Mayster. *I2(1904)135.*
COMPTON, Sir William. *XK 129.*
COMPTON, Sir William. *GutchWdU. (window given by him, Balliol Coll Chapel; qr 1).*
Or lion regard crowned betw 3 hearts Gu
— *Arch Journ (Chichester 1853) 95. c1530. (painting, Amberly Castle, Suss; ?arms of 1 of the Sibyls).*

Lion betw mullets
Lion betw 3 mullets
WOLVEY, Thomas de. *Bow LVIII 4. (sl on grant of land in Wolvey & Withybrook, Warws).*
Or lion betw 3 mullets Sa
WOLVEY. *L1 688, 5.*
WOLVEY. *XL 485. (or Wolney).*
WOLVEY. *DV 46b, 1828.*
Lion betw 4 mullets
GODYNGG, Philip. *PRO-sls.* 1392-3. *(or Jn Drinkwater).*

Lion betw pheons
Lion betw 3 pheons
EGERTON. *?source. (capitals, Gt Budworth, Ches).*
Arg lion Gu betw 3 pheons Sa
BECKET. *L1 77, 5; L2 64, 7. (armed Sa; Egerton in L1 margin).*
BEKET. *CC 233b, 383.*
BEKET. *L10 28, 12. (a&l Az).*
EGERTON. *XL 56.*
EGERTON. *?source. (War Memorial, Chester Cathedral).*
EGGERTON. *WK 789.*
EGGERTON, of Ches. *L2 180, 1.*
EGGERTON, M Rauffe, of Rydley, Ches. *I2(1904)197. (cresc for diffce on lion).*

Lion betw roundels &c
Az lion pg Arg betw 3 roundels Or
HULSON, John, of London. *L9 27b, 6.*
Gu lion Or betw 3 roundels Arg each ch with cross Gu
HOUNSLOW PRIORY. *LH 141.*
HOUNSLOW PRIORY. *L10 68, 20. (?lion Arg).*
Az lion sejt erect Arg a&l Gu betw 4 roundels (3, 1) Arg
— *BA 737. (unfinished painting).*
Lion dormant in centre of 2 squares interlaced
HAUVIE, Robert. *Stevenson.* 1296. *(lion described as coiled).*
Lion dormant in 2 equilateral triangles interlaced
POSSI, Colin de. *Birch 12810.* 1361. *(countersl used by Wm Fraunceys, of Multon, Norf).*
Sa lion Arg in 2 equilateral triangles interlaced Or in each angle roundel Gu all betw 3 spear heads 2, 1 Gu (sic)
— *PLN 1810. (qtd 2 by Philip Byflete).*

Beast (other) between
Beast betw 2 mullets in pale
TULLIDAFF, Andrew, of Rannieston. *Stevenson.* 1536. *(?stag lodged).*
Sa beast passt betw 3 birds close those in chf respectant Arg
GREENLAND, K of. *LO B 49. (?polar bear).*
Vt bear stat betw 3 martlets Arg
GREENLAND, K of. *WLN 77.*
Qtly boar betw 3 ?escallops
GLASBROK, William de. *Pudsay Deeds 233d, Yorks-sls 54.* 1365.
Stag courant to sin betw 3 5foils
STRACHAN, John. *Stevenson.* 1309.
Stag betw 3 pheons pts upwards
DAVIDSON, John. *Stevenson.*
Sa greyhound courant Or betw 2 bars Untinc
HAYNE. *LH 122. (?or fox).*

?Dog at foot of tree betw 2 5foils
OGILVIE, Patrick. *Stevenson.* 1295.

?Elephant & castle facing to sin betw in dex chf cresc & in sin mullet
GATE, Agnes atte. *LonBH G 35.* 1332. *(charges uncertain; w of Simon, butcher).*

Rabbit couchant betw cresc & mullet in chf & cresc in base
TULLIDAFF, Andrew, of that ilk. *Stevenson.* 1519.

Hare passt to sin betw 3 cups & on either side letters B & S
— *?source. (letters indistinct, could be R or D; shield on fragment of late 15 cent altar tomb, Pershore Abbey Ch, Worcs).*

?Otter salient in dex chf Erm spot & in sin flank mullet of 6 pts
MELDRUM, Alexdr, of Segie. *Stevenson.* 1455.

Cow betw 5 crosses (3, 2)
COWTON, Roger de. *Yorks Deeds VI 115.* 1353.

Paschal Lamb betw 2 pd mullets in chf & mascle in base
LAMB, John, bailie of Edinburgh. *Stevenson.* 1451-2.

Paschal Lamb betw 3 mullets
NEWSUM, John de. *PRO-sls.* 1333-4. *(Keeper of the King's horses).*

Beast (lion) in orle of

Arg lion Sa in orle of unident charges Gu
PIERPONT, Sir Henry. *BD 86. (4th N window, York Palace, Southwell).*

Sa lion Arg in orle of 8 annulets Or
FULTHORP. *CC 228b, 222.*

Sa lion Arg crowned Or in orle of annulets Arg
MALTON, Mons' Henry de. *TJ 1510. (armed Gu).*

Lion in orle of 9 annulets each enclosing letter S
SOTTONE, Thomas. *Birch 13590.* 1382. *(Merchant of Bristol).*

Lion in orle of billets
NEYRNUVHT, John, Kt. *AylesburyM-sls 28, 49.* 1363. *(?border gobony).*

Lion passt in orle of martlets all to sin
[VALOINS]. *Farrer II 344. (on font, Barney Ch, Norf).*

Gu lion passt in orle of martlets Arg
VALOYNES, Sr. *RB 180.*

Gu lion passt Or in orle of martlets Arg
VALOMYS. *L1 659, 5.*
VALOYNES. *XL 465.*

Az lion in orle of crescs Arg
WANDESFORD. *XL 463.*

Gu lion in orle of crescs Arg
BEAMONT, Ric, of Whytley, Yorks. *I2(1904)149.*

BEAUMONT. *L10 29b, 6. (a&l Az).*
BEAUMONT. *WK 836.*
BEAUMONT, William. *XL 323.*
BEAUMONT, of Yorks. *XO 86.*

Gu lion Arg in orle of 8 crescs Sa
BEAUMONT, of Whitley, Yorks. *L2 76, 2. (a&l Sa).*

Lion in orle of crosses

Sa lion in orle of crosses botonny fitchy Or
CAPELL. *LD 133.* ('armiger de Com Suff').

Lion in orle of crosslets
BAUD, John, Rector of St Nicholas Cole Abbey, London. *PRO-sls E40 A4889 4896.* S'IOHIS BAVOA E NORTE PORNE. 1375-6.

Arg lion Az in orle of crosslets Gu
MOUNTFORT, Sir Wylyam. *RH, Ancestor iv 246.*

Az lion in orle of crosslets Arg
BRAYTOFT, Sir William. *PCL I 558.*

Az lion in orle of crosslets Or
— *L10 36, 17. (qtd 2 by Cockesey).*
[?BRAOSE, of Gower]. *Dingley ccccxxxi. (qtd 3 by [Zouche of Haringworth], all imp Capel; St Bartholomew's, London).*
[?BREWES]. *Dingley cxlvi. (8 crosslets; S chancel window, Erdestland Ch, Herefs).*

Or lion in orle of crosslets Az
— *BA 1092. (a&l Gu; qtd 3 by St Maur).*

Sa lion in orle of crosslets Arg
LANGE, Robarde, of Wilts. *RH, Ancestor v 175.*
LONG. *L1 388, 2; L2 300, 5. (a&l Gu).*

Arg lion qf & crossed in salt in orle of crosslets Gu
BREWYS, Ro. *NS 141.*

Sa lion passt in orle of crosslets Arg
CHASTELION. *XL 515.*

Gu lion gard Arg in orle of 8 crosslets Or
ASTELEY. *L1 2, 3; L2 3, 7.* ('passt' in marginal note in L2).

Gu lion stat gard Arg crowned & in orle of crosslets Or
LISLE, Gerard de. *XL 398.*

Sa lion stat gard Arg crowned Or in orle of crosslets Arg
CHASTELEON, Maklow. *XL 401.*

Lion in orle of crosslets fitchy
WEST, Reginald, Ld de la Warr. *PRO-sls.* 1444-5.
WEST, Thomas, Ld la Warr. *PRO-sls.* 1501-2.

Arg lion in orle of crosslets fitchy Gu
BRETT, John. *LY A 61. (ch on shldr with estoile).*

Arg lion in orle of crosslets fitchy Sa
HAUTEVILLE, Sr de. *CKO a 47.*

Gu lion in orle of crosslets fitchy Arg
WARRE, Thomas la, KG. *Arch Journ xxxvi*
82. (a&l Az; d1525; qtg [Cantelupe]; tomb,
chancel, Broadwater Ch, Suss).
WEST, Sir Thomas. *WGA 280.*
Gu lion in orle of 6 crosslets fitchy Or
— *L2 138, 12. (qtd 2&3 by Sir Ric Corbet).*
Gu lion Or in orle of 8 crosslets fitchy Arg
HOBURY. *L1 316, 3; L2 253, 3.*
Arg lion stat regard Sa in orle of crosslets fitchy
Gu
HEIGHAM. *LH 1023.*
Lion pg in orle of crosses formy
[PEDERTON]. *DevonNQ VI i 225. c1500.*
(qtd 2&3 by St Maur, all imp by Bamfylde, of
Poltimore; early Tudor glass now in
Bamfylde Ho, Exeter).
Lion pg in orle of crosses potent
— *DevonNQ VI i 225. c1500. (imp by*
Bamfylde, of Poltimore; panel 5 of early
Tudor glass now in Bamfylde Ho, Exeter).

Lion in orle of escallops &c
Lion in orle of escallops
BAUD, John. *PRO-sls. 1375-6. (Rector of St*
Nicholas Cole Abbey, London).
Az lion in orle of escallops Arg
— *BA 36, 340. (qtd 2 by Sir Thos Molyneux,*
of Sefton).
Sa lion in orle of escallops Arg
HOLAND, Mons' Richard. *TJ 78.*
HOLLAND, Sir Richard. *LH 272.*
HOWLAND, Monsire Richard de. *CG 101.*
Sa lion gard in orle of escallops Arg
HOLLAND. *LH 996.*
Arg lion in orle of fleurs de lis Sa
BUCKMYNSTER. *L10 24, 8.*
Az lion in orle of fleurs de lis Arg
— *WK 199. (qtd 2&3 by [Sir] Pers*
[Eg]gecombe).
[HOLAND]. *ML II 51. (qtd 2&3 by Ld Lovel,*
of Titchmarsh).
Az lion in orle of fleurs de lis Or
BEAMONT, Le Ct. *BD 86. (1st N window,*
hall of York Palace, Southwell).
Sa lion Erm in orle of fleurs de lis Or
PHILLIPPS. *L2 408, 10. (ch on shldr with*
mullet).
Az lion gard in orle of fleurs de lis Arg
HOLAND. *ML I 52. (qtd by Lovel, of Tich-*
marsh).
Lion in orle of 8 roses
[MARCH]. *Edinburgh XV 123 & 132. (qtd by*
[Alexander, D of Albany]; stone, Trinity Col-
lege Hospital, Edinburgh).
Arg lion Sa in orle of roses Gu
PERPOYNT, Syr Nycoll, of Derbys. *RH,*
Ancestor v 178.
PIERPONT. *SK 296. (name added by*

Gibbon).
PIREPOUND, Sire Robert de. *N 1074.*
('.. od la bordure de roses de goules').
Sa lion in orle of roses Arg
CLIFTON, Sir Gerveis. *BW 19, 131.*

Lion in orle of foils
Vt lion pg Arg in orle of 3foils Or
VAUGHAN, Morgan. *XL 471. (?cat).*
Lion in orle of 5foils
CLIFTON, John, chivaler. *PRO-sls.* 6 May
1393.
CLIFTUN, T de. *Birch 8680.* T' DE CLIFTV.
1351.
CLYFTON, Sir John. *BA 652.*
PIERPOINT, Anna de. *Harl Soc IV 45.*
PIERPOINT, Edmund, Kt. *Harl Soc IV 46.*
1385.
PIERPOINT, Henry, Kt. *Harl Soc IV 47.*
1440-1. *(qtg Manners).*
PIERPOINT, Robert de, Kt. *Harl Soc IV 46.*
1328.
PIERPOINT, Robt de, Kt. *Harl Soc IV 47.*
1317-18.
RASEN, Anna. *Harl Soc IV 46.*
Arg lion in orle of 5foils Gu
PERPOUNTZ. *L9 104b, 6. (10 5foils).*
PIERPOUNT. *XL 550.*
Arg lion Sa in orle of 5foils Gu
MAWSEY. *L9 52a, 7. (als Pierpount; 13*
5foils).
PERPOUND, Esmond. *XL 157.*
PERPOUNT. *L9 98a, 12.*
PIERPOINT, Monsire de. *CG 47.*
PIERPOUNT, Monsire de. *CG 485.*
PURPUNDE, Mons Esmun. *WJ 316.*
Arg lion Sa in orle of pd 5foils Gu
PERPOINTZ. *L1 492, 6; L2 408, 9. (a&l Gu).*
PERPOUNTS. *SK 668.*
PIERPOINT. *PLN 1873. (qtg 2 Manours [Arg*
6 annulets Sa], 3 Heryne [Az 3 boars passt
Or]).
Arg lion in orle of 5foils Sa
CLIFTON, John. *S 363.*
CLIFTON, John de. *S 365.*
CLYFTON. *L10 41, 11.*
CLYFTON, Mons Gervase de. *WJ 331.*
Arg lion in orle of pd 5foils Sa
CLIFTON. *L1 140, 6. (a&l Gu).*
CLIFTON, Gervaise de. *XL 165.*
PERPONT, Edmund. *SES 47.*
Arg lion Vt in orle of pd 5foils Gu
— *CKO a 79.*
Az lion Or in orle of 8 5foils Arg
ANDROWEY. *L2 22, 3.*
Or lion in orle of 8 pd 5foils Untinc
CLIFVEDON. *L2 102, 2.*

Or lion Sa in orle of 5foils Gu
    MAWSEY, Richard, of Suss. *CY 170, 680.*
Sa lion Untinc in orle of 5foils Arg
    ?CLIFTON. *Coll T&G ii 96.* 1530. *(coat very indistinct; imp by Babington, ?for Bernard, (s of Sir Anthony B) & his w, dau of Sir Gervaise C, KB; Dethick Chapel, Ashover, Derbys).*
Sa lion in orle of 5foils Arg
    CLIFTON. *CB 25.*
    CLIFTON, Sir Gervaise. *XL 581. (qrs 1&4).*
    CLIFTON, Sir Gervase. *BD 86. (5th N window, hall of York Palace, Southwell).*
    CLIFTON, Sir Gervase. *CRK 429. (a&l Gu).*
    CLYFFTON, Sir Garways of, of Notts. *RH, Ancestor iv 243.*
    CLYFTON, Sir G. *WB I 41, 16.*
    CLYFTON, Gervaise. *SES 65.*
    PERPOYNT. *L9 97a, 1.*
    PIERPOND, Mons Edmond. *S 355.*
Sa lion in orle of pd 5foils Arg
    CLYFTON, Sir Gerveis. *WK 189.*
    CLYFTON, of Yorks. *L2 136, 11. (8 5foils).*
    PIERPONT, Edmond. *S 357.*
Gu lion Or head & mane Arg in orle of 5foils Arg
    GRACE. *CC 228, 195. (6 5foils).*
    GRACE, of Glams. *L9 27b, 10. (lion drawn as if head erased Arg had been set on lion Or; 5 5foils).*
Az lion gard Or in orle of pd 5foils Arg
    ANDROWEY. *CRK 1414.*

Lion in orle of 6foils
Lion in orle of 6foils
    PIRPOUNT, Robert de, Kt. *Wentworth 71.* 1323. *(sl).*
Arg lion Sa in orle of 6foils Gu
    DARCI, S' John, le Fiz. *R 20.*
    PEREPOUNT, Monsr de. *AS 378.*
    PERPOUND, S' Emond. *PO 279.*
    PERPOUNT, Mons' Henry. *TJ 77. ('..ourle de sytfoilles..').*
    PERPOUNT, Mons Thomas. *TJ 1014. (painted Arg lion Sa in border Arg ch with 10 6foils Gu).*
    PERPOUNT, Mons Thomas. *TJ 1015.*
Arg lion in orle of 6foils Sa
    POINS, Sir Harry. *BW 19, 130. (9 6foils).*
Sa lion in orle of pd 6foils Arg
    CLYFTON, Sr Gervis. *PO 266.*

Lion in orle of mullets &c
Arg lion Gu in orle of mullets Sa
    — *L9 44b, 4. (qtd 2 by Humfrey Lloyd).*
Or lion qf in salt Gu in orle of mullets Sa
    MELUSYN, E of. *WGB 138. (pedigree of Eliz Widvill).*

Gu lion Arg crowned Or in orle of roundels Or
    HAMELYN, of Leics. *BA 30b, 256.*
Vt lion in orle of 6 broom sprigs Or
    JONES, Robert, of Burton in Bromfield. *L9 4b, 9. (a&l Gu).*

Beast (other) in orle of
Ram standing before bush in orle of 6 billets
    TYLIO, Arnald de. *PRO-sls.* 1338-9. *(Rector of Ellington, Lincoln).*

Beast betw ... & label
Gu lion Arg betw 3 crosslets fitchy Or label Arg
    CAPEL, Sir Giles. *XK 138.*
Gu lion betw 3 crosslets fitchy Or label Untinc
    CAPELL, Syr Gyles, de Stebbyng, Essex. *I2(1904)205.*
Gu lion betw 3 crosslets fitchy Or label Arg
    CAPELL. *WK 834.*
Lion betw 7 crosslets & in chf label
    WARE, John, Kt, of Northants. *Birch 14262.*
    sigillvm IOHANNIS LA WAR(R)E. 1309.

Beast betw ... & chief
Gu cat pg Arg spotted Sa betw 3 annulets Arg on chf Or pale Az ch with mitre Or betw 2 pd 5foils Sa
    BROND, alias Catton. *L10 73b, 8. (Prior of Norwich & Abbott of St Albans; sin imp).*
    BROND, Robert, prior of Norwich. *L10 98, 2. (?cat stat).*
Gu goat courant betw 3 demi mill wheels Arg on chf Or 3 pd mullets Az
    MA[LENBECK], Joh. *L10 61, 4. (?Catherine wheels).*
    MALENBECK, Johannes. *WK 423. ('de Dantzich terre prusie').*
    MALENBECK, Johes. *L9 68b, 1. ('de Dantzike, terre prusse dicionis regni polonie').*
Or bull stat Gu armed Arg betw 3 roachs' heads erased & erect Vt langued Gu chf checky Arg and Az
    ROCHE. *XPat 214, Arch 69, 86. ('of London' added).*
Or bull stat Gu armed unguled & membered Arg betw 3 dragons' heads erased & erect Vt chf checky Arg and Az
    ROCHE. *WK 829.*

Beast betw ... & in chief
Arg lion passt Gu betw 2 bars Sa ch with 3 roundels (2, 1) Or in chf 3 stags' faces Sa
    PARKER, Henry, Ld Morley. *WK 500.*

Gu greyhound courant Or betw 2 bars Arg ch
with 3 martlets (2, 1) Sa in chf 2 roundels
Arg
MOYLE, John, of Estwell, Kent. *XF 823.*
(imp Darcy).
MOYLE, de Stephenton, Devon. *XF 821.*
MOYLE, Sir Walter. *XF 822. (imp Luc-
combe).*
MOYLE, Walter. *XF 824. (imp Stanley).*
Gu greyhound courant Or betw 2 bars Arg ch
with 3 martlets (2, 1) Sa in chf 3 roundels
Arg
— *L10 92, 1. (qtd 2&3 by Sir Walter
Moyle).*
MOYLE. *WB II 53, 8.*
Gu greyhound courant Or betw 2 bars Arg ch
with 3 mullets (2, 1) Sa in chf 3 roundels
Arg
— *L10 92, 2. (qtd 2 by Jn Moyle, of Estwell,
Kent).*

Beast betw ... & over all
Arg lion Gu a&l Az betw in chf 2 estoiles above
2 crescs & in base cresc betw 3 estoiles Gu
over all fess Az
DULON, Baron, of Irld & Chymwete, Devon.
L2 162, 4.
Arg semy of estoiles & lion betw in chf 2 crescs
Gu over all fess Az
DILLON, John, of Irld. *PLN 1703. (rays vary
from 9 to 12).*

BEAST IN BORDER

Demi-lion in border
Arg demi-lion Purp border gobony Or and Az
STOCKLEY. *XL 277. (a&l Gu).*
Demi-lion border roundelly
[LYNNE]. *Farrer I 60. (carved in stone over
W doorway, New Buckenham Ch, Norf).*
Gu demi-lion Arg border Sa roundelly Or
LYMME. *XL 282.*
LYNDEY. *L9 41b, 7.*
LYNNE. *XL 62.*
STOKES. *FK II 529.*
STOKES. *LS 117. (8 roundels).*
STOKES. *LS 139. (8 roundels).*
Gu demi-lion erased Arg border Sa roundelly Or
— *XL 279.*
LYONS. *XL 567. (rectius Lynne).*
STOKES. *FK II 530.*
Gu demi-lion Or border Sa roundelly Or
— *SHY 378 & 380-1. (imp [Ottelyng]).*

Demi-lion qf in border roundelly
STOKE, Thomas, of Asscheby Leger. *PRO-sls
E40 A6078.* 1405-6.
Gu demi-lion qf Arg border Sa roundelly Or
STOKES. *CRK 307. (a&l Az).*
Gu demi-lion with 2 tails couped Arg border Sa
roundelly Or
STOKES. *CRK 1476. (qrs 1&4).*
STOKNOR, of Kent. *MY A2 219.*
STOKUS, of Kent. *MY 219.*

Lion in plain border
Lion & border
— *WB I 14b, 22. (qr 2 on escutch of Stapul-
ton).*
— *Lawrance 53.* c1330. *(effigy from unk-
nown Ch, perhaps St Thomas, or one of the
Friaries; now in Scarborough Museum,
Yorks).*
— *Birch 4271, 33 & 1961. (on sl of Jn
Bettesworth, Vicar General & official Princi-
pal, See of London; qtd by B, all imp by the
See).*
— *PRO-sls.* 1391-2. *(imp by Baryngton).*
— *Lawrance 53.* c1310. *(unidentified;
known as 'Sir Robert Pounderling, once Con-
stable of Dyserth Castle'; effigy Tremeir-
chion, Flint).*
BELISME. *Birch 13848.* 1456. *(qr 1 on dex
side of 1 of 2 shields in sl of Mgt Talbot, wid
of 1st E of Shrewsbury).*
BROCAS, Arnald. *PRO-sls.* 1377.
BROCAS, Arnald, clerk. *Burrows 309-10.*
FRAMEYS, Katharine. *AnstisAsp I 216, 71.*
1373-4. *(3rd of 3 shields).*
INGHAM, John de, of Suff. *Birch 10960.*
S'I.OH.I'D.E.IN.GH.A.M. temp Edw 3.
LONGHE, Robert, of Dorset. *Birch 11379.* LE
SEAL ROBERD LONGH. 1361.
MADOC AP LLEWELYN AP GRUFFYDD.
*Lawrance 27. (d1331; effigy, Gresford, Den-
bigh).*
MEAUX, Thomas de. *PRO-sls.* 1378-9. *(sin
shield of 2 on sl).*
PERCY, Thomas. *Birch 2043.* 1366. *(Bp of
Norwich, 1356-69).*
PERCY, Thomas, Bp of Norwich. *AnstisAsp I
209, 52.* 1366.
PERCY, Thos, Bp of Norwich. *HB-SND.*
1366. *(2nd of 2 shields on sl).*
STEWART, Sir Richard, Kt. *Laing-sls II 943;
Stevenson.* 14 cent. *(qtg 2&3 checky).*
TALBOT, Margaret. *Bk of Sls 229.* 1456.
*(nee Beauchamp, w of Jn Talbot, E of
Shrewsbury).*
TALBOT, E of Shrewsbury. *WB I 35b, 1.*
WEMES, Michael de, Kt. *PRO-sls.* 1336-7.

Untinc lion ch on shldr with mullet Untinc
  border Arg
  FELDE. *PLN 818.*
Untinc lion Sa border Az
  — *WB I 15, 25. (qr 1 of coat imp by*
  Ratclyffe).
Arg lion Gu border Sa
  SEIN CLER, William de. *E I 239; E II 241.*
  SENCLER, Willm de. *WLN 783.*
Arg lion Purp border Gu
  CHEPSTOW, Henry de. *XL 449. (a&l Az).*
Arg lion Sa border Az
  — *WK 239. (qtd 2&3 by Sir Jn Hunger-*
  ford).
  — *PLN 2019. (a&l Gu; qtd 2&3 by Sir*
  Walter Hungerford).
  — *WGA 229. (escutch of Francis, Ld*
  Lovell).
  — *WGA 222. (qtd 2&3 by Ld Burnell).*
  — *I2(1904)102. (a&l Gu; qtd II 3 by [Sir*
  Bryan] Stapulton).
  BURNELL, le Sire. *TJ 954. (qtg 2&3 Or salt*
  engr Sa).
Arg lion Sa border Gu
  — *SK 908.*
  LICHTENBERG. *XL 620.*
Arg lion & border Sa
  BURNELL, Ld. *RH, Ancestor iii 202. (border*
  Az put over in later hand; [Lds Burnell by
  writ 1311-1420]).
  [MOWAT]. *Berry; Stodart pl 4. (qtd by [the*
  Ld of Leslie]; border unclear).

Az lion in border
Az lion Arg border Or
  TALBOT, 'Therl of Shrawsbery'. *I2(1904)66.*
  (qtg Talbot, Neville, Furnival & Strange).
Az lion & border Or
  [BELESME], Count de Shosber. *CN 29.*
  BELESME, E of Shrewsbury. *DX 65.*
  BELESME, Le Count of Shrosbury. *WLN 196.*
  TALBOT, Sir George, E of Shrewsbury.
  PR(1512)49; PR(1515)11. (qtg Nevill, Fur-
  nival, Verdon & Strange).
  TALBOT, George, E of Shrewsbury. *XB 16.*
  (KG 1488, d 1538).
  TALBOT, George, E of Shrewsbury. *XK 34.*
  (qr 1).
  TALBOT, Sir Gilbert. *XK 45. (qr 1).*
  TALBOT, E of Shrewsbury. *XK 214.*
Az lion Or border Gu
  — *Suff HN 2. (Sudbury College).*
Az lion & border Or
  — *WK 428. (qtd V 1&4 by Visct Lisle).*
  BELEM, Sir Roger de, 'Comes Salop'. *CV-*
  BM 172.
  BELISMO, Roger de, Salop. *CY 79, 314.*
  BELYSMO. *L10 28b, 4.*
  POICTOU, Roger de. *?source.* c1194. *(in*

window, *St Mary's Ch, Lancaster to com-*
memorate his association with the county; in
castle his arms are given as Erm 3 chevs
Gu).
  SCHROSBERY. *TB 35.*
  SHALVESBURY, Therll of. *I2(1904)49.*
  (Banner; qtg Talbot).
  SHREWESBURY, Le C de. *NB 27. (tinct of*
  border unclear).
  TALBOT, Sir Geo, E of Shrewsbury. *WGA*
  47.
  TALBOT, George, E of Shrewsbury. *WGA*
  107. (qtg Talbot, Strange & Furnival).
  TALBOT, Gilbert. *WK 15.*
  TALBOT, Sir Gilbert. *PLN 1721. (qr 1; imp*
  Sa chev betw 3 griffins' heads erased Arg).
  TALBOT, Sir Gilbert. *WB V 83. (Kt 1485).*
  TALBOT, Sir Gilbert. *WK 53.*
  [TALBOT, Sir Gilbert]. *WK 141.*
  TALBOT, John, 2nd E of Shrewsbury. *Leake.*
  c1453. *(d1460).*
  TALBOT, John, E of Salop. *CRK 1380. (qr*
  1).
  TALBOT, Ld John, E of Shrewsbury. *WGA*
  261.
  TALBOT, Ld John, E of Shrewsbury. *WGA*
  262. (s of WGA 261).
Az lion & border Or cresc Arg on cresc Az for
  diffce
  TALBOT, Sir John. *XK 188.*
Az lion Or ch on shldr with annulet Sa border
  Or
  LISLE. *CRK 255. (qr 1).*

Gu lion in border
Gu lion & border Untinc
  — *WK 744. (qtd II 3 by Sir Brian Stapilton).*
Gu lion & border Arg
  — *WLN 106.*
  MOUBREY, Geffrey de. *WJ 157.*
  MOWBRAY. *L9 69b, 4. (a&l Az).*
  MOWBRAY, Geoffrey de. *XL 329.*
  TALBOT, Sir. *WB IV 15b, 514.*
  TALBOT, Richard, E of Shrewsbury. *DX 66.*

Or lion in border
Or lion Az border Gu
  PERCY, Algernon, Bp of Norwich. *XL 406.*
  PERCY, Thomas. *WJ 97. (Bp of Norwich,*
  1356-69).
Or lion & border Gu
  — *WLN 53.*
Or lion Gu border Sa
  — *FK II 330. (qtd 2&3 by Arnaldus Buada).*
Or lion Sa border Gu
  GOURNEY, Robert de. *B 193.*
  NESLE, John III de, Count of Soissons. *C 38.*
  (d1284).
  TOURCY, Mons Willm de. *WJ 362.*

TOURNEY, William de. *XL 442.*

Field patterned lion in border
Erm lion & border Untinc
    CRONWELL, Roger de, of Burford. *Bow XXX 26.* 1423-4.
Billetty lion border
    [GISORS]. *Mill Steph.* 1524. *(qtd 2 by Berners; brass to Constance, dau of Jn B, of Writtle, Essex).*
Gu crusily & lion Or border Arg
    KNELL. *L9 12, 12. (?lion Arg).*
Gu crusily fitchy & lion Or border Arg
    KNILL. *XL 14.*

Lion crowned in border
Lion crowned & border
    BURNELL, Hugo, dns de Holcot. *Vinc 88, 48.* +SIGILLUM HVGONIS BVRNELL.
    HENLOW, Godfrey de, Kt. *PRO-sls.* 1335-6. *(shield betw oak branches).*
Untinc lion Sa crowned Or border Az
    BURNELL, Ld. *WB I 37, 11.*
Arg lion Az crowned Or border Az
    BURNELLE, Ld. *BR VI 22.*
Arg lion Sa crowned Untinc border Az
    — *I2(1904)176. (qtd 2 by Sir Jn Hungerford).*
Arg lion Sa crowned Arg border Az
    — *WK 127. (qtd 2&3 by Thos Hungerford).*
    LOVELL. *WLN 229.*
Arg lion Sa crowned Or border Arg
    MORLEY, Thomas, Ld. *WGA 112.*
Arg lion Sa crowned Or border Az
    — *I2(1904)212. (qtd 3 by 'The Lord Fytzwater').*
    — *D4 23. (escutch of [Lovell] on coat qtd by Stapilton of Notts).*
    — *XK 21. (qtd 2 by Robt Radcliffe, E of Sussex).*
    — *XK 95. (qtd 3 by Rob Radcliffe, Ld Fitzwalter).*
    — *XK 79. (qtd 3 by Radcliffe, Ld Fitzwater, KG).*
    — *BA 864. (qtd 2 by Sir Jn Hungerford, of Down Amney).*
    — *WK 416-7. (qtd 5 by Stapleton).*
    — *L10 94, 4. (qtd III 3 by Norreys).*
    — *XF 302. (qtd 3 by [Lovel]).*
    BURNEL, Ld. *PLN 107. (membered Gu; qtg 2&3 Or salt engr Sa).*
    BURNEL, le Sr le. *S 70.*
    BURNELL. *CRK 197. (qrs 1&4; tail inwards).*
    BURNELL. *Leake. (qtd 2 by Robt Radcliffe, Baron B, KG, d1542).*
    BURNELL. *L1 39, 1; L2 49, 7. (a&l Or).*
    BURNELL. *LH 834. (qtd II&III 1&4 by Sir Thos Hungerford).*

BURNELL. *LH 835. (qtd II&III 1&4 by Sir Jn Hungerford).*
BURNELL, Ld. *WB II 50, 3.*
BURNELL, Ld. *XL 189.*
BURNELL, Ld. *XL 244.*
BURNELL, Ld. *FK I 112. (qrs 1&4).*
BURNELL, Ld. *KB 307. (qrs 1&4).*
BURNELL, Ld. *AY 41.*
BURNELL, Sir .... *PLN 1572. (qtg 2&3 [Botetourt] Or salt engr Sa).*
BURNELL, Hugh, Ld. *S 72. (a&l Or).*
BURNELL, Margery. *LH 833. (imp by Sir Edm Hungerford).*
LOVEL, le S', of Salop. *CY 80, 319.*
LOVELL, le Sr de. *CN 65.*
Arg lion Sa crowned Or border Gu
    HUREHOUENE, Gerard de. *CA 118. (or Humkoven).*
Arg lion crowned Sa border Az
    BURNEL, Hugh, KG. *Leake. (d1420; qtg 2&3 Botetourt).*
Gu lion Arg crowned & in border Or
    GAUCE. *L2 224, 11.*
Or lion Sa crowned Or border Az
    BURNELL. *CT 33.*
Arg lion Sa crowned & ch on shldr with lion Or border Gu
    HUREHOUENE, Mons Gofrey. *CA 119.*

Lion qf &c in border
Az lion qf & border Arg
    CHICCHE, T, of Kent. *CRK 535.*
Arg lion qf Sa crowned Or border Az
    BURNELL. *L10 82, 1. (a&l Gu).*
Gu lion passt Arg border Az
    LEO, King of. *XL 422.*
Or lion salient border Gu
    FELBRIDGE, Geor. *NS 132.*

Lion gard &c in border
Sa lion gard Or border Arg
    BROKEYS. *PT 860.*
Or lion pg Sa border Gu
    LEMLE, Pers de. *Q 490.*
Lion pg crowned & border
    OGILVIE, Sir Andrew, of Inchmartin. *Stevenson.* 1439-40.
Or lion stat gard Sa border Gu
    — *WLN 899.*
Az semy de lis & lion regard Arg border Untinc
    HOLLAND. *L1 300, 3. (border not blazoned & only roughly tricked in painting).*
Gu lion 2corp Or crowned Az border Untinc
    — *WB I 42, 9. (qtd III 1&4 by ...).*
Gu lion 2corp Or crowned Az border Arg
    KELHAM, James. *CRK 1999. (lions sejt, comb, gard, coward).*
    KELLAM. *L2 295, 11. (tails coward).*

Vt lion 2corp coward sejt in border Arg
ATWATER. *L2 8, 11.*
Gu lion Or holding axe betw his paws border Or
NORWEYE, le Roy de. *AS 17. (Irish axe).*

Lion in patterned border

Lion in border Erm
Arg lion Az border Erm
LOUNDRES. *Nichols Leics III 328. (brass to Sir Thos Chaworth (d1458), Lound Ch).*
Arg lion Sa border Erm
— *DIG 10. (qtd by Preston, Visct of Gormanstone).*
Az lion Arg border Erm
KARE, The Baron of, of Balymackarl. *DIG 34.*
Az lion Or border Erm
LAUNDRES. *L9 35b, 10.*
LONDRES, William de. *XL 328.*
LOURDRES, Mons Willm de. *WJ 140.*

Lion in border gobony
Lion in border gobony
[NERNUIT]. *Mill Steph.* 1544. *(qtd 2&3 by Harvey; brass to Jn Leigh & w Isabel H, Addington, Surr).*
NEYRNUGHT, John, Kt. *AylesburyM-sls 28, 49.* 1363. *(?orle of billets).*
[?NIERNUIT]. *Mill Steph. (qtd by ?Harvey & imp chf indented; brass to Dame Eliz H, Abbess of Elstow, Beds, 1501-24; d1527).*
Arg lion Untinc border gobony Az and Or
TALBOT, Thomas, (of Malahide). *PLN 814.*
Arg lion Gu border gobony Arg and Gu
TALBOT, of Irld. *XL 69.*
Arg lion Gu border gobony Gu and Az
DUNHED. *L2 152, 10.*
Gu lion Arg maned Or border gobony Arg and Or
CHAMNOY, of Calthorpe. *L2 129, 12.*
Gu lion Arg border gobony Arg and Vt
MOUBRAY. *D4 25b. (qtd 3 by Gascoyn, of Galthrop, Yorks).*
Gu lion Arg border gobony Or and Arg
MOWBRAY, John, of Northd. *RH, Ancestor iv 241.*
Gu lion Arg border gobony Or and Gu
— *E6. (qtd by Gascoyn, of Galthrop, Yorks).*
Sa lion Arg border gobony Sa and Arg
— *I2(1904)114. (qtd 2&3 by George Harvey, of Thurleigh, Beds).*
— *D13 86. (qtd 4 by Leygh, of Addington, Surrey).*
— *XV I 1119. (qtd 2&3 by Wm Hartshorn, of Beds).*
— *LH 759. (qtd 2&3 by Wm Hartshorn, of Beds).*

— *WB III 117, 1. (qtd 2&3 by Whillyam Herrishorn, of Beds).*
— *XK 194. (qtd 2&3 by Sir George Harvey).*
— *WB I 20b, 6. (qtd 2&3 by Hervy).*
NERNEWT. *XFB 57. (qtd 2&3 by George Hervy, of Thyrley, Beds).*
NERNEWT, Richard. *XL 583.*
NERNEWTE. *SK 439.*
Per bend Or and Arg lion Sa border gobony Arg and Vt
PHILIP, Sir David. *Soc Jers 1928. (Governor of Jersey, 1486).*
PHILLIPP, Sir Davy. *WK 437.*
Lion gutty crowned in border gobony
WALDBY, Robert, Ld of Hexham. *Birch 2328. (Archbp of York 1397-98).*
Untinc lion Erm crowned in border gobony
Untinc
WALDEBY. *Proc Soc Antiq V 2S 58. (imp by See of York; sl of Rob W, Archbp of York 1396-8, for jurisdiction of Hexham).*

Lion in border party indented
Gu lion Arg border indented Or (outside) & Sa
— *I2(1904)274. (qtd 3 by Wyllm Ingleby, of Ripley, Yorks).*
— *L10 96b, 2. (qtd 3 by Sir Wm Gascoigne).*
— *D4 51. (qtd 3 by Gascoigne).*
— *H21 50. (qtd by Constable, of Flamborough, Yorks).*
MOUBRAY, Mons Alisandre le fitz. *WJ 200. (lion ch on shldr with mullet Sa).*
MOUBRAY, Mons J de. *WJ 199.*
MOUBRAYE, Sir Alexander. *L9 70a, 12. (a&l Az; s of Sir Jn M).*
MOWBRAY. *XFB 236. (qtd 3 by Wm Ingelby, of Ripley, Yorks).*
Gu lion Arg border indented Sa (outside) & Or
— *D4 39b. (qtd by Constable, of Flamboro, Yorks).*
— *BA 596. (border unclear; qtd 3 by Gascoyne).*
— *BA 722. (qtd 3 by Sir Wm Ingelby).*
MOWBRAY. *L9 5, 1; L9 5, 7-12. (qtd by Sir Wm Ingelby, of Rippley, Yorks).*
MOWBRAY. *L9 5, 6. (imp by Ingelby).*
MOWBRAY, Alexander de. *XL 344.*

Lion in border per fess
Per fess Arg and Gu lion & border counterch
CERNE, Philip. *E I 611; E II 613.*
CTIC, Phil' de. *WLN 589. (Cerne, Ferne or Crick).*
OORNE, Philip. *L9 88b, 8.*

Lion in border semy of annulets &c

Sa lion crowned Arg in border Arg semy of
annulets Sa
MALTON, Henry de. *XL 155.* *(a&l Or).*

Sa lion Arg crowned Or border Arg semy of
annulets Sa
MALTON. *L9 50b, 9.*
MALTON, Mons Henr' de. *WJ 308.*
MALTONE, S' Henry de. *PO 489.*
MOLTON, Henly de. *CA 20.*

Gu lion Arg ch on shldr with annulet Or border
Arg billetty Or
— *FK II 350. (8 billets).*

Az lion in border Arg semy of round buckles Az
OUTHERLONY. *SC 60.*

Az lion Or border Arg semy of round buckles
Az
OTHERLOWNY. *L2 393, 10.*

Arg lion Sa border Gu semy of castles Or
— *WLN 70.*

Arg lion Gu border Sa ch with 8 crosslets Or
— *L10 36, 12. (a&l Az).*
ST CLERE. *LS 342.*

Gyronny of 8 Gu and Sa lion Arg border Az ch
with 8 crosslets Or
MATTHEW. *XL 78.*

Gyronny of 8 Gu and Sa lion Or border Az
crusily Or
MATHEW. *L2 343, 8.*

Gyronny of 8 Sa and Gu lion Or border Az
crusily Or
MATHEW. *XPat 315, Arch 69, 93.*

Arg lion Gu crowned Or border Sa crusily Or
SENCLER, William de. *F 436.*

Arg lion Purp border Gu crusily fitchy Arg
CHEPSTOWE, H de. *WJ 360.*

Arg lion Sa border Gu crusily fitchy Or
CHEPSTOWE, H de. *WJ B 360.*

Arg lion Gu border Sa ch with 8 crosses formy
Or
ST CLERE. *LS 338.*

Lion in border semy of escallops

OXENBRIDGE. *Arch Cant iv 119.* 1400. *(qtd
2&3 by fretty & imp by Barry; brass to Mgt,
w of Edw B, Sevington, Kent).*
OXENBRIDGE. *Lawrance 35.* ante 1350.
*(adopted by Oxenbridge after marriage with
heiress of Alard, whose arms these were;
effigy, Winchelsea, Suss).*

Gu lion Arg border Vt semy of escallops Arg
OXENBRIDGE. *PLN 1307. (qtg 2&3 by Arg
lion Sa border Arg roundelly Gu).*
OXENBRIDGE. *Lambarde 52-3.* 1537. *(8
escallops; various qtgs; tomb of Sir Godard
O, Oxenbridge Chapel).*
OXONBRIGGE. *L2 388, 1. (9 escallops).*

Gu lion Arg border Vt semy of escallops Or
OXENBRIDGE. *XL 10.*
OXHAMBRIGE. *L1 483, 4. (9 escallops).*

OXHONBRIGE. *L9 89a, 9. (a&l Az; 9 escallops).*
OXYNBRYGE, Sir Godard, Kt. *D13 40d. (&
his issue; 10 escallops).*

Lion to sin & border ch with 6 escallops
BRANGWEN, John. *Birch 7750.* +S' IOHANNIS
FILII IOHANNIS. 1249-50.

Gu lion qf Arg border Vt semy of escallops Or
OXENBRIDGE. *XL 11.*
OXENBRIDGE, Sir Goddard, Kt. *XK 119. (qrs
1&4).*
OXENBRIGGE. *L9 90b, 5. (a&l Az; 9 escal-
lops).*
OXINBRUGE, Sir Godard. *WK 481.*

Lion in border ch with 8 estoiles
DUNBAR, Sir David de, Ld of Cockburn.
Stevenson. 14 cent.

Arg lion Az border semy of estoiles Untinc
BAGENHOLT, S Gefroy de. *GA 34.*

Lion in border semy of flowers

Gu lion Arg border flory Untinc
[MOWBRAY]. *Nichols Leics II 248. (Swan
Inn, Melton Mowbray).*

Or lion Gu border flory cf Gu
ALEXANDER II, K of Scotland. *MP I 85.
(d1249).*
SCOTLAND, K of. *C 15. ('dor a un lion de
goules a un bordure dor flurette de goules').*
SCOTLAND, Alexander K of. *MP Hist Min iii
65.* 1249. *('scutum regis Scociae').*

Arg lion per fess Sa and Az crowned Gu border
counterch semy de lis Or
SAUNDER, of London. *L1 618, 5. (a&l Gu).*

Lion in border ch with 8 roses
DUNBAR. *Stevenson.* 1515. *(qtd by Jn
Stewart, D of Albany; d1536; 2nd, 3rd & 4th
sls).*
DUNBAR. *Stevenson.* 1367. *(marshalled by
Agnes Randolph, 2nd w of Patrick D, 9th E
of March).*
DUNBAR, Chapter of Collegiate Ch of. *Birch
15274.* SIGILLUM COMUNE CAPITULI DUN BAR-
NENSIS. 16 May 1453. *(Indent betw Abbey
of Melrose & Coll Ch of Dunbar re teinds of
Edmonston).*
DUNBAR & March, Patrick, E of. *PRO-sls
Homage; Bain II 488, HB-SND.*
DUNBAR, Patrick, 2nd E of March. *Steven-
son.* c1340. *(5th sl).*
DUNBAR, Patrick, 1st E of March. *Stevenson.*
c1285. *(2nd sl; d1308).*
MARCH, Earldom of. *Stevenson.* 1475. *(qtd
by Alexander Stewart, 2nd s of James 2, E of
March).*

Lion in border ch with 11 roses
DUNBAR, Patrick, 2nd E of March. *Stevenson.* 1320. *(1st sl).*

Lion in border ch with 13 roses
DUNBAR, Patrick, 2nd E of March. *Stevenson*. 1334. *(2nd sl)*.
DUNBAR, Patrick V, E of March. *Arch Journ xxxvii 200-1*. 13 May 1334.
Lion in border ch with 14 roses
DUNBAR, Patrick, 1st E of March. *Stevenson*. c1285. *(1st sl; d1308)*.
Lion in border ch with 16 roses
DUNBAR, George, 3rd E of March. *Stevenson*. 1369. *(d c1420)*.
Lion in tressure of roses
DUNBAR, Patrick, 7th E of Dunbar. *Stevenson*. 1261. *(3rd sl)*.
Lion in border semy of roses
DUNBAR & March, Patrick, E of. *PRO-sls Ex Treas of Rcpt Misc 4/30; Bain III 1126, HB-SND*. 1334.
DUNBAR & March, Patrick, E of. *Birch 15687*. 1309-68. *(border unclear)*.
DUNBAR & March, Patrick, E of. *Laing-sls I 292, HB-SND*. 1320.
DUNBAR & March, Patrick, E of. *PRO-sls Chap House 36, 9, Bain III 1657, HB-SND*. 1357.
DUNBAR, Patrick, E of March. *PRO-sls Ex QR 10/28, HB-SND*. 1357.
Gu lion Arg border Arg semy of roses Gu
DUNBAR. *Berry; Stodart pl 2*. *(6 roses)*.
[DUNBAR]. *Lyndsay 50*. *(8 roses; qtd by Steuert, D of Albany)*.
DUNBAR, of Kynhownquhar. *Lyndsay 227*. *(8 roses)*.
DUNBAR, E of Marche. *Lyndsay 57*. *(10 roses)*.
DUNBAR, Patrick, E of. *LMS 37*. *(1289-1309)*.
[DUNBAR, Patrick, E of]. *Proc Soc Antiq XVII 2S 277*. 1290-1330. *(on stole, Leagram Hall, Lancs)*.
[DUNBAR], Patrick, E of Lennox. *K 342*.
DUNBAR, le Conte Patrik. *P 70; H 23*.
DUNBARRE, Patrick, Conte de. *TJ 20*.
LAONOIS, le Conte de. *K 51*.
LAONOSIS, le Comte Patrick de. *GA 35*. *('.... poudre de rosetz de gueules')*.
MARCH, le Comte de. *Gelre; Stodart pl B5*. *(8 roses)*.

Lion in border semy of foils &c
Lion in border semy of 3foils
SAUVAGE, Sir James le. *PRO-sls*. 1265-6.
Gu lion Arg border Arg ch with 8 5foils Gu
— *SC 11*. *(?8 roses; qtd 2 by E of March & Ld of Man)*.
[DUNBAR]. *L9 104a, 4*. *('Le Conte de Patrick')*.
DUNBAR, Sir David. *SC 54*. *(lion ch on shldr with 5foil Gu)*.

[DUNBAR], E of March. *SC 13*.
DUNBAR, Cunte Patrik. *D 238*.
MARCHE, le Conte de la. *BL A 4*. *(pd 5foils)*.
Lion in border semy of 5foils
DUNBAR, Patrick de, E of March. *PRO-sls AS 269*. SIGILLUM ...COMITIS DE MARCHIA. 1334-5.
Gu lion Arg border Arg semy of 5foils Gu
DUNBAR, Cunte Patrik. *FW 88*.
MARCHE, counte de la. *LM 47*.
Gu lion Arg border Arg semy of 6foils Gu
DUNBAR, Conte Patrik. *H 60*. *(?lion Or)*.
Arg lion Az border Gu semy of pomegranates Or
GARNET, 'Le Roy de'. *XL 593*.
Per pale Gu and Az lion pg Or supporting a crozier erect encircled near head by mitre all Or border Arg ch with 8 letters 'B' Sa
BERMONDSEY ABBEY. *L10 66b, 19*.
Per pale Gu and Az lion stat gard Or roundelly Sa supporting with forepaws crozier erect enfiled near head by mitre Or border Arg semy of letters 'B' Sa
BERMONDSEY ABBEY. *WK 802*. *(imp Abbot Jn Marlow)*.

Lion in border semy of mullets
Gu lion Arg border Arg semy of mullets Gu
DUNBAR. *WLN 132*. *(mullets of 8 pts)*.
Or semy of mullets & lion Gu border Or semy of mullets alternately Gu and Az
MESSINA. *PLN 604*. *(mullets of 8 pts)*.

Lion in border semy of roundels
Lion in border roundelly
— *Birch 2893*. 15 cent. *(sl of Abbot of Cerne, Dorset)*.
CLIFTON, Gervais. *Clairambault 2628*. 1 Feb 1430. *(qrs 1&4)*.
CLIFTON, Gervaise. *Roman PO 3266*. 7 May 1430. *(qrs 1&4)*.
CORNEWAILE, Elizabeth de, Lady of Kynlet. *BirmCL-sls 475234*. 1354.
CORNUBIA, Elizabeth de. *Birch 8964*. 1355. *(7 roundels; imp by 2 lions passt [Brompton]; alias Cornewaile; wid of Esmond de C, Lady of Kynlet, Salop)*.
CORNWALL, Richard, E of. *Selborne 7, 49*. Sigillum Ricardi co ....nubie. c1250. *(14 roundels)*.
CORNWALL, Richard, E of. *Arch Journ xxxiv 181-2*. SIG[ILLUM] RICARDI COMITIS [CORN]UBIE. 1256. *(sl obv attached to charter among deeds at Claydon House)*.
CORNWALL, Richard, E of. *PRO-sls AS 270*. +S'...OMITIS RICARDI. 1257.
[CORNWALL, Richard, E of]. *Birch 4953*. *(11 roundels; sl of Mayor & Burgesses of Grampound, Cornw)*.

MEAUX, Thomas de. *PRO-sls E40 A279.*
1378-9.
SALTASH, Town of, Cornw. *Birch 5374.*
SIGILLUM SALTASCHE IN CORNWAILE. 14
cent. *(13 roundels).*
Lion to sin & border roundelly
[CORNWALL, Edmund, E of]. *Birch 5190.* 13
cent. *(sl of Newcastle-under-Lyme).*
Arg lion Gu border Az roundelly Or
CORNEWAYLL, Mons George de, dyrland. *WJ
219.*
Arg lion Gu border Sa roundelly Arg
CORNUBIAE, Comes. *Q II 3. (tinct of roun-
dels unclear).*
Arg lion Gu border Sa roundelly Or
— *WLN 99.*
CORNEWALLE, the erle of. *CT 17.*
CORNEWAYLL, le Contt de. *WJ 209.*
CORNEWAYLL, Mons J de. *WJ 212.*
CORNUBIE, Ducis. *NB 2.*
CORNUBIE, Dux. *SM 155, 28; SM 244, 39.*
CORNWAILL, E of. *E II 14.*
CORNWALL, le Conte. *FW 40.*
[CORNWALL]. *OxfRS I 29. (glass Banbury;
imp by Lovell).*
CORNWAYLLE, the Duc of. *WB IV 128b, 49.
(a&l Az).*
ST ROBERT'S MONASTERY, Knaresborough,
Yorks. *D4 25. (& Ric, E of Cornwall).*
Arg lion Sa border Arg roundelly Gu
— *PLN 1307. (qtd 2&3 by Oxenbridge).*
Arg lion Sa border Gu roundelly Or
PYKERINGE, Sire Thomas de. *N 1073.*
Or lion Gu border Sa roundelly Or
BACHET. *L10 22b, 15. (8 roundels).*
BACHET. *L1 58, 1; L2 75, 1.*
BACHOT. *RB 474.*
Or lion Sa border Arg roundelly Purp
LOWNDRESSE, Baron of the Naasse. *DIG 35.*
Erm lion Gu border Sa roundelly Or
CORNWALL, John de. *XL 347.*
Per fess indented lion in border roundelly
BURNELL, Margaret. *Mill Steph.* 1529.
*(brass to Mgt, dau of Roger North, haber-
dasher of London, & w of Thos B, mercer of
London, West Drayton, Middx).*
Per fess indented Or and Arg lion Sa in border
Gu ch with 8 roundels Arg
BURNELL, Merchant, of London. *L1 115, 1;
L2 81, 7. (a&l Gu).*
Per pale Erm and Az lion Untinc border roun-
delly Sa
MERKS. *Suff HN 48. (imp by Shelton; Met-
tingham Castle or College).*

Lion collared in border roundelly
Or lion Gu collared Or border Vt roundelly Or
TALBOT, Richard. *C 172.*

Lion crowned in border roundelly
Lion crowned in border roundelly
CORNWALL, E of. *CK a 14.*
CORNWALL, Edmund, E of. *Birch 6307-8.*
1275. *(s of Ric Plantagenet, K of the
Romans; equestr sl, obv & rev).*
CORNWALL, Edmund, E of. *Dugd 17, 70.*
1282. *(8 roundels).*
CORNWALL, Edward, de Alemannia, E of.
PRO-sls. 1274-5.
CORNWALL, Richard, E of. *Lawrance 11.*
1272. *(K of the Romans, bro of Hen 3,
d1272; effigy, Hayles Abbey, Gloucs).*
CORNWALL, Richard, E of. *Birch 6328.*
SIG[ILLVM;]RICARDI: COMITIS: PICTAVIE:. 13
cent. *(Count of Poitou, 2nd s of K Jn &
afterwards K of the Romans; equestr sl obv).*
CORNWALL, Richard, E of. *PRO-sls AS 22.*
+: S' SECRETI: COMITIS: RICARDI. 1256.
CORNWALL, Richard, E of. *PRO-sls.* 1256 &
57.
GRAMPOUND, defunct Borough of. *Proc Soc
Antiq XII 2S 56.* SIGILLUM MAIORIS & BUR-
GENSIUM BURGH DE GRANDPONT ALS
PONSMUR.
PLANTAGENET, Richard, E of Cornwall,
Count of Poitou. *Birch 6330.* [Obv]SIGILL'M
RICARDI FI....
[Rev]+.....TAVIENSIS. 1227. *(9 roundels;
equestr sl obv & rev).*
Arg lion Gu crowned Az border Sa semy of
roundels Arg
LEICES, Hammerl. *A 288.*
Arg lion Gu crowned Or border Sa roundelly Or
CORNEWAILL. *L10 35b, 4. (a&l Az).*
CORNEWAILL, E of. *E I 14.*
CORNEWAILLE, le Conte de. *P 46.*
CORNEWAILLE, le Counte de. *TJ 17.*
CORNEWALLE. *SK 41.*
CORNEWAYLE. *L1 152, 3; L2 101, 10.*
CORNEWAYLE, Erle of. *RH, Ancestor iii 201.*
CORNEWAYLE, S' Edmund. *PO 384.*
CORNWAILLE, le Counte de. *LM 35.*
CORNWAL, Edmund de. *CA 72.*
CORNWALE, Erle of. *BR IV 91.*
CORNWALL. *ME 8. (ch on shldr with mullet
Arg; a&l Or).*
CORNWALL. *LY A 128. (ch on shldr with
mullet Arg).*
CORNWALL, Count de. *CN 37.*
CORNWALL, Count of. *BG 336.*
CORNWALL, Counte de. *Q 4.*
CORNWALL, E of. *B 3.*
CORNWALL, E of. *BR V a 21.*
CORNWALL, E of. *WNS 25, 17. ('Le Cnte de
Cornewait por dar ou un lion degou crone
dor ou une border sa .... dor').*
CORNWALL, E of. *CRK 262.*
CORNWALL, de. *SP A 26.*

CORNWALL, le Conte. *C 124; F 12; D 34;
HE 10; G 30; J 12; N 1042.*
CORNWALL, D of. *XL 319. (a&l Az).*
CORNWALL, D of. *BR II 21.*
CORNWALL, D of. *BA 927. (a&l Or).*
CORNWALL, D of. *PLN 40. (a&l Or).*
CORNWALL, D of. *KB 231.*
CORNWALL, Edmund, E of. *LMS 20.
(d1300).*
CORNWALL, Mons John. *T b 55.*
CORNWALL, E of, Richard. *Lawrance 37.
(on tomb of Edm Crouchback, E of Lancs,
d1296).*
CORNWALL, Richard, E of. *Sandford 95.*
CORNWALL, Richard, E of. *WestmAbb.*
c1260. *(15 cent inscription).*
CORNWALL, Richard, E of. *Keepe 242; Neale
& Brayley II 155.* 1296. *(enamelled shield
formerly on ledge of tomb of Wm de
Valence).*
[CORNWALL, Richard of]. *Inventory.* 1296.
(mont to Edmund, E of Lancs).
[CORNWALL, Richard of]. *Lethaby 235-9.* 13
cent. *(glass, E Clerestory window).*
CORNWAYLE, D of. *PCL IV 80.*
CORNWAYLE, D of. *AY 15. (ducally
crowned; armed Or).*
CORNWAYLLE, Co. *DV 45b, 1797.*
Az lion Gu crowned Or border Sa roundelly Or
CORNUWAYLE, C de. *WNR 38.*
Erm lion ducally crowned in border roundelly
Untinc
CORNWAILLE, John, Chev, Ld of Faireholt.
Birch 8973. SIG...NNIS CORNEWA.....TIS. 1440.
Erm lion Gu crowned Or border Sa roundelly Or
CORNEVAYLE, Sir John, S' de Wanhoppe. *BB
84. (d1443).*
CORNUAYLL. *L2 101, 8.*
[CORNWALL], Ld Fanhopp. *WB II 48, 10.*
CORNWALL, Mons John. *T d 55.*
GRENCORNWAIL. *CV-BM 177.*

Lion qf in border roundelly
Lion qf crowned in border roundelly
CORNWALL, Richard, E of. *MP Hist Min ii
269.*
Arg lion qf Gu crowned Or border Sa roundelly
Or
CORNWALL, Richard, E of. *MP I 38.*

Lion passant in border roundelly
Arg lion passt Gu border Sa roundelly Arg
GRENADO, le Rey de. *LM 22.*

Lion in border Vair
Arg lion Az border Vair
— *I2(1904)298. (qtd 2 by Sir Ric de Penys-
ton).*
— *BA 837. (qtd 2 by [Peniston]).*

FAWEDBRIDGE. *L1 253, 7.*
Arg lion Gu border Vair
— *PLN 1452.*

Lion in border modified
Lion border engr
— *?source.* 1436. *(?Beler; sl or deed).*
— *WB I 35b, 1. (qtd 2 by E of Shrewsbury).*
— *Mill Steph.* c1475. *(qtd by [Furnival];
brass to Nicholas Kniveton & w Joan Maul-
everer, Muffington, Derbys).*
— *C3 7.* April 1404. *(... & w Maria; imp
by 2 bars in chf 3 mullets of 6 pts; c' seal
demi-woman affronte holding in both hands
whip with 5 knotted thongs).*
— *Bow XXXIII 6.* 1396-7. *(imp Grendon).*
— *Vinc 88, 6, 11.* 1329-30. *(imp by Thos
de Kyngeston, s of Sir Jn de K; sl).*
ACTON, William. *Ash-sls 799, 42.* 1351. *(s
of Wm A, of ...).*
AMBESAS, or Aumbesas, Willelmus, of
Carshalton, Surr. *Birch 5638.* S' WIL....
1307. *(equestr sl).*
ANNAN, Elena, w of Willm de Amnaud &
after his death of Geo de Wellame. *Steven-
son 229.* 1442.
BELER, Roger. *PRO-sls.* 14 cent.
BURNELL, Edward, Ld of El. *Bow XXX 33.*
1370-1.
CARRU, Eleanor de. *AnstisAsp I 213, 61.*
SIGILLUM: ELIANORE: DE: CARRU. 1338-9.
[CLEVEDON, of Clevedon]. *Vinc 88, 11.*
(dimid by Kingston; sl).
CORNEWAYLE, Richard, Ld of Burford.
BirmCL-sls Hagley Hall 351335. 1418.
GATEGANG, Richard. *PRO-sls Anc Deeds B
3912.* 1342. *(s of Jn G).*
GRAY, John. *Roman PO 5423.* 6 Jan 1434.
GRAY, John. *Durham-sls 1108. (used by
others in 1353).*
GRAY, John. *Clairambault 4230.* 2 Nov
1433.
GRAY, Sir Patrick. *Stevenson.* 1418. *(&
others).*
GRAY, Ralph. *Clairambault 4233.* 30 Sept
1441.
GRAY, Thomas. *Birch 10217.* SIGILLUM
THOME GRAY. 1407.
GRAY, Thomas. *Durham-sls 1112.* 1346.
GRAY, Sir Thos of Heton, Ld of Wark.
Durham-sls 1113. 1407.
GREY, Andrew, Ld. *PRO-sls.* 1483.
GREY, Henry, [E of Tankerville]. *Clairam-
bault 8801-2, HB-SND.* 1440. *(qtg 2&3 lion
[Cherleton of Powys]; over all escutch).*
?GREY, John de. *Birch 10265.* SIGILLUM:
IOH'IS....E. 1418.
GREY, Sir John. *Clairambault 4231-2.* 1434

& 1438. *(s of Sir Th G, of Heton, exec, 1415, Southampton).*

GREY, Sir John, E of Torberville. *?source.* 1411-8. *(sl).*

GREY, Sir Ralph. *Greenwich 14 K5, HB-SND.* 1506.

GREY, Ralph, Chivaler. *PRO-sls.* 1436.

GREY, Thomas. *Waterford 50, HB-SND.* 1428-9.

[GREY, Sir Thomas, of Heton]. *Blair D II 141, 307. (W front, gatehouse, Hilton Castle).*

HARPER. *?source.* 1421. *(mullet for diffce on lion's shldr; brass to ?Wm H & w ... Arderne, Latton, Essex).*

HETON, Alan of. *Arch Ael NS xxv pl V 3, HB-SND.* 1347.

HETON, Alan of. *Arch Ael NS xxv pl V 4, HB-SND.* 1384.

?HETON, Sir Alan. *Blair N II 148, 305. (built into wall, Stamfordham Castle).*

HETON, Margery. *Arch Ael xxv pl V 5, HB-SND.* 1384. *(w of Alan of H).*

HETON, Thomas of. *Dodsworth 45, 113, HB-SND.* 1348.

MOREL, Martin. *PRO-sls.* s' MARTIN MOREL DOSEU. 1349-50.

MOUBRAY, John, s of William M. *Birch 11999.* s' IOH'IS FILI WILL'I MOUBRAY. 1347.

MOWBRAY, John. *Durham-sls 1836. (s of Wm M).* c1348-66.

POMERAY, Johan de la, of Berry Pomeray. *CombeAsp II 184.* 1375-6.

POMEROY, William, Esq of Collaton, Devon. *PRO-sls.* 1597-8.

POUMERAI, Henry de la. *Birch 12777.* s' HENRICI DE LA POVMERAI. 1351. *(s of Amicia de la P, Ld of Byry, of Berry Pomeroy, Devon).*

RIDEL, William. *PRO-sls EX QR Misc 37/1, HB-SND.* 1318.

STAPLETON, John of. *Durham-sls 2306.* 1375.

TALBOT. *Proc Soc Antiq XXIII 2S 105.* SIGILLUM THOME DE ROKEBY. late 14 cent. *(silver sl).*

TALBOT, Beatrice. *Coll T&G ii 86-9. (qtg Strange & imp qtly 1&4 5 escutchs (Portugal sans border) 2&3 5 crescs).* SIGILLVM: BEATRICIS: TALBOT: DNE: DE: BLAKEMERE.

TALBOT, Beatrice. *Bow L 8.* Sigillum Beatrice dne Talbot et de Blakemere. 1420-1.

TALBOT, Gilbert. *PRO-sls.* 1415-16. *('seigneur de Irchenfelde and de Blakemore').*

TALBOT, Gilbert, 5th Baron, d1419. *Birch 13829.* s' GILBERTI DNI DE TALBOT ET DE ARCHYNFELD. temp Hen 5. *(qtg 2&3 2 lions passt [Strange]).*

TALBOT, John, Ld of Furnival & Wesford, E

of Shrewsbury, Marshal of France. *Birch 13836.* SIGILLU IOHIS DNI ...LBOT & DE.... 1437. *(qtg 2&3 bend betw 6 martlets [Furnival]).*

TALBOT, John, Ld of Furnival & Wexford, E of Shrewsbury, Marshal of France. *Birch 13833.* SIGILL' IOH'IS TALBOT DNI DE FFURNYVALL. 1409-21.

TALBOT, John, E of Shrewsbury. *PRO-sls.* 1443-4.

TALBOT, Margaret. *Birch 13848.* 1456. *(wid of Sir Jn T, 1st E of Shrewsbury; 2nd qr on dex side of 1st of 2 shields).*

TALBOT, Rich, Ld of Trehenfield. *Dugd 17, 72.* 1349.

TALBOT, Richard. *PRO-sls.* 1301 & 1336-7.

TALBOT, Richard, Ld. *PRO-sls.* 1389-90.

TALBOT, Richard, Ld of Eccleswall. *Barons Letter.*

TALBOT, of Shrewsbury. *Birch 9004.* 1428. *(imp by Courtenay in arms of Anne, w of Hugh C, E of Devon, & dau of Ric, Ld Talbot).*

TALEBOT, Richard. *Birch 13850.* RICARDUS TALEBOT. early 14 cent.

TYREL, Hugh, Esq, of the King's chamber. *PRO-sls.* 1336-7.

WALEWYN, Master John de. *PRO-sls.* 1315-16.

WASTNEIS, Thomas de. *Bow XXXII 24.* 1334-5. *(s&h of Wm W).*

Arg lion border engrailed

Arg lion & border engr Az voided Arg
    RANTOUNE, of Bylle. *Lyndsay 280.*

Arg lion & border engr Az
    CREYCHTOUN, of Brounstoune. *Lyndsay 306.*

Arg lion border engr Gu
    — *WB I 16, 20. (qtd 2&3 Arg fess engr & in chf 5foil Gu).*
    — *WB II 70, 15. (qtg II: qtly 1&4 Arg bend cotised Sa 2: Arg 3: Sa 5 fusils in pale Arg III: qtly 1&4 Gu 3 bars Arg 2&3 Arg).*
    — *WB IV 172b, 838. (qtd 2&3 by Corbett).*
    — *PLN 1665. (a&l Az).*
    DUNHEAD. *BG 411.*
    DUNHED. *L10 63, 8. (a&l Az).*
    DUNHED. *FK II 852.*
    DUNHED, John. *PLN 555.*

Arg lion & border engr Or
    SCHREWISBERY, E of. *BR II 38.*

Arg lion Gu border engr Sa
    — *BA 1004. (qtd 2&3 by Tregarthyn).*
    — *PT 609.*
    POMERY. *PT 168. (in dex chf mullet Untinc).*
    ROLAND, Leschu. *HE 44.*

Arg lion & border engr Sa
  BERNEN, Lancelot de. *LE 268.*
  BERVEN. *L10 30, 7.*
  BOVILE. *XL 32.*
  BOWCLES. *L1 97, 3. (a&l Gu).*
  BOWELLS. *L1 46, 6. (a&l Gu).*
  BOWELS. *L10 84, 12. (a&l Gu).*
  DOWELLS. *BA 32, 310.*
  DOWELS. *L10 64, 10.*
  DOWELLS, Sir Hugh, Staffs. *WB III 75b, 2. (a&l Gu).*
  HARPER. *Nichols Leics IV 341.* 1428. *(window to Willm H, Nisterton Ch).*
  HARPER. *L2 269, 9.*

Az lion in border engr
Az lion Arg border engr Arg
  TYRRELL, Mons Hugh. *WJ 292.*
Az lion Arg border engr Or
  CREW. *L2 114, 12. (armed Or, langued Gu, mullet Sa pd Or on shldr, border noted in margin not painted).*
  TERELL. *CT 192.*
  TYROL, Roger. *WB I 19, 4.*
  TYRRELL, Hugh. *XL 147.*
  TYRRELL, Mons Hugh. *WJ 292.*
Az lion Or border engr Arg
  NEVILL, Mons Hugh de. *WJ 124.*
  SEEVYLL', Mons Hugh de. *XL 647.*
Az lion Or border engr Gu
  PYKENHAM. *Suff HN 2.*
Az lion & border engr Or
  — *WB III 122b, 2. (qtd by Untinc fess betw 2 chevs Untinc all imp by Gu 3 crescs Arg in chf mullet Or).*
  TIRELL, S Roger. *GA 221.*

Gu lion Arg in border engr
Gu lion & border engr Arg
  — *WB II 57, 10.*
  GRAY, Ld. *Lyndsay 108.*
  GRAY, Baster. *R 9.*
  GRAY, Henry. *LY A 27. (cresc Sa on shldr).*
  GRAY, Sir ... of ?Otley. *WB IV 145b 357. (dex imp).*
  GRAY, Sir R. *WB I 39, 8.*
  GRAY, Sir Rauff. *WK 431.*
  GRAY, Sir Rauffe. *BW 16, 108.*
  GRAY, Mons Th de. *WJ 159.*
  GRAY, S Thom, Norreys. *PO 237.*
  GRAY, Mons Thomas. *S 116.*
  GRAY, William, Bp of Ely. *Lambeth 759. (d1478).*
  GRAYE, the Lord. *SC 40. (a&l Or).*
  GRAYE, Sir John. *WGA 28.*
  GREY. *CRK 592.*
  GREY, Sr Edward. *CKO 41.*
  GREY, of Etton, Ld Powis. *L1 268, 2; L2 215, 4.*

GREY, Henry, Ld Powis. *Sandford 319. (m Antigone, nat dau of Humphrey, D of Gloucester).*
GREY, of Heton & Chillingham, Northd. *Blair N II 112, 230. (on bosses of roof of nave, Bothal Church, Northd).*
GREY, Ld John. *BD 157b. (Garter badge on mantle; E window, St George's Ch, Stanford, Lincs).*
GREY, Sir John, E of Thankerville KG. *Leake. (d1420-1).*
GREY DE NORTHD. *PT 843.*
GREY, de Northd. *PLN 740.*
GREY, Thomas. *S 118.*
GREY, Thomas. *XL 331.*
GREY, Thomas le. *BG 317.*
GREY, Will, Bp of Ely. *GutchWdU. (library window, Balliol College).*
GREYE. *LD 17. (a&l Az).*
KNOLLYS, Sir Robarde, of Northd. *RH, Ancestor iv 232. (?error for Grey).*
RIDELL, Monsire William. *CG 82.*
RYDELL, Sir William. *CV-BM 213.*
TALBOT, Monsire de. *AN 41.*
Gu lion Arg border engr Az
  — *PLN 1279. (a&l Az; qtd 2&3 by Ld Powys).*
  GRANDFORD. *L1 282, 5; L2 225, 2.*
  GRAY, Mons Thomas, de Heton. *TJ 46.*
  MARKES, Sir John. *BR V 231.*
  MERC, John de. *E I 396; E II 398.*
  MERK, S Jehan de. *GA 8.*
  MERK, Sire Johan de. *N 439. ('...la bordure enderte de').*
  MOWBRAY. *L9 69b, 5. (a&l Az).*
Gu lion Arg border engr Or
  GREY, Monsire Thomas de. *CG 81.*
Gu lion Arg border engr Sa
  GRAUMFORD, Suss. *PLN 634.*
  GRAUNSFORD. *DV 44b, 1745.*
  GRAUNSFORD. *CC 227, 169.*
  GRAUNSSFORD, Sir John, of Suss. *WB III 82, 7. (a&l Az).*

Gu lion Or in border engr
Gu lion border engr Or
  — *Leake. (qtd 2 by Jn, E of Shrewsbury KG (d1460)).*
  — *XB 16. (qtd by Talbot).*
  — *XK 224. (qtd 2 by Sir Gilbert Talbot).*
  — *XK 188. (qtd 2 by Sir Jn Talbot).*
  — *XK 34. (qtd 2 by Geo Talbot, E of Shrewsbury).*
  — *XK 45. (qtd 2 by Sir Gilbert Talbot).*
  — *XK 78. (qtr 4 of escutch of Arthur Plantagenet, KG).*
  — *WK 53. (qtd 2 by Sir Gilbert Talbot).*
  — *WK 15. (qtd 2 by Gilbert Talbot).*
  — *WK 428. (qtd V 2&3 by Visct Lisle).*

— *Leake. (qtd 2 by Sir Francis Talbot, KG (d1559) with 8 other qtgs)*.

— *XC 318. (qtd 3 by Anne Ingelby, all imp by Wriothesley qtg Dunstanville & Lusthill)*.

— *WGA 261-2. (qtd 2 by Jn Talbot, E of Shrewsbury)*.

— *ML II 15. (qtd 2 by Talbot, E of Shrewsbury)*.

— *ML II 15. (qtd 2 by Talbot, 'Erle of Shrewsbury')*.

— *WGA 47. (qtd 2 by Sir Geo Talbot, E of Shrewsbury)*.

— *CRK 1380. (qtd 2 by Jn Talbot, E of Salop)*.

— *WK 141. (qtd 2 by Sir ?Gilbert Talbot)*.

— *PLN 1721. (qtd 2 by Sir Gilbert Talbot)*.

— *Leake. (qtd 2 by Sir Geo Talbot, KG [d1541])*.

— *WB V 83. (qtd 2 by Sir Gilbert Talbot)*.

— *CRK 255. (qtd 4 by Lisle)*.

ARUNDEL, Thomas. *RH, Ancestor iii 186. (Archbp of Canterbury 1397-1414)*.

LISLE, Ld. *BR VI 45*.

SCHROWSBURY, Count de. *RH, Ancestor iv 227*.

TALBOT. *1H7 27d; D13 102. (qtd 4 by Grey on escutch of Sir Arthur Plantagenet, KG)*.

TALBOT. *Dingley. (qtg Arg 2 lions passt Gu, amp Woodstock; E window, Whitchurch Ch, Salop)*.

TALBOT. *Arch Journ xcii 91. (wall painting, All Saints, Chalgrave, Beds)*.

TALBOT. *AS 126*.

TALBOT. *CRK 228. (tail turned inwards)*.

TALBOT. *BB 25. ('s' jelbarde s' de talbotte' d1419)*.

TALBOT. *PLN 105. (membered Az; qtg 2&3 Furnival)*.

TALBOT. *PLN 1580*.

TALBOT. *PV 3*.

TALBOT. *PO 24*.

TALBOT. *Sandford 448. (qr 4 of escutch of Arthur Plantagenet, Visct Lisle, d1542)*.

TALBOT. *XL 215*.

TALBOT. *TB 1-15 & 22. (a&l Az)*.

TALBOT, Baron of Schrewysbery. *AY 30*.

TALBOT, Ld. *RH, Ancestor iv 228*.

TALBOT, Ld. *BW 8, 41. (qrs I&IV 1&4)*.

TALBOT, Ld. *FK I 111*.

TALBOT, Ld. *ML II 57*.

TALBOT, le Sire. *TJ 28*.

TALBOT, Monsire de. *CG 62*.

TALBOT, Gilbert, Ld. *Sandford 242. (m Joan Plantagenet)*.

TALBOT, Gilbert, Ld, KG. *Leake. (d1419-20)*.

TALBOT, Gylbert, Ld. *WGA 27. (buried at Whitchurch)*.

TALBOT, Mons J. *WJ 243*.

TALBOT, John.

TALBOT, Gilbert. *BD 13. (great South Window, Lichfield Cathedral)*.

TALBOT, Sir John, KG. *BB 154, 11. (qtg Strange & imp Furnival; d1453)*.

TALBOT, Mons Rich. *WJ 241*.

TALBOT, Richard, Ld. *S 71. (qtg Arg 2 lions passt Gu)*.

TALBOT, E of Shrewsbury. *WB II 49, 11. (imp Furnival)*.

TALBOT, E of Shrewsbury. *PLN 84. (qtg 2&3 Strange)*.

TALBOTT. *CT 285*.

TALBOTT, Ld. *KB 289*.

TALBOTT, Sr de. *CKO a 60*.

TALBOTT, le Sr de. *T c 28. (qtg Arg 2 lions passt Gu)*.

TALBOTT, E of Shrewsberie. *KB 267*.

Or lion in border engr

Or lion Untinc border engr Sa

POLE. *CT 157*.

Or lion Az border engr Gu

PERCY. *DV 64b, 2550*.

PERCY. *CKO 70*.

PERCY, Mons Gilberd de. *WJ 105*.

PERCY, Monsire William de. *CG 97*.

Or lion Az border engr Sa

POMERAI, Edward, of Devon. *WB III 114b, 6*.

Or lion Gu border engr Az

— *PLN 1759. (qtd 2 by Sir T Leyton)*.

Or lion & border engr Gu

FILBREGGE, 'Chevalier'. *SK 622. (lion bendwise)*.

Or lion Gu border engr Sa

POLE, de la. *E I 151; E II 151*.

POMBRAY, Edward, of Devon. *RH, Ancestor v 175. (Edward P, of Berry, d1446)*.

POMER', S' Henr'. *PO 325*.

POMERAY. *BA 1096*.

POMERAY, John. *BG 370. (a&l Az)*.

POMERAY, Mons John. *S 175*.

POMERAY, Mons Th de. *WJ 268*.

POMERCY, Monsire Henry de la. *AN 317*.

POMERE. *L9 107a, 7. (a&l Az)*.

POMEREY, Sir Thomas. *WK 129*.

POMEREYE, Mons Henry de la. *TJ 52*.

POMEROY. *XL 258*.

POMEROY, John. *S 177*.

POMEROY, Thomas de. *XL 127*.

POMERY. *PT 115*.

POMERY. *DV 68a, 2700*.

POMERY. *L1 491, 3. (a&l Az)*.

POMERY, Sir Edward. *WK 433*.

POMMERY. *WB IV 174b, 879*.

ROULAND, Leschu. *FW 61*.

Sa &c lion in border engr

Sa lion & border engr Or
    ST GEORGE. *XL 113.*
    ST JORGE. *RB 488.*
    SAMCTGEORGE. *Ll 606, 6. (armed Gu).*
Vt lion Arg border engr Untinc
    GRAY, Mons Thomas de. *TJ 47.*
Vt lion & border engr Arg
    HETON. *Ll 314, 4; L2 252, 10.*
    HETON. *XL 26.*
    HETON. *LH 87.*
    HETON, Sir Robert. *LH 349.*
    HETON, Mons Thomas de. *TJ 5555.*

Lion in border engr field patterned

Erm lion border engr Untinc
    STAPILTON, John of. *Durham-sls 2305.*
    1343.
Az billetty & lion Or border engr Arg
    GISORS, 'Jesore'. *L9 2b, 6.*
    JEFOURS. *Ll 360, 4; L2 278, 7.*
    JESORE. *FK II 328.*
Az billetty lion & border engr Or
    GISORS, Johan. *XL 61.*
Az crusily lion Or border engr Arg
    — *PO 639.*
Gu crusily & lion Arg border engr Untinc
    WARR. *Gerard 60. (Kingston St Mary).*
Gu crusily fitchy & lion Arg border engr Sa
    WARR, Sir Richard de la. *XL 239.*
    WARRE, Sir Richard. *WK 325.*
    WARRE, Sir Richard. *BA 761.*
Arg semy of 3foils lion Sa border engr Gu
    HERFORD, Sire Symon de. *PV 40.*

Lion patterned or charged in plain border engr

Or lion Gu ch on shldr with annulet Or border engr Sa
    POMEROY. *CRK 2077.*
Sa crusily & lion Arg ch on shldr with annulet Sa border engr Or
    — *L9 26a, 9. (a&l Gu).*
Gu lion Or ch on shldr with cresc Az border engr Arg
    — *XK 303. (qtd 3 by Sir Jn Dudley).*
Or lion Gu ch on shldr with cresc Arg border engr Sa
    POMEROY. *SK 904.*
Vt lion Arg ch on shldr with cresc Sa border engr Arg
    HETON, Edward de. *LY A 71.*
    HETONE. *FK II 411.*
Lion Or ch on shldr with escallop Az border engr Sa
    TALBOT, Mons J. *WJ 243.*
Gu lion Arg ch on shldr with boar's head Sa border engr Arg
    GREY, of Horton. *CRK 440.*

Gu lion Or ch on shldr with mullet Arg border engr Or
    TALBOT, Mons' Joon. *TJ 92.*
Vt lion per fess Arg and Sa border engr Arg
    — *LY A 74.*
    — *FK II 973.*
Per fess Sa and Arg lion counterch border engr Gu
    CRONE, William, of Essex & tailor of London. *LD 55. (a&l Gu).*
    GREEN, of Essex, 'Taylour of London'. *Ll 295, 5; L2 229, 3. (a&l Gu).*
Arg lion Vt gutty Arg border engr Vt
    MUCKLESTONE, Staffs. *XL 206. (a&l Gu).*
Gu lion Arg vulned on shldr Gu border engr Arg
    GRAY, S' John, de Heton. *BB 26 K 3. (d1421).*
    POWYS. *CRK 212.*

Lion in patterned border engr

Arg lion Az border engr Az ch with tressure Arg
    RANTOUNE, of Bylle. *Lyndsay 280. (armed Gu).*
Gu lion & border engr Erm
    BENET, S' Rich'. *PO 656.*

Lion in border engr gobony &c

Arg lion Gu border engr gobony Gu and Az
    DUNHED. *Ll 193, 6.*
Gu lion Arg border engr gobony Arg and Or
    GRAY, Yorks. *MY 253. (a&l Az).*
Gu lion Arg border engr gobony Arg and Vt
    — *H21 8. (qtd by Gascoigne [of Galthrop, Yorks]).*
Gu lion Arg border engr gobony Or and Arg
    CHAUMON, Mons' John, de Colthorpe. *TJ 164.*
    GREY, Sir .... *CRK 1342.*
Gu lion Arg border engr gobony Or and Gu
    — *WK 123. (qtd 3 by Gascon).*
    — *PLN 2017. (qtd 3 by Sir Wm Gascoigne).*
Gu lion Or border engr gobony Or and Gu
    — *WB III 117, 8. (qtd 2&3 by Gascoyne).*
Gu lion Arg border engr party indented Or and Sa
    — *E6. (qtd by Constable).*
Per pale Arg and Sa lion Gu border engr per pale Sa and Arg
    CHAMPENEY. *Ll 170, 3; L2 111, 6.*
    CHAMPNEYS. *L2 140, 12.*
Per pale Arg and Sa lion per pale Gu and Or border engr per pale Sa and Arg
    CHAMPNEY. *XL 518. (a&l Az).*
    CHAMPENEYS. *L10 38, 3.*
Per pale Arg and Sa lion Gu gutty Or border engr per pale Sa and Arg
    CHAMPNEY. *XL 519; L10, 38. (a&l Az).*

Lion in border engr semy &c
Sa lion Arg border engr Arg semy of cloves Sa
— *SK 331.*

Lion & border engr roundelly
    CORNEWAILLE, John, Chev. *Birch 8971.*
    SIGILLUM: IOH'IS: CORNEWAILLE. 1418.
Arg lion Gu border engr Sa roundelly Or
    CORNEWAYLE, Mons Esmon de. *WJ 210.*
Erm lion Gu border engr Sa roundelly Or
    CORNWAILE, Fanhop. *CB 51.*
    CORNWALL, 'The Baron of Burford'. *BA 17b.*
Az semy de lis Arg border engr Gu roundelly Or
    HOLAND, Mons Thomas de. *CA 82.*

Lion crowned in border engr
Lion crowned & border engr
    — *Mill Steph.* 1527. *(qtd 2&3 by Leventhorpe; brass to Thos L & w Joan dau of Geo Dallison, Sawbridgeworth, Herts).*
    FOXTON, Robert de, of Draughton, Northants. *Birch 9921.* ...OBE....DE.FOXTON. 1324.
Arg lion Sa crowned Or border Az
    — *BA 16.* (qtd 2&3 by 'Lord Burnell Ratcliffe').
    BURNELLS. *L10 81b, 1.* (a&l Gu).
Gu lion Arg crowned Or border engr Arg
    GERNET. *SK 102.* (imp by Gildisburgh).
Gu lion Arg crowned & border engr Or
    GARNET. *CB 149.*
    GARNET. *XL 535.*
    GAUCE. *L1 280, 4.*
    GERNET. *SK 195.*
Or lion Gu crowned Untinc border engr Sa
    POMEROY, Sir Thomas. *PLN 2023.*

Lion crowned in patterned border engr
Lion crowned & border engr roundelly
    CORNEWAYLLE, Dame Elizab. *Mill Steph.* c1370. *(w of Mons Esmon de C; brass, Burford, Salop).*
Arg lion Gu crowned Or border engr Sa roundelly Or
    ALMAIN, Edmond de, E of Cornwall. *Sandford 101, 94.* (d1299-1300).
    CORNWALL. *WB II 59, 8.*
    CORNWALL, Ld. *PLN 106.* (a&l Sa).
    CORNWALL, Edmond, of Herts. *CRK 990.* (a&l Or).
    CORNWALL, Sir Geoffrey. *Sandford 99.* (arms borne before he took D of Brittany prisoner).
    FANHOPE, Ld. *KB 328.* (estoile Or on shldr).
    FANOPE, Ld. *CB 7.* (a&l Or).
Erm lion Gu crowned Or border engr Sa roundelly Or
    — *WK 91.* (qtd 2&3 by Sir Thos Blount).
    BARDOLF, Ld. *BR VI 14.* (armed Or).

    CORNEWALL, Brian. *S 395.*
    CORNWALL, Sir Thomas, Knight. *I2(1904)74.*
    CORNWAL, of Burford, Salop & Berington, Herefs. *Sandford 99.*
    CORNWAL, Sir John. *Sandford 258.*
    CORNWALL. *L10 36b, 5.*
    CORNWALL, Bryan. *S 397.*
    CORNWALL, Edmund D of. *XL 320.* (a&l Az).
    CORNWALL, Ld Fanhope. *CRK 1320.* (estoile Or on shldr, a&l Or).
    CORNWALL, Sir John, KG. *Leake.* c1421. (estoile Or on shldr). (d1443).
    CORNWALL, Sir John, Ld Fanhope. *WGA 129.* (a&l Or).
    CORNWALL, Sir Thomas. *WK 222.* (a&l Or).
    FANHOPE, Ld. *BW 12, 74.* (armed Or).
    FANHOPE, Ld. *RH, Ancestor iv 229.*
    FANHOPE, Ld. *WB I 37, 8.*
    GRENE. *SK 62.*

Lion qf in border engr
Gu lion qf Or border engr Arg
    BORNE, Thomas. *CA 43.*
    BOURNE, Monsr Thomas. *SD 9.*
    BOURNE, S' Thomas de. *R 73.*

Lion passant &c in border engr
Arg lion passt border engr Sa
    LANERYN. *L9 42b, 10.*
    LAVERING. *XL 25.*
    LAWRYN. *L1 406, 1; L2 304, 12.* (a&l Gu).
Lion salient border engr
    CRICHTON, John, of Innernyte. *Stevenson.* 1520.
Arg lion salient border engr Sa
    DOWELL. *XL 192.*
Or lion salient border engr Gu
    FELBRIGGE. *XL 544.*
Or lion salient Gu border engr Sa
    POMERY. *LEP 47.* (langued Az).
Az crusily Arg lion ramp gard Arg border engr Or
    DALTON, Mons J de, of Kirby Misperton. *WJ 404.*
    DALTON, John de. *XL 459.*
Gu crusily Or lion gard & border engr Arg
    LUDELOWE, s' Th'm. *PO 644.*
Gu crusily & lion pg Arg border engr Arg
    LODELAWE, Mons' Thomas. *SD 48.*

Lion bicorporate in border engr
Az lion 2corp border engr Arg
    ATWATER, William. *CRK 881.*
Vt lion 2corp sejt & border engr Arg
    ATWATER. *L1 15, 1.*
    ATWATER. *XL 29.*
    ATWATER. *L1 15, 1; L2 8, 11.*

Lion in border indented

Lion & border indented
> [GREY]. *Blair N I 71, 129. (qtd 2&3 by Surtees, of Newcastle; tomb, St Nicholas Cathedral, Newcastle).*

Arg lion Az border indented Or
> TIRELL, S Roger. *ST 21.*

Arg lion & border indented Gu
> DUNHEAD. *CC 233b, 370.*
> TYRELL, Sir Roger. *Lawrance 45. (d1316). (effigy, Dilwyn, Herefs).*

Az lion Arg border indented Or
> TYREL, S' Roger. *PO 357.*
> TYREL, Sire Roger. *M 937.*
> TYREL, Sr Roger. *L 4.*

Gu lion border indented Arg
> RIDEL, Sire Willame. *N 1021.*
> RIDELL, Mons' William. *TJ 87.*
> RYDEL, Sire William. *O 153.*
> RYDELL. *L1 563, 6.*
> RYDELL, Sr Wm. *L 52.*

Gu lion Arg border indented Or
> MEERK, S Johan de. *ST 99.*
> MERK, Johan de. *LM 546.*
> MERKE, Essex. *L1 438, 4; L2 336, 6.*

Gu lion & border indented Or
> TALBOT, Gilbert. *CA 145.*
> TALBOT, Mons Gilbert. *SD 2.*
> TALBOT, Sr Gilbert. *L 39.*
> TALEBOT, Sire Gilberd. *N 893.*
> TALERT. *L1 639, 3.*

Or lion & border indented Gu
> ARMENIA, K of. *C 20.*

Vt lion & border indented Arg
> [HETON, Thomas of]. *Blair N I 75, 142. (S window, St Nicholas Cathedral, Newcastle).*

Arg lion Az crowned & gutty border indented Gu
> HANTON, Mons Richard. *CA 196.*

Lion in border wavy &c

Arg lion Gu border wavy Az
> — *CRK 1092.*
> SOMAYNE. *CB 17 & 18.*

Arg lion Gu border nebuly Az
> SOMAYNE. *SK 141. (imp by Moyne).*
> SOMAYNE. *SK 142.*

Gu lion gard border wavy Or
> — *WLN 160.*

Other Beast in border

Arg bear passt Sa muzzle chain & border engr Gu
> — *CRK 17.*

Arg bear Sa muzzled & border engr Gu
> BARMYHAM. *PT 1176.*

Dog in plain border

Arg talbot sejt border Sa
> FORNAYS. *PLN 1369.*
> FORNAYS. *DV 46a, 1810.*
> FORNEYS. *L1 261, 2; L2 196, 1. (?bloodhound).*
> [FURNESS]. *WB I 32b, 15.*

Dog in patterned border

Or levrier Gu collared Sa border Sa roundelly Or
> BOURDEUX, Peres de. *Ha 92. (prob foreign).*
> BUREUX, Sr Perez. *H b 92. (prob foreign).*

Dog in modified border

Per fess Arg and Sa greyhound courant in chf Sa border engr counterch
> FORD. *WB II 68, 9.*

Sa talbot passt border engr Arg
> SUDBERY. *L1 594, 3.*

Sa greyhound ramp border engr Arg
> PONERTON. *L2 404, 4.*

Arg greyhound salient border engr Sa
> — *WB II 67, 13. (qtg 2 Arg griffin segr Sa beak & forelegs Gu, 3 Barry Sa and Or on chf Or 2 pales Sa, 4 Arg 3 choughs Ppr).*

Talbot sejt border engr
> SUDBURY. *Birch 1227. 1380-1. (sl ad causas as Archbp of Canterbury).*
> SUDBURY. *Birch 4123.* SIG'CO.... GREGORII DE SUDBURY. *1528. (sl of Coll of St Gregory, Sudbury, Suff; founded by him).*
> TYBALD, Simon, Bp of London 1362-75. *Birch 1925. (alias Sudbury; privy sl).*
> TYBALD, Simon. *Birch 1923.*

Sa talbot sejt border engr Arg
> SUDBERY. *DV 45a, 1857.*
> SUDBERY. *Suff HN 2. (imp Counby; St Gregory's Ch, Sudbury).*
> SUDBURY. *LS 33.*
> SUDBURY, Simon, Archbp of Canterbury. *CVK 665.*
> SUDBURY, Sir Symon, Bp. *Suff HN 2. ('in the colledge of Sudbury').*

Goat &c in border

Az goat passt Arg armed collared & belled Or border gobony Arg and Az
> POLLAYN. *L2 410, 3.*

Gu mule passt Arg border Untinc
> MOYLE. *XF 821a.*

Gu mule stat & border Arg
> MOYLE, Kent. *L2 346, 4.*

Ox (bull) &c in border

Bull passt & border roundelly
> COLE, John. *Birch 8791.* SIGILL': IOHANNIS : COLE. *1425.*
> LYHERT, Walter, Bp of Norwich. *Birch 2055. 1466.*

Arg bull passt Gu border Sa roundelly Or
    COOLEY, of Devon. *L1 180, 2; L2 127, 10.*
    (armed Or).

Arg bull passt & border Sa roundelly Or
    COLE, Sir Adam, of Devon. *WB III 73, 4.*
    (langued Gu armed & unguled Or).
    COLE, of Tewkesbury. *BA 874.*
    COLEE. *L1 139, 2; L2 117, 1. (?bull passt).*
    COLEE. *L10 37, 6.*
    COLEE. *XPat 83, Arch 69, 75. (?bull passt).*
    COLEE, Robert, Gloucs. *WK 764.*
    HART, Walter, Provost of Oriel, Oxf, Bp of
    Norwich. *GutchWdU II 2, 781. (armed Or,*
    mitre Or in centre chf of border; or Lyhart,
    N window, Divinity School).
    [LYHART]. *Farrer III 15. 1472. (armed &*
    unguled Or; shield, Norwich Cathedral).
    LYHERT, Walter, Provost of Oriel, Bp of
    Norwich. *GutchWdU. (armed & unguled*
    Or, mitre Or in centre chf of border; in
    accompt-house, Oriel College, Oxf).

Arg bull salient & border Sa roundelly Or
    LIARD. *L9 42a, 9. (armed & unguled Or).*

Bull stat & border roundelly
    COLE, Frances. *Mill Steph. 1640. (imp*
    Thornhill; w of Ric T; brass, Aston Rowant,
    Oxfords).
    COLE, Jane. *Mill Steph. 1643. (imp Bligh;*
    w of Gregory C & dau of Wm B, of
    Botathan, Cornw; brass, Aston Rowant,
    Oxfords).
    LYHERT, Walter, Bp of Norwich. *Arch Journ*
    lxxi 236. c1480-3. (ceiling boss, Divinity
    School, Oxf).

Arg bull stat Gu border Sa roundelly Or
    COLE. *BA 1161. (armed & unguled Or; bull*
    tricked Sa).

Or squirrel salient & border engr Az
    LOVELL. *CC 224b, 91.*

Arg wolf & border engr Gu
    — *WB I 16, 18. (?wolf erect).*

Or wolf ramp Az border engr Sa
    LOVEL. *L1 407, 6; L2 301, 7. (armed Gu).*
    LOVELL. *L9 38a, 5.*

Arg wolf salient Az border Sa roundelly Or
    KYMER, Mayster Gylbert, Dorset. *RH, Ances-*
    tor vii 195.

Or wolf salient Az border engr Sa
    LOVELL. *RB 257.*
    LOVELL, John. *PLN 1327.*

Arg wolf salient Sa collar Arg ch with 3 roun-
    dels Gu border engr Sa roundelly Or
    ATWODE. *XPat 5, Arch 69, 69. (a&l Gu).*
    ATWOOD. *L2 15, 3. (a&l Gu).*

Arg wolf salient Sa collar Or ch with 3 roundels
    Gu border engr Sa roundelly Or
    ATWOOD. *L10 6b, 16. (imp Or eagle's leg*
    erased at thigh Sa on chf indented Az 3 roun-
    dels Arg [Tarbock]).

Beast & label in border

Gu lion & border Arg label Az
    MOUBRAY, son ffitz de. *WJ 158.*

Az lion & border Or label Arg & cresc Az for
    diffce
    TALBOT, Sir Gilbert. *XK 224.*

Lion border ch with 8 roses label
    DUNBAR, George, E of March. *Laing-sls I*
    1009 pl vii 4. SIGILL COMUNE CAPITULI DUN
    BARNENSIS. 16 May 1453. *(chapter sl, Dun-*
    bar College, church founded by him).

Lion in border ch with 12 roses in chf label
    DUNBAR, George, 11th E of. *Stevenson.*
    1404.

Gu lion Arg border Arg ch with roses Gu label
    Az
    DUNBAR, Patrick de, s of Count of Lennox.
    K 345.
    DUNBAR, Patrike 'fiz le conte'. *H 36; K 52.*

Lion border engr & label
    GRAY, Sir Andrew, 2nd Ld. *Stevenson.*
    1460.
    GRAY, Sir Patrick, of Kinneff. *Stevenson.*
    1461. *(?label of 5; s of 1st Ld Gray).*
    TALBOT, Gilbert, Ld of Irchenefeld, Herefs,
    3rd Baron. *Birch 13827.* SIGILLUM GILBERTI
    TALBOT. 1376.
    TALBOT, Richard. *PRO-sls.* ?temp Edw 3.
    TALBOT, Richard. *Dugd 17, 18.* 1385.

Arg lion & border engr Sa label Gu
    HARPAR, William. *LY A 51.*

Gu lion & border engr Arg label Az
    GRAY, Visct Lile. *PLN 374. (imp qtly 1&4*
    Beauchamp 2&3 Neville, cresc Sa).
    GRAY, W.. le fitz. *WJ 160.*

Gu lion & border engr Or label Az
    TALBOT. *SK 873.*
    [TALBOT]. *Proc Soc Antiq XXII 2S 465.*
    (armorial pendant).
    TALBOT, Gilbt. *WJ 242.*
    TALBOTT, Mons Richard. *SD 3.*

Gu lion & border engr Or label of 5 Arg
    TALBOTT. *CT 288. (?label Az).*

Or lion Gu border engr Sa label Arg
    POMERCY, Monsire Henry de la, le filtz. *AN*
    320.
    POMERY, le fitz. *PT 116.*
    POMERY, fitz. *DV 68b, 2701.*

Gu lion & border indented Or label Az
    TALBOT, S Wm. *ST 24.*

Beast & in base in border

Per fess Arg and Sa in chf greyhound courant &
    in base owl border engr all counterch
    FORD. *XPat 298, Arch 69, 92; Stowe 692,*
    41. (of Devon added later).
    FORD, Devon. *L2 208, 11.*
    FORD, Joh, of Ashburton, Devon. *L10 94b, 4.*

(owl b&l Or).
FORD, John, of Ashburton, Devon. *WK 513.*
(owl b&l Or).
FORDE, John, of Ashburton, Devon. *BA 1046. (owl b&l Or).*
Per pale Sa and Arg in chf greyhound courant & in base owl border engr all counterch
AYSHEBERTON. *L2 19, 2.*

Beast & in chief in border

Erm lion Gu border Sa roundelly Or in chf lion pg Arg
CORNEWAYLL, Mons Edward. *WJ 211.*
Gu lion & border in dex chf cresc Or
— *WK 427. (qtd 9 by Ld Ambros Dudeley).*
Gu lion gard border indented Arg in dex chf pd 5foil Or
RIDDEL, Sir William. *XL 288.*
Gu mule stat in sin chf mullet border Arg
MOYLE, Joh, of Eastwell, Kent. *L10 93b, 2.*
MOYLE, Sir Walter. *L10 93b, 1.*

Beast & over all in border

Lion & bend in border

Lion & bend in border
BROMFLETE, Edward. *Dugd 17, 67.* 1427.
LINDSAY, John de, Bp of Glasgow 1323-35. *Stevenson 111. (heir of Sir Philip L, of Strathgorton).*
Gu lion Or bend Erm border Az
FICHETT, of Stringston. *Gerard 32.*
Arg lion Gu bend raguly gobony Or and Vt border Az
STYWARD, Norf. *LS 180.*
Gu lion Arg bend Sa border engr Arg
GREY, Sir J. *LY A 73. (bendlet).*
Gu lion Or bend Az border engr Or
TALBOT, S John. *R 124.*
Sa lion Arg bend Gu border engr Or
RIDYDELL. *CT 365.*
Erm lion Untinc bend Or border engr Sa
— *PT 141.*
Gu lion Arg bend gobony Or and Sa border engr Arg
— *LE 456.*
Arg lion Gu crowned Or on bend Sa 3 roundels Or border engr Sa
— *CRK 559. (qtd 2&3 by Wm Boys).*
Gu lion Arg bend Az border indented Arg
GRAY, S Thomas de. *GA 40.*
GRAY, Sr Thomas. *M 24.*
Arg lion Gu 3 bends Az border engr Gu
— *LE 267.*

Lion & fess in border

Per fess Arg and Sa lion counterch fess counter gobony & border gobony Arg and Sa
— *RL 336, 2.*
[?HARPER]. *RL 62.*
Arg lion Sa fess embattled counter-emb Az border engr Gu
— *L10 47b, 3. (a&l Gu).*
CHRE TAWNES, William, of Herts. *WB III 103b, 6. (a&l Gu).*

Beast betw ... & border

Lion betw ... & border

Arg lion Gu betw 2 bends Az each ch with 3 crosslets Or border engr Gu
MARSHAM, Thomas. *LE 178.*
Lion betw 3 buckles border roundelly
TREWARTHEN. *Mill Steph; Baker Northants 224. (blazoned Gu lion betw 3 buckles Or border ?Sa roundelly Or; brass to Jn Samwell, who m dau&h of T, Cottisford, Oxfords).*
Az lion Arg betw 2 crosses formy fitchy 1 in either flank border engr Or
PYKENHAM. *L9 106a, 5. (a&l Or, 3 more crosses painted out).*
Qtly Gu and Sa lion betw 3 crosses formy fitchy at the foot Or on collar Az 3 roundels Or border Arg roundelly Sa
ALIEFF, of Colsoll, Kent. *L2 16, 2.*
Qtly Gu and Sa lion betw 3 crosses formy fitchy at the foot Or on collar Az 3 roundels Or border Arg roundelly Sa and Gu
AYLOFF, Thos, of Colsoll, Kent. *L10 94, 2.*
Or lion betw 6 roses Gu border Arg
MAITLAND, of Lethington. *Berry; Stodart 6. (?should roses be in border; 'Ceulx de Bediton').*
Az lion passt Or betw 3 dex gauntlets backs outward Arg border engr Or
CONWEY. *BA 31b, 302.*
Az lion pg betw 3 dex gauntlets backs showing Arg border engr Or
CONWEY, Henry. *L10 111, 10.*
Az lion pg paly Or and Arg betw 3 gauntlets Arg border engr Or
CONWAY. *L10 38, 8. (a&l Gu; dex gauntlets ?aversant).*
CONWAY. *WB II 65, 15.*
CONWAY. *PLN 1915. (dex gauntlets aversant).*
CONWAY. *XPat 89, Arch 69 75. (langued Gu).*
CONWAY, Henre. *WK 663. (dex gauntlets).*
CONWAYE. *L2 132, 3. (dex gauntlets).*

Arg lion in orle engr on inner side & border Az
RANTOUNE, of Bylle. *Lyndsay 280.*
Or lion qf Az in orle Gu & border Arg lozy Az
— *Proc Soc Antiq XVII 2S 278.* 1290-1330.
*(in base of panel 2 lions Arg; maniple,
Leagram Hall, Lancs).*

Buck or Stag betw ... & border

Qtly Gu and Vt buck passt betw 3 pheons Arg
border engr Or
[BUCK]. *XBM 180.* d1520-1. *(imp Kyrtton,
Fun Cert of Dame Mgt Kyrtton, wid of Sir
Stephen Jennyns, Mayor of London).*
BUCKE, Thomas, de London. *WK 625.*
BUCKE, Thos de London. *L10 110, 7.*
Qtly Gu and Vt buck stat betw 3 pheons Arg
border engr Or
BUCKE. *XPat 60, Arch 69.73.* temp Hen 8.
BUCKE. *L2 86, 5.*
Sa buck stat Arg betw 3 pheons border engr Or
roundelly Sa
PARKER. *XPat 240, Arch 69, 88.*
PARKER, Abbot of Gloucester. *L9 104b, 7.*
PARKER, Abbot of Gloucester. *L10 72, 7.*
(or hart; alias Malverne; imp Gloucs Abbey).
PARKER, Ld Will'm. *WK 638. (alias Mal-
verne, Abbot of Gloucester).*
PARKER, Ld William, Abbot of Gloucester.
L9 122a, 12.
PARKER, Wm, Abbot of Gloucester. *L10 99,
3. (alias Malvern; buck attired Or).*
Buck tripp betw 3 pheons border engr
[PARKER, Abbot of Gloucester]. *Arch Journ
xlvii 312. (tile, Gloucester Castle).*
Sa stag stat Arg betw 3 roundels Or each ch with
pheon Sa border gobony Or and Gu
FORSTER, London. *L2 210, 7.*
FORSTER, Thomas, Lond. *WK 676.*
FORSTER, Thos, London. *L10 101b, 5.*

Hind betw ... & border

Gu hind stat betw 3 pheons Or border Arg roun-
delly Sa
HUNT, de Paddon. *WK 773.*
Gu hind stat betw 3 pheons Or border engr Arg
roundelly Sa
HUNT, of Paddon, Devon. *LH 940.*
HUNT, of Padon, Devon. *LH 15.*
Gu hind tripp Arg betw 3 pheons Or border engr
Arg roundelly Sa
HUNT. *L2 253, 10.*
Gu hind tripp betw 3 pheons Or border engr Arg
roundelly Sa
HUNT, of Paddon. *L1 322, 2.*
HUNT, John, of Paddon. *BA 1319.*

Dog betw ... in border

Arg greyhound courant betw 3 choughs Sa on
border engr Gu 4 crosses formy & 4 roundels
Or alternately
WILLIAMS, Joh, of Dorchester, Dorset. *L10
93, 3.*
WILLIAMS, John, Dorset. *WK 532. (b&l Gu).*
WILLIAMS, John, of Dorset. *BA 1050. (b&l
Gu).*
Arg greyhound courant betw 3 martlets Sa
border engr Gu roundelly Or
WILLMS. *XPat 165, Arch 69, 81.*
Or greyhound courant Sa betw 3 foxes' heads
erased Az border engr Gu
HENEGE, of Hynton, Lincs. *L2 262, 4.*
(greyhound armed Gu, foxes or wolves).
Or greyhound courant betw 3 leopards' faces Az
border engr Gu
HENEGE, John, de Heynton. *WK 610.*
Or greyhound courant Sa betw 3 leopards' faces
Az border engr Gu
HENEAGE. *LH 1115.*
HENEAGE. *LH 83.*
HENEAGE. *WB I 30, 7. (?faces Sa).*
HENEGE, Joh de Heynton. *L10 110, 1.*
HENEGE, John. *WK 506. (imp Skypwithe).*
Arg greyhound courant Sa betw 3 wolves' heads
erased Gu on border Az 8 6foils Arg
HENEGE, de Heynton, Lincs. *XPat 155, Arch
69, 80.*

BEAST IN TRESSURE

Lion in single tressure

Arg lion in single tressure Sa
— *Lyndsay 164. (qtd by Wemyss).*
Or lion in single tressure Gu
WEMYS, of Reras. *Lyndsay 169. (qrs 1&4).*
Lion in tressure flory on outside
RENTON, David, of Bille. *Stevenson.* 1464.
Or lion Gu in tressure flory Vt
DUMBART, S Jehan. *GA 37. ('... ou ung
tressour fleurete de vert').*

Lion in double tressure untinc

Lion in 2tressure
SCOTLAND. *Stevenson.* 23 June 1372. *(sl of
Mgt Drummond, 2nd Q of K David 2 of
Scotld).*
Lion in 2tressure flory cf
ALBANY, Robert, D of, Regent of Scotland.
Brit Arch Assoc xlv 239. 1406-19. *(sl &
c'seal).*
[ALEXANDER, D of Albany]. *Edinburgh XV,
123 & 132. (stone, Trinity College Hospital,
Edinburgh, [pulled down 1845]).*
ALEXANDER 3, K of Scotld. *Brit Arch Assoc*

xlv 109. 1249-86. (sl).

BALLIOL, Edward. *Brit Arch Assoc xlv 237. 1332-56. (c'seal).*

BALLIOL, John, K of Scotland. *Brit Arch Assoc xlv 110-11. 1292-6. (c'seal & 2nd sl).*

BEAUFORT, Joan. *Stevenson.* 4 Sept 1439. *(imp qtly 1&4 France Modern, 2&3 3 lions pg, ?all in border gobony; loz; Q of Jas 1, dau of Jn, 1st E of Som, d1445; privy sl).*

BEAUFORT, Joan. *Stevenson. (imp qtly France & England all in border gobony; Q of Jas 2).*

BRUCE, Robert, K of Scotland. *Brit Arch Assoc xlv 235-6. 1306-29. (c'seal & 2nd sl).*

DAVID II, K of Scotland. *Brit Arch Assoc xlv 236-7. 1329-70. (1st & 2nd c'seals).*

DUNBAR, Sir Alexander of. *PRO-sls, Bain II 541, 103, HB-SND.* 1289. *(loose sl).*

DUNBAR, Alexr. *Stevenson.* 1289. *(f of Sir Patrick D & 3rd s of Patrick, 7th E of D).*

DUNBLANE, Maurice Bp of. *Stevenson 137.* 1321-47.

DUNDEE, Preceptory of St Anthony. *Stevenson 217.* S. OFFICI PRECEPTORII...NCTI A TEGU N SCO. 1443.

GUELDRES, Marie of, Q of Jas 2. *Panmure Charter, Stevenson.* 1459. *(imp per pale dex Gueldres & sin [Juliers]; 1st sl, m1449, d1462).*

INVERKEITHING. *Stevenson.* 14 cent.

JAMES I, K of Scotland. *Brit Arch Assoc xlv 240.* 1406-37. *(sl & c'seal).*

JAMES II, K of Scotland. *Brit Arch Assoc xlv 248.* 1567-1625. *(1st & 2nd c'seals & 3rd sl).*

LOTHIAN, Officialate of. *Stevenson 103.* (4th sl).

LYON, Patrick. *Stevenson.* 1449. *(cr Ld Glamis c1445, d1459).*

MARY, Q of Scots. *Brit Arch Assoc xlv 247.* 1542-68. *(dimid by France; 4th & 5th c'seals).*

MARY, Q of Scots. *Brit Arch Assoc xlv 246.* 1542-68. *(imp by per fess France & England; 3rd c'seal).*

MARY, Qu of Scots. *Brit Arch Assoc xlv 242-5.* 1542-68. *(1st & 2nd 'cseals).*

OGILVIE, Isabella. *Stevenson.* c1480. *(for her 1st husb Patrick Lyon, 1st Ld Glamis).*

RANDOLPH, Isabella. *Stevenson.* 1351. *(w of Sir Patrick Dunbar, 3rd son of Patrick, 7th E of Dunbar).*

RENTON, John. *Stevenson; Laing-sls II 842; Durham-sls 2966. (lion ch on shldr with ?buckle, lis round outside of shield).*

ROBERT II, K of Scotland. *Brit Arch Assoc xlv 238.* 1371-90. *(sl & c'seal).*

ROBERT III, K of Scotland. 1390-1406. *(sl & 1st & 2nd c'seals).*

SCONE. *Stevenson Rely Ho 200.* S' ECCE SCE TRINITATIS ET SCI MICHAELIS DE SCONA.

SCOTLAND. *Brit Arch Assoc xlv 241. (James 2, 3, 4 & 5, Ks of).*

SCOTLAND. *Stevenson 1. (end of tail inwards; attrib to K Malcolm III 1057-93, but rejected as forgery).*

SCOTLAND, K Alexander III. *Stevenson 15.* 1249-86. *(1st great sl).*

SCOTLAND, K David I. *Stevenson 6. (forged sl of K David I 1124-53).*

SCOTLAND, Guardians of. *Stevenson 18. (after death of Alexander 3, 1292; obv of Great Sl).*

SCOTLAND, Guardians of. *Brit Arch Assoc xlv 109.* 1286-92. *(sl).*

SCOTLAND, John Balliol, K of. *Stevenson 22. (obv of sl probably made in France after king's flight & capture of 1st Great Sl.Arms embroidered on robe of seated king).*

SCOTLAND, John Balliol, K of. *Stevenson 21. (rev of Great Sl).*

SCOTLAND, K Malcolm III. *Stevenson.* 14 cent. *(obv of sl of Dunfermline beside figure of St Mgt).*

SCOTLAND, K Malcolm III. *Stevenson.* 14 cent.

SHOREWOOD, Geo, Bp of Brechin (1454-1462/3). *Stevenson 131. (imp lion to sin & lion; of Bedshiel family, Berwicks).*

ST ANDREWS, University of. *Stevenson 106.*

ST ANDREWS, Vicar General of. *Stevenson 105.* c1500.

STEWART, Alex. *Laing-sls pl XI 4; Stevenson 90.* 1505-13. *(above this saltire cross raguly flory).* *(2nd Round Sl of Alex S, Archbp of St Andrews, k at Flodden, nat s of Jas 4 & Mary Boyd).*

STEWART, James. *Stevenson 89.* 1497-1504. *(Archbp of St Andrews, 2nd son of Jas 3).*

STEWART, James. *Stevenson.* c1480. *(d1503-4, 2nd son of Jas 3).*

STEWART, Marjory. *Stevenson.* 1390. *(dau of K Robt 2 of Scotl & w of Jn of Dunbar, cr E of Moray 1371).*

Arg &c lion in double tressure

Arg lion Az in 2tressure flory cf Az
  GLAMIS, Ld. *SC 42.* (a&l Gu).
  LYOUN, Ld of Glamys. *Lyndsay 109.* (a&l & ears Gu).

Gu lion 'tail inturned' in 2tressure flory on outside only Arg
  — *PLN 1659.*

Gu lion in 2tressure flory cf Arg
  DUNBAR, Sir Patrick, of Biel. *Berry; Stodart 8. (ambassador to Engld, 1423).*

Gu lion Arg in 2tressure flory cf Or
— WLN 146.

Or lion in double tressure Gu
Or lion in 2tressure Gu
    ALBANACTUS, King. *XL 413. (not flory).*
    ALBANACTUS, 1st K of Scotland. *L2 16, 7. (not flory).*
    BAILOLL, Edward, Roy d'Scoce. *BL A 1.*
    BRITAIN, Albinactus, 3rd s of Brutus.
    ALBANACTUS. *BA 911. (not flory).*
    SCOTLAND. *Brit Arch Assoc xxxiv 23.* Scutum regis Scotie. *c1400-20. (Nave ceiling, St Alban's Abbey).*
Or lion in 2tressure flory Gu
    [BALLIOL], K of Scotland. *Antiq Journ xxi 203. (Sicile Roll).*
    SCOTLAND, Kyng of. *BR I 19. (both lines of tressure embellished on outer edge with demi fleurs de lis).*
Or lion 2 tressure flory cf Gu
    — *DIG 4. (broad tressure; qtd by Burke, f of Ric B, E of Clan Rycarde).*
    ALEXANDER II, K of Scotland. *MP II 48; MP IV 80.*
    DESCOCE, le Roy. *P 16.*
    ECHOS, Le Rei de. *WNR 10.*
    ESCOCE, Rey de. *G 15.*
    ESCOCE, Rey de. *D 9a. (lion & tressure faint).*
    ESCOSE, le roy de. *LM 6.*
    ECOSSE, le Roi d'. *Gelre; Stodart pl A. (a&l Az; field outside tressure uncoloured).*
    MARCH, E of. *SC 11. (Ld of Man).*
    SCHOCE, le Roy de. *FW 12.*
    SCOCE, Le Roy de. *AS 12.*
    SCOTELANDE, le Roy de. *WLN 10.*
    SCOTLAND. *Wroxton A4, 337. ('The Kyng of Scottes is the Reede lyon').*
    SCOTLAND. *XL 414.*
    SCOTLAND. *Proc Soc Antiq XI 2S 37. (imp England; on great mace of City of Westm).*
    SCOTLAND. *SP A 11.*
    SCOTLAND. *WNS 25, 6.*
    SCOTLAND. *LMS 18.*
    SCOTLAND. *Proc Soc Antiq XVII 2S 278. 1290-1330. (maniple, Leagram Hall, Lancs).*
    SCOTLAND, K of. *ML I 111.*
    SCOTLAND, K of. *RH, Ancestor iii 198. ('Roy de Scottys').*
    SCOTLAND, K of. *PLN 25.*
    SCOTLAND, K of. *FK I 34.*
    SCOTLANDE, Kyng of. *PCL IV 67.*
    SCOTLAND, K of. *CRK 1359.*
    SCOTLAND, K of. *E I 3; E II 2.*
    SCOTLAND, K of. *LMRO 18. ('Roy descoce porte de or et une leon rampant de gules a une tressur florette de gulys').*
    SCOTLAND, K of. *AY 104.*

    SCOTLAND, K of. *ML I 508.*
    SCOTLAND, King of. *Lyndsay 1 & 18.*
    SCOTLAND, Alexander II, K of. *Sandford 86.*
    SCOTLAND, Alexander III, K of. *Keepe.*
    ALEXANDER TERTIUS REX SCOTORUM. *c1260.*
    SCOTLAND, K James I of. *Sandford 325. (m Joan Beaufort).*
    SCOTLAND, James V, K of. *Leake. 1542. (in Garter).*
    SCOTLAND, James V, K of. *XK 93. (KG, 1535).*
    SCOTLAND, Q Maud of. *Sandford 2. (w of Hen 1 of Engld; anachronistically imp by 'Normandy', Hen 7 Chapel, Westm).*
    SCOTLAND, Roy de. *WJ 75.*
    SCOTTES, the Kyng of. *SC 1.*
    SCOTTES, Ye Kyng of. *SHY 591. (lion blazoned crowned).*
    SCOTTS, K of. *KB 27.*
    SCOTTZ, King of. *BS 1.*
    SKOCIE, Rex. *SM 14, 111.*
    STEUERT, D of Albany. *Lyndsay 50. (qtg 2 Gu lion Arg border Arg ch with 8 roses Gu [Dunbar], 3 Gu 3 legs of Man Arg [Man], 4 Or salt & chf Gu [Bruce]).*
    STEUERT, D of Ross. *Lyndsay 49. (qtg 2 [Ross] & 3 [Brechin]).*
    STEWART, Ld of Avyndall. *Lyndsay 133. (qtg 2 Stewart, 3 Lennox, all in border gobony Arg and Az).*
    STEWART, Sir Andrew. *LS 211.*
    STEWART, Sir Andrew. *SC 64.*
    STEWART, James, D of Ross, Archbp of St Andrews 1497-1503. *HB-SND. (ensigned with an Archepiscopal cross & a crown).*
    STEWART, John. *Stevenson. 1423. (qtg 3 garbs; cr E of Buchan, 1406).*
    STEWART, Ld of Meffane. *Lyndsay 139. (qtg: 2 Steward, 3 Lennox, 4 Or lion Gu border gobony Arg and Az & over all Gu lion Or holding tower Arg).*
    STEWERT, E of Mar. *Lyndsay 56. (qtg Az bend betw 6 crosslets fitchy Or [Mar] over all riband engr Sa).*
    STEWERT, E of Mare. *Lyndsay 52. (qtg 2&3 Az bend betw 6 crosslets fitchy Or[Mar]; over all Or fess checky Arg and Az betw 3 crowns Gu [Stewart of Garioch]).*
    STEWERT, E of Moray. *Lyndsay 73. (qtg 2&3 Arg 3 lozenge-cushions in tressure flory cf Gu [Randolph] over all riband Sa).*
    TUDOR, Margaret. *Stevenson. (imp per fess France modern & Engld; signet sl; Q of Jas 4 & dau of Hen 7).*

Or lion in double tressure Sa &c
Or lion in double tressure flory cf Sa
    BOUCHQUHENNANE, of that ilk. *Lyndsay 400. (a&l Gu).*

Or lion in double tressure flory cf Vt
   ?GOMMS, The Lord of. *SC 112. (a&l Gu).*
Or lion Sa gutty Or in double tressure flory cf Sa
   BATHANANE. *SC 58.*

Lion dormant in tressure
Lion dormant in 2tressure
   FERINDRAUCH, Henry de. *Stevenson.*
Lion dormant in 2tressure flory
   FRENDRAUCHT, Henry. *Stevenson. 1292.*
   (not on shield).

Beast (other) in tressure
Paschal lamb in tressure flory cf
   PERTH. *Birch 15590; Stevenson.* ?*1378.*
   (2nd & 3rd Privy sls).

Lion & label in tressure
Lion in 2tressure flory cf & label
   CARRICK, John, E of. *Stevenson. (succeeded*
   to throne 1390 as K Robt 3).
   ROTHESAY, David Stewart, D of. *Stevenson.*
   (eldest s of Robt 3, cr D of Rothesay 1398,
   d1402).
   STEWART, David, Count Palatine of Strath-
   erne &c. *Stevenson. 1375. (eldest s of Robt*
   2, by Euphemia Ross; 1st sl).
Or lion in 2tressure flory cf Gu label Az
   ROTHESAY, D of, Prince of Scotland.
   Lyndsay 48.
   ROTISSAY, The Prince of. *SC 2.*
Arg lion Gu in 2tressure flory cf Sa label Arg pts
   checky Arg and Az
   CARRICK, Le Comte de. *Gelre; Stodart B 1.*

Lion & in chief in tressure
Lion in chf 3 estoiles all in 2tressure flory cf
   LYON, Wm, of Estir Ogil. *Stevenson. 1512.*

Lion & over all in tressure
Lion & bend in 2tressure
   STEWART, Francis, Ld of Badenach & Enzie.
   Ash-sls. SIGILLUM: FRANCISCI.DNI: DE
   BADZENACH.ET.EYNGZE. *(baston).*
Lion & bend in 2tressure flory cf
   STEWART, James. *Stevenson. c1550. (rib-*
   bon; nat s of Jas 5, Commendator of Kelso &
   Melrose, d1558; 2nd sl).
   STEWART, John. *Stevenson. (bend a ribbon;*
   Commendator of Coldingham; Swinton Ch, 4
   March 1559-60).
Lion to sin & bend in 2tressure flory cf
   STEWART, Margaret. *Stevenson. 1520. (nat*
   dau of Jas 4, w of Jn, Ld Gordon).
Lion & bend sin in tressure flory cf
   — *Stevenson. 1520. (ribbon; qtd by Jas*
   Stewart, d1544, nat s of Jas 4, E of Moray).
   STEWART, John, of Conoraigy. *Stevenson.*
   1483.

Lion & bend c'gobony in 2tressure flory cf
   STEWART, Thomas. *Stevenson. 1404. (nat s*
   of Robt 2, Archdeacon of St Andrews,
   dc1411).
Lion & bend raguly in tressure flory cf
   LYON, Sir John, of Glamis. *Stevenson. 1423.*
   (d1435; baton raguly).
Arg lion Gu chev Arg & fess checky Az and
   Arg in 2tressure flory cf Gu
   STRATHERN, Le Comte de. *Gelre; Stodart E*
   9.
Arg lion Gu fess checky Az and Arg in 2 tres-
   sure flory cf Gu
   ROSS, le comte de. *Gelre; Stodart B 8.*

Lion betw ...in tressure
Arg lion passt Sa ch with 2 pales Or betw 3 dol-
   phins naiant enbowed Gu each ch with 3
   roundels Or all in 2tressure flory cf Purp
   CAUNTON, J'hon, de Warwick. *WK 512.*
   (a&l Gu).
   CAUNTON, Joh de Warwick. *L10 94b, 3.*
   (a&l Gu).
   CAUNTON, John, de Warwick. *L10 44b, 5.*
   (a&l Gu).
Arg lion passt Sa ch with 3 pales Or betw 3 dol-
   phins Gu each ch with 3 roundels Or all in
   2tressure flory cf Gu
   CAUNTON, of London. *L2 131, 7.*
Arg lion passt paly Sa and Or betw 3 dolphins
   Gu each ch with 3 roundels Or all in 2tres-
   sure flory cf Purp
   CAUNTON, John, of Warwicks. *XPat 71,*
   Arch 69, 73. (armed Gu; grant).

Lion in tressure in border
Lion in tressure flory cf & border checky
   STEWART, Walter. *Stevenson. 1389. (2nd s*
   of Robt 2, E of Atholl, d1437; 1st sl).

BEAST (LION) WITH OTHER BEAST OR MONSTER
Az lion preying on wolf Arg
   — *ML I 227. ('A lyon mordawnt un wolfe';*
   lion ramp holding up wolf by back of shldrs).
Lion & dragon combatant
   WENALI, Geoffrey de. *Stevenson. 1296.*
Lion crowned & dragon ramp combatant
   TAME. *Mill Steph. 1500. (brass to Jn Tame*
   & his w Alice Tyringham).
   TAME. *Mill Steph. 1534. (cresc in chf;*
   brass to Sir Edm T & his 2 ws Agnes Gre-
   ville & Elizabeth Tyringham, Fairford,
   Gloucs).
Arg dragon Vt fighting lion Az crowned Purp
   THAME, Sir Edmund. *XK 290.*

Arg dragon Vt & lion Az crowned Gu combatant
each a&l & in centre chf cresc Gu
TAME, Edmund, of Fairford. *BA 865. (imp Grevell)*.

Arg lion Az & griffin Vt combatant
TAME, John. *?source. (d1500; Mont, Fairford Ch, Gloucs)*.

Arg lion Az crowned & armed Gu & griffin Vt
armed Gu
TAME, of Fairford, Gloucs. *Brit Arch Assoc xxvii 140*.

Lion & wyvern combatant
DAUNTESEY. *Arch Journ iv 364*. SIGILL:
IOHIS: DAVNTESEY.AR. *?c1600. (sl)*.
DUNBAR, Wm. *Stevenson. c1240. (2nd s of Patrick, 5th E of D)*.

Gu lion Or tearing at wyvern reversed in chf Ppr
— *LO 51. (wyvern has 2 heads & wings addorsed; qtd 2&3 by Jn Langrich, draper of London)*.
LANGREGE. *L9 421, 2*.

2 BEASTS (LIONS)

2 demi-lions
2 demi-lions combatant
VIPONT, Wm. *Stevenson. late 12 cent. (c'seal, not on sh)*.

Gu 2 demi-lions pg couped Or
ACHE. *L2 17, 9. (armed Sa)*.
HACCHE, J, of Devon. *CRK 1170*.

2 lions rampant
2 lions
BURTON, Alice. *PRO-sls. 1368-9. (round shield)*.
[ROLLESLEY]. *Arch Journ lxxviii 13. (imp 3 leopards' faces; on shield below feet of effigies; incised slab to Jn & Agnes R, Darley Dale, Derby; betw heads of effigies is another shield [Gu fess & border Erm] also for R)*.
SEXTEYN, John. *PRO-sls. 1384-5*.

Erm 2 lions Untinc
BURES, Michael de, of Raydon, Suff. *Birch 7927. 1338*.

Barry Arg and Gu 2 lions Sa
STOTEVYLE, Sr Nichol de. *GA 21*.

Qtly Arg and Vt 2 lions Gu
ROUS. *XL 545*.

Gu 2 lions Arg crowned Or
STRANGE, Mons Fouke le. *SD 106*.

2 lions combatant
2 lions combatant
— *Stevenson 131. (imp by Geo Shorewood, Bp of Brechin 1454-62/3)*.
VIPONT, Wm. *Stevenson. c1200. (?not on sh)*.

Arg 2 lions combatant dex Az sin Or
LUCAS. *L1 406, 3; L2 306, 10*.

Arg 2 lions combatant Sa
SOMERTON. *L1 587, 5. (armed Gu)*.
SOMERTON. *DV 49b, 1943*.
SOMERTON. *XL 528. (a&l Gu)*.

Az 2 lions combatant Arg
— *ML I 224. ('ii lyons rampawnt combatawnt')*.
HECTOR, of Troy. *Llanstephan 46, 110, 23. (the 1st of the Conquerors 'y naw Kwnkwerwr; yn gyntaf Egtor o Droin ap Priaf ap Lamaden'; 'vaes o assura dau lew Rrampant o arian wynet yn wynet', ie blue or azure with 2 lions ramp face to face)*.
HECTOR, of Troy. *BG 21*.

Az 2 lions combatant Or
HECTOR, of Troy. *ML II 108*.
HECTOR, of Troy. *ML I 129*.
OSTRYCHE, Duke of. *PCL IV 136*.

Or 2 lions combatant Gu
WYCOMBE. *WB I 44, 1*.

Or 2 lions combatant Sa
TROIE, Hector de. *LMRO 20, 32*.
TROYE, le Roy de. *WLN 81*.

Sa 2 lions combatant Or
— *Nichols Leics II 670. (Thorpe Langton Ch)*.
HECTOR. *L2 239, 2*.
HECTOR, prince of Troye. *Lyndsay 11*.
HECTOR OF TROY. *LH 33*.
HECTOR, of Troy. *RH, Ancestor iii 194*.
PRIAM, K of Troy. *KB 345. ('King Priamus & his sonne Ector')*.

Field patterned 2 lions combatant
Per pale Arg and Az 2 lions combatant dex Az
sin Or
GELDERLAND, William, Duc de. *MK 2. (temp Ric 2)*.

Per pale Az and Or 2 lions combatant dex Or sin
Sa
GELDRES, Mary of. *Sandford 326. (w of Jas II of Scotld)*.

Per pale indented Arg and Sa 2 lions combatant
counterch
[SHOTBOLT]. *CRK 149. (imp ...)*.

2 lions combatant coward &c
Arg 2 lions combatant coward dex Az sin Gu
LUCAS. *L9 39a, 4*.
LUCAS. *XL 530. (mouths closed)*.

Sa 2 lions combatant Arg crowned Or
   PRALL. *BA 1177.*
   PRALLE. *XL 263.*
   PRALLE. *L9 109a, 3.*
   PRATT. *L1 495, 6. (armed Or).*
2 lions facing each other supporting ?flaming
staff
   — *?source.* c1500. *(qr 2; carved on capital,
Mold, Flint).*

2 lions addorsed

Arg 2 lions addorsed Sa
   — *ML I 199. ('Argent ii lionsewys comme
rampant per assent').*
Az 2 lions addorsed Arg
   — *ML I 225. ('ii lyons indorsyd, or ii lyons
the iid indorsyd et hoc meliuos est. Som call
them ii lyons rampaunt per assent orper
lassent').*
Az 2 lions addorsed Or
   ACHILLES. *ML II 118.*
   ACHILLES. *ML I 149. (a&l Gu).*
Gu 2 lions addorsed Arg
   — *L10 46, 8. (tails intertwined; qtd 2&3 by
Chipnam).*
   — *WB III 108b, 7. (tails intertwined; qtd
2&3 by Thos Chypnam, of Hants).*
   ROGERS, John. *LR 54.*
Per pale Arg and Az 2 lions addorsed & coun-
terch
   GREGORY, William. *RH, Ancestor iii 190.
(arms generally given for Wm G, Ld Mayor
of London, 1451).*

2 lions dormant

2 lions dormant in base facing each other
   ALLESLEE, Richard de, rector of Harrietsham.
PRO-sls AS 71, 81 & 106. S' RICARDI-
.ALLISLEYE. *1356-7.*

2 lions passant

2 lions passt
   — *Dugd 17, 91.* 1375. *(imp by Joan de Sut-
tone).*
   — *PRO-sls.* 1389-90. *(qtd by Ric, Ld Tal-
bot).*
   — *WB I 35b, 1. (qtd 9 by E of Shrewsbury).*
   — *Dugd 17, 98.* 1237. *(imp by Roger de
Grafton).*
   — *Brit Arch Assoc NS xxiii 8.* early 14 cent.
*(qtg (2) Bendy of 10 (3) 2 bars & bend;
difficult to tell whether lions are passt or pg;
mont, Seaton, Rutl).*
   — *Brit Arch Assoc vii 433. (sin sh on sl of
Hawisia, Princess of Powys, dau of Owain de
Kevelioc).*
, Isabella. *Birch 12943.* S' ISABELLA. *(used*

by *Thos, s of Gilbert de Redehough, of Newcastle, Northd).*
ABEDETOCK, Geoffrey de, Ld of Hyndelepth.
Hist MSS Comm 5th Rep 302. 13 cent.
*(mullet at top & another on either side of
shield; broken sl giving to Prior & Convent
of Worcester right of way in road from Worc
to Coderugge).*
ABELL, Adam of Brogreve. *Bow XXVIII 14,
5. (party to deed concerning land in Sher-
stoke. T: Th Gibb, parsona de Shustoke,
Simone le Botilev, Willelmo de Blithe, Simone
de Meteley).*
ASCOLOC, Hector. *Stevenson 232.* 1296.
BELLO CAMPO, Walter de. *PRO-sls.* 13 cent.
BERKELEY, Henry de. *BGAS xiii 191.* 1220.
BISSET, Margaret. *Brit Arch Assoc xi 219.*
SIGILLUM MARGARETAE DE RIPARIS. *(dau &
coh of Jn, Ld B, w of Ric de Redvers, E of
Devon, d1184).*
BROMPTON. *Birch 8964.* 1355. *(imp by
Cornwall in arms of Elizabeth de Cornubia,
Lady of Kynlet, Salop, wid of Esmond de C).*
BROMTONE, Cecilia de. *Birch 7847.* S' CECI-
LIE [DE] BROMTONE. *14 cent.*
CAMPVILLE, Henry de. *Dugd 17, 77.* 1311.
CARRU, Eleanor de.
[STRANGE]. *AnstisAsp I 213, 61.* SIGILLUM:
ELIANORE: DE: CARRV. *1338-9.*
CATESBY, John. *PRO-sls E40 A4545 &
10832.* I.C. 1436-7. *(s of Emma de
Catesby).*
CATESBY, John. *PRO-sls E40 A4288 & 4371.*
I.C. 1416-17.
CAUNVILLE, Sir William de. *PRO-sls.* 31
Dec 1331. *(shield betw 3 5foils).*
CURSUN, John. *Birch 9144.* S' IOHANNIS
CURSOUN. *1412. (qtg 2 bend checky betw 2
?annulets, 3 Erm bend checky; s of Jn C, Kt,
of Suff).*
DARNOWLL. *Mill Steph; Belcher II 106.*
c1520. *(imp Fagger & Silverloch; found
under seats, inscription lost, Penshurst,
Kent).*
DARNOWLL. *Mill Steph; Belcher II 106.*
c1520. *(?lions pg, in chf with 2 wolves'
heads erased in base; found under seats,
inscription lost, Penshurst, Kent).*
DARNOWLL. *Mill Steph; Belcher II 106.*
1507. *(imp Stedolf: on chf 2 wolves' heads
erased; brass to Walter D & his wives
Johane & Anne).*
[DELAMERE]. *Arch Journ xxxx 37-8.* 1450-
82. *(imp 3 roaches in pale all in border
semy de lis [Roche]; 2nd shield on sl of Ric
Beauchamp, said to be for his mother).*
DUDELEY, John, de Kyngstonlisle. *WK 674.
(qrs I 1&4).*
DUDLEY, Bp of Durham. *?source.* c1480.

(sl).

DUDLEY, John. *Birch 9045.* 1521. *(qr I (of V) 1&4; qtg Malpas, Beauchamp, Newborough, Berkeley, Lisle, Gerard, Guilford, Haldon).*

DUDLEY, John, Ld. *Bow XXX 13.* 1443-4. *(central of 3 shields).*

DUDLEY, John, D of Northumberland, E of Warwick, E Marshal, KG. *Birch 9345.* 1521. *(qrs I 1&4 of V qrs; qtg Malpas, Beauchamp, Newburgh, Berkeley, Lisle, Gerard, Dudley, Guildford, Halden).*

DUDLEY, Robert, E of Leicester. *PRO-sls.* 18 June 1566. *(within garter, coronet above).*

DUDLEY, William. *Birch 2479. (privy sl, Bp of Durham, 1476-83; Birch does not definitely assign these arms to Dudley).*

DUDLEY, William. *Durham-sls 3159-61. (qtg Sutton; Bp of Durham, 1476-83).*

DUDLEY, William, Bp of Durham. *Birch 2480.* 1483. *(qtg 2&3 cross patonce [Sutton]).*

DUDLEY, William, Bp of Durham. *Keepe.* 1483. *(imp by See; Mont, Westm Abbey, since defaced).*

DUDLEY, Wm. *Arch Journ lxxi 23502. (qtd 2&3 by qtly 1&4: 3 5foils 2&3: barry & chf; Bp of Durham; Chancellor of Oxford 1483; ceiling boss, Divinity school, Oxf).*

DYMOKE, Sir John. *Dugd 17, 19.* 1355.

ENGLAND, John K of, Count of Mortaigne. *Sandford 55; Birch 6323.* +SIGILLU[M: IOH]ANNIS: FILII: REGIS: ANGLIE: D[OMINI: HIB'NIE.]. *(equestr sl obv; Birch misread this sl, beasts are passt with heads in profile & not gard).*

ERDINGTON, Thomas de. *Dugd 17, 7.* 1411 & 41.

ERDINGTON, Thomas, Kt. *PRO-sls.* 1457-8.

ESSEBY, William de. *Birch 9508.* SIGILL'WILL'I.FIL' ROBERTI.. temp Hen 3. *(s of Dominus Willelmus Robert, de Magna Esseby, Yorks).*

ESTRANGE, John, of Kuskin. *Dugd 17, 9.* 1308. *(on each side of shield lacertine beast).*

ESTRANGE, John l', of Knockin, Salop. *Bow LX 1a.* 1308-9.

ESTRANGE, Matilda L'. *Bow LX 1b.* 1308-9. *(imp by 3 lions crowned; w of Jn L'E).*

FARANFULF. *Nichols Leics III 328. (brass to Sir Thos Chaworth (d1458), Lound Ch, Leics).*

FELTON, Hamo de, Kt. *PRO-sls.* 1362-3.

FELTON, John de. *PRO-sls.* 1315-16. *(Warden of Alnwick Castle).*

FELTON, Thomas de. *PRO-sls.* 1375.

FERRERS, Elizabeth de, Lady of Chartley.

BrookeAsp I 4, 1. +SIGILLUM: ELIZABETHAE: DE: FERRARIIS:. 1371-2.

FREVILE, Dame Ide de. *Bow LVII 24.* IDE DE FREVILE. 1352-3. *(1st of 3 shields).*

GOLDINGTON, John, Ld of Hunsdon. *Bow 14.* 1407-8.

GOLDINGTONE, John. *Birch 10143.* S'IOHIS GOLDINGTONE. 1362. *(s & heir of Jn de G, of Essex).*

GOLDYNGTON, John. *PRO-sls AS 143.* S'IOHANNIS GOLDYNGTON . 1420-1.

GOLDYNGTON, John de. *PRO-sls AS 61, 131 & 143.* S IOHANNIS: GOLDYNGTON. 1400-1.

GOLDYNGTONE, John de, of Essex, Kt. *Birch 10147.* +S'[IO]H'[IS: DE:]GOLDY[NGT]ONE FORTUNE. 1336.

GORRAN, Robinus de. *Birch 10184.* +SIGIL'ROBINI DE GORRAN. 1227.

LESTRANGE, Hamo. *PRO-sls.* 1272-3.

LESTRANGE, Hamo. *PRO-sls.* 1268-9.

LESTRAUNGE, Fulk. *PRO-sls.* 1302-3.

MARE, Robert de la. SIGILL': ROBERTI DE LA MAR'.. 1364.

MIRFIELD, Adam de. *Yorks Deeds VII 146.* 1388.

MORITON, John, Count of. *Sandford 81. (John 'Sans-terre').*

MORITON, John E of, Ld of Ireland. *Sandford 49.*

PAGANELL, Gervase. *CombeAsp II 184.* +SIGILLUM GERVASII PAGNELL. *(equestr sl).*

PEDEWARDIN, Roger de, of Heref. *Birch 12454.* S' ROG'... L'.... 1300.

PEDEWARDIN, Walter de. *Birch 12458.* S' WALTERI DE PADEWARDIN. late 14 cent.

PEDWARDYN, Robert, Ld of. *Birch 12452.* SIGILLU ROBERTI PEDWARDYN. 1431.

PEDWARDYN, Roger. *Vinc 88, 55.* 1441-2. *(sl).*

PEDWARDYN, Roger, of Lincs, Esq. *Birch 12455.* SIGILLUM ROGERI PEDWARDYN. 1442.

RINGESDUNE, Hugh de, of Lincs, Kt. *Birch 12992.* SIGILL HVGONIS D'RINGESDUVE. temp Edw 1 or 2.

RIPARIIS, Margaret de. *Vinc 88, 29.* +SECRETUM MARGARETAE DE RIPARIS. *(sl).*

SANCTO VALERIO, Thomas de. *CombeAsp II 206. (equestr sl).*

SANCTO WALERIO, Tomas de. *Birch 6408-9.* +SIGILLUM: TOME DE SCO WALERIO. temp K John. *(s of Bernard, 3rd Baron St V; equestr sl obv).*

SOMERI, John. *Bow L 1.* S JOHIS DE SOMERI. 1317-8. *(grant of land in Horhull).*

SOMERY. *CT 36.*

SOMERY. *Fryer 38.* 1581. *(2 shields; qtd 3 by Sir Maurice Berkely, of Bruton, Som, on mont there).*

SOMERY, Agnes de, Lady of Northfield.

Dugd 17, 30. early 13 cent. *(w of Rog de S).*

SOMERY, John de. *PRO-sls.* 1313-14.

SOMERY, John de. *Dugd 17, 30.* 1246. *(s&h of Roger S; fan crest).*

SOMERY, Radulf de. *Dugd 17, 31.*

SOMERY, Ralph de. *Hist Coll Staffs 10 pl 10a.* +SIGILLUM RAD[ULFI] DE SUMERI. 1194-1206. *(Wodehouse, Wombone Deeds).*

SOMERY, Roger de. *Bk of Sls 12.* mid 13 cent.

SOMERY, Roger de. *Dugd 17, 30.* ?c1200. *(?his s Jn sealed in 1246).*

SOMERY, Roger de. *Bk of Sls 411.* 1269.

SOMERY, Sir Roger de. *PRO-sls.* 1270-1.

SOMERY, William de. *Dugd 17, 31.*

SPRENGHOSE, Roger. *PRO-sls.* 13 cent.

ST VALERI, Thomas de. *Bow XX 6a, b.* 1280. *(equestr sl & c'seal).*

STRANGE. *Arch Journ x 143-4.* S' HAWISIE DNE DE KEVEOLOC. late 13 cent. *(shield held in left hand by effigy; silver matrix).*

STRANGE. *Bow L 8.* 1420-1. *(qtd 2&3 by Beatrice Talbot).*

STRANGE. *PRO-sls.* 1415-16. *(qtd by Gilbert Talbot, 'seigneur de Irchenfelde and de Blakemore').*

STRANGE. *Birch 13829.* temp Hen 5. *(qtd 2&3 by Gilbert, 5th Ld Talbot, d1419).*

STRANGE. *Bow XXXIV 13.* +SIGILLUM ELIZA-BETHEA DOMINAE DE FERRARIIS. 1371-2. *(1 of 3 shields; Elizabeth de Ferrers, dau of Ralph, E of Stafford, w of: 1 Fulke, Ld Strange of Blackmere, 2 Jn, Ld F of Chartley, d1367).*

STRANGE. *Bk of Sls 229.* 1456.

STRANGE. *Birch 13848.* 1456. *(qr 3 on dex side of 1st of 2 shields in sl of Mgt, wid of Sir Jn Talbot, 1st E of Shrewsbury).*

STRANGE, le. *Farrer III 6.* *(imp by Heydon; shield on stalls, Norwich Cath).*

STRANGE, le. *Farrer III 5.* *(imp by Hoo; shield on stalls, Norwich Cath).*

[STRANGE]. *Birch 6670.* S' HAWISIE DNE DE KEVELOC. early 14 cent. *(sl of Hawisia, Domina de Keveoloc, ?Merioneth; Birch says Hawisie dau of Owen de la Pole & w of Sir Jn Charlton of Powys, marginal note corrects to 'd of John le Strange & w of Gruffyd ap Gwenwynwyn, Ld of Powys who d1289').*

STRANGE, Fulk le, Ld of Corsham. *Barons Letter Ancestor lxxxvi.*

STRANGE, John le, of Knokyn. *Barons Letter Ancestor lix.* 1301. *(on sl, shield & horse-trappers).*

STRANGE, Sir Richard le, Ld of Knokyn & Mohun. *Dugd 17, 68.* 1440. *(qrs 1&4).*

STRANGE, Sir Roger.

STRANGE, Sir Haman le. *Mill Steph.* 1506.

(qtg Mohun; brass, Hunstanton, Norf).

STRAUNGE, John le. *PRO-sls.* 1302-3. *(shield & trapper of equestr sl).*

STRAUNGGE, John le, Ld of Knokyn. *Birch 6444.* S': IOHANNIS LE STRAUNGE. 1301. *(1st Baron S, 1299-1309; equestr sl).*

SULTOR, of Dudley. *Wrottesley 256.* 1521. *(imp by Ric Wrottesley; tomb, Wrottesley Chapel, Tethenhall).*

SUMARY, John de, Ld of Newport Pagnell. *PRO-sls.* 1315-16.

SUMERI, William de. *Bow L 114.* SIGILLUM.-..ILLELMI DE SUMERI. *(equestr sl; grant to Roger fil Wm Albi one assert of Lindeswelle. Test: Rodberto Paganello tunc seneschallo, Radulfo Pamill, Johanne Russell, Ernaldo Alan Aurifabio, Ricardo de Rueleg, Ranulfo de Loos, Adamo de Harfield).*

SUMERY, Roger de. *PRO-sls.* 1268-9.

SUTTON, of Dudley. *Proc Soc Antiq II 2S 190.* *(brass to Sir Jn Ratcliffe, d1527 & w Alice [dau of Sir Edm Sutton, of Dudley], Crosthwaite Ch, Cumb).*

SUTTON, John de. *Bow L 15.* S Johannis de Sutton. 1360-1. *(sl used by Ric Seigneur de Dudley, granting lands in Kinges Swinford which he held of Jn de Sutton).*

SUTTON, John de. *Dugd 17, 31.* 1364. *(s&h of Jn de S, Ld of Duddeley).*

SUTTON, John de. *Bow L 2.* S JOHIS DE SUTTON. 1360-1. *(s of Jn de S, Kt, sometime Ld of Dudley; grant of reversion of Stowe Medowe).*

SUTTON, John de. *Dugd 17, 31.* 1344.

SUTTON, John de. *Dugd 17, 80.* 1337.

SUTTON, John de, Ld of Dudley. *PRO-sls.* 1349.

2 lions passt to sin

ESSEBY, William de. *Dugd 17, 8.* SIGILL....

PONTEFRACTO, Adam de. *Yorks Deeds I 118.* 1303.

RINGESDUNE, Ralph de, of Lincoln. *Birch 12995.* S' RADVLPHI DE RINGESDVNE. temp Edw 1 or 2.

Arg 2 lions passt Az &c

Arg 2 lions passt Az

  — *CRK 1142.*

FENYS, Sir R. *WB I 41, 22.*

GOLDINGTON, Sire Rauf de. *N 395.*

SOMERY. *XL 307.* *(& Dudley).*

SOMERY, Johan de. *LM 73.*

SOMERY, Sir John. *ML I 100; ML II 91.*

Arg 2 lions passt Gu

  — *CRK 1380.* *(qtd 3 by Jn Talbot, E of Salop).*

  — *WK 53.* *(qtd 3 by Sir Gilbert Talbot).*

  — *XK 45.* *(qtd 6 by Sir Gilbert Talbot, KG).*

  — *BW 8, 41.* *(qtd I&IV 2&3 by Ld Talbot).*

— *ML II 15. (qtd 6 by Talbot, E of Shrews-bury).*
— *PLN 1721. (qtd 6 by Sir Gilbert Talbot).*
— *ML 15. (qtd 6 by Talbot 'Erle of Shres-bury').*
— *XK 224. (qtd 6 by Sir Gilbert Talbot).*
— *WK 141. (qtd 6 by Sir Gilbert Talbot).*
— *WB II 49, 11. (qtd 2&3 by Talbot, E of Shrewsberie, all imp Furnival).*
— *WK 15. (qtd 3 by Gilbert Talbot).*
— *WGA 261-2. (qtd 3 by Ld Jn Talbot, E of Shrewsbury).*
— *BR II 38. (qtd II&III 1&4 by Erle of Schrewisbery).*
— *XB 16. (qtd by Talbot).*
— *WB V 83. (qtd 3 by Sir Gilbert Talbot, Kt 1485).*
— *XK 188. (qtd 6 by Sir Jn Talbot).*
— *XK 34. (qtd 6 by George Talbot, E of Shrewsbury).*
— *T c 28. (qtd by Talbot).*
— *WGA 47. (qtd 6 by Sir George Talbot, E of Shrewsbury).*
BRUNTON, Walter de. *WLN 390.*
ESTRANGE. *LE 18. (a&l Az; 'blackmer, Ej').*
ESTRANGE, Sire Fouk le. *N 72.*
ESTRANGE, Johan le. *D 74a.*
ESTRAUNG, Sir Fake. *BR V 36.*
ESTRONGE, John le. *FW 148.*
FRANDOL[F]. *L1 254, 5; L2 205, 1. (a&l Gu; marginal note L1: 'Strang').*
LESTRANGE, Sr Fouk. *L 159.*
LESTRANGE, Joh. *B 165.*
LESTRANGE, Munsire Johan. *D 74b.*
LESTRANGE, Mons John, Baron de Knokyn. *TJ 125.*
LESTRANGE, de Knockin. *CKO 445.*
LESTRANGE, Le Sr, baron de Knokyng. *AS 67.*
LESTRAUNGE, S Fuke. *GA 180.*
STRANGE. *PLN 84. (qtd 2&3 by Talbot, E of Shrewsbury).*
STRANGE. *TB 23. (a&l Az).*
STRANGE. *RH, Ancestor iv 227. (qtd I&IV 2&3 by Jn Talbot, Count de Schrowysbury).*
STRANGE. *TB 10. (qtd by Talbot).*
STRANGE. *Nichols Leics III 504. (Wymeswold Ch).*
[STRANGE]. *S 71. (qtd 2 by Mons Ric Talbot).*
STRANGE, Monsire le, de Blackmere. *CG 471.*
STRANGE, Sir ..., of Blackmere. *CRK 1445.*
STRANGE, of Blackmere. *LS 181. (a&l Az).*
STRANGE, of Blackmere. *Sandford 242. (qtd by Gilbert, Ld Talbot).*
STRANGE, of Blackmere. *Leake. c1453. (qtd 3 by Jn Talbot, E of Shrewsbury, KG, d1460).*

STRANGE, Sir, of Blackmore. *WB IV 154b, 515. (a&l Az).*
STRANGE, Elizabeth le. *Sandford 210. (d 1384, w of Thos Mowbray, D of Norf).*
STRANGE, Mons I, de Blak'ne. *WJ 213.*
STRANGE, Jan le. *Q 116.*
STRANGE, Joan de. *E I 150; E II 150.*
STRANGE, Sir John. *DX 67.*
STRANGE, John de, of Blackmere. *XL 314.*
STRANGE, John le, of Blackmere. *Sandford 210.*
STRANGE, John, of Blackmere. *XL 53.*
STRANGE, Jon le. *F 49.*
STRANGE, Jon le. *A 158.*
STRANGE, Sire Jon le. *PO 198.*
STRANGE, Le S' de Talbot. *WLN 222.*
STRANGE, Le Sr Talbot. *NB 69.*
STRANGE, le Sr de Talbot. *CN 46.*
STRAUNGE, Sire Johan de. *J 79.*
STRAUNGE, Johannes le. *Q II 355.*
TALBOT, 'Le Sr', Salop. *CY 81, 322.*

Arg 2 lions passt Sa &c
Arg 2 lions passt Sa
— *WB IV 168b, 766. (imp by Teryngham, of Buck Sher).*
— *PLN 616. (qtd 2&3 by 'Wat Halysnakys').*
— *PLN 946. (imp by Harrowden).*
GOLDINGAM, S' John de. *R 111.*
HERUYLL. *L1 308, 5; L2 246, 5.*
PETTENIM. *CT 402.*
STRANGE, of Gloucs. *LS 183. (a&l Gu).*
STRANGE, Perys. *XL 317.*
STRAUNGE, Mons Peris. *WJ 329.*
Arg 2 lions passt Vt
MERYFELD. *L1 432, 3; L2 332, 4.*

Az 2 lions passt
Az 2 lions passt Arg
BERKELEY, Nicol de. *XL 308.*
BERKELEYE. *L10 29b, 12. (a&l Gu; ?lions Or).*
MERFELDE, Sir J. *WB I 40, 17.*
Az 2 lions passt Or
— *WB III 86, 3. (qtd 2&3 by Sir Jn Grainder, of Walis).*
ARDYNGTON. *BA 32, 317.*
ARDYNGTON. *L1 21, 6; L2 12, 1. (armed Gu).*
ARDYNGTON, Sir Robert, of Warws. *WB III 76, 5. (a&l Gu).*
BERKLYE, Mons Nicoll de. *WJ 135.*
[ERDINGTOM]. *Nichols Leics II 558. (Evington Ch).*
ERDINGTON. *XL 45.*
ERDINGTON. *XL 512.*
ERDINGTON. *L1 230, 1; L2 179, 7.*
ERDINGTON. *PT 457.*

[ERDINGTON]. *Nichols Leics II 657. (Knoss-ington Ch).*

ERDINGTON, Sir T. *CRK 1467.*

ERDINGTON, Thomas de. *S 353.*

ERDYNGTON. *DV 50b, 2000.*

HERDINTONE, Henr de. *WLN 410.*

HERDINTONE, Henri de. *F 338.*

SOMERI, Sire Perceval de. *N 856.*

SOMERI, Roger de. *E I 185.*

SOMERY, Perceval. *BA 30, 234. (als Arding-ton).*

SOMERY, Perseval de. *Q 231.*

Gu 2 lions passt

Gu 2 lions passt Untinc

FELTONE, H. *NS 7.*

Gu 2 lions passt Arg

— *I2(1904)224. (qtd 2 by Sir Edw Gaynton, Kt).*

— *XK 37. (qrs 1&4 on escutch of Thos [Stanley], Ld Strange, KG).*

— *WLN 100.*

— *WK 186. (qtd IV 1&4 by Sir Thos Stan-ley).*

— *PLN 969. (escutch of Ld Strange).*

— *BR VI 6. (marshalled by Ric, Ld Strange, d1449).*

BEAUCHAMP, Richard, Bp of Salisbury. *PLN 186. (qtg 2 Gu fess Or betw 6 martlets Arg border Arg [roundelly Sa]).*

BODYLSGATE. *Ll 64, 6. (blazoned crowned Or).*

C'AMUL, Gerardus de. *Q II 116. (Strange superscribed in similar hand).*

DALAMARE. *PLN 1908. (qtd 3 by St John).*

DELAMARE. *Mill Steph. 1432. (imp on brass to Nicholas Carew, husband of Mercy, dau of Stephen D, Beddington, Surr).*

DELAMARE. *CRK 1643. (a&l Az).*

[DELAMARE]. *Spokes; Berks Arch Journ 42, 1. (14 cent glass in Lower Heyford, Oxfords).*

DELAMARE, (of Aldermaston). *PLN 199. (?lions pg; qtg 2&3 Achard Or bend lozy Sa).*

EREBY, of Ches. *LE 51.*

ESTRANGE. *LE 17.*

ESTRANGE. *Ll 230, 3.*

ESTRANGE, Eube le. *G 177.*

ESTRANGE, Sire Johan le. *N 70.*

ESTRANGE, Johans le. *K 61.*

ESTRANUNGE, Fulco de. *LM 322.*

ESTRAUNGE, Le. *SP A 51.*

ESTRAUNGE, Sir John. *BR V 63.*

FELTON. *PLN 292. (qtd 2&3 by Sir Jn Cur-son, of Felton).*

FELTON. *WB IV 171, 818.*

LESTRANGE, Le Sire. *TJ 124.*

LESTRANGE, Le Sr. *AS 66.*

LESTRANGE, Sr. *CKO 444.*

LESTRANGE, S Jehan. *GA 76.*

LESTRAUNGE, Sr Fuke. *RB 89.*

ORBY, Mons John. *TJ 133.*

PEDEWARDYN, Walterus. *Q II 207.*

PEDWARDYN, Walter. *XL 315.*

SPRYNGEHOSE, John, of Salop. *CY 83, 331.*

SPRYNGHOSE, Sir ..., of Salop. *CV-BM 166.*

STRANGE. *LS 57.*

STRANGE. *WB I 20, 2.*

STRANGE. *RB 345. (qrs 1&4)*

STRANGE. *XL 46.*

STRANGE. *CRK 216.*

STRANGE. *Ll 573, 3. (armed Az).*

STRANGE. *DV 69b, 2752. (on upper lion fleur de lis Gu).*

STRANGE. *WB V 31.*

STRANGE, Ld. *WLN 271.*

STRANGE, Ld. *PLN 129. (armed Az).*

STRANGE, Ld. *KB 295.*

STRANGE, Ld. *BW 11b, 71.*

STRANGE, Le. *AY 30. (qtd I&IV 2&3 by Talbot, B[aron], [Earl] of Schrewysbery).*

STRANGE, Le Sr. *NB 71.*

STRANGE, Monsire le. *CG 470.*

STRANGE, Ld, of Cokayne. *WB II 50, 12.*

STRANGE, Hamund le. *E I 174; E II 174.*

STRANGE, John le. *K 378.*

STRANGE, John le. *S 352.*

STRANGE, John le. *HE 124.*

STRANGE, Mons John. *T b 97. (upper lion ch on shldr with fleur de lis Sa).*

STRANGE, John, Ld of Knockyn. *S 53.*

STRANGE, John, Ld of Knokyn. *LMS 67. (1299-1310).*

STRANGE, of Knockin. *ML I 54; ML II 52.*

STRANGE, Ld, of Knocking. *FK I 99.*

STRANGE, Ld, of Knockyn. *ML I 104; ML II 93.*

STRANGE, of Knockyn. *XL 309.*

STRANGE, of Knockyn. *Lancs 1533 CS 110, 110. (qtd IV 1&4 by Stanley).*

STRANGE, le S'r de. *T c 18.*

STRANGE, Sire Roger le. *PO 197.*

STRAUNGE. *SM 333, 59.*

STRAUNGE. *DV 54b, 2144. (a&l Az).*

[STRANGE]. *RH, Ancestor iv 228. (qtd by Ld Talbot; Arg in later hand).*

STRAUNGE, Ld. *RH, Ancestor iv 229. (armed Az).*

STRAUNGE, Le Sr. *CN 83.*

STRAUNGE, Monsire de. *AN 59.*

STRAUNGE, Sire Fuke les. *HA 62.*

STRAUNGE, Mons Rog. *WJ 165.*

STRAWNGE, Le Sr, of Salop. *CY 81, 321.*

Gu 2 lions passt Or

Gu 2 lions passt Or
— *L9 29a, 1. (qtd II&III 1&4 by Vane).*
— *L1 115, 3. (qtd 2 by Baynton).*
— *WB I 27b, 10. (qrs 1&4 of coat imp by Untinc .... chev Erm).*
CAMVIL, Gerard de. *Q 509.*
DELAMARE. *Batt. (qtd by St John; tomb, Draycot Cerne, Wilts).*
ERDINGTONE. *LE 112. (tincts unclear).*
PATEWARDYN, S Roger de. *GA 187.*
PEDEWARDEN, Walt. *Q 521.*
PEDWARDIN, Monsire de. *CG 475.*
PEDWARDIN, Sir Walter de. *Durham-sls 1952. 1386.*
PEDWARDINE. *CRK 1796. (a&l Az).*
[PEDWARDINE]. *TZ 9.*
PEDWARDYN. *XL 55.*
PEDWARDYN. *SK 568.*
PEDWARDYN. *LP 22.*
PEDWARDYN, Sr de. *CKO 456.*
PEDWARDYN, Mons' Thomas. *TJ 143.*
PEDWARDYN, Walter. *S 364.*
PEDWARDYN, Walter de. *E I 603; E II 605.*
PEDWARDYN, Mons Waut'. *WJ 254.*
PEDWARDYN, Willm de. *WLN 436.*
PEDWORDIN. *F 388.*
PETEWARDEM. *L9 107b, 7.*
PETEWARDYN. *L1 492, 5. (a&l Az).*
PEWARDYA. *WB I 44, 12.*

Or 2 lions passt Az

Or 2 lions passt Az
— *WK 122. (qtd II 1&4 by Sir Edw Sutton, Ld Dodeley).*
— *WK 427. (qtd 7 by Ld Ambros Dudeley).*
— *XK 303. (qtd I 2&3 by Sir Jn Dudley).*
— *WGA 100. (qtd II 1&4 by Edw, Ld Dudley).*
— *L10 62b, 6. (qtd II 1&4 by Baron Dudley).*
— *XL 43.*
— *XK 23. (qtd 3 by Edw, Ld Dudley).*
— *LS 24. (qtd II 1&4 by Sutton, Ld Dudley).*
— *XK 64. (qtd II 1&4 by Edw Sutton, Ld Dudley, KG).*
DODDELEYE, Barun de. *PO 202.*
DODDLEY, Ld. *RH, Ancestor iv 229. (qrs 1&4).*
DUDELEY. *WB I 52, 12. (qrs 1&4).*
DUDLEY. *FK II 641. (qrs 1&4).*
DUDLEY, Baron. *KB 342. (qrs 1&4).*
DUDLEY, Ld. *AY 72.*
DUDLEY, Ld. *PLN 95. (armed Gu; qtg 2&3 Arg cross patonce Az).*
DUDLEY, Ld. *CRK 1308. (qrs 1&4).*
DUDLEY, John, KG. *I2(1904)288. (qtg 2 barry Arg and Az in chf 3 roundels Gu & label, 3 Gu lion & border engr Or, 4 checky*

Or and Az chev Erm, 5 Gu fess betw 6 crosslets Or, 6 Gu chev betw 10 crosses formy (6, 4) Arg, 7 Or fess betw 2 chevs Sa, 8 Gu lion pg Arg crowned Or; cr D of Northd 1551, beheaded 1553; encircled by garter & ensigned with duke's coronet).
DUDLEY, John, Ld. *WGA 106.*
DUDLEY, le Baron de, of Staffs. *CY 96, 382. (qtg Arg cross formy Az).*
SOMEREY. *CV-BM 34.*
SOMEREY, Roger de. *F 180.*
SOMEREY, Roger of. *Keepe.* ROGERUS DE SOMEREY. *15 cent.*
SOMERI, Johan de. *G 192.*
SOMERI, Sire Johan de. *N 52.*
SOMERI, [Roger] de. *E I 163; E II 163.*
SOMERY. *PT 863.*
SOMERY. *WB IV 131, 94. (qtd 1&4 by Baron of Dodele, Somery & Malpasse).*
SOMERY. *L1 574, 4.*
SOMERY. *Nichols Leics IV 929. (Shepey Magna Ch).*
SOMERY, Sir John. *WNS 26, 71. ('... por dor ii lions passanz dazur').*
SOMERY, Sir John. *BR V 27.*
SOMERY, Rog de. *Q 142.*
SOMERY, Mons Roger. *TJ 148.*
SOMERY, Roger de. *B II 97.*
SOMERY, Roger de. *WLN 686.*
SOMERY, Roger de. *C 95.*
SOMERY, Sir Roger. *PCL I 455.*
SOMERY, Sir Thomas, of Sutton. *CV-BM 51.*
SUMERI, Sire Johan. *J 40.*
SUMERY, Roger de. *FW 111.*
SUMERY, Roger de. *HE 88.*
SUMERY, Roger de. *A 213.*
SUTTON, S' Tho, of Staffs. *CY 108, 432.*
WENNE, le Baron de. *WJ 126.*

Or 2 lions passt Gu &c

Or 2 lions passt Gu
BRAMPTON. *XL 496.*
BRAMPTON, Brian de. *LM 146.*
BRAMPTON, Brian de. *E I 176; E II 176.*
BRAMPTON, Sir Bryan. *PCL I 468.*
BRAMPTON, of Oxfords. *L1 98, 2; L2 50, 7. (a&l Az).*
BRAMTON. *L10 78b, 4.*
BRAMTON, Brian de. *Q 144.*
BROMPTON, Brian de. *TJ 149.*
BROMTON, Brian de. *F 86.*
PEDEWARDYN, Water de. *FW 626.*
SAMTWALLIE. *L1 604, 5.*
ST VALLERY, Oxford. *LS 289.*
ST WALERY, Sir Richard de. *XL 247.*
ST WALY, Sire Richard de. *N 339.*
THORUNTON. *CT 329. (tincts unclear).*

Or 2 lions passt Sa
— *Neale & Brayley. (mont to Lewis Robes-*
sart d1431; qtg Arg cross formy Az, all in
border Gu; also qtg [Ferrers]).
— *Suff HN 1. (imp by Arg on bend Sa*
cotised Or 3 eagles displd Or; Braintree Ch).
GOLDINGTON. *CKO 455.*
GOLDINGTON, Monsire de. *CG 476.*

Sa &c 2 lions passt
Sa 2 lions passt Arg
— *L10 77b, 10. (qtd 2&3 by Brocas).*
— *BA 749. (qtd 2&3 by Sir Bernard Bro-*
cas).
— *XL 238. (qtd 2&3 by Sir Bernard Bro-*
cas).
STRANGE, John, of Norf. *XL 316.*
STRANGE, of Norf. *LS 182. (a&l Gu).*
STRANGWAYS, of Lancs. *CY 63, 252.*
STRAUNGE, Mons J, de Norf. *WJ 306.*
Sa 2 lions passt Or
NEOPOLITAN, Rex. *KB 354. (qrs 1&4).*
Vt 2 lions passt Arg
MYREFELD. *L9 67b, 9.*
MYRFELDE. *PT 1175.*

Field patterned 2 lions passt
Paly of 4 Arg and Vt 2 lions passt Gu
LOUTHWIKE. *L2 306, 4. (a&l Or).*
Paly of 4 Erm and Vt 2 lions passt Gu
LOUTHEWYK. *DV 66a, 2618.*
LOUTHWICKE. *L1 395, 1. (armed Or).*
LOUTHWYKES. *PT 811.*
Per pale 2 lions passt
HAYMOND, Agnes, of Aylesbury. *BirmCL-sls*
494347. 1402.
Gu semy of martlets Or 2 lions passt Arg
LESTRAUNGE, Sire Johan le. *N 881. ('de*
goules a les merelas de or e ii lions passanz
de argent').
Gu crusily fitchy 2 lions passt Arg
STRANGE, Robert le. *E I 194; E II 194.*
Sa semy of crosses botonny fitchy Or 2 lions
passt Arg
WYBURY, John. *PLN 716. (imp Arg chev Sa*
betw 3 round buckles tongues to dex Or;
?crosses pommy).
Sa semy of crosses pommy fitchy Or 2 lions
passt Arg
WYBERY, John. *WB IV 149, 421. (a&l Gu).*
Az semy of estoiles 2 lions passt Or
CHEYNY, Robert. *TJ 163. ('latine de*
Caisneto').
Arg gutty 2 lions passt Gu
DATTE, Thomas. *XL 385.*

2 lions passt charged or patterned
Gu 2 lions passt Arg 1st ch on shldr with cresc
Untinc
— *XL 48.*
Gu 2 lions passt Arg 1st ch on shldr with cresc
Az
[STRANGE, Roger]. *WJ 170. ('le second*
frere').
Gu 2 lions passt Arg each ch on shldr with fleur
de lis Gu
LESTRANGE. *PT 170.*
Az 2 lions passt Or 1st ch on shldr with 5foil Gu
ERDINGTON. *L1 230, 1.*
Az 2 lions passt Or 1st ch on shldr with mullet
Sa
ERDINGTON, Hugh. *CRK 407.*
Sa 2 lions passt Arg each ch with 2 pales Gu
STRANGWAYS. *CVL 353.*
Sa 2 lions passt Arg each ch with 3 pales Gu
STRANGWISHE, Sir James. *ML II 79.*
Untinc 2 lions passt Erm
FELTON, John of. *PRO-sls WS 253.* 1315.
FELTON, John of. *PRO-sls Ex KR 15/19.*
1318.
Gu 2 lions passt Erm
FALTON, Monsire. *CG 472.*
FELBRIGE, Gloucs. *L1 244, 4; L2 202, 2.*
(Marginal note in L2 says Felton).
FELTON. *L1 251, 1.*
FELTON. *CT 360.*
FELTON. *PLN 1195. (a&l Az).*
FELTON. *CKO 454.*
FELTON. *SP A 54.*
FELTON, Hamond de. *XL 50.*
FELTON, Hamond de. *XL 311.*
FELTON, Mons Hamond de. *WJ 178.*
FELTON, Monsire Hamond de. *AN 121.*
FELTON, Sir John, of Hunts. *WK A 16.*
FELTON, le S'r de. *T e 38.*
FELTON, S Robert de. *GA 78.*
FELTON, Sir Robert. *Q II 599.*
FELTON, S' th'. *PO 63. (above is written*
Ammonde).
FELTONE, de. *SK 301.*
FELTONE, Sire Robert de. *N 882.*
Sa 2 lions passt paly Arg and Gu
STRANGEWAYS. *LS 64. (a&l Or).*
STRANGWAIIS, John, of Lancs. *WB III 108,8.*
STRANGWAYES. *BA 719.*
STRANGWAYES. *PT 1188.*
STRANGWAYS. *FK II 332.*
STRANGWAYS. *XL 218 & 220.*
STRANGWAYS. *L1 577, 3.*
STRANGWAYS, Sir James. *XL 217. (a&l Or).*
STRANGWAYS, Sir James. *CRK 992. (qrs*
1&4).
STRANGWAYS, Sir Jamys, Yorks. *RH, Ances-*
tor iv 233. (gobbone sylvyr and gowlys).
STRANGWAYS, Mayster Gilys, de Stynysford,

Dorset. *I2(1904)233. (qtg 2&3 Or chev Gu border engr Sa).*
STRANGWAYS, of Middle Channock, Soms, & Melbury, Dors. *Gerard 85.*
STRANGWEYS. *L9 5, 9 & 10. (imp by Ingelby, qtg Rowelyff & Mowbray).*
STRANGWEYS, Sir James. *BA 597.*
Sa 2 lions passt paly of 8 Arg and Gu
STRANGEWAYS, Mayster. *I2(1904)81. (qtg Or chev Gu border engr Sa).*
STRANGWEYS. *CB 267.*

2 lions counter-passt
2 lions counter-passt
ERDINGTON, Henry de, Kt. *PRO-sls.* 1280-1.
2 lions passt addorsed
EXETER, Provosts of. *Birch 4923.*
S'PREPOSITORUM CIVITATIS DE EXONIA. 13 cent. *(in base of sl; not on shield).*

2 lions passt collared
2 lions passt collared
MARE, Philip de la. *Vinc 88, 150.* 1388-9. *(sl).*
Gu 2 lions passt Arg collared Az
DELAMAR. *L1 208, 5; L2 152, 3.*

2 lions passt crowned
2 lions passt crowned
— *Dugd 17, 20.* 1356. *(with Lucy on sl of Phillipa wid of Thos L, of Cherlcote; ?arms of her father).*
— *Dugd 17, 22.* 1387. *(qtd 2&3 by Jn de Catesby).*
CATESBY. *Mill Steph.* c1503. *(imp by Wake; brass to Rog W & his w Eliz dau of Sir Wm C, Blisworth, Northants).*
CATESBY, Geo. *Mill Steph.* c1505. *(lions ch on shldr with cresc; brass, Ashby St Legers, Northants).*
CATESBY, John de, of Assheby Leger, Northants. *PRO-sls E40 A10832, 8361, 10883, 10934 & 11101.* I.L. 1418-19.
CATESBY, Mary. *Mill Steph.* 1508. *(?crowned; brass to Mary, dau of Jn Tyringham & w of Anthony C, Tyringham, Bucks).*
CATESBY, William. *Mill Steph.* c1494. *(lions ch on shldr with cresc; qtg 2 Month-forth, of Lapworth, 3 Bishopsdon, 4 Cranford; brass to Wm C, d 20 Aug 1485 & w Margaret [Zouch]).*
CURSON, John, Kt. *PRO-sls.* 1436-7. *(qtg semy of ...).*
DYMOKE. *Mill Steph.* c1538. *(qtg 2 Wells, 3 Engaine, 4 Waterton, 5 Marmion, 6 Hebden & imp by Coffyn; brass to Sir Wm C, husband of Mgt, dau of Robt D, wid of 1 Sir Ric Vernon, 2 Hon Ric Manners, Standon, Herts).*
DYMOKE, Sir Lionel. *Mill Steph.* 1519.

(brass, Horncastle, Linc).
DYMOKE, Margaret. *Mill Steph.* 1472. *(brass to Robt Ingleton & 1st w Mgt D, Thornton, Bucks).*
FELTON. *Farrer II 65. (qtd by Jn Curson, Kt, d1471; brass, Bylaugh Ch, Norf).*
FELTON. *Birch 14047.* 1393. *(imp by Alianore de Ufford, wid of Sir Robt de U, dau of Sir Thos F, Kt).*
STRANGE, Sir Thos le, Constable of Ireld. *Mill Steph.* 1426. *(brass [modern restoration], Wellesbourne Hastings, Warws).*

Arg &c 2 lions passt crowned
Arg 2 lions passt Sa crowned Or
— *PLN 951. (imp by Terringham, [Bucks]).*
CATESBY. *PLN 428. (a&l Or).*
CATESBY. *CRK 622. (a&l Or).*
CATESBY. *FK a 447. ('Cranford otherwise Catesby').*
CATESBY, of Catesby, Northants. *FK II C 447.*
CATESBY, Mr. *WB I 24, 6. (?or cats).*
CATTYSBY, Sir H. *WB I 41, 21. (?or cats).*
CATYSBE. *I2(1904)225. (armed Gu & langued Or).*
GOLDINGTON. *XL 568. (a&l Gu).*
GRAUMFORD. *L1 281, 3.*
HARVYLE, Henr, of Staffs. *CY 103, 409.*
HARWELL, Henry. *LH 522. (or Catesby). (armed Gu & langued Or).*
Az 2 lions passt Arg crowned Or
HERWILL. *ME 96; LY A 221. (tincts given in Merton).*

Gu &c 2 lions passt crowned
Gu 2 lions passt crowned Arg
BODYLSGATES. *L10 85b, 11.*
Gu 2 lions passt Arg crowned Or
— *LS 8. (qtd 6 by Strange).*
BODELGATE, of Cornwall. *L1 112, 1; L2 76, 11. (armed Or).*
BODULGATE. *BA 951.*
BODYLSGATE. *L1 64, 6. (armed Or; painted sans crown).*
FELTON. *SHY 355. (imp by Breton).*
FELTON, le S'r de. *T e 38.*
FELTON, Sir T. *WB I 37b, 1.*
FELTON, Sir Thomas. *WGA 93.*
Gu 2 lions passt crowned Or
— *LO A 41. (imp [Wellysburne] Gu chf checky Or and Gu over all griffin segt Or & over all bend [?Az or ?Erm]).*
FELTON, Hamond de. *CA 97.*
Or 2 lions passt Sa crowned Gu
GOLDINGTON, Sir William, of Essex. *WB III 78b, 2. (a&l Gu).*

Or 2 lions passt Sa crowned Or
　GOLDINGTONE. *FK II 539.*

Sa 2 lions passt crowned
Sa 2 lions passt Arg crowned Gu
　DYMMOK, Philippus. *Q II 367.*
Sa 2 lions passt Arg crowned Or
　DEMOCK, ... *WB I 42, 3. (dau of Sir Robt
　D).*
　DIMMOCKE. *Gerard 79.*
　DIMOCK, John. *XL 318. (a&l Or).*
　DIMOCK, Sir Lionel. *XK 196. (qr 1).*
　DYMMOK. *L10 59, 15. (a&l Or; qrs 1&4).*
　DYMMOK. *L1 189, 3; L2 164, 10. (armed
　Or).*
　DYMMOK. *L10 56b, 8. (a&l Or).*
　DYMMOK, Mons John. *TJ 154.*
　DYMMOK, Mons John. *WJ 336.*
　DYMMOKE, Mayster. *I2(1904)182. (qr 1 of
　5).*
　DYMOKE. *BA 1325. (imp by Wm Coffyn).*
　DYMOKE. *L10 59b, 8. (a&l Or; qr 1 of 6).*
　DYMOKE, John. *S 515.*
　DYMOKE, John. *S 520. (armed Or langued
　Gu).*
　DYMOKE, Sir Robert. *XFB 128.*
　HAREWELL. *PLN 1853.*
　HERUNVILE, Jon de. *F 354.*
　HERUNVYLE, John de. *WLN 426.*
　HERVILLE. *SK 864. (a&l Or).*
　HERWILL. *L1 309, 2; L2 246, 4. (armed Or;
　marginal note L1 ' Demok').*
　SKURBY, Thomas, of Lincs. *WB III 119b, 4.
　(armed Or langued Gu).*

2 lions passt charged or patterned & crowned
Sa 2 lions passt Arg ch with 3 pales Purp
crowned Or
　STRANGWAYS, Giles. *PLN 1388. (a&l Gu).*
Untinc 2 lions passt Erm crowned Untinc
　[FELTON]. *Mill Steph. (qtg Erm bend checky
　Untinc on brass to Sir Jn C, & w Joan
　?Drury, Wylaugh, Norf).*
Az 2 lions passt Erm crowned Or
　MERFELDE, Sir W. *WB I 40b, 3. (?field Vt).*
Gu 2 lions passt Erm crowned Or
　FELTON. *DV 67a, 2642.*
　FELTON, de. *PT 546.*
　FELTON, Sir John. *L10 38, 19. (a&l Or; qtg
　Curson).*
　FELTON, Sir John de. *L 192. (le fiz de).*
　FELTON, Mons Th. *WJ 189.*
　FELTON, Monsire Thomas de. *AN 123.*
　FELTON, Thomas de. *XL 52.*
　FELTON, Thomas de. *XL 313.*
　FELTON, S' Thos. *PO 78.*
　FELTON, Sir Thomas, KG. *Leake.* c1421.
　(armed Or langued Az; ?d1397).
　FELTON, Monsr Tomas. *BB 63. (a&l Or).*

FELTONE, Sire John de. *N 883.*
FELTONE, Tho. *NS 82.*
Sa 2 lions passt crowned gobony of 6 Arg and
Gu
　STRANGWAYS, Robard, Yorks. *RH, Ancestor
　v 183.*

2 lions passt crowned holding
Sa 2 lions passt Arg crowned Or each holding
fleur de lis Az
　HERONYLL, Thomas de. *Ancestor ix 216. (by
　inheritance from his brother).*
　HEROVILL, Thomas de. *Dugd 17, 9. 1367-8.
　(armed Or; 'escquchoun de sable ou deux
　Leonns passantz D'argent coronez et ruglez
　D'or, ou une fleur deliz de Azure dens pies';
　s of Sir Jn de H).*
　WYRLEY, Roger de. *Ancestor ix 216. (by grt
　of Thos de Heronyll).*

2 lions statant
2 lions stat
　— *Mill Steph.* c1370. *(imp by Mons
　Esmond de Cornewaylle; brass to his w
　Dame Eliz, Burford, Salop).*

2 lions guardant
2 lions ramp gard with 1 head crowned
　NORTHAMPTON, John. *Birch 12218.* SIGIL-
　LUM IOHANNIS NORTHAMPTON. 1375.
Az 2 lions ramp gard respect Arg gutty Az hold-
ing in their forepaws crown Or
　CASSIBELLANUS, K of Great Britain. *L2 99,
　2. (tails unfeathered & couped).*
Sa 2 lions couchant gard Arg
　— *PLN 452. (qtd 2&3 by Bernard Brocas;
　armed Gu).*
　MORRELL. *WB IV 175b, 895. (qtd 2&3 by
　Barnard Brokeys).*

2 lions pg Untinc
2 lions pg
　— *Birch 8515.* 1419. *(subsidiary shield in
　sl of Thos Chaworth, of Pyghteslay Manor,
　Northants).*
　— *Brit Arch Assoc NS xxiii 8.* ?14 cent.
　*(qrs 1&4 of shield from old mont, now in S
　wall of Ch, Seaton, Rutl).*
　BEAUCHAMP, Richard. *Birch 2207.* 1470.
　*(imp 3 fishes naiant border semy of roses; Bp
　of Salisbury, 1450-81).*
　BEAUCHAMP, Walter de. *Birch 7270.*
　+SIGILL'WALTERI.DE.BELOCAMPO. 13 cent.
　BELLO CAMPO, Guido de, 9th E of Warwick.
　Birch 5658. ...AMPO COM' WARREWYK. 1301.
　CATESBY, John de. *PRO-sls.* 1420-1.
　(letters I.C. above shield).

DARNOWLL. *Mill Steph.* c1520. *(in chf, with 2 wolves' heads erased in base; found in 1922 under seats at Penshurst, Kent, inscription lost; ?for combination of D & Stedolf).*

[DELAMARE]. *?source.* 15 cent. *(qtd by Achard; on brass [inscription lost], Aldermaston, Berks).*

DENSTON. *Mill Steph.* 1495. *(coat per fess, D in base, all imp by Rog Drury on brass to him & his 3 ws Agnes, Anne & Felice, [?dau of Wm Denston], Hawstead, Suff).*

[DENSTONE]. *Mill Steph.* 1524. *(qtd 4 by Broughton; brass to H Everard & his w Mgt D, Denstone, Suff).*

ESTRAUNGE, Fulcho le, 1st Baron. *Birch 9521.* S' FULCHONIS.LE ESTRAUNGE. 1301.

ESTRAUNGE, John le. *Birch 9522.* S' IOHANNIS LE ESTRAUNGE. temp Edw 1. *(s of Jn le E, [?of Norf]).*

FELTON, Sir John, Ld of Ochiltree. *Stevenson.* 1302.

FELTON, Sir Wm de. *Stevenson.* 1333.

FITZGEROLD, Warin. *Bk of Sls 307.* 1193-1216.

MARE, Peter La. *Birch 11591.* SECR...... (P)ETRI: FIL': ROB'TI: D': MARA. 1279. *(s of Robt de la M).*

MARE, Robert de la, Kt. *PRO-sls.* 1364.

MARE, Robt de la. *Bk of Sls 414.* 1279.

MARTAIN, John, Count of. *Bk of Sls 82.* 1189-90.

MORTAIN, John, E of. *Bow XXXIX 1.* SIGILLUM IOHIS COM MOROTONII FRATRIS REGIS ANGLIE DOMINI HIBERNIE. 1189-99. *(equestr sl).*

REDVERIS, Margaret de. *Birch 12949.* SECRETUM MARG ... E DE REDVERIIS. early Hen 3. *(dau & h of Warine, s of Gerold Ripariis & wid of 1 Baldwin de Redvers, s of Wm de Vernun [de Redvers], E of Devon, 2 Fulk de Breaute, d1252; above shield cresc enclosing blazing sun or estoile wavy).*

[ROCHE]. *Burrows 350.* 1354. *(1 of 3 shields on sl of Ida, wid of Sir Jn de Plecy).*

[ROCHES]. *Mill Steph.* 1488. *(qtd 2&3 by Brocas; brass to Bernard B, Sherborne St John, Hants).*

[ROCHES]. *Mill Steph.* 1492. *(qtd 2&3 by Brocas; brass to Jn B, Sherborne St John, Hants).*

[ROCHES]. *Mill Steph.* c1540. *(qtd 2&3 by Brocas; brass to Wm B, [d1506], Sherborne St John, Hants).*

ROCHES, Joanna de. *Burrows 342.* SIGILLU IOH..NE...O.HES. 1357. *(on 3 shields on sl of Joanna, wid of Sir Jn de R).*

STRANGE, Fulk de. *PRO-sls.* 1301.

WAREN, Richard de. *Birch 14270.* SIGILLUM RICARDI DE WAREN. late 12 cent.

WARENNE, Richard de. *BrookeAsp I 10, 3.* SIGILLUM.RICARDI DE VARENNE.

2 lions pg to sin

BURTON, Alice. *PRO-sls E40 A1500.* 1368-9. *(?lions gard; dimidg pale lozy; late w of Wm de B).*

CHALTON, John of London. *PRO-sls E40 A1525.* ...DE...AND. 1365-6. *(?3 lions; imp fretty).*

Untinc 2 lions pg Sa

CATESBY, Wm, of Ashby Ledgers. *Arch Ael 28, 460.* temp Hen 7. *(qtg Cranford, Ladbrok & Bishopston & imp Zouche; illuminated psalter; d1485, husb of Margaret, dau of Wm, Ld Zouche of Haringworth).*

Arg 2 lions pg

Arg 2 lions pg Gu

DELAMERE. *WB I 23b, 6.* *(qtd by Baynton).*

ELAND, of Kingston on Hull, Yorks. *D4 40.*

FOLIOT, M de. *WNR 134.*

FOLIOT, Samson. *PCL I 457.* *(or Vneffray Litylbere).*

FOLIOT, Sansem. *Q 152.*

FOLIOTT, Saunsum. *E II 220.*

FOLYOTH, Rauf. *LM 569.*

LITILBURY. *L1 391, 6; L2 303, 4.* *(armed Az).*

LITTLEBURY. *PLN 1291.* *(a&l Az).*

LITTLEBURY, John. *S 362.*

LITTLEBURY, Sir John. *CRK 1413.*

LITTLEBURY, of Lincs. *PT 459.*

LITTLEBURY, R de. *XL 382.*

LITTLIBURY, Mons R de. *WJ 393.*

LYTTILBURY. *L9 36b, 10.*

LYTTYLBERY. *DV 51a, 2002.*

Arg 2 lions pg Sa

FELTWICK, David. *TJ 197.*

FLEETWICK, David de. *XL 386.*

FLETEWICKE. *PT 220.*

FLETEWIK, Monsire David de. *AN 185.*

FLETEWYK. *DV 46a, 1817.* *(upper lion ch on breast with annulet Or).*

FLETWICK. *DV 56a, 2206.*

FLETWYK, Mons David de. *WJ 401.*

FLETWYKE, Beds. *L1 249, 5; L2 200, 3.*

FLITTEWIK, Sire David de. *N 394.* *(' ... a ii lunars passanz de sable').*

GOODRICH, William. *S 361.*

HOLOCH, Count of. *XL 436.* *(coward).*

OSWALDKIRKE. *CRK 791.*

Arg 2 lions pg Vt

MIRFELD. *L9 67b, 6.*

MIRFELD. *CC 228, 198.*

Az 2 lions pg

Az 2 lions pg Arg

BARNE. *L10 86, 4.* *(a&l Gu).*

BARNE. *L10 22, 9.* *(a&l Gu).*

BARNE, of Northendston, ?Bucks. *L10 76, 16. (langued Gu, sans claws).*
BORNE, of Norf. *FK II 445.*
BRITLEY, Mons Robt de. *WJ 407.*
Az 2 lions pg Or
— *CT 263.*
— *WJ 1330.*
BARRI. *L10 19b, 20. (a&l Gu).*
BARRI, Bobert. *F 242.*
BARRI, Robert de. *E I 365.*
BARRI, Sire Robert. *N 362.*
BARRY. *L1 79, 6; L2 65, 6.*
BARRY. *DV 41b, 1630.*
BARRY, Robt. *WLN 458; F 242.*
BURCY. *CV-BM 232.*
DENSTON. *L10 57, 3.*
DENSTON. *XL 74.*
NAPLYS, Kyng of. *PCL IV 14. (qrs 1&4).*
SOMERI, Peynall. *E II 185.*

Gu 2 lions pg
Gu 2 lions pg Arg
— *D5 5b. (qtd by Hamon).*
— *WB IV 136, 187. (qtd 2&3 by 'the lorde bechampe').*
— *CRK 1481. (qtd 2&3 by Baynton).*
— *BA 1033. (qtd 4 by Ld St Amand).*
— *WK 420. (qtd 5 by Pawlet).*
— *1H7 44d; D13 119. (qtd 2 by Gu 3 lions Or imp by Pawlet).*
— *LS 295. (qtd 4 by Ld Ric St Amand).*
— *L10 26b, 11. (qtd 2 by Beawchamp).*
BARNE, Robert le. *XL 388.*
DALAMER, Sir Thomas. *WB V 55.*
DELAMARE. *PT 881.*
DELAMARE. *XL 57.*
DELAMARE, Piers. *XL 381.*
DELAMARE, Sir Rauff, of Gloucs. *WB III 72b, 1. (a&l Az).*
DELAMERE. *WB I 23b, 8. (imp by Vuedale).*
[DELAMERE]. *Arch lvi 331. 15 cent. (qtd 2 by Ric Beauchamp, Bp, Salisbury, 1450-81, all in border Arg semy of tonsure caps Sa; window of Ockwells Manor House, Berks).*
MAR, Monsire Robert de la. *AN 315.*
MARE, Mons John de la. *S 498.*
MARE, S' Per' de la. *R 55.*
MARE, Pierce de la. *E I 538; E II 540.*
MARE, Mons Piers de la. *WJ 389.*
MARE, Piers de le. *F 264.*
MARE, Mons' Robert de la. *TJ 196.*
MARE, Sire Robert de la. *N 237.*
MARESHALL, Wilts. *L1 442, 5; L2 335, 8.*
STRANG. *BA 811. (qtd 2 by Ric Beauchamp, Bp of Salisbury).*
Gu 2 lions pg Or
— *WB II 58, 11-12. (qrs 2&3 of coat [Or 2 bars Gu] imp by Blacknall).*
— *PLN 1951. (in chf, in base Sa 3 boars'*

heads couped Or, all imp by Sa fess Gu [sic] betw 3 'shovellers' Arg b&l Gu).*
BRONNESWYE. *L10 76, 2. (a&l Az).*
BRUNSWICK, D of. *XL 306.*
BRUNSWICK, Le D de. *WJ 91.*
[BRUNSWICK]. *XL 42.*
DOUVRE, Richard de. *B 82.*
ENGLAND, ?Henry I. *Neale & Brayley. 1606. (Mont to Q Elizabeth & Q Mary).*
NORM'NDY, D of. *PCL IV 133.*
NORMANDY. *CRK 263.*
NORMANDY, D of. *KB 228.*
NORMANDY, D of. *AY 10. (a&l Az).*
NORMANDY, Rollo, D of. *Sandford I 13. (& other Dukes of Normandy & early Kings of Engld; no contemporary evidence - attributed by later writers to distinguish from arms of Plantagenets, 3 lions pg being 2 of Normandy & 1 of Aquitaine).*
REY, Richard fiz le. *A 1.*
WILLIAM THE CONQUEROR. *KB 224.*
WILLIMUS CONQUESTOR. *BW 10, 4.*

Or 2 lions pg
Or 2 lions pg Az
— *CT 150.*
— *Lyndsay 20. (qtd on escutch of K of Denmark).*
— *ML I 276. (qtd 3 by Sweden).*
— *BR VI 52. (marshalled by Ld Dudley).*
DABYTOT. *L2 16, 7. (a&l Gu).*
DENMARK, K of. *Lyndsay 43. (imp by Jas III for his w Mgt, dau of K of Denmark).*
GOMORY. *L1 274, 4; L2 220, 1. (marginal note L1 'Somery'; marginal note L2 'Goldington of Beds').*
SOMERY, Roger de. *B 97.*
Or 2 lions pg 1st Az 2nd Gu
SALTENOR, Geffray. *WB I 19, 1.*
Or 2 lions pg Gu
CAMBER. *L2 99, 1. (3rd s of 'Brut', & 1st K of Wales).*
CAMBER, King. *XL 412.*
LOCRIN. *L2 299, 1. (qtg 2&3 Az 3 crowns in bend Or; 1st s of 'Brut').*
PEDWARDYN. *CT 80.*
SAINT VALERY, John de. *WLN 431.*
SEIN WALERY, John de. *E I 561; E II 563.*
SEINT VALERI, John de. *WLN 36; F 359.*
Or 2 lions pg 1st Gu 2nd Az
ABITOT, Geoffrey. *WLN 727.*
DABITOT, Gefrai. *F 295.*
DABITOTT, Gefrai. *E I 297; E II 299.*
DABYTOT. *L2 165, 7.*
DEABETOT. *L10 56b, 12.*
Or 2 lions passt Gu 1st gard 2nd regard
BRITAIN, Cambrius. *BA 910. (2nd s of Brutus).*

Sa &c 2 lions pg

Sa 2 lions pg Arg
— Neale & Brayley. *(imp by Brocas; mont to Sir Bernard B, d1400)*.
— WB III 103, 7. *(qtd 2&3 by Jn Ponde, of Herts)*.
— CRK 754. *(qtd 2&3 by Sir ... Brocas)*.
— 1H7 43. *(qtd by Brokas & all imp by Pexsall, of Beaurepaire)*.
BOCHYS. *L2 82, 5. (a&l Gu)*.
BROCAS. *PLN 1824. (qtd 2&3 by Stokes)*.
FORTHE. *BG 407*.
ROCHE. *XL 552*.
ROCHES. *L1 555, 5*.
ROCHES. *SK 741*.
ROCHES. *PLN 1144*.
ROCHES, Monsire de. *AN 47*.
ROCHES, John de. *Burrows 329; Soc Jers 1929. (Keeper of Jersey 1326-7 & 1328-30)*.
ROCHES, John de. *TJ 198*.

Vt 2 lions pg Arg
MIRFELD, Ricardus. *Q II 500*.
MYRFELD, Richard. *SES 27*.

Field patterned 2 plain lions pg

Per pale Gu and Vt 2 lions pg Arg
ABITOTE, Geffrey de. *WLN 532*.
DABITOT, Geffrai. *F 170*.

Per pale Gu and Vt 2 lions pg Or
— CT 258.

2 lions pg charged or patterned

Gu 2 lions pg Arg 1st lion ch on shldr with mullet Sa
MARE, Mons Th la de. *WJ 391*.

Sa 2 lions pg Arg ch with 3 pales Gu
STRANGWAYS, Jacobus. *ML I 172*.

Gu 2 lions pg Erm
SORRELL, Enquerreau de. *XL 596*.

Sa 2 lions pg per pale Arg and Or
— WB I 16, 11.

2 lions pg coward

Sa 2 lions pg coward Arg
MORRELL. *L2 348, 2*.

2 lions pg collared &c

Gu 2 lions pg Arg collared Az
— BA 806. *(qtd 2 by Forester)*.
DELAMARE. *Leake. (qtd 5 by Sir Wm Paulet, KG, d1511-2)*.
DELAMARE. *L10 57b, 10*.
POWLET, Sir John, of Hants. *WB III 72b, 5. (a&l Az)*.

Arg semy of crosses Gu 2 lions pg Sa collared Or
GOODRICH. *XL 287. (armed Gu)*.

2 lions pg crowned

CATESBY. *Mill Steph; Belcher I 73, 139 & II 78, 238. 1528. (imp by Clement on brass to Sir Ric Clement & 1st w Anne, dau of Sir Wm Catesby, Ightham, Kent)*.
POULETT, John. *Bow L 5a. 1456-7. (banner, 2nd of 2; s of Sir Jn P)*.

Arg 2 lions pg Sa crowned Or
CATESBY. *L10 37, 7. (qr 1)*.
CATESBY. *LH 381. (qr 1)*.
CATESBY. *L2 138, 11. (a&l Gu)*.
CATESBY, George. *WK 772. (1st lion ch on shldr with cresc Or)*.
DYMOCK, Sir T. *PLN 926. (membered Gu)*.

Gu 2 lions pg Arg crowned Or
FULTON. *PLN 1191. (a&l Az)*.

Gu 2 lions pg Erm crowned Or
FELTON, Sir .... *CRK 735. (a&l Az)*.

2 lions regardant

Arg 2 lions regard Gu
BRITAIN. *BW 3, 3. (Camber, K of)*.

2 lions ramp addorsed regard
— ML II 132.

Arg 2 lions addorsed regard Sa
— ML I 197. *('Argent ii lionsewys comme rampant par assent & contre-veszed sabill')*.

Az 2 lions addorsed regard Arg tails intertwined
JUDAS MACCABAEUS. *KB 6*.

2 lions combatant regard
— ML II 133.

Arg 2 lions combatant regard Sa
— ML I 198. *('[Miles] quintus argent ii lionsewys eventryd regardaunt')*.

Arg gutty Sa 2 lions combatant regard Or
— SK 962.

Per pale Or and Az 2 lions addorsed regard counterch
— XF 216. *(imp by [?Mgt Croke] Az fess engr Erm betw 3 eagles Arg)*.

Arg 2 lions passt regard Sa
BABELAM, J (sic). *CRK 784*.
FOTHRYNGAY, Mons' John. *TJ 201*.
FOTHRYNGAY, Monsr John. *TJ 200. (painted with tincts reversed)*.
HERVILE. *XL 540*.
HERVILE. *SK 526*.
HERWELL. *LH 682*.
HOWELL. *LH 1021*.

Arg 2 lions passt regard Sa crowned Or
HERWELL. *LH 683*.
HOWELL. *LH 1022. (a&l Or)*.

2 BEASTS (OTHER)

2 beasts passt
GOLDINGTON, John de. *PRO-sls AS 131.*
S'IOHANNIS GOLDYNGTON. 1400-1.

Sa 2 antelopes passt respectant in fess Arg
COTINGHAM. *L2 130, 7.*

2 bears passt
MERYNGTON, Thomas de. *PRO-sls.* 1406-7.

Or 2 bears passt Sa
FITZURSE, Sir Reginald. *CV-BM 3.*

Qtly Sa and Arg bear salient Arg in qrs 2&3
(sic)
— *WK 240. (small shield added below that
of Sir Robt Payton).*

Vair 2 bears Untinc
WALKYNGHAM, John de, Ld of Balteby, Kt.
*Birch 14221. ...S DE WALK .... 1330. (s of Ld
Alan de W, of Yorks, Kt).*

Per pale Arg and Gu 2 beavers counterch
BARNEWELL, Tomas, Surr. *RH, Ancestor vii
186.*

Erm 2 boars passt Gu
WHICHECOTE, Johannes. *Q II 618.*

Lozy 2 camels in bend sin
CAMELL, John de. *PRO-sls.* 1363-4.

Per bend Gu and Or 2 camels Sa
CRACOW, K of. *SHY 583.*
CRACOWS, K of. *AY 105. (?dromedaries).*
GRAYCOWE, Rex. *KB 353.*

Arg 2 cats passt Gu
CATTE. *L10 41, 14. (a&l & spotted with
small rings Sa).*

2 deer

2 bucks courant
BUCKESKYN, Peter, of 'Fyschele'. *PRO-sls
AS 102 & 275.* SIGILL'PETRI BVCKESKYN.
1338-9.
BUCKESKYN, Peter, of Fyschelee. *PRO-sls.*
1338-9.

Arg 2 bucks courant Sa attired Or
BUSKYN, Ro. *NS 66.*

Sa 2 bucks courant Arg
BUCKSYN, Sire Robert. *PV 16.*

Sa 2 hinds counter-passt Arg
COTINGHAM. *BA 38b, 373.*
COTTINGHAM. *Lancs 1533 CS 110, 228. (qtd
3 by Calveley).*

2 dogs &c

2 dogs courant
POTTER, Robert, of Boreham. *PRO-sls AS
94.* SLAHA SAVI CVRETE. *1373-4. (?wolves).*

Arg 2 greyhounds courant Sa
[ALFORD]. *WB II 53, 10.*

Sa 2 greyhounds courant Arg
MALEVERER, of Stenecliffe. *PT 1043.*

Az 2 greyhounds Arg collared Sa
[ROW]. *ML I 235.*

Erm 2 hounds courant regard & collared per pale
Gu and Sa
— *(?John Pene or Peue). RH, Ancestor vii
203.*

Arg 2 dogs passt Gu
BRETON. *RH, Ancestor iv 250. ('mongrelys';
qtd by Jn Quartermain).*

Az 2 greyhounds combatant Sa
(?)ENT. *WB I 18, 9.*

2 talbots stat
BRETON, Guido, dominus de Friereton. *Bow
XXXV 30.* 1401-2.
[BRETTON]. *Mill Steph.* c1460. *(stat; qtd
2&3 by Quatremain; brass to Ric Q & his w
Sibil [Englefield], Thame, Oxfords).*
MALLORRE, Stephen. *Vinc 88, 23.* 1335.
*(passt; livery to Stephen M 'filio et heredi
Simonis'; [Winwick, Northants]; sl).*

Sa 2 greyhounds ramp regard addorsed Arg collared ?Gu
BARNARD, Nycolas. *RH, Ancestor ix 160.*

2 foxes passt
— *PRO-sls E40 A11603 & A11608.* SIG HA
AV DVNETE?. *1378-80. (used by divers peo-
ple of Borham, Essex).*

Gu 2 leopards Or spotted Sa
— *WK B 48. (qtd 8 by Hen 7).*
NORMANDIE, D of. *WB II 48, 9.*
NORMANDY. *L9 86b, 7. (a&l Az).*

Sa 2 leopards salient in salt Arg spotted Untinc
— *RH, Ancestor vii 186. ('de Galeys').*

Arg 2 otters stat Sa
MELDRUM. *Berry; Stodart pl 9. ('ceulx de
melledron').*

2 oxen &c

Or 2 bulls coucht Gu
— *PLN 603. (qtd 2&3 by Count de Foix).*

Or 2 cows passt Gu collared Or belled Az
— *WGA 105. (marshalled by Gaston de
Foix, Capt de la Bouche, E of Longueville).*

2 cows
— *Lawrance 19.* post 1302, ante 1350. *(qtg
2&3 3 garbs; heraldry foreign, ?tomb of Sir
Arnaud de Gaveston, Winchester Cathedral).*

2 bulls or cows collared & belled
— *Brit Arch Assoc i 216. (qtg 2&3 3 garbs,
overall cross throughout dividing grand qrs;
all qtg 3 lions pg, 6 spread eagles, Old
France, Castile & Leon; shield of effigy, N
aisle, Winchester, commonly attributed to Wm
de Foix, said to have been Earl 'de insula
Vana alias Winsall').*

Or 2 cows pg armed gorged & belled Az
BEARNE. *Leake.* c1440. *(qtd by Gaston de
Foix, KG, c1458).*

2 ?pigs
— *Bk of Sls 499.* 1333-5. *(?Jn, Abbot of Combe, Warwicks).*

Az 2 rams combatant gard Arg horned & unguled Or
— *CB 273. (qtd 2&3 by Colyngborne).*

Per chev Gu & paly Or and Arg in chf 2 squirrels sejt respectant Or
ADOTTI. *L2 18, 3.*

Arg 2 ?wolves courant Sa
— *XC 307. (qtd 3 by Wall).*

2 wolves passt
— *Gerola 76, 226. (15 cent shield on tower of English, Bodrum, Asia Minor).*
[AYALA]. *Mill Steph.* c1475. *(qtg Sanchet, Blount, Beauchamp, border omitted; brass to Nicholas Kniveton & w Joan [Mauleverer], Mugginton, Derbys).*

Arg 2 wolves passt Az
— *RH, Ancestor iv 250. (qtd by Jn Nanfan, of Cornw).*

Arg (or ?Gu) 2 wolves passt Gu (or ?Arg)
— *PT 866. (tincts have no guide lines).*

Arg 2 ?wolves passt Sa
— *LO B 2.*

Gu 2 wolves passt Arg
LEU, Nicole de. *A 262.*
LOU, Nichole le. *FW 191.*

Sa 2 wolves passt Arg
WOLFE, Sir W. *WB I 42b, 18.*

Az 2 wolves passt coward Or
PANELL. *L9 97a, 4.*

Arg 2 ?wolves stat Gu
— *WK 107. (qtd 4 by Sir Wm Litilton).*

Az 2 wolves passt regard coward Or
PANELE. *L1 499, 1; L2 404, 2.*

2 BEASTS & LABEL

2 lions passt & label

2 lions passt & label
[?EKENEY]. *Lawrance 39.* mid 14 cent. *(on tomb of Thos Reynes, Clifton Reynes, Bucks).*
ORREBY, John de, of Lincs. *Birch 12319.*
...LLUM IOH(A)NNIS DE ORBY. 1346.
PEDEWARDIN, Walter de, of Northants, Knt. *Birch 12456.* SIGILLUM WALTERI DE PEDEWARDIN. 1370.

2 lions passt & label of 5
GOLDYNGTONE, John de, of Essex, Kt. *Birch 10146.* ..OV.... 1332.

Arg 2 lions passt Gu label Az
— *CRK 255. (qtd 3 by Lisle).*
LESTRANGE, John. *B 162. ('son fitz').*
STRANGE, John. *XL 54.*
STRAUNGE, Fitz a. *WJ 214.*

Arg 2 lions passt Sa label of 5 Gu
POLEFORD, Hugo de. *Q 500.*

Az 2 lions passt Arg label Gu
LEYBOURNE, S Thomas de. *GA 212.*

Az 2 lions passt Or label Arg
— *(...eney, S' Rich). PO 647.*

Gu 2 lions passt Arg label of 4 Arg
STRANGE. *WLN 285. (qtd 2 by Brereton).*

Gu 2 lions passt Arg label Az
[STRANGE], Jason, fitz. *WJ 166.*

Gu 2 lions passt Arg label of 5 Az
SPRINGHOSE, Roger. *E I 388; E II 390.*
SPRINGHOSE, Roger. *F 251.*
SPRINGHOSE, Roger de. *WLN 467.*

Gu 2 lions passt Arg label Or
EREBY, Ches. *L2 178, 4.*
EREBY, Sr Johan. *N 955.*
ERREBY, S Jeh de. *GA 106.*
ORBY. *XL 47.*
ORBY. *L1 483, 2.*
ORBY. *SK 736.*
ORBY, Monsire de. *AN 64.*
ORREBY. *PO 407. ('Erreby' written above in Elizabethan hand).*
STRAUNGE. *WJ 169.*

Gu 2 lions passt Arg label of 5 Or
LESTRANGE, Sire Ible. *PV 41.*
ORBY. *L9 89a, 6.*

Gu 2 lions passt Or label Arg
PEDWARDYN, Robert. *S 366.*

Gu 2 lions passt Or label Az
PEDWARDYN, le fitz. *WJ 255.*
PEDWARDYN, Robert. *XL 56.*

Gu 2 lions passt Or label of 5 Az
PEDWARDYN. *L9 100a, 61. (a&l Az).*

Or 2 lions passt Az label Gu
— *XL 44.*
WENNE, ... au Baron de. *WJ 127.*

Or 2 lions passt Gu label Az
BRAMTON, Petr de. *Q 554.*

Or 2 lions passt Gu label of 5 Az
BRAMPTON, Peres de. *Q 361.*

Or 2 lions passt Gu label Sa
BROMTON, Walter. *F 379.*

Or 2 lions passt Gu label of 5 Sa
BRANTONE, Walter de. *E I 597.*
BROMTONE, Walter de. *E II 599.*

Or 2 lions passt Sa label Gu
GOLDINTOUN, Sire Johan de. *O 209.*

Gu 2 lions passt Erm label of 5 Az
FELTON. *CT 362.*

Gu 2 lions passt Erm crowned Or label Az
FELTON, Fitz a. *WJ 190.*

2 lions gard &c & label

Arg 2 lions pg Gu label Az
LYTTELBURY, S' Rob. *PO 552.*

Arg 2 lions pg Sa label Gu
    FLETWYK, Mons David de, le fitz. *WJ 402.*
Az 2 lions pg Or label Arg
    — *XK 155. (qtd 4 by Sir Edw Chamberlain).*
    EKENEY, Mons Rich de. *WJ 398.*
    EKENEYE, Richard. *XL 387.*
    [GIFFARD]. *I2(1904)89. (qtd 3 by 'Syr
    Edward Chamberlayn of Sherborne in
    Oxfords').*
    OKENEY. *XFB 212. (qtd 3 by Edw Cham-
    berlayn, of Shyrborne, Oxfords).*
    OKENEY. *L2 397, 4.*
Gu 2 lions pg Arg label Az
    MARE, Mons R de la. *WJ 390.*
Sa 2 lions pg Or label Arg
    EKENY. *L2 152, 8.*
Gu 2 lions 1 behind the other Arg label Or
    ORBY. *L2 394, 4.*

2 lions & charged label

2 lions passt & label ch with 3 lions
    LESTRAUNGE, Eble. *PRO-sls.* ?temp Edw 3.
Gu 2 lions passt Arg on label Or 3 lions ?Az
    STRANGE. *WJ 177.*
Gu 2 lions passt Arg on label Or 3 lions Purp
    — *XL 49.*

2 BEASTS & IN BASE

2 lions & in base

Per chev Az and Arg in chf 2 lions combatant &
    in base fleur de lis counterch
    — *PLN 1115.*
Per chev Gu and Az in chf 2 lions combatant &
    in base fleur de lis Or
    CLARENCE, Sir B of. *WB I 38, 13.*
    CLARENCE, bastard of. *RH, Ancestor iv 227.*
    CLARENCE, Sir John of, 'the Bastard'. *Sand-
    ford 309 & 311.*
Per chev Gu and Az in chf 2 lions combatant
    gard & in base fleur de lis Or
    CLARENC, Basterd. *WB I 18, 17.*
    CLARENCE, bastard of. *XPat 111, Arch 69,
    77.*
    CLARENCE, le bastard de. *CN 102.*
    CLARRAUNCE, Bastard of. *RH, Ancestor v
    182.*
2 lions pg & in base fleur de lis
    CLARENCE, John, bastard of. *Roman PO
    3167.* 17 July 1430.
Per fess indented Gu and Sa in chf 2 lions pg &
    in base 2 wolves' heads erased Or
    STUDOLPHE. *WK 426. (qrs 1&4; cresc Arg
    in fess pt).*

2 other beasts & in base

Per chev Az and Gu in chf 2 harts Or drinking
    from well in base Arg
    HART, William. *LH 27.*
    HARTE. *L2 26, 4.*
Per chev Az and Gu 2 stags in chf drinking at
    well in base Arg water Az
    HERT, Syr persevall. *WB I 19b, 11.*
Per chev Az and Gu in chf 2 stags Or regarding
    well Arg in base
    HART. *XPat 125, Arch 69, 77.*

2 BEASTS BESIDE

Qtly Arg and Sa in 1 & 4 a lion passt, in 2 & 3
    a mullet counterchanged
    BRETON. *L1 52, 6; L2 60, 6.*
    BRETON. *L10 78, 4.*
    BRETON. *XL 513.*

2 BEASTS & CANTON

2 lions & canton
    LUTERINGTON, Richard de. *Yorks Deeds IV
    27.* 1230. *(?3 lions).*

2 lions canton charged

Arg 2 lions rampt Gu on canton Sa fret Or
    BUCKLAND, John de. *XL 363.*
    BUKELAND. *L10 81b, 12. (canton of Mal-
    travers).*
Gu 2 lions rampt Arg on canton Or fret Sa
    BOKELOND. *L1 66, 5.*
Gu 2 lions rampt Arg on canton Sa fret Or
    BOKELOND. *L2 51, 1.*
    BUKLOND. *L10 85b, 2. (1 lion in sin chf
    other in base; canton of Maltravers).*
Gu 2 lions passt Erm on canton mullet Or
    FELTON, Sire Roger de. *O 168.*

2 lions canton patterned

Arg 2 lions rampt Gu canton Sa fretty Or
    BUKELAND, Mons J de. *WJ 230.*
    BUKELAND, Mons Th de. *WJ 231. (cresc Or
    on upper lion).*
Gu 2 lions rampt Arg canton Sa fretty Or
    BIKELONDE, Mons John. *TJ 119.*
    BUCKLAND, Sir .... *CRK 827.*
    BUKLONDE, John de. *TJ 152.*
    ROKLANDE. *DV 56a, 2205. (?3 lions).*
    WROTH, Sir John. *PLN 469.*

2 wolves & canton

Gu 2 wolves passt Or on canton Arg demi-rose
    Gu seeded Or
    VEILLELOBOS, Sir Ferdinand de. *L10 108b, 3.
    (sin half of rose).*

VEILLELOBOS, Sir Ferdinande de. *WK 389.*
(rose b&s Ppr).

VILLA LOBOS, Ferdinando de. *XPat 203,
Arch 69, 85. (Metcalfe Bk of Kts 37 notes
Sir Ferdinando de Villa Lobos, a Spaniard
knighted at marriage of Prince Arthur 14
Nov 1501).*

2 BEASTS & CHIEF

2 lions passt & chf
ALNWICK. *?source. (sl of Bp Alnwick of
Lincoln [1436-49], ?Sanehurst).*

2 lions pg & chf
ALNWICK, William of, Bp of Lincoln. *Arch
65 pl 30, 8. (qtg cross patonce, [?Vesci]).*

Az 2 lions pg & chf Arg
— *Nichols Leics II 268. (window, Melton
Mowbray Ch).*

Per pale dex lion sin ?dragon on chf fish
FELDE, John atte, of London, fishmonger.
*PRO-sls E40 A7859. ..ATE.... 1316-17. (very
poor workmanship; doubtful heraldry).*

Gu 2 lions passt Or on chf Az fleur de lis Or
— *GutchWdU.* before 1669. *(window, Old
Hall, University College, built 1450, demol-
ished 1669).*

2 lions pg on chf Virgin & Child
LINCOLN, See of. *Birch 1758.* 1511. *(sl of
Wm Smith, Bp of Lincoln, 1496-1514).*
LINCOLN, See of. *Birch 1757.* 1496. *(sl of
Wm Smith, Bp of Lincoln, 1496-1514).*
LINCOLN, See of. *PRO-sls AS 436.* SIG ...
SMYTH: D ....LINCOLNIENSIS.CPI....A.D: C. 1506.
(sl of Wm Smyth, Bp of Lincoln).

Untinc 2 lions pg Untinc on chf Az Virgin &
Child enthroned Untinc
LINCOLN, See of. *SHY 313.*

Gu 2 lions pg Or on chf Az Virgin & Child
enthroned Or
LINCOLN, See of. *PR(1515)18. (imp Attwa-
ter).*

Per fess Az and Gu in chf Virgin crowned &
Child seated on a settle & in base 2 lions pg
Or
LINCOLN, See of. *C3 41. (St Bennetts Ch,
Huntingdon).*

Gu 2 lions pg Or on chf Az Virgin crowned &
nimbed & Child seated on altar tomb Or
LINCOLN, Bp of. *L10 66, 12.*

Per pale Sa and Arg 2 lions combatant counterch
on chf Sa 5 roundels Or in salt
WHAPLODE. *CRK 142.*

2 BEASTS & IN CHIEF

2 lions & in chf

Arg 2 lions passt Az in chf cresc Gu
FENYS, Sir J. *WB I 41, 23.*

Sa 2 lions passt paly of 8 Arg and Gu in chf
cresc Or
STRANGWAYS, Gylys, of Styngsford. *BTN
19.*

Gu 2 lions pg in chf 2 crowns Or
ST BARTHOLOMEW THE GREAT, Priory of.
*Dingley cccclxvii. (Stone shield on Rahere's
mont in St Bartholomew's Ch, London).*
ST BARTHOLOMEW'S PRIORY. *L10 66b, 23.*

Per pale 2 lions & in chf 3 escallops
ALBRYGHTON, Roger, clerk. *PRO-sls.* 1405-
6.

Per pale 2 lions & in chf pike
FELDE, John atte, fishmonger of London.
PRO-sls E40 A11788. S IOHIS ATE FELDE.
1317-18.

2 lions pg crowned in chf fleur de lis
FELTON. *Suff HN 2. (imp Lewsy [?Lucy]; St
Gregory's Ch, Sudbery).*

2 lions passt bendwise in sin chf flower
ILKETSHALL, John, of Suff. *Farrer Bacon 2.*
1284. *(?or Morgan).*

Gu 2 lions passt in chf mullet Or ch with cresc
Sa
PEDWARDYN. *WB I 25b, 4.*

2 lions in chf 2 mullets
YELAND, Richard of. *?source.* late 15 cent.
(sl).

2 bears &c & in chf

2 bears in chf an uncertain object
BOUCE, Soyer. *PRO-sls.* 1 Dec 1336.

Az 2 cats ramp regard Arg supporting betw them
in chf crown Or
CASSIBELLANUS, King. *L10 45b, 11.*

Sa 2 hounds erect addorsed regard & in chf
hind's face Arg
BERNARD, Robert. *PLN 457.*

Sa 2 greyhounds ramp addorsed regard Arg in
centre chf hind's head Or
BARNARD. *LD 107.*
BARNARD, of Hants. *L1 112, 4; L2 77, 4.*

Sa 2 bushy tailed hounds addorsed erect regard
& in chf bull's head cab Arg
BARNARD, Roberd. *WB IV 148b, 412.*

2 horses passt to sin in sin chf fleur de lis
AGNIS, Radulphus de. *Bow 9. (not on
shield).*

Az 2 wolves ramp supporting betw them in chf
crown Or
BRITAIN, K Cassibelan. *KB 38.*

2 BEASTS & OVER ALL

2 lions passt & bend

2 lions passt bend

CORBET, Thomas, Kt. *Vinc 88, 188.* SIGILL'
THOME CORBET. 1298-9. *(sl).*
CORBET, Thomas, Kt, of Brug. *Bow LV 3.*
SIGILL THOMAE CORBET. 1298-9. *(of
Bridgnorth, ?Salop).*
ERDINGTON, Egidius de. *Dugd 17, 7.* 1357-8.
FITZ-Payne. *Birch 14131.* 1366. *(incorporated in design of sl of Matildis de Vere,
Ctess of Oxf).*
STRANGE, le. *Farrer II 311-15. (Hunstanton
Ch, Norf).*
STRANGE, Hy le. *Mill Steph.* 1485. *(brass
to Hy le S & w Kath [Drury], Hunstanton,
Norf).*
STRANGE, John le, Kt. *Bow XVIII 18.*
STRANGE, Sir Roger le. *Mill Steph.* 1506.
(brass to Sir Rog le S, Hunstanton, Norf).
VERE, Joan de, Ctess of Oxford. *AnstisAsp I
220, 82.* SIG IOANE COMITISSE OXFORD.
1362-3. *(2 of 4 lozs grouped round shield).*

Arg 2 lions passt Gu bend Az
LITTLEBURY, Mons Roberte. *SD 121.*

Gu 2 lions passt Arg bend Az
STRANGE, Sir .... *WK 178.*

Gu 2 lions passt Arg bend Or
DYSTRANGE, Henry. *CT 375.*
ESTRAUNGE, Hamond, of Gloucs. *LE 49.*
ESTRAUNGE, Sire Hamoun le. *N 880.*
LESTRANGE. *L9 40a, 9.*
LESTRAUNGE, Sr Hamond. *L 173.*
STRANGE. *LS 151. (a&l Az).*
STRANGE. *WB I 15, 21.*
STRANGE, Le. *SHY 97.*
STRANGE, Le. *SK 753.*
STRANGE, John le. *S 354.*
STRAUNGE. *NS 149.*
STRAUNGE, Le. *SK 755. (cresc Az in chf).*
STRAUNGE, Sir Roger. *WK 320. (riband).*

Or 2 lions passt Gu bend Az
BRAMPTON, Brian de. *Q 367.*

Or 2 lions passt Gu bend Sa
BROMTON, Jon. *F 380.*
BROMTONE. *L10 75b, 22. (a&l Az).*
BROMTONE, John de. *E I 599; E II 601.*

2 lions passt bend charged or patterned

Arg 2 lions passt Gu on bend Vt 3 eagles displ
Or
LETILBURY. *L1 409, 2; L2 303, 5.*

Or 2 lions passt Gu on bend Sa 3 escallops Arg
BROMTONE. *L10 75b, 23. (a&l Az).*
BROMTONE, Brian de. *E I 601; E II 603.*

Or 2 lions passt Gu on bend Sa 3 escallops Or
BROMTON, Bauduin. *F 381.*

Az 2 lions ?passt Or bend Erm
CALTHORPE, John de. *XL 327.*

2 lions passt bend gobony
FELTON, William of. *Dodsworth 49, 45b,
HB-SND.* 1314.
FELTON, William of. *PRO-sls Ex QR 9/30.*
1303.

Gu 2 lions passt Arg bend gobony Or and Az
FELTON, Gloucs. *L2 209, 8.*
FELTON, Sire Willame. *N 884.*

Gu 2 lions passt Arg bend gobony Or and Sa
FELTON, S William de. *GA 13.*

2 lions pg &c & over all bend

2 lions pg bend
CRAMBETH, Matthew de, Bp of Dunblane
1288-1309. *Stevenson 141.* c1290. *(2nd sl).*

Gu 2 lions pg Arg bend Az
MARE, Piers de la. *XL 384.*
MARE, Piers de la. *WJ 392.*

Gu 2 lions pg Or bend Az
DUNSTANVILLE, Reginald de, E of Cornwall.
*Sandford 50. (baston for diffce for bastardy
not normally found until over a century
later).*

Arg 2 lions pg Gu on bend Vt 3 eagles Or
LITELBURY. *L9 42b, 3.*
LITTILBURY, Mons Humphrey de. *AS 453.*
(?or bend betw lions).
LITTLEBURY. *XL 12.*
LITTLEBURY, Sir Humphrey de. *CV-BM 217.*
(eagles displ).
LYTTELBURY, Sr de. *CKO 198. (b&l Gu).*

2 lions passt regard bend
SCOT, William, of Yorks. *Birch 13343.* SEL
PRIVE SVY APELE. 1331. *(?or bend betw
lions).*

2 lions over all cross

2 lions passt over all cross
GRISINAKE, Bernard de. *PRO-sls.* 1303.

2 lions over all ... & label

Gu 2 lions passt Arg bend Or label Az
STRAUNGE, Sir Roger. *SK 754.*

2 BEASTS BETWEEN

Arg 2 lions pg in bend Sa betw 2 bends Gu
— WB II 69, 5. (qtd 2&3 by Arg 3 bars
gemel Gu).

Sa 2 lions combatant betw 2 chevs Arg
CHIPPENHAM. L10 40, 19. (qrs 1&4).
CHIPPENHAM. XL 118.
CHIPPENHAM. RB 185.
CHIPPENHAM, Berks. L1 150, 3; L2 123, 11.
CHIPPENHAM. XV II 126.
SHIPPENHAM, William. CRK 71.

Sa 2 lions combatant Or betw 2 chevs Arg
CHIPNAM. L10 46, 8. (qrs 1&4).

Sa 2 lions passt counter-passt betw 2 chevs Arg
SHIPMAN. PLN 1575.

Sa 2 lions passt counter-passt betw 2 chevs Or
CHYPNAM, Thomas, of Hants. WB III 108b,
7. (qrs 1&4).

Sa 2 lions passt betw 2 flaunches Arg each ch
with fess Az
STEDE, William. PLN 1789.

Az 2 lions pg betw 4 demi-lis Or isst from edges
of shield
— Sandford 489. (qtd 4 by Q Catherine
Howard).

2 lions passt to sin betw 2 fleurs de lis
PAGANELL, Fulco. Birch 12342. SIGILL....DE
BAMP...E. late 12 cent. (not on shield).

2 lions passt crowned betw 3 swords
DYMOCKE, Thomas. Birch 9397.
S: THOME: : DYMMOK. 1408.

2 BEASTS IN ORLE

Gu 2 lions passt Arg in orle of martlets Or
ESTRAUNGE, Sire Johan le. N 881. ('de
goules a les merelos de or e ii lions passant
de argent').
LESTRANGE, Sr John. L 160. ('... a la border
merelottes de or').

2 BEASTS IN BORDER

2 lions in border

2 lions in plain border

2 lions passt & border
ALBANO, Gaucelin, Bp of. PRO-sls AS 318.
SIGILLUM GAUCELINI DEL GRACIA ... OPI
ALBANENSIS. 1333.
LESTRAUNGE, Hamo, Kt. PRO-sls. 1267-8.

Az 2 lions passt Or border Gu
ERDINGTON, Sr Henri. N 857.
ERDINGTONE, Berks. L2 186, 5.

Az 2 lions passt border Or
ERDYNGTONE, of Warws. LE 44.

Gu 2 lions passt Or border Az
GERNONS. FK II 725.

Arg 2 lions passt Sa crowned Or border Gu
CATESBY. FK II B 447. (Gibbon adds 'of
Catesby, Northants').
HARVILLE. LH 710.

2 lions passt border semy of martlets: see under Escutcheon

2 lions in patterned border

Az 2 lions passt Or border gobony Or and Gu
ERDYNGTON. BA 30, 235.

Arg 2 lions pg Gu border Vt semy of eagles Or
LITTLEBURY, Humphrey de. XL 383.
LYTTILBURYE, Mons Umfray de. WJ 394.
LYTTYLBURY. L9 36b, 11.

2 lions passt border roundelly
ERDINGTON, Henry de, Kt. PRO-sls. 1279-
80. (12 roundels).

Arg 2 lions passt Sa border Or semy of salts Gu
[AYALA]. AY 65. (qtd 1 by Blount, Ld
Mountjoy).

2 lions in engrailed border

Per fess Az and Gu 1 lion in chf & 1 in base all
in border engr Or
TALBOT. BD 34b. (E window, St Mary's
Chapel, Collegiate Ch of Warwick; mantle of
lady kneeling to dex).

2 lions passt & border engr
LESTRANGE, Roger, of Ellesmere, 1st Baron.
Birch 11315. 14 cent.
PEDWARDYN, John de, of Herefs. Birch
12450. S' IOH'IS DE PEDWARDYN. 1335.
STRANGE. CT 85.
STRANGE, Roger le, of Ellesmere. Barons
Letter Ancestor lviii.
SYMOND, Thomas. PRO-sls AS 191. SIGIL-
LUM THOME SIMOND. 1380-1.

Arg 2 lions passt Sa border engr Gu
CATESBY. L10 36b, 10. (a&l Gu).
CATESBY, Sir Humphrey. WK 289. (a&l
Gu).

Az 2 lions passt border engr Arg
SIMON, Thomas. XL 312.

Az 2 lions passt Arg border engr Or
SEYMOUR. CRK 1818.

Az 2 lions passt border engr Or
SEYMOUR. XL 589.

Gu 2 lions passt border engr Arg
SIMON, Thomas. XL 51.
SYMONND, Mons Th. WJ 179.

Gu 2 lions passt Arg border engr Or
ESTRANG, Sir Roger. PCL I 523.
ESTRANGE, Roger le. FW 628; FW 628c.
ESTRANGE, Sire Roger le. N 71.

ESTRAUNGE, Sire Johan le. *N 885.*
ESTRAUNGE, Rogerus Le. *Q II 24.*
LESTRAUNGE, S Jehan. *GA 184.*
LESTRAUNGE, Sire Roger de. *J 118.*
SALL. *GutchWdU. (imp Beckingham; S window, Chapel, University Coll, demolished 1668).*
STRANGE. *CT 111.*
STRANGE, Roger le. *E I 220; E II 222.*
STRANGE, Sir Roger. *BR V 77.*
STRAUNGE, Sire Johan. *HA 84.*
STRAUNGE, Sr John. *RB 112.*
STRAUNGE, Roger le. *G 65.*
TALBOT. *L1 628, 5. (armed Az).*
TALBOT. *PT 869.*

Az 2 lions pg Arg border engr Or
[?SEYMOUR], Sir Thomas. *WB III 86, 4. (a&l Gu; name in MS illegible).*
Az 2 lions pg border engr Or
BARRY, Mons William. *S 361.*
Gu 2 lions pg Arg border engr Sa
SALL, Emond, of Devon. *WB III 115b, 2. (qrs 1&4).*
Gu 2 lions pg Or border engr Sa
— *PLN 917. (a&l Az).*

2 lions in border indented
Gu 2 lions passt border indented Arg
ESTRAINGE, Rogg' le. *LM 80.*
LESTRANGE, Mons Hamond. *CA 146.*
Gu 2 lions passt Arg border indented Or
STRANGE, Rog' le. *Q 26.*

2 other beasts in border
2 beasts passt & border
— *WB I 22b, 5. (qr 1 of escutch on coat imp by Sir Geo Putnam).*
Vt 2 boars Or border Arg flory Az
POWYS, Morys de fitz Rogier de. *Fouke 34, 24. (dc1200).*
Per chev Sa and Erm in ch 2 greyhounds combatant Arg collared Gu border Az flory Or
BLEDLOWE. *PLN 1898.*
2 squirrels addorsed & border
SAMWELL, John. *OxfRS II 102; Baker Northants 224; Mill Steph. c1500. (brass, Cottisford, Oxfords).*
Per chev Sa and Erm in chf 2 wolves combatant Arg border Az ch with 8 fleur de lis Or
BLEDLOWE, Thos. *Hutton 87.*
Arg 2 wolves passt Sa border Or ch with 8 pairs of lions' paws erased in salt Gu
AYALA. *Leake. c1472. (tincts of border erroneously transposed by artist; qr 1 of Blount, KG, d1474-5).*
Arg 2 wolves passt Sa border Arg fretty Gu
BLOUNT, Sir James, Kt 1485. *WB V 72. (?border Arg semy of salts Gu).*

Arg 2 wolves courant Sa border Or semy of salts Gu
BLOUNT, Sir James. *PLN 1985. (qtg 2 Or tower 3 turreted Az, 3 Barry wavy Sa and Or, 4 [Beauchamp] Vair).*
Arg 2 wolves passt Sa border Arg semy of salts Gu
BLONT, James. *WK 7. (qr 1; in fess pt mullet Sa).*
BLOUNT, Sir James. *WK 60.*
Arg 2 wolves passt Sa border Or semy of salts Gu
BLOUNT, Thomas. *PLN 1904. ('...entoyre of saltorelles Gu'; qtg 2 Or tower 3 turreted Az, 3 Sa 2 bars wavy Or, 4 Vair, over all cresc Gu).*
2 wolves stat border semy of salts
AYALA. *Mill Steph. 1508. (qtg Sanchet, Blount & Beauchamp of Hache; brass to Ric Blount, & w Eliz [Forde], Iver, Bucks).*

— *I2(1904)289. (qtd 2 by Blount; added by later hand).*
— *XK 85. (qtd 2 by Wm Blount, Ld Mountjoy, KG, 1526).*
— *XK 98. (qtd 2 by Blount, Ld Mountjoy, Kt, 1509).*
— *WK 460. (qtd 2 by Blount, Ld Monjoie).*
BLUNTTE. *PLN 158. (qtg 2 Or tower 3-turreted Az, 3 Sa 3 bars wavy Or, 4 Vair [Beauchamp]).*

2 beasts & label in border
Gu 2 lions passt Arg label of 5 Az border Vt
SPRINGHOSE. *XL 198.*
Vt 2 lions passt Arg label of 5 Az border Gu
SPRINGHOSE, Roger. *XL 195.*
Gu 2 lions passt Arg label of 5 Az border gobony Or and Vt
SPRINGHOSE. *XL 196.*

2 beasts & in base in border
Per chev Arg and Sa in chf 2 antelopes combatant Gu in base 4 crosslets Arg border Vt gutty Or
ANTELFELD, of Herts. *L1 353, 4; L2 244, 3. (qtd 4 by Edwd Hall, of Gray's Inn).*
Per chev wavy Arg and Sa in chf 2 antelopes combatant Gu attired Or in base 4 crosslets Arg border Vt gutty Or
— *XV I 774.*
Per chev wavy Arg and Sa in chf 2 stags combatant Gu attired Or in base 4 crosses formy Arg border Vt gutty Or
— *LH 632. (qtd 4 by Jn Hall).*

Per chev nebuly Arg and Sa 2 stags counter-
salient in chf Gu attired Or in base 4 crosses
formy Arg border Vt gutty Arg
— *L10 92, 1. (qtd 4 by Hall, of Gray's Inn).*

2 beasts & over all in border

Gu 2 lions passt Arg border engr Or bend Az
ESTRAUNGE, John, of Gloucs. *LE 50.*

2 beasts betw in border

Arg 2 greyhounds combatant Sa betw 2 chev Sa
border engr Gu
— *WB I 17, 1. (imp by Haydon).*
Per pale Arg and Sa 2 wolves courant betw 3
4foils counterch border per pale Gu and Or
HORDEN, Kent. *L10 102, 8.*
HORDEN, of Kent. *L2 265, 2.*
Per pale Arg and Sa 2 wolves passt betw 3 4foils
counterch border per pale Gu and Or
HORDEN. *XPat 286, Arch 69, 91. (grant to
Thos H, of Kent, 24 May 1523, by Wriothes-
ley).*

2 BEASTS IN TRESSURE

Gu 2 lions combatant Arg in 2tressure flory cf
Or
DOLAND, Richard, of Lancs. *PLN 2069.*
2 lions passt in tressure
FELTON, William of. *Balliol E 7, 5. 1340.
(sl).*
2 lions passt in tressure flory cf
FELTON, William of. *Durham-sls 959. 1345.*
Gu 2 lions passt Arg in tressure flory Or
FELTON, Mons John de. *S 422.*
Gu 2 lions passt in 2tressure flory outwards only
Untinc
FELTON. *SK 653.*
Gu 2 lions passt in 2 tressure flory outwards only
Arg
FELTON, Mons William. *TJ 136.*
2 lions passt in 2tressure flory cf
FELTON, Sir William. *Blair N II 124, 254.
(nave, Edlingham Ch).*
Arg 2 lions passt in 2tressure flory cf Gu
KINTHORPE. *CRK 181. (qtd by Hastings).*
Gu 2 lions passt in 2tressure flory cf Arg
— *XFB 153. (qtd 2&3 by Thos Salter, of
'Westd').*
FELTON. *L1 243, 6; L2 198, 10.*
FELTON, George de. *XL 310.*
FELTON, John de. *S 427.*
FELTON, Mons John de. *TJ 1453.*
FELTON, Mons W de. *WJ 185.*
FELTON, Mons William. *TJ 137.*
FELTON, Sir Wylyam. *RH, Ancestor vii 214.*

2 beasts in tressure & label

Gu 2 lions passt in tressure Arg label Az
FELTON, Monsire William de. *AN 125.*
Gu 2 lions passt in 2tressure flory Untinc label
Az
FELTONE. *SK 654.*

3 BEASTS (LIONS)

3 demi-lions

**For demi-lions in the form of lions pg dimidi-
ated see also 3 lions pg**

3 demi-lions ramp
3 demi-lions
— *Birch 4896. 12-13 cent. (blazon unclear;
on lance flag on ship; Corporation sl of
Dunwich, Suff).*
PANCEFOT, Richard. *PRO-sls. 13 cent.*
PONCEFOT, Richard. *Birch 12779. S' RICARDI
PONCEFOT. 14 cent.*
STURMY, Henry. *PRO-sls E40 A13641.
1373-4. (Sheriff of Wilts).*
STURMY, Henry, Ld of Figheldean, Wilts.
Birch 13754. 1355.
TAIND?, William, of Chilverston, Warws.
Bow XVIII 1. 1404-5.
Arg 3 demi-lions Untinc
— *WB I 8, 3. (qtd 3 by [Seymour]).*
Arg 3 demi-lions Gu
— *XB 2. (qtd by Q Jane Seymour).*
— *WB II 56, 1. (qtd 3 by Sir Jn Seymer).*
— *I2(1904)118. (qtd 4 by Sir Jn Semer).*
— *XK 14. (qtd 4 by Q Jane Seymour).*
LERMIT, Henry. *E II 674.*
STIMY. *Sandford 488. (qtd 4 by Q Jane Sey-
mour).*
STURMAN, Sir William, of Oxfords. *WB III
84, 7. (a&l Az).*
STURMI, le. *E I 672. (or le Mervw; 'scriptus
le Mervin sed dubio').*
STURMY. *Gerard 149.*
STURMY. *LS 82. (a&l Az).*
STURMY, Sir William, of Worcs. *RH, Ances-
tor iv 247.*
STURMY, Sir Wylyam, of Hants. *RH, Ances-
tor v 182.*
STURMYN. *CRK 1558.*
STURMYN. *L1 611, 5. (armed Az).*
STURMYN. *PT 655.*
STURMYN, Sir William. *XL 585.*
Gu 3 demi-lions Arg
BENET. *CB 63.*
BENET. *L10 26, 15. (a&l Az).*

BENET, Thomas. *WJ 235.*
BENNET, Thomas. *XL 27.*
BENNET, Thomas. *XL 368.*
BENNETT, of Berks. *Suff HN 46. (imp by Browne; monastery house, Layston).*
Per fess Sa and Arg pale counterch 3 demi-lions Arg
— *CRK 664. (a&l Gu).*
— *RH, Ancestor ix 171.*
Az 3 demi-lions Erm
NEWMAN, Tomas, Northants. *RH, Ancestor vii 187.*
Gu 3 demi-lions Arg crowned Or
— *PT 618.*
BENNET, Robert. *CRK 310. (tails out-turned).*

3 demi-lions passt
3 ldemi-ions passt
KNETON, Agnes. *PRO-sls AS 12. S' ISA-BIAVDEI SUPIAVS. 1371-2. (wid of Ralph de K; dimidg 3 leopards heads).*
Gu 3 demi-lions passt in pale Or
HAYCH, of Devon. *L1 349, 5. (qtd by Or fretty Sa).*
HAYCH, of Devon. *L2 262, 8.*

3 demi-lions pg
3 demi-lions pg
CHESTER, City of. *Hope 174. 1283. (dimidg 3 garbs; on Statute Merchant sl).*
CINQUE PORTS. *Hope 175. 1305. (dimidg 3 hulls of ships; on sl of Dover).*
CINQUE PORTS. *Mill Steph. c1520. (dimidg 3 hulls of ships; brass to civilian & w, Ipswich, St Mary le Tower).*
CINQUE PORTS. *Mill Steph. (dimidg 3 hulls of ships; Canterbury Museum).*
CINQUE PORTS. *Mill Steph. 1533. (dimidg 3 hulls of ships; brass to Hy Hatche, Favers-ham Kent).*
ELAND, Wm of. *Visit Northd 44, HB-SND. 1426.*
ENGLAND. *Proc Soc Antiq V 2S 261; Arch Journ xiii 134. c1300. (dimidg France with label; for Isabella, w of Prince of Wales (later Edw 2); on shrine-shaped silver casket).*
ENGLAND, Q of. *Brit Arch Assoc vii 421. (dimidg France; w of Edw 1; sl [sans legend] attached to document dd Woodstock, 1301).*
ENGLAND, Edw 1 or 2. *Proc Soc Antiq III 2S 468. (dimidg France; on fragment of paper found when restoring 15 cent screen betw Presbyter & Chapel of St Edw, Westm Abbey).*
ENGLAND, Mary. *PRO-sls. 1300-1. (dimidg Castile & Leon; dau of Edw 1).*
ENGLAND, Mgt, Q of. *Proc Soc Antiq V 2S*

261; Arch Journ xiii 134. c1300. *(dimidg France; 2nd w of Edw 1; on shrine-shaped casket). Sandford 120, 133 & 137. (dimidg France anct).*
NEWENHAM, Edmund. *PRO-sls. 1467-8. (mullet in fess pt).*
OTHO, Holy Roman Emperor. *MP Hist Min ii 65. (dimidg eagle; outline only; 'Scutum Othonis imperatoris, cujus medietas de scuto est imperii alia vero de scuto regis Angliae').*
3 demi-lions pg to sin
— *Bk of Sls 367.* early 13 cent. *(?dimid by fleur de lis on sl of Ric de Coombe).*
Gu 3 demi-lions pg Or
CESTRIAE. *CVC 593. (dimidg Az 3 garbs Or).*
CESTRIE. *WLN 913. (dimidg Gu 3 garbs Or; 'Arma civitatis').*
CHESTER CITY. *WLN 935. (dimidg Az 3 garbs Or).*
CINQUE PORTS. *CY 171, 681. (dimidg Az 3 ships Or hulls masoned Sa; 'Arma de Synk-portes co Sx').*
CINQUE PORTS. *WLN 936. (dimidg Az 3 ships Or; 'Quinque portuum, Arma').*
CINQUE PORTS. *RH, Ancestor vii 204. (dimidg Az 3 hulls Or; 'The Armys of V Por-tys').*
CINQUE PORTS. *PLN 54. (dimidg Az 3 ships Or; imp by Calais).*
CINQUE PORTS. *ML I 128. (dimidg Az 3 ships Or).*
CINQUE PORTS. *T c 41. (dimidg Az 3 ships Or).*
CINQUE PORTS. *CVK 731. (dimidg Az 3 ships' hulls Arg).*
CINQUE PORTS. *SK 10. (dimidg Az 3 ships Or; name added by Gibbon).*
ENGLAND. *Mp VI 7. (dimidg the Empire, viz. Or a double eagle displ Sa, for Henry s of Fredrick 2).*
ENGLAND, Q of. *HE 7; FW 38. (dimidg [Aragon?]).*
ENGLAND, Q of. *HE6; FW 36. (dimidg Cas-tile above Leon).*
ENGLAND, Hen . *MP III 13. (dimidg Sa plain; 'the young king' s of Hen 2).*
HAYCH. *BA 1108.*
OTHO IV, Holy Roman Emperor. *MP Hist Min ii 83. (dimidg Or eagle Sa; elected 1199; above shield 3 crowns, overwritten: 'Argentea Aurea Ferrea').*
OTTO IV. *MP I 21; MP IV 5. (dimidg the Empire).*
REYENE, La weyle. *HE 8. (dimidg Pro-vence).*
REYNE, la. *HE 6. (dimidg Castile above Leon).*

Per pale Or and Az 3 demi-lions pg counterch
HAMON, of Kent. *L9 27b, 11.*

3 lions rampant

3 lions
— *Mill Steph.* 1477. *(imp by Strangbon on
brass to Joan dau of Thos Walrond & w of
Rob S, Childrey, Berks).*
— *Dugd 17, 9.* 1308. *(imp by Estrange, for
Maud, w of Jn E, of Kuskin).*
— *Antiq Journ vi 152-3. (arms in loz of w of
member of Ruyhales family; glassBirtsmorton
Court).*
— *Birch 7591.* 15 cent. *(qtd 2&3 by Wm
Boneville, Kt).*
— *Mill Steph.* 1475. *(on mantle of 1st w of
Philip Mede on brass to him & 2 wives at St
Mary Redcliffe, Bristol, Gloucs).*
ARUNDEL, William de. *Selborne 4, 2.* Sigill'
Willi de Arundel. *(2, 1; s of Hugh de A).*
BELHOUS, Isolda de. *Birch 7341.* SIGILLU
ISEUDE BELHOUS. 1336. *(sin of 2; wid of Jn
de B, Kt, of Barnwell, Northants & Rayleigh,
Essex; dau & coh of Lady Alicia de Beau-
mont).*
BELHOUS, Thomas de, Kt. *PRO-sls.* 1345-6.
?BYKER. *Birch 3686.* 14 cent. *(?lions in
pale; sl of Whitefriars, Newcastle).*
CALESTHORPE, Sir William de. *Stowe-Bard
1s ii 6.* +SECRETA WILL D CALESTHORP. temp
Hen 3.
CHUDDELEGH, James de. *Exeter D&C 405.*
sigil.iacobi.chiddele. 1375.
CHAMBERLEYN, Edward, of Kent. *Birch
8454.* 1529. *(2, 1; rectangular).*
COUNBY. *Suff HN 2. (imp by Sudbery; St
Gregory's Ch, Sudbury).*
DESPENCER, John le. *Proc Soc Antiq I 2S
196.* S IOHIS LE DE SPENSER D'ALDEBERY.
1343-4.
?DYNELEY. *Brit Arch ....Assoc x 184.*
1444. *(brass to Mgt, w of Wm D, St Denys,
Stanford Dingley, Berks).*
FENIS, James. *Clairambault 3552.* 14 April
1424.
FENIS, Thomas, Ld Dacre. *PRO-sls.*
FITZ HERBERT, Reginald fitz Peter. *Vinc 88,
51.* Sig reginaldi filii Petri filii herberti. *(sl).*
?FITZHERBERT. *Mill Steph.* 1444. *(lower sin
shield (3 others lost) on brass to Mgt, w of
Wm Dyneley, Stanford Dingley, Berks).*
FITZHERBERT. *Bow XXXIII 8.* Sigillum filii Her-
berti.
FITZHERBERT, Reginald. *Bk of Sls 237.*
1248-86. *(s of Peter F).*
FITZJOHN, Matthew. *PRO-sls.* S' MATHEI
FII'IOHANNIS. 1301. *(2, 1).*
FITZPETER, John fitz Reginald. *PRO-sls E40*

A4610. SIGILLUM SECRETI. 1287-8.
FITZREGINALD, John. *Bow XIX 5.* temp Edw
1. *(equestr sl).*
FITZREINALD, John. *Bow 9. (equestr sl).*
[FITZREYNOLD]. *Birch 5999.* S' IOH'IS FIL'I
REGINALDI. 1301. *(Johannis filius Reginaldi
[Ld of Blakeney, Norf]; equestr sl).*
FITZREYNOLD, John. *Barons Letter.*
FITZROGER, Sir Henry le. *Heneage 1399.*
SIGILLUM HENRICI FILII ROGERI. 1349.
FYNES. *WB I 16b, 12.*
FYNES, Sir Thomas, 8th Baron Dacre, Kt.
Birch 9998. ...DNI: +: DACRE: +: .... 1530. *(2,
1; qtg 2&3 3 escallops [Dacre]).*
GORAN, Robertus de. *Birch 10163.*
S'ROBERTI GORAN. *(2, 1).* 1235.
GRIFFITH, Thomas ap. *Dodsworth 49, 29,
HB-SND.* 1405. *(qtg 2&3 fess dancetty).*
HACHE, Avice la. *Bow XXX 7b.* 1361-2. *(1
of 3 shields; wid of Eustace la H).*
[KIRKHAM]. *DevonNQ VII ii 18-19.* ?15
cent. *(2 in chf ramp & 1 in base passt [sic
for 3 lions ramp]; carved on capital, nave
pillar, Ashcombe, Devon).*
LESTRAUNGE, John. *CassPk 323.* 9 Sept
1354. *(remains of sl).*
MACDONALD OF THE ISLES. *Stevenson;
Laing-sls I 452; Birch 16404.* 1454. *(qtg
lymphad under sail; all in tressure flory cf;
Jn, 11th E of Ross, d1498).*
MOELYS, Alice. *PRO-sls.* 1330-1. *(1 of 3
shields; w of Rog de M).*
MOELYS, Alice. *PRO-sls E40 A6829.* ALICIE
DE. 1330-1. *(1 of 3 shields; late w of Rog
de M).*
MORTAIN, Roger de, Ld of Walishale. *Dugd
17, 11.* 1309.
PAUNCEFOT, Eymer. *Dugd 17, 21.* 1318.
PAUNCEFOT, Thomas. *Birch 12414.* SIGILL
THOME PAUNCEFOT. 1472. *(2, 1; qtg lion
crowned).*
PETER, John. *PRO-sls.* 1287-8. *(s of
Reginald s of Peter).*
POULETT, John. *Bow L 5a.* Sigillum armorum
Johanis Pouleti domini de Basing et de Noney. 1456-
7. *(banner, 1 of 2; s of Sir Jn P).*
ROGER. *Stevenson 161.* 1304. *(Bp of Ross
1325-50).*
[ROSS]. *Stevenson.* 1440. *(qtd by Mac-
donald, Ld of the Isles, 10th E of Ross).*
[ROSS]. *Stevenson.* 1420. *(imp by Leslie,
Mgt, dau of Sir Walter Leslie & Euphemia,
Ctess of Ross & w of Donald, Ld of the
Isles).*
[ROSS]. *Stevenson.* 1379. *(qtd by Leslie, Sir
Walter, Ld of Ross).*
ROSS, Euphemia. *Glamis Charter, Stevenson.*
1375. *(d1387, wid of Jn Randolph, 3rd E of
Moray, 2nd w of Robt, E of Stratherne*

[afterwards K Robt II], dau of Hugh, 4th E of Ross).
ROSS, John. *Stevenson.* 1431. *(apparently to sin).*
ROSS, William, 3rd E of. *Stevenson.* 1292. *(3 sls).*
ROUS, William, of East Chalfield, Wilts. *Isbury.* SIGILLUM WILLM ROUS. 1433.
SUGUN, Reymond de. *PRO-sls.* SIGILLUM REMONDI DE SUGUN. 1340-1. *('Pincerna? dni Regis').*
THEDEMERHS, John de. *PRO-sls.* 1340-1.
THEDEMERSSH, Nicholas. *PRO-sls.* SIGILLUM NIC OLAI TEDYMERSCH. 1383-4.

Arg 3 lions Gu
Arg 3 lions Gu
— *FB 33. (imp by Pevere).*
B[OLLYNS], Sr John de. *L 10.*
BAARD. *L2 95, 2.*
BAARDE. *L10 22b, 13. (a&l Az).*
BARD. *XL 85.*
BELHOUS. *L10 26, 12.*
BELHOUS, Sr de. *CKO 608.*
BELHOUS, Mons Thomas de. *WJ 222.*
BELHOUS, Thomas. *XL 25.*
BELHOUSE, Thomas de. *XL 362.*
BELLEHOUS, Sir Johan de. *N 428.*
BOLHOUS, Essex. *L1 69, 5; L2 71, 3.*
BULLEHOUS. *L10 86b, 15. (a&l Az).*
COUMBE, Rychard de. *LM 531.*
CROYLY. *L1 149, 1; L2 123, 5.*
CROYLY. *RB 499.*
CROYLY. *L2 123, 5. (marginal note gives Gosholme).*
CROYLY. *L1 149, 1. (marginal note gives Baylhowes, Essex).*
GOSHOLME. *L1 293, 1; L2 227, 11. ('Bayherst of Essex' in margin).*
KIRHAM, of Devon. *L1 384, 6; L2 292, 11.*
KIRKHAM. *XL 260.*
TALBOT, Sir W. *BW 20b, 144.*

Arg 3 lions Or &c
Arg 3 lions Or (sic)
— *PT 143.*
COSHALME. *DV 69a, 2727.*
Arg 3 lions Purp
BAYNS. *PT 338.*
BAYOUS, Richard de. *XL 34.*
BAYOUS, Robert de. *XL 441. (a&l Az).*
BAYOUS, Sire Robert de. *N 750.*
BAYOUSSE. *L10 20b, 14.*
BAYOUSSE, Mons R de. *WJ 358.*
BAYS, John, of Hunts. *WB III 91, 7.*
BAYUS, Hunts. *L1 66, 6; L2 45, 11. (Talbot, of Bashaw, Lancs in marginal note).*
TALBOT. *PCL IV 132. ('Erele of Schrwyshere').*

TALBOT. *L1 629, 5. (armed Gu).*
TALBOT. *XL 70. (langued Az).*
TALBOT, Bryan. *PLN 188. (2, 1).*
TALBOT, Sir Edmond. *CRK 716.*
TALBOT, Sir Edward. *CVL 428. (2, 1).*
TALBOT, Mons Esmond. *TJ 158.*
TALBOT, Sir John, of Salesbury. *BA 38, 366. (qtd by Cliderhou).*
TALBOT, Suss. *MY 325.*
TALBOT, Sir Thomas. *CVL 384. (tricked Sa but Purp added).*
TALBOT, Sir Thomas, of Basha. *BA 37b, 359.*
TALBOT, Sir Thomas, of Bashall, Lancs. *XL 252. (a&l Az).*
TALBOT, Thomas, of Bashall & Salesbury. *S 124.*
TALBOTT. *PT 1054.*
TALBOTT, Sr Edmond. *L 111.*
TALBOTT, Mons Thomas. *S 122.*
TALEBOT, Sire Edmon. *N 1024.*

Arg 3 lions Sa
Arg 3 lions Sa
BAYOUSSE, Mons R de. *WJ 358.*
CHEVEREL. *XL 577.*
CHEVEREL, Sr Alexander. *AN 56; S 63; N 205.*
CHEVEREL, Sr Alissaunder. *RB 83.*
CHEVEREL, Sire Alissaundre. *HA 42, 16b.*
CHEVERELL, S Alexander. *GA 169.*
CHEVEROYL. *FK II 960. (a&l Gu).*
CHIUEROLL, of Wilts & Hants. *L1 167, 1; L2 117, 12. (a&l Gu).*
GENNE, William le. *A 34.*
JOV, William le. *FW 696.*
JOVE, William le. *FW 694c.*
MOHAWT, Sr H. *ME 49; LY A 169.*

Az 3 lions
Az 3 lions Arg
— *D4 30b. (qtd by Mydylton, of Newcastle, Northd; armed Sa langued Gu).*
— *RH, Ancestor ix 173. ('azure 3 ounces (or leopards after their kind) ramp silver').*
— *D13 21. (qtd 8 by Monyngs).*
CANBILL. *L1 126, 4; L2 104, 7. (armed Gu).*
CANVILL. *L10 43, 7.*
CHICHE. *PT 23.*
CHICHE, John. *PLN 879.*
CHYCHE. *L1 174, 5; L2 125, 7.*
CHYCHE. *DV 58b, 2307.*
FENES, Mons Rogier. *TJ 203. (lions passt in blazon).*
MOHAUTE, Mons Rich de. *WJ 287.*
MOLIANT. *L1 126, 4. (armed Gu; marginal note 'against Canbill').*
MONHANCE, Richard de. *XL 30.*
MONHANCE, Richard de. *XL 143.*
MONHAUTE. *L9 70b, 3.*

MORTEYN, Sire Roger de. *J 127.*
SURDELLE, Le Conte de. *Berry; Stodart pl 1.*
(Macdonald, E of Ross, Ld of The Isles).
THOMAS, Rychard ap Hawett ap. *BA 22b,*
192.
WARWICK, John de. *XL 35.*

Az 3 lions Or
— *Proc Soc Antiq xvii 2S 276.* c1310.
(shield on stole, Leagram Hall, Lancs).
— *WLN 171.*
DACRE, Ld. *PLN 2035. (qtg 2&3 Gu 3*
escallops Arg).
DACRE, Thomas, Ld. *SussASColl iv 192-3.*
(mont, Hurstmonceaux to Thos, Ld Dacre,
d1534 & his s Thos, Ld Dacre, d1541).
DACRES, Ld of the South. *XFB 70. (qrs*
1&4).
FEENES. *PT 501.*
FENYS, Mr, of Oxfords. *WB II 56, 11. (qr*
1).
FENYS, Sir Thomas. *BA 757 & 759. (Ld*
Dacre of the South).
FENYS, Sir Thomas, Kt 1501. *WK 279.*
(cresc Arg).
FENZ. *L1 250, 4.*
FEYNES, of Hurstmonceaux, Suss, **Baron**
Dacre of the South. *L2 202, 5.*
FFORDE, Mons Adam de. *WJ 132.*
[FIENNES]. *RH, Ancestor iv 231. (qtd 2&3*
by Ld Saye).
FIENNES, Ld Dacre. *PR(1512)62. (qtg*
Dacre).
FIENNES, the Lord Dacre of the South. *WK*
185.
FIENNES, Sir James. *CRK 756.*
FIENNES, James, Ld Say & Sale. *ML I 36.*
FIENNES, Roger. *CV-BM 30.*
FIENNES, Sir Thomas, Ld Dacre. *XL 241.*
(qrs 1&4).
FINES, of Martock. *Gerard 126.*
FITZ PIERS. *XL 548.*
FORD, Adam de. *XL 326.*
FORD, Adam le. *XL 23.*
FYNELES. *DV 63a, 2485. (armed Gu).*
FYNES, Sir Thomas, Ld Dacre, of Clavarham,
Suss. *D13 42d & 45.*
FYNNYS, The Lord Dacre, of the South.
I2(1904)192. (qtg 2 Gu 3 scallops Arg, 3 Az
3 chevs interlaced & chf Or, 4 Vair fess Gu).
FYNNYS, The Lord Dacre, of the South.
I2(1904)187. (qtd by 2: Gu 3 scallops Arg 3:
Az 3 chevs interlaced & chief Or).
LUMESIN. *PLN 595. (a&l Gu; France).*
SAY, Ld. *BR VI 56. (noted in later hand*
against arms of Ld Clynton).

Gu 3 lions Arg
Gu 3 lions Arg
— *WB I 35, 8.*
— *PT 1094. (qtd by Redman, of Thorne-*
tone).
— *SC 5. (qtd 2&3 by [Ross] 'Erle of*
Rosse').
BARNABE, Sir George of, of Yorks. *WB III*
71, 5. (a&l Az).
BERNARD, Th Fitz. *WJ 256.*
DELAWACHE, Bucks. *L2 163, 12.*
FELTON, le S'r de. *T c 38.*
FITZ HERBERT, Sire Johan le fitz Reinald. *J*
125.
FITZBARNARD, Thomas. *XL 124. (a&l Or).*
PANCEFOT, Grymbald. *TJ 105.*
PANSEVOT. *CT 251.*
PANSFOUT, Thos. *BA 20, 166.*
PAUNCEFOTE. *L1 501, 3.*
PAUNCEFOTE. *XL 245.*
PAUNCEFOTE. *CRK 1550.*
PAUNCEVOT, Grimbaud. *E I 300; E II 302.*
PAUNSFOT, Grimbaud. *WLN 691.*
PAUNSFOTE, Sir Humfrey, of Gloucs. *WB III*
73b, 7. (a&l Az).
PAUNSFOTT. *BA 850.*
PAUNSOTTE. *L9 93b, 2.*
R..., le counte de. *LM 49. (Ros added).*
ROS, Counte de. *Q 17.*
ROS, Le Conte de. *BL A 6.*
ROSS, E of. *Lyndsay 38. (imp by K Robt II*
for his 1st w Euphemia, dau of E of Ross).
[ROSS]. *Lyndsay 49. (qtd 2 by Steuert, D of*
Ross).
ROSS, E of, of Auld. *Lyndsay 88.*
ROSS, Le Comte de. *Gelre; Stodart pl E5.*
ROSS, Earldom of. *Neale & Brayley. (qtd 2*
by: D'Aubigny qtg Stuart, of Davingstone,
Lenox on escutch).
ROSS, Richard, E of. *Inventory.* R COMES
ROTHESAIAE. c1260. *(15 cent inscription).*
[VACHE, de la]. *LD 139.*
VACHE, of Bucks. *CB 48. (3-tailed pennon;*
16 cent blazon makes lions Arg crowned Or).
VACHE, Mons Hugh de. *TJ 105.*
VACHEZ. *FK II 867.*
WACHE, Fellepe le. *BB 24. (d1408).*

Gu 3 lions Or
Gu 3 lions Or
— *WB I 23b, 3. (qr 3 of coat imp by Baker).*
— *WB I 38b, 5. (qtd 2&3 by Sir W Bon-*
vyle).
— *XL 301.*
— *LS 171. (qtd 2&3 by Stucley).*
— *PLN 1803. (qtd 2&3 by Thos Dingley).*
— *PLN 1908. (qtd 2 by St John).*
— *CRK 1124. (qtd 2&3 by ?Elwat).*
— *WB I 23b, 4. (qtd II&III 2 iv by Baker).*

— *BA 1086.* *(langued Az; qtd 2&3 by Ld Bonvyle).*
— *WB I 24b, 11.* *(qtd 2 by Dyngley).*
— *WB I 20, 18.* *(qr 3 of coat imp by Sir Jn Baker).*
— *BA 1038.* *(qtd 4 by Thos Stukeley, of Aston).*
BARNARD. *L10 20b, 8.* *(a&l Az).*
BARRNARD. *CT 450.* *(charges obliterated).*
BERNARD, Th fitz. *WJ 256.*
BONVILE. *CRK 579.* *(qrs 1&4).*
BONVILE, Ld. *PLN 178.* *(qtd 2&3 by Sa 6 mullets 3, 2, 1 Arg pd Gu).*
FITZ BARNARD, Thomas. *XL 551.*
FITZ HERBERD. *SK 687.*
FITZ HERBERT, Sir Nicol. *CRK 448.*
FITZ PERS, Renaud le. *E I 47; E II 47.*
FITZ PIERS, Reginald. *XL 538.*
FITZ REYNOLD, Sir John. *BR V 50.*
FITZBARNARD, Thomas. *XL 29.*
FITZBERNARD. *BA 1101.* *(qtd 2&3 by Stukele).*
FITZHERBERD. *L2 193, 8.* *(marginal note 'Fitzrenold').*
FITZPERYS. *WB I 15b, 3.*
FYTZHERBERDE. *Suff HN 24.* *(imp by Comberforde; Linstead Ch).*
HERBERD, Monsire Mayhu filtz. *AN 302.*
HERBERT. *PO 366.* *(fiez [later hand]).*
KNYLES, Hona ap. *WK A 33.*
PAUNSEVOTE. *CT 56.*
PERES. *L9 104a, 6.*
PERES, Renaud le fiz. *Q 164.*
PIERS, Mons Reynald fitz. *TJ 146.*
REINAULD, le fitz Piers. *B 77.* *('... a trois lionseux rampant d'or').*
RENAUD, Sire Johan le fiz. *N 73.*
REYNAUD, le fiz Pers. *D 135a & b.*
REYNOLD, fitz Piers. *A 75; B 98.*

Or 3 lions
Or 3 lions Az
REPELEY .... *R 121.*
Or 3 lions Purp
TALBOT, Sir T. *WB I 39b, 1.*
Or 3 lions Sa
— *Lyndsay 27.* *(qtd by the 'Kyng off Romanes').*
HELION, John, of Essex. *LH 762.*
HILION, John, of Essex. *WB III 105b, 1.* *(a&l Gu).*
MAILLORE. *L9 49b, 9.*
MAILLORR, Mons John. *XL 175.*
MAKDONELL, Sr Dunkan, d'Escoce. *M 66.*
MALORY, John. *XL 32.*
MAYLLORYE, Mons J de. *WJ 343.*

Sa 3 lions
Sa 3 lions Arg
AIGLES. *L1 19, 4; L2 10, 12.*
COWN, Thomas de. *ME 56.* *(a&l Gu).*
ENGLEYS, Sr Johan. *N 1013.*
ENGLEYS, of North.... *LE 53.*
ENGLEYS, s' Rob'. *PO 634.*
ENGLEYS, S Robert de. *ST 50.*
ENGLISH. *FK II 576.* *('Aiglis', name added by Gibbon).*
ENGLISH, Thomas. *XL 31.*
ENGLISH, Thomas. *XL 151.*
ENGLYS, Mons Thomas. *WJ 303.*
INGLISSH, Mons' William. *TJ 159.*
MAYLER. *CRK 983.* *(qtd 2&3 by Orton).*
SANDFORDE. *PT 1247.*
[TALBOT]. *Bellasis II 306-8.* *(qtg [Harington] Sa fretty Arg, label Gu; E window, Windermere Ch).*
Sa 3 lions Or
COMBE. *XL 18.* *(qrs 1&4).*
COUMBE. *L1 148, 3; L2 123, 2.*
COUMBE. *L10 39b, 10.*
[TORPERVILLE?]. *BG 80.* *('Th Torpell?').*
TURBERVILE, Gefrai. *E I 371; E II 373.*
WYKETON, Mons J de. *WJ 348.*

Vt 3 lions
Vt 3 lions Arg
LYMBRYKE. *CB 194.* *(a&l Gu).*
WARDEWIKES, Monsire John. *AN 329.*
WARDWYCKE. *L1 665, 2.* *(a&l Gu).*
WARDWYKE, Mons J de. *WJ 359.*
WARWICK. *XL 464.*
WARWICK. *CRK 1889.* *(a&l Gu).*
WARWICKE. *PT 1239.*

Barry 3 lions
Barry of 10 Arg and Az 3 lions Gu
STODEBINT, Mons Rauf. *TJ 60.*
STODEBYNT, Sir Rauf. *RH, Ancestor vii 214.* *(?Stobeuynt).*
WODBOURNE, Mons John. *TJ 127.*
WODEBOURNE. *RB 268.*
WODEBRIRE. *F 453; Arch 39, 416.* *(Arch gives blazon as 'Arg 6 bars Az 3 lions Gu').*
WODEBURGH, Sr de. *CKO 576.*
WODEBURNE, Monsr de. *AS 342.*
WOLDEBURGH, Thomas. *TJ 582.*
WOODBOROUGH, Ralph de. *XF 379.* *(blazoned burely).*
WOODBURGH, Monsire de. *CG 541.*
WOODBURGH, Ralph de. *E I 477; E II 479.*
WOODBURN, John de. *XL 28.*
Barry of 12 Arg and Az 3 lions Gu
WOODBURN, John de. *XL 359.*
Barry of 14 Arg and Az 3 lions Gu
WODBOURNE. *L1 691, 2.*

Burely Arg and Az 3 lions Purp
  STODEBINT, Rauf. *TJ 587.*
Barry of 10 Arg and Gu 3 lions Sa
  ESTOUTEUILLE. *L2 177, 12 87.*
  STOTEUYLE, Sir Nichol. *BR V 141.*
  STOTEVILE. *LS 87.*
Barry of 12 Arg and Gu 3 lions Sa
  ESTOTEVILE, Nicolas, of Norf. *LE 24.*
Barry Arg and Sa 3 lions Gu
  — *F 272; Arch 39, 409. (blazoned Arg 6 bars Sa 3 lions Gu in Arch 39, 409).*
Burely Arg and Sa 3 lions Gu
  WOODBOROUGH, William. *XF 374.*
  WOODBURGH, William de. *E I 479; E II 481.*

Checky 3 lions
Checky Gu and Az (sic) 3 lions Az
  BARKESWORTH, Sir Robert. *BR V 207. (rectius checky Gu and Arg on bend Az 3 lions Arg).*

Erm 3 lions
Erm 3 lions Gu
  BELHOUS. *L10 26, 13.*
  BELHOUS, R de. *WJ 223.*
  BELHOUS, Richard. *XL 26.*
  BELHOUSE, Richard de. *XL 366.*
  CHIDLEGH. *L10 46, 19.*
  CHIDLEGH, James, of Devon. *WB III 114b, 9.*
  CHIDLEY, of Devon. *L1 179, 2; L2 127, 4.*
  CHUDLEIGH. *DevonNQ VII ii 22.* late 15 cent. *(on font & elsewhere, Ashton Ch).*
  CHYDELEY. *BA 1136.*

Per bend &c 3 lions
Per bend wavy Or and Az 3 lions counterch
  LAURENCE, Rece, of Kydenend. *BA 24b, 208.*
Per chev Arg and Az 3 lions counterch
  HOLKER. *LH 950. ('Hulke').*
Per chev Or and Az 3 lions counterch
  [WARMINGTON?]. *WB I 33b, 24. (lions in chf combattant).*
Per chev embattled Arg and Az 3 lions counterch
  HOLKER. *LH 469. ('Hulk').*
  [HOLKER]. *XV 867. ('Hulke').*
  HULKE. *L1 347, 2; L2 252, 4.*
Per chev embattled Gu and Or 3 lions counterch
  WIFOLDE, Nich. *Hutton 86.*
  WYFOLD. *XPat 391, Arch 69, 98.* temp Hen 5.
  WYFOLD. *XL 477.*
  WYFOLD. *XV 894.*
  WYFOLD, N. *CRK 1717. (a&l Az).*
  WYFOLD, Nicholas. *LV 64.*
  WYWOLDE. *RH, Ancestor ix 174.*

Per chev embattled Sa and Or 3 lions counterch
  — *RH, Ancestor ix 168.*
Per fess in chf 3 lions
  FIENNES, Sir Roger. *SussASColl iv 172.* c1440. *(on banner supported by alant or wolfdog; carved on gateway, S front, Hurstmonceaux Castle).*
  [FITZHERBERT]. *Berks Arch Journ 38, 154. (brass to Mgt Dyneley, N aisle, Stanford Dingley Ch, Berks).*
  FYNES. *Mill Steph.* c1510. *(qtd by Dacre & imp by Gaynesford on brass to Anne dau of Sir Thos F, Ld Dacre of the South & 3rd w of Jn [afterwards Sir Jn] G, Crowhurst, Surr).*
  PAUNCEFOOT. *Mill Steph.* c1390-1400. *(imp by Herl on incised slab to Sir Andrew H & w Joan P, Allensmere, Herefs).*
  PAUNCEFOTE, Sir Grimbald. *Lawrance 35. (effigies of Sir G, d1292, Crickhowell, Breck & his s Sir G, d1314, Much Cowarne, Herefs).*
  PROUS, Alice le. *AnstisAsp I 217, 73.* SIG ALICIE LE PROUS. 1320-1. *(wid of Wm le P).*
  SKEVYNTON, Sir John, Sheriff of London. *CY 175, 698. (only 2 lions drawn & space for 3rd on sin).*
  YDEN, Paewl. *Belcher I 91 & II 107; Mill Steph.* 1514. *(brass, Penshurst, Kent).*
Per fess Az and Or pale counterch 3 lions Or
  WHEATLEY. *XL 457.*
  WHETELL. *L1 674, 1.*
  WHETHILL, Sir John. *XK 201.*
  WHETHYLL. *XPat 388, Arch 69, 98.*
Per fess Sa and Erm 3 lions Or
  DANYEL, 'of Gloucest'. *L1 215, 1; L2 160, 8.*

Per pale &c 3 lions
Per pale 3 lions 2, 1
  FITZ-John, Matthew, Ld of Stokeham. *Birch 9738.* S MATHEI FIL IOHANNIS. 1301.
Per pale Az and Gu 3 lions Untinc
  HARBARD, The Lord. *L1 354, 1. (armed Untinc).*
Per pale Az and Gu 3 lions Arg
  — *SHY 435. (imp by Percy, E of Northd).*
  — *WGA 82. (Borne in pretence by Sir Chas Somerset).*
  ESTENE, Rychard. *RH, Ancestor vii 210.*
  FITZ HERBERT. *XL 584.*
  FITZHERBERT, in Wales. *L2 193, 9. (Baron Herbert).*
  HARBARD, Ld. *L1 553, 6.*
  HARBARTH, 'The Lord Chamberlayn'. *?source. (escutch of Somerset [France & England in border gobony Arg and Az]).*
  HARBERD, Ld. *WB I 20, 7.*
  HERBERT. *Sandford 342. (qtd 2 by Hen*

Somerset, E of Worcester, d1549).
HERBERT. *FK II 666.*
HERBERT. *WGA 254. (escutch of Sir Chas Somerset, afterwards Ld Herbert).*
HERBERT, Sir George. *WK 404.*
HERBERT, E of Huntyngdon. *AY 82.*
HERBERT, Maude. *XL 210. (imp by [?Gwillim] ap David, of Sengheuith).*
HERBERT, Sir Walter. *PLN 2015. (a&l counterch).*
HERBERT, Ld William, E of Pembroke. *WGA 226.*
ROUS, John. *CA 222.*

Per pale Az and Gu 3 lions Or
FITZ MAHEU, Herberd. *B 78.*
FITZHERBERT, Mahu fiz Johan. *G 170.*
HERBERT. *PO 367. (name added in later hand).*

Per pale Gu and Untinc 3 lions Untinc
FITZ MAHEU. *WLN 411. (unfinished).*

Per pale Gu and Az 3 lions Arg
HERBERT. *XK 48. (escutch over all, Sir Chas Somerset, Ld Herbert, KG temp Henry 7).*
HERBERT. *WB II 53, 12. (imp by Ellis).*
HERBERT. *Sandford 246, 337 & 339. (escutch of Chas Beaufort (sic), E of Worc, d1526).*
HERBERT. *LH 1096.*
HERBERT, Ld. *PLN 1278. (a&l counterch).*
HERBERT, of Gower. *Leake. (imp by Sir Chas Somerset, KG, d1526).*
[HERBERT]. *CT 104. ('Gerbertt').*
ROUS, Gile le. *LR 40.*
ROUS, Gile le. *E I 309; E II 311.*
RUS, Gile le. *F 372.*
WILLIAM UP THOMAS, of Walis, Sir. *WB III 86b, 9. (qrs 1&4).*

Per pale Gu and Az 3 lions Or
FITZ MATTHEW, Herbert. *MP Hist Min ii 500. ('Obiit Herbertus filius Mathei in Wallia, miles strennuus, lapide obrutus').*
FITZ RANAULD. *CT 2555.*
FITZHERBERT, Matthew. *MP I 74.*

Per pale Gu and Sa 3 lions Arg
ROUS, Giles le. *WLN 384.*

Per pale Gu and Sa 3 lions Or
— *TZ 8.*
HERBERT. *CRK 455.*

Per pale Gu and Vt 3 lions Or
— *CRK 1435.*

Per pale Or and Az 3 lions Gu
ROUS, Sire Roger le. *N 904.*

Qtly Gu and Az 3 lions Arg
MORGAN, William. *CRK 290.*

Semy 3 lions
Gu semy of billets 3 lions Arg
HERONDY, John le. *WLN 437.*
Gu semy of billets Or 3 lions Arg
HOND. *LH 878.*
HOND, John. *LH 262.*
HOND, John de. *E I 587; E II 589. (or Bond).*
Gu semy of billets 3 lions Or
HERONDI, Jon de. *F 389.*
Gu crusily Or 3 lions Arg
PREUZ. *L9 101b, 1.*
PREUZ, Sire Willame le. *N 180.*
Sa crusily Or 3 lions Arg
ENGLET. *L1 528, 4.*
Crusily fitchy 3 lions
[BELHOUSE]. *Mill Steph. c1520. (imp qtly, 1&4 [Dynley] 2&3 3 eagles displ; brass, Aveley, Essex).*
Arg crusily fitchy Sa 3 lions Gu
[BELHOUS]. *CRK 933.*
Sa crusily fitchy Or 3 lions Arg
WIBBURY. *DV 46b, 1822.*
WILBURY. *XL 484.*
WYLBURY. *PLN 284. (a&l Gu).*
Sa 3 lions betw 7 crosslets fitchy Or
WIBBURY. *L1 688, 6.*
Sa flory 3 lions Arg
— *CRK 573.*

3 lions charged or patterned
Gu 3 lions Or each ch on shldr with mullet Sa
— *FK II 267-8. (qtd 2&3 by Stukely).*
Gu 3 lions Erm
LUNDERTHORP, Sr de. *CKO 613.*
Sa 3 lions Erm
SUGLES. *PO 177.*
Per pale Az and Gu 3 lions Erm
HARBARD, Ld. *L1 553, 6. (Marginal note 'Arg not Erm').*
ROUS, Mons Geffray le. *TJ 72.*
ROUS, Sire Johan le. *N 905.*
ROUS, Richard le. *Q 215.*
ROUSE. *LH 1095. (lions painted Arg gutty Sa).*
Per pale Gu and Az 3 lions Erm
ESTENEY. *L2 184, 6.*
[MABEU], le fitz. *F 339.*
MAHEU, Philip le Fitz. *E I 307; E II 309.*
Sa 3 lions Or fretty Az
WICKTON, John. *XL 179.*
WYBOTON. *XL 33.*
Sa 3 lions lozy Or and Az
WYKETON, Mons J de. *WJ 348.*
Az 3 lions per pale Arg and Gu
TOMASYNE, Bartholomewe. *RH, Ancestor vii 212. (ARW notes 'The parting runs straight down from the middle of the lion's head but reaching the tail follows it round and so*

ends').

Per pale Az and Gu 3 lions Arg gutty Untinc
HERBERT. *LH 806.*

Per pale Az and Gu 3 lions Arg gutty Sa
ROUS. *LH 1095. ('Herbert or' struck
through).*

3 lions collared

Arg 3 lions Gu collared Or
REDDISH, Ralph. *CRK 1967.*

3 lions crowned

3 lions crowned
FOXCOTE, Thomas, of Stanford Manor, Berks.
Birch 9920. SIGILLUM THOME FOXCOTE.
1420. *(2, 1).*
L'ESTRANGE, Matilda. *Bow LX 1b.* 1308-9.
(imp 2 lions passt; w of Jn L'E).

Arg 3 lions crowned Gu
WALYS, Prince of. *RH, Ancestor v 181. (in
a later hand 'HO'LL DDA').*

Arg 3 lions Sa crowned Or
HALWEYN. *XL 521. (a&l Or).*

Az 3 lions Arg crowned Or
VACHE, Sr Richard de la. *I 38.*
WARWICK, John de. *XL 445.*

Az 3 lions crowned Or
DELAFORD, Wilts. *L2 164, 4.*
FORD, Adam de la. *K 788.*
FORDE, Adam de la. *K 97. ('de trois lyon-
ceaus couronnez keil ot rampans en inde
nez').*
FORDE, Sire Adam de la. *N 206.*
FORDE, Sr Adam de la. *GA 196.
('...rampans dor coronez dor').*
FORDE, of Kingston on Thames, Surr & Hart-
ing, Suss. *D13 56. (2, 1; qtg per fess Or
and Erm lion per fess Az & fretty Arg and
Gu).*
FOURD. *L1 250, 5.*

Gu 3 lions Arg crowned Or
CODERUGE. *L2 130, 2.*
LACHE, de. *PT 97.*
LAVASSE, Sir Philip. *WGA 26.*
LAVASSE, Sir Richard. *WGA 40.*
VACHE, de la. *ME 102; LY A 227.*
VACHE, of Bucks. *CB 48. (acc to 16 cent
blazon but as painted crowns omitted; 3-
tailed pennon).*
VACHE, Essex. *MY 146.*
VACHE, Mons Philip la. *S 426.*
VACHE, Philip la. *S 431.*
VACHE, Sir Philip de la. *WGA 140.*
VACHE, S' Ric la. *PO 341.*
VACHE, Mons Rich de la. *WJ 180.*
LA VACHE, Richard. *CRK 2028.*
VACHE, Richard de la. *XL 249.*
VACHE, Richard la. *XL 24.*
VACHE, Sir Richard de la, KG. *Leake.*

c1421. *(annulet Or pd Az in centre pt).*
WACHE, de la. *DV 68a, 2683.*
WACHE, S Rescharde de. *BB 33. (d1366).*

Sa 3 lions Arg crowned Or
— *FK II 579.*

Burely Arg and Az 3 lions Gu crowned Or
WODEBURCH, Rauf de. *A 284.*
WODEBURGH, Rauf de. *FW 349.*
WODEBURGH, Willame de. *FW 350.*

3 lions qf

3 lions qf
MORTEIN, Roger de, Ld of Walsall, Staffs, Kt.
Birch 11946. S' ROGERI DE MORTAIN. temp
Edw 2.

Az 3 lions qf Arg
CHYCHE. *PLN 1266.*

Gu 3 lions qf Arg
AVENEBURI, Osbern de. *F 287.*

Or 3 lions qf in salt Gu
— *WLN 155.*

Vt 3 lions qf Arg
WARDEWIK, Mons John. *TJ 151.*
WARDEWITH. *PT 98.*
WARDWYKE. *DV 68a, 2684.*

3 lions couchant

Az 3 lions couchant in pale Or
— *ML I 18. (armed Sa; 'Asur iii lyon sewys
seyawnt in cowche gold enarmyd sabyll').*

Arg gutty Gu 3 lions coucht & coward Sa
crowned Gu ch with 6 roundels 3, 2, 1 Arg
FAYREFORD. *PLN 1236.*

3 lions passant

3 lions passt
— *Birch 11534.* 1315. *(1 of 6 coats in sl of
Nicholas Malemayns, of Lincs).*
— *PRO-sls.* 1393-4. *(qtd by Constance
Martin).*
— *Bow XXX 8a.* 1348-9. *(imp by fretty can-
ton [Mathilda de Vernon]).*
BURG', Hubert de, Chamberlain of the King.
PRO-sls. early 13 cent.
[CAMVILLE]. *Keepe; Inventory.* 1505. *(qtd 4
on brass to Sir Humphrey Stanley).*
CANVILLE, William de, Ld of LLanstephan.
PRO-sls. 1325-6.
CAREW. *Mill Steph. (brass to Philipe, dau
of Nich & Mercy C, with 7 bros & 6 sis;
Beddington, Surr).*
CAREW. *Mill Steph.* 1432. *(3 brasses (a)
alone (b) imp 3 catharine wheels (c) imp
[Delamare]; brasses to Nich Carew & 1st w
Isabel [?Roet], Beddington, Surr).*
CAREW, John. *Mill Steph.* 1520. *(brass to
Jn Carew & w Mgt, St Mary's, Bury St

Edmunds, Suff).

CAREW, Nicholas. *Mill Steph.* 1469. *(brass, Haccombe, Devon).*

CAREW, Nicholas de. *PRO-sls.* 1301.

CAREW, Nicholas, Baron. *Keepe. (d1470; indent only remains).*

CAREW, Sir Nicholas, of Mitcham & Morden, Surr, Kt. *Birch 8354.* 1530.

CAREW, Nicholas de, Ld of Mulesford. *Barons Letter, Ancestor xcii.* 1301.

CAREW, Thomas de, Kt. *Brymore 30.* S' TH-...AS CAREW. 1423.

CAREW, Sir Thos. *PlymouthCL-sls 81/R.* sigill: thome: ch..w:.

CARREU, Nicholas de. *PRO-sls E40 A5292, 5295.* SIG.LVM NICHOLAI DE CARREV. 1374-5.

CARREU, Sir Nicholas. *PRO-sls AS 303, A5292, A5295 & B11699.* SIGILLUM NICHO-LAI DE CARREV. 1381-2.

CARREU, Nicholas de, Ld of Muleford. *Birch 8351.* S NICHOLAI DE CARREV. 1301.

CARREW, John de, Ld of. *PRO-sls.* 1314.

CARREW, Sir Nicholas. *PRO-sls.* 1381-2.

CARREW, Nicholas, of Nutfield Manor & Beddington &c, Surr. *Birch 8352.* SIGILLUM NICHOL[AI] DE CARREV. 1420.

CARRU, Eleanor de. *AnstisAsp I 213, 61.* SIGILLUM ELIANORE DE CARRU. 1338-9.

CARRU, John de. *Birch 8349.* SIGILLUM IOHANNIS DE CARRV. temp Edw 3.

CARRU, Nicholas de, Constable of the Castle of 'Bothvile'. *PRO-sls.* 1302-3.

COMBE, Richard de. *PRO-sls.* 1352-3 & 1357-8.

CONSTANTINE, Sir Robert. *Waiting iv 12.* temp Edw 1. *(Memo of Search by G King, Jan 1682-3).*

CURZON, Richard. *Birch 9147.* 1499.

DISNEY. *Lawrance 15.* ante 1350. *(effigy, Norton Disney, Lincs).*

EDINGTONE. *PT 764.*

ERDINGTON, S' Giles, Staffs. *CY a 98, 391.*

GEFFORDE, George. *WB I 20b, 2. (unclear whether lions are passt or gard; qrs 1&4; 1st lion in qr 1 ch with cresc on shldr).*

[GIFFARD]. *Brit Arch Assoc 3S iii 207.* 1671. *(imp by Lane; mont, Stoke Newington, Oxfords).*

GIFFARD, John, of Brymesfield. *Dugd 17, 18.* 1318.

GIFFORD. *Mill Steph.* 1400. *(brass to Sir Jn Casey, Chief Baron of the Exchequer & w Alice G, Deerhurst, Gloucs).*

GIFFORD, of Brimsfieldd. *Brit Arch Assoc vi 139.* 1315. *(sl of Mgt Nevil, 2nd w of Jn, Ld G of B, on effigy's robe & on dex shield, sin shield has lion for Neville).*

GIFFORD, Osbert. *PRO-sls E40 A249.* 1301-

2.

GYFFARD, Margaret. *Arch Journ xciii 32.* S MARGARETI GYFFARD. c1298. *(loz; ?sl of Lady Mgt, 2nd w of Jn, Ld G, of Brimsfield, d1299; sl Matrix 59, Nelson Coll).*

GYFFARD, Margaret. *SarumM-sls.* S MAR-GARETI GYFFARD. c1298. *(sl from silver matrix in collection of Dr Philip Nelson).*

GYFFORD, Margaret. *Birch 10095.* S' MAR-GARETI GYFFARD. 14 cent.

HARINGTON, Richard. *Roman PO 5714.* 27 Feb 1437. *(qrs 2&3).*

HARINGTON, Richard. *Roman PO 5713.* 5 Aug 1434. *(qrs 2&3).*

HARYNGTON, Richard. *Clairambault 4523.* 2 March 1436. *(qrs 2&3).*

LEDEBURN, Isabella de. *Birch 11273.* ISA-BEL' DE LEDEBURN. 1441. *(sl used by Jn Sewell, of Beds).*

LEDHAM, Isabel de. *PRO-sls.* 1432-3.

MALORRE, Peter. *Vinc 88, 22.* (obv)S' PETRI MALORRE DE WYNEWYK. 1308. *(rev of equestr sl).*

MARTIN, Margaret. *AnstisAsp I 214, 67.* 1343-4. *(roundel, 1 of 3 on shield).*

NEVILL, the Lady Margaret de. *PRO-sls.* 1314-15. *(shield, 1 of 2 on sl).*

NEVILLE, Margaret. *PRO-sls LS, 68.* 1315. *(qtd 2 by 1 lion; w of Jn N, of Essex).*

NEVYLE, Dame Margareta de, of London. *Birch 6690.* S' MARGA..... 1315. *(Giffard; on dress with heraldic bearings & shield).*

PEYTEVYN, Bartholomew le, Kt. *PRO-sls.* 13 cent. *(?blazon incorrect).*

RAYMONT, Garda. *PRO-sls.* 1373.

STAFFORD, Isabella. *Bow XXX 8.* 1348-9. *(loz, 1 of 3; w of Sir Ric de S).*

?STAFFORD, Isobel de. *Bow XXXIII 12a.* 1348-9. *(imp by [...] fretty; w of Ric de S).*

TUKE, Brian, Kt. *PRO-sls.* temp Hen 8.

VERNON, Maude de. *Bow XXXIII 12.* Sigillum Matildis de Vernon. 1348-9. *(shield, 1 of 3).*

3 lions passt to sin

CHESTER, William de. *Dugd 17, 72.*

Arg 3 lions passt

Arg 3 lions passt Az

— *Q II 491.* *(a&l Gu).*

CAMVILLE, Geffery. *FW 196.*

CAMVILLE, Geffrey. *A 153.*

Arg 3 lions passt Gu

— *LM 533.*

— *PLN 768. (qtd by 2 Arg chev Gu betw 3 nails Sa, 3 Gu griffin segr Or in border engr Arg, 4 Arg billetty & chev Sa).*

BROGRAVE. *LD 102. (qr 1).*

DALNY, Monsire de. *CG 462.*

DISNEY, R. *XL 19.*

DISNEY, William. *S 574.*

DISNEY, William. *S 580.*

DISVI. *L1 210, 5. (marginal note: 'Desency').*

DYNSEY. *L1 189, 4; L2 151, 1. (armed Az; marginal notes Dynseyn & Dysoy).*

DYSNY. *L10 57b, 4.*

DYSNY. *RB 145.*

DYSNY, Sr. *CKO 449.*

EASTNEY, John. *(or ?Disney). CRK 915.*

FAUCOMBRIGE. *L1 260, 2; L2 202, 8. (marginal note in L1 'Desynay').*

GIFFARD, of Claydon. *XL 302.*

GYFFORD, de Claydon. *WJ 218.*

ISNEY, Johannes de. *Q II 482.*

LYTYLBERY, Thomas. *WB IV 152, 473. (qr 1).*

ST YVE, John de. *WLN 816.*

LE STRAUNGE, Sr Fouke. *RB 60.*

WALES, 'Le princ de gales'. *Vermandois, Antiq Journ xxi 205. ('dargent iii lions de gueules passans savoir lun sur lautre a queue entortillie dedans lune des jambes du lion de derriere).*

Arg 3 lions passt Sa
— *D a 84. (unclear whether Arg or Or; poss foreign).*

CHAVERILL, Mons Rauf. *WJ 332.*

CHEVERELL, Ralph. *XL 21.*

CHEVERELL, Ralph. *XL 304.*

CHEVERILL. *CC 222b, 21.*

CHEVERYLL. *L10 41, 13.*

MERVILLE, Sir John. *PLN 912.*

Az 3 lions passt

Az 3 lions passt Untinc
GENNIVILLE. *CT 88.*

Az 3 lions passt Arg
— *WK 152. (qtd 2 by Sir Harry Vernon).*
— *WB I 36b, 5. (?lions pg; qtd 7 by Ric Bolles).*
— *WK 488. (qtd 2 by Jn Vernon).*
— *PLN 2030. (qtd 2 by Sir Harry Vernon).*
— *I2(1904)216. (qtd 2 by Thos Vernon, of Stokesay, Salop).*
— *I2(1904)272. (qtd 2 by Sir Hen Vernon).*

CAMMVILLE, Mons J. *WJ 286.*

CAMVILE. *L10 36, 1.*

CAMVILE, of Charlton Horethorne. *Gerard 156. (anciently Charlton Camvile).*

CAMVILE, Geffrai de.

CAMVILE, Geffray. *F 470.*

CAMVILE, Sr Geffrey. *N 137.*

CAMVILE, John. *XL 303.*

CAMVILE, John. *XL 141.*

CAMVILE, John. *XL 20.*

CAMVILE, William. *G 188.*

CAMVILE, Wm de. *SF 10.*

CANVYLE, Thomas de. *E I 649; E II 651.*

CAUMVILE. *CV-BM 56.*

CAUMVILE. *RB 271.*

CAUMVILE, Monsire de. *CG 468.*

CAUMVILE, Mons Hugh de. *TJ 142.*

CAUMVILLE. *L2 104, 7. (a&l Gu).*

CAUMVILLE. *CKO 452.*

CAUNVILE, de. *SP A 66.*

COMBUILE. *L1 131, 2. (marginal note Cannyl).*

LODELOW. *L2 318, 6.*

Az 3 lions pass Or
— *PLN 803.*

ENGLAND, K of. *LO (B) 30. (lions passt not gard; 'Anguli, Rex').*

FENES, Mons Rogier. *TJ 204. ('dazure a trois leonceaux rampauntes passantz dor').*

FIENNES, James, Ld Say & Sele. *ML II 35.*

HANGEST. *WB IV 155, 526.*

Gu 3 lions passt

Gu 3 lions passt Untinc
ENGLAND, K of. *Llanstephan 46, 108, 11. (qtd 2&3 by Az 3 fleurs de lis Untinc; imperial crown over shield).*

Gu 3 lions passt Arg
— *FB 73. (qtd 2&3 by Ld Poynings).*
— *WB IV 131b, 105. (qtd 2&3 by Ld Ponyng).*
— *WB V 89. (qtd 4 by Sir Humphrey Stanley, Kt 1485).*
— *WB V 71. (qtd 2&3 by Sir Edw Ponynges, Kt 1485).*
— *BA 951. (qtd 2&3 by Bodulgate).*
— *WB I 33b, 14. (qtd 4 by Geo Vernon, of Nether Haddon).*
— *XF 824. (qtd 4 by Isabell Stanley, imp by Walter Moyle).*
— *WB II 53, 8. (qtd 4 by Stanley, imp by Moyle).*
— *WK 19. (qtd 4 by Sir Humfrey Stanley).*
— *WK 62. (qtd 4 by Sir Humfrey Stanley).*
— *PLN 1976. (qtd 2&3 by Sir Edw Poynings; on escutch Or 3 piles pts in base Az).*
— *WK 6. (qtd by Sir Edw Poynynges).*

BODULGATE, Sir John, of Cornw. *WB III 80b, 4. (a&l Az).*

BRIMFFEL. *L10 78b, 16.*

BRUMESFELD. *PT 125.*

BRYMESFYLDE. *DV 68b, 2710.*

BRYMMESFELD. *L1 66, 4; L2 70, 1. (marginal note 'Gefford of Oxfordshire').*

FITZ PAIN, Sir Robert. *BR V 51.*

GEFFARD, Sir Joh. *FF 24.*

GEFFARDE. *CT 24.*

GIFFARD. *WJ 173. (...Gifferd de...feild).*

GIFFARD. *OxfRS II 10. (imp by Harringwell; on steeple North Aston).*

GIFFARD, Monsire. *CG 464.*

GIFFARD, le. *CKO 446.*

[GIFFARD]. *OxfRS II 15. 14 cent. (glass,*

Marsh Baldon, Oxfords).
[GIFFARD]. *Brit Arch Assoc 3S iii 207.*
c1330. *(wall painting, South Newington, Oxfords).*
GIFFARD, Monsire Gilbert, de Brymmesfeld. *AN 279. (1st lion ch with annulet Az for diffce).*
GIFFARD, Johan. *LM 78.*
GIFFARD, Johan. *D 86a.*
GIFFARD, Johan. *C 145a.*
GIFFARD, Johan. *D 65a.*
GIFFARD, Johan. *F 29.*
GIFFARD, Johan. *G 49.*
GIFFARD, Munsire Johan. *D 65b.*
GIFFARD, Sire Johan. *N 35.*
GIFFARD, John. *XL 14.*
GIFFARD, John. *E 25.*
GIFFARD, John. *FW 113.*
GIFFARD, John. *XL 298.*
GIFFARD, John. *C 105b.*
GIFFARD, S John. *WLN 361.*
GIFFARD, Sir John. *WNS 26, 76. ('Sire Jon Giffard por de gou iii lions passans dar').*
GIFFARD, Sir John. *ML I 83.*
GIFFARD, Monsire John, de Brymmesfeld. *AN 278.*
GIFFARD, Jon. *HE 90.*
GIFFARD, Sir Thomas. *CRK 443.*
GIFFARD, Mons' William. *TJ 122.*
GIFFARDE, le Sr. *AS 64.*
GIFFORD. *PLN 1648. (a&l Az).*
GYFFARD, le. *SP A 49.*
GYFFARD, Johan. *Q 27.*
GYFFARD, Sir John. *PCL I 524.*
STRANGE, de Knokynge. *CT 43.*

Gu 3 lions passt Or
Gu 3 lions passt Or
  — *D4 24. (imp by Hercy, of Grove, Notts).*
ALICANDER, Rex. *LO A 5. (?lions pg).*
ENGLAND, K of. *RH, Ancestor iii 199.*
ENGLAND, Richard I. *ML I 407.*

Or 3 lions passt Az &c
Or 3 lions passt Az
DENMARK. *Brit Arch Assoc xxxiv 22.*
c1400-20. *('Scutu regis Danie'; Nave ceiling St Alban's Abbey).*
DENMARK, K of. *CRK 1358. (qr 1).*
DENMARK, Kyng of. *BR I 8. (qr 1).*
SOMERY, Sr John. *L 85.*
Or 3 lions passt Gu
ST YVE, John de. *F 324.*

Or 3 lions passt Sa
Or 3 lions passt Sa
  — *PLN 992. (qtd 2&3 by Mallory).*
  — *WB IV 139b, 245. (qtd 2&3 by Sir Jorge Darell).*

CAREW. *SK A 599.*
CAREW. *DV 63a, 2497.*
CAREW. *PT 514.*
CAREW. *SK B 599. (mullet Arg on upper lion).*
CAREW, Baron. *CRK 1307.*
CAREW, Baron of. *BA 1087. (eyed & langued Gu).*
CAREW, Monsire de. *CG 467.*
CAREW, Monsire de. *AN 42.*
CAREW, The Baron of. *RH, Ancestor iv 231.*
CAREW, Barone of. *PLN 133. (a&l Gu).*
CAREW, of Crowcombe. *Gerard 47. ('a difference').*
CAREW, Sir J. *WB I 37b, 9.*
CAREW, Johan. *G 147.*
CAREW, John. *XL 22.*
CAREW, John. *XL 305.*
CAREW, John. *CA 237.*
CAREW, S' Jon. *PO 285.*
CAREW, Mayster. *I2(1904)109. (mullet Arg on shldr of upper lion; qtd 2&3 by qtly Sa and Arg).*
CAREW, Montgomery. *L10 36, 20.*
CAREW, of Mounsausery, Devon. *L1 142, 6; L2 120, 1.*
CAREW, Sir Nich de. *WNS 26, 79. ('Sire Nich de Caruw por dor iii lions passans de sable').*
CAREW, Sir Nich, KG 1536. *XK 94. (qr 1).*
CAREW, Nicholas de. *K 179.*
CAREW, Sr Nicholas. *N 140.*
CAREW, Syr John. *I2(1904)67. (a&l Gu).*
CAREW, Monsire William. *AN 325.*
CAREW, Syr Wylliam, of Devon. *I2(1904)275.*
CAREW, Sir William. *PLN 2009.*
CAREW, Sir William. *WK 82.*
CAREW, William. *BA 1321. (a&l Gu).*
CAREWE. *WB II 52, 10. (mullet Arg on upper lion).*
CAREWE. *LY A 5.*
CAREWE, le Seigneure de. *T b 21.*
CAROW. *CT 344.*
CAROW, Sir Nich', of Bodington, Surr. *L1 183, 3.*
CARREU. *CKO 450.*
CARREU, Le Baron de. *TJ 131.*
CARREWE, Mons John de. *WJ 341. (written at side: 'Mountgomeri dit Carew').*
CARROU, Mons John de. *CA 237.*
CARU, Sir Richard. *WK 267. (a&l Gu).*
CARY. *SK C 599.*
CURREU, Mons de. *AS 408.*
DENMARK, K of. *LO B 33.*
MALLORE, Peris. *LM 436.*
MALOURGOMER, Leics. *BA 30b, 251. (a&l Gu).*
MAULORIE, Perus. *Q 407.*

MONGOMERY, Adam de. *F 459.*
MONTGOMERY, Adam. *E I 377; E II 379.*

Sa 3 lions passt
Sa 3 lions passt Arg
— *PLN 1275. (qtd 2 by Sir Simon Mont-ford).*
— *Lancs 1533 CS 98, 104. (qrs 2&3 of coat imp by Standish).*
— *CRK 1786. (qtd 2&3 by Sir Ric Haring-ton).*
— *LH 105. (qtd 2&3 by Haringworth).*
ENGLISH. *XL 39.*
ENGLISHE, Staffs. *L1 223, 6; L2 171, 10. (Pilston in L1 margin).*
PELSTONE, of Wales. *CRK 2003. (a&l Gu).*
ENGLISH, of Staffs. *CRK 2003. (a&l Gu).*
Sa 3 lions passt Or
— *PLN 244. (qtd 2 by Sir George Carew).*
ARDERN, William de. *F 440.*
ARDERNE, William de. *E I 531; E II 533.*
ARDERNE, William de. *WLN 787.*
COMBE. *L1 133, 2; L2 106, 10.*
COMBE. *L10 43b, 14.*
MALFORD. *CRK 5. (or Combe).*

Field patterned 3 lions passt
Erm 3 lions passt Gu
COMBE. *DV 59b, 2344.*
COMBE. *PT 62.*
COMBE. *L2 130, 3.*
COMBE, Richard de. *TJ 134.*
COMBE, Richard de. *TJ 160. ('dermyn a trois leopardes leonceaux passantz de goules').*
COMBE, Richard de. *AN 252.*
Arg gutty Sa 3 lions passt Gu
COMBE. *XL 857.*
Or semy of hearts Gu 3 lions passt Az
DENMARK & Norway, John, King of. *Sand-ford 276. (qtg Norway; m Philippa, dau of Hen 4).*

3 lions passt charged or patterned
Gu 3 lions passt Arg upper lion ch with annulet Sa
BRYMESFYLDE. *DV 68b, 271.*
Gu 3 lions passt Arg centre lion ch on shldr with annulet Sa
BRYNMESFELD. *PT 126.*
Gu 3 lions passt Arg upper lion ch with mullet Az
[GIFFARD?]. *XL 17.*
GYFFARD, Mons Gill'. *WJ 182. (mullet of 6 pts).*

3 lions passt crowned
Arg 3 lions passt Sa crowned Or
GRAUMFORD. *L2 225, 1.*
HERVYLE, Sir John. *WB IV 158, 584. (a&l Or; Halwyn overwritten).*
Az 3 lions passt Arg crowned Or
GIFFARD, Water. *FW 662.*
GIFFORD, Walter. *A 145.*
Arg gutty Gu 3 lions passt Sa crowned Or
FAIRFORD. *LS 278. (imp by Savery).*
FAIRFORD. *XL 65.*
Or semy of hearts Gu 3 lions passt Az crowned Or
DENMARK, Margaret of. *Sandford 326. (m1469 Jas 3 of Scotld).*
Gu 3 lions passt Erm crowned Or
FELTON, Tomas. *RH, Ancestor ix 160.*

3 lions rampant guardant
Per fess Az and Arg pale counterch 3 lions gard 2, 1 Arg
WHETLEY. *PLN 1761. (imp by Pimpe).*
Per fess Az and Or pale counterch 3 lions gard 2, 1 Or
WETHYLLE, Richard. *PLN 1127.*
Per pale 3 lions gard
GATE, Geoffrey, Kt. *Birch 10039.* SIGILLUM GALFRIDI GATE. late 14 or early 15 cent.
MORTEIN, Roger de, Ld of Dunnesby. *Bow LIII 1.* S ROGERI DE MORTEIN. 1338-9.
Per pale Az and Gu 3 lions gard Or
GATE, Sir Jeferay. *WB IV 173, 855.*

England dimidg another coat: see under 3 demi-lions

England qtd by France: see in later volume under fleurs de lis

3 lions passant guardant
3 lions pg
BURGO, Elizabeth de, Lady de Clare. *Birch 7934.* 1333. *(decoration on sl; dau of Gil-bert de Clare, E of Hertford, m (1) Jn de Burgo (2) Theobald de Verdone, Ld Verdon (3) Sir Rog Damory).*
BURGO, Elizabeth de, Lady of Clare. *PRO-sls E40 A14054.* 1323. *(1 leopard on either side of shield & 1 above).*
CANTERBURY, Archbp Reynolds of. *Birch 1217.* 1320. *(obv of sl).*
CARLINGSONE, Richard. *Durham-sls 561.* 1431.
ENGAYN, Katharine. *AnstisAsp I 223, 93.* 1384-5. *(shield, 2nd of 4).*
ENGAYNE, Catherine d', of Axminster, Devon. *Bow 2.* 1384-5. *(wid of Sir Thos*

d'E).

ENGAYNE, Katherine. *BrookeAsp I 32, 2.*
Sigill Katherine engayne. *(shield, 1 of 4).*
ENGLAND. *Inventory; WestmAbb. (On 14 or 15 cent tile set in wall of house SE of Infirmary Chapel).*
ENGLAND. *Inventory; WestmAbb. (Tile ?late 14 cent pavement of Muniment Room).*
ENGLAND. *Inventory; WestmAbb.* 13 cent tile in gallery over the W end of St Faith's Chapel.
ENGLAND. *WestmAbb. c1510. (gilt bronze in panel of gates, Henry VII Chapel).*
ENGLAND. *Antiq Journ vi 449-50.* 13 cent. *(on shield on Stalyard weights).*
ENGLAND, Edw 1. *Sandford 120, 127, 129 & 137.*
ENGLAND, Edw 1. *WestmAbb.* 1291. *(carved shield in canopied niche on side of tomb of Eleanor of Castile).*
ENGLAND, Edw 1. *Stevenson 24.* SIGILLUM EDWARDI DEI GRACIA REG [IS ANGLIE DNI HIBERI] E. *(Rev of Great Sl for Government of Scotland 1296-1306; legend cont on rev: [ET DUCIS AQUITANIE AD R]EGIMEN REGNI SOCIE DEPUTATUM).*
ENGLAND, Edw 1. *Bow LVI 1.* +Edwardus dei grati rex Angliae dominus Hyberniae dux Aquitaniae 'per breve de privato sigillo'. 1280-1. *(Privy Sl).*
ENGLAND, Richard 1. *Sandford 73. (2nd sl).*
FIFE, Mary, Ctess of. *PRO-sls.* 1336-7. *(on gown of lady).*
KING'S HALL, Camb. *Proc Soc Antiq X 2S 232.* SIGILLO COMUNE CUST [ODIS ET SC] OLARIUM AULE R [EGIS IN C] ANTERBRIGGIE. *(on shield on dex side of sl of King's Hall, Camb [now Trinity College]).*
HENRY III. *WestmAbb.* c1255. *(shield on tiles, four tiles to each shield, set in rows in the pavement of the chapter house).*
HENRY III. *CT 1.*
HEREFORD. *Birch 4993.* SIGILL COMMUNE CIVIUM HEREFORD. 12 cent. *(enfiling banner flag, shield described as 'of early form').*
HEREFORD, City of. *Birch 4997.* S' BALLIVORUM CIVITATIS HEREFORDIE. 18 cent.
HEREFORD, City of. *Birch 4996.* S' BALLIVORUM CIVITATIS HEREFORDIE. 14 cent.
HOLAND, Eleanor. *Arch Journ lxxi 236.* 1480-3. *(imp by fretty; nat dau of Thos H, E of Kent by Constance dau of Edm, D of York; m 1430 Jas, Ld Audley; Ceiling boss, Divinity School, Oxf).*
LANCASTRE, Maude de, Ctess of Ulster. *PRO-sls.* 1336-7. *(1 of 4 roundels).*
MARTYN, Margaret. *AnstisAsp I 219, 78. (roundel, 1 of 3).*
NEVILL, Margaret de. *AnstisAsp I 218, 77.* SIGILLUM MARGARETE DE NEVILL. *(2nd of 3 shields; wid of Jn N).*

PLANTAGENET. *Birch 12728.* 14 cent.
RASEN, Anna de. *Harl Soc IV 46.* 1364. *(sl; Visit Notts).*
RATCLIFF, John de, Kt. *PRO-sls.* 1430. *(banner of arms of England; ?as Constable of Bordeaux).*
STAFFORD, Anne, Ctess of. *PRO-sls.* 1437-8.
TUTBURY, Peter, Prior of. *Bow XLIX 13.* 1356-7. *(shield, 1st of 2).*
VALE, William de. *Birch 14075.* QVIC...PON-..(uncertain). 1480. *(Banner flag on lance, beneath banner bear passt).*
VALENCE, William de. *Neale & Brayley II 155.* 1296. *(carved shield).*
VYNCENT, Richard, Rector of St Benet, Sherehog, London. *PRO-sls.* 1361-2.
WALTHAM ABBEY. *Proc Soc Antiq XXVIII 2S 98, 5 & 99.* 7 May 1337. *(dex side of countersl of Waltham Abbey).*
WALTHAM CROSS, Abbot of. *AnstisAsp I 176.* 1537.
WARRE, Alianor la. *Proc Soc Antiq IV 2S 389. (only fragment of uppermost beast remains; roundel on sl of Alianor, w of Sir Roger la Warre; poss Engld with label to show lady's descent from Thos of Brotherton).*
YORK, St Mary's Abbey. *Durham-sls 3568.* 1519. *(sl on dex, ?for Wm Rufus).*

Arg 3 lions pg Gu
Arg 3 lions pg Gu
DISNEY. *L10 56b, 9.*
DISNEY, R. *XL 380.*
DYSNY, Mons R. *WJ 396.*
FAUCOMBERGE, del South. *TJ 186.*
FAUCONBERG, Sir Wm. *WNS 26, 82.* ('Sire Will Faucrdberge por dar iii leopards passanz de gou').
FAUCONBERGE. *CC 222b, 27.*
FAUCONBERGE, du Sir. *CKO 453.*
FAUCONBRIG, de South, Monsr. *AS 397.*
FAUKENBERGE, S' William. *R 57.*
GIFFORD, of Claydon. *XL 12.*
IRELAND, King of. *Uffenbach 267, Antiq Journ xxi 206.* ('Hybernia, Kunig von').

Az 3 lions pg
Az 3 lions pg Arg
— *FK II 792. (qtd 2&3 by Dymoke).*
— *FK a 792. (qtd by Marmion).*
— *XF 692. (qtd 2&3 by Marmion).*
— *PLN 1628. (qtd II&III 2&3 by Sir Richard Vernon).*
BARNE. *Ll 106, 2. (langued Gu).*
?CAMVILLE. *Harl MSS 6592, 69b; Ussher 28, pl x. (qtd by [Curzon]; glass, Croxhall*

Church).
LODELAW, Salop. *L2 316, 8.*
LODELAWE, Sire Thomas de. *N 972.*
LODELOWE. *L9 43b, 3.*
LODELOWE, of Salop. *FK II 481.* ('of
Shropshire' add Gibbon).
LODILAWE. *CKO 448.*
LODLOWE, Mons de. *AS 407.*
LUDLAWE, Monsire de. *CG 463.*
LUDLOW. *XL 564.*
LUDLOWE, Mons John de. *TJ 185.*
LUDLOWE, Salop. *L2 317, 8.*
Az 3 lions pg Or
BARRI, Robert de. *E II 367.*
BEUVES, de Hampton. *FW 62.*
BEYVES, of Hampton. *HE 45.*
HANGEST. *TB 16. (a&l Gu).*
HANGEST. *TB 14. (a&l Gu; qtd by Talbot).*

Gu 3 lions pg Arg
Gu 3 lions pg Arg
— *BR VI 33. (marshalled by [Fitzpayne], Ld
Ponynges).*
— *PLN 819. (imp by Master Anne).*
— *WB IV 155b, 537. (imp by Master Anne).*
FELTON, le S. *PLN 184.*
GIFFARD, Sir John. *ML I 71.*
GIFFORD, Sir J. *PLN 411.*
GYFFORD, of Oxfords. *L1 268, 3; L2 216,
11. (armed Az).*
GYFORDE, La boff, of Bucks. *WB IV 147,
385.*
HEREFORD, City of. *Hope 181. (on state
sword, late 15 cent).*
HEREFORD, City of. *Proc Soc Antiq XII 2S
314. (on state sword, 15 or early 16 cent).*
HERRIARD, Thomas. *LH 771.*
HERRIARD, Thomas, of Hants. *WB III 114, 8.*

Gu 3 lions pg Or (England)
Gu 3 lions pg Or
— *Nichols Leics II 145. (Coston Ch).*
— *C3 19b. (Aulkmondbury Ch, Hunts).*
— *Nichols Leics II 95. (Bottesford Ch).*
ACRE, Joan of. *CR 3. (dau of Edw 1 & w of
Gilbert, E of Clare).*
ANGLETERRE, le Roy de. *AS 4.*
ANGLETERRE, Roy d'. *WJ 44. (Edw 1 or 2).*
ANGLIAE, le Roy. *RL 28, 2.*
ANGLIAE, le Roy. *RL 18.*
BERWICK-upon-Tweed. *PRO-sls, HB-SND.
1315. (common sl; on banner above bear led
by man).*
DANGLETERRE, le Roy. *P 2.*
DENGLETERRE, Le Roy. *TJ 170.*
DERBY, le C de.
PLANTAGENET. *NB 16. (?coat imcomplete).*
DURHAM, City of. *HB-SND. (1 of 2 shields,
2nd cross fimbr; sl matric at Durham).*

EDWARD OF GLOUCESTER. *XL 4.*
EDWARD I. *FC I 67.*
EDWARD III. *FC I 12, 14-15.*
EDWARD III. *FC I 45.*
ENGLAND. *LMS 2.*
ENGLAND. *BR V a 1. (a&l Az).*
ENGLAND. *Antiq Journ iv 384-5. 15 cent.
(tile in Llangatock-nigh-Usk Ch).*
ENGLAND. *SP A 3.*
ENGLAND. *XL 1.*
ENGLAND. *MP Hist Min iii 88. 1250.*
ENGLAND. *MP Hist Min iii 95. 1250. ('Scu-
tum regis Anglorum cruce signets').*
ENGLAND. *ML I 1.*
ENGLAND. *LMRO 2. ('Roy de Engeultor de
gules of iii lepars passans de or').*
ENGLAND,. *CY a 1, 3. (Henricus Secundus;
Willelmus Conquestor Rex Anglie).*
ENGLAND, K of. *FK I 18.*
ENGLAND, K of. *H a 50.*
ENGLAND, K of. *K 31.*
ENGLAND, K of. *J 1.*
ENGLAND, K of. *G 7.*
ENGLAND, K of. *FW 9.*
ENGLAND, K of. *C 3.*
ENGLAND, K of. *D b.*
ENGLAND, K of. *N 1.*
ENGLAND, K of. *CA 101.*
ENGLAND, K of. *XL 289.*
ENGLAND, K of. *D a 7.*
ENGLAND, K of. *DX 3.*
ENGLAND, K of. *E 1.*
ENGLAND, King of. *CKO a 1.*
[ENGLAND]. *Neale & Brayley II 155. 1296.
(enamelled sh on roundel on ledge of tomb of
Wm de Valence).*
ENGLAND, K Edw 1. *K 220.*
ENGLAND, K Edward 1. *FC II 119, 121-2.*
ENGLAND, K Edward 3. *FC II 94.*
ENGLAND, K Edward 3. *FC II 99.*
ENGLAND, 'K Henry ..'. *FC I 27-8.*
ENGLAND, K Henry 2. *FC II 115.*
ENGLAND, K Henry 3. *FC II 106.*
ENGLAND, K Henry 3. *FC II 92.*
ENGLAND, K John. *FC I 33.*
ENGLAND, K John. *MP I 23 & 27; MP IV 4
& 12; MP VI 5.*
ENGLAND, K John. *MP Hist Min ii 78 &
193. 1199 & 1216.*
ENGLAND, K John. *FC II 90.*
ENGLAND, K Richard. *MP I 19 & 22; MP IV
2 & 3; MP VI 4.*
ENGLAND, Roy de. *Q 1.*
ENGLAND, K Stephen. *MP I 11 & 13; MP
III 9 & 10.*
ENGLETERE, le Roy de. *WLN 2.*
ENGLETERRE, le Roy d'. *GA 1.*
HENRY. *MP I 17. (s of Hen 2).*
HENRY I. *MP Hist Min i 176 & 250. 1100*

& 1135.

HENRY I. *FC I 2.*

HENRY I. *MP I 5 & 10; MP II 7 & 8; MP VI 2.*

HENRY II. *FC I 56.*

HENRY II. *BW 12, 4.*

HENRY II. *MP Hist Min i 300 & 426.* 1154 & 1183.

HENRY II. *MP I 14 & 18; MP III 10; MP IV 1.*

HENRY II. *FC I 7 & 23.*

HENRY III. *MP Hist Min ii 196.* 1216.

HENRY III. *FC I 9, 24-6.*

HENRY III. *MP I 28 & 99; MP II 2 & 98; MP IV 1; MP VIII 2, 13 & 20.*

HENRY III. *B 1.*

HENRY III. *WestmAbb.* HENRICUS TERTIUS REX ANGLIAE. c1260. *(15 cent inscription).*

[HENRY III]. *Lethaby 235-9. (glass 13 cent E Clerestory window).*

HENRY VII. *WK B, 48.*

[HOLLAND, E of Kent]. *Farrer I 183. (on tomb of Sir Edm de Thorp, d1417; Ashwell Thorpe Ch, Norf).*

JOHN, K of England. *Sandford 81. (on Great Sl).*

JOHN, K of England. *FC II 141.*

LANCASTER, Henry, Erle off. *WB I 34, 20. ('& dowghter off Chaworth'; imp burely orle of martlets).*

LANCASTRE, Duc. *NB 3. (tinct of lions unclear).*

LANCASTRE, duc. *NB 3.*

MARIA, Princess. *Birch 11608.* 1303. *(on eagle displd; Maria, dau of Edw 3, nun at Amesbury, Wilts).*

MORTAIN, John E of. *FC I 22.*

O'BRIAN, thearle of Tomonde. *DIG 6.*

OBRYEN. *L2 396, 3. (lions poss spotted).*

RICHARD I. *FC I 8, 20-1.*

RICHARD I. *MP Hist Min ii 3 & 76.* 1189.

SHREWSBURY. *HB-SND, sl-Cast BG. (1st of 3 shields, (2) Cross of St. George, (3) 3 leopards faces).*

ST EDWARD. *WJ 24. ('Le Roy Sante Edward qui gist A...').*

STEPHEN, K. *FC I 3.*

STEPHEN, K of England. *MP Hist Min i 251 & 299.* 1136.

VALE ROYAL ABBEY. *WLN 915. (unfinished, no crozier or border).*

WILLIAM I. *MP I 2 & 3; MP III 3 & 4.*

WILLIAM I. *MP Hist Min i 7 & 35.* 1067 & 1087.

WILLIAM II. *MP I 4; MP III 5 & 6; MP VI 1.*

WILLIAM RUFUS. *MP Hist Min i 35.* 1087.

YNGLAND, Kyng of. *BR IV 73.*

Gu 3 lions pg to sin Or

— *C3 19b. (Aulkmondbury Ch, Hunts).*

— *Proc Soc Antiq XI 2S 37. (imp Scotld on Great Mace of City of Westm).*

[VALENCE, Wm, E of Pembroke]. *Proc Soc Antiq XVIII 2S 411. (qtg Valence; sh of Limoges enamel on copper 'in style of late 13 cent work').*

Or 3 lions pg

Or 3 lions pg Arg

HENRY III. *MP VIII 12. (banner on castle).*

Or 3 lions pg Az

DACYE, Roy de. *RH, Ancestor iii 192.*

DANEMARK, le Roy de. *P 13.*

DANEMARKE, le Roy de. *TJ 171. (armed Gu).*

DENMARK. *LMS 13.*

DENMARK. *LMRO 13. ('Le Roy de Danmark port lescu de or of trais lepars passant de azur').*

DENMARK, K of. *XL 379.*

DENMARK, K of. *XL 11.*

DENMARK, K of. *RH, Ancestor iii 200.*

DENMARK, K of. *FK I 40.*

DENMARK, Roy de. *WJ 67.*

DENMARKE, le Roy de. *WLN 30.*

DENMARKE, le Roy de. *L10 58b, 1.*

JERUSALEM, K of. *?source.* c1450. *(on ceiling, St Albans Abbey).*

SCANDINAVIA, K of. *PLN 32. (qtg, 2 Az 3 crowns 2, 1 Or, 3 Arg griffin segr Gu, 4 Gu lion Or holding axe erect Arg shaft Az; over all cross Arg).*

Or 3 lions pg Gu

[ENGLAND]. *Antiq Journ xxi 206. (unnamed coat on Zurich roll 1335-45).*

HIBERNIA, Konig von. *Antiq Journ xxi 206. (Wappenbuch of Conrad von Grunenberg, 1483).*

LOCRINUS. *BA 209. (eldest s of Brutus; qtg 2&3 Az 3 crowns in bend Or).*

LOCRINUS, K of Britain. *XL 411.*

Or 3 lions pg Sa

BERUCH, Duc de. *XL 428.*

CAREW. *Brit Arch Assoc xviii 182-4.* 1469-1656. *(a&l Gu; 5 Carew brasses, Haccombe, Devon).*

CAROWE, Baron of. *BW 15, 100.*

DENMARK, Roy de. *BB 56. (d c1459).*

[MALOURE]. *Nichols Leics IV 883. (Ratby Ch).*

MALOURE, of Leics. *L1 440, 2; L2 329, 7.*

Vt 3 lions pg Arg

Vt 3 lions pg Arg

— *WB I 34, 15. (qtg 2; Untinc bend Arg betw 6 ? Untinc?, 3; Untinc bend betw 6 crosslets fitchy Arg; all imp by [Seymour]).*

3 lions pg field patterned

Barry Arg and Sa 3 lions pg Or (1 on each Sa bar)
   TREGOYSE, John. *WB III 104b, 6.*

Erm 3 lions pg Gu
   COMBE, of Combe in Crewkerne. *Gerard 67.*
   COMBE, Richard de. *TJ 160.* ('*d'ermyn a trois leopardes leonceaux passantz de goules'*).
   FAUCONBERGE, Monsire de Sa. *CG 469.*

Per pale 3 lions pg to sin 2, 1
   — *Arch Journ xxxvi 101-2.* (carved on stone with 2 other shields, apparently front of tomb which was built, face inward, into London Inn at Warminster).

Per pale Gu and Az 3 lions pg Arg
   LAUNDE, Henri de la. *G 89.*

Per pale Gu and Az 3 lions pg Or
   LAUNDE, Nycolle de la. *CT 149.*

Or semy of hearts Gu 3 lions pg Az
   DANEMARCHE, le Roy de. *AS 18.* (semy of '*papmous de voces*'; armed Gu).
   DENMARK, K of. *PLN 24.*
   DENMARK, K of. *WGA 77.*
   DENMARK, K of. *Lyndsay 43.* (imp by Jas 3 for his w Mgt, dau of K of Denmark).
   DENMARKE, K of. *KB 22.* (qr 1, over all cross Arg).
   SWYTHIN, K of. *KB 26.*

Or semy of hearts Gu 3 lions pg Sa
   DENMARK, K of. *SHY 596.* (qtg, 2 Az 3 crowns Or, 3 Gu lion sitting in chair & brandishing axe [Arg or Or?], 4 Arg griffin segr Gu; over all cross Arg and on escutch Or 2 lions pg Az).

3 lions pg crowned

Arg 3 lions pg Az crowned Or
   DYNAN, Joce de. *Fouke 13, 5.* (d c1166; Recension c1310 of poem c1260).

Or semy of hearts Gu 3 lions pg Az crowned Or
   SWEDEN. *ML I 276.* (qr 1, over all cross Arg fimbr Sa).

3 lions regardant

3 lions passt regard tails coward & reflexed over back
   WALES, Principality of North. *Birch 5559.*
   SIG HENRICI DEI GRA REGIS ANGL FRANC' DNI HIBNIE PRINCIPALITAT'SUI NORTH WALLIE.

Arg 3 lions passt regard coward Gu
   WALES. *CRK 265.*
   WALES, Prince of. *KB 229.*
   WALES, Prince of. *PLN 47.* (a&l Az).
   WALES, Prince of North. *WB II 48, 7.*
   WALES, Prynce of. *RH, Ancestor v 181.* ('Ho'll dda' added in later hand).
   WALLIS, Prins of North. *BA 15b.*

Vt 3 lions regard 2, 1 Arg crowned Or
   TYSON. *North 1558 122, 124.* (qtd by Eure).

Arg gutty Gu 3 lions passt regard coward Sa crowned Or
   FAIRFORD. *L1 237, 6.* (blazoned bezanty but none painted).

Arg gutty Gu 3 lions passt regard coward Gu semy of roundels & crowned Or
   FAIRFORD. *L2 196, 8.*

3 BEASTS (OTHER)

3 indistinct beasts
   BURGH, Hubert de. ...TL.RGO[D[D[D.RGO. *AnstisAsp I 195, 26.* (?3 lions passt; 'Dni Regis Camerarius').

3 beasts (?bulls)
   — *Proc Soc Antiq III 2S 146.* 3 July 1362. (sl attached to letter of Agnes, wid of Ric F, of Coventry, making Wm Frebern of Coventry her attorney etc).

Arg 3 badgers Gu
   TRAVERS, of Lancs. *CY a 51, 203.*

Arg 3 badgers passt Sa
   BROCHALIS. *WB I 19, 16.*

3 bats displ
   — *Brit Arch Assoc xxxiv 18.* (brass to Jn & Eliz Heyworth, Wheathamstead Ch, near St Albans).
   HEYWORTH. *Mill Steph.* 1520. (qtg [Bostock]; brass to Jn H & w Eliz, Wheathamstead, Herts).
   HEYWORTH. *Mill Steph.* c1480. (brass to Hugh Bostock & w Mgt [H], Wheathamstead, Herts).
   HEYWORTH. *Mill Steph.* 1520. (brass to Jn H & w Elizabeth).
   MACRY. *Brit Arch Assoc xxxiv 18.* (brass to Hugh Bostock & w Mgt M, placed by their s Jn Wheathamstead, Abbot of St Albans 1421-60; Wheathamstead Ch, near St Albans).

Sa 3 bats Arg
   BURNYNGHILL, Hugh de. *TJ 1440.* ('... & trois chausoriz dargent').

3 bears

Untinc 3 bears ?passt Sa
   [BERHAM]. *Arch Cant xxii 231.* 14 cent. (on W face of Cranbrook Ch tower).

Arg 3 bears ?passt Sa
   HERBOTYLL. *DV 71b, 2833.* (bears smudged out).

Arg 3 bears passt in pale Sa
   TRAVERS. *CVL 350.*

Arg 3 bears ?passt Sa muzzled Gu
   DICHFYLD. *DV 64b, 2553.* (name added in later hand).

Arg 3 bears passt Sa muzzled Or
  BEARCROFT, Katherine. *Coll T&G iii 327.*
  (d 20 Sept 1507, w of Robt B; mont, Carshalton, Surr).
  BERHALGH, Richard. *TJ 1445.*
  HENBOTYLL. *PT 718.*
  HERBOTYLL. *L1 349, 2; L2 262, 3.*
Az 3 bears passt Arg muzzled Or
  BERWICK. *L10 91, 4. (qtd 4 by Ric Twedy, of Sharford Stoke, Essex).*
Per pale Arg and Sa 3 bears passt counterch
  BERE. *L2 63, 9.*
Per pale Sa and Arg 3 bears passt counterch muzzled Gu
  BERE. *L1 79, 2.*
  BERE. *L10 26b, 16.*
Qtly of 6 3 bears ramp muzzled lined & ringed
  MILL, Richd. *Mill Steph.* 1478. *(s&h of Edm Mills, brass, Pulborough, Suss).*
3 bears salient collared & chained
  — *Mill Steph.* 1473. *(imp Erdeswick; tomb of Hugh E, Sandon, Staffs).*
Qtly of 6 Arg and Sa 3 bears salient Sa muzzled, lined & ringed Or collared Gu
  MILL, Edmund. *Lambarde 221.* 1452. *(mont to Edm M & w Martha, Pulborough, Suss).*
  MILL, Richard. *Lambarde 221.* 1478. *(s&h to Edm M, mont, Pulborough, Suss).*
3 bears stat muzzled
  BERECROFT. *Mill Steph.* 1507. *(brass to Kath, w of Robt B & sis Eliz, wid of Wm Barton, (both d1507), Beddington, Surr).*
Arg 3 bears stat 2, 1 Sa muzzled Or
  — *PT 242.*
Az 3 bears stat Arg muzzled Or
  BERWYCKE. *L10 90b, 11. (qtd 2&3 by Wyngyngton).*
  BERWYKE. *L10 90b, 9. (qtd 3 by Twedy).*
  BERWYKE. *L10 90b, 10. (imp by Wyngyngton).*
Gu 3 bears stat Arg
  BARLINGHAM, Sire Richard de. *N 1086.*
  BARLYNGHAM. *L2 87, 7. (2, 1).*
  BERMINGHAM, Sr Richard. *L 213.*

3 boars
3 boars
  [SWINHOE]. *Blair N II 147, 303. (N wall of Chancel, Rock Ch, Northd).*
3 boars passt
  BACON, George. *Mill Steph.* c1500. *(annulet in chf; s of Thos B, Esq; brass, Hardwick, Norf).*
  BACON, John, of Norf & Suff. *Birch 7063.* Sigillum iohis bacon. 1435.
  BACOUN, Thomas, of Methwold, Norf. *Birch 7066.* SIGILL'THOM......... 1366.

Arg 3 boars 2, 1 Az
  ELWIK. *L2 181, 7.*
Arg 3 boars passt in pale Gu
  WHYCHECOTE, of Lincs. *RH, Ancestor ix 165. (O Barron notes 'the shield is crossed out').*
Arg 3 boars passt Sa
  — *Lancs 1533 CS 98, 53. (in the mouth of each a piece of gristle; qtd 2 by Hoult of Gresellhurst).*
  BOTELER. *SK 620. (1st boar ch on shldr with mullet Or).*
  BOTELER. *SK 619. (2, 1).*
  BUTELER. *L1 32, 1; L2 43, 6.*
  ELWICK. *CRK 555.*
  SWYNE. *L1 611, 1. (armed Or; field not blazoned).*
  SWYNOWE, John of, of Northd. *RH, Ancestor iv 244. (armed Or).*
  SWYNOWE, Robert, of Northd. *WB III 103, 9. (a&l Or).*
Az 3 boars passt Arg
  GAGHE, Matheu. *WB I 18, 9.*
  GOCH, Mathew. *CRK 967. (armed & unguled Or).*
  ORTON. *CRK 983. (armed & unguled Or; qrs 1&4).*
Az 3 boars Or
  BACON. *L10 22, 6.*
  BACON. *Suff HN 24. (imp by Everard; Cheston Ch).*
  BACON. *WB I 27b, 14. (?stat).*
Az 3 boars passt Or
  BACON. *L1 100, 2. (in pale).*
  BACON. *L2 59, 8. (2, 1).*
  [BACON]. *SHY 25. (2, 1).*
  HERYNE. *PLN 1873. (HS London notes 'they might be boars but surely hedgehogs are meant'; qtd 3 by Pierpoint).*
  SWELINGTON. *LD 31. (qtd 4).*
Gu 3 boars Arg
  SWINE. *LS 31. (armed Or).*
Or 3 boars passt Sa
  NAUTON, Wylyam, of Yorks. *RH, Ancestor vii, 197. (armed Arg).*
Sa 3 boars Arg
  SWYNHOWE, Robert. *TJ 1446. ('...a trois porcs dargent').*
Sa 3 boars passt Arg
  SWYNES. *CC 227b, 191.*
Gu 3 boars Erm
  BARDE, Edmund de. *CA 91.*

3 camels
3 camels
  — *I2(1904)245. (qtd 2&3 by Syr Rychard Weston).*

Arg 3 camels passt Sa
— *XFB 239.* *(qtd 2&3 by [Weston]).*
— *I2(1904)55.* *(qtd 2&3 by 'Weston Lord Sent Jones'; banner).*
— *WK 530.* *(qtd 2&3 by Ld Wm Weston, Great Prior of St Johns).*
— *PLN 2067.* *(qtd 2&3 by Sir Thos Weston).*
— *L9 25a, 9.* *(qtd 3 by Erle).*
CAMMELL, of Som. *1H7 8; D13 76d.* *(qtd by Weston).*

3 cats
3 cats
CATRIK, John. *Birch 2268.* 1411. *(Archdeacon of Surrey 1410-14).*
3 wild cats passt in pale
LOTHIAN, Officialite of. *Stevenson 103.* *(qtg 2&3 on cross circularly voided at fess pt therein estoile; 3rd sl).*
ST ANDREW'S, Vicar General of. *Stevenson 104.* *(qtg 2&3 on cross circularly voided at fess pt therein estoile; round sl; 1478-96).*
SHIVAS, Willm. *Stevenson 89.* *(qtg 2&3 on cross qr pd estoile; Archbp of St Andrews 1478-96/7).*
SHIVAS, Wm. *Stevenson 99.* *(qtg 2&3 on cross circularly voided at fess pt therein estoile; Archdeacon of St Andrew's 1477).*
SHIVAS, Wm. *Stevenson.* c1478. *(Archbp of St Andrews 1478-96; 2 s; s).*
Arg 3 cats pg in pale Sa
CATTE. *L2 142, 11.*
CATTE. *L10 46b, 17.*
Gu 3 cats pg in pale Arg
CATTE. *SHY 92.*
3 cats passt in border roundelly
KEYMER, Dr Gilbert. *Helyar 915.* SIGILL' GILBERTI KEYMER DOCTORI[S]. 1439. *(Attorney to Jn Kymer to receive seisin of messuages in Langport & elsewhere in Som).*

3 deer courant &c
Arg 3 stags courant Gu
— *I2(1904)280.* *(qtd 4 by Cokayne).*
Az 3 stags lodged Or
APPULBY, W. *PLN 1065.*

3 deer passant
3 bucks passt
[LEATHERSELLERS' CO]. *Her & Gen i 278.* early or mid 16 cent. *(qtg ?Tregoz; on tomb in Sompting Ch).*
3 bucks 2, 1
BUCTON, Thomas de, of Great Harrowden, Northants. *Birch 7569.* +SIGILLVM THOME DE BVCTON'. 1324.

3 stags passt
— *Birch 10219.* 1404. *(2, 1; qtd 2&3 by Ralph Green).*
[GREEN]. *Mill Steph.* *(in round tomb of man in chainmail & w ...., Reynes, Clifton Reynes, Bucks).*
[GREEN]. *Bellasis II 49; Whitaker ii 327.* *(qtg Gu chev betw 3 crosses botony Or on chf lion passt Arg [Mablethorpe]; on kneeling figure of lady, tomb of Sir T Parr, KG, d11 Nov 1517, Kendal).*
GREENE. *Hutton 80.* *(on mont of Wm Bedell for his w, dau of Rob G, Kt, Westm Abbey).*
GRENE, Sir Thomas. *Dugd 17, 33.* *(sl, mid 14 cent style).*
Arg 3 harts passt Gu
WHALLEY, of Suss. *L1 698, 3.* *(attired Or).*
Arg 3 stags passt Gu attired Or
WHALLEY. *CRK 1695.*
WHALLEY. *MY 316.*
Az 3 harts Arg
— *RH, Ancestor ix 173.*
Az 3 stags passt Arg attired Or
TRELOP, Sir W. *WB I 42, 22.*
Az 3 bucks passt Or
— *WB I 21b, 6.* *(qtd 2 by Ld Vauz).*
GREEN. *PLN 940.* *(imp Throckmorton).*
GREEN. *PLN 945.* *(imp by Trussell).*
GREEN, Sir Thomas. *PLN 2003.* *(qtg 2&3 Gu chev betw 3 crosslets Or in chf lion passt Arg).*
GREEN, Thomas. *BG 212.*
GREN, of Norton, Northants. *L1 293, 3; L2 223, 1.*
GRENE. *WB IV 159, 600.*
GRENE. *WB IV 159b, 604.* *(imp by Trussell).*
[GRENE]. *PLN 1718.* *(imp by Sir Edw Rawle).*
GRENE, Sir Tomas, of Northants. *RH, Ancestor vii 197.*
Az 3 harts passt Or
GREEN. *GutchWdU.* *(qtd 9 by Jn Mordaunt; formerly in window in BNC, Oxf).*
GRENE, Sir Henry, of Northants. *CVM 790.*
Az 3 roebucks passt Or
GRENE. *SHY 316.*
Az 3 stags passt Or
GREEN. *GutchWdU.* *(qtd 9 by Jn Mordaunt; formerly in BNC Hall).*
Sa 3 stags passt Or
RODERHAM. *XPat 211, Arch 69, 86.* *('of Hertfordsh'' added).*
Vt 3 bucks passt Arg
[?ROTHERHAM, Archbp of York]. *PLN 1133.*
SCOTT. *Stamford 5.* c1480. *(or Rotherham, Archbp of York, 1480-1500).*
[TROLLOPE, of Morden & Thornley]. *Blair D II 195, 405.* *(attired Or; imp Harpyn; Thornley Hall, Durham).*

TROLLOPPE, Tomas. *RH, Ancestor vii 211.*
Vt 3 harts passt Arg
SCOTT. *Proc Soc Antiq XIX 2S 99. (imp by
See of York for Thos S, Archbp of York
1480-50; sh on illuminated border of original
statutes of Jesus College, Rotherham, of
which he was founder).*
Vt 3 bucks passt Or
ROTHERHAM, Thomas, Bishop of Lincoln.
*GutchWdU. (d1500; window, Lincoln Coll
Hall).*
Vt 3 harts passt Or
ROTHERHAM, of Beds. *L1 566, 1.*
Erm 3 stags passt Gu attired Or
BLYTHE, Wm, of Norton, Derby. *BA 423.*

3 deer salient
Az 3 roebucks salient Or
ROTHERHAM. *L1 548, 1.*
Vt 3 harts salient Arg attired Or
TROLLEHOP. *L1 640, 2.*
TROLLEHOPP. *LY A 91.*
Per chev Sa and Arg 3 harts salient counterch
HERSTON, Fraunceys, of Surr. *RH, Ancestor
v 186. (attired Or; 2 in chf respectant).*

3 deer statant
3 bucks stat
GREEN, Sir Thomas. *Mill Steph. 1462. (qtg
[Mablethorpe]; brass to Sir Thos G, Ld of
Norton, & his wid Maud Throckmorton,
Green's Norton, Northants).*
GREEN, Sir Thomas. *Mill Steph. 1462. (imp
[Ferrers of Chartley]; brass to Sir Thos G,
Ld of Norton, & his wid Maud Throckmorton,
Green's Norton, Northants).*
Az 3 bucks stat Or
GREEN, Thomas. *S 514.*
GREN, Sir Thomas. *WK 73.*
GRENE. *DV 59b, 2357.*
Az 3 harts stat Or
GRENE, Mons Thomas. *S 509.*
Az 3 stags stat Or
GRENE, of Northants. *PT 75.*
GRENE, Sir Thomas. *WK 214.*
Vt 3 roebucks stat Or
RODERHAM, Sir Thomas. *WK 260.*

3 deer guardant &c
3 harts at gaze
[GREENE]. *RH, Ancestor xi 90.* late 14 cent.
(tomb of Reynes, Clifton Reynes, Bucks).
Vt 3 bucks at gaze Or
GREEN. *Leake. (qtd 10 by Sir Wm Parr, KG
d1571).*
GREEN. *Sandford 490. (qtd 6 by Qu Catherine Parr).*

Arg 3 roebucks passt regard Gu
LEATHERSELLERS' CO. *Welch; Wallis.
(attired Sa; grant by Jn More, Norroy, 1479).*
LEATHERSELLERS' CO OF LONDON. *1H7 60.
(attired & unguled Sa).*
OSYN, John. *RH, Ancestor ix 172.*

3 dogs courant
3 greyhounds courant
HALL, Elizabeth. *SarumC-sls M74/W205
Drawer 1.* 1456.
MAULEVERER, James. *Yorks Deeds VI 83.*
1627.
MAULEVERER, Oliver, of Lincs. *Birch 11683.*
S: OLYUERI MAULEVERER. 1401. *(in pale).*
MAULEVERER, Peter. *Yorks Deeds II 115.*
1373.
MAULEVERER, Peter, Kt. *Yorks Deeds X 137.*
...Petri Maulevev.... 1382.
Arg 3 greyhounds courant Az
PENPANE. *L9 100a, 10. (in pale).*
PENPANS, of Cornwall. *L1 513, 5. (1st ch
with roundel Gu).*
PENPONS, of Cornwall. *L2 404, 1.*
Arg 3 hounds courant in pale Az
NANFAN. *BA 962.*
Arg 3 greyhounds Gu
MAULEVERER, Sire Willame. *N 1093. ('de
argent a iii leverers de goules').*
Arg 3 greyhounds courant Sa
WYGMORE, Sir T. *WB I 41, 11.*
Az 3 greyhounds courant Arg
HUNGARIE, Rex. *SM 127, 20.*
Az 3 hounds courant in pale Or
— *Nichols Leics II 262. (imp Sa bend betw
6 crosslets Arg; window formerly (1583) in
Melton Mowbray Ch).*
Gu 3 greyhounds ?courant Arg
MAULEVERERE, Monsr. *AS 341.*
Gu 3 greyhounds courant Arg
GEROUYS. *L1 275, 1; L2 220, 11.*
MALEUERER. *L1 424, 1; L2 326, 8.*
MALEVERE, Thomas, of Lincs. *WB III 119b,
6. (in pale).*
MALEVERER, William. *F 245.*
MALEVERER, William. *WLN 461.*
MALLEUERER, William. *Kent Gentry 217,
396. ('with his difference').*
MALURERE, Willm. *WLN 467.*
MAULEVERER. *L9 50a, 12. (in pale).*
MAULEVERER. *CRK 191. (in pale).*
MAULEVERER, John. *E I 676; E II 678.*
MAULEVERER, Mons' William. *S 431.*
MAULEVERER, William. *S 436. (in pale).*
MAWLYVEREY, of Kent. *MY 232.*
Sa 3 greyhounds courant Arg
MAULEV'ER, Sir J. *WB I 39, 11.*
MAULEVERE. *L9 50b, 1. (in pale).*

Gu 3 hunting dogs ?courant Arg
   KENETZ, N de. *MP II 50*. (*'scutum de gules
   [3] caniculi de argents'*).
Gu 3 kenets questing Arg
   KENETTE, Pers de. *F 101*. (*'gules 3 kenets
   running silver'*).

3 dogs courant collared
3 greyhounds ?courant collared in pale
   [MAULEVERER]. *Mill Steph*. c1475. (*imp by
   Kniveton; brass to Nicholas K & w Joan
   [M], Mugginton, Derbys*).
   [MAULEVERER]. *Mill Steph*. c1475. (*imp by
   qtly Calverley & Scott; brass to Nicholas
   Kniveton & w Joan [M], Mugginton, Derbys*).
3 greyhounds courant collared
   [MAULEVERER]. *Mill Steph*. (*1 of 12 small
   shs round sides of tomb of Sir Thos de
   Ingilby, d c1369, Justice of K's Bench, Rip-
   ley, West Riding Yorks*).
   MAULEVERERE, Sir John. *Mill Steph*. 1400.
   (*brass to Sir Jn M & w Eleanor Middleton,
   Allerton Mauleverer, Yorks*).
Arg 3 greyhounds courant Gu collared Or
   WHELPEDALE. *PT 1168*.
Az 3 greyhounds courant in pale Arg collared Or
   CROWAN, Thomas, of Cornw. *WB III 120b,
   5*.
Gu 3 greyhounds Arg collared Untinc
   MAULYVERER, John. *SES 56*.
Gu 3 greyhounds courant & collared Arg chapes
   ?Or
   MALEVERER, Sir .... *PLN 329*. (*in pale*).
Gu 3 greyhounds courant Arg collared Az
   MALLEVERER, of Alderton, Yorks. *D4 35b*.
Gu 3 greyhounds courant in pale Arg collared
   Gu studded & ringed Or
   MALEVERER, Sir Alnoth. *WK 290*.
Gu 3 greyhounds ?courant Arg collared Or
   MALEVERER, of Allerton. *PT 1225*.
Gu 3 greyhounds courant Arg collared Or
   MALVER. *DV 46a, 1819*.
   MAULEVERER, Sir John. *S&G II 299*. (*in
   pale*).
   MAULEVERER, Oliver. *S 438*. (*in pale*).
   MAULEVERER, Mons Olyver. *S 433*.
   MAULYVERER, Sir G. *BA 634*.
   MAULYVERER, Johannes. *Q II 598*.
Sa 3 greyhounds courant in pale Arg collared
   Untinc
   MAULEVERER, John, of Allyrton. *RH, Ances-
   tor vii 196*.
   MAULEVERERE, Hopkyne, of Yorks. *RH,
   Ancestor iv 240*.
Sa 3 greyhounds courant in pale Arg collared Gu
   MICHELL, John, Westmld. *WB III 101b, 4*.
   WIGMORE. *CRK 1351*. (*studded & ringed
   Or*).
   WYGMORE. *SK 898*. (*'of Herefortshire'*

added*).
Sa 3 greyhounds courant in pale Az collared Sa
   [MACHELL]. *Bellasis II 153*. (*tincts
   incorrect; imp by [Wharton]; Corbel, altar
   table, Kirkby Thorpe*).

Patterned field 3 dogs courant collared
Arg semy of crosses fitchy 3 greyhounds courant
   Sa collared Or
   [SMYTH, Sir Walter]. *Proc Soc Antiq XXIX
   2S 204 & XXX 2S 232-4*. early 16 cent. (*qtg
   2; [Graunt] & 3; [Ruding of Worc] all imp
   [Ferrers] qtly of 8*).
Arg semy of crosses formy fitchy 3 greyhounds
   courant in pale Sa collared Or
   SMYTHE. *WK 691*.
   SMYTHE. *XPat 414, Arch 69, 100*.
   SMYTHE. *L10 111, 12*.
Per pale Vt and Arg 3 greyhounds courant coun-
   terch collared Or
   TOMLINSON, Ric. *Hutton 69*. (*in Wapping
   Ch*).

3 dogs passant
3 greyhounds passt in pale
   [MAULEVERER]. *Arch Journ xxxi 382*. (*upper
   sin sh on brass to Nicholas Kniveton, [Sheriff
   of Derby 1494], & w Joan M, Mugginton,
   Derbys*).
3 talbots ?passt
   TALBOT, Thomas. *PRO-sls KR 73/2, 34*.
   1385.
3 talbots passt
   TALBOT, Thomas, Kt. *PRO-sls*. 1386.
3 talbots passt to sin
   [BROWNE]. *Farrer II 444*. (*sh on font,
   Sustead Ch, Norf*).
Arg 3 ?dogs passt Az
   — *WK 584*. (*qtd 2&3 by Sir Ric Nanfant*).
Arg 3 talbots passt Or
   — *H18 38d; D13 148*. (*qtd by Assheley, of
   St Giles, Wymborne, Dorset*).
Arg 3 mastiffs ?passt Sa
   MARTYNE, John, of Kent. *RH, Ancestor v
   180*.
Arg 3 talbots passt Sa
   — *WB I 42, 11*. (*talbots unclear; qtd 3 by
   Yeo, of Braunton, Devon*).
   TALBOT, Sir William. *BW 18, 124*.
Gu 3 greyhounds passt Arg
   MAULEVERER, Sir Thos. *BA 41, 403*. (*in
   pale*).
   MAULEVERES, Mons John. *TJ 1211*.
   (*'...a trois leverers passantz...'*).
Sa 3 greyhounds passt Arg
   MAULEVERER, Robert. *TJ 1212*. (*'...a trois
   leverers passantz...'*).

Vt 3 hounds passt Arg
    HOUNDHILL. *LH 993.*

3 dogs passant collared

Arg 3 greyhounds passt 2, 1 Sa collared Gu
    MORE, of Liverpool. *L2 343, 5.*
Arg 3 hounds ?passt Sa collared Or
    MAUCHELL, John. *TJ 1385.* *('...a trois lever-
    ers de sable colers dor').*
Az 3 greyhounds passt Gu collared Arg
    MALEUER, S Ric. *GA 16.*
    ('...iii leuriers...').
Gu 3 greyhounds passt Arg collared gobony Or
    and Sa
    QUIXLEY, Adam de. *TJ 1212a. (ch on each
    shldr with escallop Sa).*
    QUIXLEY, John de. *TJ 1213. ('..a trois
    levereres dargent passant les colers gobonez
    dor & de sable').*

3 dogs statant

3 ?dogs ?stat
    CRIKETOT, Simon. *PRO-sls E40 A6814.*
    1315-16.
3 kenets stat
    KENNETT, Nicholas of, [Cambs]. *Bk of Sls
    381.* 1252-3. *(s of Peter of K).*
Gu 3 bloodhounds ?stat Arg
    RAGON. *L1 545, 6.*
Gu 3 ?ratch-hounds stat Arg
    RAGON. *PT 238.*
Gu 3 talbots ?stat Arg
    RAGOUN. *DV 64b, 2551.*

3 elephants

Az 3 elephants standing on crowns Or
    ALYZAUNDRE, Rex, de Almayne. *RH, Ances-
    tor vii 199.*

3 foxes

3 foxes
    [WALES]. *WK A 29. (Kadrohe, Harthe, of I
    of 'Angruyshe').*
3 foxes passt
    NANFAN, John. *Clairambault 6647.* 2 Jan
    1438. *(qtd 2&3).*
3 foxes ?passt in bend
    [MORGAN, John, of Gt Kitshall, Suff]. *Farrer
    Bacon 1.* 1316 or earlier. *(sl on charter of
    1316).*
Arg 3 foxes passt Sa
    PYLE, Richard. *CRK 1921. (charge unclear).*

3 goats

Sa 3 goats courant in pale Arg
    MULLYNG. *BA 974.*
Gu 3 goats passt Arg
    — *D4 42b. (qtd by Reresby of Yorks).*
    CHEYNEY. *LQ 105.*

Sa 3 goats passt Arg
    DYER. *L1 208, 2; L2 157, 9.*
    MULLYNG, of Cornw. *L1 459, 3; L2 341, 12.*
Sa 3 goats passt in pale Arg collared & belled
    Untinc
    STANSFELDE, Jamys. *RH, Ancestor ix 166.*
3 goats salient
    [GAYEFOR ALIAS GOATFORD]. *Proc Soc Antiq
    X 2S 15. (silver sl of Ric Townley 1628-60).*
    GAYTEFORD. *PT 343.*
Sa 3 goats salient Arg
    GAITFORD. *L1 278, 1; L2 223, 9.*
    GAYTEFORD. *PT 343.*
    GAYTFORDE, John. *RH, Ancestor ix 159.*
Sa 3 goats ?stat Arg
    DYAR. *DV 47a, 1841.*
Sa 3 goats stat Arg
    DYER. *L10 57b, 11.*
    DYER, Stephen. *PLN 1645.*

3 hares, conies &c

3 leverets
    LEVRE, Nicholas le. *Durham-sls 1589.*
    c1331.
Arg 3 conies courant Az
    ARNODE. *L10 5b, 18.*
Arg 3 hares courant Az
    ARWOD. *L1 2, 6; L2 3, 11.*
Gu 3 hares courant in pale Arg
    — *WNR 7. (Le Rei...).*
Gu 3 conies courant in pale Or
    [CONINBRE, Rex]. *FK I 45.*
Sa 3 conies courant Arg
    CUNCLIFFE. *L2 129, 6. (2&1).*
    CUNCLYFFE, of Oxfords. *MY 297.*
    CUNLIFFE, of Lancs, Bart. *CRK 1576.*
Az 3 hares in pairle Or ears conjoined
    HAREWELLE. *RH, Ancestor vii 202. (name
    added in later hand).*
3 conies passt in pale
    — *Birch 9674.* 1367. *(conies unclear; imp
    by Johanna de Ferres).*
3 conies
    CONYNGSBY, William. *PRO-sls E40 A6853.*
    SIGILLV WILLELMI ...... 1365-6. *(s of Jn de
    C).*
3 conies sejt
    CONYNGSBY, Johanna. *Vinc 88, 53.* 1320-1.
    (sl; w of Rog de C).
Arg 3 conies ?sejt Sa
    CONYNGSTON. *L1 141, 4; L2 119, 7.*
Gu 3 conies sejt Arg
    CONISBYE. *Nichols Leics IV 929. (Shepey
    Magna Ch).*
3 hares playing on bagpipes
    FITZ-ercald. *Mill Steph.* c1525. *(qtd 2&3 by
    Sacheverell; brass to Jn S (d1485) & w Joan
    Stathum, Morley, Derbys).*

Arg 3 hares sejt playing bagpipes Gu
— *L10 97b, 3. (qtd 4 by Sir Hen
Sacheverel).*
— *XFB 51. (qtd 3 by Ric Sacheverel, of
Sadington).*
— *XX 117. (qtd 4 by Sacheverel).*
— *WK 482. (qtd 4 by Sir Hen Sacheverell).*
FITZ-ercald. *Mill Steph. (qtd 2&3 by
Sacheverell; alabaster tomb to Kath Babing-
ton, nee Sacheverell; Morley, Derby).*
SACHEVEREL, Sir Henry. *XK 120. (Kt 1509).*

3 horses &c

Az 3 demi horses courant in pale Untinc
— *RH, Ancestor vii 208. (sin side is blank).*
Arg 3 asses passt Sa
STEWKLEY, Thomas. *PLN 695.*
Arg 3 horses Sa
— *?source. (imp by Sir Thos More).*
Gu 3 horses courant in pale Arg bridles Or
FRYE, of Devon. *L2 211, 4.*

3 moles

Arg 3 moles Sa
— *PT 1088. (qtd by Redman, of Twiseltone).*

3 otters

Az 3 otters passt Or
OTTYR, Robade. *RH, Ancestor vii 196.*
3 otters passt in pale each with fish in mouth
PRUDE, Thos. *Belcher II 23; Gent Mag NS
19 483. 1468. (brass, Canterbury, St
Alpheys, Kent).*

3 oxen

3 oxen in pale
BERWICK, Gilbert de. *PRO-sls. 1357-8.*
3 calves passt
CALF, Roesia. *Wells D&C II 617, 322. S'
ROESIE DE WELLESLEYE. 1351. (in pale).
(wid of Sir Jn de Willesleye).*
VEELE, Walter de. *KildareAS VII 355. 1300.
(sl; Bp of Kildare 1300-32).*
Arg 3 calves Gu
CALVE. *FK II 483.*
Arg 3 calves passt Gu
CALF. *L1 164, 1; L2 116, 4.*
Arg 3 calves passt Sa
— *D4 33b. (imp by Conyers, of Maske,
Yorks).*
METCALFE. *Nichols Leics II 720. (Med-
bourne Ch).*
METCALFE, of Richmond, Yorks. *D4 32b.
(cresc Gu for diffce).*
Arg 3 bulls passt Sa
— *PLN 1605. (qtd 2&3 by Hampton).*
HAMELYN. *L1 313, 3; L2 251, 8. (armed
Or).*
HAMELYN. *FK II 274. (armed Or;*

'*Hamelyn' named by Gibbon, 'Redmeld' by
Charles; qtd 2&3 by Camoys).*
HAMELYN. *FK II 271. (armed Or).*
STYKLEWEY, Thomas. *WB IV 166b, 733.*
Arg 3 bulls stat Sa
— *LH 496. (qtd 2&3 by Hampton).*
Or 3 cows Gu collared & belled Sa
— *WLN 158. (qtd 2&3 by Or 3 pales Gu).*

3 rats

Arg 3 ?rats bendwise 2, 1 Sa
[OSBORNE]. *PLN 1687.*

3 sheep (lambs)

3 lambs stat
AGNIS, Thomas de, of Chalfont St Giles & St
Peter, Bucks. *Birch 6774.* S' THOME DE
AGNIS. *1286.*
Arg 3 ?lambs Sa
— *CC 234, 395. (qtd 2&3 by Stamton).*

3 sheep (rams)

Arg 3 rams passt Sa
— *WB I 16b, 2. (qr 2 of coat imp by [Cour-
tenay]).*
SIDENHAM, of Brympton d'Evercy. *Gerard
107. (armed Or).*
SIDNAM, John, of Som. *WB III 119, 5.*
SYDENHAM, Simon. *SussASColl xxix 10. (Bp
of Chichester 1429-37).*
Qtly of 6 Sa and Arg on Sa ram salient Arg
GLOVERS' CO. *Welch; Wallis. (armed &
unguled Or; grant by Jn Smert, Garter, 20
Oct 1464).*
MORTON, of Glower, (Gloucs). *PLN 977.
(armed & pudenda Or).*
Arg 3 rams stat Sa
SYDENHAM. *SK 950.*

3 Squirrels

3 squirrels
— *Stevenson. 1388. (squirrels unclear; qtd
by Robt Maners).*
MARTHEBY, Richard de. *Birch 11638.* S'
RICARDI DE...... *14 cent. (2, 1).*
Arg 3 squirrels Purp
TALBOTT, Sir Emond, of Lancs. *RH, Ances-
tor iv 239. ('silver iii squareleys of porpell').*
Vt 3 squirrels Arg
— *CRK 723. (qtd 2&3 by Sir Thos
Manners).*
Vt 3 squirrels erect Arg
— *L9 52a, 2. (qtd 2&3 by Manners).*
BAXTERD, Tomas, Northd. *RH, Ancestor v
183.*
Vt 3 squirrels sejt Arg
— *PLN 1283. (qtd 2&3 by Sir Robt
Manners).*

Vt 3 squirrels sejt Or
— LD 120. (qtd 2&3 by Manners of Ithol,
Cumb).
Arg 3 squirrels playing bagpipes ?Gu
— D5 3. (qtd by Sacheverell).
Vt 3 squirrels Ppr eating nuts Arg
SWAFIELD. ML I 481.

3 urchins, hedgehogs, &c
3 hedgehogs
CLAXTON, Robert. Greenwich 14 K8, HB-
SND. 1459.
CLAXTON, Sir Robt. Durham-sls 611. 1474.
HERIZ, Sir John. Lawrance 23. 1299.
(effigy, Gonalston, Notts).
Arg 3 hedgehogs Sa
HEREISS, Ld, of Terreglis. Lyndsay 123.
HERRIES. Berry; Stodart pl 5. ('Ceulx de
Nesegles'; qtd 2&3 by Lindsay).
HERYSS, Ld. SC 48.
Az 3 hedgehogs Or
— I2(1904)139. (qtd 3 by Sir Wyllm Pier-
pount).
— H21 85. (qtd by Perpoynt).
HERICE, Sr de. CKO 600.
HERIZ. Nichols Leics II 854. (glass in
Abbot's Chapel, Stoughton).
HERIZ, Monsr J. AS 193.
HERRIES. LH 1072.
HERYS. WK 441. (urcheons; qtd 3 by Sir
Wm Perpont).
HERYZ. SK 763.
SWELINTON, Sir Roger, of Derbys. CV-BM
163.
SWELYNTON, S' Roger, of Derbys. CY a 70,
278.
SWILLINGTON, Sir Roger. CRK 1018.
(urcheons).
Or 3 hedgehogs Sa
HERICE, Henri de. FW 93.
HERICE, Henri de. A 263.

3 wolves courant
3 wolves courant
LOVETT, Thos. Mill Steph. c1500. (brass to
Thos L, d1542, s of Thos L, Esq, & w Eliz
dau of Jn Butler, Wappenham, Northants).
LOVETT, Thos. Mill Steph. ('Arma moderna
Lovettorum'; 18 cent brass to Thos Lovett,
d1491).
Arg 3 wolves courant Az
NANFANT, of Cornw. L1 476, 2. (in pale).
Arg 3 wolves Az
— WK 136. (?wolves unclear; qtd 2&3 by
Sir Ric Nanfant).
Arg 3 wolves courant in pale Sa
LOVELL. NS 140.

Purp 3 wolves courant in pale Arg collared Or
CROWAN. L2 143, 2.
Az 3 wolves courant in pale Or 1st couped pale-
ways the 2 halves separated by roundel Or
PENPONS. L9 103b, 4.

3 wolves passant &c
Arg 3 wolves passt Az
— PLN 2026. (langued Gu; qtd 2&3 by Sir
Ric Nanfan).
[LOWE]. PLN 1009. (langued Gu).
NANFAN, Sir Richard. PLN 1306. (2, 1; qtg
2&3 Sa on chev betw 3 wings Arg 3 Erm
spots; of Herefs added).
PENPONS. BA 958.
[PENPONS]. Arch lvi 334. (in pale; qtd by
[Sir Ric Nanfan]; window, Ockwells Manor
House, Berks).
PENSONS. L9 108a, 10. (in pale).
Arg 3 wolves passt Gu
WHELPDALE, Roger. GutchWdU. (1st ch on
shldr with mullet Or; Fellow of Balliol, Bp of
Carlisle, d1422).
Arg 3 wolves passt Sa
LEVETT, of Irld. LQ 71.
Sa 3 wolves passt 2, 1 Arg
PALMER, Tomas. RH, Ancestor vii 203.
Vt 3 wolves passt Or
STANHOP. L1 585, 5.
STANHOPE. PT 1267. (Maulovell added
later).
STANHOPE. LS 76.
STANHOPP, Sir Edward. WK 224. (in pale).
Az 3 wolves passt in pale Arg collared Or
CROWAN. L10 46b, 8.
Arg 3 ?wolves passt in pale Az 1st collared
around middle Gu
PENPANS, Robert, of Cornw. WB III 120b, 8.
Arg 3 wolves passt Sa each couped paleways &
the 2 halves separated by roundels Or
PENPONS. ML I 528.
3 wolves 2 in chf counter-rampant 1 in base
courant
CLAY, John. Clairambault 2564. 4 Aug
1446.
Arg 3 wolves Sa 2 in chf facing each other
— WK 614. (?lions; qtd by [Green], all imp
by Wm Bedell).
Arg 3 wolves 2 in chf combattant 1 in base passt
Sa
CLEY, Sir John. PLN 1145. (qtg 2&3
[Thweng] Arg fess Vt betw 3 popinjays Ppr,
all imp [Astley] & [Harcourt]).
Barry Arg and Gu 3 wolves ramp 2 in chf Sa 1
in base Az
ESTUDELEY. LE 66.
Arg 3 wolves stat 2, 1 Az
[PENPONS]. BA 1015. (qtd 2 by Sir Ric Nan-
fan).

3 BEASTS (LIONS) & LABEL

3 lions rampant & label
3 lions & label
BAYHOUSE, Richard de. *PRO-sls.* 9 Oct 1340-1.
HOLTE, Sir John de. *Heneage 2419.*
+S' IOHANNIS DE HOLTE. 1297.
VACHE, Richard de la, Oxfords. *Birch 14070.*
SIGILL'RICARDI DELAVACHE. 1277.
Arg 3 lions Purp label Gu
BAIHOUSE, Monsire Robert le filtz. *AN 222.*
BAYNS. *PT 210.*
RAYNES. *DV 57b, 2276.*
Arg 3 lions Sa label of 5 Gu
CHEVEREL, Alisaunder. *LM 201.*
Az 3 lions Or label Gu
FENES, Giles de. *FW 271.*
FENZ, Sire Giles de. *N 256.*
Gu 3 lions Or label Arg
CODERUGE, Mons Baudewyn de. *TJ 65.*
CODERUGGE, Baudwyn. *F 423.*
Gu 3 lions Or label of 5 Arg
CODERUGGE, Baldwyn de. *E I 555; E II 557.*
Arg 3 lions Sa crowned Or label of 5 Gu
CHEVEREL, Aleysand. *Q 381.*
Gu 3 lions Arg label checky Or and Az
VACHE, Sire Richard de la. *N 351.* *('...iii lioncels...').*

3 lions passant & label
3 lions passt & label
DABETON, Hugo. *Vinc 88, 44.* temp Edw 3. *(sl).*
GIFFORD. *Lawrance 19.* before 1350. *(effigy, Boynton, Wilts).*
GYFFARD, Thomas. *SarumM-sls.* Sigillum: thome: Gyffard.
GYFFARD, Thomas. *Nelson 83, Arch Journ xciii 39.* sigillum: thome: gyffard. c1380.
Az 3 lions passt Arg label of 5 Gu
CAMVYLE, William de. *E I 647; E II 649.*
Gu 3 lions passt Arg label Az
GIFFARD, de Bef. *A 221.*
GIFFARD, Sire Johan le boef. *N 345.*
GIFFARD, John le boef. *FW 303.*
Gu 3 lions passt Arg label of 5 Az
GIFFARD, John de Bef. *E I 650; E II 652.*
Gu 3 lions passt Arg label Sa
GIFFARD, Sire Esmoun. *N 895.*
GIFFORD, of Hinton [St George]. *Gerard 90.*
Or 3 lions passt Sa label Gu
CAREW, Sire Johan. *N 926.*

3 lions passant guardant & label
3 lions pg & label
BROTHERTON. *Smyth B II 213.* SIGILLVM MAVRICIE BERKELEY MILITIS. 1506-23. *(imp by Maurice de Berkeley).*
[BROTHERTON]. *Smyth B II 183; Birch 7401.* S' HONORABILIS DNI WILL'I DE BERKELEY ET WOTTON. 1470. *(imp Wm, 7th Baron Berkeley).*
[BROTHERTON, Thomas of]. *Bow XLIV 2.* *(imp by [Edward the Confessor] on sl of Thos Mowbray, D of Norf, E of Nottingham, Marshal of Engld).*
BYLAND ABBEY. *Bk of Sls 450.* 1426. *('arms of Brotherton which, with another Mowbray shield form arms of Byland Abbey').*
ENGLAND. *WestmAbb.* *(small sh carved in white marble; imp by France ancient for [Joan, Princess of Wales]; in 4foil panel under niche containing figure of woman on N side of tomb of [Philippa of Hainault, Qu of Edw 3]).*
JUYNER, David. *Birch 2960.* S'.DAVID.-JUYNER.ABBATIS.DE.CLEYUA. 1435. *(Abbot of Cleeve, Som).*
LANCASTER, D of. *Farrer II 444.* *(on font Sustead Ch, Norf).*
[LANCASTER, Duchy of]. *Birch 5315.* 1376. *(sl of Preston, Lancs).*
LANCASTER, Henry, E of. *PRO-sls E40 A351.* ...ICI.DE.LANC.S.RE COMITIS.LEYCEST. 1328-9. *(& E of Leicester).*
LANCASTER, Thomas, E of. *PRO-sls.* 1301 & 1311-12.
LANCASTER, Thomas, E of. *Vinc 88, 61.* ...thomas conte .... 1302. *(sl).*
LANCASTER, Thomas, E of. *Bow XLVIII 12.* +S Thome Comitis de Lancaster. 1306-7.
LANCASTRE, Maude de, Ctess of Ulster. *PRO-sls.* 1347-8 & 1336-7. *(1 of 4 shields arr in cross & imp by De Burgh).*
MOWBRAY, Elizabeth, Duchess of Norf, etc. *Birch 11990.* SIGILLUM DNE ELIZABETH DUCISSE-NORFOLCHIE COMITISSE (MARESCH'DNE DE) BRETBY & DE KNAPP. 1397. *(imp qtly 1&4 checky (Warren), 2&3 lion (Mowbray); w of Thos de M & dau of Ric, E of Arundel).*
MOWBRAY, John. *Birch 12000.* ...(C)OMIT' MAR(ESCALLI).... 1442. *(3rd D of Norf, E of Nottingham, EM).*
MOWBRAY, John. *Birch 12004.* 1457. *(3rd D of Norf, E of Nottingham, EM, Ld of Mowbray, Segrave & Gower).*
MOWBRAY, John, D of Norf. *Harl 5804, 108b.* 1461.
MOWBRAY, John, Duke of Norf. *Farrer Bacon 91.* 11 Feb 1448.

MOWBRAY, John, E of Nottingham & D of Norf. *Vinc 88, 180. (sl).*

MOWBRAY, Thomas, E of Nottingham. *Birch 12007.* SIG THOME CO'ITIS NOTYNGHAM & MARESCALLI ANGLIE DNI DE ... & SEGRAUE. 1396.

MOWBRAY. *Bow XXII 1. (imp by [Edward the Confessor]).*

[NEWARK, College of, Leics]. *Birch 3450.* 1528. *(from Hen, D of Lancaster; sl of Dean & Chapter of College).*

NORFOLK, Elizabeth, Duchess of. *Baker-sls.* 1416-17. *(sl; imp qtly Fitzalan & Warenne).*

NORFOLK, Margaret, Ctess of. *BrookeAsp I 36, 1.* S: Margarerte : Mareschall comitisse norfolchie. 1385.

NORFOLK, Thomas, E of, Marshal of England. *PRO-sls.* 1320 & 1332-3.

PLANTAGENET. *Birch 12729.*

PLANTAGENET, Edmund. *PRO-sls.* 1296. *(s of Hen 3).*

PLANTAGENET, Edward, D of Aquitaine & E of Chester. *Birch 6316.* +EDWARDVS PRIMO-GENIT' REGIS ANGLIE DVX AQVITANIE.COMES CESTRIE.PONTIVI.MONTISSROLII. 1325. *(afterwards Edw 3; equestr sl obv).*

PLANTAGENET, Henry. *Birch 12680.* S' HEN-RICI COMITIS LANCASTRIE DERBYE LEICESTRIE ET SENESCALL ANGLIE. 1347. *(E of Lancaster, Derby & Leicester, Seneschal of Engld).*

[PLANTAGENET], Thomas, [of Brotherton]. *Birch 6333.* 1322. *(E of Norf, Marshal of Engld; equestr sl).*

ULSTER, Maud, Ctess of. *Bow XLIII 2.* SIGILLVM MATILDIS COMITISSE VLTONIE. 1347. *(loz; dau of Hen, E of Lancaster, 1281-1345).*

WALES, Edward, Prince of. *Birch 5549. (afterwards Edw 2; sl obv).*

3 lions pg & label of 5
— *PRO-sls.* 1391-2. *(qtd by [Mowbray] on sl of Thos M, Earl Marshal).*

COMBE ABBEY, Warws. *Birch 2989.* SIGILL COMUNE CAPITULI MONACHOR DE CUBA. 13 cent. *(Chapter sl).*

COMBE, Thomas, Abbot of. *Bow LVII 15.* 1472-3.

EDWARD. *Bk of Sls 64.* 1262. *(eldest s of Hen 3).*

EDWARD I. *Birch 6310 & 6315.* EADWARDUS PRIMOGENITUS ET HERES DOMINI REGIS ANGLIE(obv); SIGILLUM EADWARDI FILII HEN-RICI ILLVSTRIS REGIS ANGLIE(rev). 1259. *(as heir apparent; equestr sl obv & rev).*

ENGLAND. *Sandford 120, 122-4, 127, 129, 137, 145 & 157. (Edw 1 as heir apparent; label of 3 or 5; label of 5 interwoven with tail of upper lion).*

ENGLAND, John, K of. *WB I 33b, 4. (imp*

France ancient; m [Isabella] dau of E of Angouleme).

PLANTAGENET, Edward, E of Chester & D of Aquitaine. *Birch 6316.* S'EDWARDI.-P'MOGINITI.REGIS.ANGLIE.DUCIS.AQVITANNIE: COMITIS: CESTRIE.PONTIVI.MONTISSOROLLII. 1325. *(afterwards Edw 3).*

PLANTAGENET, Edward, E of Chester. *Birch 12673.* SIGILLUM EDWARD FIL'REGIS ANGL'COMITIS CESTR'. *('s of Hen 3 afterward Edw 1' deleted by HS Kingsford and corrected to Edw 3; ante 1272).*

WALES, Edward, Prince of. *Birch 5549. (afterwards Edw 2; sl rev).*

Gu 3 lions pg & label Arg &c
Gu 3 lions pg & label Arg
— *XB 7, 38. (qtd by Howard).*
Gu 3 lions pg Or label Untinc
BROTHERTON, Sir Thomas. *BR V 1.*
Gu 3 lions pg Or label Arg
— *XL 291.*
— *XK 257. (qtd 2 by Sir Edm Howard).*
— *XK 102. (qtd 2 by Sir Maurice Berkeley; Kt 1509).*
— *XK 66. (qtd 2 by Thos Howard, KG).*
— *WK 464. (qtd 2 by Sir Morice Barkeley).*
— *1H7 1. (qtd 2 by Barkley in 2&3 of Dennys; at Master Westons).*
— *WGA 194. (qtd 2&3 by Thos [Howard], E of Surrey).*
BROTHERTON. *Leake. (qtd 2 by Thos Howard, KG, d1554).*
BROTHERTON. *Sandford 487. (qtd 5 by Qu Anne Bullen).*
BROTHERTON. *D13 104. (qtd 2 by Howard).*
BROTHERTON, Marshall of England. *Sandford 209.*
BROTHERTON, Sir Thomas (of). *BR IV 97.*
[BROTHERTON, Thomas of]. *WNS 25, 23. ('le Cunte Mareschal porte les armes dengletre ou un label dar').*
BROTHERTON, Thomas of, Comes Mareschall. *LMO 48.*
ENGLAND, Q Anne Boleyn. *XK 17. (qrs 1&5).*
[HOWARD], John, D of Norfolk. *WGA 45.*
MARESCHAL, le Conte. *AS 26.*
MARESCHAL, le Conte. *TJ 178.*
MARESCHALL, Le Counte. *SD 21.*
MARSHALL, Counte. *FK I 77.*
MOWBRAY, Anne. *Sandford 415. (w of Ric, D of York, 2nd s of Edw 4; Brotherton coat assumed by Mowbrays in preference to their own).*
MOWBRAY, D of Norf. *CRK 1367. (prob Jn, d1461).*
[MOWBRAY], D of Northfolk. *BR II 30.*
MOWBRAY, John de, D of Northfolke. *RH,*

Ancestor iv 226.

MWBRAY, John, E.M. *Leake.* c1421. *(KG, d1432).*

MOWBRAY, le Conte Maryschall, Sr de. *S 33. (qtg Mowbray Gu lion Arg).*

[MOWBRAY], le Duc de Northfolk. *BW 5, 18.*

MOWBRAY, Thomas, Ld. *ML I 53. (inherited from Brotherton).*

NORFOLK, D of. *PLN 59.*

NORFOLK, Thomas, E of. *Sandford 205.*

NORFOLKE, Dewke of. *WB IV 128, 42.*

NORTHFOLKE, Duke of. *AY 101.*

NORTHFOLKE, D of. *PCL IV 82.*

SURREY, D of. *KB 237.*

Gu 3 lions pg Or label of 5 Untinc

LANCASTER, Edmund, E of. *Neale & Brayley.* *(d1296; charges modelled in gesso, painted & gilded).*

Gu 3 lions pg Or label of 5 Arg

— *FK I 80. (qtg 2&3 Hastings & Valence qtly).*

BROTHERTON, Thomas de. *FK I 65. (5th s of Edw I).*

MOUBRAY, of Kent. *MY A2 233. (no name in original).*

MOWBRAY. *Nichols Leics III 412 pl 61. (hatched sl of Mgt [M], Duchess of Norf).* •

MOWBRAY. *BB 27. ('contte de Marschall' Joh'n, duc de norfolke' (d1432)).*

[MOWBRAY], E.M. *WGA 29. ('Brotherton' added in later hand).*

MOWBRAY, Thomas, Ld. *S 35.*

MOWBRAY, Sir Thomas, E of Nottingham. *WGA 211.*

NORFOLK, Mgt, Duchess of. *Sandford 122 & 207. (d1399).*

NORFOLKE, the D of. *BK 54. (bar Gu in chf).*

Gu 3 lions pg Or label Az &c

Gu 3 lions pg Or label Az

— *WJ 43. (Prince of Wales).*

AUNFOUR, Sire. *D b.*

EDEWARS, le fielz le Roy. *K 66.*

EDMUND, Sire. *HE 35.*

EDMUND, Sire, frere le Roy. *FW 52.*

EDMUND, Sire, frere le roy. *LM 33.*

EDWARD, le fitz le Rey. *B 2; J 2.*

GALES, le Prince de. *CKO 442. (banner).*

LANCASTER, Duke of. *WB II 48, 12.*

LANCASTER, E of. *PLN 48.*

LANCASTER, Seinte Thomas de. *WJ 26.*

LANCASTER, Thomas of. *XL 2.*

LANCASTER, Thomas, E of. *XL 290. (d1322).*

LANCASTRE, Counte de. *PO 5.*

LANCASTRE, Cunte de. *E 5.*

MARESCHALL, Comes. *LMRO 20b, 48. (Thos de Brotherton).*

WALES, Edward, Prince of. *K 408. (afterwards Edw II).*

Gu 3 lions pg Or label of 5 Az

DENGLETERRE, le fitz Eyre le Roy. *SP A 10.*

ENGLAND, le Prince. *Q 2.*

Gu 3 lions pg & label Or

ENGLAND, D of Cornwall. *XL 3.*

3 lions pg label charged

3 lions pg on label unident charges

HOLAND, Elizabeth. *BarronMS AS 19.* 1395. *(w of Jn H, E of Huntingdon; imp by Engld & border of France).*

Gu 3 lions pg Or label Arg each pt ch with eagle Gu

MOUBRAY, Mons Thos. *S 79. (qtg 2&3 Gu lion Or label Az).*

MOWBRAY, Thomas. *S 81. (qrs 1&4).*

3 lions pg label semy de lis

3 lions pg label each pt ch with fleur de lis

LANCASTER, Henry, D of. *Bow 12.*

LANCASTER, Thomas, E of. *Birch 6332.* +S' THOME.....IS: LAN.....IE: LEYCESTRIE: ET: FERRARIIS. *(E of Lancs, Leics, Derby, Lincoln & Ferrers; equestr sl obv).*

Gu 3 lions pg Or label each pt ch with fleur de lis Untinc

LANCASTER, Aveline, Ctess of. *Neale & Brayley.* 13 cent. *(d1273).*

Gu 3 lions pg Or label each pt ch with 2 fleurs de lis Untinc

[LANCASTER, Edmund, E of]. *Neale & Brayley.* 1324.

Gu 3 lions pg Or label Arg each pt ch with 2 fleurs de lis Or

LANCASTIRE, D of. *BR II 29.*

Gu 3 lions pg Or label Az each pt ch with 2 fleurs de lis Or

LANCASTER, Edmund, E of. *FC II 93.*

LANCASTER, Henry, E of. *FC II 95.*

LANCASTER, Henry, D of. *FC II 98.*

3 lions pg label each pt ch with 3 fleurs de lis

LANCASTER, Henry, E of. *Farrer II 68. (on figure, Elsing Ch, Norf).*

LANCASTER, Henry, D of. *Birch 12676.* SIGLLL HENRICI DVCIS LANCASTR'. 1351-62. *(E of Derby, Leicester & Lincoln, Seneschal of Engld).*

LANCASTER, Henry, D of. *Sandford 102 & 112. (d1361-2).*

LANCASTER, Henry, 4th E of. *Birch 12675.* SIGILLVM HENRICI COMITIS LANCASTRIE. 1345-51.

LANCASTER, Thomas, E of. *Birch 6331; Sandford 102.* SIGILLVM: THOME: COMITIS: LANCASTRII...EYCESTRIE: SENESCALLI: ANG'LIE. post 1307. *(E of Lancs, Leicester, Derby, Lincoln & Ferrers, Steward of Engld;*

equestr sl obv).
LANCASTER, Thomas, 2nd E of. *Birch 12718.*
S' THOME COMI........TRIE. 1314.
PLANTAGENET, Edmond. *Birch 12665.*
...DM...IS ANGLIE D(N)S MONEM .... 1283. *(E of
Lanc, Leics, Derby & Champagne, Ld of
Monmouth, Steward of Engld, 'Crouchback',
2nd s of Hen 3, d1256).*
[PLANTAGENET], Thomas, E of Lancaster.
Bow XXXII 22. 1302-3.

Gu 3 lions pg Or label Az each pt ch with 3
fleurs de lis Or
ENGLAND, Q Anne Bullen. *Sandford 487.
(qr 1).*
LANCASTER. *XL 292. (?Hen, cr D of Lan-
caster in 1351, d1362).*
LANCASTER, Blanch of. *Sandford 249. (w of
Jn of Gaunt).*
LANCASTER, Dame Blanch of. *BA 1062.
(imp by Jn of Gaunt).*
LANCASTER, D of. *AY 95. (a&l Az).*
[LANCASTER, Edmund, E of]. *Neale & Bray-
ley. 1296. (canopy of Mont).*
LANCASTER, Thomas, E of. *D4 43b.*
LANCASTER, Thomas, E of. *Sandford 107.
(eldest s of Edmond 'Crouchback').*
LANCASTRIE, Comes. *SM 38, 421.*
LANGCASTUR, D of. *PCL IV 78.*

3 lions pg label semy de lis
CROUCHBACK, Edmund, E of Lancaster.
Lawrance 37. 1296. *(younger s of Hen 3;
tomb, Westm Abbey).*
ENGLAND, Q Anne Boleyn. *I2(1904)17. (qtg
2; Angouleme, 3; Guyenne, 4; Butler &
Rochfort qtly, 5; Brotherton, 6; Warren; all
imp by France modern & Engld qtly).*
LANCASTER, E of. *WNS 25, 11. ('Le Contee
de Lancastre porte les armes denglete un
label de France').*
LANCASTER, Edmund, E of. *HB-SND.
(d1296).*
LANCASTER, Henry, E of. *PRO-sls Anc
Deeds L 982.* 1338.
LANCASTER, Henry, E of. *Birch 12680.*
1347. *(cr D of Lancs 1351).*
LANCASTER, Henry, D of, E of Derby &c.
PRO-sls. 1356-7.
LANCASTER & Leicester, Henry, E of. *PRO-
sls.* 1329-30 & 1333-4.
LANCASTER, Thomas, E of. *Barons Letter
58a & 58b, HB-SND.*
LANCASTER, Thomas, E of. *Durham-sls
1537.* 1298.
LANCASTERE, ...of. *CT 2. (?Edmund, 2nd s
of Hen, E of Lancaster 1267-96).*

Gu 3 lions pg Or label Az semy de lis Or
EDMUND, Sire, frere le Rey. *G 26.*
HUNTYNGTON, John, E of. *BA 1067.*
LANCASTER, le Conte de. *GA 201.*

LANCASTER, le Conte de. *J 7.*
[LANCASTER]. *Neale & Brayley. (qr 1 of
coat imp by qtly France modern & Engld;
mont erected 1606 to Qus Eliz & Mary).*
LANCASTER, D of. *RH, Ancestor iii 199.
(1st assumed by Edm, 2nd s of Hen 3, 1267-
96).*
LANCASTER, Edmund, E of. *CRK 261.*
LANCASTER, Edmund Crouchback, E of.
LMS 19. (1267-96, or his s Thos).
LANCASTER, Edmund, frere du roy, Conte de.
P 43.
LANCASTER, Henry of. *XL 9.*
LANCASTER, Henry, D of, KG. *WGA 10.*
LANCASTER, Henry, 1st D of. *XK 9.*
LANCASTER, Thomas, E of. *BR V a 5.
(d1322).*
LANCASTER, Thomas Plantagenet, E of. *K
461.*
LANCASTRE, Erle of. *BR IV 74.*
LANCASTRE, le Conte de. *L 92.*
LANCASTRE, le Conte de. *AS 23.*
LANCASTRE, le Counte de. *N 5.*
LANCASTRE, le Duc de. *AN 1.*
LANCASTRE, D of. *WJ 45.*
LANCASTRE, Esmond fitz du roy, Conte de.
TJ 173.
LANCASTRE, Thomas Counte de. *H 51a.*
LANGCASTRE, Thomas de. *K 73-4.*
LONCASTRE, Sr Thomas le Counte de. *H
51b. ('...enchecun lable 3 floures de lyz
d'or').*

Gu 3 lions pg Or label of 5 Az each pt ch with
fleur de lis Or
ENGLAND, Wm, E of Boulogne & Martain.
FC I 19. c1412.
MORETON, John, E of. *FC I 63.* c1412.

3 lions pg label of 5 each pt ch with 3 fleurs de
lis
LANCASTER, Thomas, E of. *Birch 6331;
Sandford 102.* SIGILLVM: THOME: COMITIS:
LANCASTRIE...YCESTRIE: SENESCALLI: ANGLIE.
post 1307. *(E of Lancs, Leics, Derby, Lincoln & Ferrers, Steward of Engld).*

Gu 3 lions pg Or label of 5 Az each pt ch with 3
fleurs de lis Or
BOULOGNE & Mortain, Wm, E of. *FC I 4-6.
(s of Stephen, K of Engld).*
ENGLAND, Edmond of. *Sandford 102. (2nd s
of Hen 3).*
ENGLAND, Wm, E of Warenne, Boulogne &
Mortain. *FC II 91.*
LANCASTER, The Duc. *WB IV 128b, 50.*
LANCASTER, Comes. *L9 34a, 2.*
LANCASTER, Edmund, E of. *Keepe.*
EDMUNDUS COMES LANCASTRIAE. 15 cent.
(painted sh now defaced).
LEYCESTRE, le Cosyn le Roy de. *SP A 30.*
MORTAIN & Boulogne, Stephen, E of. *FC I*

1.
3 lions pg label of 5 semy de lis
 LANCASTER, Thomas of. *Lawrance 37.*
 1296. *(s of Edm Crouchback, E of Lancs,
 who d1296; tomb, Westm Abbey).*

England & France qtly label
Qtly 1&4 Gu 3 lions pg Or 2&3 Az semy de lis
 Or over all label Arg
 ENGLAND. *Brit Arch Assoc xxxiv 22.*
 c1400-20. *(Hen 5 as Prince of Wales; 'Scu-
 tum He'r'ci p'is Wallie'; nave ceiling, St
 Alban's Abbey).*
Qtly 1&4 Gu 3 lions pg Or 2&3 Az semy de lis
 Or over all label Arg each pt ch with 3 roun-
 dels Gu
 PLANTAGENET, Isabel. *Sandford 385-6. (dau
 of Ric, E of Cambridge & w of Hen Bour-
 chier, E of Essex).*
 YORK, D of. *BR II 25.*
 YORK, D of. *Brit Arch Assoc xxxiv 23, 28.*
 c1400-20. *('Scutum duci Eboraci'; nave ceil-
 ing, St Alban's Abbey).*
 YORK, Edmund, D of. *Keepe; Neale & Bray-
 ley.* 1431. *(mont to Philippa, Duchess of
 Kent, St Nicholas Chapel).*
Qtly 1&4 Gu 3 lions pg Or 2&3 Az semy de lis
 Or label Untinc ch on fillet with 5 roundels
 & on each pt with 2 roundels Gu
 YORK, [Richard], le Duke de. *BW 5, 17.
 (qrs I & IV).*
Qtly 1&4 Gu 3 lions pg Or 2&3 Az semy de lis
 Or over all label Erm
 CLARENCE, D of. *BR II 20. (label does not
 quite reach edges).*
 LANCASTER, D of. *Brit Arch Assoc xxxiv 22,
 28.* c1400-20. *('Scutu ducis Lancastrie';
 nave ceiling, St Alban's Abbey).*
Qtly 1&4 Gu 3 lions pg Or 2&3 Az semy de lis
 Or over all label of 5 per pale Az and Erm
 BEDFORD, D of. *BR II 24.*

3 BEASTS (OTHER) & LABEL
Sa 3 greyhounds Arg collared Gu label Gu
 WYGGEMORE. *CC 229b, 251.*

3 BEASTS & IN BASE
Per fess in chf per chev Or and Az 3 lions counterch in base Sa fess wavy Or semy of
 martlets Sa
 BRITAIN, K Urstull. *KB 80.*

3 BEASTS & CANTON
3 lions on canton fret
 BOKELAND, John de. *PRO-sls.* 1361-2. *(2
 oak trees on either side of shield).*
 BUCKLAND, Matilda de. *Birch 4337.* 1376.
 (Abbess of Wilton, Wilts).
 WROTHE, John, Kt. *PRO-sls.* 1403-4.
3 lions canton ch with mullet above cresc
 ?source.
 LYNN, John. c1250. *(sl penes HL Bradfer
 Lawrence; s of Gilbert of Lynn).*
Untinc 3 lions 2, 1 Untinc canton Erm
 FORSTEBURI, Henry de. *Birch 9881.* S' HENRI
 DE FORSTESBVRI. 14 cent.
Az 3 lions 1, 2 Arg canton Erm
 SCHENNE, of Schepay, Kent. *MY 196.*
Gu 3 lions Arg canton Sa fretty Or
 BOKELAND, Monsire John. *AN 175.*
 BOKELANDE. *PT 219.*
 BUCKLAND. *Gerard 107.*

3 BEASTS (LIONS) & CHIEF

3 lions ramp & chf
Arg 3 lions & chf Gu
 YELVERTON. *L9 3b, 2.*
 YELVERTON. *WB IV 173, 847.*
Az 3 lions & chf Arg
 GRAS, Nicholas le. *HE 180.*
 GRAS, Nichole le. *FW 222.*
Az 3 lions Or chf Arg
 GRAS. *ME 64; LY A 189.*
 GRAS, Nichole le. *A 74.*
 GRAS, Nichole le. *FW 222c.*

3 lions passt & chf
Arg 3 lions passt Sa chf Erm
 JENKENSONN. *L10 24, 9.*

3 lions gard &c & chf
3 lions gard & chf
 YELVERTON. *Farrer II 120-2. (in Rougham
 Ch, Norf).*
 [YELVERTON]. *Mill Steph.* 1516. *(imp by
 Palgrave; brass to Hy P & w Anne Flemham,
 Barningham Northwood, Norf).*

Arg 3 lions gard & chf Gu
    YELVERTON. *Suff HN 42.* (*'Mr Rowsse's Rolle'*).
Per chev Az and Or 3 lions pg in pale counterch chf Arg
    CATELYN. *L10 47b, 11.*
    CATLYN, Sir Robert, Lord Chief Justys. *L9 26b, 8.*
Arg 3 lions regard & chief Gu
    [ZELVERTON]. *SHY 231.* (*imp by Gleman*).
    [ZELVERTON]. *SHY 235.* (*imp Morley*).

3 BEASTS (OTHER) & CHIEF
Sa 3 rams Arg chf Or
    CHRISTMAS. *ML I 424.*

3 BEASTS (LIONS) & ON CHIEF
Az 3 lions Arg on chf Gu demi-lion Or
    GORE. *L1 279, 6; L2 224, 9.*
Az 3 lions Arg on chf Gu demi-lion isst Or
    GARE, Sir Simon atte. *CVK 712.*
    GORE. *XL 542.*
    GORE. *SK 602.*
Gu 3 lions Arg on chf Az demi-lion isst Or
    GAYE, S Simo, of Kent. *CY a 153, 612.*
Arg 3 lions 2, 1 & on chf Gu mullet Arg
    YELVERTON, of Norf. *PLN 1753.*
Gu 3 lions pg Or on chf Az Virgin & Child Arg
    [LINCOLN, See of]. *PLN 925.*
Gu 3 lions pg Or on chf Az Virgin & Child seated on throne Or
    [LINCOLN, See of]. *Stamford 38.*

3 BEASTS (OTHER) & ON CHIEF
Erm 3 stags passt Gu attired Or on chf indented per pale Or and Az cross formy counterch betw 2 roses dex Gu & sin Arg both seeded Ppr
    BLYTHE, Galfridus, Bp of Coventry & Lichfield. *L10 98b, 5.*
    BLYTHE, Bp of Lichfield. *BA 428.* (*imp by arms of See*).
Erm 3 roebucks stat Gu on chf indented per pale Or and Az cross paty betw 2 roses counterch
    BLYTHE. *XV II 47.*
3 talbots on chf lion passt
    TALBOT, Peter. *Stowe-Bard ls viii 4.*
    +SIGILLVM PETRI TALBOT. 1325-6.
3 ?rats courant on chf moon & estoile
    HARDHETHE, William de. *PRO-sls.* S'WILL'I HARDETHE. 1302-3.

3 BEASTS & IN CHIEF
Per pale Az and Gu 3 lions Arg in chf annulet Sa
    EASTNEY, Richard. *CRK 1017.* (*a&l Sa; annulet in honour pt*).
Per fess Gu and Az in base 3 lions Arg in chf demi-lion isst Or
    GORE. *XL 542.* (*as drawn*).
Erm 3 lions in chf estoile Gu
    HONDESACRE, William. *E II 474.* (*lions & estoile in later hand*).
Az 3 lions Arg in chf mullet Untinc
    JAYNKYN, Thomas, of Lawmy Angwell. *BA 19a.*
3 lions 2, 1 in chf 3 mullets of 6 pts
    MUIR, Reginald. *Stevenson.* 1330. (*Chamberlain of Scotland 1329-40*).

3 BEASTS & OVER ALL

3 lions & over all bend

3 lions ramp & bend
3 lions bend
    SIMEON, Percival. *PRO-sls.* 1304.
Gu 3 lions Arg bend Az
    FFITZ PAYNE. *PO 243.* (*Ffitz Payne written above an earlier name, now undecipherable, which perhaps began with W*).

3 lions passt & bend
3 lions passt bend
    BATALYE, Robert, of Sweningtone. *PRO-sls E40 A2852.* ante 1279.
    FITZ-Paeyn, Robert le. *Birch 9753.* S': ROBERTI: FIL'IL'...PAYN. 1335.
    FITZ PAYN. *PRO-sls.* 1528-9 & 1536-7. (*qtd 4 by Hen Algernon Percy, 6th E of Northd*).
    [FITZ PAYN]. *PRO-sls E40 A4104.* ALGERNUS PERCY COIT NO..ONBRIE HONORV DE COKERMUTH ET PETWOTH. 1528-9. (*qtd by Hen Algernon Percy, 6th E of Northd (1489-1527)*).
    FITZ PAYNE. *CT 102.*
    FITZ-payne. *Birch 12550.* 1527-37. (*qtd 4 by Hen Algernon Percy, 6th E of Northd, KG*).
    [FITZ-Payne]. *Birch 12786.* 1412. (*qtd 2&3 by Rob, 5th Baron de Ponynges, Kt*).
    FITZ PAYNE, Robert. *Barons Letter.*
    [FITZPAYNE]. *Coll T&G iii 258.* (*qtd 2&3 by Poynynges*).
    FITZPAYNE, Robert, Kt. *Vinc 88, 39.* 1319-20. (*sl; 'fil et heres dni Roberti fil Pagani quondam domini de Frampton'*).

FUIZ-Paien, Roberti. *Birch 9752.* S':
ROBERTI: FIL'IL'...PAYN. 1316.
PAGANI, Isabella. *Vinc 88, 39.* +Sigillum Isa-
belle .... 1319-20. *(4 armorial panels meeting
in centre in shape of cross; 'dna de
Frampton-super-Sabienam, uxor quondam dni
Roberti filii Pagani').*
Gu 3 lions passt Arg bend Az
— *WK 553. (qtd 4 by Percy).*
— *CRK 1306. (qtd II & III 2&3 by Percy).*
— *WGA 207. (qtd 4 by Hen Percy, 6th E of
Northd).*
— *D4 41b. (qtd by Percy).*
— *LEP 44. (qtd by Poynings).*
— *XF 569. (qtd 2&3 by Sir Edw Poynings).*
— *XF 741. (qtd 4 by [Percy]).*
— *XK 256. (qtd by Sir Wm Percy).*
— *LE 346. (qtd 2&3 by Ponynges).*
— *WGA 186. (qtd 4 by Hen Percy, E of
Northd).*
— *BW 9b, 54. (qtd 2&3 by Ld Ponynges).*
— *AY 51. (qtd 2&3 by Ld Ponyngs).*
— *T c 20. (qtd by Poynings).*
— *WK 138. (qtd 4 by E of Northd).*
— *WGA 266. (qtd 2 by Ponyng).*
— *WB I 37, 3. (qtd 2&3 by Ld Ponyngges).*
— *WB V 33. (qtd 2&3 by [Poynings]).*
— *XB 15. (qtd by Percy).*
[FITZ PAINE]. *Nichols Leics II 558. (Evington
Ch).*
FITZ PAYN. *DV 54a, 2128.*
FITZ PAYN, le Sr de. *AS 65.*
FITZ PAYNE. *I2(1904)258. (qtd 4 by Percy).*
FITZ PAYNE. *Gerard 36, 91.*
FITZ PAYNE. *CRK 1174.*
[FITZ PAYNE]. *Lambarde 210. (qtd by Percy
& imp by Howard; tomb of Thos, E of Arun-
del, Norfolk Chapel, Arundel, Suss).*
[FITZ PAYNE]. *Blair N I 100, 211. (qtd 4 [of
5] by Percy, 6th E of Northd; in Hexham
Priory, Northd).*
[FITZ PAYNE]. *RH, Ancestor iv 229. (qtd by
Ld Ponynges).*
FITZ PAYNE, Mons' John. *TJ 123.*
FITZ PAYNE, Monsire Robert. *CG 465.*
FITZ PAYNE, Robert. *XL 15.*
FITZ-Payne, Robert. *K 161.*
[FITZPAIN]. *WK 6. (qtd by Sir Ed Poy-
nynges).*
FITZPAINE. *Leake. (qtd 4 by Hen, E of
Northd).*
FITZPAYN. *PLN 108. (qtd 2&3 by Ld Poyn-
ings).*
FITZPAYN, Gloucs. *L2 195, 1. (a&l Sa).*
FITZPAYNE, Robert de. *XL 299.*
FIZPAEN, le. *CKO 447.*
FIZPAIN, Sr R. *RB 29.*
PAIEN, Robert le fiz. *K 19.* ('rouge a pas-
sans lyons de blanc trois de un baston bleu

surgettez').
PAIN, Sire Roberd le fiz. *N 77.*
PAIN, Sire Robert le fitz. *J 119.*
PAIN, Robert le fiz. *H 67a.*
PAINE, Roberd fitz. *G 69.*
PAYN, Monsire le filtes. *AN 48.*
PAYN, Sr le fitz. *H 67b.*
PAYNE, le Fiz. *SP A 98.* temp Edw 1.
PEYNE, Mons Robt le fitz. *WJ 181.*
Gu 3 lions passt Arg bend Gu
— *XK 90. (qtd 4 by Hen Percy, E of
Northd, KG 1531).*

3 lions gard & bend
3 lions pg bend
— *PRO-sls.* 1351. *(on sl of Hen de Walton,
Archdeacon of Richmond & keeper of King's
Wardrobe).*
DERBY, E of. *CVL 324.*
FITZPAYN, Robert. *PRO-sls.* S' ROBERTI FIL
PAGANI. 1367-8.
FITZPAYNE, Robert. *Bow 13.* 1288.
LANCASTER, Henry, E of Derby. *PRO-sls
Anc Deeds L 983, HB-SND.* 14 cent.
LANCASTER, Henry, E of Derby. *PRO-sls.*
1341-2.
LANCASTER, Henry de, Ld of Monmouth.
PRO-sls. 1301.
LANCASTER, Henry de, Ld of Monmouth, 1st
Baron. *Birch 11211.* +S' HENRICI.DE
LANCASTIR.DOMIN[I.D]E.MONEMVTA. 1301.
LANCASTER, Henry of, Ld of Monmouth.
Barons Letter. (bro of E Thos, d1345).
LANCASTRE, E of. *CT 22.*
LANCASTRE, Henry de, 1st Baron (?). *Birch
11213.* [SIG]IL.LUM.H.ENRI.CI.DE.LANCA.STRE.
*(Kingsford deletes '1st Baron' & substitutes
?3rd E of Lancaster).*
LANCASTRIA, Henry de, 9th E of Derby.
Birch 11212. +S' HENRICI.DELANCASTRIA.-
COMITIS.DERBYE.. 1337-45.
LANCASTRIE, Henry of, E of Derby. *Arch
Journ x 329.* S' HENRICI LANCASTRIE COMITIS
DERBYEY. *(sl found 1810 near 'the Green
Man' on Lincoln Heath, 9 miles S of Lin-
coln).*
LEIC', Henry de, Ld of Monmouth &
Beaufort. *PRO-sls.* 1322.
PAGANI, Robert, Ld of Lammer, 1st Baron
Fitz-Payne. *Birch 9751.* +S'ROBERTI
FIL'PAGANI. 1301. *(bend narrow).*
PLANTAGENET, Henry. *Lawrance 37.* 1296.
*(younger s of Thomas, E of Lancaster; tomb,
Westm Abbey).*
POINYNGES, Robert, Ld of. *CombeAsp II
184.* Sigillum Roberti domini de Poinynges.

Gu &c 3 lions pg & bend

Gu 3 lions pg Arg bend Az
— *WB II 52, 9. (qtd 2&3 by Ponyngh).*

Gu 3 lions pg Or bend Az
DARBY, le Count de. *CG 461. (baston).*
DERBY. *PLN 36. (baston).*
DERBY, Count de. *WJ 49. (Hen of Lancaster).*
DERBY, Cunte de. *CN 34. (baston).*
DERBY, le Conte de. *CKO 443. (banner; baston).*
JOHN LACKLAND. *Dingley cccxxxv. (Tewkesbury Abbey).*
LANCASTER, Cunte de. *F 40.*
LANCASTER & Derby, Henry, E of. *CRK 259. (baston).*
LANCASTER, Mons Henri de. *SD 19. (baston).*
LANCASTER, Sir Henri (of). *BR IV 99. (bend narrow).*
LANCASTER, Sire Henri de. *J 17. (baston).*
LANCASTER, Henry E of. *Inventory.* 1296. *(mont to Edm, E of Lancaster).*
LANCASTER, Henry of. *K 466. (baston).*
LANCASTER, Henry, E of. *Sandford 109.* 1345. *(bend narrow; E of Leics, Derby & Provence, Ld of Monmouth & Steward of Engld).*
LANCASTER, S Henry de. *GA 211. (baston).*
LANCASTER, Sir Henry of. *BR V 3. ('croste azure').*
LANCASTER, Henry, D of. *CA 62. (baston).*
LANCASTRE, le fitz, Le Sr de. *AS 58. (bend a baston).*
LANCASTRE, Henri. *K 73-4. ('portoit les armes de son frere au bleu bastoun sanz le label').*
LANCASTRE, Sire Henri de. *N 20. (baston).*
LANCASTRE, Henry. *TJ 179. (frere a Thomas, Conte de Lancastre).*
LANCASTRE, Henry de. *SP A 93. (bend narrow).*
LANCASTRE, Henry de. *H 53a. (baston).*
LANCASTRE, Sr Henry de. *H 53b. (baston).*
MONMOUTH, Henry of. *Neale & Brayley. (2nd s of Crouchback; bend narrow; Mont to Aveline of Lancaster, d1273).*

Gu 3 lions pg Or bend Sa
DERBY, E of. *XL 10.*
DERBY, C of. *XL 297.*

Sa 3 lions pg Or bend Gu
— *XL 597.*

3 lions regard & bend

Arg 3 lions passt regard coward Gu bend Az
WALES. *WB I 23b, 5. (baston).*

3 lions & over all bend patterned

Gu 3 lions passt Arg bend gobony Or and Az
FITZPAYN. *L9 101b, 10.*
PAYN, Sire Robert le. *N 879. (baston).*

Gu 3 lions pg Or bend Az semy de lis Arg
LANCASTER, E of. *ML I 4.*

3 lions and over all bend charged

Gu 3 lions Arg on bend Az 3 mullets Or
PALLY. *L1 502, 1.*
STRATTON, S' Walter Pauly. *PO 246.*

Gu 3 lions Arg on bend Az fimbr Or 3 mullets Or
PALLY. *L9 97b, 3.*

Gu 3 lions passt Arg on bend Sa 3 stags' heads cab Or
BECHE. *L10 26, 9.*
BECHE, John de. *XL 300.*
BECHE, John de. *XL 16.*
BECHE, Mons John de. *WJ 174.*

Gu 3 lions passt Arg on bend Untinc 3 mullets Or
PAVELY, Monsire Walter de. *CG 466.*

Gu 3 lions passt Arg on bend Az 3 mullets Or
GIFFARD, 'de Paules'. *XL 301.*
PAULES, Mons G de. *XL 18.*
PAULY. *L9 98b, 11.*
PAULY. *PT 127.*
PAULY, Monsire Walter de. *AN 280.*
PAVELEY, Mons G de. *WJ 183.*
PAVELI, S' Wat'. *R 95.*
PAVELY. *CKO 451.*
PAVILLY, Mons Wauter de. *AS 435.*
PAWLYE. *DV 68b, 2712.*

3 lions & over all crozier &c

Gu 3 lions pg Or over all crozier in pale crook to sin Arg
VALERYAL, Abbot of. *CVC 592.*

Gu 3 lions pg Or each with crosslet Or betw forepaws over all crozier in pale Arg headed Or
VALE ROYAL ABBEY. *L10 67b, 24.*

Gu 3 lions pg Or dimid by 3 hulks of ships Arg over all in pale crozier erect Arg head Or
FAVERSHAM ABBEY. *L10 67, 19.*

Gu 3 lions pg Or over all escarbuncle of 8 rays Az
NORMANDY, Robert 'Courthose', D of. *XL 294.*

Gu 3 lions pg over all escarbuncle Or
ELTHAM, John of. *XL 6.*
NORMANDY, Robert 'Courthose'. *WJ 47.*

3 lions over all fess checky
STEWART, Alex, Bp of Ross. *Stevenson 161.*

Arg 3 lions passt Sa over all fretty Az
ALWEN. *L1 26, 2; L2 14, 3. (qtg per pale Or and Az 3 eaglets counterch).*

ALWEN, Nich. *LD 114. (qrs 1&4).*
Gu 3 lions pg Or over all sword erect Ppr hilt
  Gu pomel & quillons Or
  LONGSPEE, Dame Maud. *PLN 1156.*

3 lions over all ... & label
Gu 3 lions pg Or bend Sa label Arg
  MARSHALL, Count. *XL 296.*
  MOWBRAY, John, E Marshall. *XL 8.*
Gu 3 lions pg Or bend Untinc label Arg
  MARCHALE, Mons John Counte. *WJ 51.*

3 lions over all ... & in chief
3 lions bend & canton
  BATELSFELD, Thomas de. *PRO-sls.* 1329.
  (baston).

3 BEASTS (LIONS) BETWEEN
Sa 3 lions ramp betw 2 bends Arg
  BROWNE, of Surr. *L1 44, 5.*
Untinc 3 lions passt betw 2 bends Sa
  HAWTRE, Joh'n. *LO A 23. (bastons).*
Arg 3 lions passt betw 2 bends Arg [sic]
  BROWNE, Sir Anthony. *WK 80. (qrs 1&4,
  cresc Arg in centre of qrs).*
Sa 3 lions passt betw 2 bends Arg
  BROWN. *LE 135.*
  BROWNE. *L10 76b, 6.*
  BROWNE, Sir Anthony. *PLN 2010.*
  BROWNE, Sir Anthony, KG, d1548. *Leake.
  (qtly with Fitzalan-Maltravers & 6 other
  qtgs).*
  CARNET, Nycholas. *RH, Ancestor vii 214.*
Arg 3 lions pg betw 2 bends Gu
  [KEKEWICH]. *BA 1028.*
  PATRICK, Ric', of Galles. *L10 112b, 12.
  (a&l Gu).*
Gu 3 lions ramp Arg betw 2 bends gobony Arg
  and Az
  — *D4 37. (qtd 2&3 by Borton).*
Sa 3 lions ramp betw 2 bends engr Arg
  BROWN, of Kent. *L2 42, 10.*
  BROWN, Sir Thomas. *WB IV 153, 491.*
  BROWN, William. *BG 75.*
  BROWNE, George. *PLN 786.*
3 lions passt betw 2 bends engr
  BROWNE. *Arch Cant ii 108.* c1512. *(imp by
  Fogge; brass, formerly in Ashford Ch, to
  Thos F & w Eleanor B).*
3 lions ramp betw 4 bends
  BROWNE, Sir Anthony, KG. *WB I 8, 2.*
Arg 3 lions ramp betw 4 bends Sa
  HAWTRE. *WB II 58, 13. (imp Blaknall).*

Sa 3 lions passt betw 4 bends Arg
  BROWN, Sir Anthony. *Sandford 342.*
Sa 3 lions passt betw 4 bends Arg (outer bends
  engr on outer edge)
  BROWNE. *L10 77b, 7.*
Arg 3 lions 2, 1 Gu betw 3 crosslets 1, 2 Sa
  — *L10 23b, 2. (qtd 2 by Baret).*
3 lions betw 6 crosslets fitchy
  GAY. *Mill Steph. (qtg lion, mullet for diffce
  in dex chf; brass to Christopher G, Elmsted,
  Kent).*
  GAY. *Belcher II 46; Mill Steph.* 1507. *(qtg
  Bewberry & imp lion, estoile for diffce in dex
  chf; brass to Christopher G & wives Agnes &
  Johan, Elmsted, Kent).*

3 BEASTS (OTHER) BETWEEN
Arg 3 boars passt 2, 1 Sa betw 3 crosses formy
  in pale Gu
  BOTELER. *L10 80, 7.*

3 BEASTS IN ORLE OF
Az 3 lions pg Arg orle of roundels Or
  LODELOWE. *FK a 481.*

3 BEASTS BETW ... & IN CHF
Sa 3 lions betw 2 bends engr Arg in sin chf
  eagle's head erased Or
  BROUNE, Tomas, Kent. *MY A2 195.*
Sa 3 lions betw 2 bends engr Arg in sin chf
  griffin's head erased Or
  BROUNE, Tomas, Kent. *MY 195.*
  BROWN, Thomas, of Kent. *WB III 110, 3.*
  BROWNE, Sir T. *CRK 1607.*
  BROWNE, Thomas. *Kent Gentry 217b, 397.*

3 BEASTS IN BORDER

3 Lions in plain border

3 lions ramp in plain border
3 lions & border
  CHICCHE, Thomas, of the Isle of Thanet,
  Kent. *Birch 8567.* SIGILL': THE: DE: BOY....
  1418.
  VACHE, Philip la, Kt. *PRO-sls.* 1391.
Arg 3 lions Gu border Sa
  KIRKHAM, Nichol de. *F 195.*
  KIRKHAM, William de. *E I 564; E II 566.*

KYRHAM, Nicol de. *WLN 615.*
Az 3 lions & border Arg
— *D13 18d. (qtd by Kempe).*
CHICHCHE, John. *CVK 709.*
CHICHE. *CY 152, 608.*
CHICHE. *WB I 17b, 6.*
Per pale 3 lions & border
HERBERT, William, E of Pembroke.
BrookeAsp I 73. c1617.

3 lions passt in plain border
Gu 3 lions passt Arg border Or
GIFFARD, Elis. *A 157.*
GYFFARD, Elys. *FW 201.*
Gu 3 lions passt Or border Arg
— *PLN 1936. (qtd 2 by Nevill).*

3 lions gard in plain border
3 lions pg border
BROMFLET, Joanna. *Birch 7842.* S: IOH, :
DUCISSE: EBORA..: ET: COMITISSE: CANTERBR.
1434. *(imp Engld & France qtly for
Johanna, dau of Thos Holand, E of Kent, w
of Hen B, Chevr, & wid of Edm, D of York;
supporters: dex eagle, sin bear).*
HOLAND, Johanna de. *Birch 10766.*
S'IOHANNE: COMITISSE: ..: DNI: DE: WAKE.
1437. *(imp chev [Stafford]; dau of Hugh, E
of Stafford & w of Thos de H, 3rd E of Kent,
Lady of Wake).*
HOLAND, Sir Thomas. *Antiq Journ ii 144.
(2nd s of Sir Ric de H, used after his marr
with Joan of Kent).*
HOLAND, Thomas de, E of Kent. *Birch
10774.* SIGILLUM THOME DE HOLAND COMITIS
...... *(shield on shldr of hind lodged ducally
gorged).*
HOLAND, Thomas de, E of Kent. *Birch
10773.* 1381-97.
HOLAND, Thomas, [E of Kent]. *HB-SND.*
HOLAND, Thomas, E of Kent. *PRO-sls E40
A3209.* SIGILLUM....HOLAND. 1380-1.
HOLLAND. *PRO-sls.* c1525. *(qtd III 1 by
Manners, E of Rutland).*
HOLLAND. *Mill Steph.* c1470. *(tierced in
pale with Tiptoft in dex & Charleton in sin;
brass to Joyce C, Lady T, Enfield, Middx).*
HOLLAND. *Mill Steph.* c1470. *(qtd 2&3 by
Charleton; brass to Joyce, Lady Tiptoft,
Enfield, Middx).*
HOLLAND, Lucy, Ctess of Kent. *PRO-sls.*
1412.
HOLLAND, Thomas, D of Surrey. *Bow XL 2.*
1399. *(imp by cross formy betw 5 martlets).*
HOLLAND, Thos, E of Kent, d1397.
Durham-sls 1489.
JULERS, Elizabeth, Ctess of Kent. *PRO-sls.*
1393-5. *(?lions gard).*
PLANTAGENET, Edmund, Baron of Wodstoke,

4th E of Kent. *Birch 12669.* S' EAD...DI FILII
EDWARDI...NGL... . 1321-30.
PLANTAGENET, Edmund, of Woodstock, E of
Kent. *Birch 12688.* 1380. *(imp by Joan
Plantagenet, Princess of Wales, w of Edw
(Black Prince), Duchess of Cornw, Ctess of
Chester & Kent, & Lady of Wake).*
PLANTAGENET, John, 3rd E of Kent. *Birch
12690.* SIGILL...IOHANNIS COMITIS K(A)NCIE.
1332-52.
PLANTAGENET, Margaret, Ctess of Kent.
Birch 12701. 1349. *(imp 2 bars in chf 3
roundels; dau of Jn, Ld Wake, & w of Edm
of Woodstock, E of Kent).*
STAFFORD, Humphrey, 6th E of. *Birch
13636.* c1450. *(E of Buckingham,
Northampton & Perche, Captain of the town
of Calais & Lieutenant of the Marches of
Picardy; qtd 2&3 [in border in qr 1] by
France Modern & qtg II Bohun, III Bohun of
Northampton, IV Stafford; qr 1 borne for
Thos of Woodstock).*
Per chev Az and Or 3 lions pg counterch border
Arg
CATELYN, of Raude, Northants. *L10 47b, 17.*
CATELYN, Rob, of Rands, Northants. *L10 91,
3.*

Gu 3 lions pg Or border Arg
Gu 3 lions pg Or border Arg
— *XK 83. (qtd 2 by Ralph Nevill, KG).*
— *XB 44. (qtd by Neville).*
— *PLN 1964.*
— *D4 29b. (qtd 4 by Nevill).*
— *XK 86. (qtd III 1 by Wm Fitz William,
KG).*
— *XK 84. (qtd III by Manners, KG).*
— *XL 23. (qtd II 1 by Dudley).*
— *BA 15b. (escutch of Ric, D of York).*
BROTHERTON, Sir Edmond. *BR V 2.*
[CLARELL]. *1H7 7d; D13 76. (qtd 3 by
Fitzwilliams).*
[HOLAND]. *FK I 79.*
HOLAND, C of Kent. *XL 295.*
HOLAND, Edmund, E of Kent. *FK I 54.*
HOLAND, Eleanor. *CR 7.*
HOLAND, Kent, E of. *XL 7.*
[HOLAND], E of Kent. *KB 240.*
HOLAND, Margaret. *Sandford 322 & 324. (w
of Jn Beaufort).*
HOLAND, Thomas. *Blair D I 65, 173. (E of
Kent, D of Surrey; qtg 2 Neville; E window
of Chancel, Staincrop Ch).*
HOLAND, Thomas, E of Kent. *DX 50.*
HOLAND, Thomas, E of Kent. *S 36.*
HOLLAND, Thomas, E of Kent. *WGA 198.*
HOLLAND, Edmond, E of Kent. *WGA 53.*
HOLLAND, Joan, of Kent. *Sandford 378.
(2nd w of Edm, D of York).*

HOLLAND, E of Kent. *Neale & Brayley.*
(imp by Beaufort; mont erected 1606 to Qus
Eliz & Mary, Hen 7 Chapel).
HOLLAND, E of Kent. *?source. 1530. (glass*
of Thos, E of Rutland, Enfield Ch, Middx).
HOLLAND, E of Kent. *Sandford 205.*
HOLLAND, Thomas, E of Kent. *GutchWdU.*
(imp Fitzalan & Warren qtly; formerly in N
Window old Chapel (demol 1620) Oriel
Coll).
JOAN OF KENT, Princess of Wales. *Sandford*
184. (imp by her husb Edward, 'Black
Prince').
KENT, Count de. *RH, Ancestor iii 213.*
KENT, Counte de. *PO 6.*
KENT, E of. *PLN 79.*
KENT, E of. *PLN 1153.*
KENT, E of. *WNS 25, 24.*
KENT, Le Conte de. *AS 27.*
KENT, le Conte de. *TJ 177.*
KENT, le Conte de. *S 34.*
KENT, le Conte de. *WJ 48.*
KENT, le Conte de. *AN 18.*
KENT, Edmon, E of. *Sandford 215.*
KENT, Edmond E of. *BB 41.*
KENT, Edmond E of. *Sandford 216.*
KENT, Thomas E of. *BB 121, 6.*
PLANTAGENET, (E of Kent). *Leake. (qtd III*
1 by Thos Manners, KG).
STAFFORD, Henry, E of Wiltshire, KG. *XB*
18. (qtd by France; d1523; qr 1, for
Edmund of Woodstock).
WODDESTOK, Sir Edmund (of). *BR IV 98.*

Gu 3 lions pg Or border Az

Gu 3 lions pg Or border Az
CESTRE, le Conte de. *AS 25.*
CHESTRE, Contee de. *TJ 181.*
EXETER, John, D of. *BA 1065.*
KENT, Erle off. *WB II 48, 13.*

3 lions in patterned border

3 lions in border Erm

Untinc 3 lions Untinc border Erm
BOTELEYR, Robert le?. *Birch 7638. 1303.*
BOTELYER, Robert le. *PRO-sls. 1303-4.*

3 lions ramp in border gobony

Sa 3 lions Arg border gobony Or and Arg
ENGLISH. *FK II 578.*

3 lions gard in border gobony

3 lions pg border gobony
— *PRO-sls. 1436-7. (qtd 2&3 by Edmund*
Beaufort, Count of Mortain).
BEAUFORT, Thomas, D of Exeter. *PRO-sls.*
1424-5. (qrs 2&3).

Gu 3 lions pg Or border gobony Az and Arg
BEAUFORT, D of Somerset. *SHY 5. (unclear*
whether border Az and Arg or Az and Erm).
Gu 3 lions pg Or border gobony Or and Gu
COURTNEY, E of Devonshire, 1st M of
Exeter. *L2 101, 1. (qr 1).*

3 lions gard in border per pale

Per pale Or and Gu 3 lions pg & border coun-
terch
WHITIPOLL. *XPat 222, Arch 69, 86.*
WITHYPOLE, Paul. *XL 476.*
[WITHYPOLE, Paul]. *XL 13.*
WYTHYPOLLE, Paule, de Loundres. *WK 782.*
WYTHYPOLLES, Polle. *WK 786. (imp Cuis-*
sac).

3 lions in border semy of birds

3 lions pg border semy of martlets
[TUDOR], Jasper, D of Bedford & Ld of Bergavenny. *Birch 6485.* (rev)Sigillum excellentissimi
principis iasperis ... patrui regum; (obv) D[ucis] bedfordie
comitis .....o.... dom ..... de bergevenny. *1485-95.*
(qrs 2&3 [1&4 France modern]).
[TUDOR], Jasper, E of Pembroke, [D of Bed-
ford]. *Birch 6483.* Sig[illum] domini jasparis comi-
tid penbrochie. *1459. (qrs 2&3 [1&4 France*
modern]).

3 lions passt in border semy de lis

3 lions passt to sin border semy de lis
WYDVILLE. *Arch Journ xlv 38. (dex shield,*
sin effaced, on sl of Lionel W, Bp of Salis-
bury, 1482-5).

3 lions gard in border semy de lis

3 lions pg border semy de lis
ELTHAM, John of, E of Cornwall. *Lawrance*
37. 1334. (effigy, Westm Abbey).
HOLAND. *Gerola 220. (15 cent shield,*
Bodrum, Asia Minor).
HOLAND, Elizabeth. *PRO-sls AS 19. 1394-5.*
(imp Lancaster; w of Jn H, E of Huntingdon).
HOLAND, Elizabeth. *BarronMS AS 19. 1395.*
(w of Jn, E of Huntingdon).
HOLAND, Henry de. *Birch 10757. 1455.*
(4th D of Exeter, E of Huntingdon & of
Ivory, Admiral of Engld, Irld & Aquitaine, Ld
Lespar, Constable of the Tower of London).
HOLAND, Henry, Duke of Exeter. *Ash-sls*
234. S' henrici ducis exone admiralli angl hiber acqui-
tanie. *(sail of a man of war; Admiral of*
Engld, Irld, Aquitaine).
HOLAND, John de. *Birch 10763. 1431. (E*
of Huntingdon, Captain of Gournay &
Gisors).
HOLAND, John de. *Birch 10764.* SIGILLUM:
IOH'IS: DUCIS: EXONIE: ...COMITIS: HUNTYNG-
DON: ...: YUERI: AC: DNI: DE SPARRE. *1445.*

(3rd D of Exeter, E of Huntingdon & of Ivory, Admiral of England, Irld & Aquitaine, Ld of la Sparre).

HOLAND, John, E of Huntingdon. *PRO-sls. 1392-5.*

HOLAND, John, E of Huntingdon. *PRO-sls E40 A3234.* SIGILLV....HOLAND COMITIS HVNTYNGDONE. 1389-90.

HOLAND, John, E of Huntingdon. *PRO-sls AS 19.* 1394-5. *(sl fragment).*

HOLAND, John, E of Huntingdon. *BarronMS AS 6.* 1395.

HOLAND, John, E of Huntingdon & D of Exeter. *Antiq Journ ii 144. (younger s of Sir Ric de H).*

HOLAND, John de, 1st D of Exeter. *Birch 10758.* SIGILL........... 1380-1.

HOLAND, John de, 1st E of Huntingdon. *Birch 10761.* ....HOLAND: COMITIS: HUN-TYNGDON: CO........ 1396.

HOLAND, John de, [1st or 2nd] E of Hunting-don. *Birch 10762.* SIGILL..........

[HOLLAND], John. *Bow XLIV 4.* 1443-7. *(D of Exeter, E of Huntingdon & Ivory etc, Constable of the Tower).*

HOLLOND, John, E of Hundon. *PRO-sls. 1437-40. (Admiral of Engld, Irld & Aquitaine).*

Gu 3 lions pg Or border Arg semy de lis Or
— *BA 1067. (qtd 2&3 by Jn, E of Hunting-don).*

[HOLAND, John]. *FK I 53. (11 lis in border).*

HOLLAND, John. *AG 56b. (14 lis in border).*

LANCASTER, Dame Elizabeth, Duchess of Exeter. *BA 1066. (imp Jn of Gaunt).*

Gu 3 lions pg Or border Az semy de lis Or
— *D4 29b. (qtd 2 by Nevill).*
— *?source. (in St Bennetts Ch, Huntingdon, 28 Aug 1613).*

CORNEWAILLE, Le Conte de. *TJ 180.*

CORNEWAILLE, le Conte de. *AS 24.*

CORNWALL, E of. *KB 236.*

CORNWALL, E of. *SD 1.*

CORNWAYLLE, Comes de. *WJ 45. (Jn of El-tham, cr 1330).*

ELTHAM, John of. *Keepe.* 1337. *(mont St Edmund's Chapel).*

EXCETERE, D of. *BR II 32.*

EXCETUR, D of. *PCL IV 77.*

EXCETYR, D[uke] of. *AY 100. (a&l B).*

EXETER, Duke of. *PLN 58.*

EXETER, D of. *BA 1075.*

EXETER, Henry, D of. *BA 1069.*

EXETER, John, D of. *BA 1068.*

HOLAND. *BB 31. ('Contte de Nontyngton' [Huntingdon]).*

HOLAND, C of Huntingdon. *XL 293.*

HOLAND, C of Huntingdon. *XL 5.*

HOLAND, D of Exeter. *CRK 1368. (either Jn*

d1446 or his s Hen d1473).

HOLAND, Henry, D of Exeter. *Sandford 219.*

HOLAND, Henry, D of Exeter. *Sandford 394. (imp Anne of York).*

HOLAND, E of Huntingdon. *KB 241.*

HOLAND, John de. *RH, Ancestor iii 200. (Erle of Hontyngeton).*

HOLAND, John, D of Exeter. *Sandford 258.*

HOLAND, John, D of Exeter. *DV 58a, 2281.*

HOLAND, John de, Deuke of Excestyr. *RH, Ancestor iv 225.*

HOLAND, Thomas, E of Huntingdon. *S 38. (8 lis in border).*

HOLLAND, Erle Huntington. *BW 5, 19.*

HUNTYNGDON, le Conte de. *S 36. (8 lis in border).*

PLANTAGENET, John. *Sandford 153. (2nd s of Edw 2).*

3 lions ramp in border semy of roundels

3 lions border semy of roundels

SALAMONIS, Petrus. *Durham-sls 2164. 1370-2.*

3 lions gard in border semy of roundels

3 lions pg border roundelly

CORNWALL, D of. *Blair N I 18, 40. (Edward the 'Black' Prince, as D of Cornw; beneath battlements of Bothal Castle).*

CORNWALL, Richard, E of. *BarronMS AS 22.* S' SECRETI: COMITIS: RICARDI. 1256-7.

Gu 3 lions pg Or border roundelly Az

O'NEIL, Baron of Inyscheroune Oneyle. *DIG 24.*

3 lions in border modified

3 lions ramp in border engr

3 lions & border engr

FITZ-Herberd, Johanna, of Rype Manor, Suss. *Birch 9727.* SIGILLU.IOH'NE FITZ.HERBERD. 1391. *(imp 3 clarions 2, 1).*

FITZHERBERD, Edmund, Chev, of Offyngton &c, Suss. *Birch 9724.* SIGILLU.EDMUNDI.-FITZ.HE......D. 1381. *(qtg 2&3 gyronny of 12 border roundelly).*

GLOUCESTER, Walter. *PRO-sls E40 A95.* ...ILEU.... 1308-9.

Arg 3 lions Gu border engr Az

GLOUCESTRE, Mousire de. *CG 550.*

Arg 3 lions Gu border engr Sa

KERKHAM, Syr John, of Blakedon, Devon. *I2(1904)243.*

KIRKHAM, of Blackadon, Devon. *L9 24, 8.*

KIRKHAM, Sir John, of Blackendon, Devon. *BA 1043.*

KYRHAM. *BA 1137.*

Gu 3 lions & border engr Arg
  PEVERELL. *LEP 30.*
Gu 3 lions Or border engr Arg
  FITZ HUERDE, Edmund. *BG 135.*
  FITZ HUGH, Edmond. *S 288.*
  HUGH, Mons Edmond fitz. *S 286.*
  PEUEREL. *L1 517, 2.*
  PEVEREL. *CRK 615.*
  [PEVERELL]. *Lambarde 263. (qtd 5 by West;
  Mont to Thos West, Ld La Warr, & w Eliz
  Bonville, Boxgrove, Suss).*
  REYNALD, Sire Reynald le fiz. *O 190.*
Gu 3 lions & border engr Or
  PEVEREL. *XL 580.*
Sa 3 lions Arg border engr Or
  [ENGLISH]. *FK II 757.*
Erm 3 lions Gu border engr Sa
  KYRKEHAM. *BA 1313.*
Untinc semy de lis 3 lions Or border engr Untinc
  — *H18 45. (qtd 8 by Copleston, of Coples-
  ton, Devon).*

3 lions passt in border engr
Or 3 lions passt Sa border engr Gu
  CAREW. *L10 40, 4.*
Or 3 lions passt & border engr Sa
  CAREW. *XL 36.*

3 lions in border indented
Arg 3 lions ramp Gu border indented Az
  GLOUCESTRE, Sire Walter de. *N 892; O 94.*
  GLOWCESTRE. *L2 226, 9.*
Arg 3 lions ramp Gu border indented Sa
  BELLEHOUS, Sire Willame de. *N 429.*

3 lions in border invected
3 lions pg border invected
  [ORIEL COLLEGE, Oxf]. *Birch 5270.* 15 cent.

3 beasts (other) in border
3 beasts passt 2, 1 border gobony
  ABBOT, Isabella. *Birch 6751.* 1362. *(wid of
  Ric Abbot, tailor, of Carshalton, Surr).*
  SWINHOE, Walter of. *PRO-sls KR 73/2, 22,
  HB-SND.* SIGILLUM WALTERI DE SWYNHOW.
  1379.
3 stags passt border
  GREEN. *Mill Steph.* 1523. *(qtd by Verney;
  brass, Compton Verney, Warws).*
Az 3 stags passt Or border Arg
  — *PLN 1294. (qtd 4 by Varney).*
Sa 3 goats courant & border engr Arg
  CHAMBER, Thomas. *WB IV 180b, 986.*
  CHAMBERS, Thomas. *PLN 525.*
Sa 3 goats courant Arg armed Or border engr
  Arg roundelly Sa
  STAMFFELD, Richard, of Shipley, Yorks. *BA
  741.*

3 swine border engr
Gu 3 conies & border engr Arg
  CONYNGSBY. *L10 37b, 11.*
3 wolves passt border roundelly
  KYMER, Gilbert, clerk. *Helyar 915.*
3 wolves passt regard border roundelly
  KEYMER, Dr Gilbert. *Helyar 915.*
  SIGILL'GILBERTI KEYMER DOCTORIS. 1439.

**3 BEASTS & IN BASE &c ... IN
BORDER**
3 lions in base mullet border semy of escallops
  ROSS, Hugh, of Rarichies, 1st of Blanagowan
  (Ld of Philorth). *Stevenson.* 1351. *(escal-
  lops or ermine spots).*
Arg 3 lions & chf Gu border engr Or
  — *CRK 1141.*
3 lions pg bend all in border semy de lis
  LANCASTER, Henry of. *Sandford 102.* 1305.
  (sl).

3 beasts impaling ... in border
Gu 3 lions pg to sin Or
  HOLAND, Lucy de. *Birch 10768.* ...KENT.
  *(imp Milan, with bordure Arg for Thomas of
  Woodstock; dau of Barnabas, D of Milan &
  wid of Edmund de Holand, E of Kent).*

3 beasts qtg ... in border

England & France qtly in border
Qtly 1&4 Gu 3 lions pg Or 2&3 Az 3 fleurs de
  lis Or border Arg
  GLOWCESTRE, Duke of. *BR II 23.*
  [STAFFORD], Duke of Bokyngham. *BR II 35.*
  (qtd 1 for 'Glowcestr').
Qtly 1&4 3 lions pg 2&3 3 fleurs de lis &
  border gobony
  BEAUFORT.
  RICHMOND, Margaret, Ctess of. *WestmAbb.
  (imp by Edm, E of Richmond on mont to his
  w Mgt; S Aisle, Hen 7 Chapel).*
Qtly 1&4 Gu 3 lions pg Or 2&3 Az 3 fleurs de
  lis Or border gobony Az and Arg
  BEAUFORT, D of Somerset. *BR II 27.*
Qtly 1&4 Gu 3 lions pg Or 2&3 Az 3 fleurs de
  lis Or border gobony Az and Erm
  BEAFORD, Marcus, M of Dorsett. *BR II 26.
  (last D of Exeter).*

3 BEASTS & ... & LABEL IN BORDER

Qtly 1&4 Gu 3 lions pg Or 2&3 Az 3 fleurs de
lis Or label & border Arg
    CLARENCE, Thomas, D of. *Brit Arch Assoc
xxxiv 22.* c1400-20. *(2nd s of Hen 4; 'Scutum dni thome filii regis'; Nave ceiling, St
Alban's Abbey).*

3 BEASTS (LIONS) IN TRESSURE

3 lions in tressure flory cf
    ROSS, Euphemia. *Stevenson.* c1370.
    ROSS, Wm, 5th E of. *Stevenson.* 1364.
Or 3 lions in double tressure flory cf Gu
    DILLES, le Conte. *Berry, Stodart pl 1. (field
should be Gu lions Arg & tressure prob Or;
E of Ross, Ld of the Isles).*
Gu 3 lions passt in double tressure flory cf Or
    — *WB I 42b, 17. (qtd 2 by Sir G Mas-
tyngges).*

4 BEASTS

4 beasts (lions)

4 lions
    FITZALAN, Richard, E of Arundel. *PRO-sls.*
1296-7.
    FRISE, William, Sire de. *Proc Soc Antiq II
2S 89.* SEEL WILLAUME SIRE DE FRISE.
(Count of Holland).
    [?HAINAULT]. *Proc Soc Antiq XXIV 2S 126.
('Square banner shaped shields'; on fragment
of brass which, M Stephenson says, may be
dated about 1360).*
    [HAINAULT]. *Birch 5271.* 1340. *(sl of
Queen's Coll, Oxf).*
Gu 4 lions Arg
    FREMONDE, Thomas. *WB III 90, 1.* (2, 2).
    FREMUND. *FK II 389.* (2, 2).
Gu 4 lions Or
    — *XX 105. (in cross; qtd 5 by Windsor).*
    BENTWORTH. *XL 569. (in cross).*
Or 4 lions 1&4 Gu 2&3 Sa
    HOLAND, Duke of. *LO B 62.*
Or 4 lions 1&4 Sa 2&3 Gu
    HAINAULT. *WLN 38.*
    HAINAULT, Philippa of. *Sandford 158. (w of
Edw 3).*
    HOLLONDE, Deuke of. *RH, Ancestor ix 177.*
    STRAVANT, William, E of. *WGA 153.*
Or 4 lions 1&4 Sa 2&3 in umbre
    HAINAULT. *ML I 538.*

Sa 4 lions 1&4 Or 2&3 Az
    MOUNT, de la. *ML I 521.*
Checky of 9 Arg and Az 4 lions Or on the Arg
    STOKLEY. *RH, Ancestor ix 174. (blazon
unclear).*

Qtly 4 lions

Qtly 4 lions
    GLYNDOUR, Owen. *Arch xxv 619.*
    GREY, Henry, E of Tankerville & Ld Powys.
Brit Arch Assoc xvii 77899.
    LYDD, Kent. *Birch 5143.* S COMMUNE
BARONU DOMINI REGIS ANGLIE DE LYDE. 13
cent.
    MAUNDEVILLE, Thomas de. *PRO-sls E40
A447. ... vill....* 1283-4.
    RETHERY, Thomas, of Surr. *Birch 12961.* S'
THOME RETHERY. 1357.
    WALES, ?Yenri? de. *Clairambault 3914.* 12
Aug 1376.
    WENTWORTH. *Mill Steph.* 1513. *(qtd 2&3
by Willoughby on brass to Hugh W & w
Anne Wentworth, Wilne, Derby).*
Per cross Or (sic) 4 lions 1&4 Gu 2&3 Sa
    HAINAULT, Count of. *PLN 582.*
Qtly Arg and Az 4 lions counterch
    PIPARD, of West Chinnock. *Gerard 85.*
    PIPARD, William. *XL 137.*
    PYPARD, Mons de. *WJ 284.*
Qtly Gu and Or 4 lions counterch
    AFFABELLUS, Sanctus. *L10 65b, 23. ('St
Amphibalus' added in later hand).*
Qtly Or and Az 4 lions counterch
    LUTTELEY. *?source. (glass, Enrike, Staffs).*
Qtly Or and Gu 4 lions counterch
    LLEWELIN AP GRIFFITH. *C 13. (?lions pg).*
    WALLYS, Prynce of. *PCL IV 72.*
    WALYS, Prince of. *BR II 22.*
    WALYS, Prince of. *AY 16.*
    WALYS, Prince off. *BA 15b.*
Qtly per pale & per chev Arg and Gu 4 lions
counterch
    LAURENCE, John. *CRK 1195.*

4 lions crowned

Checky of 9 Sa & Arg 4 lions Sa crowned Gu
    — *XC 259.*

4 lions passt

Qtly Arg and Az 4 lions passt counterch
    DAVID, frere of P of Wales. *LM 31.*
Qtly Gu and Or 4 lions passt counterch
    WALLIE, Princeps. *SM 23, 140.*
Qtly Or and Gu 4 lions passt counterch
    GALES, Prince de. *G 25.*
    GLADIUS. *PLN 1160. (dau of Prince of
Wales).*
    GRUFFYD. *MP IV 59. (s of Llywelyn, Prince
of Wales).*

WALEIS. *PO 598.*
WALES, David, Prince of. *MP IV 68.*
WALES, Prince of. *LM 30.*
WALES, Prince of. *NB 1.*

4 lions gard
Qtly 4 lions pg
WALES, Prince of. *SP A 22.*
Qtly Gu and Or 4 lions pg counterch
GALES, le Prince de. *TJ 172.*
GALES, le Prynce de. *WJ 361.*
GRIFFITH, William ap. *E II 7.*
Qtly Or and Az 4 lions pg counterch
DAVID AP GRIFFITH. *E I 26; E II 26.*
Qtly Or and Gu 4 lions pg counterch
GALES, Prince de. *D 28.*
GALES, le Prince de. *FW 27.*
GALLES, Prince de. *HE 22.*
GRIFFID, Th' lin ap. *E I 7.*
LLEWELIN AP GRIFFIN. *C 13.*
WALES. *WLN 64.*
WALES. *XB 33.*
Qtly Or and Az 4 lions stat gard counterch
DAVID AP GRIFFID. *L10 2, 7.*
Qtly Or and Gu 4 lions stat gard counterch
WALES, North. *I2(1904)22. (banner supported by wyvern).*

4 beasts (other)
Qtly Or and Az 4 stags stat counterch
LLOYD, Humphrey. *L9 46b, 4. ('Humphrey LLoyd fils Rossynhall Denbigh'; qr 1, all in narrow border Gu).*
Gu 4 conies Arg
— *ML I 240. ('gules iiii conys in quadrangyll comme parturyng sylver. Hyt may be called non urnell because yt goth nat about the feld. Yf the feld were vert theys conys myght be callyd pasturyng').*

4 beasts (lions) & ...
Gu 4 lions Or on canton Arg cresc Gu
— *RH, Ancestor ix 161.*
Az 4 lions 1, 2, 1 Arg canton Erm
CHEYNEY. *ME 84; LY A 209.*
Qtly Az and Gu 4 lions pg Or on chf indented Arg 3 roundels Sa
PERT. *XPat 220, Arch 69, 85.*
PERT. *L1 533, 3.*
PERT. *L9 106a, 11.*
PERT, Dr Thomas. *L10 73, 5.*
PERT, Dr Thomas. *BA 577.*
PERT, Dr Thomas. *WK 768.*
Qtly Gu and Sa 4 lions Or in chf crosslet formy fitchy Or
?COFFOL, of Kent. *L2 140, 9.*

Az 4 lions 1, 2, 1 & canton Erm border engr Or
LAYBURNE, Mons Rog' de. *WJ 290.*

5 BEASTS
Az 5 demi-lions Arg gutty Gu
NOWENHM. *L2 366, 1.*
Gu 5 lions 2, 2, 1 Arg
— *CC 230, 269. (qtd 2 by Beauchampe).*
Gu 5 lions in cross Or
— *WK 466. (qtd 5 by Wyndesore).*
— *I2(1904)181. (qtd 5 by Sir Andrew Wyndesere).*
— *D13 123d. (qtd 5 by Wyndesor).*
— *XK 104. (qtd 5 by Sir Andrew Windsor).*
BENTWORTH. *PLN 1949. (qtd by Sir Harry, Ld Windsor & imp by Sir Ric Fowler).*
BYNCWORTH. *L1 96, 4; L2 56, 6.*
BYNTWORTH. *L10 32, 5.*

5 lions & canton
5 lions canton
CHEYNE. *Farrer II 18.* 1485. *(imp [Boleyn]; brass, Blickling Ch, Norf).*
CHEYNE, William, of Sheppy, Kent. *Birch 8564.* S' WILL...CHEYNE. 1435. *(2, 2, 1).*
SHIRLAND. *Mill Steph.* c1485. *(afterwards Cheyne or Cheyney; on brass to Jn Estbury, Lambourne, Berks).*
Az 5 lions Or canton Arg
— *SK 909. (1, 3, 1).*
Sa 5 lions & canton Arg
CHEYNEY, of Shepey. *ME 43; LY A 163. (2, 2, 1).*

5 lions canton charged or patterned
Az 5 lions Arg on canton Or mullet Gu
— *PLN 1735. (qtd 2 by Sir Wm Stonor; 2, 3).*
— *WK 55. (qtd 2 by Stoner).*
KYRCKBY, of Horton Kyrkby, Kent. *L9 24, 7. (2, 3).*
Az 5 lions Or on canton Arg mullet Arg [sic]
KYRCKBY, de Kent. *L9 12, 8. (1, 3, 1).*
Az 5 lions Or on canton Arg pd mullet Gu
KYRKBY. *L1 379, 5; L2 288, 8.*
KYRKEBY. *SK 663. (1, 3, 1).*
Az 5 lions Or on canton Or mullet Az
— *PLN 880. (qtd 2&3 by Jn Martin; ?canton Arg; 2, 3).*
Az 5 lions Or on canton Or pd mullet Gu
KIRKBY. *XL 547. (1, 3, 1).*
Untinc 5 lions Untinc canton Erm
CHEYNE, Richard. *Arch Cant ii 42, 12.* Sigullum: ricardi: cheyne. 1393.
Az 5 lions Arg canton Erm
ASSIRLONDE, Roger. *E II 529.*
[CH]EYNE, .. Robert. *WK 101. (qrs 1&4,*

mullet Or in centre of qrs).
CHAYNE, Sir John. *RH, Ancestor ix 159.*
CHEYNE. *L1 150, 6; L2 110, 8.*
CHEYNE, Sir John, of Kent. *WB III 74, 9. (a&l Gu; 2, 2, 1).*
CHEYNEY. *XL 243.*
CHEYNEY, Sir John. *WK 4.*
CHEYNEY, Sir John. *XK 41.*
CHEYNEY, Sir John. *WGA 277. (2, 3).*
CHEYNEY, Sir John. *WB V 69. (2, 3; Kt 1485).*
CHEYNEY, de Lanc. *PT 637. (Shurelande added by later hand; 3, 2).*
CHEYNEY, Sir Thomas, KG. *Leake. (d1496; qtg 2&3 Shottesbroke).*
CHEYNEY, Sir William, of Kent. *CRK 965.*
CHEYNEY, of Wilts & Shyppay. *L10 36, 7.*
CHEYNY, Sir John. *WK 54. (cresc Arg in centre of various other qrs).*
CHEYNY, Sir John. *PLN 1980. (qtg 2&3 [Shotesbrook]).*
CHEYNY, of Sheppey. *Kent Gentry 216, 394. (qtg 2&3 Erm chf per pale Or and Gu rose Gu in dex).*
LAYBURNE, Mons' Thomas. *TJ 108.*
LEYBORNE, Sr de Kent. *CKO 423.*
LILBORN. *CB 346. (arms taken by Cheney, of Kent).*
SCHERLOND. *CT 353.*
SCHEYNY, Sir T. *WB I 40b, 25. (2, 3).*
SCHIRELANDE, Mons Rogier de. *TJ 62.*
SCHIRLONDE, Roger de. *F 298.*
SCIRLANDE, Sire Robert de. *N 266.*
SCIRLANDE, Roger de. *D 223a.*
SHERLAND. *RB 468.*
SHERLAND, of Kent. *L1 150, 6. (marginal note: 'against Cheyne').*
SHERLAND, Roger. *HE 166.*
SHIRLAND, Sir Roger. *CVK 677.*
SHIRLOND. *L1 597, 6.*
SHIRLONDE, Roger de. *FW 208.*
SHURLAND, Sr Robert de. *L 143.*
SIRELANDE, Roger de. *A 20.*
SIRELONDE, Sire Robert de. *HA 63.*
SIRELONDE, Sire Robert de. *HA 50, 17.*
SIRLONDE, Roger de. *E II 531.*
Az 5 lions Or canton Erm
[CHEYNEY, Sir Thomas]. *WB I 8, 1. (2, 3; KG 1539).*
SHERLAND, Robt. *ME 62; LY A 187. (2, 2, 1).*

Az 5 lions & canton Erm
CHEYNEY, John de. *XL 139. (1, 2, 2).*

5 lions & on chf &c

Or 5 lions Sa on chf Gu 3 mullets Or
MORTON, John, de London, esquier. *XPat 247, Arch 68, 89.*

Az 5 lions Arg border engr Or
— *CG 551. (Monsire John ...).*
Az 5 lions Arg canton Erm border engr Or
LAYBURNE, du Contee de Salesbury. *TJ 109.*
LEYBORNE. *DV 40a, 1567.*
LEYBORNE, Sr J de. *CKO 422.*
LEYBOURNE, Roger de. *XL 142. (1, 2, 2).*

6 BEASTS

6 beasts (lions)

6 lions
— *PRO-sls. 1322-3. (imp by Alice, 'late the wife of' Thos, E of Lancaster, & dau of Hen, E of Lincoln).*
— *PRO-sls. 1324-5. (imp by Alisia Lestraunge, w of Ebulo L).*
BASSET, Ela. *Birch 6579; Bowles 162 pl iii.* +S'ELE BASSET COMITISSE WAREWYKIE. *post 1242. (dau of Wm Longespee I, wid of Thos de Newburgh, E of Warwick & w of Philip B, of Hedesdon).*
CLINTON, Juliana de. *PRO-sls AS 139. 1342-3. (imp by Hastings, for Juliana, dau of Thos de Leybourne & w of (1) Jn de H (2) Wm de C).*
CLINTON, William de. *BrookeAsp I 2, 5.* SIGILLVM WILLEMI DE CLINTVN. *1347.*
CLINTON, William de, E of Huntingdon. *PRO-sls AS 139.* X SIGILLVM WILLEMI DE CLINTVN. *1342-3. (lions taken from arms of his w Juliana de Leybourne).*
CLINTONE, Juliana de. *Birch 8684. post 1330. (imp by Hastings in sl of Juliana de C, dau of Thos de Leybourne, w of (1) Jn de H & (2) Wm de C, E of Huntingdon).*
CLYNTON, William de, E of Huntingdon. *PRO-sls E40 A11954, B11091.* SIGILLUM WILLELMI DE CLINTVN. *1352.*
DETTLINGE, Sir Wm de. *Arch Cant viii 273. 1284. (secretum on deed, Cumbwell Priory charters in Col Arm).*
DEVEREUX, Wm. *(or Wm Fitzpatrick, E of Salisbury). Sandford 114. (Plaque in Le Mans Cathedral).*
ESCRIUEN, William de, of Calne. *Vinc 88, 152. 1331. (sl).*
GODSALM, Richard, of Horndon, Essex, Kt. *Birch 10128.* S' RICA-RDLGO-DSALM. *1342.*
HESLERTON, Eufemia. *Yorks Deeds IV 160. 1374. (wid of Sir Walter de H).*
HESLERTON, Eupheme. *Bk of Sls 202. 1369. (wid of Walter H, & dau of Ralf Neville).*
KAMVILE, Idonia. *Isbury.* SIGILLVM YDONIE DE KAVMVILE. *c1225. (w of Wm Longespee).*

LESTRAUNGE, Alesia. *PRO-sls AS 253.*
1344-5. *(imp by lion; w of Ebulo L).*
LEYBORNE, William, Ld of. *Barons Letter.*
[LEYBOURNE]. *Mill Steph.* 1553. *(qtd 4 by
Hampden on brass to Sir Jn H & 2 wives,
Hampden, Bucks).*
[LEYBOURNE]. *Mill Steph.* 1496. *(qtd 4 by
Hampden on brass to Jn H & w Eliz Sidney,
Hampden, Bucks).*
LEYBOURNE, Roger de. *Arch Cant v 219-20.*
c1270. *(sl on deed, Cumbwell priory char-
ters in Col Arm).*
LEYBURNE, Idonea. *Durham-sls 1594.* late
13 cent.
LEYBURNE, Juliana de. *Birch 11339.*
SIGILLVM: IVLIANE: DE: LEYBVRNE. 14 cent.
LEYBURNE, Juliane de. *BrookeAsp I 5, 2.*
SIGILLVM: IULIANE: DE: LEYBVRNE.
LEYBURNE, Roger de. *BrookeAsp I 5, 4.*
SIGILLVM: ROGERI: DE: LEYBVRNE.
LEYBURNE, Roger de. *Birch 11337.*
+SIGILLVM.ROGERI.DE.LEYBVRNE. 14 cent.
LEYBURNE, Roger de. *PRO-sls AS 34.*
+SIGILLVM: ROGERI.DE.LEYBVRNE. 1271.
LEYBURNE, William, 1st Baron. *Birch 11338.*
S' WILL'I.LEYBVRNE. 1301.
LONGESPEE, Ela. *Bk of Sls 62.* 1226-36.
*(dau & h of Wm, E of Salisbury, w of Wm L,
E of Salisbury).*
LONGESPEE, Ela. *Dugd 17, 26. (w of Thos
Newburgh, E of Warwick).*
LONGESPEE, Ela. *Sandford 114, 57. (dau of
Wm Devereux or Fitzpatrick, w of Wm L).*
LONGESPEE, Emelina. *Birch 6680.* S' EME-
LINE LVNGESPEIE. 1250. *(dau of Maurice
Fitzgerald & w of Stephen L).*
LONGESPEE, Nicholas, Bp of Salisbury. *Arch
Journ xlv 31. (episcopal sl).*
[LONGESPEE, E of Salisbury]. *Arch Journ ix
300 & 385. (qtd 2&3 by [Montagu]).*
LONGESPEE, William. *Bk of Sls 56.* 1246.
LONGESPEE, William. *Isbury.*
+S'....: ...LLELMI: ...ESPEIE.
LONGESPEE, Wm de. *Bk of Sls 429.* Dec
1154-Jan 1164. *(on trappings, equestr sl).*
LONGESPEE, William. *PRO-sls.* 1246-56.
[LONGESPEE, William, E of Salisbury].
Lawrance 25. 1286. *(effigy, Salisbury
Cathedral).*
LONGESPEE, William, E of Salisbury. *Sand-
ford 57 & 117.* c1249.
LONGESPEIE, William de, E of Salisbury.
Birch 11375. ...ILELM...EI.... c1226.
LONGESPEYE, Ela, Countess of Warwick.
Selborne 4, 72. S' Elie Lungespeye. 1285.
LUNGESPEE, Stephen. *Birch 11462.* +SIGI.......-
EPHANI: LVNGGESPE. 1245-50.
LUNGHESPEIE, William, of Berks. *Birch
11464.* +SIGILLVM.WILL......GESPEIE. c1250.

NEVILLE, Richard, E of Salisbury. *PRO-sls.*
1440-1.
PAVILLY, Robert. *Bk of Sls 400.* 1245-6.
*(imp by lion on 2nd of 2 sls on charter of
Robt de P & Maud his mother).*
SARESBERIE, Ela Comitissa. *Birch 6678.*
+SECRETV ELE COMITISSE SARESBERIE. 1226.
*(dau of Wm d'Evereux, 2nd E of Salisbury;
wid of Wm Longespee).*
[SAVAGE]. *Birch 8656.* S ALEXAND' CLIF-
FORD. 1452. *(imp by Alexander Clyfford, of
Shorne Manor, Kent).*
SAVAGE, Arnald. *Birch 13286.* (S)IGILLUM
ARNALDI SAUAGE. 1372.
SAVAGE, Arnald, of Kent, Kt. *Birch 13285.*
SIGILLVM.....A....AVV. 1329.
SAVAGE, Ernald. *PRO-sls.* 1382-3.
SAVAGE, Ronald. *PRO-sls.* 1360.
SHIRLAND, Sir Robert. *Lawrance 41.* ante
1350. *(effigy, Minster, Isle of Sheppey).*
VILERS, Pagan de, of Notts. *Birch 14169.*
SIGILLVM PAGANI DE VILERS. 1321.
VIPONT, Robert. *?source.* 1223-8. *(sl).*
WARWICK, Ela, Countess of. *AnstisAsp I 225,
94.* SIGILL'ELE: COMITISSE: WAREWYCLIEX.
13 cent. *(dau of Will Longespee).*
WARWICK, Ela, Ctess of. *Bk of Sls 327.*
1284-90.

Arg 6 lions

Arg 6 lions Gu
  VYLERS, Sr Payn de. *CKO 619.*
Arg 6 lions Sa
  LEYBOURNE, Sir William. *ML I 97; ML II
88.*
  LITTLE. *LQ 100. (lions 2, 2, 2 on fore
trapper & 3, 3 on hind).*
  OTERINGBIRI, Rauf de. *D 268a.*
  SAUAGE, Mons Arnalde. *CA 65.*
  SAUAIGE. *L1 604, 6.*
  SAUVADGE, Mons Ernaud. *SD 38.*
  SAUVAGE, Sr. *CKO 636.*
  SAUVAGE, Sir Arnaud. *CVK 688. (or Sir Jn
de Sharsted).*
  SAUVAGE, S Roger. *GA 155.*
  SAUVAGE, Sire Roger. *N 271.*
  SAVAGE. *LS 258.*
  SAVAGE, Sir .... *CRK 1546.*
  SAVAGE, le. *SK 345.*
  SAVAGE, Mons Arnald. *WJ 325.*
  SAVAGE, Mons Arnald. *S 353.*
  SAVAGE, S' Arnald. *PO 375.*
  SAVAGE, Arnold. *XL 161.*
  SAVAGE, Arnold. *S 355.*
  SAVAGE, Sir Arnold. *PLN 201.*
  SAVAGE, S' Arnold, Kent. *CY 147, 588.*
  SAVAGE, Sir John, of Ches. *WB III 84b, 1.
(a&l Gu).*
  SHORSTEDE, Simunt de. *LM 427.*

WATRINGBERI, Bertelmeu de. *A 52.*
WOTERINGEBERIE, Bertilmeu de. *FW 215.*
[WRIGEL'], Bartelemew de. *HE 176.*

Az 6 lions Arg
Az 6 lions Arg
— *D4 35b. (a&l Gu; escutch of Plompton, of Plompton, Yorks).*
BEYBORNE. *L10 30, 14.*
DETTLING, Sir John. *PLN 837. (3, 3).*
LAYBORNE, Sir William. *BR V 74.*
LAYBOURN, of Consewyk. *D4 48b.*
LAYBURN, Mons John, de Kent. *TJ 106.*
LEIBORNE, Roger de. *A 5.*
LEIBURNE, William de. *FW 149.*
LEYBORNE. *FK II 566.*
LEYBORNE. *L2 315, 8.*
LEYBORNE, Roger de. *B 34.*
LEYBORNE, Sire Willame de. *N 60.*
LEYBOUNRE, Sir William de. *GA 188.*
LEYBOURN, Sr Thomas de. *RB 41.*
LEYBOURNE. *CT 73.*
LEYBOURNE, Ld de. *XL 138.*
LEYBOURNE, M de. *WNR 18.*
LEYBOURNE, Guillemes de. *K 71.*
LEYBOURNE, Sir J, of Westmld. *CRK 403.*
LEYBOURNE, Sir William. *ML I 101.*
LEYBOURNE, William de. *K 433.*
LEYBURNE. *L9 34a, 7.*
LEYBURNE, Mons de. *WJ 285. (2, 2, 2).*
LEYBURNE, Roger de. *C 74.*
LEYBURNE, Sir Roger. *CVK 675.*
LEYBURNE, Munsire William de. *D 121b.*
LEYBURNE, William de. *E I 86; E II 86.*
LEYBURNE, William de. *LM 81.*
LEYBURNE, William de. *G 75.*
LEYBURNE, Wyllem de. *HE 125.*
LONGESPEE. *LS 275. (langued Gu).*
LONGESPEE, William, E of Salisbury. *DX 20. (drawn sejt).*

Az 6 lions Or
Az 6 lions Or
ANJOU, Geoffrey, E of. *Sandford 24. (?field Gu).*
LONGAESPATA, Comitis Wilelmi. *MP Hist Min iii 84.*
LONGA SPATA, Willemi. *MP II 99. ('scutum azureum [6] leones aurei').*
LONGESPEE. *L1 411, 6; L2 300, 10.*
LONGESPEE. *RH, Ancestor ix 162.*
[LONGESPEE]. *CN 13.*
[LONGESPEE], E of Salisbery. *BR V a 18.*
LONGESPEE, de Saresburie. *SP A 38.*
LONGESPEE, le C de Salesbury. *NB 19. (lions have disappeared).*
LONGESPEE, William. *MP I 90; MP II 8. (s of Wm, E of Salisbury).*
LONGESPEE, Mons William, Conte de

Salesbury. *TJ 102.*
LONGESPEE, William de, E of Salisbury. *MP I 40.*
LONGESPEE, William III, E of Salisbury. SANDFORD 118.
LONGESPEE, William, E of Salisbury. *Keepe. (repainted shield).*
LONGESPEY. *RB 278.*
LONGESPEYE, Comes Sary. *L9 37b, 11.*
LONGSPE, Gul. *C 75.*
PLANTAGENET, Arthur. *Sandford 68. (s of Geoffrey, E of Anjou).*
SALEBURS. *N 1036.*
SALEBURS, le Counte de. *WNR 19.*
SALESBIRE. *D 221a.*
SALESBUR', [Longespee], Count de. *WJ 125. (3, 3).*
SALESBURI, Counte. *F 1.*
SALESBURI, le Cunte de. *FW 44.*
SALESBURI, le Cunte de. *G 38.*
SALESBURY, le Conte de. *B 22.*
SALISBURY, William, E of. *Sandford 117.*
SALISBERY. *HE 28.*
SALISBURY, Cunte de. *E I 20; E II 20.*
SALISBURY, Erle of. *BR IV 86.*
SALISBURY, le Conte de. *P 66.*
[SALISBURY, Cunte de]. *D 221c.*
SALSBURYE. *KB 258. (3, 3; or Savage).*
SARESBIRIENSIS, Willelmus, Comes. *MP Hist Min ii 281.*

Gu 6 lions
Gu 6 lions Arg
ESHARTON, Mons Thomas de. *AS 431.*
FITZRENAUD. *L2 195, 2.*
HASELHALTON, Sir Thomas de. *CV-BM 216.*
HESCLARTON, Sr Thomas de. *CKO 601.*
HESLARTON, Sr. *CC 222, 11. (written below: 'Leyborne').*
LAYBORN, of Yorks. *D9; E6.*
LAYBORNE. *R 130.*
[LEYBORNE]. *Bellasis II 306-8. (imp by [Bardsey], Arg 2 bars on canton Gu maunch Or; Windermere E window).*
LEYBORNE, Sire Richard de. *N 722.*
LEYBOURN, Yorks. *L1 391, 5; L2 303, 2.*
LEYBOURNE. *DV 55b, 2194.*
LEYBOURNE, Mons' Thomas. *S 354.*
LEYBURNE, Robert de. *FC I 39.*
PAUNCEFORT, Grimbaud. *HE 163.*
PAUNCEFOT, Grimbaud. *A 231.*
PAUNCEFOT, Grimbaud. *F 186.*
PAUNCEFOT, Grumbald. *FW 177.*
PAUNCEVOT, Grimbaud. *E 300.*
SAVAGE, Sr John. *Kent Gentry 217b, 397. (armed Az).*
SAVAGE, Sir John, Kent. *WB III 74, 6. (a&l Az).*
SAYBURNE, of Kendall. *PT 1096.*

SEINT HELENE, Jon. *E 335.*
SEINT HELYN, John de. *WLN 839.*
(unfinished - lions not painted in).
ST CLERE, John. *E II 494.*
ST HELENE, John. *E I 492.*
TILMANSTONE, Roger de. *FW 298.*
VAUNCEVOD, Sire Gilberd. *N 878.*
WYBARNE, Sir Richard. *PT 1011.*
Gu 6 lions Or
— *WLN 55.*

Or 6 lions
Or 6 lions Az
MORTIMER, Roger. *L9 70a, 1.*
MORTIMER, Roger. *XL 325.*
Or 6 lions Sa
DETLYNG, Sir William de. *CVK 720.*
DETTELYNGE. *L10 58b, 3.*
DETTELYNGE, S' John de. *CY 157, 628.*
DORCESTRE, Mons Oliv' de. *WJ 342.*
DORCHESTER, Oliver de. *XL 172.*
LAYBURN, Mons John de, du North. *TJ 104.*
LEIBORNE, William de. *A 4.*
LEIBURNE. *L9 35a, 8.*
LEIBURNE, Roger de. *FW 209.*
LEYBORNE, sr de, du Nor(th). *CKO 637.*
LEYBORNE, Roger de. *HE 167.*
LEYBOURNE. *L2 315, 9.*
LEYBOURNE, Roger de. *E I 496; E II 498.*
LEYBOURNE, Sire Willame de. *N 106.*
LEYBOURNE, Sire William. *J 146.*
LEYBURN, William de. *D 121a.*
LEYBURNE, Munsire Roger de. *D 116b.*
LEYBURNE, Roger de. *D 116a.*
MORTEYNE, Robert de. *ML I 25.*
[STRONGBOW]. *DX 44. (2, 2, 2).*

Sa 6 lions Arg
Sa 6 lions Arg
— *LH 609. (qtd 4 by Hampden, imp Savage).*
— *LH 607. (qtd 2&3 by Popham, all imp by Hampden).*
DETLINGE, William. *F 315.*
DETLINGE, William. *FW 214.*
DETLINGE, William. *HE 177.*
DETLINGE, William. *D 205.*
DETLINGE, William. *A 37.*
ECLINGES, William de. *E I 415.*
ECLINNGES. *LE 115.*
ECLYNGE, Mons William de. *TJ 64.*
ENGLISH, William. *XL 150.*
ENGLYS, of Tawne. *L2 180, 4.*
ENGLYS, Mons Willm. *WJ 302.*
GELING, S William de. *GA 136.*
GELINGES, William de. *E II 417.*
SAVAGE, Mons Laurence. *TJ 107.*
SAVAGE, Mons R. *AS 403.*
TAWNE. *XL 23.*

TAWNE. *L1 640, 3. (a&l Gu).*
TOWNE, Thomas de. *LY A 181.*
Sa 6 lions coward 3, 2, 1 Arg
— *PLN 1858. (3rd of 4 qrs on coat imp by Sir Jn Green).*

Sa 6 lions Gu &c
Sa 6 lions Gu
SEINT MARTIN, William de. *F 309.*
Sa 6 lions Or
— *LH 601. (qtd 4 by Hampden).*
— *BA 806. (qtd 5 by Forester).*
— *BA 1045 & 1057. (qtd 5 by Sir Nicholas Wadham).*
— *WB I 16b, 3. (qtd 5 by Wadham, of West Devon).*
— *PLN 244. (qtd 3 by Sir George Carew).*
COLINGTON, John, Suss. *RH, Ancestor v 175.*
SAINT MARTEN. *L1 572, 4.*
SAINT MARTIN. *PT 37.*
SAINT MARTIN. *Gerard 51.*
SAINT MARTIN, Lawrence. *XL 177.*
SAINT MARTIN, Wm. *E I 389; E II 391.*
SAYNTE MARTYN. *DV 59a, 2321.*
SEIN MARTIN, Sire Renaud de. *N 218.*
SEINT MARTIN, Mons' John de. *TJ 110.*
SEINT MARTYNE, Mons Laurence. *WJ 340.*
SEYNT MARTYN, Monsire Laurence. *AN 253.*
Sa 6 lions coward Or
CARINGTON. *CRK 53.*

Vt 6 lions
Vt 6 lions Arg
— *RH, Ancestor ix 163.*
Vt 6 lions Or
LANGEFORD, Sire Nicholas de. *O 138.*

6 lions patterned
Untinc 6 lions Erm
TILMANSTONE, Roger de. *A 53.*
Gu 6 lions Erm
— *ME 72; LY A 196.*

6 lions crowned
6 lions crowned
HESLERTON. *Birch 11436. 1369. (1 of 4 shields in sl of Euphemia, dau of Ralph 2nd Baron Neville).*
Gu 6 lions Arg crowned Or
HASELARTON. *PT 278. (name added).*
HASELARTONE, S' Walter. *PO 263.*
HASELERTON, Yorks. *L1 327, 2; L2 256, 12.*
HESELARTONE, Sire Thomas de. *N 724.*
HESLARTON. *LH 1119.*
HESLARTON, Mons Th de. *WJ 186.*
HESLARTON, Thomas. *XL 351.*
HESLARTON, Sir Thomas de, of Durham. *LH 653.*
HESLARTON, Sir Walter de. *LH 654. (imp*

Percy).
HESLARTON, Mons Wautier de. *TJ 63.*
HESLERTON, Mons Waut'. *WJ 198.*
HUSTURTON, Sir Thomas. *PT 1013.*

6 lions qf
Or 6 lions qf Az
MORTAIGN, Rogeirs de. *K 56. ('jaune leot o sis bleus lyons dont les coues double dioms').*
MORTAIGNE, Roger le. *K 363. (3, 2, 1).*
MORTEYN, S' Roger de. *GA 141.*
MORTIMER, Robert de. *WJ 128.*
Or 6 lions qf Sa
MARTIN. *L2 347, 7.*
MORTEYN, S'Roger de. *BR I 41.*
MORTEYN, Sire Roger. *N 93.*
MORTON. *L2 345, 3.*

6 lions couchant &c
6 lions ?couchant
— *WB I 33b, 17. (qtd 7 by [?Clisold]).*
Az 6 lions passt Arg
[STRANGE, Ld]. *PLN 969. (2, 1, 2, 1; 5 other qtgs).*
Or 6 lions passt Sa
MORTEYNE, Robert de. *ML I 26; ML II 26. (lions 2, 2, 2 should be ramp).*

6 beasts (other)
Vt 6 ?bears passt Arg
HOUWELL, Harri, of Staffs. *WB III 99, 1.*
Vt 6 dogs stat Arg
HOWNHILL, Harry, of Staffs. *LH 781.*
Vt 6 talbots passt Arg
HOUNDHYL, of Houndhil, Staffs. *L2 269, 10.*
Per fess Gu and Az in chf 6 ermines passt Arg
— *ML II 123.*

6 beasts & label

6 lions & label
6 lions & label
ALDITHLEYA, Ela de. *Birch 6573.* SIGILLVM ELE DE AVDELE'. *(dau of Wm Longespee II, wid of Jas de A, of Wretchwick, Oxfords).*
LEYBOURNE. *Lawrance 25.* ante 1350. *(effigy, Calder Abbey, Cumb).*
6 lions & label of 4
LEYBOURNE, Sarra de. *PRO-sls.* 1328-9.
LEYBURNE, Robert de. *PRO-sls.* 1302-3.
LONGESPEE. *Bk of Sls 192.* +SIGIL........ 1245-6.
Az 6 lions Arg label Gu
LEYBOURNE, Sr Henry de. *L 78.*
LEYBOURNE, S' Thos. *ST 13.*
LEYBURNE. *RB 417.*
LEYBURNE. *HA 108, 23.*

Az 6 lions Untinc label of 5 Gu
LEYBOURNE. *CT 115.*
LEYBURNE, Roger de. *G 68.*
LEYBURNE, Thomas de. *G 70.*
— *(...urne). HA 88.*
Az 6 lions Or label Gu
LONGESPEE, Estienne. *B 187.*
Gu 6 lions Arg label Az
— *FK II 184.*
LABOURNE, Sir Nicholas. *PT 1012.*
LEYBOURNE, Sire Nicholas. *N 723.*
Az 6 lions Arg label gobony Or and Gu
LEYBURNE, Sire Henri de. *N 265.*
Az 6 lions Arg label of 5 gobony Or and Gu
LEYBOURNE. *CT 167.*

6 beasts & canton

6 lions canton charged
Az 6 lions Arg on canton Erm annulet Gu
CHEYNYE, of Kent. *RB 318.*
6 lions on canton mullet
[KIRBY]. *Mill Steph. (imp [Stonor]; brass, Horton Kirby, Kent).*
[KIRBY]. *Mill Steph. (imp [Drayton]; brass, Horton Kirby, Kent).*
6 lions on canton pd mullet of 6 pts
KIRKABY, Wm. *Mill Steph.* 1458. *(brass to Wm K, priest, Theydon Gernon, Essex).*
Az 6 lions Arg on canton Or mullet Gu
— *XF 570. (3, 3; qtd 2 by Sir Wm Stoner).*
Az 6 lions Arg on canton Erm mullet Gu
CHEYNE. *RB 319.*

6 lions canton patterned
Untinc 6 lions Untinc canton Erm
FOXCOTE, Thomas, Ld of. *PRO-sls.* 1323-4.
SHURLAND. *Proc Soc Antiq XIII 2S 224. (cresc for diffce; on 15 cent silver roundel; arms of Shurland in Isle of Sheppey were assumed by Cheney family on m of Wm Ch, d1323, with Mgt dau & h of Sir Robt de S).*
Az 6 lions Arg canton Erm
CHEYNE. *PLN 838. (3, 3).*
CHEYNE. *WB IV 156b, 554.*
CHEYNE, Sr John. *Kent Gentry 217b, 397.*
CHEYNEY, Sir Francis. *XK 109. (1st lion's feet show below canton).*
CHEYNEY, Sir John. *BA 824.*
CHEYNY, Edward, Dean of Salisbury. *BA 813. (imp by Salisbury deanery, & qtg 2&3 Erm chf indented per pale Or and Gu rose Gu in dex chf).*
CHEYNY, Sir Franceys. *WK 471.*
LAYBOURNE, Mons John de. *WJ 289. (2, 2, 2).*
LAYBURNE. *L9 36b, 3.*
[LEIGHBURNE]. *Nichols Leics II 558.*

(Errington Ch).
SIRLANDE, Sr Robert de. *RB 90.*
Az 6 lions Or canton Erm
LONGESPEE, 'son frere'. *C 76.*

6 beasts canton & label
Az 6 lions Arg canton Erm label gobony Or and Gu
SHERLAND. *LS 190. (langued Gu).*

6 beasts & chief
Or 6 lions Sa on chf Gu 3 5foils Or
MARTON, Joh, de London, Esquier. *L10 61, 8.*

6 beasts & over all
Gu 6 lions Arg bend Az
HESLARTON. *LH 1121.*
HESLARTON, Mons .... *WJ 188.*
HESLARTON, Simon. *XL 352.*
Az 6 lions Arg fess Or
ROKESLEY. *XF 526.*

6 beasts in border

6 lions in border
6 lions border
HESELARTON, Walter de. *PRO-sls.* 1339-40.
Az 6 lions & border Arg
LEYBORN, de. *SK 859.*
LEYBOURNE. *L9 40a, 12.*
Az 6 lions & border engr Arg
LEYBORN, de. *SK 860.*
LEYBOURNE. *L9 40a, 11.*
Az 6 lions Arg border engr Gu
LEYBOURNE, S Henry de. *GA 190.*
Az 6 lions Arg border engr Or
LEIBOURN, S Jo de. *R 93.*
LEYBOURNE, S Simon de. *GA 189.*
LEYBOURNE, Sire Simon de. *N 264.*
LEYBOURNE, Symon de. *G 103.*
LOIBORNE, Mons Johan de. *AS 106.*
Az 6 lions & border engr Or
LEYBOURNE. *CT 107.*
Gu 6 lions & border engr Arg
HERWARE, Walter de. *XL 341.*
HESLARTON, Mons Rauf. *WJ 187.*
Gu 6 lions Arg border engr Or
HESELARTON, Sr Wauter de. *CKO 602.*
Gu 6 lions Or border engr Arg
FITZHERBERT, Reginald. *XL 374.*
FITZHERBERT, Mons Reginald. *WJ 248.*

6 lions crowned in border
Gu 6 lions Arg crowned Or border engr Arg
HASELARTONE. *PO 262.*
HERWARE. *LH 1120.*
HERWARE, Sir Walter de. *LH 652.*

6 beasts & canton in border
Az 6 lions Arg canton Erm & border engr Or
LAYBURNE. *L9 36b, 4.*
LEYBORNE. *RB 289.*

12 BEASTS OR MORE
Cordon of 12 lions pg in 6 pairs counterpasst
DOVER. *Birch 4883.* SIGILLUM COMMUNE BARONUM DE DOVORIA. 1305.
Semy of lions pg
HENRY 3. *WestmAbb. (on gilt bronze plate on which effigy of Hen 3 is placed, each beast within one of the diamonds formed by diagonal lines engraved across the plate; Confessor's Chapel).*
Az flock of sheep Arg in fold of wattle fencing supported by 5 forked props issuing from base Or
ISAAC, patriarcha. *L9 5b, 7.*

BELL
Bell
BELNE, Henry de, of Belne, Worcs. *Bow XXXV 28.* 1316-17.
Bell ensigned with mullet
BELL, Andrew, burgess of Edinburgh. *Stevenson.* 1462.
Church bell betw 3 boars' heads couped
SOUTHDALTON, Richard. *Birch 13593.* 1386.
Church bell betw letters RL in chf & a mark in base
— *SussASColl xvi 144. (on old church bell at Findon with the inscr : Sancte gabrielis).*
— *SussASColl lvii 57 & pl IV (3). (prob mark of Rog Landen, of Wokingham, bell-founder, mentioned in Eton Coll 1448; mark found on bells at Cocking & Eastbourne, Suss).*
Church bell betw letters TB
— *SussASColl lvii 42-3. (found on a number of church bells in Suss & elsewhere c1500; prob mark of Bullisdon, mentioned as bell-founder in London in 1510).*
2 bells in base stag's head erased
BELL, Bernard, of Melros ?Monastery, & of Leith. *Stevenson.* 1510.

3 bells

3 bells

BELL, Robert, juror at Coldingham. *Stevenson.* 1430.

BELL, Will, Master of Balliol. *GutchWdU. (or Jn Bell, Bp of Worcester; formerly on Wainscot in Hall, Balliol Coll [Prior to 1786]).*

Arg 3 bells Sa

BENET, Willimus. *Q II 642. (Ch bells).*

BENETT, Wm. *SES 86. (door bells; clappers Arg).*

HAYTON. *CRK 515. (Ch bells).*

HAYTON. *PT 712. (Ch bells).*

HAYTON. *DV 71b, 2827. (Ch bells).*

HAYTON. *L1 320, 6; L2 249, 2. (Ch bells).*

PORTER. *Nichols Leics II 285. (Ch bells; Welby Chapel).*

Gu 3 bells Arg

BELL. *PLN 1311. (hawk's bells).*

PORTER, Irld. *L9 92a, 9. (Ch bells).*

Sa 3 bells Untinc

PORTER, Sir Wm. *Pierpont Morgan 105. (door bells; illumination in MS).*

Sa 3 bells Arg

PORTER. *L1 503, 3.*

PORTER. *SK 726. (door bells; 'of Gloucestershire' added by Gibbon).*

PORTER. *WGB 102, 18. (door bells).*

PORTER. *L9 97b, 11. (Ch bells).*

PORTER. *LEP 60. (door bells).*

PORTER, Sir William. *PLN 205. (clappers Sa; on 2nd bell letters WAR).*

PORTER, Sir William. *BW 14b, 96.*

PORTER, Sir William. *CRK 1035. (door bells).*

PORTER, William. *BG 127. (door bells).*

PORTER, Willimus. *Q II 641. (door or Ch bells; clappers Sa).*

PORTER, Wm. *SES 85. (door bells; clappers Sa).*

PORTER, Sir Wylyam. *RH, Ancestor iv 249. (of Lincs).*

Sa 3 bells Or

BELCHAMBER. *PLN 896. (hawk's bells; imp Kowefold, Or 3 bulls' heads cab Gu).*

Gu semy of 3foils Or 3 hawk's bells Or

OLEPHERNUS. *RH, Ancestor ix 174.*

3 bells in chf lion pg

CHAUMPAYNE, William. *PRO-sls.* 1354.

Arg 3 church bells Sa in chf cresc Sa

HAYTON. *PT 713.*

10 bells

Az 10 hawk's bells Or in border Gu ?8 female heads

— Arch Journ (Chichester 1853) 95. c1530. *(painting, Amberley Castle, Suss).*

BELLOWS

Arg 3 pairs of bellows Sa

SHYPTON, John. *RH, Ancestor ix 160.*

Az 3 pairs of bellows Or piped Arg

— RH, Ancestor ix 175.

Erm 3 pairs of bellows Gu

— RH, Ancestor ix 167.

BELTS &c

Garter buckled betw 3 buckles with tongues erect

[BUCKLAND]. *Mill Steph.* 1471. *(imp by [?Whittingham] on tomb of Sir Robt W, Aldbury, Herts).*

Sa garter buckled betw 3 buckles Untinc

BOKELAND, John. *RH, Ancestor ix 161.*

Gu 2 straps buckles up Or

PELHAM. *L2 408, 2.*

Arg 3 demi-garters Az buckled & garnished Or

NERBONNE. *XPat 354, Arch 69, 96.*

See also buckles

BEND

Per bend

Per bend Az and Or

— ME 30; LY A 150. (imp by Hall).

Per bend Or and Az

— CRK 1731. (imp by Matthew Hall).

[?CRANE]. *LH 509. (imp by Hall).*

Per bend Or and Vt

— CVL 408.

HAL. *L1 336, 3; L2 244, 1.*

HALL. *LH 481.*

HALL. *LH 86.*

Per bend Sa and Arg

— ML I 2. ('Sabyll & silver party per bende').

WYNNE. *PLN 872. (imp by Drayton).*

Per bend Gu & bendy Or and Gu

— 1H7 42; D13 116d. (qtd 3 by George West, 3rd bro of Ld Lawarre).

Per bend modified

Per bend with 1 point to sin Sa and Arg

CHAMBERLAIN. *ML I 233.*

Per bend embattled Arg and Gu

BOYLE. *L1 45, 6; L2 72, 4.*

Per bend embattled Arg and Sa

DENEWGAT. *L1 201, 1; L2 155, 5.*

DEUNGATE. *L10 57b, 20.*

DUMGATE. *ML I 887. (or Deungate).*

ELLAM. *DV 68a, 2690.*
Per bend embattled Gu and Arg
BEAULY, John, de South. *TJ 1539.* (*'de goules & dargent embelis bataillee'*).
BOYLEY. *L10 85, 7.*
Per bend sin embattled Gu and Arg
BOYLE. *CRK 901.*
BOYLE. *FK II 535.*
Per bend embattled Sa and Arg
— *WB I 36, 1.* (*?Deungate or Kenley*).
COWLEY. *PLN 1509.*
KENLEY. *FK II 635.*
KENLEY. *L2 295, 8.*
KENLEY. *L9 11b, 9.*
KENLEY. *L1 377, 1; L2 290, 6.*
KOULAY, Tomas. *RH, Ancestor vii 215.*
Per bend indented Arg and Sa
KENDALE, of Ripon. *PT 1240.*
WARNER, Thomas. *PLN 976.* (*qtg 2&3 Az lis Gu*).
Per bend indented Gu and Arg
— *SK 430.*
Per bend indented Gu and Or
FRENES, Sir Walter, of Herts. *L2 210, 12.*
Per bend indented Or and Gu
HYLAND. *LH 31.*
Per bend indented Sa and Arg
GILLIOT, Nicholas de Markyngton. *TJ 1259.*
HOLWAY. *BR IV 49.*
WARNER. *PT 982.*
Per bend indented Sa and Gu
HARSSYKE. *SHY 86.* (*4 indents*).
Per bend indented Gu and Erm
— *LE 454.*

1 BEND

Untinc 1 bend
Bend
— *Stevenson.* 1518. (*qtd by Jn Erskine*).
AUNTCROU, John. *Stowe-Bard ls xiii 9.* 1348-9. (*3rd shield on sl*).
— *C3 56b.* (*imp by cross formy fitchy on chf 5 roundels; sl on Deed dd 1348-9 of Alice wid of Hugh, of the Stok of Stivecle Magna*).
— *?source.* 1410. (*imp by qtly Reynsford & [Wilcotes]; brass Great Tew, Oxfords*).
— *Clairambault 4529.* 28 Feb 1438. (*qtd 2&3 by Jn Hasting*).
— *PRO-sls E40 A8394.* SIG.. ..LELM EWELL. 1462-3. (*?..ewell, Wm; used by Thos Reynold, of Buckley*).
— *PlymouthCL-sls 107, 71.* 1427. (*qtd by Sir Jn Arundel*).
— *Stevenson.* 1473. (*qtd 2&3 by Sir Thos Wemyss, of Reres, on sl of his w Mgt, nee Vaus*).

— *PRO-sls E40 13720-1.* S HENRICI DE .....-TON. 1332-3. (*Hen de ...; used by Adam de Sudberi, chaplain, or Hen le Aundre*).
— *SHY 411.* (*qtd 2&3 by Hastynges imp Denh[am]*).
ARUNDEL, Katherine. *CombeAsp II 124.* Sigillum Katerine Arundel. 1526. (*qtg 6 martlets & imp orle of martlets*).
ATTEMORE, William. *Birch 7003.* Sigillum Will'i.atte more. 1343. (*diapered lozy a bend*).
BAYS, John. *PRO-sls.* 1372-3.
[BEAUPRE]. *Farrer II 88.* (*qtd by [Brigg]; Sall Ch, Norf*).
BISSET. *Stevenson.* 1455. (*qtd by Sir Thos Wemyss of Reres, Kt & others*).
BISSET, Elizabeth. *Stevenson.* 1280. (*'domina de Kelrevock, w of Lord Andre de Bosco'*).
BONVILE, Wm de. *Stevenson.* 1390.
BORRESDEN, Sir John de. *Lawrance 5.* c1329. (*on edge of slab to Sir Jn de B, d1329; tomb, Amotherby, Yorks*).
BOTENCUMBE, Thomas, Kt. *PRO-sls.* 1 July 1323.
BRADEWELLE, John de. *Heneage 2156.* S ... DE ... WELLE. 1351-2. (*sl on Lease of lands in Woodborough, Wilts*).
BRAKENBURY, Peter de. *Durham-sls 366.* 1340.
BRET, Bertrucat le, of Gascony. *PRO-sls AS 52.* 1383.
BRIMSTATH, John de. *Baker-sls.* 1379. (*?on bend 2 eagles; Parson of Modberlegh [Mobberley], Ches; sl on deed relating to Brimstath & Oxton, Ches*).
BULINGTONA, Matildis. *Birch 7915.* S' MATILDIE FILIE NORMAN. 13 cent. (*charge indistinct; wid of Osbert B, of Lincs*).
CARMINOU, Roger de. *PRO-sls E40 A10318.* OGERI DE CA.M.... 1348-9.
CARMYNOU, Thomas de, Kt. *PRO-sls AS 113.* SIGILLVM THOME DE CARMYNOU. 1357-8.
CHESEWICK, Robert de. *PRO-sls E40 A8035.* S' ROBER.....WIK. 1308-9.
CHESEWIK, Robert de. *PRO-sls.* 1308.
COKER, Richard, [of Bridgwater]. *Bridgwater 448, 1179.* SIGILLUM.RICARDI.COKER. 1389. (*sl*).
COKESEYE, Walter. *PRO-sls.* 1380-1.
CONSTABLE, of Flamborough. *Mill Steph.* 1491. (*imp by Clifton; brass to Sir Gervis C, Clifton, Notts; rectius qtly UntincVair over all bend Untinc, but bend is not in qrs 2&3*).
CURSON, John, Sir. *Farrer II 65.* (*qtg Felton; brass Bylaugh Ch, Norf*).
DAULTON, Henry. *PRO-sls AS 233.* S' HENRICI FIL'THOME DAVLTONE. 1324-5. (*s of Thos D; used by Jn le Wodeward de*

Coventrie).

DAULTON, Henry. *PRO-sls.* 1324-5. *(s of Thos D).*

DEMARIE, John. *PRO-sls.* S' IEH-N DEMARIE. 1377-8.

[DENNISTON]. *Stevenson.* 1471. *(qtd by Jn Maxwell, of Calderwood).*

[LE DESPENCER]. *Farrer III 37. (stone shield outside St Andrew's Ch, Norwich).*

FAUCONBERGH, Isabella de. *2D5 59b; BrookeAsp I.* Sigillum Isabelle de Fauconberge. 1383-4. *(dex shield of 5).*

FENLES, S' Will, of Suss. *CY 165, 660.*

FILGERIIS, William de. *Birch 9701.* +SIG....- WILL'I.DE FILGERIIS. 1200. *(shield diapered with sprigs of fern-like foliage (fougere) springing from base; bend is considered by JR Planche to be a diffce & 'one of the earliest instances of this mark of cadency').*

FILLE, Richard. *PRO-sls.* 1340. *(indistinct; baston).*

FOLIOT, Jordan. *Harl 2044, 112b; BrookeAsp I 51, 3.* SIGILLVM .IORDANI .FOLIOT.. temp K John & Hen 3.

FOLIOT, Jordan, of Ingham, Lincs. *Birch 9848.* +SIGILLVM: IORDANI.FOLIOT. early Hen 3.

FOLLIOT. *Antiq Journ xix. (on brass to Sir Hugh Hastings, d1347, in Elsing Ch, Norfolk, cited by his great-grandson Sir Edward H in 'Grey v Hastings' at Court of Chivalry 1407-17).*

FOUGERES, Wm de. *Bk of Sls 236.* 1200.

FRAMPTON, John, esq. *PRO-sls.* 20 May 1391-2.

FROST, Emma. *PRO-sls.* SIGILLUM EMME FROST. 1348-9. *(wid of Jn F).*

FYTON, Johanne. *BirmCL-sls Hagley Hall 351276.* 1384. *(wid of Ric F, Kt).*

GOSEHALE, John de. *(or Jn Sharreve, of Isle of Thanet, Kent). Birch 10189.* S' EL...REV DE BERTI(?). 1340.

GROSVENOR, Robert. *Birch 10310.* S ROBERTI GROSVENOR. 1378.

HAGGERSTONE, Robert of. *PRO-sls Ex KR 16/26, 70.* 1322. *(charge unclear).*

HAKELUT, Edmund, Kt. *PRO-sls.* 1315-16.

HALIBURTON, Henry. *PRO-sls Homage, Bain II 816, HB-SND.* 1322.

HALIBURTON, Henry, of Edinburgh. *Stevenson.* 1296.

HEPBURN, Patrick, E of Bothwell. *Roman PO 1822.* 15 March 1497. *(qrs 1&4).*

HEREWARD, Elizabeth. *AnstisAsp I 221, 84.* 1341-2. *(1 of 3 shields; sl).*

[LAVALL]. *Mill Steph. (qtd 2&3 by Sherington; brass to Robt Southwell & w Cecily, dau of Thos Sherington of Barham, Suff).*

LENTHALE, Roland, Kt. *Baker-sls.* S...

Leynthale: milit. 1416-17. *(qtd by bend lozy; grant with others of Manors of [Trafford] &c, Ches).*

LEVYNG, John. *PRO-sls.* 1358-9.

LUMLEY, Patrick, of that Ilk. *Stevenson.* 1397. *(one of the Scottish Commissioners).*

MALORY, Elizabeth. *PRO-sls E40 A9657.* 1429-30. *(w of Jn M, of Welton).*

MARBULL, Hugh. *PRO-sls E40 A1864.* 1528-9.

[MAULEY]. *Mill Steph.* 1418. *(imp by Sir Thos St Quintin for his w Agnes de M; brass, Harpham, Yorks).*

[MAULEY]. *Mill Steph.* 1418. *(brass to Sir Thos Quintin & w Agnes [de M], Harpham, Yorks).*

MAULEY, Peter de. *PRO-sls.* S' PETRI DE MALO LACU TERCII. 1301. *(shield & trapper on obv).*

MAULEY, Sir Peter de. *PRO-sls.* SIGILLUM PETRI DE MAULEY. 1380. *(banneret).*

MAULEY, Peter de, Chivaler. *PRO-sls.* 1369.

MAULEY, Peter de, Ld of Mulgrave. *Barons Letter. (sl & c'sl).*

MAULEY, Piers. *PRO-sls Ex KR 73/1, 18, 24, HB-SND.* 1369.

MAULEY, Piers. *PRO-sls Ex KR 73/1, 16, HB-SND.* 1369. *(bend diapered).*

[MAULEY, Sir Piers]. *Blair N I 11, 20.* 1355. *(beneath battlements of W tower of inner gateway, Alnwick Castle).*

MERIET, Lucy de. *Birch 11734.* SIGILLV....- CIE: ...E: MERIET. 1309. *(only traces remain; dau of Wm Malet & wid of Hugh de Meryet, of Kent).*

MONCEAUS, Waleran de. *Bk of Sls 479.* 1256.

MONCEUX. *CY 163, 652. ('Mownsews' of Suss).*

RUMMYLOWE, Stephen. *PRO-sls.* S' STEPHANI DE ROMELOWE. 1390.

SANDILANDS, Sir John, of Calder. *Stevenson.* 1471. *(d ante 1487, & others down to 1604).*

SARRE, Jehan de. *PRO-sls.* 1340. *(poss French).*

SCROOPE. *Mill Steph.* 1514. *(cresc in chf for diffce; qtg [Tiptoft] & imp by Brewse; brass to Thos B & w Jane S, Little Wenham, Suff).*

SCROP, Richard le. *PRO-sls E40 A10312.* S' Ricardi le Scrop. 1371.

SCROP, Stephen le, Ld of Oxendon, Gloucs. *Birch 13372.* SIGILLUM STEPHANI LE SCROP. 1449. *(qtg 2&3 [Tiptoft] salt engr).*

SCROPE. *S&G II 272. (sls on charter, Abbey of Rievaulx).*

[SCROPE]. *Mill Steph.* 1470. *(imp by Rochford; brass to Hen Rochforth, Stoke Rochford, Lincs).*

SCROPE, of Bolton, Yorks. *Blair D II 162,
342*. *(qtg 2&3 salt engr & imp qtly 1&4 3
escallops 2&3 checky; S gable, E wall, Langley Hall).*

SCROPE, Geo. *Mill Steph.* 1614. *(cresc for
diffce; brass to Geo S, Hambleden, Bucks).*

SCROPE, Geoffrey de. *Birch 13351.* S' GAL-
FRIDI DE SCRO... early 14 cent.

SCROPE, Geoffrey le. *Durham-sls 2196.*

SCROPE, Sir Geoffrey. *S&G II 273.* *(sl on
undated release, Abbey of Jervaulx).*

SCROPE, Sir Geoffrey. *S&G II 343.* ?temp
Edw 1. *(on document in Abbey of St Mary of
York).*

SCROPE, Sir Henry. *S&G II 280-1.* *(sl on
document at Priory of Newburgh).*

SCROPE, Sir Henry. *S&G II 272.* *(sl on
charter 'beyond memory of man', Abbey of
Rievaulx).*

SCROPE, John, Ld le. *PRO-sls E40 A6808.*
1471-2. VM: JOHANNIS: DOMINI: LESCROPE.
(qrs 1&4; baston).

SCROPE, Margery, lady de, & of Masham.
PRO-sls. 1417-18.

SCROPE, Richard de. *?source.* 1388. *(sl).*

SCROPE, Richard le. *PRO-sls E40 A6351.*
1378-9.

SCROPE, Richard le, Ld of Bolton. *PRO-sls
AS 4.* Sigillu: rici: le Scrop: domini: de: bolton.
1399.

SCROPE, Richard le, Chevr. *Birch 11306.* S':
RICARDI: LE: SCROPE. 1379.

SCROPE, Sir Richd le, 1st Ld Scrope of Bolton. *Durham-sls 2201.* 1383.

SCROPE, Robert. *Mill Steph.* 1500. *(brass to
Robt S & w, Hambleden, Bucks).*

SCROPE, Sr Wm. *S&G II 275.* *(tomb, Abbey
of St Agatha, Richmondshire).*

SEYNPERE, Ralph de, of Mercaston, Derbys.
Birch 13426. PREVE SV..... 1371. *(shield
betw antlers of stag's head cab).*

SORELL, Luke, of Lapworth, Warws. *Vinc
88, 20.* +SIGIL' LVCAE DE SORELL. *(grant to
Wm de Bishopston, T Walt de Daquilla,
Ricardo Trussello, Fretherico de Bishopston,
Johanne de Loddington, Fretherico de
Dukeforde).*

SPARWE, Robert, of Braunforde, Suff. *Birch
13599.* 1343. *(imp dolphin hauriant).*

SPICER, William. *PRO-sls.* 1352-3. *(s of
Ric S).*

STAFFORD, John de. *Bow XLVII 16.* 1362-3.
(sl on grant of land in Tutbury, Staffs).

STANDEN, Thomas of. *Dodsworth 49, 4b,
HB-SND.* 1346.

SUTTON, Johes de, Ld of Duddeleye.
BirmCL-sls Hagley Hall 351157. 1339.

TAPTON, William. *PRO-sls.* temp Ric 2.

TREHAMPTON, Radulfus. *Birch 6478.* S....-

ADVL......TO... 12 cent. *(s of Dom Ricardi de
T, of Leymarsh, Lincs; equestr sl).*

TURNHAM, Stephen, Kt. *Birch 6488.*
+SIGILLVM: STEPHANI: DE: TVRNAHAM. temp
K John. *(Baron T of Kent & Suss, Seneschal
of Anjou; ob ante 1214; equestr sl).*

[TYRINGTON]. *Farrer II 221.* *(in battlements
of Terrington St Clement Ch, Norf).*

VALLIBUS, John de. *Stevenson.* early 13
cent. *(s of Wm de V).*

VAUX, de, of Dirleton. *Stevenson.* 1439.
*(qtd by Walter Haliburton, Ld of Dirleton &
others).*

VAUX, John. *PRO-sls.* 1438.

VAUX, John de. *Durham-sls 2529.*

VENIS, ... de. *PRO-sls.* 1405-6.

VERNOUN, Ralph. *PRO-sls.* 1340-1.

WENDESLEY, Thos de. *?source.* 1403. *(on
surcoat of mont, Bakewell, Derbys).*

Bend sin

ARDERN, Radulf de. *Dugd 17, 15.* S. Radude
Ardeme.

BURSTALL, Robert de. *Bow LXXVIII 2.*
SIGILLVM ROBERTI DE BVRSTALL. *(equestr sl;
grant to Robt, s of Alan de B of croft Luthekestove & land in moor of Belegravia near
Burstall & Luthekestove).*

DENNISTON. *Stevenson.* 1508. *(qtd by Robt
Maxwell, of Calderwood).*

[HASTINGS]. *Proc Soc Antiq XIX 2S 241.*
temp Edw 1. *(nave, Cogenhoe Ch,
Northants).*

MORDINGTON, Sir Wm, Kt, ?Berwicks.
Stevenson. 1246.

SCHAU...t, John. *Baker-sls.* Iohis Schau...t.
1349-50. *(qtg cross engr).*

WAWE, John. *PRO-sls.* S' IOHAN UVA...
1376-7.

Bend enhanced
— *SHY 194.* *(imp lozy Or and Az).*

Untinc bend Arg
FOLIOTT. *CT 241.*

Untinc bend Gu
— *CT 298.*

Arg bend Az
Arg bend Az
— *WGA 287.*
— *D4 23.* *(qtd 3 by [Remston] all qtd IV by
Stapilton, Notts).*
— *LE 377.* *(qtd 2&3 by Gu 3 hatchets Or).*
— *WB II 69, 4.* *(qtd 2&3 by qtly Arg and
Gu & border engr Sa).*
— *LD 28.* *(qtd 2&3 by Gu maunche Or).*
BADBY, John of. *WB III 91b, 6.*
BADEUE, S' Hugo de, Essex. *CY 140, 557.*
BUSET. *L1 56, 4.*
[CENDR'?], Mons Hew. *WJ 1589.*
FENYS, S Will of Suss. *CY 162, 648.*

GISSYNG. *FB 25.*
RITHER, Mons John de. *TJ 265. (blazon adds 3 crescs Or on bend).*
SANDELANDIS, of Chalder. *Lyndsay 238.*
SANDILANDS, of Calder. *Stodart 7. (qtd 1&4 by Douglas).*
SANDILANS, le Sire de. *Stodart, pl D6.*
STANLEI, Thomas, of Staffs. *WB III 99, 9. (qrs 1&4).*
STANLEY, Johannes. *Q II 684.*
STANLEY, John. *WJ 1564.*
STANLEY, S' John de of Ches. *CY 17, 67.*
[STANLY], John. *SES 119.*
TATESHALL, le sieur. *BG 34.*
TRAVERS. *PLN 1004.*

Arg bend Gu
Arg bend Gu
— *WJ 1445. (name illegible).*
— *LS 54. (qtd 2&3 by Pole & imp Stafford).*
— *S 535. (?Tyrington).*
— *BG 268.*
— *A 256. (?Or bend Gu; Will'...).*
— *WB II 55, 12.*
— *SC 31. (qtd 3 by Ld Halybarton).*
— *PLN 104 & 146. (?qtly Arg and Gu bend Gu; qtd 2&3 by Ld Harington).*
— *Q 588.*
— *ML I 535. ('Quartly silver wit a bende upon the first asur').*
AVERYNE, Huwe de. *LM 545.*
BODRUGAN, Mons Wm. *SD 60.*
CHIDCROFT, John de. *CVK 722.*
CREAMTONE, Lincs. *L2 144, 5.*
CRUMWELL, Rauf de. *LM 417.*
DEPDEN. *LE 334.*
DEPDEN. *L1 209, 5; L2 149, 3. (L1 margin: 'Treanton of co Linc').*
DEPDEN. *RB 273.*
DEPDEN. *L10 57b, 7.*
GRABON, William. *WLN 430.*
HARINGTON. *LD 18. (?qtly Arg and Gu bend Gu, or else qtg 2&3 Gu plain).*
STOPHAM, Sr William de. *M 28. ('dargent ... de gules').*
TENDIRDEN. *LY A 48. (qrs 1&4).*
TIRENTON or TREHAMPTON. *Nichols Leics IV 641. (Higham Ch).*
TIRENTONE, Raf de. *F 110.*
TIRRINGTON, Ralph de. *WLN 403.*
TRAYHAMPTON, Rauf de. *P 117.*
TREANTON, Sr Ry. *ME 101; LY A 226.*
TREAUNTONE, Sire Rauf de. *N 680.*
TREAUNTONE, Sir Rauff. *CB 281.*
TREHAMPTON, Rauf de. *LM 178.*
TREHAMTON, Rauf de. *B 170.*
TREHAUNT, Radulfus de. *Q II 533.*
TREHAUNTON, Rauf. *Q 559.*
VAUS, Sr de. *BL A 26.*

VAUX, Ld Dirleton. *Lyndsay 129. (qtd by Haliburton).*
WAUSS. *Lyndsay 138. ('Lord of Dyrltoun of auld').*
WYNCESTRE, Richard de. *LM 512. (bend narrow).*

Arg bend Purp &c
Arg bend Purp
MALMANS, Sr Nicholas. *M 10.*
Arg bend Sa
— *D5 249. (qtd by Vavasor, of Newton & Weston, [Yorks]).*
— *WB II 66, 14. (qtd 3 by Sir Jn Mordaunt).*
— *BW 5b, 24. (qtd II&III 2&3 i&iv by Beauchamp, E Warwick).*
— *SHY 210. (qtd 2&3 by Sir Thos P... Or 3 eagles claws erased Sa).*
— *XFB 133. (qtd 4 on pennon of Johannes Mordaunt).*
— *LM 383.*
COLLEBRONE. *LO B 25.*
CRWELL. *L10 46b, 6.*
CURSON, John, of Staffs. *WB III 99b, 9. (shield badly damaged).*
[DENNISTON]. *Berry, Stodart pl 2. (qtd 1&4 by Cunningham).*
DENNISTOUN, of that Ilk. *Lyndsay 247.*
DESPENCER. *DX 62.*
DESPENCER. *BW 5b, 24. (qtd II&III 2&3 by Gu fret Or).*
LE DESPENCER. *SP A 58. (qtd by Gu fretty Or).*
[DRAYTON]. *PLN 872. (imp Wynne, Per bend Sa and Arg).*
DYTTON. *CVL 347.*
DYTTON. *L10 58b, 1.*
DYTTON, Lancs. *CY 50, 199.*
ERDSWICK, Thos. *GutchWdU. (imp by Stafford Arg on chev Gu 5 roundels Or; window, Library, Balliol College, Oxf).*
MOUNCEUX. *SK 232.*
OLDEG[RA]VE, Ric de. *Q 595.*
PAYNE, Rauf. *TJ 295.*
PAYNEL. *L1 506, 4. (?St Low).*
PAYNEL. *L9 96a, 5.*
PAYNELL. *PT 419.*
PAYNELL. *DV 56a, 2213.*
PAYNELL, Monsire Ralph, de Kaythorp. *CG 357.*
PAYNELL, Sr Rauf. *TJ 256. (gloss on Thos Stopham - 'lez armes sont en debate').*
PAYNELL, Sir Rauff. *CB 280.*
PAYNELL, Mons Rf. *WJ 1504.*
POPHAM, Sir William de. *PT 1017.*
SCOPHAM. *L1 614, 5.*
SEINTLOU. *CB 182.*
SEYNTLOWE, le S' de. *WJ 1481.*

SPENCER, Ld. *BW 7, 34. (qrs 1&4).*
SPENCER, Ld. *BR VI 12. (qtd 2&3 by Gu fret Or).*
SPENCER, Sr Herri. *BR V 12. (qtg Gu fretty Or).*
ST LOW, Sir T. *CRK 245. (qrs 1&4).*
STAPHAM. *LS 100.*
STAPHAM, Monsire de. *CG 356.*
STEPHAM, le Sr de. *AS 201.*
STEPHANT. *L1 612, 3.*
STOPHAM. *CT 130.*
MOUNSEAULX. *Suff HN 26. (Sotterley Ch).*
STOPHAM. *XPat 254, Arch 69, 89.*
STOPHAM, Sr de. *CKO 208.*
STOPHAM, John. *TJ 296. (baston).*
STOPHAM, Sir Thomas. *CB 276.*
STOPHAM, Thomas. *TJ 256.*
STOPHAM, Sire Willame. *N 728.*
STOPHAM, Willeme de. *LM 174.*
STOPHAM, Sir William. *LS 192.*
STOPHAM, Sire Wyllame de. *HA 6.*
Arg bend Vt
KENDALE. *L9 24, 2.*
KENDALL. *DV 64a, 2530.*

Az bend Arg
Az bend Arg
— *WJ 1599. (name illegible).*
— *WJ 1600. (name illegible).*
— *SC 67. (qtd 2&3 by Wemis).*
— *SK 911.*
BELGRAVE, Thomas. *LV 57.*
BISSART, Lord of Bewfort of auld. *Lyndsay 150.*
BISSET. *Berry, Stodart pl 4. (qtd 1&4 by Wemyss).*
[BISSET, of Rires]. *Lyndsay 169. (qtd by Wemys, of Reras).*
BUSELL, S'g'r. *RB 132.*
BUSET. *LE 313.*
BUSETT. *L1 87, 3; L2 67, 12.*
BUSTTES. *L10 85b, 4.*
LANWELL, Sir John. *(or [Lavall]). CRK 1286.*
LAWALL. *L9 37b, 2.*
LAWALLE, Mons J. *WJ 1577.*
LUTEREL, Sr. *CKO 195.*
NOYERS. *L2 367, 12.*
YORK. *L9 4, 9. (imp Az bend Arg; ?poss Az bend rompu Arg).*

Az bend Or
Az bend Or
— *CRK 457. (qtd 2&3 by Arundel, of Cornw).*
— *PLN 2039. (qtd 2&3 by Sir Jn Arundel).*
— *D4 29. (imp by Lumley, Durham).*
CARMENOW. *PLN 1011.*
[CARMINOW]. *Batt. (imp by qtly Arundel &*

Dauntsey; canopied tomb, Dauntsey Ch, Wilts).
CARMYNOWE, Devon. *RH, Ancestor iv 248. (cresc for diffce).*
[S]CROPE, Ld, of Bolton. *RH, Ancestor iv 230.*
DOYLY. *L1 200, 5; L2 155, 4. ('Doyly' erased & 'Scrope' noted in margin).*
GROSVENOR, Sr Robert. *WLN 295.*
GROSVENOR, S' Robert le, Ches. *CY 6, 24.*
SCROBE, Ld. *PCL IV 140.*
SCROOP, le Sr de. *CN 89.*
SCROOPE. *CB 35.*
SCROOPE, Galfredus. *Q II 15.*
SCROP, le C'r. *BD 86. (5th S window, hall, York Palace, Southwell).*
SCROP, L. *BR V a 29.*
SCROP, Sir William. *WGA 165.*
SCROPE. *WLN 254.*
SCROPE. *S&G II 278. (Sub-prior of Wartre).*
SCROPE. *WB I 29b, 4.*
SCROPE. *S&G II 271. (painted & named in old book 'the making of which is beyond memory' in Selby Abbey).*
SCROPE. *S&G II 276. (painted on wall of chapel of St Mary Magdalene nr gate of Abbey of Byland).*
SCROPE. *WB II 51, 8. (qrs 1&4).*
SCROPE, Ld. *WB I 32, 14.*
SCROPE, Ld. *BR IV 33.*
SCROPE, Ld. *FK I 104.*
SCROPE, Ld. *WB I 35b, 17.*
SCROPE, Ld. *KB 303.*
SCROPE, Ld de. *WLN 255.*
SCROPE, the Lord. *LD 4. (qrs 1&4).*
[?SCROPE]. *Dingley ccccxxxi. (qtd 3 by Arundel & imp by Capel; St Bartholomew's behind Royal Exchange, London).*
[SCROPE]. *ML I 11.*
[SCROPE]. *SHY 62. (imp [Tiptoft]).*
SCROPE, Ld [of Bolton]. *BR VI 28.*
SCROPE, Ld, of Bolton. *CRK 1305. (qrs 1&4).*
SCROPE, Ld, of Bolton. *PLN 109. (qtg 2&3 Tiptoft).*
SCROPE, Ld, of Bolton. *BW 8, 42.*
SCROPE, Ld, of Bolton. *AY 37.*
SCROPE, of Bolton. *ML I 58; ML II 55.*
SCROPE, of Bolton, Yorks. *D4 30b.*
[SCROPE, of Boulton]. *Nichols Leics II 178. (Edmondthorpe Ch).*
SCROPE, Sir Geoffrey. *S&G II 445. (s of Sir Hen S; on memorial tablet in Konigsberg Cathedral [Evidence of Sir Hen Ferrers]).*
SCROPE, Sir Henry. *S&G II 275. (painted on tomb of Sir Hen S, a founder of Abbey of St Agatha, Richmondshire).*
SCROPE, the Lord Henry, [of Bolton]. *PR(1512)64. (qtg Tibetot, Scrope of Masham*

overall).
SCROPE, John, Ld. *WGA 88.*
SCROPE, Sir John le, KG. *Proc Soc Antiq XVIII 2S 150. (5th Ld S of Bolton, d1498; qtg [Tiptoft]).*
SCROPE, Sir John, KG. *Leake. c1461. (d1494; qtg Tiptoft).*
SCROPE, Margaret. *Sandford 401. (w of Edmond de la Pole, 2nd E of Suffolk, d1513).*
SCROPE, Margaret. *S&G II 305. (imp by Chauncy Gu cross formy Arg & on chf Or lion pg Az; w of Robt de C, buried at Skirpenbeck).*
SCROPE, Ld Richard, of Bolton. *S 101.*
SCROPE, Sir Richd. *S&G II 264. (Sir Ric S & his father, ?both lawyers, said to be 1st Scropes to bear these arms; evidence of Sir Jn Massy, of Tatton, cousin of Sir Rob Grosvenor).*
SCROPE, Thomas. *S&G II 274. (monk & abbot of Jerveaulx; on tablet in Abbey).*
SCROPE, Sir William. *S&G II 309. (borne at siege of Vaunes; elder bro of Sir Ric S).*
SCROPE, Sir Wm. *S&G II 349-50. (f of Hen & Geoffrey S, 'always tourneyed in the above arms').*
SCROPE, Sir Wm. *S&G II 426-27. (gdfather of Sir Ric S; said by f of Jn Thirlewalle to have been killed at Falkirk).*
SCROPP, Ld. *BA 720.*
SCROPP, the Lord. *WK 458.*
SCROPP, Sir John, of Castlecombe. *BA 833.*
SCROPPE. *LD 106. (qrs 1&4).*
SCROPPE, Ld. *LO B 10.*
SCROPPE, the Lord. *BA 588.*
SCROPPE, Mons'r Wyll'm. *BB 101. (d1399).*
SCROUP, Ld. *BA 728.*
SCROUPE. *L1 570, 3.*
SCROWPE, ... *WJ 1603. (name illegible).*
SCROWPE, ... *WJ 1598. (name illegible).*
SCROWPE, ... *WJ 1604. (name illegible).*
SKROP, Mons Richard le. *S 99.*
SKROWP, the Lord. *I2(1904)104. (qtg Arg saltire engr Gu).*

Gu bend Arg
Gu bend Arg
— *NS 124. (qtd 2&3 by Ed Hastyng).*
— *WK 18. (qtd 2&3 by Sir Rob Poyntz Or plain).*
— *XK 111. (qtd 2&3 by Sir George Hastings, Kt 1509).*
— *CRK 196. (qtd 2&3 by Hastings).*
— *SHY 85. (qtd 2&3 by Hastings).*
— *T c 35. (qtd by le S'r de Hastings).*
— *LH 28. (qtd 2&3 by Hastings).*
— *LH 502. (qtd 2&3 by Hastings).*
— *CKO 187. (original worn away, Sr Bryn-..?, or Pryn...?, in 16 cent hand; Copy A*

gives Sr de Follyott).
— *KB 296. (qtd 2&3 by Ld Hastings).*
— *WB I 32, 12. (qtd 2&3 by Ld Hastynges).*
— *WK 473. (qtd 2&3 by Sir George Hastingis).*
— *WB II 54, 8. (qtd 2&3 by Hastings).*
— *WB II 50, 2. (qtd 2&3 by Ld Hastynges).*
— *WK 153. (qtd 2&3 by Sir Jn Hastynges).*
— *PLN 119. (qtd 2&3 by Ld Hastings Or maunch Arg).*
— *BA 608. (qtd 2&3 by Sir Jn Hastynges).*
— *SHY 196. (qrs 1&4, imp by Scales).*
— *SHY 225. (imp Scales).*
BAYNTON, Sir John. *CRK 742. (qrs 1&4).*
CAMOIS, John de. *CA 213.*
CHAURS, Hervey de. *WLN 825.*
EGSTALE, Whilliam, of Staffs. *WB III 99b, 1. (qrs I&IV 1&4).*
FALIOT, John, de Norf. *WJ 1421.*
FFOLYOT, Walter. *WLN 705.*
FILIOT. *FK II 405.*
FILIOT, Monsr de. *AS 170.*
[FOLIOT]. *AY 62. (qtd 1&2 by L[ord] Hastyngys).*
FOLIOT, Norff. *L1 248, 1; L2 203, 5.*
FOLIOT, Richard. *Q 131.*
FOLIOT, Richard. *E 59.*
FOLIOT, Rychard. *PCL I 505.*
FOLIOTT. *SP A 138.*
[FOLIOTT]. *PLN 2032. (qtd 2&3 by Sir Jn Hastings).*
FOLIOTT, Richard. *B 172.*
FOLLIOT, Monsire. *CG 352.*
[FOLLIOT]. *LMO 59.*
[FOLLIOTT]. *Farrer I 315. (qtd by [Hastyngs]; shield, Mattishall Ch, Norf).*
[FOLLYOT]. *SHY 471-483. (qtd by Hastings).*
FOLYOT. *CV-BM 44.*
FOLYOT, Mons' Richard. *TJ 253.*
FOLYOTT. *Suff HN 7. (Lavenham Ch).*
FOLYOTT, Robt, of Suss. *CY 164, 65b.*
FYLYOTT, Sir Richard. *BR V 92.*
HARCOURT, Sir Symon. *WB II 67, 1. (qrs 1&4).*
HASTINGES, Ld. *BW 12, 75. (qrs 1&4).*
HASTYNGES, Ld. *WB I 37, 20.*
HOWARD, S' Johan. *BR IV 68.*
HOWARDE, Sir J. *WB I 41b, 1.*
MARTHAM. *L2 331, 8.*
NEUFCHASTEL, Jehan de, Seigneur de Montagu. *CB 417.*
PRENDERGAST, Robarde, of Northd. *RH, Ancestor iv 243.*
ROYE, Reignante de. *LE 253.*
SCHASTOWE. *LE 392.*
Gu bend sin Arg
— *BR VI 15. (qtd by Ld Hastynges, of Kent).*

Gu bend Or &c
Gu bend Or
— *D4 27b. (imp by Cholmundeley of Golston, Yorks & by Husse, of Hurswell, Yorks).*
— *D4 37b. (imp by Gowre, of Seydnam, Yorks).*
— *CKO a 73.*
— *WLN 54.*
— *D5 155. (qtd by Legerd, of Aulabye, Yorks).*
— *WB V 88. (qtd 2&3 Or plain by Sir Robt Pointz Kt, 1485).*
CHALON, le Counte. *C 69.*
CLARENDON, Roger de. *S 135.*
COLUMBARS. *L1 163, 2; L2 118, 7.*
COLUMBERIS. *LY A 212.*
COLUMBERS. *L9 22b, 6.*
COLUMBERS. *L10 39b, 16.*
COLUMBS. *LE 148.*
CONSTABLE. *Gelre 58. (for the Constable-ship; qtg 2&3 Vair; rectius qtly GuVair bend Or).*
CONSTABLE, of Flamborough, Yorks. *D4 39b.*
FRESSE, Duke of. *PCL IV 94.*
KELOMBERIS, Mons J. *WJ 1569-70. (& his s).*
KOLOMBERRIE. *ME 87.*
Gu bend Sa
GERMAN, Mons P. *WJ 1547.*
MAULE, S Piers de. *ST 92.*

Or bend Az
Or bend Az
— *XK 136. (qtd 4 by Sir Thos Fairfax).*
— *CRK 774.*
[CALTHORPE]. *D4 35b; E6. ('Carthorpe in E6; qtd by Farfax, of Walton, Yorks).*
CARTHORP. *L10 42, 19.*
CARTHORPE. *PT 1046.*
CARTHORPP. *LE 306.*
CRY, Matheu de. *SK 467. (acc to Gibbon this is Trye).*
GERNONE. *WJ 1597, 1601 & 1605. (& 2 illegible names).*
GRY. *L1 284, 3; L2 225, 7.*
LORN, ceulx de. *Berry, Stodart pl 10. (qtd 1&4 by Or chf Sa).*
VARNON, S' Warinus le, Ches. *CY 6, 21.*
[?VAUX]. *Lyndsay 72. (qtd by Hepburn, E of Bothwell).*
VERNON, S' Nicol de. *WLN 329.*
VERNON, S' Warren le. *WLN 297.*
VERNON, Warren le. *CVC 453. (note in Glover's hand 'Az fess Or').*

Or bend Gu
Or bend Gu
— *SK 360.*
— *WJ 1557 & 1561. (name illegible).*
— *WB V 17. (qtd 1&4 by Az fess Or).*
— *WB II 55, 10.*
COTEL, Sir Elis. *CB 277.*
COTEL, Syr Elys. *N 201.*
COTEL, Thomas. *TJ 321.*
COTELL. *CT 223.*
COTELL, Dorset & Som. *L2 135, 3.*
DANSEL. *L1 197, 3. (in margin 'Cotel of Som').*
DANSELL. *L10 53, 13.*
DENESELLE. *L10 59, 11.*
DENSELL. *BA 1115.*
DREVSELL, Devonshire. *L2 160, 10.*
MORELL. *L9 70b, 10.*

Or bend Sa &c
Or bend Sa
— *D4 39b. (qtd by Bygode, of Settrington, Yorks).*
— *D4 28b. (qtd 2&3 by Salven, of Newbiggin, Yorks).*
— *WJ 1540.*
BIGOD, ... *TJ 1233b. (gloss on TJ 1233 'le Se' de Maulay port le m & Bigod').*
FOSSARD, Mons' Rob't. *TJ 1233.*
FOSSARD, Will, Baro de Mulgrave. *Vinc 5, 21.*
FOSSARDE, Robert. *P 114.*
GWYTFELD, Mons Math. *WJ 1536.*
HALHORN. *WB II 63, 12.*
[ILLAKE]. *Neale & Brayley. 1296. (Canopy of mont to Edm, E of Lancs).*
MALOLAZO. *(alias Mauley). Vinc 5, 26. (arms of Petrus de M alias dictus Mawley (d1278-9)).*
MANLEE. *L2 347, 5.*
MANLEY, Sr de. *CKO 185.*
MANNE. *ML II 72. (name mistaken for Mauley).*
MAULAIT, Monsire de. *CG 337.*
MAULAY, le Sire de. *TJ 232.*
MAULAY, le Sr de. *TJ 1233a. (gloss on: Mons' Robert Fossard).*
MAULAY, Peres de. *H 26a.*
MAULE. *L2 345, 1.*
MAULE, Sr Jo' de. *RB 57.*
MAULEE, Sire Peres de. *N 61.*
MAULEY. *CT 302.*
MAULEY. *LD 16.*
MAULEY. *CRK 218.*
MAULEY, ... *WJ 1533.*
MAULEY, Ld. *PLN 163.*
MAULEY, Ld. *RH, Ancestor iii 211. ('golde a bend sabyll'; altered from Wasteneys).*
MAULEY, Ld. *PLN 112. (qtd 2 by Or lion*

Az, 3 Az bend gobony Arg and Gu).
MAULEY, Monsire de. *AN 53.*
MAULEY, le Sr de. *T c 31.*
MAULEY, le Sr de. *AS 38.*
MAULEY, Peres de. *Q 119.*
MAULEY, Sr Peres de. *H 26b.*
MAULEY, Peris de. *LM 122.*
MAULEY, Peris de. *FF 28.*
MAULEY, Sire Peris de. *J 71.*
MAULEY, Pers de. *G 137.*
MAULEY, S' Pers. *PO 674.*
MAULEY, Sir Pers. *ML I 102.*
MAULEY, Sir Philip. *PCL I 491.*
MAULEY, Piers. *LMS 75.*
MAWLE, Ld. *WB I 37, 17.*
MAWLE, Sir Pierce. *BR V 30.*
MAWLEY. *L9 51a, 5.*
MAWLEY, ... de. *SP A 60.*
MAWLEY, Baron. *CKO a 23.*
MAWLEY, Ld. *KB 318. (qrs 1&4).*
MAWLZ. *SK 124.*
MAWOLE, L[ord]. *AY 55.*
[MORLEY, Ld. *WB V 45.*
Or bend sin Sa
— *ML I 53. ('Gold a fyssur sabyll or a sem-blawnt sabyll. Et potest ingradari sed berule non possunt').*
MAWLE, Ld. *BR VI 21.*
Or bend Vt
BRAHAM. *L2 97, 11.*
BRAHAM. *L1 118, 5. (Rougecroix; marginal note gives Browne, of Norf).*

Sa bend Arg &c
Sa bend Arg
— *LE 263. (qtd 2&3 by Fredericus de Foll-zatis).*
— *PLN 1178.*
— *LE 470.*
ANTINGHAM. *DV 57b, 2273.*
ANTINGHAM. *PT 211.*
ANTINGHAM, Bar'. *NS 11.*
ANTYNGHAM. *PO 183.*
ANTYNGHAM. *L10 5, 3.*
ANTYNGHAM. *L1 21, 2; L2 5, 9.*
ANTYNGHAM, Monsire Bartholomew de. *AN 135.*
ANTYNGHAM, Mons Bertr. *WJ 1517-8.*
AUTINGHAM. *L1 10, 6.*
GRIF, Miles. *LE 276. (Anteright added by another hand).*
HELLES, Rauf de. *FW 618.*
MONSEDLA. *WB II 55, 6. (or Ansingham or Riviere).*
RIVIERE, de la.
AUTINGHAM. *LE 259.*
TROWEU, James de. *LM 535.*

Sa bend Or
BROMFLETE. *L2 67, 11.*
[FOLJAMBE], son fitz. *WJ 1550.*
HANVILE, Ric de. *Q 529.*
HOARE. *LH 137.*
[HOARE]. *LD 27.*
HORE, Mons Ger. *WJ 1551.*

Vt bend Arg &c
Vt bend Arg
— *FK II 616. (qtd 2&3 by Strickland).*
— *LS 176. (qtd 2&3 by Strickland).*
MAR, le Counte de. *LM 46.*
Vt bend Or
— *PT 904.*
— *LH 638. (qtd 2 by Ric Hunt, of Badley, Suss).*
HINTON. *L1 345, 1; L2 248, 4.*
HYNTON. *DV 69b, 2768.*

1 BEND FIELD PATTERNED

Barry of 4 & bend
Barry of 4 Arg and Sa bend Gu
DRONSFEILD. *XPat 309, Arch 69, 92.*
Barry of 4 Az and Arg bend Gu
POWEYS, Ld. *BW 12b, 80. (qrs 1&4).*

Barry of 6 & bend
Barry of 6 & bend
— *Exeter D&C 405. 1375. (?bend charged; sl used by Wm Wyke, legend illegible may include 'Wyke').*
BOYS, Sir Roger de. *Farrer Bacon 12. 1383.*
DANBY, William, of Stoke Daubeny, Northants. *Birch 9178.* [SI]GILL': WILLI': DANBI. *1400. (dex of imp coat, sin uncertain).*
[FINCHAM]. *Farrer II 155. (Feltwell St Mary Ch, Norf).*
GANT, Gilbert de. *Bk of Sls 298.* before June 1210. *(nephew of Gilbert de G, E of Lincoln).*
GRAY, Amice de. *Harl 2117 F275b; BrookeAsp I 22, 3.* SIGILLVM: AMICIAE: DE: GRAY. *1366-7. (wid of Jn de G of Rotherfield, Kt; grant of lands in West Tanfeld, Thornbargh & Byncehow).*
GREY, Sir John de. *Dugd 17, 76. 1303. (sl).*
GREY, John de, of Rotherfield. *AnstisAsp I 207, 48. 1329-30.*
GREY, John de, of Rotherfield, Yorks. *Birch 10263.* SIG': IOHIS: DE: RETHERFELD. *1361.*
GREY, Richard. *Roman PO 5451.* 21 Jan 1428.
[GREY, of Rotherfield]. *Mill Steph. c1460. (baston; brass to Ric Quatremaynes,*

Councillor to Ric, D of York & to Edw 4 & his w Sibil, dau of Nich Englefeld, Thame, Oxfords).

HAWE, Roger. *Vinc 88, 51.* 1362-3. *(sl).*

MERIET, Simon de. *PRO-sls.* 1363-4. *(baston).*

MERYET. *PRO-sls.* 1354-5. *(baston).*

[MONCHENSY]. *Birch 3332.* 15 cent. *(2nd sl of Priory of St Mary, Ixworth, Suff).*

PAPENHAM, Mond.Laurence de, of Northants, Hunts & Essex. *Birch 12376.* SIG...AVRENCII DE P...PENHAM. 1372.

PENBRIGGE, Richard de, Kt. *PRO-sls.* 1362-3.

PENBRUGGE, Henry de. *PRO-sls AS 20.* S'H.-..CI: DE: PEN...GE. 1302-3. *(shield placed on lion).*

PENBRUGGE, Henry de, Kt. *PRO-sls E40 A943.* S' HENRICI DE PENEBRVGE. 1302-3.

POINYNGES, Robert, Ld of. *CombeAsp II 184.* Sigillum roberti domini de Poinynges. *(qtg 2&4 3 lions pg surmounted by bend).*

PONYNGES, Robert, Ld de, of Suss, 5th Baron. *Birch 12786.* SIGILLUM ROBERTI? DOMINI DE PONIGGES. 1412. *(qtg 2&3 [Fitz-Payne?] 3 lions passt & bend).*

PONYNGGES, Thomas de. *Birch 12789.* SIGILLV THOME DE PONYNGES. 14 cent. *(bend ch with annulet for diffce).*

PONYNGS, Michael de. *PRO-sls.* .... DE PORVOUS. 1326-7. *(baston).*

POWNINGS, Eliz. *Faussett 1759.* c1528. *(dau of Sir Jn Scott & w of Sir Edw P; qtg 2&3 3 piles [Brian]; shield, now lost, on brass, chancel, Brabourne, Kent).*

POYNINGS. *Birch 12550.* 1527-37. *(qtd 3 by Hen Algernon Percy, 6th E of Northd, KG).*

POYNINGS. *PRO-sls.* 1528-9 & 1536-7. *(baston; qtd 3 by Hen Percy, 6th E of Northd, 1489-1527).*

[POYNINGS]. *Farrer Bacon 47.* 14 cent. *(on sl, detached, with [Beauchamp] fess & 6 mullets).*

QUAPLODE, John. *Birch 12881.* A ION EST CEO SEL DE QVAPPEL LEL (Motto). 1361. *(s of Edm de Q, of Norf, Kt).*

SHEPMAN, Robert. *(called Hynedon). SarumC-sls M74/W205 Drawer E.* 1378.

SONLES, John de. *Clairambault 8684.* 10 Feb 1298-9.

SOULES, John of. *Bain pl III 6, HB-SND.* 1289-90.

SOULES, Sir John de. *Stevenson 22.* S' IOH'IS DE SOULES MILITIS.

SOULIS, Sir John, Kt. *Stevenson.* 1292.

VERNON, John, of Somerton, Norf, Kt. *Birch 14155.* S' IOH'IS VERN.... 1357.

Barry of 6 Arg & Az bend

Barry Arg and Az bend Az

[GREY, of Rotherfield]. *Stamford 35. (bendlet Gu according to Holles).*

Barry Arg and Az bend Gu

— *XK 90.* (qtd I 4 by Hen Percy, E of Northd, KG 1531).

— *D4 23.* (qtd IV 1&4 by [Lovell]).

BARREY. *L10 21, 8.* *(baston; qrs 2&3).*

DANCORT, Lovell, of Staffs. *WB III 99b, 2.*

GAMTS, of Yorks. *XF 29.*

GAUNT. *L2 220, 6.*

GAUNT, Gilbert de. *LM 101.*

GAUNT, William de. *B 72.*

GRAY, Mons Barth. *WJ 506.*

GRAY DE BOWTONE. *PT 1249.* *(baston).*

GRAY, Mons Esmound de, de .... *WJ 508.*

GRAY, Sr John. *H 38b.*

GRAY, Mons John de, of Retherfeld. *WJ 505.*

GRAY, Sr Jon, Rotherfeld. *PO 210.*

GRAY, Mons Ric' de. *WJ 507.*

GRAY, Robert le. *WLN 797.*

GRAY, de Rotherfeld, Sr J. *CKO 305.* *(baston).*

GRAY, le Sire, de Stylyngflete. *TJ 571.* *(baston).*

GRAY, Sir Thomas, of Horton. *BA 659.*

GREY, Monsire de. *AN 72.*

GREY, Monsire, de Barton. *CG 222.*

GREY, le Sr de, Sr de Estmelingflete. *AS 99. (baston).*

GREY, Johan de. *H 38a.* *('vi pieces dasure et dargent ad le baston de goules').*

GREY, Sire Johan de. *N 448.*

GREY, Mons John. *CA 217.* *(baston).*

GREY, Mons' John, de Rotherfeld. *SD 24.*

GREY, John, Ld, of Rotherfeld. *S 66.*

GREY, Maud. *?source.* 1394. *(imp by Sir Thos Harcourt; tomb, Stanton Harcourt, Oxfords).*

GREY, Mons' Richard. *S 344.* *(Grey 'with a bend gules').*

GREY, Richard. *S 346.*

GREY, Robert de. *E 285.*

GREY, Robert de. *XF 958.*

GREY, Robert de. *F 281.*

GREY, Robertus. *Q II 158.*

GREY, of Rotherfeild. *Leake.* *(baston; qtd 4 by Francis Lovell, KG, d1483).*

GREY, le Sr le, de Rotherfeld. *S 64.* *(Grey 'with a bend gules').*

GREY, Ld, (of) Rotherfeld. *FK I 131.*

GREY, of Rotherfeld. *CRK 230.* *(baston).*

GREYE, the Lorde, of Rotherfeld. *WK B 25.*

HORBIN. *LH 992.* *(blazoned burely).*

HORBOURNE, Sire Johan de. *J 108.*

HORBURI, Sire Johan de. *N 738.*

ORE, Richard de. *FW 655.*

PABEHAM, Jan de. *Q 230.*

PARTHENAY. *C 174.* *('dit l'Archeveque').*
PAYN, Mons Robert. *WJ 495.* *(baston; son frere le fitz).*
PENBRYGE. *L1 502, 5.* *(baston).*
PONYNGES, Ld. *BW 9b, 54.* *(bend passes under Az bars; qrs 1&4).*
QUAPPELAND, Emund de. *Q 292.*
STANGAL, Mons Rauf de. *WJ 1151.* *(baston).*
STANGATE, Ralph. *XF 418.*
WALEYS, Henry le. *(or Stangate or Gaunt).* *XF 966.*
Barry Arg and Az bend sin Gu
— *BR VI 46.* *(marshalled by Ld Powis).*
Barry Arg and Az bend Or
— *PCL IV 143.* *(qtd 4 by Ld Lowell).*
GRAYE. *PT 453.* *(baston).*
GREY. *DV 50b, 1996.*

Barry Arg & Gu bend
Barry Arg and Gu bend Arg
— *Nichols Leics II 436.* *(Billesdon Church).*
MALKASTRE, S' Rob'. *PO 492.* *(baston).*
Barry Arg and Gu bend Az
MALCASTRE, Robert le. *CA 23.* *(baston).*
MANCESTRE. *L9 50b, 3.* *(blazoned burely).*
MANCHESTER. *XF 414.* *(blazoned burely).*
MONCASTRE, Mons Robert. *S 526.* *(baston, blazoned burely).*
MULCASTER. *PT 1257.* *(baston).*
MULCHESTRE, ... *WJ 1162.* *(blazoned burely).*
MUNCASTRE. *L1 427, 2; L2 330, 2.* *(blazoned burely).*
Barry Arg and Gu bend Sa
— *LE 275.*
CHAWORTH, Henry de. *TJ 1581.* *(blazoned burely).*
CHAWORTH, Mons Henry. *TJ 589.* *(blazoned burely).*
MARTYNDALE, William de. *TJ 1599.* *(baston).*

Barry Arg & Sa &c bend
Barry Arg and Sa bend Gu
[GREY, of Rotherfield]. *OxfRS IV 215; OxfAS 83, 13.* 1455. *(qtd 4 by Lovel; tomb Minster Lovel, Oxfords).*
HOGHTON. *PT 533.* *(baston).*
Barry Arg and Vt bend Gu
— *WGA 186.* *(qtd 3 by Hen Percy, E of Northd).*

Barry Az &c bend
Barry Az and Or bend Gu
— *WB III 121b, 9.* *(qtd 2&3 by Sir Johan Bare, of Herts).*
PENBRUGGE, Mons Richard. *WJ 814.* *(baston).*

Barry Gu and Arg bend Az
MULCASTRE, David de. *FC II 138.* *(baston).*

Barry Or & Arg &c bend
Barry Or and Arg bend Gu
— *Q 569.* *(unfinished).*
Barry Or and Az bend Gu
— *S 270.* *(qtd 2&3 by Thos Barry).*
— *PLN 1068.* *(qr 3 of coat imp by Sir Thos Bourchier).*
— *PLN 238.* *(baston; qtd 2&3 by Sir Thos Barre).*
— *CRK 749.* *(baston; qtd 2&3 by Sir Thos Barry).*
— *WK 553.* *(qtd I 4 by Percy).*
— *I2(1904)74.* *(qtd III, 2&3 by Sir Thos Cornwall).*
— *S 465.* *(qtd 2&3 by Mons Thos Barr).*
GAUNT. *L1 273, 4; L2 220, 5.*
GAUNT. *HA 126.*
GAUNT. *HA 138, 26.*
[GAUNT]. *Neale & Brayley.* 1296. *(canopy of mont to Edm, E of Lancs).*
GAUNT, G. *RB 396.*
GAUNT, Geffrey de. *C 86.*
GAUNT, Mons' Gilb't de, de Swaldale. *TJ 1231.*
GAUNT, Sire Gilberd de. *P 1044.*
GAUNT, Gilbert. *XF 960.*
GAUNT, Gilbert de. *P 102.*
GAUNT, Sir Gilbert. *CRK 604.* *(baston).*
GAUNTZ, Mons Gilbert. *WJ 1001.* *(baston).*
PEMBRIDGE. *XF 713.*
PEMBRUGE. *LEP 7.*
PEMBRUGE, Henri de. *E I 291; E II 293.*
PENBRIGE. *L9 97b, 7.*
PENBRUGE, Sire Henri de. *N 945.*
PENBRUGGE. *DV 63a, 2499.*
PENBRUGGE. *PT 516.* *(baston).*
PENBRUGGE. *CT 293.*
PENBRUGGE, Henr' de. *WLN 800.*
PENBRUGGE, Henri de. *F 285.*
PENBRUGGE, Monsire Richard. *AN 197.* *(baston).*
PENBRYGE. *L1 502, 5.*
PENEBRUGGE, S Henry de. *GA 215.* *(baston).*
PENNEBRIGGE, Sr Henry de. *L 5.*
[PONYNGS]. *I2(1904)258.* *(marshalled by [Percy] E of Northd).*
PONYNGS, Mons Lucas de. *WJ 842.* *(barry poss Or and Vt; baston).*
[POYNINGS]. *WB V 33.* *(baston).*
QUAPLAD, Monseur. *AS 491.*
QUAPPELAD, Ed'us de. *Q II 304.*
QUAPPOLOD, Tohmas. *PCL I 418.*
Barry Or and Az bend sin Gu
— *BR VI 33.* *(qtd by Ld Ponynges).*
QUAPLADE, Nicholas. *GutchWdU.* *(Abbot of*

Reading Monastery, Benefactor of Balliol
College, c1327; window, Balliol Coll
Library).

Barry Or & Gu &c bend
Barry Or and Gu bend Gu
SAYNT OWEN, Joan de. *E II 289.*
Barry Or and Vt bend Gu
— *WK 553. (baston; qtd III by Percy).*
— *WK 138. (baston; qtd 2 by E of Northd).*
— *WGA 207. (baston; qtd 3 by Hen Percy,*
6th E of Northd).
— *XF 741. (baston; qtd 3 by Percy).*
— *CRK 1306. (riband; qtd II&III 1&4 by*
Percy).
— *XK 90. (baston; qtd 3 by Hen Percy, E of*
Northd, KG 1531).
— *XK 47. (baston; qtd 3 by Hen Percy, E of*
Northd, KG).
— *D4 41b. (qtd by [Percy]).*
— *XK 256. (baston; qtd 3 by Sir Wm*
Percy).
— *WK 420. (baston; qtd 3 by Pawlet).*
— *XB 15. (baston; qtd by Percy).*
POINYNGES, le Sr de. *S 66.*
PONGYNG, S'r de, of Suss. *MY 310.*
PONIGES, S' John de. *R 47. (baston).*
PONINGES. *BG 64. (baston).*
PONINGES, Sire Michel de. *N 238.*
PONINGES, Sr Michel. *L 135.*
PONINGGES, Mons Thomas de. *CA 53. (bas-*
ton).
PONYNG, Sir Edward. *WGA 266. (baston).*
PONYNGE. *Suff HN 4. (Acton Ch).*
PONYNGE, le Sr de. *CN 52. (baston).*
PONYNGE, Sire Michel de. *HA 3. (baston).*
PONYNGE, le Sr de, of Suss. *CY 159, 636.*
(baston).
PONYNGE, Syr Edward. *I2(1904)107. (qtg, 2*
Gu 3 lions passt A bend Az, 3 Or 3 piles Az).
PONYNGES. *LE 346.*
PONYNGES, Ld. *RH, Ancestor iv 229. (bas-*
ton).
PONYNGES, Monsr de. *AS 297. (baston).*
PONYNGES, Sr de. *CKO 306. (baston).*
PONYNGES, le Sr. *NB 80. (baston).*
PONYNGES, Sir Edward. *WB V 71. (baston;*
Kt 1485).
PONYNGES, Sir Michael. *CV-BM 309. (bas-*
ton).
PONYNGES, Sire Michael de. *HA 11, 13.*
(baston).
PONYNGES, Sir Michel. *CB 293.*
PONYNGES, Sr Michol de. *RB 19. (baston).*
PONYNGES, Rogerus. *Q II 481.*
PONYNGES, Mons' Thomas. *SD 33.*
PONYNGGES, Ld. *WB I 37, 3. (baston).*
PONYNGH. *WB II 52, 9. (qrs 1&4).*
PONYNGIS. *L1 490, 1.*

PONYNGIS. *L9 107a, 1. (baston).*
PONYNGS. *I2(1904)258. (qtd 3 by Percy).*
PONYNGS. *DV 54a, 2127. (baston).*
PONYNGS, Mons Thoms. *WJ 841.*
POWNYNGGES, Monsire de. *AN 30.*
POYNENGES, le S'r de. *T c 20. (qtg Gu 3*
lions passt Arg bend Az).
POYNINGS. *XF 454. (baston).*
POYNINGS. *Leake. (qtd 3 by Hen, E of*
Northd, KG).
POYNINGS. *LEP 44. (baston).*
POYNINGS. *WLN 228.*
POYNINGS. *Gerard 36.*
POYNINGS, Ld. *FK I 125.*
POYNINGS, Ld. *PLN 108. (riband which HS*
London notes is Sa; qtd 2&3 by Fitzpayne).
POYNINGS, Ld. *KB 335. (qrs 1&4; baston).*
POYNINGS, Ld. *FB 73. (baston).*
[POYNINGS]. *Lambarde 210. (qtd by [Percy],*
imp by Howard; tomb of Thos, E of Arundel,
Norfolk Chapel, Arundel, Suss).
[POYNINGS]. *Blair N I 100, 211. (baston;*
qtd 3 by Percy, 6th E of Northd; Hexham
Priory, Northd).
POYNINGS, Sir Edward. *XF 569. (baston;*
qrs 1&4).
POYNINGS, Sir Edward. *PLN 1976. (qtg*
2&3 Gu 3 lions passt Arg on escutch Or 3
piles meeting in base Az).
POYNINGS, Sir Edward, KG. *XK 43. (bas-*
ton; qrs 1&4).
POYNINGS, John, Ld St John. *Sandford 225.*
(3rd husb of Philippa Mortimer, 2nd dau of
Edm, E of March).
POYNINGS, the Lorde. *WK B 26. (baston).*
POYNINGS, Lucas. *A 106.*
POYNINGS, Robert, Ld. *S 68.*
POYNYNGES, Sir Edwd. *WK 6.*
POYNYNGES, Mons' John. *TJ 565. (baston).*
POYNYNGES, Mons' Thomas. *TJ 573. (bas-*
ton).
Barry Or and Vt bend Sa
PONYNG, the Lorde. *WB IV 131b, 105. (bas-*
ton; qrs 1&4).

Barry Sa &c bend
Barry Sa and Arg bend Az
— *ML I 516. ('Sylver & sabyll barryd in vi*
a bende asur upon the same').
Barry Vt and Or bend Gu
PONYNGES. *PO 30. (baston).*
PONYNGS, L[ord]. *AY 51.*
Barry Gu and Vair bend Or
CONSTABLE, Sir Marmaduke. *WK B 33.*
(baston).
Barry Vair and Gu bend Or
COSCY, Thomas de. *C 180.*

Barry of 8 or more & bend
Barry of 8 & bend
  GYSBURN, John de. *PRO-sls.* 1377-8.
Barry of 8 Arg and Az bend Gu
  — *Neale & Brayley; Inventory. (imp by Lewis Robessart, d1431).*
  — *WK 168. (qtd II 2 by Sir Thos Cheyny).*
  GREY, Sir John. *BR V 256.*
  RYTHERISFELDE. *PO 29. (baston).*
Barry of 8 Or and Az bend Untinc
  PEMBRUGE. *LEP 6.*
Barry of 8 Or and Az bend Gu
  — *WB IV 139, 239. (baston; qtd 3 by Sir Thos Barre).*
  GAUNT, Gilb't de. *Q 95.*
Barry of 10 bend
  BURTON, Henry of. *Exeter D&C 270.* sigillum : heurici : d : burtone. 1380-1.
  [PABENHAM]. *Proc Soc Antiq XIX 2S 240.* temp Edw 1. *(on nave pier, Cogenhoe Ch, Northants).*
Barry of 10 Arg and Az bend Gu
  — *Keepe 241.* 1296.
Barry of 12 Arg and Az bend Untinc
  — *WB I 14b, 22. (qtd II 4 by Stapulton).*
Barry of 12 Arg and Az bend Gu
  MUNCASTER, Robert. *S 531.*
  STANGATE. *LS 199. (baston).*
Barry of 14 Arg and Az bend Gu
  NORBURY, Sir John de. *PT 1027. (baston).*
Burely Arg and Az bend Gu
  WALEIS, Henri le. *E I 304; E II 306.*
Burely Az and Arg bend Gu
  BAVER, le Duc de. *P 39.*

Barry wavy or nebuly & bend
Barry nebuly bend
  CLARE, Elizabeth de. *Birch 7934.* 1333. *(dau of Gilbert de Clare & Joan, dau of Edw 1 & Eleanor of Castile; w of (1) Jn de Burgo, (2) Theobald de Verdon, (3) Sir Rog Damory).*
  CLARE, Elizabeth de. *Birch 7940.* 1353. *(armorial roundel on sl).*
  DAMORY, Roger. *Yorks Deeds VII 196.* 1317. *(?Vair bend Untinc).*
Barry wavy bend
  BURGO, Elizabeth de, Lady of Clare. *PRO-sls.* 1326-7. *(baston).*
  [DAMORY]. *Stowe-Bard ls ix 5.* 1336-7. *(central sh on sl of Lady Eliz Clare for 3rd husb Sir Rog D).*
  BURGH, Elizabeth de, Lady of Clare. *AnstisAsp I 219, 79.* 1332-3.
  [POYNINGS]. *PRO-sls E40 A4104.*
  ALGERNNVS PERCYCOIT NO...ONB RIE HONORV DE COKERMOTH ET PETWORTH DNS NRI. 1528-9. *(baston; qtd 3 by Hen Algernon Percy, 6th E of Northd).*

Barry wavy Arg and Gu bend Az
  DAMERE, Sir John. *L 11. (baston).*
  DAMMORE. *CC 226, 131.*
  DAMMORT. *DV 43a, 1685.*
  DAMORY. *L1 192, 3. (baston).*
Barry nebuly Arg and Gu bend Sa
  AMMORY. *L10 6, 16.*
Barry wavy Arg and Gu bend Sa
  AMMORI, Sire Roger. *N 329.*
  AUMARY. *L2 12, 12. (baston).*
  PURCEL. *L9 98a, 11.*
Barry nebuly Or and Gu bend Az
  LOVELL. *PO 178. (baston).*
Barry wavy Or and Gu bend Az
  LOVEL, Sr Tho. *L 13. (baston).*
  LOVEL, Sire Thomas. *N 330.*
  LOVELL, S Thomas. *ST 58. (baston; s of Sir Joh Lovell).*
Barry wavy Or and Gu bend Sa
  — *D 244c.*
  LOVEL, Johan. *D 191a.*
  LOVEL, Jon. *F 476. (baston).*
Barry wavy Or and Sa bend Arg
  PAVELE, Sire Walter le. *N 335.*
  PONELEY. *L1 526, 4.*
Barry wavy Erm and Sa bend Gu
  — *SK 861.*
Barry wavy of 8 Arg and Sa bend Gu
  LEKEBORNE, Johannes de. *Q II 527.*

Checky & bend
Checky & bend
  — *LE 330. (imp by Barkeley, of Coberly, Gloucs).*
  — *Birch 8679.* CLYFTO.... 1427. *(qtd 2&3 by Jn Clifton, of Topcroft, Norf, Kt).*
  BEKERING, Thomas de, of Bolington, Lincs, Kt. *Birch 7324.* ...GILLVM...ME.DE.B.... 1348.
  BEKERYNG, Thomas de. *PRO-sls.* 1346. *(baston).*
  BEKERYNG, Thomas, esquire. *PRO-sls.* 1420-1. *(baston).*
  BRUT, Thomas, Kt. *PRO-sls.* 1410. *(baston).*
  CAILLI, Edmund de. *Stowe-Bard ls x 3.* S': EDMUNDI...D CAILI. 1333-4.
  CLIFFORD, Sir J. *Bk of Sls 321 & 340.* 1241.
  CLIFFORD, Walter de. *Birch 8670.* +SECRET.- ..WALTERI: D'CLIFFOR (rev); +SIGILL'M WA....- ..FORD (obv). *(d1264, s of Walter de C, Ld of Buckingham).*
  CLIFTON, John de. *Farrer I 76.* temp Edw 3. *(carved over W doorway, Hilborough Ch, Norf).*
  KYNARDESL', Hugh de. *PRO-sls. (baston).*
  ROOS, John de, of Pinchbeck. *PRO-sls.* 1347-8.

Checky Arg and Az bend Az
BEKERING. *L10 27, 15.*
BEKERYNG, Sir Thomas de. *CB 282.*
Checky Arg and Az bend Gu
BRUTTE, Robert. *SES 44.*
Checky Arg and Gu bend Az
BEKERING. *L1 89, 2; L2 68, 9.*
BEKERING, Sr Thom de. *CKO 431. (baston).*
BEKERING, Sire Thomas. *N 1060.*
BEKERING, Thomas. *M 60.*
BEKERYNG, Mons' Thomas. *TJ 1121.*
PYKERYNG, Monsr Thomas de. *AS 388. (baston).*
ROOS, Sir John. *LR 5. (baston).*
Checky Arg and Gu bend Sa
— *D4 23. (qtd 2 by [Remston] all qtd IV by Stapilton, Notts).*
— *WB I 14b, 22. (qtd IV 2 by Stapulton).*
BEKENGES, S' Th. *R 127.*
BEKERING. *L10 26, 1. (baston).*
BEKERING, Mons Thomas de. *WJ 1139. (baston).*
BEKERING, William de. *WJ 1140. (cresc Or in dex chf; baston).*
BEKERYNG. *CT 317.*
BEKERYNG, Mons Thomas de. *AS 440. (baston).*
BLOUNT. *LE 322.*
BLOUNT, Mons' William. *TJ 1131. (baston).*
BLOUNTE, S'g'r. *RB 168.*
BLUNT. *L1 55, 6; L2 40, 12.*
Checky Arg and Sa bend Gu
— *WB I 14b, 19.*
BELSTANES, Stevene de. *LM 208.*
BRUT. *L10 75b, 24.*
BRUT, Richard de. *E I 606; E II 608.*
BRUTTE, Robertus. *Q II 580.*
ELMEBRIGG, John de, of Kent. *WJ 1144.*
PARTRIDGE. *LEP 18.*
PERICYCHE. *DV 61b, 2428.*
PERTRICHE. *L1 521, 2. (Helmebreg, Gloucs in margin).*
PERTRYCHE. *LE 396.*
PERTRYGE. *L9 102b, 4.*
Checky Az and Or bend Arg
WARWICK. *MP II 104.*
Checky Az and Or bend Gu
CLIFFORD, Walter de. *WLN 725. (baston).*
CLYFFORD, Sir J. *PCL I 553. MP I 70; MP II 13; MP IV 54.*
Checky Gu and Arg bend Az
ROOS, Mons John de. *WJ 1138.*
Checky Gu and Or bend Sa
MULTON. *DV 66b, 2627. (baston).*
Checky Or and Az bend Gu
CLIFFORD. *L10 36, 10.*
CLIFFORD, S Johan. *N 200.*
CLIFFORD, Reinaud de. *E I 233; E II 235.*
CLIFFORD, Roger. *P 93. (tricked fess Gu).*

CLIFFORD, Walter. *F 293.*
CLIFFORD, Walter de. *B 30.*
CLIFFORDE, Gautier de. *P 94.*
CLYFFORD. *CT 349.*
GLYNTON, Mons Robert de. *WJ 1127. (baston).*
Checky Or and Gu bend Sa
MULTON, de. *PT 820. (baston).*
Checky Sa and Arg bend Gu
[PARTRIDGE]. *PLN 1612.*
Checky Vair and Gu bend Or
— *SK 464. (baston).*

Erm & bend
Erm & bend
— *PRO-sls.* 1303. *(... de Ch...; used by Geoffrey de Monterevell).*
BALUN, Johannes de of Merkeley, Heref. *Birch 5646.* SIGILLUM IOHANNIS ......UN. 1210-45. *(Birch says 'arms indistinct, perhaps as above'; equestr sl).*
BATHE, Eleanor de. *AnstisAsp I 211, 55.* 1349-50. *(2nd of 3 shields; sl).*
BERNAK, Robert de. *PRO-sls.* 1354-5.
BOURNE, Johan de. *LM 543.*
FERNYNGHAM, John de. *Arch Cant iii 144.* S Johis de Fernnyngha. 1375-6.
FOTHERINGHAM, David, of Powie. *Stevenson.* c1450.
[FRENINGHAM]. *Mill Steph; Belcher II 132.* 1518. *(qtd by Isly; brass to Thos I & w Eliz Guldeford, Sundridge, Kent).*
[FRENINGHAM]. *Mill Steph; Belcher II 130.* 1429. *(imp by Isly; brass to Rog Isly, Ld of manors of 'Sondresshe & ffrenyngham', Sundridge, Kent).*
LODEWYK, Hugh, of Kent. *Birch 11360.* 1364.
VAUS, Sir Wm, Kt. *Stevenson.* c1240.
WEYN, William le. *Birch 14432.* SIGILLI WILLELMI DE WEYN. temp Edw 1. *(s of Rob le W, of Wirksworth, Derbys).*
Erm bend Az
— *LE 130.*
BOWRNE. *L10 87, 15.*
BOWRNE, Jacob de, of Kent. *CY 144, 575.*
BOWRNE, Jacobus de. *CVK 686.*
DEUER, Sr H. *ME 54; LY A 179.*
ENGLISCHE. *L1 226, 2; L2 170, 11.*

Erm bend Gu
Erm bend Gu
— *LE 455. (qtd 2&3 by Moreton).*
— *D13 6d. (qtd by Isley, all imp by Jas Peckham, of Wrotham, Kent).*
— *L9 72b, 11. (qtd 2&3 by Moreton).*
— *LY A 46. (qtd 4 by Jn Baset).*
— *1H7 47. (qtd by Isley, all imp by Hill).*
— *I2(1904)180. (qtd 5 by Wm Holand, of*

Weare, Devon; added by Jos Holand c1630).
ALEPTREFEUD, Henry de. *FW 290.*
APULDERFEILD, Henry de. *A a 38.*
BACOT, Mons W. *WJ 1567.*
BAGOT, S' William. *PO 622.*
BARNAK. *L10 20b, 19.*
BERNAK, Mons R. *WJ 1446.*
BURY. *LE 221.*
BURY. *L1 99, 3. (baston; qtg Az falcon rising Gu).*
ELMESTED, John. *WB IV 183b, 1043.*
FREMIGHAM, Wallis, of Som. *L1 253, 2; L2 201, 11.*
FREMYNGHAM, John, of Waleis. *ME 55; LY A 180.*
FRENYNGHAM, of Kent. *SK 720.*
ISELE, ... of Suss. *CY 174, 696.*
ISELEY. *L9 3, 6.*
ISELEY, (Kent). *PLN 654.*
ISLE, John de. *CVK 701.*
WALAYS, John de. *CT 377.*
WALEYS, Sire Johan le. *N 193.*
WALEYS, Johnes le. *LM 317.*
WALEYS, Willm le. *WLN 594.*
WALLEYS, Sir John de. *CB 277.*
WALLEYZ, Sr John de. *L 179.*
WELSE, Sire Johan. *HA 89, 21.*
WELSE, Sire Johan. *HA 19.*
WELSE, Sr John. *RB 124.*

Erm bend Sa
Erm bend Sa
— *WLN 173.*
— *WB I 29b, 16. (qtd 2 by Untinc on bend Sa 3 leopards' faces Or border engr Sa).*
KELLESHALLE, Johannes. *Q II 677.*
KELSALL. *L9 10, 5.*
KELSALL, S Jolf de, of Ches. *CY 7, 25.*
LETLESHALL, John. *SES 113.*
[WALLEYS]. *SHY 82.*
WALLIS. *CRK 1800.*

Gyronny & bend
Gyronny of 6 Arg and Gu bend Az
BASSINGBOURNE, Monsire Giles. *CG 519. (baston).*

Lozengy & bend
Lozy bend
MEYDENE, Gilbert, of Bulverhithe, Suss. *Birch 11770.* S' L SIMON DE .... early 14 cent. *(blazon unclear).*
RYBBESFORD, Robert de. *PRO-sls. 1359-60. (blazon unclear).*
Lozy Arg and Gu bend Untinc
ROKELEE. *CT 369.*
Lozy Arg and Gu bend Az
ROKELE, Richard de la. *E I 677; E II 679.*

Lozy Arg and Gu bend Sa
ROKELEY. *Nichols Leics III 934. (Ravenston Ch).*
Lozy Az and Or bend Gu
ALVEHAM, Mons' Rauf de. *TJ 642. ('dazure endnete [struck out & velengrele written above] dor et une bende de goules').*
Lozy Gu and Arg bend Az
ROKELEY, Richard. *LR 49.*
Lozy Gu & Vair bend Or
SKEYTOUN, Ra. *NS 27.*

Paly & bend
Paly & bend
— *Vinc 88, 38.* +SIGILLUM ELENAE BAKEPUS. 1384-5. *(sl of Elena, dau of Thos Bakepuz, of Barton Bakepuz, Derbys; Power of attorney for seisin in Barton Bakepuz to Wm Hyde).*
— *Birch 7073.* SIGILLVM EMME DE BAKEPUS. *(imp Bakepuz; sl of Emma de B; used by Alicia, dau of Thos Adam, of Ashbourne, Derbys).*
ANNESLEY, Hugh. *PRO-sls. 1421-2. (baston).*
ANNESLEY, Hugh de. *PRO-sls. 1398-9.*
ANNESLEY, Thos of. *Durham-sls 78. 1375-83.*
GRANDISON. *Birch 3810. (Bp of Exeter; founder, 1337, of Collegiate Ch of Ottery St Mary, Devon; collegiate sl).*
GRANDISON, John. *Birch 1560. (Bp of Exeter 1327-69).*
HAUTEVILLE, Rodurphus de. *PRO-sls. 1337-8.*
JAKKESON, John. *PRO-sls. 1394-5. (baston; s of Ric Jakkeson, of Hungerton).*
?LONGFORD. *Bow XXXV 2.* +Sigillum Elene Bakepuz. 1384-5. *(imp Bakepuz; sl of Helena, dau of Thos B, of Barton Bakepuz, Derbys).*
LONGFORD, Alice de. *Bow XXX 23. 1373-4. (wid of Nicholas de Longford, Kt).*
LONGFORDE, Nicholas, of Longforde, Derbys. *Birch 11378. 1572.*
LUNDY, Alexander of. *Durham-sls 1679. 1330. (1 of 2 coats on sl, other 3 lozs; sl used by Eustace Fitzrobert, of Brandon).*
Paly of 10 bend sin Untinc
BURGHULLE, Roger de, of Carey, Herefs. *Birch 7955.* +S...OR..ULLE.

Paly Arg & Az bend Gu
Paly Arg and Az bend Gu
— *WB I 42, 15. (qtd 2&3 by Sir E Gradlyng).*
— *FK II 765. (qtd 2&3 by Coytyffes).*
— *XO 120. (qtd 2&3 by Coytif).*
ANDESLE, Sir John. *WB III 83b, 3. (baston).*
ANNESLEY. *L1 3, 6; L2 4, 10. (baston).*

ANNESLEY. *L10 4b, 20.*

ANNESLEY, Sir Hewe, of Anysley. *RH, Ancestor iv 237.*

ANNESLEY, John. *BG 388.*

ANNESLEY, Mons John de. *S 182. (baston).*

ANNYSLEY. *L1 109, 6. (marginal note 'against Borowell').*

ANSLE, Sir John. *CV-BM 248.*

AUNSELL, John. *TJ 1302. (baston).*

BOROWELL. *L1 109, 6; L2 79, 7.*

BOROWELL, Yorks. *MY 266.*

BURGHILL. *CRK 1581.*

GRANNSUN. *SK 40.*

GRANSON, Peres de. *SP A 108.*

GRAUNSON. *CV-BM 45.*

GRAUNSON, Otys de. *CA 171.*

GRAUNZUN, S Piers de. *GA 203.*

Paly Arg & Gu &c bend Arg &c

Paly Arg and Gu bend Arg

LANGFORDE, Sir John. *WK 246.*

Paly Arg and Gu bend Az

— *FK II 988.*

Paly of 4 Arg and Gu bend Sa

RYDELLE, Sir John. *BR V 268.*

Paly Arg and Gu bend Sa

ENEBY. *L2 183, 12.*

ENEBY, Robert. *FW 347; A 260.*

MALIOLOGRE, le. *LM 7.*

RIDEL, Sire Johan. *N 382.*

RYDELL. *L1 553, 3.*

Paly Arg and Sa bend Gu

— *WLN 891.*

BURGHILL. *BA 19.*

Paly of 10 Arg and Sa bend Gu

BURGHULL, Roger de. *E I 669; E II 671.*

BURGHULLE. *CT 137.*

BURHHULL. *L2 95, 12.*

BURNHULLE, Roger de. *L10 34, 3.*

Paly Arg and Vt bend Gu

BAUNFELD. *L10 20, 15.*

STAMFELD, Mons Thom de. *WJ 451.*

Paly Or & Az bend Gu

Paly Or and Az bend Gu

GRAUNTSON. *CT 48.*

PENBRUGE. *CB 46. (baston; pennon with 3 black tails).*

SHERLEY, William de. *F 437.*

SHIRLEY, William de. *WLN 784.*

Paly of 10 Or and Az bend Gu

SOLERS, Henry de. *E I 483; E II 485. (baston).*

Paly Or & Gu bend Arg

Paly Or and Gu bend Arg

DRAYCOTT. *Nichols Leics III 491. (East Norton Chapel).*

LANFORD, Sire Nicholas de. *PV 20.*

(baston).

LANGEFORD, Sire Johan. *N 623.*

LANGEFORD, S John de. *GA 225. (baston).*

LANGEFORD, Monsire Nichall de. *CG 502. (baston).*

LANGEFORD, Sire Nicholas de. *O 144.*

LANGEFORD, Sr Nicholas. *R 11.*

LANGEFORD, William. *BG 271.*

LANGEFORDE, S Nicol. *PO 515.*

LANGFORD. *FK II 831; FK II 832.*

LANGFORD. *L9 43a, 8.*

LANGFORD, Mons Nichol de. *AS 363. (baston).*

LANGFORD, Mons Nicholas de. *SD 52.*

LANGFORD, Mons Nicol de. *CA 129.*

LANGFORD, Sir R. *PCL I 548.*

LANGFORTH, Mons Nich de. *WJ 443.*

LONGEFORD, Mons Nichol de. *TJ 1069. (baston).*

LONGEFORD, Mons Nicolas de. *S 220. (baston).*

LONGFORD. *Nichols Leics III 781. (imp by Staunton; S window, Castle Donington Ch).*

LONGFORD, of Derbys & Notts. *L1 393, 5; L2 300, 6.*

LONGFORD, S Nich de, of Lancs. *CY 64, 254.*

LONGFORD, Nicholas de. *S 222.*

LONGFORD, Sir Nicol. *CRK 1002. (qrs 1&4).*

LONGFORD, Sir Rauff. *BA 41b, 410. (baston).*

MAJORCA, Roy de. *WJ 76.*

Paly Or & Gu &c bend Az &c

Paly Or and Gu bend Az

— *SK 123. (baston).*

LONGFFORDE. *WB I 33, 13. (qtg 2&3 qtly Arg and Gu).*

LONGFORD, Sir Ralph. *PLN 1315. (qtg 2&3 qtly Arg and Gu).*

MAJORCA, Roy de. *WJ 76.*

Paly Or and Gu bend Sa

BYRTON. *LE 356.*

BYRTON. *CC 222b, 20.*

HUNTINGDON. *LH 998.*

HUNTINGDON, le Conte de. *TJ 1220.*

HUNTINGDON, le Conte de. *P 62. ('paale dor et de goules ove une bende de sable').*

HUNTINGDON, le Comte de. *B 14. (pale d'or et de goules ung bende noir; 'John Scot ... in the lyffe of Davyd his father and Randolff erle of Chester his uncule').*

Paly Or and Vt bend Gu

BAMFELD, of Som. *L2 97, 8.*

See also under 1, 2, 3 pales &c and over all

Per bend sin &c bend

Per bend sin Az and Gu bend Or
?CASSE. *SHY 207.*

Per fess Gu and Or bend Az
— *PT 844. (baston).*

Per fess dancetty bend
NEVILE, John de. *PRO-sls.* 13 cent. *(baston).*

Per fess indented Gu and Vt bend Or
NEVILLE, Hugh de. *MP IV 19. (shield reversed).*

Per fess indented Gu and Vt bend Sa
NEVILLE, John de, Chief Forester, 1246. *MP IV 69. (shield reversed, above it hunting horn hanging from hook [one of the earliest official badges]).*

Per pale bend

Per pale bend
— *BD 42b. (imp by Hageford on tomb of Thos H, d23 April 1469 & w Mgt; S side, Warwick Collegiate Ch).*
CHAUCER, Geoffrey. *?source. (sl).*
CHAUCER, Thomas. *Bow 12.*
CHAUCER, Thomas, Esq. *PRO-sls.* 1408-9.
HEYDONE, Richard de. *BerksCRO-sls Isbury D/Q1/T14.* S RICARDI DE HEYDONE. 1319-20. *('filius domini Ricardi de Heydon, Kt').*
ORREBY, John de, Clerk. *PRO-sls.* 1314-5. *(on 2 of 4 shields set in legend on sl of Orreby).*
WALDEGRAVE, Richard de. *Bow 16b.*

Per pale Arg and Gu bend Az
WALDEGRAVE. *SK 105. (baston).*

Per pale Arg and Gu bend Sa
HEMENHALES, Sir Rauf. *BR V 142.*
WALDEGRAVE, Rics de. *LM 312.*

Per pale Arg and Sa bend Gu
— *LE 283.*

Per pale Gu and Sa bend Arg
WELLS, John. *PLN 694.*

Per pale Or and Gu bend Sa
HUNTINGDON, E of. *LH 324.*

Per pale Gu and Az bend Arg on Gu
— *PLN 1925. (qtd 2 by Sir Jn Dawtry).*

Per pale Gu and Az bend sin Arg on Gu
— *PLN 1925. (qtd 3 by Sir Jn Dawtry).*

Per pale indent Arg and Gu bend Az
EGEBALSTOUN, Henricus de. *Q II 254.*

Per pale indent Arg and Gu bend Or
— *Q 204.*

Per pale indent Arg and Gu bend Sa
EGEBASTON, Henr' de. *Q 517.*

Per pale dex Az chf indent Or sin per bend Or and Az over all bend Gu
?BLUNVY. *SHY 69. (?for Blundevill, qtly per fess indent Or and Az bend Gu).*

Pily & bend

Pily of 4 Arg and Gu bend Sa
GRUNARKE. *BG 1. (name added in later hand).*

Barry pily bend
SMYTH, Walter, of Ingham, Suff. *Birch 13550.* ...SME.... 1352.

Qtly bend

Qtly bend
— *BrookeAsp I 31, 2.* SIGILLUM ELIZABETH DARCIE DOMINE DE WHERLTON. *(loz 1 of 5; sl of Eliz Darcy, Lady of Wherlton).*
— *PRO-sls E40 A1567.* ..HANNI... 1365-6. *(baston; used by Wm de Sutton).*
— *Vinc 88, 51.* +SIGILLUM ELIZABETH DAR-CIE DOMINE DE WHERLTON. 1346-7. *(loz, 4th of 5, on sl of Eliz Darcy, domina de Wherl-ton).*
BALIOL, Ada. *BM Harl 245, 123b, HB-SND. (1 of 2 shields, other is an orle).*
BERKELE, Sir Giles de. *PRO-sls.* 1265-90. *(baston; equestr figure deeply cut from a gem; 1 of 4 shields in legend).*
BISKELE, Richard de, of Frostenden, Suff. *Birch 7485.* SIGILL' RICARDI D' BISKEL. 1349.
BLOUNT, Hugh. *Bow 14. (s of Hugo le B).*
BROK, Hugh de. *Arch Cant iii 143.* S' HUGONIS DE BROK. 1276-7. *(baston).*
CASTRIE, Robert de, of Killingholm, Lincs. *Birch 8415.* SIGILL R..TI CASTRIE. temp Hen 3.
CHEDLE, Geoffrey de, Kt. *PRO-sls.* S' GAL-FRIDI DE DUTTONE. 13 cent. *(baston).*
?CLAVERING. *Farrer II 250. (battlements, Harpley Ch, Norf).*
CLAVERING, Eva. *Birch 8611.* 1334. *(dau of Johan de C).*
CLAVERING, John. *Balliol D6, 38, HB-SND.* 1328.
CLERICUS, Walter, dictus de Lynleye, ?Herts. *Birch 8632.* 1346. *(blazon unclear, legend indistinct).*
EUER, Hugh de. *Birch 9534.* SIGILL' HUGONIS D' EUER. 13 cent.
EURE, Hugh of. *Balliol D6, 27, HB-SND.* 1267.
EURE, Sir Hugh of. *Durham-sls 929.* 1273.
EURE, Sir Robt of. *Durham-sls 933.* 1367.
EVERINGHAM, Sir Adam de. *Yorks Deeds I 155.* 1347.
EVERINGHAM, Sir Adam de. *Yorks Deeds I 144.* 1317.
EVERINGHAM, Sir Adam de. *Yorks Deeds I 190.* 1357. *(crest: crab).*
FASTOLF, Hugh. *PRO-sls E40 A6910.* 1375-6.
FITZNICHOLL, Thomas, Kt. *PRO-sls.* 22

November 1418. *(baston)*.
FITZROBERT, John. *Durham-sls 1002*.
FITZROGER, Robert. *Durham-sls 1003*. *(?f of Jn Fitzrobert)*.
FRAUNCEYS, Alan le. *Yorks Deeds III 30*. 1293.
GARSALE, Thomas de, Kt, Warws. *Birch 10035*. S...ME DE GARSH.L. 1309.
GARSALE, Sir Thos de. *Dugd 17, 73*. 1309.
GROS, John. *Birch 10308*. SIGILLUM IOHANNIS GROS. 1396. *(used by Oliver Groos, of Norf)*.
HANAM, Thomas. *PRO-sls*. 1592. *(baston)*.
HOO, T de. *Birch 10806*. 1341.
HOO, Thomas de. *PRO-sls*. 1358. *(baston)*.
ROCHEFORD, Waleran de, Kt. *PRO-sls E40 A2726*. S' WALERAN DE ...HEFORD. 1329-30.
ROCKELEE, Richard de la. *Bow XVII 14*.
ROGERI, Nicholas fil, of Gloucs. *Birch 9757*. SIGILLUM NICOLAI FILII ROGERI. temp Hen 3 or Edw 1.
ROGERI, Robertus filius. *Birch 6006*. late 13 cent.
ROGERI, Robertus filius. *Birch 6005*. SIGILLUM ROBERTI FILII ROGERI. 12 cent.
SAKEVILE, Edward, Esq, of Lincs. *Birch 13198*. SIGILLUM EDWARDI SACK..E. 15 cent.
WALEYS. *Yorks Arch Journ iii 60*. 1401. *(qtd 2&3 by Fitzaucher, Erm on chf 3 lions Untinc; sl of Sir Jn Depden)*.
WIDDRINGTON, Gerard of. *Dodsworth 45, 94, HB-SND*. 1361.
WIDDRINGTON, Sir Gerard of. *Durham-sls 2651*. 1466. *(baston)*.
WIDDRINGTON, Roger. *Dodsworth 49, 43b, HB-SND*. 1280.
WIDDRINGTON, Roger of. *Durham-sls 2653*. 1369. *(baston)*.
WIDDRINGTON, Roger of. *Durham-sls 2652*. 1357. *(baston)*.
WIDDRINGTON, Roger of. *Durham-sls 2654*. 1357. *(baston)*.
WIDDRINGTON, Roger of. *HB-SND*. 1345.
WIDERINGTON, Roger de. *Birch 14465*. SIGILL ROGERI DE WIDERINGTON. 1345. *(bro of Gerard de W, Kt, of Northd)*.
WODRINGTON, John de. *?source*. 1393. *(sl)*.
WODRINGTON, John de. *Bow LVI 8*. 1392-3.
WYDERINGTON, Roger de. *Vinc 88, 66*. SIG ROGERI DE WYDERINGTON. 1351. *(grant of land in Great Heton)*.
WYDERINGTON, Roger de. *Bow LVI 2*. +Sigill Rogeri de Widerington. 1351. *(grant of land in Great Heton, Lancs)*.

Qtly bend sin
— *Cleeve*. 14 cent. *([Fitznicholas or W Beauchamp])*.

Qtly Arg & Az bend Gu
Qtly Arg and Az bend Gu
BRAY. *LE 315*.
BRAY. *RB 136*.
BRAY. *L10 77b, 13*.

Qtly Arg & Gu bend Az
Qtly Arg and Gu bend Az
HELERS. *L1 303, 1; L2 243, 12*.
HELLERS. *LH 1013*. *(baston)*.
MASCY, Hugo, of Tympeley, Ches. *CY 23, 92*. *(baston)*.
MASCY, de Tynperley. *CVC 614*. *(baston)*.
MASSY, Hugh le, of Timperley. *WLN 662*. *(baston)*.
MASSY, de Temperle. *LE 228*.
MASSY, of Temperley. *CRK 1080*. *(baston)*.
MASSY, de Tymperley. *L9 53a, 11*.
ROBELEY. *L1 546, 2*.
ROKELE. *PT 401*. *(baston)*.
ROKELL. *DV 62a, 2450*. *(baston)*.

Qtly Arg & Gu bend Gu &c
Qtly Arg and Gu bend Gu
— *WB II 49, 12*. *(qtd 2&3 by Ld Haryngton)*.
— *CRK 193*. *(baston; qtd 2&3 by Harington)*.
— *PLN 104; PLN 146*. *(qtd 2&3 by Harington; painted qtly 1&4 Arg bend Gu 2&3 Gu plain)*.
— *XFB 48*. *(qtd 4 by Sir Jn Harington)*.
— *LD 18*. *(painted qtly 1&4 Arg bend Gu 2&3 Gu; qtd 2&3 by Harington)*.
LOREYN, Sir N. *WB I 37b, 3*.
LORING, Sire Peres. *N 397*.
LORINGE, Sir Nycoll. *WK B, 28*. *(baston)*.
?LORYNG. *Arch Journ xcii 89 & 91*. c1300. *(2 wall paintings ?for Sir Peter Loryng who was granted charity by Dunstable Priory in 1273 & for his son Peter who d1302; All Saints, Chalgrave, Beds)*.
LORYNG, Monsire Nel. *AN 210*.
LORYNGES. *L9 39b, 2*.
LORYNGES, Nel. *SK 272*. *(baston)*.
LOZENGE, of Beds. *L1 389, 2; L2 309, 4*.
Qtly Arg and Gu bend Or
— *WB I 29b, 15*. *(qtd II&III 2&3 by Warton)*.
WALEYS, Mons Richard. *TJ 937*. *('quartle dargent & de goules & 1 baston dor permy le goules')*.
WALEYS, Mons Richard. *TJ 936*.
Qtly Arg and Gu bend sin Or
WALEYS, Monsire. *CG 407*. *(baston)*.

Qtly Arg & Gu bend Sa

Qtly Arg and Gu bend Sa

— PLN 1964. (baston; qtd II&III 8 by qtly Az and Gu).

ASCHELEY, of Ches. L2 14, 5. (baston).

BEKERING. L10 27b, 19.

DESPENSER, le Sr. NB 50. (gold frets in 2&3 have disappeared).

DESPENSER, Hughe. SD 101. (baston).

?DUTTON. PCL II 49.

WEDRINGTON. PT 234. (baston).

WEDRYGTON. L1 669, 5.

WEDRYNGTON, Sir John of. BA 641. (baston).

?WIDDRINGTON. Blair N II 233. (baston; roof bosses, nave, Bothel Ch, Northd).

WIDERINGTON. Nichols Leics III 934. (Ravenston Ch).

WITHERINGTON, Gerard de. S 576. (baston).

WITHERINGTON, R. CRK 1752. (baston).

WYD, Sr Gerard of. PO 264. (written above in Elizabethan hand 'S' Gerard of Widerinton').

WYDERINGTON. DV 64b, 2542. (baston).

WYDRYNGTON, Sir Henry. WK 447. (baston).

WYDRYNGTON, Mons John de. TJ 941. (baston).

WYTHERINGTON, Sr de. CKO 467.

WYTHERYTON, Monsr de. AS 226. (baston).

WYTHRINGTON, Sir Gerard. WK 31. (baston).

WYTHRYNGTON, Mons Gerrard de. S 570. (baston).

Qtly Arg & Sa bend Gu &c

Qtly Arg and Sa bend Gu

— LE 429.

DUCKET, Sir Hugh, of Lincs. Her & Gen vii 255. SIGILL HUGONIS DUKET. 1275. (tincts from a shield in Hathern Ch for Hugh Duket, Rector in 1298; sl on bond, in Westm Abbey muniments).

DUCKET, Hugh, Rector. Nichols Leics III 845. 1298. (Hathern Ch).

EUNYNGHLI. DV 54a, 2134.

EVERINGHAM. RB 335.

EVERINGHAM, Sir Adame. WK B, 32. (baston).

EVERINGHAM, Robert, Norf. WB III 107b, 5.

EVERINGHAM, Monsire de, de Rokeley. CG 411.

EVERINGHAM, de Rokkele. CKO 468. (baston).

EVERYNGAM, Sr Adam. PO 509. (baston; written above in contemporary hand 'Rokkele').

EVERYNGHAM. L1 229, 2.

EVERYNGHAM. LE 347.

EVERYNGHAM. L2 172, 7. (3 mullets shown in ink on bend).

EVERYNGHAM. LE 101.

EVERYNGHAM, Sire Adam de. PV 46. (baston).

EVERYNGHAM, Johannes. Q II 247. (baston).

EVERYNGHAM, Sir John. PCL I 434.

EVERYNGHAM, Mons John, de Roklay. TJ 942. ('...i baston de goules permy').

EVERYNGHAM, Monsr de, de Rokeley. AS 236. (baston).

EVINGHAM, Adam. BG 221. (baston).

GARSALE, Berks. L2 232, 1.

HEVERINGHAM. PT 1102. (baston).

HOO, Beds. L2 270, 6.

Qtly Arg and Sa bend Or

HOO, Robert. LH 250.

HOO, Sire Robert de. N 388.

Qtly Arg & Sa bend Sa

Qtly Arg and Sa bend Sa

?EVERINGHAM, Lawrans. S 285. (baston).

EVERINGHAM, Lawrence. LE 110. (baston).

EVERINGHAM, Lawrence. S 287. (baston).

LERUS. L2 315, 5.

ROUS. LR 82. (baston).

ROUS. L1 564, 2.

ROUS, Mons Richard le. TJ 945. ('.. un baston permy largent de sable').

ROUS, Monsire Richard le. CG 414.

ROUS, Sire Richard le. N 386.

ROUS, Sr Richard le. CKO 474. (baston).

Qtly Az & Or bend Gu

Qtly Az and Or bend Gu

BURG. SK 363. (baston).

BURGGES. L10 84, 7. (baston).

BURGH. L1 83, 3.

LANGTON, Robert. PLN 702. (baston).

Qtly Gu & Untinc &c bend Or &c

Qtly Gu and Untinc bend Or

CONESTABLE, Wills de. LM 325. (baston).

Qtly Gu and Arg bend Arg

— WB II 70, 9. (?qtly 1&4 Gu bend Arg 2&3 Arg).

SAKEVILE, Andr de. Q II 220.

WALEYS. DV 55b, 2190. (baston).

Qtly Gu and Arg bend Az

— PCL II 15. (baston).

MASSY, de Tymperle. SK 1036. (baston).

Qtly Gu and Arg bend Or

— Q 577.

— XFB 244. (qtd II 2&3 by Sir Thos Wharton, of Westmld).

HOO, Robert de. WLN 398. (baston).

WALEYS. LE 353. (baston).

WALEYS. CC 222, 7.

WALEYS, Sr. CKO 463. (baston).

WALEYS, Sire Richard le. *N 1069. ('quartile de argent e de goules a une bende de or').*
WALEYS, Stephen de. *E I 392; E II 394.*
WALEYS, Stephen le. *WLN 874.*
WALEYS, Stephs le. *LM 329. (baston).*
WALLYS. *L1 671, 4.*

Qtly Gu & Or &c bend Arg &c

Qtly Gu and Or bend Arg
— *WB I 20b, 12. (qtd 4 by Poynes).*
— *CK a 84.*
— *BA 846. (baston; qtd 2&3 by Sir Robt Pointz).*
FITZ NICOL. *XF 443. (baston; qtd 4 by Poyntz).*
FITZMEOL. *L1 260, 4.*
FITZNICOL. *L2 193, 3.*
FITZNICOLE. *RB 314.*
NICOL, fitz. *DV 40b, 1591.*
NICOL, Mons Thomas fitz. *S 256. (baston).*
NICOL, Thomas fitz. *S 258.*
NYCHOLL, fitz. *LE 340.*
NYCOL, Sir Thomas fittes. *WK B 30. (baston).*

Qtly Gu and Or bend Az
FELLE. *FK II 474.*
SAKEVYLE, Aundreu de. *LM 520. (tinct of bend unclear).*

Qtly Gu and Or bend Gu
BEACHAMP, John de, de Bedford. *E II 360.*

Qtly Gu and Or bend Or
SACKEALL. *PT 853. (baston).*

Qtly Gu and Or bend Sa
ROGER, Robert le fitz. *E II 49.*

Qtly Gu and Vt bend Arg
CONSTABLE, of Flamborough. *Lawrance 45. 1344. (on tomb of Sir Edm Thwing, d1344; effigy, Sheriff Hutton, Yorks).*

Qtly Or & Az bend Gu

Qtly Or and Az bend Gu
BERKELEY, Giles. *F 387.*
BERKELEY, Giles de. *WLN 435. (baston).*
BURGH. *L2 49, 11.*
FASTOLF, Nicholas. *SES 146. (baston).*
FASTOLF, Nicholaus. *Q II 714. (baston).*
SOMERI, Sire Johan de. *N 408.*
SOMERY. *L1 604, 4.*
SOMERY, Sir John. *CB 286.*
SOMERY, Sir John. *BR V 274.*
SUNRY, Sr Jo, de Kent. *L 216. (baston).*
WULTIRTON, Jo. *NS 96.*

Qtly Or & Gu bend Arg &c

Qtly Or and Gu bend Arg
BEAUCHAMP. *FK a 261.*
SAKEVYLLE, Essex. *MY 122.*

Qtly Or and Gu bend Az
STURMYN, Sir Roger. *LS 84. (baston).*

Qtly Or and Gu bend Gu
— *WK 486. (qtd 3 by Sir Wm Gascoigne, of Cardington, Beds).*
BEACHAMP, John de, of Bedford. *E I 358. (baston).*
BEAUCHAMP. *L1 75, 5; L2 38, 9.*
BEAUCHAMP, of Bedford. *L10 25b, 9.*
BEAUCHAMP, Ld Bedford. *BR IV 9.*
BEAUCHAMP, Ld, of Bedford. *BR V a 28.*
BEAUCHAMP, Will'm. *B 54.*
BEAUCHAMP, William de. *MP II 28.*
BEAUCHAMP, William, of Bedford. *P 79.*
BEDFORD. *L2 87, 9.*
BEDFORD, Ld. *BR VI 61.*
BEDFORD, Ld. *BR IV 35.*
BELECHAUMP, Walter. *C 147.*
LORYNGE, Mons Neal. *BG 165.*

Qtly Or & Gu bend Sa &c

Qtly Or and Gu bend Sa
— *WB II 59, 3. (baston).*
BEAUCHAMP. *FK II 261.*
BEAUCHAMP, Ld of Bedford. *CRK 1314. (baston).*
BEWCHAMPE. *BirmCL-sls I 168241.*
CHAVERYNG, Sr John. *BR V 10.*
CLAVERING. *L10 42, 16. (baston).*
CLAVERING. *FB 28. (baston).*
CLAVERING. *OxfRS I 22. (riband).*
CLAVERING. *CT 59. (baston).*
CLAVERING, Sr de. *CKO 476. (baston).*
[CLAVERING]. *Brit Arch Assoc 3S iii 207-8.* 14 cent. *(glass, South Newington, Oxfords).*
CLAVERING, of Essex. *L1 140, 5.*
CLAVERING, Sir John. *ML I 81; ML II 70.*
CLAVERING, Robert. *S 246.*
CLAVERING, Mons Robert fitz Roger de. *TJ 958.*
CLAVERING, Robert fitz Roger de. *P 116.*
CLAVERYNG, Sir Robert. *WK B 29. (baston).*
CLAVERYNGE, S Jon. *PO 623. (baston).*
CLAVERYNGES. *SK 116. (baston).*
CLAVING, Robert. *BG 326.*
EUERS, Henry de. *WLN 381. (baston).*
EURE, Roger de, le Fitzjohn. *B 169.*
FITZ-Roger, Robert. *K 96. (his sons took name Clavering).*
LACY, E of Lincoln. *NB 10. (baston).*
LACY, E of Lincoln. *Q II 27. (baston).*
MALBON, Sir Hugh, Founder of Combermere. *CVC 504. (baston).*
MALBON, Hugo, Ches. *CY 20, 79. (baston).*
MALBONE, S Hugh de. *WLN 355. (baston).*
POMFRET. *L1 518, 2.*
ROBERT, John fitz, of Clavering. *MP IV 39. ('hoc etiam anno obiit Johannis filius Roberti, vir nobilis et unus de praecipiis*

baronibus in plaga Anglie borealis').
ROGER, Robert fitz. *D 89; K 12; N 26.*
ROGER, Robert fitz. *F 94; H 5; S 244. (baston).*
ROGER, Robert le fitz. *E I 49. (baston).*
ROGER, Robert le fitz. *Dodsworth 49, 43b, HB-SND. 1280. (baston).*
ROGER, Sir Robert fitz. *CB 287.*
ROGER, Sir Robt fiz. *FF 21. (baston).*
ROGERE, le fiz. *SP A 104. (baston).*
RONDOLF, M fiz. *WNR 140.*
ROY, Robert le fitz. *L10 30, 9.*

Qtly Or and Gu bend Vt
FAGEUILLE. *L1 248, 6.*
SACEUYLE, Sir Andrew. *BR V 197. (Vt sic for Vair).*

Qtly Or & Sa &c bend Gu &c
Qtly Or and Sa bend Gu
BYSLEY. *CRK 104. (baston).*
EVERRYNGHAM, Adam. *LE 63. (baston).*
ULSTON, Jo. *NS 70. (baston).*
WLUNSDON. *L1 671, 1.*

Qtly Or and Sa bend Sa
LEROWSSE, of Knoddishall, Suff. *Suff HN 22. (imp by Jenney).*

Qtly Or and Vt bend Arg
POMERELL. *LEP 54. (riband).*

Qtly Or and Vt bend Gu
— *LE 208.*
— *SK 932. (baston).*

Qtly Sa & Arg bend Arg &c
Qtly Sa and Arg bend Arg
HOO. *PT 607. (baston).*

Qtly Sa and Arg bend Az
— *ML I 347. ('Quartly sabyll & sylver a bend asur upon the same. Thou mayst nat say upon bothe in thys scocheon ut prius').*

Qtly Sa and Arg bend Or
HO, Robert de. *F 105. (baston; below this shield written 'Robert de Champaine').*
HOO, Robert de. *LH 838. (baston).*
HOO, Robert de. *E I 445; E II 447. (baston).*
HOO, S Willm de, of Suss. *CY 160, 637. (baston).*

Qtly 1&4 fretty &c over all bend
Qtly Gu fretty Or & Arg bend sin Sa
SPENCER. *BR II 33. (baston; qtd I&IV 2 & II&III 3 by D of Warwyk).*

Qtly Or fretty Sa & Arg bend sin Sa
DESPENSER, Geoffrey le. *MP IV 79. (shield rev).*

Qtly 1&4 paly Or and Gu 2&3 qtly Arg and Gu bend Az
LONGFFORDE. *WB I 33, 13.*

Qtly Vair & Untinc bend Untinc
CONSTABLE, John, Dean of Lincoln, 1514-28. *Birch 1812.*

Qtly Vair and Gu bend Or
CONSTABLE, Sir John. *I 36.*
CONSTABLE, Richd. *S 372.*
CONSTABLE, Sr Wm. *M 77.*

Qtly Or & checky Arg and Gu bend Az
— *Proc Soc Antiq XVII 2S 275. c1310. (shield on stole, Leagram Hall, Lancs).*

Qtly 2&3 fretty over all bend
Qtly 2&3 fret bend
— *Birch 12099. 1529. (qtd IV 2&4 by Sir George Neville, 4th B Bergavenny).*
CHENEY. *Birch 3292. 1301. (Chapter sl of Priory of St Faith, Horsham, Norf).*
?DESPENCER. *Birch 6938. 1368. (roundel, base of 4; sl of Sibilla d'Arundell).*
DESPENCER. *Birch 7252-3. 1430. (qtd 2&3 on escutch of Ric de Beauchamp, 13th E of Warwick; sl used after his 2nd marriage with Isabel, dau & coh of Thos le D, E of Gloucester).*
DESPENCER, le. *Cleeve. ?14 cent.*
DESPENCER, Elizabeth. *Birch 9274 & 9276.* LE: SEAL: ELIZABET: DAME: LA: DESPENSERE. *1401. (imp Burghersh, lion qf; above shield griffin couchant; dau of Bartholomew, 4th Baron B & wid of Edw, Baron D).*
DESPENCER, Hugh le, of Solihull, Warws, Kt. *Birch 9280.* SIGILLU HUG...E SPENCER. *1385. (martlet for diffce in qr 1).*
DESPENSER, Anne. *PRO-sls AS 21.* S' ANNE LE DESPENSER. *1363-4. (wid of Edw le D, Kt).*
DESPENSER, Constance. *AnstisAsp I 223, 88.* +SIGILLUM CONSTANS DAME DISPENCER. *(qr 4 of loz; w of Thos Despencer, E of Gloucester).*
DESPENSER, Edward le. *Bk of Sls 481. 1364.*
DESPENSER, Hugh le. *Birch 9281.* S' HUGONIS LE DESPENSER. *1436.*
DESPENSER, Thomas le, Kt. *PRO-sls E40 A11046.* SIGILLV: THOME: SPENCER. *1363-4. (baston).*
DESPENSER, Thomas le, E of Gloucester. *Birch 9283.* SIGILLUM: THOME: : DNI: LE: DESPENSER. *1397.*
DESPENSIER, Hugh le, Kt. *Birch 9277.* SIGILLUM HVGONIS LE DESPENSER. *1304.*
[SPENCER]. *SHY 419. (baston; imp by [Hastynges]).*

Qtly 2&3 fretty bend
[DESPENSEIER, Hue le]. *Farrer I 338. 1529. (brass to Robt Clere; Ormesby St Margaret Ch, Norf).*
DESPENSER, Anne. *PRO-sls. 1363-4. (baston; shield betw 4 roundels; wid of Edw le*

Despenser, Kt).

DESPENSER, Anne. *BarronMS AS 21.* 1356. *(3 charges on bend; wid of Edw le D, Kt).*

DESPENSER, Anne le. *PRO-sls E40 A4785, 4792 & 4795.* S' ANNE LE DESPENSER. 1363-4. *(imp 4 voided lozs; wid of Edw D).*

DESPENSER, Hugh. *PRO-sls.* 13 cent. *(baston; 'dispensarius').*

DESPENSER, Hugh. *PRO-sls AS 98.* +SIG....ISPENSARII. 13 cent. *(baston).*

DESPENSER, Hugh. *PRO-sls E40 A6877.* ..-.NSATOR.... 13 cent.

DESPENSER, Hugh le. *PRO-sls.* 1307-8. *(baston; the elder).*

DESPENSER, Hugh le. *PRO-sls.* 13 cent. *(baston).*

DESPENSER, Hugh le, Kt. *PRO-sls AS 63 A6847.* S' HUGONIS LE DESPENSER. 1293-4. *(baston).*

DESPENSER, Hugh le, Kt. *PRO-sls E40 A6847.* ...LE DE...ER. 13-14 cent.

DESPENSER, Hugh le, Kt. *PRO-sls.* 1293-4 & 1304-5. *(baston).*

DESPENSER, Thomas le, Kt. *PRO-sls.* 1363-4. *(baston).*

DESPENSER, Thomas le, E of Gloucester. *PRO-sls.* 1397-8. *(baston).*

LITLINGTON, Abbot Nicholas, d1386. *Neale & Brayley; Inventory. (vaulting boss, outer division of entry from Dean's Yard to Cloister; arms indistinct).*

SPENCER, Baron. *CK a 18.*

Qtly Arg and Gu in 2&3 fret Or bend Sa
— *XK 147. (baston; qtd VIII 2&3 by Sir Hen Pole).*
— *FK I 78. (qtd 2&3 by Clare, E of Gloucester).*
— *XK 69. (riband; qtd 3 by George Nevile, Ld Bergavenny, KG).*
— *KB 253. (qtd 7 by Nevyll, E of Warwkye).*

DESPENCER. *Neale & Brayley.* 1296. *(on canopy of mont to Edm, E of Lancaster).*

DESPENCER. *XK 7. (qtd 4 by Anne Nevile, w of Ric 3).*

DESPENCER, Le. *GutchWdU. (Rector's lodgings, Lincoln Coll).*

DESPENCER, Monsire le. *CG 412.*

DESPENCER, le. *Proc Soc Antiq XVII 2S 276.* c1310. *(shield on stole at Leagram Hall, Lancs).*

DESPENCER, le. *Sandford 332. (escutch of Eleanor Beauchamp, d1467).*

DESPENCER, Sr. *BB 13. (d1375; bend only in qrs 1&4).*

DESPENCER, Ld Edward. *XK 10. (baston).*

DESPENCER, Thomas le, E of Gloucester. *Sandford 379. (qtd 2&3 by Clare; husb of Constance, dau of Edm, D of York).*

DESPENCER, Thomas, E of Gloucester. *S 44.*

(baston).

DESPENCER, le, Counte of Wyncester. *RB 6.*

DESPENCER, le. *Sandford 441. (qtd 6 by Mgt Plantagenet, d1541).*

DESPENCER, le. *Sandford 372 & 442. (qtd 8 by Hen Pole, Ld Montague, d1539).*

[DESPENSER]. *D13 4. (qtd 3 by Nevill).*

[DESPENSER]. *D13 3d. (baston; imp by Clare).*

DESPENSER, Hugh le. *Sandford 140. (banished 1322, m Eleanor de Clare).*

DESPENSER, S Hugh le. *GA 61. (baston).*

SPENCER. *L1 570, 2.*

SPENCER. *SHY 151. (baston).*

Qtly Arg & Gu fretty Untinc bend Sa
DESPENSERE, le Sr de. *AS 100. ('quartere dargent et de goul le goul frette sur layent un baston de sable').*

Qtly Arg & Gu fretty Or bend Untinc
SPENCER. *CT 25.*

Qtly Arg & Gu fretty Or bend Or
DESPENSER, Hugh' le. *B 114.*

Qtly Arg & Gu fretty Or bend Sa
— *WGA 234. (baston; qtd 3 by Sir George Neville, Ld Abergavenny).*
— *WB IV 131b, 108. (baston; qtd 2&3 by Ld Bergavenny).*
— *L10 45, 12. (baston; qtd VII 2&3 by Mgt, dau of Geo, E of Clarence).*
— *CRK 1371. (baston; qtd 3 by Hen Beauchamp, D of Warw).*
— *WGA 238. (baston; qrs 2&3 of escutch of Ric Beauchamp, E of Warw).*
— *WB II 49, 14. (baston; qtd 2&3 by Beauchamp, E of 'Worceter').*
— *WK 142. (baston; qtd 3 by [Neville]).*

DEPENSER, H le. *WNR 51.*

DESPENCER. *BD 36. (baston; gown of (Isabella, 2nd w of Ric, E of Warw), kneeling to sin, also on gown of (Eleanor, Duchess of Som); window, St Mary's Chapel, Collegiate Ch of Warw).*

DESPENCER. *WB V 41. (baston).*

DESPENCER, le Sr de. *CN 47. (baston).*

DESPENCER, Hewe le. *LM 66.*

DESPENCER. *WLN 223.*

DESPENCER. *PLN 192. (qtd 2&3 by Clare).*

DESPENSER, Ld. *RH, Ancestor iv 228. (baston).*

DESPENSER, Ld. *FK I 86. (baston).*

DESPENSER, Sr le. *CKO 462. (baston).*

DESPENSER, le. *Habrington ii 242. (qtd by Clare, all imp by Beauchamp qtg Warwick; glass, Pershore Abbey Ch, Worcs).*

DESPENSER, le Mons de. *AN 98.*

DESPENSER, le Sr. *S 42.*

[DESPENSER]. *PLN 111. (qtd 2&3 by [Beauchamp]; cresc Sa for diffce).*

[DESPENSER]. *PLN 1053. (riband; imp by*

'My Lord of Clarence').
DESPENSER, Sr Henri. *J 19.*
DESPENSER, Henry, Bp of Norwich. *RH, Ancestor iii 207. (cresc for diffce in qr 1).*
DESPENSER, Hue le. *Q 46.*
DESPENSER, Hue le. *E II 196; E I 196. (baston).*
DESPENSER, Hugh. *D 145b; HE 100; FW 119; A 214; G 48; H 56; K 41; N 24.*
DESPENSER, Hugh. *S 125. (baston, martlet Sa in chf).*
DESPENSER, Hugh. *MP II 58. ('album ubi nigra gules a or frette').*
DESPENSER, Hugh le. *P 90.*
DESPENSER, Hugh le. *K 306. (baston, not in qrs 2&3).*
DESPENSER, Mons Hugh le. *TJ 943. (baston).*
DESPENSER, Hugh, E of Winchester. *LMS 56. (d1326).*
DESPENSER, Robert, de Staindone. *F 474.*
DESPENSER, Thomas, E of Gloucester. *ML II 18.*
SPENCER. *WB IV 161b, 648. (baston).*
SPENCER. *PV 71. (baston).*
SPENCER, Ld. *KB 281. (baston).*
SPENCER, Ld. *WK B 7. (baston).*
SPENCER, Edward, Ld, KG. *WGA 12. (baston).*
SPENCER, of Gloucs. *Nichols Leics I 854. (glass, Abbot's Chapel, Stoughton).*
SPENSER, Ld. *BR IV 104.*
SPENSER, Sir. *FF 14. (baston).*
SPENSER, Sir Hewe. *PCL I 540.*
Qtly Or and Gu in 2&3 fret Or bend Sa
SPENSER, Sire. *PO 22. (baston).*
Qtly Or & Gu fretty Or bend Sa
DESPENSER, Hue. *D 145a. (baston).*

Qtly 2&3 semy over all bend
Qtly Or & Gu semy of annulets Arg bend Sa
BORGYLOUN, Sire Robert. *N 583.*
Qtly Or & Gu roundelly Arg bend Sa
BOURGYTON. *L2 70, 3.*

Qtly 2&3 Vair over all bend
Qtly Untinc & Vair bend Untinc
CONSTABLE, Margaret. *Bk of Sls 489.* 1428. *(wid of Marmaduke C, Kt & dau of Robt Cumberworth).*
CONSTABLE, Marmaduke. *PRO-sls.* 8 November 1363. *(baston; Sheriff of York).*
CONSTABLE, Marmaduke, of Flamborough. *Bk of Sls 488.* 1369.
CONSTABLE, Robert, of Hamboro, Yorks, Kt. *BrookeAsp I 43, 3.* 1343-4. *(qrs 1&4).*
CONSTABLE, Wm, of Flamborough. *Bk of Sls 524.* c1200.
PEVERELL. *Mill Steph; Belcher II 61.* 1491.

(imp by Colard on brass to Jn C & w Margery, Lower Halling, Kent).
Qtly Gu & Vair bend Arg
CONSTABLE, Monsire le, seigneur de Flamburgh. *CG 408. (baston).*
GOVIZ. *Gerard 227.*
Qtly Gu & Vair bend Or
CONESTABYLL, of Flaynborowe. *RH, Ancestor v 178.*
CONETABLE, M le. *WNR 150.*
CONSTABLE. *SK 398. (baston).*
CONSTABLE. *L9 5, 12. (imp by Ingelby qtg Rowclyff & Mowbray).*
CONSTABLE. *L9 5b, 3. (imp Ingleby).*
[CONSTABLE]. *Proc Soc Antiq XVII 2S 276.* c1310. *(shield on stole, Leagram Hall, Lancs).*
[CONSTABLE]. *SHY 9.*
CONSTABLE, of Flamborough, Yorks. *L1 123, 3; L2 101, 6. (baston).*
CONSTABLE, of Flamburgh, Yorks. *L10 36b, 7.*
CONSTABLE, John, Dean of Lincoln, 1514-28. *Durham-sls 3321.*
CONSTABLE, S Marmaduke. *PO 383. (baston).*
CONSTABLE, Sir Marmaduke. *BA 600.*
CONSTABLE, Sir Marmaduke. *XK 260. (cresc Sa for diffce).*
CONSTABLE, Mons Richard. *BG 166.*
CONSTABLE, Richard. *S 374. (baston).*
CONSTABLE, Mons Robert. *TJ 938. ('...de goules & de ver ove un baston dor').*
CONSTABLE, Sir Robert. *CV-BM 199. (baston).*
CONSTABLE, Sir Robert. *CRK 430. (baston).*
CONSTABLE, Sir Robert. *WK 251. (baston).*
CONSTABLE, Sr Robert le. *CKO 479.*
CONSTABLE, Syr Marmaduke, of Everingham, Yorks. *I2(1904)241. (cresc Sa on bend for diffce).*
Qtly Gu & vairy Or and Vt bend Arg
PEUERELL. *L1 500, 5.*
PEVERELL. *L9 106a, 6. (baston).*
Qtly Gu & vairy Vt and Or bend Arg
PEVERELL, Hu. *NS 34.*

Qtly modified & bend
Qtly per fess dancetty bend
BELHOUS, Isolda de. *Birch 7341.* 1336. *(dex of 2; dau & coh of Lady Alicia de Beaumont & wid of Jn de Belhous, Kt, of Barnwell, Northants & Rayleigh, Essex).*
Qtly indent Az and Gu bend Arg
WEST. *LE 345.*
WEST. *RB 327.*
WEST. *DV 54a, 2125. (baston).*

Qtly per fess indent Az and Gu bend Arg
    WEST. *L1 690, 4.*
Qtly per fess indent Az and Or bend Gu
    BERKLAIE, Giles de. *E II 259.*
Qtly per fess indent Gu and Or bend Or
    BENDLOW. *GutchWdU. (window, Old Hall,*
    University Coll, built 1450 demolished 1669).
Qtly indent Gu and Vt bend Or
    NEVILLE, Hugh de. *MP II 32.*
Qtly per fess indent Or and Az bend Gu
    BERKELAIE. *L10 21b, 8.*
    BERKLAIE, Giles de. *E I 257. (baston).*
Qtly per fess indent Or and Gu bend Az
    — *CT 201.*
Qtly per pale & per chev reversed Arg and Az
    bend Sa
    — *PLN 1707.*

Semy of billets & bend
Billety bend
    CLAXTON, John de. *PRO-sls.* 1324-5.
Az billety & bend Or
    MARRE, le Counte de. *C 63.*
Sa billety & bend Arg
    BOULERS, Baldwin de. *E I 466; E II 468.*
    (baston).
    BOULERS, Baudwin. *A a 280.*
    BOULERS, Baudwyn. *F 208.*
Sa billety & bend Or
    COLENTIER, S Jehan de. *GA 20.*
    FOULCHAMP, Mons Godfr. *WJ 1549. (field*
    unclear).
    KALENTERS, S John de. *ST 97.*

Semy of crosses & bend
Crusily bend
    BURNYGHEM, William. *Roman PO 2344.* 19
    Sept 1365. *(crosses unclear).*
Arg crusily & bend Gu
    HUNTINGFEILD, Sr William de. *I 32.*
Az crusily Arg bend Or
    FIF, C de. *WNR 45.*
Az crusily Or bend Arg
    EUSTACE, Sire Thomas fitz. *N 658.*
Az crusily & bend Or
    MARE, Counte de. *Q 15.*
Gu semy of crosses bottony & bend Arg
    HORNESBY, Mons John. *TJ 244.*
Gu crusily & bend Arg
    HAUWARD, Monsire de. *AN 114.*
    HAWARDE, Mons John. *S 200.*
    HAUWARD, Sire Johan. *N 566.*
    HAUWARD, Sire William. *O 49.*
    HOWARD, Sir de. *F 405.*
    HUNTINGFEILD, Cael de. *A 257.*
    HUNTINGFEILD, 'Lere'. *LH 844.*
    HUNTINGFIELD, Saer de. *E I 524; E II 526.*

Gu crusily & bend Or
    CHAIRS, Herevi de. *F 455.*
    PRESTON, Sr William de. *I 39.*
    PRESTON, William de. *A 259.*
Or crusily Sa bend Gu
    NEVILL, John de, le Forster. *B 178.*
Sa crusily & bend Arg
    LONGEVILERS, Sire Thomas de. *O 142.*

Semy of crosses fitchy & bend
Crusily fitchy bend
    CHEIN, Reginald, Ld of Inverugie. *Stevenson.*
    1296.
    HOWARD, Edmund, Archdeacon of Northd
    1340. *Durham-sls 3273.*
    HOWARD, Edmund, Master of Kepier in 1341.
    Blair D II 119, 275. (6 crosses; above front
    of Gateway, Kepier Hospital, Durham).
    HOWARD, John, Kt. *BrookeAsp I 25, 1.* S.-
    IOHANNIS: HOWARD: MILITIS. 1396-7.
Az crusily fitchy & bend Or
    MAR ET GARNONCH, Conte de. *BS 4.*
Gu crusily fitchy & bend Arg
    HOUHARD. *PO 45.*
Sa semy of crosses formy fitchy Arg bend Or
    HANVILE, Elyas de. *Q 530. (?crosses*
    potent).
Sa crusily fitchy & bend Or
    HAMVILE, Ellis de. *E I 523; E II 525. (or*
    Henri de Haumvill).

Semy de lis & bend
Arg semy de lis Sa bend Gu
    PEYFRER, S Fuke. *GA 192. (baston).*
Az semy de lis & bend Gu
    BURBUN, Dewke de. *RH, Ancestor ix 177.*
    (struck out).
Az semy de lis Or bend Gu
    — *WLN 43.*
    BOURBON. *PLN 580. (baston).*
    BOURBON, le Duc de. *LE 245. (baston).*

Semy of foils &c & bend
Semy of 5foils bend
    RODEVILE. *?source.* 1381. *(sl on deed).*
Gutty bend
    LONG, William de. *PRO-sls.* 1366-7.
Arg gutty & bend Sa
    VYLYIS. *SHY 168.*
Gu roundelly Or bend Arg
    SOUCHE, Sire Amery la. *O 22.*
    SOUCHE, Sire Amory la. *N 819.*
    SOUCHE, of Leics. *BA 31, 269.*
    SOWCHE. *BA 556.*
Gu roundelly Or bend Az
    SOUCH, Sire Amery de la. *L 183.*

Vair & bend

Vair bend Untinc

COLEWORTH, Elizabeth de. *Birch 6617.* +S'
ELIZABETH DE COLEWORTHE. temp Hen 3 or
Edw 1. *(w of Sir Hugh C, of Horndon-on-
the-hill, Essex).*

COLEWORTHE, Hugh de, of Horndon-on-the-
hill, Essex, Kt. *Birch 8806.* S' HVGONIS DE
COLEWORTHE. temp Hen 3.

DAMORY, Roger. *Yorks Deeds VII 196.*
1317. *(?barry nebuly).*

GRESLEYE, Robert de, Kt. *PRO-sls.* 1350-1.
(shield betw 9 salts; baston).

MANCESTER, Guy de. *Bow XXXI 11.* 1350-1.

MANCESTRE, Guy de, Kt. *Bow LXXIV 3.*
SIGILLVM GVIDONIS. DE. MANCESTRE. 1316.
*(grant to Erneburga, Abbess of Polesworth,
of land in Aldeburgh).*

MANCESTRE, Guydon de. *Dugd 17, 7.* Sy.
Guydonis de Mancestre.

MANCESTRE, John de. *Nichols Leics IV 1034.*
c1285.

NORTON, Juliana. *Birch 6692.* 1344. *(1 of 2
shields; wid of Ric de N, of Long Itchington,
Warws).*

Vair bend Gu

DELAMOTE. *L1 205, 6; L2 157, 2.*
MANCESTER. *Lancs 1533 CS 53. (qtd 5 by
Hoult of Gristlehurst).*

MANCESTRE, Sire Guy de. *O 139. (baston).*
MANCHESTER, G. *RB 397.*
MANCHESTER, John de. *E II 456.*
MAUNCESTRE. *L9 50a, 9.*
MOTE, Monsr W de la. *AS 264.*
MOTTE, de la. *XF 67.*

Vairy & bend

Vairy Arg and Gu bend Sa

— *I2(1904)299. (qtd 5 by Sir Phelipe
Herres).*

BECH, S William. *R 65. (baston).*

Vairy Arg and Sa bend Gu

MANCESTRE, G. *HA 127.*
MANCESTRE, G. *HA 26, 139.*
MANCESTRE, Johan de. *LM 256.*
MANCHESTER, John de. *E I 454.*
MANCHESTER, John de. *XF 369.*
MAUNCESTRE. *SK 739. (baston).*
MAUNCESTRE, Monsire Esmon. *AN 330. ('...
a baston gules').*

MAUNCHETTER, S' Gy de. *PO 479. (baston).*
MAUSUER. *L1 424, 6; L2 326, 8. (marginal
note in L1: 'Mancester of Warwicks').*

MONTIOY, Monsire Raufe de. *CG 436. (baston).*

MONTIOYE, Sr Rauf de. *CKO 517. (baston).*

Vairy Arg and Sa bend Or

GRANDONE. *BA 29b, 221.*
GRANDONE, Sire Johan de. *N 842.*

GRAUNDON, Sr John de. *L 89. (baston).*
GRAUNDOWNE, Lincs. *L2 231, 12.*
GRENDON, S John. *ST 40. (baston).*
GRENDON, S' Jon. *PO 628. (baston).*

Vairy Or and Gu bend Az

FERERS, Sire Thomas de. *N 936. (baston).*

Vairy Sa and Arg bend Gu

MANCESTRE, Radolfus. *Q II 267.*
MANECESTRE, Jan de. *Q 216.*

1 BEND PATTERNED

Bend barry

Arg bend barry of 4 indent Or and Gu
HATTON. *PLN 1055.*

Bend bendy

Arg bend bendy of 3 Az and Or & Sa
HARDY, William, of Yorks. *RH, Ancestor v
178. (qtg 2&3 Arg chev Gu betw 3 spearheads Sa).*

Gu bend bendy of 3 Arg and Sa
BENDYSH. *ML I 289.*

Erm bend bendy of 8 Arg and Sa
— *ML I 369. ('Hermyn a bend sylver &
sabyll costyd in viii').*

Bend checky or counter gobony

Bend checky

KENDALE, John. *Birch 4540.* S Armoru Iohis
Kendale Prioris Sanctis Iohis Iherusal.... *(Prior of St
Johns, Clerkenwell, 1491-1501).*

MENTEITH, Sir Wm, of West Kerse, Kt.
Stevenson. 1497. *(?Sir Jn).*

Untinc bend checky Arg and Gu
VAUX, John de. *B 33.*

Arg bend checky Arg and Gu
VAUX, Roland. *TJ 1390.*

Arg bend checky Arg and Sa
SAPRAM. *CB 73. (?bend counter-emb).*

Arg bend checky Gu and Or
VAUX. *PT 1155.*

Arg bend checky Or and Gu
VAUX. *CT 459. (qrs 1, 3&5; Clerk of the
Green cloth).*

VAUX, Rawleyn, of Cumb. *RH, Ancestor iv
244.*

Az bend checky Arg and Az
WELLYS. *CB 83.*

Or bend checky Arg and Sa
MONTECH. *SC 89.*

?MONTEITH. *Lyndsay 351. (drawn as lozy
paly bendy; qtd by Haldane of Gleneagles).*

Or bend checky Or and Gu
— *WK 114. (qtd 3 by Sir Ric Salkeld,
according to trick in later hand).*

Or bend checky Sa and Arg
MENTEITH, of the Carse. *Lyndsay 386.*
Sa bend checky Arg and Az
FOURNES ABBEY. *D4 47b.*
Or bend checky Sa and Erm
STYLE. *LS 159.*
STYLE. *CRK 1958.*
Or bend checky Erm & Az ermined Arg
STYLE. *DV 61a, 2413.*
Or bend checky Erm and Sa
STYLE. *L1 598, 1.*
Or bend countergobony Erm and Sa
STYLE. *LE 393.*

Erm bend checky &c
Erm bend checky Untinc
CURSON, John. *Birch 9144.* 1412. *(qtd 4 by Jn Cursun, or Cursoun, s of Jn Cursun, Kt, of Suff).*
CURSOUN, Wm of Byntree, Norf. *Birch 9148.* 1370.
?CURSUN. *Mill Steph.* 1471. *(qtd 2&3 by Felton, all imp qtly Swynford & Drury on brass to Sir Jn Curson & w Joan ?Drury, Bylaugh, Norf).*
Erm bend checky Arg and Sa
CORSUM. *DV 46a, 1812.*
CUISSAC, de Norf. *WK 786. (imp by Polle Wythypolles).*
CURSON. *Farrer I 328. (roof, Yaxham Ch, Norf).*
CURSON, Mons. *T b 87. (martlet Gu in sin chf for diffce).*
CURSON, Mons John. *T b 86.*
CURSSUM. *L1 131, 4; L2 107, 10.*
CURSUN, de Brightwell, Suff. *LE 448.*
Erm bend counter gobony Arg and Sa
CURSON, Sir John. *PLN 396.*
CURSON, Sir John, of Felton. *PLN 292. (qtd 2&3 by Felton).*
Erm bend checky Sa and Arg
?CURSON. *L10 38, 19. (qtd by 2&3 Sir Jn Felton).*
CURSSUM. *L10 43b, 4.*
CURZON. *CRK 82.*

Fretty &c bend checky
Arg fretty Sa bend checky Or and Gu
REYNES, Roger de. *FW 187.*
Gu crusily Arg bend checky Or and Az
ORNESBY. *L9 89b, 6.*
ORNESBY, Sire Willame de. *N 564.*

Bend chevronny
Erm bend chevronny Untinc
— *WB I 33b, 16. (qr 2 of coat imp by ?Wilcocks).*

Erm bend chevronny of 6 Gu and Or
— *PLN 935. (imp by Mauntell).*
Erm bend chevronny of 8 Or and Gu
BRAILY. *CRK 1462. (or Bruley).*

Bend Erm
Untinc bend Erm
BITILISGATE, Thomas de. *Birch 7489.* SIG THOME DE BITILISGATE. *(sl used by Wentelina, w of Jn de Ralegh, Chev).*
BUCTON, William. *Clairambault 1677.* 6 June 1430. *(qrs 1&4).*
ESSEBI, Jordan. *Birch 9507.* S'....ANI DE ESEB. *(s of Wm de Essebi, of Lincs).*
PHILPOT. *PT 583.*
WALWAYN, Philip. *PRO-sls.* 1400.
Az bend Erm
— *SK 998.*
PRYOURE, Charles. *LE 219.*

Gu bend Erm
Gu bend Erm
— *WJ 1429. (name illegible).*
— *PLN 1347. (spots reversed).*
— *WB I 32, 18. (spots reversed).*
MOREWS. *L9 72b, 6.*
PHILPOT. *L9 98a, 4.*
RIPON, Monsire William de. *CG 375. (label Or).*
RY, Rannlyhs de. *Q 495.*
RYE. *L1 545, 1.*
RYE. *DV 57a, 2256.*
RYE. *PT 193.*
RYE, Sr de. *CKO 228.*
RYE, Sir Michael. *LR 28.*
RYLE, Rondulf du. *LM 525.*
WALWAYNE, John. *RH, Ancestor vii 192.*
WALWAYNE, Nicol. *CRK 1664.*
WALWEIN, Sr John. *R 118.*

Sa &c bend Erm
Sa bend Erm
PHELIPOT, Sir John. *CV-BM 295.*
PHILIPOTT, Sir Joh. *Hutton 86.*
PHILPOT. *CC 230, 257. (qtg 2&3 Arg on cross Sa leopard's face Or).*
PHILPOT. *L1 504, 1.*
PHILPOT, of Hants. *PLN 1296.*
PHILPOT, J. *CRK 2021.*
PHILPOTT, Sir John. *WK 297.*
PHYLPOT, Sir John, of Middx. *WB III 121, 4.*
PHYLPOTT. *DV 67b, 2678.*
Vt bend Erm
— *WB I 19b, 8. (qrs 1&4 of coat imp by Waller).*
WETENALE, Sir Thomas. *CVC 456.*
WETENALL, Sr Thomas de, Ches. *CY 12, 46.*
WETNALE. *BA 4b.*
WETNALE, Sir Thomas de. *CVC 556.*

WETNALL, Sir T de. *LE 222.*
WETNALL, Sir T de. *SK 1009.*
WETNALL, Sr Thomas de. *WLN 311.*
WETTENHALL. *PCL II 2.*
WETTENHALL, Wm. *Hutton 86.*
WHETENHALE, Sir Thomas. *CRK 1077.*
WHETENHALL, William. *LV 46.*

Barry bend Erm
Barry Untinc bend Erm
HORTON, Waleran of. *Durham-sls 1381.*
c1250. *(unclear whether bend charged or Erm).*
MERIET, Simon, of Som, Kt. *Birch 11738.*
S...ERIET NOUE SARUM. 1368. *(?of New Sarum).*
MERIETH, Simon de. *Birch 11736.* S'
SIMONIS DE MERIET. 1368.
Barry Arg and Sa bend Erm
— *H21 87. (qtd by Bourchier).*
Barry Or and Az bend Erm
STANHOW, Hervey de. *XF 372.*
STANHOW, Hervey de. *WLN 867.*
STANHOWE, Hervy de. *E I 462; E II 464.*
Barry Or and Gu bend Erm
MULCHESTOR. *Q 542.*
Barry Or and Sa bend Erm
— *WLN 904.*
— *PLN 1920. (qtd 2&3 by Master Franceys).*
EMERIKE, Monsire John. *CG 227.*
EMERYKE, Sr. *CKO 330. (baston).*
MERIELT, of Hestercombe. *Gerard 60.*
MERIET. *XF 791.*
MERIET. *DV 55a, 2165. (baston).*
MERIET. *LE 351.*
MERIET. *L9 54a, 11.*
MERIET, Sire Johan de. *N 208. (le neveu).*
MERIET, Johes de. *Q 457.*
MERIET, Sir John. *WNS 25b, 46. ('Sire Jon Meriot por barre de vi peces dor et de sa ou un baston dermine').*
MERIET, Sir John de. *CB 292.*
MERIET, of Som. *L1 425, 2; L2 327, 10.*
MERIETTES. *RB 366.*
MERRIET, Sir John, of Hestercombe. *Lawrance 29. (d1327; effigy, Combe Flory, Som).*
MERYET. *CT 267.*

Barry wavy &c bend Erm
Barry nebuly Gu and Or bend Erm
AMORI, M de. *WNR 113.*
Barry wavy Or and Sa bend Erm
POVELEY. *L9 101a, 9.*
Barry nebuly Or and Sa bend Erm
PAVELEY. *XF 802.*

Barry nebuly Vt and Gu bend Erm
AMORI, M de. *WNR 111.*

Checky bend Erm
Checky Untinc bend Erm
— *XFB 150. (qtd IV 2&3 by Christopher Knyvett).*
— *WLN 330. (qtd 4 by Jn Legh, of Rudge).*
— *Birch 8678.* SIGILLU IOHANNIS CL...ARMIG. 15 cent. *(qtd 2&3 by Jn de Clifton, Kt).*
?CLIFFORD. *Mill Steph.* 1518. *(qtd 2&3 by Cayley, all qtd IV by Knevett on brass to Eliz, dau of Sir Wm K, Eastington, Gloucs).*
CLIFTON, Adam de. *PRO-sls.* 1363.
CLIFTON, Constantine. *Farrer II 29. (Cawston Ch, Norf).*
CLIFTON, John de. *Bow 15.*
Checky Arg and Gu bend Erm
— *L9 22b, 8. (qtd II&III by Knevet).*
Checky Az and Or bend Erm
WARWICK, E of. *MP Hist Min ii 468. (d1242; 'Scutum comitis de Warewic').*
WARWICK, Thomas, E of. *MP I 70; MP II 13; MP IV 54.*
Checky Gu and Or bend Erm
CLIFFTON, Sir John, of Norf. *WB I 89b, 3.*
CLIFTON. *Farrer I 58. (qtd by Cayley). (Old Buckenham Ch, Norf).*
KAYLLY, Adam de. *LM 304.*
Checky Or and Az bend Erm
CLIFTON, Adam. *AN 75.*
CLIFTON, Sir Adam, of Norf. *Nichols Leics II 882. (Newton Harcourt Ch).*
CLIFTON, Sir John. *PLN 233.*
WARWICK, Thomas E of. *MP II 104. ('scutum eschekeratum dor et dazur bende ermine').*
Checky Or and Gu bend Erm
— *LE 160. (qtd 2&3 by Gu bendy of 5 Arg [Clyfton]).*
— *WB II 59, 14.*
— *XK 103. (qtd II&III 4 by Sir Thos Knyvet, Kt, 1509).*
CALY, of Norf. *L2 101, 12.*
CAYLI, Sr Adam. *N 534.*
CAYLY. *WK 465. (qtd II&III 4 by Sir Thos Knyvet).*
CAYLY. *LE 233.*
?CLIFTON. *Farrer I 183.* c1425. *(tomb of Sir Edm Thorp, Ashwellthorpe Ch, Norf).*
CLIFTON. *L1 127, 6; L2 101, 12.*
CLIFTON. *PO 47.*
CLIFTON. *Farrer I 104. (Heckingham Ch, Norf).*
CLIFTON. *L10 39, 8.*
CLIFTON. *FB 27. (imp by Mawteby).*
CLIFTON. *FB 7. (imp Mortimer).*
CLIFTON. *PLN 788. (imp by Knyvet, of Buckenham).*

CLIFTON, Adam de. *TJ 289.*
CLIFTON, Sir John. *PLN 1411.* *(Erm tails in bend sin).*
CLIFTON, Sir Robert. *BW 19, 132. (annulet Gu in dex chf).*
CLYFFTUN. *WB I 34b, 6.*
CLYFTON, Adam de. *TJ 1281.*
CLYFTON, Mons Adam de. *WJ 1142.*
CLYFTON, Sir J. *WB I 37b, 7.*
CLYFTON, Sir J. *BW 16b, 110.*
CLYFTON, John. *NS A 125.*
CLYFTONNE. *SK 117.*
KINGSTON. *L1 375, 1.*

Paly &c bend Erm

Paly Or and Gu bend Erm
LANGFORD, Mons Rich. *WJ 444.*
LANGFORTHE. *L9 36a, 3.*
Per pale Gu and Or bend Erm
LONGFORD. *LE 385.*
LONGFORD. *DV 60a, 2368.*
LONGFORD. *L9 38a, 10.*
LONGFORD. *CC 235, 419.*
LONGFORD. *L2 300, 8.*
Qtly Gu vairy Or and Vt bend Erm
PEVERELL. *PT 742. (baston).*
Untinc crusily fitchy Untinc bend Erm
COMBE, William de. *Birch 4082.* S FRIS WIL-..E COMBE ...BIS DE STA.... *(Abbot of Stanley, Wilts).*
Gu roundelly Or bend Erm
SOUCH, Wille la. *Q 449.*
Vairy Or and Az bend Erm
COCK, Henry. *PLN 765. (qtg 2&3 Gu on bend Arg cotised Az 3 lozs Gu).*
Vairy Or and Vt bend Erm
KOCK, Hary. *WB IV 152, 470.*

Bend Ermines

Arg bend Ermines
HENSLEY, Thos. *WB III 104b, 3.*

Bend fimbriated

Gu bend Az fimbriated Arg
— *ML I 493. ('Goules a bend sylver voyded wit asur comme gartercy').*
Gu bend checky Or and Az fimbr Arg
— *ML I 494. ('Ther ys I beryth theys armys goules a bend sylver voyded wit asur comme garterey thus voyded wit asur & gold chekke').*
Or bend gobony Arg and Az fimbr Gu
ROYDON. *LE 285.*
Sa bend Erm fimbr Gu
BEYNTON, John, of Wilts. *WB III 91b, 1.*
Checky Arg and Gu bend Az fimbr Or
— *WLN 729. (Fouc de ...).*

Az crusily Or bend Gu fimbr Or
ESTONE. *LE 117.*
ESTONE, Ric de. *WLN 620.*
ESTONE, Richard de. *E I 419; E II 421.*
ESTONE, Richard. *E 419.*
ESTONE, Richard. *F 150.*

Bend fretty

Untinc bend fretty Untinc
— *Arch Cant iv 119.* c1400. *(qtd by Oxenbridge, all imp by Barry on brass to Margareta, w of Edw B, Sevington, Kent; from Sir Ed Dering's Church notes taken 1628).*
— *Lawrance 51.* 1340-50. *(effigy, Bamburgh, Northd).*
MATROS, Maurice de. *PRO-sls.* 1247-8.
ORE, Robert de, Suss. *Birch 12310.* SIGILLUM ROBERTI DE ORE. 1378.
WYGHT, Nicholas de. *PRO-sls.* 1335.
Arg bend Gu fretty Or
ROTELLWELL, William. *WJ 1468.*
ROTELWELL, William. *LR 33.*
Gu bend Arg fretty Sa
— *XK 119. (qtd 3 by Sir Goddard Oxenbridge, Kt 1509).*
— *WK 481. (qtd 3 by Sir Godard Oxinbruge).*
Gu bend Az fretty Arg
DORE, Sr Robt de, Suss. *CY 166, 661.*
Or bend Az fretty Arg
ORE, Robert de. *CV-BM 302.*
Barry Or and Az bend Gu fretty Arg
MELTON, Thoroldus de. *PE II 6. ('in Cletham in Yelthorp, Lincs').*
MILTON, Galfridus de. *PE I 7.*
Checky Or and Az bend Gu fretty Arg
CHEYNE. *L10 43b, 16.*
Checky Or and Az bend Gu fretty Erm
CHEYNE. *L2 110, 4.*
Qtly bend fretty Untinc
PORTER. *CassPk 316.* 21 Oct 1400. *(imp by Wauton on grant by Ismania, wid of Sir Wm W & dau&h of Jn Porter, of Stebbing).*

Bend gobony

Bend gobony
BUYRLEYE, Roger. *Birch 7957.* ...OGERI DE BVRLE.... *(s of Jn, Ld of Buyrleye).*
FITZ WARYN, Pieres le. *Birch 9788.* SIGILL ..-.TRI LE FIZ WARIN. 1332. *(lines in bend sin alternately plain & indented; peculiarity in charge of bend is in reference to arms of Fitz-Warren, viz qtly per fess indented).*
SOULES, Thomas de. *PRO-sls.* c1230.
Arg bend gobony Az and Gu
PARYS. *LE 431.*
PARYS. *L1 519, 6; L2 406, 8.*
PARYS. *L9 102b, 7.*
PARYS. *WB II 63, 3.*

Or bend gobony Arg and Az
  TRIE, le Signeur de Bilebatia de. *C 128.* *('..
  d'or a une bende gobone d'argent et
  d'azur').*

Barry bend gobony
Barry Arg and Az bend gobony Or and Gu
  GRAY. *PLN 392.*
  GRAY, Mons Robert, de Barton en Rydale.
  TJ 570. (baston).
  GRAYE. *PT 452. (baston).*
  GREY. *CB 209.*
  GREY. *PLN 933. (barry of 8).*
  GREY. *DV 50b, 1995.*
  GREY, Sir Nichol. *CV-BM 252. (bend
  gobony of 7).*
Barry Arg & Az roundelly Or bend gobony Or
  and Gu
  GREY. *Nichols Leics II 558. (Evington Ch).*
Barry Az and Arg bend gobony Arg and Gu
  GREY, Sire Nichol de. *O 96.*
Barry Az and Arg bend gobony Or and Gu
  GRAY, Sr Nicolas de. *M 13.*
  GREY, Sire Nicholas de. *N 415. ('les armes
  de Grey a un baston gobonne de or e de
  goules').*
Barry Or and Vt bend gobony Arg and Gu
  PONIG, Sr Th. *R 48.*

Checky &c bend gobony
Checky bend gobony
  MICHELL, Henry. *PRO-sls.* 1371-2.
  (unclear).
Erm bend gobony Untinc
  CURZON. *Proc Soc Antiq VII 2S 213. (qtd
  by Wm Norman; sl matrix).*
Lozy Gu and Or bend gobony Arg and Az
  GRAYE. *L2 231, 3. (of Lancs or Westmld).*
  GREY, Sire Thomas de. *N 1022.*
  (baston; '..a les lozenges de or ...').

Paly bend gobony
Paly bend gobony
  HAUTEVILLE, Ralph de, Banneret. *PRO-sls.*
  1341-2.
  HAUTEVILLE, Rodurphus de. *PRO-sls.*
  1337-8. *(bend unclear).*
Paly Arg and Az bend gobony Gu and Or
  LEVET, Sir Walter. *CVC 506.*
  LEVET, Sr Walter. *WLN 291. (Mayor of
  Chester).*
  LEVET, S' Water, of Ches. *CY 8, 29.*
  LEVET, Walterus. *Q II 676.*
Paly Arg and Az bend gobony Or and Gu
  LEVETT, Walter. *SES 112. (baston).*
Paly Az and Arg bend gobony Or and Gu
  ANNESLE, Mons John. *TJ 1068.*
  ANNESLEY, Monsr de. *AS 315.*

Paly Gu and Arg bend gobony Or and Gu
  ANNESLEY. *LE 165.*

Qtly &c bend gobony
Qtly bend gobony
  — *PRO-sls.* ...Hanni.... 1365-6. *(baston; used
  by Wm de Sutton).*
Crusily bend gobony
  TOLTHORP, Alice. *Birch 13956.* 1324. *(wid
  of Thos de T, of Yorks; 2nd of 3 shields).*
Az semy de lis Or bend gobony Arg and Gu
  — *LE 254.*
  BOURBON. *PLN 597. (qtd 2&3 by Navarre).*
  BURGUNDY. *RH, Ancestor iii 197. (qtd by
  Navarre-perhaps Jn, 1425-79).*
  NAVARRE, K of. *WB IV 127, 33. (baston).*
  NAVARRE, K of. *CRK 1400. (qrs 1&4).*
  NAVERN, le Roy de. *LE 243.*
Az semy de lis Or bend gobony Gu and Arg
  NAVARRE, K of. *BR I 13. (qrs 1&4).*
Az semy de lis Or bend gobony Erm and Gu
  TAMPES, le Comte de. *LE 256. (le Comte
  d'Etampes).*

Bend lozengy &c
Untinc bend lozy Untinc
  BERMYNGEHAM, William de. *Birch 7413.*
  S...lelmi bermyngham. 1399-1412. *(qtd by per
  pale indent).*
  DEINCOURT, Isabel. *Wentworth.* 1345-6.
  (blazon unclear; wid of Sir Wm Fitzwilliam).
  MARESCHAL, Anselm, Kt. *Birch 11603.*
  SIGILLUM ANSELMI MARESCHAL. 1337.
  WALDYVE, Thomas, of Oxfords. *Birch
  14215.* 1441.
Arg bend lozy Gu and Arg
  WYNSELOWE, de Cozheche. *WB IV 179b,
  967.*
Arg bend lozy Or and Gu
  HAREWEDON. *CC 232, 329.*
Gu bend lozy Arg and Gu
  WINSLOW. *PLN 542.*
Or bend lozy Gu and Arg
  BELHOUS, Thomas de. *LM 454.*
Or bend lozy Gu & Vair
  BELHOUSE, Theobald de. *E I 536; E II 538.*
  BELLEHOUS, Thom del. *Q 285.*
Sa bend lozy Arg and Gu
  URSWICK, Sir William. *CRK 999.*
Arg bend paly Gu and Erm
  — *ML I 502. ('Sylver a bend goules & her-
  myn palyd in vi quarters. Or in vi quarters
  paley').*
Paly Arg and Az bend paly Gu and Or
  ANNESLE, Sr de. *CKO 618.*
Paly Gu and Arg bend counterch
  — *D4 42b. (qtd by Wentworth, of Went-
  worth, Yorks).*
  WODROFFE. *D9. (qtd by Wentworth, of*

Wentworth, Yorks).

Bend per bend &c

Vt bend per bend sin lengthwise Sa and Arg
— *ML I 451. ('Vert a bend sabyll & sylver pyled in ii le iid de southe. On vert a band sabyll & sylver bendy le iid de south. Le iid de south that ys to say the iid color that ys sabyll he ys undyr the sylver for he is next the poynt ther for thou must say le iid de south for he myght ber a bend sabyll & sylver bende & yet sabyll should be above as thus [fig 451A Per bend bevilled Sa and Arg] and ther for thou must say le iid de south, but her le iiid de south as yf the feld wer of an other color').*

Per bend Arg and Sa bend counterch
WILLIAM DAVID, Morgan ap. *BA 22, 184.*

Per bend sin Sa and Arg bend counterch
ULSTAN, K, pa'. *KB 67. (K of Britain).*

Arg bend per bend Erm and Sa
— *ML I 474. ('Sylver a bende hermyn & sabyll bendey').*

Gu bend per bend indent Or and Az
FRENES, Sir Walter, of Herts. *L2 210, 12. (as blazoned).*

Per fess Untinc and Untinc bend Gu
GREY, Robert de. *LM 581.*

Per fess Arg and Gu bend counterch
— *FK II 495.*

Per pale bend counterch

Per pale Arg and Gu bend counterch
CHASERS. *L10 37b, 20.*
CHAUCER. *CRK 1601.*
CHAUCER. *FK II 836.*
CHAUCER, Geoffrey, d1400. *Keepe; Neale & Brayley. (N&B do not give tincts; shield has recently been correctly repainted as blazoned above).*
CHAUSER. *L1 131, 5; L2 108, 2.*
CHAUSER. *DV 48a, 1888.*
CHAUSER. *RH, Ancestor ix 166. (name added in later hand).*
CHAUSERS. *XPat 94, Arch 69, 75.*
CHAWSER. *LY A 3.*
CHAWSERYS, Jafferey, of Oxfs. *RH, Ancestor iv 250.*

Per pale Arg and Gu bend sin counterch
?CHAUCER. *CRK 872.*

Per pale Gu and Arg bend counterch
CHAUCER, Geoffrey, d1400. *Dingley ccccxxxvii.*
CHAUCERS, John, of Berks. *WB III 101b, 1.*

Per pale Gu and Az bend counterch
— *Neale & Brayley; Inventory. 1431. (N&B reverse tincts & attribute coat to Chaucer; canopy of mont of Lewis Robessart).*

Bend qtly

Az bend qtly bendwise Arg and Gu
HURTES, John, of Northd. *LH 791.*

Az bend qtly bendwise Gu and Arg
— *CRK 1939.*
HURTES, John, of Northd. *WB III 94b, 3.*

Gu bend qtly Sa and Arg
— *CRK 64.*

Or bend qtly bendwise Az and Gu
— *LE 274.*

Vt bend qtly bendwise Arg and Sa
— *ML I 277.*

Per salt Gu and Sa bend qtly Gu and Erm
— *RH, Ancestor ix 160.*

Per salt Or and Az bend qtly Erm and Az
— *ML I 415. ('Gold & asur in geron a bend quarterly hermyn & in umbre. Or a bend quartly hermyn & of the iid'; blue pieces of bend fall on blue parts of field).*

Bend billety

Bend semy of billets
BRETT. *L10 76b, 15.*
MORIENX, Thomas de, of Suff, Chevr. *Birch 11925.* Sigillvm Thome de Morienx. *1364.*
MORIEUX. *Mill Steph. 1485. (qtd 2&3 by Hy le Strange on brass, Hunstanton, Norf).*
MORIEUX. *Mill Steph. 1508. (qtd 2&3 by Sir Rog le Strange on brass, Hunstanton, Norf).*
MORIEUX. *Mill Steph. 1506. (qr 4 of tabard of Sir Rog le Strange's effigy on his brass, Hunstanton, Norf).*
MORIEUX. *Mill Steph. 1506. (qtd 2&3 by Walkefare as imp by Strange on effigy of 'Jn le Strange, Knt, Walkefare & Morieux' on brass to Sir Rog le Strang, Hunstanton, Norf).*

Arg bend Gu semy of billets Arg
BRETT. *NS A 50.*

Gu bend Arg semy of billets Sa
— *LS 8. (qtd 3 by Strange).*
BRET. *CV-BM 69.*
MARROWS. *L1 428, 2; L2 330, 12.*
MORIEUX. *Proc Soc Antiq XVI 2S 169.* 14 cent. *(?Sir Thos who took an active part against the rebels in 1381; banner, Norwich Cathedral).*
MORIEUX. *PLN 1214.*
MORIEUX. *Farrer III 9.* 14 cent. *(Norwich Cathedral).*
MORREWES, Mons Thomas. *S 565. (7 billets).*
MORREWES, S Thos. *PO 76.*
MORYENS. *CB 176. (billets 1, 2, 1, 2, 1).*
MORYEWIS, Tho. *NS A 48.*
MORYNEUS. *L9 70b, 9.*
MORYNEUS, Mons T de. *WJ 1428.*
MORYS, Sir Thomas, of Suff. *WB III 71b, 6.*

MURREUX. *SK 236.*
MURREUX. *SK 226.*
MURREUX, Monsire Thomas. *AN 157.*
MURZEUX. *L2 341, 11.*

Bend semy of cross crosslets
Untinc bend Sa crusily Arg
— *WB I 21b, 6. (marshalled by Cheyney, all imp by Ld Vauz).*
Arg bend Az crusily Or
LOUDHAM, Sire Johan de. *N 637.*
LOWDAM. *L9 44a, 8.*
LOWDHAM, Sir John. *Lawrance 27. (d1318; about 24 crosslets in pairs on bend; effigy, Lowdham, Notts).*
Arg bend Sa crusily fitchy Or
— *SK 302.*

Bend semy de lis
Arg bend Az semy de lis Or
DEYWYLYM. *L2 165, 3.*
Or bend Az semy de lis Or
GOLDINGTON. *CRK 1431.*
GOLDYNGTON. *L2 217, 10.*
GOLDYNGTON, of Yorks. *MY 288. (lis in bend sin).*

Bend roundelly
Arg bend Gu roundelly Or
CURZON, Sir John. *N 591.*
Barry wavy Arg and Gu bend Sa roundelly Or
GOLOPE, Mons John. *TJ 598. (baston).*
Qtly Arg and Gu bend Sa roundelly Or
BOXSTEDE, Sire Rauf de. *N 438.*
Qtly Or and Gu bend Az roundelly Arg
STORMYN, Sire Roger. *N 523.*
Qtly Or and Gu bend Sa roundelly Or
ROCHEFORDE, John. *BG 258.*

Bend Vair
Untinc bend Vair
— *PRO-sls E40 A16633.* S Radulphi de ....
1354-5. *(Ralph de ...; used by Simon de Sekkyndon, Parson of Thorpe Constantine).*
SHELREYE, Edmund de. *Vinc 88, 54.* +SiG EDM... DE SHELREYE. 1372-3. *(sl).*
THENFORD, Nicholas de. *PRO-sls.* 1367-8.
Untinc bend vairy Erm and Untinc
HAVOUR, Richard. *Birch 10591.* SIGILLUM RICARDI ...OUR. 1475.

Gu bend Vair
Gu bend Vair
— *PLN 1109. (qtd 2&3 by Arg cross moline Gu).*
— *LE 294.*
— *CT 202.*
BEAUCHAMP. *LE 386.*
BEAUCHAMP. *CC 235, 420.*

BEAUCHAMP. *DV 60a, 2371.*
BEAUPELL. *L1 77, 1; L2 39, 6.*
BEUPEL, Sire Robert. *O 103.*
BEUPEL, Sir Robt. *WNS 26b, 112.*
RALE, Henry de. *FW 317.*
RALEE, Mons John. *TJ 262. (blazoned Gu bend Vair crusily Arg).*
RALEIGH, Henry de. *WLN 543.*
RASE. *L1 557, 6.*
WYNDLESORE, Hugh de. *FW 680.*

Checky &c bend Vair
Checky Or and Gu bend Vair
BOTEREUX, Monsire de. *CG 331.*
BOTEREUX, Sr de. *CKO 189.*
BOTEREUX, Mons W. *AS 474.*
BOTERUX. *L10 84b, 15.*
BOTREAUX, le Sire. *TJ 231.*
BOTREAUX, Mons William. *TJ 1119.*
BOUTREUX. *L1 98, 4; L2 47, 11.*

Erm bend Vair
Erm bend Vair
APULDREFELD, John de. *BarronMS. (E window, Warhome Ch, also noted in Challock Ch by Le Neve).*
RALLE, Henri de. *A 185.*
Erm bend vairy Or and Gu
APELTREFEUD, Henry. *FW 291.*
APELTREFEUD, Henry. *A a 40.*

Fretty bend Vair
Untinc fret Untinc bend Vair
— *PLN 2064. (qtly in qr III).*
Gu fret Arg bend vairy Arg and Gu
NORVILL. *L2 369, 6.*
Gu fret Arg bend vairy Gu and Or
— *WB I 17, 8. (qrs 2&3 of coat imp by Arg on chev betw 3 lions Sa 3 roundels Or [?Delwood]).*
NORTON. *L9 85a, 6.*

Paly bend Vair
Paly Untinc and Untinc bend vairy Or and Sa
NELSUN, Henri le. *F 471. (?paly Or and Purp or Arg and Vt).*
Paly Arg and Gu bend vairy Arg and Sa
ANNESLE, Sr de. *CKO 502.*
ANNESLEY, Monsire de. *CG 501.*

Qtly bend Vair
Qtly Untinc bend Vair
ROCHEFORD, Alice de, wid of Sir Hen de Greville. *LonBH G3.* S ALISIE DE ROCHEFORD. 1334.
SACKVILLE. *Bow XVI 12.*
SAKEVILLA, Andrew de. *PRO-sls.* 1356-7. *(Seneschal of household of E of March).*
SAUUKEVILL, Andrew de. *PRO-sls.* c1300.

Qtly Gu and Arg bend Vair
    SAKEUYLE, Sr Andrew. *PO 400.*

Qtly Gu & Or bend Vair
Qtly Gu and Or bend Vair
    SACKVILE. *CRK 459.*
    SACKVILE, Thomas. *BG 277.*
    SACKVILLE. *LS 255.*
    SACKVILLE, Thomas. *S 260.*
    SAKEVILE. *FK II 823.*
    SAKEVILLE, Andreu de. *Q 244.*
    SAKEVILLE, Geffray de, Suss. *TJ 1394.*
    SAKEVILLE, Mons Thom. *S 258.*
    SAKVYLE, Suff. *MY 60.*

Qtly Or & Gu bend Vair
Qtly Or and Gu bend Vair
    FITZJOHN, Essex. *L2 192, 8.*
    LEKENOR, Mons Tomas, Suss. *MY 315.*
    SACKEUILLE. *L1 606, 2.*
    SACKVILLE, Andrew. *CA 56. (baston).*
    SAGEVILE, Sire Andrew de. *N 526.*
    SAKALL, Monsr de. *AS 380. (baston).*
    SAKEVELE. *Suff HN 49. (Mettingham Castle or College).*
    SAKEVILE, Monsire de. *CG 417.*
    SAKEVILE, Sr de. *CKO 466.*
    SAKEVILE, Andrew de. *FW 645. (outline of bend drawn in later hand).*
    SAKEVILLE, Baron. *CK a 35.*
    SAKEVILLE, Andreu de. *A 134.*
    SAKEVYLE. *WB I 14b, 7.*
    SAKEVYLE, Sr Tho, Suss. *CY 160, 638.*
    SAKEVYLL, Sir. *PLN 303.*
    SAKEVYLLE, Essex. *MY 122.*
    SAKVILL, Mons Andrew. *SD 35.*
    SAKVILLE, Mons John. *TJ 948. (baston).*
    SAKVYLE, Rychard. *WB II 65, 13.*

Semy bend Vair
Gu semy of billets Or bend Vair
    CAUDRAY. *PO 320. (in later hand).*
Gu crusily Arg bend Vair
    RAFE, Mons J de. *AS 477.*
    RALEE, John de. *CA 40.*
    RALEE, Mons John. *TJ 262. (painting omits crosslets).*
    RALEY, Monsire de. *CG 364.*
Gu crusily Or bend Vair
    RALE, Sr Jon de. *PO 498.*
    RALEIGH, Henry. *LR 44.*
    RALEIGH, Henry de. *E I 407; E II 409.*
Gu semy of escallops Arg bend Vair
    BEUPEL, Sire Robert. *N 179.*

1 BEND MODIFIED

Bend arched
Arg bend arched Sa
    STOPHAM, Sr Willm de. *RB 22.*
    STOPHAM, Sire Wyll de. *HA 13b, 14.*
Barry Arg and Az bend arched Vt
    SAXONY, D of. *LO B 61.*
Erm bend arched Gu
    — *CV-BM 52.*

Bend couped
Checky Or and Az bend couped Gu
    — *BA 843. (checky in 2 top rows are like billets fessways, in lower part they are paleways; qtd 5 by Sir Thos Cokesey).*

Bend dancetty
Bend dancetty
    — *Birch 12356.* 15 cent. *(imp by Robt Pakingham or ?Pakeman, Esq).*
    BLAKET, Bartholomew. *PRO-sls.* 1368.
    CAILY, Richard. *Birch 8011.* ...Rica(?)....
    1368. *(Rector of Sampford Parva, Essex).*
    GAMELIN, Laurence. *Stevenson.* 1317. *('filius Gamelini').*
    MALYN, John. *Birch 11559. (dimid eagle; s&h of Wm M, jun, of Ipswich, Suff).*
    WIVERESTON, William de. *Bow XXVII 14.* 1351-2 & 1376-7.
    WIVERISTON, William de. *Dugd 17, 45.* 1351-2.
    WRIGHTE, John le. *PRO-sls E40 A16735.* s Johannis ....weyne. 1348-9.
Arg bend dancetty Az
    — *D4 49. (qtd by Skelton, of Bramford, Cumb).*
    BRAMPTON. *L10 76, 19.*
Arg bend dancetty Gu
    HACTON. *LH 569. (?Acton).*
    HACTON. *CC 235b, 436.*
Arg bend dancetty Sa
    ASTON, Roger de. *TJ 1475.*
    LYSTONE, Mons Ric de. *WJ 1513.*
Erm bend dancetty Or
    CHAUMP.., Thomas. *BG 354.*
Qtly Arg and Sa bend dancetty Gu
    — *LM 433. (baston).*

Bend embattled
Bend emb
    ESH, Roger of. *Durham-sls 919.* 1322-46. *(in base of 4 shields arranged in cross).*
    ESH, Simon of. *Durham-sls 918.* 1322-46. *(in base of 4 shields arranged in cross).*

MANSTON. *Lawrance 27.* pre 1350. *(?betw cotises; effigy, Leeds, Yorks).*
Arg bend emb Sa
SANTON, Monsrie Henry de. *CG 346.*
STANTON, Mons Henry de. *AS 444.*
STAUNDON, Henry de. *TJ 247.*
STAUNTON, Henry de. *TJ 1251.*
Gu bend emb Arg
PENZRET, Sire Johan de. *N 1014.* *('...bende bataille...').*

Bend embattled counter-embattled
Bend embattled counter-emb
— *Birch 9513.* 1348. *(3rd of 4 shields in sl of Symond de Esshe, of Seaton & Seaham, co Durham).*
CHERLTON, Robert de, of West Wittenham, Berks. *Birch 8529.* 1381.
RYNGBOURNE, William, of Berks. *Birch 13191.* 1384.
Arg bend embattled counter-emb Sa
SABRAM. *CRK 1901.*
SAPRAM. *CB 73.* *(?bend checky of 2 tires).*
SAPY, Sr de. *CKO 201.* *(& H de Stanton, both names given in original hand).*
STAINTON. *LS 204.* *(grady).*
STANTON, Sir Henry de. *CV-BM 250.*
STANTONE. *SK 457.*
STAUNTON. *LS 164.*
STOYNTON, Henry de. *WJ 1515.* *(grady).*
Gu bend embattled counter-emb Arg
ALEYNSCHERLYS, Sir Thomas. *L10 6b, 12.*
PENZERT. *L1 527, 5.*
PENZRET. *L9 102a, 6.*
SCHERLLIS, Mons Aleyn. *WJ 1439.*
Sa bend embattled counter-emb Arg
MANSTON. *DV 69a, 2722.*
MANSTON. *CRK 927.*
MANSTONE. *PT 1197.*
MASTON. *L1 433, 1; L2 333, 7.*
MAYNSTON, John. *RH, Ancestor vii 189.*
WAUSTON. *PT 138.*
Erm bend embattled counter-emb Untinc
ROUS, Alis de la. *Birch 13143.* S ALIS DE JAROUS. 1409. *(1 of 2 shields in sl; sl used by Johanna, wid of Sir Jn Cary, Kt).*
Gu bend embattled counter-emb Erm
— *WJ 1440.*

Bend engrailed
Bend engr
— *CombeAsp II 203.* *(qtd by Philip Tylney, a chevron).*
— *PRO-sls.* 1483. *(qtd by Rog Dynley).*
— *Birch 8874.* 1407. *(qtd 2&3 by Thos Colpepir, Ld of Hardreshull, Warws, Kt).*
ACHARD, Joan. *Selborne 4, 87.* 1319. *(dau*

& h of Sir Adam Gurdon).
ACHARD, Robert, Kt, Ld of Aldermaston. *Aldermaston.* SIGILL RO... ACHARD. 1349-50.
COLEPEPER. *Birch 8816.* 1512. *(imp by Hardyshull in arms of Alexander Colepepyr, of Goudhurst, Kent, Kt).*
COLEPEPER, Peter, of Kent. *Birch 8873.* SIGILLUM PETRI COLEPEPR. 1411.
COLEPEPIR, John, of Northants, Kt. *Birch 8872. ....IS.....* 1429. *(qtg 2&3 chev betw 9 martlets [Hardyshull], over all label).*
COLEPEPER, Sir John. *Arch Cant iii 144.* S.-.ILLU. .ANNIS COLEPEPER. 1484-5.
COLPEPIR, Geoffrey, of Peckham parva, Kent. *Birch 8867.* SIG GALFRIDI COLPEPIR. 1369. *(annulet for diffce).*
CULPEPER. *Mill Steph.* 1525. *(brass to Reynold Peckham & w Joyce C, Wrotham, Kent).*
CULPEPER. *Mill Steph; Belcher II 57.* c1520. *(brass prob for Walter C, 1462, & w Agnes Roper, 1457).*
DURHAM, John. *Stevenson.* 1320. *(?or Durant).*
FORTESCU, Sir John. *Proc Soc Antiq III 2S 348.* SIGILLUM DOMINI IOHANNIS FORTESCU MILITIS. 28 Nov 1450. *(signet sl attached to letter of attorney from certain feoffees of Sir Jn Fastolf).*
GROVE, Richard. *Birch 10312.* 1431. *(Armourer & Citizen of London).*
MANSTON. *Yorks Deeds II 112.* 1549. *(qtd 2&3 by Rog Dyneley).*
MANSTON. *Yorks Deeds II 108.* 1516. *(qtd 2&3 by Rog Dyneley).*
MANSTON. *Yorks Deeds II 106.* 1488. *(qtd 2&3 by Rog Dyneley).*
MEULARD, Katherine. *Birch 11767.* 1350. *(executrix of will of Jn de Aldeburgh, late Burgess of Reading).*
MORYEUX, Thomas, Kt. *Bow XXXI 13a.* temp Edw 2.
QUAREL, Hamo. *PRO-sls.* S HAMONIS QUAREL. 1319. *(used by Edm Q).*
RADCLIF, Ralph de. *Birch 12896.* S REDVLPHI RADCLIF. c1390.
RADCLIFF. *Mill Steph; Thornley 203.* 1531. *(imp Ashton, of Middleton; brass to Alice A & her 3 husbs (1) Jn Laurence, (2) Rich Radcliff, of Tower, (3) Thos Booth, of Hakensall; Middleton, Lancs).*
RADCLIFFE. *Mill Steph; Thornley 155.* 1524. *(qtd 2&3 by Harington; on wife's mantle; brass to Hy Norris, of Speke, & w Clemence H, Aughton, Lancs).*
RADCLIFFE, Sir George. *Greenwich 19 K36, HB-SND.* 1547. *(imp fess betw 3 cartwheels).*
RATCLIFFE, Sir John. *Proc Soc Antiq II 2S 190.* *(d1527; shield also appears reversed*

with rose in sin chf; brass to Sir Jn R & his
w Alice, dau of Sir Edm Sutton, of Dudley;
Crosthwaite Ch, Cumb).
RATCLYFF, Lord Fitzwarter. *I2(1904)53.*
(banner).
WANE, Martin. *Stevenson.* 1468. *(Great
Almoner & Confessor of Jas III & Chancel-
lor of diocese of Glasgow).*
WARNER, Thomas, of Winchester, Hants.
Birch 14280. ...OME WARNER. *1398.*
Bend sin engr
FORTESCUE, John. *Birch 9884.* +S' M.D.
IOH'IS FFORTESCHU.M. *(Chief Justice of the
King's Bench, Kt).*

Arg bend engr Az
Arg bend engr Az
RAYGATE, Mons John, de Houke. *TJ 271.*
RAYGUT, Monsr de. *AS 371.*
ROIGATE, Monsire. *CG 382.*

Arg bend engr Gu
Arg bend engr Gu
— *XFB 48. (qtd 2 by Sir Jn Haryngton).*
— *CRK 734. (qtd 2&3 by Sir Thos Cul-
peper).*
— *S 120. (qtd 2&3 by Culpeper).*
COLEPEPER. *S 118. (qtd by Thos Har-
dreshull).*
COLEPEPER. *DV 61a, 2410.*
COLEPEPER, Alexander. *Kent Gentry 216,
395. (qtg Hardehull).*
COLEPEPHER. *GY 15.*
COLPEPER. *Hutton 16.* 1523. *(imp by Legh;
window, Lambeth Ch).*
CULPEPER. *Mill Steph.* 1420. *(imp by Cob-
ham, of Starborough; brass to Dame Eleanor,
dau of Sir Thos Colepeper & 1st w of Sir
Reginald Cobham of South Leigh, Surr).*
CULPEPER. *L9 22b, 7.*
CULPEPER. *LH 377. (qr 1 of coat imp by
Harington).*
CULPEPER. *LH 389. (qtd 2 by Harington, all
imp Moton).*
CULPEPER. *WB I 22b, 9-13.*
CULPEPER. *LH 378. (qtd 2 by Harington).*
CULPEPER, Sir John, Kent. *L10 44b, 8.*
CULPEPER, Sir John, of Kent. *WB III 74, 3.*
CULPEPER, of Kent. *L2 140, 2.*
CULPEPER, Sir Thomas. *PLN 211.*
CULPEPPER. *Lambarde 184. (imp by Hals-
ham; mont to Sir Hugh H, 1442, & Joyce
dau of Sir Jn C, 1421, West Grinstead, Suss).*
CULPEPPER, Thomas. *BG 225.*
GREY, John de. *E I 140.*
KNEFFET, Essex. *MY 120.*
KULPEPER, Mons Waut, of Kent. *WJ 1575.*
WALERAND, Robert. *B 156.*
WALROND, Robert. *F 76. ('argent a bend

fusilly gules').*
WAUCAR.., Sir R. *WB I 41, 1. (name
unclear).*
Arg bend sin engr Gu
CHITECROFT, Piers. *CVK 708.*
CHYPCROFTE, P... de, Kent. *CY 156, 623.*
COLEPEPR. *PT 698. (qtd by Hardshull).*
WROTESLEY, Lord Hugh de. *BD 161. (3rd
window, St Georges Ch, Stanford, Lincs).*

Arg bend engr Purp
Arg bend engr Purp
MALEIS, Sir Nycholas. *CB 279. (or
Maleyns).*
MALEMEIS, Sire Nicholas. *N 296.*
MALEMYS. *L1 439, 4; L2 337, 1.*
MALEUREUVES, Sr Michel. *L 139.*
MALMAYES. *CG 381.*
MALMEYNS, Nichol. *TJ 312.*
MELEMEYNS, Mons Nicholl. *AS 372.*

Arg bend engr Sa
Arg bend engr Sa
CULPEPER, Sir Alexander, Kent. *WB II 67, 6.*
GLASINGBURY, Sr Henry de. *L 147.*
GLASTINBERI. *HA 27, 150.*
GLASTINBURI. *HA 138.*
GLASTINBURI. *RB 405.*
GLASTINGBURS, Sire Henri de. *N 195.*
GLASTYNBURY, S Henry de. *GA 216.*
GRENALD. *CT 452.*
LORING, Nigel. *BD 153. (qtg 2&3 Arg bend
Sa; 2nd window, St Georges Ch, Stanford,
Lincs).*
RADCLEIFFE. *WB II 55, 7.*
RADCLIF, Sir John. *BW 14, 90.*
RADCLIFF, of the Tour. *BA 41b, 407.*
?RADCLIFFE. *Hill IV 3, 292; Bellasis II 161.
(windows with clear glass field, Long Marton,
Westmld).*
RADCLIFFE, Sir .... *CVL 362.*
RADCLIFFE, Lord Fitzwater, KG. *XK 79.*
RADCLIFFE, James. *CRK 1070.*
RADCLIFFE, Sir John. *PLN 240. (cresc Arg
for diffce).*
RADCLIFFE, Sir John. *WGA 273.*
RADCLIFFE, Robert, KG. *Leake.* 1542. *(qtly
with Fitzwalter & qtg 2 Burnell, 3 Lucy, 4
Molton of Egremont).*
RADCLIFFE, Robert, E of Sussex. *XK 21.
(qrs I 1&4).*
RADCLYF. *CC 233, 361.*
RADCLYFFE. *PT 1073.*
RADCLYFFE, Sir John, Lancs. *RH, Ancestor
iv 238.*
RATCLEVE. *SHY 31.*
RATCLIFFE. *LR 57.*
RATCLIFFE, Sir Alexander. *XK 238.*
RATCLIFFE, Ld Fitzwalter. *PLN 1840. (qtg 2

Fitzwalter Or fess betw 2 chevs Gu, 3 Burnell Gu lion Sa crowned Or, 4 Arg 3 bars Gu).
RATCLIFFE, Ld Fytzwater. *I2(1904)212. (qtg 2 Or fess betw 2 chevs Gu, 3 Arg lion Sa crowned Or border Az, 4 Arg 3 bars Arg).*
RATCLIFFE, Sir Robert, Ld Fitz Walter. *PR(12)57; PR(15)27. (qtg Fitzwalter, Burnell & Melton of Egremont).*
RATCLYF. *CB 74. (& Bynnyng).*
RATCLYFF. *LE 295.*
RATLEFFE, Mayster. *I2(1904)211. (cresc for diffce; qtg 2 Or fess betw 2 chevs Gu, 3 Arg 3 bars Gu).*

Az bend engr Arg &c
Az bend engr Arg
HALES. *CRK 1620.*
Az bend engr Or
BERMINGHAM, Sr Thomas. *L 230.*
BERMINGHAM, Water. *E 143. (or Wm B).*
BERMINGHAM, Sire William. *J 135.*
BERMINGHAM, Sire William. *N 132.*
BERMINGHAM, Sire William. *O 15.*
BERMINGHAM, William. *F 163.*
BERMYNGHAM. *L1 63, 4.*
BERMYNGHAM, Sir William de. *CB 291.*
BURMINGHAM, Willam de. *Q 86.*
BURMYNGHAM, Sir William. *PCL I 521.*

Gu bend engr Arg
Gu bend engr Arg
RALEE. *L1 554, 1.*
RALEE, Sire Symon de. *N 181.*

Gu bend engr Or
Gu bend engr Or
CRAYETH. *CV-BM 37.*
MARCHALL. *FB 30.*
MARCHALLE, Sire William. *BR V 80.*
MARESCHAL, Mons William. *TJ 272.*
MARESCHALL, William le. *SP A 113.*
MARESHALL. *DV 54a, 2135.*
MARESHALL. *LE 348.*
MARESHALL, John. *PCL I 515.*
MARESHALLE, Johannes le. *Q II 75.*
MARESTANS, Gwillim le. *CB 284.*
MARISCHALL. *L9 49b, 1.*
MARSHALL. *RB 336.*
MARSHALL. *L1 449, 6; L2 335, 12.*
MARSHALL. *RH, Ancestor ix 162.*
MARSHALL, Sr John. *RB 82.*
MARSHALL, Sir W. *ML I 91; ML II 82. (?bend lozy).*
MARSHALLE, Sr Willm de. *RB 38.*
RATCLYFFE. *WB I 15, 25.*

Or bend engr Az
Or bend engr Az
FOKERAM, Berks. *L1 250, 2; L2 204, 2.*
FOKERAM, Richard. *BA 793.*
FOKERAM, Sir Richard. *CB 275.*
FOKERAM, Sire Richard. *N 313.*
FOKERAM, Willimus de. *Q II 462.*
FUKERAM, Richard. *E 602.*
GROVE. *L1 282, 2; L2 222, 9.*
GROVE. *CC 230b, 280.*

Or bend engr Gu
Or bend engr Gu
?COTELE. *E 530.*
KULPEPER, Mons Waut, of Kent. *WJ B 1575.*
WROTTESLEY, Hugh de. *S 19.*
WROTTESLEY, Sir Hugh. *BB 62. (d1381).*
WRYOTTESLEY. *L1 678, 3.*
WRYOTTESLEY, Mons Hugh de, KG. *S 17.*
WRYTESLEY, Sir Hugh. *WGA 92.*

Or bend engr Sa
Or bend engr Sa
ACHARD, Sir Richard. *CB 274.*
ACHARD, Robert. *L10 6, 18.*
ACHARD, Robert. *BA 792.*
ACHARD, Sire Robert. *N 312.*
ARCHARD, Berks. *L2 15, 9.*
GLASTINGBURY, Monsire de. *CG 384.*
MAULAY, Thomas de. *Q II 425.*

Sa bend engr Arg
Sa bend engr Arg
BEREFORD, Mons Roberte. *SD 110.*
BRADDEN, Willimus de. *Q II 477.*
BRADDENE. *L10 79b, 2.*
BRADDENE, Sire Geffrey. *N 770.*
BRADDENE, Northants & Rutld. *L2 88, 11.*
BRADDENE, William. *G 108.*
BRADDENE, William. *TJ 1397.*
CUSANNS, William de. *CA 36.*
WELYNTON, Mons Emmori de. *WJ 1522.*

Sa bend engr Or
Sa bend engr Or
WETTEFELDE, Richard de. *F 373. (?lozy).*
WITEFELD, Robert de. *FW 328.*
WITEVILDE, Sire Witt de. *WNS 25b, 48. (...por de sa ou un bende engle de v poinz dor).*

Barry bend engr
Barry Arg and Az bend engr Gu
GRAY, Johan de. *K 62. ('barree de argent e de asur entallie a bende rouge engreellie').*
GREY. *XF 662.*
GREY. *FK I 143.*
GREY, J de. *SP A 78. ('Filz Reginaldi').*
GREY, S Jehan de. *GA 103.*
GREY, Johannes de. *Q II 206.*

GREY, John de. *K 382.*
GREY, John de. *FW 599.*
GREY, Renaud de. *CA 44. (baston).*

Barry wavy bend engr
Barry wavy bend engr
POURE, Nicholas. *Bow LIX 8.* Sigillum Nicholai Poure. 1343-4.

Checky bend engr
Checky bend engr
— *WB I 21b, 6. (marshalled by Chequl, all imp by Ld Vauz).*
Checky Or and Gu bend engr Sa
— *WK 168. (qtd III 1 by Sir Thos Cheyny).*

Erm bend engr Az &c
Erm bend engr Az
DENNER, Sir Henry. *Q II 584.*
Erm bend engr Gu
COOLPEPER, John. *CVK 707.*
COOLPEPER, John, Kent. *CY 152, 606.*
PLOKENET, Aleyn de. *D 128a & 128b.*
PLOKENET, Sire Aleyn. *N 53.*
PLOKENET, Sire Aleyn. *J 39.*
PLOKENETT. *G 76.*
PLOKENETT, Alain. *E I 138.*
PLOKENETT, Sir Aleyn. *CB 289.*
PLONKENET, Sir Alan. *WNS 25b, 31. ('Sire Alein Plokenet por deremine ou un bende engrele de gout').*
PLUCKENET, Alanus. *Q II 105.*
PLUGENET, Alan. *LMS 90.*
PLUKENET, le Sr de. *AS 103.*
PLUKENET, Alayn. *FW 165.*
PLUKENET, Aleyn. *HE 131.*
PLUKNETT. *SP A 125.*
PLUKNETT, Monsire. *CG 380.*
PLUKNETT, Mons Aleyn. *TJ 311.*
PLUMBNET, Sir Aleyn. *BR V 44.*
Erm bend sin engr Gu
PLOKENET, Alain. *A 82.*

Erm bend engr Sa
Erm bend engr Sa
KELSALLE. *BA 5.*
KENSALL, S Golf de. *WLN 358.*

Per pale bend engr
Per pale bend engr
— *Birch 12318. 1314-15. (arms in panel in sl of Jn de Orrebi).*
Per pale Arg and Gu bend engr Sa
WALDEGRAVE, S Ric. *PO 500.*
WALGRAVE, Richard. *CA 37. (baston).*

Qtly bend engr
Qtly bend engr
LORING, William. *PRO-sls.* 1381.
Qtly Arg and Gu bend engr Gu
LORRYNG, Mons Neel, KG. *S 18. ('...a bend engrailed gules').*
LORYNG, Monsire Roger. *AN 221. (baston).*
LORYNGES. *SK 273. (baston).*
Qtly Arg and Gu bend engr Sa
LORENGE, Sir Noel. *WGA 246.*
LORING, Neil. *S 20.*
LORINGE, S Neel. *BB 10, 144. (d1386).*
LORYNG, Sir Nele. *Leake.* (on scroll) Mons neall loryng p'm fund. *(1st Founder KG, d1385-6).*
LORYNGES. *L9 39b, 3.*
Qtly Gu and Arg bend engr Or
WALEYS, Mons Richard. *TJ 968. (baston).*
Qtly Sa and Arg bend engr Gu
— *PT 834.*

Qtly 1&4 patterned bend engr
Qtly Vair and Gu bend engr Or
CONSTABLE, Sr Robert. *M 78; N 1105. (baston).*
MONTGOMERY, Walter. *CA 79. (baston).*

Qtly 2&3 patterned bend engr
Qtly Untinc & fretty Untinc bend engr Untinc
DISPENSATOR, Anne le. *Bow XXXIII 14.* 1348-9. *(imp 4 lozs).*
Qtly Arg & Gu fretty Untinc bend engr Sa
DESPENSERE, Sr E. *AS 101. (baston; bro of le Sr de Despensere).*
Qtly Or & Gu fretty Or bend engr Sa
SPENSER, S Gilberd. *PO 549.*

Billety bend engr
Billety bend engr
ALINGTON. *Mill Steph.* 1490. *(qtg Argentine, all imp by Clonville; brass to Jn C & w Margery dau of Sir Wm A; West Hanningfield, Essex).*
Sa billety bend engr Arg
ALINGTON. *LH 566 & 596.*
ALINGTON, William. *PLN 1264. (qtg 2&3 Gu 3 covered cups Arg, imp Despenser & others).*
ALYNGTON. *LE 439.*

Semy of crosses bend engr
Sa crusily bend engr Arg
WERFEILD, Robert de. *A 278. (?bend lozy).*

Vair bend engr
Vair bend engr Untinc
FACY, Thomas. *PlymouthCL-sls T 6/33. (?bend indented).*
GONYS, John. *PRO-sls.* 1353-4. *(?bend indent).*

GRESELE, Robert de, of Ealinghol, **Staffs.**
Bow XXXIII 10. 1355-6.
GRESELEY, Sir Robert. *Dugd 17, 44.* 1360-1.
Vair bend engr Gu
    GOUNTS, Brian de. *E I 106.*
    MOTE, Mons William de la. *TJ 622.*

Bend engr & patterned or fimbriated
Az bend engr Erm
    — *SK 13.*
Gu bend engr Erm
    — *LE 415.*
Per pale Arg and Gu bend engr Erm
    — *FK II 299.*
Arg bend engr Az fimbriated Or
    BRESEY. *L10 23b', 18.*
Untinc bend engr Vair
    TONKE, John de la. *PRO-sls.* 1364-5.

Bend flory

Bend flory
    CARNABY, William of. *Harl 1448, 57b, 24,*
    HB-SND. 1387. *(imp 2 bars in chf 3 roun-*
    dels).
Bend sin flory
    CARNABY, William of. *Dodsworth 45, 78,*
    HB-SND. 1346-7. *(imp 2 bars).*
Bend flory c'flory
    BROMFLEET, Margaret. *Mill Steph.* 1407.
    (w of Sir Thos B; brass, Wymington, Beds).
    BROMFLEET, Sir Thomas. *Mill Steph.* 1430.
    (brass, Wymington, Beds).
    BROMFLET, Henry, Chevr. *Birch 7840.*
    1434. *(afterwards Baron B, of Vescy; qtg 2*
    Vescy, 3 Aton, 4 ?St John).
    BROMFLETE. *PRO-sls. (qtd by Hen, Ld*
    Clifford).
Or bend flory Az
    GODYNGTON. *L2 233, 6.*
Or bend flory c'flory Az
    GOLDYNGTON. *L1 270, 3.*

Sa bend flory Or
Sa bend flory c'flory Or
    — *D4 31b. (sub-imp by Tonge, of Ekylsall,*
    co Durham).
    — *D4 46. (qtd by Clifford, E of Cumb).*
    BROMEFLETE. *DV 65b, 2594. (heads of lis*
    only).
    BROMFLET. *PT 283.*
    BROMFLET. *WGB 102, 11.*
    BROMFLET. *L1 87, 2.*
    BROMFLET, Dns Henricus. *LE 265.*
    BROMFLETE. *L10 79, 15.*
    BROMFLETE. *LD 118.*
    BROMFLETE. *Leake. (qtd 3 by Hen Clifford,*
    KG, d1542-3).
    BROMFLETE, Sir Henry. *CRK 1028.*

BROMFLETT. *L10 80, 9. (qr 1 of 4).*
BROMFLETT. *WK 539. (qtd 2 by Ld*
Clyfford).
BRONFLETTE, Sir Harry. *BW 16, 107. (qrs*
1&4).
BROWNFLETE, Sir H. *WB I 37b, 18.*
VESSIE, Lorde. *KB 331. (qrs 1&4;*
'Bromflett' added in another hand).
WESSEY, Lord. *RH, Ancestor iv 231. (qtg*
Aton).

Barry bend flory
Barry of 10 Or and Sa bend flory on upper side
Vt
    SAXONIE, D de. *LE 250.*

Bend fracted or rompu

Az bend rompu Arg
    YORK. *L9 4, 9. (?per pale Az bend Arg).*
Az bend fracted & lower half enhanced Arg
    ZORKES. *FK II 917.*
Az bend rompu lower half dropped Arg
    YORKE. *CRK 1721.*
Erm bend fracted Az
    PLOKENET, Aleyn de. *LM 150.*
Per bend Az and Arg bend rompu Erm lower
half removed towards dex base
    — *ML I 454. ('Hec non sunt arma sed*
    quoddam fictum quia hec benda est contra
    gemetriam eo qoud est fracta & nullum
    firmans potest esse fractum quia est incon-
    veniens eo quod est quasi oppositum in
    obiecto & specialiter nullum firmans quod
    pertinet ad gemetriam ut benda vel barr vel
    copula nullum istorum potest esse fractum,
    quod nota').
Per bend Or and Az bend rompu Vt lower half
removed towards dex base
    — *ML I 455. ('Asur & or ii bendes con-*
    trevectyd i upon the feld an other in the fyrst.
    Yt appereth be the blesyng howgh the asur &
    gold ys born. A bend may not be brokeyn ne
    barr ne cheveron be cause they be chef that
    go thorowe the schocon').

Bend indented

Bend indented
    — *Durham-sls 1638.* 1337. *(used by Robt*
    Lucas).
    CLIFTON, Henry of. *Durham-sls 642.* 1258.
    1374-5.
    LYNDE, Robert atte. *PRO-sls E40 A4101.*
    1374-5. *(imp Erm ?fess dancetty; or Ric*
    Lynde).
    VANNE, Perottus. *PRO-sls E40 A7848.* SIGIL-
    LUM ... SI. 1338-9. *(executor of will of Jn V,*
    of London).

Arg bend indented Gu
    GREY, Sir John de. *E II 140.*
    WALRANT, John. *TJ 325.*
Arg bend indented Sa
    GLASTINGBYRY, John. *TJ 321. (as blazoned; over [endentee] is interlined, in original hand, 'vel lozengee vel engrelee'; painted bend of 8 lozs).*
    GLASTINGBYRY, John. *TJ 322.*
Az bend indented Or
    BERMGHAM, Wm de. *E II 143; E I 143.*
Gu bend indented Or
    MARECHAL, Sire Willame le. *N 84.*
    MARESCAL, Jon le. *A 238.*
    MARESCAUS, Guillems le. *K 3.*
    MARESCHAL, Sire Ancel le. *O 135.*
    MARESCHALL, Sire William le. *J 75.*
    MARESCHALL, Sr William. *L 71.*
    MARSCAL, John le. *FW 631.*
    MARTEL, Sire Johan. *HA 55.*
Or bend indented Az
    FOUKESHAM, Thomas. *TJ 320. ('...une bende endentee dazure', vel engrelee vel losengee son alias).*
Sa bend indented on upper edge Arg
    — *CB 213.*

Field patterned bend indented
Barry bend indented
    GRAY, John de. *PRO-sls.* late 13 cent.
Barry Arg and Az bend indented Gu
    HEMYNGTON, Robert de, of Ches. *CY 16, 63.*
Erm bend indented Untinc
    BOHUN, Joan de. *CombeAsp II 126.* SI: IOHANNE: DE: BOHOUN. *(1 of 3 shields).*
Erm bend indented Gu
    PLOKENETT, Adam. *E II 138.*
Per bend Arg and Az bend indented on lowerside Vt
    — *ML I 401. ('Asur & sylver a bend indentyd into the fyrst vert').*
Qtly bend indented
    BEAUMER, Adomar de. *PRO-sls.* 1341-2.
Vair bend indented Gu
    GOUNIS, Brian de. *E II 106.*
    GOUVIS, Mons Brian de. *TJ 327.*

Bend indented patterned
Vt bend indented Erm
    SUMNER. *LS 296.*

Bend lozengy

Bend of demi-lozenges
Arg bend of demi-lozs Gu
    — *ML I 431. (?9 demi-lozs; 'Sylver a bend demi-losenge goules. They wer geve & awardyd for mylpykkes').*

Arg bend of 8 demi-lozs Sa
    — *SK 930.*
Arg bend of 9 demi-lozs Sa
    — *FK II 803. (qtd 2&3 by Gu 6 roundels Or).*
Arg bend of 11 demi-lozs Sa
    — *LE 206.*

See below for bend of 3, 4 or more lozenges (number specified)

Bend lozengy
Bend lozy
    — *Birch 11302.* 1449-50. *(qrs 1&4 of coat imp by Roland Lenthall, Ld of Haverfordwest, Pembs, Kt).*
    — *Birch 11301.* 1416. *(qtd 2&3 by Rowland Leynthale, of Hampton Court, Kt, Master of the Robes to Hen 4, a Commander at Agincourt).*
    [ACHARD]. *Mill Steph.* 15 cent. *(qtg [Delamare]; inscription lost; brass, Aldermaston, Berks).*
    ALEYN, John, of Tacolneston, Norf. *Birch 6804.* 1375. *(imp 6 eagles displd 3, 2, 1, on canton indistinct charge).*
    BAINTON. *Mill Steph.* 1516. *(qtg [Delamare & Roche] on brass to Jn B, Bromham, Wilts).*
    BAINTON. *Mill Steph.* 1516. *(qtg [Delamare & Roche] & imp Digges on brass to Jn B & w Jane Digges, Bromham, Wilts).*
    BAYNTON, John. *Dingley xxxv.* 1517. *(qtg 2 Roche, 3 Delamere, all imp Digges; brass, Bromham Ch, Wilts).*
    CHENEY. *Birch 3294.* 1281-93. *(sl of Priory of St Faith, Horsham, Norf).*
    CULNHATH, Richard of. *Dodsworth 45, 96, HB-SND.*
    GLASTINGBURY, Henry de, Kt. *PRO-sls.* 1316-17.
    LENTHALE. *Baker-sls.* 1416-17. *(qtd by bend; grant with others of manors of Trafford, Stonydunham & Mole, Ches).*
    LINDON, Simon de, Kt. *PRO-sls.* 13 cent.
    MARECHALL. *Farrer I 276. (imp by Morley; Hingham Ch, Norf).*
    MARECHALL, of Hingham. *Farrer I 269. (Brandon Parva Ch, Norf).*
    MARECHALL, of Hingham. *Farrer I 297. (Wymondham Ch, Norf).*
    MENNEL, Alan. *Arch Ael NS iii 83, HB-SND.* 1357.
    ?RALEGH. *Arch Journ viii 319.* c1300. *(effigy of Sir Matthew Furneaux, Ld of Ashington, who married 1305-6 Maud, dau of Sir Warini de Ralegh, of Nettlecombe; incised slab, Ashington, Som, inscription lost).*
    TAVERNER. *Farrer I 222. (Wickhampton Ch, Norf).*

TAVERNER, John. *Farrer II 104. (d1548; Brisley Ch, Norf).*
WALERAND, Robert. *PRO-sls.* 1268-9.

Bend sin lozy
— *Cleeve.* 14 cent. *(Raleigh or Sydenham).*

Bend lozy of 3
ARDINGEL, Robert, Mechant of the Bardi. *PRO-sls E40 A6970.* +ARDINGELLI: D': SOTIE-TATE: BARDOR:. 1317-18.
MARUM, Nicholas. *Birch 11653.* S' : NICOLAI : LA.... 1336.

Bend lozy of 4
— *SHY 454. (qtd 2&3 by ...nyett, all imp Letice).*
FOKERAM, Robert. *Birch 9843.* S' ROB'TI FOKERAM. 1323.
MARSHAL, John. *Bk of Sls 313.* early 13 cent.

Bend lozy of 5
— *Mill Steph. (imp by Philip; brass to Dame Christine, d 25 May 1470, w of Sir Matthew P, Citizen & Goldsmith, Mayor of London; Herne, Kent).*
ARCHARD, Robert. *Bow 2.*
BENTON, Nicholas. *PRO-sls.* 1410-11.
BERMINGHAM, William, Ld of. *Dugd 17, 41.* 1329.
BERMYNGHAM, Isabella de. *Dugd 17, 77.* 1304. *(1 of 3 shields on sl).*
BRADDENE, Geoffrey. *Birch 7724.* S' GAL-FRIDI DE BRADDENE. 14 cent. *(s of Wm de B, of Thornborough, Bucks & Blakesly, Northants, Kt).*
FOKERAM, Richard, of Som, Kt. *Birch 9840.* S' RICARDI F[OK]ERAM. 1279.
GALES, Jakelyne. *Birch 10015.* S' JAKELYNE VX' IOH'IS GALESI. 1418. *(imp lion; w of Jn G; sl used by Robt Louthe, Citizen of London).*
HERFORD, Warinus de. *AnstisAsp I 228, 101.* S' WARINI DE HERFORDIE. 1282.
KNYGHT, of 'Northsher'. *CY 46, 182.*
MARESCHAL, Sir Anceline le, Kt. *NorfHo I 52 & 53.* 1337-8.
MARSHAL, William, of Hingham. *PRO-sls.* 1301.
MARSHALL, William. *Barons Letter. (baton on each side of shield).*
RALE, Warine de, of King's Walden, Herts. *Birch 12901.* S' WAR[INI] DE R.... 1331.
RAYGATE, William. *Birch 12935.* SIGILL' WILL'I DE RAYGATE. 1338. *(s of Robt de R, of Lincs, Kt).*
TOKY, Richard, of London. *PRO-sls E40 A2222.* ...TOKY. 1387-8.
WALERAND, Robert. *Bk of Sls 94.* 1267.
WALERAND, Robert. *Bk of Sls 411.* 1269.
WYTEFELD, Sir William de. *Heneage 301.*
+SIGILLUM ....ELD. 1276. *(acknowledgement*

of fealty for tenement in Batheuston, Som).

Bend lozy of 6
MARSHALL, Anselm le. *Bow XXXII 25.* Sigillum Anselmi le Marshall. 1310-11.

Arg bend lozengy Arg (sic)
Arg bend lozy of 4 Arg
LENTHALL. *LE 344. (sic; qr 4; in 1st qr 5 lozs).*
Arg bend lozy of 5 Arg
LENTHALL. *LE 344. (qr 1; 4 lozs in qr 4; sic).*

Arg bend lozengy Az
Arg bend lozy Az
— *Leake. (qtd 8 by Sir Will Fitzwilliam, KG, d1543).*
Arg bend lozy of 5 Az
— *PLN 1957. (qtd III 6 by Sir Wm Fitz Williams).*
— *CRK 1883.*
— *PLN 1958. (qtd 5 by lozy Arg and Gu, all imp by Gardner, of Lincs).*
REYGATE, Sr de. *CKO 235.*
REYGATE, Mons Ro. *WJ 1532.*
RIGATE, Mons John. *WJ 1586.*
RYGATE. *DV 57b, 2269.*
RYGATE. *PT 205.*
RYGATE. *L1 562, 1.*

Arg bend lozengy Gu &c
Arg bend lozy Gu
CHEYNY, Sir Thomas. *WK 168.*
Arg bend lozy of 4 Gu
STACHAM. *L1 590, 6.*
STATHAM. *LS 122. (2 lozs & 2 halves).*
STATHAM. *BA 1298.*
STATHAM. *ME 111; LY A 236.*
STATHHAN. *LE 134.*
Arg bend lozy of 5 Gu
BRADESTON. *L1 55, 2.*
MALEMEYNS. *L9 52b, 7.*
MALEMEYNS. *BA 1285.*
MAULEMAYNS. *L1 444, 1; L2 337, 2.*
WALERAND, Robert. *B 156.*
[WALROND]. *CRK 1267.*
Arg bend lozy of 6 Gu
WALROND, Robert. *CV-BM 249.*
Arg bend lozy of 5 Purp
MALEMAYNES, Sr. *CKO 234.*

Arg bend lozengy Sa
Arg bend lozy Sa
— *1H7 7d; D13 76. (qtd 5 by Fitzwilliam).*
— *XK 144. (qtd III 4 by Sir Wm Fitzwilliam).*
C...ing, Th. *CT 289. (field ?Or).*
GLASTONBURY, Sir Henry de. *CB 283.*
WHITTON. *Gerard 107.*

WHYTON, John de. *Gerard 15.* temp Edw 3.
Arg bend lozy of 5 Sa
— *BA 806. (qtd 4 by Forester).*
— *WB III 119, 5. (qtd 2 by Jn Sidnam, Som).*
— *WB I 16b, 1 & 2. (no 2 imp by [Courtenay]).*
— *WB I 16b, 1.*
— *XK 86. (qtd IV 4 by Wm Fitz William, KG, 1526).*
— *LE 301.*
DYCONS. *WJ 1509.*
GLASTIGB, Sr Henry. *R 40.*
GLASTINGBURY. *LE 323.*
GLASTINGBURY, of Dorset & Som. *L1 290, 3; L2 226, 11.*
GLASTINGBURY, Sgr. *RB 173.*
GLASTONBURY, Sir Hy. *WNS 26b, 98.*
Arg bend lozy of 6 Sa
GLASTONBURY. *BA 1286. (4 & 2 half lozs).*
GRENEFELD, M de. *WNR 142.*
REIGATE, Sir Robert. *LR 37.*
Arg bend lozy of 8 Sa
GLASTINGBYRY, John. *TJ 321. (blazoned bend indented or engr).*

Az bend lozengy Arg
Az bend lozy of 5 Arg
— *CRK 1836. (qtg 2&3 Arg 2head eagle Gu).*

Az bend lozengy Or
Az bend lozy Or
BIRMYNGHAM, Willame de. *LM 130. (field unclear).*
Az bend lozy of 5 Or
— *CRK 1126. (qtd 2&3 by Birmingham, all in border Or).*
BERMINGHAM, Sir William. *Lawrance 5. 1324. (St Martin, Birmingham, Warws).*
BIRMINGHAM. *BA 1269.*
BIRNIGHAM. *L10 31b, 4.*
Az bend lozy of 6 Or
BERMINGHAM, William de. *WLN 561.*

Gu bend lozengy Untinc &c
Gu bend lozy of 6 Untinc
MARESHALLE, Johannes le. *Q II 75. (pencilled over original Gu bend engr Or).*
Gu bend lozy Arg
DAWBANEY, Sir Gyles. *RH, Ancestor v 181. (?engr).*
RALEIGH, Sir Simon. *Lawrance 37. 1306. (effigy, Nettlecombe, Som).*
RALEY, of Nettlecombe. *Gerard 25.*
Gu bend lozy of 3 Arg
— *LY A 93.*

Gu bend lozy of 5 Arg
— *WK 331. (qtd 3 by Sir Jn Trevelian).*
— *WLN 895.*
— *L9 49a 10.*
FRESFORD, Mons. *WJ 1438.*
MARSCHAL. *L1 448, 3; L2 335, 10.*
[MARSHALL]. *TJ 1542. ('Les armes del office du Mareschal Dirlande').*
MARSHALL, Sir Thomas, of Norf. *WB III 74b, 9.*
RALE, Devon. *L1 564, 6.*
RALEY. *LE 182. (or Marchall).*
RALEY. *BA 1148.*
RAYLIGHE. *BA 1283.*

Gu bend lozengy Or
Gu bend lozy Or
MARESCHALL, le Sr de. *AS 84. (?engr).*
MARESHAL, Jon le. *LM 149.*
MARSHALL, Wm le. *K 48. ('engreellie').*
Gu bend lozy of 4 Or
MARTEL, Sire Johan. *HA 16, 41.*
Gu bend lozy of 5 Or
— *WJ 1573.*
— *WK 500. (qtd 4 by Hen Parker, Ld Morley).*
CHRACHETH. *WLN 386.*
MARCHALL, ?Ann'. *NS 17.*
MARESCHAL. *L9 49a, 8.*
MARESHALL, Monsire. *CG 379. (?engr).*
MARISHALL. *BA 1282. (tinct of bend unclear).*
MARSHALL. *FK II 245.*
MARSHALL, Sr de. *CKO 232.*
MARSHALL, John le. *E I 635; E II 637.*
MERSHALL. *PO 99.*
Gu bend lozy of 7 Or
MARECHALE, Jan le. *Q 75.*

Or bend lozengy Az
Or bend lozy Az
FOKERAM. *CC 223, 35.*
FOKERAM, Wills de. *Q 480.*
Or bend lozy of 5 Az
FOKERAM. *LE 357.*
FOKERAM. *L1 260, 1; L2 204, 3.*
FOKERAM. *BA 1288.*
FOKERAN, M de. *WNR 97.*
FOKERANDE, Mons. *AS 458.*
FUKERAM, Richard. *E I 602; E II 604.*
Or bend lozy of 7 Az
FAUKERHAM. *CT 189.*
Or bend lozy of 8 Az
FOUKERHAM, Thomas. *TJ 319.*

Or bend lozengy Gu
Or bend lozy of 4 Gu
SORNELIER. *BA 1219.*

Or bend lozy of 5 Gu
— *FK II 819.*
[PINCKNEY]. *E I 530; E II 532.*
SORNELIER. *BA 1209. (4 1/2 lozs).*

Or bend lozengy Sa
Or bend lozy Sa
[ACHARD]. *PLN 799. (qtd 2&3 by de la Mare, of Aldermaston).*
C...ing, Th. *CT 289. (?field Arg).*
?GLASTENBURY. *ML I 562.*
GLASTINGBURY, Monsr de. *AS 331.*
TALBOT, of Bossington. *Gerard 14.*
Or bend lozy of 5 Sa
— *Q 437.*
ACHARD. *Berks Arch Journ 42, 1.* 14 cent. *(Lower Heyford, Oxfords).*
ACHARD, Mons Richard. *WJ 1545.*
ACHART, Robt. *Q 241.*
ARCHARDE. *PT 1042.*
ARCHERD. *L10 6b, 8.*
ARCHERD. *BA 1274.*
DACHERD. *SK 442.*
DACHERD. *L10 53b, 4.*
GLASTINGBYRY, Sr de. *CKO 237.*
Or bend lozy of 6 Sa
ACHARD, Roberd. *LM 350.*

Sa bend lozengy Arg
Sa bend lozy Arg
— *I2(1904)74. (qtd II 3 by Sir Thos Cornwall, Kt).*
BAYNTON. *L1 115, 3. (qtg 2 Gu 2 lions passt Or, 3 Az 3 ?fish naiant in pale Arg).*
BAYNTON. *CRK 1481.*
BAYNTON, Sir Edward, Kt. *I2(1904)224. (qtg 2 Gu 2 lions passt Arg, 3 Az 3 roach naiant in pale Arg).*
BEINTON. *BA 1281. (qrs 1&4 of Lenthall).*
BEYNTON. *Suff HN 42. (qtg 2&3 [Sulyard] Az 3 fishes naiant in pale Arg).*
BRADDEN, Wills de. *Q 498.*
CUSANOR. *L1 156, 5; L2 112, 11.*
LENTHALE. *DV 54a, 2121.*
MALEMEYNS. *CT 133.*
PLUNCKNETT, Baron of Donsary, Irld. *Gerard 78.*
Sa bend lozy of 5 Arg
— *WJ 1529. (name illegible).*
— *WB I 39b, 7. (qtd 2&3 by Sir A Lentall).*
— *L9 41a 12. (qtd 2&3 by Lenthall).*
— *WB II 60, 4. (qtg 2&3 Sa on bend Arg cotised Or 3 mullets Or).*
— *L9 44a 9. (qtd 2&3 by Rowland Lenthall).*
— *BA 18b. (qtd 2 by Rowland Lentall).*
BAYNTON. *WB I 23b, 6.*
BAYNTON, Sir John. *CRK 727.*
BENTON. *L10 28, 2.*

BENTON. *SK 261.*
BENTON. *L1 104, 2.*
BERFORD, Sr Robert. *R 41.*
BEYNTON. *L1 33, 5; L2 40, 3.*
BEYNTON. *BA 1268.*
BRYITTON, Sir John, Wilts. *WB III 100, 8.*
HERTFORD. *LH 873. (or Baynton).*
HERTFORD, Tho. *NS 16.*
LENTHAL, Sir Rowland. *PLN 204. (qtg 2&3 Arg on bend Sa cotised Or 3 mullets Or).*
LENTHALE. *L9 37b, 12.*
LENTHALL. *L1 410, 3; L2 311, 10.*
LENTHALL. *RB 324. (qrs 1&4).*
LENTHALL. *SK 351.*
LENTHALL, Sir Roland. *CB 231.*
LENTHALL, Sir Roland. *CRK 1520.*
LENTHALLE. *CT 433. (qrs 1&4).*
Sa bend lozy of 6 Arg
— *DV 42a, 1649. (qtd 2&3 by Lentale).*
BRADDENE, Wills de. *LM 321.*
Sa bend lozy of 9 Arg
MALEMAYNES, Thomas. *TJ 1340. ('Sable a une bende mascle de argent de noef ').*
Sa bend lozy of 10 Arg
BEYNTON, Sir John. *BA 834.*

Sa bend lozengy Or
Sa bend lozy Or
HERFORD. *L1 320, 1; L2 253, 12.*
HERFORD, Monsire Thomas. *AN 189.*
WYTFELD, Sire William de. *O 62. (?engr).*
Sa bend lozy of 4 Or
HERFORDE. *DV 57a, 2246.*
Sa bend lozy of 5 Or & Arg
HEREFORD. *LH 1132.*
Sa bend lozy of 5 Or
— *(Mons...). WJ 1553.*
EREFORD. *L2 179, 9.*
HEREFORD, Thomas. *BA 1227.*
HEREFORD, Sir Thomas, Cornw. *LH 666.*
HERTFORD. *PO 110.*
PLONKETT, Irld. *L2 408, 5. (qtg 2&3 Gu tower ported Or).*
ST OLMERS, Sir Edward. *BA 1299. (4 1/2 lozs).*
ST OMER. *CRK 1875. (rectius Whitfield).*
WHITFIELD, Richard de. *WLN 385.*
Sa bend lozy of 6 Or
HEREFORD. *PT 86.*

Vt bend lozengy Or
Vt bend lozy of 5 Or
KNIGHT. *LD 94.*
[KNIGHT]. *BA 1210.*

Field patterned bend lozengy
Barry bend lozy
GREY, Jn de, of Beds. *Birch 10262.* s
IOHAN[NIS] DE GREY. 1293.

Barry Arg and Az bend lozy of 6 Gu
  HEMINGTON. *LH 1088.*
  HEMYNGTON. *BA 1307.*
Barry Arg and Az bend lozy of 7 Gu
  GREY. *CT 214.*
  HEMINGTON, Robert de. *WLN 844.*
  HEMINGTON, William le. *CVL 392.*
  HEMYNGTON, Robert. *PCL II 82.*
Barry Arg and Az bend lozy of 8 Gu
  HEMYNGTON, William. *CVC 482.*
Barry Arg and Gu bend lozy of 6 Az
  ROS, Mons John de, de Tyd. *WJ 614.*
Barry Arg and Gu bend lozy of 8 Az
  ROOS, Sir John, of Tyd. *LR 10.*

Erm bend lozengy
Erm bend lozy Untinc
  BOHUN, Johanna de, Domina de Kelpek.
  Vinc 88, 54. +SIGILL. 1345-6. *(sl).*
  PLOKENET, Alan. *PRO-sls E40 A3186 &
  3187.* 1308-9.
Erm bend lozy Gu
  PLUNEKNETT, of Haselbury. *Gerard 79.*
Erm bend lozy of 5 Gu
  — *PLN 1749. (qtd 2&3 by Mynors).*
  PLOKENET, Sr Aleyn. *CKO 233.*
  PLONKET. *WJ 1461-2.*
  PLUCKNET. *FK II 660.*
  PLUKENET. *Dingley clxvii. (mont of Joan,
  d1327, w of Humphrey Bohun, & dau of Alan
  P, Heref Cathedral).*
  PLUKENET. *BA 1291.*
Erm bend lozy of 6 Gu
  — *WNR 102.*
  PLOKNETT. *CT 62.*
  PLUKENET. *L1 504, 6.*
  PLUKENET, Aleyn de. *Q 105.*
  PLUKNENET. *L9 98a, 10.*
Erm bend lozy of 7 Gu
  PLUKNETT, Sr Aleyn. *ME 108; LY A 235.*
Erm bend lozy of 5 Sa
  WITWILL, William. *BA 1228.*
  WYTNYL, Mons W. *WJ 1510.*

Qtly bend lozengy
Qtly bend lozy
  CHENE, John. *Birch 8521.* S.IOHIS...CHENE.
  1376. *(sl used by Wm C, of Boxford, Suff,
  Kt).*
  [CHEYNE]. *Mill Steph.* c1480. *(dex pale of
  shield (now lost), Engaine in centre &
  Pabenham in sin; brass, inscription
  mutilated, to Sir Jn Sage & 1st w Eliz C,
  Broxbourne, Herts).*
Qtly Arg and Sa bend lozy Untinc
  CHEYNE, of Cambs. *CB 347.*
Qtly Arg and Sa bend lozy Gu
  CHEYNE. *CC 230, 268. (mullet Untinc in sin
  chf).*

CHEYNEY. *LS 281. (imp by Say).*
CHEYNEY, Elizabeth. *LH 612. (dau of Sir Jn
C; imp by Haselton).*
Qtly Arg and Sa bend lozy of 3 Gu
  CHEYNE, Cambs. *L1 168, 2. (not
  throughout; as painted).*
Qtly Arg and Sa bend lozy of 5 Gu
  CHEYNE. *L1 168, 2; L2 110, 5.*
Qtly Arg and Sa bend lozy of 6 Gu
  — *WB I 21b, 6. (qrs 1&4 of coat imp by Ld
  Vauz).*
  CHENY, of Cambs. *DV 70a, 2769.*
  CHEYNE, Essex. *MY 133.*
  CHEYNE, Lawrence. *CRK 1837.*
  CHEYNEY, of Cambs. *BA 1270.*
  CHEYNEY, of Cambs. *L10 36, 6.*
Qtly Arg and Sa bend lozy of 7 Gu
  CHENEY, of Cambs. *PT 905.*
Qtly Arg and Sa bend lozy of 6 Sa
  — *CRK 42.*

Semy bend lozengy
Sa crusily Or bend lozy of 7 Arg
  WHITFIELD. *BA 1309.*
Sa crusily & bend lozy Or
  WYTEFEELD, Robarte de. *FW 328c. ('sable
  crusilly gold with a bend fusilly gold').*
Sa crusily & bend lozy of 7 Or
  WHITFIELD, Robert de. *E I 525; E II 527.*

Vair bend lozengy
Vair bend lozy of 5 Untinc
  BOWERE, Elisabeth. *CombeAsp II 130.* S.
  ELISABETH: BOWERE. 1337.
Vair bend lozy Gu
  GOVIZ, Brian de. *Gerard 227.*
  MOTE, Sr William de la. *CKO 622.*
Vair bend lozy of 6 Gu
  GOUIL, Brian de. *BA 1214.*
  GOVIS. *XF 787.*

Bend lozengy patterned
Gu bend lozy Erm
  HELE. *Gerard 48. (alias Hawey or Hals-
  way).*
Gu bend lozy of 5 Erm
  — *WB I 16b, 3. (qtd 3 by Wadham, of West
  Devon).*
  — *BA 1045 & 1057. (one spot on each loz;
  qtd 3 by Sir Nicholas Wadham).*
Per bend Sa and Arg bend lozy of 8 counterch
  — *SK 353.*

Bend masculy
Gu bend masculy of 5 Arg
  FREFORD. *L1 236, 2; L2 195, 9.*
  FREFORD. *FK II 839.*
  FREFORD. *BA 1293.*

FREFORD, Mons le. *AS 463.*

Bend raguly

Bend raguly
FORTON, John de. *PRO-sls.* 16 March 1422.
PENRICH, John de, Kt, Keeper of Harbottle
Castle. *PRO-sls.* 1340-1.
PREYERS, Thomas, of Dersynton, ?Gloucs. Zat
I Ne Were (Motto). *Birch 12845.* 1380. *(mar-*
ginal note by HS Kingsford: 'This is sl below
shield of Birch 12831 when latter has been
screwed out and off').
Bend sin raguly
BURY, Edward, of Farleigh, Wilts. 1544.
Birch 7971.
Arg bend raguly one branch on each side in chf
Gu
STYWARD. *ML I 402.*
Arg bend raguly Sa
SAUNTON. *ML I 461.*
SAUNTON. *L1 609, 2.*
Az bend raguly Gu
— *CC 235, 414.* *(qtd 2&3 by Cokayn).*
Az bend raguly Or
— *LE 383.* *(qtd 2&3 by Cokayn).*
Gu bend raguly Sa
— *WLN 857.* *(?partly raguly).*
Fretty bend raguly
— *Arch xxix 406.* *(sl belonging to Earl*
Ferrers).
Lozy with dot in each loz bend raguly
— *Arch Journ iv 251.* 14 cent. *(lozs*
diapered; on a secret revealed when centre
of matrix of sl of Thos de Prayers is
unscrewed; inscribed 'Zat Ine Were').

Bend voided: see bend fimbriated

Bend wavy or nebuly

Bend nebuly
[GOLDINGHAM]. *Mill Steph.* 1518. *(imp Lis-*
ter on brass to [Jn G] & 2nd w Thomasin
Lister, Belstead, Suff).
[GOLDINGHAM]. *Mill Steph.* 1518. *(imp*
[Lowthe] on brass to [Jn G] & 1st w [Joan
Lowthe], Belstead, Suff).
[GOLDINGHAM]. *Mill Steph.* 1518. *(brass to*
[Jn G], Belstead, Suff).
Bend wavy
REDE, Robert, Kt. *PRO-sls.* 1503. *(unclear*
blazon).
SWALE, W. *PE II 22.* *('a Newton juxta*
Ripeley in Chartis Will').
WALLOP. *Whitmore.* *(qtg [Valoynes]; on*
mont of Thos Hampton, d1483; Stoke Char-
ity, Hants).

Untinc bend wavy Sa
WALLUP, Syr John. *WB I 24b, 13.*
Arg bend wavy Gu
— *LE 305.*
GOLDINGHAM. *FK II 754.*
GOLDINGHAM. *Suff HN 41.* *('Mr Rowsse's*
Rolle').
[GOLDINGHAM, Sir Alex]. *PLN 309.*
GOLDYNGEHAN, Suff. *MY 30.*
GOLDYNGHAM, Suff. *L1 280, 6; L2 228, 10.*
GOLDYNGHAM, Sir Water of, of Essex. *WB*
III 78, 7.

Arg bend wavy Sa

Arg bend wavy Sa
— *I2(1904)234.* *(qtd 7 by Sir Thos Boleyn,*
Kt).
BOURTON, of Kynsley, Yorks. *D4 43b.*
BURTON. *XPat 310, Arch 69, 93.* *(name*
almost obliterated).
BURTON. *L10 86b, 9.*
BURTON, John de. *S 596.*
BURTTON. *DV 62a, 2443.*
DEBENHAM. *CRK 1485.*
WALLOP, Sir John. *Leake.* *(KG, d1551-2;*
qtg 2&3 paly wavy Arg and Sa on chf Or salt
Gu).
WALLOPP, Sir John. *WB I 42, 4 & 8.*

Gu &c bend wavy

Gu bend wavy Arg
COLHET, Mons Richard. *CA 231.*
Gu bend nebuly Arg
CULUET, S' Ric'. *PO 560.*
Gu bend wavy Or
BERTHORPE. *BG 450.*
Or bend wavy Sa
— *CRK 1234.* *(qtd 2&3 by Riddell).*
WALOPPE. *PT 800.* *(name in later hand).*
Arg crusily & bend wavy Gu
BOKKYNG, John de. *TJ 236.*
Sa bend wavy bendy wavy Arg and Az
STANDEN. *CRK 1577.*
Sa bend wavy bendy wavy of 8 Arg and Az
STANDEN. *RB 525.*
Gu bend wavy Erm
NOTBEAME. *SK 424.*
Per pale Sa and Arg bend wavy counterch
— *FK II 869.*

BEND & LABEL

Bend & label

— *Lawrance 24. (on tomb of Sir Edm Mauley, k at Bannockburn, 1314; Bainton, Yorks).*

— *PRO-sls.* S' ELIANOR DE GISTING.... temp Edw 3. *(4 identical shields; used by Eleanor de Columbers).*

CARMINOW, Alice de. *AnstisAsp I 213, 60.* SIGILL ALICIE: DE: CARMINO. 1376-7.

CONGALTON, Richard, of that Ilk. *Stevenson.* 1463.

S...cre, John de. *Birch 13194.* SIGILLVM IOHANNIS DE S...CRE. 1332.

DUNRE, Richard de. *Birch 9371.* 1345. *(Ld of Dunre, Dinedor, Herefs).*

DUNRE, Richard, Ld of. *Dugd 17, 53.* 1344.

LONDON, John de. *Birch 11367.* SIGILLVM IOHANNES. 1340. *(Rector of Elmestede Ch, Kent).*

MOREBY, William de. *Birch 11914.* S' WILL'I DE MOREB.... 1348. *(s of Robt de M, of Warws, Kt).*

SANCTO PETRO, John de. *PRO-sls.* 1332-3. *(any charge on bend defaced).*

SCROOPE, Richard. *Birch 1640. (Bp of Lichfield & Coventry 1386-98).*

SCROP, Guffrey de. *PRO-sls.* 1328-9.

SCROP, Henry le, Kt. *Birch 13353.* SIGILLVM HENRICI LE SCROP. 1355. *(hand isst from dex of shield holding lance with triangular flag ch with 2 bars, on sin 2 3foils slipped; s&h of Geoffrey le S, Kt, of London).*

SCROP, Stephen, 2nd Baron, of Masham. BIRCH 13307. S' STEPH'I LESCROP DNI DE MASHAM. 1391.

SCROP, William le, Ld of Man & the Isles. *Birch 13379.* S...DE..CROP. 1393. *(beheaded 1399).*

SCROPE, Sir Geoffrey. *S&G II 280. (sl on documents at Priory of Newburgh).*

SCROPE, Sir Geoffrey le. *Yorks Deeds VII 191.* 1334.

SCROPE, Henry le, Kt. *PRO-sls.* 1363-5 & 72-3. *('Governor of Our Seignours').*

SCROPE, Sir Henry le. *Yorks Deeds VII 191.* 1362.

SCROPE, Sir Henry le. *Durham-sls 2199.* 1341. *(1st Ld S, of Masham).*

SCROPE, Henry le. *Bowes 3, HB-SND.* 1388. *(d1391).*

SCROPE, Henry le. *Yorks Arch Journ xii 258, HB-SND.* 1384. *(d1391).*

SCROPE, Joan. *Yorks Deeds VI 38.* 1376. *(imp Fitzhugh).*

SCROPE, John le. *Yorks Deeds VII 191.* 1384.

SCROPE, Richard le. *PRO-sls.* 1358-9 & 1379-80.

SCROPE, Stephen le. *Birch 13367 & 13371.*

1395.

SCROPE, Thomas, 6th Baron, of Masham. *Birch 13377.* SIGILLU...OME DNI LESCROOP DE MASHAM. 1462.

SCROPE, William le, Kt. *PRO-sls.* 1386.

[ST LOE]. *Vinc 88, 45.* +++SIGILLVM ELAE DE SANCTO MAURO DOMINAE DE CASTLE CARY. 1409. *(qtg [Pavely] & imp by St Maur, used by Ela, wid of Ric de St Maur, Kt, of Castle Cary, Soms & dau of Sir Jn St Loe; seisin of land in Swanskote to her s Nicholas).*

?ST PIERRE. *Ussher 28 pl X. (imp by Jn Horton, of Catton, d1521; glass, Croxhall Ch).*

WORVELY, Thomas, gent. *Bow XLVII 20.* 1461-2. *(grant of land in Nourbourne iuxta Branicham).*

Bend sin & label

WALEWAYNE, Thomas, of Herefs. *PRO-sls.* 1402-3.

Bend & label of 5

— *Bk of Sls 226.* 1332. *(on sl used by Isabel de Buleye, dau of Thos de B).*

BATHE, Eleanor de. *AnstisAsp I 211, 55.* 1349-50.

BISCET, William. *Birch 7483.* +S' WILLELMI BISCET. 1292.

BISCET, William. *PRO-sls.* 1290.

BISSET, Wm. *Stevenson.* 1296.

CALIN, Phelipe de, ?clerk. *Birch 8017.* +S' PHELIPE DE CALINCLE. 1372. *(sl used by Robt Fynch, s of Wm F, of Snape, Suff).*

EMNEBURGH, Richard de, Soms, Kt. *WellsM-sls 99, 32.* ....EB..... 1260.

FOLIOT, Jordan. *PRO-sls.* late 13 cent. *(s of Ld Ric F).*

FOLIOT, Jordan. *Dugd 17, 19. (s of Ld Ric F).*

FOLIOT, Jordan. *Birch 9851.* SIG[ILLVM]: IORDANI: FOLIOT. 13 cent.

FOLIOT, Jordan. *PRO-sls AS 235.* SIGILL IORDANI FOLIOT. late 13 cent. *(s of Dan Richard).*

KNYVETON, William. *Birch 11135.* SI...L'.-.RIC'. 1324. *(s of Hen de K, Lincs).*

MACNAUGHTON, Gilchrist. *Stevenson.* c1247. *(s of Malcolm M).*

RUNGETON, Nigel of. *Durham-sls 2137. (fl 1230).*

VERNON, Esmond. *Dodsworth 45, 103b, HB-SND.* 1361.

Arg bend Az label Gu

Arg bend Az label Gu

— *WJ 1552.*

— *WB V 95. (?bend Sa; qtd 4 by Sir Thos Cokesey, KB, 1485).*

HOVEL, Hugh. *LH 258.*

HOVILE, Hugo de. *F 202.*

KENDALE, Mons Ed. *WJ B 1472.*
MORE, S Estevene de la. *GA 49.*
Arg bend Az label of 5 Gu
    HOVEL, Hugh de. *LH 843.*
    HOVILE, Hugh. *E I 522; E II 524.*

Arg bend Sa label Gu
Arg bend Sa label Gu
    — *BW 12, 73. (qtd 2&3 by Ld Botrews).*
    — *L9 22b, 4. (qtd 4 by Kokesey).*
    — *L10 36, 17. (qtd 4 by Cookesey).*
    — *BA 16. (qtd 2&3 by Ld Botreux).*
    — *WK 57. (qtd 4 by Sir Thos Cookesey, alias Grevell).*
    — *WK 31. (qtd 4 by Sir Thos Cokesey).*
    — *PLN 1988. (qtd 4 by Sir Thos Cokesey).*
    — *WB V 95. (?bend Az; qtd 4 by Sir Thos Cokesey, KB, 1485).*
    — *BA 843. (qtd 4 by Sir Thos Cokesey).*
    MAULEY, Sr Peres de. *M 38.*
    SAINT PERE, Sr Brian de. *L 110.*
    SEIN PERE, Uriel de. *FW 633.*
    SEIN PERE, Sire Urien de. *N 131.*
    SEINPER, Hurien de. *F 94.*
    SEINT LOWE. *WJ 1484.*
    SEINT PERE. *WJ 1483.*
    SEMPER, Sir Brian de. *CB 290.*
    SEYN PERE, S' Jh'n. *PO 454.*
    SEYTLOWE. *WJ 1482.*
    ST LOW. *Gerard 54.*
    ST PIERE. *CRK 1279. (qrs 1&4).*
    STOPHAM, Johan de. *G 179.*
Arg bend Sa label of 4 Gu
    SEYNPERE. *L1 575, 4.*
Arg bend Sa label of 5 Gu
    SAUNPERE, Sir John. *CV-BM 455.*
    SAYNT PERE, Sr John, of Ches. *CY 9, 35.*
    SEIN PIERE, Uriel de. *LM 74.*
    SEINTE PERE, Urien de. *Q 78.*
    SEYNPERE, Sir John. *WLN 319.*
    SEYNT PERE, Brieu de. *PCL I 517.*
    ST PERE, Hurian de. *E II 92.*
    ST PIERE. *DV 49b, 1941. (baston).*
    ST PIERE, Sir John, of Ches. *CRK 1076.*

Arg bend Sa label Or
Arg bend Sa label Or
    — *XE 113. (qtd 4 by Cooksey).*
    POPHAM, Sir John de. *PT 1019.*
    STOPHAM, Sire Johan de. *N 729.*

Arg bend Vt label Gu
Arg bend Vt label Gu
    — *PT 189.*
    CENDALE, Sr Robert de. *L 67.*
    KENDAL. *L1 378, 3; L2 290, 9.*
    KENDAL, Edward de. *CA 39.*
    KENDALE, Monsr de. *AS 214.*
    KENDALE, Sr de. *CKO 200.*

KENDALE, Mons Ed. *WJ 1472. (?bend Az).*
KENDALE, Mons Edmond de. *SD 31.*
KENDALE, Richard de. *TJ 245.*
KENDALE, Mons' Robert de. *TJ 323.*
KENDALE, Sir Robert. *BR V 265.*
KENDALE, Sire Robert de. *N 404.*
KENDALL, Monsire. *CG 345.*
[KENDALL]. *WB I 30b, 12.*
KENDALLE, Sir Robert de. *CB 285.*
Arg bend Vt label of 5 Gu
    KENDAL, Sir Robert. *WNS 25b, 55. ('Sire Rob de Kendale per dor ou une bende de vert label de gou').*
    KENDALL. *SK 259.*
    KENDALL, of Beds. *CB 229.*

Az bend Or label Arg
Az bend Or label Arg
    — *WK 458. (escutch of the Ld Scropp).*
    — *D4 34. (qtd by Dransfeld, of Yorks).*
    — *BA 719. (qtd 2 by Strangways).*
    — *1H7 7d; D13 76. (qtd 2 by Fitzwilliams).*
    — *XK 96. (escutch of Ld Scrope, Kt, 1509).*
    LESCROP, Mons' Geffray. *TJ 248.*
    LESCROP, Monsr Geffray. *AS 157.*
    SCROP, Sr Geffrey le. *CKO 203.*
    SCROP, Ld, Upsalle. *BW 9, 52.*
    SCROPE. *S&G II 279-80. (on morse of cope 'beyond memory' at Kirk Oswald).*
    SCROPE, Ld. *BR VI 28. (of Upsale).*
    SCROPE, Sir Geoffrey, Abbot of Coverham. *S&G II 277. (effigy on tomb, Coverham).*
    SCROPE, Sir Geoffrey, Abbot of Roche. *S&G II 276. (in window of Abbey of Roche since 'beyond the time of memory').*
    SCROPE, Sir Henry. *S&G II 292-3. (cousin of Sir Ric Scrope).*
    SCROPE, Henry, Ld, of Masham. *S 84.*
    SCROPE, John. *BG 300.*
    SCROPE, K of Man. *FK I 72. (qrs 2&3).*
    SCROPE, of Masham. *LD 6.*
    SCROPE, Richard, Archbp of York. *RH, Ancestor iii 207.*
    SCROPE, Sir Stephen. *S&G II 324. (in Cyprus before K of Cyprus' intended expedition to Alexandria; evidence of Nicholas Sabraham).*
    SCROPE, Stephen. *BG 296.*
    SCROPE, of Upsala. *CRK 226.*
    SCROPE, Ld, of Upsale. *XK 255.*
    SCROPE, Ld, of Upsale. *RH, Ancestor iv 230.*
    SCROPE, Ld, of Upsall. *KB 336.*
    SCROPE, of Upsall. *Nichols Leics II 178. (Edmondthorpe Ch).*
    SCROPE, Sir Wm. *S&G II 291. (elder bro of Sir Ric S).*
    SCROPPE, Ld, of Upsall. *BA 589.*
    SCROUP, Sire Henri. *PO 229.*
    SCROUPE. *SK 853.*

SKROP, Mons Henr le. *S 82.*

Az bend Or label of 5 Arg
SCROPE, Sir Geoffrey. *WNS 25b, 54.* ('Sire *Geffrei Scrop per dazur ou une bende dor label dar'*).

Az bend Or label Gu &c
Az bend Or label Gu
— *I2(1904)180.* (*qtd 15 by Sir Rychard Grenevile, Kt; added by Jos Holland c1630*).
— *I2(1904)67.* (*qtd 4 by Syr Jn Carew, Kt*).
— *I2(1904)183.* (*qtd 4 by 'Mayster Arron-dyll'*).
— *BA 1321.* (*qtd 5 by Wm Carew*).
— *S 144.* (*qtd 2&3 by Wm le Scrope*).
— *I2(1904)275.* (*qtd 5 by Sir Wm Carew, Kt, of Devon*).
— *WK 187.* (*qtd 2&3 by Sir Jn Arundell*).
CARMINOU, Monsire de. *CG 361.*
CARMINOW. *CRK 1472.*
CARMINOW, of Cornw. *L1 177, 4; L2 126, 6.*
CARMYNAW. *L10 38b, 5.*
CARMYNOU, Mons Thomas. *TJ 261.*
CARMYNOUN, Sr de. *CKO 215.*
CARMYNOW. *BA 935.*
CARMYNOW. *WJ 1602.* (*?bend Arg*).
CARMYON. *XFB 129.* (*qtd 4 on pennon*).
GERMYNOUN, Monsr de. *AS 195.*
SCROPE, William. *BG 294.*
Az bend & label Or
DESTRON, Monsire Jefferey. *CG 349.*

Gu bend & label
Gu bend Arg label Az
FOLYOT, Jordan. *Q 505.*
Gu bend Arg label Or
— *LE 281.* (*trick only*).
FOLIOT, Sire Edmon. *N 681.*
Gu bend Or label Arg
COLLUMBERS, Sir Philip de. *Gerard 53.* (*qtg 2&3 Sa cross formy fitchy Or*).
COLUMBERS. *DV 42a, 1650.*
Gu bend Or label of 5 Arg
— *WB IV 161b, 646.* (*qtd 2&3 by Sir Jn Hacklewen*).
— *PLN 1082.* (*qtd 2&3 by Sir Jn Harlwin*).

Or bend & label
Or bend Az label Gu
TRIE, Renaud de. *C 129.*
Or bend Gu label Az
— *LE 280.*
CONGILTOWN, of that Ilk. *Lyndsay 261.*
Or bend Sa label Gu
[MAULEY]. *WJ 1537.*

Field patterned bend & label

Barry &c bend & label
Barry Arg and Gu bend Az label Or
MULCHESTRE. *WJ 1164.*
Erm bend Sa label of 5 Gu
SEYN PERE, Jhon de. *Q 426.*

Qtly Untinc bend & label
Qtly bend & label
CALEY, William, of Scratby, Norf, Kt. *Birch 8292.* S' WILLELMI....Y. 1372.
LACY, Henry de, E of Lincoln, Constable of Chester. *Bow XX 2.* (*deed mentions w Mgt; equestr sl*).
LACY, Henry de, E of Lincoln, Constable of Chester. *Bow XLIV 6.* (*equestr sl*).
LASCY, John de, Constable of Chester. *PRO-sls.* 13 cent. (*baston*).
Qtly bend & label of 4
LACY, John de, E of Lincoln. *Arch Journ (Lincoln 1848)* 272. +SECRETV IOH'IS DE LASCI COM LINC ET COSTAB' CESTE. (*countersl*).
LACY, John de, E of Lincoln, 1232-40. *Arch Journ (Lincoln 1848)* 272. +: S': IOHIS: DE: LASCY: COMITIS: LINCOLN': ET: CONSTABVL 'CESTRIE. (*equestr sl*).
LASCY, John de, E of Lincoln & Constable of Chester. *PRO-sls.* 13 cent.
LORYNG, Master William. *PRO-sls.* 1392-3.
Qtly over all bend sin & label of 4
HO, Robert de. *Vinc 88, 84.* +S' ROBER....O. (*sl on grant of lands in Botegue to Hugh de Capes*).
Qtly bend & label of 5
LACI, Henry de. *Birch 11194.* +SECRETVM HENRICI DE LACI.
LACI, Henry de, E of Lincoln &c. *PRO-sls.* 13 cent. (*?label of 4; obv, shield & trapper*).
LACI, Henry de, E of Lincoln &c. *PRO-sls AS 199.* S' HENRICI: DE: LACI: COMITIS LINC.- ..STABVLAR: CESTR'. 13 cent. (*equestr sl*).
LACY, Edmund de. *Bk of Sls 452.* 1251.
LACY, Henry de. *PRO-sls E40 A2154.* SECRETV.... 1271-2.
LACY, Henry de, E of Lincoln & Constable of Chester. *PRO-sls AS 199.* SECRETVM: HENRICI: DE: LACI. 13 cent. (*baston; countersl*).
LACY, Roger de, Constable of Chester. *Bk of Sls 71.* 1207-11.
LASCY, Edmund de. *Yorks Deeds I 68.* 1251.
Qtly over all bend sin & label of 5
HO, Robert de, of Norf. *Birch 10718.* +S' ROBERTI...AT...O. 13 cent.

Qtly bend & label of 7
  LASCI, Roger de, Constable of Chester. *Birch 11198.* +SIGILL' [RO]GERI DE....B[VL]ARII CESTRIE. 1179-1211.

Qtly Arg &c bend & label
Qtly Arg and Gu bend Untinc label Arg
  CLAVERING, J. *RB 418.*
Qtly Gu and Or bend Sa label Arg
  FORMI, Sire. *J 89. (baston).*
Qtly Gu and Or bend Sa label of 5 Arg
  [LACY, E of Lincoln]. *E II 9.*
Qtly Gu and Or bend sin Sa label of 5 Arg
  LACY, Henry of, E of Lincoln. *Keepe.* c1260. HENRICUS DE LACY COMES LINCOLNIAE. *(15 cent inscription; ?Lacy arms reversed).*

Qtly Or &c bend & label
Qtly Or and Gu bend Untinc label Arg
  CLAVERYNG. *CC 224, 78.*
  CLAVERYNGE. *RB 341.*
Qtly Or and Gu bend Sa label Arg
  CLAVERING, J. *HA 23, 109. (baston).*
  CLAVERING, J. *HA 89. (baston).*
  CLAVERING, John. *S 248.*
  CLAVERING, John. *S 246. (baston).*
  CLAVERYNG. *LE 363. (baston).*
  LACY. *MP II 90.*
  LACY, John de, E of Lincoln. *MP IV 37.*
  TRUMPINTON, Rog de. *Q 34. (baston).*
Qtly Or and Gu bend Sa label of 5 Arg
  LACY, John de, E of Lincoln. *MP I 63; MP II 20.*
  LACY, E of Lincoln. *L9 34a, 3.*
  LACY, E of Lincoln. *L9 103a, 1. (& Pomfreyt).*
  LACY, E of Lincoln. *E I 9. (baston).*
  LINCOLE, Counte de. *F 13.*
  LINCOLN, Earl of. *WLN 186. (baston).*
  LINCOLN, le Conte de. *CN 5.*
  LINCOLN, Jn, E of. *MP Hist Min ii 436.* 1240. *('Comes Lincolniae et Cestriae Johannes'; d1240; shield reversed).*
  LYNCOLN, Erle of. *WB II 49, 5. (baston).*
  NICHOLE, Counte de. *D 25b.*
  NICHOLE, le Comte de. *B 9.*
  NICOLE. *G 46. (baston Sa; 'le veyle escu de Nicole').*
  NICOLE, Cunte de. *D 25a.*
  NICOLLE, le Cunte de. *FW 45. (baston Sa).*
  PONTEFRACT. *CRK 270. (baston).*
  WORCESTER, E. *SM 151, 27. (baston).*
Qtly Or and Gu bend Sa label Az
  CLAVERING, Johan. *H 17. (baston).*
  TRAMPINTON, Sir Raffe. *PCL I 537.*
Qtly Or and Gu bend Sa label of 5 Az
  CLAVERING, de. *SP A 137.*
  TRUMPINTON, Roger. *Q II 34.*

Qtly Or and Gu bend Sa label Vt
  CLAVERING, Johan. *K 13; N 27. (baston).*
  CLAVERING, John de. *K 100. (s of Robt Fitzroger).*
  CLAVERYNG, Sir John de. *CB 288.*

Qtly 2&3 fretty bend & label
Qtly in 2&3 fret over all bend & label of 5
  DESPENCER, Hugh le. *Birch 9279.* S' HVGONIS LE DESPE[NC]ER.
Qtly 2&3 fretty over all bend label of 5
  DESPENSER, Hugh le. *PRO-sls.* 1318-19. *(shield hanging from leopard's head; baston).*
  DESPENSER, Hugh le, the younger. *PRO-sls E40 A4887.* ...ONIS DE DES...ER. 1322-2.
Qtly Arg & Gu fretty Or bend Sa label Az
  DESPENSER, Sr Hue fitz. *N 25.*
  SEMPHILL, Sr Hewe. *BR V 6. (le Despenser).*
Qtly Arg & Gu fretty Or bend & label Sa
  DESPENSER, Sr Hugh. *L 61.*

Semy &c bend & label
Az semy de lis Or bend Arg label Gu
  MORIE, le Prince de la. *WJ 89.*
Az semy de lis Or bend Arg label of 4 Gu
  — *WLN 87.*
Vair bend Gu label Arg
  MOTE, Sr de la. *CKO 264.*
  MOTE, Mons William del. *TJ 250.*
Vairy Or and Az bend Gu label Arg
  DELAOURS, Monsire William. *CG 350.*

Bend patterned & label
Gu bend Erm label Az
  RYE, Sr William de. *M 29.*
Gu bend Erm label Or
  RISERE. *L1 554, 2.*
  RYE, Mons William de. *TJ 276.*
  RYE, Sr William de. *L 54.*
  RYZERE, Sire Willame de. *N 674.*
Gu bend Arg semy of billets Sa label Gu
  MURREUX. *SK 235.*
Gu bend Arg semy of billets Sa label Or
  MORYNEUS, Mons T. *WJ 1432. ('son fitz').*
Sa bend semy de lis Or label Arg
  BRONFLETTE, le Sieur Herre. *BG 357.*
Qtly Untinc and Untinc bend Vair label Untinc
  SAUKEVILE, Andrew, of Wilts & Berks. *Birch 13196.* SIG ANDREE DE SAUKEVILE FILII. 1365. *(alias Sakeville le Fitz).*

Bend modified & label
Qtly bend dancetty label
  LONGVILLERS, Margaret de. *Yorks Deeds III 29.* late 13 cent.

Qtly bend dancetty label of 5
  NEVILLE, Margaret. *PRO-sls.* 1308. *(wid of
  Sir Geoffrey N).*

Bend engr & label
Bend engr label
  COLEPEPER, Thomas, Kt. *PRO-sls.* 1330-1.
  CULPEPPER. *?source.* 14 cent. *(tomb, S
  Luffenham Ch, Rutl).*
Arg bend engr Gu label Az
  COLEPEPER. *L1 172, 4; L2 124, 8.*
  COLEPEPER. *LE 395.*
  CULPEPPER. *PLN 1559.*
  SAINT MARD, Lancelot. *C 178.*
Arg bend engr Sa label Untinc
  RADCLIF. *CC 233, 366. (tincts unclear; qtg
  2&3 paly Arg and Az mullet Untinc in dex
  chf).*
Arg bend engr Sa label Gu
  BECONUS, Monsire Walter de. *CG 383.*
  BEKUNS, Walter. *TJ 313. ('...labelles de
  goules').*
  RADCLIF. *CC 233, 362.*
Az bend engr Or label Gu
  BERMINGHAM, Sire Thomas. *N 868.*
  BERMYGHAM. *L10 28b, 20.*
  BERMYNGHAM. *L2 43, 4.*
  BIRMINGAN, S Thomas de. *GA 93.*
Gu bend engr Or label Arg
  BRAIBEF. *F 374.*
  MARESCHAL, Sire Auncel le. *N 540.*
  MARESCHALL, Sr Ancell de. *L 73.*
  MARSHALL, Norf. *L1 437, 2; L2 335, 6.*
  MERHAS, Sir Ansel. *BR V 102.*
Gu bend engr Or label of 5 Arg
  MARSHALL, Mons Ancell, of Norf. *WJ 1571.*
Gu bend engr Or label of 5 Or
  MARSHALL, Mons Ancell, of Norf. *WJ B
  1571.*
Or bend engr Az label of 5 Gu
  FOKERAM, Sir Rauf de. *WNS 26b, 89. ('Sire
  Rauf de Fokeram por dor bende eng le dazur
  label de gou').*
Sa bend engr Arg label Gu
  CUSANCE, W. *SD 15.*
  GIFFARD, Sr Robert. *GA 60.*
Bend flory c'flory label
  BROMFLEET, Margaret. *Mill Steph.* 1417.
  *(qr 3; qr 2 is bend flory counterfl; w of Sir
  Thos B, of Wymington, Beds).*
Sa bend flory c'flory Or label Arg
  BROMFLET. *DV 65b, 2596.*
Sa bend flory c'flory & label Or
  BROMFLETE. *PT 285.*
Bend indented label of 5
  CUSANCIA, William de. *PRO-sls.* 1350-1.
  (Keeper of the King's Wardrobe).
  CUSAUNCE, William de. *PRO-sls.* 1341-2.

Bend lozengy & label
Bend lozy of 5 label of 5
  BERMINGHAM, Sir Fulk. *Dugd 17, 41.* 1341.
  BERMYNGHAM, Fulk de, Chev, of Tamworth,
  Warws & Staffs. *Birch 7407.* S[IGILL]VM
  FOVKE DE BVRMIGHAM. 1342.
  RALEGH, John de, of Devon, Chevr. *Birch
  12902.* SIGILLU IOHANNIS DE RALEGH. 1381.
Arg bend lozy of 5 Sa label of 5 Gu
  BECONUS, Sr de. *CKO 236.*
  COSANZ, Sr William. *R 39.*
Gu bend lozy of 5 Or label of 5 Arg
  BRAIBOEF, John de. *E I 534; E II 536.*
  BRAYBEC. *L10 75b, 19.*
  BRAYBEC. *BA 1276. (?label Or).*
  MARSHALL, Baron. *CK a 43.*
Or bend lozy of 5 Gu label Az
  — *SK 982.*
  MARSHALL, Rye. *LE 242.*
Or bend lozy Sa label of 5 Untinc
  GLASTONBURY, Henry de. *Gerard 15.* 14
  cent. *(right of his w Alice dau & h of
  Laurence Talbot, of Bossington).*
Sa bend lozy of 5 Arg label Gu
  — *CRK 558.*
Sa bend lozy of 5 Arg label of 5 Gu
  BENTON. *SK 262.*

Bend & label charged or patterned
Az bend Or on label Arg annulet Sa
  SCROP, Mons Thomas le. *S 136.*
  SCROPE, Thomas le. *S 138.*
Az bend Or on label Untinc 3 roundels Gu
  SCROPE. *S&G II 324. (mont in ch at
  Messembre to ... Scrope; ?to Sir Geoffrey, s
  of Sir Hen S, who was buried at Konigsberg,
  Prussia, or Sir Wm who died 'over the Great
  Sea'; evidence of Nicholas Sabraham).*
Az bend Or label Erm
  SCROPE, Sir Geoffrey. *S&G II 447. (s of Sir
  Hen Scrope).*
  SCROPE, John le. *S 146.*
  SCROPE, Sir Wm. *S&G II 373-4. (at Siege
  of Calais & at Crecy).*
  SCROUP, le. *RB 207.*
Az bend Or label of 5 gobony Arg and Gu
  SCROP, Sr de. *RB 178.*
Az bend Or label gobony Gu and Arg
  LESCROP, Monsr le Fiz. *AS 209.*
  SCROP, Mons Henri le. *S 144.*
  SCROP, Henry de. *CA 236.*
  SCROPE, Sir Geoffrey. *S&G II 353. (glass,
  Konigsberg; evidence of Jn Rither).*
  SCROPE, Sir Geoffrey. *S&G II 353. (s of Sir
  Hen S; buried at Konigsberg; evidence of Jn
  Rither).*
  SCROPE, Henry le. *S 148.*

Or bend Gu label gobony Arg and Az
  SULLEYE, S William de. *GA 48.*

BEND & IN BASE
Bend sin in base lion passt crowned
  OGILVIE, John, Sheriff-depute of Inverness.
  Stevenson. 1499.
Bend sin in sin base mullet
  DENNISTON, Robert, of Balgarrane. *Steven-*
  son. 1499. *(or Danielston).*
Bend in base cross formy over all label of 5
  LAUDO, John de Sancto, of Som, Kt. *Birch*
  13236. ..OH'IS DE SA..Y LOV... late Hen 3.

BEND & CANTON
Az bend & sin canton Arg
  — *ML I 393. ('asur a bend wit a quater*
  senestre sylver'; canton is about 2/5ths of
  shield's width).
Arg bend engr & canton Sa
  DALBY. *L1 200, 1; L2 154, 12.*
  DALBY. *FK II 787.*
  DALBY. *L10 53, 17.*
Bend canton paly
  PLATYN, John. *?source.* 14 cent. *(sl at*
  Penshurst).
Checky bend on canton lion passt
  CLYFFORDE, Richard de. *Vinc 88, 39.*
  RICHARDI DE CLYFFORDE. *(s of Ric de C; sl*
  on grant of land in Frampton-on-Severn,
  Gloucs, to Ric de Cantelowe).
Bend on canton lion on mount
  SCROPE, Sir Henry. *S&G II 333.* 1320-1.
  ('en la caunton p. amount un petit leoncell';
  charter at Marygg, evidence of chaplain of
  M. Jn de Brereton).
Arg bend sin lozy of 5 Gu on canton Gu crozier
erect Or
  BOXLEY ABBEY. *L10 67, 12.*

BEND & CHIEF
Bend & chf
  — *WB I 14b, 22. (qtd III 3 ii of Stapulton).*
  BASSET, Margaret. *Birch 6586.* [+S]IGILLVM
  SECRETI. 13 cent. *(wid, of Quorndon, Leics;*
  2nd of 2 shields).
  BRIENE, Dame Alice de. *PRO-sls.* 1387-8.
  (sin of 2 on sl; or Thos Walewyn).
  MARSHALL, Sir Peter. *Lawrance 29.* 1322.
  (?d1322; effigy, Newcastle Cath).
Arg bend Az chf Gu
  [CROMWELL]. *PLN 1130. (qtd I&IV 4 by*
  [Berners]).

Arg bend Gu chf Az
  CROMWELL, Mons Rauf. *TJ 325. (painted*
  bend Gu over all).
  CROMWELL, Mons Rauf. *TJ 326.*
Az bend & chf Or
  CARMENAW. *L2 142, 4.*
  CARMINAW. *L10 46, 18.*
  CARMINAW, Thomas, of Devon. *WB III*
  114b, 5.
Gu bend & chf Arg
  HANSTED. *L2 247, 3. (or Hampsted).*
Or bend Az chf Gu
  HARINGTON, Sir John. *LH 193.*
  HARINGTONE, Sire Johan de. *N 638.*
Or bend Sa chf Gu
  HARINGTON, Sir John. *LH 286.*
  HARYNGTON, Mons John de. *TJ 316.*
Sa bend & chf Or
  — *Dingley ccccxl. ('cut in stone in N part of*
  Westm Abbey').
Erm bend Az chf Gu
  CHAMPAIGNE. *L2 141, 3.*
  CHAMPAIGNE. *L10 39, 16.*
Vairy Arg and Sa bend Gu chf Or
  MOUNTENY, Mons Rauf. *TJ 603. (baston).*

Bend patterned chief plain
Gu bend gobony Az and Arg chf Or
  MAULEVERER, Mons John. *TJ 329.*
Barry Arg and Az bend gobony Arg and Gu chf
Gu
  GRAYE, Sir Edmond. *CKO 301a. (baston;*
  banner; prob 16 cent addition).

Bend modified chief plain
Bend engr chf
  ?HALDEN. *Mill Steph; Belcher I 91 & II 107.*
  1514. *(imp by Iden on brass to Pawle Yden,*
  Penshurst, Kent).
  HALDEN, William de, citizen of London.
  PRO-sls BS 13. SIGILL WILLELMI DE HAL-
  DENE. 1377-8.
Arg bend engr & chf Sa
  — *L10 96b, 6. (qtd 2&3 by Sir Jn Per-*
  ceval).
Bend indented chf
  ROTHEWELL, Thomas. *PRO-sls.* 1412-13.
  (the Elder; ch with a ?? in dex chf).
  ROTHEWELLE, Thomas de, of Southmorton,
  Esq. *PRO-sls.* 1423-4. *(martlet in in dex*
  chf).
Arg bend indented Gu chf Az
  GAYVAGE, Mons Payn de. *TJ 328.*
Bend lozy of 6 chf
  [ROCHEWELL]. *Mill Steph.* 1499. *(qtd 2&3*
  by Leyneham on brass to Mgt Wode, formerly
  w of Robt Lyneham, Tidmarsh, Berks).
  [ROCHEWELL]. *Mill Steph.* 1517. *(qtd 2&3*
  by Leyneham on brass to Hen Lynham,

Tidmarsh, Berks).
Arg bend lozy of 3 Gu chf Az
    GAMAGE, Raffe. *WB IV 170b, 803. (qrs 1&4).*
Arg bend lozy of 5 Gu chf Az
    HERRY, Thomas ap. *BA 19b, 159.*
Gu bend lozy Arg chf Or
    — *I2(1904)177. (qtd 2&3 by Hen Leynham, 'de Tydmarshe in coun Barkshire').*

Bend & patterned chief
Arg bend Sa chf barry wavy Gu and Or
    NORBERY, of Yorks. *MY 290.*
Arg bend Sa chf barry wavy of 4 Or and Gu
    NORBURY, of Derbys. *CRK 988.*
Gu bend Arg chf countergobony Or and Az
    HAWSTEAD, Sir John. *LH 320.*
Gu bend Erm chf countergobony Or and Az
    HAWSTEAD, Sir John. *LH 313.*
Arg bend Sa chf vairy Or and Gu
    FITZHERBERT, A. *CRK 1193. (?chf per fess wavy; ?Norbury).*

Bend & modified chief
Or bend Gu chf indented Vt
    NEVIL. *L1 473, 4; L2 360, 3.*

Bend chief & label
Arg bend engr Gu on chf Az label Arg
    GAMAGE, Adam de. *F 300.*
Arg bend lozy of 5 Gu on chf Az label of 5 Sa
    GAMAGE, Adam de. *WLN 732.*

Bend & on chief
Bend engr indistinct charges on chf
    HALDENNE, William de. *Birch 10382.*
    SIGILL' WILLEMI DE HALDENNE.
Arg bend Sa on chf Gu 2 bars wavy Or
    NORBERY. *L1 477, 2; L2 369, 9.*
    NORBERY. *L2 361, 11.*
Gu bend engr Erm on chf Or lion passt Sa
    — *SK 491.*
Arg bend countergobony Or and Az on chf Gu 2 lions passt Or
    CURSON. *Suff HN 5. (Long Melford Ch).*
Arg bend countergobony Az and Or on chf Gu 2 lions pg Or
    CURSON. *L10 38b, 13.*
    CURZON, Thomas, of Bellingford, Norf. *XL 82.*
Arg bend of 7 demi-lozs Sa on chf Or bend betw 6 martlets Sa
    — *SK 929. ('bend of Lutterell').*
Arg bend of 9 demi-lozs Sa on chf Or bend betw 6 martlets Sa
    — *LE 205.*
Or bend Az on chf Gu eagle Arg
    — *L10 103, 9. (eagle displd, sans legs).*
    — *LE 151.*

Or bend Az on chf Gu eagle betw 2 annulets Arg
    — *L10 103b, 19.*
    — *LE 147.*
Bend checky on chf cross
    ST JOHN'S HOSPITAL, Clerkenwell. *Birch 4540.* S'ARMORU IOHIS KENDALE PRIORIS SANCTI IOHIS IHERUSAL..... *(imp fretty, on chf per fess in base 3 escallops & in chf cross; sl of Jn Kendale, Prior, 1491-1501).*

Bend & on chief escallops &c
Bend lozy of 3 on chf 3 escallops
    [GAMAGE]. *Mill Steph. 1493. (qtg [Turberville]; all imp by Conquest on brass to Jn C, his s Ric, & his w Isabel [Gamage], Houghton Conquest, Beds).*
Arg bend lozy of 3 Gu on chf Az 3 escallops Or
    GAMAGE. *LE 193.*
    GAMAGE, Ralph. *PLN 1046. (qtg checky Or and Gu fess Erm).*
    GAMAIGE, of Wales. *L1 288, 2.*
    GAMMAGE. *BA 21, 125. (qtg Vt on bend Arg 3 martlets Gu).*
    GAMMAGE, Morgan. *BA 23b, 202. (qtg checky Or and Gu fess Erm).*
    GAMMAGE, Robert. *BA 23b, 203. (qtg checky Or and Gu fess Erm; cresc for diffce).*
Arg bend lozy of 5 Gu on chf Az 3 escallops Arg
    — *WB I 24b, 2. (imp by Ld Wm [Howard]).*
    GAMAIGE. *L2 226, 2.*
Erm bend engr Arg gutty Gu on chf Az stag's head coupd Or attired Arg
    HEADINGHAM, Robert. *PLN 827.*

Bend on chief mullets
Bend on chf 2 mullets
    — *PRO-sls E40 A6808. 1471-2. (qtd 3 by Eliz, w of Jn, Ld le Scrope).*
Bend on chf 2 pd mullets
    — *Arch Cant xiii 378. (imp by [Rufford]; in N Chantry, founded by a Rufford in 15 cent, Orpington, Kent).*
    ST JOHN, of Bletso. *Proc Soc Antiq XVII 2S 56. (sin part of tierced shield with Zouch in centre & Seymour qtg Lovel in dex; Oker memorial brass, Okeover, Staffs).*
    ST JOHN, Elizabeth. *Mill Steph. (dau of Sir Oliver St J, of Bletso; marshalled in base, Beauchamp, of Bletso imp Patshull, of Bletso in chf on brass to Wm, Ld Zouch, of Haringworth & 2 ws Alice Seymour & Eliz St J, Okeover, Staffs).*
Untinc bend Gu on chf Sa 2 pd mullets Or
    ST JOHN. *WB I 42, 8.*
Arg bend & on chf Az 2 mullets Or pd Vt
    ST JOHN. *L9 4, 6.*

Arg bend & on chf Gu 2 pd mullets Untinc
 ST JOHN, Sir John. *WB I 19b, 16.*
Arg bend & on chf Gu 2 mullets Or
 HOLWER. *L2 268, 4. (marginal note 'St John'.)*
 ST JOHN, Sir John. *WK 213.*
 ST JOHN, John, of Penmawr. *BA 22b, 190.*
Arg bend & on chf Gu 2 pd mullets Or
 SENT JOHN, Sir ... de. *WB IV 144, 333.*
 ST JOHN. *CB 58. (mullets of 6 pts).*
 ST JOHN. *XK 184. (marshalled by Sir Hen Owen).*
 ST JOHN, Sir John. *WK 151.*
Arg bend & on chf Gu 2 mullets Or pd Vt
 ST JOHN. *FK II 296.*
 ST JOHN. *LS 249.*
Arg bend & on chf Gu 2 mullets Vt
 [ST JOHN]. *PLN 350.*
Bend lozy on chf 2 pd mullets
 BACOUN, Sire Edmoun. *Lawrance 1. c1320. (brass, Gorleston, Suff).*
Bend on chf 3 mullets
 HARIETESHAM, Alexander. *PRO-sls. 1391-2.*
Arg bend engr Sa on chf Gu 3 mullets Or pd Sa
 TRERISE. *WK 296. (name added in later hand; qtd 2 by Sir ... Arundell, of Treryse).*

Bend & on chief roundels &c
Sa bend Erm on chf Arg 3 roundels Gu
 BROME. *LE 142.*
 BROUN. *L1 46, 1; L2 42, 12.*
 BROUN. *BA 516.*
 BROUN. *L10 77, 17.*
Arg bend of demi-lozs Sa on chf Gu 6 roundels Or
 — *SK 931. (7 demi-lozs).*
 — *LE 207. (9 demi-lozs).*
Az bend Or on chf Arg salt engr Gu betw 2 Cornish choughs Ppr
 VYNOR, Henry, of London. *L9 25a, 10.*

Bend & on chief & label
Arg bend & on chf Gu 2 mullets Or label Az
 HOLEWERE. *WB I 32b, 7.*
 OLIVER. *PLN 1361.*

BEND & IN CHIEF
Bend & indistinct charge in chf
 JEDWORTH, Patrick, of Gamylschelis. *Stevenson. 1464.*
Bend Vair indistinct charge in chf
 SCROPE, John, King's Paymaster in Irld. *PRO-sls. 1368-9.*
Bend & in sin chf annulet
 COKE, John, of Lilburne. *Bow XXVII 7. 1405-6.*
 COKE, John, of Lilleburne. *Vinc 88, 50. 1405-6. (sl).*
 FRAUNCEYS, Adam. *PRO-sls. 1371-2.*
Arg bend & in sin chf annulet Az
 — *Nichols Leics IV 313. 1428. (imp by Harper in window of Wm H; Misterton Ch).*
 COK, John, of Lilborne. *Bow XXX 25. 1423-4.*
Arg bend & in sin chf annulet Sa
 OTWAY, Richard. *CRK 610.*
Sa bend Arg in sin chf annulet Gu
 ANTINGHAM, Nycho'. *NS 102.*
Qtly Arg & Gu fretty Or bend Sa in dex chf annulet Or
 SPENCER. *SK 23.*
Qtly Untinc & Vair bend in dex chf annulet
 CONSTABLE, Robt. *Mill Steph. 1454. (brass to Robt Constable, Chancellor of Durham, Borsall, Yorks).*
Bend gobony in chf annulet
 STEWART, Alan, of Paisley. *Stevenson.*
Gu bend Vair in dex chf annulet Untinc
 BEAUCHAMP. *CC 232b, 346.*
Gu bend Vair in sin chf annulet Arg
 BEAUCHAMP. *L10 16b, 12.*
Az bend Gu lion Or isst in chf
 — *ML I 478. ('Asur a lyon rampaunt gold defetyd wit a bend gowlys').*
Gu bend Arg in chf lion Or
 ARMENIA, Roy de. *WJ 73.*

Bend & in chief bird
Gu bend Sa in sin chf bird Az
 GERMAN, Mons P... *WJ 1547.*
Bend checky in sin chf bird
 VAUX, John. *Dodsworth 49, 26, HB-SND. 1425. (?bend lozy).*
Arg bend Gu in sin chf corbie Sa
 SHOLE, Robert. *WJ 1452.*
Erm bend checky Sa and Arg in sin chf eagle Gu
 CURSUN, Robert. *LY A 100.*
Bend & in sin chf martlet
 WALDEN, Roger, Archbp of Canterbury. *PRO-sls E40 A6975 & 7888. 1398-9.*
 WALDEN, Roger, Archbp of Canterbury. *PRO-sls E40 H6975.* ...GRI CANTUAR ARCHIEPI. *1398-9.*
 WALDENE, Roger, clerk. *Vinc 88, 37.* 1382-

3. *(sl).*
WESTWYKE, Hugh de. *Vinc 88, 69.* 1363.
*(sl on grant of land in Eslington, Whitting-
ham, Throunton, Barton, Northd).*
Gu bend Az in sin chf martlet Arg
WALDEN, Sir Alex, of Essex. *CY 137, 546.*
Gu bend Az in sin chf martlet Or
WALDEN, Roger. *Chron Usk 35.* ('*de rubio
cum ligamine blodio et una merinula aurea*';
Bp of London 1404-6).
WALDEN, Roger, Archbp of Canterbury. *CVK
668.*
Qtly Arg & Gu fretty Or bend Sa in dex chf
martlet Sa
SPENCER. *SK 24.*
SPENCER, Hugh le. *S 127.*
SPENSER, Hugh de. *BG 295.*
Qtly Or and Gu bend Vair in sin chf martlet Arg
SACKVILE. *LS 220.*
SAKEVYLE. *LE 141.*
Arg bend engr Sa in sin chf martlet Sa
WYLILE, Symkyn. *WB III 104b, 2.*
Bend lozy in sin chf martlet
FREFORD, John de, Kt. *Bow XXVIII 17a.* +S'
JOHANNIS DE FREFORD. 1364-5. *(grant of
mill in Cumberford & 'sectam molendini' in
Serescole, Staffs).*
FREFORD, John de, Kt. *Vinc 88, 188.*
+SIGILL' IOHANNIS DE FREFORD. 1364-5. *(sl).*
FREFORD, John de, of Staffs, Kt. *Birch 9946.*
S' IOHA...ORD. 1345. *(?lozy of 5).*

Bend & in chief book &c
Bend in chf book
PEVERELL, Thomas, Bp of Llandaff, 1398-
1407. *Birch 1884. (?billet).*
Bend in chf buckle
SLEICH, Richard. *Stevenson.* 1431.
Bend gobony in chf buckle
STEWART, Alan, of the Frelande. *Stevenson.*
1438.

Bend & in chief castle
Arg bend & in sin chf tower triple-turreted Sa
PLUNKET, of Dunsany, Irld. *L9 106b, 4.*
[PLUNKET], Sir ..., of Irld. *WB III 86b, 5.*
(name illegible, page torn).
Sa bend & in sin chf castle Arg
PLUNKET. *L1 498, 6.*
PLUNKET. *L9 103a, 12. (3-turrets).*
PLUNKET, Ld of Kylleyne. *DIG 16.* (3
turrets; within circular wall).
PLUNKETT, of Irld. *LQ 98.* (*castle 3 towers
2, 1 joined by embattled wall).*
Qtly Gu & vairy Or and Vt bend Arg in dex chf
castle triple-turretted Arg
PEUVERELL, Count of Nottingham. *L9 97a,
2.*

Sa bend lozy & castle in chf Arg
PLUNKETT, Baron of Lowth. *Gerard 78.*

Bend & in chief crescent
Bend & in sin chf cresc
HOUTON, William de. *PRO-sls.* 1383-4.
Sa bend & in sin chf cresc Arg
ANTYNGHAM. *CC 228b, 224.*
Gu bend Erm in sin chf cresc Arg
— *BG 374.*
Arg bend Az semy of lis Or in sin chf cresc Sa
DOYVILL. *L10 64, 15.* ('*Clapham' added in
later hand).*
Arg bend engr Sa in chf cresc Arg
RADCLIFFE, Robert, Ld Fitzwalter. *XK 95.*
(qr 1).
RADCLYF. *DV 61a, 2415.*
RADCLYFF. *LE 394.*
RADCLYFF. *WK 457. (qrs 1&4 of Ld Robt
Fitzwater).*
RADCLYFF. *L1 559, 3.*
Arg bend lozy & in sin chf cresc Sa
LYE. *CRK 1575. (lozy of 6).*
LYE. *L1 414, 4; L2 312, 11.*
LYE, Yorks. *MY 264.*
Or bend lozy of 6 Sa in sin chf cresc Gu
ARCHARD. *L10 74, 12. (qtd 2&3 by Ford-
ham).*
Bend nebuly in sin chf cresc
DEEN, Richard le. *PRO-sls.* 27 Feb 1327.
(6foil above shield).
Gu bend Arg in sin chf cresc Erm
— *LE 154.*

Bend & in chief cross &c
Bend & in sin chf cross
HATHELOK, Robert. *PRO-sls.* 1391-2.
Arg bend dancetty Sa in sin chf cross botonny
Gu
LYSTON. *L9 37b, 1.*
Bend dancetty in sin chf crosslet
— *CY 142, 565. (qtd 2&3 by per pale chev;
'... Bremston' crossed out).*
Arg bend & in chf crosslet fitchy Sa
— *LE 335.*
Bend & in sin chf cross formy
WARENDER, John. *Birch 14260.* A MERCI
GOD. 1357. *(or Hen Colle; Citizens &
Woolmen of London).*
Arg bend engr Sa in chf escallop Gu
RADCLIFFE, Sir Richard. *CRK 442.*
RADCLYFE. *PT 788.*
Arg bend Sa in dex chf on escutch Arg lion Gu
STOPHAM, Willam de. *Q 257.*
Bend in chf estoile
FLEMING, John. *Birch 9829.* S' IOHANNIS
FLEMING. late 13 cent. *(?or mullet of 6 pts).*
[?H]..rston, John de. *Birch 10379.* SIG ... H'IS.
DE ....TON. 1366. *(sl used by Wm de*

Haldenby).
PLEMING, John. *Stevenson.* 13 cent. *(mullet of 6 pts).*

Bend sin in dex chf estoile
— *Stevenson.* post 1513. *(?arms reversed in cutting?; qtd by Janet Hepburn, w of George, 3rd Ld Seton).*

Crusily fitchy bend in sin chf estoile
MAR, Sir Donald. *Stevenson. (later 12th E of Mar, d c1297; 2nd sl).*

Per bend Sa and Arg bend counterch & estoile Gu
GAWEN, Johne. *BA 22, 185. (Jn Gawen ap William ap Davit).*

Bend engr in sin chf estoile
WALLERE, William, of Suff. *Birch 14227.* SIGILLUM WILL[ELM]I WALLERE. 1431.

Gu bend Or in chf fleur de lis Arg
— *WJ 1437.*

Bend & in chief head

Bend in sin chf lion's face
FRAUNCEYS, Adam, Citizen & Mercer of London. *Birch 9935.* SIGILLVM ADE FRAUNCEYS. 1351.

Bend in sin chf ?lion's head erased
LYELL, John. *Stevenson.*

Bend in sin chf leopard's face
BUSCRE, John. *Birch 7972.* SIGILL' ... HIS: DE: B.... 1332. *(s of Hen B, de Malyns, of London).*

Arg bend Gu in sin chf ?camel's head couped Gu muzzled Sa
LEVINGTOUN, of Saltcottis. *Lyndsay 295.* 1542. *(alias Lethington).*

Qtly Gu & vairy Or and Az bend Arg in dex chf stag's face Or
PEVEREL, Count of Nottingham. *L9 107b, 6.*

Bend in sin chf wolf's head erased & to sin
LIVINGTON, Jas, Bp of Dunkeld 1476-83. *Stevenson 143. (s of Levington, of Saltcoats, E Lothian).*

Bend & in chief horn &c

Bend engr in sin chf stag's attires
PEEBLES, Janet. *Stevenson.* 1522. *(w of Jn Curror, burgess of Edinburgh).*

Bend in sin chf hunting horn stringed
BOURHILL, Laurence, Sheriff of Lanark. *Stevenson.* 1456.

Az bend Or in sin chf loz Erm
SCROP, Mons le. *S 148.*

Bend in sin chf mascle
VAUS, Robert, burgess of Edinburgh. *Stevenson.* 1506. *('owner of the mills at Drumsheugh').*

Bend & in chief mullet &c

Bend in sin chf mullet
HOLLOND, Peter de. *PRO-sls E40 A6985.* S' PETRI DE HOLLOND. 1453-4. *(mullet of 6 pts; used by Morgan ap Llewelyn ap Jevan).*

Az bend & in sin chf mullet Arg
BUSET, de. *PT 288.*
BUSETT. *DV 1883. (mullet pd in outline only).*

Arg bend countergobony Gu and Sa in dex chf mullet Sa
WHYCHSALE, Heylyn, of Salop. *CV-BM 171.*

Arg bend countergobony Sa and Arg in sin chf mullet Sa
WHYKSALE, Haylin, of Salop. *CY 87, 348.*

Bend per bend indented in chf mullet
HEREFORDE, Walter de. *Dugd 17, 95.* 1357.

Gu bend Arg billety Sa in sin chf mullet Or pd Gu
MURREUX. *SK 236.*

Arg bend dancetty Sa in sin chf mullet Gu
DOUNHOLT. *L1 211, 4. (as painted; marginal note 'Sir Richard Lyston').*
LYSTONE, Pers de. *WJ 1514.*

Or bend dancetty Sa in sin chf pd mullet Gu
DOUNHOLT. *L10 63b, 12.*
DOUNHOLT. *L1 211, 4; L2 159, 2. (as blazoned; marginal note 'Sir Richard Lyston').*

Arg bend engr & in sin chf pd mullet Gu
ARTIN, Sarlo, of Essex. *WB III 88b, 3. (name unclear).*

Arg bend engr & in sin chf mullet Sa
RADCLYFE. *PT 787.*

Gu bend engr & in sin chf mullet Arg
FENTOUNE, of that ilk. *Lyndsay 271.*

Arg bend lozy of 5 & in sin chf mullet Sa
TOUKY. *L1 641, 3. (mullet of 6 pts).*

Az bend Or in sin chf mullet Erm
SCROP, Mons' Steven le. *S 150.*

Bend lozy in chf roundel
COLLACE, John. *Stevenson.* c1340.

BEND & OVER ALL

Bend & lion
— *Stevenson.* 1410. *(qtd by Alexander Lindsay, 2nd E of Crawford, d1439).*
WALLACE, Sir Richard, Kt, of Barmer & Goderick. *Stevenson.* 1220.

Arg bend Sa fretty Or cotised Gu lion Untinc
DENHAM, John de. *CA 74.*

Arg bend Az over all bend sin Gu
— *ML I 446. ('Silver a sawtry asur & gowlys senglyd comme bend de south a fyssur. Or he beryth silver a fyssur gules upon a bend asur. Or a semblaunt gules etc').*

Arg bend Gu over all orle of martlets Sa
— WJ 1465. (name illegible).
HAY. LH 135.
HAY, Sir Henry. LH 588.

Bend & over all cross &c
Bend sin cross raguly
CRAUNFORD, Robert. PRO-sls E40 A5053.
....RENVS.... 1347-8. (s of Nicholas C; bend
has curious top).
CRAUNFORD, Robert. PRO-sls. 1347. (s of
Nicholas C).
Bend sin cross voided ch in centre with
peacock's head erased
COLVILLE, Henry, bailie of St Andrews.
Stevenson. 1468.
Bend mill-rind in fess
FONTIBUS, Richard de, of Kilwingholm etc,
Lincs. Birch 9855. +SIGILLM RICARDI DE
FONTIB'. early 13 cent.
Gu bend Erm voided escutch Arg
QUYXLEY. L1 536, 2; L2 417, 3.
Az bend Arg on escutch Or bend engr Sa
LYDEVUSORS, Sire Johan de, Franceis. O 7.
('dasur ove i bend dargent ove i escuchon
dor ove i bend engrelee de sable').
Bend over all 3 escutchs
HAY, Wm, of Mayne. Stevenson. 1520.
(escutch in dex chf over bend; Superior of
Culcabok, &c).
Bend sin over all estoile
GRAY, Robert. Stevenson. 1451. (?mullet of
6 pts; Common measurer in Leith).

Bend & over all fess &c
Bend sin over all fess
BODEL, John de, of Burwell, Lincs. Birch
7524. +SIG ... IOHANNIS DE BODEL. c1240.
Gu bend Arg over all fess Or
FITZ OSBORNE, William, E of Herefod. Brit
Arch Assoc xxvii 189-190. (posthumous
invention. From this derived (a) Gu 2 bends
Or and Arg of Milo, E of Gloucester, (b)
Bohun's bend cotised).
Checky bend over all fess
CLYFFORDE, John, Bastard of, Esq. Birch
8663. SIGILLUM IOHIS BASTARDI DE CLYF-
FORD ARMIG. 15 cent.
Or bend Gu fess checky Arg and Az
CHASTELMONT, le Sr de. Berry; Stodart pl 4.
(Stewart of Castlemilk).
Bend & on fess 3 roundels
HUNTINGFELD, John de. PRO-sls. 13 cent.
YREYS, Sir Galfrid le. Dugd 17, 76. 1309.
Arg bend Gu over all stag's head cab Sa
— FK II 410.
Gu bend & over all 7 voided lozs 3, 3, 1 Or
GRAYE, Herr Jan. Gelre 58b. c1380.

Sa bend Or over all 3 picks Arg
HONDE. LH 926.
Qtly bend in centre pt roundel
CLAVERING, Alan. PRO-sls Ex KR 16/26, 28,
HB-SND. 1323-4. (baston).

Bend & over all staff
Az bend & over all crosier in bend sin Or
COMBERMERE, Abbas de, Salop. CY 88, 352.
ST AGGAS MONASTERY, Richmond, Yorks.
D4 32b.

BEND BETWEEN
Bend betw 2 indistinct charges
TOTEL, Roger, junior. Stowe-Bard ls ix 4.
S' ROGERI DE TOTEL IUNIORI. 1337-8.
Bend betw 6 indistinct charges
GRIFFITH, Rees ap. Dodsworth 49, 29b, HB-
SND. 1411.
Bend betw indistinct charges
GARELYNE, John, of Suthgivel. PRO-sls E40
A9596. 1325-6.
MORYN, John. Birch 11986. 1340. (s of
Robt Moryn, of Kylvyngton, Notts).
WALDEN, John, armiger. PRO-sls E40
A7888. 1398-9. (bro of Rog Walden, Archbp
of Canterbury).
Bend sin betw indistinct charges
HOWARD, Lady Anne. PRO-sls E40 A13566.
1510-11. (w of Thos, Ld Howard).
Bend betw indistinct object in sin chf & bird in
base on staff
TILLY, John, of Okewelle, Yorks. Birch
13945. 1342.
Az bend Or fretty Untinc betw indistinct charges
Untinc
[BRETON], ... WJ 1606.
Bend engr betw indistinct charges
KENNEDY, David, of Pennyglen. Stevenson.
1529. (charges perished).
Bend lozy betw 6 indistinct charges
PLUCKENET, Alan. PRO-sls. 1303. (charged
on breast of eagle displd).
Bend raguly betw 2 indistinct charges
WALLEWORTH, Thomas, Canon of York.
Yorks Deeds X 80. ...WALLWOR... 1409.

Bend betw annulets
Qtly bend betw annulet in qr 2 & ?4foil in qr 3
CALLE, Thomas. Stowe-Bard ls xi 7 MS ii
90. SIGILLVM THOME CALIEI. 1383-4 or ear-
lier. (appended to various deeds).
Qtly Or and Gu bend Sa betw 2 annulets Arg
BOURGYTON. L1 67, 4.
Bend checky betw 2 annulets
— Birch 9144. (annulets unclear; ?qtd 2 by
Jn Cursun, s of Jn C, Kt, of Suff).

Bend betw 3 annulets
MULES, Margaret de. *AnstisAsp I 224, 92.*
+SIGILLVM: MARGARETE: MEOLES. 1347. *(sin of 2 shields).*
Sa bend betw 6 annulets Or
LEKE. *L9 40a, 3.*
LEKE, de. *SK 590.*
LEYKE. *L1 404, 2; L2 301, 11.*
Qtly bend betw 6 annulets
BURGULION. *Birch 13466.* 15 cent. *(alias Borgonion; qtd 2&3 by Ralph Sheltun, Esq).*
Qtly Or and Gu bend Sa betw 6 annulets Arg
BURGOLION. *SK 99.* *(baston; imp by Shelton; names added by Gibbon).*
BURGOLYONE. *FK II 392.* *(baston).*
Arg bend Sa semy of feathers Arg betw 6 annulets Sa
— *ML I 511.* *('Sylver a bend sabyll & of the fyrst plume bendee betwyx vi pelettes in ii tryanglys. Thou shalt sett sylver before quia hic quantitas coloris habet locum that ys to say because there ys more sabyll than sylver').*
Bend lozy of 6 betw 6 annulets
WYOTT, John. *Yorks Deeds VIII 94.* 1426.
Qtly Or and Gu bend Sa betw 10 annulets Arg
BURGELON, Sir Robert. *BR V 124.*

Bend betw 2 beasts
Bend betw 2 lions
BOHUN, Henry de, E of Heref & Ld Constable. *Dugd 17, 71.* late 12 cent. *(equestr sl).*
BOXE, Henry de la. *Heneage 772.* +SI HENRICI DE LA BOX. 1336. *(s of Sir Hen de la B; lease of tenement in Box, Wilts).*
THURMOND, Nicholas. *PRO-sls.* 1392-3.
Az bend betw 2 lions Or
DILLINGEN, Hartman V, Count of. *C 53.*
Gu bend betw 2 lions Or
ARMENIA, K of. *XL 418.*
KYBURG, Count of. *C 117.*
Gu bend Erm betw 2 lions Or
— *FK I 36.*
Bend engr betw 2 lions
STRANGBON. *Mill Steph.* *(brass to Joan, dau of Thos Walrond & w of Rich S; Childrey, Berks).*

Bend betw 2 lions passt &c
Bend fretty betw 2 lions passt
BOXA, Henry de, Kt. *PRO-sls.* S' HENRICI DE LA BOX. 13 cent. *(lions indistinct).*
Gu bend Or betw 2 lions passt Arg
STRANGE. *LS 8.* *(qr 1).*
Bend betw 2 lions passt regard
SCOT, William, of Yorks. *Birch 13343.* SEL PRIVE SVY APELE. 1331. *(?surmounted by bend).*

Sa bend Gu betw 2 leopards sejt Arg spotted Sa
WODEVYLE, Sir Thomas, of Lancs. *WB III 73b, 6.*
Gu bend engr Or betw 2 hinds stat Arg
— *WB I 30b, 13.*
Sa bend betw 2 talbots Arg
HOLLES, William, of London. *LH 356.*

Bend betw 3 beasts
Bend betw 3 lions
BATHE, Eleanor de. *AnstisAsp I 211, 55.* 1349-50.
Checky Arg and Gu bend Az betw 3 lions Arg
BARKESWORTH, Suff. *L1 70, 1; L2 70, 9.*
Arg bend Gu betw 3 lions passt Sa
SOTFORD, John, of Devon. *WB III 115, 8.*
Gu bend Az betw 3 lions passt Arg
— *T c 20.* *(qtd by barry Or and Vt bend Gu [Poynings]).*

Bend betw 4 beasts
Qtly Or and Arg in qrs 1&4 2 lions Gu over all bend sin Sa
BUXSELL. *L10 84, 5.*

Bend betw 6 beasts (lions)
Bend betw 6 lions
— *PRO-sls.* 1357-8. *(1 of 4 roundels of arms on sl of Ida de la Warde, Lady of Nevile).*
[BOHUN]. *PRO-sls E41 AA58 & 59.*
SIGILLVM DOMINI HENRICI STAFFORD. 1519-20. *(qtd 2 by Hen Stafford, E of Wiltshire).*
[BOHUN]. *AnstisAsp I 225, 93.* 1384-5. *(3rd & 4th shields of 4 of Katharine Engayn).*
BOHUN, Humfrey de, E of Heref & Essex. *Vinc 88, 151.* *(sl).*
BOHUN, Humphrey de, (6th) E of Heref. *Birch 7529.* +SIGIL' HVMFRIDI DEBVHVN. 1238.
BOHUN, John de, E of Heref & Northamp. *CombeAsp II 158.* S' Iohanne de bohun comit de herford norhamt.
GRENVILL, Adam de. *Dugd 17, 18.* Sigill Ade de Greinvill.
GREYVYLE, William de. *PRO-sls.* 1328-9.
LEGER, Joan. *Heneage 771.* 1336. *(w of Rog L; lease of tenement in Boxe, Wilts, sometime held by Alice, sis of Sir Hen de la Boxe).*
THURMOND, Nicholas. *PRO-sls BS 58.* Sigill': nicholai: thurmond. 1392-3. *(?5 or 6 lions).*
Arg bend Sa betw 6 lions Gu
BANN. *RB 479.*
BANY. *L10 22b, 16.*
BANY. *L2 95, 1.*
BARM, de. *LE 310.*

Az bend Arg betw 6 lions Or
— WB IV 128, 43. (qtd 2&3 by 'Dewke of
Bokyngham').
BOHUN. MP II 95.
BOHUN, Sire Edmon. O 74.
BOHUN, Henry de, E of Hereford. MP I 33.
BOHUN, Humphrey de, E of Hereford. MP II
9. (s of Hen, E of Hereford).
BOOUN, Henricus de, comes Herefordiae. MP
Hist Min ii 243. 1220. ('Scutum de azuro,
leones de auro, benda alba').
HERFORD, Erl of. BR IV 78.
Gu bend betw 6 lions Arg
MARTHAM. L1 428, 5.
Or bend Arg betw 6 lions Gu
BOX, Sire Henri. N 259. (?bend Az).
Or bend betw 6 lions Gu
BOX, Suss & Surr. L2 88, 5.
Sa bend betw 6 lions Arg
SNAVES, Johannes de. FW 686.

Bend patterned &c betw 6 lions
Bend crusily betw 6 lions
BOHUN, Humphrey de. PRO-sls. 13 cent.
(the younger).
Per bend Arg and Sa bend lozy of 4 Or betw 6
lions counterch
TOTESBERY, Bawedewyn. WB IV 179b, 968.
TYTTISBURY. BA 1296.
Arg bend lozy of 5 Gu betw 6 lions Sa
TITTESBURY. XL 574.
TYTTISBURY. FK a 926.
Arg bend lozy of 5 Or betw 6 lions Sa
TYTTISBURY. FK II 926.
Per bend Arg and Sa bend lozy of 5 Or betw 6
lions counterch
TITISBOROUGH. L1 629, 6. (armed Gu).
TITSBURY. CRK 1726.
TITTESBURY. XL 526.
TUKSBURY, Baldwin. PLN 543.
TUTISBURY. DV 49a, 1936.

Bend betw 6 other beasts
Bend betw 6 bats displd
COLNE, William de, of Steyning. Steyning 6.
1342. (sl on grant of land in Steyning in
parish of Stogursey, Som).
Sa bend betw 6 goats ramp Arg
GAYTEFORDE, T. WB I 43, 1.

Bend betw bendlets: see bend cotised

Bend betw billets
Bend betw 2 billets
LIVINGSTON, Alexander, 2nd of Dunipace.
Stevenson. 1518.
Bend betw 3 billets
— Stevenson. (qrs 2&3 of coat imp by
Arthur Erskine).

LIVINGTON, Alexander, 2nd of Dunipace.
Stevenson. 1521. (2nd sl).

Bend plain betw 6 billets
Bend betw 6 billets
— Stevenson. 1465. (qtd by Jas Living-
stone, cr Ld L, 1458).
MAUDUYT, John. Heneage 409. 1343. (Par-
son of Wynterbourne Earl, Wilts).
Az bend betw 6 billets Arg
SMITH, Mons' John, of Norf. WJ 799.
Az bend Arg betw 6 billets Or
[SMYTH]. WB I 18b, 14. (qtd by Marschall).
[SMYTH]. WB I 18b, 8.
Sa bend betw 6 billets Arg
— LE 423.
ALYNGTON. L1 12, 1. (painted 8 billets).
ALYNGTON. ME 110; LY A 234.
Sa bend betw 6 billets Or
[CALLANDER]. Lyndsay 106. (qtd by Living-
stone, Ld of C).
[CALLANDER]. SC 53. (qtd 2&3 by Lewyns-
ton, of C).
CALLANDER, of that ilk. Lyndsay 393.

Bend engr &c betw 6 billets
Bend engr betw 6 billets
ALINGTON. Arch Journ xiv 290. (martlet on
cresc for diffce; qtg [Argentine, FitzSymons
& Gardiner]; engraved on 2 silver drinking
cups presented to Lyon's Inn by Giles A,
1580).
ALINGTON. Mill Steph. c1530. (brass to
Ursula Drury, w of Giles A, Hawstead, Suff).
ALINGTON. Mill Steph. c1530. (imp Gar-
diner on brass to Ursula Drury, w of Giles A,
Hawstead, Suff).
ALINGTON. Mill Steph. c1530. (imp Drury
on brass to Ursula Drury, w of Giles A,
Hawstead, Suff).
ALINGTON. Mill Steph. 1522. (brass to Jn
Newport, Furneux Pelham, Herts).
ALINGTON. Mill Steph. 1518. (brass to Robt
Newport & w Mary [A], Furneux Pelham,
Herts).
Az bend engr betw 6 billets Arg
ALYNGTON. L1 20, 1; L2 11, 3.
Gu bend engr betw 6 billets Or
— WB III 123, 6. (qtd by Sir Jn le Grays, of
Cambs).
Sa bend engr betw 6 billets Arg
ALINGTON. Coll T&G iv 33-40. (sundry
monts [1522-1691], Horseheath, Cambs).
ALINGTON, Sir Giles. XK 115. (qrs 1&4).
ALYNGTON. L10 5, 4. (qtg 2&3 Gu 3
covered cups Arg [Argentine]).
ALYNGTON. Suff HN 43. (qtg 2&3 Gu 3
covered cups Arg).
ALYNGTON, Essex. MY A2 161.

ALYNGTON, Sir Giles. *WK 477.*
HALINGTON. *RB 548.*
Bend lozy of 5 betw 6 billets
　BOURNE, Isabella de. *Birch 7671.* SIGILLVM
　ISABELLE DE BOVRNE. 1346. *(sin of 2
　shields; wid of Thos de B, of Stanford Rivers
　Manor, Essex).*

Bend betw 7 billets or more
Or bend Gu betw 7 billets Sa
　— *FK II 686.*
Sa bend betw 7 billets Arg
　BOULERS, Baldewin de. *WLN 544.*
Sa bend Arg betw 7 billets Or
　SMYTH. *L1 582, 2.*
Sa bend betw 8 billets Arg
　ALYNGTON. *L1 12, 1. (blazoned 6 billets).*
Sa bend engr betw 8 billets Arg
　ALINGTON. *CRK 1204.*
　ALINGTON, of Cambr. *L2 7, 4.*
　ALYNGTON, Essex. *MY 161.*
Sa bend betw 10 billets Arg
　BONVILERS, Baudewyn de. *L10 34, 8.*

Bend betw bird &
Bend betw eagle displd & crosslet
　RISHWORTH, John. *Yorks Deeds I 227 & III
　121.* 1457.
Arg bend Az betw bird rising in chf Az &
crosslet in base Sa
　— *D4 43b. (qtd by Savell, of Yorks).*

Bend betw 2 birds
Arg bend betw 2 birds Gu
　?STAUODON. *CC 227b, 184.*
Az bend betw 2 eagles Arg
　— *L10 105, 2.*
Qtly Erm and Vt bend Gu betw 2 falcons Or
　BURY. *L10 85, 2.*
Bend betw 2 ?geese
　RENTE, Alice. *Birch 12957.* 1337. *(wid of
　Thos de la R, of Ipswich, Suff or Jn Rodlond,
　of Ipswich).*
Arg bend betw 2 martlets Az
　— *FK II 430.*
Arg bend betw 2 martlets Gu
　STAVERDON. *LS 91.*
Gu bend betw 2 martlets Arg
　— *LE 462.*
Gu bend betw 2 martlets Or
　RAHERE. *Dingley cccclxviii. (tomb, Ch of St
　Bartholomew the Great, London).*
Arg bend engr betw 2 martlets Gu
　STANDON. *LS 200.*
　STAUERDON. *L1 594, 6.*
　STAVERDON. *LE 436.*
Arg bend engr betw 2 martlets Sa
　— *DV 249.*

Sa bend betw 2 owls Arg
　— *WK 145. (qtd 4 by Savage).*
Bend engr on upper side betw swan & duck
　FLEMYNG, Martin. *PRO-sls.* 1328-9.
Bend betw 2 swans
　SWANLUND, Thomas de. *PRO-sls.* 1335-6.
　SWANLUND, Thomas de, of London. *Birch
　13792.* SIGILLVM THOME DE SWANLVND.
　1335.
Or bend lozy Sa betw 2 swans Untinc
　DURBURGH, John de. *Gerard 14.*

Bend betw 3 birds
Bend betw 3 birds facing to sin
　BASSINGBORNE, Thomas de. *Birch 7206.* +S'
　THOME DE BASSINGB'. 14 cent.
Bend betw 3 falcons
　HORDENE, Geoffrey de. *Birch 10821.*
　+SIGILLVM: GAVFRIDI: :HORDENE:. 12 cent.
Arg bend betw 3 martlets Gu
　STAUERDON. *L1 616, 6.*
Or bend betw 3 martlets Gu
　— *E6. (subqtd by Stapilton, of Wyghell,
　Yorks).*
Gu bend Az betw 3 owls Arg b&l Or
　SLEY. *PT 484.*
Az bend engr Or betw 3 owls Arg b&l Gu each
standing on tun fessways Or
　CATTON, James. *CRK 1792.*

Bend betw 6 birds
Bend betw 6 birds
　CLAY, John de. *PRO-sls.* 1307.
　TEMPEST, Richard. *PRO-sls.* 1360, 1362 &
　1386.
　URSFLETE, Gerard, Kt. *PRO-sls.* 1417.
Gu bend betw 6 birds Or
　HELAND, Sir John. *LH 667. (?martlets).*

Bend betw 6 eagles
Or bend Gu betw 6 eagles displd Sa
　VERLAY, Sire Felip de. *N 456. ('de or a vi
　eglis de sable).*
　VERLY, Sir Philip. *BR V 235.*

Bend betw 6 geese
Arg bend betw 6 brangeese Ppr
　BURNELL, of Newton, in Yeovil, Poynington.
　Gerard 170.

Bend betw 6 martlets
Bend betw 6 martlets
　— *WB I 35b, 1. (qtd 7 by E of Shrewsbury).*
　CARNOT, William, Visct. *Dugd 17, 62.*
　?early 13 cent.
　CICESTRE, Peter de. *PRO-sls.* 1308-9.
　(Clerk of pantry & buttery to Edw 1).
　ECCLESHALE, Robert de. *Birch 9423.*
　S' ROBERTI DE ECCLESHALE. 1328. *(betw 4*

wyverns).

FAUCONBERGH, Isabella de. *BrookeAsp I.* SIGILLUM ISABELLE DE FAUCONBERGE. 1383-4.

FERRERS, William de. *Bow LXVII 1.* +S. GVILLMI VICEDNI CARNOT. *(grant to ch of St Mary of Broc).*

FORNIVALE, Gerard de, of Staffs. *Birch 9978.* +SIGILLVM GERARDI DE FORNIVALE. late 12 cent. *(on bend the word 'Maria').*

FOURNIVAL, Thomas. *Birch 9912.* SIGILLVM: THOME: FOVRNIVAL. late 13 cent.

FURNEFAL, Thomas de, Ld of Sheffield, 1st Baron Furnival. *Birch 9983.* SIGILLUM: THOME DE FURNEFAL. ?1301.

FURNIAL, William. *Birch 9987.* SIGIL' WILLI DE FORNEUALLE. 1366. *(s of Thos, Ld of Hallamshire).*

?FURNIVAL. *?source.* 1376. *(sl of hospital of St Giles of Brompton Bridge).*

FURNIVAL. *Bk of Sls 229.* 1456.

FURNIVAL. *Birch 13836.* 1437. *(qtd 2&3 by Jn Talbot, Ld of F & Wesford, E of Shrewsbury, Marshal of France).*

[FURNIVAL]. *Birch 13848.* 1456. *(qtd 4 on dex side of 1st of 2 shields in sl of Mgt Talbot, wid of Sir Jn T, 1st E of Shrewsbury).*

[FURNIVAL]. *Mill Steph.* 1475. *(qtd 2&3 by Talbot on brass to Nicholas Knivaston & w Joan [Mauleverer], Mugginton, Derbys).*

FURNIVAL, Gerard de. *Dugd 17, 32.* ?mid 13 cent. *(s of Gerard de F).*

FURNIVAL, Thomas de. *Barons Letter.*

FURNIVAL, Thomas de. *CombeAsp II 148.* +SIGILLVM THOME DE FVRNEFAL.

FURNIVAL, Thos. *Her & Gen iii 334.* 1274.

FURNIVALL, Gerard de. *Bow LXXVII 1.* *(s of Gerard de F; equestr sl).*

FURNIVALL, Thomas de, Ld of Hallamshire. *Birch 9985 & 9986.* AGLA BERONYX GRADIEL TETRAGRAMATON (the magical words). 1347 & 1361.

[FURNIVALLE], Gerard. *Birch 6048.* S' GERARDI FILII GERA.... late 13 cent. *(s of Gerard F, of Caldecote Manor, Herts).*

FURNIVALLO, Thomas. *Birch 9981.* +S': THOME: [D]E F..... 13 cent. *(s of Thos de F, of Yorks).*

GERY. *Mill Steph.* c1455. *(brass to Rog G, Vicar of Whitchurch, Oxfords).*

LECHEFORD, Nicholas de. *Birch 11271.* SIGILLV: NICHOLAY: DE: LECHEFORD. 1352. *(sl used by Johanna, dau of Walter de Bray, of Henewyk, Bedf).*

LOUTERELL, Geoffrey, Ld of Irneham, Lincs, Kt. *Birch 11476.* SIGILLUM GALFRIDI LOUTERELL. 1417.

LOUTERELL, Haurie. *PRO-sls.* 1421-2. *(w of Andrew of Tonsham).*

LUTERAL, Geoffrey. *Yorks Deeds II 199.* 1317.

LUTRELL, John, Kt. *PRO-sls.* 1429-30.

MONYPENY, David, of Petworth, Suss. *Birch 11898.* 15 cent. *(qtg 2&3 on fess 3 fleurs de lis).*

MOUNTNEY. *Mill Steph.* 1526. *(imp by Appleton; brass to Robt A & w Mary, 2nd dau&coh of Thos M, Little Waldingfield, Suff).*

MOYNE, John le. *PRO-sls E40 A6184.* S'IOHIS LE MOINE FIL' NICHOL' LE MOINE. 1260-68. *(equestr sl).*

MUNTENI, Ernulph de, of Suff & Essex, Kt. *Birch 12035.* S' ERNVLPHI DE KVNTENI. 1311.

MUNTENO, Arnulf de, of Diss, Norf. *Birch 12032.* SIGILL' ARNVLFI DE MVNTENI. late 13 cent.

NASSYNGTON, Robert de. *Birch 3876.* *(Abbot of Ramsey, 1342-9).*

OLYVERE, Robert, of Essex. *Birch 12300.* S' ROBERT OLIUER. 1432. *(qtg 2&3 eagle rising betw ?3 indistinct charges).*

?ORFLETE, Gerard. *Birch 12313.* 1416. *(qtg 2&3 on fess 3 fleurs de lis).*

SEITONE, Nicholas de, of Maydewell, Northants, Kt. *Birch 13443.* ......NE. 13 cent.

SETONE, John de, Ld of Maydewell, Morthants. *Birch 13438.* SIGILL' IOHANNIS DE SETONE. 1402. *(s&h of Jn de Seyton, Kt).*

[SEYTON]. *RH, Ancestor xi 90.* c1390. *(on tomb of Reynes, Clifton Reynes, Bucks).*

SEYTON, Henry de, Kt. *PRO-sls.* 1352-3.

SEYTON, Thomas. *Vinc 88, 32.* 1446-7. *(sl; dominus de Maydewell, Northants).*

SEYTOUN, John de, of Maydewell, Northants, Kt. *Birch 13432.* SIGI[LLU]M IOHANNIS DE SEYTOUN. 1383.

WYNCESTRE, Henry de. *PRO-sls.* 1328-9.

Arg bend betw 6 martlets Gu
Arg bend betw 6 martlets Gu

— *XK 45 & 224.* *(qtd 4 by Sir Gilbert Talbot).*

— *WGA 261-2.* *(qtd 4 by Jn, Ld Talbot, E of Shrewsbury).*

— *D4 24b.* *(qtd 2&3 by Worsop Abbey, Notts).*

— *XK 188.* *(qtd 4 by Sir Jn Talbot).*

— *XK 34.* *(qtd 4 by Geo Talbot, E of Shrewsbury).*

— *WGA 47.* *(qtd 4 by Sir Geo Talbot, E of Shrewsbury).*

— *WK 15.* *(qtd 4 by Gilbert Talbot).*

— *BR II 38.* *(qtd II&III 1&4 by [Talbot], E of Shrewsbury).*

— *KB 267.* *(qtd 2&3 by Talbot, E of Shrewsbury).*

— ML II 15. (qtd 4 by Talbot, Erle of Shrewsbury).

— WB V 83. (qtd 4 by Sir Gilbert Talbot, Kt, 1485).

— PLN 1721. (qtd 4 by Sir Gilbert Talbot).

— WK 53 & 141. (qtd 4 by Sir Gilbert Talbot).

— CRK 1380. (qtd 4 by Jn Talbot, E of Shrewsbury).

FFURNIVAL, Thomas de. LM 126.

FFURNIVALL, Thom de. LMRO 315.

FORNEVALE, Sir. WB IV 154b, 516.

FORNEVALE, Sr de. CKO 186.

FORNIVAL, le Sr. NB 64.

FORNIVAL, Thom de. Q 136.

FORNIVAL, Sire Thomas de. N 102.

FORNIVALE, le Sr de. AS 69.

FORNIVALE, S Thomas. BR IV 16.

FORNIVALE, Thomas de. H 70a.

FORNIVALL, le Sr de. CN 55.

FORNYWALE, Ld. RH, Ancestor iii 204.

FOURNEVAL, Thomas de. K 59.

FOURNIVALL. WJ 1449.

FOURNIVALL, de. SP A 61.

FOURNIVALL, Sir Thomas. H 70b.

FOURNYVALE, le Sire de. TJ 239.

FOURNYVALL. TB 24.

FOURNYVALL. PV 84.

FURNAVYLE, Sir Robert. BR V 71.

FURNEVALL, Monsire de. CG 340.

FURNEWALE, Ld. AY 56.

FURNIVAL. Arch Journ xcii 92. c1300. (tinct of field unclear; Wall painting, All Saints, Chalgrave, Beds).

FURNIVAL. BB 154, 11. (imp by Sir Jn Talbot, KG).

FURNIVAL. WB II 49, 11. (qrs 1&4, imp by E of Shrewsbury).

FURNIVAL. Leake. c1453. (qtd 4 by Jn Talbot, E of Shrewsbury, d1460).

FURNIVAL. XX II 100. (qtd 2&3 by Nevile, Ld Furnival).

FURNIVAL. CRK 233.

FURNIVAL. MP II 45 & 77.

FURNIVAL. AY 30. (qtd II&III 1&4 by [Talbot] B of Shrewsbury).

FURNIVAL. Neale & Brayley. 1296. (canopy of mont to Edm, E of Lancaster).

FURNIVAL, Ld. PLN 105. (qtd 2&3 by [Talbot]).

FURNIVAL, Ld de. WLN 243.

[FURNIVAL]. PLN 1968. (qtd 4 by E of Shrewsbury).

[FURNIVAL]. PLN 1979. (qtd by Sir Gilbert Talbot).

[FURNIVAL]. RH, Ancestor iv 227. (qtd II&III 1&4 Jn Talbot, 1st E of Shrewsbury).

FURNIVAL, Thomas de. K 374.

FURNIVAL, Thos de. SF 2. (succeeded as Ld Alton, 1316, jure uxoris).

FURNIVAL, William de. ML I 29; ML II 30.

FURNIVALE, Sir Tomas. PCL I 452.

FURNIVALL. DV 62b, 2476.

FURNIVALL, Gerard de. E I 210; E II 208.

FURNIVALL, Sire Thomas de. J 64.

FURNIVALLE, Walter de. C 81.

FURNUYVALL, Sir Thomas de. GA 130.

FURNYVAL. L1 262, 3; L2 197, 3.

FURNYVALE. PT 492.

FURNYVALE, Ld. BR VI 18. (qtd by E of Shrewsbury).

FURNYVALE, Monsieur de. AN 82.

FURNYVALL, Gerard de. FW c 611.

FURNYVALL, Lorde. KB 312.

FURNYVALL, Thomas. B 147.

FURNYVALLE, Ld. WB I 37, 18.

TALBOT, Ld. BW 8, 41. (qtd II&III 1&4).

TALBOT, Ld Furnival. ML I 60. (martlets misblazoned molettes).

Arg bend betw 6 martlets Sa

Arg bend Gu betw 6 martlets Sa

— Q 412.

Arg bend betw 6 martlets Sa

— XB 16. (qtd by Talbot).

LOUTERELL. PLN 1221.

TEMPEST. Suff HN 49. (Mettingham Castle or College).

TEMPEST. L1 629, 3.

TEMPEST. WJ 1494. ('son fitz').

TEMPEST, of Craven. PT 1049.

TEMPEST, Sir John. CRK 759.

TEMPEST, Sir John, of Yorks. WB III 76b, 2. (qrs 1&4).

TEMPEST, Petrus. Q II 612.

TEMPEST, Mons Ric. WJ 1493. (?storm finches).

TEMPEST, Mons Richard. S 219.

TEMPEST, Richard. S 221.

TEMPEST, Richard. BG 202.

TEMPEST, Sir Richard. XK 171.

TEMPEST, Sir Richard. BK 64 & 402. (qtg 2&3 Erm fess lozy of 5 Gu [Hepden]; in margin against standard of Sir Ric T).

TEMPEST, Sir Richard, of Bracewell, Yorks. BA 606. (beaked Gu).

TEMPEST, Mons' William. TJ 335.

TEMPEST, of Yorks. D4 45.

TEMPESTE. PT 360.

Az bend betw 6 martlets Arg

Az bend betw 6 martlets Arg

— PLN 1839. (in base of coat per fess, all imp by Bruarne, of Lincs).

GOBAUD, John. Q 515.

[L]UTTERELL, Hew. WK 133.

LOTEREL, Sir Hugh. CRK 840.

LOTERELL. L9 35b, 4.

LOTERELL. *L1 401, 2; L2 317, 1.*
LOTERELL, Monsire. *CG 342.*
LOTERELL, Thomas. *E I 640; E II 642.*
[LOTERELLE, Robertus]. *Q II 494. (names of 494 & 495 have been interchanged).*
LOTREL, Andrew. *BG 206.*
LOUTERELL, Sir Hugh. *PLN 1739.*
LUTEREL, Mons Geffray. *AS 139.*
LUTRELL, Mons Robert. *TJ 240.*
LUTTEREL. *PLN 1664.*
LUTTERELLE. *DV 59b, 2350.*
LUTTRELL, Andrew. *S 250.*
LUTTRELL, Sir Geoffrey. *Arch Journ xxxviii 62-63. (in Luttrell Psalter &c; on sl of Sir Geoffrey L, last Baron of Irnham).*

Az bend betw 6 martlets Or
Az bend Arg betw 6 martlets Or
— *WLN 900.*
  LUTTRELL. *PT 68.*
  MONTENAY. *WB IV 172, 831.*
  MONTENY, Robert de. *FW 164.*
  MUNTENY, Robert de. *D 67a & b.*
Az bend betw 6 martlets Or
— *RH, Ancestor ix 162.*
— *LE 87. (qtd 2&3 by Elveden).*
  LUTTRELL, Mons Andr. *WJ 1582.*
  MONTONI, Robert de. *F 179.*
  MONWTENY, Sir James. *BR V 252.*
  MOUNCENEYE, Monsieur Robert. *S 217.*
  MOUNTEIN, S Ernaud de. *GA 97.*
  MOUNTENEY, Sir .... *CRK 1545.*
  MOUNTENEY, Ernaud de. *B 145.*
  MOUNTENEY, Essex. *MY 169.*
  MOUNTENEY, Essex. *L1 421, 6; L2 324, 2.*
  MOUNTENEY, Robert. *S 219.*
  MOUNTENEY, Robert de. *WLN 685.*
  MOUNTENY, Ernald de. *MP IV 82. (shield reversed with broken spear; k at tournament, 1252).*
  MOUNTENY, Ernaud de. *Q 148.*
  MOUNTENY, Sire Ernauf de. *N 418.*
  MOUNTNEY, Sire Ernaud de. *J 114.*
  MOUNTNEY, Robert de. *E 36.*
  MOWNTENEY, Sir William. *PLN 226.*
  MUNTEIN, Robert de. *A 199.*
  MUNTENY, Roberd de. *HE 140.*
  MUNTENY, Robert de. *D 222a.*
  PICOT. *L1 528, 3. (marginal note, 'Menteney').*
  SERTON, John de. *BG 207.*

Gu bend betw 6 martlets
Gu bend betw 6 martlets Arg
  LOTEREL, M. *WNR 92.*
  SETON, Mons J de. *WJ 1435.*
Gu bend Arg betw 6 martlets Or
— *PLN 1878.*
  MOUNTENY, Robert. *BG 210. (also Secton).*

SECOUNE, S' Jon. *PO 334. (written above in Elizabethan hand 'Setoun').*
SETON. *PT 6115.*
SETON. *DV 51b, 2028.*
SETON, John de. *S 220.*
SETON, John de. *TJ 294.*
SETON, Monsire John de. *AN 218.*
SEYTON. *LS 327.*
SEYTON. *L1 610, 4.*
SEYTON, Johan de. *LM 200.*
SEYTON, Mons' John de. *S 218.*
Gu bend Or betw 6 martlets Arg
  HELAND, Mons J. *WJ 1555.*
Gu bend betw 6 martlets Or
  BRET. *L1 80, 3; L2 53, 12.*
  BRETTE. *L10 76, 24.*
  BRETTE, John. *BG 205.*
  FOURNYALE, Tomas. *PCL I 443.*
  FURNEUS, Maheu de. *G 183.*
  MONTANY, Sir Thomas. *BR V 98. (mullet Arg for diffce).*
  MONTENEY. *L2 347, 12.*
  MONTNEY, Monsire. *CG 343.*
  MOUNCENEYE, Mons John. *S 216.*
  MOUNTENEY. *PT 1051.*
  MOUNTENEY, John. *S 218.*
  MOUNTENEY, Mons Thomas. *TJ 241.*
  MOUNTENEY, Sr Thomas de. *CKO 196.*
  MOUNTENEYE. *L9 73a, 12.*
  MOUNTNEY, Everarde de. *Q II 148.*
  MOUNTONY, Sire Thomas de. *O 4.*

Or bend betw 6 martlets
Or bend betw 6 martlets Az
— *LE 268. (qtd 2&3 by Lancelot de Bernen).*
Or bend betw 6 martlets Gu
— *WLN 58.*
— *LE 341. (qtd 2&3 by Ufflett).*
— *L10 30, 7. (qtd 2&3 by Berven).*
— *PLN 168. (qtd 2&3 by Arg on fess Az 3 fleurs de lis Or [S. Gerard Urflete]).*
  FURNEVAL, Gerard de. *FW 611b.*
  FURNIVAL. *Arch Journ xii 92. c1300. (tinct of field unclear; wall painting, All Saints Chalgrave, Beds).*
  FURNIVAL, Gerard, of Munden. *Proc Soc Antiq XVII 2S 277. c1310. (shield on mainiple, Leagram Hall, Lancs).*
  FURNIVALL, Gerard. *B 149.*
  FURNIVALL, Thomas de. *E I 208; E II 206.*
  UFFLET. *L1 656, 3.*
  UFFLETE. *SK 658.*
  UFFLETE, Gerard. *S 464. (qrs 1&4).*
  UFFLETE, Gerard. *BG 201.*
  UFFLETE, Mons Gerrard. *S 459. (qtg 2&3 Arg on fess Az 3 fleurs de lis Or).*
  VPFLITE. *RB 316. (qrs 2&3).*

Or bend betw 6 martlets Sa
— *LH 576. (qtd 2&3 by Harleston).*
LOTEREL, Sire Andreu. *N 644.*
LOTEREL, Sir Hugh. *CRK 1514.*
LOTERELL. *L1 390, 6; L2 302, 8.*
LOTERELL. *L9 42a, 7.*
LOTERELL. *BA 1102.*
LOTERELL. *LE 204.*
LOTTERELL, Lincs. *L2 317, 7.*
LOTTRELL, Sir H. *WB I 39, 20.*
LUTERELL. *FK II 313.*
LUTHERELL. *WB II 59, 11.*
LUTRELL, Sir Hugh, of Som. *WB III 100b, 6.*
LUTTERELL. *SK 928-9.*
LUTTRELL, of East Quantockhead & Dunster. *Arch Journ xxxviii 63.* early 14 cent.
LUTTRELL, Sir Hugh. *PLN 217.*

Sa bend betw 6 martlets
Sa bend betw 6 martlets Arg
SMITH, of Hilton. *Her & Gen v 33. (Jos Morris of Shrewsbury's MS).*
SOMERI, Henry de. *E I 464.*
SOMERY, Henry de. *WLN 546.*
SOMRI, Henri de. *F 210.*
Sa bend betw 6 martlets Or
ECCLESHALE, Sir Robert. *N 1102.*
EKELSALL. *L2 182, 7.*
EKELYSHALL. *L2 177, 10.*
EKLESCHALE, Sir Robert. *BR V 107.*
SOMERY, Henry de. *E II 466.*

Bend modified betw 6 martlets
Arg bend arched betw 6 martlets Gu
FORNIVAL, M. *WNR 90.*
Bend dancetty betw 6 martlets
?RUSSELL, Peter de, of Southampton. *Birch 13175.* ...etri.... 13 cent.
Arg bend engr betw 6 martlets Sa
— *D4 35. (qtd 3 by Malore, of Hutton Conyers, Yorks).*
— *FK II 391.*
[TEMPEST]. *Blair D II 195, 412. (imp by Trollope qtg Harpyn; Thornely Hall, co Durham).*
TEMPEST, of Studeley. *BA 672.*
TEMPEST, Sir William. *PLN 754.*
TEMPEST, Sir William. *PLN 364.*
Az bend engr betw 6 martlets Or
PICOT, Pers. *F 478.*
PIGOD, Piers. *E I 549; E II 551.*
PIGOT, Piers. *TJ 1275.*
PIGOTT, Perys. *C 83. ('d'azur a sis merlot d'or a une bende d'or engrale').*
PYCOT, Sire Peres. *N 629.*
PYKET, Sir Piers. *GA 209.*
Arg bend indented betw 6 martlets Sa
TEMPEST, Mons' Richard. *TJ 336.*

Az bend indented betw 6 martlets Or
PICOT, Jan. *Q 184.*
PIGOT, Piers. *TJ 330.*
Arg bend lozy betw 6 martlets Or
PYCOTT. *Gerard 3.*
Az bend lozy betw 6 martlets Or
PIGOT, Piers. *WLN 494.*

Bend betw 6 owls &c
Sa bend Erm betw 6 owls Arg
— *WB I 25b, 5-6. (qtd 2 by Newell).*
Bend betw 6 stormfinches
TEMPEST, Richard. *PRO-sls Ex KR 73/2, 34, HB-SND.* 1386.
TEMPEST, Sir Richard. *Durham-sls 2390.* 1397.
TEMPEST, Sir Richard. *PRO-sls Ex KR 73/1, 13, HB-SND.* 1362.
Bend engr betw 6 stormfinches
TEMPEST, Sir Thomas. *?source.* 1540.

Bend betw bougets &c
Bend sin betw 2 bougets
FARRILE, Richard de, bailie of Edinburgh. *Stevenson.* 1451.
Arg bend Az betw 3 loz-shaped buckles Gu
BARRET, John, of Suff. *WB III 109, 9.*
Arg bend betw 6 buckles Az
HADHAM, Thomas. *TJ 337.*
Arg bend betw 6 round buckles Sa
HADHAM, Thomas. *LH 289.*

Bend betw castles &c
Bend betw 2 castles
DONCASTRE, William. *Birch 9303.* S' WILL'I F ELIE DE D...CASTRE. 1430. *(?coat poss 3 5foils over all bend; s of Elias de D; used by Jn Attilburghe, Chaplain of Norwich, Norf).*
Bend betw 2 coins
— *Bow XXX 36.* 1422-3. *(imp by Rog de Wirley, s of Cornelius W, of Houndesworth, Staffs).*

Bend betw cotises or bendlets: see bend cotised

Bend betw 2 crescents
Bend betw 2 crescs
— *SHY 456. (imp Bowser).*
— *SHY 416. (imp [Hastings]).*
— *SHY 417. (imp Brews).*
[DEBENHAM]. *Mill Steph.* 1514. *(qtd 2&3 by Brewes on brass to Thos B, Little Wenham, Suff).*
[DEBENHAM]. *Mill Steph.* 1514. *(imp by Brewes, for his grandparents on brass to Thos B & w Jane [Scroope], Little Wenham).*
DEBENHAM, Gilbert. *Farrer Bacon 20.* 1414. *(sl).*

DEBENHAM, Gilbert de. *PRO-sls.* 1361.
DEBENHAM, Gilbert, of Essex & Suff. *Birch 9261.* 1413. *(or Depenham).*
Untinc bend betw 2 crescs Or
— *SHY 284. (imp Jarnygham).*
— *SHY 285. (imp Soche).*
Bend betw 2 increscs
GOBIOUN, William. *Birch 10122.* SIGILL' WILLELMI GOBIOUN. 1397.

Sa bend betw 2 crescents
Sa bend Or betw 2 crescs Arg
DEBENHAM. *WB IV 170, 797.*
Sa bend betw 2 crescs Or
DEBBEN, Sir Gilbert. *WK 586.*
DEBEHAM. *SHY 453. (imp by Brewes).*
DEBENHAM. *Suff HN 22.*
DEBENHAM. *XO 93.*
DEBENHAM. *Suff HN 41.*
[DEBENHAM]. *SHY 58 & 61.*
DEBENHAM, Sir Gilbert. *PLN 1040. (imp [Beauchamp] Gu crusilly & fess Or).*
DEBENHAM, Sir Gilbert, Suff. *PLN 1741. (qtg 2&3 Or crusilly & chev Gu).*
DEBNAM. *L10 57, 4.*
DEBNAM. *Suff HN 48. (imp by Brewse).*
DEBNAM. *MY 331. (qtd 2&3 by Debnam, Suss).*
DEBYNHAM. *Suff HN 47.*
DEBYNHAM, Suff. *L1 196, 1; L2 153, 7.*

Bend engr betw 2 crescents
Arg bend engr betw 2 crescs Sa
CANT. *Lyndsay 471.*
HEDILHAM. *LE 241.*
HEDILSHAM. *LE 180.*
HEDILSHAM. *XO 82.*
HEDISHAM. *LH 116 & 1039.*
HEDISHAM. *L1 316, 5; L2 253, 4.*

Bend betw 3 crescents
Bend betw 3 crescs
WATERTON, William de. *Birch 14310.* S' WILL'I DE WATERTON. 1338. *(sl used by Matillis, dau of Jn, s of Robt de Raynberghe, of Yorks).*
Bend bretessed betw 3 crescs
GRENLEYE, William. *Birch 10241.* ..ILL'I.- ..IOHANNIS.... 1347. *(s of Jn de G, of Notts).*

Bend betw 6 crescents
Bend betw 6 crescs
DESPENSER, Hugh le, kt. *PRO-sls E40 A10910.* 1314.
FOLIOT, Edmund. *PRO-sls.* 1303-4.
HAUDLOE, John. *PRO-sls.* temp Edw 2.
Arg bend betw 6 crescs Sa
TROYS, Harman. *XO 90.*
TROYS, Herman. *WJ 1512.*

Gu bend betw 6 crescs Arg
FOLIET, S Edmond. *GA 131.*
FOLIOT, Edmound. *Q 513.*
FOLIOT, Esmond. *TJ 990.*
FOLYOTT, Sr Edmund. *M 15.*
Gu bend betw 6 decrescs Arg
FOLLIOT, Gerard. *LMS 74. (?or Jordan).*
Gu bend Arg betw 6 increscs Or
FOLIOT, Esmond. *TJ 298. ('...sys cressantz pendantz dor').*
Gu bend Or betw 6 crescs Arg
LEALL. *L2 309, 6.*
Sa bend betw 6 crescs Arg
STANHOPE, Sir Edw. *GY 11.*
Gu bend gobony Arg and Az betw 6 crescs Arg
LYOLL, Thomas. *Q II 135. (?crescs Or).*
Gu bend gobony Or and Az betw 6 crescs Arg
WELLE, Sire Johan de. *N 297.*
Az bend arched betw 6 crescs Arg
GRECI, M de. *WNR 91.*

Bend betw cronels
Arg bend betw 6 cronels Sa
— *ST 315.*

Bend betw 1 cross &
Bend betw cross couped in chf & in base annulet
HILLE, Richard, d1440. *SussASColl lvii 24. (? & border; bellfounder; found on bells cast by Hille & on others by his wid Johanna who m 2ndly Jn Sturdy).*
Arg bend betw crosslet fitchy in chf & in base round buckle Sa
— *LE 333.*

Bend betw 2 crosses
Or bend betw 2 crosslets Sa
BORNAM. *WB I 34b, 3.*
BORNAM. *PLN 1408.*
BURNAM. *LE 379.*
BURNAM. *L2 81, 10.*
BURNAM. *L10 83b, 10.*
BURNAM. *CC 234, 398.*
Bend engr betw 2 crosslets
TYDESDON, Roger. *PRO-sls.* 1387-8.
Arg bend lozy of 5 betw 2 crosslets fitchy Sa
DYTONES. *BA 1223.*
DYTONS, Mons gautte. *L10 58b, 11.*
Bend betw 2 crosses patonce
FOLIOT, Richard. *Yorks Deeds I 68.* 13 cent. *(s of Jordan F).*

Bend betw 3 crosses
Gu bend Vair betw 3 crosses trefly Arg
KASE, de. *LE 163. (or Rase).*
Az bend betw 3 crosses trefly fitchy Or
BLAKET, Sir Emond, Gloucs. *WB III 73b, 8. (qrs 1&4).*

Bend betw 3 crosslets fitchy
— *Stevenson.* 1517. *(qtd by Jn Erskine, 5th Ld E; 3rd sl).*
Arg bend betw 3 crosslets fitchy Sa
KAWSTON. *PO 102.*
Az bend betw 3 crosslets fitchy Or
BLAKET, fitz Edmond. *L10 74b, 1. (qrs 1&4).*
MAR, Cunte de. *HE 56.*
Gu bend betw 3 crosslets fitchy Arg
HOWARD, Ld. *LH 476.*
Gu bend betw 3 crosses formy Arg
RERESBY. *L1 549, 2.*
Sa bend engr betw 3 crosses formy Or
KENYON. *CRK 189.*

Bend betw 3 crosses & ...
Bend sin betw 3 crosslets in chf & 3 mullets of 8 pts in base
NISBET, John, of Dalzell. *Stevenson.* c1513. *(m Mgt Somerville, whose arms he seems to have adopted).*
Bend sin betw 3 crosses formy in chf & salt couped in base
MECKFEN, Robert, of Mekven, Lord of that ilk. *Stevenson.* 1443.

Bend betw 4 crosses
Gu bend betw 4 couped crosses Arg
HUNTINGFELD, Her de. *Q 456.*
Gu bend betw 4 crosslets fitchy Arg
HUNTYNGFELD, Petrus de. *Q II 444.*

Bend betw 6 crosses
Bend betw 6 crosses
— *WB I 9, 1. (qtd 2 by Vere on escutch of Sir Anthony Wingfield, KG 1541).*
Arg bend betw 6 crosses couped Gu
[EUSTACE]. *Proc Soc Antiq XVII 2S 276.* c1310. *(on stole, Leagram Hall, Lancs).*
Sa bend betw 6 crosses couped fitchy Or
HAUVYLE, Elys de. *LM 482.*
Bend betw 3 crosses fitchy & 3 crosses within crescs
PAGE, Robert. *Durham-sls 1931.* 1366-8.

Bend betw 6 crosses botonny
Arg bend betw 6 crosses trefly Gu
BOKKYNGES. *LE 167.*
Gu bend betw 6 crosses trefly Arg
HAWARD, Mons William. *TJ 152.*
Gu bend betw 6 crosses trefly Or
FURNEAUX, Sir Simon. *WNS 26b, 93. ('Sire Simon Forneaus por de gou ou une bende vi croiz boton dor').*
UMFREVYLE, Sir R. *WB I 38b, 4.*
Sa bend betw 6 crosses trefly Arg
LONNGEVELIERS. *LE 317.*
LUNGUILLERS. *L1 411, 2.*

Arg bend wavy betw 6 crosses trefly Gu
BORKYNGES. *LE 320.*
Bend betw 6 crosslets trefly fitchy
DRAYTON, Sir John. *OxfRS IV 119.* 1417. *(d1417; brass, Dorchester, Oxfs).*
Arg bend betw 6 crosses trefly fitchy Sa
LONGVILLARS. *CT 355.*
Az bend betw 6 crosses trefly fitchy Or
DRAYTON. *XFB 109. (qtd 2 by Barantin).*
DRAYTON, Sir John. *LE 121.*
Gu bend betw 6 crosses botonny fitchy Arg
[HOWARD]. *BG 397.*
HOWEARD, the Lorde. *WB IV 135b, 176.*

6 crosses formy &c follow 6 cross crosslets fitchy

Bend betw 6 cross crosslets
Bend betw 6 crosslets
— *DerbysAS XIV 90/91.* 1500. *(imp by Shelley on tomb of John S, at Shelley).*
CHEYNE, John, Parson of Hanbury, Staffs. *Birch 8550. ...HEYNE....* 1383. *(unclear).*
FURNEAUX. *AnstisAsp I 217, 74. +SIGILLVM: MARGARETE: DE: BELLO: PRATO.* 1330-1. *(imp by Mgt, wid of Ralph de Beaupre & dau of Matilda de F).*
LONGVILERS, John de, Kt. *Birch 11381. SIGILL' IOHANNIS DE LONGVILERS.* 1358. *(alias Lungvilers; s of Thomas de L, Kt).*
ORMONDE, Anne, Ctess of. *BirmCL-sls 492083.* 1397. *(qrs 1&4).*
STANHOP, Richard, of Northants, Kt. *Birch 13658. SIGILLU RICI STANHOP.* 1433.
STANHOPE. *Coll T&G ii 96.* 1530. *(Longvilliers coat, sometimes used by Stanhopes; imp by Jn Babington who m Sanctia, dau&h of Sir Jn S, of Ramptons). (Dethick Chapel, Ashover, Derbys).*
STANHOPE, Richard. *Dugd 17, 38.* 1408.
STANHOPE, Richard, Kt. *Bow LXI 2.* Sigillu rici Stanhop. 1422. *(grant of Manor of Dunton in Arden).*
STRECCHE, Thomas. *Wells D&C II 644, 456.* 1388-9. *(bro&h of Robt S; seisin of lands in Ediston, Som).*
TYE, Robert. *Weston 18.* SIEIL LUM R TR. 1375-6. *(s of Sir Peter Ty, Kt; sl on grant of Manors of Lonewade & Tyttleshall).*

Arg bend betw 6 cross crosslets
Arg bend betw 6 crosslets Gu
BOKKING, Monsire de. *CG 334.*
Arg bend betw 6 crosslets Sa
KAWSTON, Mons R. *WJ 1496.*
STANHOP, Ricardus. *Q II 571.*

Az bend betw 6 cross crosslets
Az bend Arg betw 6 crosslets Or
FITZEUSTACE, Lincs. *L2 192, 4.*
Az bend betw 6 crosslets Or
DRAYTON. *L1 216, 5; L2 161, 6.*
EVSTAFF. *L2 185, 12.*
FITZEUSTACE. *Proc Soc Antiq XVII 2S 276.*
c1310. *(on stole, Leagram Hall, Lancs).*
HOO, Sir T. *WB I 42, 21.*

Gu bend betw 6 cross crosslets
Gu bend betw 6 crosslets Arg
— *WGA 46. (qtd 2&3 by Jn de Vere, E of Oxf).*
— *WGA 45. (qtd 2&3 by Jn Howard, D of Norf).*
HAUWARDE, Mons J. *AS 360.*
HAWARD, Sr Wil. *CKO 206.*
HAWARDE, Mons John. *TJ 251. ('de goules une bende dargent & vi croiseletz dargent').*
HOWARD. *WGA 172. (?Flodden augmentation on bend; qr 2).*
[HOWARD]. *PLN 1270. (qtd 2&3 by E of Oxford).*
HUNTINGFIELD, Saer. *LH 260.*
RALE, Sr Johan de. *CKO 217.*
Gu bend Or betw 6 crosslets Arg
RATRI, Ceulx de. *Berry; Stodart 10.*
Gu bend betw 6 crosslets Or
FORNEAUS. *DV 43a, 1698.*
FORNEUS, Sir Maheu. *RB 76.*
FORNEUS, Sir Maue. *HA 15b, 33.*
FOURNEAUX. *L1 237, 2; L2 195, 11.*
FURNEAUX, of Kilve. *Gerard 31.*
FURNEUS, Sire Maeu. *HA 40.*
PRESTON, Piers de. *P 130. ('ioust Windeslawe').*

Or bend betw 6 cross crosslets
Or bend betw 6 crosslets Sa
NEVILLE, John, le Forestier. *Brit Arch Assoc xxii 285-8.* ?c1250. *('dor ung bend de goules croiselles noire'; Planche thinks this is not a Neville coat but adopted on marriage to some heiress).*

Sa bend betw 6 cross crosslets
Sa bend betw 6 crosslets Arg
— *Nichols Leics II 262. (imp by Az 3 hounds courant in pale Or; window, Melton Mowbray Ch).*
— *S 87. (qtd by Reynold Everyngham).*
— *LE 108. (qtd 2&3 by Everingham).*
— *S 89. (qtd 2&3 by Raynold de Everingham).*
LONGEUYLER, Jon. *PO 277. (written above in Elizabethan hand 'Longewillers').*
LONGVILERS, Monsr de. *AS 338.*
LONGVILERS, Sir Thomas. *CV-BM 225.*

LONGVILLERS. *PT 1266.*
LONGVILLERS. *WK 224.*
LONGVILLERS. *L2 311, 12.*
LUNGEVILERS, Monsire de. *CG 369.*
LUNGVILERS. *L9 37a, 5.*
LUNGVILERS, Sgr. *RB 140.*
LUNGVILERS, Mons Thomas. *TJ 168.*
STANHOPE, Sir Edw. *(d1511). GY B 11.*
STANHOPE, Ralph. *GutchWdU. (Fellow of Balliol, ?living post 1431).*
Sa bend Or betw 6 crosslets Arg
STANHOPE, Sir Richard. *BD 86. (4th N window, Hall of York Palace, Southwell).*

Bend patterned betw 6 cross crosslets
Bend checky betw 6 crosslets
ORMESBY, William de, Kt. *PRO-sls.* 1304-5.
Gu bend checky Or and Az betw 6 crosslets Untinc
— *FB 37.*
Gu bend checky Or and Az betw 6 crosslets Arg
ORNESBY, Norf. *L1 486, 3; L2 390, 6.*
Bend Vair betw 6 crosslets
KNIVETON, Henry de. *Bow XXIV 17.* Sigillum Henrici de Norbury. 1364-5. *(Rector of Norbury; grant of manor of R..., Staffs).*
KNYVETON, Henricus de. *Vinc 88, 3.*
+SIGILLVM HENRICI DE KNYVETON. 1374-5. *(rector ecclesiae de Northburye; sl).*
Gu bend Vair betw 6 crosslets Arg
— *WB I 33b, 2. (qtd 2 by Chechester).*
RALEIGH, Sir John. *LR 30.*
RALPH. *LR 94.*
RAYLE, Mons John. *WJ 1427. (alias Raylegh).*
Gu bend Vair betw 6 crosslets Or
RALEY, Henry de. *FW 317c.*

Bend modified betw 6 cross crosslets
Arg bend engr betw 6 crosslets Gu
BOKKYNG. *L10 85, 14.*
Arg bend lozy of 3 betw 6 crosslets Sa
CORNWALL. *L1 135, 5; L2 101, 9.*
Gu bend lozy of 3 Erm betw 6 crosslets Or
AUBEMARLE. *L1 9, 4.*
Arg bend nebuly betw 6 crosslets Gu
BORKYNGES. *L10 83b, 2.*
Arg bend wavy betw 6 crosslets Gu
BELLYNG, Sr de. *CKO a 192.*
BOCKINGE, S'g'r. *RB 157.*
BOKKYNG, Mons de. *AS 285. ('le pe de sable le pe de goul').*
BOKKYNG, Sr de. *CKO 192.*
BORKINGE. *L1 56, 2; L2 74, 10.*

Bend betw 6 cross crosslets fitchy
Bend betw 6 crosslets fitchy
— *SHY 8. (qtd 2&3 by Spencer).*
— *Stevenson.* 1454. *(qtd by Robt Lyle, Ld*

of Duchale; 2nd sl).
— *Birch 14125. 1496. (qtd 2&3 by Jn de Vere, 13th E of Oxford, Grand Chamberlain & Admiral of Engld).*
— *Stevenson. (qtd by Jn, 4th Ld Lyle, dc1469; 2nd sl).*
— *Birch 13856. 1359. (2nd of 3 shields in sl of ... Talworthe).*
— *WB I 24b, 17. (qtd 2 of Vere).*
— *Stevenson. 1440. (qtd by Robt Erskine, 1st Ld E, dc1452).*
BERE, John de la. *PRO-sls.* 1461.
CHEIN, John, of Essilmont. *Stevenson.* 1495.
GARRIOCH, James, of Kynstare. *Stevenson.* 1454.
[HOWARD]. *Arch Journ ix 28. (qtd 2&3 on sl of Jn Vere, 13th E of Oxf, 1417-61).*
[HOWARD]. *Arch 66, 305. (qtd 2&3 by Vere).*
[HOWARD]. *Farrer I 222. (mont, Wickhampton Ch, Norf).*
[HOWARD]. *Farrer II 220. (on battlements, Terrington St Clements Ch, Norf).*
[HOWARD]. *Farrer I 33. (West front of tower, Fersfield Ch, Norf).*
HOWARD, Elizabeth. *Birch 14119. 1463. (qr 1 of coat imp by Jn de Vere, 14th E of Oxf for his w Elizabeth H).*
HOWARD, John, Kt. *Birch 10872.* SIGILLUM IOHANNIS HOWARD MILITIS. *15 cent. (qtg 2&3 Palis).*
HOWARD, John, Kt. *PRO-sls.* 1349.
HOWARD, John, Kt. *Vinc 88, 154.* SIGILLVM IOANNIS HOWARD MILITIS. *(qtg Mowbray; sl).*
HOWARD, John, Kt. *PRO-sls.* 1464-5.
HOWARD, John, Ld of, of Essex, Kt. *Birch 10871.* HOWARD. *1479.*
HOWARD, John, of Essex, Kt. *Birch 10868.* S': IOHANNIS: HOWARD: MILITIS. *1431. (qtg 2&3 lion passt [Plais]).*
HOWARD, Sir Robert. *Farrer Bacon 10.* 1383.
HOWARD, Thomas. *Birch 10877.* SIGIL THOME HOWARD. *c1400.*
HOWARD, Thomas. *Birch 10878.* SIGILLVM TH...HOWARD...OLCIE. *1518. (2nd D of Norf, EM, KG &c; qtg, 2 Brotherton, 3 Warren, 4 Mowbray; shield encircled with Garter).*
MAR. *Stevenson. c1380. (qtd by Wm Douglas, 1st E of D, dc1384; 3rd sl).*
MAR. *Stevenson. 1378. (borne by Mgt Stewart, w of Thos, 13th E of Mar, d post 1417; 2nd sl).*
MAR, Donald, 12th E of. *Stevenson. (d1332).*
MAR, Thomas, 13th E of. *Stevenson. 1332. (d c1377).*
STACI, Thomas. *Birch 13618.* S' THOME FILI THOME STACI. *14 cent. (s of Thos S).*

TALWORTH, Joan de. *PRO-sls BS 8.* S'IOHE DE TALWORTHE. *1350-1. (2nd of 3 shields; w of Arnold de Monteneye).*
TALWORTH, Joan de. *PRO-sls.* S' IOHE DE TALWORTHE. *1350-1. (1st of 3 shields). (w of Arnold de Monteneye).*
TY, Robert. *Birch 14033.* SIGILLUM ROBERTI TY. *1378.*

Arg bend betw 6 cross crosslets fitchy
Arg bend betw 6 crosslets fitchy Gu
   BLAKET. *LE 376.*
Arg bend betw 6 crosslets fitchy Or
   BLAKET, Sr. *CC 234, 396.*
Arg bend betw 6 crosslets fitchy Sa
   ICHINGHAM. *FB 68. (or Tye).*
   LUMHUNLERS. *Q II 559.*
   LUNGUILLERYS. *L9 37a, 12.*
   LUNGVILERIS, Mons J. *WJ 1489.*
   TYE. *Suff HN 27. (Sotherley Ch).*

Az bend betw 6 cross crosslets fitchy
Az bend betw 6 crosslets fitchy Arg
   CHEYNE, of Essilmont. *Lyndsay 384.*
   EWSTAS. *Suff HN 6. (imp by Clopton; Long Melford Ch).*
   HORNSBY, Sir John. *LH 280.*
Az bend Arg betw 6 crosslets fitchy Or
   EUSTACE, Fitz. *CRK 532.*
Az bend betw 6 crosslets fitchy Or
   — *I2(1904)254. (qtd 2 by Sir Wm Barentyn).*
   — *XK 190. (qtd 2 by Sir Wm Barantine).*
   — *LE 371. (qtd 4 by Mylborne, all imp by Rudhall).*
   — *WB I 16b, 11-12. (qtd 2 by Sir W Barontyne).*
   DRAYTON, Sir John. *CRK 1470.*
   GRAYTUN, Suss. *MY 323.*
   MAR, le Conte de. *BL A 16.*
   MAR, le Cunte de. *FW 84. (tinct of crosses unclear).*
   [MAR]. *SC 96. (qtd by Douglas).*
   [MAR]. *Lyndsay 303. (qtd by Douglas, of Drumlanrig).*
   [MAR]. *Lyndsay 96. (qtd by Erskine, E of Mar).*
   [MAR]. *Lyndsay 52 & 56. (qtd by Steuert, E of Mar).*
   [MAR]. *Lyndsay 111. (qtd by Ld Lyle).*
   MAR, le Comte de. *Berry; Stodart B 4.*
   MARE, le Conte de. *Stodart 1.*
   MARE, Mons Daland de la. *TJ 1254.*
   MARRE, E of. *SC 17.*
   SONCIULE, Sr Simon de. *R 102.*

Gu bend betw 6 cross crosslets fitchy
Gu bend betw 6 crosslets fitchy Arg
   — *XK 33. (qtd 2&3 by Jn Vere, E of Oxf, KG).*

— *D4 27b. (qtd 5 by Nevell, Ld Latimer).*
— *XB 14. (qtd by Vere).*
— *Hutton 24. (qtd 10 by Ric Wingfield; N Window, Gray's Inn Hall).*
HAUWARD. *SK 748. (qrs 1&4).*
HAWARD. *PT 87.*
HAWARD, Monsire. *CG 351.*
HAWARD, Sr. *CKO 205.*
HAWARD, Mons Richard. *WJ 1430.*
HAWARD, Sir, Suff. *MY 40.*
HAWARD, E of Surr. *L1 300, 1.*
HAWARDE. *DV 57a, 2249.*
HAWARDE, L[ord]. *AY 64.*
HOUWARD, Sir J. *BW 15, 97. (?crosses formy fitchy).*
HOWARD. *Dingley ccclxv. (qtd by Vere; chancel window, St Andrews in the Wardrobe, London).*
HOWARD. *FB 2. (imp by 'E of Oxf').*
HOWARD. *LH 599. (qrs 1&4).*
HOWARD. *Leake. (qtd 2 by Vere on escutch of Sir Anthony Wingfield, KG, d1553).*
HOWARD. *PLN 1966. (qtd 2&3 by E of Oxf).*
HOWARD, the Lord. *I2(1904)105. (qtg 2 Gu 3 lions pg Or label Arg, 3 Checky Or and Az, 4 Gu lion Arg langued Az; cresc for diffce over all in fess pt; k at Bosworth, 22 Aug 1485).*
[HOWARD]. *Farrer III 9.* 14 cent. *(painted panel, Norwich Cath).*
[HOWARD]. *Proc Soc Antiq XVI 2S 170. (?for Sir Jn H, of Fersfield, fl 1388; banner on 14 cent retable at Norwich Cath).*
[HOWARD]. *PLN 1241. (imp by Lady Mary ...).*
HOWARD, Sir Edmund. *XK 257. (cresc for diffce).*
HOWARD, John. *S 202.*
HOWARD, Sir John. *LH 325.*
HOWARD, Sir John. *PLN 175.*
HOWARD, Sir John. *LH 290.*
HOWARD, Sir John. *CRK 1045.*
HOWARD, Sir John. *LH 153.*
HOWARD, Sir Richard. *LH 586.*
HOWARD, Sir Richard, of Essex. *LH 731.*
HOWARD, Robert de. *WLN 453.*
HOWARD, Sir Robert. *Sandford 212. (m Mgt, dau of Thos Mowbray, D of Norf, d1432).*
HOWARD, E of Surr. *AY 83. (qr 1).*
HOWARD, Sir Thomas, KG. *XK 66.*
HOWARD, Thomas, E of Surr. *WGA 194.*
HOWARD, Thomas, E of Surr. *N 48. (qtg Brotherton, Warren & Mowbray).*
HOWARDE. *Suff HN 2. (imp by 'Oxforde'; College of Sudbury).*
HUNTINGFELD, Saer de. *FW 345.*

Gu bend Arg betw 6 crosslets fitchy Sa
  HAWARDE, S John, Norf. *CY 113, 451.*
Gu bend Az betw 6 crosslets fitchy Or
  — *SK 760.*
Gu bend betw 6 crosslets fitchy Or
  FORNEAUX. *Leake. (qtd 5 by Wm Parr, KG, d1571).*
  FURNEAUX. *CC 226, 140.*
  HANVILLE, Ellis. *LH 259.*
  HAWARD, Mons John. *TJ 1248.*
  PRESTONE, Willame de. *FW 346.*

Sa bend betw 6 cross crosslets fitchy
Sa bend betw 6 crosslets fitchy Or
  BEESTOUN, W. *HA 146.*
  BEESTOUN, W. *RB 414.*
  BEESTOUN, W. *HA 28, 159.*
  BYSTON. *D5 7.*

Bend patterned &c betw 6 cross crosslets fitchy
Az bend countergobony Or and Gu betw 6 crosslets fitchy Or
  — *XF 134. (qtd 2&3 by Az fess Or).*
Gu bend Vair betw 6 crosslets fitchy Arg
  RASE. *L1 557, 6.*
Arg bend lozy of 3 betw 6 crosslets fitchy Sa
  CORNEWALL, John. *S 544.*
  CORNEWAYLLE. *L10 42, 18.*
  CORNWALL. *BA 1271.*
  CORNWALL, John de. *S 550.*

Bend betw 6 crosses formy &c
Sa bend betw 6 crosses formy Arg
  LUNGUILERS, Sr de. *CKO 221.*
Az bend Gu cotised betw 6 crosses formy Or
  — *PLN 1954. (imp by bend Gu 3 ?roses or ?leopards' faces Or).*
Gu bend betw 6 crosses moline Untinc
  — *LS 345. (qtd II&III 2&3 by Strode).*
Per pale bend betw 6 crosses patonce
  — *Cleeve.* 14 cent.
Gu bend Vair betw 6 crosses potent Arg
  PALE, Sr John de. *R 114.*

Bend betw 7 or more crosses
Arg bend Or betw 7 crosslets Az
  DOUGLAS, le Comte de. *Berry; Stodart B 2.*
Gu bend betw 8 crosslets Arg
  HOWARD, Sir John. *BR V 139.*
Gu bend checky Az and Or betw 8 crosslets Arg
  ERUSBY, Sir William. *BR V 148.*
  ORNSBY, Sir John. *BR V 122. (mullet Sa for diffce).*
Az bend betw 8 crosslets fitchy Arg
  CHEYNE. *Lyndsay 485.*
Gu bend of 4 mascles Erm betw 12 crosslets Or
  AUBEMARLE, Dorset. *L2 10, 1.*

Bend betw 3 cups &c

Az bend betw 3 covered cups Arg
   BUTLER, John. *S 289. (as painted)*.
Az bend betw 3 covered cups Or
   BOTTLER, de Beausey, Lancs. *CY 53, 211.*
   BOTTLER, Sir Thos, of Beausey. *BA 36, 341.*
   BUTLER, John. *S 289. (as tricked)*.
Arg bend Sa roundelly Or betw 3 pots Gu
   MONBOUCHER, Sir Barthelmew. *L2 347, 9.*

Bend betw 6 cups

Bend betw 6 covered cups
   BUTLER, Sir Thos. *Mill Steph. 1522. (brass
   to Sir Thos B & w Mgt Delves, Warrington,
   Lancs, now in Warrington Museum)*.
Arg bend betw 6 covered cups Sa
   BOTELER, of Wilts. *PLN 1043. (qtg 2&3 Or
   3 leopards' faces Sa)*.
   BOTELER, of Wilts. *WB IV 170, 799. (qrs
   1&4)*.

Az bend betw 6 cups Or

Az bend Arg betw 6 covered cups Or
   BOTELER, Mons John. *S 287.*
Az bend betw 6 covered cups Or
   BOTELER. *FK II 749. (qrs 1&4; 'of Salop'
   added by Gibbon)*.
   BOTELER. *WB I 33, 16.*
   BOTELER. *PT 880.*
   BOTELER, John. *PLN 1492.*
   BOTELER, Sir John, of Beausy. *CVL 363.*
   BOTELER, of Warrington, & Wem, Salop. *L1
   107, 1; L2 43, 9.*
   BOTELER, William, of Wereinton. *CA 75.*
   BOTILER, Sire Willame le, de Wemme. *N
   962.*
   BOTTELER. *L10 85, 11.*
   BOTYLER. *PO 218.*
   BUTELER, of Werington. *PT 1063.*
   BUTLER. *BG 303.*
   BUTLER. *GY 9.*
   [BUTLER]. *LD 25. (qrs 1&4)*.
   BUTLER, of Beawsey, Lancs. *LY A 4. (qrs
   1&4)*.
   BUTLER, Sir Richard, Lancs. *RH, Ancestor iv
   238.*
   BUTLER, Sir Thomas. *PLN 2018.*
   BUTLER, Sir Thomas. *PLN 1318. (qtg 2&3
   Or lion Gu)*.
   BUTLER, of Warrington. *CRK 254.*
   BUTTELER, Sir Thomas, of Warrington. *WK
   124.*
   WERINTONE. *RB 402.*
   WERINTONE. *HA 132. (used by Boteler
   Grammar School, Warrington)*.
   WERINTONE. *HA 26b, 144.*

Bend betw escallops

Arg bend betw 3 escallops Sa
   COTERELL. *L1 148, 1.*
Sa bend betw 3 escallops Or
   FOLJAMBE, Godfrey. *S 309.*
Barry Or and Az bend Arg betw 3 escallops Gu
   KYNGESHEMEDE. *L1 378, 6.*
Bend betw 5 escallops
   — *Mill Steph. 1493. (qtd 2&3 by Plumpton
   on brass to Jn Southill & w Eliz P, Stokers-
   ton, Leics)*.

Bend betw 6 escallops

Bend betw 6 escallops
   — *Lawrance 21. c1329. (?Sir Ric Gyver-
   ney, dc1329; effigy, Limington, Som)*.
   — *CT 146.*
   [DANIEL]. *Mill Steph. 1462. (brass to Sir
   Sampson Meverell, Tideswell, Derbys)*.
   DESPENSER, Hugh le. *PRO-sls E40 A10910.
   c1310. (sl on will of Sir Robt de Burgerse,
   Demesne of Manor of Tremewnthe to Jn de
   Handlo)*.
   FOLJAMBE. *Arch Journ lxxx 1, 5. 1376.
   (mont of Sir Godfrey F & w Bakewell)*.
   FOLJAMBE. *Mill Steph. 1529. (brass to Sir
   Godfrey F, Chesterfield, Derbys)*.
   FOLJAMBE. *Brit Arch ....Assoc vii 324-5.
   (dex shield on mont of Sir Godfrey F, d1378
   & w Avena, d1383, Bakewell Ch)*.
   FRECHENVILE, Ralph de, of Cruche. *Birch
   9945.* CREDE MICHI. *temp Edw 2.*
   FRECHWELL. *Mill Steph. 1480. (tomb &
   brass to Peter F, of Staveley, Derbys)*.
   VYLERS, Matthew, Warws. *Birch 14190.
   1321.*

Arg bend betw 6 escallops

Arg bend betw 6 escallops Arg (sic)
   FRECHEVILE, Sr de. *CKO 222.*
Arg bend betw 6 escallops Sa
   COTERELL. *L2 141, 7.*
   COTERELL. *L1 148, 1; L2 122, 12.*
   COTERELL. *LE 461.*
   COTERELL. *L10 40, 3.*
   ?WALTON. *CRK 878.*
   WALTON, Whilliam. *WB III 104b, 1.*
   WALTON, William. *CRK 115.*

Az bend betw 6 escallops

Az bend betw 6 escallops Arg
   FRECHELIVE, Anker de. *FW 189.*
   FRECHEUILLE. *L1 243, 2; L2 199, 4.*
   FRECHEVELE. *LE 372.*
   FRECHEVILE. *Coll T&G i 35-37. 1503-1682.
   (Staveley Ch)*.
   FRECHEVILL, Monsr de. *AS 382.*
   FRECHEVILLE, Monsire de. *CG 370.*
   FRECHEVILLE, S'g'r. *RB 162.*

FRECHVILE. *PT 1271.*

FRECHVILE. *CRK 1711.*

FRECHVILE, John. *TJ 269.*

FRECHVYLL, of Staley, Derbys. *CY 73, 290.*

FRESSHVILLE, le Sr. *WJ 1578.*

FRETCHVYLE. *ME 90; LY A 215.*

GUNORA. *BG 88.*

Az bend betw 6 escallops Or

— *BD 86. (qtd by Sir Wm Plumton; window, Hall of York Palace, Southwell).*

DANIEL. *L10 52b, 6.*

DANIELL, John. *E I 574; E II 576.*

FOLJAMBE. *H21 3. (imp by Donham, of Notts).*

Gu bend betw 6 escallops

Gu bend betw 6 escallops Arg

— *LE 402.*

— *PLN 1520. (mullet Gu for diffce).*

Gu bend betw 6 escallops Or

CHAMBERLEYN, Alyn le. *Q 165.*

CHAMRESLEY, Johannes le. *Q II 165.*

CHAUMBLEYN, Johan le. *LM 241.*

Gu bend Vt betw 6 escallops Arg

BRANPEL, Sir Robert. *GA 68.*

Sa bend betw 6 escallops

Sa bend betw 6 escallops Arg

— *CT 312.*

FOLGAMBE. *L1 242, 6; L2 198, 11.*

Sa bend Or betw 6 escallops Arg

— *CVK 767.*

FOLJAMBE, Mons Godfrey. *S 307.*

Sa bend betw 6 escallops Or

— *WB I 41, 15. (qtd 2&3 by Sir W Plumton).*

— *D4 35b. (qtd 2&3 by Plompton, of Plompton, Yorks).*

— *D4 23b. (imp by Donham, of Kerlyngton, Notts).*

FOLCHAMP, Robt de, Derbys. *CY 72, 287.*

FOLEIAMBE, of Walton, Derbys. *L2 211, 2.*

FOLEJAMBE, Sir Godifree, de Watton, Derbys. *I2(1904)148. (qtg, 2 Arg on bend Az 4 crosses formy Or, 3 Arg chev betw 3 escallops Gu).*

FOLGEHAM. *SK 983.*

FOLGHAM. *LE 213.*

FOLGHAM, Sir Alysaundyr, Derbys. *RH, Ancestor iv 234.*

FOLGHAM, Sir R. *WB I 39, 13.*

FOLIAMB, Godefridus. *Q II 606.*

FOLIAMBE. *PT 1207.*

FOLIAMBE, Godfridus. *SES 64.*

FOLJAMBE, Sir ..., Derbys. *CRK 871.*

FOLJAMBE, Godfrey. *BG 233.*

FOLJAMBE, Thomas. *E I 580; E II 582.*

FULCHAMP. *CV-BM 179.*

Bend patterned &c betw 6 escallops

Bend gobony betw 6 escallops

REUDE, Elys de. *Burrows 290 & 308, pl 44.*

...EL...VDE.. *1334.*

Az bend gobony Arg and Gu betw 6 escallops Arg

— *Nichols Leics II 673. (Tur Langton Ch).*

Az bend gobony Sa and Gu betw 6 escallops Arg

— *PLN 664.*

Gu bend Vair betw 6 escallops Arg

BEAUPELE. *SK 277.*

BEOPELL, Devon & Cornw. *L1 81, 3; L2 66, 4.*

BEOPELLE. *CB 243.*

BEUPELL. *L10 28, 14.*

Gu bend Vair betw 6 escallops Or

BEAWPELL. *WB I 19b, 25. (or Saxilby).*

WYLTON, Harry, of Wilts. *RH, Ancestor vii 193.*

Az bend indent Or and Gu betw 6 escallops Arg

CRUS, Mons Robert. *CA 32. (name & blazon tampered with by later hand).*

Az bend voided betw 6 escallops Arg

CRUSE, of Irld. *L2 131, 1. (?2 bendlets).*

Bend betw 8 escallops

Gu bend betw 8 escallops Or

CHAMERSLEY. *Suff HN 42. (imp by Phelipe).*

Bend betw escutcheons

Az bend Or betw 3 escutchs Arg

— *LE 468.*

Bend betw estoile &

Bend engr betw estoile & cresc

BALNE, Henry de. *PRO-sls. 1348-9.*

BINNING, Simon. *Stevenson. 1399.*

Bend betw 2 or more estoiles

Bend betw 2 estoiles

RELTON, Henry de. *PRO-sls.* S HENRICI DE RELTON.

Bend sin betw 2 estoiles

PROFEIT, Mariote, of Gothimes. *Stevenson. 1454. (prob reversed in cutting).*

Bend sin indent on lower side betw 2 estoiles

WILLIAMSON, John, in Petrynole. *Stevenson. 1455.*

Bend betw 3 estoiles

MACGAHAN, Roland, of Wigtons. *Stevenson. 1296.*

Bend sin betw 3 estoiles

COMRIE, John, of Comrie. *Stevenson. 1530.*

Bend sin engr betw 3 estoiles

LUMSDEN, Gilbert. *Stevenson. 1420.*

Sa bend betw 3 estoiles Or

— *WB I 42, 2-3. (qtd 5 by Sir Jn Skypwith).*

Bend betw 6 estoiles
  HETTON, Henry de. *Baker-sls.* Sigillum Henrici de Hetton. 1391. *(name does not appear in deed which relates to Mobberley, Ches, but one of witnesses is Ralph de Hattun, Sheriff of Chester).*
Arg bend betw 6 estoiles Gu
  SHYPMAN, John de, Kent. *CY 158, 630.*
Sa bend betw 6 estoiles Or
  ESTEBY. *L2 184, 12.*
Az bend dancy betw 6 estoiles Arg
  — *CRK 936.*

Bend betw fish
Bend betw 2 fish hauriant
  FREK, William. *Vinc 88, 44. (sl).*
Sa bend betw 2 dolphins hauriant Arg
  — *L10 54b, 2. (fish unclear; qtd 3 by Dawes, of Sharpham, Devon).*
  — *WB I 23b, 15.*
  FRENCHE. *L1 239, 5; L2 198, 2.*
Sa bend Arg betw 2 dolphins hauriant Or
  FRENSHE, of Canterbury. *L1 265, 4; L2 211.*
Gu bend wavy betw 2 dolphins hauriant embowed Arg
  MARTHAM. *CB 139.*
  MARTHAM. *L9 51b, 4.*
  MARTHAM. *L2 341, 10.*
  MARTHAM. *SK 185.*
  SERIANT, Andreas. *CVK 758. (fish unclear).*

Bend betw fleurs de lis
Qtly Gu and Sa bend Untinc betw 2 fleurs de lis Arg
  — *WB I 19b, 8. (qtd 2 by Vt bend Erm, all imp by Waller).*
Bend engr betw 2 fleurs de lis
  — *Keepe. (qtd by Sir Thos Vaughan, d1483; brass [indent only remains]).*
Bend betw 3 fleurs de lis
  REVILL, William. *Yorks Deeds VIII 8. 1528.*
Gu bend Arg betw 3 fleurs de lis Or
  CAUNTELO, Salop. *L2 136, 6.*
Sa bend betw 3 fleurs de lis Or
  SCARBER. *L1 611, 2.*
Qtly Gu and Arg in dex chief bend Or betw 3 fleurs de lis counterch
  — *LE 297.*

Bend betw 6 fleurs de lis
Bend betw 6 fleurs de lis
  — *Bow XXX 1. (qtd 3 on sl by Samson Meverell, Kt, of Throwley, Staffs).*
  — *Durham-sls 2269. 14 cent. (1 of 4 coats on lady's sl; qtd 1 by Clifford, qr 3 Segrave).*
  CROK, Reginald. *PRO-sls. 1322-3.*
  GAYTON, Ralph de. *PRO-sls E40 A1955.*
  SIGILL' RADULFI DE AIT. 1231-2.
  GEYTON, Ralph de. *PRO-sls.* SIGILL RADULFI

D CRI. 1231.
  HAMPTON, John. *Bridgwater 512, 1025.*
  S' IOHANNIS HAMPTON. 1401. *(grant of land in Huyssche).*
  MUNREVEL, Geoffrey de. *PRO-sls.* 1307.
  RUNTYNGES, Robert. *Birch 13164.* S' GREG.-..T...WOD'. 1327. *(s of Reginald R, of Horncastle, Lincs).*
Arg bend betw 6 fleurs de lis Gu
  ELEZ, Sire Robert le fiz. *WNS 26, 57.*
  ELLIS, Fytz. *DV 50a, 1966.*
  ELYS, B Roberte le fitz. *PT 295.*
  ELYS, Fitz. *CV-BM 78.*
  FITZELLYS. *L1 262, 2; L2 193, 6.*
  FITZELY, Robert. *?source.* 1470. *(glass, Waterperry, Oxfords).*
Az bend Or betw 6 fleurs de lis Arg
  — *ME 106; LY A 231.*
Sa bend betw 6 fleurs de lis Arg
  REDMER. *LE 391.*
Sa bend Arg betw 6 fleurs de lis Or
  REDEMER. *PLN 1597.*
  REDMER. *L1 559, 2.*
  REDMER. *DV 61a, 2408.*
  REDMORE. *CRK 833.*
Bend gobony betw 6 fleurs de lis
  TAYLOR, Thomas. *Birch 13881.* ..OV..E.BIEN ME L.... 1312. *(s of Robt le T, of Chatesham, Suff).*
Bend sin gobony betw 6 fleurs de lis
  ALBON, William. *PRO-sls.* 1384-5.
Arg bend of 7 lozs Gu betw 6 fleurs de lis Az
  BELLAN. *L10 23b, 16. (roundel Or on 3rd loz).*

Bend betw flowers
Bend betw 2 roses
  BLUNDE, Rosamund. *Durham-sls 2283. (styled Rosamund of Spen, w of Sir Jn of Egleston).*
Bend betw 2 roses pd
  PARIS, Simon de. *Birch 12381.* SIGILLUM SIMONIS DE PARIS. 1349.
Gu bend betw 2 roses Arg
  — *SK 321.*
Arg bend Az betw 6 roses Gu
  — *CB 19.*
Or bend Az betw 6 roses Gu
  MOOTLOWE, Sir Henry. *CVC 516.*
  MOTLOW, Henry de, Ches. *CY 38, 151.*
Bend engr betw 6 roses
  DENTON, John. *PRO-sls RS 149, HB-SND.* 1364. *(s of Jn of D).*
Or bend engr betw 6 roses Gu seeded Or
  WARNER, Essex. *L1 696, 4.*
  WARNER, of Essex. *CB 31.*

Bend betw foils

Bend betw 6 3foils slipped
HAUVILLE, Robert de, of London. *Birch 10587.* SIGILL' ROB... 1314.

Bend betw pd 5foils
BYDYK, Anthony de, Parcener of Silton Manor, Dorset. *Birch 7993.* 1314. *(5foils indistinct).*

Bend betw 2 5foils
VAUS, Sir John. *Stevenson.* 1396. *(5foils indistinct).*

Arg bend betw 2 pd 5foils Sa
— *PLN 1959.* *(imp Arg fess Az).*

Gu bend engr betw 2 pd 5foils Arg
— *FK II 292.*

Gu bend engr Erm betw 2 pd 5foils Arg
— *FK II 720.*

Bend sin engr betw 3 5foils
FRASER, James, of Frendraught. *Stevenson.* 1402. *('fraises').*

Bend betw 6 5foils
FRISELLE, William. *PRO-sls Ex QR Misc 38/22, HB-SND.* 1323. *('fraises'; baston).*

Bend gobony betw 6 5foils
RODVILE, John, of Lindley, Leics. *Bow XLVII 4.* 1381-2.

Or bend engr betw 6 5foils Gu
WARNERE. *FK II 593.*

Bend betw 6 6foils
CAMBHOUSE, William. *PRO-sls.* 1323. *(s of Jn de C).*

Bend engr betw 6 pd 6foils
WALEYS. *CassPk 317.* SIGILLUM JOHAN .... 18 June 1346. *(indenture of agreement betw Wm Porter, of Stetting & Jn W, of Gt Waltham, re marriage of their children Hen P & Joan W).*

Bend betw frets: see qtly 2&3 fretty over all bend

Bend betw garbs

Bend sin betw garb & unident charge
LEGAT, Thomas, Burgess of Irvine. *Stevenson.* 1512. *(?plant or flames of fire).*

Arg bend Sa betw 2 garbs Gu
QUITFURD. *Lyndsay 383.*

Az bend Arg betw 2 garbs per fess Or and Arg
ALDIS. *FK II 500.*

Bend raguly betw 2 garbs
WALWORTH, William de, Citizen of London. *PRO-sls BS 3.* : Sigillum: Willi: de: Walleworth. 1377-8. *(?bend charged).*

Gu bend raguly Arg betw 2 garbs Or in chf & Arg in base
WALWORTH, Sir Wm, Mayor. *Hutton 118.* 1374 & 1380.

Gu bend raguly Arg betw 2 garbs Or
WALWORTH. *XPat 392, Arch 69, 98.* temp Edw 4.
WALWORTHE. *RB 234.*
WALWORTHE. *LE 328.*
WALWOURTH. *L1 691, 5.*

Gu bend raguly betw 2 garbs Or
WALWURTH, Suss. *MY 344.*

Gu bend raguly Sa betw 2 garbs Or
— *PT 357.*

Gu bend raguly betw 3 garbs Or
RYLLYNGHAULE, Cumb. *L2 296, 1.*

Az bend betw 6 garbs Or
SANDBACH. *Lancs 1533 CS 98, 64.* *(qrs 1&4 of Sir Alexander Radcliffe).*

Bend betw hands

Bend betw 2 dex hands & arms couped
BRAZ, John, of Wyke, Dorset. *Birch 7770.* Sigill iohanis braz. 1417.

Sa bend betw 2 dex hands Arg
BRASE. *FK II 1027.*

Bend betw 1 head (beasts) &

Bend lozy betw stag's head & palm branch
SALIB, Joan. *PRO-sls.* 1365-6.

Sa bend betw ?doe's head in chf & roundel in base Arg
— *Blair N V 217, 456.* *(roof bosses, S transept, Cathedral Ch of St Nicholas, Newcastle-upon-Tyne).*

Bend engr betw cow's head cab in chf & garb in base
CANT, John, Bailie of Montrose. *Stevenson.* 1506.

Bend betw 2 heads (beasts)

Bend checky betw 2 boars' heads couped
FREELAND, Robert. *Stevenson.* ?16 cent.

Bend engr betw 2 boars' heads erased
FLEMING, David, Burgess of Perth. *Stevenson.* 1465.

Bend engr betw 2 stags' heads cab
?NEEDHAM. *Mill Steph.* 1470. *(qtd 2&3 by Urswick on brass to Thos U, Chief Baron of the Exchequer, Dagenham, Essex).*

Arg bend engr Az betw 2 bucks' heads cab Sa
NEDAM, Sir John. *BA 4.*
NEDHAM. *L2 259, 8.*
NEEDHAM, J. *CRK 1738.*
NYDAM, of Shenton. *PT 985.*

Bend engr betw 2 bulls' heads
NETEHAM, Richard. *Birch 12079.* SIGILL' RICARDI NETEHAM. 14 cent.

Bend engr betw 2 bulls' heads erased cab
STRASACKER, Richard de. *Birch 13720.* SIGILL' RICARDI STRESAKIR. early 15 cent.

Vt bend engr betw 2 bulls' heads erased Arg
　　STEERFACE. *LS 174.*
　　STERESACRE. *FK II 546.*
　　STERESACRE, Rychard. *LY A 37.*
Vt bend engr betw 2 bulls' heads erased Or
　　STERYSACRE. *WB I 15, 9.*
Gu bend wavy betw 2 wolves' heads erased Arg
　　— *SK 1116.*

Bend betw 2 heads (birds)

Az bend per bend wavy Or and Gu betw 2 birds'
　　heads erased Arg
　　STALBROOK. *LS 137. (?storks).*
Az bend per bend nebuly Or and Gu betw 2
　　storks' heads erased Arg
　　STALBROOK. *LV 54.*
Az bend vairy Or and Gu betw 2 storks' heads
　　erased Arg
　　STALBROKE, London. *L1 618, 6.*

Bend betw 3 heads (lions) &c

Arg bend Gu betw 3 lions' heads erased Sa
　　PEDERTON. *Gerard 198.*
Arg bend Gu betw 3 lions' heads erased Sa
　　crowned Gu
　　— *I2(1904)180. (qtd 5 by Bamfeld, of Pol-
　　timore, Devon; added by Jos Holand c1630).*
Arg bend Gu betw 3 lions' heads erased Sa
　　crowned Or
　　PEDERTON, Cornw. *L2 409, 11.*
Bend betw 3 leopards' faces
　　FULSHAM, Benet de. *PRO-sls.* 6 Apr 1327.
　　TIMURTHE, Richard de, Surr. *Birch 13947.* S'
　　RICARDI DE TIMVRTHE. 1380. *(alias
　　Tymworthe).*
Bend engr betw 3 leopards' faces jesst de lis
　　DENYS, Sir Walter, d1506. *?source. (brass,
　　Olverton Ch, Gloucs).*

Bend betw 3 heads (other beasts)

Az bend betw 3 boars' heads couped Or
　　GORDOUNE, of Lochinver. *Lyndsay 427.*
Or bend betw 3 boars' heads Sa
　　— *WB IV 170b, 805. (imp by Drew Lysle).*
　　CAMERY. *L1 154, 2. (armed Arg).*
Bend wavy betw 3 boars' heads ?erased
　　ALLARDICE, Jas. *Stevenson 227. (Provost of
　　Collegiate Ch of BVM of the Rock, nr St
　　Andrews, 1497-1506).*
Bend sin betw 3 bucks' heads cab
　　DOYLEY. *Graveney V 1452. ?1453. (qtd by
　　Lewknor; palimpsest brass shield, prob from
　　brass at Stepham, Suss to Jn Bertelot).*
Arg bend betw 3 harts' heads cab per pale Or
　　and Sa
　　BECHE, de. *BA 810.*
Gu bend engr betw 3 bulls' heads erased Arg
　　STERESACRE. *CRK 1606.*

Bend betw 3 heads (birds)

Az bend betw 3 hawks' heads erased Arg
　　CHARTSEY. *L1 154, 4; L2 115, 8.*
Sa bend betw 3 herons' heads erased Arg
　　GELOUER. *L1 281, 1; L2 219, 2.*
Sa bend Gu betw 3 storks' heads erased Arg
　　GELOUER. *FK II 667.*
Sa bend Or betw 3 storks' heads erased Arg
　　GELOVER. *FK a 667.*

Bend betw 3 heads (monsters)

Arg bend Gu betw 3 dragons' heads erased Sa
　　MASSY. *L1 449, 3; L2 330, 11. (langued
　　Gu).*
　　MASSY. *LE 156.*
　　MASSY. *L9 53a, 2.*
　　MASSY, Thomas. *LY A 114.*
Arg bend betw 3 griffins' heads erased Sa
　　— *LE 420.*
　　WALDERN. *L1 688, 4.*
　　WALDERNE, William, of Middx. *WB III 111,
　　9.*
　　WALDRON. *CRK 1603.*

Bend betw 4 heads (beasts)

Bend indent betw 4 boars' heads couped & 2
　　crosslets fitchy
　　GORDON, Janet, Lady Dunachton. *Stevenson.*
　　1528.

Bend betw 6 heads (beasts)

Bend betw 6 lions' heads erased
　　FLAMBARD, Philip. *Birch 9826.* S': PHILIPPI
　　FLAMBARD. 1363.
Arg bend Ermines betw 6 lions' heads erased Or
　　HENSLEY, Thos. *WB III 104b, 3.*
Az bend Arg betw 6 leopards' faces Or
　　FYNCHINFELD. *L1 238, 6; L2 196, 5.*
Bend engr betw 6 leopards' heads
　　DENTON, John de. *PRO-sls.* 1323. *(?this-
　　tles).*
　　DENTON, John de. *Bow LV 19.* Sigillum
　　Johannis de Denton. 1370. *(s of Jn de D, of
　　Newcastle-on-Tyne).*
Bend indent betw 6 boars' heads
　　OLIVER, Robert. *PRO-sls.* 1309-10.
Vt bend Gu betw 6 bulls' heads Arg
　　— *RH, Ancestor vii 231.*

Bend betw 6 heads (monsters)

Gu bend Or betw 6 unicorns' heads couped Or
　　WOMWELL. *PT 1099.*

Bend betw horseshoes

Arg bend wavy Gu betw 2 horseshoes Az
　　HODDESDON, Robert. *LH 769.*
Or bend betw 3 horseshoes Sa
　　CHAUMBRUN. *RH, Ancestor v 177.*

Bend betw insects &c

Bend betw 6 bees

BESTON, Henry de. *Birch 7442.* +Sigillum henrici de beston. 14 cent.

Arg bend betw 6 bees volant Sa

BEESTON. *CRK 1562.*

BEESTON. *BA 3.*

BEESTON, Henry de. *WLN 679.*

BESTON. *L10 27b, 20.*

BESTON. *L1 99, 2; L2 58, 4.*

BESTON. *LE 214.*

BESTONE. *SK 989.*

Arg bend betw 10 bees 4, 6 Sa

BESTON, Henry de, Ches. *CY 34, 135.*

Bend betw knives

Bend betw 6 cheese-knives

HONINGTON, Roger. *Birch 10800.* +S' ROG'I HONIGTO'. 1399. *(sl used by Mgt Pykyng, of Norwich, Norf).*

Bend betw leaves

Bend engr betw 6 ?leaves

DENTON, John of. *Durham-sls 782.* 1332-41. *(?non heraldic).*

Bend betw letters &c

Bend betw letter R & mullet

NEWTON, Robt. *Durham-sls 1888.* 1431. *(?merchant's mark).*

Bend betw lozenges or mascles

Bend betw mascle & cresc

IRELAND, Richard. *Stevenson.* 1464. *(s of Andrew I, Burgess of Perth).*

Bend betw 2 mascles

DURAUNT, Denise. *PRO-sls.* 1348-9. *(wid of Jn D).*

Arg bend betw 3 lozs in chf & 3 picks in base Sa

BOLRON. *BA 38, 364.*

Arg bend betw 5 lozs 3, 2 in chf & 3 picks in base Sa

BOLRON. *L10 86, 11.*

Arg bend betw 5 lozs 3 in chf & 2 in base & 3 hammers 1 in chf & 2 base Sa

BOLRON. *L1 95, 3.*

Arg bend betw 5 lozs in chf & 3 hammers in base Sa

BOLRON. *L2 55, 12.*

Gu bend betw 5 mascles Arg

FREFORD, Mons de. *AS 463.*

Bend betw 6 lozenges or mascles

Bend betw 6 lozs

— *Birch 10470.* 1482. *(used by Rob Hardy, Hurer, Rob Auon, Brewer, Will Edwardes, Woolpacker, & Will Caton, Grey-Tower, all of London).*

Gu bend betw 6 mascles Arg

FREFORD, John. *TJ 1037.*

Gu bend betw 6 lozs Or

— *I2(1904)180.* *(qtd 14 by Sir Ric Grenevile, Kt; added by Jos Holland c1630).*

FITZIVE. *Gerard 54.*

Arg bend engr Sa betw 6 lozs Vt

— *CRK 804.*

— *PT 166.*

Bend Vair betw 7 lozs

BOGHELEGHE, Thomas, of Boycomb in Fareweye, Devon. *Birch 7526.* S' R...... 1386.

Bend betw monsters

Arg bend betw 3 wyverns Az

CREKE, Wautier. *SD 58.*

Sa bend betw 6 wyverns Arg

BENHALE, Mons Roberte. *SD 86.*

Bend betw mullet & ...

Arg bend betw mullet in chf & cresc in base Sa

BESSEMBY. *SHY 293.* *(?field Or).*

Bend betw mullet & roundel

FAUMER, William of. *Durham-sls 956.* 1364.

Bend betw 2 mullets

Bend betw 2 mullets

BELTON, Henry of. *Durham-sls 193.* 1328-36.

?WYGHTMAN. *Mill Steph.* c1455. *(imp [Golofre] on brass to man in armour & w, Wytham, Berks).*

?WYGHTMAN. *Mill Steph.* c1455. *(brass to man in armour & w, Wytham, Berks).*

Bend betw 2 pd mullets

PYEL, John, citizen & merchant of London. *PRO-sls BS 26.* Sigillum iohis pyel. 1329-30 & 1359-60.

Arg bend betw 2 mullets Az

— *ML I 372.* *('sylver a bend asur betwyx ii close molettes of the same').*

Arg bend betw 2 mullets Sa

— *CRK 1216.* *(qtd 3 by Hodelston).*

PEEL. *L1 498, 5.*

PEELL. *L9 97a, 3.*

Arg bend betw 2 pd mullets Sa

— *PLN 936.* *(qtd 2&3 by Hudleston).*

PYEL. *L9 100a, 9.*

PYHELL. *LE 477.* *(or Pygel).*

Arg bend countergobony Arg and Sa betw 2 mullets Sa

HAYLYNWIKE. *LH 707.*

Bend Erm betw 2 pd mullets

PIEL, John, citizen & merchant of London. *Birch 12634.* SIGIL...MI PYEL. 1369.

Gu bend Arg gutty Sa betw 2 pd mullets Arg
   BANGOR, Bishop of. *L10 66b, 2.*
   BANGOR, See of. *N 14. (imp Skevington).*
Gu bend betw 2 pd mullets Erm
   HODENET. *FK II 647.*

Bend betw 3 mullets
Bend betw 3 mullets
   FOWKES, Richard, Rector of Birdbrook.
   PRO-sls. 1393-4.
   STOKE, Richard, Rector of Birdbrook. *PRO-sls.* : DEV: REGTERE: CES: ARMES: T: L: ??.
   1386-7.
Bend betw 3 pd mullets
   PIEL, John. *PRO-sls.* 1371-2.
Arg bend Az betw 3 mullets Gu
   LANGLEY. *Suff HN 39. (imp by Smyth).*
   ('Mr Kempe's house at Cavendish').
   LARGE. *L1 397, 3; L2 307, 5.*
   LARGE. *LE 469.*
   LARGE. *L9 42b, 12.*

Bend betw 6 mullets
Bend betw 6 mullets
   BRETON, Sir Robt. *Lawrance 7. (?d c1345;*
   effigy, Panton, Lincs).
   CROK, Nicholas. *PRO-sls.* 3 May 1374.
   [FURNIVAL]. *PRO-sls.* 1443-4. *(qtd by Jn*
   Talbot, E of Shrewsbury).
   GALEYS, William le. *PRO-sls.* 1347-8.
Bend betw 6 pd mullets
   — *AylesburyM-sls 612/39.* 1365. *(6 pts; sl*
   used by either Wm Clerke or Edm Attewelle,
   of Hertwell).
   GALEYS, William le. *PRO-sls E40 A6971.*
   1347-8.
   HANSARD, John. *Bow XXX 7a.* 1361-2. *(6*
   pts).
   WALTON, Richard de, Parson of Rocheford.
   PRO-sls. 1357-8.

Arg bend betw 6 mullets
Arg bend betw 6 mullets Gu
   BRETON, Piers. *TJ 1168.*
   MOYNE, John. *TJ 1593.*
Arg bend Gu betw 6 mullets Sa
   — *LE 200. (6 pts).*
Arg bend betw 6 mullets Sa
   ARDIS. *L10 5, 8.*
   ARDYS. *L1 5, 4; L2 7, 1.*

Az bend betw 6 mullets
Az bend betw 6 mullets Arg
   HANBY, Anthony. *CRK 541.*
   SAYETON. *L1 581, 1. (Howbye in margin).*
Az bend betw 6 pd mullets Arg
   BRETON, Sr Robt. *CKO 226.*
   HOLBE, Leics. *L2 270, 5.*
   HOUBY, Gilbert de. *Q II 524.*

   HOUBY, Gillis de. *Q 548. (6 pts).*
Az bend Arg betw 6 mullets Or
   BRETON, Mons Robt. *WJ B 710. (6 pts).*
Az bend betw 6 mullets Or
   — *WB I 35, 24.*
   — *PLN 1862. (qtd by Skevington, Staffs).*
   BRETON. *L10 76, 17. (6 pts).*
   BRETON. *PLN 1500.*
   BRETON, Mons. *AS 392.*
   BRETON, Monsire John. *CG 373.*
   BRETON, Mons Robt. *WJ 710. (6 pts).*
   BRETON, Mons Robt. *TJ 274.*
   BRETON, Robt. *TJ 1167.*
   BRETON, Sire Robt. *O 93.*
   BRETON, Sire William. *N 685.*
Az bend betw 6 pd mullets Or
   BRETON, Robert. *S 441.*
   BRETON, Mons Robt. *S 436.*
   HOWBY. *Nichols Leics III 1095. (qtd 2&3*
   by Kynnyan; Ulvescroft Priory).
Az bend betw 6 mullets Or pd Gu
   BRETON, Lincs. *L1 105, 1; L2 60, 3.*
   BRETONNE. *FK II 601. (6 pts).*

Gu &c bend betw 6 mullets
Gu bend betw 6 mullets Arg
   HANSARD, Sire Johan. *N 1019.*
   HANSARD, Sir John. *LH 206.*
   HANSARD, of Westmld. *L1 326, 6; L2 248,*
   12.
Gu bend Arg betw 6 mullets Or
   SETONE, Mons John de. *CA 71.*
Gu bend betw 6 mullets Or
   MONTENEY. *Farrer II 149. (nave roof,*
   Threxton Ch, Norf).
Vt bend betw 6 pd mullets Arg
   PUDSEY. *SK C 737.*
Vt bend Or betw 6 pd mullets Arg
   PUDSEY. *L1 517, 1.*
Vt bend betw 6 pd mullets Or
   PUDSEY. *L9 105b, 6.*
   PUDSEY. *SK A&B 737.*
Per pale Sa and Gu bend Arg betw 6 mullets Or
   — *CB 28.*
Arg bend wavy betw 6 mullets of 6 pts Gu
   FODRYNGEY, Mons J. *WJ 1463.*

Bend betw nails
Vt bend Arg betw 6 nails Or
   TYLER, Sir Wm. *WK 14.*
   TYLER, Sir Wm. *XPat 205, Arch 69, 85.*
   (ktd at Milford Haven 1485).

Bend betw pheons
Bend betw 6 pheons
   WYCHTON, John de. *PRO-sls.* S' IOHIS SPAR
   ?. 1316.

Bend betw picks

Gu bend betw 3 picks Arg
  PIKWORTH, Mons John. *TJ 259.* (*'de goules un bende dargent & trois picois dargent'*).
Bend betw 6 picks
  PICKWORTH, Sir Hugh, of Holme, Selby, Yorks. *Lawrance 35.* c1325. (*effigy, Selby Abbey, Yorks*).
Arg bend betw 6 picks Sa
  PIGOTT. *L2 405, 8.*
  PYGOTT, Mons Randolf. *WJ 1576.*
Gu bend betw 6 picks Arg
  PICKWORTH, Mons de. *CG 360.*
  PIKWORTH, Mons Philip. *WJ 1580.*
  PYKEWORTH, Sr de. *CKO 213.*
Gu bend Arg betw 6 picks Or
  PYCWORTH. *LE 181.* (*?picks Arg*).
Gu bend Or betw 6 picks Arg
  PICKWORTH. *CRK 1822.*
Gu bend betw 6 picks Or
  PICKEWORTH. *L1 518, 6.*
  PIKWORTH, Mons Philip. *WJ B 1580.*
  PIKWORTH, Thomas. *TJ 1319.* (*'...a une bende & vi picois dor'*).
  PYCWORTHE. *L9 103b, 2.*

Bend betw roundels

Arg bend of 5 lozs Az each ch with salt Gu betw 2 roundels Az
  — *ML I 514.* (*'sylver a bend losenge asur sawtryd goules betwyx ii hurtes'*).
Arg bend Az betw 3 roundels Gu
  KAROE, Robt, Middx. *WB III 111, 7.* (*?or Robt Large*).
Arg bend Gu betw 3 roundels Sa
  COTTON. *WLN 286.* (*on escutch of Venables*).
Or bend Az betw 3 roundels Gu
  COURTENEY, of Dorset & Som. *L2 134, 12.*
Or bend betw 3 roundels Gu
  WARNER, John, of Essex. *WB III 106b, 9.*
Sa bend Or betw 3 roundels Arg
  — *WB III 119, 5.* (*?fountains; qtd 3 by Jn Sidnam, Som*).

Bend betw 3 fountains

Sa bend Or betw 3 fountains Ppr
  STORTON. *WB I 29b, 20.*
  STOURTON. *LS 138.*
  STURTON, Sir John. *T b 104.*

Bend betw 6 roundels

Bend betw 6 roundels
  GALEYS, William le. *PRO-sls E40 A4349 & 4351.* 1347-8.
  MEREWORTH, John de. *PRO-sls.* 1340-1.
  PIERS, William, of Odiham, Hants. *Birch 12637.* S' .... 1450.
  STOURTON, Wm, Kt. *SarumC-sls M74/W205*

Drawer I. 1496.
  STOWTON, William. *PRO-sls.* 1542-3.
  WENSLEY, John. *Yorks Deeds VI 116.* 1528.
  WENSLEY, Peter de. *Yorks Deeds VI 115.* 1357.
Arg bend betw 6 roundels Gu
  — *Lancs 1533 CS 110, 202.* (*qtd by Orell*).
Az bend betw 6 roundels Or
  BUKLE. *WB I 43b, 22.*
  [LULLE]. *CRK 1673.*

Gu bend betw 6 roundels

Gu bend betw 6 roundels Arg
  FITZWARYN, de Totley. *BA 473.*
  ZOUCHE, Aymer la. *TJ 277.*
Gu bend Arg betw 6 roundels Or
  CARISIT, Devon. *L1 180, 1; L2 127, 9.*
  FITZWARREN, of Toppley. *L2 210, 3.*
  FITZWARREN, of Totley. *BA 1159.*
  SOUCHE, la. *HA 92.*
  SOUCHE, Amerye la. *HA 23b, 112.*
  SOWCHE, Mons le. *WJ 1424.*
  ZOUCH, Monsire la. *CG 377.*
  ZOUCHE, Sr la. *CKO 230.*
  ZOUCHE, Aumeri la. *RB 422.*
  ZOWCHE, le. *L9 37a, 11.*

Sa bend betw 6 roundels

Sa bend Or betw 6 roundels Arg
  STORTON, Ld. *RH, Ancestor iv 231.*
  STOURTON, Ld. *PLN 172.*
  STURTON, Ld. *AY 66.*

Bend betw 6 fountains

Bend betw 6 fountains
  STOURTON, Edward, 6th Ld. *?source.* 1535. (*imp [Fauntleroy]; tomb, St Peters, Stourton, Wilts*).
  STOURTON, William, of Stourton, Wilts. *Helyar 960/961.* SIGILLUM WILLELMI STOURTON. 1411.
Gu bend Or betw 6 fountains Ppr
  STOURTON, Ld [William]. *PR(1512)68.*
Sa bend Or betw 6 fountains Ppr
  [ST]URTON, Ld. *WK 149.*
  STORTON, Sir. *WB IV 170, 795.*
  STOURETON. *PT 921.*
  STOURTON. *L1 587, 4.*
  STOURTON. *DV 70b, 2783.*
  STOURTON. *CRK 241.*
  STOURTON, Ld. *PLN 2031.* (*fountains painted light blue blotched with white & crossed by wavy lines, all are of more than 6 & some odd in number of divisions & those to dex of bend drawn bendy wavy*).
  [STOURTON]. *WB I 30, 14.*
  STOURTON, Sir J. *BW 14b, 94.*
  STURTON. *BA 463.*
  STURTON, Ld. *BA 818.* (*fountains bendy*

wavy).
STURTON, Sir J. *WB I 37b, 4.*
STURTON, Sir John. *T e 104.*

Bend modified betw 6 roundels
Sa bend Or embattled counter-emb betw 6 roundels Arg
— *SK 423.*
Sa bend raguly Arg betw 6 roundels Or
WALLWORTH. *BA 492.*

Bend betw 10 roundels
Gu bend Arg betw 10 roundels Or
SOWCHE. *FK II 704.*
Gu bend engr Erm betw 10 roundels Or
ZOUCH. *Nichols Leics II 228. (Kirkby Beler Ch).*

Bend betw saltire & ...
Bend engr betw salt couped & boar's head erased
DUDDINGSTON, Thomas, of Kilduncane, Fife. *Stevenson.* 1525.
Bend sin betw salt couped & mullet
WINTER, David, of Abernethy, Perths. *Stevenson.* 1439.
Arg bend betw 6 salts couped Gu
— *CB 24.*

Bend betw staves &c
Arg bend betw 3 croziers Gu
DENHOLLS. *L10 59, 12.*
DONSELL, Devon. *L1 215, 4; L2 160, 11.*
Arg bend Gu betw 3 croziers erect Or
DENSYLL. *BA 1152.*
Arg bend betw 3 ragged staves Az
— *ML I 438. ('sylver a bend betwyx iii raggyd stavys bendey').*

Bend betw wings
Arg bend betw 3 wings Az
BACHELER. *L10 22, 10.*
BACHLER. *L1 106, 6.*

Bend betw wreaths
Arg bend Sa betw 2 chaplets each ch with 4 4foils Gu
STEPHANT, William. *LS 85.*

BEND BETWEEN & LABEL
Arg bend betw 6 martlets Gu label Az
FURNIVAL, William. *B 144.*
[FURNIVALL], Mons Th, son fitz. *WJ 1450.*
FURNIVALL, Wm. *B 148.*
Arg bend betw 6 martlets Gu label of 5 Az
FORNYVAL, Sir Thomas, 'le Filz'. *CV-BM 227.*
Az bend betw 6 martlets Or label of 5 Gu
MUNCEUU. *L9 75a, 4.*
MUNTENY, Ernaud. *E I 642; E II 644.*
Gu bend betw 6 crosslets Arg label Or
HAWARD, Mons John. *CA 178.*
Gu bend betw 6 crosslets fitchy Arg label Or
HAWARD. *LE 291. (label unclear).*

BEND BETWEEN & CHIEF
Arg bend Gu gutty Arg betw 2 birds close Gu chf countergobony Or and Sa
PLAYDELL. *L9 92b, 3.*
PLAYDELL. *XPat 217, Arch 69, 86.*
PLAYDELL. *L10 112b, 3.*
Arg bend Gu gutty Arg betw 2 birds close Ppr chf countergobony Or and Sa
PLAYDELL. *WK 711. (birds have greenish breast with yellow spots & red wings, tail & head).*
Arg bend Gu gutty Arg betw 2 birds close Erm chf countergobony Or and Sa
PLAYDELL, Thomas. *BA 780. (?birds Cornish coughs).*
Bend betw 6 ermine spots ?& chf
GARDA, G de la, of France. *Birch 10021. 1385. (used by Bartholomew Castre, Citizen & Goldsmith of London).*
Bend between 2 mullets chf
PROUSZ, John. *PRO-sls E40 A6964.*
...LAV?. 1395-6. *(mullets of 6 pts).*

BEND BETWEEN & ON CHIEF
Arg bend betw 5 martlets & on chf Gu lion pg Or
BASSINGBOURNE, John de. *MP II 29. ('scutum superius de gules leo aureus, inferius scutum de albo fesse de gules aves de gules').*
Arg bend checky Sa & Erminois betw 2 lions' heads erased Gu on chf Az 3 billets Arg
STYLE. *LS 133. (langued Az).*
STYLE, John, de Tenyrton, Devon. *WK 787.*
Arg bend checky Erm & Ermines betw 2 lions' heads erased Gu on chf Az 3 billets Arg
STYLE. *XPat 227, Arch 69, 87.*

Gu bend Vair betw 2 garbs Or on chf Arg 3 chessrooks Sa
   RICHARD. *LR 79-80. (imp Rokeby).*
   RYCCARDE, Thos, of Yorks. *L10 100, 7-8.*
   RYECARDE, Thomas, de Herteffeld, Yorks. *WK 666.*
   RYECARDE, Thomas, of Herteffeld, Yorks. *BA 711.*
   ?RYETARDE. *LE 484.*
Sa bend Vair betw 2 shovellers & on chf Or 3 5foils Gu
   RAYMOND, Master. *PLN 2066. (qtg II&III 1&4 Gu chev betw 3 [gryphons'] heads erased Or 2&3 Arg fess betw 2 chevs; over all annulet for diffce).*
   REYMOND. *XPat 213, Arch 69, 86. ('of London' added; 5foils pd).*
   REYMONDE. *L10 60b, 7. (5foils pd).*
Bend betw 6 ?choughs on chf 3 ?horses' heads
   GOSTWIKE, John, Kt. *PRO-sls. 1544-5. (Treasurer to Hen 8).*
Bend lozy betw 2 mullets on chf ?roundels
   CHELARDESTON, Roger de, Rector of St Benet Gracechurch, London. *PRO-sls. [1354-5].*
Or bend betw 2 bulls' heads Sa on chf barry of 4 Arg and Gu prior's staff Az bendways
   HOLLATE, Robert, of Holmesworth, Yorks, Bp of Llandaff. *Hare I R36, 157.*

BEND BETWEEN & IN CHIEF

Bend engr betw 3 fleurs de lis in chf annulet
   CLARYNGDON, Robert de, Kt. *PRO-sls E40 A6774. 1379-80.*
Bend betw crosslets in chf cresc
   CLUN, Hospital of. *HB-SND. (sl Cast BG).*
Az bend betw 6 escallops Arg pd mullet Gu in dex chf
   FRESCHEVILE, Mons Rauff. *S 373.*
Arg bend betw 3 wings Az 1, 2 in dex chf mullet Arg
   BACHELER. *FK II 600.*

BEND IN BORDER

Bend in border
   — *Clairambault 2637. 27 Feb 1427. (qtd 2&3 by Thos Clynghin).*
   CLINGHIN, Thomas. *Roman PO 3265. 18 Sept 1436.*
Arg bend Gu border Sa
   FANNEL, of Northants. *L2 209, 7.*
Arg bend Sa border Az
   LAMKYN. *WB IV 161, 637. (qrs 1&4).*
Arg bend in border Sa
   SHY 289. *(qtg 2&3 Gu hart's head couped Or; annulet Or in centre of qrs; 1 or 2 letters cut away from name [presumably Lamkyn]).*
Az bend in border Arg
   OVERTON, of Westmld. *L2 390, 2.*
Az bend in border Or
   SCROPE. *S&G II 279. (glass, Lanercost Priory, ch & refectory).*
Gu bend in border Or
   — *CB 30.*
Qtly Arg & Gu fretty Or bend Az border Arg
   NOERFWIC, Die Bisscop van. *Gelre 57b. c1380. (ie Hy Despencer, Bp of Norwich 1370-1406).*

Bend patterned or modified in plain border

Arg bend dancetty per bend dancetty Or and Az border Gu
   BODIAM, Willame. *FW 657.*
Sa bend flory Or border Arg
   BROMFLETE. *L10 78, 8.*
   BRUMFLETE. *CC 235, 428.*
Bend indented & border
   ACHARD, Robert, Ld of Aldermaston. *PRO-sls. 1335-6. (blazon unclear).*
Gu bend lozy of 5 in border Or
   — *BA 839. (qtd 4 by Sir Philip Herres).*
   MARESCHALL. *L9 73b, 6.*
   MARESCHALL, Sir Ralph. *BA 853.*
Gu bend lozy of 5 Erm border Az
   READ, of S Bradon [in Puckington]. *Gerard 152.*

Bend in patterned border

Arg bend Gu border Erm
   FAUVELL, Mons. *AS 461.*
Bend border gobony
   TREHAMPTON, Sir John. *Lawrance 45. c1350. (shield badly restored & unclear; effigy, Lea, Lincs).*
Bend border countergobony
   — *Birch 12277. 1378. (imp in arms of Mgt de Nuthille, w of Peter de N, of Lincs).*
Arg bend Gu border countergobony Arg and Az
   — *L10 36, 17. (qtd 5 by Cokesey).*
Arg bend Gu border countergobony Or and Az
   — *WB V 95. (?border Or and Sa; qtd 5 by Sir Thos Cokesey, KB 1485).*
   — *WK 31. (qtd 5 by Sir Thos Cokesey).*
   — *WK 57. (qtd 5 by Sir Thos Cookesey, alias Grevell).*
   — *PLN 1988. (qtd 5 by Sir Thos Cokesey).*
   — *XE 113. (qtd 5 by Cooksey).*
   — *L9 22b, 4. (qtd 5 by Kokesey).*
   BREWYS. *PLN 558. (qtg 2&3 by crusily lion Or).*
   BRUESE. *PT 564. (or Brewes).*

Arg bend Gu border countergobony Or and Gu
— *C2 250b. (Chancel windows, Reigate, Surr).*

Bend in border semy &c
Bend in border ch with 8 martlets
ENEFELD, Thomas de. *PRO-sls.* 1336-7.
Arg bend Gu border Sa semy of escallops Or
— *(Sir Hugh ..., of Oxf). WB III 82, 4.*
Arg bend engr Sa border Gu ch with 8 escallops Arg
RADCLIFF, Sir Richard. *WGA 119.*
Qtly 2&3 fretty bend border semy of mitres
SPENCER, Henry. *Birch 2045 & 2047. (Bp of Norwich 1370-1406).*
Arg bend Gu border Sa roundelly Or
FAUREL, Sr. *CKO 190.*
FAUVEL, Hugo. *PT I 8.*
FAUVEL, Mons Roger. *TJ 233.*
FAUVEL, Sire Willame. *N 771.*
FAUVELL, Monsire. *CG 332.*
FAVELL, Gilbertus. *PT II 7.*
Or bend dancetty Or and Az border Gu roundelly Or
BODIAM, William. *A a 139. (query blazon).*
Arg bend lozy of 6 Gu border Sa roundelly Or
BOURRE. *L10 34b, 5.*
Arg bend lozy of 7 Gu border Sa roundelly Or
BOURRE. *L10 23b, 17.*
Untinc bend Untinc border Vair
HUNTERCOMBE, John de, of Bucks, Kt. *Birch 10928. ...HVNTERCVM....* 1362.

Bend in border modified
Bend border engr
— *SHY 345. (imp by [Thwayte]).*
KNEVETT. *Mill Steph.* 1518. *(qtg Cromwell; brass to Eliz, dau of Sir Wm K, Eastington, Gloucs).*
KNYVET, John. *Birch 11111.* SIGILLUM IOHAN... KNYUET. 14 cent.
KNYVET, John, chevalier. *PRO-sls.* 1376.
KNYVET, John, of Essex, Chevr. *Birch 11112.* SIGILLUM: IOHANNIS: KNYUET. 1376.
KNYVET, John, of Northants. *Birch 11114.* SIGILLUM IOHANNIS KNYVET. 1410.
KNYVET, Richard. *PRO-sls.* 1342.
KNYVET, Robert, of Kent, Esq. *Birch 11120.* SIGILLU: ROBERTI: KNYUET. 1396. *(in chf annulet for diffce).*
KNYVET, Thomas, of Essex, Esq. *Birch 11122.* SIGILLU: THOME: KNYUET: ARMIG':. 1421. *(qtg 2&3 3 escutchs each ch with lion [?Harlow]; annulet in chf in qr 1 for diffce).*
[KNYVETT]. *Farrer I 60. (qtg [Cailly] 5 bends; carved in stone over W doorway, New Buckenham Ch, Norf).*
[KNYVETT]. *Farrer I 60. (qtg [Basset];*

carved in stone over W doorway, New Buckenham Ch, Norf).
SWINITHWAITE, William de. *Yorks Deeds II 102.* 1365.

Arg bend in border engr
Arg bend in border engr Gu
— *D4 34b. (qtd by Wandysford).*
MUSTERS, of Yorks. *D5 132.*
Arg bend Gu border engr Or
BILLEMORE, Monsr Roberte. *SD 61.*
Arg bend Sa border engr Az
KNEVET. *?source. (mont of Eliz, d1518, dau of Sir Wm K, Eastington Ch, Gloucs).*
Arg bend in border engr Sa
KNEVET, Sir John, of Essex. *WB III 78, 8. (qrs 1&4).*
KNEVET, Sir Thomas. *L9 22, 8. (qr 1 of 6).*
KNYVET. *WB IV 153, 95. (qrs 1&4).*
KNYVET. *L9 9b, 7.*
KNYVET. *CC 233b, 381.*
KNYVET. *L2 287, 3.*
KNYVET, of Bokenham. *PLN 788. (qtg 2&3 [Clyfton] checky Or and Gu bend Erm).*
KNYVET, Sir Thomas. *XK 103. (Kt 1509; qr 1).*
KNYVET, Sir Thomas. *WK 465. (qr 1, label Az over all qrs).*
KNYVET, of Weldon. *PLN 790. (qtg 2&3 [Fitz Oles] bendy Or and Az canton Erm).*
KNYVET, of Weldon, Northants. *PLN 789. (qtg 2&3 [Bassett, of Weldon] Or 3 pales Gu border Az roundelly Or).*
KNYVETT. *Farrer I 185. (on font, Ashwellthorpe Ch, Norf).*
[KNYVETT]. *Farrer I 58. ((a) alone, (b) qtg Arg [Clifton] checky Gu and Or bend Erm; window, Old Buckenham Ch, Norf).*
KNYVETT, Christopher de. *XFB 150. (qr 1).*
KNYVETT, Sir Ottomarus. *BR II 36. (?Tudor addition).*

Az &c bend in border engr
Az bend Or border engr Arg
WARD. *L1 695, 6.*
WARDE. *PT 745.*
Az bend Or border engr Gu
WARD. *CRK 1983.*
Gu bend in border engr Arg
BECKMOR, Mons Richard de. *WJ 1422.*
BELKEMORE, John. *TJ 280. ('de goules une bende dargent une bordure dargent recercelee').*
BILKEMORE, Monsire de. *CG 339.*
BILKEMORE, Sr Ro[bt] de. *CKO 238.*
BURD, Sr de. *CKO a 238.*
BYKENOR, Robert. *CA 47.*
REWMORE, Sir Richard. *LR 29.*

Or bend in border engr
Or bend in border engr Gu
  MOSTINES. *H21 34b.*

Field patterned bend plain in border engr
Barry Or and Vt bend Gu border engr Arg
  PONYNGS, Mons Nich de. *WJ 843.*
Barry Or and Vt bend Gu border engr Sa
  PONYNGES. *L9 93a, 10.*
Barry Or and Vt bend Gu border engr Erm
  [PONINGES], Mons Michael. *SD 34.* (*'son frere').*
  POYNINGS, Michael. *CA 54.* (*baston).*

Bend patterned in border engr
Bend barry border engr
  DAUNE, Richard. *Durham-sls 775.* c1380.
Gu bend Erm border engr Az
  WALWAYN. *CRK 1157.*
Or bend Vair border engr Gu
  — *RH, Ancestor ix 162.* (*one of the 'olde lordys of tyme past').*

Bend patterned in border engr & patterned
Az bend per pale Gu and Or border engr per pale Or and Gu
  PRYORE, Emonde. *RH, Ancestor ix 167.*

Bend modified in border engr
Bend engr border engr
  RADCLIVE, Robert de. *PRO-sls.* S' ROBERTI DE RADCLIF. 1340-1.
Arg bend engr in border engr Sa
  KNYUET. *L1 372, 1.*

Bend in border indented &c
Bend in border indented
  — *YPhil-sls.* 1361. (*sin of 2 shields on sl of Oliver de Holme, dex: cross formy label).*
Arg bend in border indented Sa
  KNEVET. *WB II 56, 16.*
Gu bend in border wavy Arg
  ?BELKMORE. *ML I 364.*

BEND & IN CHIEF IN BORDER
Bend & in chf annulet in border engr
  KNEVET, Thomas. *PRO-sls.* 1430-1.
Gu bend Erm in sin chf lion Or border Erm
  WALWYN, Elizabeth. (*imp by Humphrey Tyrrell).* *XV I 450.*
Gu bend Erm in chf talbot courant Or in border Erm
  WALLEWEYN, of Longford, Herefs. *LE 290.*
Gu bend Arg in sin chf martlet Or border engr Or
  DANELL. *FK II 629.*
  DANIEL. *FK a 629.*

Gu bend Az in sin chf martlet Or border engr Or
  DANIELL. *PLN 1554.*
Gu bend Or in sin chf martlet Or border engr Or
  DANEL. *L1 199, 4; L2 154, 10.*

BEND BETWEEN ... IN BORDER

Bend betw ... in plain border
Bend betw 6 martlets border
  MONTENEYE, Arnold de. *PRO-sls BS 8.*
  ...RN/VLPDV/S. DE.... 1350-1.
  MOUNTEN, Aernulphus de. *Birch 12034.*
  S' ARNVLPHVS DE MOVNTEN'. 1359. (*alias Mounteney).*

Bend betw ... in border engr
Bend betw 6 martlets border engr
  LUTERELL, Elizabeth. *PRO-sls.* 1380-1. (*formerly w of Andrew L, Kt).*
  LUTRELL, Hugh, of Essex, Suff &c. *Birch 11478.* SIGILLUM: HUG.... 1406.
  LUTTRELL. *Arch Journ xxxviii 63.* (*imp Courtenay on sl of Lady Eliz L, nee Courtenay & sis of Archbp of Canterbury).*
  LUTTRELL, John. *Arch Journ xxxviii 65.* (*traces of label appear to be hanging from top of the shield; s of Sir Hugh L, d1428).*
Arg bend betw 6 martlets in border engr Sa
  LOTTERELL. *PT 848.*
Or bend betw 6 martlets in border engr Sa
  LOTERELLE, Mons Andr. *WJ 1534.*
  LUTREL, Mons Hue. *S 214.*
  LUTTRELL, Hugh. *S 216.*
  LUTTRELL, Sir Hugh. *Arch Journ xxxviii 63.* (*at siege of Rouen, d1428).*
Arg bend engr betw 2 crescs in border engr Sa
  HEDILSHAM. *LE 180.*
  HEDILSHAM. *XO 81.*
  HEDISHAM. *LH 115.*
  HEDISHAM. *LH 1102.*
  HEDYLHAM. *LE 240.*
Bend engr betw 3 crescs border engr
  MOSELL, Thomas. *Stowe-Bard 2s iv 5.* Sigill thome: Mosyll. 1404-5. (*s of Robt M).*
Gu bend betw 2 roses Arg border engr Sa
  — *SK 322.*
Bend engr betw 3 ?cocks' heads border engr
  FLEMMING, William. *PRO-sls.* 1360-1.

BEND IN TRESSURE
Bend checky tressure flory c'flory
   MENTEITH, Sir John, Kt. *Stevenson.* 1343.
   (Ld of Arran, Skipness & Knapdale).

Index of Names

ABBERNON, Rogo de; 108
ABBOT, Isabella; 309
ABEDETOCK, Geoffrey de, Ld of Hyndelepth;
  254
ABEL, John; 45
ABELL, Adam of Brogreve; 254
ABELYN; 2
ABERNETHY; 135, 217, 219
—, Alex, 4th Ld, of Saltoun; 224
—, Sir Alexander; 217
—, The Ld, of Alton; 135
—, Sir Geo, 4th of Saltoun; 108
—, Geo, of Ugstone; 224
—, Sir George, 5th of Saltoun; 217
—, Jean d'; 224
—, Laurence; 217
ABERNYCHEL, Patryk' de; 219
ABIRNETHY, the lord of; 219
—, Ld Saltown; 135
ABITOT, Geoffrey; 264
ABITOTE, Geffrey de; 265
ABRAHAM, Patryark; 212
ABRENTHY, le S'g'r de; 219
ABRISCOURT; 63
—, Sir Sancett de; 63
ACBEECH; 20
ACHARD; 355, 358
—, Joan; 350
—, Mons Richard; 358
—, Sir Richard; 352
—, Roberd; 358
—, Robert; 352
—, Sire Robert; 352
—, Robert, Kt, Ld of Aldermaston; 350
—, Robert, Ld of Aldermaston; 393
ACHART, Piers; 94
—, Robt; 358
ACHE; 253
ACHILLES; 254
ACRE, Joan of; 287
ACTON, Lawrence of; 108
—, Maud of; 108
—, Nicholas; 204
—, Richard de; 141, 153
—, William; 240
ADAM, John; 187
—, Thomas, fitz; 185
ADMER; 68
ADOTTI; 267
AFFABELLUS, Sanctus; 310
AGENALL; 190, 193
AGLIONBY, of Aglionby, Cumb; 37
AGLIONBYE; 37
AGLOMBY, Johan; 37
AGNIS, Radulphus de; 269
—, Thomas de, of Chalfont St Giles & St
  Peter, Bucks; 295
AIGLES; 278
AILNER; 214

AIRTH, Elizabeth; 108
ALAYN, Bryan le fiz; 60
ALBANACTUS; 251
—, King; 251
—, K of Britain; 135
—, 1st K of Scotland; 251
ALBANIACO, Francis de; 135
ALBANO, Gaucelin, Bp of; 271
ALBANY, Duc of; 135
—, d'; 131
—, Robert, D of; 108
—, Robert, D of, Regent of Scotland; 249
ALBARTON; 53
ALBENI, William de; 108, 196
ALBON, William; 386
ALBRYGHTON, Roger, clerk; 269
ALCMADE, Florencius; 108
ALDBURGH, Hugh de; 155
ALDEBURGH, Elizabeth; 109
—, Ivo de, Kt; 109
ALDEBURGHE, William de, of Kirkby Over-
  blow Manor, Yorks, Kt; 109
ALDEFELDE, Mons Robert de; 223
ALDEHAM; 45
ALDER, Robert; 76
ALDINGTON, Henry de; 49
ALDIS; 387
ALDITHLEYA, Ela de; 316
ALDRINGTON; 49
ALEIN; 41
ALEPTREFEUD, Henry de; 332
ALEXANDER; 198
ALEXANDER 3, K of Scotld; 249
ALEXANDER, D of Albany; 249
—, King of Macedon; 198
ALEXANDER THE GREAT; 197-8
ALEXANDER II, K of Scotland; 237, 251
ALEYN, Sire Brian fiz; 60
—, John, of Tacolneston, Norf; 355
ALEYNSCHERLYS, Sir Thomas; 350
ALFORD; 266
ALFREYD, Kynd; 48
ALGERNOUNS, Baron Erll Percy; 133
ALGERNOWE; 133
ALICANDER, Rex; 284
ALIEFF, of Colsoll, Kent; 248
ALINGTON; 353, 373-4
—, of Cambr; 374
—, Sir Giles; 373
—, John; 109
—, William; 353
ALLARDICE, Jas; 388
ALLERTON; 53, 82
ALLESLEE, Richard de, rector of Harrietsham;
  254
ALMAIN, Edmond de, E of Cornwall; 245
ALMAYE, Rex Welmarie d'; 76
ALNWICK; 269
—, William of, Bp of Lincoln; 269

ALTOBOSCO, Peter de; 109
ALVEHAM, Mons' Rauf de; 332
ALVINGHAM, Michael; 30
ALWEN; 304
—, Nich; 305
ALYNGTON; 353, 373-4
—, Essex; 373-4
—, Sir Giles; 374
ALYZAUNDRE, Rex, de Almayne; 294
AMANDE; 196
AMARLE; 63
AMBESAS, or Aumbesas, Willelmus, of
    Carshalton, Surr; 240
AMERLE, le H; 63
AMMARLE; 63
AMMARY; 94
AMMORI, Sire Richard; 94
—, Sire Roger; 330
AMMORY; 330
AMORI, M de; 344
AMUNDEVILLE, Ralph de; 40
—, Richard de; 64
ANDERSON, David; 1
ANDESLE, Sir John; 332
ANDREW, Ralph, of Burenham; 122
—, Wm, of Estbury, Glam; 57
ANDROWEY; 231-2
ANGLE, Mons John d'; 209
ANGLETERRE, le Roy de; 287
—, Roy d'; 287
ANGLIA; 186
ANGLIAE, le Roy; 287
ANGUS, E of; 129
—, Le Conte de; 129
—, Malcolm, 5th E of, 1214-42; 192
ANJOU, Geoffrey, E of; 314
—, Margaret of; 58, 88
—, Q Margaret of; 97-8
ANK, Mons Gregere; 36
—, Mons Gregor de; 36
ANLET; 4
ANLETT; 4-5
ANNAN, Elena, w of Willm de Amnaud &
    after his death of Geo de Wellame; 240
ANNELET; 4-5
ANNESLE, Sr de; 346, 348
—, Mons John; 346
ANNESLEY; 332-3, 346
—, Monsire de; 348
—, Monsr de; 346
—, Sir Hewe, of Anysley; 333
—, Hugh; 332
—, Hugh de; 332
—, John; 333
—, Mons John de; 333
—, Thos of; 332
ANNYSLEY; 333
ANSLE, Sir John; 333
ANSTABETH, Moles de; 37

ANTELFELD, of Herts; 272
ANTINGHAM; 326
—, Bar'; 326
—, Nycho'; 368
ANTYNGHAM; 326, 369
—, Monsire Bartholomew de; 326
—, Mons Bertr; 326
APELTREFEUD, Henry; 348
APHOEL, Cygnen; 200
APLETON; 200
APPELBI, Isabella de; 85
APPELTON; 200
APPELTONE; 200
APPOLTON; 200
APPULBY, W; 291
APPULTON; 200
APSLE, John; 66
APSLEY; 66
APULDERFEILD, Henry de; 332
APULDREFELD, John de; 348
ARABIE, le roy de; 153
ARAGON, King of; 87
ARANDELL, E of, of Suss; 131
ARCHALL, of Salop; 17
ARCHARD; 11, 34, 369
—, Berks; 352
—, Robert; 356
ARCHARDE; 358
ARCHBOLD; 151
ARCHER; 10-11, 139
—, Bro Thos le; 10
—, John of Tamworth, Warws; 10
—, Nicholas le; 11, 139
—, Richard le; 10
—, Richard, Ld of Midleton Hugeford; 10
—, Richard, of Warws; 11
—, Warws; 11
ARCHERD; 358
ARCHIER, Bro Thos le; 10
ARCOURTE, Sr John de; 19
ARCULET, Guille; 59
ARDARN, Randulf de; 148
ARDEN, Waukelinus de; 137
—, Waukelynus de; 133
ARDENA, William de, of Hampton-in-Arden,
    Warws; 122
ARDERN; 148, 169
—, John de; 199
—, Radulf de; 321
—, William de; 285
ARDERNE; 149
—, M de; 138
—, Baudebyn de; 137
—, of Irld; 143
—, Randolf de; 149
—, Randolph de; 150
—, Monsr' Wakelyn a; 139
—, Mons' Wakelyn d'; 139
—, [Sr Wakelyn d'; 139

—, Waklin de; 138
—, Waukelyn de; 138
—, William de; 285
ARDINGEL, Robert, Mechant of the Bardi; 356
ARDIS; 390
ARDREN; 139
ARDYNGTON; 257
—, Sir Robert, of Warws; 257
ARDYS; 390
ARENDEAL, Die Grave van; 131
ARMENIA, K of; 135, 167-8, 246, 372
—, Roy de; 368
ARMENTERS, Johan de; 141
—, Munsire Johan de; 141
ARMONIE, K of; 124, 169
—, Rex; 81
ARMYNE, Le Roy de; 167
ARNALD, Vicar of Ecclesfield, Yorks; 213
ARNALE, M de; 100
ARNODE; 294
ARONDEL, Richart, le Conte de; 131
ARONDELL, Conte de; 131
—, le Counte de; 131
—, Richard de, of Brandon Manor, Warws, Kt; 109
ARONDELLE, E of; 131
AROUNDEL, Hen de; 222
—, Johannes de; 222
ARRONDELL, E of; 131
—, Co de; 131
ARRONDELLE, the erle of; 109
ARRUNDELL, Count le; 131
—, Mons Esm d'; 208
ARTHUR; 63
ARTIN, Sarlo, of Essex; 370
ARTOYE, Janico de; 76
ARUNDEL; 109, 131, 154
—, Counte de; 131
—, E of; 123, 131
—, le Counte de; 131
—, Beatrice, Ctess of Arundel; 109
—, Comes de; 131
—, E of, KG 1525, d1544; 131
—, le Conte d'; 131
—, le Count d'; 131
—, Edmund de; 109
—, Edmund Fitzalan, E of; 131
—, J; 219
—, John, Count of; 131
—, John, E of; 131
—, John, Earl of; 109
—, John de, of Ayno, [Aynho, Northants]; 109
—, John d'; 109
—, Katherine; 319
—, off Warren; 131
—, R' filtz au Count; 208
—, Ricardus, E of; 109
—, Rich E of; 109

—, Richard, E of; 109, 131
—, Richard d'; 109
—, Thomas; 243
—, Thomas, E of; 131
—, Thomas, Archbp of Canterbury; 109
—, Thomas, Archbp of Canterbury, 1397-1414; 109
—, Thomas Fitzalan of, Archbp of Canterbury 1397-1414; 131
—, Thos, E of; 131
—, Thos, Archbp of Canterbury, 1397-1414; 109
—, Sir William of; 131
—, Sir William of, KG; 131
—, William de; 275
—, William, E of; 131
—, William, E of, & Ld Mautravers; 109
—, William, E of, KG; 131
—, Sir William, KG, d1400; 131
—, S Willm de, d1400; 131
ARUNDELL; 122, 131, 222
—, Cont de; 131
—, de; 131
—, E; 131
—, E of; 131
—, le counte de; 129
—, Comes de; 131
—, le Comte d'; 131
—, Le Counte d'; 131
—, Sir Edward de, Kt; 109
—, Fitzallen; 131
—, Sir John; 109
—, Sir John of; 131
—, Ric, E of; 109
—, Mons Rich; 131
—, Thomas, E of; 131
—, Thomas, Archbp of Canterbury; 131
ARUNDELLE, John, Kt; 109
—, William de, chivaler; 109
ARWOD; 294
ASCHEBY; 154
ASCHELEY, of Ches; 336
ASCHETON, Mons Robert de; 46
ASCHFELD, of Suss; 99
ASCHTON, Robert de; 46
ASCHWELL, Elyanora; 185
ASCOLOC, Hector; 254
ASHBURNE, John de, of Lichfield; 1
ASHBY; 14, 18
ASHDOWN; 162
ASHEBY, Sir Robert; 154
ASHENDEN; 162
ASHENDENE; 162
ASHTON, Sir Robert; 46
ASHWAY, Stephen; 158
ASHWEY, Stephen de; 57, 192
ASK, Conan de; 60
—, Conan of; 57, 109
ASKBY, Mons W de; 154

—, William de; 154
ASKE; 57-8, 60, 73, 85
—, of Acton, Yorks; 60
—, of Actone; 60
—, of Aughton, Yorks; 73
—, of Aughtone; 19
—, Mons Conand d'; 59, 98
—, of Eastrington, Yorks; 59
—, Elizabeth; 73
—, Jn of; 57
—, John de; 70
—, Sir John of; 60
—, Katherine; 60
—, Reynold; 59
—, Richd of; 57
—, 'son fitz'; 70
—, of Yorks; 73
ASKEBY, Monsire Robert de; 154
—, S Robert de; 160
—, Mons' Roger de; 154
—, Monsr Roger de; 154
—, Sir Roger de; 154
ASLEBY, Sgr de; 154
ASPOLE, John; 66
ASSCHEBY, Sire Robert de; 154
ASSH'WY, Mons Esteven; 158
ASSHEDON, Robert de; 46
ASSHEFELD; 95
ASSHTON, Monsire Robert de; 46
ASSIRLONDE, Roger; 311
ASSKEBY, s' Rob'; 154
ASTEL; 193
ASTELE, Mons' Thomas; 156
ASTELEY; 124, 190, 230
—, Robert; 193
ASTELL, William of; 229
ASTERLEY, Alice de; 109
ASTLEY; 193
—, Aegidius de; 208
—, Guy de; 195
—, Mons Gye de; 193
—, Sr Robert de; 193
—, Monsire Thos de; 156
—, William de; 109
ASTLY; 193
—, Mons Robert de; 193
ASTON; 222
—, John de, Kt; 3
—, Sir John; 3
—, Robert de; 46
—, Roger de; 349
ASTONE, Sire Richard de; 222
ASTROP; 62
AT WOD; 177
ATHERTON; 53
ATHOL, Sir Aymer of; 186
ATLEE; 128, 176
ATMORE, Henry & his w Johanna; 50
ATON; 30, 67

ATTE HALL, William, of Heyemedwestret; 10
ATTE WODE, Mons John; 177
ATTELLE; 128
ATTEMORE, William; 319
ATTEWODE, John; 109
ATTLODGE, of Chardstock, Dorset; 159
ATTWODE; 202
ATTWOOD; 183
ATWATER; 236, 245
—, William; 245
ATWOD; 177
ATWODE; 247
—, Sr; 177
ATWOOD; 177, 196, 247
—, John; 177, 183
—, [of Worcs]; 177
AUBEMARLE; 381
—, Dorset; 383
AUBERVILLE; 2
AUBRAI; 220
AUBREY, Thomas, of Walton, Surr; 109
AUCHTERGAVIN, Robert of; 109
AUHNO, Wm de; 34
AUK, de; 36
—, Mons' Gregoir de; 36
—, Gregoire de; 36
AUKE, de; 36
AULDMAULDEN, Wm; 202
AUMARY; 94, 330
—, de; 94
AUNFOUR, Sire; 299
AUNGEVYN, William de; 42
—, Willimus; 42
AUNSELL, John; 333
AUNTCROU, John; 319
AUTINGHAM; 326
AVENEBURI, Osbern de; 281
AVENEBURY, Osbern de; 1
AVENEL, William; 204
AVERYNE, Huwe de; 322
AYALA; 267, 271-2
AYLAND; 50
AYLEWARD, Rychard; 50
AYLOFF, de Britagne, Essex; 227
—, of Britsynt, Essex; 227
—, Essex; 227
—, Thos, of Colsoll, Kent; 248
—, William, de Bretains, Essex; 227
—, William, of Bretayne, Essex; 227
AYS, Eustace de, clerk; 205
AYSHEBERTON; 248
AYSSELDON; 162
BOLLYNS, Sr John de; 276
BAA; 168
BAARD; 276
BAARDE; 276
BABELAM, J (sic); 265
BACHELER; 392-3
BACHEPUIS, John de; 109

BACHET; 239
BACHLER; 392
BACHOT; 239
BACKPUS, John de, miles, of Barton, Derbys; 39
BACON; 23, 88, 290
—, George; 290
—, John, of Norf & Suff; 290
BACONTHORP, S' Barth, Norf; 183
BACOT, Mons W; 332
BACOUN, Sire Edmoun; 368
—, Thomas, of Methwold, Norf; 290
BADBY, John of; 321
BADEUE, S' Hugo de, Essex; 321
BADLESMERE; 100
BADSULL, John; 202
BAGENHOLT, S Gefroy de; 237
—, Sr Raulf, of Staffs; 144
BAGOT, S' William; 332
BAGSSHAM; 11
BAIHOUSE, Monsire Robert le filtz; 297
BAILOLL, Edward, Roy d'Scoce; 251
BAINBRIDGE, Christopher, Bp of Durham 1507-08; 12
—, Christopher, Archbp of York 1508-14; 12
BAINTON; 355
BAIOUS, Sr de; 38
BAIOUSE, Mons Goselyn de; 150
BAKEPUCE, Sire Johan de; 40
BAKEPUIZ, John de; 39
BAKEPUS, Emma de; 39
—, Johannes de, dns de Barton; 39
—, Nicholas, of Barton-Bakepuz; 39
BAKEPUZ, Helena; 39
—, Johan de, of Allexton, Leics; 109
—, Dame Johanna, of Bailston, Derbys; 39
—, John de; 39
BAKER, Jennequin; 109
—, John, of Morpeth; 1
BAKON, Maut; 200
BAKPUCE, of Northants & Rutld; 40
BALBIRNY, Alexr, of Inverychty; 192
BALDERSTON, Mons Richard; 125
BALDERSTONE, Richard de, of Preston, Lancs; 195
BALDIRSTONE; 125
BALDRESTON, Mons Richard de; 125
BALDYRSTON, Rycharde; 176
BALIOL, Ada; 334
—, Guy; 1
BALLARD, Tomas; 159
BALLIOL, Edw; 109
—, Edward; 250
—, John; 109
—, John, K of Scotland; 250
—, K of Scotland; 251
BALNE, Henry de; 385
BALOUN, Thomas; 92
BALSHAM, R de; 99

BALUN; 92
—, Johannes de of Merkeley, Heref; 331
—, John de; 92, 98
—, Jon de; 63
—, Reginald de, Ld of Magna Markeleyn, Herefs; 63
—, Sir Walter de; 92
—, Walter de; 92
—, Water de; 92
BAMFELD, of Som; 333
BANBRYG, Edward; 12
BAND, John, Rector of St Nicholas, Cole Abbey; 229
BANESAR, Wat' de; 176
BANGOR, Bishop of; 390
—, See of; 390
BANN; 372
BANY; 372
BAR; 62
—, S Ernaud de; 27
—, S Jehan de; 53
—, Mons Thomas; 62
BARANTYNE; 176
BARBITONSOR, John, burgess of Montrose; 205
BARBY, Thomas, of Irld; 225
BARD; 276
BARDE, Edmund de; 290
BARDEWELL; 82, 204
—, Wyll'm, of Suff; 204
BARDEWELLE; 82
BARDOLF, Ld; 245
BARDSEY; 32
BARDULF, William; 185
BARDWELL; 81-2, 204
—, of Norf; 204
BARE, Mons John de; 53
—, Sir John, of Herefs; 20
—, Tomas, de Calays; 200
BARET; 90
—, de belhows in alvithley Essx; 85
—, William; 99
—, Wm; 90
BARETT, Nicholas, clerk; 57
BAREWASSHE; 177
BARFORD, Master; 200
BARINGETUN, Sr Phil de; 180
BARINGTONE, Sire Felip de; 180
BARKESWORTH, Sir Robert; 279
—, Suff; 372
BARLE; 62, 65, 76, 95, 97
BARLEE, of Derbys; 67
BARLEY; 65, 67
—, Derby; 67
—, Herts; 65
—, of Herts; 97
—, John; 65
—, Ralph; 205
—, Robert, de Barley, Derbys; 67

BARLINGHAM, Sire Richard de; 290
BARLOW; 65
BARLYE, Essex; 99
BARLYNGHAM; 290
BARM, de; 372
BARMYHAM; 246
BARNABE, Sir George of, of Yorks; 277
BARNAK; 332
BARNARD; 200, 269, 278
—, of Hants; 269
—, Sir J; 200
—, Jhon, of Suff; 200
—, Jonh'n, of Suffolk; 200
—, Nycolas; 266
—, le S'r de; 152
—, Roberd; 269
BARNARD CASTLE, Richard of; 201
BARNARDE; 2, 200
BARNARDESON; 81
BARNE; 263, 286
—, of Northendston, ?Bucks; 264
—, Robert le; 264
BARNES, Joh; 52
BARNEWELL, Tomas, Surr; 266
BARNS; 100
BARR, Sir John; 62
—, Mons Thomas; 62
BARRE; 62-3, 66
—, Mons John; 63
—, Sir John; 62, 74
—, Sir John, of Herefs; 62
—, Mons' Robert; 63
—, Syr Johne; 21
—, Sir T; 62
—, Sir Thomas; 62, 90
BARRENKTON, Mons W de; 181
BARRES, Jean de, Seigneur d'Oissorey; 128
BARRET, John, of Suff; 378
—, Sire Stevene; 171
—, William; 99
BARRETT, S'; 22
—, of Irld; 21
BARREY; 62, 327
—, Viscount of; 87
BARRI; 264
—, Bobert; 264
—, Robert de; 264, 287
—, Sire Robert; 264
BARRINGTON, William de; 160
BARRNARD; 278
BARROW; 5
BARRY; 62, 100, 264
—, of Irld; 87
—, John de; 74
—, Mons' John; 75
—, Sir John B; 74
—, Robert; 63
—, Robt; 264
—, Sir Thomas; 21

—, Thomas; 62
—, Sir W; 81
—, Mons William; 272
BARTHOLUS, of Saxo Ferrato; 184
BARTON, Robert, of Overbarnton; 64
BARTUN; 3
BARWARD, S' Johan; 200
BARYNGTON; 181
—, Leics; 180
—, of Leics; 155
—, S Phelip de; 180
BASET, Phelip; 96
BASQUER; 214
—, of Fflytte, IOW; 214
—, Matthew; 214
BASSAT, Adam; 99
BASSET; 45, 63-4, 94-5, 98
—, M; 95
—, Alan; 92
—, Alan, of Wilts; 23, 25
—, of Cornw; 92
—, Ela; 312
—, Ela, Ctess of Warwick; 64
—, Fulk; 93
—, Fulk, Bp of London 1244-1259; 64
—, Gilbert; 93, 96
—, Gilebertus; 143
—, Helewisa; 93
—, Jan Philipp; 64
—, S' Laur'; 92
—, Laurence; 94
—, Lawrence; 94
—, of Leics; 94
—, Margaret; 366
—, Phelip; 96
—, Phelipe; 96
—, Philip; 93, 95-6
—, Philip, of Little Stambridge, Essex; 93
—, Ralph, of Chedle, Kt; 93
—, Sire Rauf; 65
—, S Ric; 45
—, de Sapecote; 95
—, Simon; 25, 95, 99
—, Simon, Kt; 93
—, Symon; 65, 94
—, Thomas, of Cornw; 92
—, Mons W de, de Cornaile; 92
—, Willa; 45
—, Sire Willame; 45
—, Mons' William; 95
—, Sr William, de Cornwail; 92
—, Willimus; 36
—, Wm; 45
BASSETH, Alan; 93
—, Symon; 93
BASSETT; 25, 92-3, 95-7
—, Gilbert; 93
—, S' Joh; 97
—, Sir John; 92

—, Phillip; 96
—, Thomas, de Cornewaille; 92
—, of Umberleigh, Devon; 96
BASSINGBORNE, Thomas de; 374
BASSINGBOURNE, Monsire Giles; 332
—, John de; 392
BASTARD, John; 217
BASTON, Monsire de; 171
BATALYE, Robert, of Sweningtone; 302
BATELSFELD, Thomas de; 305
BATH, Peter of; 46
BATHANANE; 252
BATHE, Eleanor de; 26, 221, 331, 361, 372
—, John, of Wallington, Surr; 109
BAUD, John; 231
—, John, Rector of St Nicholas Cole Abbey;
  152
—, John, Rector of St Nicholas Cole Abbey,
  London; 230
BAUESAR, Walter de; 176
BAUNFELD; 333
BAUSE, Thomas de; 123
—, Sire William; 38
BAVANT, Walter; 55
BAVAUNT; 20
—, Mons Waut; 20
BAVENT; 222
—, Mons Rob; 222
—, Robert de; 174
—, S Robert de; 222
—, Robert, of Forsett, Lincs; 222
BAVER, le Duc de; 330
BAWDE, John; 155
BAWLE, Sir H; 196
BAXBY; 20
BAXTER, Geoffrey, of Lossithe, Co Forfar;
  216
BAXTERD, Tomas, Northd; 295
BAYEMAN; 222
BAYENAM; 187
BAYHOUSE, Richard de; 297
BAYHUSE, S' John de; 38
BAYMONT; 91
BAYNBRYG, Edward; 12
BAYNS; 276, 297
BAYNTON; 358
—, Sir Edward, Kt; 358
—, John; 355
—, Sir John; 324, 358
BAYONS; 38, 87
—, Lincs; 38
—, William de; 38
BAYOUES, Sr William; 38
BAYOUS; 38
—, Monsire de; 38
—, le, de la Marche; 87
—, Richard de; 276
—, Robert de; 276
—, Sire Robert de; 276

—, Mons Waut' de; 38
—, Sir William, dc1327; 38
BAYOUSE; 87
—, Mons Rauf; 87
—, Sire Willame de; 38
BAYOUSSE; 276
—, Mons R de; 276
BAYS, John; 319
—, John, of Hunts; 276
BAYUS, Hunts; 276
BEACHAMP, John de, de Bedford; 337
—, John de, of Bedford; 337
BEAFORD, Marcus, M of Dorsett; 309
BEAMME, King of; 182
BEAMOND; 155
BEAMONDE, Mons John; 226
BEAMONT; 222
—, Le Ct; 231
—, Ld, of Devon; 90
—, le Sire de, of Devon; 89
—, Sir Jean, Viconte; 152
—, Ric, of Whytley, Yorks; 230
BEAMOUND; 152
—, Mons Henry de; 224
BEAMOUNT; 152
—, Ld, of Devon; 90
BEARCROFT, Katherine; 290
BEARNE; 266
BEAUBRAS, Mons Robert de, S' de Porches-
  tre; 100
BEAUCHAMP; 337, 348, 368
—, Ld Bedford; 337
—, Ld of Bedford; 337
—, Ld, of Bedford; 337
—, of Bedford; 337
—, S Jehan, of Essex; 168
—, Sir Jn, of [Fifiel]d; 164
—, Sire Johan de, of Fifelde; 168
—, Johanna de, Lady of Abergavenny; 109
—, Richard; 262
—, Richard, Bp of Salisbury; 258
—, Walter de; 262
—, Will'm; 337
—, William de; 337
—, William, of Bedford; 337
BEAUCHAMPE, John; 168
BEAUFORT; 309
—, D of Somerset; 307, 309
—, Joan; 250
—, Thomas, D of Exeter; 307
—, Thomas de, 2nd D of Exeter; 195
BEAULY, John, de South; 319
BEAUME, le Roy de; 182, 192
BEAUMER, Adomar de; 355
BEAUMOND; 2, 91
—, Le Sire de; 152
—, Andr'; 223
—, le, of Devon; 89
—, Sir Hy de; 220

—, J de; 226
—, Mons J de, of Devon; 89
—, Mons' John, of Devon; 89
—, Mons' Lowys; 222
—, W; 211
—, La Wyscount de; 152
BEAUMONT; 91, 151-2, 155, 222, 226, 230
—, Ld; 152
—, Ld de; 153
—, Le Sr; 123
—, Le Sr de; 152
—, le Sr de; 152, 222
—, Monsire de; 222
—, Sire de; 222
—, Visct; 152
—, Alice de; 220
—, Hen, Ld; 152
—, Sire Henri; 222
—, Henry de, Kt; 151, 220
—, Henry, Ld; 151
—, S Henry; 222
—, S Henry de; 222
—, Sir Henry de; 220
—, Sire Henry; 222
—, Sr Henry; 222
—, Henry de, Count de Buchan; 151
—, Henry, E of Buchan; 222
—, Henry de, Constable of Engld; 220
—, Sr Hy de; 222
—, Isabel de; 109
—, Sr J de, de [devensh']; 90
—, Jn, Ld; 152
—, Johanna; 91
—, John; 91
—, Mons John; 91
—, Sir John, KG; 152
—, John de, 4th Baron; 151
—, John, Visc; 151
—, Katherine de; 220
—, Lewis de; 151
—, Lewis, Bp of Durham 1318-33; 151
—, T de; 222
—, Thomas; 91
—, Thomas de; 151, 222
—, Thomas, Ld of Basqueville; 151
—, Thomas, miles; 91
—, Sir Tomas, of Devon; 22
—, Vicecomes; 152
—, of Whitley, Yorks; 230
—, S William de; 211
—, William; 109, 230
—, William de; 109
—, of Yorks; 230
BEAUMONT & Folkingham, John, Visc; 151
BEAUPELE; 385
BEAUPELL; 348
BEAUPRE; 219, 319
—, Sr de; 219
—, Monsire Ralph de; 220

—, Monsr Rauf de; 219
BEAUPREE; 219
—, Mons' Rauf de; 219
BEAUUER, William de; 109
BEAWPELL; 385
BEBYLEY; 205
BECH, S William; 342
BECHE; 304
—, de; 388
—, John de; 304
—, Mons John de; 304
BECK, Thomas; 34
BECKER, [Lambert]; 109
BECKET; 229
BECKINGHAM; 76
BECKMOR, Mons Richard de; 394
BECONUS, Sr de; 365
—, Monsire Walter de; 365
BEDFFORD, James, co Durham; 62
BEDFORD; 337
—, Ld; 337
—, D of; 301
—, Wylyam; 101
BEDLAM HOSPITAL; 36
BEESTON; 169, 389
—, Henry de; 389
—, Ralph de; 142
—, William de; 220
BEESTOUN, W; 383
BEHAIGRE, le Rey de; 177
BEINTON; 358
BEK, Anthony; 192
BEKE; 34
—, of Berks; 34
—, Thomas; 34
BEKENGES, S' Th; 331
BEKERING; 331, 336
—, Sr Thom de; 331
—, Mons Thomas de; 331
—, Sire Thomas; 331
—, Thomas; 331
—, Thomas de, of Bolington, Lincs, Kt; 330
—, William de; 331
BEKERYNG; 331
—, Mons' Thomas; 331
—, Mons Thomas de; 331
—, Sir Thomas de; 331
—, Thomas de; 330
—, Thomas, esquire; 330
BEKET; 229
BEKINGHAM; 31
—, Thomas; 76
BEKUNS, Walter; 365
BEKYNGHAM; 76
BEKYSWELLE, John; 9
BELCHAMBER; 318
BELEBOCHE, Alexander; 123
BELECHAUMP, Walter; 337
BELEM, Sir Roger de, 'Comes Salop'; 234

BELER; 143
—, Roger; 240
BELESME, Count de Shosber; 234
—, E of Shrewsbury; 234
—, Le Count of Shrosbury; 234
BELGRAVE, Thomas; 323
BELHOUS; 276, 279-80
—, Sr de; 276
—, Isolda de; 275, 340
—, R de; 279
—, Richard; 279
—, Mons Thomas de; 276
—, Thomas; 276
—, Thomas de; 346
—, Thomas de, Kt; 275
BELHOUSE; 280
—, Richard de; 279
—, Theobald de; 346
—, Thomas de; 276
BELISME; 233
BELISMO, Roger de, Salop; 234
BELKEMORE, John; 394
BELKMORE; 395
BELL; 318
—, Andrew, burgess of Edinburgh; 317
—, Bernard, of Melros ?Monastery, & of
  Leith; 317
—, Robert, juror at Coldingham; 318
—, Will, Master of Balliol; 318
BELLAN; 386
BELLE, Stephen; 4
BELLEHOUS, Sir Johan de; 276
—, Thom del; 346
—, Sire Willame de; 309
BELLER, Jacobus; 143
—, James; 143
BELLERS; 143-4, 170, 182
—, Harry, of Stoke; 144
—, James; 143
—, Mons' James; 143
—, John, of Kettleby; 143
—, of Leicester; 170
—, of Leics; 143
—, Mons' Rog' de; 143
—, Roger de; 143, 170
—, Mons Roger de, le fitz; 170
BELLERYS, Sir J; 170
BELLO CAMPO, Guido de, 9th E of
  Warwick; 262
—, Walter de; 254
BELLO MONTE, Henry de, Kt; 151
BELLOCAMPO, Ric de; 164
BELLOMONTE, Henry de; 220
—, Henry de, E of Buchan, 1st B Beaumont;
  220
BELLYNG, Sr de; 381
BELNE, Henry de, of Belne, Worcs; 317
BELSTANES, Stevene de; 331
BELTON, Henry of; 389

—, Richard de; 11
BELYSMO; 234
BEMCLER, Suff; 181
BEME, K of; 182, 184
—, Ye Kyng of; 184
BEMOND, Sir Thomas, of Devon; 62
BEMONDE, le Sour de; 222
BEMOUNDE, Ld; 152
BEMOUNT, Ld; 152
—, Vicount; 152
BEMUND, S' henr; 222
BENDENGES, Peter de; 57
BENDING, Adam de; 57
—, Peter de; 57
BENDLOW; 341
BENDYSH; 342
BENESTED, John of; 74
BENET; 273
—, Betkyn; 107
—, S' Rich'; 244
—, Thomas; 274
—, Willimus; 318
BENETT, Wm; 318
BENGES, John de; 110
BENGHAM, Sire Thomas; 143
BENHALE, Mons Roberte; 389
BENINGEWRD, Walter; 110
BENINGWORTH, Walter de; 110
BENNET, Robert; 274
—, Thomas; 274
BENNETT, of Berks; 274
BENSTEAD, Sir Edward; 81
BENSTED; 81-2
—, Jane Parnel; 81
BENSTEDE; 60, 82
—, Edmund de; 81
—, Edward de, chivaler; 81
—, of Essex; 60
—, John de; 74
—, Sir John; 81
—, Pernella de; 81
BENSTEED; 60
BENTON; 358, 365
—, Nicholas; 356
BENTWORTH; 310-11
BENUS, Robert de; 92
BEOPELL, Devon & Cornw; 385
BEOPELLE; 385
BER; 200
—, of Cornw; 200
BERDESEY, Gilbert de; 32
BERDEWELL; 204
—, William, of Bardwell & Norton; 204
—, Wm; 204
BERDEWELLE, Wy; 204
BERDON, Robert; 3
BERDSEY; 27, 32
BERDWELL; 204
—, Whilliam, of Suff; 204

—, William; 204
—, Sir Wm; 204
BERE; 200, 290
—, John de la; 382
BERECROFT; 290
BEREFORD, Mons Roberte; 352
BERELEY, John; 69
BERELY, John; 101
BERENGER, Sir Ingelram, Kt; 41
BERESFORD; 200
BEREWYK, Hugh de, of Beaconsfield, Bucks, Kt; 110
BERFORD, Sr Robert; 358
BERGHERSH; 177
BERHALGH, Richard; 290
BERHAM; 289
BERKELAIE; 341
BERKELE, Sir Giles de; 334
BERKELEY, Giles; 337
—, Giles de; 337
—, Henry de; 254
—, Nicol de; 257
—, Thomas, of Yorks, Kt; 110
BERKELEYE; 257
BERKLAIE, Giles de; 341
BERKLYE, Mons Nicoll de; 257
BERLAY, Mons' John, d1383; 101
BERMGHAM, Wm de; 355
BERMINGHAM, Sir Fulk; 365
—, Sr Richard; 290
—, Sire Thomas; 365
—, Sr Thomas; 352
—, Water; 352
—, Sir William; 357
—, Sire William; 352
—, William; 352
—, William de; 357
—, William, Ld of; 356
BERMONDSEY ABBEY; 238
BERMYGHAM; 365
BERMYNGEHAM, William de; 346
BERMYNGHAM; 352, 365
—, Fulk de, Chev, of Tamworth, Warws & Staffs; 365
—, Isabella de; 217, 356
—, Sir William de; 352
BERNAK, Mons R; 332
—, Robert de; 331
BERNARD; 200
—, Sir John, of Jersey; 200
—, Robert; 269
—, Th Fitz; 277
—, Th fitz; 278
BERNARDCASTIELL, Richard de, Clerk; 205
BERNARDUS, Clericus Episcopi; 123
BERNEN, Lancelot de; 242
BERNER, John; 217
BERNERS, John, of Bepeden; 217
—, Nicholas, ld of Amberden; 24

—, Thomas, of Essex; 24
BERNES; 45
—, of Cambs; 45
BERNYNGHAM, Richard de; 57
BEROHERSSH, S' Barth, Kent; 177
BERTHORPE; 360
BERTRAM; 138
—, Robert; 138
BERUCH, Duc de; 288
BERVEN; 242
BERWICK; 290
—, Gilbert de; 295
BERWICK-upon-Tweed; 287
BERWYCKE; 290
BERWYKE; 290
BERY; 89
—, John de; 10
—, Raynald de, Kt; 90
BESSEMBY; 389
BESTNEY; 192
—, Mons Edward de; 192
BESTON; 169, 389
—, Sr de; 182
—, Henry de; 389
—, Henry de, Ches; 389
—, Myles de; 169
—, Sir T; 167
BESTONE; 389
BETKYNDENET; 107
BEUCHAMP, of Essex; 168
—, of Fyfelde; 168
—, Johan de; 168
—, Sir John; 168
—, Jon de; 168
BEUERLEY; 101
BEUERLY; 101
BEUMONDE; 155
BEUPEL, Sire Robert; 348-9
—, Sir Robt; 348
BEUPELL; 385
BEUPREY, of Cornw; 218
BEURLY, Mons' reschard, d1387; 101
BEUVES, de Hampton; 287
BEUYLLE; 205
BEVERIDGE, Sir John; 143
BEVERLEY; 101, 105
—, Richard; 105
—, Simond de; 105
BEVILLE, Joan; 205
—, Reginald de; 205
BEVYLE, of Wolston; 205
BEVYLEY, ?of Gowlowris; 205
BEVYLLE, of Woolston; 205
BEWCHAMP, Sir T; 22
BEWCHAMPE; 337
BEWET, John; 205
BEWLEY; 31
BEWME, The Kyng off; 167
BEWMONT, Sir T; 92

BEWYS, Ld; 139
BEXWELL; 9
—, of Norf; 9
BEXWELLE; 9
BEYBORNE; 314
BEYNTON; 358
—, Sir John; 358
—, John, of Wilts; 345
BEYVES, of Hampton; 287
BIGHAM; 143
BIGOD, ...; 325
—, Ld; 143
—, Hugh; 186
—, Erle Marshal; 144
—, Mon' Roger, le Counte de Northfolk; 144
—, Raf; 220
—, Rauf; 144, 220
—, Roger; 142
—, Roger, E of Norfolk, Marshal of England; 144
—, Roger, of Scotld; 142
—, Roger [7th] E of Norfolk, Marshall of England; 110
BIGOT, Erle; 144
—, Roger, Conte de Norfolk; 144
—, Roger, E of Norfolk; 185
BIJGOT, S' Water; 144
BIKELONDE, Mons John; 268
BILKEMORE, Monsire de; 394
—, Sr Ro[bt] de; 394
BILLEMORE, Monsr Roberte; 394
BILLERS; 170
—, of Leics; 143
BILNEVOWE, S Piers de; 128
BILNEY; 30
BINGHAM; 144
BINLEY; 30
—, Sir John; 28
BINNING, Simon; 385
BINOLE, Lambert de; 14
BIRCH 13307; 361
BIRMINGAN, S Thomas de; 365
BIRMINGHAM; 357
BIRMYNGHAM, Willame de; 357
BIRNIGHAM; 357
BISCET, William; 361
BISE, John de la; 202
BISKELE, Richard de, of Frostenden, Suff; 334
BISSART, Lord of Bewfort of auld; 323
BISSET; 319, 323
—, Elizabeth; 319
—, John, of Garmouth; 66
—, Margaret; 254
—, of Rires; 323
—, Wm; 361
BITILISGATE, Thomas de; 343
BLACBORNE, Nycolas, of Yorks; 172
BLACKFORD; 73

BLACKHAM, Benet de; 18
—, Bennet de; 20
BLACKWALL, Richard; 214
BLADWELL; 143
BLAKBORNE, Richard, of Lancs; 173
BLAKE, John 'of the [Walysh]'; 126
BLAKEBORNE, John de; 216
BLAKEFORD; 60, 73
BLAKEHAM, Beges; 20
—, Bennet de; 20
—, Sire Thomas; 21
BLAKELIG, Thomas; 20
BLAKENGHAM; 51
BLAKENHAM, Sr Thomas; 21
BLAKET; 382
—, Sr; 382
—, Bartholomew; 349
—, Sir Emond, Gloucs; 379
—, fitz Edmond; 380
BLAKISTON, Roger of; 37
BLAMMONSTER, Mons Rauf; 209
BLANDE, Mons John; 51
BLANKLEY; 74
BLANSEILE, Robert, burgess of Aberdeen; 56
BLANSON; 4-5
BLAUNFRONT, Sire Thomas; 106
—, Thomas, of Ramenham, Berks; 213
BLAUPRE, Margaret de; 217
BLAUXTON, Wylyam; 37
BLAYKESTON, Roger de; 37
BLEDERYKE, Thomas phyllyp ap, of Wales; 163
BLEDLOWE; 272
—, Thos; 272
BLEMCANSOP, Sir Thomas of; 9
BLENKENSOP; 9
—, Thomas, de Helbek; 9
BLENKENSOPPE; 9
BLENKINSOP; 9
BLISSWORTH; 42
BLODWELL; 142
BLONT, James; 272
—, of Mangersfield; 48
—, Sr William; 96
BLOUND, Walter; 96
BLOUNT; 95-6, 99, 331
—, William le; 95
—, Sir Edward; 65
—, Felipa; 97
—, Hugh; 334
—, Sir James; 272
—, Sir James, Kt 1485; 272
—, Mons John; 25
—, John of Button, Gloucs; 48
—, John le, of ?Sheprigge, Wilts; 93
—, of Mangersfield, Gloucs; 48
—, Mgt, of Mangersfield; 48
—, Baron Mottoye; 96
—, Sir Thomas; 96

—, Thomas; 272
—, Sir Thomas, of Staffs; 97
—, Mons' W; 96
—, Mons Walt; 99
—, Sir Walter; 99
—, Walter, chev, of Burton-on-Trent, [Staffs];
  93
—, Walter, Ld Montjoy; 96
—, Sire Willame; 96
—, Mons William; 96
—, Mons' William; 331
—, Monsire William; 96
—, Sr William; 96
—, William; 95-6
—, William le; 93
BLOUNTE, S'g'r; 331
BLOUT, Edmund; 48
BLUND, William le; 93
BLUNDE, Rosamund; 386
BLUNDEVILLE, Ranulph de, E of Chester;
  110
—, Ranulph, 7th E of Chester; 110
BLUNDUS, William; 3
BLUNT; 93, 96, 331
—, Ld Monjoie; 96
—, William le; 96
—, William le, Kt; 93
BLUNTTE; 65, 272
—, Sir J; 85, 96
BLUNVY; 334
BLYTHE; 302
—, of Blythe, Lincs; 227
—, Galfridus, Bp of Coventry & Lichfield; 302
—, Bp of Lichfield; 302
—, Wm, of Norton, Derby; 292
BOCHE; 98
BOCHYS; 265
BOCKEMESTRE, S' Will'; 151
BOCKINGE, S'g'r; 381
BOCKMINSTER, Monsire; 151
BOCMESTRE, Mons William de; 151
BODEL, John de, of Burwell, Lincs; 371
BODELGATE, of Cornwall; 261
BODIAM, Willame; 393
—, William; 394
BODRUGAN, Mons Wm; 322
BODULGATE; 261
—, Sir John, of Cornw; 283
BODYLSGATE; 258, 261
BODYLSGATES; 261
BOELLES, ... de; 192
BOFTON, Milis de; 169
BOGHELEGHE, Thomas, of Boycomb in
  Fareweye, Devon; 389
BOGREBARIN, William (called); 142
BOGWRTH; 163
BOHAYME, le Roy de; 182
BOHEMIA; 181-2, 184
—, K of; 131, 182, 184

—, King of; 182-3, 187
—, Anne of; 183
BOHUN; 372-3
—, Sire Edmon; 373
—, Henry de, E of Heref & Ld Constable; 372
—, Henry de, E of Hereford; 110, 373
—, Humfrey de, E of Heref & Essex; 372
—, Humphrey de; 192, 373
—, Humphrey de, E of Hereford; 373
—, Humphrey de, (6th) E of Heref; 372
—, Joan de; 355
—, Johanna de, Domina de Kelpek; 359
—, John de, E of Heref & Northamp; 372
BOIS, de; 29
—, Ernaldus de; 27
—, J del; 27
—, J. deu; 18
—, Jehan de; 27
—, Joan du; 27
—, Richard de; 104
—, Richard du; 104
BOKELAND, S Jehan de; 89
—, John; 318
—, John de; 301
—, Monsire John; 301
BOKELANDE; 301
BOKELOND; 268
BOKENHAM; 176, 223
—, John de; 223
BOKESELL, Alan de; 110
BOKESHULL, Sire Alan; 158
—, Sire Alleyn; 158
—, Monsire Mayn; 158
BOKINGHAM, Sgr de; 223
BOKKING, Monsire de; 380
BOKKYNG; 381
—, Mons de; 381
—, Sr de; 381
—, John de; 360
BOKKYNGES; 380
BOKMONSTRE, Sire Willame; 151
—, Sire William; 147
BOKMYNSTER, Monsr de; 151
BOKNOM; 223
BOKSELLE; 158
BOKYNGHAM, of Suff; 124
—, of Suss; 125
BOLBEC; 110, 172
BOLBEK, le Baron Sr Hugh de; 139
BOLE; 205
BOLEBEC; 139, 172
BOLEBEK, Hugh; 157
BOLEGH, of Cornw; 204
BOLHOUS, Essex; 276
BOLKEWORTH, Sr William de; 163
BOLMEER, Die here van; 131
BOLMER, Sire Rauff; 146
BOLMERE; 145
BOLRON; 389

BOLTESHAM, Sire Thomas; 11
BOLTON; 215
BONDE, Simon, Citizen of London; 110
BONERES, Robt of, Merchewood Valley, Dorset, priest; 1
BONNEVAL; 198
BONVILE; 278
—, Ld; 278
—, Wm de; 319
BONVILERS, Baudewyn de; 374
BONYUET; 82
BOOLS; 205
BOOR; 200
BOOUN, Henricus de, comes Herefordiae; 373
BORDET, Leics; 54
—, of Leics; 18
BORDIT, Mons Richard; 18
BORDYT, Mons Roger; 54
BORE; 200
BOREWASCHE; 177
BOREWASHE, Bertelmo de; 177
BOREWASSHE; 177
BORGYLOUN, Sire Robert; 340
BORHUNTE, William de; 14
BORKINGE; 381
BORKYNGES; 380-1
BORNAM; 379
BORNBY, Thomas, of Northants; 36
BORNE, of Norf; 264
—, Thomas; 245
BORNEL; 166
BORNELL, Sr de; 147
BOROWASH; 178
BOROWASHE, Sir Bartholomew; 178
BOROWELL; 333
—, Yorks; 333
BORRESDEN, Sir John de; 319
BORS; 104
—, Nicolas de; 28
—, Richard de; 104-5
BORSE, Nicoll; 28
—, Nicoll de; 28
BORWASTHE; 177
BOSAN; 10-11
BOSARD, Sire Hugh; 53
BOSCO, Ernald de; 28-9
—, Ernaldus de; 14
—, John de, Kt; 27
—, Richard de, Kt; 101
—, Willim de; 27
BOSOM; 11
BOSON; 10
BOSOUN; 11
—, John; 11
—, Sr Jon; 11
—, Ralph; 11
—, Rauf; 11
BOSSON; 11
BOSTON; 169

BOSUM; 11
—, of Devon; 11
—, of Norf; 11
BOTBARNE; 156
BOTBERNE; 156
BOTELER; 21, 37, 290, 305, 384
—, John; 384
—, Mons John; 384
—, Sir John, of Beausy; 384
—, of Warrington, & Wem, Salop; 384
—, William, of Wereinton; 384
—, of Wilts; 384
BOTELEYR, Robert le?; 307
BOTELYER, Robert le; 307
BOTENCUMBE, Thomas, Kt; 319
BOTERELL; 142
BOTEREUX, Monsire de; 348
—, Sr de; 348
—, Mons W; 348
BOTERUX; 348
BOTERWYK, John; 202
BOTEVILLE, Richard; 185
BOTHE, Sr Robt de, of Ches; 3
BOTILER, Sire Willame le, de Wemme; 384
BOTREAUX, le Sire; 348
—, Elizabeth; 110
—, Mons William; 348
BOTTELER; 384
BOTTELLEN; 21
BOTTLER, de Beausey, Lancs; 384
—, Sir Thos, of Beausey; 384
BOTYLER; 384
BOUCE, Soyer; 269
BOUCHQUHENNANE, of that ilk; 251
BOUGHTON; 204
—, Mons' Peris de; 204
—, Piers de; 204
BOULERS, Baldewin de; 374
—, Baldwin de; 341
—, Baudwin; 341
—, Baudwyn; 341
BOULMER, Sr de; 146
BOULOGNE; 129
—, Reynold de; 9
BOULOGNE & Mortain, Wm, E of; 300
BOULTUM, Rauff de; 11
BOURBON; 341, 346
—, le Duc de; 341
BOURDEUX, Peres de; 246
BOURG, Elizabeth de, Lady of Clare; 94
BOURGERISE, Poinsars; 187
BOURGHERSHE, Sir Bartholomew; 177
BOURGHEYCHT; 178
BOURGULYON; 9
BOURGYTON; 340, 371
BOURHILL, Laurence, Sheriff of Lanark; 370
BOURNE, Isabella de; 374
—, Johan de; 331
—, Monsr Thomas; 245

—, S' Thomas de; 245
BOURNUS, of Seygraw; 131
BOURRE; 394
BOURSY, Thomas; 2
BOURTON, of Kynsley, Yorks; 360
BOUTHIN, John de; 212
BOUTREUX; 348
BOVILE; 242
—, John de, of Ardleche; 185
BOWCLES; 242
—, Clo; 201
BOWELES, John, of Colmorde, Beds; 186
BOWELLS; 242
BOWELS; 242
—, John, of Colmorde, Beds; 186
BOWER, Matthew; 91
BOWERE, Elisabeth; 359
BOWES, John of; 203
BOWLMAR, Sir Rowfe, of Yorks; 146
BOWRNE; 331
—, Jacob de, of Kent; 331
—, Jacobus de; 331
BOX, Sire Henri; 373
—, Suss & Surr; 373
BOXA, Henry de, Kt; 372
BOXE, Henry de la; 372
BOXHILL, Monsire; 133
—, Mons Alain de; 158
—, Alan de; 180
—, Sir Alan; 180
—, Mons Rauf; 158
BOXHUL, Suss & Surr; 158
BOXHULL; 158
—, Sir Alan; 180
BOXHYLL, Sir Robard; 158
BOXLEY ABBEY; 366
BOXSTEDE, Sire Rauf de; 348
BOXWELL; 9
BOXWORTH, Sir William; 163
—, Sir Wm, of Cambs; 163
BOXWORZE; 163
BOXWURTH; 163
BOYDELL, of Ches; 1
BOYES; 27
—, Sir Roger; 28
—, Ryc'; 28
BOYLAND; 170
BOYLE; 318-19
BOYLEY; 319
BOYLOND, Sir Robert, of Suff; 128
BOYNTON, William of; 203
BOYS; 27-8
—, Ernald de; 27
—, Ernaldi de; 27
—, Ernaud; 27
—, Mons Henry de; 27
—, Hugh; 28
—, James de; 27
—, James du; 27

—, Jamis deu; 27
—, Jamus de; 27
—, Johan; 27
—, Johannes de; 28
—, John; 27
—, John de; 27
—, John, Kt; 174
—, Sir John; 27
—, S John, of Essex; 27
—, John, of Felmingham, Norf; 28
—, Jon; 27
—, Jon de; 28
—, of Lincs; 27
—, Sir Reynold de; 27
—, Ricard; 104
—, Ricard de; 104
—, Richard; 104
—, Richard de; 105
—, Richard du; 104
—, Richard du, Kt; 105
—, Richard du, of La Seete Manor, Ludlow,
   Salop; 101
—, Roger; 46
—, Roger le; 28
—, Sir Roger; 27
—, Sir Roger de; 326
—, Roger de, of Farnham, Suff; 28
—, Thos, Ld of Manor of Honyng; 14
—, Walter, of Aldham, Yaldham Manor, Kent,
   Kt; 110
BOYSE, Nicolas du; 28
BOYVILE, William; 186
BOYWORTHE, Sire Willame de; 163
BOZAM; 11
BOZOM; 11
BOZOME; 11
BOZON; 11
—, Dominus Wm; 11
—, Johannes; 11
—, Sire Peres; 11
—, Raf; 11
BOZOUN; 11
BRABAN, D of; 139
BRABANT; 139
—, Count of; 209
—, Duke de; 110
—, Henry, D of; 139
—, John, D of; 110, 139
—, Margaret, Duchess of; 139
BRABANT & Louvain, Ancient Duchy of; 110
BRACKLEY; 22-3
BRADDEN, Willimus de; 352
—, Wills de; 358
BRADDENE; 352
—, Sire Geffrey; 352
—, Geoffrey; 356
—, Northants & Rutld; 352
—, William; 352
—, Wills de; 358

BRADESTON; 356
BRADEWARDYN; 91
BRADEWELL, Thomas, of London, Chev; 82
BRADEWELLE, John de; 319
BRADWARDYN; 90-1
BRADWELLE, Th; 82
BRAGDEN; 228
BRAHAM; 326
BRAIBEF; 365
BRAIBOEF, John de; 365
BRAILE, Willm de; 17
BRAILY; 343
BRAIOSE; 110
BRAKELEY; 22-3
BRAKENBURY, Peter de; 319
BRAKINBERI, Cecilia de; 110
BRAMBULLE; 3
BRAMPTON; 110, 128, 259, 349
—, Brian de; 259, 270
—, Sir Bryan; 259
—, of Oxfords; 259
—, Peres de; 267
BRAMSTON, Hue de; 19
BRAMTON; 128, 259
—, Brian de; 259
—, Petr de; 267
BRANC, Robert le, of Magna Shepey; 110
BRANCEPETH; 67
BRANCH; 218
BRANCHE; 218, 223
BRANCHYS; 218
BRAND, Robert; 147
BRANDON; 140, 169-70, 181
—, KG; 172
—, Sir Charles, KG; 169
—, Sir Charles, D of Suff; 169
—, Charles, D of Suff; 169, 179
—, Charles, 1st D of Suff, KG; 182
—, D of Suff; 170
—, Sir Robert; 169
—, Sir Thomas; 169-70, 172
—, Sir Thomas, KG; 169
—, Sir William; 169-70
BRANE; 100
BRANGWEN, John; 237
BRANNCHE; 218
BRANNDESTON, Hugo de; 46
BRANPEL, Sir Robert; 385
BRANSPATH; 67
BRANTONE, Walter de; 267
BRANTYNTHORPE, Laur de; 181
BRAOSE; 182
—, Ld; 148
—, Sir Gilbert; 147
—, of Gower; 230
—, Sir Thos; 146
—, William de; 147
BRASE; 387
BRAUNCH; 218

BRAUNCHE; 218
—, Philip; 217
—, Sir Philip, of Lincs; 218
BRAUNDESTON, Hugh de, Ld of Lapmouth; 46
—, Hugo de; 46
BRAUNDESTONE, Hugo; 46
BRAUNEPATH, John, of Westmld; 32
BRAUSA, ... de; 91
BRAWNE; 67
BRAY; 335
BRAYBEC; 365
BRAYE; 89
—, Gilbert de; 204
—, Mons Reynald de; 89
BRAYLFORD; 30
BRAYLSFORD; 31
BRAYNE, conte; 149
—, de Ponzet; 149
BRAYTOFT; 123, 149
—, Mons de; 147
—, Sr de; 147
—, Le bone W; 123
—, of Braytoft Hall, Lincs; 147
—, Jane; 148
—, Sir William; 230
—, William; 123
BRAYTOFTE; 190
BRAZ, John, of Wyke, Dorset; 387
BREAUS; 146
BREAUSE, Gloucs; 180
BRECKNOCK; 81
BREDEKIRKE, John of; 72
BREDERODE; 135
—, Regnault, seigneur de; 168
BREERTON, Sir John; 17
BREEUS, Johanna le; 170
BREHOUSE, de; 149
BREMBER; 3
—, Sir Nicholas; 4
—, Sir Nicholas, Kt; 3
—, Sir Nicol; 3
BREMBRE, Thomas de, Dean of St.
   Cathberga's Coll Ch, Wimborne, Dorset; 4
BREMBURE, Sir Nichol, Middx; 3
BRENESIN, Margaret; 217
BREOUSE, Norf; 183
—, William de; 147
—, William de, Ld of Gower; 146
—, Wm de; 147
BRERETON; 17
—, Sir ...; 17
—, of Ches; 17
—, Joan; 14
—, Sir John; 17
—, Sr John; 20
—, Randle, of Brereton; 37
—, Sir Randolfe; 17, 54
—, Sir Randolph; 17

—, Syr Randolf, of Ipston; 17
—, Sir William; 17
—, Sir William de; 17
—, Sr William de; 17
—, S' William de, of Ches; 17
—, Sir Wylliam; 17
BRERTON, Andrew of; 17
—, Sir John; 20
—, Thomas, of Ches; 17
—, Mons Will; 17
—, Sir William de; 17
BRERTUN, of Kent; 17
BRESEY; 354
BRESYNGHAM, John; 1
BRET; 149, 155, 347, 377
—, Bertrucat le, of Gascony; 319
—, Ralph le, of Crockerne Stoke, ?Dorset; 110
—, Simon le; 194
—, Walter le; 122
BRETE, Sr Emenuy de la; 1
BRETON, ...; 371
—; 266, 268, 390
—, Mons; 390
—, Guido, dominus de Friereton; 266
—, Monsire John; 390
—, Lincs; 390
—, Piers; 390
—, Robert; 390
—, Mons Robt; 390
—, Robt; 390
—, Sir Robt; 390
—, Sire Robt; 390
—, Sr Robt; 390
—, Sire William; 390
BRETONNE; 390
BRETT; 135, 149, 155, 347
—, Bernard le; 193
—, John; 230
BRETTE; 193, 377
—, Mons Bernard le; 193
—, Edmund de la; 1
—, Eurmenions de la; 1
—, John; 377
—, son fitz de la; 210
BRETTON; 266
BREUS; 62, 183
—, Sir Richard of; 179
BREUSE; 148
—, Monsire de; 148
—, Sir Giles; 183
—, Sire Giles; 155
—, Monsr John; 180
—, Monsire Peres; 171
—, Sire Peres; 183
—, Reynald; 23
—, Reynaud; 23
—, Sire Richard; 183
—, Monsr Thomas; 148
—, Willam; 180

—, Willem; 148
—, Munsire William; 148
—, Sire William; 148
—, Sr William; 180
—, William; 92, 148
—, William de; 92, 95
—, Wm de; 148
BREUUSE, M de; 131
BREUX; 171
BREWASE, William de; 148
BREWES; 146, 170-1, 183-4, 209, 230
—, le Sire de; 148
—, Sir Brian; 148
—, J de, le fitz; 209
—, John; 180
—, John de; 182
—, S' John de; 148
—, Piers de; 171
—, Mons' Reynald; 91
—, Mons' Reynald de; 91
—, Sire Thom'; 149
—, Thomas le; 149
—, Thos; 184
—, Willa de; 146
—, William de; 92, 147
—, S Wm de; 148
—, Wm; 184
BREWIS, Johes de; 21
BREWNE, Sir Tomas; 153
BREWOS, Wm de, Ld of Bramber & Gower; 147
BREWOSE; 148
—, Monsr de; 148
—, John de, of Hasketon Manor, Suff, Kt; 180
BREWOUSE, John de, Ld of Buckingham, Kt; 110
BREWS; 148, 180, 183-4
—, of Bucks; 148
—, Mons John de; 183
—, Mons Piers de; 171
—, S Tho de, of Norf; 128
BREWSE; 147-8, 171, 184
—, Monsire de; 149
—, Johanna le; 174
—, Sir John, of Suss; 146, 148
—, Mons' Thomas; 149
BREWSE OF SUSS; 171
BREWTE; 186
BREWYS; 147, 393
—, Ro; 230
BREYSY, Sr Peres de; 160
BRIAN, M de; 128
BRIDDELESHALA; 79
BRIDDESHALE, S Gilbert de; 40
BRIDESALE, Sire Gilberd; 79
BRIDESHAL, Gilbt de; 69
BRIDGE, John at the; 110
BRIENE, Alice; 110
—, Dame Alice de; 366

BRIENNE; 145
BRIERTON; 17
—, of Brierton, Ches; 17
BRIGG; 82
BRIGHT, William; 149
BRILIANS, S Galiard de; 100
BRIMFFEL; 283
BRIMSTATH, John de; 319
BRINN; 172
BRINTON, Adam de; 180
BRINTONE, Adam de; 180
BRIQUEBEC, Bertram, Sire de, Constable of
  France; 138
BRIRTON, Reynold; 17
BRISBURGH, John, of Suff; 207
BRISEWORTH, John; 218
BRITAIN; 265
—, Albinactus, 3rd s of Brutus; 251
—, K Albrygh of; 213
—, K Alphened of; 213
—, K Alwolfe of; 213
—, K Brecyrall of; 5
—, Brut, 1st K of; 193
—, Brutus, K of; 193
—, K Brutus; 135
—, Brutus, 1st K of; 193
—, Cambrius; 264
—, K Cassibelan; 269
—, K Eguerd of; 213
—, K Engest panim; 129
—, K Engest Panim; 167
—, K Erpenwolde; 157
—, K Erpewolde; 137
—, K Gowan Saracin of; 131
—, K Hungan of; 131
—, K Ida pa'; 200
—, K Kemelyn; 102
—, K Kenwolff; 102
—, K Knoght of; 131
—, K Leyr panim; 142
—, K Mercelyn of; 213
—, K Offred of; 213
—, K Redbald p; 70
—, K Saber of; 5
—, K Sewarde of; 5
—, K Sexrode of; 5
—, K Sweyn of; 131
—, K Sygbert; 157
—, K Urstull; 301
—, K Wylden of; 213
BRITAIN K ARDULFE OF; 213
BRITAINK MARCELYN OF; 213
BRITCHEBURY, Mons' Avery; 29
BRITLEY, Mons Robt de; 264
BRIUS; 194
—, Roberte; 194
BRIUYS, Mons Robert de; 192
BRIWES, Robert de; 192
—, Robt de; 192

BRIWYS, Mons Robert de; 194
—, Mons' Robert de; 194
BROCAS; 110, 190, 265
—, Sir ...; 190
—, Arnald; 233
—, Arnald, clerk; 233
—, Bernard; 188, 190, 210
—, Mons' Bernard; 210
—, Monsire Bernard; 190
—, Monsr Bernard; 190
—, Sir Bernard; 188, 190-1
—, Bernard, of Little Weldon, Northants &c,
  Kt; 188
—, John; 110, 188
—, John de; 110
—, Monsire John; 190
—, Sir John de; 188
—, John, of Basing, Hants, Kt; 110
—, Oliver; 188
—, Wm; 188
—, Wm, of Beaurepaire; 190
BROCHALIS; 289
BROCKEYS; 190
BROCKHULL, Thomas; 211
BROCUS, Barnard; 190
BROGHTON; 27
—, John de; 30
—, of Lancs; 27
—, Nych'; 30
—, Thomas; 30
BROGRAVE; 282
BROK, Hugh de; 334
BROKAS; 190
—, Bernard; 190
—, Mons Bernard; 191
—, Mons' John; 190
BROKE, Thos; 226
BROKES; 188
—, Mons; 190
BROKESBY; 67
BROKEYS; 190-1, 235
—, Barnard; 190
BROKUNBERWG, Edmund de; 110
BROKYSBY, Sir J; 32
—, Notts; 66
BROME; 368
—, William, Vicar of Bakewell, Derbys; 20
BROMEFLETE; 354
BROMEHALL; 155
BROMFLEET, Margaret; 354, 365
—, Sir Thomas; 354
BROMFLET; 354, 365
—, Dns Henricus; 354
—, Henry, Chevr; 354
—, Joanna; 306
BROMFLETE; 326, 354, 365, 393
—, Edward; 248
—, Sir Henry; 354
BROMFLETT; 354

BROMHALE; 139, 154, 156
BROMHALL; 139
BROMPTON; 254
—, Brian de; 259
BROMTON; 157
—, Bauduin; 270
—, Brian de; 259
—, Jon; 270
—, Th de; 157
—, Walter; 267
BROMTONE; 270
—, Brian de; 270
—, Cecilia de; 254
—, John de; 270
—, Walter de; 267
BROMWECHE; 161
BROMWICH; 137, 161
—, John de; 161
BROMWYCH; 161
—, Mons John de; 161
—, Sir John; 161
BROND, alias Catton; 232
—, Robert, prior of Norwich; 232
BRONEBY, S' Nich'; 36
BRONFLETTE, Sir Harry; 354
—, le Sieur Herre; 364
BRONNESWYE; 264
BRONWYCHE; 161
BROOK, Thomas de, Ld of Holditch, Devon; 207
—, Thomas, of Som, Kt; 211
BROOKE; 136
BROTHERTON; 297-8
—, Sir Edmond; 306
—, Marshall of England; 298
—, Sir Thomas; 298
—, Sir Thomas (of); 298
—, Thomas de; 299
—, Thomas of; 297-8
—, Thomas of, Comes Mareschall; 298
BROUGHTON; 16, 30
—, J, of Staffs & Warws; 30
—, Nicholas de; 30
—, Richard; 30
—, Richard de; 30
BROUN; 368
BROUNE, Tomas, Kent; 305
BROUNFLETE, Henry, Kt; 174
BROUNING, of Melbury Sampford; 65
BROUNYNG; 65
BROUNZ, Thomas, of Harwell; 82
BROUSE, Mons John de; 183
BROUTON; 30
BROUTONE; 30
BROWES, Sir Giles; 155
BROWN; 305
—, Sir Anthony; 305
—, David, of Cumbrycolstoun; 110
—, Gilbert, Bailie of Perth; 185

—, Janet; 217
—, of Kent; 305
—, Sir Thomas; 305
—, Thomas, of Kent; 305
—, William; 305
BROWNE; 293, 305
—, Sir Anthony; 305
—, Sir Anthony, KG; 305
—, Sir Anthony, KG, d1548; 305
—, George; 305
—, Stephen; 28
—, of Surr; 305
—, Sir T; 305
—, Thomas; 305
BROWNFLETE, Sir H; 354
BROWNING, of Dorset; 64
BROWNYNG; 65
—, John; 64
BROWNYNGE; 64
BROWTON; 30
BRUCE, Peter, 1st of Skelton; 110
—, Sir Robert; 145
—, Robert, K of Scotland; 250
—, Robt; 110, 192
BRUCE OF SKELTON; 171
BRUCOURT, John de; 89
BRUCURT, John de; 89
BRUEN, Roger de, of [Bruen] Stapleford; 200
BRUESE; 393
BRUITOFT, William; 123
BRUMESFELD; 283
BRUMFLETE; 393
BRUMPTON, John de; 110, 174
BRUN; 161
—, Sr de; 161
—, Sire Richard; 128
—, Mons William; 145
BRUNE, Monsire de; 128
—, Mons Thomas; 153, 161
—, Mons' William; 145
BRUNNE, John, of Wyvelingham, [Willingham, Cambs]; 110
BRUNSWICK; 264
—, D of; 264
—, Le D de; 264
BRUNTOFT, Philip de; 123
—, Philip of; 110
BRUNTON, Walter de; 257
BRUS; 110
—, Peter; 110
—, Peter de; 123
—, Peter of; 110
—, Peter, d1272; 110
—, Piers; 123
—, Simon; 217
—, William; 193
BRUSELL, S. Jamys; 224
BRUT; 195, 331
—, Richard de; 331

—, Thomas, Kt; 330
BRUTE, K; 193
—, Rex; 193
BRUTTE, Robert; 331
—, Robertus; 331
BRUTUS, King; 195
—, K of Britain; 195
—, le roy; 195
BRUYN, J of Cumb; 160
—, John, of Cumb; 160
—, Robert; 110
BRUYNE; 160
—, Johan, of Cumb; 160
BRUYS, Ld of Annandale; 85
—, Mons', de Skelton; 123
—, Ld of Skelton, Yorks; 123
BRWS; 148
—, Suff; 184
BRYDDELSHALE; 41
BRYERTON; 17
BRYEYLSHALL, of Lincs; 79
BRYITTON, Sir John, Wilts; 358
BRYME; 161
BRYMESFYLDE; 283, 285
BRYMMESFELD; 283
BRYNMESFELD; 285
BRYNTONE; 177
BRYS, Monsr Richard; 180
BRYTO, Sir Roger; 19
BRYTTE, Wyllm; 149
BUCK; 249
BUCKE; 249
—, Thomas, de London; 249
—, Thos de London; 249
BUCKESKYN, Peter, of 'Fyschele'; 266
—, Peter, of Fyschelee; 266
BUCKLAND; 301, 318
—, Sir ...; 268
—, John de; 268
—, Matilda de; 301
BUCKMASTER, William; 151
BUCKMOUSTZ, Sr de; 151
BUCKMYNSTER; 231
BUCKSYN, Sire Robert; 266
BUCKTON; 82-3, 204
—, John; 201
BUCTON, John de; 204
—, Thomas de, of Great Harrowden,
  Northants; 291
—, Sir W; 204
—, William; 343
BUERLY, Sir Simon de; 105
BUKCULL, Mons Aleyn; 180
BUKCYLL, Mons Aleyn; 180
BUKELAND; 268
—, Mons J de; 268
—, Mons Th de; 268
BUKES, Walter; 147
BUKESHYLL, Sir Alleyne de; 181

BUKLE; 391
BUKLOND; 268
BUKLONDE, John de; 268
BUKMENSTER; 151
BUKMYNSTER; 151
—, Mons Willm; 151
BUKSTON; 29
BUKTON; 76, 82
—, John de; 204
—, Robert de; 83
BUKTONE, Robert, of Newenton, Suff; 83
BULBEC; 173
BULBECK, Sir Hugh; 64
—, de Sandfort; 99
BULBECKE; 162
—, John, of Kingeston; 70
BULINGTONA, Matildis; 319
BULLEHOUS; 276
BULLMAN; 68
—, John; 68
BULLMER; 146
BULMER; 146, 160, 215
—, Sir de; 146
—, Mons Ansketil, de Shirefhoton; 160
—, Hugh of; 145
—, Johan; 153
—, Sir John; 145
—, Mons' John, de Bulmer; 146
—, Sir R; 145
—, Ralph; 146
—, Ralph, Ld; 146
—, Ralph of; 145
—, Sir Ralph; 142, 146
—, Sir Ralph of; 145
—, Mons Rauf de; 146
—, Monsr Rauf; 146
—, S Rauf; 146
—, Sire Rauf; 146
—, Sir Rauff; 146
—, Sr Rauff; 146
—, Sire Roger; 145
—, of Sherriff Hutton, Yorks; 160
—, Tiphaine; 146
—, William, of Uppisland, Yorks; 228
—, Wm, of Vppisland, Yorks; 228
—, of Yorks; 146, 160
BUR; 145
—, William; 145
BURBUN, Dewke de; 341
BURCESTER, Austin Priory of St Edburga,
  Oxfords; 93
BURCY; 264
BURD, Sr de; 394
BURDEIT, John; 18
—, Robt; 54
BURDET; 54
—, Mons John; 54
—, Sir John; 54
—, Nicolas; 192

—, Sir Oliver; 18, 54
—, Monsire Richard; 18
—, Richard; 18
—, Sr Richard; 18
—, Roberd; 54
—, Sire Robert; 54
—, Robt; 54
—, Monsire Roger; 50
—, Sr Roger; 54
—, Syr John, de Bromcot, Warw, d1528; 54
—, Sir Thomas, of Irld; 54
—, Sire Willame; 18
—, Willame; 18
—, William; 14
BURDETT; 18, 54, 59
—, of Bromcot; 54
—, Nicolas; 185
BURDEUX; 36
BURDEYT, Mons' Richard; 18
—, Mons Roger; 54
BURDON, Nicholas, Kt; 80
BURDUN, of Gloucs, Kt; 80
BURES, Adam de; 52
—, Michael de, of Raydon, Suff; 253
BUREUX, Sr Perez; 246
BUREWASH, Mons Bertelmew de; 177
BUREWASSH, Mons B le fitz de; 210
—, Mons J de; 221
BUREWASSHE; 177, 221
BURG; 336
BURG', Hubert de, Chamberlain of the King; 281
BURGELON, Sir Robert; 372
BURGGES; 336
BURGH; 336-7
—, Elizabeth de, Lady of Clare; 330
—, Hubert de; 289
—, Thomas; 2
BURGHASCH, Barth; 177
BURGHE; 3, 104
BURGHECHE, Monsr de; 177
BURGHERSH; 132, 174, 181, 210
—, Monsire de; 210
—, Barthelmew; 210
—, Mons Barthelmew; 177
—, Bartholomew; 177
—, Bartholomew de; 174, 177
—, Sire Berth; 177
—, Sire Bertilineo; 177
—, Sr Esteven; 177
—, Hereberd; 177
—, John de; 174, 221
—, John de, Kt; 174
—, Margaret de; 145, 174
—, Robt; 174
BURGHERSHE, Mons John; 177
BURGHERSSH, Bartholomew de; 174
—, Bartholomew de, Kt; 174
—, Bartholus; 177

BURGHILL; 333
BURGHULL, Roger de; 333
BURGHULLE; 333
—, Roger de, of Carey, Herefs; 332
BURGO, Eliz de, Lady of Clare; 110
—, Elizabeth de, Lady de Clare; 285
—, Elizabeth de, Lady of Clare; 285, 330
BURGOGNE; 170
BURGOIGN; 202
BURGOLION; 372
BURGOLYONE; 372
BURGON; 11
BURGOYNE; 202-3
—, John; 202
BURGULION; 372
BURGUNDY; 346
—, Palatinate; 128
BURGWASHE; 174
BURHHULL; 333
BURLAY, Mons' Symon; 105
BURLAYE, Mons Simon; 101
BURLAYES, Mons Joh de; 101
BURLEY; 65, 101, 105, 225
—, Sir...; 105
—, John de; 69
—, Sir John; 101
—, Sir John, KG; 101
—, John de, of Salop; 225
—, Mons'r Symond, d1388; 101
—, Mons Rich; 101
—, Sir Simon; 104
—, Simon, KG d1388; 101
—, Thomas de; 73
BURLEYE, Sir John; 101
BURLY, Sir Simon; 101
BURMINGHAM, Willam de; 352
BURMYNGHAM, Sir William; 352
BURNABY; 36
BURNAM; 379
BURNBY; 36
BURNEBY, Eustace; 45
—, George; 36
—, T; 193
BURNEL; 166
—, Ld; 235
—, le Sr le; 235
—, Alicia; 110
—, Edward; 164
—, S. Edward; 166
—, Sire Edward; 166
—, Hue; 218
—, Hugh, KG; 235
—, of Irld; 223
—, Sire Nich'; 173
—, Phelip; 166, 218, 223
—, Phelipe; 218
—, Philip; 166
—, Philippus; 126
—, Robert, Ld of Hodenhulle; 224

—, Robt; 224
—, William, Constable of Dublin Castle; 223
BURNELL; 166, 168, 183, 235
—, Ld; 183, 234-5
—, Ld le; 183
—, le Sire; 234
—, le Sr de; 183
—, Sir ...; 160, 235
—, Sir Edward; 166
—, Edward, Ld of El; 240
—, Hue de; 218
—, Hugh; 218
—, Hugh de, Kt; 110
—, Hugh, Ld; 235
—, Hugh de, Kt, Ld of Holgate & Weolygh; 110
—, Hugh, Kt, Ld of Wyleye; 110
—, Hugo; 110, 218
—, Hugo, dns de Holcot; 235
—, Margaret; 239
—, Margery; 235
—, Merchant, of London; 239
—, of Newton, in Yeovil, Poynington; 374
—, Phelip; 126, 223
—, Philip le; 218
—, Philipp de; 223
—, le Sr, Salop; 182
—, of Staple [Fitzpaine, Som]; 166
—, Walter; 223
—, Willame; 208
BURNELLE; 166
—, Ld; 235
—, Le Sr; 176
—, Hugh, of Great Bradley, Suff, Kt; 164
BURNELLS; 245
BURNHULLE, Roger de; 333
BURNYGHEM, William; 341
BURNYNGHILL, Hugh de; 289
BURSTALL, Robert de; 321
BURTON; 79, 360
—, Alice; 253, 263
—, Henry of; 330
—, John de; 360
—, Thomas of; 51
—, Wathyn; 110
BURTRESSE, Monsire Bartholomew de; 177
BURTTON; 360
BURWACHE; 132
BURWASH, Henry; 174
BURWASSHE; 177
BURY; 332, 374
—, Edward, of Farleigh, Wilts; 360
BUSCHE, Sir J; 59
BUSCRE, John; 370
BUSCY, Oliver de; 217
—, William de, kt; 110
BUSELL, S'g'r; 323
BUSET; 321, 323
—, de; 370

BUSETT; 323, 370
BUSEY, Oliver de; 217
BUSKYN, Ro; 266
BUSSCHON, Bartholomew de; 174
BUSSE; 59
—, Mons William de, of Lincs; 88
BUSSEBY, Sir Myles, Kt; 59
BUSSEY; 59
BUSSY; 59
—, le Sire de; 59
—, Monsr de; 59
—, Sire Huge; 59
—, Sir Hugh de; 57
—, Johannes; 59
—, Mons' John; 59
—, Monsr John; 59
—, Sir John; 59
—, John, of Bernardeston & Kedyngton Manors, Suff & Essex, Kt; 57
—, Sir Miles; 59
—, Sir Mylys; 59
BUSTTES; 323
BUSY, Sr de; 41
BUT'COMBE; 75
BUTELER; 290
—, of Werington; 384
BUTLER; 384
—, of Beawsey, Lancs; 384
—, John; 384
—, Sir John; 176
—, Ralph; 21
—, Sir Richard, Lancs; 384
—, Sir Thomas; 384
—, Sir Thos; 384
—, of Warrington; 384
BUTTELER, of Bedmaton; 21
—, Sir Thomas, of Warrington; 384
BUTTON, Rodger; 142
BUXHULLE, Mons allen; 158
BUXHYLL, Sir Alen; 158
—, Sr Aleyn, Suss; 178
BUXSELL; 372
BUXSTON, Salop; 29
BUXTON; 82
BUYRLEYE, Roger; 345
BUZCI, Oliver de, of Notts, Yorks, &c; 217
BUZOUN, John of Exeter, Devon; 11
BYDYK, Anthony de, Parcener of Silton Manor, Dorset; 387
BYGOD, erll Marishall; 144
—, E Marshal; 144
—, Count Marshall; 145
—, Roger le; 142
—, of Setterington, Yorks; 143
BYGODD, of Setteryngton, Yorks; 144
BYGODE, erle of Norfolk; 144
—, of Setteryngton, Yorks; 143
BYGOT; 144
—, Comes; 144

—, Hugh' le; 132
—, Duke of Northefolk; 144
—, R, comit mareschall; 144
—, Rauf; 220
—, Richard, Count Marshall; 144
BYGOTT; 144
—, Erle of Cambre; 144
—, Comes; 144
BYKENOR, Robert; 394
BYKER; 275
—, Robert of; 32
BYLAND ABBEY; 297
BYLAND MONASTERY, Yorks; 226
BYLLYNGFORTH; 12
BYLSDEN; 79
BYNCWORTH; 311
BYNGHAM; 143
BYNLEY; 27
BYNTWORTH; 311
BYRNELL; 124
—, Mons J; 209
—, Mons Nicoll de; 160
BYRTE; 147
BYRTON; 333
BYSLEY; 338
BYSTON; 383
BYTHEMORE, William, of Nailsea, Som; 142
C'AMUL, Gerardus de; 258
C...hille, Thomas; 40
C...ing, Th; 356, 358
CABELL; 205
CABLE, John, of Frome, Som; 25
CADURCIS, Thomas de, Kt; 72
CAILLI, Edmund de; 330
CAILY, Richard; 349
CALAIS, Mayoralty of; 200
CALESTHORPE, Sir William de; 275
CALETOFT, Philip de; 77
CALEY, William, of Scratby, Norf, Kt; 363
CALEYS, [Town of]; 79
CALF; 295
—, Roesia; 295
CALFOURE, Hugh de, of Bathequelle,
  [Bakewell], Derbys; 111
CALIN, Phelipe de, ?clerk; 361
CALLANDER; 373
—, of that ilk; 373
CALLE, Thomas; 371
CALSTON; 37
—, Thomas; 36
—, Thomas, of Wilts; 37
CALTHORP; 221
—, Isabel; 25
—, Mons John de; 218
CALTHORPE; 325
—, John de; 270
CALTOFT, Monsire de; 161
CALVE; 295
CALVERLAY, John de, of Calverley, Yorks;

225
CALVERLEY, Walter, of Stanley, Yorks; 203
CALY, of Norf; 344
CAMAYL; 201
CAMBER; 264
—, King; 264
CAMBHOUSE, William; 387
CAMBRIDGE, Wm; 23
CAMELL; 201
—, of Queen Camel, Som; 201
—, John de; 266
CAMERA, Johannes de; 111
CAMERON; 58
—, of Ballegarno; 58
—, E of Gowrye; 89
—, John, Bp of Glasgow, 1427-46; 58
—, Sir Robert, of Balegrenack, Kt; 58
—, Robert, of Balegrenach; 65
—, Wm; 79
—, Wm, Prior of St Andrews, 1469-82; 58
CAMERY; 388
CAMMELL, of Som; 291
CAMMVILLE, Mons J; 283
CAMOIS, John de; 324
CAMPEGIUS, Laurence, Bp of Salisbury; 226
CAMPVILLE, Henry de; 254
CAMVIL, Gerard de; 259
CAMVILE; 283
—, of Charlton Horethorne; 283
—, Geffrai de; 283
—, Geffray; 283
—, Sr Geffrey; 283
—, John; 283
—, William; 283
—, Wm de; 283
CAMVILLE; 281, 286
—, Geffery; 282
—, Geffrey; 282
—, Geoffrey de; 1
—, Willelmus de; 188
CAMVYLE, William de; 297
CANBELLANUS, Philip; 123
CANBILL; 276
CANFELD; 66
CANT; 379
—, Sir Charles, parson of Orphir; 215
—, John, Bailie of Montrose; 387
CANTERBURY, Archbp Reynolds of; 285
CANTWELL; 5
—, of Irld; 5
CANVILL; 276
CANVILLE, William de, Ld of LLanstephan;
  281
CANVYLE, Thomas de; 283
CANYS; 62
CAPEL; 150, 227
—, Sir Giles; 232
—, of Stibbyng, Essex; 227
—, Sir William; 227

CAPELL; 227, 230, 232
—, Henry de, of Denham, Bucks; 26
—, Syr Gyles, de Stebbyng, Essex; 232
—, Sir William; 150
—, Sir Wm; 227
CAPELLA, John de la; 204
CAPELLE, [Sir William; 150
CAPRAVILLA, Wm de, of Reydon, Suff; 204
CARESSWELLE, S' William; 81
CARESVILLE, Jhon; 81
CARESWALL, Sir Piers de, Notts; 57
CARESWELL; 81
—, Mons William de; 82
CARESWOLL; 82
CAREW; 281, 284, 288, 309
—, Baron; 284
—, Baron of; 284
—, Monsire de; 284
—, The Baron of; 284
—, Barone of; 284
—, of Crowcombe; 284
—, Sir George; 167
—, Sir J; 284
—, Johan; 284
—, Sire Johan; 297
—, John; 281, 284
—, S' Jon; 284
—, Mayster; 284
—, Montgomery; 284
—, of Mounsausery, Devon; 284
—, Sir Nich de; 284
—, Sir Nich, KG 1536; 284
—, Nicholas; 282
—, Nicholas, Baron; 282
—, Nicholas de; 282, 284
—, Sr Nicholas; 284
—, Sir Nicholas, of Mitcham & Morden, Surr,
   Kt; 282
—, Nicholas de, Ld of Mulesford; 282
—, Monsr Pers de; 81
—, Robert of; 111
—, Syr John; 284
—, Syr Wylliam, of Devon; 284
—, Thomas de, Kt; 282
—, Sir Thos; 282
—, Monsire William; 284
—, Sir William; 284
—, William; 284
CAREWE; 284
—, le Seigneure de; 284
CARINGTON; 315
CARISIT, Devon; 391
CARKOWE, Kyng of; 64
CARLINGSONE, Richard; 285
CARLIOL, Henry of; 205
—, John of; 184
CARMENAW; 366
CARMENOW; 323
CARMINAW; 366

—, Thomas, of Devon; 366
CARMINOU, Monsire de; 363
—, Roger de; 319
CARMINOW; 323, 363
—, Alice de; 361
—, of Cornw; 363
CARMYNAW; 363
CARMYNOU, Mons Thomas; 363
—, Thomas de, Kt; 319
CARMYNOUN, Sr de; 363
CARMYNOW; 363
CARMYNOWE, Devon; 323
CARMYON; 363
CARNABE, Sir Renold; 42
CARNABY, Sir Reynald, Kt, of Northd; 49
—, Mons William; 42
—, William of; 354
CARNET, Nycholas; 305
CARNOT, William, Visct; 374
CAROW; 284
—, Sir Nich', of Bodington, Surr; 284
CAROWE, Baron of; 288
CARREU; 284
—, Le Baron de; 284
—, Nicholas de; 282
—, Sir Nicholas; 282
—, Nicholas de, Ld of Muleford; 282
CARREW, John de, Ld of; 282
—, Sir Nicholas; 282
—, Nicholas, of Nutfield Manor & Beddington
   &c, Surr; 282
CARREWE, Mons John de; 284
CARRICK, Le Comte de; 252
—, John, E of; 252
CARROU, Mons John de; 284
CARRU, Eleanor de; 240, 254, 282
—, John de; 282
—, Nicholas de, Constable of the Castle of
   'Bothvile'; 282
CARSWELL; 75
CARSWELLE; 81
CARTHORP; 325
CARTHORPE; 325
CARTHORPP; 325
CARTMEL PRIORY; 123
CARTMELL MONASTERY, Yorks; 144
CARU, Sir Richard; 284
CARY; 284
CARYSWALL, of Staffs; 57
CASSATT; 92
CASSE; 334
CASSIBELLANUS, King; 269
—, K of Great Britain; 262
CASTEL; 22
CASTELL; 22
CASTELLO, William de; 29
CASTEN, le Sire de; 62
CASTERTON, Geoffrey de; 85
CASTILE, K of; 125

CASTRE, William of; 212
CASTRIE, Robert de, of Killingholm, Lincs; 334
CATELYN; 302
—, of Raude, Northants; 306
—, Rob, of Rands, Northants; 306
CATESBY; 261, 265, 271
—, of Catesby, Northants; 261
—, Geo; 261
—, George; 265
—, Sir Humphrey; 271
—, John; 254
—, John de; 262
—, John de, of Assheby Leger, Northants; 261
—, Mary; 261
—, Mr; 261
—, William; 261
—, Wm, of Ashby Ledgers; 263
CATHCART, James, of Carbiston; 2
CATLYN, Sir Robert, Lord Chief Justys; 302
CATRIK, John; 291
CATTE; 266, 291
CATTON, James; 374
CATTYSBY, Sir H; 261
CATYSBE; 261
CATZENELENBOGEN, Count of; 192
CAUDRAY; 349
CAUFELD; 72
CAUMVILE; 283
—, Monsire de; 283
—, Mons Hugh de; 283
CAUMVILLE; 283
CAUNDYS; 178
CAUNTELO, Salop; 386
CAUNTON, J'hon, de Warwick; 252
—, Joh de Warwick; 252
—, John, de Warwick; 252
—, John, of Warwicks; 252
—, of Leics; 40
—, of London; 252
CAUNTONE, Sr Johan; 40
CAUNVILE, de; 283
CAUNVILL, Richard de; 185
CAUNVILLE, Sir William de; 254
CAVERSHAM; 2
CAVYS; 62
CAWNE; 158
—, Mons Th; 158
—, S Tho; 179
—, S Tho, Staffs; 179
—, Sir Tho, Staffs; 179
—, Sir Thomas; 179
CAYLI, Sr Adam; 344
CAYLY; 344
CAYNES; 62
—, Robert de; 90
—, Robert de, Kt; 91
CELY; 228
CENDALE, Sr Robert de; 362

CENDR', Mons Hew; 321
CERNE, Philip; 236
CESTRE, le Conte de; 307
CESTRIAE; 274
CESTRIE; 274
CHAIRS, Herevi de; 341
CHALLONS; 50
—, of Devon; 50
CHALMERS, Robert; 111
—, Wm; 225
CHALON; 19, 56
—, le Counte; 325
CHALOND, Sir John; 50
CHALONDE; 50
CHALONS; 50
—, Devon; 50
—, Mons Robert; 49
—, Sir Robert; 50, 57
CHALOUNS; 50
CHALOURS, Sir Robt, of Devon; 50
CHALOUYS, Sir Robt; 50
CHALTON, John of London; 263
—, Thomas; 196
CHAM; 59
CHAMBER, Thomas; 309
CHAMBERLAIN; 318
CHAMBERLEYN, Alyn le; 385
—, Edward, of Kent; 275
CHAMBERS, Thomas; 309
CHAMBRE, Ambrose del; 111
CHAMERSLEY; 385
CHAMNOY, of Calthorpe; 236
CHAMPAIGNE; 366
CHAMPAIN, John, of Kent; 25
CHAMPAINE; 95
—, Robert de; 94
CHAMPAYN, John; 25
—, John, of Kent; 25
CHAMPAYNE, S Jehn de; 64
—, Johan; 64
—, Mons John; 23
—, Robert; 64
CHAMPENEY; 244
—, of Kent; 64
—, Robert; 64
CHAMPENEYS; 64, 244
CHAMPNEY; 244
CHAMPNEYE, hasard; 64
CHAMPNEYS; 73, 128-9, 176, 180, 244
CHAMRESLEY, Johannes le; 385
CHANDOS, Monsire de; 178
—, Ches; 178
—, Sr Roger; 178
CHANDOYS; 178
CHANI, Lucas; 59
CHAORCIIS, Paganus de; 97
CHARBONE, Johan de; 155
CHARITE, Henry de la; 38
CHARLETON, Sr de; 135

—, Alan de; 217
—, of Kent; 135
—, Baron of Powis, Wales; 135
—, Ld Powys; 135
CHARLETOUN, Eliz; 111
CHARLILTON, le Sr; 133
CHARLTON; 135, 155
—, le Sr de; 135
—, Monsire de; 135
—, de Appllee, Salop; 156
—, Edward, Ld Powis; 111
—, Edward, Ld Powis, KG; 135
—, Howell de; 156
—, Mons J de; 135
—, J le fitz de; 209
—, John de; 135
—, John, Ld, of Powys; 135
—, Ld Powis; 135
—, of Powys; 111
—, le S'r de; 135
—, Thomas, Bp of Hereford; 147
CHARTSEY; 388
CHASERS; 347
CHASTEL; 30
—, Rychard, Sr de; 62
—, Sr William; 30
—, Wills den; 28
CHASTELEON, Maklow; 230
CHASTELION; 230
CHASTELL, of Berks; 30
CHASTELMONT, le Sr de; 371
CHASTELON; 195
CHASTELPER; 213
CHASTILEON, Mons Maklou; 195
CHASTILOUN, Hugh; 195
CHASTON, Mons' Thomas; 63
CHATEAUVILLAIN, John de; 146
CHAUCER; 174, 347
—, Geoffrey; 334
—, Geoffrey, d1400; 347
—, Henry; 184
—, Thomas; 334
—, Thomas, Esq; 334
CHAUCERS, John, of Berks; 347
CHAUMBLEYN, Johan le; 385
CHAUMBRUN; 388
CHAUMON, Mons' John, de Colthorpe; 244
CHAUMP.., Thomas; 349
CHAUMPAIGNE, Margerie, Dame de, of
   Kent; 64
CHAUMPAYNE, William; 318
CHAUNDAS, Mons John; 178
CHAUNDOS; 178
CHAUNTTE; 21
CHAURI; 21
CHAURS, Hervey de; 324
—, Payn de; 84
CHAURSEY, Patrick de; 87
CHAURY; 21

CHAUSER; 347
CHAUSERS; 347
CHAUSI, Thomas de; 140
CHAVERILL, Mons Rauf; 283
CHAVERYNG, Sr John; 337
CHAWORTH, Henry de; 328
—, Mons Henry; 328
—, Pain de; 100
—, Patrik; 100
CHAWRY; 21
CHAWSER; 347
CHAWSERYS, Jafferey, of Oxfs; 347
CHAYNE, Sir John; 312
CHEDLE, Geoffrey de, Kt; 334
CHEDNEDUIT, William de; 196
CHEFREVILL, Sir Adam, of Reydon, Suff;
   204
CHEIN, John, of Essilmont; 382
—, Reginald, Ld of Inverugie; 341
CHELARDESTON, Roger de, Rector of St
   Benet Gracechurch, London; 393
CHELLERY; 5
CHENE, John; 359
CHENEY; 338, 355
—, of Cambs; 359
—, Nicolas; 59
CHENY, of Cambs; 359
CHEPSTOW, Henry de; 234
CHEPSTOWE, H de; 237
CHERCHEMAN; 52
CHERLATON, John de; 111
CHERLETON; 111
—, Humfrey, of Yorks; 135
—, Humphrey de, Archdeacon of Richmond;
   111
—, Sire Joh de; 135
—, Ld Powys; 135
—, mons'r Eduard, s'r de powis; 135
CHERLETONE, John de, Ld of Powys,
   Montgomers; 111
CHERLTON; 111
—, Robert de, of West Wittenham, Berks; 350
CHESEWICK, Robert de; 319
CHESEWIK, Robert de; 319
CHESTER, City of; 274
—, Ralph, Earl of; 111
—, Ranulf, E of; 207
—, Ranulph, E of; 111, 135
—, Ranulph E of; 185
—, William de; 282
CHESTER CITY; 274
CHESTERFIELD, Richard; 193
CHESTRE, Contee de; 307
CHETEHAM, John; 211
CHETEWODE, John, Kt; 111
—, John, of Warkworth, Northants, Kt; 111
CHETEWOOD, Thomas; 111
CHEVEREL; 276
—, Sr Alexander; 276

—, Aleysand; 297
—, Alisaunder; 297
—, Sr Alissaunder; 276
—, Sire Alissaundre; 276
CHEVERELL, S Alexander; 276
—, Ralph; 283
CHEVERILL; 283
CHEVEROYL; 276
CHEVERSTUN, John de; 111
CHEVERYLL; 283
CHEYGNE; 168, 172
CHEYNDUYT; 196
CHEYNE; 94, 311-12, 316, 345, 359, 383
—, Cambs; 359
—, of Cambs; 359
—, Essex; 359
—, of Essilmont; 382
—, Mons John; 135, 159
—, Sr John; 316
—, Sir John, of Kent; 312
—, John, Parson of Hanbury, Staffs; 380
—, Lawrence; 359
—, Richard; 311
—, .. Robert; 311
—, William, of Sheppy, Kent; 311
CHEYNEY; 294, 311-12, 359
—, of Cambs; 359
—, Elizabeth; 359
—, Sir Francis; 316
—, John de; 312
—, Sir John; 312, 316
—, de Lanc; 312
—, of Shepey; 311
—, Sir Thomas; 312
—, Sir Thomas, KG; 312
—, Sir William, of Kent; 312
—, of Wilts & Shyppay; 312
CHEYNY, Edward, Dean of Salisbury; 316
—, Sir Franceys; 316
—, Sir John; 312
—, Robert; 260
—, of Sheppey; 312
—, Sir Thomas; 356
CHEYNYE, of Kent; 316
CHICCHE, T, of Kent; 235
—, Thomas, of the Isle of Thanet, Kent; 305
CHICHCHE, John; 306
CHICHE; 276, 306
—, John; 276
—, Ralph, of Kent, Gent; 111
CHICHESTER, City of; 211
CHIDCROFT, John de; 322
CHIDLEGH; 279
—, James, of Devon; 279
CHIDLEY, of Devon; 279
CHIPNAM; 271
CHIPPENHAM; 271
—, Berks; 271
CHISHULLE, William de, of Grant Lawefare,

[?Great Laver, Essex]; 111
CHITECROFT, Piers; 351
CHIUEROLL, of Wilts & Hants; 276
CHOKE, John; 64
CHORLETON, of Salop; 135
CHRACHETH; 357
CHRE TAWNES, William, of Herts; 248
CHRIKINGHAM, S Wat de; 49
CHRIST, 'our Lord Jesus'; 206
CHRISTISON, Richard; 216
CHRISTMAS; 302
CHUDDELEGH, James de; 275
CHUDLEIGH; 279
CHURCHILL; 219, 223
CHURCHMAN; 41, 52
CHYCHE; 276, 281
CHYDELEY; 279
CHYPCROFTE, P... de, Kent; 351
CHYPNAM, Thomas, of Hants; 271
CHYPRE, le roy de; 140
CICESTRE, Peter de; 374
CIFREWAST, le Sr; 83
CINQUE PORTS; 197, 274
CIPRES, Kyng of; 170
—, le Roy de; 169
CLAPAN, of Glaslogy; 210
CLARE, Elizabeth de; 330
CLARELL; 306
CLARENC, Basterd; 268
CLARENCE, Sir B of; 268
—, bastard of; 268
—, le bastard de; 268
—, D of; 301
—, Sir John of, 'the Bastard'; 268
—, John, bastard of; 268
—, Thomas, D of; 310
CLARENDON, Roger de; 325
CLARK, John; 38
—, Thomas; 38
CLARRAUNCE, Bastard of; 268
CLARYNGDON, Robert de, Kt; 393
CLAVERING; 334, 337
—, de; 364
—, Sr de; 337
—, Alan; 371
—, of Essex; 337
—, Eva; 334
—, J; 364
—, Johan; 364
—, John; 334, 364
—, John de; 364
—, Sir John; 337
—, Robert; 337
—, Mons Robert fitz Roger de; 337
—, Robert fitz Roger de; 337
CLAVERYNG; 364
—, Johannes de; 208
—, Sir John de; 364
—, Sir Robert; 337

CLAVERYNGE; 364
—, Jhon de; 124
—, S Jon; 337
CLAVERYNGES; 337
CLAVING, Robert; 337
CLAXTON, John de; 341
—, Robert; 296
—, Sir Robt; 296
CLAY, John; 296
—, John de; 374
CLEDFORD, Richard de; 111
CLEMSBY, Leics; 166
CLERICUS, Walter, dictus de Lynleye, ?Herts;
  334
CLERK; 38
—, John; 63
CLERKE; 49
CLERVAUS, John de; 111
CLERVAUX, John; 111
CLEUEDON; 168
CLEVEDON, of Clevedon; 240
—, Hugh de; 168
—, Mons Hugh de; 168
CLEVISBY, Sire Johan; 166
—, Sir Johan, de Dene; 125
CLEY, Sir John; 296
CLICE; 207
CLIFDONE, S'Edmond; 168
CLIFFDON; 168
CLIFFORD; 331, 344
—, Sir J; 330
—, S Johan; 331
—, Reinaud de; 331
—, Robert de; 111
—, Roger; 331
—, Rogerus de; 18
—, Walter; 331
—, Walter de; 330-1
CLIFFORDE, Gautier de; 331
CLIFFTON, Sir John, of Norf; 344
CLIFTON; 152, 231-2, 344
—, Adam; 344
—, Adam de; 344-5
—, Sir Adam, of Norf; 344
—, of Barrington; 152
—, Constantine; 344
—, Gervais; 238
—, Gervaise; 238
—, Gervaise de; 231
—, Mons' Gervaise de; 155
—, Sir Gervaise; 160, 232
—, Sir Gervase; 232
—, Monsr Gervays de; 155
—, Sir Gerveis; 231
—, Sir Gervis; 152
—, Henry of; 354
—, Monsire Jervis de; 198
—, John; 231
—, John de; 231, 330, 344

—, Sir John; 344-5
—, John, chivaler; 231
—, Sir Robert; 345
—, Sir Robt; 152
CLIFTUN, T de; 231
CLIFVEDON; 231
CLINGHIN, Thomas; 393
CLINTON, Alice de; 111
—, of Irld; 226
—, Juliana de; 312
—, William de; 312
—, William de, E of Huntingdon; 312
CLINTONE, Juliana de; 312
CLISSON; 167
CLIVEDON, Esmon; 168
—, Sr Jo; 168
—, Sire Johan; 168
—, Reginald de; 137
—, Renaud de; 168
CLODSHALE, Richard, Esq; 51
CLOPTON; 21-2
—, Joan; 21
—, Johanna; 22
CLUN, Hospital of; 393
CLYFDON; 168
CLYFFORD; 331
—, Sir J; 331
—, Wylyam, of Gloucs; 12
CLYFFORDE, John, Bastard of, Esq; 371
—, Richard de; 366
CLYFFTON, Sir Garways of, of Notts; 232
CLYFFTUN; 345
CLYFTON; 152, 231
—, Adam de; 345
—, Mons Adam de; 345
—, of co Durham; 229
—, Sir G; 232
—, Sir Gereys of, of Notts; 152
—, Gervaise; 232
—, Mons Gervase de; 231
—, Gervasius de; 152
—, Sir Gerveis; 232
—, Sr Gervis; 232
—, Sir J; 345
—, John; 345
—, Sir John; 231
—, of Yorks; 232
CLYFTONNE; 345
CLYNTON; 2
—, William de, E of Huntingdon; 312
CLYSE; 203, 207
CLYSSON, le Sr de; 167
CLYVDONER; 137
CLYVEDON, Edmund de; 111
—, Sir John de; 168
—, Mons' Reymunde de; 168
COBHAM, Mons J de; 157
—, John; 157
—, John de; 157

—, s' Jon; 157
—, Sir Rauf; 157
—, Sir Rawfe de; 157
COCK, Henry; 345
—, John; 9
COCKAYN, Sir John; 14
COCKAYNE, Edmund; 2
—, Sir John; 14
CODENHAM, Oliver; 64
CODENORE, Mons Henry fitz a; 87
CODERUGE; 281
—, Mons Baudewyn de; 297
CODERUGGE, Baldwyn de; 297
—, Baudwyn; 297
CODYNGTON, William de; 220
COFFLAN, Hugh de; 145
COFFOL, of Kent; 311
COFTYN, Sir T; 24
COK, John, of Lilborne; 368
COKAIN, Richard, of Derbys; 20
COKAYN; 2, 20
COKAYNE; 2
—, Sir John, of Derbys; 20
COKE, John, of Lilburne; 368
—, John, of Lilleburne; 368
COKEHAM; 157
COKER, Richard, [of Bridgwater]; 319
COKESEYE, Walter; 319
COKHAM; 157
COLBRET; 226
COLE; 247
—, Sir Adam, of Devon; 247
—, Frances; 247
—, Jane; 247
—, John; 246
—, of Tewkesbury; 247
COLEBROOKE; 226
COLEE; 247
—, Robert, Gloucs; 247
COLENTIER, S Jehan de; 341
COLEPEPER; 350-1, 365
—, Alexander; 351
—, Peter, of Kent; 350
—, Thomas, Kt; 365
COLEPEPHER; 351
COLEPEPIR, John, of Northants, Kt; 350
COLEPEPR; 351
COLESHULL, Lawrence de; 212
COLEUILLE, Sire Rob of Blakan; 43
COLEVILE, Geffrai; 208
—, John; 128
—, Roger de; 207
—, Willm de; 24
COLEVYLE, John de; 208
COLEWORTH, Elizabeth de; 342
COLEWORTHE, Hugh de, of Horndon-on-
the-hill, Essex, Kt; 342
COLGRYM, Laurence, of Watyndon, Surr; 205
COLHET, Mons Richard; 360

COLINGTON, John, Suss; 315
QUEEN'S COLL, Cambridge; 85
COLLACE, John; 370
COLLEBRONE; 322
COLLUMBERS, Sir Philip de; 363
COLNE, John de, of Steyning, Som; 216
—, William de, of Steyning; 373
COLPEPER; 351
—, Sir John; 350
COLPEPIR, Geoffrey, of Peckham parva,
Kent; 350
COLUERLEY, of Marsland, Lincs; 208
COLUILE, Geffrey; 208
COLUMBARS; 325
COLUMBERIS; 325
COLUMBERS; 325, 363
—, Eleanor de; 14
COLUMBS; 325
COLVILE, Sir Jn, of Norf; 163
—, John; 128
—, John de; 218
—, de Mershlande; 208
COLVILLE, Henry, bailie of St Andrews; 371
—, Mons' John, de Mershland; 208
COLVYLE, Sir John, of Norf; 128
COLVYLL, Mons J; 218
COLYNGRYGGE, W; 132
COMALE; 151
—, Robart; 151
—, Robarte; 150
COMBE; 278, 285
—, of Combe in Crewkerne; 289
—, Richard de; 282, 285, 289
—, Thomas, Abbot of; 298
—, William de; 345
COMBE ABBEY, Warws; 298
COMBERFORD, John; 202
—, John de; 202
COMBERMERE, Abbas de, Salop; 371
COMBERTON; 197
COMBES, William; 224
COMBLANDIE, Comes; 132
COMBUILE; 283
COMPTON; 229
—, of Compton; 229
—, Henry; 229
—, Mayster; 229
—, Sir William; 229
COMRIE, John, of Comrie; 385
COMYN; 3
CONESTABLE, Mons le, de Holdrenesse; 88
—, Robert, de Holdrenesse; 88
—, Wills de; 336
CONESTABYLL, of Flaynborowe; 340
CONETABLE, M le; 340
CONEY, Robert de; 92
CONGALTON, Richard, of that Ilk; 361
CONGILTOWN, of that Ilk; 363
CONINBRE, Rex; 294

CONISBYE; 294
CONNIBRE, le Roy de; 204
CONNSTALB, Sir J, of ...; 59
CONSTABLE; 86, 88, 325, 340
—, of Flamborough; 319, 337
—, of Flamborough, Yorks; 325, 340
—, of Flamburgh, Yorks; 340
—, 'de halshame'; 87
—, of Holderness; 88
—, of Holderness, Yorks; 88
—, of Holdernesse; 88
—, Sir J; 18
—, Sir John; 338
—, John the, of Chester; 123
—, John, Dean of Lincoln, 1514-28; 338, 340
—, Mons John, [of] Halsham; 88
—, Sir John, of Holderness; 88
—, Sir John, of Holdernesse; 88
—, Margaret; 340
—, Marmaduke; 340
—, S Marmaduke; 340
—, Sir Marmaduke; 329, 340
—, Marmaduke, of Flamborough; 340
—, Mons Richard; 340
—, Richard; 340
—, Richd; 338
—, Mons Robert; 340
—, Sir Robert; 340
—, Sr Robert; 353
—, Sr Robert le; 340
—, Robert, of Hamboro, Yorks, Kt; 340
—, Robt; 368
—, Monsire le, seigneur de Flamburgh; 340
—, Syr Marmaduke, of Everingham, Yorks; 340
—, Sr Wm; 338
—, Wm, of Flamborough; 340
CONSTABYLL, Sir J; 99
—, Sir John, Yorks; 88
—, Ser John, Yorks; 60
—, Tomas, of Cattys fosse, Yorks; 24
CONSTANTINE, Sir Robert; 282
CONSTANTINOPLE, Emperor of; 5
CONWAY; 248
—, Henre; 248
CONWAYE; 248
CONWEY; 248
—, Henry; 248
CONYNGSBY; 309
—, Johanna; 294
—, William; 294
CONYNGSTON; 294
COOCUTRE, Walter of; 214
COOK; 68
COOKE; 68
COOKES; 68
COOKHAM, J; 157
COOLEY, of Devon; 247
COOLPEPER, John; 353

—, John, Kent; 353
COOMBES; 225
COOVIN, Bartholomew de; 111
COPELAND; 28
—, Alan de; 28
—, Sir Richard; 28
—, Sautone; 28
COPLAND; 28
—, of Stanton; 28
CORBET; 27-8, 149, 189, 203
—, Agnes; 29
—, de Hadley, Salop; 27
—, Sr Johan; 28
—, John; 29
—, Nicholas; 111
—, R; 27
—, S' Rob'; 27
—, Robert; 26-8, 53
—, Robert, of Ebrington, Gloucs, Chev; 29
—, Robert, of Hadley, Salop; 28
—, S' Rog; 31
—, Roger, Kt, Ld of Hadley, Salop; 29
—, Thomas, Kt; 270
—, Thomas, Kt, of Brug; 270
CORBETES; 27
CORBETT; 27, 111
CORDER, Mons Gauweyn; 5
CORNEVAYLE, Sir John, S' de Wanhoppe; 240
CORNEWAILE; 220
—, Elizabeth de, Lady of Kynlet; 238
CORNEWAILL; 239
—, E of; 239
CORNEWAILLE, le Conte de; 239
—, Le Conte de; 308
—, le Conte de; 308
—, le Counte de; 239
—, John, Chev; 245
CORNEWALE, Monsire Jeffrey de; 223
CORNEWALL; 245
—, Brian; 245
—, Sire Edmund; 223
—, Sire Geffray; 223
—, John; 383
CORNEWALLE; 239
—, the erle of; 239
CORNEWAYLE; 239
—, Erle of; 239
—, S' Edmund; 239
—, Mons Esmon de; 245
—, Richard, Ld of Burford; 240
CORNEWAYLL, le Contt de; 239
—, Mons Edward; 248
—, Mons George de, dyrland; 239
—, Mons J de; 239
CORNEWAYLLE; 383
—, Dame Elizab; 245
CORNNWALL, Sir Thomas, Knight; 245
CORNUALL; 223

CORNUAYLL; 240
CORNUBIA, Elizabeth de; 238
CORNUBIAE, Comes; 239
CORNUBIE, Ducis; 239
—, Dux; 239
CORNUK; 68
CORNUWAYLE, C de; 240
CORNWAILE, Fanhop; 245
CORNWAILL, E of; 239
CORNWAILLE, le Counte de; 239
—, John, Chev, Ld of Faireholt; 240
CORNWAL, of Burford, Salop & Berington, Herefs; 245
—, Edmund de; 239
—, Sir John; 245
CORNWALE, Erle of; 239
—, Monsire Symond de; 223
CORNWALL; 239, 245, 381, 383
—, Count de; 239
—, Count of; 239
—, Counte de; 239
—, de; 239
—, E of; 239, 308
—, Ld; 245
—, le Conte; 239-40
—, Bryan; 245
—, 'The Baron of Burford'; 245
—, D of; 240, 308
—, Edmond, of Herts; 245
—, Edmund, E of; 239-40
—, Sir Edmund; 223
—, Edmund D of; 245
—, Edward, de Alemannia, E of; 239
—, Ld Fanhope; 245
—, Ld Fanhopp; 240
—, S' Geffray; 223
—, Sir Geoffrey; 223, 245
—, John de; 239, 383
—, Mons John; 240
—, Sir John, KG; 245
—, Sir John, Ld Fanhope; 245
—, E of, Richard; 240
—, Richard, E of; 238-40, 308
—, Richard of; 240
—, Sir Thomas; 245
CORNWAYL, Sir Edmur,¹; 224
CORNWAYLE, D of; 240
CORNWAYLLE, the Duc of; 239
—, Co; 240
—, Comes de; 308
CORSUM; 343
CORVYLL; 218
COSANZ, Sr William; 365
COSCY, Thomas de; 329
COSHALME; 276
COSSINGTON, Stephen; 43
COSTER; 93
COSYN; 184
—, Dorset; 183

—, of Dorset; 173
—, Thomas; 183
COTEL, Sir Elis; 325
—, Syr Elys; 325
—, Thomas; 325
COTELE; 352
COTELL; 325
—, Dorset & Som; 325
COTENHAM, John de; 98
COTENOR, Ld G'y; 88
COTERELL; 384
COTINGHAM; 266
COTTESFORD; 53
COTTINGHAM; 266
COTTINGHAM PRIOR, E Riding Yorks; 41
COTTON; 391
—, Thomas, of Staffs; 191
COTTUN; 191
—, Yorks; 191
COUCI; 89, 92
COUCY, de; 21
—, Earle of Bedford; 75
—, Engeram de; 91
—, Enguerrand de; 98
—, Enguerraud, Sire de; 91
—, Enguerraud de, E of Bedford; 91
—, Enquerrand Sire de; 86
—, Ingeham, Ld of, E of Bedford; 91
—, Ingelram; 91
—, Ingelram de; 92
—, Ingelram, Ld of; 62
—, Ingleram de; 91
—, Ingram, sire de; 91
COUMBE; 278
—, Rychard de; 276
COUNBY; 275
COUNTONE, of Leics; 40
COUPELAND; 28
COUPLAND, Alan de; 28
—, Sir Alan de; 28
—, Richard; 28
—, Sir Richard; 28
COURCY; 21
—, Ld; 92
—, E of Bedford; 92
COURTENAY, E of Devon; 133
—, John de; 21
COURTENEY, of Dorset & Som; 391
COURTNEY, E of Devonshire, 1st M of Exeter; 307
COUSI; 92
COUSSY; 92
COVENTRY, Town of; 203
COVENTRY CITY; 203
COWCYE; 22
COWFFOLD; 80
—, of Essex; 76, 80
COWLEY; 319
COWN, Thomas de; 278

COWNE; 158
—, Sir Thomas; 158
COWTON, Roger de; 230
COX; 67
CRACOW, K of; 266
CRACOWS, K of; 266
CRAMBETH, Matthew de, Bp of Dunblane 1288-1309; 270
CRANE; 318
CRANEBURA; 18, 54
CRANEBURY, Mons Rauf de; 18
—, Mons Willm de; 54
CRAUNFORD, Robert; 371
CRAWFORD, Reginald; 111
CRAYETH; 352
CREAMTONE, Lincs; 322
CRECY, Mons Thomas; 176
CREICHTON, Ld; 124
CREIGHTON, Robt, Bp of Bath & Wells; 141
CREKE, Wautier; 389
CREKINGHAM; 43, 48
CREKYNGHAM; 49
—, Mons Wauter de; 52
CREKYNGHM; 49
CREPPINGE, Johan; 153
—, Johan de; 146
—, Sr Johan; 146
CREPYNG, of Lincs; 146
CREPYNGE, Jon de; 146
CRESCQUES, Robert de; 83
CRESCY, Sir Edmond; 181
CRESEY, Esmond de; 174
CRESIGNES; 83
CRESPIN, William; 64
CRESSE, Hew; 183
CRESSEWELL, Alexander; 3
—, Robert de; 206
CRESSI, Monsire de; 176
CRESSIE, Sr de; 176
CRESSWELL, Robert of; 206
CRESSY; 126, 176
—, Monsr; 176
—, Hugh de; 111
—, Sir Joh, Northants; 175
—, John de; 176
—, Mons John de; 176
—, Sir John; 174
—, Sir John de; 176
—, Sir John, Northd; 175
—, Sir Roger; 210
—, Sr Roger; 210
—, William; 176
—, William de; 176
—, Willm de; 176
—, Yorks; 176
CRESTY, Sir J; 103
CRESWELL; 81
CRETHON, the Lord; 124
CREW; 156, 242

CREWE; 156
—, of Northants; 156
—, Thos de [d1418] & w Julian [Sesin] 1411; 111
CREYCHTOUN, of Brounstoune; 241
—, of Strathurde; 124
CRICHTON; 111, 124
—, of Cairns; 124
—, Edw, of Kirtilhous; 111
—, John, of Innernyte; 245
—, Laurence, of Rosse; 215
—, Marion; 215
—, of Nachtane; 124
—, Robert, 2nd Ld C of Sanquhar; 111
—, of Sanquhar; 154
CRIKETOT, Simon; 294
CRIOLL, Nichole; 3
CRISTON, ceulx de; 124
CROCHTON, of Sanchar; 124
CROK, Nicholas; 390
—, Reginald; 386
CROKE, Piers; 12-13
CROMELL; 7
CROMMEL; 9
CROMMVELLE; 7
CROMWELL; 7, 53, 138, 366
—, John; 6, 182
—, John de; 182
—, S John de; 7
—, Sir John; 176
—, Sr John; 7
—, John de, of Arnold Manor, Notts, Kt; 6
—, Jon de; 7
—, Mons Rauf; 366
—, Sir Richard; 138
CRONE, William, of Essex & tailor of London; 244
CRONWELL; 9
—, Roger de, of Burford; 235
CROSWELL; 75
CROUCHBACK, Edmund, E of Lancaster; 300
CROWAN; 296
—, Thomas, of Cornw; 293
CROWELL, Thomas, of Herts; 53
CROWHYRST, de Scotney, Suss; 76
CROY, Anthony, Ld de, C of Porcien; 12
—, Jehan de, Seigneur de Chimay; 12
CROYDON, Joan; 111
CROYLY; 276
CRUMBEWELL, John de, Constable of Tower of London; 6
CRUMWELL; 8
—, Monsr de; 7
—, Sr de; 7
—, S Jeh de; 182
—, Mons John; 7
—, Rauf de; 322
CRUS, Mons Robert; 385
CRUSE, of Irld; 385

CRWE; 156
CRWELL; 322
CRY, Matheu de; 325
CTIC, Phil' de; 236
CUDEHAM, John; 64
CUISSAC, de Norf; 343
CULNHATH, Richard of; 355
CULPEPER; 350-1
—, Sir Alexander, Kent; 351
—, Sir John, Kent; 351
—, Sir John, of Kent; 351
—, of Kent; 351
—, Sir Thomas; 351
CULPEPPER; 351, 365
—, Thomas; 351
CULUET, S' Ric'; 360
CUMBERFORD, John de; 202
CUMBERTON; 197
CUMBES, Edmund de; 217
CUNCLIFFE; 294
CUNCLYFFE, of Oxfords; 294
CUNLIFFE, of Lancs, Bart; 294
CURDEN; 9
CURREU, Mons de; 284
CURSON; 343, 367
—, Mons; 343
—, John; 343
—, John, Kt; 261
—, John, Sir; 319
—, Mons John; 343
—, Sir John; 343
—, Sir John, of Felton; 343
—, John, of Staffs; 322
CURSOUN, Wm of Byntree, Norf; 343
CURSSUM; 343
CURSUN; 343
—, de Brightwell, Suff; 343
—, John; 254
—, Robert; 368
CURZON; 343, 346
—, Sir John; 348
—, Richard; 282
—, Thomas, of Bellingford, Norf; 367
CUSACK, of Irld; 21, 90
CUSANCE, W; 365
CUSANCIA, William de; 365
CUSANNS, William de; 352
CUSANOR; 358
CUSAUNCE, William de; 365
CUSCI, Engelrami de; 75
CUTTE, John, Kt; 202
CUYSY, Thomas; 91
CYFERWAST, Mons John; 83
CYFREWAST; 58, 77
—, le Sr de; 83
CYPRES, K of; 140
—, Rex de; 140
CYPRESS, The Kyng off; 140
CYPRUS; 70, 140, 169

—, K of; 140
—, King of; 99, 169
CYTRIK PANYM, King; 198
CYTRYK, King in England; 198
CYTRYL, King; 198
D'ACHERES, Rigaud, Bp of Winchester,
   1320-23; 111
D'AINCURT, Sir Ralph, of Sizergh; 27
D'ANGLE, Sir Gyggard, Count de
   Hon[tingdon; 146
D'ARTOIS; 94
D'AUBECHECOURT, Mons Nichol; 73
D'AUBIGNY, William, E of Arundel; 177
D'AUMERY; 94
D'EVEREUX, Amauricus or Almaric, 4th E of
   Gloucester; 93
DABERYCHCORT, Sir Nicoll; 73
DABETON, Hugo; 297
DABITOT, Geffrai; 265
—, Gefrai; 264
DABITOTT, Gefrai; 264
DABREGECOURT; 63, 73
DABRICHCOURT; 63
DABRICHECOURT; 52, 63
—, Eustace; 63, 73
—, John; 73
—, John de; 73
—, Nichol; 63
—, Nicol; 63
—, Sir Sanchet de, KG, d1348-9; 63
—, Sir Sanset; 63
—, Sansett; 63
DABRIDGCOURT; 63
DABRIDGECOURT; 63
—, John; 73
—, Sir John; 63
DABRIGECOURT; 69
DABRISCOURTE; 63
DABRYCHCORTE, Essex; 63
DABRYCHYIRRTTE, Sir Sanset; 63
DABRYGECOURT; 63
DABRYSCOURT; 73
DABYTOT; 264
DACHERD; 358
DACRE, Ld; 277
—, Thomas, Ld; 277
DACRES, Ld of the South; 277
DACUS, Thomas; 13
DACYE, Roy de; 288
DALAMARE; 258
DALAMER, Sir Thomas; 264
DALARNARE, Peter, Kt, of Parva, Heref; 63
DALAVALE, Mons' John; 77
—, Monsr John; 21
DALAWARE, Ld; 150
DALBY; 366
DALDEBURGH, Mons Hugh; 155
DALEWELL, of Northd; 21
DALLE, Richard; 58

—, of Wychy...; 52
DALNY, Monsire de; 282
DALTON; 56, 128, 151, 167, 190-1, 196, 210
—, Monsire de; 148
—, Sr de; 190
—, Mons J de; 210
—, Mons J de, of Kirby Misperton; 245
—, John; 210
—, John de; 245
—, Sir John; 167
—, of Lancs; 172
—, Mons R de; 190
—, Richard de; 190
—, Robert de; 189
—, Sr Robert; 193
—, Mons Rog de; 167
—, S'Thos, of Lancs; 167
—, W de; 191
—, of Yorks; 191
DALTONE, S' Rob'; 190
DALTUN; 190
DAMARY, Mons' Richard; 95
DAMERE, Sir John; 330
DAMMARI; 94
DAMMARTIN, Galiena de; 192
DAMMORE; 330
DAMMORT; 330
DAMMORY; 66, 94
DAMOCKE, Sir ...; 4
DAMORI, Roger; 47
DAMORY; 330
—, Sir Richard; 94
—, Richard, Chevr, of Bucks; 93
—, Roger; 330, 342
DAMPMARTIN; 87
DANBY, Thomas; 111
—, William, of Stoke Daubeny, Northants; 326
DANCORT, Lovell, of Staffs; 327
DANDELEIGH, Sir Philip; 54
DANDESEY; 65
—, John; 65
DANDUERS; 208
DANEL; 395
DANELL; 395
DANEMARCHE, le Roy de; 289
DANEMARK, le Roy de; 288
DANEMARKE, le Roy de; 288
DANERNER, Mons Gerard; 225
DANESTON, John, of Suff; 13
—, of Suff; 12
DANEYS; 13
—, Elizabeth; 12
DANGLETERRE, le Roy; 287
DANIEL; 384-5, 395
—, Hugh; 33
DANIELL; 395
—, John; 385
DANIELLE, John; 206
DANMARCHIE, King; 13

DANNDELEGH; 73
DANSEL; 325
DANSELL; 325
DANYEL, 'of Gloucest'; 279
DANYELL, John; 207
DANYERS, Thomas; 46
DANYS, Le Sieur; 13
DAPISCORTE; 63
DARBY, le Count de; 304
DARCI, S' John, le Fiz; 232
DARCK, Roger; 206
DARCY, Elizabeth; 83
—, Elizabeth, Lady of Wherlton; 83
DARDERN, Monsire Wakehide; 161
DAREL; 167
—, Marmaduke; 111
DARELL; 168, 171-2, 182
—, Sir Edw, of Hilcot, Wilts; 173
—, Sir Edward; 162, 167, 171-3
—, Sir Edward, of Littlecote, Wilts; 167
—, John; 111, 172
—, Sir John; 166-7, 172
—, Sir Jorge; 129
—, of Littlecot; 171
—, of Suff; 167
—, Thomas; 73
DARELLE, Marmaduke, Ld of Sesay, Yorks;
   164
DARESBURY; 206
DARNOWLL; 254, 263
DARONDELL, le Count; 132
—, le Conte de, et de Warren; 132
DARRALL, Sir Emonde, of Yorks; 129
DARREL, of Kent; 171
—, Sir Richard; 167
DARRELL; 129, 167, 199
—, Thomas, of Yorks; 167
—, William; 171
DARRUNDELL, le Counte; 132
DARTEYS, of Irld; 95
DARUNDEL, Le Conte; 132
—, le Conte; 132
—, le Conte de; 132
—, Monsire Edmon, le filtz; 208
DARUNDELL, le Counte; 132
—, Sibilla; 111, 208
DARYNDELL, Le Cont; 132
DATTE, Thomas; 260
DAUBENY, Hugh; 132
—, William; 132
DAUBRIGCOURT, Mons Eustace; 73
—, Mons Gafry; 73
DAULTON; 151
—, Henry; 319-20
DAUMARY; 94
—, Monsire; 94
—, Sr; 94
—, Mons Richard; 95
—, Robert; 66

DAUMORI; 71
DAUNDELEGH; 55
—, Mons Philip; 55
—, Mons Philip de; 55
—, Philip; 16, 55
DAUNDELEIGH; 54-5
DAUNDELEY, S' Rob'; 73
DAUNDESEY; 65
—, John; 65
DAUNDESEYE, Water; 26
DAUNDYSE, Water; 26
DAUNDYSLAYE, Mons John; 25
DAUNE, Richard; 395
DAUNT, T; 106
DAUNTESEY; 253
—, John, Kt; 94
DAUNTESEYE, John; 65
—, Sr Richard; 97
DAUNTSEY; 65
—, of Dauntsey; 25
DAVELL, William; 51
DAVERS, of Beds; 132
DAVERSCOURTE, Sir J; 63
DAVID; 55
—, frere of P of Wales; 310
—, [Gwillim] ap, of Sengheuyth; 163
DAVID AP GRIFFID; 311
DAVID AP GRIFFITH; 311
DAVID II; 196
—, K of Scotland; 250
DAVIDSON, John; 229
DAVY, John, of Multon, Suff; 111
DAWBANEY, Sir Gyles; 357
DAWBRICHCOURT, Nicholas; 63
DAWES, of Sharpham, Devon; 186
DAWNE; 47
—, John, of Ches; 47
DEABETOT; 264
DEANE; 27
DEAUMARY; 94
DEBBEN, Sir Gilbert; 379
DEBEHAM; 379
DEBENHAM; 360, 378-9
—, Gilbert; 378
—, Gilbert de; 379
—, Sir Gilbert; 379
—, Gilbert, of Essex & Suff; 379
—, Sir Gilbert, Suff; 379
DEBNAM; 379
DEBYNHAM; 379
—, Suff; 379
DEDENE; 27
DEEN, Johan de; 55
—, Richard le; 369
DEINCOURT, Isabel; 346
DELAFELD, of Irld; 135
DELAFELDE; 135
DELAFIELD, Sir Gylberd; 97
DELAFORD, Wilts; 281

DELALAWNDE, Thomas; 75
DELAMAR; 261
DELAMARE; 63, 92, 258-9, 263-5
—, (of Aldermaston); 258
—, Piers; 264
—, Sir Rauff, of Gloucs; 264
DELAMER; 23
—, of Berks; 23
DELAMERE; 254, 263-4
DELAMOTE; 342
DELAOURS, Monsire William; 364
DELAPLAUNCHE, of Bucks; 170
DELAPOLE; 135
DELAREVER, Sir R; 23
—, Tomas, of Berks; 23
DELARIVIERE, Sir John, of Berks; 23
DELAVAL; 21
—, Hugh; 46
—, Robert; 20, 70, 204
—, of Seaton-Delaval; 20
DELAWACHE, Bucks; 277
DELAWARE; 150
DELAWARR, Ld; 150
DELAWARRE; 150
DELLESFELDE, Mons' Gilbert; 95
DEMARIE, John; 320
DEMOCK, ...; 262
DEMPSTER, John, of Caraldston; 217
DEN, of Hunts; 55
—, Jan de; 55
—, Monsire Richard le; 155
DENARDESTONE, Sr Peres; 35
DENARDSTON; 12
—, Sir Piers; 35
—, Sir Thomas, of Suff; 12
DENARSTON; 12
—, Sir Rob, of Suff; 34
DENDUN, John; 172
DENE; 27, 125
—, de; 27
—, Sire ...; 22
—, Mons J de; 67
—, Sr J de; 54
—, Sire Johan; 22
—, Sr Johan; 125
—, Mons' John; 67
—, of Leics; 125
DENEIS, of Sock Dennis, Ilchester; 13
DENEMACHE, le Rei de; 13
DENESELLE; 325
DENESTON; 36
DENET; 107
—, Betkin; 107
DENEWGAT; 318
DENGLETERRE, le fitz Eyre le Roy; 299
—, Le Roy; 287
DENHAM, John de; 370
DENHOLLS; 392
DENMARK; 19, 284, 288

—, K of; 12, 197, 264, 284, 288-9
—, Eric V, K of; 205
—, Kyng of; 284
—, Margaret of; 285
—, Roy de; 288
—, K Sweyn of; 12
DENMARK & Norway, John, King of; 285
DENMARKE, K of; 197, 289
—, le Roy de; 288
DENNARDESTON, Suff; 35
DENNER, Sir Henry; 353
DENNIS, Sir ...; 13
DENNISTON; 320-2
—, Robert, of Balgarrane; 366
DENNISTOUN, of that Ilk; 322
DENSELL; 325
DENSTON; 263-4
DENSTONE; 263
DENSYLL; 392
DENTON; 37-40, 122
—, John; 38, 386
—, John de; 388
—, John of; 58, 389
—, Mons Ric' de; 38
—, S' Ric' de; 38
DENTONE; 37-9
DENTTON, Wm; 39
—, Wylyam; 38
DENYE, of Devon; 13
DENYS; 13
—, of Devon; 13
—, of Holcombe, Devon; 13
—, Sir Thomas; 13
—, Thomas, of Holcombe, Devon; 13
—, Sir Walter, d1506; 388
DEPDEN; 322
DEPENSER, H le; 339
DERBY; 211, 304
—, Count de; 304
—, Cunte de; 304
—, E of; 303-4
—, le Conte de; 304
—, C of; 304
—, le C de; 287
—, John de; 111
DERWENTWATER; 27, 30-2
—, Sr de; 32
—, Adam de; 31
—, John; 31
—, Mons' John; 30
—, Sir John; 31
—, John de, of Cumb, mil; 30
DERWENTWATRE, John; 31
DERWINTWATER, le Sire de; 30
DESCOCE, le Roy; 251
DESMAREYS, Sr Herbert; 126
DESNEY; 153
DESPAGNE, Le Roy; 126
DESPAYNE; 33

DESPENCER; 322, 338-9
—, le; 338
—, Le; 339
—, le; 339
—, le Sr de; 339
—, Monsire le; 339
—, Sr; 339
LE DESPENCER; 320, 322
DESPENCER, Ld Edward; 339
—, Elizabeth; 338
—, Hewe le; 339
—, Hugh le; 364
—, Hugh le, of Solihull, Warws, Kt; 338
—, John le; 275
—, Thomas le, E of Gloucester; 339
—, Thomas, E of Gloucester; 339
—, le, Counte of Wyncester; 339
DESPENSEIER, Hue le; 338
DESPENSER; 339
—, Ld; 339
—, le; 339
—, le Mons de; 339
—, le Sr; 336, 339
—, Sr le; 339
—, Anne; 111, 184, 338-9
—, Anne le; 164, 339
—, Constance; 338
—, Edward le; 338
—, Geoffrey le; 338
—, Sr Henri; 340
—, Henry, Bp of Norwich; 340
—, Hue; 340
—, Hue le; 340
—, Sr Hue fitz; 364
—, Hugh; 339-40
—, Hugh le; 338-9
—, Hugh' le; 339
—, Hugh le; 340, 364, 384
—, Hugh le, Kt; 339
—, Hugh le, kt; 379
—, Mons Hugh le; 340
—, S Hugh le; 339
—, Sr Hugh; 364
—, Hugh, E of Winchester; 340
—, Hugh le, the younger; 364
—, Hughe; 336
—, Robert, de Staindone; 340
—, Thomas le, Kt; 338-9
—, Thomas le, E of Gloucester; 338-9
—, Thomas, E of Gloucester; 340
DESPENSERE, le Sr de; 339
—, Sr E; 353
DESPENSIER, Hugh le, Kt; 338
DESTANLADE, Sire Rauf; 183
DESTRON, Monsire Jefferey; 363
DETLING, William de; 1
DETLINGE, William; 315
DETLYNG, Sir William de; 315
DETTELYNGE; 315

—, S' John de; 315
DETTLING, Sir John; 314
DETTLINGE, Sir Wm de; 312
DEUER, Sr H; 331
DEUESCHIRE, Erle of; 133
DEUNGATE; 318
DEVENYSCHIRE, le Counte de; 133
DEVEREUS, John, Ld of East Harptree; 111
DEVEREUX, Wm; 312
DEVON, E of; 133
—, Earl of; 133
—, Amice, Countess of; 174
—, Amicia, Ctess of; 112
—, Baldwin, E of; 178
DEVONSCHIRE, le Conte de; 133
DEWILLE, Devon; 152
DEWY; 227
DEYSTERE, Richard; 112
DEYVILE, Sr Johan; 152
DEYWELLE, Sir John; 142
DEYWYLYM; 348
DICHFYLD; 289
DICWARD; 4
DILLES, le Conte; 310
DILLINGEN, Hartman V, Count of; 372
DILLON, John, of Irld; 233
DIMMOCKE; 262
DIMOCK, John; 262
—, Sir Lionel; 262
DIPER; 219
DISNEY; 282, 286
—, R; 282, 286
—, William; 282-3
DISPENSATOR, Anne le; 353
DISSINGTON, Nicholas of; 205
DISVI; 283
DOBRICHECOURT, Sir John; 63
DOCKESSAY, of Salop; 222
DODDELEYE, Barun de; 259
DODDLEY, Ld; 259
DODELEY, the Lord; 179
DODYTON, Monsr de; 43
DOK, William; 3
DOKESEYE, S Richard; 221
DOLAND, Richard, of Lancs; 273
DOLYNG, Sir J; 23
DOMMVIL, John, of Modberlegh; 162
DOMVILE; 163
—, de Lymme; 163
DOMVILLE, John; 112
—, John de; 163
DOMVYLE, John, of Ches; 163
DON, Sir Edward; 207
—, John; 207
DONCASTER, Borough of; 211
DONCASTRE, William; 378
DONDAS, Ceulx de; 125
DONE, Sir John, of Utkington; 47
DONET, Matilda; 112

DONEVILL; 218
DONEWYCO, John; 112
DONN, Griffyth; 207
DONNVILE, of Limme, Ches; 163
DONNVILLE; 163
DONSELL, Devon; 392
DOON; 207
DORCESTRE, Mons Oliv' de; 315
DORCHESTER, Bailiffs of; 194
—, Oliver de; 315
DORE, Sr Robt de, Suss; 345
DORKALEWE; 81
M'DOUGAL; 166
DOUGLAS, E of Angus; 129
—, le Comte de; 383
—, Gavin, Bp of Dunkeld; 112, 217
—, Wm, 2nd E of Angus (1402-37); 112
—, Wm, 2nd Earl of Angus (1402-1437); 112
DOUMUILL, John, of Modberlegh; 162
DOUMVYLE; 163
DOUN; 207
DOUNHOLT; 370
DOUNWILE, John; 112
DOUVRE, Richard de; 264
DOVER; 317
—, Mayoralty of Port of; 197
DOWELL; 245
DOWELLS; 242
—, Sir Hugh, Staffs; 242
DOWELS; 242
DOWNE; 47
—, John; 47
DOWNES; 201
—, of Ches; 201
—, of 'Shrigley'; 201
DOWNYS, de Chest; 201
DOYLEY; 388
DOYLY; 323
DOYN, Artaut de; 196
DOYVILL; 369
DRATON; 36
DRAYCOTT; 333
DRAYTON; 36, 144, 322, 380-1
—, Jane; 143
—, Sir John; 380, 382
—, of London; 144
—, Robard; 144
—, of Salop; 18
DREVSELL, Devonshire; 325
DREW; 186
—, Mons de, of Devon; 186
DREWE, of Sharpham, Devon; 186
DRONSFEILD; 326
DROWMUND, Ld; 65
DRU, Thomas; 186, 196
DRUEL, John, Sheriff of Northants; 112
DRUMMOND; 93
—, Ld; 96
—, Anabell; 96

—, Harry; 69
—, James; 66
—, John; 64, 76
—, John, 1st Ld; 25, 64, 202
DRW, of Devon; 186
DUBOIS; 27
DUBU..., John; 70
DUCKET, Sir Hugh, of Lincs; 336
—, Hugh, Rector; 336
DUDDINGSTON, Thomas, of Kilduncane, Fife; 392
DUDELEY; 259
—, John, de Kyngstonlisle; 254
DUDELLEY, Ld Ambros; 138
DUDLEY; 179, 259
—, Baron; 259
—, Ld; 259
—, de Dudeley, Baro; 183
—, Bp of Durham; 254
—, Edw, Ld; 179
—, Edward, Ld; 179
—, John; 194, 255
—, John, KG; 259
—, John, Ld; 174, 255, 259
—, Sir John; 179
—, John, D of Northumberland, E of Warwick, E Marshal, KG; 255
—, Robert, E of Leicester; 255
—, le Baron de, of Staffs; 259
—, William; 255
—, William, Bp of Durham; 255
—, Wm; 255
DUDLYE; 179
DULON, Baron, of Irld & Chymwete, Devon; 233
DUMBART, S Jehan; 249
DUMGATE; 318
DUNBAR; 237-8
—, Sir Alexander of; 250
—, Alexr; 250
—, Chapter of Collegiate Ch of; 237
—, Sir David; 238
—, Sir David de, Ld of Cockburn; 237
—, George, E of March; 247
—, George, 3rd E of March; 238
—, George, 11th E of; 247
—, of Kynhownquhar; 238
—, E of March; 238
—, E of Marche; 238
—, Cunte Patrick; 238
—, Patrick de, s of Count of Lennox; 247
—, Patrick, E of; 112, 238
—, Sir Patrick, of Biel; 250
—, Patrick, E of Lennox; 238
—, Patrick de, E of March; 238
—, Patrick, E of March; 238
—, Patrick, 2nd E of March; 237-8
—, Patrick, 1st E of March; 237-8
—, Patrick, 7th E of, 1248-89; 123
—, Patrick, 5th E of Dunbar (1182-1232); 112
—, Patrick, 7th E of Dunbar; 238
—, Patrick V, E of March; 238
—, Conte Patrik; 238
—, Cunte Patrik; 238
—, le Conte Patrik; 238
—, Patrike 'fiz le conte'; 247
—, le Counte Patriz; 129
—, Wm; 253
DUNBAR & March, Patrick, E of; 237-8
DUNBARRE, Patrick, Conte de; 238
DUNBLANE, John, Bp of; 213
—, Maurice Bp of; 250
DUNDAS, James of that ilk; 112
—, o yt ilk; 125
—, of that ilk; 125
DUNDEE, John de; 213
—, Preceptory of St Anthony; 250
DUNDUN; 157
DUNHEAD; 241, 246
DUNHED; 236, 241, 244
—, John; 241
DUNHEUED, John de; 112
DUNMERE, Richard de; 51
DUNN, Owen; 207
DUNRE, Richard de; 361
—, Richard, Ld of; 361
DUNSTANVILLE, Reginald de, E of Cornwall; 270
DURANT, Peter, Esq; 203
DURAS, Gaillard, Ld; 163
DURAUNT, Denise; 389
DURBURGH, John de; 374
DURHAM, City of; 287
—, John; 350
DURRANT, John; 185
DUTTON; 336
DYAR; 294
DYCHANT, John; 77
—, Robert; 57
DYCONS; 357
DYER; 294
—, Stephen; 294
DYKESONE, of Ormistoun; 215
DYMMOK; 262
—, Mons John; 262
—, Philippus; 262
DYMMOKE, Mayster; 262
DYMOCK, Sir T; 265
DYMOCKE, Thomas; 271
DYMOKE; 261-2
—, John; 262
—, Sir John; 255
—, Sir Lionel; 261
—, Margaret; 261
—, Sir Robert; 262
DYNAN, Joce de; 289
DYNELEY; 275
DYNSEY; 283

DYPRE; 224
DYSNY; 283
—, Sr; 283
—, Mons R; 286
DYSTRANGE, Henry; 270
DYTONES; 379
DYTONS, Mons gautte; 379
DYTTON; 322
—, Lancs; 322
DYVA, William de; 195
EASTNEY, John; 283
—, Richard; 302
ECCLES, John de; 185
ECCLESHALE, Robert de; 374
—, Sir Robert; 378
ECHEBASTON, Sr Richard; 220
ECHELASTONE; 155
ECHINGHAM; 2
ECHOS, Le Rei de; 251
ECLELASTON, of Leics; 220
ECLELASTONE, of Leics; 220
ECLINGES, William de; 315
ECLINNGES; 315
ECLYNGE, Mons William de; 315
ECOSSE, le Roi d'; 251
ECTON, Sir Milis, of Hants; 76
EDE, Majory; 199
EDEFYN, Sir E; 104
EDEWARS, le fielz le Roy; 299
EDINGTONE; 282
EDLINGHAM, John; 63
—, Walter of; 112
EDMONSTON, of Duntroch; 2
—, Sir Wm of Duntreath, Justice-General of
  Scotland; 3
EDMUND, Sire; 299
—, Sire, frere le Rey; 300
—, Sire, frere le Roy; 299
—, Sire, frere le roy; 299
EDWARD; 298
EDWARD I; 287, 298
EDWARD, le fitz le Rey; 299
EDWARD OF GLOUCESTER; 287
EDWARD III; 287
EDYNGTONE, Gilbert de; 81
EGBASTON; 218
—, Mons Rich de; 218
EGEBALSTOUN, Henricus de; 334
EGEBASTON, Henr' de; 334
EGERTON; 229
EGGERTON; 229
—, of Ches; 229
—, M Rauffe, of Rydley, Ches; 229
EGIPT; 13
EGLINTON; 3-4
—, Sir Hugh; 4
EGREMOND; 124
EGREMOYNE, Ld; 155
EGRENHALE; 72

EGRENHALL; 67, 72
EGREVALE, Robert; 223
EGREYNALL; 223
EGRYNALE, Mons Robt; 223
EGSTALE, Whilliam, of Staffs; 324
EIRLIEHEYM; 169
EKELSALL; 378
EKELYSHALL; 378
EKENEY; 267
—, Mons Rich de; 268
EKENEYE, Richard; 268
EKENY; 268
EKERYNGE, Mons Rich de; 43
EKLESCHALE, Sir Robert; 378
ELAND, Sr de; 50
—, J; 50
—, Sir John de; 50
—, John de, of Wrenthorpe, Yorks, Kt; 50
—, of Kingston on Hull, Yorks; 263
—, Robt, of Lincs; 50
—, Thomas de; 50
—, Wm of; 274
ELANDE, John; 50
ELCHEFELD; 95
ELCHEFFELD, Oxfords; 25
ELCHESFELD, of Oxfords; 95
ELEANOR, Queen; 99
ELEFELD, Monsr Gilbert de; 97
ELEFETE, of Oxon; 95
ELESFELD; 95
—, s'gilberd; 95
ELEZ, Sire Robert le fiz; 386
ELFRIDE, K of England; 48
—, K in England; 48
ELFRIDUS, Rx; 48
—, K of Britain; 48
ELKESFELD; 95
ELKYSFELDE; 65
ELLAM; 319
ELLEM, Alexr; 199
ELLESFELD; 95
—, M de; 96
—, Sir; 95
—, Sr Gilbert; 95
—, Sr Johan; 25, 95
ELLESFIELD, Monsire de; 95
ELLINGTON; 5, 9
ELLIS; 155
—, Fytz; 386
ELLON, Robert; 217
ELMEBRIGG, John de, of Kent; 331
ELMES; 55
ELMESTED, John; 332
ELSEFELD, Gilbert de, Kt; 63
—, Sire Gilbert de; 95
ELSTED, Mons Gilbert de; 141
ELTHAM, John of; 304, 308
—, John of, E of Cornwall; 307
ELTON, Sir John, of Yorks; 80

ELWICK; 290
ELWIK; 290
ELYS, B Roberte le fitz; 386
—, Fitz; 386
ELYSDON; 168
EMERIKE, Monsire John; 344
EMERYKE, Sr; 344
EMNEBURGH, Richard de, Soms, Kt; 361
EMRIK; 89
EMRYK, Mons John; 89
ENDERBY; 63, 69
—, John, of Stratton, Beds, Esq; 69
ENEBY; 333
—, Robert; 333
ENEFELD, Thomas de; 394
ENGAYN, Katharine; 285
ENGAYNE, Catherine d', of Axminster,
   Devon; 285
—, Katherine; 286
ENGELFELD, Sir Thomas, of Berks; 68
ENGHAM, William; 48
ENGHM; 48
ENGLAND; 193, 274, 286-8, 297-8, 301
—, K of; 283-4, 287
—, King of; 287
—, D of Cornwall; 299
—, Edmond of; 300
—, Edw 1; 286
—, K Edw 1; 287
—, Edw 1 or 2; 274
—, K Edward 1; 287
—, K Edward 3; 287
—, K Erpewold in; 137
—, Hen ; 274
—, ?Henry I; 264
—, 'K Henry ..'; 287
—, K Henry 2; 287
—, K Henry 3; 287
—, John, K of; 298
—, John K of, Count of Mortaigne; 255
—, K John; 287
—, Mary; 274
—, Mgt, Q of; 274
—, le Prince; 299
—, Q of; 274
—, Q Anne Boleyn; 298, 300
—, Q Anne Bullen; 300
—, K Richard; 287
—, K Richard I; 123
—, Richard 1; 286
—, Richard I; 284
—, Roy de; 287
—, K Stephen; 287
—, William I; 88
—, Wm, E of Boulogne & Martain; 300
—, Wm, E of Warenne, Boulogne & Mortain;
   300
ENGLEFELD, John; 210
—, John de; 68

—, Philip de, Kt; 67-8
—, Robert; 68
—, Roger de; 36
—, William de, of Englefield, Berks; 186
ENGLEFEUD, William de; 78
ENGLEFIELD; 34, 68, 186
—, Philip; 68
ENGLET; 280
ENGLETERE, le Roy de; 287
ENGLETERRE, le Roy d'; 287
ENGLEYS, Sr Johan; 278
—, of North...; 278
—, s' Rob'; 278
—, S Robert de; 278
ENGLISCHE; 331
ENGLISH; 278, 285, 307, 309
—, of Staffs; 285
—, Thomas; 278
—, William; 315
ENGLISHE, Staffs; 285
ENGLYS, of Tawne; 315
—, Mons Thomas; 278
—, Mons Willm; 315
()ENT; 266
ENTWISLE, Sir Bertyn of; 168
EPPYNGE, Matilda de; 75
ERCALEW, Sir John; 81
ERCALEWE, Sr Willame; 81
ERCALWE, Sire William de; 81
ERCEDECNE, Matilda; 41
ERCEDEKNE, Matilda; 36, 41
ERDINGTOM; 257
ERDINGTON; 257-8, 260
—, Egidius de; 270
—, S' Giles, Staffs; 282
—, Sr Henri; 271
—, Henry de, Kt; 261, 271
—, Hugh; 260
—, Sir T; 258
—, Thomas de; 255, 258
—, Thomas, Kt; 255
ERDINGTONE; 259
—, Berks; 271
ERDSWICK, Thos; 322
ERDYNGTON; 258, 271
ERDYNGTONE, of Warws; 271
EREBY, Ches; 267
—, of Ches; 258
—, Sr Johan; 267
EREFORD; 358
ERELINGTON, Monsire d'; 165
ERINGSTON, William; 69
ERLHAM, John de; 52
ERMENIE, Rex; 157
ERMENYE, King of; 168
—, le Roy de; 135
ERMONYE, Kyng of; 226
—, Roy de; 164
ERPEWOLD, King; 190

—, Rx; 190
ERREBY, S Jeh de; 267
ERRINGTON; 38
ERUSBY, Sir William; 383
ERYNGTON, Gerard, of London; 86
—, John de; 38
ESCOCE, Rey de; 251
ESCOSE, le roy de; 251
ESCOTEVILL, Baron; 140
ESCRIUEN, William de, of Calne; 312
ESH, Roger of; 217, 349
—, Simon of; 349
ESHARTON, Mons Thomas de; 314
ESLINGTON; 40
—, John de; 40
—, Robert of; 40
—, Robert of, Kt; 40
—, Robert, of Eslington, Northd, Kt; 40
ESMTON; 148
ESPAINE, le roy d'; 124
ESSEBI, Jordan; 343
ESSEBY, William de; 255-6
ESSELINGTON, Robert; 38
—, Robert de, Kt; 40
ESSELYNGTON, Mons John de; 52
—, Thomas de; 53
ESSEX, John of; 112
—, Roy de; 1
ESTBURY; 95
ESTEBY; 386
ESTELEY, Ld; 156
—, Sr Andrew de; 155
ESTENE, Rychard; 279
ESTENEY; 280
ESTENGRAVE, Sire Johan; 141
ESTENGREVE, Joan de; 141
—, Mons' John; 141
ESTHELASTON; 155
ESTHEYE, Andrew de, Kt; 112
ESTINGGREFE; 141
ESTLE; 125, 209
—, of Leics; 209
ESTLEE, Giles de; 209
—, Sire Nicholas de; 155
ESTLEYE, Andreu de; 155
ESTONE; 345
—, Johan; 148
—, John de; 148
—, Ric de; 345
—, Richard; 345
—, Richard de; 345
ESTOTEVILE, Nicolas, of Norf; 279
—, Robert, of Norf; 140
ESTOTEVILLE, Estond de; 140
—, Robert d'; 100
ESTOUN, John de; 132
ESTOUTEUILLE; 279
ESTOUTEVILLA, Jn de; 140
ESTRAINGE, Rogg' le; 272

ESTRANG, Sir Roger; 271
ESTRANGE; 257-8
—, Eube le; 258
—, Sire Fouk le; 257
—, Johan le; 257
—, Sire Johan le; 258
—, Johans le; 258
—, John, of Kuskin; 255
—, John l', of Knockin, Salop; 255
—, Matilda L'; 255
—, Roger le; 271
—, Sire Roger le; 271
ESTRANUNGE, Fulco de; 258
ESTRAUNG, Sir Fake; 257
ESTRAUNGE, Le; 258
—, Fulcho le, 1st Baron; 263
—, Hamond, of Gloucs; 270
—, Sire Hamoun le; 270
—, Sire Johan le; 271-2
—, John le; 263
—, Sir John; 258
—, John, of Gloucs; 273
—, Rogerus Le; 272
ESTRONGE, John le; 257
ESTUDELEY; 296
ESTWODE, Richard; 185
ETHEL; 112
ETHERESSETE; 189
ETHERESSETTE; 191
ETHRESSETT; 191
ETTON; 3
—, Sir J of; 76
EU, le Counte d'; 145
—, Ralph de Yssondin, Count of; 80
EUER, Hugh de; 334
EUERS, Henry de; 337
EUERYNGHAM, S' Edmund; 154
EUGEYS, John d'; 112
EUNYNGHLI; 336
EURE, Hugh of; 112, 334
—, Sir Hugh of; 334
—, Sir Robt of; 334
—, Roger de, le Fitzjohn; 337
EUSTACE; 380
—, Fitz; 382
—, Sire Thomas fitz; 341
EVERINGHAM; 161, 173, 336
—, Sr de; 173
—, Adam; 161, 173
—, Adam de; 161
—, Sir Adam; 161
—, Sir Adam de; 112, 161, 334
—, Sir Adame; 336
—, Sir John; 228
—, Lawrans; 336
—, Lawrence; 336
—, Raynold de; 161
—, Reynold; 161
—, Robert, of Devon; 161

—, Robert, Norf; 336
—, Monsire de, de Rokeley; 336
—, de Rokkele; 336
—, Sir Thomas d'; 220
—, Monsire Thos de; 220
EVERRYNGHAM, Adam; 338
EVERYGHAM, Mons Reyn'; 161
EVERYNGAM, Sr Adam; 336
EVERYNGHAM; 161, 336
—, Mons Ad; 161
—, Sire Ad'; 161
—, Adam; 161
—, Adam de; 161, 173
—, Sire Adam de; 336
—, Johannes; 336
—, Mons John de; 161
—, Sir John; 161, 336
—, Mons John, de Roklay; 336
—, Robert de; 123
—, Robts de; 161
—, Monsr de, de Rokeley; 336
—, Mons W, son filtz; 209
EVINGHAM, Adam; 336
EVSTAFF; 381
EWERYNGHAM, Sir John; 161
EWSTAS; 382
EXCETERE, D of; 308
EXCETUR, D of; 308
EXCETYR, D[uke] of; 308
EXETER; 195
—, Duke of; 308
—, D of; 308
—, Henry, D of; 308
—, John, D of; 307-8
—, Provosts of; 261
EYLAND; 50
EYLANDE; 50
EYRE; 200
—, Mayor of London; 206
—, Simon; 206
—, Symkin; 206
—, Thomas; 211
EYSSELDONE, of Devon; 162
EYSTON, William, of Istelworth; 14
FACOMBERGE, Monsire de; 124
FACONBERGE; 124
—, Monsire de; 124
—, Monsire Walter de; 221
FACONBREGE, Le Sr de; 124
FACY, Thomas; 353
FACYNEL, William; 86
FAGEUILLE; 338
FAIRFAX; 84, 216
—, Sir Guy; 216
—, Sir Thomas; 216
—, Sir Thos; 70
—, of Walton, Yorks; 216
FAIRFORD; 285, 289
FAIRLE, of that ilke Braide (sic); 224

FAIRLIE, Archibald, friar of Braid; 224
—, James; 217
—, John; 205
—, Wm, of Braid; 224
FALCON; 221
FALCONBRIDGE; 147
—, Roger; 155
—, Wm Nevil, Ld; 124
FALERON; 221
FALIOT, John, de Norf; 324
FALLAGE; 106
FALTON, Monsire; 260
FALYNGBROME; 204
FANHOPE, Ld; 245
FANNEL, of Northants; 393
FANOPE, Ld; 245
FARANFULF; 255
FARRILE, Richard de, bailie of Edinburgh; 378
FARRYNGES, Richard de; 78
FASTOLF; 82
—, Hugh; 334
—, Nicholas; 337
—, Nicholaus; 337
FAUCO(n)berge, S Walter; 124
FAUCOMBERGE; 24, 161
—, del South; 286
—, Mons' Henry; 24
—, Mons' Henry de; 24
—, John de; 112
—, Sr Waultre; 221
FAUCOMBERGES; 24
FAUCOMBRIGE; 283
—, Essex; 24
FAUCONBERG; 23-4, 124
—, John de; 222
—, Monsr John; 221
—, Sir John de; 112
—, Roger; 155
—, Thos; 112
—, Walter de; 124
—, Sir Water de; 112
—, William; 221
—, William de; 24
—, Sir William, of Catfoss, d1294; 24
—, Sir Wm; 286
FAUCONBERGE; 24, 286
—, du Sir; 286
—, Sr de; 221
—, Sire Henri; 24
—, Sr Henry de; 24
—, J de; 222
—, Mons' Roger; 155
—, Monsire de Sa; 289
—, Sire Walter; 221
—, Mons Waut'; 24
FAUCONBERGH, Isabella de; 112, 320, 375
FAUCONBREGE; 24
FAUCONBRIDGE, The Lorde; 124

FAUCONBRIG, de South, Monsr; 286
FAUCOUNBERGE, Sire Wauter; 124
FAUCUNBERG, Wm de; 24
FAUCUNBERGE, William de; 24
FAUCUNBRUGH, Monsr Henry; 24
FAUKENBERGE, S' William; 286
FAUKERHAM; 357
FAUKONBERGE, Le Sr de; 124
FAUMER, William of; 389
FAUREL, Sr; 394
FAUVEL, Hugo; 394
—, Mons Roger; 394
—, Sire Willame; 394
FAUVELL, Mons; 393
—, Monsire; 394
FAVELL, Gilbertus; 394
FAVERSHAM; 197
FAVERSHAM ABBEY; 304
FAWCOMBRYGE; 124
FAWCONBERGH, Ld; 124
FAWEDBRIDGE; 240
FAWKENER, John; 73
FAYERFAX, of Yorks; 216
FAYPOW, R'; 17
FAYREFORD; 281
FAYRFAX, Sir Thomas; 216
—, of Yorks; 84
FAYRFORD; 95
FECKENHAM, Henricus de, of Kidderminster,
  Worcs; 58
FEENES; 277
FELBREKE, Sir Symond, d1442; 187
FELBRIDGE, Geor; 235
—, George; 112
—, Sire Robert de; 135
FELBRIGE, Mons' George; 156
—, Gloucs; 260
—, Mons Gorg; 187
—, Norf; 187
—, S' Roger; 135
FELBRIGG; 112, 156, 187
—, Robert de; 112
—, Simon de, Kt; 112
—, Sy; 135
FELBRIGGE; 112, 135, 187, 245
—, George; 156, 187
—, George de, of Mildenhall, Suff; 112
—, Mons John; 187
—, Sire Rogert; 188
—, Simon; 135
—, Simon, Kt; 187
—, Sir Simon; 135, 188
—, Sir Simon, KG; 135
—, Simon de, of Felbrigg, Norf, Kt; 112
—, Sir Symond; 135
—, Symond de; 187
FELBRYDGE; 135, 156
—, Mons; 135, 141
—, Sir; 135

FELBRYG, Emond; 135
—, George; 188
—, Sir Roger; 188
FELBRYGGE; 188
—, Sir Simon, Kt; 112
—, Sir Symon, KG; 187
FELBRYGGS, Sir S; 135
FELDE; 234
—, John atte, fishmonger of London; 269
—, John atte, of London, fishmonger; 269
FELLBRUGGE, Sir Symon; 132
FELLE; 337
FELTON; 144, 258, 260-2, 267, 269, 273
—, de; 262
—, le S; 287
—, Sir ...; 265
—, Fitz a; 267
—, George de; 273
—, Gloucs; 270
—, Hamo de, Kt; 255
—, Hamond de; 260-1
—, Mons Hamond de; 260
—, Monsire Hamond de; 260
—, John de; 255, 273
—, John of; 260
—, Mons John de; 273
—, Sir John; 262
—, Sir John de; 262
—, Sir John, of Hunts; 260
—, Sir John, Ld of Ochiltree; 263
—, le S'r de; 260-1, 277
—, S Robert de; 260
—, Sir Robert; 260
—, Sire Roger de; 268
—, Sir T; 261
—, Mons Th; 262
—, S' th'; 260
—, Monsire Thomas de; 262
—, Sir Thomas; 261
—, Sir Thomas, KG; 262
—, Thomas de; 255, 262
—, S' Thos; 262
—, Monsr Tomas; 262
—, Tomas; 285
—, Mons W de; 273
—, Sire Willame; 270
—, Mons William; 273
—, Monsire William de; 273
—, S William de; 270
—, Sir William; 273
—, William of; 270, 273
—, Sir Wm de; 263
—, Sir Wylyam; 273
FELTONE; 273
—, de; 260
—, H; 258
—, Sire John de; 262
—, Sire Robert de; 260
—, Tho; 262

FELTWICK, David; 263
FENER, Monsire Thalman; 210
FENES, Giles de; 297
—, Sire Johan de; 126
—, Mons Rogier; 276, 283
FENIS, James; 275
—, Thomas, Ld Dacre; 275
FENLES, S' Will, of Suss; 320
FENTON; 31
FENTOUNE, of that ilk; 370
FENYS, Sir J; 269
—, Mr, of Oxfords; 277
—, Sir R; 256
—, Sir Thomas; 277
—, Sir Thomas, Kt 1501; 277
—, S Will of Suss; 321
FENZ; 277
—, Sire Giles de; 297
FERERS; 25
—, Sire Thomas de; 342
FERIBY, Wm de; 197
FERINDRAUCH, Henry de; 252
FERINGES, Richard; 78
FERNYNGHAM, John de; 331
FERRERS; 177
—, Erle of; 95
—, Elizabeth de, Lady of Chartley; 255
—, Mons' Robert, Baron de Wemme; 194
—, William de; 375
FEYCE, William; 74
FEYNES, of Hurstmonceaux, Suss, Baron
  Dacre of the South; 277
FFAUCONBERGE, Rog'; 156
—, Mons Th; 208
—, Mons W; 221
FFAUCONBRGE, Mons Waut; 124
FFAUCUNBERGE, Sire Walter; 124
FFELBRIG, S Sim; 188
FFITZ PAYNE; 302
FFLAUNDRES, le Count de; 137
FFOLUYLE, S' Matthew; 28
FFOLYOT, Walter; 324
FFORDE, Mons Adam de; 277
FFURNIVAL, Thomas de; 376
FFURNIVALL, Thom de; 376
FFYCHET, S' Tho'; 219
FFYENLL, Jn; 164
FICHET; 219, 221
—, Thomas; 221
—, Thomas, Kt; 217, 221
FICHETT, of Spaxton; 221
—, of Stringston; 248
FIENNES; 277
—, Ld Dacre; 277
—, the Lord Dacre of the South; 277
—, Sir James; 277
—, James, Ld Say & Sale; 277
—, James, Ld Say & Sele; 283
—, Roger; 277

—, Sir Roger; 279
—, Sir Thomas, Ld Dacre; 277
FIF, C de; 341
FIFE; 112
—, le Comte de; 135
—, Duncan, 10th E of Fife; 112
—, Mary, Ctess of; 112, 286
FILBREGGE; 188
—, 'Chevalier'; 243
FILBRIDGE; 209
FILDYNG, William, of Lutterworth; 55
FILEBRIGG, Monsire Roger; 210
FILGERIIS, William de; 320
FILIOT; 97, 324
—, Monsr de; 324
FILLE, Richard; 320
FILMER; 69
FINCH; 74
FINCHAM; 71, 326
—, John; 217
—, Simon; 71
FINES, of Martock; 277
FINEUX, of Essex; 126
FIT, le Conte de; 135
FITCH; 13
FITCHET; 219
—, Monsire Thomas; 221
FITZ ALAIN, Sr Richard, Counte de Arundell;
  132
FITZ-alan, Alianora; 112
FITZ ALAN, Brian; 89
—, Brian, de Bedale; 98
—, Bryan; 89
FITZ-alan, family of; 112
—, Jn, 16th E of Arundel, Captain of Rouen,
  &c; 112
—, Richard, 10th E of Arundel & Surrey; 112
—, Richard, 9th E of Arundel; 112-13
—, Thomas, 11th E of Arundel & Surrey; 113
FITZ ALAYN, Sr Bryan le; 89
FITZ ALEIN, Joh le; 132
FITZ ALEYN, Brian le; 89
—, Bryan de; 87
—, Sire Bryan le; 89
FITZ BARNARD, Thomas; 278
FITZ BRIAN, Alein le; 89
FITZ-ercald; 294-5
FITZ GERARD; 192
FITZ HERBERD; 278
FITZ-Herberd, Johanna, of Rype Manor, Suss;
  308
FITZ HERBERT; 279
—, Sire Johan le fitz Reinald; 277
—, Sir Nicol; 278
—, Reginald fitz Peter; 275
FITZ HUERDE, Edmund; 309
FITZ HUGH, Edmond; 309
FITZ-John, Matthew, Ld of Stokeham; 279
FITZ MABEU, ... le; 143

FITZ MAHEU; 280
—, Herberd; 280
FITZ MARY; 26
FITZ MATTHEW, Herbert; 280
FITZ NICOL; 337
FITZ OSBORNE, William, E of Herefod; 371
FITZ-Paeyn, Robert le; 302
FITZ PAIN, Sir Robert; 283
FITZ PAINE; 303
FITZ PAYN; 302-3
—, le Sr de; 303
FITZ PAYNE; 302-3
FITZ-Payne; 270
FITZ-PAYNE; 302
FITZ-payne; 302
FITZ PAYNE, Mons' John; 303
—, Monsire Robert; 303
—, Robert; 302-3
FITZ-Payne, Robert; 303
FITZ PERS, Renaud le; 278
FITZ PIERS; 277
—, Reginald; 278
FITZ RANAULD; 280
FITZ REYNOLD, Sir John; 278
FITZ-Roger, Robert; 337
FITZ WARYN, Pieres le; 345
FITZ WILLIAM, S' Will'; 92
FITZAERUS, Sir John; 192
FITZALAN; 81, 113, 129, 132
—, 'Le Count de Arondelle'; 132
—, E of Arundel; 132
—, E of Arundell; 132
—, of Bedale; 89
—, Sir Brian; 60
—, Brian, d 1306; 86
—, 'Contte de Aronde' John', d1436; 132
—, 'Contte de Arundell Reschard'; 132
—, Edmund, E of Arundel; 113
—, Henry, KG, E of Arundel; 132
—, Henry, E of Arundel; 132
—, John, E of Arundel; 132, 168
—, John, E of Arundel, Marshal of Engld; 113
—, Richard; 132
—, Richard, E of Arundel; 113, 132, 310
—, Thomas, Archbp of Canterbury; 113
—, Thomas, E of Arundel; 132
—, Thomas, of Arundel, Archbp of York,
  1388-96; 113
—, 'Tomas Conte de Arondell'', d1415; 132
—, William, KG; 132
FITZALURED, of Irld; 98
FITZALYN, Bryan; 60
FITZAWBERNE; 82
FITZBALDWIN, Gilbert; 192
FITZBARNARD, Thomas; 277-8
FITZBERNARD; 278
FITZBRIAN; 86
FITZELLYS; 386
FITZELY, Robert; 386

FITZEUSTACE; 381
—, Lincs; 381
FITZGEFFRY, John; 216
FITZGERALD; 194
FITZGERARD; 192
—, Warin le; 194
FITZGEROLD, Warin; 263
FITZHAMON, Robert; 188-9
FITZHERBERD; 278
—, Edmund, Chev, of Offyngton &c, Suss; 308
FITZHERBERT; 275, 279
—, A; 367
—, in Wales; 279
—, Mahu fiz Johan; 280
—, Matthew; 280
—, Mons Reginald; 317
—, Reginald; 275, 317
FITZIVE; 389
FITZJOHN; 72
—, Essex; 349
—, Lincs; 44
—, Matthew; 275
FITZMEOL; 337
FITZNICHOLL, Thomas, Kt; 334
FITZNICOL; 337
FITZNICOLE; 337
FITZODO, Gilbert; 215
FITZOSBORN; 82
FITZOSBORNE, of Suff & Essex; 82
FITZPAIN; 303
FITZPAINE; 303
FITZPAYN; 303-4
—, Gloucs; 303
—, Robert; 303
FITZPAYNE; 302
—, Robert; 303
—, Robert de; 303
—, Robert, Kt; 302
FITZPERYS; 278
FITZPETER, John fitz Reginald; 275
FITZPIERS, John; 217
FITZRADULF, Nicholas; 14, 74
FITZRALPH; 14
FITZRAUF, Sir Symon; 157
FITZRAUFFE; 100
FITZREGINALD, John; 275
FITZREINALD, John; 275
FITZRENAUD; 314
FITZRERY, Irld; 166
FITZREYNOLD; 275
—, John; 275
FITZROBERT, John; 335
FITZROGER, Sir Henry le; 275
—, Robert; 335
FITZSIMON, Hugh; 113
FITZSYMOUND, Mons Rauf; 128
FITZURSE, Reginald; 199
—, Sir Reginald; 266
—, Robert; 199

FITZWARREN, of Toppley; 391
—, of Totley; 391
FITZWARYN, de Totley; 391
FIZ ALAIN, Jon le; 132
FIZ ALEYN, Richard le, Counte Darundel; 132
FIZ URS, Reygnald; 200
—, Reynold; 200
FIZPAEN, le; 303
FIZPAIN, Sr R; 303
FLAGUIERAN, Richard de la; 11
FLAMANK, Peter; 147
FLAMBARD, Philip; 388
FLANDERS; 113, 137
—, Count of; 137
—, Guy de Dampierre, Count of; 137
—, Philip of Alsatia, E of; 137
—, Robt the Frison, E of; 137
—, Thomas, Count of; 139
FLANDRES, C de; 137
FLAUNDERS, Louis; 113
FLAWNDRYN; 211
FLEET; 55, 223
—, Lawrence de; 218
—, Richard, Ld of; 185
FLEETWICK, David de; 263
FLEMING; 35, 51
—, David, Burgess of Perth; 387
—, Gilbert; 113
—, John; 369
FLEMMING, William; 395
FLEMMYNG, [Rich], Bp of Lincoln; 69
FLEMYNG, Bp of Lincoln; 40
—, Martin; 374
FLEMYNGE, de Wath; 35
FLEMYNGES; 35, 51
FLESCHER, David; 1
FLETE; 55-6, 218
—, John; 224
—, Laurence de, of Wisbeach, Cambs, Kt; 217
—, Laurens; 224
FLETEWICKE; 263
FLETEWIK, Monsire David de; 263
FLETEWYK; 263
FLETWICK; 263
FLETWYK, Mons David de; 263
—, Mons David de, le fitz; 268
FLETWYKE, Beds; 263
FLITTEWIK, Sire David de; 263
FLORIMUND, Ld of Spa...; 212
FLOTE; 55
—, Guillermus; 86
FODRINGHAME, of Powrye; 61
FODRYNGEY, Mons J; 390
FOGGE, Sir ...; 41
FOKERAM; 357
—, Berks; 352
—, Sir Rauf de; 365
—, Richard; 352
—, Sir Richard; 352

—, Sire Richard; 352
—, Richard, of Som, Kt; 356
—, Robert; 356
—, Willimus de; 352
—, Wills de; 357
FOKERAN, M de; 357
FOKERANDE, Mons; 357
FOKINGTONE, Hugh de; 185
FOLCHAMP, Robt de, Derbys; 385
FOLEIAMBE, of Walton, Derbys; 385
FOLEJAMBE, Sir Godifree, de Watton, Derbys; 385
FOLGAMBE; 385
FOLGEHAM; 385
FOLGHAM; 385
—, Sir Alysaundyr, Derbys; 385
—, Sir R; 385
FOLIAMB, Godefridus; 385
FOLIAMBE; 385
—, Godfridus; 385
FOLIET, S Edmond; 379
FOLIOT; 324
—, Bishop; 166
—, M de; 263
—, Sire Edmon; 363
—, Edmound; 379
—, Edmund; 379
—, Esmond; 379
—, Jordan; 320, 361
—, Jordan, of Ingham, Lincs; 320
—, Norff; 324
—, Richard; 113, 324, 379
—, Rychard; 324
—, Samson; 263
—, Sansem; 263
FOLIOTT; 321, 324
—, Richard; 324
—, Saunsum; 263
FOLJAMBE; 384-5
—, Sir ..., Derbys; 385
—, Godfrey; 384-5
—, Mons Godfrey; 385
—, son fitz; 326
—, Thomas; 385
FOLLIOT; 320, 324
—, Monsire; 324
—, Sir Geoffrey; 97
—, Gerard; 379
—, Sir Jeffry; 65
FOLLIOTT; 324
FOLLYOT; 324
FOLVILLE; 67
FOLYOT; 324
—, Jordan; 363
—, of Kent; 7
—, Mons' Richard; 324
FOLYOTH, Rauf; 263
FOLYOTT; 324
—, Sr Edmund; 379

—, Robt, of Suss; 324
FONTIBUS, Richard de, of Kilwingholm etc, Lincs; 371
FORD; 246-7
—, Adam de; 277
—, Adam de la; 281
—, Adam le; 277
—, Devon; 247
—, Joh, of Ashburton, Devon; 247
—, John, of Ashburton, Devon; 248
FORD ABBEY, Devon; 91
FORDE; 160
—, Adam de la; 281
—, Sire Adam de la; 281
—, Sr Adam de la; 281
—, John, of Ashburton, Devon; 248
—, of Kingston on Thames; 160
—, of Kingston on Thames, Surr & Harting, Suss; 281
FORDHAM; 34
—, Willimus; 34
FORDHM; 34
FORDWICH, Kent, Mayor of; 192
FOREST; 10
—, Guaston de; 58
FORESTER, Mons John Neville le; 161
—, John le, of Stony-Stratford, Bucks; 217
FORMAN; 48
FORMI, Sire; 364
FORNAYS; 246
FORNEAUS; 381
FORNEAUX; 383
FORNEUS, Sir Maheu; 381
—, Sir Maue; 381
FORNEVALE, Sir; 376
—, Sr de; 376
FORNEYS; 246
FORNIVAL, le Sr; 376
—, M; 378
—, Thom de; 376
—, Sire Thomas de; 376
FORNIVALE, le Sr de; 376
—, Gerard de, of Staffs; 375
—, S Thomas; 376
—, Thomas de; 376
FORNIVALL, le Sr de; 376
FORNYVAL, Sir Thomas, 'le Filz'; 392
FORNYWALE, Ld; 376
FORSTEBURI, Henry de; 301
FORSTER, London; 249
—, Thomas, Lond; 249
—, Thos, London; 249
FORTESCU, Sir John; 350
FORTESCUE, John; 351
FORTHE; 265
FORTON, John de; 360
FOSSADE, Mons Emery de; 82
FOSSARD, Mons' Rob't; 325
—, Will, Baro de Mulgrave; 325

FOSSARDE, Robert; 325
FOTHERINGHAM, David, of Powie; 331
—, Sir Hugh, Kt; 89
—, Margaret; 75
—, Thomas, of Powrie Wester; 75
—, Thos; 89
—, Wm; 69
FOTHRYNGAY, Mons' John; 265
—, Monsr John; 265
FOUGERES, Wm de; 320
FOUKERHAM, Thomas; 357
FOUKESHAM, Thomas; 355
FOULCHAMP, Mons Godfr; 341
FOULDON, Simon de; 49
FOULISHURST, Matthew de; 21
FOULKES, de Penebrugge; 88
FOULS; 88
FOULTES, Willame de; 87
FOURD; 281
FOURDHAM; 34
FOURNEAUX; 381
FOURNES ABBEY; 343
FOURNEVAL, Thomas de; 376
FOURNIVAL, Thomas; 375
FOURNIVALL; 376
—, de; 376
—, Sir Thomas; 376
FOURNYALE, Tomas; 377
FOURNYVALE, le Sire de; 376
FOURNYVALL; 376
FOWKES, Richard, Rector of Birdbrook; 390
FOWRYS, S' John of; 84
FOX, William, of Colde Ascheby, Northants; 113
FOXCOTE, Thomas, Ld of; 316
—, Thomas, of Stanford Manor, Berks; 281
FOXLE, John de; 14
—, Mons' John de; 18
—, Sir John de; 14
—, of Suss; 19
FOXLEY; 14, 19, 56
—, of Northants; 18
—, Thomas; 14
FOXLLE, Sire Johan de; 18
FOXTON, Robert de, of Draughton, Northants; 245
FRAMEYS, Katharine; 233
FRAMPTON, John, esq; 320
FRANCEIS, Mons Adam; 158
FRANCES, John; 61
FRANCEYS, Sir Thomas; 142
FRANCIS, Sir Adam; 159
—, John; 61
—, Wm; 113
FRANDOLF; 257
FRASER, James, of Frendraught; 387
—, Wm, of Philorth; 113
FRAUNCES, Adam; 159
—, Sir Adam; 159

FRAUNCEYS; 61, 158-9
—, Adam; 159, 368
—, Mons Adam; 158
—, Adam, Citizen & Mercer of London; 370
—, Sir Adam, of Middx; 159
—, Alan le; 335
—, Sir G; 158
—, Mabell; 158
—, Mayor of London; 159
—, Nicholaus le, of Wridelyngton, or Worlington, Suff; 113
FRAUNCYS, Sir Adame; 159
FRAUNKTON, Multon de; 60
FRAYN, Monsire de; 22
FRECH; 207
FRECHELIVE, Anker de; 384
FRECHENVILE, Ralph de, of Cruche; 384
FRECHEUILLE; 384
FRECHEVELE; 384
FRECHEVILE; 384
—, Sr de; 384
FRECHEVILL, Monsr de; 384
FRECHEVILLE, Monsire de; 384
—, S'g'r; 384
FRECHVILE; 385
—, John; 385
FRECHVYLL, of Staley, Derbys; 385
FRECHWELL; 384
FREELAND, Robert; 387
FREFORD; 359
—, Mons de; 389
—, Mons le; 360
—, John; 389
—, John de, Kt; 369
—, John de, of Staffs, Kt; 369
FREGENHALL, Richard; 73
FREK, William; 386
FREMELESWORTH, William de; 34
FREMIGHAM, Wallis, of Som; 332
FREMLINGHAM, Ralph de; 192
—, Mons Rauf de; 192
FREMONDE, Thomas; 310
FREMUND; 310
FREMYNGHAM, John, of Waleis; 332
FREN', Mons Hag' de; 22
FREN, S' Hugh; 22
FRENCH; 203
FRENCHE; 386
FRENDRAUCHT, Henry; 252
FRENE; 22
—, de; 22
—, Sr de; 22
—, Hugh; 22
—, Hugh de; 22
—, Mons' Hugh de; 22
—, Walter de; 22
FRENES, Sir Walter, of Herts; 319, 347
FRENINGHAM; 331
FRENSHE, of Canterbury; 386

FRENYNGHAM, of Kent; 332
FRERE, Walter, of Sawbridgworth, Herts; 20
FRESCHEVILE, Mons Rauff; 393
FRESFORD, Mons; 357
FRESLANDE, Roy de; 226
FRESNE, Hugh de; 22
FRESNES; 126
FRESSE, Duke of; 325
FRESSHVILLE, le Sr; 385
FRETCHVYLE; 385
FREVILE, Dame Ide de; 255
FREVYLLE, Baldewine; 99
FREWEN, Fulke; 78
FREWKESMERE; 227
FREY, William, of Warws &c; 212
FREYNE; 78
—, Mons Fowk la; 78
—, Roger la; 79
FREYNEE, Mons' Hugh; 22
—, Mons' Rauf; 22
FRISE, William, Sire de; 310
FRISELLE, William; 387
FROGENALLE, of Kent; 33
FROGENHALE; 35
FROGENHALL; 32
FROGGENHALL, Sir John; 33
FROGHALE; 33, 35
FROGHALL; 33
FROGNAL; 33
FROGNALE, Sir Rychard; 35
FROGNALL, Edmond; 33
—, John; 33
—, John, of Kent; 33
—, Thomas; 33
FROME; 150
FROST, Emma; 320
FRY; 59
FRYE, of Devon; 295
FRYS; 59
FUIZ-Paien, Roberti; 303
FUKERAM, Richard; 352, 357
FULCHAMP; 385
FULHAM, William, Fishmonger of London; 211
FULLER; 66
—, Rob, Abbot of Waltham; 80
—, Rob, Abbot of Waltham 1526-38; 80
FULLERTON, John, of that Ilk; 206
FULSHAM, Benet de; 388
FULTHORP; 145, 230
FULTON; 221, 265
FULYOTT, Sir John; 7
FURNAVYLE, Sir Robert; 376
FURNEAUX; 380, 383
—, of Kilve; 381
—, Sir Simon; 380
FURNEFAL, Thomas de, Ld of Sheffield, 1st Baron Furnival; 375
FURNES, Michael de; 30

FURNESS; 246
FURNEUS, Sire Maeu; 381
—, Maheu de; 377
FURNEVAL, Gerard de; 377
FURNEVALL, Monsire de; 376
FURNEWALE, Ld; 376
FURNIAL, William; 375
FURNIVAL; 375-7, 390
—, Ld; 376
—, Ld de; 376
—, Gerard de; 375
—, Gerard, of Munden; 377
—, Thomas de; 375-6
—, Thos; 375
—, Thos de; 376
—, William; 392
—, William de; 376
FURNIVALE, Sir Tomas; 376
FURNIVALL; 376
—, Gerard; 377
—, Gerard de; 375-6
—, Mons Th, son fitz; 392
—, Sire Thomas de; 376
—, Thomas de; 377
—, Thomas de, Ld of Hallamshire; 375
—, Wm; 392
FURNIVALLE, Gerard; 375
—, Walter de; 376
FURNIVALLO, Thomas; 375
FURNUYVALL, Sir Thomas de; 376
FURNYVAL; 376
FURNYVALE; 376
—, Ld; 376
—, Monsieur de; 376
FURNYVALL, Gerard de; 376
—, Lorde; 376
—, Thomas; 376
FURNYVALLE, Ld; 376
FYCHET, Mons Th; 221
—, Thomas Kt; 217
FYCHETES; 221
FYCHETT; 221
FYF, le conte de; 132
FYLBREGG; 209
FYLYOTT, Sir Richard; 324
FYNCH, Margaret; 74
FYNCHAM; 71, 89
FYNCHAN; 71
FYNCHE; 74
—, Elizabeth; 74
—, of London; 74
FYNCHEHAM; 62
FYNCHINFELD; 388
FYNCHYN; 71
FYNELES; 277
FYNES; 218, 275, 279
—, Sir Thomas, Ld Dacre, of Clavarham, Suss;
277
—, Sir Thomas, 8th Baron Dacre, Kt; 275

FYNEUX, John; 132
FYNNYS, The Lord Dacre, of the South; 277
FYTON, Johanne; 320
FYTTON; 3
FYTZ ALLYN, E of Aroundel; 132
FYTZHERBERDE; 278
GADDESDEN; 41
GAGHE, Matheu; 290
GAINCTE, Sir Gylbert of; 222
GAITFORD; 294
GALES, Jakelyne; 356
—, le Prince de; 299, 311
—, Prince de; 310-11
—, le Prynce de; 311
GALEYS, William le; 390-1
GALLE, John de; 73
GALLES, Prince de; 311
GALLEWAIT, Le Cont de; 124
GALLOWAY; 113, 128, 164
—, Thos of; 192
—, ye lord of, of auld; 167
GALWAY, Alan, Sire de; 167
GAMAGE; 367
—, Adam de; 367
—, Raffe; 367
—, Ralph; 367
GAMAIGE; 367
—, of Wales; 367
GAMELIN, Laurence; 349
GAMMAGE; 367
—, Morgan; 367
—, Robert; 367
GAMTS, of Yorks; 327
GANT, Gilbert de; 326
—, Gilbert de, E of Lincoln; 86
GARDA, G de la, of France; 392
GARDINS, William de, of Oxfords, Kt; 26
GARDYN, Cambs; 26
—, of Cambs; 26
—, Sire Thomas de; 26
GARE, Sir Simon atte; 302
GARELYNE, John, of Suthgivel; 371
GARGRAVE; 47
GARNET; 245
—, 'Le Roy de'; 238
GARNON; 195
GARNONS, Sir Randol; 129
GARRFELD, de ...; 72
GARRIOCH, James, of Kynstare; 382
GARSALE, Berks; 336
—, Thomas de, Kt, Warws; 335
—, Sir Thos de; 335
GASTNEIS; 162
—, John de; 162
—, John de, Rector of Cranewik; 162
—, Thomas de, Kt; 162
—, William de, Kt; 162
GATE, Agnes atte; 230
—, Geoffrey, Kt; 285

—, Sir Jeferay; 285
GATEGANG, John; 113
—, Richard; 240
GATESDON, John de; 14
GAUCE; 235, 245
GAUFELD; 66
GAUFELDE; 72
GAUNT; 84, 327-8
—, G; 328
—, Geffrey de; 328
—, Gilb't de; 330
—, Mons' Gilb't de, de Swaldale; 328
—, Sire Gilberd de; 328
—, Gilbert; 328
—, Gilbert de; 70, 327-8
—, Sir Gilbert; 328
—, Gilbert de, E of Lincoln; 90
—, William de; 327
GAUNTZ, Mons Gilbert; 328
GAWEN, Johne; 370
GAWSELL, Nycolas; 66
GAY; 305
GAYE, S Simo, of Kent; 302
GAYEFOR ALIAS GOATFORD; 294
GAYNES; 61-2
GAYTEFORD; 294
GAYTEFORDE, T; 373
GAYTFORDE, John; 294
GAYTON, Ralph de; 386
GAYVAGE, Mons Payn de; 366
GEFFARD, Sir Joh; 283
GEFFARDE; 283
GEFFORDE, George; 282
GEI, Water de; 223
GELDEFORD, Johan de; 75
GELDER, Wm, D of; 137
GELDERLAND, William, Duc de; 253
GELDERS, Reynald II, E of; 182
GELDO, Adam de; 57
GELDRES, Mary of; 253
GELING, S William de; 315
GELINGES, William de; 315
GELLERS, le Conte de; 145
—, le conte de; 145
GELOUER; 388
GELOVER; 388
GELRE, le Duc de; 146
GENEURE, Petrus de; 138
GENEVA, Peter de; 126, 138
GENEVRE, Eble de; 138
—, Piers de; 179
GENEWELL; 51
GENNE, William le; 276
GENNIVILLE; 283
GENOESE, the; 3
GEOFFREY ATTE HACCHE; 76
GEORGE, Mons' Baudewyn Seint; 213
GERARD; 157, 187
—, John; 217-18

—, Sir Pers; 172
—, Piers; 172
—, T; 215
—, Sir Thomas; 172
—, Thomas; 113
—, Sir Thomas, of the Brym; 172
—, Sir Thomas 'of the Brymme'; 172
GERMAN, Mons P; 325
—, Mons P..; 368
GERMEYN, Joh'n, of Suff; 189
GERMIN, John, of Suff; 189
GERMYN; 189
—, of Suff; 189
GERMYNOUN, Monsr de; 363
GERNEGAN FIZ HUGHE; 140
GERNET; 245
GERNONE; 325
GERNONS; 271
—, Randle, E of Chester; 129
—, Randolf; 129
GERNUZ, Ranulph; 129
GEROLDI, Warinus filius; 194
GEROUYS; 292
GERRADE, Thomas; 128
GERRARD; 169
GERY; 375
—, Willm, de Berkeway; 56
—, Willyam; 56
GEY, Walter de; 218, 223
GEYTON, Ralph de; 386
GIBBON; 223
GIBES; 13
GIBON; 226
GIBTHORPE; 52
GIFFARD; 268, 282-5
—, le; 283
—, Monsire; 283
—, de Bef; 297
—, of Claydon; 283
—, Elis; 306
—, Sire Esmoun; 297
—, Monsire Gilbert, de Brymmesfeld; 284
—, Holekirn; 35
—, Hossebarn; 76
—, Johan; 284
—, Munsire Johan; 284
—, Sire Johan; 284
—, Sire Johan le boef; 297
—, John; 284
—, S John; 284
—, Sir John; 284, 287
—, John de Bef; 297
—, John le boef; 297
—, Monsire John, de Brymmesfeld; 284
—, John, of Brymesfield; 282
—, Jon; 284
—, Osbert; 68
—, Sir Osbert; 34
—, Osborne; 35

—, Mons' Oubarne; 35
—, Mons' Oubern; 35
—, 'de Paules'; 304
—, Sr Robert; 365
—, Sir Thomas; 284
—, Water; 285
—, Mons' William; 284
—, William; 147
GIFFARDE, le Sr; 284
GIFFORD; 282, 284, 297
—, Alexr, Parson of Newlands; 69
—, of Brimsfieldd; 282
—, of Claydon; 286
—, of Hinton [St George]; 297
—, Sir J; 287
—, James, of Sheriffhall; 89
—, Jas, of Sheriffhall; 61
—, John, Ld of Yester; 62
—, Osbert; 282
—, Thomas; 69
—, Walter; 285
—, of Yester; 62, 90
GIFFORDE, Osbarn; 77
GILBERTUS, Canonicus; 98
GILDEFORD, Jan de; 75
GILL; 190
GILLIOT, Nicholas de Markyngton; 319
GILPIN; 212
GIMIGIS, Nicholas de; 38
GISORS; 146, 235
—, 'Jesore'; 244
—, Johan; 244
GISSYNG; 322
GLADIUS; 310
GLADSTONE, John; 113
—, Sir Wm, Kt; 196
GLAMIS, Ld; 250
GLASBROK, William de; 229
GLASINGBURY, Sr Henry de; 351
GLASTENBURY; 358
GLASTIGB, Sr Henry; 357
GLASTINBERI; 351
GLASTINBURI; 351
GLASTINGBURS, Sire Henri de; 351
GLASTINGBURY; 357
—, Monsire de; 352
—, Monsr de; 358
—, of Dorset & Som; 357
—, Henry de, Kt; 355
—, Sgr; 357
GLASTINGBYRY, Sr de; 358
—, John; 355, 357
GLASTONBURY; 357
—, Henry de; 365
—, Sir Henry de; 356
—, Sir Hy; 357
GLASTYNBURY, S Henry de; 351
GLENDOUR, Owen; 142
GLOUCESTER, Walter; 308

GLOUCESTRE, Mousire de; 308
—, Sire Walter de; 309
GLOVERS' CO; 295
GLOWCESTRE; 309
—, Duke of; 309
GLYNDOUR, Owen; 310
GLYNTON, Mons Robert de; 331
GOBAND; 43
—, John; 41
—, of Lincs; 43
GOBANDE; 43
—, Mons; 43
GOBAUD, Monsire; 43
—, Sr; 43
—, Johan; 43
—, Sire Johan; 43
—, Johannes; 43
—, John; 376
GOBAUDE, Mons le; 43
GOBIOUN, William; 379
GOCH, Mathew; 290
—, Morgan; 58
GODALE, William, of St Albans; 113
GODSALM, Richard, of Horndon, Essex, Kt;
   312
GODYNGG, Philip; 229
GODYNGTON; 354
GOLAFRE, Isabella; 113
GOLD, of Stowemarket, Suff; 212
GOLDE, of Suff; 160
GOLDINGAM, S' John de; 257
GOLDINGEHAM, William de; 65
GOLDINGHAM, Aleyn de; 65
—; 97, 360
—, Sir Alex; 360
—, Alexander; 97
—, Mons' Alexander; 97
—, Sir Walter; 65
—, Walter; 93
GOLDINGTON; 260-1, 348
—, Monsire de; 260
—, John de; 266
—, John, Ld of Hunsdon; 255
—, Sire Rauf de; 256
—, William de, Kt, of Essex & Berks; 78
—, Sir William, of Essex; 261
GOLDINGTONE; 262
—, John; 255
GOLDINTOUN, Sire Johan de; 267
GOLDSBOROUGH; 69
GOLDWELL; 113, 160
—, James; 142
GOLDYNGEHAN, Suff; 360
GOLDYNGHAM; 65
—, Suff; 360
—, Walter, Kt; 93
—, Sir Water of, of Essex; 360
GOLDYNGHM, of Norf; 25
GOLDYNGTON; 348, 354

—, John; 255
—, John de; 255
—, of Yorks; 348
GOLDYNGTONE, John de, of Essex, Kt; 255, 267
GOLDYSBOROW, of Oxfords; 69
GOLLOFFYR, Tomas, Oxfords; 47
GOLOPE, Mons John; 348
GOMER; 94
GOMMS, The Lord of; 252
GOMORY; 264
GONNEBY, S Robert de; 124
GONSON; 56, 74
—, William; 74
GONYS, John; 353
GOODRICH; 265
—, William; 263
GORAN, Robertus de; 275
GORDON, Janet, Lady Dunachton; 388
GORDOUNE, of Lochinver; 388
GORE; 302
GORGES; 73
—, Raf de; 5
GORGYS; 89
GORNAY, M Mauys; 2
GORRAN, Robinus de; 255
GOSEHALE, Johan de; 147
—, John de; 320
—, Margaret de, of Kent; 113
GOSELL; 66
GOSHALL, Sir John; 171
GOSHOLME; 276
GOSPELAWE, Richard de; 215
GOSTWIKE, John, Kt; 393
GOSWICK, John of; 200
GOTEHILL; 39
GOTEHURST; 211
GOTISLE; 226
GOUBAD, Les Armes; 43
GOUIL, Brian de; 359
GOULD; 160
GOUNIS, Brian de; 355
GOUNSTON, Mayster; 74
GOUNTS, Brian de; 354
GOURLAY, Wm, of Bagally, Angus; 113
GOURNAY, Mons Maheu de; 2
GOURNEY, Robert de; 234
GOUSSILL; 66
GOUVIS, Mons Brian de; 355
GOVIS; 359
GOVIZ; 340
—, Brian de; 359
GOVYS; 76
GOWER; 69
—, of Stydhm; 79
—, of Stytenam; 79
GOWOWRIS, of Cornw; 205
GOWRE, of Seydnam, Yorks; 79
GOWSELL; 227

GRABON, William; 322
GRACE; 132, 153, 219, 232
—, of Glams; 232
—, William; 4
GRAFTON, of London; 144
GRAI, Henri de; 87
—, Richard de, of Codnor; 59
GRAMARY; 146
—, Sr de; 146
—, Mons' Henry; 146
—, Mons' William; 146
—, Monsire William; 146
—, Sir William; 113
GRAMARYE; 145
—, Mons W; 146
GRAMMARY, William; 146
GRAMORI, s'Welliam; 146
GRAMPOUND, defunct Borough of; 239
GRANDFORD; 242
GRANDISON; 332
—, John; 332
GRANDONE; 342
—, Sire Johan de; 342
GRANDPRE, Henry, Count of; 89
GRANNSUN; 333
GRANSON, Peres de; 333
GRAPER, Peter; 164
GRAS; 301
—, de; 132, 153
—, Nicholas le; 301
—, Nichole le; 301
GRASELL; 24
GRAUMFORD; 261, 285
—, Suss; 242
GRAUNDON, Sr John de; 342
GRAUNDOWNE, Lincs; 342
GRAUNSFORD; 242
GRAUNSON; 333
—, Otys de; 333
GRAUNSSFORD, Sir John, of Suss; 242
GRAUNTSON; 333
GRAUNZUN, S Piers de; 333
GRAY; 71, 87, 113, 162, 346
—, de; 87
—, Ld; 87, 242
—, le Sr de; 88
—, S' de; 87
—, Sr de; 87
—, Amice de; 326
—, Sir Andrew, 2nd Ld; 247
—, Mons Barth; 327
—, Baster; 242
—, Codenore; 87
—, le Sr, de Codnore; 87
—, Ld, of Cotenor; 87
—, Mons Esmound de, de ...; 327
—, Henri le; 87
—, Henry; 242
—, Henry de; 87

—, Sr Henry; 87
—, of Hilton; 16
—, Janet, lady of West Wemyss; 113
—, Johan de; 352
—, John; 240
—, John de; 86, 355
—, Sr John; 327
—, Mons John de, of Codenore; 87
—, S' John, de Heton; 244
—, Mons John de, of Retherfeld; 327
—, Sr Jon, Rotherfeld; 327
—, Visct Lile; 247
—, Master of; 129
—, Sr Nicolas de; 346
—, Sir ... of ?Otley; 242
—, Sir Patrick; 240
—, Sir Patrick, of Kinneff; 247
—, Sir R; 242
—, Ralph; 240
—, Sir Rauff; 242
—, Sir Rauffe; 242
—, Mons Ric' de; 327
—, Mons Richard; 87
—, Monsire Richard; 88
—, Richard de; 87
—, Sire Richard de; 87
—, Sr Richard de; 91
—, Robert; 371
—, Robert le; 327
—, Mons Robert, de Barton en Rydale; 346
—, de Rotherfeld, Sr J; 327
—, le Sire, de Stylyngflete; 327
—, Mons Th de; 242
—, S Thom, Norreys; 242
—, Mons Thomas; 242
—, Mons Thomas de; 167, 244
—, S Thomas de; 248
—, Sr Thomas; 248
—, Thomas; 240
—, Mons Thomas, de Heton; 242
—, Sir Thomas, of Horton; 327
—, Sir Thos of Heton, Ld of Wark; 240
—, W.. le fitz; 247
—, William, Bp of Ely; 242
—, Yorks; 244
GRAY DE BOWTONE; 327
GRAYCOWE, Rex; 266
GRAYE; 328, 346
—, the Lord; 242
—, Sir Edmond; 366
—, Herr Jan; 371
—, Sir John; 242
GRAYTUN, Suss; 382
GREAI, Richard de; 86
GRECI, M de; 379
GREECE, King of; 75
GREEN; 173, 291-2, 309
—, of Essex, 'Taylour of London'; 244
—, Sir John; 173

—, Sir Thomas; 291-2
—, Thomas; 291-2
GREENE; 173, 291-2
—, John; 173
GREENLAND, K of; 229
GREGOR; 78
GREGORY, Monsire, de Suss; 78
—, William; 34, 254
GREISELEY, Margaret de; 6
GREISTOCK; 72
GREN, of Norton, Northants; 291
—, Sir Thomas; 292
GRENACRE, Mons Robert; 2
GRENADO, le Rey de; 240
GRENALD; 351
GRENAM, John; 79
GRENCORNWAIL; 240
GRENDON, S John; 342
—, S' Jon; 342
GRENE; 173, 245, 291-2
—, Sir Henry, of Northants; 291
—, Sir John, of Essex; 173
—, of Northants; 292
—, of Saufford, Essex; 173
—, Mons Thomas; 292
—, Sir Thomas; 291-2
—, Sir Tomas, of Northants; 291
GRENEFELD, M de; 357
GRENEFERD, Mons John; 139
GRENFERD; 159
GRENLEYE, William; 379
GRENVILL, Adam de; 372
GRESELE, Robert de, of Ealinghol, Staffs; 354
GRESELEY, Sir Robert; 354
GRESLEYE, Robert de, Kt; 342
GREY; 87, 91, 97, 162, 242, 246, 328, 346, 352, 359
—, Baron; 87
—, Ld; 87-8, 128
—, Monsire de; 87, 327
—, Munsire de; 87
—, Sir ...; 244
—, Andrew, Ld; 240
—, Monsire, de Barton; 327
—, le Sr, de Codenore; 87
—, Ld, of Codnor; 87
—, le Sr, de Codnor; 87
—, of Codnor; 59, 87
—, of Codnor, Richard, Ld; 86
—, Ld, of Codnore; 87
—, of Codnore; 87
—, Ld Edmund, Ld of Hastings, Weysford & Ruthyn; 68
—, Edward; 35
—, Sr Edward; 242
—, le Sr de, Sr de Estmelingflete; 327
—, of Etton, Ld Powis; 242
—, Henry de; 87
—, Henry, Ld; 86

—, Henry le; 87
—, Sire Henry de; 87
—, Sr Henry de; 87
—, Henry de, Ld of Codnor; 86
—, Henry de, of Codnor; 86
—, Henry, of Codnor, d 1308; 87
—, Henry, 2nd E of Tankerville; 113
—, Henry, Ld Powis; 242
—, Henry, [E of Tankerville]; 240
—, Henry, E of Tankerville & Ld Powys; 310
—, of Heton & Chillingham, Northd; 242
—, of Horton; 244
—, J de; 352
—, Sir J; 248
—, Jan de; 71
—, S Jehan de; 352
—, Jn de, of Beds; 358
—, Joan de; 87
—, Johan de; 87, 327
—, Sire Johan de; 327
—, Johannes de; 352
—, John de; 87, 240, 351, 353
—, Ld John; 242
—, Mons John; 327
—, Mons' John [KG]; 87
—, Sir John; 240, 330
—, Sir John de; 326, 355
—, John, Ld [of Codnor]; 86
—, Mons' John, de Rotherfeld; 327
—, John de, of Rotherfield; 326
—, John de, of Rotherfield, Yorks; 326
—, John, Ld, of Rotherfield; 327
—, Sir John, E of Thankerville KG; 242
—, Sir John, E of Torberville; 241
—, [L]ord; 97
—, Maud; 327
—, Sir Nichol; 346
—, Sire Nichol de; 346
—, Sire Nicholas de; 346
—, de Northd; 242
—, le S'r de; 87
—, Sir Ralph; 241
—, Ralph, Chivaler; 241
—, Reginald, Ld Hastings, Weyford & Ruthyn; 4
—, Renaud de; 353
—, Reynaud de; 66, 87
—, Ricard de; 66
—, Ricardus de; 87
—, Mons' Richard; 327
—, Richard; 326-7
—, Richard de; 58, 71, 87
—, Richard de, Kt; 86
—, Richard, Ld; 86
—, Richard, Ld de; 86
—, Sir Richard; 86
—, Sir Richard, Ld, of Codnor, KG; 87
—, Richard, Ld, of Codnor; 87
—, Richard, of Codnor, KG; 87

—, Richard de, of Derbys, Kt; 72
—, Richard, Kt, E of Kent; 69
—, Richart de; 87
—, Robert de; 88, 327, 347
—, Robertus; 327
—, Robt de; 70
—, of Rotherfeild; 327
—, le Sr le, de Rotherfeld; 327
—, Ld, (of) Rotherfield; 327
—, of Rotherfield; 326-8
—, Le Sieur; 87
—, Monsire Thomas de; 242
—, Sire Thomas de; 346
—, Thomas; 241-2
—, Thomas le; 242
—, Sir Thomas, of Heton; 241
—, Will, Bp of Ely; 242
—, Ld, de Wilton; 87
—, of Wilton; 70
GREY DE NORTHD; 242
GREY OF RUTHEN, Roger de; 42
GREYE; 242
—, the Lorde, of Rotherfeld; 327
—, Sir Rechart; 86
GREYSTOCK; 56
GREYVYLE, William de; 372
GRIERSON, Gilbert, of Lag?; 192
GRIF, Miles; 326
GRIFFID, Th' lin ap; 311
GRIFFITH, Jeovan ap; 135
—, Rees ap; 371
—, Thomas ap; 275
—, William ap; 311
GRIMBALD; 72
GRIMBAUD, Robt, Ld of Houghton, Northants; 52
GRIMOND, 'de la seure'; 135
GRIMSTEDE, Sire Andreu; 63
GRISINAKE, Bernard de; 270
GRISLEY, Mons de; 91
GROS, John; 335
GROSVENOR, Robert; 320
—, Sr Robert; 323
—, S' Robert le, Ches; 323
GROUSTEL, Emond; 32
GROVE; 352
—, Richard; 350
GRUFFYD; 310
GRUNARKE; 334
GRUWEL, John, sen, of Cawes, Salop; 225
GRY; 325
GRYFFYTH, Mathew, of Herts; 129
GRYMSTED, of Dorset; 63
GRYNE; 164
GUARNE, Sir Raynold; 91
GUBIONE, Sir Hugh; 84
GUBWARTON, Ralph of; 188
GUELDRES; 167
—, Duke of; 167

—, D of; 1
—, Marie of; 181
—, Marie of, Q of Jas 2; 250
GUILDEFORD, of Staffs; 75
GUINES, Le Conte de; 76
GUISNES, Bailieship of the Town; 113
—, Baldwin de; 3
GULDEFORD, Sire Johan de; 75
GUMBERWORTH, Robert de, of Lincs; 24
GUNDELL; 55
GUNDREINLE, S Gerard; 1
GUNORA; 385
GUNSTORP, Elizabeth, Dame de; 214
GUNTHORPE, Thomas; 35
GUTHRIE, John; 113
GUY; 87
GUYAN, Duk off; 193
GUYANE, D of; 193
GUYEN; 193
GUYENNE; 193
—, D of; 193
GWERRY; 32
GWYEN, Duke of; 193
GWYTFELD, Mons Math; 325
GYAN, the armys of; 193
GYBBES; 12
GYBBYS; 12
GYBES, of Devon; 12
GYBON; 226
GYBSON, Thomas, Grocer of London; 211
GYBTHORP; 52
GYFFARD; 35
—, le; 284
—, Elys; 306
—, Mons Gill'; 285
—, Johan; 284
—, Sir John; 284
—, Margaret; 282
—, Richard; 123
—, Thomas; 297
GYFFERT, Ld, of Auld; 90
GYFFORD, de Claydon; 283
—, Margaret; 282
—, of Oxfords; 287
GYFORDE, La boff, of Bucks; 287
GYGGES, Robert, of Wigton; 26
GYL, [of] Devon; 190
GYLDER, D of; 167
GYLLE; 190
GYSBOROW MONASTERY, Yorks; 218
GYSBURN, John de; 330
H..RSTON, John de; 369
HAAG, Baron Sigismund; 205
HAB, Monsire Godard de; 166
HACCHE, J, of Devon; 253
HACCOMBE, Sir Stephen; 59
HACHE, Avice la; 275
HACHETON; 158
HACHETUN, Henry de; 192

HACHUTT; 13
HACKET; 12
HACLUIT, Ralph, d1527; 12
HACLUT, Mons de; 23
HACON, Sir Hubert; 23
—, of Norf; 23
HACTON; 349
HADERSETT, Nicholas de; 170
HADESTOKE, ...tinus de; 208
HADHAM, Thomas; 378
HAGELEY; 105
HAGGELEYE, Robert; 113
HAGGERSTONE, Robert of; 320
HAGLEY; 103, 105
—, Henry; 105
—, T; 105
HAIG, Peter, Ld of Bemerside; 58
HAILL; 126
HAINAULT; 113, 137, 310
—, Count of; 310
—, Philippa of; 137, 310
HAINTON, John le; 220
HAIWARDE, de; 167
HAK-BECHE, Sir Robert; 19
HAKBECHE; 19
HAKE; 73
—, Mons' Andreu; 73
HAKEBECH, Sir Robert, of Norf; 14
HAKEBECHE; 14
HAKEBICHE; 19
HAKELUT, Edmund, Kt; 320
HAKENBECH, Sir Reynold; 19
HAKENBECHE; 19
—, Mons' Reynald; 19
HAKON, Sir Hubert; 22
HAL; 318
HALDEN; 366
—, William de, citizen of London; 366
HALDENNE, William de; 367
HALE, Frank de, Kt, Ld of Rocheford; 164
HALES; 352
—, Nicolas; 11
HALEWETON, S' Thomas de; 167
HALFORD, John de, of Ches; 202
HALGHTON, le S' de; 38
—, John de, Kt; 38
—, le Sieur de Shasta de; 185, 188
HALHORN; 325
HALIBURTON, Henry; 320
—, Henry, of Edinburgh; 320
HALINGTON; 374
HALL; 39, 48, 81, 84, 318
KING'S HALL, Camb; 286
HALL, Elizabeth; 292
—, Pyersse of; 48
HALOM; 160
—, Sr de; 160
—, Mons Johan de; 160
HALON, Monsire John; 160

HALOUGHTON, Mons Thomas de; 167
HALSAL, Sir Gilbert; 52
HALSALL; 16
—, S' Gilbert de, Lancs; 16
HALSWELL, of Halswell [in Goathurst]; 71
—, Nicholas; 71
HALTON, le Sire de; 38
—, Henry de; 190
—, Sir Henry de; 190
—, John of; 38
—, Mons John de; 38
—, Mons Robert de; 42
—, Sir Robert; 42
HALTUN; 221
HALUGHTON, Thomas; 211
—, Thomas de, Kt; 114
HALWETONE, s'th'm; 167
HALWEYN; 281
HALYS; 52
—, Mastyr; 52
HAMELYN; 157, 172, 295
—, Sr; 161
—, S Jehan; 220
—, Sire Joham; 172
—, Sire Johan; 172
—, Sr John; 172
—, S'Jon; 172
—, of Leics; 172, 232
HAMLON, of Oxfords; 160
HAMLYN, Monsire; 161
—, Sir John; 220
HAMMORE, Sr Richard de; 95
HAMO, s of Richard; 58
HAMON, of Kent; 275
HAMPTON, John; 199, 386
HAMVILE, Ellis de; 341
HANAM, Thomas; 335
HANBY, Anthony; 390
HANDLE; 173
HANDLO; 173
—, John de, of Borstall, Kent, Kt; 114
—, Sire Jon de; 173
HANDLON, Sir John; 160
HANGELTON, Richard de; 25
HANGEST; 283, 287
HANLO; 165
HANLON, Sir John; 124, 160
HANLOW, Monsire John de; 160
HANMEL, Gilbert; 123
HANSAKER, John; 114
HANSARD, Sire Johan; 390
—, John; 390
—, Sir John; 390
—, of Westmld; 390
HANSBERCH; 100
HANSTED; 366
HANTEUILLE; 149
HANTON, Mons Richard; 246
HANVILE, Elyas de; 341

—, Ric de; 326
HANVILLE, Ellis; 383
HARALDE, Kynge; 51
HARAULDE, King; 51
HARBARD, Ld; 279-80
—, The Lord; 279
HARBARTH, 'The Lord Chamberlayn'; 279
HARBERD, Ld; 279
HARCCOURT, S Jeh de; 44
HARCORT, Sire Johan de; 19
HARCOURT; 14, 16, 19, 37
—, Sir ...; 19
—, Anthony, d1541; 37
—, of Devon & Cornw; 19
—, de, of Guernsey; 19
—, Sir Harry; 19
—, Johan de; 19
—, John; 26
—, Sir John; 19, 44
—, John de, of Ellenhall, d1330; 19
—, Sir John, of Staffs; 19
—, Lo; 60
—, S'r de; 19
—, Richard de; 19, 86
—, Sir Richard; 14
—, Sir Robard, Oxfords; 19
—, Sir Robert; 19
—, Sir Robert, KG, d1470; 19
—, Simon de; 114
—, Sir Simon; 19
—, of Stanton Harcourt, Oxfords; 19
—, Sir Symon; 324
—, Mons Th de; 19
—, Sir Thomas; 19
—, Thomas; 19
—, Sir William; 19
—, William; 19
—, William de; 46
HARCOURTE, Sir R.; 19
HARDES, Edmond, of Kent; 224
HARDHETHE, William de; 302
HARDIS, Edmund; 224
—, Emond, of Kent; 224
HARDRES; 224
—, Edmond, of Kent; 224
—, Edmund; 224
—, Edmund de, of Kent; 224
—, Emond, of Kent; 224
—, Robert de; 224
HARDRYS, John, of Kent; 195
HARDUS, Kent; 224
HARDY, William, of Yorks; 342
HARECOURT; 37
—, le Sire de; 26
—, Mons de; 19
—, Sr de; 19
—, Alice de; 14
—, le Comte de; 19
—, J; 19

—, Sr Jo de, le fitz; 26
—, Sire Johan de; 19
—, John de; 19
—, Sr John de; 19
—, Richard; 20
—, Richard de; 14
—, Sr Roger de; 37
—, Sir Thomas; 14
—, Thomas de; 14
—, Thos, Esq; 14
—, Mons' William; 20
—, Sir William de; 14
HARECOURTE; 20
—, Mons' Thomas; 20
—, William de; 20
HARECURT, John de; 19
—, Richard de, of Bosworth; 14
—, Richard de, of Staffs; 15
—, Richart de; 20
—, Sayer de; 15
—, Thomas, Kt; 15
—, William; 20
HAREWEDON; 346
HAREWELL; 262
HAREWELLE; 294
HARIETESHAM, Alexander; 368
HARINGTON; 322
—, Sir John; 366
—, Richard; 282
HARINGTONE, Sire Johan de; 366
HARMANVILLE; 20
HARNAGE; 215
HARNALL; 4
HAROLD, K; 51
—, King; 51
—, K of Engld; 176
—, King of Man & the Isles; 185
—, le Roy; 51
HAROWDON; 28
HARPAR, William; 247
HARPELEY; 81
HARPER; 241-2, 248
HARPERLEY, of Suff; 81
HARPUR, of Bambery; 55
HARRECOURT; 19
—, Sir Robert; 19
HARRENCOURT, Sir Robert; 19
HARROLDE, K; 51
HARROWDEN; 28
HARSSYKE; 319
HARSYK; 2
HART; 268
—, Walter, Provost of Oriel, Oxf, Bp of
   Norwich; 247
—, William; 268
HARTE; 268
HARTELYNGTON; 149
HARTHILL; 17
HARTHULL, Sir Richard; 17

HARTLEPOOL; 211
—, Town of; 211
HARTLINGTON, Sir Henry; 165
—, William; 114
HARTLYNGTON, Henry; 114
HARVEY, Thomas; 212
HARVILLE; 271
HARVY; 35
HARVYLE, Henr, of Staffs; 261
HARWELL, Henry; 261
HARYETE, Henry de; 48
HARYNGTON, Mons John de; 366
—, Richard; 282
HASARD, Thomas, of Wilts; 64
HASELARTON; 315
HASELARTONE; 317
—, S' Walter; 315
HASELERTON, Yorks; 315
HASELHALTON, Sir Thomas de; 314
HASELWOOD; 213
HASTANG; 159
—, Robert; 225
—, Sir Robert; 213
—, Sir Robert de; 114
—, Thomas, of Warws; 114
HASTINGES, Ld; 324
HASTINGS; 321
—, Sir Drewe; 205
—, Edmund de; 94
—, Edmund of; 94
—, Sir Robert; 180
HASTYNG, Mons Dreuve de; 205
HASTYNGES, Ld; 324
HASTYNS, Sir Robert; 142
HASWELL, Wm, of Roxburghs; 114
HATHELOK, Robert; 369
HATHEWICK; 62
HATTELYFF, Lincs; 45
HATTON; 342
—, Elena de; 114
HAUBERK, Sir Nicol; 96
HAUDLO, John de, Kt; 114
—, John de, of Essex, Kt; 114
HAUDLOE, John; 379
HAUERING; 125
HAUIRINGE; 210
HAUKBECK, S; 19
HAUKWODE, John de, of Sible Hedingham;
   217
HAULE; 10
HAULON, Sire Johan de; 161
HAULOU, Mons John; 161
—, Mon John; 161
HAULOW, Sir John; 161
HAULOWE, Sr John de; 161
HAULTON, Sr de; 38
HAUTE, Henry de; 225
HAUTEUILLE; 147
—, Cornw & Devon; 149

HAUTEVILE; 149
—, Monsire de; 149
—, Sire Geffrei de; 149
—, Sir Jeoffrey; 146
HAUTEVILL, Monsr de; 149
HAUTEVILLE; 149
—, Sr de; 230
—, Sire Geffrey; 149
—, Sir Geoffrey; 149
—, Ralph de, Banneret; 346
—, Rodurphus de; 332, 346
—, Mons' Thomas; 149
—, Sir Thomas; 147
HAUTTE, Sir Wm, of Kent; 158
HAUTUILE, de; 149
HAUTVILE, de; 149
HAUVIE, Robert; 229
HAUVILLE, Robert de, of London; 387
HAUVYLE, Elys de; 380
HAUWARD; 383
—, Monsire de; 341
—, Sire Johan; 341
—, Sire William; 341
HAUWARDE, Mons J; 381
HAVERCOURT; 19
HAVEREYNGDOON, Dominus de; 49
HAVERING; 176
—, John de; 174
—, John de, Baron; 174
—, John of; 174
—, Sir John; 181
—, Sr John de; 162
—, Mons Rich; 176
—, Richard; 176
—, Sir Richard; 176
—, Sir William; 176
—, Wilts; 176
HAVERINGE; 176
—, Monsire de; 176
—, Johan de; 162
—, Sire Johan de; 181
HAVERINGES; 176
HAVERINGGE, Richard of, Archdeacon of
  Chester; 208
HAVERLEY, Johan de; 181
HAVERS, Sir Robt; 33
HAVERYNG; 176
—, Monsr de; 176
—, Fitz a; 210
—, Mons' Guilliam de; 176
—, S' John; 183
HAVERYNGES, Fitz a; 210
—, Monsire Richard; 176
—, Richard de; 176
HAVOUR, Richard; 348
HAWARD; 383, 392
—, Monsire; 383
—, Sr; 383
—, Mons John; 383, 392

—, Mons Richard; 383
—, Sir, Suff; 383
—, E of Surr; 383
—, Sr Wil; 381
—, Mons William; 380
HAWARDE; 383
—, Mons John; 341, 381
—, S John, Norf; 383
—, L[ord]; 383
HAWBERK, Sir Nicol; 25
HAWE, Roger; 327
HAWGHTON, Sir Rycharde, of Lancs; 61
HAWSTEAD, Sir John; 367
HAWTE, Henry de; 225
HAWTON, Sir T; 2
HAWTRE; 305
—, Joh'n; 305
HAY; 371
—, Sir Henry; 371
—, Matilde de la, d1484; 53
—, Wm, of Mayne; 371
HAYCH; 274
—, of Devon; 274
HAYE, Balthasar de la; 173
—, Juliana de la; 70
HAYLARD; 57
HAYLES; 10
HAYLYNWIKE; 389
HAYME, John, of Irld; 20
HAYMOND, Agnes, of Aylesbury; 260
HAYNE; 229
HAYNTONE, John, Abbot of Bardney, Lincs;
  220
HAYOE, John, of Irld; 20
HAYTON; 318
—, John of; 192
—, Robert; 186
HAYWARD; 71
HEADINGHAM, Robert; 367
HECTOR; 253
—, prince of Troye; 253
—, of Troy; 253
HECTOR OF TROY; 253
HEDERISHEVED, Sir John de; 189
HEDERSET, John de, of Wymondham, Norf,
  Kt; 189
HEDILHAM; 379
HEDILSHAM; 379, 395
HEDISHAM; 379, 395
HEDRISHENED, Mons Esmon; 191
—, Mons Johs de; 189
HEDRISHERED, Sir Estienne; 191
HEDRISHEVED; 189
HEDYLHAM; 395
HEIDELBERG, Count of; 169
HEIGHAM; 228, 231
HELAND, Mons J; 377
—, Sir John; 374
HELAUNDE, Ric' de; 17

HELBECK, of Helbeck, Westmld; 5
HELBEK, S Thomas de; 8
HELBEKE, Sir Thomas; 8
HELE; 359
HELERS; 335
HELION, John, of Essex; 278
HELLERS; 335
HELLES, Rauf de; 326
HELPISTO', Joan de; 51
HELPISTONE, Johannis de; 51
HELTON, John, of Westmld; 5
HELTONE; 4
HELYNGSALE; 23
HEMENHALES, Sir Rauf; 334
HEMINGTON; 359
—, Robert de; 359
—, William le; 359
HEMYNGTON; 359
—, Robert; 359
—, Robert de, of Ches; 355
—, William; 359
HENAUDE, le Count de; 137
HENBOTYLL; 290
HENEAGE; 249
HENEGE, de Heynton, Lincs; 249
—, of Hynton, Lincs; 249
—, Joh de Heynton; 249
—, John; 249
—, John, de Heynton; 249
HENGEBACH, 'Monsire Johan de Heyn-
   baugh'; 219
HENHALE, Edmund de; 114
HENLOW, Godfrey de, Kt; 235
HENLOYN; 211
HENRY; 287
HENRY 3; 317
HENRY I; 287-8
HENRY, John ap, of Kilpeck; 76
HENRY II; 288
HENRY III; 286, 288
HENRY VII; 288
HENSLEY, Thos; 345, 388
HEPBURN, Patrick, E of Bothwell; 320
HEPKALE, John de; 189
HER..., le Roy de; 185
HERBERD, Monsire Mayhu filtz; 278
HERBERT; 278-81
—, Ld; 280
—, Sir George; 280
—, of Gower; 280
—, E of Huntyngdon; 280
—, Maude; 280
—, Sir Walter; 280
—, Ld William, E of Pembroke; 280
—, William, E of Pembroke; 306
HERBOTYLL; 289-90
HERCEBOY, Martin; 174
HERCOURTT; 20
HERDINTONE, Henr de; 258

—, Henri de; 258
HEREFORD; 286, 358
—, City of; 286-7
—, Thomas; 358
—, Sir Thomas, Cornw; 358
HEREFORDE, Walter de; 370
HEREISS, Ld, of Terreglis; 296
HEREWARD; 226
—, Elizabeth; 320
HEREWARDE, of Suss; 226
HERFORD; 358
—, Erl of; 373
—, Sire Symon de; 244
—, Monsire Thomas; 358
—, Warinus de; 356
HERFORDE; 358
HERICE, Sr de; 296
—, Henri de; 296
HERIZ; 6, 296
—, Monsr J; 296
—, Sir John; 296
HERMENVILE, Sir Simon de; 15
HERON, Messire Jehan; 16
HERONDI, Jon de; 280
HERONDY, John le; 280
HERONYLL, Thomas de; 262
HEROVILL, Thomas de; 262
HERRES, Robert, of Auchtorabyth; 205
HERRIARD, Thomas; 287
—, Thomas, of Hants; 287
HERRIES; 296
HERRING, Hugh & William; 184
—, Katrine; 215
—, Patrick; 89
HERRY, Thomas ap; 367
HERSTON, Fraunceys, of Surr; 292
HERT, Syr persevall; 268
HERTECOMBE, Richard; 174
HERTFORD; 358
—, Tho; 358
—, Sir Thomas, of Badesworth; 153
—, William; 114
HERTFORDE, Mons Thomas, de Bad-
   desworthe; 161
—, Sir Tomas; 161
HERTHILL; 17
HERTHILL', Mons de; 18
HERTHILL, Mons' John; 22
HERTHULE, of Derbys; 18
HERTHULL; 18
—, Sir Richard; 15
—, Sir Richard de; 15
HERTHULLE, Richard de; 15
—, Sir Richard; 18
—, Sir Richard de; 15
—, Sir Richard de, of Derbys; 15
—, Sire Richard de; 18
HERTLOU, S' William; 81
HERTLYNGTON; 165

—, Mons Henry; 165
—, Monsr Herry de; 165
HERTTYLL, Tomas; 89
HERUNVILE, Jon de; 262
HERUNVYLE, John de; 262
HERUYLL; 257
HERVILE; 265
HERVILLE; 262
HERVY, Nycolas; 35
HERVYLE, Sir John; 285
HERWARE; 317
—, Sir Walter de; 317
—, Walter de; 317
HERWELL; 265
HERWILL; 261-2
HERYNE; 290
HERYS; 296
HERYSS, Ld; 296
HERYZ; 296
HESCLARTON, Sr Thomas de; 314
HESE; 90
—, Henry; 61, 88, 90
HESELARTON, Walter de; 317
—, Sr Wauter de; 317
HESELARTONE, Sire Thomas de; 315
HESLARTON; 315, 317
—, Mons ...; 317
—, Sr; 314
—, Mons Rauf; 317
—, Simon; 317
—, Mons Th de; 315
—, Thomas; 315
—, Sir Thomas de, of Durham; 315
—, Sir Walter de; 315
—, Mons Wautier de; 316
HESLERTON; 315
—, Eufemia; 312
—, Eupheme; 312
—, Mons Waut'; 316
HESSE, Landgrave of; 154
HETERSETE; 183
HETHE, Robert de, of Surr; 52
HETHERESSETE, Monsire Esmon; 191
HETHERFEL; 189
HETHERFIELD; 192
HETHERSET; 189
—, Sir Edmund; 156
—, John de; 189
HETHERSETE; 189
HETHERSETT; 189
HETHERSETTE; 191
HETHIRSETE; 189
HETIRSETE, Ed'; 189
HETON; 139, 216, 244
—, Alain de; 139
—, Alan of; 241
—, Sir Alan; 241
—, Aleyn de; 139
—, Mons Aleyn de; 139

—, Edward de; 244
—, Mons Henry de; 128
—, Sir Henry, of Heton; 114
—, John de; 15
—, Margery; 241
—, Sir Robert; 244
—, Mons Thomas de; 244
—, Thomas; 186
—, Thomas de; 17, 186
—, Thomas of; 241, 246
HETONE; 244
HETSCHETE, Agneta; 114
HETTON, Henry de; 386
HETYRSETT, Tho'; 192
HEULE; 58
HEUSE, Henri; 61
HEVERINGHAM; 336
HEWERING; 176
HEWICK; 153
—, Monsire de; 153
—, Nicol; 153
—, Sir Nicol, Ches; 153
HEWIKE, Sir de; 153
HEWYK; 153
—, Mons' Nichol; 153
—, Mons Nicol; 153
—, s' nicole; 153
—, Monsr Nychol de; 153
—, Sir Nycoll; 153
HEWYKE, Sir Nicol; 153
HEYDONE, Richard de; 334
HEYTON; 11
HEYWARD, John; 114
—, John, of Cannington, Som; 188
HEYWORTH; 289
HIBERNIA, Konig von; 288
HIDE, Roger de; 58
—, Thomas de la; 114
HIGHAM; 228
—, of Kent; 228
HIKLYN; 69
HILDESLEY; 78-9
HILION, John, of Essex; 278
HILL, John, of Trill; 223
HILLE, Richard, d1440; 379
HILTON; 15-16, 18, 125, 154, 165, 176
—, Baro de; 16
—, Baron; 16
—, Baron de; 16
—, de; 16
—, Ld; 16
—, le Baron de; 16
—, le Sire de; 16
—, le Sr de; 16
—, Sr de; 16, 165
—, the Barron of; 16
—, Adam; 114, 215
—, Mons Alex de; 16, 26
—, Alexander, Ld of; 15

—, Alexander of; 185
—, Aley de; 26
—, Sir Bartholomew, Cumb; 176
—, Die here van; 16
—, ?Edward; 16
—, of Hilton, co Durham; 15
—, Hochequin; 114
—, Sir John; 38
—, Sir Jordan; 16
—, Jurdan de; 16
—, Lancs; 176
—, Maykin; 114
—, Mons Robert de; 16
—, Robert; 16
—, Robert de; 16
—, Robert of; 26
—, Sir Robert; 16
—, Sr Robert of; 16
—, Sir Robert, of York; 16
—, Robt de; 15
—, Thomas; 15
—, William de, Ld; 15
—, William, of Hilton, co Durham; 15
—, Wm of; 15
HILTONE, Robert de; 16
HILTYN; 156
HINDE, John; 228
HINETONE, John de; 114
HINTON; 326
HO, Robert de; 338, 363
—, Robert de, of Norf; 363
HOARE; 326
HOBURY; 149-50, 231
HOCKLEY; 219
HODDESDON, Robert; 388
HODENET; 390
HODERINGO, Barth; 1
HOEUSE, Henry, Kt; 61
HOGHTON; 61, 70, 74, 328
—, Monsire Adam de; 61
—, Sir Adam de; 61
—, Sir Alexander, of Hoghton; 61
—, of Houghton; 61
—, of Houghton, Ches; 61
—, John; 74
—, John de; 72
—, of Lancs; 59
—, Mons Ric de; 61
—, Mons' Richard de; 61
—, Sir Richard; 61
—, of Yorks; 98
—, Yorks; 61
HOKELEY; 135-6, 219
HOLAND; 151, 190-1, 210, 221, 228, 231,
    306-8
—, Duke of; 310
—, Monsire de; 191
—, Sir Alan de; 191
—, Mons Aleyn de; 191

—, Sir Aleyn de; 191
—, C of Huntingdon; 308
—, C of Kent; 306
—, D of Exeter; 308
—, Edmund, E of Kent; 306
—, Eleanor; 286, 306
—, Elizabeth; 299, 307
—, Henry de; 307
—, Mons' Henry de; 191
—, Henry, D of Exeter; 308
—, Henry, Duke of Exeter; 307
—, E of Huntingdon; 308
—, Johanna de; 306
—, John; 308
—, John de; 307-8
—, John, D of Exeter; 308
—, John de, Deuke of Excestyr; 308
—, John, E of Huntingdon; 308
—, John, E of Huntingdon & D of Exeter; 308
—, John de, 1st D of Exeter; 308
—, John de, 1st E of Huntingdon; 308
—, John de, [1st or 2nd] E of Huntingdon; 308
—, E of Kent; 306
—, Kent, E of; 306
—, of Lancs; 191, 221
—, Lucy de; 309
—, Margaret; 306
—, Maud de; 114, 151
—, Mons Otes de; 191
—, Mons' Otes [KG]; 191
—, Sir Otis; 191
—, Mons R de, le fitz; 210
—, Mons' Richard; 231
—, Robert de; 191
—, Robert de, Kt; 114
—, Sir Robert; 151, 191
—, Mons Robt de; 191
—, Sir Roger, of Lancs; 225
—, Mons Thomas de; 245
—, Mons' Thomas [KG]; 191
—, Sir Thomas; 227, 306
—, Thomas; 306
—, Thomas, E of Huntingdon; 308
—, Thomas de, E of Kent; 306
—, Thomas, [E of Kent]; 306
—, Wylliam; 191
HOLANDE, D of; 136
—, Sir Henry de; 190
—, James; 2
—, Sir John; 190
—, Mons Th de; 191
HOLANDIAE, Willelmus, Comes; 136
HOLANDSWAYN, Robert de; 114
HOLAUND, Mons Robert de; 191
—, Robert de; 151
HOLBE, Leics; 390
HOLCAM; 26
HOLDHALLE; 157
HOLDYCH; 79

HOLDYCHE; 79
HOLEWELL, Lady Johanna de, wid of Sir
  Walter de H, of Herts; 51
HOLEWERE; 368
HOLFORD; 202
—, Sir George; 202
—, John de; 202
—, Sir John; 202
—, William de; 202
HOLFORDE; 202
—, John de; 202
HOLKAM; 26
HOLKER; 279
HOLKHAM; 26
—, Sir ...; 26
HOLLAND; 114, 136, 151-2, 156, 189, 191,
  231, 235, 306
—, Charlis; 221
—, Earls of Kent; 191
—, Edmond, E of Kent; 306
—, Monsire Henry de; 193
—, Sir Henry; 194
—, Erle Huntington; 308
—, Joan, of Kent; 306
—, John; 308
—, John I, E of; 136
—, Sir John; 189
—, Sir John, of Thorpwater, Northhants; 191
—, E of Kent; 288, 307
—, Lucy, Ctess of Kent; 306
—, E of Ostrevaunt; 137
—, Sir Richard; 231
—, Robert de; 190
—, Sr Robert; 191
—, Robt of; 190
—, Robt of, 1st Ld; 191
—, Sgr Richard de; 151
—, Thomas, D of Surrey; 306
—, Sir Thomas, E of Kent; 191
—, Thomas, E of Kent; 307
—, Thos of, E of Kent; 191
—, Thos, E of Kent, d1397; 306
—, William, Count of; 136
—, William of; 178
HOLLANDE; 1, 191
—, Mons' John de; 191
HOLLANT, Her Thomas van; 191
HOLLATE, Robert, of Holmesworth, Yorks,
  Bp of Llandaff; 393
HOLLES, William, of London; 372
HOLLOND, John, E of Hundon; 308
—, Peter de; 370
HOLLONDE, D of; 136
—, Deuke of; 310
HOLME; 154
—, Robert; 33
—, Robert, of York; 32
—, Robert, of Yorks; 32
—, Roger; 114

—, of Suff; 154
—, William de; 67
—, of Yorks; 201
HOLME COLTRAN ABBEY, Cumb; 137
HOLNERNES, le Conestable de; 88
HOLOCH, Count of; 263
HOLOND, Sire Huwe; 50
—, Sir Thomas; 191
HOLONDE, D of; 136
—, John de; 191
—, Sir Ottes; 191
—, Robt de, of Lancs; 191
HOLSTENE, William; 46
HOLT; 3, 21, 37
HOLTE; 69
—, Sir John de; 297
HOLWAY; 319
HOLWER; 368
HOME, of Aittoune; 139
—, Sir Alex, of that ilk, d c1460; 114
—, ceulx de dunegles; 129
HOND; 280
—, John; 280
—, John de; 280
HONDE; 371
HONDESACRE, William; 302
HONGEFORD, 'Mons Wauter, S de'; 44
HONGERFORD; 44
HONINGTON, Roger; 389
HONTERCOMB; 75
HONTERCOMBE; 75
—, Sire Wauter de; 75
HONTERKUMBE, Water de; 75
HOO; 338
—, Beds; 336
—, John; 80
—, Robert; 336
—, Robert de; 336, 338
—, Sire Robert de; 336
—, Sir T; 381
—, T de; 335
—, Thomas de; 335
—, S Willm de, of Suss; 338
HOPETON, Water de; 148
HOPTON; 55
—, Sir Arthur; 55
—, Mayster; 56
—, Nicholas de; 55
—, Robert; 55
—, Sir Walter; 148
—, Walter; 148
HOPTONE; 55
—, Walter de; 148
—, S' Water; 150
HOPTTON, of Gloucs; 148
HORBIN; 327
HORBIRI, Johan de; 70
HORBOURNE, Sire Johan de; 327
HORBUN, of Yorks; 100

HORBURI, Sire Johan de; 327
HORBYN; 100
HORDEN; 273
—, Kent; 273
—, of Kent; 273
HORDENE, Geoffrey de; 374
HORE, Mons Ger; 326
HORECOURT, Sir Thomas; 15
—, William de; 15
HORNE, Gerard; 189
HORNEDEN, Sir Wm, of Horneden, Berwicks;
 189
HORNESBY, Mons John; 341
HORNSBY, Sir John; 382
HORTON; 206
—, Waleran of; 344
HORUM, Mons Gerrarde; 189
HORWOD, of Hunts; 74
—, John, of Hunts; 74
HOSCARLE, Sr Thm; 12
HOSEE; 61
HOSEY; 61
HOSTERLE; 88
HOSTERLEY; 88
HOTOFT; 43
HOTUN, Richd of; 114
HOUBY, Gilbert de; 390
—, Gillis de; 390
HOUEL; 114, 207
HOUERCOMB; 75
HOUGHTON; 86
—, Monsire Ric' de; 61
—, Monsire Richard de; 66
—, Sir Richard; 61
HOUGHTONE; 61
HOUHARD; 341
HOULAND, Mons Henry de; 148
—, Sir Richard de; 194
HOUNDHILL; 294
HOUNDHYL, of Houndhil, Staffs; 316
HOUNS, John; 125
HOUNSLOW PRIORY; 229
HOUNTERCOMBE, Sire Wauter de; 75
HOURON; 210
HOURTONE, S' ad'; 59
HOURUN, Gerard; 189
HOUSE; 58
—, Sir Henry, of Suss; 61
HOUTON, William de; 369
HOUWARD, Sir J; 383
HOUWELL, Harri, of Staffs; 316
HOVEL, Hugh; 361
—, Hugh de; 362
HOVILE, Hugh; 362
—, Hugo de; 361
HOWARD; 380-3
—, Ld; 380
—, Sir de; 341
—, the Lord; 383

—, Sir Edmund; 383
—, Edmund, Archdeacon of Northd 1340; 341
—, Edmund, Master of Kepier in 1341; 341
—, Elizabeth; 382
—, S' Johan; 324
—, John; 383
—, John, Kt; 341, 382
—, Sir John; 114, 383
—, John, D of Norfolk; 298
—, John, Ld of, of Essex, Kt; 382
—, John, of Essex, Kt; 382
—, Lady Anne; 371
—, Sir Richard; 383
—, Sir Richard, of Essex; 383
—, Robert de; 383
—, Sir Robert; 382-3
—, E of Surr; 383
—, Sir Thomas, KG; 383
—, Thomas; 382
—, Thomas, E of Norf; 114
—, Thomas, E of Surr; 383
HOWARDE; 383
—, Sir J; 324
HOWBY; 390
HOWEARD, the Lorde; 380
HOWELL; 265
—, Davy; 197
HOWLAND, Monsire Richard de; 231
HOWNHILL, Harry, of Staffs; 316
HOYCOURT, Walran de; 182
HOYLANDE, Sire Robert de; 191
HUBAND, John, Ld Ipsley; 114
HUGH, Mons Edmond fitz; 309
HUGHES; 143
HUGRIE, le rey de; 192
HUKLENG; 69
HULKE; 279
HULL, Robert; 221
HULSON, John, of London; 229
HULTON; 176
—, of Farneworth; 165
—, of the Park, Lancs; 176
—, Thomas, of Farnworth; 165
—, William; 154
HUM; 189
—, Maister; 189
HUME, Ld; 139
—, Patrick; 114
HUMES; 189
HUMME; 139
HUMSCHALTES, William; 12
HUMSHALTS, William de; 13
HUNDURCOMBE, Sire Water; 75
HUNGARFORTH, Ld; 44
HUNGARIE, K of; 98
—, Rex; 292
—, le Roy de; 75, 87
HUNGARY; 60, 87, 97-100
—, K of; 80, 100

—, King of; 58, 87, 98
—, Roy de; 98
HUNGAYTE, William, of Saxton, Yorks, Esq;
 215
HUNGERFORD; 41, 44-5, 69
—, Baron of; 44
—, Ld; 44
—, Mons; 44
—, Sir Edw; 45
—, Sir Edward; 45
—, Sir John; 45
—, Sir John, of Down Amney; 45
—, Margaret; 41
—, Ld Moleyns; 45
—, Sir R; 45
—, Robert; 38
—, Robert de; 26
—, Robert, Ld of; 45
—, Robert, Chivaler; 36
—, Mons Walter; 43
—, Sir Walter; 45
—, Sir Walter, KG; 45
—, Sir Walter, Kt 1485; 45
—, Walter; 42
—, Walter de, KG; 45
—, Walter de, Kt, ?1st Baron; 42
—, Walter, Kt; 42
—, Sir Walter, of Heytesbury; 42
—, Walter, Ld of Heytesbury & Hommet; 42
—, Walter, 1st Ld; 45
—, Mons Water; 45
—, Sir Water; 45
HUNGERFORDE, Sir ?G; 45
HUNGREFORD, Baron; 45
—, Ld; 45
—, Sir R; 45
HUNGREFORDE, Sir Edmonde; 45
HUNGRY, Ye Kyng of; 98
HUNGYRFORDE, Ld; 45
HUNT; 32, 249
—, John, of Paddon; 249
—, de Paddon; 249
—, of Paddon; 249
—, of Paddon, Devon; 249
—, of Padon, Devon; 249
HUNTERCUMBE, Wauter de; 75
HUNTERCOMBE; 57, 75, 82
—, Le Sire de; 75
—, Sr de; 75
—, John de, of Bucks, Kt; 394
—, Ralph; 75
—, Ralph de; 75
—, Sir Walter; 20, 75, 82
—, Walter; 57, 75
—, Walter de; 57, 75
—, Walter of; 75
—, Sir Waut' de; 75
—, Wauter de; 75
HUNTERCOMDE, Sir Walter; 76

HUNTERCUMBE, M de; 82
—, Walt de; 75
—, Walter de; 75
—, Walter de, Kt; 20
—, Wautier; 75
HUNTERTOMBE, William; 75
HUNTINGDON; 333
—, E of; 334
—, le Cont de; 146
—, le Conte de; 333
—, le Comte de; 333
HUNTINGFEILD, Cael de; 341
—, Sr William de; 341
HUNTINGFELD, Her de; 380
—, John de; 371
—, Saer de; 383
HUNTINGFIELD, 'Lere'; 341
—, Saer; 381
—, Saer de; 341
HUNTINGTON, Waltheof, Erle of; 213
HUNTRECOMBE, Ralph; 75
HUNTYNGDON, le Conte de; 308
HUNTYNGFELD, Petrus de; 380
HUNTYNGTON, John, E of; 300
HUNTYRCOUMP, Sr Waultier; 75
HUNTYRCUMBE, Mons Waut' de; 75
HUREHOUENE, Gerard de; 235
—, Mons Gofrey; 235
HURSTAL, William; 13
HURSTHALE, William de; 13
HURSTHALL, William; 13
HURTES, John, of Northd; 347
HUSCARL, Thomas, of Beddington, Surr; 12
HUSCARLE, Thomas; 13
HUSE; 61-2, 90
—, Le S; 61
—, Sr de; 61
—, Henr'; 61
—, Henry; 61
—, Henry de, Ld of Harting; 61
—, Henry, Ld of Harting, Suss, Kt; 61
—, Mons Mark de; 20, 61
—, Mons' Thomas; 61
HUSEE; 61, 90
—, Sire Henri; 61
—, Matilda; 89
—, Mons' Tho; 61
HUSER, Henry, Ld of Hertyng; 61
HUSEY, Monsire Henry; 61
—, S' Henry; 61
—, Margaret; 89
HUSSE; 90
HUSSEE, Henre, of Suss; 61
HUSSEY; 61-2, 86, 89-90
—, Sir ...; 90
—, Baron of Galltram; 61
—, Sir Harry; 61
—, Henry; 90
—, Henry de; 90

—, Sir Henry; 61
—, Sir Henry, of Suss; 61
—, Hubert; 21
—, Hugh le; 90
—, of Kenersey Hall; 39
—, Maryon; 21
—, Sir Thomas; 61
HUSSY, le Sire; 61
HUSTURTON, Sir Thomas; 316
HUTTOFT, Henry, of Southampton; 67
—, de Southampton; 67
HUTTON; 150
—, Robert; 114
HUYLTON, le Baron de, of Lancs; 16
HUYSE, Mons Hug' de; 21
—, Mons Hug de; 61
HYDDE, Wyllyam; 70
HYDE, de la; 70
—, Alan, Kt, of Beds; 114
—, Roger de; 86
HYDE ABBEY; 214
—, Winchester; 214
HYETT; 213
HYLAND; 319
HYLDESLEY; 79
—, Wm; 79
HYLL, Wylyam, of Som; 222
HYLLE, John, Ld of Esterpostrugge; 223
HYLLES, William; 206
HYLLTUN, of Lancs; 165
HYLTON; 37
—, de; 16
—, Ld; 16
—, the baron of; 16
—, le Baroun de; 16
—, of Durham; 16
—, Godfrey; 16
—, Baron off; 16
—, Sr Robert de; 16
—, Thos, de Farworth, Lancs; 165
HYLTONE; 125
—, Sire Robert de; 16
HYLTUSLE, S' Rob' de; 79
HYNGGELOSE; 82
HYNKEPENNE; 77
HYNKPENNE; 77
HYNTON; 326
HYTHE, Kent, Customs of; 197
HYZHAM; 228
ICHINGHAM; 382
IDLE, Sire Johan del; 186
—, Sire Warin del; 187
IFORD, William de; 65
ILDEVER P., King; 198
ILDLE, Cunte del; 133
—, Munsire Gerard de; 194
—, Gerard del; 194
ILE, Gerard del; 187
ILKETSHALL, John, of Suff; 269

ILLAKE; 325
ILLE, le Counte del; 60
ILLESLEY; 89
ILSTED, K; 47
ILYS, Ld of; 13
INCHMARTIN; 114
—, Sir Henry, Ld of that ilk; 114
—, John of, Ld of that ilk; 145
INGELOSE; 82
—, Monsire John; 82
INGHAM, John de, of Suff; 233
INGHAMES, Sir Henry; 82
INGLEFELD, Robert, Esq; 68
INGLEFYLDE; 67
INGLESFIELD; 67
INGLIS, Alex, of Tarvet; 214
—, Master Alexr, Doctor of Decrees & Master
   of Requests; 215
—, Patrick, of Perth; 214
—, of Terwat; 214
—, Thomas, portioner of Duddingston; 214
INGLISFELD; 67
INGLISSH, Mons' William; 278
INGLONS, Sir; 82
INGLOS; 82
—, Henry; 67
INGLOSE; 82-3
—, He; 82
—, Henry, Kt; 76
—, Henry, Kt, of Norf; 82
INGLOSSE, Sir Henry; 82
—, of Norf; 82
INGLOYS; 83
INGOLFYLDE, Sir Thomas, of Berks; 68
INGPEN; 33
INKPEN; 77
INKPENNE; 77
INSULA, Baldwin de, E of Devon; 114
—, Gerard de; 195
—, Robert; 208
INVERKEITHING; 250
IRELAND, King of; 286
—, Andrew, burgess of Perth; 38
—, Master John; 199
—, Richard; 389
ISAAC, patriarcha; 317
ISELE, ... of Suss; 332
ISELEY; 332
—, (Kent); 332
ISLE, John de; 332
ISNEY, Johannes de; 283
ISSODUN, Ralph de, Comte d'Eu; 15
JACHLE, John; 114
JACSON; 160
JAKKESON, John; 332
JAMES I, K of Scotland; 250
JAMES II, K of Scotland; 250
JAUNEBY, S.Robert de; 165
JAYNKYN, Thomas, of Lawmy Angwell; 302

JEDWORTH, Patrick, of Gamylschelis; 368
JEFORS; 146
JEFOURS; 244
JENKENSONN; 301
JENKES; 57
JERARD; 157
JERARDE; 172
JERMY; 189
—, [Sir] John; 189
JERMYN; 189, 193
JERUSALEM, K of; 288
JESORE; 146, 244
JESORS, Sir John; 146
JEU, Mons' Richard le; 155
—, Sr Richard le; 155
JEVAN AP GRIFIT; 136
JOAN OF KENT, Princess of Wales; 307
JOHAN, Sire Adam le fiz; 45
JOHN, Mons Adam fitz; 45
—, K of England; 288
JOHN LACKLAND; 304
JON, Monsr Rich le; 155
JONES, Robert, of Burton in Bromfield; 232
JORDAN; 148
JOSKYN; 11
JOV, William le; 276
JOVE, William le; 276
JUDAS MACCABAEUS; 265
JULERS, le Counte de; 137
—, Elizabeth, Ctess of Kent; 306
JULIERS; 114, 137, 168
—, Eliz; 137
—, of Gulick; 137
—, William, Marquess of; 114
JUNTROID; 210
JURDEYNE; 148
JUSTICE, Reginald, of Kent; 92
JUYNER, David; 297
KAINES; 62
KALENTERS, S John de; 341
KAMVILE, Idonia; 312
—, Idonia de; 114
KARDOYLL; 6
—, Mons Rauf de; 6
KARE, The Baron of, of Balymackarl; 236
KARESWILL, Monsire de; 81
KARKENTON; 60
KARNABY; 42-3
—, William de; 42
KAROE, Robt, Middx; 391
KARVELL, Robert, of Northants; 67
KASE, de; 379
KATCHEBURY; 29
KATHERMA; 2
KAVERNER, Mons' Gerard; 225
KAWSTON; 380
—, Mons R; 380
KAYLLY, Adam de; 344
KAYNES; 91

—, John de; 91
KEKEWICH; 305
KEKITMORE, Piers de; 1
KELHAM, James; 235
KELLAM; 235
KELLAWE FAMILY; 114
KELLESHALLE, Johannes; 332
KELOMBERIS, Mons J; 325
KELSALL; 332
—, S Jolf de, of Ches; 332
KELSALLE; 353
KELYNGEINCHE; 159
KELYNGMARCH; 160
KEMIS, Robertus de; 92
KEMPSER, Petronilla; 174
KENAN, Blethyn ap; 129
—, Grefithe ap, P of Gwemothe; 162
KENARDESLEYE, Simon de; 227
KENDAL; 362
—, Edward de; 362
—, Peter de; 114
—, Sir Robert; 362
KENDALE; 323
—, Monsr de; 362
—, Sr de; 362
—, Mons Ed; 362
—, Mons Edmond de; 362
—, John; 342
—, Richard de; 362
—, of Ripon; 319
—, Mons' Robert de; 362
—, Sir Robert; 362
—, Sire Robert de; 362
KENDALL; 323, 362
—, Monsire; 362
—, of Beds; 362
KENDALLE, Sir Robert de; 362
KENEL, Robert de; 92
KENELMUS, Sanctus; 105
KENERSEY; 39
KENETTE, Pers de; 293
KENETZ, N de; 293
KENEZ, Robert de; 92
KENLEY; 319
KENNEDY, David, of Pennyglen; 371
KENNETT, Nicholas of, [Cambs]; 294
KENNITON, Ine de; 69
KENNTONE, Hue de; 69
KENSALL, S Golf de; 353
KENT, Count de; 307
—, Counte de; 307
—, E of; 307
—, Le Conte de; 307
—, le Conte de; 307
—, Edmon, E of; 307
—, Edmond E of; 307
—, Erle off; 307
—, Thomas E of; 307
KENULFUS, Rx; 102

—, King in England; 102
KENULPH, King; 102
KENYON; 380
KERKBY; 30
KERKENTON; 62
KERKETON, Monsr Jehan de; 62
KERKHAM, Syr John, of Blakedon, Devon; 308
KERNABY; 32
—, of Northd; 42
KETERICH, Richard, of Cambs; 139
KETTESED; 53
KETTESSED; 53
KEVELIOC; 114
KEVELL, Robert de; 92
KEVEOLOC, Hawisia, Domina de; 114
KEYMER, Dr Gilbert; 291, 309
KEYNES, S' Jon; 92
—, Robt; 62
—, Sir Robt, d1318; 62
KICHARD; 146
KIDEWELLY, Geoffrey; 207
KIDWELLY; 207
—, David; 207
KILKENNY, William; 115
KILLINGMARCH; 160
—, J; 160
KILLINGWORTH, William; 38
KINARDSLEIE, Jehan de; 148
—, Richard de; 148
KINDERTON, Baro de, of Ches; 18
KINGESTON, Sr de; 179
—, John de; 174
—, John, Ld of; 174
—, Sire Nicholas de; 210
KINGESTONE, Sire Walter de; 221
KINGGESTONE; 179
—, J de; 179
KINGSTON; 174, 345
—, John de; 175
—, Sir John; 115
—, Sir Nicholas; 210
—, Thomas de; 179
—, Sir Walter de; 221
—, Walter de; 3
KINKESTON, Sire Johan de; 138
KINROSS, Sir John, Kt; 115
KINTHORPE; 273
KIRBY; 143, 316
KIRCH; 201
KIRCKBY, Mons de; 138
KIRHAM, of Devon; 276
KIRKABY, Wm; 316
KIRKALAYN, Mons William de; 81
KIRKALON, Le sire de; 81
KIRKALOU, Mons Richard; 81
KIRKBY; 30, 56, 311
—, Alan de; 30
—, Alexander de; 30

—, of Kirkby Hall; 30
—, Mons' Richard de; 30
—, Richard de; 30
KIRKBY-Beller; 164
KIRKE, Adam de; 196
KIRKEBY; 30, 143
—, John, of Lancs; 30
—, John de, of Wygenthorp; 115
—, Robert; 56
—, Wills de; 143
KIRKEBYE, Richard; 30
KIRKENTON; 60, 62
KIRKETON; 62
—, Mons' John de; 62
—, Mons John de; 90
—, Monsire John de; 62
—, John de, of Balderton Gate Street, Newark; 1
—, Robert de, in Hoyland, Lincs, Kt; 86
KIRKHAM; 275-6
—, of Blackadon, Devon; 308
—, Sir John, of Blackendon, Devon; 308
—, Nichol de; 305
—, William de; 305
KIRKINGTON, Sir John de; 62
KIRKLAND; 84
KIRKTON; 62
KIRTON; 98
—, Mons John de; 62
KIVELI, Jordan de; 207
KNEFFET, Essex; 351
KNEL; 148
KNELAND, of that ilke; 204
KNELL; 150, 235
KNELLE, Edmund de; 149
—, Edmund de, of Suss, Kt; 149
KNETON, Agnes; 274
KNEVET; 394-5
—, Sir John, of Essex; 394
—, Sir Thomas; 394
—, Thomas; 395
KNEVETT; 394
KNIGHT; 358
KNIGHTCOLE, Walter de, of Leics; 115
KNILL; 150, 235
KNIVETON, Henry de; 381
KNOLLE, John, of Bridgwater; 79
KNOLLYS, Sir Robarde, of Northd; 242
KNOUGHT, K; 189
KNOWT, Nicholas; 69
KNYGHT, of 'Northsher'; 356
KNYLES, Hona ap; 278
KNYT; 18
KNYUET; 395
KNYVET; 394
—, of Bokenham; 394
—, John; 394
—, John, chevalier; 394
—, John, of Essex, Chevr; 394

—, John, of Northants; 394
—, Richard; 394
—, Robert, of Kent, Esq; 394
—, Sir Thomas; 394
—, Thomas, of Essex, Esq; 394
—, of Weldon; 394
—, of Weldon, Northants; 394
KNYVETON, Henricus de; 381
—, William; 361
KNYVETT; 394
—, Christopher de; 394
—, Sir Ottomarus; 394
KOCK, Hary; 345
KOLOMBERRIE; 325
KOTTISFORDE, Mons Rog de; 57
KOULAY, Tomas; 319
KRYNKEPENE; 77
KUC, John, Ld of; 50
KULPEPER, Mons Waut, of Kent; 351-2
KYBURG, Count of; 372
KYCHARD; 146
KYDEVELLY, Sir Morgan; 207
KYDWELLE; 203, 207
KYDWELLY; 207
KYLKENNI, William de; 153
KYMER, Gilbert, clerk; 309
—, Mayster Gylbert, Dorset; 247
KYNARDESL', Hugh de; 330
KYNARDESLE, Sire Huge de; 148
KYNARDESLEY; 128, 148
KYNARDESLEYE; 146
—, Hugh de, of Herefs, Kt; 147
KYNDERTON, le Baron du; 18
KYNGESHEMEDE; 384
KYNGESTON; 139, 219
—, de; 179
—, J de; 179
—, Johan de; 179
—, John, Ld; 175
—, Mons John de; 179
—, Sir John; 179
—, Sir John de; 175
—, Matilda de; 115
—, Nicol de; 210
—, Sir T; 179
—, Mons Th de; 179
—, Mons Thomas; 179
—, Thomas; 115, 175
—, Thomas de; 175
—, Walter de; 3
KYNGESTONE, Sire Henri de; 210
—, Thos of; 91
KYNGGESTON, Monsire de; 179
KYNGGISTON; 179
KYNGGYSTON, of Chelvey, Berks; 183
KYNGSTON; 139, 209
KYNGSTONE; 179
KYNKESTONE, Sire Johan de; 179
KYNNELMARCH; 160

KYNTZBUULER, de; 182
KYPLES; 2
KYRCKBY, of Horton Kyrkby, Kent; 311
—, de Kent; 311
KYRETON, Sir John, of Lincs; 62
KYRHAM; 308
—, Nicol de; 306
KYRKALAYN; 84
KYRKALON, Sr; 81
KYRKBY; 311
—, of Kirkby, Lancs; 30
—, of Lancs; 30
—, Wm; 143
KYRKE, Adam de; 196
KYRKEBY; 30, 311
—, John de; 30
—, Mons John de; 32
—, S' Jon; 30
—, Willam de; 143
KYRKEHAM; 309
KYRKETON; 62
—, Sr J de; 62
—, Mons Joh de; 62
—, Robert de; 62
KYRKETONE, S' Jon de; 62
—, Robert de; 62
KYRKLAY, Monsr de; 81
L'ESTRANGE, Matilda; 281
LABOURNE, Sir Nicholas; 316
LAC..., John; 204
LACHE, de; 281
LACI, Henry de; 115, 363
—, Henry de, E of Lincoln &c; 363
LACY; 136-7, 364
—, Baron; 136
—, Alice; 115
—, Edmund de; 363
—, of Hartre; 26
—, Hen, E of Lincoln; 136
—, Hen de, E of Lincoln, Constable of Chester; 115
—, Henry de; 363
—, Henry de, E of Lincoln; 115, 123
—, Henry de, E of Lincoln & Constable of Chester; 363
—, Henry de, E of Lincoln, 1257-1312; 136
—, Henry de, E of Lincoln, Constable of Chester; 363
—, Henry, E of Lincoln; 136
—, Henry of, E of Lincoln; 364
—, Henry de, Counte de Nichole; 136
—, Henry de, Conte de Nichole; 136
—, Hy de, E of Lincoln; 115
—, Sire Johan de; 97
—, John de, E of Lincoln; 363-4
—, John de, E of Lincoln, 1232-40; 363
—, Count of Lincoln; 136
—, E of Lincoln; 137, 337, 364
—, Earl of Lincoln; 177

—, of Northd; 97
—, Counte Nycoll; 206
—, erle off Lyncolne; 136
—, Roger de, Constable of Chester; 363
LAGGAGE, Wylyam; 37
LAKE, Monsire de; 8
LAMB, Bernold; 205
—, John, bailie of Edinburgh; 230
LAMBE, Alexander, [St Andrews]; 206
—, Duncan, [St Andrews]; 206
LAMERE; 125
LAMKYN; 393
LANCASTER; 29, 32, 192, 300
—, Cunte de; 304
—, Duke of; 299
—, E of; 299-300, 304
—, le Conte de; 300
—, Sir ...; 29
—, The Duc; 300
—, Alice; 115
—, Aveline, Ctess of; 299
—, Blanch of; 300
—, Dame Blanch of; 300
—, Comes; 300
—, D of; 297, 300-1
—, Duchy of; 297
—, Edmund, E of; 197, 299-300
—, Edmund Crouchback, E of; 300
—, Edmund, frere du roy, Conte de; 300
—, Dame Elizabeth, Duchess of Exeter; 308
—, Mons Henri de; 304
—, Sir Henri (of); 304
—, Sire Henri de; 304
—, Henry, E of; 297, 299-300
—, Henry E of; 304
—, Henry, E of; 304
—, Henry of; 300, 304, 309
—, S Henry de; 304
—, Sir Henry of; 304
—, Henry, D of; 299, 304
—, Henry, D of, KG; 300
—, Henry, D of, E of Derby &c; 300
—, Henry, E of Derby; 303
—, Henry de, Ld of Monmouth; 303
—, Henry de, Ld of Monmouth, 1st Baron; 303
—, Henry of, Ld of Monmouth; 303
—, Henry, Erle off; 288
—, Henry, 1st D of; 300
—, Henry, 4th E of; 299
—, J de; 29
—, Sir J de, de Helg[ill]; 29
—, John de; 29
—, John of; 29
—, John of, Ld of Grisdale; 29
—, of Milverton; 29
—, Mr Roger; 29
—, Roger de; 29
—, Seinte Thomas de; 299
—, Thomas de; 192

—, Thomas, E of; 297, 299-300
—, Thomas of; 299, 301
—, Thomas, 2nd E of; 300
—, Thomas Plantagenet, E of; 300
—, Sir William; 29
—, William; 29
—, William de; 29
LANCASTER & Derby, Henry, E of; 304
LANCASTER & Leicester, Henry, E of; 300
LANCASTERE, ...of; 300
LANCASTIRE, D of; 299
LANCASTRE; 29
—, Counte de; 299
—, Cunte de; 299
—, Duc; 288
—, duc; 288
—, E of; 303
—, Erle of; 300
—, le Conte de; 300
—, le Counte de; 300
—, le Duc de; 300
—, D of; 300
—, Esmond fitz du roy, Conte de; 300
—, le fitz, Le Sr de; 304
—, Henri; 304
—, Sire Henri de; 304
—, Henry; 304
—, Henry de; 304
—, Sr Henry de; 304
—, Henry de, 1st Baron (?); 303
—, Sire Johan de; 29
—, John; 84
—, John de; 28
—, Mons' John, de Helgill; 29
—, Maude de, Ctess of Ulster; 286, 297
—, Mons' Roger de; 29
—, Roger de; 29
—, Mons Th de; 192
—, Monsire Thomas de; 192
—, Thomas Counte de; 300
—, Wm de; 29
LANCASTRIA, Henry de, 9th E of Derby; 303
LANCASTRIE, Comes; 300
—, Henry of, E of Derby; 303
LANDALE, Thomas; 207
LANERYN; 245
LANFORD, Sire Nicholas de; 333
LANGCASTRE, Thomas de; 300
LANGCASTUR, D of; 300
LANGE, Robarde, of Wilts; 230
LANGEFORD, Sire Johan; 333
—, S John de; 333
—, Monsire Nichall de; 333
—, Sire Nicholas de; 315, 333
—, Sr Nicholas; 333
—, William; 333
LANGEFORDE, S Nicol; 333
LANGFORD; 333
—, Mons Nichol de; 333

—, Mons Nicholas de; 333
—, Mons Nicol de; 333
—, Sir R; 333
—, Mons Rich; 345
LANGFORDE, Sir John; 333
LANGFORTH, Mons Nich de; 333
LANGFORTHE; 345
LANGLE, S' Th'm; 39
LANGLEI, Robt, of Northants; 142
LANGLEY; 390
—, Robert, of Northants; 142
LANGMAN, Robert; 115
LANGREGE; 215, 253
LANGRISH, Walter; 215
LANGSTON; 160
LANGTON, David; 206
—, David of; 206
—, John de; 115
—, Nicholas of; 189
—, Robert; 336
—, Thomas, de Wyngarde; 162
—, Thos of; 115
LANWELL, Sir John; 323
LAONOIS, le Conte de; 238
LAONOSIS, le Comte Patrick de; 238
LARCHIER, Thos; 10
LARGE; 390
—, Christina le; 115
LASCELLES, Thomas de, Kt; 161
LASCI, Henry de, E of Lincoln; 115
—, Roger de, Constable of Chester; 364
LASCY; 125
—, Edmund de; 363
—, Henry de, E of Lincoln; 115
—, John de; 125
—, John de, Constable of Chester; 363
—, John de, E of Lincoln & Constable of
    Chester; 363
—, Margaret de, Ctess of Lincoln; 115
—, Margaret de, Ctess of Lincoln & Pem-
    broke; 115
—, Margareta de, Ctess of Lincoln & Pem-
    broke; 115
LATHAM, Richard; 42
LATHBURY; 29, 67
LATHE; 140
LATHEBURY; 29
LATHEBY; 29
LATOUR, William de; 55
LAUDO, John de Sancto, of Som, Kt; 366
LAUNDE, Henri de la; 289
—, Nycolle de la; 289
LAUNDRES; 236
LAURENCE; 175
—, John; 310
—, Rece, of Kydenend; 279
LAURENS AP WM AP DAVID; 188
LAUTHER, Geoffrey, Esq, of Kent; 6
LAVACHE, Richard de; 1

LAVALL; 320
LAVARE; 209
LAVASSE, Sir Philip; 281
—, Sir Richard; 281
LAVERING; 245
LAVEROK, John; 68
LAVINTONE, William de; 72
LAWALL; 323
LAWALLE, Mons J; 323
LAWARE; 148
LAWARRE; 150, 158
—, Baron; 129
—, Ld de; 150
LAWELLYN, andorch; 200
LAWRENCE, John, s of; 69
—, John, of Seton; 69
LAWRYN; 245
LAYBORN, of Yorks; 314
LAYBORNE; 314
—, Sir William; 314
LAYBOURN, of Consewyk; 314
LAYBOURNE, Mons John de; 316
LAYBURN, Mons John, de Kent; 314
—, Mons John de, du North; 315
LAYBURNE; 316-17
—, du Contee de Salesbury; 312
—, Mons Rog' de; 311
—, Mons' Thomas; 312
LAYS, Philip de, Clerk; 15
LAYSETER; 167
LAYSNE, Robert; 115
LEAKE; 7
LEALL; 379
LEATHERSELLERS' CO; 291-2
LEATHERSELLERS' CO OF LONDON; 292
LEBAUD S THOM; 188
LECHCHE, John; 20
—, John, of Suss; 20
LECHE, John; 2
LECHEFORD, Nicholas de; 375
LEDEBURN, Isabella de; 282
LEDES, Alexander de; 58
LEDHAM, Isabel de; 282
LEDYS, Mons Esmond, de Kent; 19
LEE; 47
—, of Cumberland; 47
—, John de, de Bothes; 46
—, of Lee; 136
—, Sir Robert de, of Adlington; 47
—, Sir Robert de, de Adlynton; 47
—, W Atte; 128
LEEGH, Mons William de; 47
LEEK, of Leics; 143
LEGAT; 141
—, Thomas, Burgess of Irvine; 387
—, Thomas, de Herts; 141
LEGE, D of; 183
LEGER, Joan; 196, 372
LEGET, Thomas, esquire; 141

LEGH; 46-8, 194
—, of Adlington; 47
—, de Adlyngton; 47
—, de Adlynton; 47
—, Sr de Both, Ches; 47
—, de Bothes; 46
—, of Bothes; 46
—, de Boths; 46
—, of the Bouthes; 47
—, of High Legh; 125
—, John A; 47
—, John de, of Bothes; 46
—, John de, de Legh; 125
—, John, of Legh; 136
—, John de, de Legh, Ches; 136
—, de Legh; 136
—, of Legh; 136
—, Robert; 47
—, Robert de; 47
—, of Routh; 71
LEGHE; 48
—, de Bothes; 47
LEGHVILE, Thom de; 205
LEGRE; 186
LEIBORNE, Roger de; 314
—, William de; 315
LEIBOURN, S Jo de; 317
LEIBURNE; 315
—, Roger de; 315
—, William de; 314
LEIC', Henry de, Ld of Monmouth &
  Beaufort; 303
LEICES, Hammerl; 239
LEICESTER, E of; 177
—, Earl of; 177
LEICESTRE, le Conte de; 177
LEICESTRIE; 177
LEIGH; 194
—, of Leigh; 136
—, of Leighe; 156
LEIGH OF BOOTH; 46
LEIGHBURNE; 316
LEIGHE, Mons Thomas de; 47
LEINSTER; 125
LEK; 8
—, Monsr de; 8
—, Sr J de; 8
LEKE; 372
—, de; 372
—, Mons John de; 8
LEKEBORNE, Johannes de; 330
—, Robts de; 47
LEKENOR, Mons Tomas, Suss; 349
LELBENSTEYN; 138
LEMBOURE; 181
LEMESEY; 229
LEMESEYE; 229
LEMLE, Pers de; 235
LENFANT, Walter; 147

LENTHAL, Sir Rowland; 358
LENTHALE; 355, 358
—, Roland, Kt; 320
LENTHALL; 356, 358
—, Sir Roland; 358
—, Roland, Ld of Haverfordwest, Pembr, Kt;
  115
LENTHALLE; 358
LENTOFT, Sire de; 159
LEO, King of; 235
—, Master Henry, Physician; 115
LEON; 115, 125-6
—, Isabel of Castile &; 125
LEPTON, of Cornburgh; 68
LERMIT, Henry; 273
LEROWSSE, of Knoddishall, Suff; 338
LERUS; 336
LESCOT, Walter; 115
LESCROP, Monsr le Fiz; 365
—, Mons' Geffray; 362
—, Monsr Geffray; 362
LESLIE, Thomas; 10
LESTOUTEVILLE, Robert de; 140
LESTRANGE; 260, 270
—, Le Sire; 258
—, Le Sr; 258
—, Sr; 258
—, Sr Fouk; 257
—, Hamo; 255
—, Mons Hamond; 272
—, Sire Ible; 267
—, S Jehan; 258
—, Joh; 257
—, Munsire Johan; 257
—, John; 267
—, Mons John, Baron de Knokyn; 257
—, Sr John; 271
—, Le Sr, baron de Knokyng; 257
—, de Knockin; 257
—, Roger, of Ellesmere, 1st Baron; 271
LESTRAUNGE, Alesia; 115, 313
—, Eble; 268
—, S Fuke; 257
—, Sr Fuke; 258
—, Fulk; 255
—, Hamo, Kt; 271
—, Sr Hamond; 270
—, S Jehan; 272
—, Sire Johan le; 260
—, John; 275
—, Sire Roger de; 272
LETILBURY; 270
LETLESHALL, John; 332
LETTOWE, le Roy de; 205
LEU, Nicole de; 267
LEUSANDBERGH, Cardynal; 165
LEVERER, Richard, of Suss; 203
LEVERYCH, Duk, de la Marche; 125
LEVERYCHE, Duc, de la Marche; 125

—, duc de la Marche; 125
LEVET, Sir Walter; 346
—, Sr Walter; 346
—, Walterus; 346
—, S' Water, of Ches; 346
LEVETT, of Irld; 296
—, Walter; 346
LEVINGTOUN, of Saltcottis; 370
LEVRE, Nicholas le; 294
LEVYNG, John; 320
LEWESTON OF LEWESTON, of Dors; 13
LEWESTONE, William, Esq, of Dorset; 12
LEWKENORE, Sir Roger, of Suss; 203
LEWSTON, P; 13
LEWYS, Geoffrey; 188
LEYBORN, de; 317
LEYBORNE; 312, 314, 317
—, Sr J de; 312
—, Sr de Kent; 312
—, sr de, du Nor(th); 315
—, Sire Richard de; 314
—, Roger de; 314-15
—, Sire Willame de; 314
—, William, Ld of; 313
LEYBOUNRE, Sir William de; 314
LEYBOURN, Sr Thomas de; 314
—, Yorks; 314
LEYBOURNE; 313-17
—, Ld de; 314
—, M de; 314
—, Guillemes de; 314
—, S Henry de; 317
—, Sr Henry de; 316
—, Sir J, of Westmld; 314
—, Sire Nicholas; 316
—, Roger de; 312-13, 315
—, Sarra de; 316
—, S Simon de; 317
—, Sire Simon de; 317
—, Symon de; 317
—, Mons' Thomas; 314
—, S Thomas de; 267
—, S' Thos; 316
—, Sire Willame de; 315
—, Sir William; 313-14
—, Sire William; 315
—, William de; 314
LEYBURN, William de; 315
LEYBURNE; 314, 316
—, Mons de; 314
—, Sire Henri de; 316
—, Idonea; 313
—, Juliana de; 313
—, Juliane de; 313
—, Robert de; 314, 316
—, Munsire Roger de; 315
—, Roger de; 115, 313-16
—, Sir Roger; 314
—, Thomas de; 316

—, Munsire William de; 314
—, William de; 314
—, William, 1st Baron; 313
—, Wyllem de; 314
LEYCESTR, Conte de; 177
LEYCESTR', le Comte de; 177
LEYCESTRE, le Cosyn le Roy de; 300
LEYCESTRIE, Alianore, Comitissa; 175
LEYGH, of Isel, Cumb; 47
—, of Isell, Cumb; 47
LEYKE; 372
LEYSETR, E of; 177
LEYTON, Sir J; 129
—, Sir Thos; 193
LIARD; 247
LIBAND, Thomas; 185
LICHTENBERG; 234
LIGHTFOTE, Sir John, of Essex; 71
LILBORN; 312
LILE; 178
—, Gerard de; 194
—, Jo[hn]; 194
—, S' John de; 194
—, S' Waren de; 194
LILLE; 141
—, Cunte de; 133
—, Sr Girard de; 194
LIMBURG, Count of; 176
—, D of; 183
LIMESEY; 229
LINCOLE, Counte de; 364
LINCOLN, Bp of; 269
—, E of; 133
—, Earl of; 364
—, le Conte de; 364
—, Comes; 136
—, Jn, E of; 364
—, See of; 269, 302
LINCOLNE, le Cont de; 132
—, le Counte de; 136
LINCOLNIE, Comes; 136
LINDE; 46
LINDLAWE, William de, of Beverley; 115
LINDON, Simon de, Kt; 355
LINDSAY, Herbert; 213
—, John de; 86
—, John de, Bp of Glasgow 1323-35; 248
—, Sir Wm; 89
LINLITHGOW; 211
LION, le Sr de; 218
LISELEY; 194
LISENIAN, Sr Geffrey; 141
LISLE; 187, 194-5, 234
—, de; 187
—, Ld; 243
—, le Sr de le; 194
—, Gerard de; 230
—, Gerard, Ld; 194
—, Gerard, Visct; 195

—, Monsire Gerard de; 194
—, S Gerard de; 195
—, Sir Gerard; 187
—, Sir Humphrey, of Woodburn & Felton; 141
—, John de; 141, 159
—, Lord John; 51
—, Robert; 115
—, Robert de; 141
—, Robt de; 115
—, Sir Robt, of Woodburn; 141
—, Thomas; 141
—, Walter de; 116
—, Sr Warin de; 194
—, Warren, Ld, of Kingston L'Isle; 194
—, S Waryn de; 194
LISLEY, Monsire Gerard de; 194
LISTER; 146
LITELBURY; 270
LITHGOW, Patrick, Edinburgh; 212
LITILBURY; 263
LITLINGTON, Abbot Nicholas, d1386; 339
LITTILBURY, Mons Humphrey de; 270
LITTLE; 313
LITTLEBURY; 263, 270
—, Humphrey de; 271
—, Sir Humphrey de; 270
—, John; 263
—, Sir John; 263
—, of Lincs; 263
—, R de; 263
—, Mons Roberte; 270
LITTLIBURY, Mons R de; 263
LIVET; 149
—, John; 147
—, Robert; 147
LIVINGSTON, Alexander, 2nd of Dunipace;
   373
LIVINGTON, Alexander, 2nd of Dunipace;
   373
—, Jas, Bp of Dunkeld 1476-83; 370
LLEWELIN AP GRIFFIN; 311
LLEWELIN AP GRIFFITH; 310
LLOYD, Humphrey; 311
LOCHERAYN; 187
LOCKE, Thos, of Whiteknights, Berks; 34
LOCRIN; 264
LOCRINUS; 288
—, K of Britain; 288
LODELAW, Salop; 287
LODELAWE, Sir La...; 190
—, S Th de; 126
—, Mons' Thomas; 245
—, Sire Thomas de; 287
LODELOW; 283
—, John; 116
LODELOWE; 161, 287, 305
—, Robert de, of Norf & Suff; 48
—, of Salop; 287
—, Mons Thomas de; 137

LODEWYK, Hugh, of Kent; 331
LODILAWE; 287
LODLOWE, Mons de; 287
—, Mons' John de; 137
LOIBORNE, Mons Johan de; 317
LOLT, Gundreda; 116
LONCASTER, John de, of Grisdale; 29
LONCASTOR, Rog' de; 29
LONCASTRE, Sr Thomas le Counte de; 300
LONDE, William del; 53
LONDON, Diocese of; 192
—, John de; 361
LONDRES; 8
—, William de; 236
LONDRESS; 8
LONG; 148, 230
—, of Draycot; 149
—, of Draycott; 149
—, Sir Henry; 149
—, Mayster Henry, Miltes; 149
—, Sir Thomas; 188
—, William de; 341
LONGA SPATA, Willemi; 314
LONGAESPATA, Comitis Wilelmi; 314
LONGCASTER; 193
LONGE; 149
LONGEFORD, Mons Nichol de; 333
—, Mons Nicolas de; 333
LONGESPEE; 314, 316
—, le C de Salesbury; 314
—, Ela; 313
—, Emelina; 313
—, Estienne; 316
—, Nicholas, Bp of Salisbury; 313
—, E of Salisbery; 314
—, le Count de Salisbury; 1
—, E of Salisbury; 313
—, de Saresburie; 314
—, 'son frere'; 317
—, Mons William, Conte de Salesbury; 314
—, William; 313-14
—, William III, E of Salisbury; 314
—, William de, E of Salisbury; 314
—, William, E of Salisbury; 313-14
—, Wm de; 313
LONGESPEIE, William de, E of Salisbury;
   313
LONGESPEY; 314
LONGESPEYE, Comes Sary; 314
—, Ela, Countess of Warwick; 313
LONGEUYLER, Jon; 381
LONGEVILERS, Sire Thomas de; 341
LONGFFORDE; 333, 338
LONGFORD; 332-3, 345
—, Alice de; 332
—, of Derbys & Notts; 333
—, S Nich de, of Lancs; 333
—, Nicholas de; 333
—, Sir Nicol; 333

—, Sir Ralph; 333
—, Sir Rauff; 333
LONGFORDE, Nicholas, of Longforde, Derbys; 332
LONGHE, Robert, of Dorset; 233
LONGSPE, Gul; 314
LONGSPEE, Dame Maud; 305
LONGVILERS, Monsr de; 381
—, John de, Kt; 380
—, Sir Thomas; 381
LONGVILLARS; 380
LONGVILLERS; 381
—, Margaret de; 364
LONNGEVELIERS; 380
LORAINE, John; 116
—, Patrick; 194
LORENGE, Sir Noel; 353
LOREYN, Sir N; 335
LORING, Neil; 353
—, Nigel; 351
—, Sire Peres; 335
—, William; 353
LORINGE, S Neel; 353
—, Sir Nycoll; 335
LORN, ceulx de; 325
LORRAINE; 98
LORRYNG, Mons Neel, KG; 353
LORTY; 160
LORYNG; 335
—, Master William; 363
—, Monsire Nel; 335
—, Sir Nele; 353
—, Monsire Roger; 353
LORYNGE, Mons Neal; 337
LORYNGES; 335, 353
—, Nel; 335
LOTEREL, M; 377
—, Sire Andreu; 378
—, Sir Hugh; 376, 378
—, Robts; 43
LOTERELL; 376-8
—, Monsire; 377
—, Robert; 43
—, Thomas; 377
LOTERELLE, Mons Andr; 395
—, Robertus; 377
LOTHER; 7-8
LOTHIAN, Officialate of; 250
—, Officialite of; 291
LOTREL, Andrew; 377
LOTTERELL; 395
—, Lincs; 378
LOTTRELL, Sir H; 378
LOU; 39
—, Sire Johan le; 39
—, Nichole le; 267
LOUCHE; 36
—, Adam; 36
LOUCHER, Monsire; 8

LOUCHES, Adam de; 107
—, Adam, Kt; 33
—, Adam, of Berks; 68
LOUDER, Sir Hugh; 8
LOUDHAM, Sire Johan de; 348
LOUEDAY, of Essex; 63
LOUEL; 147
—, J; 65
—, S' Jon; 95
LOUELL', John de; 159
LOUND, John de, of Hayton, Notts; 116
LOUNDRES; 236
LOURARANCE, Mons; 223
LOURDRES, Mons Willm de; 236
LOUTERELL; 376
—, Geoffrey, Ld of Irneham, Lincs, Kt; 375
—, Haurie; 375
—, Sir Hugh; 377
LOUTH; 216
—, John; 207
—, [?Nicholas de]; 202
LOUTHE; 207
—, Robert; 207
—, Robert, of Herts; 203
—, Roger, Ld of Wolverton, ?Bucks; 207
LOUTHER; 8
—, Mons Hugh de; 8
LOUTHEWYK; 260
LOUTHIER, John; 6
LOUTHIRS; 7
LOUTHRE, Monsr de; 8
—, Sr Hugh de; 8
—, John de; 8
LOUTHRES; 7
LOUTHWICKE; 260
LOUTHWIKE; 260
LOUTHWYKES; 260
LOUVEL, Sr Richard; 148
LOUVELL, Ld John; 95
LOVEDAY; 92
—, John; 92
—, Margaret; 63
—, Sir Richard; 65
—, Sire Richard; 63
—, Roger; 92
—, Roger de; 92
—, William; 92
LOVEL; 66, 95-6, 116, 147-8, 247
—, Ld; 25, 96
—, Sr; 96
—, Le Sr de, et de Holland; 96
—, J; 65, 96
—, Jan; 66
—, Johan; 95-6, 330
—, Sire Johan; 96
—, John; 93, 96, 209
—, John, Ld; 93-4, 96
—, Ld John, of Tichmersh; 95
—, Jon; 330

—, Matilda, Lady; 93
—, Maud; 93-4
—, of Oxfords; 96
—, Richard; 133, 150
—, Sire Richard; 146, 148
—, S' Richd; 133
—, Robert, esq; 94
—, le S', of Salop; 235
—, Sr Tho; 330
—, Sire Thomas; 330
—, Ld, of Titchmarsh; 25
—, of Titchmarsh; 96
—, Wm, Ld, d1455; 95
LOVELL; 65-6, 85, 95-6, 98-9, 147-8, 150,
   235, 247, 296, 330
—, Ld; 25, 96
—, le Sr; 96
—, le Sr de; 235
—, Monsire; 96
—, Ld, of [Castle] Cary; 148
—, Francis, Ld; 96
—, Francis, Ld, KG (d1483); 95
—, Sire Johan; 65
—, John; 93, 247
—, John, Kt; 94
—, John, Ld; 93
—, Mons' John; 96
—, S John; 96
—, Sr John; 96
—, John, d1408; 96
—, Mons Nicoll; 209
—, Mons Rich; 150
—, Mons' Richard; 148
—, Monsire Richard; 148
—, Monsr' Richard; 148
—, Richard; 146
—, Robert, Esq; 94
—, Robt; 93
—, Rycharde; 146
—, S Thomas; 330
—, Thomas; 71
—, Mons Thomas, de Tychemersshe; 96
—, William; 96
—, William, Ld; 85
—, William, Ld Burnell & Holand; 93
LOVELLE, le S'r de; 96
LOVENHAM; 70, 216
LOVET, Joan de; 158
LOVETOD, Jhon de; 155
LOVETOFFE; 159
LOVETOFT; 125, 159
—, Monsire de; 166
LOVETOFTE, Sgr de; 159
LOVETOFTES; 159
—, Mons J; 159
LOVETOT; 116, 159
—, M; 159
—, Jan de; 159
—, Johan de; 155, 159

—, John; 159
LOVETT, Thos; 296
LOVEYN, Henr'; 168
LOWCHE; 36
LOWDAM; 348
LOWDE, John, of Suff; 213
LOWDER, Sir H; 8
—, Jefferray, of Kent; 8
LOWDHAM, Sir John; 348
LOWE; 296
LOWELL, Ld; 25, 96
—, S'g'r, de Tichemerch; 96
—, L[ord]; 96
LOWELLE, Sir John; 99
LOWICK; 38
LOWND, Thomas de la; 80
LOWNDRESSE, Baron of the Naasse; 239
LOWTHE; 207
—, Mons Adam; 36
LOWTHER; 8-9
—, Mons Hugh de; 8
—, S Hugh; 8
—, Sir Hugh; 8
—, John of; 8
—, Mons Robert de; 8
—, Robert; 8
—, Sir Robert; 8
—, William; 7
LOWTHRE; 7-8
LOWTHUR, Sir Jefrai, of Yorks; 8
LOZENGE, of Beds; 335
LUCAS; 253
—, Willimus; 54
—, Wm; 54
LUCENBURGHT; 169
LUCIEN, Mons' Piers; 221
—, Warinus, dominus de Brokehole, Northants;
   221
—, Sir Waryn; 221
LUCION, Monsire de; 221
LUCY, Sir Wm; 99
LUCYEN; 221
—, Sr Piers; 221
LUDELOWE, s' Th'm; 245
LUDLAWE, Monsire de; 287
LUDLOW; 183, 287
—, Borough of; 228
—, John; 137
—, John de; 138
—, Sir Richard, Salop; 181
—, Salop; 228
—, Thomas de; 162
LUDLOWE; 126, 161
—, Mons' John; 138
—, Mons John de; 287
—, Sir John de; 206
—, S John de, Salop; 126
—, Sir John de, of Salop; 126
—, Salop; 287

LUKYN, Warren; 222
LULLE; 391
LUMESIN; 277
LUMHUNLERS; 382
LUMLEY, Margaret de; 151
—, Patrick, of that Ilk; 320
LUMSDEN, Gilbert; 385
LUNDERTHORP, Sr de; 280
LUNDY, Alexander of; 332
LUNEBURG, le Duke de; 153
LUNEBURGH, le Duke de; 141
—, D of; 141
LUNGESPEE, Stephen; 313
LUNGEVILERS, Monsire de; 381
LUNGHESPEIE, William, of Berks; 313
LUNGUILERS, Sr de; 383
LUNGUILLERS; 380
LUNGUILLERYS; 382
LUNGVILERIS, Mons J; 382
LUNGVILERS; 381
—, Sgr; 381
LUNGVILLERS, Mons Thomas; 381
LUSIGNAN; 100
—, Cipaus; 140
—, Comte de la Marche; 99
—, Hugh le Brun, Seigneur de, Count de la
   Marche; 87
LUSYON; 222
LUTERAL, Geoffrey; 375
LUTEREL, Sr; 323
—, Andrew, Ld of Hooton-Pagnel, Yorks; 58
—, Mons Geffray; 377
LUTERELL; 378
—, Elizabeth; 395
LUTERINGTON, Richard de; 268
LUTHERELL; 378
LUTREL, Mons Hue; 395
LUTRELL, Hugh, of Essex, Suff &c; 395
—, Sir Hugh, of Som; 378
—, John, Kt; 375
—, Mons Robert; 377
LUTTELEY; 310
LUTTEREL; 377
LUTTERELL; 378
—, Hew; 376
LUTTERELLE; 377
LUTTLETON, Matilda; 116
LUTTRELL; 377, 395
—, Mons Andr; 377
—, Andrew; 377
—, Sir Andrew; 58
—, of East Quantockhead & Dunster; 378
—, Sir Geoffrey; 377
—, Hugh; 395
—, Sir Hugh; 378, 395
—, John; 395
LUVETOT, John de; 116
—, John de, of Suff; 116
LUXEMBOURG; 116, 140, 165, 169, 181

—, Count of; 140
LUXEMBURG; 140
—, Duke of; 170
—, Jaquetta; 181
LUZER, Henry; 7
LYDD, Kent; 310
LYDEVUSORS, Sire Johan de, Franceis; 371
LYE; 369
—, Robert; 46
—, Yorks; 369
LYEGH, William; 47
LYELL, John; 370
—, Sir John; 116
LYGHT, Thewe of, of Lancs; 18
LYGNY, Sr Waleran de; 140
LYHART; 247
LYHERT, Walter; 211
—, Walter, Bp of Norwich; 246-7
—, Walter, Provost of Oriel, Bp of Norwich;
   247
LYLE; 194
—, E de; 133
—, Ld; 187
—, Monsire de; 194
—, s' Gerard; 195
—, Sr Gerard; 193
—, John, of Suss, Kt; 99
—, of Northants; 194
—, of Northd; 141
—, Sr Warin de; 194
—, Monsire Waryn de; 194
—, Waryn de le; 194
LYLLE; 195
—, Mons Gerrard; 195
—, Mons Henry; 195
—, Mons J de; 141
—, Sr Warren de; 194
—, Mons Waryn; 210
LYMBRYKE; 278
LYMESEY, of Lancs; 229
LYMME; 233
LYN..., Sir Hugh de; 12
LYNCHEFED, Terry de; 37
LYNCOLN, Counte de; 136
—, Erle of; 364
LYNCOLNE, Erle of; 190
LYND; 46
LYNDE; 46, 125
—, Robert atte; 354
—, Wylyam; 158
LYNDESEY; 200
LYNDESEYE, Willms de; 61
LYNDEY; 233
LYNDSEY; 200
LYNGCOLN, Erelle of; 136
LYNN, John; 301
LYNNE; 233
LYOLL, Thomas; 379
LYON, Sir John, of Glamis; 252

—, Patrick; 250
—, Wm, of Estir Ogil; 252
LYON KING OF ARMS; 214
LYONS; 125, 233
—, Mons J de; 125
—, John de; 125
—, Sir John; 116
—, Sir John de, of Northants; 125
LYOUN, Ld of Glamys; 250
LYOUNS; 125, 155-6
—, Mons John de; 125
LYOUNUS, S Jon; 125
LYSTON; 369
LYSTONE, Pers de; 370
—, Mons Ric de; 349
LYTTELBURY, Sr de; 270
—, S' Rob; 267
LYTTILBURY; 263
LYTTILBURYE, Mons Umfray de; 271
LYTTYLBERY; 263
LYTTYLBORNE, Sir J; 106
LYTTYLBURY; 271
LYTYLBERY, Thomas; 283
LYVETT, Robert; 147
MALENBECK, Joh; 232
MABANKES; 72
MABEU, le fitz; 280
MACDONALD OF THE ISLES; 275
MACDOWAL, Dougal; 116
—, Sir Wm, of Newrlant; 215
MACDOWALL; 167
MACDUFF, E of Fyfe; 136
MACGAHAN, Roland, of Wigtons; 385
MACHELER, Sir Grede; 95
MACHELL; 293
MACINTOSH, Farquhar, of Keppoch; 116
MACKHARTYMORE, erle of Clemkerne; 201
MACKINTOSH, Duncan; 123
MACNAUGHTON, Gilchrist; 361
MACRY; 289
MADOC AP LLEWELYN AP GRUFFYDD;
   233
MAER, de la; 63
MAERTSE, Die Grave van der; 102
MAGGESSONE; 77
MAGNEBY, Hugh de; 71, 74
MAHAUT, Mons Robt de; 155
MAHAWTE, Costantyne; 125
MAHEU, Philip le Fitz; 280
MAIDESTONE, Rychard; 12
MAIDSTONE; 12, 73
MAIDSTONE OF WARDALL; 12
MAILLORE; 278
MAILLORR, Mons John; 278
MAILORY; 173
MAINS, John le; 33
MAINWARING; 17-18, 55
—, Agnes; 15
—, of Ches; 18

—, of Ichtfeld; 54
—, John, 'de Pevyr'; 18
MAINWARINGE, de Pevor; 17
MAINWARYNG, Sir John, of Ches; 17
MAITLAND, of Lethington; 248
—, Robert, of Netherdale; 116
MAJORCA, Roy de; 333
MAKDONELL, Sr Dunkan, d'Escoce; 278
MAKDUFF, erle of Fyffe of auld; 136
MALBANKE; 48
MALBON, Sir Hugh, Founder of Combermere;
   337
—, Hugo, Ches; 337
MALBONE, S Hugh de; 337
MALCASTRE, Robert le; 328
MALDON, William de; 77
MALEFAUNT, Sir Thomas; 84
MALEIS, Sir Nycholas; 351
MALEMAYNES, Sr; 356
—, Thomas; 358
MALEMEIS, Sire Nicholas; 351
MALEMEYNS; 356, 358
MALEMYS; 351
MALENBECK, Johannes; 232
—, Johes; 232
MALEUER, S Ric; 294
MALEUERER; 292
MALEUREUVES, Sr Michel; 351
MALEVERE, Thomas, of Lincs; 292
MALEVERER, Sir ...; 293
—, of Allerton; 293
—, Sir Alnoth; 293
—, of Stenecliffe; 266
—, William; 292
MALFORD; 285
MALIOLOGRE, le; 333
MALKASTRE, S' Rob'; 328
MALLERY; 178
MALLEUERER, William; 292
MALLEVERER, of Alderton, Yorks; 293
MALLO, Anthony; 176
MALLORE, Johan; 163
—, Peris; 284
—, Robert, of Welleton, Kt; 123
MALLORRE, Stephen; 266
MALLORY; 176
—, Anthony; 178
—, Antony; 178
—, Mons Antoyn; 178
—, John; 116, 216
—, Sir Wm; 163
MALMANS, Sr Nicholas; 322
MALMAYES; 351
MALMESHILL, Sir Thomas; 36
MALMEYNS, Nichol; 351
MALMIRAN, Mariota dau of, of Glencharn;
   64
MALOIR, John; 178
MALOLAZO; 325

MALONY, John, of Welton; 116
MALORE; 178, 181
—, of Hutton Conyers, Yorks; 178
—, Joh; 163
—, John, of Welton; 106, 216
—, Sir Willm; 181
MALORRE, Anketil; 175
—, John; 106, 116
—, Peter; 282
MALORY; 106-7, 157, 177-8
—, B; 106
—, Elizabeth; 320
—, John; 278
—, John, of Welton; 116
—, John, of Welton, Northants; 106, 217
—, Stephen; 163
—, Sir William; 181
—, Sir Wm, Hunts; 178
MALORYE; 106
MALOURE; 288
—, of Leics; 288
MALOURGOMER, Leics; 284
MALTON; 237
—, Mons Henr' de; 237
—, Henry de; 237
—, Mons' Henry de; 230
—, Roger de; 167
MALTONE, S' Henry de; 237
MALURE, William; 173
MALURERE, Willm; 292
MALVER; 293
MALVESILL; 36
MALVESYLL; 36
MALVESYLLE; 36
MALVOSYLL; 36
MALYN, Rx; 213
—, John; 349
MAN, Wm; 116
MANBE, William; 150
MANBY, Mons John de; 71
MANCESTER; 342
—, Guy de; 342
MANCESTRE; 328
—, G; 342
—, Guy de, Kt; 342
—, Sire Guy de; 342
—, Guydon de; 342
—, Johan de; 342
—, John de; 342
—, Radolfus; 342
MANCHESTER; 99, 328
—, G; 342
—, John de; 342
MANCHESY; 99
MANDEUYT, Mons Th; 155
MANDEVILE, Thomas; 171
MANDEVILLE, Thos; 60
MANDEVYLL; 155
MANECESTRE, Jan de; 342

MANERS; 33
—, Sir George; 33
—, Mons' John; 33
—, Monsr R de; 33
—, Mons Rob; 33
—, Robert de; 35
—, Sr Robert de; 33
—, Robt; 58
—, of Rutl; 35
—, Sir Thomas; 35
MANERUS, S' Rob'; 33
MANERYNG; 18
MANERYS, Robarde, Northd; 33
MANFELD, Simon; 55
MANLEE; 325
MANLEY, Sr de; 325
MANNE; 325
MANNERS; 6, 19, 33, 35
—, Monsire de; 33
—, Sir George; 33
—, George, Ld Roos, d1513; 33
—, de Ithell, Cumb; 33
—, Sir John; 33
—, Michael; 6
—, Robert; 32-3
—, Robert de; 33
—, Sir Robert; 33
—, Sr Robert de; 33
—, Sir Robert, d28 Sept 1354; 33
—, Sir Thomas; 33
—, Thomas, Ld Roos, KG; 35
—, Thomas, E of Rutl, KG 1525; 35
—, Thomas, E of Rutl, Baron Roos of Ham-
  lake, Trusbut & Belvoir, KG; 35
MANNOLT; 7
MANOURS; 7
MANSTON; 160, 350
MANSTONE; 350
MANTON, Joan; 116
—, Thomas de; 213
MANVERS; 7
MANWARING, Sir John; 54
—, Sir John, of Pever; 17
MANWARYNG, of Ichfelde; 18
—, John, of Peover; 54
MANWAYRINGS, Joan; 15
MAPLETON; 47
MAPULTON; 47
MAR; 382
—, Cunte de; 380
—, le Conte de; 382
—, le Counte de; 326
—, le Cunte de; 382
MAR', S' Reginal de la; 92
MAR, le Comte de; 382
—, Sir Donald; 370
—, Donald, 12th E of; 382
—, Monsire Robert de la; 264
—, Thomas, 13th E of; 382

MAR ET GARNONCH, Conte de; 341
MARA, William de, Ld of Rendcomb, Gloucs;
  20
MARAIS, Denys de; 141
MARBULL, Hugh; 320
MARCH; 192, 231
—, Count de; 102
—, E of; 81, 102-3, 251
—, Erle of; 103
—, B[aron] of; 103
—, ...le, [Le Co.]; 102
—, le Comte de; 238
—, Earldom of; 237
—, Edmund, Count de, d1424; 102
—, Edward, E of; 103
—, Roger, E of; 103
—, 'le second fitz'; 105
—, 'son fitz eisne'; 105
MARCHAL, Cunte; 144
—, E; 144
MARCHALE, Mons John Counte; 305
MARCHALL; 352
—, ?Ann'; 357
—, John?; 151
MARCHALLE, le Count; 129
—, Sire William; 352
MARCHAM; 227
—, Sir Richard; 136
MARCHE, [Count] de la; 100
—, Counte de; 102
—, counte de la; 238
—, Erle of; 103
—, le Cont de; 102
—, le Conte de la; 238
—, Comit de la; 102
—, Erele of; 103
—, Ingraham de la; 100
—, Pain de la; 140
—, Mons Payn de la; 140
—, Payn de la; 140
—, Thomas; 222
—, Sir Wm, Kt; 116
MARDIT; 21
MARE, Counte de; 341
—, le Conte de; 382
—, Mons Daland de la; 382
—, John de la; 99
—, Mons John de la; 129
—, Mons' John de la; 189
—, Mons John de la; 264
—, S' Per' de la; 264
—, Peter La; 263
—, Philip de la; 261
—, Pierce de la; 264
—, Mons Piers de la; 92, 264
—, Piers de la; 270
—, Piers de le; 264
—, Mons R de la; 268
—, Richard de la; 92

—, Mons' Robert de la; 264
—, Robert de la; 255
—, Robert de la, Kt; 263
—, Sire Robert de la; 264
—, Robt de la; 263
—, Mons Th la de; 265
MARECHAL, Sire Willame le; 355
MARECHALE, Jan le; 357
MARECHALL; 355
—, of Hingham; 355
MAREESCALLUS, Gilebertus, Comes; 144
MAREIS, William; 97
MARESCAL, Jon le; 355
MARESCALLE, Comes; 144
MARESCALLUS, Comes; 144
—, Willelmus, comes de Penbroc; 144
MARESCAUS, Guillems le; 355
MARESCHAL; 123, 144, 357
—, Counte; 144
—, le Conte; 298
—, le counte; 143
—, le Counte; 144
—, Sire Ancel le; 355
—, Sir Anceline le, Kt; 356
—, Anselm, Kt; 346
—, Sire Auncel le; 365
—, Mons William; 352
MARESCHALE, le Conti de; 136
MARESCHALL; 393
—, Cunte; 144
—, le Conte; 144
—, Le Counte; 298
—, le Sr de; 357
—, Sr Ancell de; 365
—, le Bygod; 144
—, Comes; 299
—, Sir Ralph; 393
—, Sire William le; 355
—, Sr William; 355
—, William le; 352
MARESHAL, le Conte; 144
—, Jon le; 357
MARESHALL; 352
—, Monsire; 357
—, John; 352
—, Wilts; 264
MARESHALLE, Johannes le; 352, 357
MARESTANS, Gwillim le; 352
MAREYS; 97
—, Geoffrey de; 129
—, William de; 138
MARIA, Princess; 288
MARIES; 65
MARISCALE, Cunte; 144
MARISCHALL; 352
MARISCO, de; 138
MARISHALL; 357
MARKES, Sir John; 242
MARLAND; 74

MARLANDE; 74
MARMIEN, Sr William; 173
MARMIENN; 173
MARMION; 167
—, Sir Mansell; 171
—, Robert; 116
—, William; 173
MARMYON; 173
—, Agnes; 164
—, John, of Kyesby, Lincs; 116
—, of Lincs & Leics; 173
—, of Suff; 171
—, Mons W; 173
—, Mons William; 161
MARMYOUN, Sire Willame; 173
MARNAY, [Hen 1st Ld]; 189
MARNE; 189
MARNER; 189
MARNEY; 189
—, Ld; 189
—, Sir Harry; 192
—, Sir Henry; 189
—, Sir Henry, KG; 189
—, Sir John; 210
—, of Layer Marney, Essex; 189
—, Richard de; 189
—, Robert; 189
—, Robert de, Kt; 189
—, Robert, Kt; 116
—, William; 210
MARNY, Sir Henry; 189
—, Mons' Robert; 189
—, Robt de, of Essex, Kt; 189
—, William de, of Essex & Kent, Kt; 116
MARRE, E of; 382
—, le Counte de; 341
MARREIS, William, of Kent; 65
MARREYS, William; 99
MARROWS; 347
MARSAM; 227
MARSCAL, John le; 355
—, Mons John; 84
MARSCHAL; 357
—, C le; 144
MARSCHALL; 5
—, John, d1492; 28
MARSCHE; 103
—, Roger, Conte de la, d1360; 102
MARSHAL, Anselm, Earl; 144
—, Gilbert, E; 180
—, Gilbert, Earl; 143-4
—, John; 144, 356
—, Richard; 180
—, Richard, E; 180
—, Walter; 179
—, Walter, Earl; 144
—, William, E; 180
—, William, Earl; 144
—, William, of Hingham; 356

—, William, senior; 180
MARSHALE, Counte de; 143
MARSHALL; 142-4, 352, 357
—, Baron; 365
—, Count; 305
—, Counte; 298
—, le Cunte; 144
—, Sr de; 357
—, Mons Ancell, of Norf; 365
—, Anselm le; 356
—, John le; 357
—, Sr John; 352
—, Norf; 365
—, of Notts; 66
—, Sir Peter; 366
—, Rye; 365
—, Thomas de; 22
—, Sir Thomas, of Norf; 357
—, Sir W; 352
—, William; 356
—, William, E of Pembroke; 144
—, Wm le; 357
MARSHALLE, Sr Willm de; 352
MARSHAM, Thomas; 248
MARTAIN, John, Count of; 263
MARTEINE; 138
MARTEL, Sire Johan; 355, 357
—, Richard; 13
—, Sire Will; 43
—, Sr William; 43
MARTHAM; 324, 373, 386
MARTHEBY, Richard de; 295
MARTIGNY, Elyas de; 84
MARTIN; 15, 17, 26, 316
—, of Burton; 60
—, Constance; 15
—, Sir Constantine; 41
—, Sr, of Devon; 17
—, of Gloucs; 22
—, Sir John; 17
—, John, of Canterbury, Kent, esq; 202
—, Margaret; 15, 282
—, Nicholas fitz; 26
—, Sire Wary; 22
—, Willa; 27
—, Sire Willame; 17
—, Ld William; 17
—, Monsire William; 17
—, S' William; 17
—, Sir William; 17
—, William; 15, 17, 27
MARTON, Joh, de London, Esquier; 317
—, Ser Wyll'm; 17
MARTYDALE; 46
MARTYN; 16, 56
—, le Sr; 17
—, John; 65
—, Sir John, of Devon; 17
—, Margaret; 15, 286

—, Nichol Fitz; 26
—, Nichol le fitz; 26
—, le S' R; 17
—, Monsire Robert; 17
—, Robert, of Chideock, Dorset; 15
—, Waryn; 61
—, S Water; 56
—, Willam; 57
—, Willame; 66
—, Monsr William; 17
—, Sir William; 17
—, Sr William; 17, 27
—, Williamus; 17
—, Willimus; 26
—, S. Wm; 17
MARTYNDALE; 46
—, William de; 328
MARTYNE, John, of Kent; 293
—, Sir William; 17
MARUM, Nicholas; 356
MARY, Q of Scots; 250
—, Qu of Scots; 250
MARYNER, Robert; 189
—, William; 210
—, S' Willm, of Essex; 189
MARYON, William, Kt; 164
MASCY, Hugo, of Tympeley, Ches; 335
—, de Tynperley; 335
MASON; 160, 196
—, T; 197
MASONE, Sire John; 197
MASSON; 196-7
MASSY; 388
—, Hugh le, of Timperley; 335
—, de Temperle; 335
—, of Temperley; 335
—, Thomas; 388
—, de Tymperle; 336
—, de Tymperley; 335
MASSYDONIE, Roy de; 76
MASTON; 350
MATELAND, of Lethyntown; 162
MATHEW; 237
MATRAVERS; 116
MATREVERS, le S'or de; 132
MATROS, Maurice de; 345
MATTHEW; 237
MAUDUT, William; 17
MAUBREY, Sir Roger; 130
MAUCHELL, John; 294
MAUDEUT, Wm; 17
MAUDEYT; 58, 194
MAUDIT, Mons Rogere; 21
MAUDUIT; 17
—, Alienor; 20
—, Sir Roger; 20
—, Walter; 17
—, William; 17
—, William de, erle of Warwicke; 18

MAUDUT; 21
—, Sr de; 21
—, Monsr R. de; 21
—, Monsire Roger; 21
—, of Staffs; 21
MAUDUTT; 21
MAUDUYT, John; 373
—, Monsr Roger; 21
—, William; 17
MAUDYT, Robert, Ld, of Hanslape; 17
—, Roger, Kt; 20
—, Roger, Chev; 20
MAUFE, William; 150
—, William de; 116
—, Sr Wm, of Suss; 150
MAUFEE, Sire Willame; 150
MAULAIT, Monsire de; 325
MAULAY, le Sire de; 325
—, le Sr de; 325
—, Peres de; 325
—, Thomas de; 352
MAULE; 325
—, Sr Jo' de; 325
—, S Piers de; 325
MAULEE, Sire Peres de; 325
MAULEMAYNS; 356
MAULEON, Wm de; 116
MAULEV'ER, Sir J; 292
MAULEVERE; 292
MAULEVERER; 292-3
—, James; 292
—, John; 292
—, Mons John; 366
—, Sir John; 293
—, John, of Allyrton; 293
—, Oliver; 293
—, Oliver, of Lincs; 292
—, Mons Olyver; 293
—, Peter; 292
—, Peter, Kt; 292
—, Ralph, of Lanarks; 215
—, Robert; 293
—, Sir Thos; 293
—, Sire Willame; 292
—, Mons' William; 292
—, William; 292
MAULEVERERE, Monsr; 292
—, Hopkyne, of Yorks; 293
—, Sir John; 293
MAULEVERES, Mons John; 293
MAULEY, ...; 325
—; 320, 325, 363
—, Ld; 325
—, le Sr de; 326
—, Monsire de; 326
—, Peres de; 326
—, Sr Peres de; 326, 362
—, Peris de; 326
—, Sire Peris de; 326

—, Pers de; 326
—, S' Pers; 326
—, Sir Pers; 326
—, Peter de; 320
—, Sir Peter de; 320
—, Peter de, Chivaler; 320
—, Peter de, Ld of Mulgrave; 320
—, Sir Philip; 326
—, Piers; 320, 326
—, Sir Piers; 320
MAULORIE, Perus; 284
MAULYVERER, Sir G; 293
—, Johannes; 293
—, John; 293
MAUNBY, Mons Hugh; 71
MAUNCESTRE; 342
—, Monsire Esmon; 342
MAUNCHETTER, S' Gy de; 342
MAUNCYLL, John; 66
MAUNDEVILE, Richard; 86
MAUNDEVILLE, Ralph de, of Essex; 192
—, Mons' Thomas; 60
—, Thomas de; 310
—, Thomas, Ld of Auescote, Northants; 58
MAUNWARING, Thomas de; 15
MAUSE; 150
MAUSLEY, Sir Symond; 157
MAUSUER; 342
MAUTRAVERS, John; 1
MAWLE, Ld; 326
—, Sir Pierce; 326
MAWLEY; 326
—, ... de; 326
—, Baron; 326
—, Ld; 326
MAWLYVEREY, of Kent; 292
MAWLZ; 326
MAWOLE, L[ord]; 326
MAWRE, John, of Kryke; 58
MAWSEY; 231
—, Richard, of Suss; 232
MAXWELL, Gilbert; 226
—, John; 204
MAY, Hew; 77
—, S Reginaldi le; 51
MAYDESTON; 12
MAYDESTONE; 12, 73
MAYDYSTON, of Middx; 12
MAYLER; 278
MAYLLORYE, Mons J de; 278
MAYLORRE, Christfr; 163
—, Esteven; 163
MAYN WARON; 55
MAYNERYNG, Sir J; 17
MAYNSTON, John; 350
MAYNWARE', Sir J; 17
MAYNWARING, of Ches; 18
MAYNWARINGE; 17
MAYNWARRYNG, Sir John; 17

MAYNWARYN, Ranulf; 17
MAYNWARYNG; 15, 17
—, Sir John; 17
—, S' John, Ches; 17
—, John, of Peover, Ches; 18
MCDOUAL; 167
MEALOS, Mons John de; 43
MEAUX, Thomas de; 233, 239
—, Thomas de, Kt; 199
MECHELL, Hary; 159
MECKFEN, Robert, of Mekven, Lord of that
   ilk; 380
MEDEHOP; 141
MEDELTON ABBAY; 106
MEDFORD, Walter de; 85
MEERK, S Johan de; 246
MEINEL, M de; 83
MEINELL; 83
MEINILL, Nicholas de; 74, 83
MEISHAM, William de, of Eton & Meisham;
   208
MELDRUM; 205, 266
—, Alan; 212
—, Alexdr, of Segie; 230
—, David, Canon of Dunkeld; 216
—, George, of Petcarrie; 205
—, Master Wm; 216
—, Wm; 216
—, Wm, Bp of Brechin; 216
MELEMEYNS, Mons Nicholl; 351
MELES, M de; 45
—, Mons de; 43
—, Mons Roger de; 43
MELESE, Roger de; 38
MELSANBY, Walter de; 77
MELTON, Thoroldus de; 345
—, Sir Thos; 58
MELUSYN, E of; 232
MELVILLE, Robert; 116
MEMILE; 83
MEMPYNSON; 154
MENALL, Monsire de; 83
MENELL; 83
—, Ld; 83
MENERS, Mons' Robert; 33
MENIL, Nichol de; 83
—, Nicol de; 76
MENILE, Le Sr de; 83
—, le Sr de; 83
MENILL; 84
—, Mons Nich; 77
—, Sire Nichole de; 76
—, Nicolas de; 77, 83
MENILLE, Sr de; 77
—, Nicholl de; 83
MENIRLE, Rauf; 169
MENNEL, Alan; 355
MENTEITH, of the Carse; 343
—, Sir John, Kt; 396

—, Sir Wm, of West Kerse, Kt; 342
MENTIETH, Earldom of; 94
MENVILL, Ralph; 116
MENY; 37
MENYL, Esteven de; 83
MENYLE, le Sire de; 83
MENYLL; 83
—, le; 83
MENYLLE; 83-4
MEOLES; 43
MERC, John de; 242
—, Mons Robert de; 187
—, Will de; 130
MERCELYN, Rex; 213
—, King in England; 213
—, Rec; 213
MERDISFEN, Roger de; 70
LA MERE; 125
MERE, le; 125
MEREWORTH, John de; 391
MERFELDE, Sir J; 257
—, Sir W; 262
MERHAS, Sir Ansel; 365
MERICK, of Som; 89
MERIELT, of Hestercombe; 344
—, of Merielt; 89
MERIET; 89, 98, 344
—, Sire Johan; 89
—, Sire Johan de; 344
—, Johes de; 344
—, Sir John; 344
—, Sir John de; 344
—, Lucy de; 320
—, Matildis de; 86
—, Simon de; 327
—, Simon, of Som, Kt; 344
—, of Som; 344
MERIETH, Simon de; 344
MERIETTES; 344
MERK, Ingram del; 130
—, S Jehan de; 242
—, Johan de; 246
—, Sire Johan de; 242
MERKE, Essex; 246
—, Simon de; 217
—, Willm de; 130
MERKES, William le; 116
MERKS; 239
MERLAGE, Wm, of Derby; 142
MERNY, le fitz ... de; 210
—, Mons R de; 189
MERRIET, Sir John, of Hestercombe; 344
MERSHALL; 357
MERTON, Mons Richard de; 66
MERTONE, Edmund de; 217
MERVILLE, Sir John; 283
MERYET; 89, 327, 344
—, Sir John de; 86
—, de Somersett; 89

MERYFELD; 257
MERYNGTON, Thomas de; 266
MERYOT, John de; 89
MESCHENES, of Copland, Cumb; 136
MESCHINES, de 'Le Count de Lincolne'; 132
—, Randle, 1st E of Chester; 136
—, Sir Randol; 136
—, Randolf le tierce, Conte de Chestre; 136
—, Rannulf de, E of Chester; 116
—, Ranulph; 207
MESCHYNES, Ranulph; 136
MESSINA; 238
METCALFE; 295
—, of Richmond, Yorks; 295
METFORD; 183
—, John; 23, 85
METTE, William, of Canterbury, Kent; 211
METTINGHAM COLLEGE, Suff; 116
MEUFORD; 157
MEULAN, Amaury de; 180
MEULARD, Katherine; 350
MEULES, Monsire de; 43
—, Sr de; 43
—, Mons John; 43
—, Sr Jon; 43
MEURIC; 116
MEWFORD, Norff; 157
MEYDENE, Gilbert, of Bulverhithe, Suss; 332
MEYNEL, M de; 84
—, Sire Nicholas de; 77
MEYNELL; 2
—, de; 83
—, Nicholas, Ld; 83
—, Nicholas of; 83
MEYNILL, Sir...; 83
—, Sr Nichol de; 77
—, Nicholas de, Ld of Whorlton; 83
MEYNWARYN, Sir John; 17
MEYNWARYNGE, William de, of N Wales; 15
MICHANTE, Monsr John; 208
MICHELL, Henry; 346
—, John, Westmld; 293
MICHELSTAN; 4
MICOLL; 136
MIDDELTON, Margery; 116
MIDDILTON, Elias de; 223
MIDDLETON, Sir ...; 223
—, John, of Kilhil; 116
—, Margery; 116
—, Patrick; 116
MIKLEYE, Adam de; 116
MILDE; 225
MILL, Edmund; 290
—, Richard; 290
—, Richd; 290
MILLTONE, Rob de; 46
MILTON; 36
—, Galfridus de; 345

MILTON ABBEY; 106
MIRABIEL, Symon de; 164
MIRFELD; 263
—, Ricardus; 265
MIRFIELD, Adam de; 255
MISSENDEN MONASTERY; 48
MITFORD, of Berks; 85
—, Richard; 85
MOAUT; 128
MOBRAY; 150
MOELES, Nichol de; 43
—, Nicholas de; 41
MOELS; 43, 70
—, John de; 42
—, John de, Ld of Cadbury, Som, 1st Baron; 42
—, John de, Ld of North Cadbury; 42
—, Rog de; 43
MOELYS, Alice; 275
MOHANT, Roger; 128
MOHAUD, Sire Robert; 128
MOHAUT; 128
—, de; 128
—, le Sire de; 128
—, Ad de; 84
—, Jan de; 209
—, Johan de; 123
—, Millicent de; 116
—, Robert de; 128
—, Sr Robert; 128
—, Robert de, Ld of Hawarden; 116
—, Rog de; 128
—, Roger de; 128
—, William; 116
MOHAUTE, Mons Rich de; 276
—, Robert le; 128
MOHAWT, Sr H; 276
MOIGN; 40-1
MOIGNE, Maria; 226
—, [Sr] Will; 59
—, Mons William; 41
—, William, Kt; 38
MOIGNI, William; 41
MOILES; 56
MOINE, Guil Le; 41
MOKLOW, of Worcs; 213
MOL, of Codsall, Staffs; 2
MOLES, Nicholas de; 43
—, Roger de; 43
—, Rogg de; 43
MOLETON; 60
—, de; 87
—, Thomas, of Gilsland, Cumb; 66
MOLETONE; 60
MOLEZ, Sir John; 43
MOLIANT; 276
MOLIS, Nicholas de; 42
MOLL, Robert, of Codsall, Staffs; 2
MOLTON; 58-60

—, Alanus de, of Lincs; 65
—, Henly de; 237
—, of Lincs; 59
—, Sir Thomas; 59, 75
—, Sire Thomas de; 60, 88
—, Sr Thomas de; 88
—, Thomas de; 60
—, Mons Thos de; 70
—, Thos de; 60
MOLTONE, Thomas de; 60
MOMFORD; 116, 177
MOMPESSON; 154
MONALT; 128
MONBOUCHER, Sir Barthelmew; 384
MONCASTRE, Mons Robert; 328
MONCEAUS, Waleran de; 320
MONCEUX; 320
MONCHANESY, William de; 100
MONCHENEY, Sir William; 97
MONCHENSEY; 99
MONCHENSI, Sire Willame de; 100
MONCHENSY; 91, 100, 327
—, of Herts; 100
—, Wm de; 99
MONCHORY, the Lorde; 97
MONCRIEFF, Malcolm of; 213
MONDIDIERS, Simon; 3, 99
MONFORD, Sir John; 99
—, Mons Laur'; 149
MONFORT, s'Ailsander; 148
—, Syon, Conte de Leicestre; 177
MONGOMERY, Adam de; 285
MONHALT, D of Kent; 128
—, Millisent de; 116
MONHANCE, Richard de; 276
MONHAULT, of Lincs; 84
MONHAUT; 84, 116, 128, 209
—, Le Sr de; 128
—, Adam; 125
—, Adam de; 84
—, Sire Jemes de; 84
—, John de; 209
—, Sr R de; 128
—, Sr Robart; 128
—, Robert; 155
—, Robert de; 128
—, Sire Robert de; 128
—, Roger le; 128
MONHAUTE; 276
—, Roger de; 128
—, Sr Roger de; 128
MONMOUTH, Henry of; 304
MONORGON, Gilbert; 228
—, Gilbert, of that ilk; 228
MONPEUCON, Edmond, of Battington, Wilts; 154
MONPEYZON, Sir Gyles; 126
MONPINZON, Sire ...; 154
MONPISSONE; 154

MONPYSSON, John; 126
MONSEDLA; 326
MONTALT; 116, 128, 226
—, Robert de; 116, 128
—, Roger of; 122
MONTANY, Sir Thomas; 377
MONTCHENISY, Thomas de, of Suff, Chevr;
99
MONTE, le Counte del; 210
MONTE ALTO, Emma; 116
—, Emma de; 116
—, Milisenta de, of Barby, Northants; 117
—, Robert de; 117
—, Robert de, Ld of Hawardyn, Flints, 2nd
Baron; 117
—, Rogerus de, Seneschal of Chester; 117
—, Wm; 117
MONTE CANISY, Dionisia de; 185
—, Dionyisia de; 206
MONTEALTY; 128
MONTECH; 342
MONTEFORTE, Wellesburne de la; 199
—, Wellisburne Bellator; 199
MONTEITH; 342
MONTENACK, Robert; 139
MONTENAY; 377
MONTENDRE, William; 171
MONTENEY; 377, 390
MONTENEYE, Arnold de; 395
MONTENY, Robert de; 377
MONTFORD; 46
—, Guy de; 176
—, John de, Ld of Lunmeth; 117
—, Erle of Leycetr; 130
—, Sir Richard; 199
—, Simon de; 176
—, Simon de, E of Leicester; 175
—, Thomas; 147
—, Sir Thomas, of Yorks; 147
MONTFORT; 46, 117, 149, 177, 182
—, Alexander de; 148
—, Dorset & Som; 149
—, le Counte de Leicestre; 177
—, le Counte de Leycestre; 177
—, Counte de Leycestre; 177
—, Cunte de Leycestre; 177
—, 'de Nony'; 176
—, Peter de; 99
—, Philip de; 210
—, Simon de, Earl of Leicester; 177
—, Simon de, E of Leicester; 177
—, Simon de, E of Leicester, 1230-65; 177
—, Simon, E of Leicester; 177
—, Symon; 176
—, le Cunte Symund; 177
MONTGOMERY, Adam; 285
—, John, of Eagleshame; 2
—, Roger de; 117
—, Walter; 353

MONTHALT, Sr de; 128
MONTHAULT, Baron; 128
MONTHAUT, Ada de; 84
MONTIOY, Monsire Raufe de; 342
MONTIOYE, Sr Rauf de; 342
MONTNEY, Monsire; 377
MONTONI, Robert de; 377
MONTPYNSON, of Norf; 126
MONTRYVEL; 182
—, Monsire de; 182
MONWTENY, Sir James; 377
MONYPENY, David, of Petworth, Suss; 375
MOORTONE, Ric' de; 203
MOOTLOWE, Sir Henry; 386
MOPISSON; 80
MORAZ, Sir Bayous de; 88
MORDINGTON, Sir Wm, Kt, ?Berwicks; 321
MORE; 50, 87
—, S Estevene de la; 362
—, Hants; 50
—, of Liverpool; 294
—, Nicholas de La, of Som; 84
—, Thomas; 199
—, Thomas de la; 86
—, Thomas, clerk; 117
—, of Wydeford; 49
MOREBY, William de; 361
MOREL, Martin; 241
MORELE, Sire William; 216
MORELL; 325
MORES, Wyllyam; 65
MORETON, John, E of; 300
MOREWS; 343
MORGAN, John, of Gt Kitshall, Suff; 294
—, William; 280
MORGANBAGHAN; 201
MORHALE, Thomas; 40
MORHALL, Thomas, parson of Iverton; 15
MORHALLE, Thomas; 40
MORHAM, Adam; 69
MORIE, le Prince de la; 364
MORIENX, Thomas de, of Suff, Chevr; 347
MORIEUX; 347
MORITON, John, Count of; 255
—, John E of, Ld of Ireland; 255
MORLAY, Ld; 166
—, Tomas, Sir de; 166
MORLAYE, die here van; 164
—, R', le Fitz; 210
—, Mons Robt, of Norf; 166
—, Willam de; 176
—, Mons Willm de; 166
MORLE; 166, 172
—, Ld; 166
—, Ld de; 166
—, le Sr de; 166
—, Sir Robert; 176
—, Robt de, King's Admiral in the North; 164
—, Sire Roger de; 166

—, William de; 166
—, Wm de, Marshal of Irld (3rd Baron M); 164
MORLEE; 166
—, le Sr de; 166
—, Monsire de; 166
—, Mons Robert de; 208
—, Robert de, Kt; 117
—, Sire Robert de; 182
—, Robt de; 164
—, Sir Robt; 164
—, Robt de, Admiral of the Fleet of the North; 164
—, Robt de, Marshal of Irld; 164
—, Robt de of Suff, Kt; 164
—, Sir Wm de; 117
MORLEI, Robt de, Kt; 86
MORLENS, Sir Roger; 43
MORLES; 43
MORLEY; 99, 117, 138, 164, 166
—, Ld; 166, 326
—, Le Sire de; 126
—, le Sire de; 126, 166
—, Le Sr de; 166
—, le Sr de; 166
—, Sr de; 166
—, Anna, Lady de; 164
—, Isabella, Lady de; 164
—, of Kent; 166
—, Lorde; 166
—, Nicholas; 179
—, le Sr de, of Norf; 166
—, Norf; 182
—, le S'or de; 166
—, Monsire Rob de; 219
—, Robert de; 166, 208
—, Robert de, 2nd Ld; 117
—, S Robt; 182
—, Thomas, Ld; 166, 235
—, Thos de, Kt, Marshal of Ireld; 164
—, Thos, Kt, Ld de M (4th Baron); 164
—, Thos, Kt, Ld de M (4th Baron), Marshal of Irld; 164
—, Sir William; 182
—, Sr William de; 176
—, Wm de, 3rd Ld; 164
MORLEYE, Will de; 182
MORRELL; 262, 265
MORREWES, Mons Thomas; 347
—, S Thos; 347
MORRIS, W; 97
MORTAIGN, Rogeirs de; 316
MORTAIGNE, Roger le; 316
MORTAIN, John, E of; 263
—, John E of; 288
—, Roger de, Ld of Walishale; 275
MORTAIN & Boulogne, Stephen, E of; 300
MORTAMER, Sir Robert; 22
MORTEIN, Roger de, Ld of Dunnesby; 285

—, Roger de, Ld of Walsall, Staffs, Kt; 281
MORTEMER; 38, 41, 103-4
—, Emounde; 103
—, Geffrey de; 106
—, John; 104
—, John de; 103
—, Sir John; 104
—, Sir John, of Herefs; 105
—, Roberd, of Essex; 105
—, Robert de; 22
—, Roger de; 103-4
—, Sir Roger; 102
—, Sire Roger de; 103
—, Roger de, 4th E of March & Ulster; 101
—, Rogiers de; 104
—, Willame de; 106
MORTEMERE; 102, 106
MORTES; 35
MORTEYN, S' Roger de; 316
—, Sire Roger; 316
—, Sire Roger de; 277
—, S'Roger de; 316
MORTEYNE, Robert de; 315-16
MORTIMER, Edmund de; 103
—, Jan de; 103
MORTIM(er), Robt de; 22
—, Willam de; 51
MORTIMER; 40, 91, 101-4, 106
—, Baron; 104
—, de; 103
—, E de; 103
—, Ld; 104
—, M de; 103
—, Sir ...; 41
—, Anna; 103
—, Anne; 103
—, Earls of March; 102
—, Edmond; 103
—, Edmund; 103
—, Edmund de; 102
—, Edmund, E of March; 101-3
—, Edmund, E of March, Ld of Wigmore; 102
—, Edmund de, 3rd E of March; 102
—, Edmund de, 1st Baron, of Wigmore; 102
—, Gefrai de; 106
—, Geoffrey; 106
—, Geoffrey de; 106
—, Henri de; 104
—, Sire Henri de; 103
—, Henry de; 103, 105
—, of Herefs; 105
—, Hue de; 22
—, Hugh; 103
—, Hugh de; 102
—, Hugh de, of Salop, Kt; 102
—, Sir Hugh, of Salop; 103
—, Hughe de; 22
—, Hugo de; 102
—, Sire Hugue de; 22

—, Isabella de; 22
—, James; 123
—, Jefray; 106
—, Jehan de; 103
—, John de; 103
—, John de, Kt; 102
—, S John de; 105
—, Sir John; 103
—, Sir John [Kt 1485]; 104
—, E of March; 102-3
—, Margaret; 102
—, Maud de; 102
—, Raf de; 104
—, of Ricards' Castle; 90
—, of Richard's Castle; 91
—, Roberd de; 22
—, Munsire Robert de; 22
—, Robert; 22
—, Robert de; 22, 316
—, Robertus de; 91
—, Rog de; 104
—, Munsire Roger de; 103
—, Roger; 102, 104, 315
—, Roger de; 102-4
—, Roger of; 103
—, Sir Roger de; 104
—, Sire Roger de; 103-4
—, Sr Roger de; 102
—, Roger de, C of March; 48
—, Roger, of Chirk; 104
—, Sr Roger de, le fitz; 105
—, Roger de, E of March & Ulster; 102
—, Roger, E of March; 102-3
—, Roger de, Ld of Pentkellyn; 104
—, Roger de, Ld of Pentkellyn, 2nd Baron; 102
—, Roger de, Ld of Wigmore, Herefs; 102
—, Roger, of Wigmore, d 1328; 104
—, Rogg' de; 104
—, Thomas, burgess of Dundee; 117
—, Will' de; 106
—, Willam de; 106
—, William; 106
—, William de; 23, 106
—, Willimus de; 51
—, Wm; 208
MORTIMERE; 22
MORTMER, Ed'us de; 103
—, Sir Edmund; 102
MORTON; 316
—, Edward; 117
—, of Glower, (Gloucs); 295
—, Mons' Hugh; 22
—, John de; 117
—, John, de London, esquier; 312
—, Ld Walter de, of Bucks; 72
MORTUMER, Ld of Wigmore; 103
MORTUO MARI, John de, Kt; 105
—, Walter de, Constable of Beaumaris; 102

—, Willelmus de, of Attleborough; 22
MORTUOMARI, Edmund de; 102
—, Roger de; 102
MORTYMAR, of Fowlis; 161
MORTYMER; 41, 104
—, Monsire de; 104
—, Mons Geffray; 103
—, Sir Henry; 105
—, S' Hug de, of Salop; 103
—, Hugh; 40
—, Mons Hugh; 103
—, Mons' Hugh; 103
—, S. Hugh de; 19
—, Sir Hugh; 104
—, Sire Hugh de; 104
—, Sr Hugh de; 22
—, Sire Johan de; 105
—, Mons' John; 22
—, S John; 105
—, Erle of Marche; 103
—, Mons Rauf; 105
—, Mons' Roger le; 103
—, Roger; 103
—, Roger de; 103
—, S Roger; 104
—, Sire Roger de; 104-5
—, Sr Roger; 103
—, Sr Roger de; 104
—, Mons Th; 105
—, Mons' Walran; 35
—, S. William; 21
MORTYMERE; 104, 106
—, Sir Humfrey, of Salop; 103
MORVILE; 107
—, Bernard de; 107
MORVILLE, Wm; 185, 187
MORYENS; 347
MORYEUX, Thomas, Kt; 350
MORYEWIS, Tho; 347
MORYN, John; 371
MORYNEUS; 347
—, Mons T; 364
—, Mons T de; 347
MORYS, Sir Thomas, of Suff; 347
MOSELL, Thomas; 395
MOSGRAVE; 7
—, Sir R; 7
—, Ric; 7
MOSGROWE, John, of Westmld; 7
MOSSIETO, Peter de; 211
MOSTINES; 395
MOTE, Sr de la; 364
—, Monsr W de la; 342
—, Mons William de la; 354
—, Sr William de la; 359
—, Mons William del; 364
MOTLOW, Henry de, Ches; 386
MOTTE, de la; 342
MOUBRAY; 130, 236

—, Le Sr de; 130
—, Monsire de; 130
—, Sr de; 167
—, Alexander de; 208
—, Mons Alisandre le fitz; 236
—, Gefrey de; 208
—, Geoffrey de; 208
—, Mons J de; 236
—, Jn de, Ld of Island of Axholme, Lincs, 2nd Ld; 165
—, Jn de, 3rd Ld M; 164
—, Sr Jo de; 130
—, Sire Johann de; 130
—, John, s of William M; 241
—, of Kent; 299
—, Robert de; 130
—, S Robt de; 130
—, Rog de; 130
—, Roger; 130
—, Sir Roger; 130
—, son ffitz de; 247
—, Mons Thos; 299
—, William, Kt; 171
MOUBRAYE, Sir Alexander; 236
MOUBREY, D of Norfolk, of Leics; 130
—, Geffrey de; 234
—, Roger de; 130
MOUCHANESY, Willm de; 84
MOUHAULT, Joan de; 209
MOUHAUT, Robert de; 128
MOUKELOW, Peter; 214
MOULENT; 179
MOULES; 43
—, Sire Johan de; 43
—, Sr John de; 43
—, Wm de; 59
MOULTON; 59-60, 66, 68, 70, 72
—, le Sire de, de Fraunkton; 60
—, le Sire de, de Gillesland; 59
—, of Lincoln; 59
—, Thomas de; 60
—, Thos de; 60
MOULTONE, Thomas de; 29
MOUMBRAI; 130
MOUNBRAY, Sire Johan de; 130
MOUNCENEYE, Mons John; 377
—, Monsieur Robert; 377
MOUNCEUDYT, Mons W; 167
MOUNCEUX; 322
MOUNCHENSY, Mons' William; 100
MOUNFFORT, s' Laurence; 147
MOUNFORD; 149, 176
—, ... de; 177
—, Sr de; 176
—, Conte de Leycester; 177
—, Mons' Thomas; 147
MOUNFORT, de; 146
—, Sire ... de; 147
MOUNGUMBRY, Thomas, Ld of ?Lonlond;

140
MOUNMAREYN; 99-100
MOUNPYNSSON; 154
MOUNPYSSON, Sir John, of Essex; 154
MOUNSEAULX; 323
MOUNT, de la; 310
MOUNTEFORD; 46
MOUNTEIN, S Ernaud de; 377
MOUNTEN, Aernulphus de; 395
MOUNTENAK, Mons Robt; 139
MOUNTENAKE; 139
MOUNTENDRE; 171
MOUNTENEY; 377
—, Sir ...; 377
—, Ernaud de; 377
—, Essex; 377
—, John; 377
—, Robert; 377
—, Robert de; 377
—, Mons Thomas; 377
—, Sr Thomas de; 377
MOUNTENEYE; 377
MOUNTENY, Ernald de; 377
—, Ernaud de; 377
—, Sire Ernauf de; 377
—, Mons Rauf; 366
—, Robert; 377
MOUNTFORD, Sr de; 147
—, Thomas de; 147
MOUNTFORT, S. Alexander de; 147
—, Mons' Thomas; 147
—, Sir Wylyam; 230
MOUNTHAULT; 128
MOUNTNEY; 375
—, Sire Ernaud de; 377
—, Everarde de; 377
—, Robert de; 377
MOUNTONY, Sire Thomas de; 377
MOUSGRAVE, Sir John; 7
MOWAT; 234
—, John; 215
MOWBRAY; 117, 130, 155, 165, 167, 234, 236-7, 242, 298-9
—, de; 130
—, E.M; 299
—, Ld; 130
—, Monsire de; 130
—, Sr de; 130
—, Alexander de; 236
—, Alicia de; 117
—, Anne; 298
—, of Axholme; 130
—, of Barnbwgall; 167
—, C of Nottingham; 130
—, D of Norf; 298
—, D of Northfolk; 298
—, David, of Barnbougle; 187
—, Dukes of Norfolk; 130
—, Elizabeth, Duchess of Norf, etc; 297

—, fittz a Seignr; 208
—, Geoffrey; 208
—, Geoffrey de; 234
—, Geoffrey of; 208
—, Jn, of Barnbougle; 165
—, Jn, E of Nottingham & D of Norfolk; 117
—, John; 130, 241, 297
—, John de; 117
—, John, Ld; 117, 130
—, Sr John; 130
—, John, D of Norf; 297
—, John de, D of Northfolke; 298
—, John de, Kt, Ld of Isle of Axholme; 117
—, John de, Ld of Isle of Axholme; 117
—, John, E Marshall; 305
—, John, Duke of Norf; 297
—, John, of Northd; 236
—, John, Ld, E of Nottingham; 130
—, John, E of Nottingham & D of Norf; 298
—, le Conte Maryschall, Sr de; 299
—, Nigel; 130
—, le Duc de Northfolk; 299
—, Cont de Notingham, Count Marshall; 130
—, Sr Phillip de, d'Escoce; 224
—, Mons Roger de; 130
—, Roger; 117, 130, 208
—, Roger de; 117, 130
—, Thomas; 299
—, Thomas, Ld; 299
—, Thomas, D of Norfolk, E of Nottingham, E Marshal; 117
—, Thomas, E Marshal & E of Nottingham; 117
—, [Thomas Lord], E of Nottingham; 130
—, Sir Thomas, E of Nottingham; 299
—, Thomas, E of Nottingham; 117, 298
—, 'Sir Tomas, contte de Notyngeham'; 130
—, William de; 117, 130
MOWBRAY OF BARNBOUGAL; 167
MOWBRAYE; 130
—, E of Nottingham; 130
MOWBREY, Mons Alisant de; 208
—, John; 189
MOWERES, Sir Symond; 99
MOWMFORD, of Yorks; 147
MOWNS; 141
—, Ralph de; 141
—, Mons Rauf de; 141
MOWNTEIOYE, Ld; 25
MOWNTENEY, Sir William; 377
MOYELE; 41
MOYLE; 216, 233, 246
—, Joh, of Eastwell, Kent; 248
—, John, of Estwell, Kent; 233
—, Kent; 246
—, de Stephenton, Devon; 233
—, Sir Walter; 233, 248
—, Walter; 233
MOYLES, Sr John de; 43

MOYN; 41
—, Monsire William; 41
MOYNE; 41
—, John; 390
—, John le; 375
—, Mons John le; 60
—, S' Jon; 60
—, Mons William; 41
—, William; 41
MUBARI, Roger de; 117
MUCEGROS, Agnes de, dame de Chenmore; 117
—, Agnes de, Lady of Chinnor; 123
MUCHEGROS, Johan de; 208
MUCKLESTONE, Staffs; 244
MUCKLOW; 214
—, Wm, of Worcs; 214
MUHAUD, Wm; 117
MUHAUT, Adam de; 84
—, Mons Adam de; 84
—, Roger de; 128
MUHAUTE, Mons' John; 208
—, Mons Robert de; 128
MUILL, Nicholas; 83
MUIR, Reginald; 302
MUKLOW, William, of Worcs; 214
MUKTAN, Mons Rob de; 138
MUKTON; 138
MULCASTER; 328
MULCASTRE, David de; 328
MULCHESTOR; 344
MULCHESTRE, ...; 328
—; 363
MULES, Johan de; 43
—, Sire Johan de; 43
—, Mons John de; 43
—, Margaret de; 42, 372
MULETONE, Thomas de; 66
MULLYNG; 294
—, of Cornw; 294
MULTON; 59, 66, 68, 70-1, 331
—, de; 331
—, le S' de; 59
—, le Sr de; 59
—, Sir Edward, of Lincs; 88
—, Eliz de; 58
—, Sr, de F[raunkton]; 60
—, Sr de, de Gilesland; 59
—, Jn de; 58
—, Johannes de; 68
—, John de; 68
—, John de, Kt; 68
—, Mons John de; 36
—, Sir John; 68
—, Mons' John, de Frankton; 69
—, Mons' Rauf, de Egremond; 59
—, Rauf fitz Rauf de, de Richmundshire; 88
—, Mons Robert de; 70
—, Thomas; 26

—, Thomas de; 59, 66, 88
—, Thomas de, Forester; 66
—, Mons Thomas, de Gillesland; 66
—, Thomas de, of Kyrketon, Kt; 70
—, Thos de; 58-9
—, Thos de, Ld of Egremont, Cumb; 58
—, Mons Will de; 66
MULTONE; 66
—, S' Th'm de; 70
MUMBRAY, William de, of Yorks; 117
MUMBREY, Roger de; 130
MUNBRAI; 130
MUNBRAY, Roger de; 130
MUNCASTER, Robert; 330
MUNCASTRE; 328
MUNCES, Robert de, Lincs; 1
MUNCEUU; 392
MUNCHANESI, William de; 100
MUNCHENSI; 91
—, Joan; 91
MUNCHENSY; 91
—, Thomas; 100
—, Walter de; 100
—, Wm de; 85, 100
MUNCRIEF, of that ilke; 213
MUNDEVILLE, Ralph de, of Durham; 56
MUNDHAM, John de; 225
MUNFICHET, Wm, 'Ld of Kergill'; 106
MUNFORD, Monsire Symun de; 177
MUNFORT, Symun de; 177
MUNHAUT, Roger de; 128
MUNREVEL, Geoffrey de; 386
MUNTEIN, Robert de; 377
MUNTENI, Ernulph de, of Suff & Essex, Kt; 375
MUNTENO, Arnulf de, of Diss, Norf; 375
MUNTENY, Ernaud; 392
—, Roberd de; 377
—, Robert de; 377
MUNTHAM, de; 225
MURHOIL; 63
MURIEHT, Johan; 86
MURKEIL; 63
MURLION; 63
MURLYON; 63
MURRAY, John; 216
MURREUX; 348, 364, 370
—, Monsire Thomas; 348
MURZEUX; 348
MUSARD, John; 181
—, Malcolm; 117-18
—, Ralph, of Derby; 193
MUSCAMP, Robert of; 67
—, Robert, Berwicks; 185
MUSCEGROS, Agnes de; 118
—, Munsire Robert de; 136
—, Robert de; 136
MUSCHAMP; 60
MUSEGROS, M; 133

MUSGRAFE, Mons Thomas; 7
MUSGRAVE; 6-7
—, Monsire de; 7
—, Monsr de; 8
—, Sr de; 7
—, Fitz Louis; 7
—, of Hertlaw, Westmld; 7
—, Sir John; 7
—, Sir John, Westmld; 7
—, of Murton; 6
—, Sir R; 7
—, [Sir] Richard; 6
—, Sir Richard, of Westmld; 7
—, S Thm; 7
—, Mons Thom de; 7
—, Mons Thomas; 7
—, Sir Thomas de; 6
—, Thomas; 7
—, Thomas of; 6
—, of Yorks; 7
MUSHAMPE; 60
MUSSEGRES, Robert; 136
MUSSEGROS, Robt de; 136
MUSTERS, of Yorks; 394
MUSTHAMP; 60
MWBRAY, John, E.M; 299
MYDDILTON, Elias de; 223
MYDDYLTON, of Yorks; 223
MYDYLTON; 223
MYLDE; 225
MYLE, John, Chaplain; 213
MYLTON; 36
—, Richard, of East Greenwich; 67, 74
MYREFELD; 260
MYRFELD, Richard; 265
MYRFELDE; 260
MYRIELL, John, Clerk; 40
MYTHOP, Roger de; 170
NAIRNE; 3
NAMUR; 168
—, Sir Robert; 162
NANFAN; 292
—, John; 294
—, Sir Richard; 296
NANFANT, of Cornw; 296
NAPLES, Alphonse, K of; 99
NAPLYS, Kyng of; 264
NARFORD, Thomas de, Kt; 118
NARSTOFT, of Bucks; 146
NARTOFT; 139
NARWI, Sir; 158
NASSAU, Count of; 146
NASSYNGTON, Robert de; 375
NAUTON, Wylyam, of Yorks; 290
NAVARRE, K of; 346
NAVERN, le Roy de; 346
NEAPOLIS, Kyng of; 75
NECHE, Sir Wilham; 186
NEDAM, Sir John; 387

NEDHAM; 387
NEEDHAM; 387
—, J; 387
NEIRFORD, Mons John de; 157
—, Sire Willame de; 157
—, Mons William; 157
—, Mons William de; 157
NEIRFORDE, Monsr de; 157
NEIRMUST, of Bucks; 146
NEIVILE, Joan de; 129
—, Water de; 78
NELLO; 186
NELSUN, Henri le; 348
NEOPOLITAN, Rex; 260
NERBONNE; 318
NEREFORD; 180, 183, 187
—, William de; 157
NERFFORDE; 163
NERFORD; 118, 157, 172, 180
—, ... de; 180
—, Monsire de; 157
—, Sr de; 157
—, John de; 172
—, S' John de; 157
—, S' John, of Essex; 130
—, Reynald de; 172
—, Thomas de, Kt; 118
—, Waut' de; 172
—, Wille de; 157
—, Sir William de; 157
—, William de; 157
NERNEWT; 236
—, Richard; 236
NERNEWTE; 236
NERNUIT; 236
NESLE, John III de, Count of Soissons; 234
NESSEFIELD, Margaret; 118
NETEHAM, Richard; 387
NEUFCHASTEL, Jehan de, Seigneur de Montagu; 324
NEUVIL, Margaret de; 118
NEVELL, Sir John, of Essex; 129
NEVIL; 367
—, Ld Fauconberg; 124
NEVILE; 78
—, Ld Facombriges; 124
—, Hugo de; 129
—, John de; 334
—, John de, Kt; 208
—, John de, Kt, of Essex; 118
—, Walter de; 1, 79
NEVILL; 13
—, Monsire le, of Essex; 129
—, le ffiltz; 208
—, of France; 12
—, Mons Hugh de; 242
—, S Hugh de; 129
—, Sr Hugh de, de Essex; 129
—, Monsr J, de [?Essex]; 129

—, John de, le Forster; 341
—, Lady Margaret de; 118
—, the Lady Margaret de; 282
—, Margaret de; 118, 286
—, Sir Wm, KG; 124
—, Sir Wm, Ld Fauconberg, KG; 124
NEVILLE, George; 15
—, Hugh de; 118, 334, 341
—, Hugh de, Kt, of Darnall, Notts; 118
—, John de; 118
—, John de, Kt; 118
—, John de, Chief Forester, 1246; 334
—, John de, of Essex; 208
—, Mons John, de Essex; 129
—, John, le Forestier; 381
—, Margaret; 118, 282, 365
—, Richard de; 118
—, Richard, E of Salisbury; 313
—, William de; 53
NEVYLE, Sir Jon, of Essex; 129
—, Dame Margareta de; 118
—, Dame Margareta de, of London; 282
NEVYLL; 129
NEWARK; 68, 79
—, College of, Leics; 298
—, of Dalton; 79
NEWARKE, of Dawlton; 79
NEWBOROUGH MONASTERY, Yorks; 226
NEWBURN, Roger of; 46
NEWELL; 71
NEWENHAM, Edmund; 274
NEWERENE, Bucks; 37
NEWERKE; 79
NEWFORDE; 157
NEWMAN, Tomas, Northants; 274
NEWPORT; 145
—, of Essex; 145
—, John; 118, 142
—, Mr; 75
—, Robert; 142
—, Robt; 143
NEWSUM, John de; 230
NEWTON, Robt; 389
—, of Swell; 155
—, Thomas of; 215
—, Wm, of Newton; 118
NEWTOUN; 214
NEWYLE, Sir John; 161
NEYMYSTE; 146
NEYRMYST; 146
—, of Essex; 139
NEYRNUGHT, John, Kt; 236
NEYRNUVHT, John, Kt; 230
NEYRNUYST, Sire Johan; 146
NEYVILE, Sire Hue de; 129
NEYVILLE; 129
NICHOL, Erl of; 136
NICHOLE, Cunte de; 136-7, 364
—, le Conte de; 137

—, le counte de; 137
—, C de; 133
—, le Comte de; 364
NICHOLL, de; 137
—, Co; 133
NICOL; 118
—, fitz; 337
—, Mons Thomas fitz; 337
—, Thomas fitz; 337
NICOLE; 364
—, Cunte de; 364
—, le counte de; 126
—, Enris li bons quens de; 137
NICOLLE, le Cunte de; 364
NIDIN, Hugh de, Perthshire; 185
NIERNUIT; 236
NISBET, John, of Dalzell; 380
NITHSDALE; 138
NOBLE, William; 8
NOERFWIC, Die Bisscop van; 393
NONAUNT, Willame de; 125
NONGEDEMO; 4
NONYS APPRES; 153
NOONWERS; 37
NORAIS, Malcolm; 64
NORBERY; 367
—, of Yorks; 367
NORBURY, of Derbys; 367
—, Sir John de; 330
NORFFOLKE, Cont de; 144
NORFOLK, Erle of; 144
—, le C de; 144
—, D of; 299
—, Duchess of; 118
—, Eliz, Duchess of; 118
—, Elizabeth, Duchess of; 298
—, Margaret, Ctess of; 298
—, Mgt, Duchess of; 299
—, Thomas, E of; 299
—, Thomas, E of, Marshal of England; 298
NORFOLKE, le Count de; 144
—, the D of; 299
—, Dewke of; 299
NORM'NDY, D of; 264
NORMAN, John; 68
NORMANDIE, D of; 266
NORMANDY; 264, 266
—, D of; 264
—, Robert 'Courthose'; 304
—, Robert 'Courthose', D of; 304
—, Rollo, D of; 264
NORMANVILLE, Leo de; 185
NORMAVILLE; 75
NOROVAIGE, le roy de; 125
NORROY; 158
NORTH'LAND, le Counte de; 133
NORTHAM; 170, 173
—, Thomas de; 170
NORTHAMPTON; 197

—, John; 197, 262
—, John de; 197
NORTHAMTON; 197
NORTHD, Hen, E of, KG; 133
NORTHEHUMBERLAND, E of; 133
NORTHEWAY; 197
NORTHFFOLKE, Robarde, of Yorks; 22
NORTHFOLKE, Duke of; 299
—, D of; 299
NORTHMBRLAND, Comes; 133
NORTHTOFT, Edmund de; 118
NORTHUBRIE, Comes; 138
NORTHUMB'LAND, le Count de; 133
NORTHUMBERLAND; 118, 133
—, Conte de; 133
—, le Conte de, Sr de Lucy; 133
—, Hen, E of; 133
—, [Hen Percy] E of; 133
—, Therll of; 133
NORTHUMBERLANDE, E of; 133
NORTHUMBERLOND, Count de; 133
NORTHUMBLOND, E of; 133
NORTHUMBRIA, Comes; 133
NORTHUMBRYELAN, Comes; 133
NORTHUMBURLAND, Erle of; 133
NORTHWAY; 197
NORTHWICHE, Monsire de; 158
NORTHWYCHE; 158
NORTHWYKE, Sire Johan de; 209
NORTOFT, Sire Adam de; 139
NORTON; 348
—, Mons Gerveis de; 169
—, James de, Kt; 118
—, Juliana; 342
—, Robt de; 139
NORTONE; 139
—, Sire James de; 140
—, Joames de; 118
—, Richard de, of Waddeworth, Yorks; 184
NORTWYCHE, Mons John de; 158
NORVILL; 348
NORWAY; 197-8, 205
—, K of; 13, 197-8
—, Rex de; 198
—, K Harold Hadrada of; 13
—, the Kyng off; 198
—, le Roy de; 198
—, Roy de; 198
NORWEYE, le Roy de; 236
NORWICH; 143, 158, 220
—, City of; 211
—, John; 158
—, John de; 158
—, S' John de; 209
—, Sir John; 158
—, Sir John, Kt; 118
—, of Mettingham; 118
—, Roger; 173
—, of Suff, Chevr; 158

—, Wm de, Abbot of W Dereham; 118
NORWICH CITY; 215
NORWICHE; 158, 220
—, John; 220
—, Mons John de; 158
—, Mons' John de; 206
—, John of Essex; 158
—, Mons Water; 209
NORWITZ, Monsr de; 158
NORWYC; 158
NORWYCH, Jo; 158
—, Sir John; 158
—, John, of Yoxford, Suff; 217
NORWYCHE; 158, 172
—, Mons John; 158
—, Sir John, of Norf; 158
—, Mons.Rog.de; 173
—, Roger; 172
—, Sir W; 143
NORWYZ, Monsire de; 158
NOTBEAME; 360
NOTTINGHAM; 197
—, E of; 130
NOTYNGHAM, Le C de; 130
—, Erl of; 130
NOUWERS; 37
—, Sire ... de; 37
NOUYK, Peter de; 118
NOVEREY, John; 15
NOVEREYE, John, of Burton; 32
NOWENHM; 311
NOWERS; 37
—, John; 36-7
—, Sir John; 37
NOWFORD, Norff; 157
NOYERS; 323
NUGGE, Peter; 225
NUNFORT, Symon de; 177
NUNGEDENE; 2
NUSOUN, John; 82
NYCHOLL, Count de; 190
—, fitz; 337
NYCHOLLE, E of; 125
NYCOL, Sir Thomas fittes; 337
NYCOLL, counte; 199
NYDAM, of Shenton; 387
NYDDISDAILL, Ld of, of auld; 138
NYDYAN, Nycolas, Ld of Delven; 21
O'BRIAN, thearle of Tomonde; 288
O'BRYN, Captain Donagh; 118
O'NEIL, Baron of Inyscheroune Oneyle; 308
OBRYEN; 288
OCHTERLONYE, of Kellye; 128
OCTANION; 141
OCTOMEN; 141
OGILVIE, Alexr, Sheriff of Angus; 165
—, Sir Andrew, of Inchmartin; 235
—, David; 187
—, Sir David, Kt; 194

—, Isabella; 250
—, John; 210-11
—, John, Sheriff-depute of Inverness; 366
—, Patrick; 230
—, Sir Patrick, Kt; 210
—, Walter, of Beaufort; 193
OGILVY, of Auchterhouse; 187
—, of Findlater; 185
—, James; 193
—, Patrick, of Easter Kelor; 185
OGILWEY, Ld; 187
OGILWY; 195
—, of Ochterhouss; 125
—, of Straheryne; 194
OGLE; 41
OGYLWY, of Balefan; 195
OHENLOYN; 211
OKEHAMPTON; 21
OKENEY; 268
OLAV, King; 198
OLDCALL; 157
OLDCHALL; 158
OLDEGRAVE, Ric de; 322
OLDEHALE, Sir William, of Norf; 157
OLDEHALL, Norf; 157
OLDHALE, Sir Wylyam, Lincs; 180
OLDHALL; 130, 172
—, Sr de; 158
—, Sir William; 157
OLDHALLE, WIlliam; 118
—, William, Kt; 118
—, Sir Wm; 118
OLEPHERNUS; 318
OLIFE; 207
OLIVER; 368
—, Robert; 388
OLOM; 8
OLOUTHER, Sire Huwe; 8
OLTON; 145
—, Johannes de; 145
—, John de; 145
—, John de, Ches; 145
—, John, of Olton, Ches; 145
OLYVERE, Robert, of Essex; 375
OOKYNDONE, Nicol de; 130
OORNE, Philip; 236
OPTON; 148
OPTONE; 148
—, Sire Walter de; 148
ORBY; 267-8
—, Monsire de; 267
—, Mons John; 258
ORE, Richard de; 327
—, Robert de; 345
—, Robert de, Suss; 345
ORFLETE, Gerard; 375
ORIEL COLLEGE, Oxf; 309
ORIFLAMME, the; 1
ORMESBY, Ralph; 118

—, William de, Kt; 381
ORMONDE, Anne, Ctess of; 216, 380
ORNESBY; 343
—, Norf; 381
—, Sire Willame de; 343
ORNSBY, Sir John; 383
ORREBY; 267
—, John de, Clerk; 334
—, John de, of Lincs; 267
ORRELL, Sir John, of Som; 20
ORRETONE, M de; 195
ORTON; 165, 192, 203, 290
—, Mons J de; 192
—, John; 192
OSBORNE; 295
OSOLVESTON ABBEY, Leics; 61
OSTERLEY; 88
OSTERWIC, Baldwin de; 92
OSTON; 145
OSTOTENILE; 140
OSTREVANT, Wm E of, & D of Holland; 138
OSTRYCHE, Duke of; 253
OSWALDKIRKE; 263
OSWALSTER; 218
OSWELSTRE; 218
OSYN, John; 292
OTERINGBIRI, Rauf de; 313
OTHERLOWNY; 237
OTHO, Holy Roman Emperor; 274
OTHO IV, Holy Roman Emperor; 274
OTTEBY; 43
—, of Lincs; 44
—, Sire Randolf de; 43
OTTO IV; 274
OTTYR, Robade; 295
OTWAY, Richard; 368
OULTON; 144-5
OUNDLE; 55
—, Bucks; 57
OUTHERLONY; 237
OVER, Hugh de, Ld of Ketenes; 118
OVERTON, of Westmld; 393
OWERBY, John, of Kent; 105
OWGAN, Monsire William; 41
OWLIAMS; 75
OWLTIM; 143
OWNDEL; 55
OWONDELL; 55
OXBURGH; 45
OXENBRIDGE; 123, 237
—, Sir Goddard, Kt; 237
OXENBRIGGE; 237
OXFORD, City of; 212
—, Sr John de; 72
—, Mayoralty; 205
OXFORD UNIVERSITY; 212
OXHAMBRIGE; 237
OXHONBRIGE; 237
OXINBRUGE, Sir Godard; 237

OXONBRIGGE; 237
OXYNBRYGE, Sir Godard, Kt; 237
OYRII, Geoffrey de; 86
P..lie..; 205
PABEHAM, Jan de; 327
PABENHAM; 330
PACHE, John, of Lawford; 118
PADINGTON, Emond, of Essex; 49
PAGANELL, Fulco; 271
—, Gervase; 255
PAGANI, Isabella; 303
—, Robert, Ld of Lammer, 1st Baron Fitz-Payne; 303
PAGE, Robert; 380
PAGEMAN, Richard; 15
PAIEN, Robert le fiz; 303
PAIN, Sire Roberd le fiz; 303
—, Sire Robert le fitz; 303
—, Robert le fiz; 303
PAINE, Roberd fitz; 303
PAINEL, Hugo; 50
—, S Thomas; 51
PAINELL, Thomas; 51
—, William; 50
PAITSULL; 170
PAKEMAN; 49
—, Simon, of Warws & Lincs; 56
PAKINGHAM, Robert, Esq; 37
PAKMAN; 49
PALE, Sr John de; 383
PALGRAVE; 128, 189-90
PALIS PERCIE, Sir Gylis; 193
PALLGRAVE; 189
PALLY; 304
PALMAR, Thomas; 56
PALMER; 47, 56
—, of Steyning, Suss; 56
—, T; 46
—, Thomas; 47
—, Thomas, of Holt; 47
—, Tomas; 296
PALMERE; 47
PANCEFOT, Grymbald; 277
—, Richard; 273
PANEBRIGGE, Henri de; 98
PANEBRUGE, Henry de; 88
PANELE; 267
PANELL; 267
PANSEVOT; 277
PANSFOUT, Thos; 277
PANTON; 21, 40
—, Hugh de; 35
—, James de; 82
PANTOUF, Roger de; 118
PANTULF, William; 118
PAPENHAM, Mond.Laurence de, of Northants, Hunts & Essex; 327
PAR, Sir Thomas Kt; 52
—, Wil; 15

—, William de, Kt; 52
PARIS, Simon de; 386
PARKER; 52, 249
—, Abbot of Gloucester; 249
—, Henry, Ld Morley; 232
—, Sir James; 52
—, Sir James, Knyght; 52
—, John; 52
—, Ld Will'm; 249
—, Ld William, Abbot of Gloucester; 249
—, Wm, Abbot of Gloucester; 249
PARR, Sir Thomas; 57
PARRE, William, KG; 52
PARRY; 75
PARTENEY, le Sire; 104
PARTHENAY; 328
PARTRIDGE; 331
PARYS; 345
—, Hugh de; 118
PASCY, Mons J de; 189
PASELEY; 182
PASHELEY; 182
—, Sr John; 168
PASHLEY, John; 182
—, Sir John; 182
PASSELE; 177
—, Mons Robert de; 132
PASSELEWE, John; 185
PASSELEY, S'Robert de, of Suss; 167
PASSHELEY, John, Esq; 175
PASSLE, S' Rob de, Kent; 177
PATEL, Ralph; 24
PATELL, Rauf; 24
PATESHILL, Monsire de; 170
PATESHULL; 170
—, Mons' John; 170
PATEWARDYN, S Roger de; 259
PATISHILL', Monsr J de; 170
PATOLE; 9
PATRICK, Ric', of Galles; 305
PAULES, Mons G de; 304
PAULY; 304
—, Monsire Walter de; 304
PAUNCEFOOT; 279
PAUNCEFORT, Grimbaud; 314
PAUNCEFOT, Eymer; 275
—, Grimbaud; 314
—, Grumbald; 314
—, Thomas; 275
—, William; 18
—, Wm; 18
PAUNCEFOTE; 277
—, Sir Grimbald; 279
—, Jn, of Hasfield, Gloucs; 165
PAUNCEVOT, Grimbaud; 277, 314
PAUNSEVOTE; 278
PAUNSFOT, Grimbaud; 277
PAUNSFOTE, Sir Humfrey, of Gloucs; 277
PAUNSFOTT; 277

PAUNSOTTE; 277
PAUNTON, S Hugh de; 37
—, Sire Hugh de; 37
PAVEILLI, Reinald de; 86
PAVELE, Sire Walter le; 330
PAVELEY; 344
—, Mons G de; 304
PAVELI, S' Wat'; 304
PAVELY; 304
—, Monsire Walter de; 304
PAVILLY, Robert; 313
—, Robert de; 118
—, Mons Wauter de; 304
PAVYS, Edward Ld; 136
PAWLYE; 304
PAWNTON; 59
PAY; 83
PAYLE, Sir Raf; 138
—, Sir Robt, of Kent; 138
PAYLEN; 138
PAYLLE, Syr Raff; 129
PAYLOW; 138
PAYN, Monsire le filtes; 303
—, Sr le fitz; 303
—, Mons Robert; 328
—, Sire Robert le; 304
—, Sir Thomas; 160
PAYNE, le Fiz; 303
—, Rauf; 322
—, Mons' Walter; 177
—, Wautier; 177
PAYNEL; 50-1, 53, 322
—, Jan; 50
—, John; 50
—, John, Lord of Otley; 50
—, John, Ld of Otteleye, (?1st Baron); 50
—, Thom; 51
—, Sire Thomas; 51
—, Thomas; 51
—, Thomas, Kt; 49, 201
—, Thos; 50
—, Sire Will; 50
—, Willam; 50
—, Sire Willame; 50-1
—, Willem; 50
—, Willeme; 50
—, Sr William; 50
—, William; 50, 118
—, William de; 50
—, William, Ld of Fracyngton; 50
—, William, Ld of Fracynton; 50
PAYNELL; 37, 50-1, 322
—, Hugh; 51
—, Monsire Ralph, de Kaythorp; 322
—, Sr Rauf; 322
—, Sir Rauff; 322
—, Mons Rf; 322
—, Thomas; 51
—, Mons William; 50

—, Sr William; 69
—, William; 50
PAYNELLE, Robertus; 50
PAYON; 160
PAYTESHUL; 170
PAYTEVYN, Thomas, Kt; 118
PEARLE; 10
PECCHE; 182
—, Mons John; 182
—, Sir John; 182, 184
—, Sir John, of Kent; 157
—, Sr Thm; 4
—, William; 184
—, Sir Wm; 182
PECEHY, Sir John; 182
PECHAM, Johannes de; 7
—, Jon de; 7
—, Lora; 175
PECHCHE, Sir William; 182
—, S' Willm, of Kent; 184
PECHE; 172, 183-4
—, Sr de; 172
—, John; 184
—, Sir John; 182
—, Sir John, Kt; 182
—, Mons Thos; 4
—, Sir William; 184
PECKERINGE, Sr; 170
PEDERTON; 231, 388
—, Cornw; 388
PEDEWARDEN, Walt; 259
PEDEWARDIN, Roger de, of Heref; 255
—, Walter de; 255
—, Walter de, of Northants, Knt; 267
PEDEWARDYN, Walterus; 258
—, Water de; 259
PEDWARDIN, Monsire de; 259
—, Sir Walter de; 259
PEDWARDINE; 259
PEDWARDYN; 259, 264, 267, 269
—, Sr de; 259
—, le fitz; 267
—, John de, of Herefs; 271
—, Robert; 267
—, Robert, Ld of; 255
—, Roger; 255
—, Roger, of Lincs, Esq; 255
—, Mons' Thomas; 259
—, Walter; 258-9
—, Walter de; 259
—, Mons Waut'; 259
—, Willm de; 259
PEDWORDIN; 259
PEEBLES, Janet; 370
PEECHE, John; 182
PEEL; 389
PEELL; 389
PEITO, William de, senior; 90
PEKERING; 170

PEKERYNG, of Therkele, Cumb; 171
PELHAM; 318
PELLEGRIN, Hugh; 81
—, Raymond; 81
PELMORBA, John; 95
PELSTONE, of Wales; 285
PEMBRIDGE; 328
—, Henry de; 98
—, Sir Richard; 70
PEMBRIGGE, Fouke de; 86
PEMBROKE, le Conte de; 144
PEMBRUGE; 98, 140, 328, 330
—, Henri de; 328
—, Henry de; 86
PEMBRUGGE, Fulk de, Ld of Tonge; 86
PEMBRYGE, Fulco de, Kt; 86
PEMPROU; 81
PENBREGGE; 88
PENBRIG; 80
PENBRIGE; 88, 328
PENBRIGGE, Mons Fouke de; 88
—, Richard de, Kt; 327
PENBROKE, Le count de; 100
PENBRUGE; 333
—, S' Folco, of Staffs; 88
—, Sire Henri de; 328
PENBRUGGE; 328
—, Fulk de; 86
—, Henr' de; 328
—, Henri de; 328
—, Henry de; 327
—, Henry de, Kt; 327
—, Mons Richard; 328
—, Monsire Richard; 328
—, Sir Richard; 98
—, Staffs; 98
PENBRUGH, Sir Fulke de; 88
PENBRYGE; 328
—, Sir Rychard, of Herefs; 70
PENEBREGGE; 98
PENEBRIGE, Henr' de; 88
PENEBRUGE, Foulk de; 88
—, Henri de; 98
—, Henry; 74
—, Henry de; 98
PENEBRUGGE; 88
—, Fouke de; 98
—, Henri de; 98
—, S Henry de; 328
—, of Mouneshull Gamage; 98
PENECESTRE, Margaret de; 34
—, Maud; 34
PENEDELE, Henry de; 138
PENEDOKE, Henry de; 138
PENERE; 53
PENGELLI; 150
PENGELLY; 153
PENLE, Elizabeth de, ?of Herts; 118
PENNE, John de la; 52

PENNEBREGGE; 98
PENNEBRIGGE, Sr Henry de; 328
PENNEBROK, le counte de; 160
PENNEBRUGGE, Robert de; 86
PENPANE; 292
PENPANS, of Cornwall; 292
—, Robert, of Cornw; 296
PENPONS; 296
—, of Cornwall; 292
PENRICH, John de, Kt, Keeper of Harbottle Castle; 360
PENSONS; 296
PENZERT; 350
PENZRET; 350
—, Sire Johan de; 350
PERCHEHAY, Henry, of Devon; 211
PERCI; 133
—, Henri de; 133
—, Henry de; 118
PERCIE, E of Northumberland; 129
PERCY; 118-19, 124, 133-4, 154-6, 209, 222, 243
—, Baron; 133
—, de; 155
—, Ld; 133
—, le sire de; 133
—, le Sr de; 133
—, Monsire de; 133
—, Algernon, E of Northd; 134
—, Algernon, Bp of Norwich; 234
—, Comes Northumbria; 134
—, fitz Count; 209
—, le fitz; 162
—, Mons Gilberd de; 243
—, Sir Harry; 208
—, Hen; 134
—, Hen Algernon, 6th E of Northd; 134
—, Hen Algernon, 6th E of Northd (1489-1527); 119
—, Hen de, E of Northd; 119
—, Hen, E of Northd; 134
—, Henr' le; 134
—, Sire Henri de; 134
—, Henry; 119, 208, 225-6
—, Henry de; 119, 134, 208
—, Henry, Ld; 134
—, Henry, Ld, 1299-1315; 134
—, Mons Henry; 209
—, Sir Henry; 209
—, Sir Henry de; 134
—, Sire Henry de; 134
—, Sr Henry de; 134
—, Henry Algernon, E of Northd; 134
—, Henry Algernon, 6th E of Northd; 119
—, Henry Algernon, 6th E of Northd, KG(?); 119
—, Henry Algernon, 6th E of Northd, KG; 119
—, Henry de, Chevr; 225
—, Sir Henry de, le Fiz; 209

—, Henry de, 2nd Baron (1315-52); 119
—, Henry, 2nd Ld, of Alnwick, d1351; 119
—, Henry de, ?2nd E of Northd, Ld of Honour of Cockermouth; 119
—, Henry de, E of Northd; 119
—, Henry, E of Northd; 119, 134
—, Henry, Ld of, 3rd Baron; 119
—, Henry de, (3rd) E of Northd, Warden of East Marches towards Scotld; 119
—, Henry de, 1st E of Northd; 119
—, Henry de, 1st E of Northd & Ld of Cockermouth, Cumb; 119
—, Henry, 1st E of Northd; 119
—, Henry, 6th E of Northd; 119
—, Henry, Ld of Topcliff; 120
—, Henry de, of Wilts; 217
—, Sr Herry; 134
—, Sire Nichol; 94
—, E of Northd; 124, 134
—, R.; 219
—, Ralph; 156
—, S' Rauf de; 156
—, Mons' Rauff; 156
—, Mons Roger; 156
—, Stewyn; 35
—, T de; 155
—, Sir Thomas; 134
—, Sir Thomas de; 120
—, Thomas; 120, 233-4
—, Thomas de; 120, 209
—, Thomas, Kt; 120
—, Thomas, Lord Egremont; 120
—, Thomas de, of Essex, Kt; 120
—, Thomas, Bp of Norwich; 120, 233
—, Mons'Thos de; 134
—, Thos, Ld Egremont; 188
—, Thos, Bp of Norwich; 233
—, Thos, E of Worcester; 134
—, W; 154
—, Monsire William de; 243
—, Sir William; 134
—, William de; 129, 134
—, William of; 178
PERCYE, de; 134
—, Monsire de; 134
PEREPOUNT, Monsr de; 232
PERES; 278
—, Renaud le fiz; 278
PERICYCHE; 331
PERKER; 52
PERLL; 10
PERNESTEDE, Richard de; 120
PEROT; 200-1
PEROTE; 200-1
PERPENT, Ed'us; 152
PERPOINTZ; 231
PERPONCET, Sr Robert de; 218
PERPONT; 229
—, Edmund; 231

PERPOUND, S' Emond; 232
—, Esmond; 231
PERPOUNT; 218, 229, 231
—, le Seigneur de; 152
—, Henr' de; 219
—, Mons' Henry; 232
—, S'John, of Norf; 100
—, Mons Thomas; 232
PERPOUNTS; 231
PERPOUNTZ; 231
PERPOYNT; 145, 232
—, Syr Nycoll, of Derbys; 231
PERPUND, H; 219
PERSE; 10
PERSEHAY, Henry; 211
PERSEY; 120
PERSY, Henry de; 134
—, E of Northumberland; 134
PERT; 311
—, Dr Thomas; 311
PERTH; 252
PERTRICHE; 331
PERTRYCHE; 331
PERTRYGE; 331
PESCHCHE; 4
PESHALE, Ralph de, of Essex; 93
PESHALLE, [Sir] Hew; 60
PETER, John; 275
—, Nychol; 168
PETERSHEYN; 180
PETEWARDEM; 259
PETEWARDYN; 259
PETHERTON, Robert de; 22
PETIT; 125, 227
—, of Cornw; 156
PETO; 90
PETOWE; 90
PETTENIM; 257
PETYT; 125
PEUER, Sir Philip; 53
PEUEREL; 70, 309
PEUERELL; 340
PEULE, s' Rich'; 137
PEUVERELL, Count of Nottingham; 369
PEVENYS, Nicholas; 15
PEVER; 55
PEVERE; 20, 55
PEVEREL; 70, 145, 213, 309
—, Count of Nottingham; 72, 370
PEVERELL; 70, 140, 309, 340, 345
—, Conte; 72
—, Hu; 340
—, Thomas, Bp of Llandaff, 1398-1407; 369
PEVOR; 20
PEWARDYA; 259
PEWPE; 38
PEYFRER, S Fuke; 341
PEYNE, Mons Robt le fitz; 303
PEYTENEY; 165

PEYTEVYN, Bartholomew le, Kt; 282
—, Thomas, Kt; 208
PEYTO; 90
—, William; 90
—, William de; 90
—, Sir Wylyam; 90
PHELIP; 173
PHELIPOT, Sir John; 343
PHELIPS, Francis, of London; 120
PHILIP, Sir David; 236
PHILIPOTT, Sir Joh; 343
PHILIPPE; 152
PHILLIP, Sir Matthew; 173
PHILLIPP, Sir Davy; 236
PHILLIPPS; 231
—, Matthew; 172
PHILPOT; 343
—, of Hants; 343
—, J; 343
PHILPOTT, Sir John; 343
PHYLPOT, Sir John, of Middx; 343
PHYLPOTT; 343
PIARPOUNT, Syr Wyllm; 152
PICKERING; 141, 170
—, Sir Edward; 170
—, James; 141
—, Sir James; 170
—, Sir Jamys, of Yorks; 170
—, John; 120
—, Robert; 141
—, Theophilus, Rector of Sedgefield; 141
PICKEWORTH; 391
PICKINGHAM; 198
PICKWORTH; 391
—, Mons de; 391
—, Sir Hugh, of Holme, Selby, Yorks; 391
—, Mons' Robert; 3
PICOT; 43, 377
—, Jan; 378
—, Monsire John, de Dodington; 43
—, Pers; 378
PIEL, John; 390
—, John, citizen & merchant of London; 389
PIERPOINT; 120, 152-3, 231
—, Monsire; 218
—, Monsire de; 231
—, Anna de; 231
—, Edmund, Kt; 231
—, Henry de; 79
—, Henry, Kt; 231
—, Robert de, Kt; 231
—, Sir Robert; 152
—, Robt de, Kt; 231
PIERPOND, Mons Edmond; 232
PIERPONT; 231
—, Edmond; 232
—, Henry; 219
—, Sir Henry; 230
PIERPOUNT; 231

—, Monsire de; 231
PIERRE...nt, John de; 58
PIERREPOINT-Roucy, John III Count of; 134
PIERS, Mons Reynald fitz; 278
—, William, of Odiham, Hants; 391
PIGOD, Piers; 378
PIGOT, Sr Bawdewyne; 43
—, of Doditon; 43
—, Mons John, de Dodington; 43
—, Piers; 378
PIGOTE; 43
PIGOTT; 391
—, Perys; 378
PIKERING; 170
—, Mons' Robert; 141
PIKERINGE; 170
PIKOTT, Baldwin; 42
PIKWORTH, Mons John; 391
—, Mons Philip; 391
—, Thomas; 391
PIMPE; 33, 67
PINCKNEY; 358
PIPARD; 27, 31-2
—, M; 31
—, Sir John; 31
—, Ralph; 31
—, Mons' Rauf; 31
—, Rauf; 31
—, Sire Rauf; 31
—, of West Chinnock; 310
—, William; 310
PIPART; 31
—, Radulfus; 30
—, Ralph; 31
—, Ralph, of Derbys; 31
—, Rauff; 67
—, Sr Rauff; 31
PIPPARD; 31
—, Joan; 58
PIREPOUND, Sire Robert de; 231
PIRLY; 143
PIRPONT, Sr Robert; 218
PIRPOUNT, Robert de, Kt; 232
PIRPUND, Henry; 219
PISANS, the; 3
PLACE; 186
—, Mons John; 186
—, Monsire Richard; 186
PLACEY; 193
PLAICE, Sr; 186
—, Mons Richard de; 186
PLAIS; 185-6
PLAIZ, Hugh de; 185-6
PLANCHE, de la; 145
—, John de; 145
—, Matilda de; 145
PLANCO, Jacobus de; 145
PLANK, Sr Jake de la; 170
PLANKE, William la; 170

PLANQUE, Maillin de le; 209
PLANTAGENET; 286-7, 298
—, Arthur; 314
—, Edmond; 197, 300
—, Edmund; 298
—, Edmund, Baron of Wodstoke, 4th E of Kent; 306
—, Edmund, of Woodstock, E of Kent; 306
—, Edward, E of Chester; 298
—, Edward, E of Chester & D of Aquitaine; 298
—, Edward, D of Aquitaine & E of Chester; 298
—, Henry; 298, 303
—, Isabel; 301
—, John; 308
—, John, 3rd E of Kent; 306
—, (E of Kent); 307
—, Margaret, Ctess of Kent; 306
—, Richard, E of Cornwall, Count of Poitou; 239
—, Thomas, [of Brotherton; 298
—, Thomas, E of Lancaster; 300
PLATYN, John; 366
PLATZ; 186
PLAUNCE, Jake de la; 145
PLAUNCHE; 170
—, Sire ... de la; 145
—, Sire Jak de la; 145
—, S Jakes de la; 145
—, Sire Jakes, de la; 145
—, Sir Johes de la; 170
PLAUNK, Mons J del; 145
PLAUNKE; 170
PLAUNKYS; 170
PLAYCE, Monsr Richard; 186
PLAYDELL; 392
—, Thomas; 392
PLAYS; 186, 221
—, Sir ...; 188
—, Sire Gyles; 193
—, Sir J; 186
—, Joh; 186
—, John; 185-6
—, Mons John; 186
—, Sire Richard de; 143
PLAYSE; 186
PLAYSTOWE; 216
PLAZETIS, Johan de, E of Warwick; 6
PLECITE, de; 9
PLECY; 6
—, Hue de; 6
—, John; 6
—, Nicholas de; 8
PLEICI, Sire Edmond de; 9
PLEISE, M de; 6
PLEMING, John; 370
PLESCIS, Hue de; 6
PLESCY; 7

PLESE, Monsire Richard; 186
PLESENCE, Count of; 25
PLESEY; 8
PLESIS, Sr de; 6
PLESSETIS, Hugh de; 6
—, John; 6
—, John de, 8th E of Warwick; 6
PLESSIS; 7
—, Monsire de; 7
—, Hue de; 7
—, Sire Hugue de; 7
—, Sir John de; 7
PLESSY; 7
—, Mons Hug de; 7
—, John of; 120
—, Richard of; 120
PLESSYS, Mons John; 7
PLESY; 7
—, Monsire John de; 7
—, Monsire Nichol de; 8
PLESYE; 7
PLEYS, Sir Richard; 188
—; Sir Rychard; 186
PLOKENET, Alain; 353
—, Alan; 359
—, Aleyn de; 353-4
—, Sire Aleyn; 353
—, Sr Aleyn; 359
PLOKENETT; 353
—, Adam; 355
—, Alain; 353
—, Sir Aleyn; 353
PLOKNETT; 359
PLONKENET, Sir Alan; 353
PLONKET; 359
PLONKETT, Irld; 358
PLUCKENET, Alan; 371
—, Alanus; 353
PLUCKNET; 359
PLUGENCY, William de, of Lambourne,
  Berks; 120
PLUGENET, Alan; 353
PLUKENET; 359
—, le Sr de; 353
—, Alayn; 353
—, Aleyn; 353
—, Aleyn de; 359
PLUKNENET; 359
PLUKNETT; 353
—, Monsire; 353
—, Mons Aleyn; 353
—, Sr Aleyn; 359
PLUMBNET, Sir Aleyn; 353
PLUNCKNETT, Baron of Donsary, Irld; 358
PLUNEKNETT, of Haselbury; 359
PLUNKET; 369
—, of Dunsany, Irld; 369
—, Sir ..., of Irld; 369
—, Ld of Kylleyne; 369

PLUNKETT, of Irld; 369
—, Baron of Lowth; 369
POELE, Sir John; 25
POICTOU, Roger de; 234
POINS, Sir Harry; 232
POINTZ, of Curry Mallett; 89
—, Hugh; 75, 89
—, Hugh, Ld; 89
—, Sir Robert; 98
POINYNGES, le Sr de; 329
—, Robert, Ld of; 303, 327
POINZ, Hue; 98
POITCU; 120, 165
POKKEBORN, Roberd de; 95
POLDEGREVE, Symond; 221
POLE; 25, 95, 219, 243
—, de la; 25, 243
—, Le Sr de la; 136
—, Edmund de la, 3rd D of Suff, KG; 175
—, Eweyn; 209
—, Griffith ap Owen de la, Ld of Powis; 136
—, Sr Johan de la; 37
—, Sir John de la; 25
—, John de la, D of Suff; 175
—, John de la, D of Suff, KG; 175
—, de la, Ld of Keveoloc; 120
—, L'y Sire de la; 136
—, Lewiz de la; 218
—, Lewys de; 219
—, Sire Lowys de la; 219
—, Sr Richard de la; 25
—, Seignior de la; 136
—, Mons' William; 136
—, Mons William de; 25
—, Sir William; 151
—, Sir William de la, le Joesne; 26
POLEFORD, Hugo de; 267
POLERENE, le Roy de; 205
POLEY, Monseur de; 138
POLLARE, John, of Devon; 8
POLLAYN; 246
POLLE; 194
POLMORVA, J; 64
POLTIMORE, Richard de; 138
POMERAN, le rey de; 205
POMBRAY, Edward, of Devon; 243
POMER', S' Henr'; 243
POMERAI, Edward, of Devon; 243
POMERAY; 243
—, Johan de la, of Berry Pomeray; 241
—, John; 243
—, Mons John; 243
—, Mons Th de; 243
POMERCY, Monsire Henry de la; 243
—, Monsire Henry de la, le filtz; 247
POMERE; 243
POMERELL; 338
POMEREY, Sir Thomas; 243
POMEREYE, Mons Henry de la; 243

POMEROY; 154, 243-4
—, John; 243
—, Sir Thomas; 245
—, Thomas de; 243
—, William, Esq of Collaton, Devon; 241
POMERY; 241, 243, 245
—, Sir Edward; 243
—, fitz; 247
—, le fitz; 247
POMFRET; 337
POMMERY; 243
POMYS; 52
PONCEFOT, Richard; 273
PONDESHAM, S de; 179
PONELEY; 330
PONERTON; 246
PONGYNG, S'r de, of Suss; 329
PONIG, Sr Th; 346
PONIGES, S' John de; 329
PONINGES; 329
—, Mons Michael; 395
—, Sire Michel de; 329
—, Sr Michel; 329
PONINGGES, Mons Thomas de; 329
PONTEFRACT; 364
PONTEFRACTO, Adam de; 256
PONTIF, le conte de; 72
PONTIS, Count of; 72
PONYNG, Sir Edward; 329
—, the Lorde; 329
PONYNGE; 329
—, le Sr de; 329
—, Sire Michel de; 329
—, le Sr de, of Suss; 329
—, Syr Edward; 329
PONYNGES; 329, 395
—, Ld; 328-9
—, le Sr; 329
—, Monsr de; 329
—, Sr de; 329
—, Sir Edward; 329
—, Sir Michael; 329
—, Sire Michael de; 329
—, Sir Michel; 329
—, Sr Michol de; 329
—, Sir Robert; 70
—, Robert, Ld de, of Suss, 5th Baron; 327
—, Rogerus; 329
—, Mons' Thomas; 329
PONYNGGES, Ld; 329
—, Thomas de; 327
PONYNGH; 329
PONYNGIS; 329
PONYNGS; 328-9
—, L[ord]; 329
—, Mons Lucas de; 328
—, Michael de; 327
—, Mons Nich de; 395
—, Mons Thoms; 329

POOLE; 25, 151
—, Monsire de la; 136
—, Sir Thomas of; 151
—, Wm; 151
POOLL', Sir Thomas; 152
POOLLE; 152
POPHAM, Sir John de; 362
—, Sir William de; 322
PORCHESTER; 84, 100
PORINTONE, Gilbert de; 155
POROCE, le rey de; 125
PORTEES, Richard de; 101, 105
PORTER; 318, 345
—, Irld; 318
—, Sir William; 318
—, William; 318
—, Willimus; 318
—, Sir Wm; 318
—, Wm; 318
—, Sir Wylyam; 318
PORTES, Richard de, Ld of Bromesbergh; 101
PORTYNGTON; 41
POSSI, Colin de; 229
POTHAM, Johan de; 7
POTTER, Robert, of Boreham; 266
POTTERE, Thomas, of Bridgwater; 15
POULE; 219
POULEINE; 204
—, Rex; 204
POULETT, John; 265, 275
POULLE, Thomas; 151
POUMERAI, Henry de la; 241
POURE, Nicholas; 353
POUTONE, S William de; 151
—, S. William de; 228
POUWES, le Sr de; 136
POVELEY; 344
POWELL; 166
—, Benedict; 225
—, John; 166
POWER, Michael; 1
—, William le, Kt; 120
POWERTON; 202
POWES; 132, 136
—, Ld; 136, 178
—, The Lorde; 136
POWEYS, Ld; 326
POWIS; 136
POWLET, Sir John, of Hants; 265
POWLEY; 179
POWNINGS, Eliz; 327
POWNYNGGES, Monsire de; 329
POWYS; 72, 136, 244
—, Ld; 136
—, le Sr de; 136
—, Morys de fitz Rogier de; 272
—, le S' de, of Salop; 136
POYNENGES, le S'r de; 329
POYNES; 97-8

—, John; 97
POYNINGES; 89
POYNINGS; 70, 84, 327-30
—, Ld; 329
—, Sir Edward; 329
—, Sir Edward, KG; 329
—, Isabella de; 70
—, John, Ld St John; 329
—, the Lorde; 329
—, Lucas; 329
—, Michael; 395
—, Robert, Ld; 329
POYNIS; 89
POYNS, Hugh; 89
—, Sr Hugh; 89
—, Sire Nicholas de; 89
POYNTZ; 98
—, de; 89
—, Hugh; 76
POYNYNGES, Sir Edwd; 329
—, Mons' John; 329
—, Mons' Thomas; 329
POYNZ, Sr Nichol; 98
PRALL; 226, 254
PRALLE; 226, 254
PRATT; 254
PRENDERGAST, Robarde, of Northd; 324
PRENDERGEST, Sir Henry, Kt; 67
PRESTON; 24-5, 31
—, Eda de; 31
—, Laurence de; 24
—, Piers de; 381
—, of Preston Patrick; 67
—, Richard de; 31
—, Mons Thomas; 24
—, Sr William de; 341
—, William; 120
—, William de; 341
—, Wm, of Lancs; 31
PRESTONE, Loren de; 24
—, Willame de; 383
PRESTWOOD, George, of Whittcombe,
  Devon; 228
PREUZ; 280
—, Sire Willame le; 280
PREYERS, Thomas, of Dersynton, ?Gloucs;
  360
PRIAM, K of Troy; 253
PRILLY, Hugh; 120
PRISSONY, the Lorde; 105
PROFEIT, Mariote, of Gothimes; 385
PROFETT, 'D'; 183
PROUS, Alice le; 279
PROUSZ, John; 392
PRUDE, Thos; 295
PRYORE, Emonde; 395
PRYOURE, Charles; 343
PUDSEY; 390
PUGEYS, S Ernaud William de; 160

PUL; 151
PULHAM; 107
PULL', Sir John de; 152
PULL, Sir John de; 120, 151
—, S John de, of Ches; 128
PULLE, Sir John de; 151
PULTONOR, Richard; 139
PULTIMOR, Richard; 139
PUNDELARD, Robert; 143
PUNE, Sir J de la; 38
PUNINGE, Lucas de; 70
PUPELPENNE, Geoffrey de, of Som; 215
PURCEL; 330
PURCELL; 47
PURPUNDE, Mons Esmun; 231
PURROK, Johannes; 9
PURSELL; 47
PUSEY, Henry; 72
—, William; 71
PUYNES; 98
—, Monsire de; 89
PYCCEN, John; 120
PYCKERING; 170
PYCOT, Sire Baudewyne; 43
—, de Dodyton; 43
—, Sr Johan, de Dodington; 43
—, Sire Peres; 378
PYCOTT; 43, 378
—, Baldwin; 175
PYCWORTH; 391
PYCWORTHE; 391
PYEL; 389
—, John, citizen & merchant of London; 389
PYGOT, Mons John, of Doditon; 43
—, Walter; 90
PYGOTT, Mons Randolf; 391
PYHELL; 389
PYKENHAM; 129, 242, 248
PYKERING, Mons' James le; 141
—, Sir James; 120
—, Mons' Thomas; 170
PYKERINGE, de Illertone; 170
—, Sire Thomas de; 239
PYKERYNE, Mons James de; 170
PYKERYNG; 141, 170
—, Sir Edward; 170
—, Sir R; 167
—, Monsr Thomas de; 170, 331
PYKERYNGE, Sir Edward; 170
—, James; 170
PYKET, Sir Piers; 378
PYKEWORTH, Sr de; 391
PYKKYNHAM; 129
PYKNAM, of Essex; 198
PYKRYNG, S'Jacob de, of Lancs; 171
PYKUAM; 198
PYKWORTH, Robert; 3
PYLE, Richard; 294
PYLKYNGTON, Sir John, Kt; 120

PYMPE, Sir John, of Kent; 67
—, of Nettlestead; 33
PYNKENY, Johan de; 95
PYPARD; 31
—, Mons de; 310
—, Raf; 31
—, Ralph; 31
PYPART, Sir Raffe; 67
PYPPARD; 31
—, Ratherfeld; 31
PYPPARDE; 31
PYRELY; 160
PYRLEY, John; 143
PYRLY; 143
PYRPOYNT; 153
QIUTON; 79
QUAPLAD, Monseur; 328
QUAPLADE, Nicholas; 328
QUAPLODE, John; 327
QUAPPELAD; 70
—, Ed'us de; 328
QUAPPELAND, Emund de; 328
QUAPPOLOD, Tohmas; 328
QUAREL, Hamo; 350
QUARLTON; 193
—, le sieur de; 195
QUEENS COLL CAMB; 97
QUEMYN; 189
QUERLETON, le Sr de; 193
QUERZETON, Mons Robt, Sr de; 185
QUITFURD; 387
QUIXLEY, Adam de; 294
—, John de; 294
QUYXLEY; 371
R..., le counte de; 277
RACELLE, Raf; 24
RADCLEIFFE; 351
RADCLIF; 365
—, Sir John; 351
—, Ralph de; 350
RADCLIFF; 350
—, Sir Richard; 394
—, of the Tour; 351
RADCLIFFE; 350-1
—, Sir ...; 351
—, Lord Fitzwater, KG; 351
—, Sir George; 350
—, James; 351
—, Sir John; 351
—, Sir Richard; 369
—, Robert, KG; 351
—, Robert, Ld Fitzwalter; 369
—, Robert, E of Sussex; 351
RADCLIVE, Robert de; 395
RADCLYF; 351, 369
RADCLYFE; 369-70
RADCLYFF; 369
RADCLYFFE; 351
—, Sir John, Lancs; 351

RADICH, John, of Lancs; 162
RAE, Alexr; 201
RAFE, Mons J de; 349
RAGON; 294
RAGOUN; 294
RAHERE; 374
RALE, Devon; 357
—, Henry de; 348
—, Sr Johan de; 381
—, Sr Jon de; 349
—, Warine de, of King's Walden, Herts; 356
RALEE; 352
—, John de; 349
—, Mons John; 348-9
—, Sire Symon de; 352
RALEGH; 355
—, John de, of Devon, Chevr; 365
RALEIGH, Henry; 349
—, Henry de; 348-9
—, Sir John; 381
—, Sir Simon; 357
RALEY; 357
—, Monsire de; 349
—, Henry de; 381
—, of Nettlecombe; 357
RALLE, Henri de; 348
RALPH; 381
RANDE; 180
RANDES, Robert; 190
RANDOLPH, Isabella; 250
RANTOUNE, of Bylle; 241, 244, 249
RASE; 348, 383
RASEN, Anna; 231
—, Anna de; 286
RASSTEL, Rauf; 24
RATCLEVE; 351
RATCLIFF; 31
—, John de, Kt; 286
RATCLIFFE; 351
—, Sir Alexander; 351
—, Caryll; 31
—, Ld Fitzwalter; 351
—, Ld Fytzwater; 352
—, Sir John; 350
—, Sir Robert, Ld Fitz Walter; 352
RATCLYF; 352
RATCLYFF; 352
—, Lord Fitzwarter; 351
RATCLYFFE; 352
RATELL, Rauf; 24
RATFORDE, Sir H; 158
RATLEFFE, Mayster; 352
RATRI, Ceulx de; 381
RAWSON, Richard; 35
RAYGATE, Mons John, de Houke; 351
—, William; 356
RAYGUT, Monsr de; 351
RAYLE, Mons John; 381
RAYLIGHE; 357

RAYMOND, Master; 393
RAYMONT, Garda; 282
RAYNES; 297
RAYOUS, Monsr de; 38
READ, of S Bradon [in Puckington]; 393
REASON; 227
REDDISH, Ralph; 281
REDE, Robert, Kt; 360
REDEMER; 386
REDESDALE, Ld; 195
—, le S' de; 193
REDHAM, William de, of Norf; 120
REDMER; 386
REDMORE; 386
REDVERIS, Margaret de; 263
REDVERS; 120, 134
—, de; 120
—, Baldwin de; 120
—, Baldwin, E of Devon; 134
REFFUGE, of France; 48
REGINALDUS, Scs; 145
REIGATE, Sir Robert; 357
REINAULD, le fitz Piers; 278
REISTON, Mons Raufe de; 152, 171
REKELL, William; 49
—, Wyllm, of Kent; 49
REKETT, William, of Kent; 49
RELTON, Henry de; 385
RENAUD, Sire Johan le fiz; 278
RENE, Count Palatine de; 169
RENTE, Alice; 374
RENTON, David; 120
—, David, of Bille; 249
—, John; 250
REPELEY ...; 278
REPINGHALE, Johan de; 45
REPOND; 7
RERESBY; 380
RESKMER, Sir Rauf A, of Cornw; 68
RESKYMER, of Cornw; 68
RESOUN, Sire Johan de; 215
RESTONE; 169
RETHERY, Thomas, of Surr; 310
REUDE, Elys de; 385
REVERS; 130
REVESCROFT, Hugh de; 74
REVIERS; 134
—, Baldwin de, E of Devon; 134, 178
REVILL, William; 386
REWMORE, Sir Richard; 394
REY, Richard fiz le; 264
REYDON, Eliz; 153
REYENE, La weyle; 274
REYGATE, Sr de; 356
—, Mons Ro; 356
REYMOND; 393
REYMONDE; 393
REYNALD, Sire Reynald le fiz; 309
REYNAUD, le fiz Pers; 278

REYNE, la; 274
—, Count Palatine of de; 188
REYNES, Roger de; 343
REYNOLD, fitz Piers; 278
REYSTON, Ralph de; 171
RHEINFELDT; 139
RHODES, Prior Robt; 5
—, Robert; 5
RICHARD; 393
RICHARD I; 288
RICHARDSON, Patrick, of Drumsheugh, Burgess of Edinburgh; 10
RICHEMOND, Sr Rohaut de; 77
—, Rouald de; 77
—, Sr Thomas de; 85
RICHEMONDE, Mons' Roald de; 77
RICHEMONNDE, S Thomas de; 77
RICHEMOUND, John de; 78
RICHEMUND, Thom de; 77
RICHES; 4
RICHINGFELD, Mons de; 139
RICHMOND; 33, 77
—, Briaunt de; 77
—, Joan; 76
—, Margaret, Ctess of; 309
—, Sir Roald de; 77
—, Roald, Constable of; 77
—, Sir Roland; 77
—, Sir Thomas de; 76
—, Thos of; 67
—, William de; 77
RICHMONT, Monsire Rohaine de; 77
—, Thomas de; 77
RICHMUND, Ronant de; 77
RICHMUNDIE, Roaldus, Yorks; 33
RICKHILL; 49
RIDDEL, Sir William; 248
RIDEL, Sire Johan; 333
—, Patrick; 185
—, Sire Willame; 246
—, William; 241
RIDELL, Mons' William; 246
—, Monsire William; 242
RIDLEY; 212
RIDVERS, E of Devon; 134
RIDYDELL; 248
RIGATE, Mons John; 356
RIKHILL, Wm; 80
RILBY; 27
RINGESDUNE, Hugh de, of Lincs, Kt; 255
—, Ralph de, of Lincoln; 256
RIPAR, B de, E of Devon; 120
RIPARIIS, Alicia de, Ctess of Devon; 120
—, Margaret de; 255
RIPARIJS; 134
RIPARIO, Peter de; 15
RIPON, Monsire William de; 343
RIRPOND, Henry; 219
RISERE; 364

RISHTONE, Gilbert de, of Kent; 10
RISHWORTH, John; 374
RITHER, Mons John de; 322
RIVER, de la; 23
—, la; 23
—, Richard de la; 23
RIVERE, Sire Johan de la; 23
—, John de la, Kt; 24
RIVERES, Richard de; 23
RIVERS; 23, 120, 134
—, Richard; 23
—, Richard de; 23
RIVIERE, de la; 326
RIVVERE, Sr John de la; 23
ROANBRAS, Sir Robt, Ld Porchester; 100
ROBASSAET; 140
ROBELEY; 335
ROBERSART, Theodore, alias Canoune; 120
—, Theodore, Canon; 120
ROBERT, Hewe; 143
—, John fitz, of Clavering; 337
ROBERT II, K of Scotland; 250
ROBERT III, K of Scotland; 250
ROBERTES; 143
ROBESART; 138, 162
—, Sir Lowis, Ld Bourghshier; 162
ROBESSART, Sir Lewis, KG; 162
—, Lewis, Ld Bourchier, d1431; 120
—, Roger; 120
—, Terry, Kt; 120
ROBILARD, Thomas; 10
ROBSARD, Sir John; 140
ROBSARDE, Ld Bowrcher; 140
ROBSART; 140, 162
—, Ld; 162
—, John; 208
ROBSARTE, Sir J; 138
ROBSERD, Sir John; 140, 162
ROBSERT; 140
ROBUSSARD, Mons' John; 140
ROCEL, Raf; 24
LA ROCHE; 148
ROCHE; 232, 263, 265
ROCHEFORD, Alice de, wid of Sir Hen de
    Greville; 348
—, Waleran de, Kt; 335
ROCHEFORDE, John; 348
ROCHES; 263, 265
—, Monsire de; 265
—, Joanna de; 263
—, John de; 265
ROCHEWELL; 366
ROCHFORD; 166
—, John, Ld; 188
ROCHFORT; 188
ROCHINGES; 219
ROCHYNGE, Rauf de; 169
ROCKELEE, Richard de la; 335
RODELEY; 52

RODERHAM; 291
—, Sir Thomas; 292
RODES, John de; 120, 217
RODEVILE; 341
RODINGTON; 66
RODLEY; 63
RODVILE, John, of Lindley, Leics; 387
ROGER; 275
—, Roberd fiz; 126
—, Mons Robert le fitz; 125
—, Robert fitz; 126, 338
—, Robert le fitz; 337-8
—, Sir Robert fitz; 338
—, Sire Robert le fitz; 125
—, Robt le fiz; 126
—, Sir Robt fiz; 338
ROGERE, le fiz; 338
ROGERI, Nicholas fil, of Gloucs; 335
—, Robertus filius; 335
ROGERS, John; 254
ROIGATE, Monsire; 351
ROKELE; 335
—, Richard de la; 332
ROKELEE; 332
ROKELEY; 332
—, Richard; 332
ROKELL; 335
ROKELYS; 49
ROKESLEY; 317
ROKEWODE, William, Essex & Suff; 2
ROKLANDE; 268
ROLAND, Leschu; 241
ROLLESLEY; 253
ROMELY, Alice de; 60
ROMSERT, Sir Gery; 162
RONDOLF, M fiz; 338
ROOKES, Richard, of Bucks; 120
ROOP; 153
—, ... de; 153
ROOPE; 153
ROOS; 71
—, Beatrice de; 101
—, George, Ld; 33
—, Mons John de; 331
—, Sir John; 331
—, John de, of Pinchbeck; 330
—, Sir John, of Tyd; 359
—, Thomas, of Lutterworth; 212
ROPE; 132, 153
RORYNGE; 72
ROS; 71
—, Counte de; 277
—, Le Conte de; 277
—, Sire Johan de; 71
—, Mons John de, de Tyd; 359
ROSCOMMOUR, Cornwall; 68
ROSCOMOUR; 68
ROSEI, Baldwin de; 199
ROSELIS, John de; 120

ROSS; 275, 277
—, E of; 277
—, E of, of Auld; 277
—, le comte de; 252
—, Le Comte de; 277
—, David; 217
—, Earldom of; 277
—, Euphemia; 275, 310
—, Hugh, of Rarichies, 1st of Blanagowan (Ld of Philorth); 309
—, John; 276
—, Richard, E of; 277
—, William, 3rd E of; 276
—, Wm, 5th E of; 310
ROSSE; 71
ROTCHESFORD; 166
ROTE; 159
ROTELLWELL, William; 345
ROTELWELL, William; 345
ROTHELANE, William; 213
ROTHELEY, W; 73
ROTHERHAM; 292
—, Archbp of York; 291
—, of Beds; 292
—, Thomas, Bishop of Lincoln; 292
ROTHESAY, D of, Prince of Scotland; 252
—, David Stewart, D of; 252
ROTHEWELL, Thomas; 201, 366
ROTHEWELLE, Thomas de, of Southmorton, Esq; 366
ROTHING; 219, 224
—, S Johis de; 49
—, S Rauff de; 72
ROTHINGE, Sire Rauf de; 72
ROTHYN, de; 224
ROTHYNG, ... de; 142
ROTHYNGES; 219
ROTISSAY, The Prince of; 252
ROULAND, Leschu; 243
ROUS; 24, 161, 253, 281, 336
—, Alis de la; 350
—, Mons Geffray le; 280
—, Gile le; 280
—, Giles le; 280
—, Sire Johan le; 280
—, John; 280
—, Mons Richard le; 336
—, Monsire Richard le; 336
—, Richard le; 280
—, Sire Richard le; 336
—, Sr Richard le; 336
—, Roger le; 179
—, Sire Roger le; 280
—, Thos le, Ld of Walsall; 158
—, William, of East Chalfield, Wilts; 276
ROUSE; 280
ROUSWELL, Roger; 179
ROUTH, Amand; 196
—, Sir Amand; 196

ROUTHE, Mons Amand de; 196
ROW; 266
ROWALD; 80
ROWE, Richard; 71
ROWLAND, John; 120
ROWLEY, Thomas; 201
ROWSWELL; 143
—, of Lymington, Som & of Devon; 143
ROY, Robert le fitz; 338
ROYDON; 345
ROYE, Reignante de; 324
ROYSTON, Sir Ralph; 171
RUCKHYLL; 49
RUFFUS, David, of Forfar; 198
RUGEMOND, Sire Thomas de; 77
RUKHILL; 49
RUMMYLOWE, Stephen; 320
RUNGETON, Nigel of; 361
RUNTYNGES, Robert; 386
RUS, Gile le; 280
—, Roger le; 179
RUSSEL, Mons de; 214
—, Adam; 185
—, Ld John, KG; 214
RUSSELL; 213-14
—, Ld; 214
—, Gilbert, of Thorentone, Lincs; 154
—, Gilbert, of Thornton; 155
—, Jas; 214
—, John; 214
—, Sir John; 214
—, John, of Grafham, Hunts; 121
—, Peter de, of Southampton; 378
—, [Wm, of Chenies]; 214
RUTLAND, Thomas, E of; 35
RY, Rannlyhs de; 343
RYBBESFORD, Robert de; 332
RYCCARDE, Thos, of Yorks; 393
RYCHEMOUND, Mons Roland de; 77
RYCHFORDE, Hen; 3
RYDEL, Sire William; 246
RYDELL; 246, 333
—, Sir William; 242
—, Sr Wm; 246
RYDELLE, Sir John; 333
RYDELY; 205
RYDER, Sir Ralph; 130
—, Sir Rauff; 155
—, Sir Robert; 130
—, Sir Robt; 130
RYDLEY; 205, 212
—, of Ches; 212
RYE; 343
—, Sr de; 343
—, Sir Michael; 343
—, Mons William de; 364
—, Sr William de; 364
RYECARDE, Thomas, de Herteffeld, Yorks; 393

—, Thomas, of Herteffeld, Yorks; 393
RYETARDE; 393
RYGATE; 356
RYHULL, Michel de; 126
RYKHILL, William; 49
RYKHULL, William; 49
RYKHYLL; 49
RYLE, Rondulf du; 343
RYLLYNGHAULE, Cumb; 387
RYNGBOURNE, William, of Berks; 350
RYS, Thoms, of London; 227
RYSELEY, Sir John, [Kt 1485]; 80
RYSUM; 198
RYTFORD; 158
RYTHERISFELDE; 330
RYTHRE; 13
RYUER; 23
—, Sr Jon de la; 23
RYVER, de la; 23
—, John de la; 23
—, Mons John de la; 23
RYVERE, Mons de la; 23
—, Mons John de la; 23
—, Mons' John de la; 23
—, Sir John de la, Ld of Thormarton, Gloucs;
  23
—, Mons Rich de la; 47
—, Thomas de la; 23
RYZERE, Sire Willame de; 364
SABARNE, D of; 130
SABRAM; 350
SABRAN, D of; 130
SACEUYLE, Sir Andrew; 338
SACHEVEREL, Sir Henry; 295
SACKEALL; 337
SACKEUILLE; 349
SACKVILE; 349, 369
—, Thomas; 349
SACKVILLE; 348-9
—, Andrew; 349
—, Thomas; 349
SAGEVILE, Sire Andrew de; 349
SAINCT BRIDE, Nicholl de; 100
SAINT HOWEYN, Les Armes; 89
SAINT MARD, Lancelot; 365
SAINT MARTEN; 315
SAINT MARTIN; 315
—, Lawrence; 315
—, Wm; 315
SAINT PERE, Sr Brian de; 362
SAINT VALERY, John de; 264
SAINTLOWE, Mons Thomas de; 41
SAINTTLE, Monsire Hugh; 33
SAKALL, Monsr de; 349
SAKEUYLE, Sr Andrew; 349
SAKEVELE; 349
SAKEVILE; 349
—, Monsire de; 349
—, Sr de; 349

—, Andr de; 336
—, Andrew de; 349
—, Edward, Esq, of Lincs; 335
SAKEVILLA, Andrew de; 348
SAKEVILLE, Baron; 349
—, Andreu de; 349
—, Geffray de, Suss; 349
—, Mons Thom; 349
SAKEVYLE; 349, 369
—, Aundreu de; 337
—, Sr Tho, Suss; 349
SAKEVYLL, Sir; 349
SAKEVYLLE, Essex; 337, 349
SAKVILL, Mons Andrew; 349
SAKVILLE, Mons John; 349
SAKVYLE, Rychard; 349
—, Suff; 349
SALAMONIS, Petrus; 308
SALEBURS; 314
—, le Counte de; 314
SALESBIRE; 314
SALESBUR', [Longespee], Count de; 314
SALESBURI, Counte; 314
—, le Cunte de; 314
SALESBURY, le Conte de; 314
SALIB, Joan; 387
SALISBERY; 314
SALISBURY; 215
—, Cunte de; 314
—, Erle of; 314
—, le Conte de; 314
—, William, E of; 314
SALL; 272
—, Emond, of Devon; 272
SALLE, Sir Robert; 157
SALLEY; 142, 157
SALSBURYE; 314
SALTASH, Town of, Cornw; 239
SALTENOR, Geffray; 264
SALTU, Bernard de; 226
SAMBORNE; 139
SAMCT GEORGE; 213
SAMCTGEORGE; 244
SAMFORD; 94-5
—, de; 95
SAMORY, Sir Richard; 92
SAMPFORD; 64
—, Roger de, Kt; 64
SAMPSON; 100
—, Henry; 80
—, John; 80
—, Mons Robert; 100
SAMTWALLIE; 259
SAMWELL, John; 272
SANCTO JOHANNE, Ld of Plumpton,
  Northants, Kt; 28
SANCTO PETRO, John de; 361
SANCTO VALERIO, Thomas de; 255
SANCTO WALERIO, Tomas de; 255

SANCTUS REYNOLDUS, Myles; 142
SANCTUS SEBASTIANUS; 11
SANDACRE, Monsire de; 218
—, Monsr; 221
SANDBACH; 387
SANDEFORD; 3
SANDEFORDE, Lore de; 94
SANDELANDIS, of Chalder; 322
SANDFORD; 95
SANDFORD 118; 314
SANDFORD, Baron; 139
—, Nicholas de; 94
—, Tohmas; 65
—, William de; 94
SANDFORDE; 278
SANDIACRE; 221
—, Sr de; 221
—, Geoffrey de; 221
SANDILANDS, of Calder; 322
—, Sir John, of Calder; 320
SANDILANS, le Sire de; 322
SANFORD; 94
SANTON, Monsrie Henry de; 350
SAPI, Thomas; 145
SAPRAM; 342, 350
SAPY; 145
—, Sr de; 350
—, John de; 145
SARESBERIE, Ela, Ctess of; 196
—, Ela Comitissa; 313
SARESBIRIENSIS, Willelmus, Comes; 314
SARRE, Jehan de; 320
SARTEVILLE, S', de Cotyngham; 100
SAUAGE, Mons Arnalde; 313
SAUAIGE; 313
SAUCOIO, Ralph de; 140
SAUKEVILE, Andrew, of Wilts & Berks; 364
SAUMVYLE, John; 162
SAUNBI; 42
SAUNDER, of London; 237
SAUNDFORD, Thomas de; 65
SAUNFORD; 95
—, Gilebert de; 94
—, Lawrence de; 25, 94
—, Mons' Thomas; 95
SAUNFORDE, Tomas de; 64
SAUNPERE, Sir John; 362
SAUNTON; 360
SAUUKEVILL, Andrew de; 348
SAUVADGE, Mons Ernaud; 313
SAUVAGE, Sr; 313
—, Sir Arnaud; 313
—, Sir James le; 238
—, S Roger; 313
—, Sire Roger; 313
SAVAGE; 313
—, le; 313
—, Sir ...; 313
—, Arnald; 313

—, Mons Arnald; 313
—, S' Arnald; 313
—, Arnald, of Kent, Kt; 313
—, Arnold; 313
—, Sir Arnold; 313
—, S' Arnold, Kent; 313
—, Ernald; 313
—, Sr John; 314
—, Sir John, of Ches; 313
—, Sir John, Kent; 314
—, Mons Laurence; 315
—, Mons R; 315
—, Robert le; 89
—, Ronald; 313
SAVOY, Piers of, E of Richmond; 209
SAWTRE PRIORY; 22
SAXBEY; 71
SAXBY, of Northamp; 71
SAXNEIE, Le Snre; 167
SAXONIE, le Duke de; 81
—, D de; 354
SAXONY, D of; 349
—, Henry, D of; 98
SAY, Ld; 277
SAYBURNE, of Kendall; 314
SAYETON; 390
SAYMORE, Ld; 150
SAYNT OWEN, Joan de; 88, 329
SAYNT PERE, Sr John, of Ches; 362
SAYNTE MARTYN; 315
SAYNTOWYN, Ra'; 89
SCALEBROK, Willeme de; 31
SCANDINAVIA, K of; 198, 288
SCARBER; 386
SCARBOROUGH; 27
SCARBOURGH; 27
SCARBURGH; 27
SCARINGBOURNE; 212
SCARLET; 157-8
SCARNIGBOURNE; 212
SCARYNGBOURNE; 212
SCHARD, Roger, of Suff; 71
SCHARDLOWE, Mons Willm de; 59
SCHARINGBOURNE; 212
SCHARYNGBURNE, Mons' Andrewe de; 212
SCHASTOWE; 324
SCHAU...t, John; 321
SCHENNE, of Schepay, Kent; 301
SCHEPERWAST, Robert; 83
SCHERBOURNE; 127
SCHERLLIS, Mons Aleyn; 350
SCHERLOND; 312
SCHEYNY, Sir T; 312
SCHIRELANDE, Mons Rogier de; 312
SCHIRLONDE, Roger de; 312
SCHOCE, le Roy de; 251
SCHOTE, John; 121
SCHREWISBERY, E of; 241
SCHROSBERY; 234

SCHROWSBURY, Count de; 243
SCHWARZENBERG; 167
SCHYRINGHAM, Sr de; 157
SCHYRHYLL; 217
SCIRLANDE, Sire Robert de; 312
—, Roger de; 312
SCOCE, Le Roy de; 251
SCONE; 250
SCOPHAM; 322
SCOT, John, of Essex; 199
—, Walter, Justiciar; 165
—, William, of Yorks; 270, 372
SCOTELANDE, le Roy de; 251
SCOTENAY, John de; 121
SCOTLAND; 249-51
—, K of; 237, 251
—, King of; 251
—, Alexander K of; 237
—, Alexander II, K of; 251
—, Alexander II of; 121
—, K Alexander II; 121
—, Alexander III, K of; 251
—, Alexander III of; 121
—, K Alexander III; 250
—, K David I; 250
—, Guardians of; 250
—, K James I of; 251
—, James V, K of; 251
—, John Balliol, K of; 250
—, Kyng of; 251
—, K Malcolm III; 250
—, Q Maud of; 251
—, Roy de; 251
SCOTLANDE, Kyng of; 251
SCOTT; 291-2
SCOTTES, the Kyng of; 251
—, Ye Kyng of; 251
SCOTTS, K of; 251
SCOTTZ, King of; 251
SCREMBY, Mons' de; 70
SCROBE, Ld; 323
SCROOP, le Sr de; 323
SCROOPE; 320, 323
—, Galfredus; 323
—, Richard; 361
SCROP, Mons le; 370
—, Sr de; 365
—, le C'r; 323
—, Sr Geffrey le; 362
—, Guffrey de; 361
—, Mons Henri le; 365
—, Henry de; 365
—, Henry le, Kt; 361
—, Sir Henry le; 15
—, L; 323
—, Richard le; 320
—, Stephen, 2nd Baron, of Masham; 361
—, Stephen le, Ld of Oxendon, Gloucs; 320
—, Mons' Steven le; 370

—, Mons Thomas le; 365
—, Ld, Upsalle; 362
—, Sir William; 323
—, William le, Ld of Man & the Isles; 361
SCROPE; 320, 323, 362, 365, 393
—, Ld; 323, 362
—, Ld de; 323
—, Lord, Kt 1509; 129
—, the Lord; 323
—, Ld [of Bolton]; 323
—, Ld, of Bolton; 323
—, of Bolton; 323
—, of Bolton, Yorks; 321, 323
—, of Boulton; 323
—, Geo; 321
—, Geoffrey de; 321
—, Geoffrey le; 321
—, Sir Geoffrey; 321, 323, 361, 363, 365
—, Sir Geoffrey le; 361
—, Sir Geoffrey, Abbot of Coverham; 362
—, Sir Geoffrey, Abbot of Roche; 362
—, Henry le; 361, 365
—, Henry le, Kt; 361
—, Sir Henry; 321, 323, 362, 366
—, Sir Henry le; 361
—, the Lord Henry, [of Bolton]; 323
—, Sir Henry le, governor of our seignours; 15
—, Henry, Ld, of Masham; 362
—, Joan; 361
—, John; 362
—, John, Ld; 324
—, John, Ld le; 321
—, John le; 361, 365
—, Sir John, KG; 324
—, Sir John le, KG; 324
—, John, King's Paymaster in Irld; 368
—, K of Man; 362
—, Margaret; 324
—, Margery, lady de, & of Masham; 321
—, of Masham; 362
—, Richard de; 321
—, Richard le; 321, 361
—, Richard, Archbp of York; 362
—, Richard le, Ld of Bolton; 321
—, Ld Richard, of Bolton; 324
—, Richard le, Chevr; 321
—, Sir Richd; 324
—, Sir Richd le, 1st Ld Scrope of Bolton; 321
—, Robert; 321
—, Sir Stephen; 362
—, Stephen; 362
—, Stephen le; 361
—, Thomas; 324
—, Thomas le; 365
—, Thomas, 6th Baron, of Masham; 361
—, of Upsala; 362
—, Ld, of Upsale; 362
—, Ld, of Upsall; 362
—, of Upsall; 362

—, Sir William; 324
—, William; 363
—, William le, Kt; 361
—, Sir Wm; 324, 362, 365
—, Sr Wm; 321
SCROPP, Ld; 324
—, the Lord; 324
—, Sir John, of Castlecombe; 324
SCROPPE; 324
—, Ld; 324
—, the Lord; 324
—, Mons'r Wyll'm; 324
—, Ld, of Upsall; 362
SCROUP, Ld; 324
—, le; 365
—, Sire Henri; 362
SCROUPE; 324, 362
SCROWPE, ...; 324
SCRYMGEOUR, David, of Fardell; 215
—, James; 199, 215
—, Sir James; 199
—, James, of Kirkton; 211
—, John; 199
—, Walter, of Glaswell; 215
SCURES, Robert de; 37
SCURMY; 138
—, Monsr; 188
SEAGRAVE, John, Ld, d1354; 168
SECILIE, K of; 98
—, Kyng of; 88
SECOUNE, S' Jon; 377
SEDEM, Sir William; 64
SEE; 25
—, Martin del; 23
—, Sir Martyn of the; 25
—, Mayster Stewyn of the, of Yorks; 26
SEEGRAVE, Monsire de; 168
SEEVYLL', Mons Hugh de; 242
SEG'F, Sir Joh' de; 168
SEGRAVE, Johan de; 138
—, Nichol de; 168
SEGRAUE; 168
—, L[ord]; 168
—, le Sour de; 168
SEGRAVE; 165, 168-9, 210, 217, 220
—, Ld; 168
—, Le Sire de; 168
—, Le Sr de; 168
—, Mons de; 220
—, Monsire de; 168
—, Sr de; 168
—, Anne, Abbess of Barking, Essex; 168
—, Christina de; 121, 175
—, S Esteuen, s of Joh; 171
—, Mons Esteven de; 171-2
—, Sire Estevene de; 171
—, Sr Estienne de; 171
—, Henr de; 220
—, Sire Henri de; 220

—, Henry de; 220
—, S Henry; 220
—, Sr Henry de; 224
—, Henry de, Sheriff of Norf & Suff; 220
—, Hew; 220
—, 'How'; 220
—, Hugh; 220
—, Hugh de; 217
—, Mons Hugh de; 173
—, Hugh de, of Berks, etc, Kt; 217
—, Sir Hugo, of Oxfords; 36
—, J de; 169
—, Sr J de; 169
—, J, fitz a seign; 210
—, Jan de; 171
—, Jn de; 165
—, Jn Ld; 165
—, Jn, Ld of; 165
—, Jn de, 2nd Baron; 165
—, Jn, Ld de, ?3rd Baron; 165
—, S Joh; 169
—, Johan de; 169, 171
—, Sire Johan de; 169, 224
—, Sr Johan; 169
—, John de; 169
—, John, Ld; 169
—, John of; 121
—, Sir John; 169
—, Sir John de; 169
—, Sire John de; 169
—, Lorde; 169
—, Nichol de; 210
—, Sire Nichol de; 210
—, Sr Nichol de; 210
—, Nicholas de; 210
—, Nicholas de, Ld of Stowe; 225
—, Nichole de; 138
—, Sire Nichole de; 210
—, Mons Nicholl de; 171
—, Nicol de; 210
—, Sr Nicol de; 210
—, Nicolas de; 210
—, S Nychol de; 210
—, Monsire Simon; 186
—, Simon; 220
—, Sr Stephen de; 169
—, Sire Symon de; 220
SEGRE, John de; 195
—, Simon; 194
—, Simon de; 186
SEGRETTY; 187
SEGRETY; 187
—, Simon; 186
—, Symon; 141, 186
—, Symond; 186
SEIN BRIDE, Nichole de; 100
SEIN CLER, William de; 234
SEIN MARTIN, Sire Renaud de; 315
SEIN MARTYN, Joan de; 26

SEIN PERE, Uriel de; 362
—, Sire Urien de; 362
SEIN PIERE, Uriel de; 362
SEIN WALERY, John de; 264
SEINCLER, Sire Johan de; 181
SEINPER, Hurien de; 362
SEINT HELENE, Jon; 315
SEINT HELYN, John de; 315
SEINT JOHN, Mons' Giles; 28
SEINT LOWE; 362
SEINT MARTIN, Mons' John de; 315
—, William de; 315
SEINT MARTYNE, Mons Laurence; 315
SEINT OWEN, Raf de; 60
SEINT PERE; 362
SEINT POULE, Earl of; 183
SEINT QUINTYN, Mons' Herbert; 196
SEINT VALERI, John de; 264
SEINTE PERE, Urien de; 362
SEINTGEORGE, William, Kt, of Warws &
   Dorset; 121
SEINTLOU; 322
SEITONE, Nicholas de, of Maydewell,
   Northants, Kt; 375
SELBY; 58, 99
—, James; 86
—, John; 100
—, Walter de; 101
—, Water de; 101
—, Mons Waut' de; 101
—, S' Will'; 100
SELEYDEN, de; 152
SEMPER, Sir Brian de; 362
SEMPHILL, Sr Hewe; 364
SENCHER, Sir John; 181
SENCLER, William de; 237
—, Willm de; 234
SENDIACRE, Galfrs de; 221
SENINGVEAM, Elgenardus de; 121
SENLES, le sr de; 88
SENLYS; 38
—, Sir John, of Lincs; 39
SENT JOHN, Sir ... de; 368
SERIANT, Andreas; 386
SERTON, John de; 377
SETON; 377
—, Mons J de; 377
—, John de; 377
—, Monsire John de; 377
SETONE, Mons John de; 390
—, John de, Ld of Maydewell, Morthants; 375
SETTOUN, of Tulibody; 3
SEURMY; 188
SEXTEYN, John; 253
SEYGRAVE; 169
—, Sire Nicholas de; 210
SEYMARKE; 68
SEYMARKES; 68
SEYMOUR; 271

—, Ld; 148
—, Sir ...; 147
—, Sir Thomas; 272
SEYN PERE, S' Jh'n; 362
—, Jhon de; 363
SEYNCLER, Guydo de; 183
SEYNE, Count of; 192
SEYNPERE; 362
—, Sir John; 362
—, Ralph de, of Mercaston, Derbys; 321
SEYNT MARTYN, Monsire Laurence; 315
SEYNT OWEN; 60
SEYNT PERE, Brieu de; 362
SEYNT POWLE, Earl of; 184
SEYNTLOWE, le S' de; 322
SEYTLOWE; 362
SEYTON; 375, 377
—, Henry de, Kt; 375
—, Johan de; 377
—, Mons' John de; 377
—, Thomas; 375
SEYTOUN, John de, of Maydewell, Northants,
   Kt; 375
SHALVESBURY, Therll of; 234
SHEEPWASH, John; 212
—, William; 212
SHELFORD; 63
SHELREYE, Edmund de; 348
SHEPMAN, Robert; 327
SHERBURN, Richard de; 190
—, Sir Richard, of Stonyhurst; 127
SHERBURNE, Sir Rich, of Stonyhurst; 127
SHERINGBORNE; 212
SHERLAND; 140, 312, 317
—, of Kent; 312
—, Robt; 312
—, Roger; 312
SHERLEY, William de; 333
SHERLYNGHAM; 157
SHILFORD; 23, 63
SHIPMAN; 271
SHIPPENHAM, William; 271
SHIRBURNE, Mons R de; 190
SHIRLAND; 311
—, Sir Robert; 313
—, Sir Roger; 312
SHIRLEY; 49
—, Ralph de, Kt; 170
—, William de; 333
SHIRLOND; 312
SHIRLONDE, Roger de; 312
SHIVAS, Willm; 291
—, Wm; 291
SHOLE, Robert; 368
SHOREWOOD, Geo, Bp of Brechin (1454-
   1462/3); 250
SHORSTEDE, Simunt de; 313
SHOTBOLT; 253
SHREWESBURY, Le C de; 234

SHREWSBURY; 288
SHURLAND; 316
—, Sr Robert de; 312
SHYLFORDE, Tomas; 63, 92
SHYPMAN, John de, Kent; 386
SHYPTON, John; 318
SIBBALD, Isabella, of Balgony; 121
SIDENHAM, of Brympton d'Evercy; 295
SIDNAM, John, of Som; 295
SIFERWAST, Joh'es; 80
SIFFERWAS, Sir Robert; 83
SIFFEWAST, Monsire Roger; 76
SIFREWAST; 64, 77
—, Sr de; 83
—, Richard; 77
—, Richard de; 77
SIGOYNE, M de; 25
SIMEON, Percival; 302
SIMON, Ralph Fitz, of Ormesby; 157
—, Thomas; 271
SIMONIS, Hugh, fil; 123
SIMOUND, Hugh le; 89
SINOPIS, Queen; 134
SIRELANDE, Roger de; 312
SIRELONDE, Sire Robert de; 312
SIRIE, Rex; 76
SIRLANDE, Sr Robert de; 317
SIRLONDE, Roger de; 312
SKARLET; 160
SKELTON; 41
SKEVYNTON, Sir John, Sheriff of London; 279
SKEYTOUN, Ra; 332
SKIPTON, John de; 1
SKIPWITH; 68, 202
—, Sir William; 68
—, William; 68
—, Wm, of St Albans, Herts; 68
SKIPWYTH, Mons Will de; 202
SKOCIE, Rex; 251
SKOT, Robert, of Whitley, Ches; 121
SKROP, Mons Henr le; 363
—, Mons Richard le; 324
SKROWP, the Lord; 324
SKRYMGEOUR, of Dudupe [Dudhope]; 199
SKRYMZOUR, Ban' Man; 132
SKURBY, Thomas, of Lincs; 262
SKYPTON; 142
—, John de; 211
SKYPWITH; 68, 202
—, Sir John; 68
SKYPWITHE; 202
—, Sir John; 68
—, William, of St Alban's; 68
SKYPWYTH; 35
—, William de, of Lincs; 46
SLAKE, Nicholas, Rector of Yeovil; 121
SLANLOW, Monsire de; 138
SLEICH, Richard; 369

SLEY; 374
SMETHELAY; 50
SMETHELEY; 50
SMITH, of Hilton; 378
—, Mons' John, of Norf; 373
SMYTH; 373-4
—, of the Hough, Ches; 34
—, Messire Thomas; 34
—, Syr Thos, of the Loghem, Ches; 34
—, Thomas, of Hanewell, ?Northants; 37
—, Sir Thos, of the Hoghe, Ches; 34
—, Thos, of Kymberle; 121
—, Sir Walter; 293
—, Walter, of Ingham, Suff; 334
SMYTHE; 293
SNAVES, Johannes de; 373
SNETESHAM, Thomas de; 121
SNETTON, Simon de; 147
SNOWDEN; 129
SNOWDUN, Hugh, of Ches; 129
SOITTONE, Sire Johan de; 209
SOLERS, Henry de; 333
SOLMES, Count of; 146
SOMAYNE; 246
SOMEREY; 259
—, Roger de; 259
—, Roger of; 259
SOMERFIELD; 92
SOMERI, Henry de; 378
—, Johan de; 259
—, Sire Johan de; 259, 337
—, John; 255
—, Sire Perceval de; 258
—, Peynall; 264
—, [Roger] de; 258-9
SOMERTON; 253
SOMERVILLE; 72
SOMERY; 255-6, 259, 337
—, Agnes de, Lady of Northfield; 255
—, George de; 64, 92
—, Henry de; 378
—, Johan de; 256
—, John de; 256
—, Sir John; 256, 259, 337
—, Sr John; 284
—, Perceval; 258
—, Perseval de; 258
—, Radulf de; 256
—, Ralph de; 256
—, Rog de; 259
—, Mons Roger; 259
—, Roger de; 256, 259, 264
—, Sir Roger; 259
—, Sir Roger de; 256
—, Sir Thomas, of Sutton; 259
—, William de; 256
SOMRI, Henri de; 378
SONCIULE, Sr Simon de; 382
SONLES, John de; 327

SORELL, Luke, of Lapworth, Warws; 321
SOREWELL; 121
SORNELIER; 357-8
SORRELL, Enquerreau de; 265
SOTFORD, John, of Devon; 372
SOTTONE, Sire Johan de; 213
—, Sire Richard de; 138
—, Thomas; 230
SOUCH, Sire Amery de la; 341
—, Wille la; 345
SOUCHE, la; 391
—, Sire Amery la; 341
—, Amerye la; 391
—, Sire Amory la; 341
—, of Leics; 341
SOULES, John of; 327
—, Sir John de; 327
—, Thomas de; 345
—, Will' de; 59
—, Wm; 59
SOULIS; 70
—, Sir John, Kt; 327
—, Nicholas; 86
—, Nicholas de; 86
—, William; 86
SOULLY, Sir John; 75
SOUTHDALTON, Richard; 317
SOUTON; 179
SOUZA, de; 194
SOWCHE; 341, 392
—, Mons le; 391
SPAIN; 126
—, K of; 126
—, King of; 126
SPALDYNG, Michel de; 36
SPARWE, Robert, of Braunforde, Suff; 321
SPAYN, King of; 173
SPAYNE; 126
SPECCOT, John, of Devon; 11
SPEKE; 48
—, Sir Geo; 48
—, Sir John; 48
—, of Whitelackington; 48
SPELMAN; 40
SPENCER; 25-6, 94, 338-40, 368-9
—, Baron; 339
—, Ld; 323, 340
—, Edward, Ld, KG; 340
—, of Gloucs; 340
—, Henry; 394
—, Sr Herri; 323
—, Hugh le; 369
—, Sir Robert; 26
—, Sir Robert, of Spencercomb, Devon; 26
SPENS, John; 223
SPENSER; 94, 339
—, Ld; 340
—, Sir; 340
—, Sire; 340

—, S Gilberd; 353
—, Sir Hewe; 340
—, Hugh de; 369
—, Mons Philip; 66
SPICER, William; 321
SPIGNELL, Sir Adam; 59
SPIGORNEL, S' Rad'; 69
SPIGURNEL; 78
—, Ralph; 58
—, Thomas; 78
SPIGURNELL; 59
—, Dame Elizabeth, Lady of Wigenneure; 58
—, Radulphus, miles; 88
—, Mons' Rafe; 69
—, Sir Richard; 59
SPILMAN; 52
SPINGURNELL; 59
SPINGURNELLE, Ralph; 69
SPONDON, Agnes de; 214
SPRENGHOSE, Roger; 256
SPRIGONELL, Mons Thom; 79
SPRING; 127
—, Sire Johan; 127
—, John; 127
—, Sir John; 127
SPRINGE; 127
SPRINGES, Sir John; 139
SPRINGHOSE; 272
—, Roger; 267, 272
—, Roger de; 267
SPRYGONELL, le fitz; 79
—, Mons Rauf; 75
—, Mons Tho; 78
SPRYNGEHOSE, John, of Salop; 258
SPRYNGES, Mons J; 127
SPRYNGHOSE, Sir ..., of Salop; 258
SPYGURNEL; 59
—, Monsire Rauf; 59
SPYGURNELL; 66
SPYGURNELLE; 59
SPYPWYTH, Sir; 68
SQUIRREL; 206
SQUYRYE, Suff; 206
SQYRYE, of Suff; 206
ST AGGAS MONASTERY, Richmond, Yorks; 371
ST AMOUND, Ld; 148
ST ANDOENS, John de, Kt; 86
ST ANDREW'S, Vicar General of; 291
ST ANDREWS, House of the Friars Preachers; 216
—, University of; 250
—, Vicar General of; 250
ST BARTHOLOMEW THE GREAT, Priory of; 269
ST BARTHOLOMEW'S PRIORY; 269
ST BEYSSE ABBEY, Yorks; 134
ST BEYSSE MONASTERY, Yorks; 134
ST CLER, Guido de, Kt; 181

ST CLERE; 237
—, John; 315
ST EDMUNDS, Thomas of; 121
ST EDWARD; 288
ST FRIDESWIDE'S PRIORY; 215
ST GEORGE; 244
ST HELENE, John; 315
ST HELYN, John de; 1
ST JOHN; 367-8
—, Arnaud de, de Gartre; 94
—, of Bletso; 367
—, Elizabeth; 367
—, Sir John; 368
—, John, of Penmawr; 368
ST JOHN'S HOSPITAL, Clerkenwell; 367
ST JORGE; 244
ST LIZ; 38
—, E of Northants; 38
—, Symonde, 2nd E of Northampton; 187
ST LOE; 361
ST LOW; 362
—, Sir T; 323
ST MARTIN, William de; 1
ST MAUR; 148
ST OLMERS, Sir Edward; 358
ST OMER; 358
ST OSWOLDE ...; 198
ST OWEN; 89
—, John de; 88
—, Ralph de; 60
ST PAUL; 181
ST PERE, Hurian de; 362
ST PIERE; 362
—, Sir John, of Ches; 362
ST PIERRE; 361
ST POL, Count of; 183
ST ROBERT'S MONASTERY, Knaresbor-
ough, Yorks; 239
ST URSULA; 11
ST VALERI, Thomas de; 256
ST VALLERY, Oxford; 259
ST WALERY, Sir Richard de; 259
ST WALY, Sire Richard de; 259
ST YVE, John de; 283-4
STACHAM; 356
STACI, Thomas; 382
STAFFORD, Anne, Ctess of; 286
—, Duke of Bokyngham; 309
—, Henry, E of Wiltshire, KG; 307
—, Humphrey, 6th E of; 306
—, Isabella; 282
—, Isobel de; 282
—, John de; 321
STAINTON; 350
STAKEPOL; 162
—, Philip de; 206
—, Sire Richard de; 162
STALBROKE, London; 388
STALBROOK; 388

STALHAM; 81
STAMFELD, Mons Thom de; 333
STAMFFELD, Richard, of Shipley, Yorks; 309
STAMFORD, Hospital of; 52
STAMTON; 2
STANBERY, Harry; 160
STANDEN; 360
—, Thomas of; 321
STANDON; 2, 374
STANFORD; 94
—, Gilbert de; 94
—, Simon de; 187
STANFORT; 94
STANGAL, Mons Rauf de; 328
STANGATE; 330
—, Ralph; 328
STANGRAVE; 141
STANHOP; 296
—, Ricardus; 380
—, Richard, of Northants, Kt; 380
STANHOPE; 296, 380
—, Sir Edw; 379, 381
—, Ralph; 381
—, Richard; 380
—, Richard, Kt; 380
—, Sir Richard; 381
STANHOPP, Sir Edward; 296
STANHOW, Hervey de; 344
STANHOWE, Hervy de; 344
STANLAWE, Sire Rauf; 183
STANLEI, Thomas, of Staffs; 322
STANLEY, Johannes; 322
—, John; 322
—, S' John de of Ches; 322
—, John, 'of Wyver'; 32
STANLOW, John de; 175
STANLOWE, Mons de; 178
—, Mons Gerard; 178
—, John de, Kt; 181, 183
—, Sir Radulf de; 121
—, Ralph de; 175
—, Sr Raufe; 176
STANLY, John; 322
STANORE, Monsr de; 34
—, J, Sr de; 34
—, Mons' John; 34
—, Mons' John de; 34
STANPARD, Lord of Shyston; 10
STANSFELDE, Jamys; 294
STANTON, Mons Henry de; 350
—, Sir Henry de; 350
—, John, of Wolvelay, Yorks; 121
STANTONE; 350
STAPALTON, Mons Miles de; 126
STAPEL; 35
STAPELDOWNE, Sr Robert de; 180
STAPELEGH, Peter de; 121
STAPELLTON; 126
STAPELTON, Brian de, Kt; 121

—, Mons' Bryan de; 156
—, Miles de; 121
—, Sr Miles; 154
—, Sire Milis de; 126
—, Milo de, of Yorks, Kt; 121
—, Milys de; 181
—, Monsr Nichol de; 126
—, Mons Nicol de; 126
—, Robert de; 176
STAPELTONE, Miles; 179
—, Sire Miles de; 127
—, Robert de; 176
STAPHAM; 323
—, Monsire de; 323
STAPILLTON; 127, 155
STAPILTON; 155
—, Monsr de; 176
—, Brian; 156
—, Brian de, Kt; 121
—, Sir Brian; 121
—, Mons Bryan de; 154
—, Mons' Bryan de; 154
—, Mons Bryan de; 156
—, Sir Bryan; 127
—, Elizabeth; 208
—, John of; 244
—, Mons Miles de; 209
—, My; 127
—, Mons' Myles [KG]; 156
—, Mons Myles de, de Bedale; 154
—, Mons Myles, de Haddilsay; 127
—, Nicholas; 121
—, of Notts; 127
—, Mons' Richard; 97
—, Mons Th de; 208
—, of Wighill, Yorks; 127
STAPLETON; 121, 127, 154, 176
—, Monsire de; 176
—, Sir; 127
—, Sr de; 127
—, Sir Brian; 127, 156
—, Sir Brian de, of Wighill; 156
—, Bryan; 127
—, Sir Bryan; 127, 156
—, Sir Bryan, KG; 127
—, Sir Bryan & his bro Sir Miles S, KG; 127
—, Hugh; 182
—, John of; 241
—, Ld Miles; 127
—, Miles; 127, 154, 156, 179
—, Miles de; 127
—, Miles, Ld; 127
—, Sir Miles; 121, 127, 156
—, Monsire Miles de, de Bydal; 154
—, S Miles de, of Norf; 127
—, Monsire Nicholas de; 127
—, Sir Nicholas; 208
—, Robert de; 176
—, Sir Robert; 175

—, Robt de; 177
—, Sire Rychart de; 25
STAPLETONE, Messire Bryane; 156
STAPULTON; 121, 127, 156, 208
—, Mons Bryan; 127
—, [Sir Bryan]; 127
—, Sir Miles; 127
—, Robert; 177
—, of Suss; 127
—, Willm, of Yorks; 141
STAPULTONE, Brian; 127
—, Sir Bryan; 127
STAPYLTON; 127
—, Sir M; 127
—, Sir B; 156
—, Sir Bryan of; 127
STATHAM; 356
STATHHAN; 356
STAUBERT, Jehen de; 121
STAUERDON; 374
STAUNDON, Henry de; 350
STAUNTON; 132, 350
—, Henry de; 350
STAUODON; 374
STAVERDON; 374
STAYBER, Sir Lawrence; 214
STAYN, William de, of Lincs; 24
STAYNE; 24
—, de; 24
—, William de, of Lincs; 24
STAYNING, of Suff; 199
STAYNTON; 2
STEDE, William; 271
STEERFACE; 388
STENINGS, of Honicott [in Selworthy]; 214
STENYNG; 214
STEPELTON; 129
—, Sr; 177
STEPELTONE, Sire Robert de; 177
STEPHAM, le Sr de; 323
STEPHANT; 323
—, William; 392
STEPHEN, K; 288
—, K of England; 288
STEPLETON, Mons John; 177
—, Roberd de; 177
STEPULLTON, Robert de; 177
STEPULTON; 134, 177
STERBORGH; 38
STERESACRE; 388
—, Rychard; 388
STERLYNG, Sir T; 78
STERYSACRE; 388
STETHAM, de; 71
STEUERT, D of Albany; 251
—, D of Ross; 251
STEWARD; 224
STEWART, Alan, of the Frelande; 369
—, Alan, of Paisley; 368

—, Alex; 250
—, Alex, Bp of Ross; 304
—, Alex, 6th E of Menteith (d ante 1306); 72
—, Sir Andrew; 251
—, Andrew, 2nd Ld Avondale; 121
—, Ld of Avyndall; 251
—, David, Count Palatine of Stratherne &c; 252
—, Francis, Ld of Badenach & Enzie; 252
—, James; 250, 252
—, James, D of Ross, Archbp of St Andrews 1497-1503; 251
—, John; 251-2
—, John, of Conoraigy; 252
—, Margaret; 252
—, Marjory; 250
—, Ld of Meffane; 251
—, Sir Richard, Kt; 233
—, Robert; 121
—, Robert, D of Albany, E of Fife & Monteith; 209
—, Thomas; 252
—, Walter; 252
STEWERT, E of Mar; 251
—, E of Mare; 251
—, E of Moray; 251
STEWKLEY, Thomas; 295
STEYNGRAVE, Joan de; 141
STIENE, Conrand de; 171
STIMY; 273
STOCKLEY; 233
STODAWE, John de; 78
STODDAW, John; 78
STODEBINT, Mons Rauf; 278
—, Rauf; 279
STODEBYNT, Sir Rauf; 278
STODEHAM, M de; 71
STODHAM, Simon de; 90
STODON; 68
STODOWE; 68
STOKE, Richard, Rector of Birdbrook; 390
—, Stephanus de; 81
—, Stevin; 84
—, Thomas, of Asscheby Leger; 233
STOKES; 63, 73-4, 173, 177, 180, 192, 233
—, of Brinton, Berks; 180
—, of Devon, Alderman of London; 215
STOKKE; 52
STOKLEY; 310
STOKNOR, of Kent; 233
STOKUS, of Kent; 233
STOKYS, John; 181
STONAR, ...; 23
STONE, William de; 193
—, Willm de; 193
STONER; 34, 67
—, Sir Walter; 34
—, Sir William; 34
—, William; 34

STONHOUSE, Thos de; 121
STONNE; 192
STONOR; 33
—, John de; 34
—, Sir John; 34
STONORE; 67
—, John de; 34
—, John de, Kt; 34
—, Robert, of Oxfs; 34
—, Thomas de; 34
STONORRE, William; 35
STONORT; 34
STONTEVILLE, John, Ld of; 175
STOPHAM; 323
—, Sr de; 323
—, Johan de; 362
—, Sire Johan de; 362
—, John; 323
—, Sir Thomas; 323
—, Thomas; 323
—, Willam de; 369
—, Sire Willame; 323
—, Willeme de; 323
—, Sir William; 323
—, Sr William de; 322
—, Sr Willm de; 349
—, Sire Wyll de; 349
—, Sire Wyllame de; 323
STORMY, John; 188
—, Mons John; 195
—, S' John; 190
STORMYN, Sire Roger; 348
STORTON; 391
—, Ld; 391
—, Sir; 391
STORWYCH, Sir ...; 143
STORY; 180, 182
—, Mons Richard; 180
—, Richard; 180
—, Sir Richard; 182
—, Sr Robert; 126
—, S' William; 176
—, William; 176, 206
STORYE; 184
—, Mons Willm; 176
STOTEUYLE, Sir Nichol; 279
STOTEVILE; 99, 279
—, Robert de; 100
STOTEVILLE, John de, Ld of Ekyntona, Derbys; 140
STOTEVYLE, Sr Nichol de; 253
STOURETON; 391
STOURTON; 391
—, Ld; 391
—, Edward, 6th Ld; 391
—, Sir J; 391
—, Ld [William]; 391
—, William, of Stourton, Wilts; 391
—, Wm, Kt; 391

STOUTEUILLE; 99
STOUTEVILE, Jehan de, of Northd; 84
STOWDOW; 68
STOWTON, William; 391
STOYNTON, Henry de; 350
STRACCHE, John, Kt; 121
STRACHAN, Alexr, of Knox; 201
—, Andrew; 201
—, John; 229
—, John, of Thornton; 216
STRACHEY, Walter; 177
STRADLING, Joan; 94
STRAFFORD, William de; 185
STRAICHAUCHIN, of Thorntoun; 202
STRANG; 264
STRANGBON; 372
STRANGE; 73, 254, 256-8, 267-8, 270-2, 372
—, Ld; 258, 316
—, le; 256
—, Le; 258, 270
—, le; 270
—, Le Sr; 258
—, Monsire le; 258
—, Sir ...; 270
—, Monsire le, de Blackmere; 257
—, Sir ..., of Blackmere; 257
—, of Blackmere; 257
—, Sir, of Blackmore; 257
—, Mons I, de Blak'ne; 257
—, Ld, of Cokayne; 258
—, Elizabeth le; 257
—, Mons Fouke le; 253
—, Fulk de; 263
—, Fulk le, Ld of Corsham; 256
—, of Gloucs; 257
—, Sir Haman le; 256
—, Hamund le; 258
—, Hy le; 270
—, Jan le; 257
—, Jason, fitz; 267
—, Joan de; 257
—, John; 267
—, John le; 258, 270
—, John le, Kt; 270
—, Mons John; 258
—, Sir John; 257
—, John de, of Blackmere; 257
—, John le, of Blackmere; 257
—, John, of Blackmere; 257
—, John, Ld of Knockyn; 258
—, John, Ld of Knokyn; 258
—, John le, of Knokyn; 256
—, John, of Norf; 260
—, Jon le; 257
—, Sire Jon le; 257
—, of Knockin; 258
—, Ld, of Knocking; 258
—, Ld, of Knockyn; 258
—, of Knockyn; 258

—, de Knokynge; 284
—, of Norf; 260
—, Perys; 257
—, Sir Peter; 73
—, le S'r de; 258
—, Sir Richard le, Ld of Knokyn & Mohun; 256
—, Robert le; 260
—, Rog' le; 272
—, Roger; 260
—, Roger le; 272
—, Sir Roger; 256, 272
—, Sir Roger le; 270
—, Sire Roger le; 258
—, Roger le, of Ellesmere; 271
—, Le S' de Talbot; 257
—, le Sr de Talbot; 257
—, Le Sr Talbot; 257
—, Sir Thos le, Constable of Ireld; 261
STRANGEWAYS; 260
—, Mayster; 261
STRANGRAUE; 141
STRANGWAIIS, John, of Lancs; 260
STRANGWAYES; 260
STRANGWAYS; 260
—, Giles; 262
—, Gylys, of Styngsford; 269
—, Jacobus; 265
—, Sir James; 260
—, Sir Jamys, Yorks; 260
—, of Lancs; 260
—, Mayster Gilys, de Stynysford, Dorset; 261
—, of Middle Channock, Soms, & Melbury, Dors; 261
—, Robard, Yorks; 262
STRANGWEYS; 261
—, Sir James; 261
STRANGWISHE, Sir James; 260
STRASACKER, Richard de; 387
STRATHEARN, Robt, 4th E of; 121
STRATHERN, Le Comte de; 252
STRATTON, S' Walter Pauly; 304
STRAUNGE; 73, 258, 267, 270
—, Ld; 258
—, Le; 270
—, Le Sr; 258
—, Monsire de; 258
—, Fitz a; 267
LE STRAUNGE, Sr Fouke; 283
STRAUNGE, Sire Fuke les; 258
—, Mons J, de Norf; 260
—, Sire Johan; 272
—, Sire Johan de; 257
—, Johannes le; 257
—, John le; 256
—, Sr John; 272
—, Pe; 73
—, Mons Peris; 257
—, Mons Rog; 258

—, Roger le; 272
—, Sir Roger; 270
STRAUNGGE, John le, Ld of Knokyn; 256
STRAVANT, William, E of; 310
STRAWNGE, Le Sr, of Salop; 258
STRECCHE, Thomas; 380
STRECH; 125, 136
STRECHE; 136
—, John, of Norf, Kt; 121
STRETTUN, Richard de, Kt; 185
STRICKLAND, Sir Walter; 28, 76
STRIKELAND; 2
STRIKLANDE, Sire Walter de; 27
STROGUL, Balduin de; 223
STRONDE, Wylyam of Surr; 11
STRONGBOW; 315
STUCLE, Johan de; 219
STUDOLPHE; 268
STURI, William, Kt; 175
STURMAN, Sir William, of Oxfords; 273
STURMI, le; 273
STURMY; 193, 273
—, Henry; 273
—, Henry, Ld of Figheldean, Wilts; 273
—, John, Kt; 121
—, Mons John; 188
—, Sir William, of Worcs; 273
—, Sir Wylyam, of Hants; 273
STURMYN; 273
—, Do'; 190
—, Sir Roger; 337
—, Sir William; 273
STURTON; 391
—, Ld; 391
—, Sir J; 392
—, Sir John; 391-2
STURY, Alice; 93
—, Sir William; 176
STUTEVILE; 98
—, Johanna de; 100
—, Robert de; 140
STUTEVILLE, Joanna de; 81
—, John de; 140
—, Robert de; 86, 140
STUTEVYLE, John de; 84, 140
STUTTEVILLE, Mons' Rob't; 100
—, Mons Robert; 100
—, Mons' Robert; 100
—, Robert de; 140
STUTVYLL, Mons Robert de; 140
STYKLEWEY, Thomas; 295
STYLE; 343, 392
—, John, de Tenyrton, Devon; 392
STYWARD; 125, 224, 360
—, Mons Augustine de; 226
—, Norf; 248
—, of Norf; 224
—, Mons Robert de; 226
—, Thomas, of Swaffham; 218

—, Thomas, of Swaffham, Norf; 224
SUDBERY; 246
SUDBURY; 246
—, Simon, Archbp of Canterbury; 246
—, Sir Symon, Bp; 246
SUEBERR, le Roy de; 182
SUFFOLK, D of; 140
—, John, D of; 175
SUGLES; 280
SUGUN, Reymond de; 276
SULBYRNE; 160
SULEE, Bartholomew de; 20
—, Munsire Bartholomew de; 20
SULIE, Sir Remund, of Glam; 58
SULL', Monsr de; 20
SULLEYE, S William de; 366
SULLIA, Reimund, of Glam; 58
SULLY, Sir John; 75
—, Sir John, KG; 75
SULTON, John; 217
SULTOR, of Dudley; 256
SUMARY, John de, Ld of Newport Pagnell; 256
SUMERI, Sire Johan; 259
—, Radulfus de; 121
—, William de; 256
SUMERY, Roger de; 256, 259
SUMNER; 355
SUNRY, Sr Jo, de Kent; 337
SURDELLE, Le Conte de; 277
SURGEON, J; 207
SURIE, le Roy de; 129
SURREY, D of; 299
SUSSEX, William, E of; 121
SUTHORMESBY, Simon de, of Lincs, Kt; 123
SUTLON, de Hols; 222
—, T; 222
SUTTON; 134, 138, 156, 179-80, 209, 222
—, Sir ... de; 218
—, Sr de; 179
—, Sir Benet de; 53
—, Sr Benet de, Staffs; 53
—, Dean Robert; 159
—, of Dudeley; 179
—, of Dudley; 256
—, Edward, Ld Dudley; 179
—, Sir Edward, Ld Dudley; 179
—, Monsr Johan de; 222
—, Sire Johan de, de Holderness; 222
—, Johes de, Ld of Duddeleye; 321
—, John de; 256
—, Mons John de; 222
—, Monsire John de; 222
—, Sr John de; 213
—, John de, Ld of Dudley; 256
—, Sir John de, of Holderness; 222
—, John, 2nd Ld; 221
—, Margaret; 220
—, Nicholas de, of Threak; 121

—, Ric, Steward of Syon; 180
—, Sir Richard; 156
—, Sr Richard; 183
—, Sgr de; 222
—, S' Tho, of Staffs; 259
—, William de; 42
SUTTONE, S' Jon; 222
SUYLLY, Mons' Robert; 20
SWAFIELD; 296
SWALE, W; 360
SWANLUND, Thomas de; 374
—, Thomas de, of London; 374
SWARTENBORCH, Count of; 189
SWEDEN; 289
—, K of; 153
SWELINGTON; 130, 290
SWELINTON, Sir Roger, of Derbys; 296
SWELYNTON, S' Roger, of Derbys; 296
SWESIE, Rex; 134
SWETHERIK, le Roy de; 141
SWETHYN, Kyng of; 134
SWEYN; 121
SWILLINGTON, Sir Roger; 296
SWINE; 290
SWINHOE; 290
—, Walter of; 309
SWINITHWAITE, William de; 394
SWINTON, Alan, of that ilk; 200
SWYDYNGFELD, Tarrimus; 56
SWYNE; 290
SWYNES; 290
SWYNFORD, William; 31
SWYNHOWE, Robert; 290
SWYNOWE, John of, of Northd; 290
—, Robert, of Northd; 290
SWYTFORD, Sir Robert, Middx; 29
SWYTHIN, K of; 289
SYBILL; 206
—, John, of Kent; 206
SYDENHAM; 295
—, Simon; 295
SYFERWAST; 77
SYFFREWAST, de; 77
SYFIRWAST, John; 76
SYFREWAST; 77, 83
—, Sir John; 76
—, John, Ld of Clewer; 76
SYFREWASTE; 76
SYMON, Sire Rauf filz; 157
SYMOND, Fitz; 157
—, Thomas; 271
SYMONND, Mons Th; 271
SYMOUND, Mons Rauf fitz; 157
SYPRES, Rex de; 140
SYPRESSE, K of; 170
TABY, Sir John; 59
TAIND, William, of Chilverston, Warws; 273
TALBOT; 2, 22, 40, 99, 241, 243, 247, 271-2, 276, 278

—, Ld; 243, 376
—, le Sire; 243
—, Monsire de; 242-3
—, Sir; 234
—, Beatrice; 241
—, of Bossington; 358
—, Bryan; 276
—, Sir Edmond; 276
—, Sir Edward; 276
—, Mons Esmond; 276
—, Ld Furnival; 202, 376
—, Sir Geo, E of Shrewsbury; 234
—, Sir George, E of Shrewsbury; 234
—, George, E of Shrewsbury; 234
—, Gilbert; 40, 88, 234, 241, 243, 246
—, Gilbert, Ld; 243
—, Gilbert, Ld, KG; 243
—, Mons Gilbert; 246
—, Sir Gilbert; 234, 247
—, Sr Gilbert; 246
—, Gilbert, Ld of Irchenefeld, Herefs, 3rd Baron; 247
—, Gilbert, 5th Baron, d1419; 241
—, Gilbt; 247
—, Gylbert, Ld; 243
—, of Irld; 236
—, Mons J; 243-4
—, John; 22, 125, 243
—, Mons John; 22
—, S John; 248
—, Sir John; 234
—, Sir John, KG; 243
—, John, Ld of Furnival & Wesford, E of Shrewsbury, Marshal of France; 241
—, John, Ld of Furnival & Wexford, E of Shrewsbury, Marshal of France; 241
—, John, 2nd E of Shrewsbury; 234
—, Sir John, of Salebury; 276
—, John, E of Salop; 234
—, Ld John, E of Shrewsbury; 234
—, John, E of Shrewsbury; 241
—, S' Jon'; 22
—, Mons' Joon; 244
—, Margaret; 233, 241
—, Peter; 302
—, S' Ric'; 22
—, Mons Rich; 243
—, Rich, Ld of Trehenfield; 241
—, Richard; 239, 241, 247
—, Richard, Ld; 241, 243
—, Richard, Ld of Eccleswall; 241
—, Richard, E of Shrewsbury; 234
—, 'Le Sr', Salop; 257
—, Baron of Schrewysbery; 243
—, 'Erle of Shesbury'; 129
—, E of Shrewsbury; 233-4, 243
—, of Shrewsbury; 241
—, Suss; 276
—, Sir T; 278

—, 'Therl of Shrawsbery'; 234
—, Sir Thomas; 276
—, Thomas; 293
—, Thomas, Kt; 293
—, Sir Thomas, of Basha; 276
—, Sir Thomas, of Bashall, Lancs; 276
—, Thomas, of Bashall & Salesbury; 276
—, Thomas, (of Malahide); 236
—, Sir W; 276
—, Sir William; 293
—, William; 22
—, S Wm; 247
TALBOTES; 22, 40
TALBOTT; 22-3, 243, 247, 276
—, Ld; 243
—, le Sr de; 243
—, Sr de; 243
—, Sr Edmond; 276
—, Sir Emond, of Lancs; 295
—, Mons Gilbert; 40
—, Mons Richard; 247
—, E of Shrewsberie; 243
—, Mons Thomas; 276
TALEBOT, Sire Edmon; 276
—, Gelebert; 88
—, Sire Gilberd; 246
—, Gilleberd; 88
—, John; 22
—, John, of Gainsborough, Lincs; 208
—, Richard; 241
—, Sire Richard; 22
—, Robert; 89
TALERT; 246
TALWORTH, Joan de; 382
TAME; 252
—, Edmund, of Fairford; 253
—, of Fairford, Gloucs; 253
—, John; 253
—, William, of Hants; 17
TAMPES, le Comte de; 346
TANFELDE, Dernegan fitz Hugh de; 70
TANNE; 59
—, Sir Lucas; 59
—, Sr Lucas, of Ches; 59
—, Sir Richard; 59
TANNY, le Seignor de; 59
TANY; 59, 69
—, Monsire de; 59
—, Monsr de; 59
—, Sr de; 59
—, Sire Johan; 59
—, Mons' John; 59
—, Lucas; 59
TAPTON, William; 321
TARS, le roy de; 204
TARSSE, Rex; 204
TARSUS, K of; 212
—, King of; 204
TATE, Roy de; 204

TATESHALL, le Sieur; 62
—, le sieur; 322
TAUNE, Sir Lucas; 59
TAVERNER; 355
—, Gerard; 225
—, John; 356
TAWNE; 315
TAYLOR, Thomas; 386
TAYS, the Kyng of; 179
TEDUR; 122
TEMESE, Thomas; 25
TEMPEST; 376, 378
—, of Craven; 376
—, Sir John; 376
—, Sir John, of Yorks; 376
—, Petrus; 376
—, Mons Ric; 376
—, Mons Richard; 376
—, Mons' Richard; 378
—, Richard; 374, 376, 378
—, Sir Richard; 376, 378
—, Sir Richard, of Bracewell, Yorks; 376
—, of Studeley; 378
—, Sir Thomas; 378
—, Mons' William; 376
—, Sir William; 378
—, of Yorks; 376
TEMPESTE; 376
TEMPLE, The; 206
—, Knights of the; 206
—, Nicholas, d1551; 54
TENDIRDEN; 322
TERBERVILE, Hue de; 125
TERELL; 242
THAME, Sir Edmund; 252
THANI, Lucas; 59
THARS, K of; 204
THARSE; 204
THAWITS; 226
THEBOLD, John, of Merden, Suss; 64
THEDEMERHS, John de; 276
THEDEMERSSH, Nicholas; 276
THELVETHAM, John de, of Norf; 15
THENFORD, Nicholas de; 348
THLOD, John, of Wales; 187
THOMAS, le fitz; 76
—, Rychard ap Hawett ap; 277
—, Whilliam, of Carms; 207
THOMER; 94
—, William de, of Bridgewater; 94
—, William, of Bridgewater; 94
THOMPSON; 193
THOMSON, Joh, Esq; 193
THORNHILL, Sr Brian de; 77
THORNBERY, John de, Kt; 224
THORNBURY; 142
THORNEBERY; 142
THORNEBURY, Philip; 224
THORNEHAM, Robert; 215

THORNEHILL; 80
—, William, Esq; 76
THORNETONRUST, Elys de; 13
THORNHILL; 77, 80
—, Beatrice; 76
—, Mons' Bryan; 77
—, Monsire Bryan de; 77
—, Monsr Bryan de; 77
—, John de; 76
—, Thomas de; 80
—, William de; 76
THORNHILLE, S' bryan; 77
THORNTON, Mathe; 13
THORNY; 138
THORP; 151
—, Mons' W de; 101
—, William de; 101
THORPE; 198
—, Sir ...; 228
—, Sire William de; 100
THORUNTON; 259
THORVILL, Johannes; 77
THRECKINGHAM, Sir Walter; 48
THREKINGHAM, Sr de; 49
THREKYNGHAM, Sr de; 49
THURKINGHAM, Sire Wauter de; 52
THURMOND, Nicholas; 372
THURSTON; 74
—, Joh; 74
THWAITES; 226
TIERSTEIN, Count of; 202
TIGOT, Sr Henry; 36
TILIOL, Robert; 217
TILIOTT; 219
TILLIOL, Geoffrey; 219
—, Sir P; 219
—, Peter; 217
—, Sir Peter; 217
TILLIOLL, Mons' Piers; 219
TILLOL; 219
TILLY, John, of Okewelle, Yorks; 371
TILLYOLF, Sr Robert; 219
TILLYOLL, Mons Robt; 219
TILMANSTONE, Roger de; 315
TIMURTHE, Richard de, Surr; 388
TINGLETON; 34
TINNGLEY, Kent; 157
TIPAUT; 186
TIRELL, S Roger; 242, 246
TIRENTON or TREHAMPTON; 322
TIRENTONE, Raf de; 322
TIRRINGTON, Ralph de; 322
TITISBOROUGH; 373
TITSBURY; 373
TITTESBURY; 373
TOCHET, Sir John, of Derbys; 153
—, S' Tho', of Derbys; 141
TOCOTES, Elizabeth, Lady of St Amand; 217
TODEHAM, Oliver de; 92

TODENHAM; 92
—, Monsire; 92
—, of Devon; 64
—, John de, of Suff, Kt; 92
—, Oliver de, of Lymington; 64
TODMHAM; 92
TOKETT; 218
TOKY, Richard, of London; 356
TOLL; 56
—, Christoffer, seriant at arms; 56
—, Christopher, of Cirencester, Gloucs; 56
—, Christopher, of Cirencester, serjeant at arms; 56
TOLTHORP, Alice; 6, 346
TOMASYNE, Bartholomewe; 280
TOMLINSON, Ric; 293
TOMSON; 193
TOMSYN, Bartholomew; 160
TONKE, John de la; 354
—, Sr Robert; 88
TOPCLIFFE, Nicholas of; 121
TORAUD, John, Rector of Grytelynton, Wilts; 206
TORBEVILE, Huge de; 125
TORBURVILE, Richd, of Dorset; 165
TORELL, Sir Wm; 205
TORPERVILLE; 278
TORRELL, of Ilchester; 205
TOTEL, Roger, junior; 371
TOTENHAM; 98
TOTESBERY, Bawedewyn; 373
TOTHILL; 39
TOUCHET, Sir Thomas; 153
—, William, Ld of Levenhales; 150
TOUK, Robert; 89
—, Sire Robert; 88
TOUKE, Monsire Robert; 89
TOUKES; 88
TOUKY; 370
TOURCY, Mons Willm de; 234
TOURNEY, William de; 235
TOWCH, of that ilk; 127
TOWNE, Thomas de; 315
TRABOME; 142, 224
TRACE; 204
TRACY, Sir J; 226-7
—, Sir Wylyam; 89
TRAFFORD, Alice; 94
TRAFFORDE, Stephen, of Northants; 208
TRAGOSE, Sir John, of Suss; 36
TRAMPINTON, Sir Raffe; 364
TRANE, Sir Sandich de, KG; 178
—, Sir Sandich de la; 178
TRAU, Soudan de la; 121
TRAUE, Sir Sandich de; 136
TRAVERS; 289, 322
—, of Lancs; 289
TRAYHAMPTON, Rauf de; 322
TREANTON, Sr Ry; 322

TREAUNTONE, Sire Rauf de; 322
—, Sir Rauff; 322
TREDEK, Sir J; 204
TREDERFFE, John; 201
TREGOCE; 78
—, Sir John; 78
TREGOIZ, John; 78
TREGOLD, Thomas; 13
TREGOLZ; 78
TREGOS; 78
—, s' Henri; 78
—, Johan; 84
—, Sire Johan; 78
—, Monsire, de Suss; 78
TREGOSE, Ralph; 78
TREGOSSE, Henry; 78
TREGOT, Jan; 78
TREGOUS, Jon; 78
TREGOYS; 36
TREGOYSE, John; 289
TREGOZ; 36, 78
—, Monsire; 78
—, Geffry; 78
—, Geoffrey; 78
—, Henri; 78
—, Munsire Henri; 78
—, Sire Henri; 78
—, Henry; 78
—, Joan; 78
—, Johan; 78
—, Munsire Johan; 78
—, John; 79
—, Sr John; 78
—, Robert; 78
—, Robert de; 78
—, Sr, of Suss; 78
TREGOZE; 78
—, Sr; 78
TREHAMPTON, Sir John; 393
—, Radulfus; 321
—, Rauf de; 322
TREHAMTON, Rauf de; 322
TREHAUNT, Radulfus de; 322
TREHAUNTON, Rauf; 322
TREIGOZ, Henry; 78
—, Sire Jon; 78
TREKINGHAM, Monsire de; 49
TREKYNGHAM, Mons John de; 49
TRELOP, Sir W; 291
TREMARGAN; 143
TRENTHAM; 38
TRERISE; 368
TRERYS, Sir ...; 75
TRESUYLYON; 212
TRETHEK; 204
TREUERY; 59
TREVARTHEAN; 200
TREVELIAN, Sir John; 212
TREVELYAN; 77, 212

TREVILLIAN, of Nettlecombe; 212
TREVOS, Henre; 78
TREVRY; 73
TREVYLYON; 212
TREWARTHEN; 200, 248
TREWICK, Thomas of; 69
TREYGOS; 78
—, Henry; 78
—, Mons' John; 79
—, Mons Rauf; 78
TREYGUS; 79
—, of Kent; 78
TRIE, Renaud de; 363
—, le Signeur de Bilebatia de; 346
TRIGOT, Sire Henry; 36
TRISTRAM, Sir; 127
—, Master Mathew; 227
TROIE, Hector de; 253
TROIS, Thomas; 69
TROLLEHOP; 292
TROLLEHOPP; 292
TROLLOPE, of Morden & Thornley; 291
TROLLOPPE, Tomas; 292
TROUP, John; 205
TROUSTELL, Ed'us; 32
TROWEU, James de; 326
TROYE, le Roy de; 253
TROYS, Harman; 379
—, Herman; 379
—, Thomas; 74
TRUBLEVILE, Sir David; 165
TRUBLEVILLE; 209
TRUBLEVILLL, of Guernsey; 229
TRUMPINTON, Rog de; 364
—, Roger; 364
TRYGOWS, Sir Bernard, of Hants; 193
TUCHET, William; 149
TUDENHAM, John; 92
—, John, Kt; 24
—, Jorge de; 98
TUDOR, Jasper, D of Bedford & Ld of Bergavenny; 307
—, Jasper, E of Pembroke, [D of Bedford; 307
—, Margaret; 121, 251
TUKE, Brian, Kt; 282
—, S Robert; 88
TUKSBURY, Baldwin; 373
TULLIDAFF, Andrew, of Rannieston; 229
—, Andrew, of that ilk; 230
TUNES, le Rey de; 187
TURBERUYLE, Suss; 165
TURBERVIL; 209
—, Hugh; 165
—, John de, Kt; 121
TURBERVILE; 125, 167, 187, 209, 228
—, Gefrai; 278
—, Hue; 125
—, Munsire Hue; 125
—, Sir John; 165

—, Richard; 170
—, Robert; 165
—, Thom; 209
—, Thomas; 141
—, Thomas de; 141
TURBERVILL, Hawe de; 125
—, Herre; 125
—, Hue de; 125
—, Thom de; 165
TURBERVILLE; 125, 165
—, de; 125
—, Sr de; 170
—, Hue de; 165
—, Hugo; 125
—, Sr Hugo de; 125
—, Joan de; 23
—, Sir John; 165
—, Mon' Hugh de; 165
—, Mons' Thomas; 145
TURBERVYLE, Sir Thomas of Herefs; 170
TURBERVYLLE, Jn; 165
TURBEVILE, Huge de; 165
TURBREVILLE, John; 165
TURBULVYLE; 165
TURBURUILLE; 208
TURBURVYLE, Mons Rich; 170
—, Monsire Richard; 170
TURBURVYLL, Mons W; 209
TURBURVYLLE, Mons Th; 141
TURNBULL, Wm; 73
TURNHAM, Stephen, Kt; 321
TUTBURY, Peter, Prior of; 286
TUTISBURY; 373
TUYFORD, Sire Johan de; 31
—, of Leics; 31
TUYFORDE, Sire Johan de; 31
TWIFORD, Monsire de; 27
—, Sir Nicol; 29
TWRBYRWYLE, Sir Tomas; 145
TWYFORD; 29, 31-2, 85
—, Sr de; 31
—, le Fitz; 32
—, John de; 31, 45
—, John de, Kt; 31
—, Mons' John de; 31
—, Sir John; 31
—, Sir John de; 31
—, Sr John; 31
—, Sir John de, Derbys; 31
—, S' Jon; 31
—, Richard; 31
—, Mons' Robert; 31
—, Monsire Robert; 31
—, Robert; 31
—, Robert de, Kt, of Warws; 15
TWYFORDE; 31
—, Mons John de; 31-2
—, Sr John de, Derbys; 31
TWYNHAM, Walter, of Kingston; 69

TY, Robert; 382
TYBALD, Simon; 246
—, Simon, Bp of London 1362-75; 246
TYDESDON, Roger; 379
TYE; 382
—, Robert; 380
TYLER, Sir Wm; 390
TYLIEL; 219
TYLIO, Arnald de; 232
TYLIOL, Robert, Kt; 218
TYLIOLL; 156
TYLLIOL, S' Rob'; 219
TYLLOL, Sir Robert; 219
—, Sire Robert; 219
TYLNEY, Ralph; 193
TYLYALL, Sir Pyerssa, of Cumb; 219
TYMPERLEY, of Suss; 160
—, Suss; 158
TYMPURLEY, Suff; 158
TYMPYRLEY, Tomas; 158
TYREL, Hugh, Esq, of the King's chamber; 241
—, S' Roger; 246
—, Sire Roger; 246
—, Sr Roger; 246
TYRELL, Sir Roger; 246
TYRINGTON; 321
TYROL, Roger; 242
TYRRELL, Hugh; 242
—, Mons Hugh; 242
TYSON; 289
TYTTISBURY; 373
UFFLET; 377
UFFLETE; 377
—, Gerard; 377
—, Mons Gerrard; 377
UFFORD, Johannes; 146
ULSTAN, K, pa'; 347
ULSTER, Maud, Ctess of; 298
ULSTON, Jo; 338
ULTONIGEN, Graf von; 201
UMFREVYLE, Sir R; 380
UNDERHILL, Thomas; 6
UPTON; 15
URDENBEND, Corsill de; 5
URDENBOND, Renaud de; 4
URSFLETE, Gerard, Kt; 374
URSWICK, Sir William; 346
UTLAGE(), William; 121
VERDON, S' Ch; 138
—, S' Jo de; 138
VACHE, de la; 146, 277, 281
—, of Bucks; 277, 281
—, Essex; 281
—, Mons Hugh de; 277
—, Mons Philip la; 281
—, Philip la; 281
—, Philip la, Kt; 305
—, Sir Philip de la; 169, 281

—, S' Ric la; 281
—, Mons Rich de la; 281
LA VACHE, Richard; 281
VACHE, Richard de la; 281
—, Richard la; 281
—, Sir Richard de la, KG; 281
—, Sire Richard de la; 297
—, Sr Richard de la; 281
—, Richard de la, Oxfords; 297
VACHEZ; 277
VAGHAM, Morgan; 201
VAGHAN; 201
VAL, Sir Hugh de la; 21
—, Sir Robert de la; 20
VALCHE; 67
VALE, Mons Henry de; 20
—, Robert de la, Kt, of Northd; 20
—, Mons William de; 55
—, William de; 286
VALE ROYAL ABBEY; 288, 304
VALENCE; 84
—, Aymer de; 84
—, William de; 286
—, Wm, E of Pembroke; 288
VALENS; 87
—, erle of Penbroke; 100
VALERYAL, Abbot of; 304
VALLE CRUSIS ABBEY; 227
VALLES, Sr Adam de; 178
VALLIBUS, John de; 321
VALOINS; 230
VALOMYS; 230
VALOYNES; 92, 230
—, Sr; 230
—, Thebaude de; 96
VALUN, M de; 63
VANDERNOOTT, Jn, of London; 121
VANNE, Perottus; 354
VARDES, de; 224
VARE, De la; 209
VARNON, S' Warinus le, Ches; 325
VAUGHAN, John; 127
—, Morgan; 231
VAUNCEVOD, Sire Gilberd; 315
VAUS, Sr de; 322
—, Sir John; 387
—, Robert, burgess of Edinburgh; 370
—, Sir Wm, Kt; 331
VAUX; 325, 342
—, de, of Dirleton; 321
—, Ld Dirleton; 322
—, John; 321, 368
—, John de; 321, 342
—, Rawleyn, of Cumb; 342
—, Roland; 342
VEAUTRE, Simon; 121
VEELE, Walter de; 295
VEILLELOBOS, Sir Ferdinand de; 268
—, Sir Ferdinande de; 269

VEILLEVYLLE, Sir Rouland de; 156
VEILOND, Sire Johan de Veilond; 218
—, Sir John de; 218
VELDENS, Count of; 124
VENABLES; 2, 16, 18
—, Sir ...; 18
—, Alexander; 46
—, Bolyn; 40
—, Baron, of Hilton, co Durham; 18
—, S' Hugh; 18
—, Sir J; 18
—, of Jersey; 18
—, of Kinderton; 18
—, Sir Ric'; 18
—, Ricardus; 18
—, Sir Rich le; 18
—, Mons Richard; 47
—, Richard; 18, 37
—, Sir Richard; 18
—, Roger de; 15
—, Rogerus de; 18
—, Thos, of Golborne, Ches; 18
—, William de, Kt; 121
—, Sir William, de Bolin; 40
—, Sir William, of Bolyn; 40
—, S' William, Bolyn, of Ches; 40
—, Wm de; 121
VENABLYS, Sir J; 18
VENABYLYS; 18, 20
VENIS, ... de; 122, 321
VENNER; 180
VENNOR; 159
VENOR; 159
VENOUR; 159
—, Sire Robert le; 180
VENYS, D[uke] of; 196
VEPONT, Sir John de; 8
VEPOUND, Sire Johan de; 8
—, Sire Nicholas de; 8
VEPOUNT, Sr de; 8
—, John de; 7
—, Sr John de; 8
—, Mons John, of Westmld; 8
—, Sr Nicolas; 8
—, S Rob; 8
VERCHI, M' Giup de; 144
VERDON; 122, 138
—, Monsire de; 138
—, Sr de; 138
—, J, le fitz de; 209
—, John de; 138
—, Mons' John; 138
—, Mons John de; 138
—, Mons' John de; 139
—, Monsire John de; 139
—, Sir John de; 139
—, John de, of Norf, Kt; 122
—, Sir John, of Northants; 139
—, Mons Th de; 154

—, Mons' Thomas; 154
—, Monsire Thomas de; 198
—, Sr Thomas de; 154
—, Thomas de; 122
VERDONE; 139
VERDOUN; 139
—, Jo; 139
—, Sire Thomas de; 139
—, Thomas de; 154
—, Thomas de, of Northants, Kt; 122
VERDOUNE; 139
VERDUN, Sr Thomas de; 139
—, Thomas de, of Norf, Kt; 122
VERE, Joan de, Ctess of Oxford; 270
VERIFORD, Sir William; 157
VERLAY, Sire Felip de; 374
VERLY, Sir Philip; 374
VERNEY; 39
VERNIM; 88
VERNON, Esmond; 361
—, John, of Somerton, Norf, Kt; 327
—, Maude de; 282
—, S' Nicol de; 325
—, S' Warren le; 325
—, Warren le; 325
—, William de; 16, 187
VERNOUN, Ralph; 321
VESCQ, Mons William de; 219
VESCY, Isabella de, senior of Scorby, Yorks; 122
—, Mons' William; 219
VESEY; 219
VESSIE, Lorde; 354
VEST; 163
VETERIPONT; 7
VEUPONT, John de; 7
VEUTER, Simon; 147
VICCHERCHE, Sir Alan de; 58
VIEL, Thomas; 122
VIGOROUS; 54
VILERS, Pagan de, of Notts; 313
VILLA LOBOS, Ferdinando de; 269
VINCENT, William, of Essex, Gent; 200
VIPOINTE, Monsire de; 8
VIPONS; 8
VIPONT; 4, 6, 8
—, Ivo de; 9
—, John; 9
—, John de; 6, 9
—, Maud de; 9
—, Robert; 313
—, Robert de; 6
—, Wm; 253
VIPOUNT; 6
—, le Sire de; 8
—, Sr John de; 8
—, S Nychol de; 8
VIPOUNTE; 8
VIPOUNTES; 8

VITERIE; 8
VIVIAN; 125, 142
VPFLITE; 377
VUIYAN, of Cornw; 125
VYLERS, Matthew, Warws; 384
—, Sr Payn de; 313
VYLYIS; 341
VYNCENT, Richard, Rector of St Benet, Sherehog, London; 286
VYNOR, Henry, of London; 368
VYPOUNT, Wylyam, of the Byschopcryte of Durham; 8
VYPOUNTE; 8
WA...s, John; 122
WAC, Baldwinus; 44
—, Bawdewyn; 44
WACHE, de la; 281
—, Fellepe le; 277
—, S Rescharde de; 281
WAFRE, Alan; 122
WAGGE, Nicholas, of Rothewell, Northants; 175
WAK; 44
—, Badewyn; 44
—, Bawldwyn; 44
—, Sr Hugh de; 44
—, Sir John; 44
—, the Lorde; 44
WAKE; 42-4, 46, 53
—, Baron; 43
—, Ld; 44
—, Ld de; 79
—, le; 44
—, Le S de; 44
—, le Sire de; 44
—, Le Sr; 44
—, le Sr de; 44
—, M; 43-4
—, Monsire de; 44
—, Baldeuuinus; 44
—, Baldwin; 44
—, Baldwin de; 42
—, Sir Baldwin, of Bucks; 44
—, Baldwin, d c1282; 42
—, Baudewin; 44
—, Baudewyn; 44
—, Munsire Baudewyn; 44
—, Mons Bawdewyn; 49
—, Bawdwin; 44
—, de Bleseworth; 53
—, de Bleseworthe; 53
—, de Blisworth; 53
—, Hue; 43, 49
—, Sire Huge; 44
—, Sire Huge, le oncle; 43
—, Hugh; 42, 44
—, Hugh le; 44
—, Sir Hugh; 49
—, Hugh, of Clifton, Kt; 42

—, Hugh, of Clyfton, Kt; 42
—, Sir Hugh, le oncle; 43
—, Joan; 44
—, Johan; 44
—, Johan de; 44
—, Sire Johan; 44
—, John; 72
—, John, Ld; 44
—, Sir John; 20
—, Sr John; 44
—, Sr John de; 44
—, of Kent; 46
—, L; 44
—, Roger; 42
—, Le Seignr; 44
—, Mons T de, of Wynterburne, Yorks; 49
—, S Thom; 53
—, Mons Thom del; 53
—, Thomas; 42, 44, 53
—, Thomas, Ld; 44
—, Monsire Thomas, de Blisworthe; 53
—, Thomas, of Bliseworth, Northants, Kt; 53
—, Monsire Thomas, de Blisworth; 53
—, Mons Thomas, de Blisworth; 53
—, Thomas of Blisworth, Kt; 53
—, Thomas, of Blisworth, Northants, Esq; 42
—, Sire Thomas, de Blithesworthe; 53
—, Mons Thomas, de Blyseworth; 53
—, Mons Thomas de Depynge; 53
—, Thomas, Ld of Lidele, 3rd Baron; 42
—, Sir Thomas, Ld of Lidell; 42
—, Thomas, Ld of Lydel, Cumb; 44
—, Thos, de Bluseworth; 53
—, Thos, Ld of Lavell; 42
—, Wylyam, of Northants; 43
WAKEFARE, Sr de; 127
WAKEFAYRE; 156, 163
WAKEFELD; 69
WAKEFORD; 156
WAKELYN; 157
WAKESAYE, of Norf; 138
WAKFILDE; 69
WALAYS, John de; 332
WALDBY, Robert, Ld of Hexham; 236
WALDEBY; 236
WALDEGRAVE; 334
—, S Ric; 353
—, Richard de; 334
—, Rics de; 334
WALDEMOND, le Counte; 100
WALDEN; 39
—, Sir Alex, of Essex; 369
—, Alexander; 39
—, Mons' Alexander; 39
—, John, armiger; 371
—, Roger; 369
—, Roger, Archbp of Canterbury; 368-9
WALDENE; 39
—, Roger, clerk; 368

WALDERN; 388
WALDERNE, William, of Middx; 388
WALDEVE, John, s of; 122-3
WALDRON; 388
WALDYVE, Thomas, of Oxfords; 346
WALEDENE, R; 45
WALEIS; 311
—, Henri le; 330
WALENS, S' Jon; 140
WALERAND, Robert; 351, 356
WALES; 289, 294, 304, 311
—, of Cragy; 130
—, David, Prince of; 311
—, Edward, Prince of; 298-9
—, North; 311
—, 'Le princ de gales'; 283
—, Prince of; 289, 311
—, Prince of North; 289
—, Principality of North; 289
—, Prynce of; 289
—, ?Yenri? de; 310
WALEWAYNE, Thomas, of Herefs; 361
WALEWYN, Master John de; 241
WALEYS; 335-6, 387
—, Monsire; 335
—, Sr; 336
—, Estevene le; 67
—, Henry le; 328
—, Sire Johan le; 332
—, Johnes le; 332
—, Mons Richard; 335, 353
—, Sire Richard le; 337
—, Stephanus; 67
—, Stephen de; 337
—, Stephen le; 337
—, Stephs le; 337
—, Willame de; 79
—, Wille de; 79
—, Willimus le; 79
—, Willm le; 332
—, Wm le; 79
WALGRAVE, Richard; 353
WALKEFAR, Monsire Richard; 156
WALKEFARE; 155-6, 163
—, Mons; 155-6
—, Robert; 156
—, Sire Robert de; 156
WALKEFER, Monsire Thomas; 163
WALKELYN; 157
WALKFARE; 155
—, Mons J; 209
—, Mons Rich; 156
—, Richard; 196
—, Richd; 122
—, Robe; 171
—, Mons Robt; 156
—, Robt de, of Cambs, Kt; 122
—, Ry; 156
—, Sgr de; 155

—, Mons Th; 163
—, Tho; 156
WALKFAYRE, Monsire; 198
WALKINGHAM, S Alani; 20
—, Sire Johan de; 21
WALKYNGHAM, Mons' Aleyn, de Ridmere; 21
—, Mons' John de; 21
—, Sr John de; 21
—, John de, Ld of Balteby, Kt; 266
WALKYNGTON, Aleyn de; 138
WALLACE, of Craigie; 130
—, Duncan, Laird of Sundrum; 122
—, Lambert, of Shewalton; 215
—, Sir Richard, Kt, of Barmer & Goderick; 370
WALLAR, John; 64
WALLERE, William, of Suff; 370
WALLERRON; 68
WALLEWEYN, of Longford, Herefs; 395
WALLEWORTH, Thomas, Canon of York; 371
WALLEYS; 332
—, Sir John de; 332
WALLEYZ, Sr John de; 332
WALLIE, Princeps; 310
WALLIS; 332
—, Prins of North; 289
WALLOP; 360
—, Sir John; 360
WALLOPP, Sir John; 360
WALLUP, Syr John; 360
WALLWORTH; 392
WALLYS; 337
—, James; 227
—, Prynce of; 310
—, Symon fili; 180
WALOPPE; 360
WALRANT, John; 355
WALROND; 356
—, Robert; 351, 356
WALSALL; 67
WALSH; 59, 67
—, Thomas; 79
WALSHE; 66-7
—, Mons John; 84
—, Mons' Thomas; 79
WALTER, Thomasina; 199
WALTHAM ABBEY; 286
WALTHAM CROSS, Abbot of; 286
WALTHEOF, E of Huntington; 213
WALTON; 45, 189, 384
—, Henry de; 149
—, les Armes de; 189
—, Richard de, Parson of Rocheford; 390
—, Robert de; 122
—, Whilliam; 384
—, William; 384
WALWAYN; 395

—, Philip; 343
WALWAYNE, John; 343
—, Nicol; 343
WALWEIN, Sr John; 343
WALWORTH; 387
—, William de, Citizen of London; 387
—, Sir Wm, Mayor; 387
WALWORTHE; 387
WALWOURTH; 387
WALWURTH, Suss; 387
WALWYN, Elizabeth; 395
WALYS, Prince of; 281, 310
—, Prince off; 310
WANCY, Wm; 122
WANDACK, Thomas, dominus de Pillardynton Herci; 228
WANDESFORD; 178, 230
WANDISFORD; 178
WANDYSFORD, of Kirklinton, Yorks; 178
WANE, Martin; 351
WARD; 54, 394
—, Edmund, of Staffs; 57
—, S' William de la; 150
WARDE; 54, 394
—, Edmond, of Staffs; 57
—, John; 53
—, Monsire John; 54
—, Robert de la; 97
WARDEWIK, Mons John; 281
WARDEWIKES, Monsire John; 278
WARDEWITH; 281
WARDON; 139
WARDWYCKE; 278
WARDWYKE; 281
—, Mons J de; 278
LA WARE; 154
WARE, de la; 148
—, Ld de la; 192
—, Monsire de; 150
—, Monsire la; 150
—, Monsr le; 150
—, Henry; 227
—, J son fitz de la; 209
—, Johan de la; 150
—, Sire Johan de la; 150
DE LA WARE, John; 146
LA WARE, Mons John; 154
—, Sir John; 148
WARE, Mons' John la; 148
—, Sir John la; 148
—, John, Kt, of Northants; 232
—, Mons' Robert de la; 150
—, Mons Roger le; 150
—, Roger de la; 150
—, Roger la; 150
—, Rogers de la; 150
—, William de; 219
WAREN, Richard de; 263
WARENDER, John; 369

WARENNE, Richard de; 263
WARINGTON; 155
WARKWORTH; 122
WARMINGTON; 279
WARNER; 319
—, Essex; 386
—, of Essex; 386
—, John, of Essex; 391
—, Thomas; 319
—, Thomas, of Winchester, Hants; 351
WARNERE; 387
WARNETT; 201
—, John; 201
—, John, of Hempstead, Suss; 226
LA WARR; 150
WARR; 228, 244
—, de la; 158
—, Ld de la; 150
—, John de la; 148
—, John, Ld de la; 150
—, John, Ld la, Kt; 149
—, Sir Richard de la; 244
—, Thomas La; 150
—, [Thos] West, Ld La; 150
LA WARRE; 150
WARRE, Ld de la; 150
—, le Sr de; 150
—, le Sr de la; 130
—, le Sr la; 150
—, Lord de; 130
—, Alianor la; 286
—, Elizabeth; 227
—, John de la; 150
—, John la; 227
—, John la, Kt; 227
—, Sr John le; 209
—, John, 4th Ld La; 227
—, Sir Richard; 244
—, Robert; 227
—, Sir Roger la; 149
LA WARRE, Thomas; 148
WARRE, Thomas, Kt, Ld la; 227
—, Thomas la; 147
—, Thomas la, KG; 231
—, Thomas la, clericus, Dominus la; 227
—, Thomas la, clerk; 152
—, Thomas la, of Lincs, Clerk; 147
—, Thomas, Ld la, 5th Baron, clerk; 227
—, Thos la; 122
WARRINGTON; 156
WARTHYLL, Nicholas; 122
WARWICK; 278, 331
—, E of; 344
—, Ela, Countess of; 313
—, Ela, Ctess of; 313
—, John de; 277, 281
—, Thomas E of; 344
—, Thomas, E of; 344
WARWICKE; 278

WARYNGTON, Mons de; 155
WASHINGTON, ...; 40
—; 41
—, William de; 40
—, William of; 40
WASSENES, of Heydon, Notts; 163, 181
WASSINGTON, Mons' William de; 41
WASSTNESSE, J; 163
WASSYNGEDON, Mons Willm de; 41
WASSYNGTON, Mons ... de, du Count de
    Lancaster; 41
—, Robert de; 40
WASTENEI, Edmund de; 179
WASTENEIS, Sr William; 163
WASTENES; 181
WASTENEY, Edmun; 163
—, Sr William; 139
WASTENEYS; 163
—, le Sr de; 179
—, Mons Arnold de; 179
—, Sire Edmon; 179
—, Edmund de, Kt, of Lincs; 181
—, Johan de; 163
—, Mons Robert de; 179
—, S' Th'm; 163
—, Mons Thomas; 163
—, Thomas; 163, 181
—, Sire Willame; 163
—, William; 123, 163
—, William le; 163
—, Willm de; 163
WASTENSIS, M.le; 163
WASTENYS, Jan le; 163
WASTERNEYS, William le; 163
WASTHOUSE; 79
WASTNEIS; 163
—, Thomas de; 241
—, William de, Kt; 213
—, Wm, of Colton; 163
WASTNES, Monsire de; 179
—, of Stowe; 162
WASTNESSE, Mons Esmoigne; 181
—, Mons Th.; 163
WASTNEYES; 163
WASTNEYS; 122, 163
—, Edward, Kt; 175
—, Tomas, Notts; 179
—, William le; 163
—, William, of Ches; 163
WASTYNGES; 179
WATENYS, Willame le; 163
WATERTON; 48
—, Sir Robarde, Yorks; 71
—, William de; 379
WATFORD; 71
WATLINGTONE, Joceus de, of Suss; 122
WATRINGBERI, Bertelmeu de; 314
WATTEVILE, Agnes de; 16
WATTON; 223

—, Wylyam, of Kent; 223
WAUBOURN ABBEY; 65
WAUCAR.., Sir R; 351
WAUSS; 322
WAUSTON; 350
WAUTEVILL, Sr Geffrey; 220
WAWE, John; 321
WAY, Rog; 23
WAYLAND, Sir Rechard; 218
WAYLES, John; 84
WEAVER; 32
—, Sir...; 32
WEBERE, de; 32
WEDON, Ralph de, Kt; 37
WEDONE, Sire Rauf de; 37
WEDRINGTON; 336
WEDRYGTON; 336
WEDRYNGTON, Sir John of; 336
WEEDE, Bernard le; 90
WEEKS, Richard de; 157
WEELAND; 218
WEEVER, S' Edward de; 32
WEKYNDON, ... de; 130
WELAND; 218
—, Monsire de; 218
—, Monsr de; 218
WELE, S. Phelip de; 210
WELEGBY; 55
WELEND, Roger de; 218
WELFFORD, Thomas, of Kent; 175
WELLAME, Alexr; 23
WELLAND, Thomas de; 218
WELLE; 178
—, de; 56
—, le Sr de; 178
—, Adam de; 138, 178
—, Monsire Adam de; 178
—, S Adam de; 178
—, Adam de, 1st Baron; 175
—, Sire Johan de; 379
—, John de; 175
—, Monsire John de; 178
—, Rob de; 56
—, Mons Robert de; 43
—, Robert; 16
—, Robert de; 22
WELLES; 138, 142, 175, 177-8, 221
—, Ld; 168, 178
—, le S' de; 178
—, le Sire de; 178
—, le Sr de; 178
—, Sr de; 43
—, Adam de; 178
—, Adam, Ld; 175
—, Adam, Ld of; 175
—, Adam of; 175
—, Sir Adam; 178
—, Sire Adam de; 178
—, Sire Felip de; 221

—, John; 175
—, John, Ld; 178
—, John, Visct; 178
—, Mons John de; 221
—, le S'or de; 178
—, S Phelip de; 178
—, Willimus de; 178
—, Wills de; 138
WELLIS, Visct; 178
—, John, of Middx; 142
WELLS; 175
—, Ld; 178
—, Viscount; 178
—, Alex; 122
—, John; 178, 334
—, John, Ld; 178
—, John, Visct; 179
WELLYNG; 20
WELLYS; 142, 179, 342
—, Ld; 179
—, Ld of; 179
—, Sir; 179
—, Sr de; 179
—, the Lord; 179
—, W; 142
WELSCHE; 79
WELSE, Sire Johan; 332
—, Sr John; 332
WELSH, Thomas, d1383; 79
WELYNTON, Mons Emmori de; 352
WELYSHAM; 39
WEMES, Michael de, Kt; 233
WEMIS, of Reraff; 136
WEMYS, of Reras; 249
WEMYSS; 219
—, Andrew; 122
—, David, of Wemyss; 122
—, John; 122
—, John, of Wemyss; 122
—, of Reres; 122
—, of that ilk; 136
WENABLES; 18
WENALI, Geoffrey de; 252
WENDESLEY, Thos de; 321
WENDOR; 10
WENLOKE, Richard de; 211
WENNE, le Baron de; 259
—, ... au Baron de; 267
WENSLEY, John; 391
—, Peter de; 391
WENTWORTH; 310
WENUNWYN, ... ap; 136
—, Griffid ap; 136
WERDON; 187
WERFEILD, Robert de; 353
WERINTONE; 384
WESCHYNGTON, Tomas; 69
WESSEY, Lord; 354
WESSHYNGTON, John; 40

WESSINGTON, Sir Walter de; 221
—, Sir Wm of; 40
WESSYNGTON, Mons' Wautier de; 222
—, Mons William de; 41
WEST; 181, 227, 340-1
—, Reginald, 5th B, 6th Baron de la Warr; 228
—, Reginald, Ld de la Warr; 230
—, Sir Thomas; 150, 231
—, Thomas, Kt, Dominus de la Warr; 1
—, Thomas, 8th Ld la Warr; 228
—, Sir Thomas, Ld de la Warre; 150
—, Thomas, Ld la Warr; 230
—, Thomas, Ld La Warre; 150
—, Ld De La Warr; 149
WESTBURY, William; 189
WESTON, Mons Lambert de; 18
—, Mons Roger de; 150
—, Monsire Roger de; 224
—, Roger de; 150, 224
—, William de; 149, 208
WESTONE, John de; 122, 149
—, Thomas de; 190
WESTWYKE, Hugh de; 369
WETENALE, Sir Thomas; 343
WETENALL, Sr Thomas de, Ches; 343
WETESHAM, Mons Robert de; 37
—, Robert de; 37
WETHYLLE, Richard; 285
WETNALE; 343
—, Sir Thomas de; 343
WETNALL, Sir T de; 344
—, Sr Thomas de; 344
WETTEFELDE, Richard de; 352
WETTENHALL; 344
—, Wm; 344
WEUER; 32
WEVER, S' Edwarde, of Ches; 32
WEYLAND; 218
—, Sr de; 218
—, Sr Jo de; 218
—, S John de; 218
—, of Radwell in S Petherton; 218
WEYLANDE, Sire Johan de; 218
—, Sire Richard de; 218
WEYLAUND, Sir John de; 218
—, S' Jon; 218
WEYLOND; 220
—, Sir John; 218
WEYLONDE; 220
WEYN, William le; 331
WHADDON, William; 223
WHALLEY; 291
—, of Suss; 291
WHALLEY ABBEY; 137
WHAPLODE; 269
WHEATLEY; 279
WHELOBE, Hew; 54
WHELPDALE, Roger; 296
WHELPEDALE; 293

WHETELL; 279
WHETENHALE, Sir Thomas; 344
WHETENHALL, William; 344
WHETHILL, Sir John; 279
WHETHYLL; 279
WHETLEY; 285
WHICHECOTE, Johannes; 266
WHIT, John le; 13
WHITE, of Irld; 13
WHITFIELD; 359
—, Richard de; 358
—, Robert de; 359
WHITHEVED, Alan of; 16
WHITIPOLL; 307
WHITTINGHAM; 122
WHITTON; 356
WHITWELL; 186
WHITWORTH, Sir Thomas; 52
WHYCHECOTE, of Lincs; 290
WHYCHSALE, Heylyn, of Salop; 370
WHYKSALE, Haylin, of Salop; 370
WHYTHORSSE, Rychard; 63
WHYTON, John de; 357
WIBBURY; 280
WICKHAM, of Irld; 214
WICKTON, John; 280
WIDCOMBE, of Widcombe in Martock; 47
WIDDRINGTON; 336
—, Gerard of; 335
—, Sir Gerard of; 335
—, Roger; 335
—, Roger of; 335
WIDERINGTON; 336
—, Roger de; 335
WIDVILE, Elizabeth; 182, 184
WIFOLDE, Nich; 279
WIGHAL, John; 225
WIGMORE; 293
WIKES, Richard de; 128, 157
WILBRAHAM, William; 32
WILBURY; 280
WILFORD; 129
WILL, Johan le fitz; 21
WILLEMESCOTE, Sire Henri de; 70
WILLESBY, John; 193
WILLIAM I; 288
WILLIAM THE CONQUEROR; 264
WILLIAM DAVID, Morgan ap; 347
WILLIAM II; 288
WILLIAM RUFUS; 288
WILLIAM UP THOMAS, of Walis, Sir; 280
WILLIAMS, Joh, of Dorchester, Dorset; 249
—, John, Dorset; 249
—, John, of Dorset; 249
WILLIAMSCHOTE, Eleanor de; 122
WILLIAMSCOTE, Sir Thomas de; 70
WILLIAMSON, John, in Petrynole; 385
WILLIMUS CONQUESTOR; 264
WILLISLEY; 198

WILLMS; 249
WILLOUGHBY; 54-5
—, of Derbys; 54
—, Dorothy; 54
—, Edmond; 54
—, Hugh; 54
—, Sir Hugh; 54
—, Sir Hugh, of Notts; 54
—, Sir R; 57
—, Richard de, Kt, jun; 54
—, Richard, Judge in Assizes, Warwicks; 54
—, Richd; 54
WILMSCOTE; 45
WILOUGHBY, Sir Henry; 54
WILSON; 27, 29
WILUGHBY, Mons Richard de; 55
WINCHCOMBE, Abbey of; 105
WINCHESTER, Thomas; 122
WINDOUT; 228
—, Bartholomew, de Radiswott, Herts; 228
WINSLOW; 225, 346
—, Thomas; 225
WINTER; 186
—, David, of Abernethy, Perths; 392
WINTERHULLE; 26
WINTERSHALL, Sir ...; 20
WINTERSHULL, John de; 26
—, of Surr; 20
WIRHALE, John de; 122
WITEFELD, Robert de; 352
WITEVILDE, Sire Witt de; 352
WITHERINGTON, Gerard de; 336
—, R; 336
WITHYPOLE, Paul; 307
WITTISBURY; 42
WITWILL, William; 359
WIVERESTON, William de; 349
WIVERISTON, William de; 349
WIVILE, William de; 53
WLUNSDON; 338
WNGARIE, the Kyng off; 98
WOD; 207
WODBOURNE; 278
—, Mons John; 278
WODBRERE; 81, 100
WODBURNE, Mons J de; 79
WODDE, Mons J de; 180
WODDESTOK, Sir Edmund (of); 307
WODE; 183, 207
—, of Batterley, Staffs; 207
—, John atte; 175
—, Peter atte; 10
WODEBOURNE; 278
WODEBRIRE; 278
WODEBURCH, Rauf de; 281
WODEBURGH, Sr de; 278
—, Rauf de; 281
—, Willame de; 281
WODEBURNE, Monsr de; 278

WODELL, William; 51
WODEVILE, Sir Thomas; 27
WODEVYLE, Sir Thomas, of Lancs; 372
WODRINGTON, John de; 335
WODROFFE; 346
WODYLL; 122
WOGAHAN, Johannes de; 34
WOKENDONE, Nichol de; 167
WOKINDON', Sire Nicol de; 171
WOKINDON, Sire Nicol de; 171
—, Sr Nicol de; 171
—, Sire Thom de; 167
—, Sire Thomas de; 167
—, Sr Thomas de; 167
WOKINGDON, Monsire de; 167
WOKINGDONE, Sire Nicholas de; 167
—, Sire Thomas; 154
WOKINGTON, Nicol; 167
—, Thomas de; 154
WOKYNDON, Monsr Thomas de; 167
WOKYNDONE, Nicholaus de; 167
WOKYNGDON, Sir Michael; 153
WOKYNGDONE; 154
WOKYNGTON; 167
—, Mons Nich; 167
—, Mons Th de; 154
WOLDEBURGH, Thomas; 278
WOLF; 39, 207
—, John, clerk; 207
WOLFE; 39, 207
—, John, Ld of Frolesworth, Leics; 207
—, Sir W; 267
WOLSTONE; 9
WOLVEY; 229
—, Thomas de; 229
WOMWELL; 388
WOOD; 207
—, John; 207
—, John de; 180
—, Thomas, of Wood End, Berks; 214
WOODBOROUGH, Ralph de; 278
—, William; 279
WOODBURGH, Monsire de; 278
—, Ralph de; 278
—, William de; 279
WOODBURN, John de; 278
WOODE, John, of Kent; 203, 207
—, of London; 215
—, Rog, serjeant at law; 213
WORCESTER, E; 364
WORCESTYR, Count de; 209
WORSOP PRIORY; 159
WORTHSTEDE, Simon de; 206
WORVELY, Thomas, gent; 361
WOTERINGEBERIE, Bertilmeu de; 314
WOULFSON; 207
WRIAELEYE, Pers; 54
WRIALLEY, Piers; 54
WRIGEL', Bartelemew de; 314

WRIGHTE, John le; 349
WROKESHALE, Geffray; 21
—, Sir John of; 20
WROKESHALL, Gefferey de; 46
WROTESLEY, Lord Hugh de; 351
WROTH, Sir John; 268
WROTHE, John, Kt; 301
WROTTESLEY, Hugh de; 352
—, Sir Hugh; 352
WRYOTTESLEY; 352
—, Mons Hugh de, KG; 352
WRYTESLEY, Sir Hugh; 352
WUCY, Hugh; 122
WULTIRTON, Jo; 337
WYBARNE, Sir Richard; 315
WYBERGH; 69
WYBERY, John; 260
WYBOTON; 280
WYBURY, John; 260
WYCHTON, John de; 390
WYCOMBE; 253
WYD, Sr Gerard of; 336
WYDEFORD, Richard de; 213
WYDELOCK, John; 215
WYDERINGTON; 336
—, Roger de; 335
WYDEVILL; 165
WYDRYNGTON, Sir Henry; 336
—, Mons John de; 336
WYDVILL, Elizabeth; 182
WYDVILLE; 307
WYFOLD; 279
—, N; 279
—, Nicholas; 279
WYFORD, Sir John de; 31
WYFRINGDON, Sr Nicho. de; 167
WYGGEMORE; 301
WYGHT, de; 134
—, Nicholas de; 345
WYGHTMAN; 389
WYGMORE; 293
—, Sir T; 292
WYKE, of Northwyke & Cocktree; 12
WYKEN, William de, clerk; 122
WYKES, Richard de; 128
WYKETON, Mons J de; 278, 280
WYLBURY; 280
WYLE(s), John; 122
WYLEGHBY, Mons Richard de; 55
—, Monsr Richard de; 55
WYLILE, Symkyn; 369
WYLLOWGBY, Yorks; 54
WYLLUGOB; 54
WYLLYRGHBY, Syr Henry; 54
WYLOGHBY, Richard de; 54
WYLOUGHBY, of Notts; 54
WYLOWBY, Sir Harry; 54
WYLTON, Harry, of Wilts; 385
WYMBYSH, Thomas; 138

WYMBYSSH, Thomas; 138
WYNCESTRE, Henry de; 375
—, Richard de; 322
WYNDLESORE, Hugh de; 348
WYNDOUT, Barthelmew, de Radiswell, Herts; 228
WYNFLEW; 225
WYNNE; 318
WYNSELOWE, de Cozheche; 346
WYNSENT, Wylyam, of co Durham; 30
WYNTRESHULL, John; 26
WYNTURSALL, Sr Symond, of Surr; 20
WYOTT, John; 372
WYREHAM, Ivo de, of Thetford; 142
WYRLEY, Roger de; 262
WYTEFEELD, Robarte de; 359
WYTEFELD, Sir William de; 356
WYTER; 205
—, Thomas; 186
WYTFELD, Sire William de; 358
WYTHAM, William de, of Grimsby; 81
WYTHERINGTON, Sr de; 336
WYTHERYTON, Monsr de; 336
WYTHRINGTON, Sir Gerard; 336
WYTHRYNGTON, Mons Gerrard de; 336
WYTHYPOLLE, Paule, de Loundres; 307
WYTHYPOLLES, Polle; 307
WYTNYL, Mons W; 359
WYTTELBERY; 42
WYTTYSBURY; 42
WYVER, Edward de; 32
—, Geo de; 32
WYVERE, de; 32
WYVILE, William de; 53
WYWOLDE; 279
YDEN, Paewl; 279
YEDEFEN, Thomas; 63
YEDELISSH, Sir John; 175
YELAND, Richard of; 269
YELVERTON; 301-2
—, of Norf; 302
YELVETENE; 25
YEVELTON, of Ivelton; 25
YLE, Le Comte del; 134
—, le Cunte del; 134
—, Sire Fouk del; 194
—, Sr Fouke del; 194
—, Sire Foukes del; 195
—, Gerard de; 195
—, Sire Gerard del; 195
—, Sire Robert del; 195
—, Sire Warin del; 195
—, Sire Waryn del; 195
YLLE, Cunte del; 134
YNGELOUE, Sir H; 82
YNGLAND, Kyng of; 288
YNGLIS, of Lochende; 214
YNGLOUS, Sir Harry; 82
YNGYLFELD, Essex; 68

YORK; 323, 354
—, D of; 301
—, Edmund, D of; 301
—, [Richard], le Duke de; 301
—, St Mary's Abbey; 286
YORKE; 354
—, Sir Robert de; 166
YREYS, Sir Galfrid le; 371
ZEBELTON; 26
ZELVERTON; 302
ZEVELTON, Mons Robert de; 25
—, Robert de; 26
ZEYLONDE, Willm de; 53
ZINGEL; 10
ZINGELL, Stephen; 10
ZORKES; 354
ZOUCH; 392
—, Monsire la; 391
ZOUCHE, Sr la; 391
—, Aumeri la; 391
—, Aymer la; 391
ZOWCH, Thomas; 213
ZOWCHE, le; 391